Bits, Bytes, &  s . . .

"Exhaustive in its coverage...indispensable for anyone interested in computer-assisted biblical studies."

> Susan Hockey
> Computing in the Arts
> Oxford University

"An encyclopedic resource....up-to-date...practical; an indispensible tool for the novice and a valuable reference for the experienced."

> Peter C. Patton
> Director of the Minnesota Supercomputer Institute
> Professor at the Center for Ancient Studies
> The University of Minnesota

"An excellent new book....an accurate and detailed description, intelligent and encyclopedic, not only of scholarly uses of computers, but of how computers operate and of Bible study uses at more popular levels....An impressive accomplishment."

> Robert A. Kraft
> Professor of Religious Studies
> University of Pennsylvania

"Precise...authoritative...articulate....The scholar who hopes to use the computer in his or her biblical research can either read *Bits, Bytes, and Biblical Studies* or reinvent the wheel."

> Jeffrey William Gillette
> Senior Programmer
> Humanities Computing Facility
> Duke University

"A single, comprehensive source of all the related material....I can only hope similar texts are soon available for the remaining humanities disciplines."

> Nancy M. Ide
> Assistant Professor of Computer Science
> Department of Computer Science
> Vassar College

"Virtually exhaustive yet manages to evaluate the products with remarkable depth....I would be hard-pressed to think of any book I've read that packs in so much information for each product, consistently hitting the critical areas, providing helpful charts, additional bibliography (including reviews published elsewhere!)....No library will be able to afford to be without this book."

Moises Silva
Professor of New Testament
Westminster Theological Seminary

"An indispensable guide to sources of information on the computer-assisted study of Greek, Hebrew, Latin, and other languages needed for biblical studies....The complete, thorough documentation is very impressive."

Frank Otto
Executive Director
CALICO
Brigham Young University

"A virtual gold mine...useful both for the beginner...and also for the experienced user...a *vade mecum* in the best sense."

James F. Strange
Dean of the College of Arts and Letters
The University of South Florida

"There are now three essential tools for computer-assisted biblical studies: the Bible, a computer, and *Bits, Bytes, and Biblical Studies*."

H. Van Dyke Parunak
Ann Arbor

A Resource Guide for the Use of
Computers in Biblical and Classical Studies

BITS, BYTES & BIBLICAL & STUDIES

JOHN J. HUGHES

Academie
Books Grand Rapids,
Michigan
Zondervan Publishing House

Bits, Bytes, & Biblical Studies
Copyright © 1987 by John J. Hughes

Regency Reference Library is an imprint of Zondervan Publishing House, 1415 Lake Drive, S.E., Grand Rapids, Michigan 49506.

Library of Congress Cataloging in Publication Data

Hughes, John Jones
  Bits, bytes, and biblical studies.

  Bibliography: p.
  Includes index.
    1. Bible—Study—Data processing.   2. Electronic digital computers.   3. Classical philology—Data processing.   I. Title.
BS600.2.H83 1987   220'.028'55   87-6163
ISBN   0-310-28581-X (pbk.)

Printed in the United States of America

88 89 90 91 92 / EE / 10 9 8 7 6 5 4 3 2

For

Claire, Nell, and John

Contents

Figures

Tables

Analytical Outline

Chapter 4: Computer-Assisted Language Learning

Chapter 5: Communicating and On-Line Services

Chapter 6: Archaeological Programs

Chapter 7: Machine-Readable Ancient Texts and Text Archives

Acknowledgments

Bits, Bytes, & Biblical Studies owes many things to many people. My wife, Claire, and my three boys, John, Ryan, and Allen, deserve a special "thank you" for their patience and encouragement during the production of this book. My mother and father also deserve a special note of thanks for their generous support.

Ron Pitkin and Paul Franklin oversaw the book's early stages. Ed van der Maas and Stan Gundry of Zondervan Publishing House have been supportive and patient throughout the writing and typesetting process.

In alphabetical order, I would like to recognize the many scholars who patiently answered questions and provided material about the ways in which they have used computers to study machine-readable versions of biblical, classical, and related texts. Many thanks to: John R. Abercrombie (University of Pennsylvania), Francis I. Andersen (University of Queensland), Theodore F. Brunner (TLG Project, University of California, Irvine), Yaacov Choueka (Bar-Ilan University), Edward B. James (Imperial College, London), A. Dean Forbes (Hewlett-Packard Laboratories, Palo Alto), Timothy Friberg (formerly at the University of Minnesota), Jeffrey William Gillette (Duke University), J. Alan Groves (Westminster Theological Seminary), Robert A. Kraft (University of Pennsylvania), Paul A. Miller (Trinity Evangelical Divinity School), Peter M. K. Morris (University of Wales), Andrew Q. Morton (Fife, Scotland), David W. Packard (IBYCUS Systems), H. Van Dyke Parunak (formerly at the University of Michigan), Fr. R.-Ferdinand Poswick (Centre : Informatique et Bible—Maredsous), Yehuda T. Radday (Israel Institute of Technology), Eep Talstra (Vrije Universiteit Amsterdam), Emmanuel Tov (the Hebrew University, Jerusalem), and Gérard E. Weil (Université Jean Moulin—Lyon III).

Many friends graciously read some or all of the manuscript, caught a number of errors, and made valuable suggestions that helped to improve this book. Special thanks to John D. Hughes, James V. Mannoia, Jr., H. Van Dyke Parunak, Jeffrey William Gillette, Robert A. Kraft, Robin C. Cover, and to my wife, who served as copy editor, proofreader, and indexer.

Evelyn Barnes and Bill Spitzak provided technical assistance that enabled me to typeset this manuscript with FinalWord II™ on a Compugraphic® MCS™ 8000.

John J. Hughes
October 1987

Units of Measure

General

b	Bit, one binary digit
B	Byte, eight bits
K	Kilo, thousand, 1,000 or 1,024 (2^{10}); the latter is a measure of a computer's storage capacity.
M	Mega, million, 1,000,000 or 1,048,576 (2^{20}); the latter is a measure of a computer's storage capacity.
G	Giga, billion, 1,000,000,000 or 1,073,741,824 (2^{30}); the latter is a measure of a computer's storage capacity.
T	Tera, trillion, 1,000,000,000,000 or 1,099,511,627,776 (2^{40}); the latter is a measure of a computer's storage capacity.

Time

ms	Millisecond (.001, or 10^{-3} sec, a thousandth of a second)
μs, μsec	Microsecond (.000001, or 10^{-6} sec, millionth of a second)
ns	Nanosecond (.000000001, or 10^{-9} sec, a billionth of a second)
ps	Picosecond (.000000000001, or 10^{-12} sec, a trillionth of a second)

Speed

GFLOPS	Gigaflops, billion floating-point operations per second
MFLOPS	Megaflops, million floating-point operations per second
MIPS	Million instructions processed per second
MOPS	Million arithmetic/logical operations per second

Electricity

Hz	Hertz (cycles/sec)
KHz	Kilohertz (10^3, or 1,000 cycles/sec)
MHz	Megahertz (10^6, or 1,000,000 cycles/sec)

Units of Measure

Storage

Kb	Kilobit (10^3, or 1,000 bits)
Mb	Megabit (10^6, or 1,000,000 bits)
Gb	Gigabit (10^9, or 1,000,000,000 bits)
Tb	Terabit (10^{12}, or 1,000,000,000 bits)
KB	Kilobyte (10^3, or 1,000 bytes)
MB	Megabyte (10^6, or 1,000,000 bytes)
GB	Gigabyte (10^9, or 1,000,000,000 bytes)
TB	Terabyte (10^{12}, or 1,000,000,000,000 bytes)

Input/Output

bps	Bits per second
cps	Characters per second
Mb/sec	Megabits per second

Miscellaneous

μ	Micron (10^{-6}, or .000001 meter)
tpi	Tracks per inch

Academic Abbreviations and Acronyms

AAR	American Academy of Religion
ACH	Association for Computers and the Humanities
ACP	Aramaic Computer Project
AEP	(IBM) Advanced Education Project
AIBI	Association International Bible et Informatique
AJLC	*American Journal of Computational Linguistics*
ALLC	Association for Literary and Linguistic Computing
APA	American Philological Association
ARPANET	Advanced Research Project Agency Network
ASBL	Association Sans But Lucratif
ASV	American Standard Version
BDB	Brown, Driver, and Briggs, *Hebrew and English Lexicon of the Old Testament*
BDBHM	Base de Données Bibliques en Hebreu Massoretique
BH³	*Biblia Hebraica* (Kittle, 3d ed.)
BHS	*Biblia Hebraica Stuttgartensia*
BIBP	Bibliographical Information Bank in Patristics
BICS	*Bulletin of the Institute of Classical Studies*
BIOSCS	*Bulletin of the International Organization for Septuagint and Cognate Studies*
BITNET	Because It's Time Network
CADIR	Centre pour l'Analyse du Discours Religieux
CAL	Comprehensive Aramaic Lexicon
CAM	Computer-Aided Analysis of Mesopotamian Materials
CAMDAP	Computer and Medieval Data Processing
CARNES	*Computer Aided Research in Near Eastern Studies*
CASTLOTS	Computer-Assisted Statistical Linguistic Old Testament Studies
CATAB	Centre d'Analyse et de Traitement Automatique de la Bible et des Traditions Écrites
CATSS	Computer Assisted Tools for Septuagint Studies
CCAT	Center for Computer Analysis of Texts
CCCGI	Cornell Center for the Computerization of Greek Inscriptions
CCUA	Christian Computer Users Association
CDMB	Centre de Documentation sur les Manuscrits de la Bible
CHum	*Computers and the Humanities*
CIB	Centre : Informatique et Bible—Maredsous
CM	*Cybernetica Mesopotamica*
CNA	Neo-Assyrian Text Corpus Project
CNAS	*Corpus of Neo-Assyrian Studies*
CNRS	Centre Nationale de la Recherche Scientifique
COLOE	Computerization of Language Oriented Enterprises
CRAL	Centre de Recherche et d'Applications Linguistiques
CSHVB	*Computer Studies in the Humanities and Verbal Behavior*
CSNET	Computer Science Research Networks
CSRB	*Council on the Study of Religion Bulletin*

CTJ	*Calvin Theological Journal*
DBAGI	Data Bank for Ancient Greek Inscriptions
DDBDP	Duke Data Bank of Documentary Papyri
DHDB	Duke Humanities Data Base
DSS	Dead Sea Scrolls
DTS	Direct Translators Support
EA	Expositor's Assistant
EARN	European Academic Research Network
EBAF	Ecole Biblique et Archeologique
ECSE	*Encyclopedia of Computer Science and Engineering*
ETP	Exegetical Toolkit Project
ExpT	*Expository Times*
GJD	Global Jewish Databasae
GJD/RP	Global Jewish Database/Responsa Project
GNB	Good News Bible
GNT	Greek New Testament
GRAMCORD	Grammatical Concordance
HCCP	Harvard Classics Computer Project
HCLB	Hebrew Computational Linguistics Bulletin
HDHL	*Historical Dictionary of the Hebrew Language*
HDP	Historical Dictionary Project
IAC	Institute for Antiquity and Christianity
IAS	Institute for Advanced Study
IASEP	Institute for Advanced Study Epigraphic Project
IBR	Institute for Biblical Research
IDB	*The Interpreter's Dictionary of the Bible*
IG	*Inscriptiones Graecae*
IHRT	Institut de Recherche et d'Histoire des Textes
IIMAS	International Institute for Mesopotamian Area Studies
IL	Israel Network
IOSCS	International Organization for Septuagint and Cognate Studies
IOSOT	International Organization for the Study of the Old Testament
IPM	Information Processing and Management
IRCOL	Institution for Information Retrieval and Computational Linguistics
IRHT	Institut de Recherche et d'Histoire des Textes
IRIS	Institute for Research in Information and Scholarship
JANET	Joint Academic Network
JBL	*Journal of Biblical Literature*
JCBI	*Journal of Computer Based Instruction*
JCS	*Journal of Cuneiform Studies*
JLS	Jewish Law Service
JNSL	*Journal of Northwest Semitic Languages*
JRSS	*Journal of the Royal Statistical Society*
JSS	*Journal of Semitic Studies*
JTS	*Journal of Theological Studies*
KJV	King James Version
LIBRI	Literary Information Bases for Research and Instruction
LIMC	Lexicon Iconographicum Mythologiae Classicae
LXX	Septuagint
MARC	Machine-Readable Cataloging Record
MIT	Massachusetts Institution of Technology
MPCABS	Michigan Project for Computer-Assisted Biblical Studies
MS	Manuscript

MSS	Manuscripts
MT	Masoretic Text
NEH	The National Endowment for the Humanities of the United States of America
NIV	New International Version
NKJV	New King James Version
NT	New Testament
NTS	*New Testament Studies*
OCLC	Ohio College Library Center
OT	Old Testament
OTIK	Old Testament in the Computer
OTS	*Oudtestamentische Studien*
OUCS	Oxford University Computing Service
RIM	Royal Inscriptions of Mesopotamia Project
RIMRTH	Rutgers Inventory of Machine-Readable Texts in he Humanities
RLG	Research Libraries Group
RLIN	Research Libraries Information Network
RNS	Religious News Service
RP	Respona Project
RSV	Revised Standard Version
SAA	*State Archives of Assyria*
SAAB	*State Archives of Assyria Bulletin*
SBL	Society of Biblical Literature
SEA	Svensk Exegetisk Arsbok
SEG	*Supplementum Epigraphicum Graecum*
SIL	Summer Institute of Linguistics
SSMR	*Social Science Microcomputer Review*
SUNET	Swedish University Network
TAPA	*Transactions of the American Philological Society*
TEDS	Trinity Evangelical Divinity School
TLG	Thesaurus Linguae Graecae
TU	Texte und Untersuchungen
UA	Unité Associé
UBS	United Bible Societies
UCLA	University of California at Los Angeles
UCSD	University of California at San Diego
UUCP	Unix-to-Unix Communications Package—the Unix Network
VT	*Vetus Testamentum*
WCP	Westminster Computer Project
WUSTL	Washington University LAN
ZAW	*Zeitschrift für die alttestamentliche Wissenschaft*

Computer Abbreviations and Acronyms

AC	Alternating Current
ACIA	Asynchronous Communications Interface Adapter
ADB	Apple Desktop Bus
AEK	Apple Extended Keyboard
AFP	AppleTalk Filing Protocol
AI	Artificial Intelligence
ALGOL	Algorithmic Language
ALU	Arithmetic-Logic Unit
ANSI	American National Standards Institute
APA	All-Points-Addressable
API	Application Program Interface
APL	A Programming Language
ARLL	Advanced Run Length Limited
ARRAS	Archive Retrieval and Analysis System
ASC	Apple Sound Chip
ASCII	American Standard Code for Information Interchange
ASIC	Application-Specific Integrated Circuit
A/UX	Apple UNIX
BASIC	Beginners All-Purpose Symbolic Instruction Code
BBS	Bulletin Board Service
BCD	Binary Coded Decimal
BIOS	Basic Input-Output System
BISYNC	Binary Synchronous Communication
BITBLT	Bit-Block Transfer
BIU	Bus Instruction Unit, Bus Interface Unit
BIX	BYTE Information Exchange
BMP	Berkeley Morphology Package
BPI	Bits Per Inch
BSD	Berkeley Standard Distribution
CAD	Computer-Aided Design
CAI	Computer-Aided Instruction
CAL	Computer-Aided Learning
CALI	Computer-Assisted Language Instruction
CALIS	Computer-Assisted Language Instruction System
CALL	Computer-Assisted Language Learning
CAM	Computer-Aided Manufacturing
CAMMU	Cache/Memory Management Unit
CBBS	Computer Bulletin Board System
CCITT	Comité Consultatif International Téléphonique et Télegraphique
CD	Carrier Detect
CDC	Control Data Corporation
CD-ROM	Compact-Disk Read-Only Memory
CFM	Cubic Feet Per Minute
CGA	(IBM) Color/Graphics Adapter

CIS	CompuServe Information Service
CISC	Complex Instruction Set Computer
CLUT	Color Lookup Table
CMOS	Complementary Metal-Oxide Semiconductor
CNS	CompuServe Network Services
COBOL	Common Business Oriented Language
CPI	Characters Per Inch
CP/M	Control Program for Microprocessors (or Microcomputers)
CPS	Characters Per Second
CPU	Central Processing Unit
CR	Carriage Return
CRT	Cathode Ray Tube
CTS	Clear To Send
CU	Control Unit
D/A	Digital-to-Analog
DBMS	Database Management System
DC	Direct Current
DCA	Document Control Architecture
DCE	Data Communications Equipment
DDD	Direct Distance Dialing
DDI	Device Driver Interface
DDL	Document Description Language
DEC	Digital Equipment Corporation
DES	Data Encryption Standard
DIF	Data Interchange Format
DIP	Dual In-Line Pin (or Package)
DJN/R	Dow Jones News/Retrieval Service
DMA	Direct Memory Access
DOS	Disk Operating System
DPI	Dots Per Inch
DRAM	Dynamic Random Access Memory
DSR	Data Set Ready
DTE	Data Terminal Equipment
DTL	Diode-Transistor Logic
DTR	Data Terminal Ready
EBCDIC	Extended Binary-Coded Decimal Interchange Code
ECC	Error Correction Coding
EGA	(IBM) Enhanced Graphics Adapter
E-Mail	Electronic Mail
EMI	Electromagnetic Interference
EMM	Expanded Memory Manager
EMS	Expanded Memory Specifications
EOI	End of Interrupt
EOL	End of Line
EPLD	Erasable Programmable Logic Device
EPROM	Erasable Programmable Read-Only Memory
ERLL	Enhanced Run Length Limited
ESDI	Enhanced Small Device Interface
EU	Execution Unit
FAPI	Family Application Program Interface
FAT	File Allocation Table
FET	Field-Effect Transistor
FF	Flip-Flop
FIFO	First-In-First-Out

FORTRAN	Formula Translator
FPU	Floating-Point Unit
GEM	Graphics Environment Manager
GDT	Global Descriptor Table
GIGO	Garbage-In-Garbage-Out
GMEC	Graphics Memory Expansion Card
GND	Ground
GPIB	General-Purpose Interface Bus
HFS	Hierarchical File System
HGC	Hercules Graphics Card
HGC+	Hercules Graphics Card Plus
HMMU	H-Memory Management Unit
HP	Hewlett-Packard
IBM	International Business Machines
IC	Integrated Circuit
ICL	International Computers Ltd.
ICP	Intelligent Communications Processor
IEEE	Institute of Electrical and Electronic Engineers
I/O	Input/Output
IOPL	I/O Privilege Levels
IP	Information Provider
IPC	Inter-Process Communication
IPM	Inches Per Minute
IRS	(*PC Magazine*'s) Interactive Reader Service
ISC	Ibycus Scholarly Computer
ISO	International Standards Organization
IWM	Integrated Woz Machine
KBD	Keyboard
KDEM	Kurzweil Data Entry Machine
KIS	Kanji Interface System (aka KanjiTalk)
KMP	Knuth-Morris-Pratt
KWIC	Keyword-In-Context
KWOC	Keyword-Out-Of-Context
LAN	Local Area Network
LDT	Local Descriptor Table
LED	Light-Emitting Diode
LIFO	Last-In-First-Out
LIM	Lotus-Intel-Microsoft
LPM	Lines Per Minute
LSB	Least Significant Bit (or Byte)
LSI	Large-Scale Integration
MAP	Manufacturing Automation Protocol
MAR	Memory Address Register
MCA	Micro Channel Architecture
MCGA	Multicolor Graphics Array
MDA	IBM Monochrome Display Adapter
MFM	Modified Frequency Modulation
MicroCALIS	Microcomputer Computer-Assisted Language Instruction System
MIDI	Musical Instrument Digital Interface
MIMD	Multiple-Instruction Stream, Multiple-Data Stream
MISD	Multiple-Instruction Stream, Single-Data Stream
MITS	Micro Instrumentation and Telemetry Systems
MMA	Massed-Microprocessor Approach

MMD	Memory-Mapped Display
MMT	Massed-Microprocessor Technology
MMU	Memory Management Unit
MODEM	Modulator-Demodulator
MOS	Metal-Oxide Semiconductor
MOSFET	Metal-Oxide Semiconductor Field Effect Transistor
MOU	Mouse
MPU	Microprocessing Unit
MQ	Multiplier-Quotient
MQR	Multiplier-Quotient Register
MRT	Machine-Readable Text
MSB	Most Significant Bit (or Byte)
MS-DOS	Microsoft Disk Operating System
MSI	Medium-Scale Integration
MSS	Mass Storage System
MTBF	Mean Time Between Failures
NAND	Not and
NASA	National Aeronautic and Space Administration
NEC	Nippon Electric Company
NLP	Nonlinear Programming
NMI	Non-Maskable Interrupt
NMOS	Negative Metal-Oxide Semiconductor
NMRQ*	Non-Master Request
NOR	Not or
NTSC	National Television Standard Committee
OCP	Oxford Concordance Program
OCR	Optical Character Reader (or Recognition)
OEM	Original Equipment Manufacturer
OROM	Optical, Read-Only Memory
OS	Operating System
PACE	Processing and Control Element
PAD	Packet Assembler/Disassembler
PAL	Programmable Array Logic
PARC	Palo Alto Research Center (Xerox)
PCL	Printer Command Language
PDL	Page Description Language
PDN	Public Data Network
PDP	Programmed Data Processor
PGA	IBM Professional Graphics Adapter
PIC	Programmable Interrupt Controller
PIO	Parallel Input/Output
PIP	Page Image Processor
PLA	Programmed Logic Array
PLATO	Programmed Logic for Automatic Teaching Operations
PMMU	Paged Memory Management Unit
PMOS	Positive Metal-Oxide Semiconductor
POS	Programmable Option Select
PROM	Programmable Read-Only Memory
PSE	Packet Switching Exchange
PSS	Packet Switching Service
PTT	Postal Telephone & Telegraph
RAM	Random Access Memory
RC	Resin Coated
RCA	Radio Corporation of America

RCPM	Remote CP/M System
RD	Receive Data
RFI	Radio Frequency Interference
RGB	Red-Green-Blue
RIP	Raster Image Processor
RIS	Roman Interface System
RISC	Reduced Instruction Set Computer
RLL	Run Length Limited
ROM	Read-Only Memory
RSCS	Remote Spooling Communications Subsystem
RTS	Request To Send
R/W	Read/Write
SAA	Systems Application Architecture
SAM	Sequential Access Method
SANE	Standard Apple Numerics Environment
SCC	Serial Communications Controller
SCSI	Small Computer System Interface
SD	Send Data
SDI	Selective Dissemination of Information
SDLC	Synchronous Data Link Control
SGML	Standard Generalized Markup Language
SIG	Special Interest Group
SIMD	Single-Instruction Stream, Multiple-Data Stream
SIMM	Single In-line Memory Module
SIO	Serial Input/Output
SIP	Single In-Line Package
SISD	Single-Instruction Stream, Single-Data Stream
SLS	Strained-Layer Superlattice
SNA	Systems Network Architecture
SNOBOL	String-Oriented Symbolic Language
SPC	Scholarly Personal Computer
SRAM	Static Random Access Memory
SSI	Small-Scale Integration
STC	Source Telecomputing Corporation
SYSOP	System Operator
TDMS	Text Data Management System
TI	Texas Instruments
TOP	Technical Office Protocol
TSR	Terminate and Stay Resident
TTL	Transistor-Transistor Logic
TWX	Teletypewriter Exchange
UART	Universal Asynchronous Receiver/Transmitter
VAR	Value-Added Reseller
VAX	Virtual Address Extension
VDI	Virtual Device Interface
VGA	Video Graphics Array
VHF	Very High Frequency
VIA	Versatile Interface Adapter
VIO	Video
VLSI	Very Large-Scale Integration
VM	Virtual Memory
VRAM	Video Random Access Memory
VSAM	Virtual Storage Access Method
VTOC	Volume Table of Contents

Computer Abbreviations and Acronyms

WAN	Wide Area Network
WATS	Wide-Area Telecommunications Service
WFF	Well-formed Formula
WORM	Write-Once, Read-Many
WYSIWYG	What You See Is What You Get
XOR	Exclusive-Or

Preface

Just as the steam engine multiplied man's muscle and provided the power that made yesterday's Industrial Revolution possible, so the computer has multiplied man's mind and provided the power for today's Technological Revolution. And just as industry of a few centuries ago raced to mechanize itself by using the power steam provided, so industry today is racing to computerize itself by using the power of the integrated circuit.

The power and speed of the integrated circuit and the microprocessor are not restricted to industry; they have become part of the warp and woof of everyday life. Microprocessors control everything from washing machines to kidney dialysis machines, from billion-dollar space shuttles to five-dollar digital watches. Tiny integrated circuits that can fit on the surface area of a pencil eraser routinely perform a broad spectrum of functions that formerly required rooms full of vacuum tubes or that could not be done at all.

Bit by bit (so to speak), computers are becoming part of the warp and woof of biblical, classical, and other humanistic studies. Because of their power, speed, and ability to function as general-purpose machines, computers are causing a revolution in the way that languages and literary documents are studied. Scholars now are able to study machine-readable versions of a broad range of texts in many languages. Sophisticated programs allow texts to be searched, concorded, and analyzed in new and previously undreamed of ways. Students and scholars may study the morphology, lexicography, syntax, style, structure, and semantic features of texts faster and with more flexibility than has ever before been possible. Programs that concord *grammatical constructions* are beginning to revolutionize the writing of grammars. Sophisticated word processing programs can display multiple character sets on-screen, and flexible dot-matrix and laser printers can print nonroman characters in various fonts with near-typeset quality. Increasingly, students from the high-school to the graduate-school level are studying ancient and modern languages with the assistance of computers.

Bits, Bytes, & Biblical Studies is a review-oriented reference book and resource guide that focuses on the use of computers in biblical and classical studies. Its carefully organized information about products, projects, and resources for text-oriented computing should prove helpful for anyone using computers for word processing, literary analysis, computer-assisted language learning, or related tasks. Extensive bibliographies provide additional information. This book includes moderately technical, detailed product reviews.

Although every effort has been made to ascertain the accuracy of each fact, such things as addresses, phone numbers, prices, program specifications, and so forth are subject to change. And although every effort has been made to be as encyclopedic as is reasonable and possible, omissions are inevitable. Readers are therefore encouraged to send corrections and additions to the author so that subsequent editions of *Bits, Bytes, & Biblical Studies* may be as correct and complete as possible.[1]

Information about the **Bits & Bytes Review**™, a newsletter published by the author, may be found at the end of this book.

---

1. The author may be contacted % Zondervan Publishing House or electronically % CompuServe® (71056,1715), BITNET (XB.J24@Stanford), or MCI Mail (226-1461).

Chapter 1

The Pulse of the Machine

And now I see with eyes serene
The very pulse of the machine.
William Wordsworth[1]

1.1 Introduction

Late at night a classicist is tediously typing a scholarly paper that contains numerous citations from various Greek texts. It is nerve-wracking work. Should he leave blanks for the Greek text and write the citations in by hand when he is finished typing, or should he change typewriter elements as he proceeds and enter the Greek citations as they occur? Either way is more time consuming than typing in just one language. And he must remember to leave enough room on each page for footnotes. He begins to wonder why he hasn't purchased a microcomputer, printer, and multilingual word processing program that would enable him to display Greek and other non-roman characters on-screen, cut and paste text, automatically number and place footnotes, generate indices, and print the manuscript, foreign characters and all.

A linguist would like a list of every occurrence of every articular infinitive in ancient Greek literature and a list of every occurrence of *diathēkē* in that same literature. Without a computer it would be impossible to provide such information. With a computer the linguist can have his lists in a matter of minutes.

A student is laboring through entry after entry in a concordance to the Bible trying to locate every instance where *justice*, *mercy*, and *righteousness* occur in the same paragraph. Weary from looking up reference after reference and from trying to keep track of his progress with a pencil and paper, the student turns to his friend for help. The friend presses a few keys on his computer and in a matter of minutes has a complete set of all the occurrences of those terms, listed by book, chapter, and verse.

A scholar works for months, attempting to match a fragment of an ancient manuscript with the original text he suspects it may have come from. It's like trying to figure out where one piece of a hundred-thousand piece jigsaw puzzle that is now lost fits a reconstructed version of that puzzle. The scholar shows his fragment to a friend. In a matter of minutes, by using a computer to search an entire machine-readable ver-

---

1. William Wordsworth (1770–1850), "She Was a Phantom of Delight" (1804).

sion of the text the fragment may belong to, the friend is able to suggest several possible matches, one of which turns out to be correct.[2]

Those simple examples illustrate several of the many ways that computers can help us study and work with texts—modern as well as ancient—faster, more accurately, more easily, and more rewardingly. Before we begin to examine the vast array of products and resources that are available for helping us analyze and manipulate texts, we should learn something about the way computers work. Because this is a book about the ways *computers* are being used in classical and biblical studies, it behooves us to begin by acquiring a working knowledge of this machine. A basic understanding of computers will provide a background that will make subsequent discussions and evaluations of many programs more intelligible and meaningful, and it will enable us to read with increased understanding the literature about those programs.

When you type *Dear Claire* on a mechanical typewriter, there is little mystery. You can see how the keys on the keyboard are connected by levers to the keys that strike the paper. Typewriters are extremely helpful but not very interesting because they are fairly simple mechanical or electrical devices. When you type *Dear Claire* on a computer keyboard, there is a great deal of mystery—if you stop to ask yourself how your keystrokes resulted in those two words being displayed on the screen. Looking inside the computer will only add to the mystery! A computer is not a mechanical device, and a visual inspection of its components does not reveal how the computer works.

If we are to see "the very pulse of the machine," we must recognize that computers are *logic machines that are powered by electricity*. To understand how computers work, we must understand something about logic, mathematics, and electricity. You do not have to be a mechanic to drive your car, and you do not have to be an electrical engineer or a computer scientist to operate your computer. But just as an educated adult should have a fundamental understanding of how the internal combustion engine works, so we should acquire a basic grasp of how computers operate, and that is what we will do in this chapter. We will find out how *Dear Claire* got on the screen, and in doing so we will see something of "the very pulse of the machine!"

Arthur C. Clarke once wrote, "Any sufficiently advanced technology is indistinguishable from magic." After reading this chapter, however, computers should seem far less mysterious or magical and a great deal more logical. In fact, if we took the time, we would see that computers are completely logical, though very complex, machines.

1.2 A Matter of Words

There are two types of computers, analog and digital. An analog computer is any device that measures continuous variations of one quantity in terms of the continuous physical variations of another quantity. A glass thermometer is an analog computer because it measures the continuous variations in temperature in terms of the continuous variations in the length of the liquid in a tube. An "old-fashioned" clock is an analog computer because it measures the continuous progression of time in terms of the continuous progression of the hands on the face of the clock. And a slide rule is yet another example of an analog computing device. In an analog computer, then, one value is analogous to another value, and the latter is measured by the former as a series of continuous physical variations. Thus an analog computer performs computations by manipulating continuous physical variables that are analogs of the quantities

---

2. See Levenson, "Crunching," 81.

being subjected to computation.[3] An analog computer does not calculate numbers or by means of numbers, though it may represent its result numerically as a mark on a number line or graph. Analog computers are usually special-purpose machines.[4]

Broadly speaking, a digital computer is any device that performs calculations on numbers by means of numbers or by using discrete, not continuous, values. It is a device that computes with digits (hence *digital* computer),[5] not with pieces of wood, hands on a dial, or mercury in a tube; and it represents its results digitally, usually as numbers. In that sense, then, mechanical and electronic calculators are *types* of digital computers, and the abacus is the world's oldest digital computing device. It is more correct, however, to distinguish calculators from computers. Calculators and digital computers are similar because they both have memories, and they both operate digitally. They are different because only digital computers operate with programs that are stored in memory, and only computers are general-purpose machines. Because digital computers store the program and the data the program is to operate on together in memory, programs in a digital computer are able to branch from one instruction to another, depending on the result of a prior operation—something ordinary calculators are not able to do.[6] Because they are general-purpose machines, computers are able to perform all the arithmetic functions of calculators, as well as to run all the other types of programs we write for them.

Digital computers (hereafter simply "computers") are usually divided into three classes—mainframe, minicomputer, and microcomputer—based on several factors, including the physical size of the system, word length, CPU speed, addressable memory, and so forth.[7] As microcomputers become more and more powerful, the distinctions between them and minicomputers begin to blur.

1.3 A Machine Powered by Electricity

Before discussing the fundamental physical components of a computer and explaining how they relate to one another in a system, we should acquire a rudimentary knowledge of how computers use electricity to perform arithmetical and logical operations on data. I have said that a computer is "a logic machine that is powered by electricity." By "powered by electricity" I do not mean that computers are powered by electricity in the same mundane sense that an electric typewriter or clock is powered by electricity. In a computer electricity does more than provide the power to make mechanical parts like the disk drives turn. In a computer electrical states and patterns actually *are* the "parts." They represent all data—all the instructions and all the information the instructions are to operate on—and electricity is the means the computer uses to perform the logical and arithmetic operations called for by these instructions and made possible by the computer's architecture. In place of the hundreds of gears, wheels, and rods of early electro-mechanical computers, modern computers use electricity racing through logic circuits inside of tiny silicon chips.

To understand "powered by electricity," we must understand what a computer truly is. Strictly speaking, a computer is not a grey metal box with disk drives, a keyboard, and a screen. It is not something mechanical but something electrical and logical. Technically speaking, the computer consists of four basic components that we will shortly discuss: (1) an arithmetic-logic unit, (2) a control unit, (3) a memory, and

---

3. *Dictionary of Computing*, 12.

4. See Goldstine, *Computer*, 39–59, and ECSE, 63–85, for brief histories of analog computing devices.

5. *Digital*, of course, originally referred to fingers and toes. The decimal number system arose from using fingers for counting.

6. The programs for programmable calculators, such as the TI-59, are stored on plug-in, interchangeable, solid-state, preprogrammed software modules or on magnetic strips.

7. We will discuss these technical terms later in this chapter.

3

(4) registers, to which we need to add (5) buses, and (6) ports so that the various parts of the computer can communicate with one another and with input-output devices. None of those basic components is mechanical; none of them moves. The only "things" that move in the computer (in the narrow sense of *computer*) are electrons, because all processes and computations in the computer—from representing symbols or numbers to processing words to calculating spreadsheets to displaying graphics—are electrical. All letters, numbers, and commands—every bit of data stored in the computer's memory—are really just distinct strings of on-and-off electrical states,[8] and all the computer's arithmetic and logical operations are performed by electricity racing through the machine's logic circuits.

In order for all alphanumeric symbols[9] to be represented by electrical states that are subject to logical and arithmetic operations, all letters, numbers, symbols, and instructions must be translated into a common form that is amenable to *electrical representation* and that is suited to *arithmetic and logical operations*. The simplest and most efficient such common form is the binary number system. There are two reasons for that. First, in the binary, or base-2, number system there are only two numerical values, 0 and 1. Combinations of 0s and 1s can be made to represent *any* alphanumeric symbol, just as combinations of dots and dashes in the Morse Code can represent any letter or number.[10] Second, because the binary system uses only two symbols, the computer can represent these two symbols as one of two electrical states: on or off, or (to put it more precisely) as high or low voltage levels. Therefore the binary number system allows us to use electricity to represent any letter, number, symbol, or instruction as a combination of on-and-off electrical states that are stored in the computer's memory. For example, here are some ASCII[11] values, expressed in their full binary form, for a letter, number, and symbol: A is 01000001, 7 is 00110111, $ is 00100100, and the binary value of the op-code for the ADD instruction in IBM 8086/8088 Assembler is 00000001 (see below). The ASCII value of *Dear Claire*, expressed in its full binary form, would be: 01000100 (D), 01100101 (e), 01100001 (a), 01110010 (r), 00100000 (space), 01000011 (C), 01101100 (l), 01100001 (a), 01101001 (i), 01110010 (r), 01100101 (e), but those binary numbers could also stand for the following decimal numbers: 68, 101, 97, 114, 32, 67, 108, 97, 105, 114, and 101. Each program determines what all the combinations of binary numbers in its code and data sections mean, that is, whether 01000100 means *D* or 68.[12] In a computer, then, electrical states represent all data—the commands and the information the commands are to operate on. In a moment we will see why the binary system is well-suited for arithmetic and logical operations.

In principle, using electrical states in a binary fashion to represent all alphanumeric symbols is no different from sending *Dear Claire* in the Morse Code and having the results displayed visibly as a series of lit and unlit light bulbs. Imagine a long row of light bulbs. Every time a dot is transmitted, a bulb turns on. Every time a dash is transmitted, a bulb remains off. By reading the pattern of lit and unlit bulbs, we could translate the message that had been sent. That rough analogy illustrates how a computer's memory can meaningfully store and "understand" *everything* as strings of on-and-off electrical states.

---

8. More technically, these are high and low electrical states. See below.

9. E.g., *D, a, 1, 7, ?, ;, #,* etc.

10. Technically speaking, the Morse Code is not a *binary* system because it uses spaces to separate the dots and dashes of one letter from those of another letter.

11. *ASCII* stands for American Standard Code for Information Interchange.

12. See Osborne and Bunnell, *Introduction*, 123–26.

1.4 A Logic Machine

By "logic machine" I do not merely mean that computers are logical in design or function in the same sense that we might say that a typewriter or a telephone was logically thought out and so operates in a logical manner. That use of *logical* means something like "makes sense" or "is designed in a rational way." Computers are certainly logical in that sense of the term, but I am using *logic* more strictly to refer to actual logical operations (which we will discuss below) such as "If 0 and 0, then 0" or "if 1 and 1, then 1" or "if 1 or 0, then 1." The computer is a logic machine in the sense that *every* instruction it carries out is performed as a logical operation by means of a strictly defined set of logic circuits that are built into its processor. A computer can do *nothing* unless its task is explicitly defined not only in a logical fashion but in a way that turns every step of the task into a logical operation that the machine can perform by using its logic circuits. Computers do everything "by the book." They never operate intuitively. They do not know how to take shortcuts. They are not creative. You cannot delegate a task to them and expect them to figure out how to do it, unless that ability has been designed into the *program* the computer is running. Computers are tireless, perfectly obedient, incredibly fast, and never bored, but they are stupid. They cannot even tell you the time of day unless you have given them a program that instructs them in a step-by-step way how to do that. Computers have prodigious memories and powerful brains, but they have no minds.

A computer's ability to carry out programs by means of logical operations is an ability that is physically built into it. This logical ability is a fundamental aspect of the architecture of the computer's processor; it is an ability that is designed into the electrical circuits of that chip. Therefore those electrical circuits are also properly called "logic circuits." Thousands of such electrical circuits, made of transistors etched in silicon, combine two or more of several fundamental types of "logic gates" to form logic circuits that give the computer the ability to perform a wide variety of logical operations.[13] The complete set of logical operations the processor can perform is called its "instruction set." I will discuss logic gates, logic circuits, and instruction sets below.

Computers, then, use electricity to represent and to manipulate binary symbols by means of logical operations. The particular type of logic that computers use is known as "Boolean logic," or "Boolean algebra."[14] It is named after George Boole (1815–1864), a self-educated intellectual giant and English mathematician. Boole was the first person to reduce logic, or the laws of thought, to a rigorous set of propositions that could be expressed symbolically in the form of a calculus, or algebra. Along with Leibniz, Boole is the founder of modern symbolic logic.[15]

---

13. The Intel 8088, the microprocessor used in the IBM PC and in many other microcomputers, contains about 29,000 NMOS transistors that make up about 9,000 logic gates. All of that is contained on a sliver of silicon about a quarter of an inch square. The 8088 is housed in a 40-pin package that measures 2 inches × 9/16 inches × 1/8 inches deep. The amount of time it takes a logic gate to operate is called "propagation delay," and according to Intel literature (*Intel Product Guide* (1985), 32), the register-to-register add time, or propagation delay, for the 8088 is 0.38 millionths of a second per data word. That means that the 8088 can add two 8-bit numbers in 0.38 millionths of a second.

14. Because Boole developed an algebra of logic, *Boolean logic* and *Boolean algebra* may be used interchangeably. Boole's great achievement was to produce a mathematical, or algebraic, logic, i.e., to express logic in the form of mathematical, or algebraical, statements.

15. Goldstine (*Computer*, 35–38, 60–64) has an illuminating discussion of Boole and his contribution to logic, mathematics, and computers, though Bell's presentation is more comprehensive (*Men*, 433–47). Technically speaking, it is more accurate to describe Boole's achievement as a calculus of classes in extension, i.e., a calculus of things and sets of things, than as a calculus of pure logic. For our purposes, however, such hairsplitting is not important.

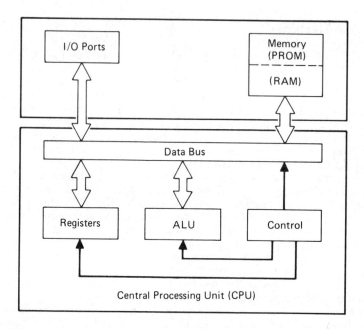

Figure 1.1: Diagrammatic representation of the central processing unit. (Reprinted by permission of Van Nostrand Reinhold Company. Taken from Anthony Ralston and Edwin D. Reilly, Jr., eds. *Encyclopedia of Computer Science and Engineering*, 2d ed., 1983, p. 971.)

If you took an introductory course in logic, you most likely learned to use Boolean "truth tables." A truth table requires that every statement be in a propositional form that is either true or false. A truth table, then, is a binary approach to problem solving, and as such it exemplifies the way electrical circuits can be designed to mimic the operations of Boolean logic. In fact, as we will see below, all the possible results of a given logic gate's operation on two operands can be expressed by using Boolean truth tables.[16]

To understand what Boole achieved and how his insights made computers possible, we need to refresh our understanding of algebra.[17] Algebra is an abstract system developed from arbitrary symbols that are combined according to operational signs whose use is specified by certain rules. Algebraic symbols do not represent numbers, and the operational signs used in algebra are not to be confused with arithmetical operational signs. An algebraic system is not concerned with numbers but with working out the results that follow from the logical use of its symbols, operational signs, and rules of application. Algebra, then, is very much concerned with logic, and so it is not surprising that Boole's first major publication was called *The Mathematical Analysis of Logic* and his second *An Investigation of the Laws of Thought on which are founded the Mathematical Theories of Logic and Probabilities*.

Boolean algebra consists of a well-defined system of symbols and the rules that specify how certain operators may be used to relate those symbols. The fundamental Boolean operators are AND, OR, and NOT. Operators operate on operands (the symbols). Operands can be (1) propositions, (2) sets, or (3) binary numbers. Sometimes those three fundamental categories of operands are "mapped" into one another

---

16. Cf. Sargent and Shoemaker, *IBM*, 183–87; Lawson, *Understanding*, 93–106; Osborne, *Introduction*, 2-4—2-12.

17. *Algebra* comes from the title of the book *Al-jabr wa'l muqabalah*, which was written in the ninth century by the famous and influential Arabic mathematician al-Khowarizmi (cf. Shurkin, *Engines*, 25).

through the correspondences TRUE = universal set = 1; FALSE = empty set = 0.[18] Propositional, set theory, and binary operands each have distinct symbols (see below), as do the operators AND, OR, and NOT when used propositionally, in set theory, and to perform binary arithmetic.

When the operands are propositions with truth values, the Boolean operators are truth-functional in nature. Propositional operands are represented by the truth-value symbols *T* (for "true") and *F* (for "false"). The Boolean operators AND, OR, and NOT are represented by the symbols ^ , v, and ~ respectively. By assigning each operand a value of *T* or *F*, and by defining the meaning of the operators ^ (AND), v (OR), and ~ (NOT), applying the operators to the operands determines the truth or falsity of the result of that application (see Table 1.1).

When the operands are sets, the Boolean operators are defined in terms of the three basic operations of set theory—intersection, union, and complement. Set theory operands are represented by various symbols that denote sets (e.g., *S* or *T*) and by other symbols that represent the elements in sets (e.g., *a*, *b*, *c*). The Boolean operators AND and OR are represented by the symbols *U* (for "union") and an inverted *U* (for "intersection"), and a bar over the symbol for a set means "negation" and represents the operator NOT. The union of two sets consists of those elements that are members of one or the other or both of the sets, that is, the combination of all the elements in both of the sets. The intersection of two sets consists of those elements that are members of both sets, that is, only those elements that are common to both sets. The complement of a set consists of those elements that do not constitute a subset of the set. For example, if *T* = {a,b,c,d,e} and if *S* = {a,b,c}, then *S* is a subset of *T* and the complement of *S* with respect to *T* is a set that consists of those elements in *T* that are not in *S*, namely the set {d,e}.[19]

When the operands are binary numbers, the Boolean operators AND, OR, and NOT are defined arithmetically as addition, multiplication, and negation.[20] Binary numbers are represented by 0s and 1s and the Boolean operators AND, OR, and NOT by the symbols "+," "•," and "−" respectively.

Boolean operators are binary and logical. An operator takes two inputs (the operands) and performs its specific logical operation on them. The result can then become an operand for another operation. Thus Boolean operators are like gates that direct operands down one path or another. Appropriately, then, because of the way they function, Boolean operators are known in the context of computer architecture as "logic gates." By using the three fundamental operators AND, OR, and NOT, a computer can perform four-function arithmetic and logical operations, such as comparing two letters, words, or numbers to see if they are the same. Because Boolean algebra is binary and its operations are all logical operations, it is easy to construct circuitry on computer chips to mimic the logical operations that Boolean gates perform,[21] as the following tables and discussion will illustrate.

In the examples in Table 1.1, *A* and *B* represent inputs (or operands), and *C* represents the output of the truth tables and logic gates. *AND*, *OR*, and *NOT* represent the three fundamental logical operators or types of logic gates; *XOR* (explained below) represents a variation of the *OR* gate. *NOR* and *NAND* represent two additional types of gates that are combinations of an AND gate or an OR gate followed by a NOT gate.

---

18. I own that insight to Dr. H. Van Dyke Parunak.

19. Goldstine (*Computer*, 63–64) gives a delightful illustration of how Boolean set theory may be used to analyze the Mosaic proposition "Clean beasts are those which divide the hoof and chew the cud" (cf. Lev. 11:3).

20. ECSE, 179.

21. In 1938, Claude E. Shannon, a student of Vannevar Bush's at MIT, wrote a masters thesis in which he showed that Boolean logic could be used in the design and analysis of electrical circuits. Shannon's insight helped to pave the way for using Boolean logic to design computer circuits and for designing computer circuits to mimic the operations of Boolean logic.

Logical Operator/Logic Gate	Truth Table Values/Signal Values		
	A	B	C
AND	0	0	0
	0	1	0
	1	0	0
	1	1	1
OR	0	0	0
	0	1	1
	1	0	1
	1	1	1
XOR	0	0	0
	0	1	1
	1	0	1
	1	1	0
NOT	0		1
	1		0
NOR	0	0	1
	0	1	0
	1	0	0
	1	1	0
NAND	0	0	1
	0	1	1
	1	0	1
	1	1	0

Table 1.1: Logical operators and their truth table values.

The value of 0 is "false," and the value of 1 is "true." I will define A to mean "The sun is shining" and B to mean "The birds are singing."

Look at the first row of the AND truth table. If "The sun is shining" is false and if "The birds are singing" is false, then "The sun is shining AND the birds are singing" is false. Look at the second row of the AND table. If "The sun is shining" is false and if "The birds are singing" is true, then "The sun is shining AND that the birds are singing" is false. Skip to the fourth row of the AND table. If "The sun is shining" is true and if "The birds are singing" is true, then and only then is "The sun is shining AND the birds are singing" true.

Look at the first row of the OR truth table. If "The sun is shining" is false and if "The birds are singing" is false, then and only then is "The sun is shining OR the birds are singing" false. Look at the second row of the OR table. If "The sun is shining" is false and if "The birds are singing" is true, then "The sun is shining OR the birds are singing" is true. Skip to the last row of the OR table. If "The sun is shining" is true and if "The birds are singing" is true, then "The sun is shining OR the birds are singing" is true.

Look at the fourth row of the XOR truth table. XOR stands for "exclusive or," whereas OR stands for "inclusive or." The difference between exclusive and inclusive "or" is simple: inclusive "or" gives a truth table value of true if *either or both* of the values of each of the two inputs is true. Exclusive "or" gives a truth table value of true only if *one but not both* of the values of each of the two inputs is true. Put another way, XOR means "one operand or the other but not both," and OR means "one operand or the other or both."[22] Thus, for example, the fourth line of the XOR table means that if "The sun is shining" is true and if "The birds are singing" is true, then "The sun is shining OR the birds are singing BUT NOT BOTH" is false.

Look at the NOT truth table. Unlike the other tables, the NOT table has a single input, and the logical operator (NOT) simply inverts the value of that input from true to false, from yes to no, from high to low, from 1 to 0, etc. A NOT gate in a computer is known as an "inverter" because it takes a *single* input and inverts it, that is, it changes a 0 to a 1, or vice versa. Look at the first column of the NOT truth table. If "The sun is shining" is false, then the operator NOT inverts the value of that statement, so that "The sun is shining" is true. The NOR and the NAND operators work in similar ways.[23]

AND yields a 1 if and only if both operands are 1, OR yields a 1 if and only if one or both operands are 1, XOR yields 1 if and only if the operands are different, and NOT inverts the value of its operand.

Of course, microcomputers do not operate with Boolean truth tables. Instead, as I noted, they use logic gates to mimic Boolean operators (as the examples in the truth table/signal table illustration indicate) and combinations of gates called "logic circuits" to perform arithmetical and other operations.

More specifically, here is how Boole constructed his algebraical logic. Boole defined logic as (1) an arbitrary system of *symbols*, or *signs* (e.g., x, y, z), that can represent things or sets of things,[24]—words, numbers, pictures, people, or whatever you wish. (2) The system consists of two *operations* that affect those signs: "+" and "•" ("=" is used to relate the results those operational signs produce), and those operations may result in other signs (for example, if x and y are signs, so are "$x + y$" and "$x \bullet y$"). (3) The behavior of the operators is governed by common algebraic rules such as "$x + y = y + x$" and "$x \bullet (y + z) = x \bullet y + x \bullet z$." In Boolean logic, the main exception to the rules of ordinary algebra is "$x^2 = x \bullet x = x$ for every x."[25] This seemingly strange rule, which is important in constructing a computer's logic circuits,[26] is really not difficult to understand if we keep in mind that Boolean logic deals with *things* or *sets of things* and not with numbers. For example, if x stands for the *set* of all golden retrievers, then we can see that "$x^2 = xx = x$" refers to the intersection[27] of the set of golden retrievers with itself, which is simply the set of golden retrievers—a delightful set to be sure!

---

22. See Sargent and Shoemaker, *IBM*, 80–82, for details.

23. See ibid., 183–87, and Lawson, *Understanding*, 93–106, for further schematics and explanations of the major types of logic gates and their truth tables; and see *ECSE*, 179–84, for a more extensive discussion of Boolean algebra.

24. I will use *set* and *class* synonymously.

25. See Goldstine, *Computer*, 60.

26. See ibid., 282–83.

27. The form of expression "xy," or "x • y," denotes the intersection of x and y, i.e., the class of members common to set x and set y.

Arithmetical Operator	Symbol		
	X	Y	Z
+	0	0	0
	0	1	1
	1	0	1
	1	1	0
●	0	0	0
	0	1	0
	1	0	0
	1	1	1

Table 1.2: Arithmetical operators and their binary values.

What Boole did next in the development of his system is what made it possible for computers to be designed so that binary arithmetic can be performed by using Boolean logic. Boole said that *any* sign, or symbol—any x or y or z—in his system has one and only one of two possible values: 0 or 1. Why did Boole assign the value 0 or 1 to every sign? Because 0 and 1 are the only values that satisfy Boole's special law of logic: "$x^2 = xx = x$." In Boolean logic, 0 and 1 have logical, not arithmetical, values; 1 represents the universal set, and 0 represents the null, or empty, set. Thus 0 and 1 are the two limits of class extension; they are the limits of the possible values of any symbol (i.e., operand). Thus in Boolean logic, "1y = y for every y" means that the set of all things (i.e., 1) contains *all* the members of *any* set. And in Boolean logic, "0y = 0 for every y" means that the set of no things (i.e., 0) does not contain any members of any set; it is an empty set. Boole expressed the complement of a set, or class, as "(1 − x)."[28] If x represents grizzly bears and 1 the universal set of all things, then "(1 − x)" is the compliment of x and represents the set of everything in the world that is not a grizzly bear. Goldstine shows that using the arithmetical operators "+" and "•" on binary numbers yields the same product as using the Boolean operators AND and OR on symbols (e.g., x, y, z), which means that "the arithmetical product [of binary arithmetic] is the same as the logical product [of Boolean algebra],"[29] as Table 1.2 illustrates.

In that table, "+" and "•" are *arithmetical* operators and mean "true sum" and "true product," the symbols X and Y represent numbers in the binary system, Z represents the result of the operations, and the values in the columns under X, Y and Z are binary ones.

The sum of binary 1 and binary 1 is binary 10. Thus the fourth row of the "+ table" should read 10. It reads 0 because there is an implied carry of the 1. Interestingly, applying the arithmetic operators "+" and "•" in the binary (base-2) number system results in a "+ table" whose values are identical to those of the XOR truth table and a "• table" whose values are identical to those of the AND truth table.

28. "$x = x^2$" is equivalent to "x(1 − x) = 0" and shows that "(1 − x)" means that a set, or class, and its complement have nothing in common.

29. Goldstine, *Computer*, 63. Goldstine (62–64) gives several interesting examples of the equivalence between the results of Boolean logic and those of binary arithmetic.

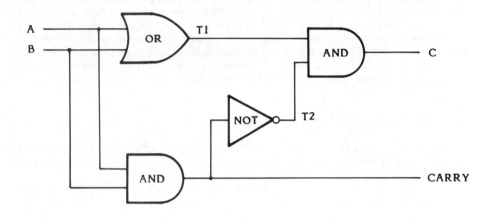

Figure 1.2: Diagrammatic representation of binary adder circuit. (Reprinted by permission of Computer Science Press, Incorporated. Taken from Harold W. Lawson, Jr., *Understanding Computer Systems*, 1982, p. 99.)

Figure 1.2 depicts the logical design of a binary adder circuit and illustrates how logic gates can be combined to form logic circuits to perform arithmetical operations, how Boolean logic can be used to perform binary arithmetic, how binary arithmetic can be performed as a series of *logical operations*, and how circuits in computer chips can be designed to carry out various types of logical operations, some of which are arithmetical. In Figure 1.2, A and B are the inputs, C the result, and T1 and T2 the temporary results. Each logic gate is labeled according to the operation it performs on the data.

Because computers use the binary system to represent all data, A and B can each have only one of two arithmetical values: 0 or 1. Thus there are only four possible combinations of values: (1) A = 0 and B = 0, (2) A = 0 and B = 1, (3) A = 1 and B = 0, and (4) A = 1 and B = 1. Let us trace the sets of values for combinations 1, 2, and 4, gate-by-gate, through this binary adder circuit to illustrate how a logic circuit can perform binary arithmetic. OR, AND, and NOT are *logical* operators, just as in the truth table example above. Take the first case. If A = 0 and B = 0, then A OR B = 0 (= T1). Here's how that works. A AND B = 0, NOT inverts that 0 to a 1 (= T2), and T1 (0) AND T2 (1) = 0 (= C). Consider the second case. If A = 0 and B = 1, then A OR B = 1 (= T1). Here's how that works. A AND B = 0, NOT inverts that 0 to a 1 (= T2), and T1 (1) AND T2 (1) = 1 (= C). Look at the fourth case. If A = 1 and B = 1, then A OR B = 1 (= T1). Here's how that works. A AND B = 1, NOT inverts that 1 to a 0 (= T2), and T1 (1) AND T2 (0) = 0. The operation of each gate was a *logical* operation, but the values of each input were *arithmetical*. That is why the results of the operations on the second and fourth sets of values are different from what those results would have been if a simple AND gate had been used to operate on those values. In the second set (A = 0 and B = 1), for example, a simple Boolean AND would yield 0, but the sum of 0 and 1 is 1, the product the adder circuit correctly gave. In the fourth set (A = 1 and B = 1), for example, a simple Boolean AND would have

11

yielded 1, but the sum of "1 + 1" in the binary system is 10, the answer the adder circuit correctly gave.[30]

All of that may sound like a lot of mathematical "mumbo jumbo" that has somehow gotten mixed up with thoughts of bears, birds, dogs, and sunny days, but Boole's ideas are among the most brilliant of the last few centuries, and they paved the way for modern computers. Because a computer is a logic machine that is powered by electricity, it is capable of doing anything that can be done by means of logical operations and doing it automatically. Therefore we may define a computer as an automatic, electronic, general-purpose, logic machine.

1.5 The Fundamental Components

We are now in a position to discuss the fundamental physical components of a computer and by doing so to understand better how computers use electricity to represent and manipulate binary symbols by means of logical operations.

Everything associated with the working of computers falls into one of three categories: hardware, software, and firmware. *Hardware* refers to the physical components from which the computer is constructed. It includes items such as disk drives, keyboards, screens, modems, and any other physical thing directly associated with the working of the computer.

If you took the cover off an IBM PC[31] and looked inside, you would see a bewildering assortment of things. You would see a large, square-shaped box that is the power supply and one or more square-shaped objects that house the disk drives. You would also see one or more rectangular printed circuit boards (also known as "cards") covered with small, black rectangular objects known as "chips." *Chip* is computer jargon for *integrated circuit*, or *semiconductor*. One board might be the disk controller board, another might be the monochrome display and printer adapter card, perhaps another would be a memory expansion board or an asynchronous communications card. All of those boards stand vertically and plug into expansion slots in a large, rectangular printed circuit board known as the "system board," or "mother board."[32] The ends of some of the cards plugged into the system board protrude out of the back of the computer chassis and have sockets in them where cables of various sorts may be attached. Those sockets are called "ports," and the cables that are plugged into them connect the boards to various input-output devices, such as the screen, keyboard, printer, and plotter.[33]

The system board has two basic types of chips plugged directly into it: logic chips and memory chips. Logic chips derive their name from the fact that they perform some logical operation or operations on data; memory chips store the data the logic chips operate on. There are many types of logic chips (see below) and two fundamental types of memory chips: read-write chips (also known as "random access memory"—RAM—chips) and read-only memory chips (ROM).[34] The largest logic

---

30. The adder circuit identified C as binary 0, and the CARRY branch of the circuit carried the binary 1.

31. In the remainder of this chapter, I will predominantly use the IBM PC (PC for short) as a point of reference when explaining how computers work. The PC is a well-known implementation of microcomputer architecture, though faster, more powerful, and more sophisticated microcomputers that use more advanced architectures are available.

32. I will use the term *system board*.

33. Additionally, some cards have ports that do not protrude from the back of the chassis but that allow cables to be run internally from the card to I/O devices that are housed within the chassis (e.g., a disk drive).

34. The data in RAM and in ROM chips can be accessed at random. RAM, however, is the conventional term for read-write memory chips.

chip is the microprocessor, the Intel 8088.[35] Next to that chip we might find its fraternal twin, the Intel 8087 math coprocessing chip. Another logic chip on the system board is the 8284A clock generator chip, which controls the speed at which data is transmitted throughout the computer system. Also plugged directly into the system board are the 8253 counter/timer circuit chip, the 8288 bus controller chip, the 8255A-5 timer chip, the 8237 direct memory access (DMA) controller, the 8255 parallel I/O chip, and the 8259A programmable interrupt controller chip. Other important logic chips in the machine include the NEC PD765 floppy disk controller chip and the 6845 CRT controller chip. Thus there are many "smart chips" in the computer. The system board also is home to five ROM chips and to varying numbers of RAM chips. All of the components mentioned in this and the preceding paragraph are part of the computer's hardware.

Software refers to the programs that the computer runs, and these are of two basic types: "system programs" and "application programs." System programs are also known as "control programs," or as "operating system programs." As the various names for this type of program suggest, the job of a system program is to operate the computer *system*. System programs help to relate application programs and input-output devices in an orderly fashion. The job of a system program, then, is an internal one; it is to maintain order within the machine. Operating systems actually consist of many separate modular programs that are designed to work together in a harmonious fashion to keep the computer system functioning smoothly. An operating system is designed around the specific parameters of a particular processor. The operating system for the Apple Macintosh, for example, will not work on IBM PCs because these two machines use different microprocessors that have different, incompatible architectures. I will discuss operating systems more thoroughly below.

Application programs,[36] as the name suggests, are programs designed to perform one of a number of different types of tasks that relate to the world outside of the computer. Word processing programs, data base management programs, and communication programs are all examples of different types of application programs.

"Soft" in *software* indicates that software is the opposite of *hardware*; *software* does not refer to something physical but to *the programs* that run the computer or that the computer runs. In the world of microcomputers, programs are usually distributed on floppy diskettes and sometimes on ROM chips, though software should not be confused with the medium on which it is distributed (i.e., the diskette or the ROM chip). Software refers to any program, and such a program may or may not exist on floppy disks or ROM chips. *Software*, then, is synonymous with *program*.

Firmware refers to software that resides in ROM chips (instead of on diskettes or elsewhere), to programs and subroutines that are fixed in the ROM's circuits.[37] ROM consists of a set of routines that the manufacturer has placed in the chips in such a way that the routines are nonvolatile (they maintain their integrity whether or not they receive any electricity), unerasable,[38] and available to the whole system at any time. ROM chips come with the computer as an integral part of it.[39] Programmable Read-Only Memory (PROM) and Erasable Programmable Read-Only Memory (EPROM)

---

35. The 8088 is a microprocessor, not a microcomputer. A microprocessor does not contain RAM or input-output (I/O) ports. Additional components, such as memory and ports, must be added to a microprocessor to make a microcomputer.

36. These are often referred to as "applications programs." I will use the singular *application*.

37. In the IBM PC, programs and subroutines that are stored in ROM chips are invoked through "interrupts," a concept we will discuss below.

38. Programs that are placed in random access memory (RAM), however, are volatile and erasable.

39. The IBM PC's ROM performs two major functions. It contains the BIOS (Basic Input-Output System), which is at the very heart of the operating system, and a complete version of interpreter BASIC, which BASIC programs must use to turn their source code statements into object code—concepts I will discuss below.

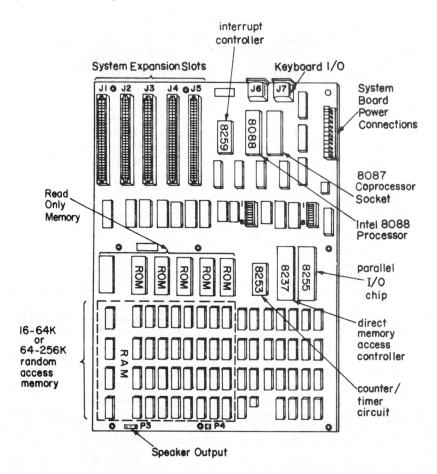

Figure 1.3: Layout of IBM PC system board. (Reprinted by permission of Addison-Wesley Publishing Company. Taken from Murray Sargent III and Richard L. Shoemaker, *The IBM Personal Computer from the Inside Out*, 1984, p. 7.)

chips are other examples of firmware.[40] To eliminate the need for power-hungry, bulky disk drives and to increase overall power and performance, the designers of many of the new "laptop," or "briefcase," computers have placed their computer's operating systems and several application programs in firmware. Because firmware is software *built into hardware*, programs and routines in firmware are nonvolatile, unerasable, and always available.

We have learned that a computer consists of four basic components: (1) an arithmetic-logic unit, (2) a control unit, (3) a memory, and (4) registers, to which we need to add (5) buses, and (6) ports so that the various parts of the computer can communicate with one another and with input-output devices. All six of those components are part of the machine's hardware, and to understand how a computer works, we will discuss each in turn. But first, here is a brief overview of a computer system.

---

40. EPROMS can be erased by exposing them to ultraviolet light of a certain wave length.

Broadly speaking,[41] a computer obtains data from an input device, performs different logical and arithmetical operations on that data, and sends the results to an output device. The various operations the computer performs are specified by instructions in the programs that have been loaded into the computer's memory. The basic operations required to run a program—fetching instructions from memory, decoding them to see what operations they call for, and executing them by notifying the appropriate devices within the computer of what they are to do—are controlled by a device called a "control unit." When an instruction is being executed, the control unit spends its time moving data between devices and performing operations on data in devices. One of the devices that the control unit controls is called the "arithmetic-logic unit." That device performs logical and arithmetical operations on data. The instructions and the data the instructions operate on[42] are loaded into the computer's memory—into its RAM chips. In an IBM PC, the computer's memory is divided into sequential locations, each of which has a unique address and each of which contains eight binary digits (1 byte) worth of information. Memory locations are grouped into larger categories known as "segments," each of which is used by a program in a distinct way. One segment is used to hold the data the program is going to operate on, another to hold the program's code (i.e., all the operations the program wants performed), and a special segment called the "stack" holds the intermediate results of operations. Special types of memory cells called "registers" (whose contents can be accessed faster than can the contents of regular memory cells) also are used to temporarily store the intermediate results of a program that is being run. A special type of register known as a "flag" provides feedback to the control unit by recording information about the results achieved by executing an instruction. Flags also help to govern the operation of the control unit. All of the information that is passed from one part of the computer to another goes through electronic "doorways" known as "ports" and travels over communication pathways known as "buses."

Morse provides the following simplified analysis of the execution of an AND instruction to illustrate how some of the components we just mentioned relate to one another.

> The control unit sends a control signal to the program area requesting the next instruction. The program area responds by sending an instruction to the control unit. The control unit then decodes the instruction and discovers it's an "add" instruction. It then sends out control signals to (1) the data area telling it to move two values to the arithmetic device, (2) the arithmetic device telling it to add the two values it received, and (3) the data area telling it to receive the result of the addition.[43]

The schematic representation of a computer's basic components in Figure 1.4 will provide further help in understanding the next several subsections.

1.5.1 The Arithmetic-Logic Unit

Because computers process binary symbols by means of logical and arithmetic operations, there must be a component in the computer to perform those operations. Because binary arithmetic can be performed as a series of logical operations, the arith-

---

41. In this paragraph, I am greatly indebted to Morse's excellent description on pages 1–3 of his book *The 8086/8088 Primer*. For the technically minded, this book is one of the clearest, easiest-to-understand, and complete explanations of how the 8086 and 8088 microprocessors work.

42. To a computer, instructions are just another type of data.

43. Morse, *Primer*, 2.

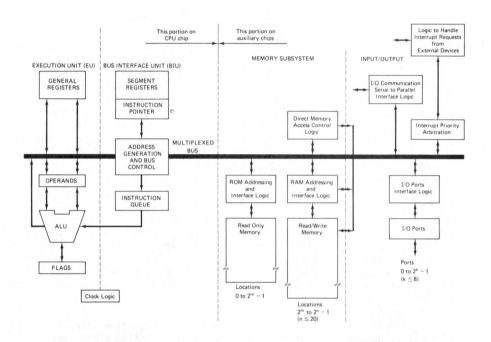

Figure 1.4: Diagrammatic representation of Intel 8086/8088 microcomputer organization. (Reprinted by permission of Intel Corporation. Copyright 1980.)

metic unit and the logical unit may be combined into one, the arithmetic-logic unit (ALU). The ALU is like a machine within a machine. It adds, subtracts, divides, multiplies, compares symbols, and performs other logical operations. The ALU is part of the microprocessor chip, which also contains the control unit (CU), the registers, and the internal data bus, all of which we will discuss below. The ALU, the CU, the registers, and the internal data bus may be referred to collectively as the "central processing unit" (CPU), or (if you wish to be technical) in a microcomputer those components are sometimes called the "microprocessing unit" (MPU) or simply "microprocessor." The idea behind "central" in *CPU* is to distinguish the main processor that is responsible for controlling and coordinating the work of the entire computer system from the auxiliary processors and peripheral devices that assist it in its task.

1.5.2 The Control Unit

Just as we must command the computer what to do, the ALU and other components of the computer system must be told what to do. Just as a busy airport needs an air-traffic controller to direct the flow of airplanes and to sequence their takeoffs and landings, so the processor needs a device that directs the flow of electrical "traffic" entering and leaving it and that sequences its operations and those of the other parts of the machine. Such a device is called the "control unit" (CU), or "execution unit" (EU),[44] and it is part of the microprocessor chip. The CU receives all the instructions issued to the computer (e.g., by its operator, by a device, or by a program), interprets them, and issues the proper commands to the appropriate circuits to carry out the instructions. The CU, then, fetches, decodes, and oversees the execution of all instructions, thereby directing and sequencing all the computer's operations. Physically, the CU consists of registers, counters, and other components that are required to control the movement of information between memory, the ALU, and other parts of the computer. Like an electrical taskmaster who unerringly supervises and instructs an army of perfectly obedient silicon slaves to do exactly what you and your programs command, the CU coordinates, manages, and oversees the working of the computer's hardware and software, insures that all instructions are properly obeyed, and makes the whole system function in a smooth and orderly fashion.

Because the CU is an electrical device, it only responds to and understands the binary, on-off "language of electricity," which is called "machine code." Machine code is the strings of 1s and 0s that the machine actually reads, and these 1s and 0s are physically represented in the computer by high and low voltage states. The CU is designed in such a way that unique, preassigned codes instruct it to perform certain operations. These preassigned codes are called "operation codes, "op-codes," or simply "codes," and they each instruct the computer to perform a distinct operation.[45] Op-codes are part of a program's instructions, which are stored in memory. An instruction for the IBM's microprocessor might contain the op-code 00000001, which would inform the CU to request the ALU to add two numbers together. The instruction that contained the op-code would also specify the addresses (the locations in memory) of the two numbers (the data, or operands)[46] that are to be added. Each instruction the computer receives, then, contains an op-code and specifies (directly or indirectly) the addresses of the operands. In addition to providing the source addresses of the operands, an instruction may also provide the destination address that specifies where the result of the operation is to be stored. Assembly language instructions[47] are written in the form "action, destination, source," so that the statement "MOV AL,8" instructs the CU to MOVe (the operation part of the instruction) the 8 into the AL register.[48]

Earlier, I referred to *instruction set*, which I defined as the complete set of logical operations the processor can perform. An instruction set usually includes the following five classes of operators: (1) logical, (2) arithmetic, (3) sequence control, (4) special control, and (5) input/output (I/O). Each of those classes contains a number of distinct instructions, or op-codes, that perform *operations* on the data, such as ADDing,

---

44. I will use the more popular term *control unit*.
45. I will use *op-code*.
46. An operand may be the data in memory that is to be operated on, the data that results from an operation, or the contents of a memory unit called a "register" (see below).
47. Assembly language, or Assembler, is a type of programming language that will be discussed below.
48. Cf. Sargent and Shoemaker, *IBM*, 23.

LOADing, and STORing—thus the "op" in *op-code*. The ways an instruction set can specify the location of an operand in memory are referred to as "addressing modes" (see below). An instruction set, then, is the list of all possible op-codes the processor can respond to and the addressing modes pertinent to each.

The processor in the IBM PC is an Intel 8088, and its instruction set consists of approximately 70 distinct instructions and twenty-four addressing modes. The instructions in the 8088's instruction set can be grouped into eight categories:[49] (1) data-transfer instructions, (2) arithmetic instructions, (3) logical instructions, (4) string instructions, (5) transfer-control instructions, (6) interrupt instructions, (7) flag instructions, and (8) synchronization instructions. Each of those categories can be broken down further into different classes, each of which contains several members. For example, the data-transfer instructions consist of (1) general-purpose transfers, (2) accumulator-specific transfers, (3) address-object transfers, and (4) flag transfer instructions. The arithmetic instructions consist of (1) addition, (2) subtraction, (3) multiplication, and (4) division instructions. The logical instructions can be broken down into (1) Boolean, (2) shift, and (3) rotate classes.[50]

The CU is assisted in its task by the system clock. The clock helps to orchestrate the functioning of the logic circuits by causing the CU to perform all its actions "in step" with the clock. Each "tick" of the clock instructs the CU to move to the next step of its operations. By operating in this precise, step-by-step fashion, the CU makes all the logic gates in the processor operate simultaneously, just as well-drilled troops in a parade all march in step with the beat of the drummer.

In a stock IBM PC the clock "ticks" 4.77 million times each second (i.e., the clock runs at 4.77 MHz), and each clock cycle lasts 210 nanoseconds (210 billionths of a second). The "tick" is really an electrical pulse that is received from the clock generator (an 8284A chip), whose pulse rate is determined by a quartz crystal.[51] The "clock rate"—also known as the "cycle rate," or "pulse rate"—is the time required to change the information in a set of registers (see below).[52] The CU requires at least four clock cycles (840 nanoseconds) for each machine cycle, which may be defined as "the series of activities that begins when the CU initiates the execution of one instruction and ends when the execution is complete, the CU being ready to start another cycle."[53] Thus a machine cycle, which is also known as an "instruction cycle," is the execution of one complete instruction, and in an IBM PC that requires at least four clock cycles.[54] The speed at which the system clock operates plays a significant role in determining the speed at which the computer operates.

1.5.3 Memory

But where do the instructions that the processor receives come from? In an ultimate sense, instructions originate from programs, which can be defined as logically arranged, fixed series of instructions that are designed to achieve particular objectives or applications. Programs are usually stored on disks, but an instruction in a program cannot be communicated to the processor unless the section of the program that contains the instruction has been loaded from the disk into the computer's memory. In a proximate sense, then, instructions originate in memory.

---

49. See Morse, *Primer*, 34.

50. See ibid., 34–98, for an excellent discussion of the 8086 and 8088 instruction set.

51. The 8284A generates one clock pulse for every three pulses from the crystal.

52. That internal cycle time is not to be confused with the main memory cycle time, which is usually several times greater than the internal clock rate.

53. Chien, *Programming*, 29.

54. Many instructions require far more than four clock cycles to execute, and therefore many machine cycles are longer than four clock cycles. See Metcalf's and Sugiyama's "Table A-2. Execution Time for 8088 Instructions" (*Guide*, 364–67).

A computer's memory is divided into discrete segments called "bytes." A byte is 8 bits, and *bit* is computer jargon for *binary* digit, the 0s and 1s of the binary number system that represent alphanumeric symbols, that is, numbers, letters, and other symbols. Each bit occupies one memory cell. The 8-bit byte has become the standard unit of information because 8 bits is the smallest even multiple of 2 that contains enough different positions (i.e., eight) to allow for enough unique combinations (i.e., $2^8 = 256$) to conveniently represent all the main symbols—numbers, letters, punctuation marks, etc.—that need to be represented. Computers operate on one or more bytes of information at a time, and the number of bytes or bits that a computer can operate on at one time is known as the computer's "word length." A 16-bit machine, for example, operates on 16 bits, or 2 bytes, of information at a time and is said to have a word length of 16 bits, or 2 bytes. Generally speaking, the longer the word length, the faster and more powerful the computer is because it can read and write more data at a time than can a computer with a shorter word length.

A computer's memory is divided into bytes for the same reason that words in sentences and letters in the Morse Code are separated by spaces. For written communication to take place, there must be some way of discriminating one word from another. Spaces do that. If Morse Code were sent with no pauses, it would be unintelligible. The computer's processor also needs to be able to discriminate one word (in the computer sense of *word*), or bit string, from another, otherwise the processor could not tell if it was looking at an op-code or at an operand. In fact, it would be totally confused. What spaces are to written communication and what spaces or pauses are to the Morse Code, byte-size *divisions* are to the computer's memory, and every piece of data in the computer's memory must occupy one or more bytes. Computer memory deals with *everything* in terms of byte-size chunks. Thus a byte is the fundamental unit in terms of which the computer actually operates.[55]

In the IBM PC, memory is organized into (1) RAM, which can be read from and written to and which is therefore more descriptively known as "read-write memory," (2) ROM, which can be read from but not written to, and (3) VRAM (video RAM)—also called display adapter memory—which stores the information that is displayed on the screen (see below). Like RAM, ROM and VRAM also may be accessed randomly, instead of serially, or sequentially. As I noted earlier, RAM and ROM are located in chips on the system board; additional RAM may be provided on add-in memory boards that plug into the system board. VRAM is located on the display adapter card, which plugs into the system board.

1.5.4 Addresses

Just having all those bytes of instructions in memory does not help the processor carry out its job any more than having someone's name and phone number helps you know where they live. All of us have had the experience of knowing that we have a piece of information but not knowing where that information is. Possessing information is futile unless you can locate the information you posses. Imagine a library that has no card file, no book numbers, no protocols for shelving books, and in which the books were constantly moved from one location to another. Such a library would be useless because you could never find what you needed. That kind of chaos also would characterize a computer's memory if the processor had no way of knowing the location of each byte of information. The problem of locating information in a computer's memory is solved by numbering every byte of memory with a unique binary number (beginning at binary 0), just as the problem of locating books in libraries is solved, in part, by assigning each book a unique number. The result of the binary numbering of

---

55. The memory of some computers is organized into larger sized units known as "paragraphs" or "pages."

the bytes in a computer's memory is known as the "memory address system." Because every byte has an address, the processor knows exactly where to find what it needs to carry out its instructions, just as knowing the call number of a book allows you to locate it in the library. Thus when the processor receives the op-code 0000001—add two numbers—in one way or another (see below under addressing modes) it is also told the address in memory of each of the two numbers it is to add.

By virtue of specifying the highest possible number a memory address may have, the architecture of a given microprocessor determines how many bytes it can address, just as specifying the highest possible address a house may have and requiring successive addresses to be incremented by a fixed number would limit the number of houses that could be located on a given street. The 8088 uses 20-bit-long addresses. Since each bit in the address may be a 0 or a 1 and since the addresses are 20 bits long, the 8088 can address 2^{20}, or 1,024K—1,048,576—different bytes of memory (a K in computer terminology means 1,000 in the base-2, or binary, number system and so means 2^{10}, or 1,024.)

The 8088 uses two numbers for each memory address.[56] The first number, which specifies a 16K segment of memory known as a "paragraph boundary," is called the "segment" part of the address, or the "segment address." The second number, which specifies an exact location in memory relative to the segment address, is called the "relative address," the "offset address," or the "effective memory address." The relative address can be up to 64K away from the segment address. Together, the segment and offset addresses specify an "absolute address." This form of addressing, known as "segmented addressing," is like a librarian telling you that the book you want is on shelf thirty-three, ninety-four books down the shelf from its left-hand end. Norton says "The segment part of an address becomes a base location for a 64K working area, which the relative part can address."[57]

Earlier I mentioned addressing modes, which were defined as the ways an instruction can specify the location of an operand. As we just learned, all 8088 memory addresses are computed by summing the contents of a segment address and an offset address. Offset addresses are specified by using one of twenty-four addressing modes, which can be divided into the following basic types: (1) immediate (an instruction specifies an immediate operand, i.e., one that is contained in the bytes immediately following the op-code), (2) register (an instruction specifies the contents of a register as an operand), (3) direct (an instruction specifies an operand by placing the operand's memory address in the data segment register—see below), (4) direct-indexed (an instruction specifies the SI or DI register as an index register and then specifies the operand's address in memory—also see below), and (5) implied-memory (an instruction specifies the SI or DI register as an index register but does not specify a memory ad-

---

56. See Norton, *Inside*, 28–30, and Morse, *Primer*, 13–18, for explanations of how the 16-bit-long words that the 8088 recognizes can be used to form 20-bit-long addresses.

57. Norton, *Inside*, 29. In this and the following subsections, I am greatly indebted to Peter Norton's excellent work *Inside the IBM PC: Access to Advanced Features and Programming*, to Murray Sargent III's and Richard L. Shoemaker's *The IBM Personal Computer from the Inside Out*, and to Stephen P. Morse's *The 8086/8088 Primer*. Robert Lafore's *Assembly Language Primer for the IBM PC & XT* and Metcalf's and Sugiyama's *Beginners Guide to Machine Language on the IBM PC & PCjr* also have been quite helpful. For those who would like to learn assembly language, understand more about the architecture of the 8088, and actually "see" the 8088 at work, I recommend *The Visible Computer: 8088—Assembly Language Teaching System*, which consists of a 337 page book and a disk that contains programs that display on-screen, in a step-by-step fashion, the way the 8088 actually executes instructions. Contact: Software Masters, P.O. Box 3638, Bryan, TX 77805; (713) 266-5771; $69.95; reviewed in *PC Tech Journal* (September 1985): 25. Editions for the 6502 (the microprocessor used in the Apple II series of computers) and the 6510 (the microprocessor in the Commodore 64) are available for $49.95 and $39.95 respectively.

dress, thereby implying that the information in the register is the operand's address). Other types include (6) base-relative and (7) stack-memory addressing modes.[58]

1.5.5 Registers

As we have learned, the processor receives, interprets, and causes instructions to be executed by issuing the proper commands to the appropriate circuits and devices, thereby directing and sequencing all the computer's operations. To assist it in executing instructions, the processor uses special memory cells called "registers." Like a scratch pad or blackboard, registers function as places where the processor can temporarily store the intermediate results of a program that is being run.[59] Like the CU and the ALU, the registers are part of the microprocessor chip. Registers in the 8088 have three major functions, and those functions distinguish registers from regular memory locations. First, the CU can command the ALU to perform logical and arithmetical operations on data in the registers. Second, the CU can use the registers to store addresses that point to locations in memory. Third, the CU can use the registers to read data from and to write data to the peripheral devices that are connected to the computer.[60] Like other memory cells, registers are organized into byte-sized units, but they are identified by distinctive names and letters that reflect their specific functions, rather than by binary addresses as are regular memory cells.

The 8088 has thirteen registers,[61] each 16 bits, or 1 word, wide.[62] These registers may be grouped into four sets: (1) general-purpose registers (AX, BX, CX, DX), (2) segment registers (CS, DS, ES, SS), (3) pointer and index registers (SP, BP, SI, DI), and (4) the instruction pointer (IP). The general-purpose registers hold the intermediate results of operations and the operands for arithmetic and logical operations, the segment registers specify segments of memory where the program's code, data, and stack

---

58. See Rector and Alexy, *Book*, 3-30—3-44, for an excellent discussion of the 8086/8088's addressing modes.

59. These results are also the immediate results of the processor's operations.

60. Lafore, *Assembly*, 57. Peripheral devices, also called "peripherals," are input-output devices, such as the printer, the screen, or the keyboard, that are not part of the computer per se and so are peripheral to its operation.

61. The flag register is, in a sense, a fourteenth register, though it does not behave like the other registers. The nine 1-bit flags in the 16-bit flag register consist of *status* flags, which report the status or results of operations in the processor (such as overflow, interrupt, parity, and the like) and *control* flags, which control the operations of the processor (such as slowing down the rate at which it executes instructions). See Chien, *Programming*, 74-75; Lafore, *Assembly*, 158-65; or Sargent and Shoemaker, *IBM*, 30, 66-74, for more details.

62. All registers in the 8088 are 16-bit registers. Therefore any 8088 computer may be called a 16-bit machine or may be said to have 16-bit architecture. That means that the 8088's registers can work with 16 bits, or 2 bytes, at a time, that is, with words that are 16 bits wide. But the 8088 is designed to communicate with the rest of the computer and with I/O devices in words that are 8 bits wide. Although the 8088's registers and internal data bus can handle 16-bit words, its external data bus is limited to 8-bit words, and that is why computers that use the 8088 are often referred to as 16/8-bit machines.

Intel introduced the 8080 (an 8-bit processor) in 1974 and released the 8086 (a true 16/16-bit processor) and the 8088 in 1978. The 8080 was a very popular 8-bit microprocessor. Supposedly, Intel introduced the 16/8-bit 8088 because in the late 1970s—due in large measure to the success of the 8080—peripheral devices that communicated with computers in 8-bit words were more reasonably priced, more readily available, and easier to design and construct than those that communicated in 16-bit words. In the late 1970s, the microcomputer was a relatively new type of computer that was not firmly established in the marketplace, and so at that time the 8088 afforded microcomputer designers (such as the IBM team at Boca Raton that designed the IBM PC) a more economical approach to constructing a microcomputer system. Today, true 16/16-bit microcomputers, such as the IBM PC AT (which uses an Intel 80286 microprocessor), are readily available and economical, and a new generation of 32-bit microcomputers, based on the Intel 80386 and on the Motorola 68020 microprocessors, is emerging.

are located, and the pointer and index registers specify exact locations within memory segments.

Each of the four general-purpose registers can be divided into two 8-bit registers. Viewed as four 16-bit registers, they are designated AX, BX, CX, and DX. When divided into 8-bit registers, they are designated AH, AL, etc. H and L stand for "high" and "low." Morse says, "The dual nature of these registers permits them to handle both byte and word quantities with equal ease."[63] Each of the general-purpose registers can be used for general storage, that is, for holding the operands for arithmetic and logical operations and for storing the intermediate results of operations. Furthermore, (generally speaking) the contents of these registers can participate in arithmetic and logical operations. The contents of two general-purpose registers, for example, could be added together and the result stored in a third such register.[64] Each general-purpose register also has a specialized use. The AX (accumulator) register is specially designed for arithmetic and logical operations. It often holds, or accumulates, the values used for various operations. The BX (base) register is specially designed to point to memory locations. It is often used to specify offset addresses relative to the DS (data segment) register. The CX (count) register is specially designed to count the number of times an operation has been performed. The DX (data) register is often used to hold the port address for a particular input or output instruction.

The four segment registers (CS, DS, ES, SS) are used to specify segment addresses. Segment registers have three different functions, and they allow the 8088 to work with blocks of memory that are larger than 64K. First, the segment registers are used to help specify the address of a program's code. The code's segment address is stored in the CS (code segment) register and its offset address in the IP (instruction pointer) register. Thus the CS and IP registers together specify the code's absolute address. Second, the segment registers are used to help specify the address of a program's data. The data's segment address is stored in the DS (data segment) register, and its offset address is often specified by using the DX, SI, or DI registers, or in other ways, as we saw above in our discussion of addressing modes. The ES (extra segment) register functions as a second data segment register and can be used to address the screen or operating system. Third, the segment registers are used to help specify the address of the program's stack, a concept to which we will return in the next subsection. The stack's segment address is held in the SS (stack segment) register, and its offset address is specified by using the SP (stack pointer) or BP (base pointer) registers. Each of these segments—code, data, and stack—can be up to 64K in size. Thus a program's code could be placed in one 64K segment of memory, the program's data in another such segment, and the program's stack in a third segment. In that manner, the 8088 can run programs that are much larger than 64K. Norton says,

> When a program is prepared to be run, the operating system . . . decides which paragraph locations will be used for the program's code, data and stack. The segment registers CS, DS and SS are set to point to those locations. When it is running, the program makes use of the segment register values to find its way through memory.[65]

Segment registers, then, let the CU know where to find the code, data, and stack it needs to execute a particular program, just as a helpful librarian could tell you the exact location of the primary and secondary materials you needed to carry out a project and where you could store the papers you had been working on.

There are five other registers in the 8088, the IP (instruction pointer) register, and the two pointer (SP and BP) and two index (SI and DI) registers. The IP (instruction

---

63. Morse, *Primer*, 19.
64. Ibid.
65. Norton, *Inside*, 30.

pointer) register always works with the CS (code segment) register to inform the processor of the absolute address of the next instruction that is to be executed. The IP register points to (i.e., contains) the address of the next instruction that is to be fetched from memory and executed.[66] The pointer and index registers are used to hold offset addresses for a program's stack, base, source, and destination. By specifying the register that contains the address of the operand, instead of specifying its address directly, an instruction can be shorter and the program "tighter" than it otherwise would be. As Morse notes,[67] this is like abbreviated telephone dialing where you store complete phone numbers under 1- or 2-digit codes and dial the complete number by entering those codes. In effect, the 1- or 2-digit code specifies which "register" holds the complete phone number you wish to dial. By using the pointer and index registers to store offset addresses that are the result of *previous* operations, a program can access those memory locations. In addition to being used to hold offset addresses, the processor can perform arithmetical and logical operations on the values contained in the pointer and index registers.[68]

The SP (stack pointer) register works with the SS (stack segment) register to inform the processor of the current stack location. The SP register always points to the last piece of data that was PUSHed[69] onto the stack. The SP register, then, specifies an offset address from the base of the segment of memory pointed to by the SS register. Similarly, the BP (base pointer) register may be used to specify an offset address from the segment of memory pointed to by the SS register. The SI (source index) and the DI (destination index) registers are "specialty registers"[70] that work with the DS (data segment) register to specify the source of the operands and the destination where the results of an operation are to be stored.

1.5.6 Interrupts and the Stack

In addition to processing, the processor must be able to interact with the world outside of itself. It does this in three ways. It uses (1) memory accesses (which I have discussed) to address its memory, (2) interrupts (which I will now discuss) to respond to requests from software and hardware, and (3) ports (which I will discuss in the next subsection) to pass data to or to receive data from the world outside of itself.

An interrupt is just what the term suggests—an interruption of the processor by hardware, software, or by some logical condition in the processor itself. The processor could discover the needs of the world outside of itself either by polling the various devices in the machine or by waiting to be interrupted by them.[71] Using interrupts is more efficient and less time consuming than polling. By using interrupts, the different parts of the system are saying to the processor, "Don't call us, we'll call you when we need a job done."

Interrupts allow the processor to respond to the needs of its hardware and software and to certain logical needs as well. When some piece of hardware or software signals the processor that it needs attention, that signal is known as an "external interrupt." When you type on the keyboard, for example, you are creating a hardware interrupt that requests the processor to stop all processing, pay attention to your demands, and

---

66. Chien says, "Once the execution process begins, the CU will fetch an instruction from the memory as dictated by the next instruction in the IP register, direct the decoded instruction to the proper functional component responsible for execution, and relinquish its control of the instruction to that particular component. When the execution of the instruction is complete, the control is returned to the CU, completing a 'machine cycle'" (Chien, *Programming*, 29).

67. Morse, *Primer*, 20.

68. Morse's explanation of registers (*Primer*, 12–33) is particularly lucid and helpful.

69. We will discuss the PUSH operation below.

70. Chien, *Programming*, 37.

71. See Sargent and Shoemaker, *IBM*, 254–70, for an in-depth discussion of polling.

carry them out. A "logical interrupt" is an internal interrupt that is generated by the processor itself. If the ALU tries to divide by zero or if the result of an arithmetical operation is too large to fit into the proper register, for example, an interrupt occurs. Software, too, can interrupt the processor. When one program needs to run another program or subroutine, it calls an interrupt that allows the appropriate program or subroutine to take control of the processor. All the services performed by the operating system (DOS) and by the ROM-BIOS (see below) are performed by using interrupts, and many of those interrupts consist of several subroutines. An interrupt, then, is a request for the processor to run one of many specific routines that are stored in memory.

In the 8088 each interrupt has an assigned number, called an "interrupt number," or "interrupt type." These numbers correspond to specific routines whose addresses are stored in a table that is located at the beginning of the computer's memory.[72] The addresses in this table are known as "interrupt vectors" (see below) and the table where they are stored as the "interrupt vector table." Thus each interrupt type corresponds to an interrupt vector (an address), and the interrupt vector table contains the list of the addresses in memory of all the routines that interrupts can request simply by providing an interrupt number, or type. Some interrupt types are used by DOS, others by the ROM-BIOS, and others by the BASIC interpreter. Altogether, there are 256 different interrupt vectors, each 4 bytes long.

Vector refers to one address that holds another address; a vector is a pointer to another memory location. The processor uses interrupt vectors to transfer control of the processor to a particular service routine that the interrupt has requested. Because each interrupt provides a number that instructs the processor where in the vector table to find the address of the routine the interrupt is calling, programs can run interrupt routines without having to know the addresses of those routines. That introduces a great deal of flexibility into the system because it makes it possible to change the contents or the address of a service routine without having to rewrite all the programs that use that routine. All that must remain constant for programs to be able to continue to use the modified service routine is the interrupt number, or type.

When an interrupt occurs, the processor finishes processing the current instruction and then PUSHes the current program's address (which is located in the CS and IP registers and which refers to the *next* instruction that is to be executed in that program) to the top of a segment of memory known as the "stack," thus saving those CS and IP values as a return address to be used when the interrupt has been handled. Saving the interrupted program's address prepares for returning control back to that program after the interrupt's needs have been serviced. In addition to being used to handle interrupts, the stack is also used when a program calls a subroutine. A "subroutine" (sometimes called a "procedure") is a program within a program, a part of a program that performs some specific task. One subroutine may call other subroutines and thus further subdivide the work the processor does, as Figure 1.5 illustrates. The stack, then, is a portion of memory where the processor keeps a record of what it was doing before it was interrupted; it is "a holding place for suspended work."[73] People often get interrupted in the midst of having a "great thought," which we frequently insist on jotting down before we deal with the interruption. We make notes about such thoughts to insure that we will not forget them and to allow ourselves to return to them after we handle the interruption. The function of the stack is identical to the note we jotted down when our thoughts were interrupted. Because the processor can be interrupted while it is handling an interrupt or subroutine, a stack's "notes" can be several deep.

According to Norton,[74] stacks are named after and work like the stacks of plates on spring-loaded platforms that may be seen in cafeterias. (1) Each new plate pushes the

---

72. This table is stored in two files that are part of DOS: IBMBIO.COM and IBMDOS.COM. The contents of those files are loaded into the computer's memory every time the machine is booted up. See below.

73. Norton, *Inside*, 43.

74. Ibid., 42.

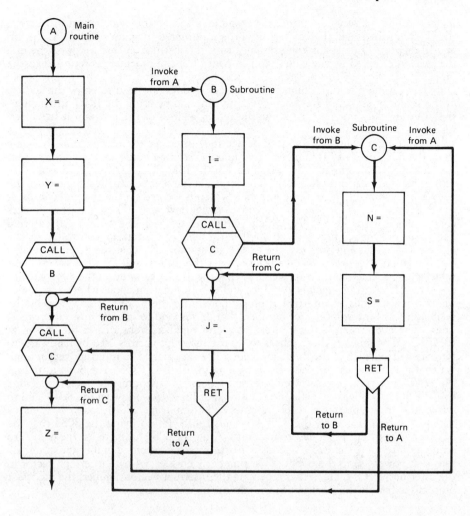

Figure 1.5: Diagrammatic representation of subroutine invocation program flow-of-control. (Reprinted by permission of Prentice-Hall, Incorporated. Taken from George W. Gorsline, *16-Bit Modern Microcomputers. The Intel I8086 Family.*, 1985, p. 94.)

others in the stack down, (2) the last plate in is the first plate out, and (3) popping the top plate off causes the next plate to rise to the top of the stack. In the 8088, an operation called PUSH places data on the stack, an operation called POP removes it, and the last instruction in is the first instruction out.[75] The SS (stack segment) register points the processor to the 64K segment of memory where the stack is located (i.e., to the stack's segment address), and the SP (stack pointer) register indicates the top of the stack (i.e., the stack's offset address). When an interrupt occurs or when a subroutine is called, the processor finishes processing the current instruction and PUSHes the current program's address from the CS and IP registers to the top of the stack. After load-

---

75. This is called Last-In-First-Out, or LIFO.

ing and running a service routine, for example, a special interrupt return instruction (IRET) POPs the stack, thereby restoring the interrupted program's address to the CS and IP registers. Processing then resumes with the instruction that followed the one that was interrupted by the caller, and so control of the processor is returned to the proper instruction in the program that was being executed when the interrupt occurred. By using interrupt numbers, the processor does not need to know the address of the interrupt service it has been called to run, and by using the IRET instruction, the interrupt does not need to know the return address of the program it has interrupted.

Because more than one external device may interrupt the processor at the same time, the 8088 needs a "traffic cop" to sequence external hardware interrupts so that they may be handled in an orderly fashion. In the IBM PC a device known as an "interrupt handler" performs this task. The interrupt handler is actually a logic chip, the 8259A programmable interrupt controller, which is located on the system board near the 8088, and it can handle up to eight external devices.[76] These external devices communicate with the 8259A, which communicates with the 8088. All external hardware interrupts, then, are channeled through the interrupt controller to the processor. To function properly, the 8259A must know: (1) what the external devices are, (2) which ones are to receive priority over the others, and (3) what each device wants when it sends an interrupt signal so that the 8259A can inform the 8088 what to do. The 8259A is a *programmable* chip, and the information about what each device wants when it sends an interrupt is programmed into the 8259A at power-up by the 8088 as a set of interrupt vector numbers that correspond to specific interrupt request lines. The 8088 receives those interrupt vector numbers from a DOS file known as IBMBIO.COM, one of whose jobs is to set the interrupt vectors used by hardware interrupts.[77] Thus each of the interrupt request lines is assigned an interrupt vector number that is stored in the 8259A. By using data in IBMBIO.COM, the 8088 initializes the 8259A to respond to hardware interrupt requests, to use interrupt vectors specified by IBMBIO.COM with specific interrupt request lines, to work with the 8088, and to reinitialize interrupts after receiving the end-of-interrupt (EOI) code.[78] When a hardware interrupt occurs, the 8259A signals the 8088, notifying the 8088 that the 8259A has an interrupt request to transmit. After the 8088 has signaled the 8259A to send the interrupt, the 8259A sends a 1-byte interrupt vector number (programmed into it at power-up) to the 8088. That number identifies a 4-byte interrupt vector in the interrupt vector table. After receiving the interrupt vector number, the processor proceeds to handle the interrupt in the manner described above.

1.5.7 Ports

We have learned that there are three ways the processor can communicate with the world outside of itself: through memory accesses, through interrupts, and through ports. The only way the 8088 can pass data to or receive data from the world outside of itself and memory is through ports. Ports are electronic "doorways" that are connected to physical devices that input data from and that output data to the world outside the microprocessor. Data from a keyboard, mouse, light pen, disk drive, or other input device can reach the processor only by means of a port. Conversely, to send data

---

76. The eight hardware interrupts are (1) the Non-Maskable Interrupt (NMI), which signals things like power failures, (2) the timer interrupt, (3) the keyboard interrupt, (4) the diskette drives interrupt, (5) the communications adapter interrupt, (6) the printer interface interrupt, and two unassigned interrupts. See Norton, *Inside*, 39–40.

77. See Morse, *Primer*, 135–37, and Sargent and Shoemaker, *IBM*, 239.

78. See Sargent and Shoemaker, *IBM*, 239.

to the screen, printer, plotter, disk drive, modem, or other output device, the processor must use a port. Thus one use of ports in the PC is as data paths.

Each port has an identifying number and is addressed in the same manner that bytes or words in memory are addressed, except that there is no port segment register. Thus all ports are considered to be in one segment.[79]

Ports can be activated by means of interrupts. Pressing a key on the keyboard, for example, causes a hardware interrupt that causes a ROM-BIOS routine to send an IN signal to the keyboard port, thereby allowing the data in the keyboard buffer into the computer. I will discuss this more fully below.

1.5.8 Buses

We have learned that the processor receives its instructions from memory where they are stored in byte-sized chunks that have distinct addresses. But how do the instructions actually get from the RAM chips to the microprocessor? How can the processor read two numbers from RAM, transfer them to the registers, operate on them, and then write the results back into memory unless the processor is able to communicate with RAM? And how can the 8259A interrupt controller and the 8088—two separate chips—communicate? Since everything happens electrically in a computer, there must be electrical "pathways," or circuits, that connect all the relevant parts of the computer to one another. These common pathways are called buses. Rather than design separate circuits that would directly connect each individual part of the computer to all the other parts, computer engineers created the bus, which is a circuit that is common to, or shared by, many parts of the computer and that connects them indirectly.

A bus is somewhat like a telephone system. The wire from your phone feeds into a common line (the trunk line) and into a system that allows you to call anyone else who has a phone, even though there is not a wire that leads directly from your house in New York to a friend's house in Tokyo. A bus, then, consists of electrical circuits that provide a common means for various parts of the computer to communicate with one another. A bus is a common data path.

There are two basic types of buses, internal and external. The internal bus is called the "internal data bus." It is 16 bits wide and is found inside the microprocessor, where it connects the ALU, the CU, and the registers. But the processor must be able to communicate with components that are external to itself, such as RAM, ROM, and all the other fundamental parts of the machine. In the 8088 various types of external buses—the control bus, the address bus, and the external data bus—make that possible.[80]

The address bus is used by the processor to transmit the address of the memory location whose contents it needs. Twenty of the 8088's forty pins, which plug into the system board and thence are connected to the address bus, are dedicated to memory addressing. Thus the address bus is 20 bits wide. That makes sense because we have learned that the 8088 uses 20-bit wide numbers to address memory. If the address bus was less than 20 bits wide, the 8088 could not send all the bits of an address to memory at the same time. In an 8088-based system (like the IBM PC), after the address has been sent to memory, that memory location responds to the processor's request by putting its contents—1 byte—on the 8-bit wide external data bus and sending that byte to the processor.[81] Because the external data bus is 8 bits wide, all 8 bits of the 1-byte

---

79. Morse, *Primer*, 18.

80. See Sargent and Shoemaker, *IBM*, 210–18, for more details.

81. In an 8086-based system, the external data bus is 16 bits wide. As I mentioned earlier, that is the fundamental difference between the 8088 and the 8086.

memory location are transmitted to the processor in parallel.[82] Although the 8-bit width of the external data bus allows a byte-sized instruction to be fetched or transmitted in one memory access, a word-sized instruction requires two memory accesses to two consecutive bytes. The control bus is used by the processor to transmit signals to all the relevant components of the computer to synchronize their use of the external data bus and of the I/O ports so that no two components are trying to transmit or receive data simultaneously.

1.6 Putting It All Together

Here is a somewhat technical but nevertheless simplified and incomplete explanation of what happens when you type *Dear Claire* on the keyboard. This explanation will illustrate most of what we have discussed in the preceding subsections. When you type on it, the keyboard does not "know" that the D that you typed is a D or that the C is a C. Inside the IBM PC keyboard is a microprocessor, an 8048. One of its main jobs is to "watch" the keys and to report keystrokes to the computer's main microprocessor, the 8088. The 8048 recognizes each key by an identifying number called a "scan code." On an IBM PC, the scan code for *Dear Claire* is 32 (D), 18 (e), 30 (a), 19 (r), 57 (space), 46 (C), 38 (l), 30 (a), 23 (i), 19 (r), 18 (e). The 8048 has its own buffer that may be used as needed to record scan codes while it interrupts the processor by sending a keyboard action interrupt (IRQ1) to the 8259A interrupt controller through the keyboard port and over the external data bus. The 8259A translates the keyboard interrupt IRQ1 into Interrupt 9 and informs the processor that the keyboard needs attention and wants to transmit some characters. The 8088 finishes processing its current instruction and then responds to the 8259A's request by stopping its processing and PUSHing the address of the next instruction (the CS and IP values) in the current program onto the stack so that when it has finished processing the interrupt, it can locate and finish processing the program it was working on when the interrupt occurred. The 8088 then notifies the 8259A that it is ready to handle the interrupt. The 8259A then transmits the 1-byte code for Interrupt 9 to the processor. That 1-byte code identifies a 4-byte interrupt vector in the interrupt vector table. Using the AH register, the processor reads from the vector table the address of the routine that the interrupt called for, locates that routine (which usually consists of several subroutines) in memory, loads it into the program address registers CS and IP, and runs it.

In the case of our example, the keyboard interrupt called for a routine (Interrupt 9) that is part of the ROM-BIOS. Having located that routine in memory by looking up its address in the vector table, the 8088 loaded it into the CS and IP address registers and then ran it. One of that routine's subroutines sent an interrupt to the keyboard buffer of the 8048 that ordered it to transmit its stored scan codes through the keyboard port into the ROM-BIOS's 32-byte buffer and then to clear its own buffer so that

---

82. Data is communicated over a bus either in serial or in parallel. *Serial* and *parallel* refer to two fundamentally different principles for communicating and for operating on data. The bits in a word can be communicated serially, one at a time (as they are in asynchronous communications; see chapter 5), or simultaneously, in parallel. Similarly, a computer can operate serially on one word or instruction at a time, or it may process several words or instructions simultaneously, that is, in parallel. Most computers (1) communicate one word at a time (i.e., serially), (2) communicate all the bits in a word in parallel, and (3) process the bits of each word in parallel. That is referred to as von Neumann architecture (after the late John M. von Neumann). The sort of parallelism just mentioned is not to be confused with parallel *processing*, which involves the use of two or more processors that simultaneously process two or more instructions, or words. Von Neumann's architecture specified that only one operation or one piece of data could be handled at one time. In a von Neumann-type machine, the processor takes one instruction from memory, processes it, and then returns the result to memory. Multiple computations cannot be performed simultaneously. To learn more about non-von Neumann architecture, read W. Daniel Hillis, *The Connection Machine* (Cambridge, Mass.: MIT Press, 1985).

it would be ready to receive more keystrokes. (Scan codes are transmitted serially from the 8048's buffer as 8-bit binary numbers.) Another of the ROM-BIOS's subroutines then translated the scan codes into their appropriate values. In the case of our example, these are the ASCII values (given in hex) 44 (D), 65 (e), 61 (a), 72 (r), 20 (space), 43 (C), 6C (l), 61 (a), 69 (i), 72 (r), 65 (e).[83] Each keystroke is stored in the ROM-BIOS's buffer as 2 bytes, and these decoded scan codes remain in the buffer until a program removes them and places them in video memory.

But *Dear Claire* has not yet been displayed on the screen. Many computers, including the IBM PC, use a technique called "memory mapping" to communicate with their screens, an approach in which each address in video memory corresponds to a specific location on the screen.[84] The computer and monitor share some addressable memory—alternately referred to as "video memory," "display adapter memory," the "frame buffer," and the "video buffer"—that is located on the display adapter. The microprocessor accesses this memory through one port and the video display controller through another—a dual-port approach that allows both the microprocessor and the video controller to access video memory rapidly. Information written to video memory is read by the "video display controller," a logic chip located on the display adapter, and written to the screen as a series of "pixels," or "dots" (see below).[85] By changing what is written in video memory, the computer changes what is written on the screen. To write to the screen, then, a program writes to video memory; to read from the screen, a program reads from video memory. In a memory-mapped display, the information on the screen can be changed as fast as the processor can write new information to video memory.[86]

Two bytes are used to map each position on the screen. The first, or character, byte specifies what symbol is to be displayed, and the second, or attribute, byte specifies how that symbol is to be displayed, that is, normal, reverse video, bold-faced, or blinking. A standard screen is twenty-five lines long and eighty columns wide, so there are 2,000 possible locations on the screen. Since it requires two bytes to map each location, 4,000 bytes are needed to map one monochrome screen.[87]

Once the ASCII values of *Dear Claire* have been placed in video memory, the video controller reads them, looks up their corresponding dot patterns in a ROM chip known as a "character generator," which is located on the display adapter, translates the ASCII codes into the proper dot patterns, and, by consulting a "row counter" (which is part of the video controller), loads those patterns, in the same order in which they appeared in memory, into a device known as a "shift register," which converts the parallel dot patterns it receives into a stream of serial dots, or data, known as a "video." The shift register, working under the direction of the video controller, then causes the dot patterns (i.e., the video) to be displayed on-screen, pixel-by-pixel, by the scanning beam of the CRT's electron gun (see below). Character-by-character, that process is repeated until *Dear Claire* is displayed.

---

83. *Hex* is short for *hexadecimal*, the base-8 number system that is used for numbering addresses in the computer's memory. See Andersen, *Visible Computer*, 15–19, for a helpful explanation of hexadecimal numbers.

84. See Ciarcia, "Color Graphics Board. Part 1." 105–13, and "Color Graphics Board. Part 2," 87–98, for an outstanding explanation of the principles and technology used to display information on CRTs. Also see Rende, "Monitors," 253–58.

85. In addition to reading what is placed in video memory and causing it to be written to the screen, the video controller provides all the timing and control signals for the monitor.

86. Information is represented in video memory either as codes that are translated into the dot patterns that represent characters (i.e., text-mode memory mapping) or as the dot patterns of the characters themselves (i.e., graphics-mode memory mapping). Thus, in a sense, there are two types of memory-mapped displays, one for text and one for graphics. See the discussion in chapter 2 for more details.

87. In chapter 2, when we discuss multilingual word processing programs and programs that generate nonroman characters on screen, I will discuss bit-mapped graphics. Also see Hughes, "LaserView," 12–18.

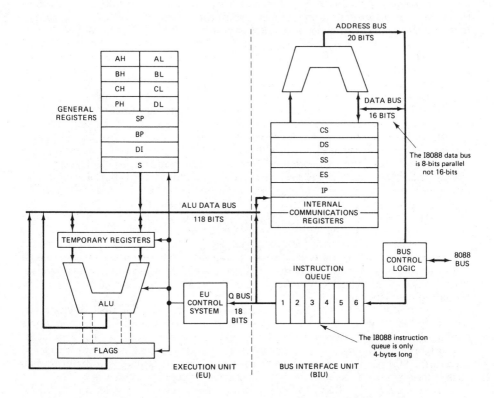

Figure 1.6: Intel 8086 block diagram. (Reprinted by permission of Intel Corporation. Copyright 1980.)

Believe it or not, that was a *simplified* explanation of how characters are displayed on a monochrome screen! But by now I imagine that you are beginning to get the point: computers are completely logical and vastly complex. Figures 1.6 and 1.7, diagrams of the main components of a microcomputer, will help us picture some of what we have learned so far.

1.7 DOS and the ROM-BIOS

Now that we are beginning to "see the very pulse of the machine," we need to explain more fully three topics I have deliberately omitted so far in our discussion. First, we need to understand more clearly what DOS and the ROM-BIOS do and how they relate to one another and to interrupts. Second, we should learn something about the way disk drives use diskettes to store information. And third, we should familiarize ourselves with the different kinds of programming languages there are and find out how they are translated into machine code.

We have learned that the operating system consists of many separate, modular programs that are designed to work together in a harmonious fashion to keep the computer system functioning smoothly. Those programs are arranged in a hierarchical fashion so that a program on any one level can ignore the details of what is happening at other levels. The primary task of the operating system is to handle the needs of

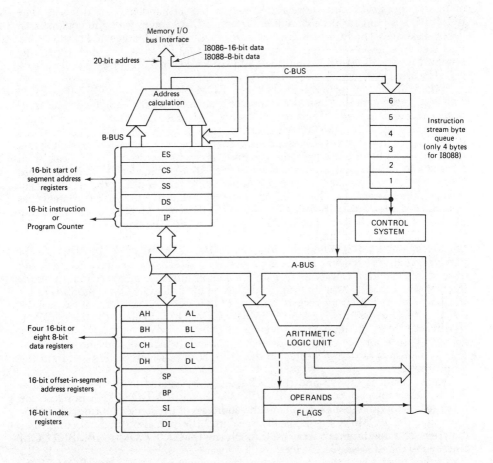

Figure 1.7: Intel 8086 detailed functional block diagram. (Reprinted by permission of Intel Corporation. Copyright 1980.)

various input-output devices, such as the printer, diskette drives, and so forth.[88] The secondary task of the operating system is to perform fundamental file-management services, such as directory searches, file copying, program loading, and the like.[89] The operating system is referred to as the "disk operating system" (DOS) because it services so many needs that are associated with the disk drives, diskettes, and the programs on the diskettes, especially moving data between memory and mass storage devices (i.e., diskettes, hard disks, optical disks).

We also have learned that the ROM-BIOS consists of a set of routines (stored in read-only memory chips and invoked through interrupts) that service the needs of various input-output devices, such as the screen, keyboard, printer, and disk drives.

---

88. For example, DOS handles all the hardware-dependent details of disk read/write operations, such as seek rates, head settle time, rotation speed, etc.

89. Cf. Norton, *Inside*, 55.

Among their other functions, then, DOS and the ROM-BIOS both handle the needs of input-output devices and so are also known as "device handlers," or "drivers." The ROM-BIOS is built into the computer on chips; DOS comes with the computer on floppy diskettes. The ROM-BIOS is not part of DOS per se, but because of their common concerns, DOS can use the services of the ROM-BIOS as part of the operating system. Like the ROM-BIOS routines, DOS service routines and function calls are invoked by using interrupts.[90]

When an IBM PC is first turned on, the ROM-BIOS runs the POST (Power-On Self-Test), a program that tests the computer's memory and the equipment that is attached to the computer. Then the ROM-BIOS locates the "boot record," a small program that resides on the floppy diskette or hard disk. After reading (i.e., loading) this program, the ROM-BIOS passes control to it. (The boot record is part of DOS and is named for its function: it pulls the computer up by its bootstraps, so to speak, from inactivity to activity, and so is also known as the "bootstrap loader.") The boot record "contains the minimal amount of program needed to read and start the main parts of the operating system."[91] The main job of the boot record is to load two system files from the diskette or disk, IBMBIO.COM and IBMDOS.COM, both of which are hidden files, that is, they are not named in directory listings, and so they cannot be erased. Among other functions, the IBMBIO.COM supplements, corrects, and provides a way of over-riding the routines in the ROM-BIOS.[92] IBMDOS.COM provides intermediate-level input-output services, which, as we have learned, are divided into function calls (which share a common interrupt number) and interrupts (each of which has its own interrupt code). One of IBMBIO.COM's chores is to set the low numbered interrupt vectors, and one of IBMDOS.COM's duties is to initialize other interrupt vectors. After IBMBIO.COM has loaded IBMDOS.COM, IBMBIO.COM loads the next component of DOS, COMMAND.COM, which is a command processor that processes internal commands (which are built into it) and external commands (which it locates on the disk), both of which are entered from the keyboard.

More specifically, DOS and the ROM-BIOS are related in the following ways. When the computer is booted up, IBMBIO.COM and IBMDOS.COM initialize the interrupt vectors and so make available the addresses of the service routines offered by DOS and the ROM-BIOS. Logically speaking, the processor channels interrupts (function calls and interrupt services) through the IBMDOS.COM to IBMBIO.COM and then to the ROM-BIOS services.

Lafore illustrates those relationships by comparing DOS, the ROM-BIOS, IBMBIO.COM, IBMDOS.COM, and COMMAND.COM to a company.[93] You, the computer operator, are the chairman of the board. COMMAND.COM is the chief executive officer (CEO), but the current application program is the *acting* CEO.

---

90. Technically speaking, service routines are divided into "DOS interrupts", which are invoked through individual interrupts, and "DOS function calls," which share a common interrupt number. Altogether, there are eight DOS interrupt services: seven "DOS interrupts" and an eighth that is used to invoke the forty-one "DOS function calls." Both types of service routines are invoked by software interrupts. I will refer to "DOS interrupts" as "interrupt services," to "DOS function calls" as "function calls," and to the contents of either or both categories as "service routines." Function calls are used to receive input from the keyboard, to output data to the screen and printer, for I/O to the asynchronous communications port, to create, erase, open and close files, for directory searches, and to read and write data. Interrupt services are used to terminate the operation of a program, to write data in system buffers to disk, to intercept the control-break signal, to catch certain trouble conditions, to read and write diskette buffers, and so forth. See Norton, *Inside*, 60–61, 64–72, for a complete list and explanation of each of the service routines.

91. Norton, *Inside*, 57.

92. The IBMBIO.COM is a "changeable extension" to the ROM-BIOS; see Norton, *Inside*, 56, 59, for details. Because IBMBIO.COM resets the interrupt vectors, it can be used to correct any errors in the ROM-BIOS routines without having to replace the ROM chips.

93. Lafore, *Assembly*, 92–96.

IBMDOS.COM is management, and IBMBIO.COM is the foreman. Who are the workers? The ROM-BIOS routines are. The ROM-BIOS, then, is the point where software interfaces with hardware, because the ROM-BIOS contains most of the input-output routines that actually communicate with peripheral devices.[94] Lafore says,

> IBMBIOS supervises the activities of the ROM routines. If IBMDOS or another program wants to use a routine in ROM, the request is "passed through" to IBMBIOS. . . . which decides what to do with it before passing it on to the appropriate ROM routine. . . . IBMDOS concerns itself with more general, less detailed problems than do ROM and IBMBIOS. . . . IBMDOS . . . contains the "entry points" for the DOS function calls . . . (entry points are simply addresses whose routines begin in memory). . . . The actual input/output routines may be in ROM, but your program must go through IBMDOS to use them.[95]

1.8 Storage

Computers store programs and information in files on a variety of media—floppy diskettes, hard disks,[96] reel-to-reel tape, and optical disks.[97] We will now take a brief look at floppy diskettes and their principles of disk storage.

Diskettes are thin, flexible plastic disks that are covered with metal oxide that can hold a magnetic charge. Because they are flexible, diskettes are sometimes called "floppys." The principle used to store information on diskettes is the same principle used to store information on magnetic recording tape. In both cases, a read/write head stores information on the surface of the magnetic medium by magnetizing that medium's iron oxide coating.

The diskette is enclosed in a felt-lined square jacket that (usually) has four openings. In the center of the jacket is a large circular hole, the hub opening, where the diskette drive mechanism engages the diskette to spin it. The two oval shaped read/write slots (on double-sided disks) are the places where the read/write heads read information from the diskette and write information to it. The index holes are small, round, superimposed holes on either side of the diskette near the hub opening that help the read/write heads locate the beginning sector on the diskette and thus find whatever file has been requested. The small, square, write-protect notch governs whether information can be written to the diskette or not.

Think of a diskette as a phonograph record. Early phonograph records were one sided, and so were early diskettes, which were known as "single-sided diskettes." They had one read/write slot, and they were designed for machines that had one read/write head. If both sides of a diskette have read/write slots and if the diskette has *two* sets of index holes and two write/protect notches, then the disk drive(s) treats the diskette as a single-sided diskette, and users must flip the diskette to access the information on the

---

94. Ibid., 94.

95. Ibid., 94–95.

96. Fixed, or hard, disks store information and operate in ways that are similar to floppy diskettes. For more information, see Norton, *Inside*, 261–63.

97. Currently, optical disks that allow users to write, erase, and record data are not yet commercially available, though CD-ROMs—Compact-Disk Read-Only Memory—are. Like songs on a record, the data on a CD-ROM can be "played" (i.e., read); unlike magnetic media, users cannot record, erase, and record data again on a CD-ROM, though write-once CD-ROMs (known as WORMs—Write-Once, Read-Many) are now beginning to appear.

second side. Such diskettes are therefore called "flippy" or "reversible" diskettes.[98] If both sides of a diskette have read/write slots and if there is only *one* set of index holes and one write/protect notch, then the diskette is known as a "double-sided" diskette, and that is the most common type. Such diskettes are designed to be used with double-sided disk *drives*, which have two read/write heads, one for each side of the double-sided diskette.

Phonograph records contain songs separated by spaces, and diskettes contain tracks separated by spaces. Each track is a full circle and is divided into sections called "sectors," or "records."[99] Unlike the recordings on phonograph records, the tracks on diskettes are uniformly spaced, are uniform in number, and contain a uniform number of sectors. Just as the computer's memory deals with everything in byte-sized chunks, so diskettes deal with all information in sector-sized units. Computers are very logical and orderly in the way they store their data.

Diskettes for the IBM PC are 5.25 inches in diameter, contain forty tracks (numbered 0 through 39) per side at a density of 48 tracks per inch, and each track has nine 512-byte sectors.[100] Thus each track can store 4,608 bytes of information, and so forty tracks can store 184,320 bytes, and a double-sided diskette can store 368,640 bytes, though not all of that space is available to users (DOS occupies some of it). Just as the data in memory has to be organized logically and uniformly, so the data on diskettes must be organized logically. The procedure that organizes the diskette in a logical way that the computer can understand is known as "formatting." When a diskette is formatted, (1) sectors are created, (2) each sector is given an address that specifies its location and size, (3) the 1-sector-long boot record is copied onto the diskette, and (4) a file allocation table (FAT) that occupies the sectors that follow the boot record is created.[101] The FAT is in charge of indicating which of the diskette's data sectors have data in them and which are free to receive data. It also informs the directory where to find each sector of a file. Finally, on a double-sided diskette, (5) the next seven sectors are reserved as a file directory that contains a list of all the files on the diskette. The directory contains the following information about each file: file name, extension, attribute, time, date, size, and starting cluster number.[102] Each file, then, consists of a directory entry, space allocation, and data sectors.

1.9 Programming Languages

We have learned that computers must be told exactly what to do and that they must receive their instructions in machine language—strings of binary 0s and 1s. And we have learned that programs are logically arranged, fixed series of instructions that are designed to accomplish certain tasks. Programs are constructed around or in accordance with one of several possible algorithms,[103] a fancy name for the formulas,

---

98. Flippy diskettes are often used to distribute programs that are aimed at a market with a significant number of older machines with single-sided drives.

99. The records on a diskette are sometimes referred to as "physical records" to distinguish them from the "logical records" of information that are recorded in the physical records.

100. Only DOS 2.0 and higher uses 9-sectored tracks. The IBM PC-AT uses 5.25-inch, 1.2-megabyte diskettes. Models 50, 60, and 80 of IBM's new PS/2 line of computers use 3.5-inch, 1.44-megabyte microfloppy diskettes. Macintoshes use 3.5-inch, 800-kilobyte microfloppy diskettes.

101. The 2-sector-long FAT occupies four sectors because it is copied twice as a sort of precautionary measure.

102. The starting cluster number points to the file's beginning point in the FAT. See Norton, *Inside*, 84–85. Double-sided diskettes pair even and odd consecutive sectors on the same track into units called "clusters." Allocating space in 2-sector-long clusters helps to keep the FAT to a manageable size, so to speak!

103. *Algorithm* can refer to the logical patterns of instructions around which and out of which programs are built or to the fixed rules that are embodied in the electrical circuits of the computer's chips. Wirth

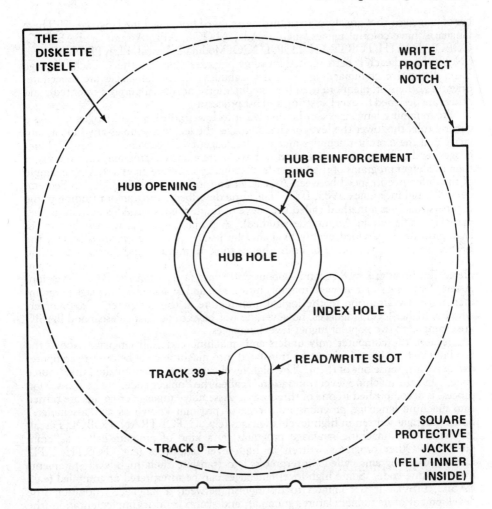

Figure 1.8: Layout of floppy diskette. (Reprinted by permission of Robert J. Brady Company. Taken from Peter Norton, *Inside the IBM PC. Access to Advanced Features and Programming*, 1983, p. 74.)

schemes, and methods that programs use to achieve their goals.

Programs are not written in machine code because that would be too tedious and demanding for human programmers. Instead, programs are written in one of any num-

---

("Data Structures," 60) refers to the second sense of the term as "hard-wired algorithms." *Algorithm* comes from *algorism*, the early name for the Arabic form of writing numbers (e.g., 1, 2, 3, . . . n). *Algorism* derives from the name of the famous Arabic mathematician al-Khowarizmi, to whom I referred earlier in this chapter when we discussed algebra. In medieval Europe, the "algorists" counted with Arabic numerals, and the "abacists" used counting boards and Roman numerals. Because Arabic numerals were a product of a Muslim country, Christian Europe strongly resisted their use. See Shurkin, *Engines*, 26–27.

ber of languages that are closer to or further removed from machine language.[104] These languages have colorful names, such as Ada, ALGOL, APL, Assembler, BASIC, C, COBOL, FORTH, FORTRAN, LISP, LOGO, Modula-2, Pascal, PL/I, PROLOG, and SNOBOL, and each is better suited for some purposes than for others. Each language has a distinctive grammar, syntax, and vocabulary. Some languages are procedure-oriented, others problem-oriented (i.e., applications- or special-purpose-oriented), and others are designed to excel at string and list processing.

Programming languages can be divided into low- and high-level languages. As a general rule, the lower the level of the language, the less it resembles any human language and the more it resembles machine language, and vice versa. Lower-level languages tend to be more concrete and to have more compact programs that run faster than the larger programs of the higher-level languages. Lafore gives a striking example of the difference in speed between Assembler and interpreted BASIC.[105] In September 1981 and in January 1983, *BYTE* magazine described a program for finding prime numbers that uses a method called the Sieve of Eratosthenes (an Alexandrian mathematician under whom Archimedes studied). A prime number is any whole number that can only be divided evenly by 1 and by itself. Running on an IBM PC, the BASIC version of the Sieve of Eratosthenes took 30 minutes and 30 seconds (1,830 seconds) to complete ten iterations of the process, but the Assembler version completed ten iterations in 8 seconds—about 230 times faster than the BASIC version! Assembler is one step removed from machine code, and so assembly language programmers must pay attention to the logical architecture of the computer. Programmers who use higher-level languages, however, do not have to do that. Pascal and BASIC are examples of two popular higher-level languages.

Because the computer only understands machine code, all languages above the level of machine language must be translated into machine code before the computer can make any sense out of them. The high-level, source program is called the "source code," and the machine-level translation is called the "object code." The translation process is accomplished in one of three ways. Assembly language programs are turned into machine language programs by a type of program known as an "assembler." Some programs written in high-level languages (e.g., C, FORTRAN, COBOL, Pascal) are turned into machine language programs by a kind of program called a "compiler."[106] Other programs written in high-level languages (e.g., FORTH, APL, LOGO) use programs called "interpreters" to translate their high-level statements into machine code. Some high-level languages can be interpreted or compiled (e.g., BASIC, LISP). It is common to distinguish between a language's notation (the development of its nomenclature, grammar, and syntax) and its implementation (the development of an interpreter or a compiler that translates the notation into machine code). What is the difference between a compiler and an interpreter? Compilers translate all of a program's source code into object code, which is then turned into a load module (a finished program that is ready to run) by a link editor. Once it has been compiled, a compiled program runs without further translation. Interpreters translate a program's source code into object code one instruction or line at a time, run that instruction, and then translate the next instruction, run it, and so forth. Needless to say, compiled programs run faster that interpreted ones. Like a compiler, an assembler produces a finished, ready-to-run program.

---

104. *Programming language* is less precise than *programming notation*. *Language* suggests dialog and communication. What programmers actually do is write various formulas that instruct, or program, the computer to function in specified ways. Programming *language* is, however, the accepted usage.

105. Lafore, *Assembly*, 472–77.

106. *Compiler* was coined by Grace Murray Hopper in 1952 to describe her first translator program. Ms. Hopper was influential in the development of COBOL.

Bibliography

Andersen, Charles. *The Visible Computer: 8088—Assembly Language Teaching System*. Bryan, Tex.: Software Masters, 1985.

Bell, E. T. *Men of Mathematics*. New York: Simon and Schuster, 1937.

Bradbeer, Robin, Peter De Bono, and Peter Laurie. *The Beginner's Guide to Computers*. Reading, Mass.: Addison-Wesley Publishing Co., 1982.

Chien, Chao C. *Programming the IBM Personal Computer: Assembly Language*. New York: Holt, Rinehart and Winston, 1984.

Ciarcia, Steve. "Build the GT180 Color Graphics Board. Part 1: Basic Technology." *BYTE* (November 1986): 105–13.

———. "Build the GT180 Color Graphics Board. Part 2: Hardware." *BYTE* (December 1986): 87–98.

Denning, Peter J., and Robert L. Brown. "Operating Systems." *Scientific American* 251 (September 1984): 94–106.

Gorsline, George W. *16-Bit Modern Computers: The Intel I8086 Family*. Englewood Cliffs, N.J.: Prentice-Hall, Inc., 1985.

Hughes, John J. "LaserView: The Master of the Raster." *Bits & Bytes Review*™ 1 (January 1987): 12–18.

Illingworth, Valerie, and Edward L. Glaser, eds. *Dictionary of Computing*. Oxford: Oxford University Press, 1983.

Kay, Alan. "Computer Software." *Scientific American* 251 (September 1984): 53–59.

Lafore, Robert. *Assembly Language Primer for the IBM PC & XT*. New York: Plume/Waite, 1984.

Laurie, Peter. *The Joy of Computers*. Boston: Little, Brown and Co., 1983.

Lawson, Harold W. Jr. *Understanding Computer Systems*. Rockville, Md.: Computer Science Press, 1982.

Lechner, H. D. *The Computer Chronicles*. Belmont, Calif.: Wadsworth Publishing Co., 1984.

Levenson, Thomas. "Crunching the Classics," *Discover* (February 1984): 81ff.

Morse, Stephen P. *The 8086/8088 Primer*. 2d ed. Hasbrouck Heights, N.J.: Hayden Book Co., Inc., 1982.

Metcalf, Christopher D., and Marc B. Sugiyama. *Compute!'s Beginner's Guide to Machine Language on the IBM PC & PCjr*. Greensboro, N.C.: Compute! Publications, Inc., 1985.

Norton, Peter. *Inside the IBM PC: Access to Advanced Features and Programming*. Bowie, Md.: Brady, 1983.

Osborne, Adam. *An Introduction to Microcomputers: Vol. 1, Basic Concepts*. 2d ed. Berkeley: OSBORNE/McGraw-Hill, 1980.

Osborne, Adam, and David Bunnell. *An Introduction to Microcomputers: Vol. 0, The Beginners Book*. 3d ed. Berkeley: OSBORNE/McGraw-Hill, 1980.

Osborne, Adam, and Jerry Kane. *An Introduction to Microcomputers: Vol. 2, Some Real Microprocessors*. Berkeley: OSBORNE/McGraw-Hill, 1978.

Ralston, Anthony, and Edwin D. Reilly, Jr., eds. *Encyclopedia of Computer Science and Engineering*. 2d ed. New York: Van Nostrand Reinhold Co., 1983.

Rector, Russell, and George Alexy. *The 8086 Book*. Berkeley: OSBORNE/McGraw-Hill, 1980.

Rende, Vincent N. "Monitors: A Look Behind the Screen." *PC Magazine* (March 6, 1984): 253–58.

Sargent, Murray III, and Richard L. Shoemaker. *The IBM Personal Computer from the Inside Out*. Reading, Mass.: Addison-Wesley Publishing Co., 1984.

Seidman, Arthur H., and Ivan Flores. *The Book of Computers and Computing*. New York: Van Nostrand Reinhold Co., 1984.

Tesler, Lawrence G. "Programming Languages." *Scientific American* 251 (September 1984): 70–78.

Wirth, Niklaus. "Data Structures and Algorithms." *Scientific American* 251 (September 1984): 60–69.

Bibliography of the History of the Computer

Readers who are interested in the history of the computer may
find the following bibliography useful.

Augarten, Stan. *Bit by Bit: An Illustrated History of Computers*. New York: Ticknor & Fields, 1984.

———. *State of the Art: A Photographic History of the Integrated Circuit*. New York: Ticknor & Fields, 1983.

Braun, Ernest, and Stuart Macdonald. *Revolution in Miniature: The History and Impact of Semiconductor Electronics*. 2d ed. Cambridge: Cambridge University Press, 1982.

Evans, Christopher. *The Making of the Micro: A History of the Computer*. New York: Van Nostrand Reinhold Co., 1981.

Freiberger, Paul, and Michael Swaine. *Fire in the Valley*. Berkeley: OSBORNE/McGraw-Hill, 1984.

Goldstine, Herman H. *The Computer: From Pascal to von Neumann*. Princeton: Princeton University Press, 1972.

Hillis, W. Daniel. *The Connection Machine*. Cambridge, Mass.: MIT Press, 1985.

Metropolis, N., J. Howlett, and Gian-Carlo Rota., eds. *A History of Computing in the Twentieth Century*. New York: Academic Press, 1980.

Moreau, R. *The Computer Comes of Age: The People, the Hardware, and the Software*. Cambridge, Mass.: MIT Press, 1984.

Moritz, Michael. *The Little Kingdom: The Story of Apple Computer*. New York: William Morrow & Co., Inc., 1984.

Randell, Brian, ed. *The Origins of Digital Computers*. New York: Springer-Verlag, 1982.

Reid, T. R. *The Chip: How Two Americans Invented the Microchip and Launched a Revolution*. New York: Simon and Schuster, Inc., 1984.

Shurkin, Joel. *Engines of the Mind: A History of the Computer*. New York: W. W. Norton & Co., 1984.

Wulforst, Harry. *Breakthrough to the Computer Age*. New York: Charles Scribner's Sons, 1982.

Chapter 2

Word Processing and Related Programs

> He who first shortened the labor of
> Copyists by device of movable types
> Was disbanding hired armies, and
> Cashiering most kings and senates,
> And creating a whole new democratic
> World: he had invented the art of
> Printing.
>
> Thomas Carlyle[1]

2.1 Introduction

Johannes Gutenberg's invention of movable type around 1440[2] revolutionized the arts of printing and bookmaking and eventually put most scribes out of work. By 1500 over 1,000 printing shops in Europe had collectively printed several million books; and by 1515, primarily through the efforts of the Venetian printer Aldus Manutius, inexpensive, pocket-sized editions of all the major Greek classics had been translated and printed,[3] thereby making available to literate Europeans a vast amount of knowledge that previously was available only to a wealthy, privileged few. Eventually, the invention of movable type helped to bring about the academic investigation of subjects, the development of agreed disciplines, the standardization of learning and spelling, the concept of "mastership" of a subject and, correspondingly, the fragmentation of knowledge into specialized areas and the rise of the "expert."[4] This "democratization" of knowledge—making the wealth of classical and contemporary learning available inexpensively in European languages in book form—was one of the key factors in and a necessary condition for the Renaissance in the sixteenth century.

In a similar way, word processors, or word processing programs,[5] have forever altered the way that everything from simple letters to the most complex manuscripts are created. Just as Gutenberg's movable type revolutionized the arts of printing and

---

1. Thomas Carlyle (1795–1881), *Sartor Resartus* (1833–1834).

2. Actually, about 1045 the Chinese printer Pi' Sheng made the first movable type, using separate pieces of clay for each character.

3. Burke, *Connections*, 105.

4. Ibid., 104.

5. I will use *word processor* as a synonym for *word processing program*, though, technically, *word processor* refers to a dedicated, special-purpose computer and *word processing program* to a program that runs on general-purpose computers.

bookmaking, so word processors have revolutionized the way that words get into type. Word processors have not, however, paved the way for a new Renaissance; their forté lies in making the processes of writing—composing, editing, rewriting—and printing easier.

Word processor is a rather plebeian term that denotes an interrelated set of programs that allow users to enter, manipulate, edit, format, display, and print text. Word processors vary from one another in many ways. Some of the major differences include the following. (1) Word processors have different interfaces: some are command-driven, others menu-driven, and some mix both strategies together.[6] (2) They have different text orientations: some are page-oriented, treating text as a linked series of discrete pages, others are document-oriented, treating text as a continuous, unified stream. (3) They have different display orientations: some display documents on-screen (more or less) the way they will look when printed,[7] others do not. (4) They have different ways of handling the commands that govern the formatting of a document: some embed formatting commands directly into the text itself (so that the commands appear as part of the text), others hide the commands. And (5) word processing programs differ in terms of their features. The more powerful programs automatically number and place footnotes and endnotes, create tables of contents and indices, allow two or more files to be edited concurrently, permit the screen to be split into two or more windows, automatically save text to disk, and so forth. And some word processors include spelling programs, text retrieval programs, and some can do simple four- or five-function arithmetic. More will be said about all of these matters later in this chapter.

In this chapter we will examine and evaluate many word processing and related programs.[8] *Related programs* refers to (1) font and printer utilities, (2) spelling, thesaurus, and grammar programs, (3) bibliography and sorting programs, (4) text retrieval programs, (5) keyboard macro utilities, and to (6) desktop publishing programs—to programs that enhance or extend the basic tasks of word processing.[9] We also will learn about generating, displaying, and printing standard and nonstandard characters.

It is neither desirable nor practical to discuss every word processing program; there are over 200 of them for the IBM PC alone! Broadly and generally speaking, word processors may be divided into three basic groups that roughly correspond to three different types of users: corporate, professional, and personal.[10] Corporate word proces-

---

6. *Interface* describes the way that users and programs interact with one another, users issuing commands to programs and receiving information from them. *Command-driven* and *menu-driven* refer to two different types of interfaces. In a command-driven program, users operate the program by issuing commands directly. In a menu-driven program, users operate the program by selecting items from a menu. Generally speaking, menu-driven programs are easier to use than command-driven ones, though being forced to move through different menu levels to invoke a desired function is often slower than issuing a command directly.

7. This is called WYSIWYG (pronounced "wizzywig"), which means "what you see is what you get," and will be discussed later in this chapter.

8. Because I am grouping all of these language-related programs together, this is a *very* long chapter. Perhaps, to conform its length to that of other chapters, this chapter should be divided into two or three chapters—or made into a book of its own! I have chosen not to divide the material in this chapter, however, because I like having similar things grouped together. Readers with different taxonomic or aesthetic sensibilities are free to disagree.

9. I have deliberately omitted "idea processors"—also known as "thought processors" or "thought organizers" or "outliners"—a type of program that is, in effect, an outliner. For those who need help in creating outlines or who are interested in this type of program, read Stallings, "Outliners," 199–220; Hershey, "Processors," 337–50; Foster, "Outliners," 74–83; Caruso, "New Ways," 79–83; Dickinson, "Outlines," 199–220. Some word processors (e.g., Microsoft Word, Lotus Manuscript) contain extensive outlining capabilities.

10. See the January 28, 1986, issue of *PC Magazine* for extensive reviews of seventy-six corporate, professional, and personal word processing programs.

sors are designed for secretarial and clerical use in the word processing departments of large corporations. Professional word processors are designed for professionals—writers, academicians, scientists, lawyers, researchers, executive secretaries—and include programs with academic, scientific, and business orientations. Personal word processors are designed for home use and for use by executives and others who do light word processing on an occasional basis. Corporate word processors include programs such as MultiMate Advantage, SAMNA Word III, and WordStar 2000 Plus, none of which we will examine in this chapter. Personal word processors include programs such as MacWrite, BankStreet Writer, Easy, and PFS Write, and we will not examine any of them, either. Instead, we will look at about three dozen programs (some in more detail than others), some of which fall into the broad category of professional word processors, others of which are members of a hybrid set I have called "dedicated multilingual programs."

Generally speaking, the word processing programs I have chosen to include in this chapter may be divided into two broad groups: professional programs with multilingual capabilities and dedicated multilingual programs. By *professional programs with multilingual capabilities* I refer to the most powerful examples of the academic, business, and scientific word processing programs that are capable of displaying or printing nonstandard characters or of doing both. *Dedicated multilingual programs* refers to word processing programs expressly designed to work with nonroman alphabets. Some of these programs are full-featured professional programs, others more closely resemble multilingual personal word processors.

Since with only several exceptions the most powerful microcomputer word processing programs are designed for IBM PCs, I have chosen that machine as my standard of reference, though this chapter will include information about a number of programs and products for the Macintosh. It is not possible to review every multilingual word processor for every make of computer, and far more multilingual word processing programs have been written for the IBM PC than for all the other popular microcomputers combined. Although at this time IBMs and IBM clones appear to be the machines of choice among scholars,[11] the recent advent of the expandable Macintosh SE (which can be purchased with an internal hard drive) and the open-architecture, high-powered Macintosh II (which contains six expansion slots)[12] may cause that situation to change. Because of their extreme power and flexibility, we will examine Gutenberg Sr., which runs on Apple IIs, and GRAMEDIT, which runs on NEC-APCs, as well as the word processor that is included with the IBYCUS Scholarly Computer.[13]

Unless stated otherwise, the programs will be reviewed on a standard IBM PC-XT running under DOS 2.1 at 4.77 MHz. This machine is equipped with a Hercules Graphics Card Plus, a Hercules Color Card, and uses an IBM monochrome monitor and a Princeton Graphic Systems HX-12 RGB color monitor. All programs will be run from the 10-megabyte MiniScribe hard disk that came with the machine, unless

---

11. See, for example, The Office of Scholarly Communication and Technology's report "A Survey of Computer Use in Projects Sponsored by the National Endowment for the Humanities" (Anne Jamieson Price, April 1986). The 36-page report is available (free) from The Office of Scholarly Communication and Technology, American Council of Learned Societies, 1717 Massachusetts Ave., N.W., Suite 401, Washington, DC 20036; (202) 328-2431.

12. The Macintosh SE and Macintosh II are reviewed in depth in the March 1987 issue of the *Bits & Bytes Review*™.

13. We will not, however, examine CP/M programs because they run on the 8-bit 8080 and Z80 microprocessors—weak processors by today's standards—because the best CP/M programs have been ported to the IBM environment, and because although it has tens of thousands of loyal users, far fewer programs of all types are being written for CP/M machines.

otherwise noted.[14] Because I find the key layout on the standard IBM keyboard unsatisfactory, I use a Key Tronic 5150 keyboard. Other, more elaborate keyboards are available from the WICO Corporation, the Key Tronic Corporation, PCD Maltron Limited, the Maxi-Switch Company, Enigma Research, and LC BLOC.[15]

Presently, one of the most explosive microcomputer markets is "desktop publishing." Broadly speaking, *desktop publishing* refers to any program (or combination of program and computer system) that enables users to produce near-camera-ready copy by using a microcomputer and (usually) a laser printer. More specifically, *desktop publishing* refers to programs that give users control over the size, attributes, and placement of text and graphics on a printed page, to programs that allow users to design and compose what each page of a document will look like when printed.[16] They are called "desktop" because they use microcomputers and laser printers. Their output is "near"-camera-ready because it is 300 or 600 dots per inch (dpi), not 1,200 to 2,400 dpi as is the case with the true camera-ready copy produced by digital phototypesetters.[17] To the extent that word processing programs give users control over the size, attributes, and placement of text and graphics on a printed page, they are like desktop publishing programs. And to the extent that desktop publishing programs allow users to enter, manipulate, edit, format, display, and print text, they are like word processing programs. Later in this chapter we will return to the topic of desktop publishing.

Although I will not evaluate computer systems in this book, to paraphrase Wallace Warfield Simpson's "You can never be too thin or too rich" (not exactly biblical or classical ideas!), it *is* true that your computer system can never be too fast, too powerful, have too much primary or secondary memory![18] Faster, more, and bigger are definitely better when it comes to computer processors, memory, and mass storage devices.

In addition to the general bibliography at the end of the chapter and the special bibliographies that follow most of the programs we will look at, the following books and articles may prove helpful.

Bagnall, Roger S. *Word Processing for the Classicist.* American Philological Association, Committee on Education, Educational Papers 2, 1985. Available from Teaching Materials and Resources Center, American Classical League, Miami University, Oxford, OH 45056.

Boudrot, Thomas E. *Byte-Sized Activities: The Generic Word Processing Book.* Glenview, Ill.: Scott, Foresman, & Co., 1985.

---

14. Because in some cases it is impossible to uninstall from a hard disk a copy-protected program that has been installed there, I have tested such programs on my floppy-disk drive, rather than be forced to reformat my entire hard disk to erase the unwanted program.

15. Apparently, IBM designed the PC's original keyboard to conform to European DIN standards (see Sargent and Shoemaker, *IBM,* 273–74). For more information on keyboards, see Rosch, "Keyboards," 203–20; Cowart, "Key Tronic," 162–70; Sandler, "Soft Touch," 347–50; and Posa, "Keyboard," 56. Especially interesting in this context are the LC BLOC keyboards, which have Liquid Crystal Display (LCD) key tops. On one model, for example, seventy-five of the 95 keytops are user-programmable LCD's that display characters in 8-by-12 pixel matrices. Standard character sets for English and Western European languages are stored in the keyboard's 16K of ROM and may be switched among with a keystroke or two. Additional character sets may be downloaded from the computer into the keyboard's 64K of RAM. This board comes with a number of predefined, software-based character sets and a font-editing utility that allows users to create additional character sets. Ninety-four of the keyboard's 95 keys can be programmed as macro keys (see below), and up to 126 keystrokes can be assigned to each key. A special "string key" (located on the numeric keypad) is used to define and to activate macros. A microprocessor in the keyboard controls the keytop display. For more information see the *Bits & Bytes Review*™ 1 (February 1987): 9–13.

16. Sometimes, because of the control they give users over the printed page, these programs are referred to as "page-composition" and as "page-design" programs. *Desktop publishing* program, however, is the more common term and the one I will use.

17. A digital phototypesetter is any computer-driven typesetting machine that stores text, graphics, and fonts in digital form and that uses a laser beam or other imaging technology (e.g., CRT) to create images on photographic film that must be processed with a developer.

18. See Bagnall, *Word Processing,* 6–19.

Dickinson, John et al. "The Business of Words: Corporate, Professional, Personal." *PC Magazine* (January 1986): 93–251.
_____. "The Business of Words: Special Purpose." *PC Magazine* (February 25, 1986): 177–214.
Fluegelman, Andrew, and Jeremy Joan Hewes. *Writing in the Computer Age: Word Processing Skills and Style for Every Writer*. New York: Anchor, 1983.
Gallagher, Brian. *Microcomputer Word Processing Programs: An Evaluation and Critique*. New York: Instructional Resource Center of CUNY, 1985.
Good, Phillip. *Choosing a Word Processor*. Mattawan, Mich.: Information Research, 1982.
Hession, William, and Malcom Rubel. *Performance Guide to Word Processing Software*. New York: McGraw-Hill, 1985.
Information Research, *Word Processing Comparison Tables*. Mattawan, Mich.: Information Research, 1985.
McGovern, Edmond. *Word Processing: A Writer's Guide*. Exeter: Globefield Press, 1985.
McKenzie, Alan T., ed. *A Grin on the Interface: Word Processing for the Academic Humanist*. New York: The Modern Language Association of America, 1984.
McWilliams, Peter A. *The Word Processing Book*. Garden City, N.Y.: Doubleday, 1984.
Marshak, R. *Word Processing Software for the IBM PC*. New York: McGraw Hill, 1985.
Martinez, Thomas E., ed. *Collected Essays on the Written Word and the Word Processor*. Villanova, Penn.: Villanova Press, 1984.
Meilach, Dona Z. *Before You Buy Word Processing Software*. New York: Crown, 1984.
Noble, David F., and Virginia Noble. *Improve Your Writing with Word Processing*. Indianapolis: Que Corporation, 1984.
Pfaffenberger, Bryan. "A Typology of Word-Processing Programs." *Research in Word Processing Newsletter* 4 (February 1986): 2–15.
Software Digest™. *The Ratings Book™: IBM PC Word Processing Programs*. Wynnewood, Penn.: Software Digest, Inc., 1984.
Waith, Mitchell, and Julie Arca. *Word Processing Primer*. Peterborough, N.H.: BYTE/McGraw-Hill, 1982.
Zinsser, William. *Writing with a Word Processor*. New York: Harper, 1983.

Additionally, Edward Mendelson's "Word Processing: A Guide for the Perplexed"[19] and his "Word Processing: A Continuing Guide for the Perplexed"[20] are witty, urbane, intelligent, opinionated, and highly recommended introductions to academic word processing.

2.2 Characters, Screens, and Printers

Before reviewing any programs, it is important to understand the parameters that computer design, monitor electronics, video hardware, and printer types establish and how these parameters require designers of word processing programs to make choices that affect the nature and behavior of their programs. Specifically, we need to learn (1) how composite characters (see below) can be created with standard keyboards, (2) how characters can be defined and represented in the computer's memory, (3) how characters are transmitted to the monitor and displayed on-screen, (4) what determines a screen's resolution, (5) what special monitors and video hardware are available for multilingual word processing, and (6) what kinds of printers are best suited for this task. By understanding these matters, we will be able to understand some of the fundamental differences in design philosophy among the programs we are about to review and how these differences affect performance.[21]

Consider, for example, the following questions that must be answered in order to design a multilingual word processing program for languages that contain composite characters.[22] (1) How can composite characters be formed with regular keyboards? (2)

---

19. *Yale Review* 74 (1985): 615–40.
20. *Yale Review* 75 (1986): 454–80.
21. See Becker, "Multilingual Word Processing," 96–107, for some general observations.
22. By *composite character*, I am referring to characters that consist of a letter and one or more diacritical marks. By *diacritical mark*, or *diacritic*, I am referring to any symbol with semantic or phonetic value (or both)

How can the computer be made to display nonroman characters? (3) How can composite characters be displayed clearly on-screen? (4) How can a program work with several hundred distinct composite characters? For example, over 400 different characters are required to form a full set of vocalized Hebrew letters,[23] and a full set of accented Greek characters requires up to 512 different composite characters.[24] (5) How can composite characters be printed? (6) How can several different alphabets be available concurrently in one program?

2.2.1 Display Modes

Computers display information on the screen in one of two basic modes—text (also known as alpha, alphanumeric, and character) and graphics—because the adapters, or video boards, that control what is displayed on the screen and how it is displayed are of two fundamental types—text and graphics. These two types may be subdivided into four classes: (1) monochrome boards without graphics capabilities, (2) monochrome boards with graphics capabilities, (3) monochrome/graphics boards, and (4) color/graphics boards.

As you may recall from our discussion in chapter 1, the IBM PC uses a memory-mapped approach to communicating with the screen. Information is represented in video memory either as codes that are translated into the dot patterns that represent characters (i.e., text-mode memory mapping) or as the dot patterns of the characters themselves (i.e., graphics-mode memory mapping). Thus, in a sense, there are two types of memory-mapped displays, one for text and one for graphics.

2.2.1.1 Text Mode

Here's how text-mode memory mapping works for the standard IBM Monochrome Display Adapter (MDA).[25] As we learned in chapter 1, when keys are pressed on the keyboard, they create keyboard scan codes that are read by an interrupt routine in the computer's Basic Input Output System (BIOS) and converted (i.e., decoded) to ASCII codes, which are stored in the BIOS's 32-byte buffer until a program causes the microprocessor to write them to video memory (there are various means that can be used to write these codes to memory). Once the ASCII codes are placed in video memory, the video controller reads them, looks up their corresponding dot patterns in the ROM-based character generator, translates the ASCII codes into the proper dot patterns, and, by consulting the row counter (which is part of the video controller), loads the patterns in the same order in which they appeared in memory into the shift register, which converts the parallel dot patterns it receives into a stream of serial dots, or data, known as a "video." The shift register, working under the direction of the video controller, then causes the dot patterns (i.e., the video) to be displayed on-screen, pixel-by-pixel, by the scanning beam of the cathode ray tube's (CRT) electron gun (see below). Like the video controller and video memory, the character generator is located on the display adapter, and it contains the dot patterns for 256 characters.

Although ROM-based character generators typically restrict users to the 256 dot patterns that have been placed in the ROM chip, by changing ROM chips users can display different characters and symbols. Thus by inserting a ROM chip that contains

---

that is not part of a language's formal alphabet (e.g., Hebrew vowels, Greek accents and breathing marks) but that is used when the language is written to influence the meaning or pronunciation (or both) of words.

23. According to "Dragonfly Memo" (February 1986): 2, a publication of Dragonfly Software, manufacturers of Nota Bene™, a multilingual word processing program (see below).

24. According to John R. Abercrombie, "Graphics Display of Foreign Scripts for Language Analysis" (August 1986): 2 (unpublished).

25. See Knorr, "Intelligence," 198–209, for a helpful summary of basic types of IBM-PC video adapters.

the dot patterns for English and Hebrew characters, for example, users can perform bilingual Hebrew-English word processing. This approach, which is used by some of the multilingual word processing programs we will review, has the advantage of allowing users to display nonstandard characters on inexpensive, high-resolution monochrome monitors.[26] A related approach is to use an adapter board that contains two or more 256-character ROMs. Information about such boards is included later in this chapter.

Some display adapters, however, such as IBM's Enhanced Graphics Adapter (EGA), are able to work in text mode with *RAM-based* character generators. Like ROM-based character generators, RAM-based character generators translate ASCII (or other) codes in video memory into dot patterns that represent characters. Unlike ROM-based character generators, RAM-based character generators are not restricted to working with fixed, unchangeable character sets. As the term suggests, the character sets in *RAM-based* character generators exist in RAM, not ROM, and therefore may be altered and changed. RAM-based character generators allow users to download character sets into the generator. These character sets may be purchased or created with a font editor. Some RAM-based character generators allow users to work with more than 256 different characters simultaneously. The EGA, for example, allows users to download four 256-character fonts and to combine any two of them into a single active font (i.e., 512 different characters). And the Hercules Graphics Card Plus (HGC+) allows users to work with up to twelve 256-character fonts simultaneously (i.e., 3,072 different characters).

Text-mode memory mapping is a very fast way to write the screen because only the byte-size ASCII code for each character position on the screen is stored in memory. Since an 80-column-by-25-line screen can display a maximum of 2,000 characters, and since IBM PCs use two bytes to define each text-mode character—one byte to specify the character and the other to specify its attribute (e.g., normal, intense video)—only 4,000 bytes (4K) of video memory are needed for monochrome, text-mode memory mapping. *Text mode*, then, refers to one way that data may be represented in video memory and translated into appropriate dot patterns.[27]

There are three main drawbacks to a ROM-based, text-mode solution to multilingual word processing. (1) ROM chips restrict the number of characters that may be displayed. (2) ROM-based character generators are inflexible; character sets can be changed only by changing ROM chips. And (3) text-mode character cells are fixed in size and tend to be too small to display characters in some alphabets clearly (e.g., vocalized Hebrew, Chinese). Although RAM-based, text-mode solutions to multilingual word processing alleviate objections *(1)* and *(2)*, RAM-based character sets are formed in fixed-size matrices that are the same size (or about the same size) as those used to form ROM-based fonts.[28]

---

26. A variation of this approach is to use a special display adapter board that allows users to load custom character sets into EPROMs (Eraseable Programmable Read-Only Memory chips) or to download RAM-based character sets onto the board or to do both.

27. Actually, there are several distinct text modes.

Throughout this chapter I will use *text mode* to refer to an 80-column-by-25-line format with 720-by-350 resolution, what the EGA refers to as mode 7.

28. I am using *font* and *character set* interchangeably. Technically speaking a *font* is "a single collection of one typeface [e.g., Elite, Courier], in one size [e.g., 12 point, 10 point], and in one variation [e.g., roman, italic, bold]" (*Personal Publishing* (December 1985): 30). All the fonts from a particular typeface are known as a *type family*. Another term for *variation* is *typestyle*. I will use *font* to refer to a set of same-sized characters of various typestyles that are unified by belonging to one typeface.

2.2.1.2 Graphics Mode

Here's how graphics-mode memory mapping works. When keys are pressed on the keyboard, they create keyboard scan codes that are read by an interrupt routine in the computer's BIOS and converted to ASCII codes, which are stored in the BIOS's 32-byte buffer. Graphics programs contain routines that translate those codes into dot patterns—pixel settings—without using a ROM- or RAM-based character generator and that write them to video memory. In graphics mode, video memory does not contain byte-size ASCII codes that represent characters but the actual bit patterns of the characters themselves. Those bit patterns correspond to pixel settings and are displayed without the intervention of a character generator.

To write characters to the screen in graphics mode, one of two basic approaches may be used. With CGA-type adapters an indirect approach is often followed that uses a special 8-byte scheme to describe how characters are to be drawn. Eight bytes are used for each character because in this mode, using this approach, characters are defined in cells that are 8 pixels wide by 8 pixels high (64 pixels in all), and each bit in the 8 bytes represents 1 pixel.[29] When a character is written to video memory using this scheme, a ROM-BIOS routine, which works in conjunction with the video controller, consults a character-drawing table that is stored in a ROM chip on the display adapter to determine how the character is to be drawn. The routine then translates the character-drawing table's description of the character into pixel-setting commands and sets the display memory bits, which the video controller reads in parallel fashion and loads into the shift register.[30] The shift register converts the parallel dot patterns into a stream of serial dots, or data—the "video"—and causes them to be displayed on-screen, pixel-by-pixel, by the scanning beam of the CRT's electron gun.

The character-drawing table only covers the first 128 ASCII characters, however, and so the upper 128 values in the table (it can hold 256) may be defined by a programmer to be whatever he or she wishes them to be—nonroman characters, for example. That is the approach some of the multilingual word processing programs we will review have adopted.[31] Unfortunately, unless the custom character-drawing table is modified so that it can dynamically switch new characters in and out and so use an infinite number of characters, such an approach limits users to 128 special (i.e., nonstandard) characters.

The second way to write characters to the screen in graphics mode is for graphics programs to set pixels directly in video memory, and some of the programs we will review use this approach.

In either case, in graphics-mode memory mapping there is at least one value in video memory for every pixel on the screen; each pixel is mapped in memory as one or more bits; there is a bit-to-pixel relationship. Thus this approach to writing the screen is often referred to as *bit-mapped* graphics. The contents of the screen exist in video memory as a map of bits, not as a set of byte-size ASCII codes; video memory is a map—an exact representation—of the screen.[32]

---

29. This approach, then, requires four times as much memory to define each character as does the text-mode approach, which defines each character with 2 bytes.

30. Using the ROM-BIOS character-handling routines to *read from* the screen in graphics mode works this way. The ROM-BIOS routine that in text mode reads the ASCII character codes, in graphics mode reads pixel settings and compares them against patterns in the character-drawing table, which, as Norton notes, is a crude form of pattern recognition or pattern matching (ibid., 181).

31. See DeLoach, "Custom Characters," 45, for a description of how to do this (a brief program listing is included), and Norton, *Inside*, 180–82.

32. See Sargent and Shoemaker, *IBM*, 293. Sometimes *bit-mapped* is used loosely as a synonym for *BITBLT*, which stands for "bit-block transfer." BITBLT refers to a type of memory mapping in which pixel settings are defined in memory sequentially as a contiguous rectangular block, starting at the top left pixel and moving left to right, row by row. The block of memory so defined may be a whole screen, a subset of a

There are three main drawbacks to a graphics-mode solution to multilingual word processing. (1) Graphics mode requires more memory than text mode. In *text* mode, as we have seen, it takes 4 kilobytes to map one video screen. To map one 640-by-200 EGA (or CGA) graphics screen in mode 6 (a two-color mode), however, requires 16 kilobytes; each pixel requires 1 bit to map, and there are 640-by-200 or 128,000 pixels.[33] Higher-resolution modes and modes that work with more colors at a time require more memory. Up to a point, however, memory can always be increased.

(2) In takes longer to redraw the screen in graphics mode than in text mode because each individual pixel must be drawn, either one at a time or in sets.[34] Slow processors (e.g., the IBM PC's 8088 running at 4.77 MHz), narrow external data busses (e.g., the IBM PC's 8-bit bus), and slow application programs exacerbate this problem. The inherent slowness of graphics displays, however, can be overcome (to a greater or lesser extent) by sophisticated programming, fast RAM, faster and more powerful processors, graphics coprocessors, wider data busses, and so forth.[35]

(3) Graphics resolution on color monitors is not as good as it is on monochrome monitors. The resolution of the CGA in graphics (or text) mode, for example, is poor when compared to that of the MDA. The CGA has a maximum resolution of 640 pixels by 200 lines in either mode. It can display 80 columns by 25 lines in the two-color (i.e., black-and-white) graphics mode with full 640-by-200 resolution, but it can only display 40 columns by 25 lines in the four-color graphics mode. In the latter mode the CGA is limited to 320-by-200 resolution, which is too poor for "serious" (i.e., extended) word processing, as is its maximum resolution. And in either mode, in any setting, when scrolling (moving the information on the screen up or down a line at a time), the CGA produces horrible, unacceptable flickering as it redraws the entire screen.[36] Although the resolution of the EGA is far superior to that of the CGA (see above), it is still somewhat inferior to that of the MDA or the Hercules Graphics Card's (HGC) 720-by-348 resolution.

Thus the main options for displaying nonstandard characters are as follows: (1) use graphics mode on the CGA, EGA, HGC, or some other board, (2) use text mode on the MDA, HGC, or some other board and change ROM character-generator chips (3) use a board like the EGA of the HGC+ that has a RAM-based character generator and that accepts downloaded character sets.

That brief description of display modes provides a glimpse of the basic ways that characters can be defined and represented in the computer's memory and how they are transmitted to the monitor. In the following discussion, we will learn how characters are displayed on-screen and about screen resolution.

---

screen, or a superset of the screen. BITBLT technology may be implemented in hardware, in software, or in both. The amount of information that can be moved to video memory in one bit-block transfer is hardware dependent and is a function of the bandwidth either of the computer's external data bus or of the graphics coprocessor's data bus (if a graphics coprocessor is being used). Programs that use BITBLT routines make one call to move the block of pixel settings. The particular implementation of BITBLT determines how the block is moved, how fast it is moved, and to what part of memory it is moved. Display adapters and programs that support BITBLT speed up screen rewriting by allowing whole blocks of pixel settings to be transferred to video memory at a time.

33. 128,000 divided by 8 bits per byte = 16,000 bytes, which is equivalent to 16K.

34. See Norton, *Inside* (Revised), 214.

35. See Norton, *Inside*, 177–82, for some details.

36. FlickerFree™, a memory-resident program available for $39 from the Gibson Research Corporation, 9 Lago Sud, Irvine, CA 92715; (714) 854-1520, eliminates flicker when scrolling on CGA monitors and speeds up screen rewriting. See Norton, "Issues," 73–75. The CGA's screen flickers because the slow dynamic RAM used in the CGA (the MDA uses fast static RAM) prohibits the screen from being refreshed while the video memory (the slow dynamic RAM) is being read from or written to by the CPU (Sargent and Shoemaker, *IBM*, 301). If the CGA's video memory were not turned off while being updated, the screen would display "snow," a more unacceptable condition than flickering (Petzold, "Achieving," 146), and the scrolling would be too slow (Sargent and Shoemaker, *IBM*, 301).

2.2.2 Raster-Scan Graphics

Text-mode characters and graphics-mode characters are displayed on-screen by a technique known as "raster-scan," or "pixel-scan," graphics. This technique is used in television sets and in most microcomputer monitors to display data on-screen and is not to be confused with bit-mapped graphics, which refers to one way that data is represented in video memory. Display adapters that represent data in video memory as ASCII codes and display adapters that represent data in video memory as bit maps both use monitors that employ raster-scan technology to display that data on-screen.

Here's how raster-scan graphics works. Raster-scan graphics contrasts with vector-scan graphics and refers to the way the monitor's electron beam traces the screen.[37] In raster-scan graphics, an electron beam scans the screen from left to right and top to bottom, creating a rectangular pattern, or "raster." A *raster* is the set of invisible, parallel lines that are *continuously* generated by the monitor's scanning electron beam. The video controller, which is synchronized with the raster, *modulates* the electron beam, so causing what is written in video memory to be displayed on-screen (see below). Raster-scan graphics also is known as "pixel-scan" graphics because when the scanning electron beam is modulated by the video controller, it lights or leaves unlit the smallest addressable areas on each scan line, which are alternatively known as "pixels" (*picture elements*) or as "dots."[38] A *pixel*, then, is the smallest addressable segment of a raster line.[39] The more pixels per inch, the more detail and definition there is, and that means a higher resolution. The higher the resolution, the more clearly complex characters can be displayed, regardless of the mode used. An IBM monochrome screen has approximately 60 pixels per inch and a Macintosh screen approximately 52. Some ultrahigh-resolution screens have 150 pixels per inch. There is a direct correspondence between pixel density and cost; the higher the resolution, the more expensive the monitor and display adapter.

---

37. In vector-scan graphics, the electron beam does not scan the screen in a fixed pattern, or raster, but draws straight lines called "vectors" between points in accordance with a program's instructions. This is a second use of *vector*, which here means "line." Vector scanning produces crisper, more precise images and so is useful for displaying architectural and engineering drawings on computer screens. But since each line (vector) of a character requires a separate command, vector-scan graphics is more complex, program intensive, and slower, though less memory hungry, than raster-scan graphics. Furthermore, because vector-scan graphics cannot display solid areas and because curves are easier to produce with raster-scan graphics, raster-scan graphics are better for drawing characters. See Van Dam, "Graphics," 146–59, for an interesting discussion of the relative strengths and weaknesses of raster-scan versus vector-scan graphics for various applications.

38. Some sources refer to these points or areas as "rels" (resolution *elements*) and define pixel (or "pel," a term IBM likes to use) as a single element in video memory that represents a set of rels.

Dot can be a misleading synonym to use for *pixel* because on monochrome screens, pixels are actually square or rectangular in shape. In fact, for a variety of reasons, square pixels are the most preferable shape. A screen that uses square pixels is easier to program, can be updated more quickly, and forms more accurate curves than one that does not. To draw proper curves, such as circles, with rectangular pixels requires programs to attempt to compensate for the tendency of rectangular pixels to form ellipses. That requires more programming and thus more time to redraw the screen than is the case with screens that use square pixels. And the curves formed by rectangular pixels are not as accurate as those formed with square pixels. Thus screens that use square pixels can display the curved portions of characters with greater accuracy than can screens that use rectangular pixels.

Pixel aspect ratio is the term used to refer to the relation between a pixel's width and height. If a pixel is square, its aspect ratio is 1:1; if it is rectangular, its aspect ratio is some other pair of numbers, such as 9:4 (IBM video cards create rectangular pixels). See the *Bits & Bytes Review*™ 1 (January 1987): 12–18, for an in-depth discussion of the preceding topics in this section. Also see Knorr, "Intelligence," 198–209.

39. Because raster lines are one pixel thick and because the pixels on each raster line are vertically aligned with the corresponding pixels on the other raster lines, the raster may be *pictured as* a grid of intersecting horizontal and vertical lines whose intersections are the pixels or as the square or rectangular areas formed, or bounded, by the intersecting lines.

There are different ways to express a screen's resolution. Screen resolution may be defined either in terms of the number of pixels per scan line and the number of scan lines per frame or in terms of the former number only. Other definitions of *resolution* are possible, but those are the ones we will use.[40] Thus, for example, a screen that has a resolution of 1,024-by-1,024 would have 1,024 pixels per scan line and 1,024 scan lines per frame. And so any measurement of screen resolution in the form N-by-M is really a measurement of pixels-by-scan lines. Sometimes both dimensions are expressed in terms of pixels, since the lines on the screen are really one-pixel thick (or, looked at another way, since the thickness—height—of a pixel is the same as the thickness of a scan line). Or a screen could be said to have a resolution of 1,024, which would refer to pixels per scan line. In some literature, however, screen resolution in pixels is reserved as a measurement of graphics-mode resolution, and text-mode resolution is expressed in terms of columns and lines.

As the CRT's electron beam strikes the screen, the video controller causes it to "ignite" or not to ignite the phosphor with which the screen is coated. Monochrome screens have a uniform phosphor coating; color screens are coated with a pattern of very small circular, rectangular, or square phosphor dots, one-third of which glow red when lit, one-third of which glow green, and one-third of which glow blue. Because color monitors use discrete phosphor dots, their resolution is inherently less than that of the uniformly coated screens of monochrome monitors. The phosphor dots on color monitors are about 0.3 to 0.6 millimeters in diameter; the smaller the dot size, the higher the resolution. Typical color monitors have three electron guns, one for each of the three phosphors.

In this subsection we have learned how characters are displayed on-screen and about screen resolution. Now we are in a position to understand the relation between character size and resolution.

2.2.3 Resolution and Character Size

In *text mode* all characters on a given screen are formed in identically sized matrices known as "character boxes" or as "pixel matrices," regardless of whether the characters are ROM-based or RAM-based. A matrix is defined as so many pixels wide by so many scan lines (or pixels) high, just as is screen resolution. A typical screen is 80 columns wide and 25 lines tall, which means that it can display 25 lines of 80 columns each. The width of each column is equal to the width of the character matrix. The resolution of characters that can be displayed on a screen is a function of the screen's resolution. Thus the number of pixels in a scan line and the number of scan lines on a screen determine how many pixels may be used to form each of the characters. For example, a 720-by-350 screen allows programs to display 25 lines of eighty 7-by-9 characters that are formed in 9-by-14 boxes. Or, looked at another way, to display 25 lines of eighty 7-by-9 characters in 9-by-14 boxes would require a screen resolution of 9 × 80 across (720) and 14 × 25 down (350), which is what the IBM monochrome screen has. The more pixels a character box contains in each dimension, the easier it is to read the characters because they are defined in greater detail than would be the case if the box were formed with fewer pixels, that is, had a lower density of pixels. For example, the Ibycus Scholarly Computer, which is specially designed for working with texts in various languages (see below), forms 16-by-16 characters in 18-by-16 boxes, which means that its 80-column-wide screen has a resolution of 1,440 and that its characters are far easier to read than those formed in smaller boxes on lower resolution screens.

Usually, but not always, characters may not be as tall or as wide as the matrices in which they are formed. Otherwise, the tops of characters with "ascenders" (e.g., *d, t*) might touch the bottoms of the "descenders" of certain characters (e.g., *y, p, q*) on the

---

40. See *Handbook of Computers and Computing*, 152–55, for an enlightening discussion of *resolution*.

line above, and the sides of wide characters (e.g., *w*) might touch the sides of adjacent wide characters. In the IBM monochrome's 9-by-14 character cell, for example, the outer columns on each side are *usually* used for spacing (thus reducing the actual character width from 9 to 7 pixels), and the upper two rows and lower row also are *usually* used for spacing (thus reducing the actual character height from 14 to 11). Thus, generally speaking, the maximum amount of space an alpha character may occupy is 7-by-11 pixels. Although some lower ASCII and box-graphics characters use all 9 columns and 14 rows, the MDA's alpha characters are referred to as 7-by-9 pixels, a reference to the main part of the character box. The "extra" 2 pixels are used for descenders. Certain alpha characters, however, (e.g., *m* and *w*) are 8 columns wide.

Working with 7-by-9 characters makes it difficult to form legible composite characters, especially in languages like Classical Hebrew where tiny diacritial marks (i.e., vowel points) can be inserted *within* letters and *grouped* below them. This small character size also makes it difficult to clearly form letters that have multiple diacritical marks above and below them, such as a Greek vowel with a smooth breathing mark, circumflex accent, and iota subscript.

Although *graphics mode*, bit-mapped characters are not formed in fixed-size matrices but may be any size, most graphics-mode word processing programs try to display twenty-five 80-character lines per screen, which on standard size screens means that the concerns expressed above about character size and screen resolution in text mode also apply to such programs. Lower-resolution graphics cards compound the problem.

Because the typical character box is too small and the typical screen resolution too poor for legibly forming the composite characters used in some languages, this chapter contains a section that lists very-high- and ultrahigh-resolution screens and adapter cards, as well as adapters that allow characters to be formed in larger-than-average boxes.

Now that we have discussed the relation between character size and resolution, we can turn our attention to a less complicated but no less important topic—how composite characters may be created with standard keyboards.[41]

2.2.4 From Keyboard Character to Screen Character

Standard US, UK, and Western European keyboards pose three major problems for multilingual word processing programs that are designed to work with languages other than the ones supported by the character-generator ROM chips in the machines to which those keyboards are attached.[42] (1) Standard key assignments are different from those needed by the multilingual programs. (2) The ninety (or so) distinct values a standard keyboard offers are too few to represent the total number of possible character combinations used by two or more distinct alphabets. And (3) standard keyboards do not allow users to create composite characters. Thus designers of multilingual word processing programs must figure out how to reassign keyboard values so that pressing *m*, for example, causes a Greek μ to be displayed on-screen, when a μ is desired. If these programs are to be *multi*lingual, their designers must figure out how to allow users to switch between two or more sets of key assignments. And if these programs are to work with languages that have many composite characters, some provision must be made for using the keyboard to create those characters.

In the following discussion, I will distinguish "physical keyboard" from "logical keyboard." A logical keyboard is any set of key assignments that may be bound to the

---

41. I would like to thank Jeffrey William Gillette, Senior Programmer at Duke University's Humanities Computing Facility, for drawing my attention to this issue and suggesting that I include a section on it.

42. To simplify matters in this discussion, by *multilingual word processing program* I am referring to a program that works with two or more distinct alphabets, e.g., the roman alphabet and the Cyrillic alphabet.

keys of a physical keyboard. The values of the key assignments on a logical keyboard may be stored in software (e.g., in a program), in firmware (e.g., in a ROM character generator), or in RAM (e.g., in a RAM-based character generator). Programs that allow users to change the standard key assignments to those for German, Italian, Greek, or Cyrillic, for example, may be said to work with different logical keyboards. Every program, multilingual or not, may be thought of as assigning one or more logical keyboards to the keys on a physical keyboard.[43]

Apart from using special physical keyboards, there are four logical options that designers of multilingual word processing programs can choose from to solve the problems listed above. These options are not mutually exclusive; two or more can be combined in one program.[44] (1) One logical-keyboard character can be mapped to one screen character, (2) one logical-keyboard character can be mapped to more than one screen character, (3) more than one logical-keyboard character can be mapped to one screen character, and (4) more than one logical-keyboard character can be mapped to more than one screen character. Numbers (2), (3), and (4) are closely related and will be discussed in terms of (2).

Standard keyboards follow option (1) and map one logical-keyboard character to one screen character. On a standard US keyboard, for example, a keyboard A maps to a screen A. This one-to-one mapping of logical keyboard characters to single screen characters works well for languages with no or few composite characters. In such cases, different logical keyboards may be used to switch from the standard lower ASCII characters, for example, to some other set of characters, such as the upper ASCII characters (which contain many Western European composite characters), or to some other set of characters, such as Cyrillic, that are available to the processor and that may be displayed on-screen.[45] One-to-one mapping makes it easy to enter composite characters since each composite character is bound to its own logical-keyboard key. When using this system, pressing a single key causes a composite character to be displayed on-screen. Programs that adopt this approach use different means to allow users to toggle among various logical keyboards. Some programs (such as Multi-Lingual Scribe) use the function keys to switch from one logical keyboard to another. Other programs (such as Nota Bene and ChiWriter) use menu sequences to switch from logical keyboard to logical keyboard.

Because languages like Classical Greek and Classical Hebrew each have *hundreds* of possible composite characters (see above), it is not practical to create several logical keyboards for each language and to assign each composite character its own logical-keyboard key. Programs that work with Classical Greek and Classical Hebrew often adopt option (2) and allow users to map one logical-keyboard character to more than one screen character. An acute accent, for example, could be represented by one character and combined with other characters to form composite characters. Option (2), then, requires users to use two (or more) keys to produce a single composite character. Programs that adopt this option allow two characters to be combined in one screen position in one of four ways: (1) by defining one key as a "dead key," (2) by defining all the diacritical keys as dead keys, (3) by defining all diacritical marks as "trailing accents" that are automatically combined on-screen with the character they follow, or (4) by inverting the order in (3). A "dead key" is any key that when pressed causes the cursor to remain stationary so that two keyboard values may be entered in the same screen position or that allows one value to be entered in a screen position al-

---

43. For more information on this topic, see the *Bits & Bytes Review*™ 1 (February 1987): 9–13.

44. My thanks to Jeffrey William Gillette for suggesting these options.

45. In text mode these characters might be available on boards that support auxiliary ROM chips or they might be available as characters that are downloaded into a RAM-based character generator. In graphics mode they might be bit mapped to the screen or they might be switched in and out of the CGA's upper, "vacant" 128 ASCII positions.

ready occupied by a character.[46] The Ibycus Scholarly Computer, for example, re-quires the Extended Character key (on its Hewlett-Packard keyboard) to be used as a dead key to enter diacritical marks in the midst of existing text but otherwise forms composite characters by treating diacritical marks as trailing accents.

2.2.5 Video Display Adapters

In this section we will examine the major types of video display adapters that allow us (1) to display nonroman characters on-screen, (2) to display characters in high-resolution graphics mode, or (3) to do both.[47] Because display adapters have different characteristics, developers of word processing programs have to write separate screen "drivers" for each video board they support.[48] Thus not every word processing program can be used with every display adapter.

As I indicated above, custom character sets are either RAM-, ROM-, or EPROM-based. ROM- and EPROM-based character sets come in a chip or chips that are inserted into the proper socket(s) on the display board. Each chip can store 256 values (characters), and some boards can hold more than one such chip. RAM-based character sets, which may be purchased or created by using a font editor (a software utility—see below), can be stored on disk and from there downloaded, as needed, into the display adapter and displayed by a RAM-resident character generator. Some of the multilingual word processing programs we will examine have their own font editors and RAM-based character generators.[49]

The boards we will now discuss are representative of various types of video display adapters in general but are by no means a complete listing of all such boards. At this moment there are, for example, well over a dozen EGA-compatible boards, each of which has a distinct combination of features,[50] as well as single boards that can emulate the CGA, EGA, and HGC![51] Furthermore, new boards and video modes continue to be introduced. IBM's new PS/2 line of computers, for example, has introduced several new video standards. To simplify matters, I will neither discuss the various color modes some of the boards support nor their graphics capabilities in general, since we are interested in these boards only with respect to their abilities to facilitate high-resolution, text-mode multilingual word processing.

---

46. If all the diacritical marks in a language are bound to dead keys, then each time a diacritical mark is entered the cursor remains stationary, and the user must enter an alpha character in the same screen location as the diacritical mark to cause the cursor to advance.

47. This section will not include information about ultrahigh-resolution video adapters that cost more than $1,000. For information on those products, see Petzold and Rosch, "Four-Figure Video," 235–74.

48. *Driver*, or *device driver*, refers to a program that controls a specific input-output device, such as a particular video card or printer. Because driver routines are very hardware-specific and deal with the real-time behavior of different devices, a program that is designed to use several video cards or several printers, for example, must include separate, specific drivers for each video card and printer supported. Although different examples of a given type of device (e.g., printer) perform similar functions, they differ in the ways those functions are evoked by the application program and operating system. Different devices use different control signals to perform similar functions. Every device in a computer system requires a specific driver. See Gibson, "Drivers," 59, for a brief but helpful discussion of device drivers.

49. On that topic, see Wilton, "Character Sets," 197–208.

50. See Alsop, "Standard," 141–43; Petzold, "Achieving the Standard," 145–82; Knorr and Koessel, "EGA," 210–19; Pappas and Murray, "EGA," 313–18; Cockerham, "EGA Spectrum," 80–86 (part 1), 147–63 (part 2).

51. E.g., the MegaGraph Plus by ATronics International, Inc., 491 Valley Way, Bldg. 1, Milpitas, CA 95035; (408) 943-6629; $549.

2.2.5.1 IBM Monochrome Adapter

We have learned that the upper 128 ASCII positions on the MDA's character-generator ROM chip contain many Western European composite characters, as well as "box graphics" and mathematical symbols, which means that this board can be used for multilingual word processing with Western European languages. As I noted earlier, the character-generator ROM chip on the MDA can be removed and a custom chip, which costs between $25 and $200, installed in its place.[52] A custom chip can contain 256 values (characters), for example, Hebrew and English characters.[53] The advantages of using a custom character-generator ROM chip in the MDA for multilingual word processing are (1) high resolution (720-by-350), (2) cost savings (you don't have to buy a new display adapter or a color monitor), and (3) high-speed screen redrawing. The disadvantages are that you have to change chips and that you are limited to 256 characters.

IBM Monochrome Adapter
IBM Corp.
100 N.W. 51 St.
Boca Raton, FL 33432
(800) 426-2468
List Price: $250

2.2.5.2 IBM Color/Graphics Adapter

As we have learned, although the IBM Color/Graphics Adapter allows users to define the upper 128 ASCII positions, this card is a poor choice for multilingual word processing for the following reasons. (1) Its character-drawing-table character size is smaller than that of the MDA, (2) its maximum resolution is considerably lower than that of monochrome screens, (3) programs that use it cause the screen to flicker unacceptably when updating video memory, and (4) it takes longer to redraw the screen in graphics mode. Nevertheless, because of its low price and widespread use, many multilingual word processing programs support this card.

IBM Color/Graphics Adapter
IBM Corp.
100 N.W. 51 St.
Boca Raton, FL 33432
(800) 426-2468
List Price: $295

---

52. Removing and installing chips can be tricky. When doing so be sure to (1) avoid transferring static electricity to the chip (ground yourself and dissipate any static buildup before touching the chip), (2) pry the chip loose with a special chip extractor or very small, flat-bladed screwdriver, applying even pressure slowly as you pry, (3) wrap uninstalled chips in conductive foam and store them in a safe, dry place away from excessive heat, cold, and moisture, and (4) (re)install chips with the semicircular indentation on one end matching the semicircular indentation on the socket (i.e., be careful not to install chips backwards).

53. Readers interested in purchasing a $25 English/Hebrew ROM chip for the IBM Monochrome Display Adapter, IBM Color/Graphics Adapter, Hercules Graphics Card, Hercules Color Card, or the video card in the Epson/Equity computers should contact Max Weinryb, 2415 Grant St., Berkeley, CA 94703; (415) 848-8996. Weinryb's chips contain a full consonantal Hebrew alphabet, no vowels, and are fully compatible with the IBM ROM chips sold in IBM's English/Hebrew versions of the MDA and CGA, with the HGC ROM, and with the Epson/Equity ROM. The Hebrew characters in Weinryb's ROMs occupy ASCII positions 128-154.

2.2.5.3 Hercules Graphics Card

There are two display adapters that are widely considered industry standards because of the volume of their sales, the number of programs that support them, and the number of board manufacturers who imitate them. These two cards are the Hercules Graphics Card and IBM's Enhanced Graphics Adapter. The HGC is compatible with the MDA and CGA, but the EGA is not compatible with the HGC. Thus programs designed for the MDA and CGA will work on the HGC, but programs designed to run *exclusively* on the EGA will not. The HGC provides 720-by-348 resolution in *both text and graphics modes*. That resolution is significantly better than the CGA's, marginally better than the EGA's, and insignificantly less than the MDA's. Because it can work with monochrome monitors in graphics mode at 720-by-348, the HGC offers an attractive low-cost, high-resolution, graphics-based solution to designers of multilingual word processing programs. T^{3TM}, for example, a scientific word processing program that works in graphics mode with the HGC and that we will review below, allows users to create as many 128-character bit-mapped fonts as there is available disk space and to display up to sixteen fonts per document (i.e., up to 2,048 different characters per document).

The advantages of the HGC for multilingual word processing are (1) high resolution in graphics mode, (2) cost savings (it works with monochrome monitors), (3) the ability (in graphics mode) to display an infinite variety of characters on-screen, and (4) the fact that a number of multilingual programs support this card. The major disadvantage of using the HGC *in graphics mode* for multilingual word processing is the increased length of time it takes in this mode to redraw the screen.

> Hercules Graphics Card
> Hercules Computer Technology
> 2550 Ninth St.
> Berkeley, CA 94710
> (800) 532-0600, in Canada: (800) 323-0601, (415) 540-6000
> List Price: $299

2.2.5.4 Hercules Graphics Card Plus

Hercules Computer Technology's Graphics Card Plus (HGC+) is fully compatible with the HGC and MDA and offers text mode, graphics mode, and a new video mode that Hercules calls RamFont™. Because the HGC+ can do everything that the HGC can do and more, the HGC+ is a "superset" of the HGC. RamFont is a hybrid mode that operates with text mode's speed and predefined character sets while allowing the simultaneous display of limited on-screen graphics. In RamFont mode the HGC+ uses a RAM-based character generator and 12-bit character definitions (see below), which means that instead of being restricted to one font of 256 different characters, RamFont allows up to twelve fonts of 256 characters each to be used concurrently in one document—up to 3,072 characters in all. And because fonts are RAM-based in RamFont mode, users may download fonts, which may be various heights and widths (see below). As in text and graphics modes, characters in RamFont mode are displayed with 720-by-348 resolution.[54] Essentially, then, RamFont combines text mode's speed

---

54. RamFont's power and flexibility result from Hercules's new, proprietary, on-board video processor (the V112) that acts to extend the internal registers of the 6845 video controller chip (see chapter 1). In effect, the V112 adds three new registers to the 6845: (1) the xMode Reg, which is programmed to select either the 4K or 48K RamFont mode or the regular text mode and to select 8-bit- or 9-bit-wide characters, (2) ScoreReg, which indicates the position in the character matrix where an underscore will be placed, and (3) StrikeReg, which determines where in the character matrix an overstrike will occur.

and ease of use with graphics mode's flexibility and versatility. Like the HGC, the HGC+ displays bit-mapped graphics with 720-by-348 resolution.[55]

Hercules also markets the Hercules InColor™ Card, a color version of the HGC+ that displays up to 16 colors from a palette of 64 at 720-by-348 resolution on Enhanced Color Display and multi-sync monitors. Like the HGC+, the InColor card operates in three modes: (1) text, (2) graphics, and (3) RamFont. When operated with two colors in the RamFont mode, the InColor card allows users to work with 12,288 characters! The InColor card is fully compatible with the HGC and HGC+ and retails for $499.

In RamFont mode character matrices *and characters* may be 4 to 16 scan lines high and 8 or 9 pixels wide.[56] FontMan™, the HGC+'s font editor, allows users to edit and create fonts in 8-by-16 matrices. Different size characters can be displayed simultaneously on-screen through software "by fragmenting larger characters into smaller elements and mapping them directly to the screen."[57] As many as 43 lines of 90 characters or as few as 21 lines of 80 characters can be displayed on a standard size screen.

The HGC+ has two distinct RamFont modes, the 4K mode and the 48K mode. Because the 4K mode uses 8-bit character codes (and 8-bit attribute codes)—just like the standard text mode—it will display all normal ASCII text-mode applications. Thus the 4K RamFont mode may be used to alter the system's normal, or standard, font to any one of the more than two dozen fonts that come with the HGC+ (or to any font created with FontMan). The altered font is displayed both at the system level and in application programs. Because the 48K RamFont mode uses 12-bit character codes (and 4-bit attribute codes), the HGC+ can display up to twelve fonts in a document.[58] By allowing the character codes to consist of 12 bits, the HGC+ permits 3,072 distinct combinations.[59] By allowing each of the 3,072 characters to have a distinct code, the HGC+ preserves the speed of text-mode character display. To display any of the 3,072 characters, a program need only write the proper code to video memory, and the video display controller will cause it to be displayed in the manner I described earlier in this chapter. The 48K RamFont mode supports the following attributes: normal, high-intensity, boldface, blink, reverse, overstrike, and underline. (The MDA's text attributes do not include boldface and overstrike.)

The HGC+ comes with screen drivers for Lotus 1-2-3 (release 2), Symphony™ (release 1.1), Framework II, and Microsoft Word (version 3.0). Other programs related to multilingual word processing that have drivers for the HGC+ (and InColor) in RamFont mode include Dragonfly Software's Nota Bene™, Lotus's Manuscript™, Design Enterprises' Alexander™, Soft Evolutions' Suprafont™, and Image Processing Software's Turbofonts™. With its ability to display 3,072 different characters at a time and with a list price of only $299 (and a street price close to $200), the HGC+ offers a

---

55. The HGC+ comes with a font editor (FontMan™), font loader, more than twenty-five sample fonts, two diagnostic and some other programs, and a parallel printer port. A downloadable, consonantal-only Hebrew character set for the HGC+ is available from the Hebrew Users' Group, B'nai B'rith Hillel Foundation, 2736 Bancroft Way, Berkeley, CA 94704; (415) 845-7793; $5. This is the same character set that Max Weinryb sells in ROM chips (see above).

56. In text mode the HGC+ creates characters on monochrome screens in boxes that are 14 scan lines high by 9 pixels wide.

57. Letter from Scott Anderson, Technical Sales Representative, Hercules Computer Technology, September 4, 1986.

58. Four of the 12 character bits in the 48K mode actually specify a font type and are known as a type pointer; the other 8 bits are the ASCII character code.

59. Although $2^{12} = 4,096$, because the RamFont's character storage area in RAM is 48K, only 3,072, not 4,096, characters may be displayed. Each character is allotted 16 bytes of storage space (regardless of the character's actual size), which means that 48K of RAM (49,152 bytes) can store 3,072 characters in 16-byte spaces. Or look at it this way: in RamFont mode each font consists of 256 16-byte characters, which is 4K per font, and $12 \times 4K = 48K$.

flexible and powerful, low-cost, high-resolution, text- and graphics-mode solution to developers of multilingual word processing programs.

The advantages of the HGC+ for multilingual word processing are (1) high resolution in text, graphics, and RamFont modes, (2) cost savings (it works with monochrome monitors), (3) high-speed screen redrawing (in text mode), (4) the ability to display 3,072 characters on-screen in 48K RamFont mode, and (5) the ability to work with downloadable fonts. The major disadvantages of using the HGC+ in RamFont mode for multilingual word processing are (1) only one font size can be displayed on-screen at one time (unless large characters are fragmented into smaller elements and mapped directly on-screen), (2) proportional spacing cannot be displayed on-screen (something that requires bit-mapped graphics), and (3) the HGC+ is not EGA compatible. In my opinion, those disadvantages are eclipsed by the HGC+'s advantages.

> Hercules Graphics Card Plus
> Hercules Computer Technology
> 2550 Ninth St.
> Berkeley, CA 94710
> (800) 532-0600, in Canada: (800) 323-0601, (415) 540-6000
> List Price: $299; $499 for InColor card
> Bibliography: Mark J. Welch, "Hercules Improves Its Monochrome Card," *InfoWorld* (September 1, 1986): 41–42; Garry Ray, "Hercules Offers Greater Potential Ability On Its Successor to the Graphics Card," *PC Week* (September 2, 1986): 83, 86–87; Rich Malloy, "The Hercules Graphics Card Plus," *BYTE* (December 1986): 249–52.

2.2.5.5 IBM *Enhanced Graphics Adapter*

It took the EGA less than two years to become an industry standard for display adapter cards, as the more than one dozen EGA clones on the market and the strong support from programmers attest.[60] The EGA has a resolution of up to 640-by-350 in graphics mode on monochrome monitors and on Enhanced Color Displays (or compatible monitors) and in text mode on Enhanced Color Displays. And it has a resolution of 720-by-350 in text mode on monochrome monitors. In graphics mode the EGA can display 7-by-9 characters in 8-by-14 matrices on monochrome monitors and on the Enhanced Color Display, as it can in text mode on Enhanced Color Displays. And in text mode the EGA can display 7-by-9 characters in 9-by-14 matrices on monochrome monitors. Bypassing the EGA's character generator and bit-mapping all characters to the screen in graphics mode allows programmers to create larger characters than the EGA's character generator allows. For example, according to Jeffrey William Gillette, the *Duke Chinese Typist* (an EGA-based, graphics-mode program) treats Chinese and English characters as 16-by-16 pixel entities.

Perhaps the most important aspect of the EGA for multilingual word processing is its RAM-resident character generator that, with adequate memory (256K RAM),[61] allows users to have up to four 256-character fonts in memory simultaneously, any two of which may be combined into one 512-character active font. Characters may be

---

60. See Petzold, "Achieving," 145–82. Petzold's very helpful article evaluates and compares many EGA clones.

61. The EGA comes with 64K of RAM on the main board. The Graphics Memory Expansion Card (GMEC), an add-on card, adds an additional 64K of RAM and the Memory Module Kit (MMK) another 128K (this 128K worth of RAM plugs into the GMEC). The GMEC is required to display two 256-character fonts and the MMK to hold four 256-character fonts in memory. Most EGA clones come standard with 256K of VRAM.

designed from 1 to 32 scan lines high and 8 pixels wide for color monitors and 9 pixels wide for monochrome monitors. When a text mode is selected, the EGA's BIOS, which contains two character sets (one 8-by-14 set for high-resolution color monitors and one 8-by-8 set for CGA displays), loads the appropriate font into the EGA's RAM-based character generator where the EGA hardware can "access it just like the old adapters did their ROM character generators."[62] By using a font editor and loader, users can create and load *custom* fonts into the EGA. Thus the EGA offers a powerful and flexible, high-resolution, text- and graphics-mode solution to designers of multilingual word processors. Duke University's *Duke Language Toolkit* (see below), for example, is designed to run exclusively on the EGA in text mode and includes an excellent font editor (FED) and loader (LOADFONT).

The advantages of the EGA for multilingual word processing are (1) high resolution, (2) the ability to display up to 512 different characters on-screen, (3) high-speed screen redrawing in text mode, (4) the ability to work with downloadable fonts, and (5) the fact that many multilingual programs support this card. The major disadvantage of this card for multilingual word processing is its high cost (see below), especially when equipped with the two memory options, an objection that is mitigated by the $200 street price of 256K EGA clones.

> IBM Enhanced Graphics Adapter
> IBM Corp.
> 100 N.W. 51 St.
> Boca Raton, FL 33432
> (800) 426-2468
> List Price: $524
> Options: Graphics Memory Expansion Card: $199; Graphics Memory Module Kit: $259
> Bibliography: Glenn A. Hart, "IBM Sets a New Standard," PC *Magazine* (December 25, 1985): 171–78; Thomas V. Hoffmann, "Graphic Enhancement," PC *Tech Journal* (April 1985): 58–77; Rolf Kallenbach, "IBM EGA Features Rainbows of Colors," *InfoWorld* (September 30, 1986): 49–52; Peter Norton, "Choosing Character Sets with EGA," PC *Magazine* (November 26, 1985): 79, 83–84; "Color Me Enhanced," PC *Magazine* (November 12, 1985): 81, 85; "The Trouble with EGA," PC *Magazine* (October 29, 1985): 79, 83–85; Mary Petrosky, "Market Looks to EGA as De Facto Standard," *InfoWorld* (August 19, 1985): 32–37; Charles Petzold, "Achieving The Standard: 12 EGA Boards," PC *Magazine* (August 1986): 145–82; "Exploring the EGA, Part 1," PC *Magazine* (August 1986): 367–84; "Exploring the EGA, Part 2," PC *Magazine* (September 16, 1986): 287–313; Karl Koesel and Darcy DiNucci, "Clearly Resolved," PC *World* (June 1985): 256–61.

2.2.5.6 *Best of Both*

The Best of Both (BoB™) display adapter from Persyst™ is a combination card that drives monochrome and color/graphics monitors and that provides very-high resolution in text (800-by-400) and color/graphics (640-by-400) modes. It does not emulate the EGA. BoB does not support IBM monitors but requires a special high-resolution monitor such as the Tatung® 1370, Taxan™ 440, NEC™ JC-1410, or NEC™ JC-1401P3A Multisync, which have the proper bandwidths, frequencies, and blanking

---

62. Hoffmann, "Enhancement," 61; cf. Petzold, "Achieving," 148.

periods.[63] Unlike the MDA and the HGC, which create 7-by-9-pixel characters in 9-by-14 boxes, and the CGA, which creates 7-by-7-pixel characters in 8-by-8 boxes, the BoB creates 8-by-11-pixel characters in 10-by-16 boxes. The optional Expanded Graphics Capability allows the BoB to display characters in graphics mode with 640-by-400 pixel resolution.

The BoB uses an EPROM as its character generator and comes with a second EPROM that can contain a second set of 256 user-defined characters. By using the Persyst SoftSet™ Utilities font editor and RAM-resident character generator, a third 256-character font can be created and downloaded. Thus, in text mode, the BoB can display three different 256-character fonts, or 768 different characters altogether.

The BoB is designed so that programs written for the MDA automatically work with the BoB and display text at 800-by-400, without the need for a special driver. Programs written for the CGA automatically work with the BoB and display text at 640-by-400 (if the Expanded Graphics Capability option is installed), without the need for a special driver.

The advantages of the BoB for multilingual word processing are (1) high resolution, (2) the ability to display up to 768 different characters on-screen in text mode, (3) fast screen redrawing in text mode, (4) the ability to work with downloadable fonts, and (5) the fact that all programs written for the MDA and CGA are compatible with this card and are displayed at higher than normal resolutions. The major disadvantage of the BoB for multilingual word processing is that it requires an expensive color monitor.

> BoB™ Display Adapter
> EMULEX-Persyst™
> Emulex Corporation
> 3545 Harbor Blvd.
> P.O. Box 6725
> Costa Mesa, CA 92626
> (800) 854-7112, (714) 662-5600
> List Price: $299
> Expanded Graphics Capability: $275

2.2.5.7 Quadvue

The Quadvue™ display adapter, a monochrome video card that operates only in text mode, comes with a font editor (Q-Scribe) that allows users to create character sets, any one of which can be downloaded to the board. Thus, as with the MDA and FTA (see below), users are restricted to working with one 256-character font at a time. Software that comes with the board allows users to switch from one font to another.

> Quadvue™
> Quadram Corporation
> 4355 International Blvd.
> Norcross, GA 30093
> (404) 923-6666
> List Price: $345

---

63. These monitors retail for around $800 each.

2.2.5.8 *FonTableaux*

The FonTableaux™ display adapter (FTA), which is specifically designed for multilingual and technical (scientific) word processing, is a combination card that drives monochrome and color/graphics monitors and that provides high resolution (720-by-350) on monochrome monitors in text and graphics modes. It does not emulate the EGA. Unlike the other display adapters we have discussed, instead of replacing the computer's video card(s), the FTA functions as a secondary video card and requires the presence of an MDA, CGA, HGC, or compatible board to work. The FTA is connected by a jumper cable to the character-generator ROM chip's socket on the primary video board, and the primary video adapter's ROM chip is moved to an empty socket on the FTA. That gives the FTA the ability to display the entire IBM character set, as well as a downloaded set, though both sets may not be used concurrently. The FTA's font editor allows users to create as many 256-character fonts as desired, only one of which, however, can be downloaded to the FTA at a time and displayed by the FTA's RAM-resident character generator. Essentially, then, the FTA is a replacement for the primary video board's character-generator ROM.

The FTA comes with a font editor, font switcher, font loader, and four fonts designed for the monochrome screen: (1) Cyrillic, (2) Classical Greek (no diacritics), (3) Arabic, and (4) Hebrew (consonants only). Included in the list of word processors supported by the FTA are (1) XyWrite, (2) Word Star, (3) PerfectWriter, (4) Word Perfect, and (5) SAMNA Word III. Printers that are supported include (1) IBM Graphics, (2) Epson FX, (3) Okidata 92/93, and (4) Gemini 10x.

The advantages of the FTA for multilingual word processing are (1) high resolution, (2) the ability to display custom character sets, (3) fast screen redrawing, and (4) the fact that it is compatible with a number of popular word processors. The major disadvantages of the FTA for multilingual word processing are (1) the fact that it does not function as a stand-alone video board (thereby taking up an extra expansion slot) and (2) the fact that it can only display one font at a time.[64]

FonTableaux™ Display Adapter
ELECTREON™
The FonTableaux Group
P.O. Box 2253
Princeton, NJ 08540-0253
(609) 683-4453, (609) 921-2131
List Price: $299.95

2.2.5.9 *Summary*

Of the different display adapters we have reviewed, for multilingual word processing the Hercules Graphics Card Plus and IBM's Enhanced Graphics Adapter are the most attractive. When combined with multilingual word processing programs that take advantage of their distinctive features, these cards offer flexible, powerful, high-resolution ways to display nonroman characters on-screen.

---

64. The MULTIFONT adapter board, a similar product from Hash-Tech (2065 Martin Avenue #103, Santa Clara, CA 95050; (408) 988-2646; $187.50), also plugs into the ROM socket on the MDA and allows users to display up to 256 custom characters that can be created with a font editor and downloaded with another utility, both of which are included with the board. Only one 256-character font—IBM's or a custom one—may be active at a time, a serious restriction.

FEATURES	MDA	CGA	EGA¹	EGA²	HGC	HGC+	BoB	FTA
Character Box Size	9x14	8x8	8x14	9x14	9x14	9x16	9x16	8x14
Character Size	7x9	7x7	7x9	7x9	7x9	9x16	9x16	7x9
Character Box Density	126	64	112	126	126	144	144	112
Character Density	63	49	63	63	63	144	144	63
Maximum Resolution	720 350	640 200	640 350	720 350	720 348	720 348	640 400	720 350
Maximum Display Size	80x25	80x25	80x25	80x25	80x25	80x25	90x43	80x25
Maximum Characters	256	256	512	512	256	3,072	768	256

Table 2.1: Adapter board parameters. MDA = IBM Monochrome Display Adapter, CGA = IBM Color/Graphics Adapter, EGA¹ = IBM Enhanced Graphics Adapter in high-resolution graphics mode F or 10, EGA² = IBM Enhanced Graphics Adapter in monochrome alpha (text) mode 7, HGC = Hercules Graphics Card, HGC+ = Hercules Graphics Card Plus in RamFont mode, BoB = Best of Both card, FTA = FonTableaux card.

2.2.6 Special Screens

There are three types of special screens that can enhance word processing: (1) over-size screens (or special adapters) that can display a whole 8.5-by-11-inch page of text (i.e., 80-by-55) or more, (2) ultrahigh-resolution screens (e.g., 1,664-by-1,200), and (3) graphics screens that offer built-in support for displaying multiple character sets. Because oversize screens are usually ultrahigh-resolution screens (and vice versa), we will combine *(1)* and *(2)* into a single category. Because most of the word processing programs we are going to review do not include drivers for these screens, I will only devote a small amount of space to this otherwise interesting topic. See the *Bits & Bytes Review*™ 1 (January 1987): 12–18, and Charles Petzold and Winn L. Rosch, "Four-Figure Video," *PC Magazine* (May 26, 1987): 235–74, for more information.

2.2.6.1 Oversize, Ultrahigh-Resolution Monitors and Special Adapters

The size of a standard display—80 columns by 25 lines—is an arbitrary size that restricts users to displaying only half of a printed 8.5-by-11-inch page of text, which is usually 80 columns across and 55 to 66 lines long (70 to 76 if using European A4 size paper).[65] The resolution of standard monochrome monitors—720-by-350—is not well-suited for displaying complex composite characters legibly. Not surprisingly, then,

---

65. See Sachs, "Big Screen," 122–33, for more information about four of the screens mentioned in this section. Also see James Felici, "Screen Tests," *Publish!* (May 1987): 50–57; James Karney, "Multi Displays," *Personal Publishing* (January 1987): 44–53; Bill Nichols, "The Big Picture," *Personal Publishing* (January 1987): 28–33.

several companies market screens that remedy one or both of those problems in one of two ways: by using oversize, ultrahigh-resolution screens (with special video cards) or by using special video cards that reduce the size of the characters so that more lines of text fit on standard size screens.

The GENIUS VHR, which comes with its own video card and which is mounted in portrait mode (i.e., vertically),[66] is one example of an oversize, high-resolution screen. (1) It allows a full page of text to be displayed—up to 66 lines on the American version, up to 76 lines on the European version (the size of an A4 page). (2) It comes with two 256-character ROMs, the second of which contains all the special characters and symbols needed for Western European languages. (3) Special custom versions of the board can contain up to eight 256-character fonts in ROMs (i.e., up to 2,048 different characters). (4) It uses square pixels (a 1:1 pixel aspect ratio), which results in faster screen updates and truer curves (see above). (5) It has up to 100 pixel-per-inch resolution both vertically and horizontally. (6) It can display up to 736-by-1,008 in graphics mode and either 80-by-25 or 80-by-66 in text mode.[67] (7) Its 8-by-12 characters (with 3 line descenders) are formed in 9-by-15 character matrices. Thus they are denser—better defined—than those formed by the MDA, CGA, EGA, or HGC, but not denser than those that can be formed by the HGC+, which allows characters in RamFont mode to be up to 9-by-16. (8) The model 402 can operate in either text mode or in graphics mode or in both at the same time.[68] (9) It can emulate the MDA and the CGA. (10) It is fully compatible with at least four multilingual word processing programs we are about to review: FinalWord II, XyWrite III, Nota Bene, and Microsoft Word.[69] (11) There is a wide range of software compatibility between the GENIUS VHR and existing IBM PC software. (12) The GENIUS VHR is a white-phosphor monitor, which means that the display is either black-on-white or white-on-black. (13) Because the GENIUS VHR is reported to redraw the screen quickly (I have no precise measure of its speed), can display text in graphics mode with 736-by-1,008 resolution, creates 8-by-12 characters, and can display a full page of text, it would make an excellent monitor for graphics-mode or text-mode multilingual word processing. Unfortunately, the GENIUS VHR and card cannot be used in the same system with another monitor and video card.[70]

The GENIUS VHR
Micro Display Systems, Inc.
1310 Vermillion St.
P.O. Box 455
Hastings, MN 55033
(800) 328-9524, (612) 437-2233
List Price: $1,595 (model 401—text only); $1,795 (model
    402—text and graphics)

Here is a list of other, oversize, white-phosphor, ultrahigh-resolution monitors for IBM PCs and for the Macintosh.

---

66. *Portrait mode* is contrasted with *landscape mode*, which refers to a monitor whose screen is mounted with the larger dimension running horizontally.

67. The MDS—Micro Display Systems—literature defines resolution in graphics mode in terms of pixels and in text mode in terms of columns-by-lines.

68. By splitting the screen into two windows, the GENIUS VHR can operate in a dual mode where one window is in text mode and the other in graphics mode.

69. According to MDS's Bill Fraser, XyWrite III can drive the GENIUS in text mode at 720-by-990 (a full 66 lines), which means that Nota Bene, an enhanced version of XyWrite III, should be able to drive it at that same resolution. I have no information about what resolution FinalWord II and Microsoft Word are capable of with this monitor.

70. Items (2), (3), (8), and (9) are not typical of oversize, high-resolution screens.

LaserView™ Display System
Sigma Designs, Inc.
46501 Landing Parkway
Fremont, CA 94538
(415) 770-0100
Basic Facts: 19-inch (landscape mode); 1,664-by-1,200 (nonin-
        terlaced); bandwidth: 160 MHz; horizontal scan
        rate: 75 KHz
Computers Supported: IBM PCs and compatibles; 15- and 19-
        inch Macintosh versions are being developed.
List Price: 15-inch: $1,895; 19-inch: $2,395; both prices in-
        clude the LDA-1200 display adapter.
Other: See the *Bits & Bytes Review*™ 1 (January 1987): 12–18,
        for an in-depth review of the LaserView™.

Viking 1
Moniterm, Inc.
5740 Green Circle Dr.
Minnetonka, MN 55343
(612) 935-4151
Basic Facts: 19-inch (landscape mode); 1,280-by-960 (noninter-
        laced); bandwidth: 110 MHz; horizontal scan rate:
        66 KHz
Computers Supported: IBM PCs and compatibles
List Price: $2,395

LM-300 and LM-301
Princeton Graphic Systems
601 Ewing Bldg. A
Princeton, NJ 08540
(800) 221-1490
Basic Facts: 15-inch; LM-300 (portrait mode), LM-301
        (landscape mode); 1,660-by-1,200 (noninterlaced);
        bandwidth: 160 MHz; horizontal scan rate: 75 KHz
Computers Supported: IBM PCs and compatibles
List Price: $750 each and $750 for the adapter

The Quadscreen®
Quadram Corporation
4355 International Blvd.
Norcross, GA 30093
(404) 923-6666
Basic Facts: 17-inch (landscape mode); 968-by-512; can display
        up to 160 columns by 64 lines.
Computers Supported: IBM PCs and compatibles
List Price: $1,995

WY-700
Wyse Technology
3571 N. 1st St.
San Jose, CA 95134
(408) 433-1000
Basic Facts: 15-inch (landscape mode); 1,280-by-800 (inter-
        laced)
Computers Supported: IBM PCs and compatibles
List Price: $999

Amdek 1280
Amdek Corp.
2201 Lively Blvd.
Elk Grove, IL 60007
(312) 364-1180
Basic Facts: 15-inch (landscape mode); 1,280-by-800 (inter-
laced)
Computers Supported: IBM PCs and compatibles
List Price: $999

Intelligent High Performance Video Adapter
Video-7
550 Sycamore Dr.
Milpitias, CA 95035
(408) 943-0101
Basic Facts: 1,024-by-1,024, 16 colors or shades of grey from
palette of 4,096; drivers for Windows, GEM,
AutoCAD, Lotus 1-2-3, Halo, PC Paintbrush Plus
List Price: Not known

ConoVision 2800
Conographics Corp.
17841 Fitch
Irvine, CA 92714
(714) 474-1188
Basic Facts: 19-inch (landscape mode); up to 2,880-by-1,024
(interlaced)
Computers Supported: IBM PCs and compatibles
List Price: $1,525; display adapter: $1,325

MegaScreen™ Plus
MicroGraphic Images
20954 Osborne St.
Canoga Park, CA 91304
(818) 407-0571
Basic Facts: 19.5-inch (landscape mode); 1,024-by-900; 75 dpi
Computers Supported: Macintosh
List Price: $2,495; the MegaScreen II, which is not compatible
with a Macintosh that uses a math coprocesor or an
internal hard disk, is available for $1,995.

The Big Picture
E-Machines
7945 Southwest Mohawk St.
Tualatin, OR 97062
(503) 692-6656
Basic Facts: 17-inch (landscape mode); 1,024-by-808; 82 dpi
Computers Supported: Macintosh
List Price: $1,995

Radius Full Page Display
Radius, Inc.
1050 E. Duane Ave., Suite F
Sunnyvale, CA 94086
(408) 732-1010
Basic Facts: 15-inch (portrait mode); 640-by-864; can display
full A4 size page plus menu bar.
Computers Supported: Macintosh
List Price: $1,995

SuperVision
California Computer Systems
2036 Concourse Dr.
San Jose, CA 95131
(408) 945-0500
Basic Facts: This is a special adapter card for IBM PCs that displays up to 132 columns by 44 lines.
List Price: $499 (without graphics); $599 (with graphics); $100
(optional add-on board)

The Graphics Master
Tecmar Incorporated
Personal Computer Products Division
6225 Cochran Rd.
Cleveland, OH 44139
(216) 349-0600
Basic Facts: This is a special adapter card for IBM PCs that dis-
plays up to 80 columns by 86 lines.
List Price: $695

2.2.6.2 Other High-Resolution Monitors

In addition to the ultrahigh-resolution monitors mentioned above, the following very-high resolution monitors should be noted.[71]

NEC JC-1401P3A Multisync
NEC Home Electronics (USA), Inc.
Personal Computer Division
1255 Micheal Dr.
Woodale, IL 60191
(312) 860-9500
Maximum Resolution: 800-by-560 pixels
List Price: $899

The Microvitec Cub
Techland Systems, Inc.
25 Waterside Plaza
New York, NY 10010
(212) 684-7788
Maximum Resolution: 895-by-585
List Price: $1,290

2.2.6.3 Special Graphics Screens

The CATAB/CALLIGRAPHE 44© is a special monitor that offers built-in hardware and software support for displaying multiple character sets and is compatible with any microcomputer, minicomputer, or mainframe that has a standard RS-232C serial (asynchronous) interface.[72] The resolution of the 14-inch, green-phosphor screen is 1,024-by-768 pixels. Over a thousand different characters[73] may be used concurrently. The CALLIGRAPHE supports RAM-based and ROM-based character gen-

---

71. As with the monitors listed above, programs must include special drivers to run these monitors at maximum resolution.

72. The CALLIGRAPHE can communicate with the computer at 300 to 19,200 baud.

73. I assume the literature means 1,024, though it does not specifically say so.

erators, as well as bit-mapped graphics.[74] Fonts and assembly-language character generators can be loaded into RAM (or into a ROM or EPROM chip) on the CALLIGRAPHE's display adapter and directly addressed by programs, or programs may work with bit-mapped fonts and write the screen pixel-by-pixel. RAM-based character generators are available for Arabic, Hebrew (vocalized), Syriac, Greek, Chinese, Cyrillic, and other fonts. The literature does not state if a font editor is included.

> CATAB/CALLIGRAPHE 44©
> UNIXSYS
> 3, Place Paul-Verlaine
> 75013 Paris
> France
> (1) 4589-8990, from North America dial 011-33-1-4589-8990
> List Price: 12,000 to 15,000 French francs, approximately US
> $1,846 to $2,307 (based on an exchange rate of 6.5
> francs/dollar)

2.2.7 Printers and Printing

And now for a very brief glimpse into Pandora's box! To benefit from the multilingual abilities of the programs we are about to review, you will need a printer that can print nonstandard characters. There are five basic types of printers, numerous different brands, and a multitude of specific models—far too many different printers for me to do more than summarize a few important facts and to describe one particular printer in some detail. For helpful explanations of the differences, strengths, and weaknesses of the basic types of printers, see Steve Rosenthal, "How PC Printers Make Their Mark," PC *Magazine* (Nov. 27, 1984): 124–29; Don Conkey and Sharyn Conkey, "A Printer Shopping List," PC *World* (November 1985): 133–43; and the April 1986 issue (vol. 2, no. 8) of the *Penn Printout*. For very helpful reviews and comparisons of over 200 printers, see the series of articles on printers in the October 1983, the November 27, 1984, the September 17, 1985, and the November 11, 1986, issues of PC *Magazine*. Also see Karen Sorensen et al., "Dot-Matrix Printers," *InfoWorld* (July 28, 1986): 29–43.

2.2.7.1 Five Basic Types of Printers

There are five basic types of printers. (1) Printers that store characters on removable daisywheels or print thimbles are known as impact or letter-quality printers because of the way they form their characters on paper and because of the quality of the characters they form. Like typewriter keys, the characters on the print wheels of these printers are fully formed and strike the ribbon with enough force to create characters of exceptionally high quality. (2) Printers whose print heads consist of anywhere from nine to twenty-four tiny wires that form characters by impacting the paper are known as dot-matrix or matrix printers because the characters they form are composed of a series of overlapping dots that are created in rectangular, fixed-size matrices.[75] Dot-matrix printers can operate by using predefined character sets or by *drawing* characters in graphics mode (a slow way to print). (3) Printers that form characters by spraying

---

74. RAM-based character generators are programmed in 8080 or Z80 assembler and operated by a Graphic Display Controller (GDC) that is powered by a NEC 7220-D graphics processor (with 128K RAM), which is controlled by an on-board Intel 8085 (code compatible with the 8080) running at 10 MHz.
 The CALLIGRAPHE literature refers to character generators as "writing generators" because they may include instructions that govern features of the screen other than the shapes of the characters that are displayed, such as the direction in which characters are displayed, that is, left-to-right or right-to-left.

75. Some dot-matrix printers allow for several different size grids to be used, though not concurrently.

dots of ink on the paper are known as ink-jet printers and can be thought of as a type of nonimpact dot-matrix printer. (4) Printers that form characters on paper by using advanced photocopier technology are known as laser printers because they use a laser beam to form characters on an electrostatically charged drum. Because they form characters as dots in matrices, they, too, may be seen as another type of nonimpact dot-matrix printer.[76] And (5) IBM produces a line of printers—Quietwriters—that form characters by using thermal-transfer technology in which a multi-pin print head heats a special heat-sensitive, layered ribbon and "melts" characters on the paper. Because their print heads consist of multiple pins, Quitewriters may be thought of as yet a third type of nonimpact dot-matrix printer. Thus, logically speaking, there are two fundamental types of printers: impact and dot-matrix.

2.2.7.2 Printer Parameters

Fundamental printer parameters include (1) speed, (2) print quality, and (3) flexibility. Noise level could be considered as a fourth parameter, but I'll not worry with that here. Laser, ink-jet, and dot-matrix printers are the fastest, letter-quality the slowest. Letter-quality printers, however, tend to have the highest quality output because they produce fully-formed characters; other printer technologies must form characters by using a series of overlapping dots. Laser printers and some ink-jet and twenty-four-pin dot matrix printers,[77] however, can produce characters that are difficult to distinguish from those created by impact printers. As is true with screen resolution (see the discussion above), the smaller and more numerous the dots, the better the resolution of the characters. Twenty-four-pin print heads, for example, produce noticeably higher quality (i.e., denser) characters than do nine-pin heads.

Flexibility refers to a printer's ability to accept downloaded fonts, to use different fonts concurrently, to display different character attributes such as italic, bold and underlined, to print sub- and superscripted characters, to perform reverse line feeds, to backspace, and so forth—topics we will discuss below.

2.2.7.3 Printers for Multilingual Word Processing

Almost any printer can be made to print nonstandard character sets. Because impact printers allow users to change print wheels, they can be used to print multilingual documents, as long as the proper print wheels are available. But because (1) they are limited to between 96 and 128 characters per print wheel, because (2) no one print wheel can hold all the necessary characters for a complete roman and a complete non-roman character set, and because (3) changing print wheels over and over again in a multilingual document is more trouble than it is worth, we can eliminate impact printers. Most laser, ink-jet, and dot-matrix printers can use nonstandard fonts, which are loaded into the printer through cartridges that contain character sets on ROM

---

76. I'm including the IBM 3812 Pageprinter and similar printers that use LED technology in this category. See the following articles for explanations of how laser printers work and for comparisons of different laser printers: Bernard, "LaserJet," 36–87; Martin, "Printers," 83–91; Dickinson, "Printers," 208–9; Harts, "Little Engine," 210–11, "Ricoh," 353–56; Christian, "Lasers," 211–14; Rosenthal, "Printers," 214–16; Burns and Venit, "Printers," 184–92; Heid, "Laserjet," 34–39; Hart, "Printer," 205–15; Roth, "JLaser," 46–50; Ulick, "HP LaserJet Plus," 52–61; Hart, "Savvy Shoppers Guide," 60–69; Felici, "Memory," 84–86; Poor, "Tag," 269–86; Poor and Machrone, "Technology," 123–45; O'Brien, "HP Laserjet," 161–73; Gardner, "LaserJet," 229–33.

77. Twenty-four-pin dot-matrix printers were developed by the Japanese to print the complex kanji characters of that language.

chips or downloaded from software in the computer into the printer's RAM.[78] Laser printers and some dot-matrix printers can draw characters in graphics mode, thereby producing *any* character (see below under "Font and Printer Utilities"), but this is a slow way to print.[79] In terms of flexibility, speed, and quality, the best types of printers for multilingual word processing are laser printers and dot-matrix printers.

The most heavily supported laser printers for microcomputers are the Apple LaserWriter and LaserWriter Plus and the Hewlett-Packard LaserJet and LaserJet Plus.[80] Because dot-matrix printers represent the best combination of flexibility and cost, however, we will focus on them. Two of the most popular brands of dot-matrix printers for multilingual word processing are Epson and Toshiba. Only certain models of each brand, however, will (1) accept downloaded fonts, (2) perform reverse line feeds, (3) backspace, and (4) allow users to work concurrently with multiple fonts. We have already discussed downloading fonts—creating character sets that can be stored on disk and downloading them as needed into the printer's RAM—and displaying different character attributes. Backspacing and reverse line feeds are necessary for placing accents over characters, thereby reducing the number of basic symbols needed to create composite characters. And working with multiple fonts concurrently is absolutely necessary for multilingual word processing.

One exceptionally flexible dot-matrix printer that accepts downloaded fonts, performs reverse line feeds, backspaces, prints italics, bold and underlined, does super- and subscripting, allows multiple fonts to be used concurrently, and supports character matrices of up to 36-by-24 dots[81] is the Toshiba P351-Model 2 (which Toshiba calls the "3-in-One"), the successor to the popular Toshiba P1351.[82] Almost every major word processing program—multilingual and otherwise—supports this printer, whose features we will now discuss.[83]

The P351, Toshiba's top-of-the-line model, has a 24-pin print head and can print 136 columns in three types of fonts: (1) resident, (2) downloadable, and (3) plug-in cartridge fonts. The three resident fonts, which are built into the printer, include a high-speed font, and two high-quality fonts (Courier and Prestige Elite). Downloadable fonts are purchased on disks or created with word processing programs and downloaded by using special "escape sequences" (special codes).[84] Cartridge fonts

---

78. Just as nonstandard character sets can be downloaded into RAM-based character generators and displayed on-screen, and just as character-generator ROM chips can be changed and different sets of characters displayed on-screen, so nonstandard fonts either must be downloaded into the printer's RAM or loaded into the printer via ROM-based font cartridges if the nonstandard characters on-screen are to be printed correctly in text mode. The printer's character sets must correspond to the character sets used on-screen. Thus for each screen font, there must be a corresponding printer font.

79. According to Abercrombie ("Graphics Display of Foreign Scripts for Language Analysis" (August 1986): 15—unpublished), an Epson FX80+ dot-matrix printer can print in graphics (or "raster") mode at 8 cps as opposed to 80 to 160 cps in text mode, i.e., when working with RAM-based character sets.

80. In the original LaserJet (not the Plus model), fonts are loaded in cartridges and may not be downloaded from disk. That makes the original model less acceptable for multilingual word processing than the Plus model, which accepts downloaded fonts.

81. Many dot-matrix printers restrict character matrices to 8-by-9 dots.

82. The P351-Model 2 corrects some of the frustrating design features of the original P351. On the Model 2, the DIP switches have been moved from the back of the printer and placed just under the printer's lift-up top cover. The Model 2 has a redesigned front panel that contains print selection switches that govern options such as pitch, font, print quality, and paper motion. The Model 2 also prints a little faster in draft mode and includes a new switch-selectable quiet mode, which slows the printer down—thereby quieting it—without affecting print quality. And the Model 2 will accept 6-part forms.

83. When run in the graphics mode, the P351 emulates Qume SPRINT 11 graphics.

84. Escape codes (also known as control codes) are nonprinting codes that are sent to the printer to alter the appearance of text that follows the escape code. To cause a printer to print text in italics, for example, an escape code is sent to the printer to inform it to print in italics until it receives another escape code that instructs it to print in some other typestyle. Escape codes are so named because they always begin with the ESCape character (decimal 27) and cause the printer to escape from printing, to switch modes, and to print

67

are available from Toshiba for $49.95 each, and each cartridge holds two 128-character fonts. In addition to the three resident fonts, two fonts can be downloaded into the printer's RAM and another two loaded from cartridges that plug into external slots on the rear of the printer. Thus up to seven different 128-character fonts may be used concurrently (i.e., 896 different characters). This means that users can work with 512 custom characters (i.e., four custom 128-character fonts) and the three resident fonts at the same time.

The Toshiba P351 can print in letter-quality mode at burst rates of up to 100 characters per second (cps) and in draft-quality mode at burst rates of up to 288 cps,[85] as well as produce dense, high-resolution (180-by-180 or 180-by-360 dpi), dot-addressable graphics. Because of its 24-pin print head, superthin wires,[86] and overlapping dots, the Toshiba P351 produces very high quality print. In my opinion—and in that of the reviewers at *PC Magazine*—because of its flexibility, speed, high-quality construction, and reasonable cost, the Toshiba P351 is the dot-matrix printer of choice, especially for multilingual word processing.

> Toshiba P351
> Toshiba America, Inc.
> Information Systems Division
> 9740 Irvine Blvd.
> Irvine, CA 92718
> (800) 457-7777, (714) 583-3000
> List Price: $1,399 (includes parallel and serial ports); some options: $199 for bidirectional tractor, $699 for electronic integrated sheet feeder, $69 per font cartridge (8 available), $35 to $69 per downloadable font set (3 to 5 fonts per set)

2.3 Word Processing Terminology

Before proceeding with our reviews of the programs, we need to master some word processing terminology. As you know by now, computer jargon has developed with little—if any—respect for the English language. Nouns such as *bug*, *chip*, *hardware*, *software*, *firmware*, and *stack* and verbs such as *debug*, *download*, and *upload* and words like *input* and *output*, which are used both as nouns and as verbs, stretch the language considerably. But nowhere is the stretching more pronounced than in the area of word processing terminology. In this area ordinary words like *widow*, *orphan*, *child*, *parent*, and *string* have been given new meanings.[87] In addition to those words, we must learn

---

in the new mode. A full escape sequence consists of three parts (three contiguous codes): (1) the ESC code, (2) a function code (e.g., a code that means change font, change pitch, change typestyle) that informs the printer what function is called for, and (3) a parameter code that specifies which particular variation of the function is to be implemented (e.g., change font to Elite, change pitch to 12 dpi, change typestyle to italics). Escape codes are usually handled automatically by word processing software and are part of the software's printer definition file.

85. According to *PC Magazine*, however, in the high-speed mode the Toshiba P351 prints at 108 cps (Dickinson, "Printers," 156).

86. The print pins on the P351's print head are only 8 mils (0.2 mm) in diameter—just twice the diameter of a human hair.

87. A *widow* is a line of text, such as the first line of a paragraph, that is left standing alone at the bottom of a page when for aesthetic reasons it belongs at the top of the following page. An *orphan* is a line of text, such as the last line of a paragraph, that is left standing alone at the top of a page when for aesthetic reasons it belongs at the bottom of the previous page. *Child* and *parent* are, I believe, *sui generis* to FinalWord II (see below) and have to do with commands whose values are relative to one another such that the value of one command (the parent) determines the values of the related commands (the children), terminology obviously developed by someone with no children!

terms such as *block move, command line, cut and paste, default, delete, delimiter, editor, environment, format, formatter, flushleft, flushright, footer, header, information line, insert mode, install program, justify, leading, macro, mark, menu, message line, microjustification, move, overstrike mode, overwrite mode, page footing, page heading, printer tables, proportional spacing, pushover mode, ruler line, search and replace, split screen, status line, strikeover mode, translation table, undelete, vertical justification, wild-card character, window, wrap, WYSIWYG,* and on and on. Although we cannot spend too much time on terminology, we should define some of the more important words.

Roughly speaking, like Gaul, all word processing terminology can be divided into three parts: (1) editing terms (words that pertain to text entry and manipulation), (2) formatting terms (words that pertain to coding text for printing), and (3) printing terminology. These three divisions correspond to the three major programs or functions of a word processing system—editing, formatting, and printing, which also are sometimes referred to as the editor, the formatter, and the print program.

2.3.1 Editing Terms

Editing terms have to do with text entry and manipulation. A basic distinction in inputting (another barbarism!) text is that between *insert* (or *pushover*) mode and *overwrite* (or *overstrike*) mode. In insert mode, text that is entered in the midst of existing text causes text to the right of the cursor to be pushed to the right (or to the left in right-to-left oriented word processors, e.g., Hebrew word processors), that is, pushed over. In overwrite mode, text that is entered in the midst of existing text overwrites the existing text, thus causing it to disappear. In either text-entry mode, most word processing programs will automatically *wrap* text from line to line without users having to enter "carriage returns."

One major part of word processing—perhaps the activity that consumes the most user time—is text manipulation: copying, deleting, moving, and changing text. Indeed, the ability to rearrange and change text on-screen—to edit a document—is one of the main reasons word processors were created in the first place. By using the appropriate commands to set *marks* at two different places in a document, users can *copy* or *delete* the block of text that intervenes between the two marks. Text that has been copied or deleted may be *undeleted* somewhere else in that or another document, something that is known as a *block move.* On some word processors, the block of text that is to be deleted is highlighted. Moving text by blocks is also referred to as *cut and paste.*

Other fundamental editing activities include search and search-and-replace. Texts may be searched for strings of symbols, and when found, those strings may be replaced automatically with other, user-specified strings. (A *string* is any combination of symbols; a *symbol* may be a letter, a number, or any other sign.) For example, "Jason" could be replaced with "Jason and the Argonauts," a procedure known as *search and replace.* If that is done globally (that is, automatically throughout a document, from the point where the cursor is to the end of the document, without user intervention), it is known as *global search and replace.* If it is done on a case-by-case basis that requires user input for each instance, it is known as *conditional search and replace.* Some word processors support *wild-card searching,* which means that the program can search for strings in which one or more characters are wild-card characters. For example, a program that supports wild-card searches might accept a command like *∗all,* which would locate all four-letter words that ended in the character string *all,* that is, "ball," "call," "fall," "hall," "mall," "pall," "tall," and "wall."

Some word processors allow users to redefine keys and to assign character strings and commands to key combinations. Redefining a key might be as simple as defining the left-hand Shift key on an old IBM keyboard to be the backslash key, and vice versa, since the "old" IBM keyboard separates ʒ from Shift by inserting the backslash key, contrary to the standard American typewriter keyboard, which has the left-hand

Shift key immediately to the left of *z*. Defining a key combination (e.g., Alt + any key) so that it prints a string of characters or performs multiple commands or does both is known as creating a *macro*. A macro is a one-keystroke combination that executes what would otherwise require multiple keystrokes.

As I mentioned earlier, word processors differ in their interfaces—the way users and the program interact. Some word processors create *ruler lines* across the top of the screen that indicate columns and that show tab settings. Some have *command lines*, at the top or bottom of the screen, to which the cursor must be moved to issue commands. Some have *message lines*, or *information lines*, at the top or bottom of the screen, where messages are displayed. Some have *status lines*, at the top or bottom of the screen, that show what row, column, line, and page the cursor is in, how much free space is on the disk, and so forth. Some combine several of those functions on one line. And some number the lines of text down the left side of the screen. Some word processors allow users to turn such features off and to operate with (virtually) a "clean screen." Most word processors have *menus*, which are lists of commands (often accompanied by instructions) on how to use the word processor. Users select from menus the commands they wish implemented. Some word processors provide context-sensitive, on-line help about their various features.

Finally, though this by no means exhausts the terminology in this category, some word processors allow users to *split*, or divide, the screen into different sections known as *windows* and to edit two or more files (documents) concurrently or to edit two or more different sections of the same file at the same time.

2.3.2 Formatting Terms

Formatting refers either to the activity of inserting coded commands into a document to specify how the document is to be printed or to the activity of the word processor whereby those coded commands are acted upon. I will use the term in the former sense. Formatting a document includes choosing a typeface (roman, italic, bold), setting margin widths, determining whether notes will be placed at the end of the document or at the foot of the page, defining running headers and footers, specifying what kind of justification to use, and so forth.

Word processors differ in the codes and formatting commands they use and in the way codes and commands are displayed (or not displayed) on-screen. For example, FinalWord, the word processor I am using to write this book, uses formatting commands that have one of two basic forms: (1) @x<yyy>, where "@" is a special code that indicates that a formatting command follows, "x" stands for the specific formatting command, "<" and ">" are *delimiters* that define the section of text that the command is to act upon, and "yyy" is the string of text that is to be acted upon, and (2) @begin(*environment*) . . . @end(*environment*), where "@" is a special code that indicates that a formatting command follows, "begin" is a command that indicates the beginning of a major environment that affects a section of text ("end" signals the end of the environment), and "environment" is a term that stands for different environments such as "level" (for automatically numbered lists), "verbatim," "quotation" (for block quotations), and so forth.[88] So in FinalWord, to print "Dear Claire" in italics, I would type "@i<Dear Claire>" ("i" is the command for italics), and "@i<Dear Claire>" would be displayed exactly that way on-screen, though the formatter would cause it to be printed correctly as *Dear Claire*.

---

88. Actually, all text in every word processing program is inside an environment, and all formatting commands can be thought of as altering the text in the environment delimited by the command. Thus the first type of command in FinalWord also can be thought of as creating an environment between the two delimiters.

Other word processing programs (e.g., Nota Bene) display text that is to be italicized in reverse video, text that is to be bold as intense video, text that is to be underlined as underlined, and so forth, without displaying the coded commands used to define those mini-environments, though such programs have a "reveal" mode that allows users to see and edit the codes that the program has inserted in the text. Thus all word processing programs insert formatting codes in the text: some embed codes so that they appear on-screen as part of the text, others hide the codes. The second type of program tends to be known as WYSIWYG (pronounced "wizzywig"), which means "what you see is what you get"—more or less.[89]

Most word processing programs come with many or most of the formatting parameters preset to certain *default values*. These values have been assigned by the manufacturer and can be altered by users. The basic values that must be set before the formatter can process text for printing include the following: (1) justification—whether the left side (flushleft) or right side (flushright) or both sides of the text are to be printed flush, (2) margins—how much white space to leave around the four sides of the text, (3) line and paragraph spacing—how much space to leave between lines and between paragraphs, (4) headers and footers—whether *running headers* and *running footers* are to be included at the top and bottom of each page, (5) type of notes—footnotes or endnotes, and (6) the default font.

2.3.3 Printing Terms

Word processing programs normally have an *install program* that is used to install the word processor for a user's (1) computer, (2) monitor, (3) keyboard, and (4) printer or printers. Typically, these programs are menu-driven. As I mentioned earlier, a word processing program must provide a driver for every input/output device it supports.

Printer drivers are part of a program's "printer tables," which are lists of printer-specific variables that work with the printer drivers to drive specific printers. Depending on the particular word processing program, printer tables are capable of being edited (of having their values changed by users). A typical printer table contains the following *logical* components: (1) attribute tables, (2) font tables, (3) width tables, (4) substitution tables (sometimes referred to as "translation tables"), and (5) the printer-driver program. The attribute tables specify which printer attributes are supported (e.g., bold, italics, superscript, overstrike) and contain the escape sequences that activate those attributes. Font tables specify which fonts are supported (e.g., Pica, Elite) and contain the escape sequences that activate those fonts. Width tables specify the width of the characters. Substitution tables specify how characters are to be printed and allow users to have the printer print nonstandard characters by redefining the values of standard characters. Printer drivers control horizontal and vertical spacing, line feeds, carriage returns, printer initialization and reset strings, overprinting, and other parameters.

Proportional spacing refers to printing characters in various widths, rather than assigning each character the same width. For example, in a proportionally spaced font, *m* and *i* would be different widths. Word processing programs that support proportionally spaced printing usually include a character width table that specifies a width for

---

89. WYSIWYG is often used loosely to refer to programs that display text attributes (e.g., italics, bold, underlined) on-screen or that show line and page breaks with a high degree of fidelity to what the printed version of the page will look like or that do both. To be WYSIWYG in a *literal* sense, however, a program would have to display on-screen (1) actual line, page and column breaks, (2) actual type size, (3) actual typeface and typestyle, (4) actual letter, word and line spacing, (5) columns in position, (6) all special characters, (7) running headers and footers, and (8) footnotes properly placed. Cf. *Personal Publishing* (October 1985): 25; Steve Roth, "What Is Wysiwyg?," *Personal Publishing* (March 1987): 26–28.

each proportionally spaced character. Unlike whole-space justification, which adds whole spaces between words to justify text, *microjustification* adds space in fractional units between characters, as well as between words, to justify text. Pages of text that have been *vertically justified* are of equal depth, that is, the vertical dimension of the text area on such pages is identical. Vertical justification is important for programs that can be used to typeset, since publishers want the text areas on facing pages to be identical heights. Like microjustification, vertical justification adds spacing (*leading*) between lines in fractional units to make the height of the text area on each page uniform.

2.4 Categories for Evaluating Programs

Programs will be evaluated in the same manner, using the same categories and criteria. Although every effort has been made to be as objective as possible, subjective judgments and personal preferences will inevitably enter in. Therefore it is only fair to share my prejudices. I prefer command-driven, document-oriented, full-featured word processing programs that are as fast and flexible as possible. I prefer programs that use mnemonic commands, that work in text mode, that allow the maximum amount of user customization, that format documents for printing at print time, and that support the automatic numbering of different levels of headings and of footnotes. WYSIWYG programs that hide formatting codes are nice, as long as they make it easy to do global search and replaces on the codes. I am ambivalent about on-line help. I prefer to spell check in batch mode with a stand-alone program after a document is created, rather than be interrupted by a built-in spell checker while I am composing. Built-in spell checkers are nice, however, for checking words or sections of a document without having to exit the word processing program.

To provide some balance to my prejudices, I have done three things. First, in this chapter and throughout this book, I have sent copies of *every* review to the companies whose product(s) I have reviewed so that the factuality of my statements and the fairness of my judgments might be assessed by those who should be the most capable of doing so. Almost every company has taken the time to read what I have written, correct it, make suggestions, and return the material to me. I have then corrected the factual inaccuracies in my reviews and, when I deemed it proper, modified my criticisms. Every effort, then, has been made to get the facts correct and to be fair.

Second, when possible I have included short bibliographies after each review or after each set of reviews. These bibliographies list all the major reviews of the program of which I am aware, as well as any books or other major learning aids that are available.

Third, in the listing of facts given with each program I have included information about Special Interest Groups (SIGs), newsletters, bulletin boards, and other sources of information.

More detailed and discursive reviews of some of the major programs and products discussed in this chapter (and in other chapters of this book) have appeared and will appear in my newsletter the **Bits & Bytes Review**™, as will reviews of many products and resources not discussed in this book (see the subscription information at the end of this book).

Many of the word processing programs reviewed in this chapter will prove daunting and frustrating to the complete novice who has no one to provide assistance. Indeed, many of the programs will challenge readers who are experienced in using word processors! My assumption, however, is that with patience and determination, any reader of this book can learn any of the programs we are about to review.

The word processing programs reviewed below will be evaluated primarily, though not exclusively, with regard to their suitability for scholarly and multilingual word processing. Because word processing programs are inherently complex, several different sets of categories will be used to evaluate them. Reviews will vary in length, depending on a program's features, flexibility, power, and sophistication.

The following categories will be used to evaluate each program in terms of its suitability for creating large, complex documents and for multilingual word processing: (1) performance and versatility, (2) documentation, (3) ease of use, (4) error handling, and (5) support.

Categories such as (1) ease of start up, (2) ease of learning, and (3) value have been omitted because they are so subjective and user-variable. A $500, complex, do-everything program may seem a terrific value to one person who may find the program easy to start and to learn, while another person may think the program is terribly overpriced, overpowered, complex, and difficult. Although also somewhat subjective, I have nevertheless included "ease of use" as a category. On the one hand, learning a program is, more or less, something that is mastered within a relatively short period of time and then is over with. On the other hand, a program's user interface—the way the program requires users to interact with it—is constant, within certain parameters. "Ease of use," then, though somewhat subjective, seems less so than the three categories I have omitted.

2.5 Programs with Multilingual Capabilities

In this subsection we will examine a number of professional programs with multilingual capabilities. In this context *professional programs* refers to commercial programs designed for professionals in the academic, scientific, and business communities. *Multilingual capabilities* means that these programs can display different fonts on-screen or print them or do both. Although most of the categories are self-explanatory, four demand a bit of explanation. (1) **Produces ASCII Files:** refers to a program's ability to output files in ASCII code (whether or not that is the default setting of the program). ASCII files can easily be read by other word processors, application programs, operating systems, printers, and so forth. (2) **Produces PostScript Files:** refers to a program's ability to output files that are formatted in the PostScript page-description language, a machine-independent language that is increasingly used for desktop and conventional publishing. Word processing programs that can produce PostScript files can drive laser printers and phototypesetters that are equipped to receive and interpret such files, thereby facilitating desktop publishing and user-controlled phototypesetting. (3) **Drives Typesetters:** refers to a program's ability to drive phototypesetters, that is, to be used in a PC (that is functioning as the "front end" for the typesetter) in such a way that the PC and the word processing program are able to treat the phototypesetter as an ordinary output device (i.e., as a printer) and so cause it to produce high-resolution (1,200 or more dpi), camera-ready copy directly from formatted word processing files, without those files having to be recoded or "massaged." (4) **SideKick Compatible:** refers to a program's ability to work with Borland International's SideKick, a popular, pop-up, memory-resident, multifaceted windowing utility that includes a calculator, calendar, note pad, telephone dialer, ASCII table, appointment scheduler, and rudimentary word processor.

For programs that operate printers in text mode (which includes most of the programs reviewed below), I have not listed the number of different printer fonts that may be specified in a single document since this figure is a function of the printer's capabilities and of the program's printer tables. Because each of the programs reviewed below works with a large number of printers, to save space I have not listed that information. For the sake of readers who wish to produce copy on laser printers, I have included information about which laser printers the programs work with. It is usually safe to assume that a word processing program will work with most (if not all) Epson, Toshiba, and NEC printers, among others.

Although copies of a few programs arrived too late to be reviewed, I have tried to include enough information about them to give readers an adequate idea of their main features. Such programs will be given proper reviews in future editions of this book or in the **Bits & Bytes Review**™ or both.

Readers who are interested in helpful and detailed charts that compare many word processing programs feature by feature should consult: Dickinson, "The Business of Words: Corporate, Professional, Personal," 93–251, "The Business of Words: Special Purpose," 177–214; Adrian, "Word Processors," 199–233; Raskin, "More Power," 127–73; Foster, "Word Processing," 35–43; and Software Digest™ *The Ratings Book*™: *IBM PC Word Processing Programs*.

2.5.1 Academically Oriented Programs

2.5.1.1 *FinalWord II*

- BASIC PRODUCT INFORMATION

Name of Program: FinalWord II™
Company Name: Mark of the Unicorn, Inc. (MOTU)
Address: 222 Third Street, Cambridge, MA 02142
Phone: (617) 576-2760
Technical Support: (617) 576-3052, Mon. – Fri.: 9:00 A.M. – 6:00 P.M., EST
Price: $395; $145 per copy for three or more copies ordered on a university purchase order
Version Tested: 2.01 and Beta version 2.02
Runs On: All MS-DOS-based computers
Memory Requirements: 192K, 256K for spelling checker, 448K for autocheck
Operating System Requirements: DOS 2.0 or greater
Disk Drive Requirements: 2
Copy Protected: No
Possible Backups: Unlimited
Hard Disk Compatible: Yes
Produces ASCII Files: Yes
Produces PostScript Files: Yes
Drives Laser Printers: Yes, LaserWriter, LaserWriter Plus, LaserJet, LaserJet Plus
Drives Typesetters: Yes, Compugraphic 8000 series, Intergraphics typesetting service
SideKick Compatible: Yes
Mnemonic Commands: Yes
User Interface: Command-driven and menu-driven
Text Display: Auto word wrap, on-screen justification
Screen Display Reformatting: Constant and automatic
Formatting Text for Printing: At print time
Text Orientation: Document
Screen Mode: Text
WYSIWYG: No
Edit Files Larger Than Memory: Yes
Uses Function Keys: Yes
Key Template or Labels: No
Product Includes: Disks, manual, quick reference card
Number of Disks: 2

- INSTRUCTIONAL MATERIALS/SOURCES

Manual: 505 pages, three-ring binder, typeset, tabbed, indexed
Tutorial: Minimal (9 pages)
Quick Reference Card: Yes

Demo Disk Available: No
On-Line Help: No
Pop-Up Command Menus: Yes
SIGs: Yes, on-line bulletin board and conferencing at (617) 484-2594; 300 or 1,200 baud; many FW II macros, program fixes, conferences, and more; all day every day, except Wednesdays, from 10:00 A.M. to 7:00 P.M., EST
Newsletters: "FinalWord II User Notes" (sporadically and occasionally) from MOTU
Major Reviews: *InfoWorld* (April 28, 1986): 54–55; *PC Magazine* (January 28, 1986): 144, 146, 148; *Research in Word Processing Newsletter* 4 (October 1986): 2–5; *Computers and Composition* 3 (August 1986): 60–71.
Other Learning Aids: None

- ## MULTILINGUAL FEATURES

Video Cards Supported: MDA, CGA, EGA, HGC, and other "standard" cards
Specify Different Fonts in Document: Yes
Print Different Fonts: Yes
Display Different Fonts On-Screen: No
Foreign Fonts Included: None
RAM-Based Character Generator: No
Font Editor: No
Number Characters Per Font: 256
Maximum Screen Fonts Per Document: 1
Mode Used to Display Nonstandard Characters: Text
Edit Right-to-Left: No
Display Entire ASCII Character Set: Yes

- ## SPECIAL FEATURES

Run DOS Commands from Program: Yes
Chain Files for Printing: Yes
Queue Files for Printing: No
Spelling Checker: Yes, approximately 70,000 words. The spell checker is Trigram System's Micro Spell.
Thesaurus: No
Windows/Split-Screen: Yes, maximum of 6
Columns: Yes, maximum of 5
Footnotes: Yes
Bibliography: No
Table of Contexts: Yes
Indices: Yes, 1 index (up to 4 levels) per file
Keyboard Macros: Yes, text and commands
Text Retrieval System: No
Internal Programming Language: Yes
Other: InfoMerge™, a mail-and-merge utility, is available for $95; FW II supports the GENIUS VHR monitor (see above) and mice.

- ## SUPPORT ETC.

Warranty: 90 days, materials only
Support: Phone, bulletin board, letter
Update Policy: Free to licensees
Other Information: Users of previous FinalWord versions may update to FW II for $95.

Introduction. All microcomputer word processors have histories, but only Final-Word II™ (hereafter FW II) and a few others have pedigrees. FW II traces its lineage back to EMACS, which stands for Editing MACroS, a powerful mainframe editor originally developed at MIT and frequently used by programmers for writing programs, and to SCRIBE, Carnegie Mellon University's text formatter.[90] With two such for-

---

90. FW II's formatting commands are, by and large, a subset of the SCRIBE commands.

midable parents, it's no wonder that FW II is as precocious, complex, powerful, and (sometimes) temperamental as it is.

Performance and Versatility. There are many reasons this program is especially well-suited for academic and multilingual word processing (version 1 has long enjoyed widespread acceptance among academicians and professional writers). FW II supports (1) odd and even headers and footers, (2) up to six horizontal windows of user-specifiable sizes, (3) editing different portions of the same file in different windows, (4) as many as twenty-four files open at once (which is like having twenty-four full-screen windows), (5) up to five columns of text, which may be "snaked" when printed (i.e., text that ends in one column is automatically carried to the top of the next) and which may contain footnotes properly placed at the bottom of the appropriate column, (6) changing typestyle (e.g., bold, italic), font, and pitch anywhere within a document, (7) unlimited end- and footnotes of unrestricted length in multiple formats and styles, with footnotes correctly wrapped from page to page, (8) wild-card search and replace, (9) files as large as 500K (approximately 250 pages of text), (10) chaining files for printing, so that pagination and footnote and outline numbers are continuous across chained files, (11) formatting files in almost any conceivable way, and (12) automatically cross referencing properly tagged information. And FW II, which supports over 100 makes and models of printers and typesetters, will automatically create (13) indices, (14) tables of contents, and (15) tables of figures. It will (16) perform multilevel sectioning, and it includes (17) a spelling checker (to which users can add additional words), and (18) a print preview feature. FW II (19) comes with its own programing language (similar to C) that allows users to write extremely complex and sophisticated macros for the editor and formatter, and FW II (20) allows its formatter style-sheet, printer-table, and keyboard-assignment files to be edited from top to bottom. FW II, then, is especially well-adapted for large, complex writing jobs—books, dissertations, theses, and such.

Although it is not a WYSIWYG program and cannot handle graphics, FW II has many powerful desktop publishing and typesetting features. In fact, FW II is so powerful that I used it to typeset this book.[91] Although other word processing programs (e.g., XyWrite III) have announced drivers for phototypesetters, at this time only FW II actually includes one (for the Compugraphic® MCS™ 8000 series). Thus FW II is the only word processing program I know of that can actually drive, that is, control, a typesetter.

As with EMACS, FW II is command-driven, though it also allows users to invoke editing, formatting, and printing commands from menus, to edit those commands, to write their own editing, formatting, and printing commands, and to create their own menus. FW II includes a true programming language (similar to C) that supports conditional statements, declaring and passing variables, setting and resetting flags, loops, exiting to DOS to run a program, inserting strings, and so forth. Thus FW II can be made to behave in almost any way users desire. In effect, then, FW II and its programming language allow users to write their own word processor!

The editor and formatter can be customized because (1) the files that govern the way they work are plain ASCII and so may be edited, and (2) the command sets for the editor and formatter are written as macros. To customize the editor or formatter, users write macros. To speed up macro execution, FW II includes a special compiler that compiles plain ASCII macros to binary code. Macros enable users to redefine the way the editor and formatter work, to redefine *all* key assignments and cursor movements, to write their own menus and error messages, and to do much, much more. To typeset this book, for example, I created a macro that read every file several times and that

---

91. This book was typeset on a Compugraphic® MCS™ 8000 phototypesetter, driven by FW II in the typesetter's "semi-slave" mode, using an IBM-compatible computer as a front end. Bill Spitzak (MOTU), Jeff King (Compugraphic Corp.), and Evelyn Barnes (Spectrum Stationary & Printing) deserve a special note of thanks for their technical expertise and assistance, which made this possible.

changed all undifferentiated double quotation marks to proper opening and closing double quotation marks and that did the same for undifferentiated single quotation marks—an exceptionally boring and tedious task that would have taken hours to do any other way. It took FW II less than thirty minutes to read approximately 2 megabytes of text and complete those tasks.

FW II also allows users to define new formatting environments and then to refer to them in a text file by using macros. To typeset this book, I defined many new environments that I then referred to with macros. The macro @BU, for example, indents a certain amount and then causes a "bullet" to be typeset. The macro @Bib, which I also created, causes the typesetter (or printer) to move to a new page, to move down several lines, to center *Bibliography*, to print it in bold in a certain font, and then to skip another line or two. The environment @SC was created to cause any text between the delimiters that follow it to be printed in small caps. Thus @SC(A.D.) results in A.D. The environment @e, also created for this book, causes everything between the delimiters that follow it to be set in 8 point type with a hanging indent value of -1.25 picas and grouped. That environment is used in bibliographies throughout the book.[92] User-created editing and formatting macros may be bound to function keys or placed in user-created, pop-up menus from which they may be selected.

All of those environments and formatting macros were defined in FW II's style sheet file, a plain ASCII file called TEXT.MAK. Because TEXT.MAX (or a custom version of it) controls *all* of FW II's formatting commands, it functions on a document globally. And custom versions of TEXT.MAK can be created for different printing and typesetting jobs. To invoke a custom style sheet, a command like the following is placed at the beginning of the file the style sheet is to be used with: @Make(BBBS.MAK), where "BBBS.MAK" is the name of a custom version of TEXT.MAK. Placing that single command at the beginning of a file causes the file to be formatted and printed in accordance with all the specifications contained in the custom .MAK file. Once users have created custom .MAK files for various printing tasks, they can forget about most formatting parameters as they create the text files that the custom .MAK files are to be used with. Thus by using custom .MAK files, users insure formatting continuity across files, thereby eliminating the need to specify formatting variables for each file. An unlimited number of custom .MAK files may be created, and .MAK files are not restricted to a fixed number of entries, as are the style-sheet files for Microsoft Word and the Ventura Publisher.

Not only can the editor and formatter files be edited, but so can the printer tables. They, too, are plain ASCII files, whose driver definitions, width tables, and so forth are compiled when users install a particular output device.[93] The printer tables, like the editor and formatter files, are obtuse and not really explained in the manual. However, with the proper knowledge of how to edit such files, users can create new fonts, alter width tables, create substitution tables, and so forth. When learning how to typeset with FW II, for example, I created seventy-two different fonts in three typefaces (Times, Goudy, and a special Symbol typeface) that used seven different width tables, two different character translation tables, two different substitution tables, and I modified the driver so that it would overprint and create a "bold bold," since Goudy bold (the typeface used to set this book) is not really very bold.[94] There is no way I could have done all of that—or been successful in getting the program to work with the typesetter in the first place—without a *lot* of technical help from one of the *programmers* at MOTU. I mention all of those things about FW II's ability to typeset not because I expect the average reader to rush out and begin to typeset documents

---

92. When creating environments, users may specify justification, leading, margins, fonts, gutter width (if working with columns), columns, spacing, indent and outdent values, and users may set counters, increment counters, and cause an environment to be numbered.

93. FW II allows an unlimited number of output devices to be installed concurrently.

94. FW II distinguishes between character translation and character substitution tables.

with this program but to illustrate FW II's truly incredible power and flexibility and because laser printers (like typesetters) can work with user-defined fonts, width tables, translation tables, and substitution tables.

Seven features allow FW II to function as a multilingual word processing program. (1) FW II allows users to create and edit keyboard files and to redefine keys and key combinations, which means that foreign-language keyboard layouts can be created. (2) FW II allows users to define one or more keys as "dead keys," which allows composite characters to be created. (3) FW II has a special overprinting command that is designed for creating and printing composite characters. (4) FW II's character translation and substitution tables can be edited, and users can create new tables, which means that foreign-language fonts can be created for printers. (5) FW II's *@font* command allows users to change typefaces, type styles, and type sizes anywhere within a document, line, or word. (6) FW II can display all 128 upper, or "extended," ASCII characters, many of which are Greek or composite Western European characters. And (7) FW II's *@tct* command allows users to have the formatter translate any character or character string to any other character or character string on output. Thus if an output device is capable of printing Hebrew and Greek, for example, FW II can be configured to do so. But since FW II operates in text mode using a ROM-based character generator, only the 256 values in the video ROM chip can be displayed on-screen. Thus FW II does not allow users to *display* foreign-language characters (other than those available in the video ROM's upper 128 ASCII positions), though presumably there is no reason why FW II could not be made to work with a multifont board such as the HGC+.

Documentation. Although clearly written for the most part, FW II's 500-page manual is intimidating, to say the least. Helpful examples are provided to illustrate most commands, but the manual contains only a brief, simplistic, 9-page tutorial—hardly enough to get a novice up and running without some headaches.[95] And (as the manual warns) the extensive, 130-page section on programming FW II's editor and formatter requires some programming expertise to understand and to implement—more expertise than many users will have, though the obvious power and flexibility of the programming language will make most users want to try to use it. Unfortunately, the section of the manual on programming contains almost no examples. Furthermore, the manual's index is woefully incomplete. Again and again, I found myself turning to it in vain for help in locating a topic. The manual fails to provide adequate documentation for many commands, and the program contains no on-line help.

Ease of Use. Although not a program for the fainthearted or raw beginner, FW II will richly reward those who are willing to invest the time and effort required to tackle its very steep and demanding learning curve, which is exacerbated by the obtuse manual, poor technical support (see below), and lack of an adequate tutorial and on-line help.

FW II's basic editing functions are cleanly implemented and easy to use. Cursor movement, deletion, block moves, file handling, and windows may all be invoked from menus. Most of FW II's editing and printing commands can be issued in any of four ways: (1) by using the function keys alone and in combination with shifting keys,[96] (2) by using shifting keys in combination with alpha keys, (3) by using the pop-up menus, or (4) by issuing commands directly. Occasionally, FW II uses a Command Line for certain functions (e.g., search and replace), though most commands are issued directly. Users can easily alter which commands are attached to which keys and attach new commands to keys to which FW II has attached no commands.

---

95. The manual for version 1.16 of FinalWord came with a separate, detailed, spiral-bound introduction and tutorial booklet. It seems strange that an even more complex version of the program lacks such a guide.

96. A shifting key is a nonprinting key that changes the value of a printing key.

Most of FW II's editing and printing commands begin with *Ctrl-X* ("X" for "Extended Functions"). *Ctrl-X* invokes a pop-up menu (which can be customized) that lists the available submenus. Menu items are selected by highlighting them with cursor keys or by typing the first letter of the item's name. Frequently, this displays a second pop-up menu. Thus many FW II commands consist of three keystrokes: *Ctrl-X*, followed by a single letter that designates one of several submenus, followed by the first letter of a particular command on the submenu.[97] *Ctrl-X-P-P*, for example, means "Extended Functions, Print Menu, Print" and is the command given from within the editor to format and print a document according to all its embedded formatting commands (as they are interpreted by the active .MAK file). *Ctrl-X-R-S* sets a marker, and *Ctrl-X-R-D* deletes the text between the cursor and the marker ("R" stands for "Regions," a particular submenu); *Ctrl-X-R-U* undeletes the last deletion. Menus can be bypassed, commands may be entered directly, and users can specify the menu pop-up-delay factor.

Although FW II's editing commands generally require more keystrokes to implement than those of many word processors, most commands are mnemonic and transparent, which facilitates quick learning and easy retention. Learning over 100 formatting and printing commands and their many combinations and permutations, however, as well as the correct syntax, which is usually straightforward but which can get complex, is a much more daunting undertaking. Fortunately, most of the major formatting and printing commands may be selected from pop-up menus. When a formatting command is selected from a menu, FW II automatically types the formatting command in the text at the place the cursor was left when the command was selected. Thus, for example, users do not have to type *@begin(Flushright) . . . @end(Flushright)*; the program does that automatically when that environment is selected from the layout menu and returns the cursor to a spot between the opening and closing delimiters so that users may enter the text that is to be flushright. That saves a lot of typing. Each formatting command begins with the @ mark and encloses the text it affects in delimiters: < >, {}, [], (), '', or "". For example, to have FW II print "Bits & Bytes" as a pageheading in the top left corner of every odd page of a document and the section title in bold as a pageheading in the top right corner of every odd page, a user would issue this command: *@pageheading(odd, left "Bits & Bytes", right "@b< @title(section)>")* at the beginning of the file. But there is an easier way to create headers and footers: customize the TEXT.MAK file so that fewer variables have to be entered in the text file. For example, I created a macro (@HF) in the custom version of the .MAK file used to format this book that specified where I wanted the headers and footers placed, what they were to contain, the size of type they were to be in, what typestyles were to be used, how much leading to use, and how far to space the elements in the headers. (Like many user-created macros, this macro uses several predefined FW II macros.) By placing @HF (for "headers and footers") at the beginning of each text file, along with the chapter title, the @HF macro caused the headers and footers you see on the pages of this book to be produced by the typesetter. Because all of FW II's formatting commands are visible, in a highly formatted document it soon becomes difficult to tell what the printed version is going to look like. To help with this difficulty, FW II includes a print preview option that displays on-screen the effect of most formatting commands.

FinalWord includes a version of Trigram's Micro Spell, an "intelligent," interactive spelling program with several unique features that make it one of the best and most flexible spell checkers available. Although listed as containing about 70,000 words, suffix-stripping algorithms effectively double this spell checker's effective size. As implemented on FinalWord, Micro Spell can be used in autocheck, "manual," and

---

97. FW II comes with three alternative command layouts: the old (version 1) FW layout, the new FW II layout, and an EMACS layout, any one of which may be loaded with the program and each of which may be edited from top to bottom.

batch modes and (1) allows users to add words to the main dictionary files, (2) to delete words from those files, and (3) to create a user file of new words. Words that are added to the main dictionary files are compressed with a special Micro Spell algorithm. Furthermore, Micro Spell allows users to (4) specify that any word or string of characters automatically be changed to any other word or string of characters, a feature that chronically poor spellers will appreciate and that allows the program to be used as a text-only macro program. (This feature works only in batch-correct mode, not in autocheck mode.) Thus, for example, users may specify that "bannana" automatically be changed to "banana" and that "tsr" automatically be changed to "terminate and stay resident." Such "word pairs" and text macros may be added to Micro Spell's main dictionary files. Micro Spell also (5) flags doubled words, for example, "the the," and gives users the chance to delete the doubled word; and Micro Spell (6) catches improper capitalization, for example, "JOhn." Unfortunately, there is no way to turn this last feature off, and so the program faithfully and annoyingly flags abbreviations such as "MHz," "KHz," and so forth. Finally, Micro Spell (7) allows users to look up words using "*" as a multi-character wild card and "?" as a single-letter wild card. Micro Spell may be set to check text as it is being entered, or it may be used to check a single word, paragraph, or the rest of a file from the cursor to the end. When used in the autocheck mode as text is being entered, on a 4.77-MHz machine it is not too difficult for fast typists to loose keystrokes while Micro Spell stops to look up a word it does not recognize.

Error Handling. FinalWord has long been famous for its crash recovery, state-save, and undelete safety features. When a file is called for editing, FW II reads as much of it as it can into RAM, where all editing takes place. Because it uses virtual-memory architecture, FW II can edit files that are much larger than memory, swapping pages of the file in and out of RAM as needed. Files are edited within the confines of a special disk file known as a "swap file," whose size, which is user-specifiable, may be as large as 512K and which may contain as many as twenty-four open files.[98] The size of the swap file determines the maximum size of files that may be edited, which is about 500K. The swap file is a disk file that functions as FW II's work space, or buffer, into which FW II places and saves all files that have been read into the editor. During periods of keyboard inactivity, at user-specified intervals, FW II automatically saves the working file (and any open files) to disk—to the swap file—a feature that is referred to as "state-save." Thus if the system crashes (because of a power failure or for some other reason), or if the program is exited before open files have been explicitly saved, no data is lost because those files have been saved in the swap file. In the case of a system crash, users recover their files from the swap file by running the FinalWord program FWRECOVE.COM.

By entering FW (with no specified filename) at the system level, FW II quickly re-enters the file that was last edited, at the exact place it was exited from, regardless of whether the file had been saved or not—another bonus of FW II's swap-file architecture. Until closed by user command, the original copies of files that have been opened for editing are not overwritten. Thus the swap file preserves the most recent editorial changes, leaving the original unaltered until overwritten when the open file is saved. Closing a file deletes it from the editor but leaves the original version unaltered. FW II allows users to undelete their last editing deletion.

Support. During the past four years, I have called MOTU technical support many times and have generally found their support personnel to be well-informed, patient, and helpful, as long as the question or problem is not too technical. Because MOTU's personnel support three or four different MS-DOS and Macintosh programs, however, they are not specialists on any one program. Occasionally, in response to a difficult but not unanswerable question, I have been told, "I haven't dealt with that problem

---

98. Since users can switch from one open file to another, each open file is like a full-screen window.

in a long time" or "I don't know, why don't you try. . . ." That's not very satisfying. MOTU seems to be a small company, and I believe that they only have two support personnel. They do not have a toll-free number, and their line is often busy. Occasionally, MOTU publishes a free newsletter for registered users. MOTU's bulletin board contains program fixes, macros, conferences, and other information.

Bibliography. Steve King, "FinalWord II Packs a Punch," *InfoWorld* (April 28, 1986): 54–55; Steve Siebert, "The Final Word Review," *PC Magazine* (January 1983): 340–44 (a review of version 1 of the FinalWord that is still quite helpful); Jared Taylor, "The Business of Words: Professional—The FinalWord 2.0," *PC Magazine* (January 28, 1986): 144, 146, 148; Gordon P. Thomas, "FinalWord II: An Authoring System for a Word Processing Program," *Computers and Composition* 3 (October 1986): 2–5; "FinalWord II: Word Processing for a College Writing Program," *Research in Word Processing Newsletter* 4 (October 1986): 2–5.

2.5.1.2 *XyWrite III Plus*

• *BASIC PRODUCT INFORMATION*

Name of Program: XyWrite III Plus™
Company Name: XyQuest, Inc.
Address: P.O. Box 372, Bedford, MA 01730
Phone: (617) 275-4439
Technical Support: (617) 275-4439, Mon. – Fri.: 9:00 A.M. – 6:00 P.M., EST
Price: $445
Version Tested: 3.1
Runs On: IBM PCs and many compatibles
Memory Requirements: 256K; 384K if using speller and thesaurus
Operating System Requirements: DOS 2.0 or greater
Disk Drive Requirements: 1
Copy Protected: No
Possible Backups: Unlimited
Hard Disk Compatible: Yes
Produces ASCII Files: Yes
Produces PostScript Files: Yes
Drives Laser Printers: Yes, LaserWriter, LaserJet, Canon LBP 8A, Blaser, Corona
Drives Typesetters: No, but drivers are under development.
SideKick Compatible: Yes
Mnemonic Commands: Yes, for the most part
User Interface: Command-driven
Text Display: Auto word wrap, no on-screen justification
Screen Display Reformatting: Constant and automatic
Formatting Text for Printing: Continuously
Text Orientation: Document
Screen Mode: Text
WYSIWYG: Yes
Edit Files Larger Than Memory: Yes
Uses Function Keys: Yes
Key Template or Labels: Yes
Product Includes: Disks, manual, three tutorial booklets, quick reference card, installation guide, function key template
Number of Disks: 5

• *INSTRUCTIONAL MATERIALS/SOURCES*

Manual: 533 pages, three-ring binder, slipcase, typeset, tabbed, indexed
Tutorial: Yes, three separate tutorial booklets: (1) Quick Start Tutorial, (2) Basic Word Processing Tutorial, (3) Applications Tutorial
Quick Reference Card: Yes
Demo Disk Available: Yes, $7

On-Line Help: Yes
Pop-Up Command Menus: No
SIGs: Not known
Newsletters: "XyWug," % Joe Russell, 120 Howard St., Suite 410, San Francisco, CA 94105, $14.50/yr (U.S.A.), $19/yr (Canada, Mexico), $25/yr elsewhere, 7 issues
Major Reviews: *InfoWorld* (April 14, 1986): 41–42; *PC Magazine* (January 28, 1986): 173–74 (XyWrite II Plus 2.0); *Personal Publishing* (September 1986): 34–42; *PC World* (August 1986): 224–29.
Other Learning Aids: David H. Rothman, *XyWrite Made Easier* (Blue Ridge Summit, Penn.: TAB Books, Inc., 1987

- ## MULTILINGUAL FEATURES

Video Cards Supported: MDA, CGA, EGA, HGC, Quadvue, and other "standard" cards
Specify Different Fonts in Document: Yes
Print Different Fonts: Yes
Display Different Fonts On-Screen: No
Foreign Fonts Included: None
RAM-Based Character Generator: No
Font Editor: No
Number Characters Per Font: 256
Maximum Screen Fonts Per Document: 1
Mode Used to Display Nonstandard Characters: Text
Edit Right-to-Left: No
Display Entire ASCII Character Set: Yes

- ## SPECIAL FEATURES

Run DOS Commands from Program: Yes
Chain Files for Printing: Yes
Queue Files for Printing: Yes
Spelling Checker: Yes, approximately 100,000 words; can add 10,000 words.
Thesaurus: Yes, 15,000 root terms, approximately 220,000 words
Windows/Split-Screen: Yes, maximum of 9
Columns: Yes, maximum of 16
Footnotes: Yes
Bibliography: No
Table of Contexts: Yes, but not automatically
Indices: Yes
Keyboard Macros: Yes, text and commands
Text Retrieval System: No
Internal Programming Language: Yes
Other: Multiple file search, on-line reference manual, mailmerge. XyWrite III supports the GENIUS VHR (monitor see above).

- ## SUPPORT ETC.

Warranty: Media only
Support: Phone, letter
Update Policy: $50 to upgrade from version 3.1 to XyWrite III Plus; $150 to upgrade from version II Plus to XyWrite III Plus
Other Information: None

Introduction. Like FinalWord™ II, XyWrite III™ (hereafter XW III) is a program with a pedigree. Just as FW II's academic lineage is revealed in its command-driven interface and embedded formatting codes, so XW III's roots in the publishing industry are revealed in its command-driven interface and WYSIWYG screen display. It is no surprise that XW III is patterned after ATEX,[99] a commercial, minicomputer page-definition and composition system for computerized typesetting and publishing that is

---

99. Atex, Inc., 32 Wiggins Ave., Bedford, MA 01730; (617) 275-8300.

used by numerous newspapers, publishing houses (e.g., Ziff-Davis), and magazines (e.g., *Time*); XW III was developed by two former ATEX systems programmers, Dave Erickson and John Hild. Just as FW II's commands, to some extent, reflect its close ties to EMACS, which is used extensively by programmers, so XW III's commands reflect its close ties with ATEX, which is used extensively by professional writers who create files for computerized typesetters. And like FW II, XW III has a strong and dedicated following of power users.

Performance and Versatility. Among the many distinguishing features that have made XW the program of choice for the editors and staff at *PC Magazine*,[100] as well as among many academicians, are its speed—a result of the fact that the program is written in assembly language (see chapter 1)—power, and flexibility. The operations of function keys and function calls (over 125 two-letter editing commands that represent basic keyboard actions) are virtually instantaneous, as are scrolling and cursor movement. Text attributes such as underline, bold, and bold underline are displayed onscreen as such, as are superscripts, subscripts, and page layout in general. XW III takes a WYSIWYG approach to word processing.

A number of other features make XW III especially attractive. XW III allows users to (1) work with up to nine horizontal or vertical windows, whose size is user-specifiable (including full-screen) and which may overlap, (2) have as many as nine files open at once, (3) work with up to sixteen columns of text and specify separate format commands for each column, (4) change typestyle, font, and pitch anywhere within a document without interfering with right justification, (5) have unlimited end- and footnotes in user-defined formats, with footnotes correctly wrapped from page to page, (6) have three-levels of footnotes per page, each with their own individual format, if desired, (7) search with six different wild-card characters, (8) work with files larger than memory, (9) chain files together for printing, so that pagination and footnote and outline numbers are continuous across chained files, (10) format files in almost any imaginable way, (11) store up to 36 keyboard macros (blocks of text) in each of an unlimited number of macro sets, (12) automatically create tables of contents and multiple indices, (13) perform ten-level sectioning of documents in user-specifiable styles, (14) queue files for printing, (15) vary the line spacing on a document to the finest degree any given printer can support, (16) bidirectionally cross reference text, and (17) specify leading automatically or by line or wherever desired.

On the one hand, unlike FW II, XW III does not support (1) editing different portions of the same file in different windows, (2) unlimited levels when automatically numbering text sections (ten levels is the limit), (3) pop-up, on-screen command menus, or (4) style sheets that globally control formatting parameters. On the other hand, unlike FW II, XW III (1) allows up to nine different indices per document, (2) has extensive, user-customizable help screens, (3) allows users to edit one document while printing another,[101] (4) supports vertical, horizontal, and overlapping windows whose sizes are user-defined, (5) includes a mail merge utility, and (6) performs onscreen math. Thus like FW II, XW III is well suited for large, complex writing jobs of the sort that academicians frequently undertake. XW III supports almost 100 different makes and models of printers.

Because it lacks pop-up command menus, XW III is one of the most purely command-driven word processors imaginable. Its great wealth of commands, though daunting at first, provide precise and extremely flexible control. Its built-in programming capabilities, though not as elaborate and extensive as FW II's, are nevertheless

---

100. In the January 28, 1986, issue of *PC Magazine*, sixteen reviewers reviewed seventy-six word processing programs. Eight of those reviewers use XyWrite, two use WordStar, two Framework, and one each use WordPerfect, FinalWord II, Volkswriter Deluxe, and Microsoft Word.

101. FW II allows editing one document while printing another, but its implementation of this feature is incredibly slow and causes huge intermediate printer output files to be created. FW II macros could be written to create multiple indices and help screens.

quite powerful and easier to understand and use. XW III's programming language supports saving values, conditional statements, passing arguments, jumping to labels, saving and inserting strings, exiting to run subroutines and programs, and more.

A keyboard macro capability allows users to assign any keystrokes and character strings to almost any key or key combination and to combine any of XW III's commands, in any order, in programs that will automatically execute from within XW III. By using XW III's macro feature, users can customize XW III's editing, formatting, and printing commands to their hearts' content.

Five features allow XW III to function as a multilingual word processing program. (1) XW III allows users to create and edit keyboard files and to redefine key combinations. Thus foreign-language keyboard layouts can be created and displayed on-screen. While in the editor, users can switch from keyboard layout to keyboard layout by using the *LDKBD* <*filename*> command (load keyboard followed by a keyboard filename). (2) XW III allows users to create character substitution tables. Character substitution tables specify how each on-screen character is printed and thus allow users to create foreign-language printer fonts. Each printer table can contain an unlimited number of separate, uniquely labeled character substitution tables. (3) XW III also allows users to modify existing printer font tables or to create new ones. A font table specifies the printer codes to access a particular character set, and each font table can include a reference to a character substitution table, which defines a particular character set. The character substitution table could define a nonstandard, "foreign" character set. Thus by defining a font in terms of a nonstandard character set, characters from that set would be printed when that font is specified in the document. From within the editor, then, users could switch from font to font, anywhere within a document, by issuing a *PT* <*number*> command (*PT* for print type, where *number* is the number of a specific print type (PT) as defined in the printer file). XW III allows an unlimited number of font tables and print types in a printer file. The print-type section of each printer file is also referred to more descriptively as the "display mode attributes" because the values specified in a printer file's attribute tables and font tables can be assigned to display modes, such as bold, underlined, and so forth.[102]

Alternatively, (4) within each print-type table, up to 256 different modes can be defined in terms of the values of that or another font table and attribute table. (Thus XW III allows up to 256 separate fonts in one document.) By properly customizing some of the mode commands in a print-type table so that specific modes are bound to foreign-language fonts and by assigning number keys in the keyboard file to specific modes, the Ctrl key could be used in combination with user-specified number keys to toggle in and out of different foreign-language character sets. For example, one or more print-type tables in a single printer file could include the definition *MD BO+FOREIGN+BOLD*, which defines the display mode "BOLD" to refer to the font table "FOREIGN," which could be whatever foreign-language character set a user had defined it to be in that font table. And (5) XW III can display all 128 upper ASCII characters. But since XW III operates in text mode using a ROM-based character generator, only the 256 values in the video ROM chip can be displayed on-screen. XW III, then, does not allow users to display foreign language characters (other than those available in the video ROM's upper 128 ASCII characters), though presumably there is no reason why XW III could not be made to work with a multifont board like the HGC+.[103]

XW III comes with Microlytics' spell checker and thesaurus. The spell checker includes 100,000 words, and users may add up to 10,000 words to a personal dictionary.

---

102. Each printer file also contains one or more user-modifiable character width tables that specify the width that characters in a particular character set will be when printed. For example, a 10-pitch Pica font has ten characters per inch, and a 12-pitch Elite font has twelve characters per inch. XW III also supports microjustification.

103. And that is exactly what Nota Bene, an enhanced version of XW III, has done (see below).

The spell checker works in autocorrect, "manual," and batch modes. In batch mode, the spell checker can check a series of files. A text-only macro feature allows the program to translate any text string into any other text string, for example, "tsr" into "terminate and stay resident." Unlike Trigram's implementation of this feature, the Microlytics version works in autocheck mode so that the transformation is made as you type, not later as you batch correct a file. The Microlytics RAM-resident Word Finder™ Thesaurus contains 15,000 root entries and over 220,000 synonyms. By placing the cursor on a word for which synonyms are desired and hitting Ctrl-T, the thesaurus pops up a window of synonyms for the selected word.

Documentation. Although very comprehensive and generally well indexed,[104] XW III's 533-page manual is dry, sparsely illustrated, and frustratingly organized. For example, both FW II and XW III show how to enter each formatting command, but only FW II shows what the printed results of each of those commands will look like. In most cases, XW III simply *describes* the results that commands produce. Fortunately, however, XW III comes with an installation guide and three excellent tutorial booklets full of clear instructions, helpful illustrations, and well-done indices. By reading the tutorial booklets and following their instructions, I learned the program quickly and found that I could then read the manual with a higher degree of comprehension. XW III includes a plastic, L-shaped template that fits around the function keys and that lists their predefined values. Unfortunately, this template is (1) hard to read, (2) contains one mistake,[105] and (3) is easily knocked off the keyboard. But having a template, even an imperfect one, is preferable to having none at all.

Ease of Use. XW III is a program for power users—for people who need maximum control, flexibility, and speed in a word processor. Like FW II, XW III has a very steep but rewarding learning curve. Cursor movement, deletion, block moves, file handling, windows, and most other editing functions are cleanly implemented, easy to learn, and execute quickly. It is difficult to understand, however, why such an intricate, complex, and powerful program, which comes with extensive menu-driven, on-line help, does not also include pop-up command menus—something that would greatly simplify life not only for the beginner but also for those who will not be using the program on a daily basis. Although most of its commands are fairly mnemonic and transparent, because of its ATEX heritage, some of XW III's commands are opaque. For example, *TYPE* means print, *TYPES* means print to screen, and *SAVE/GETS* means define and save a macro and retrieve a macro.

Editing commands are entered by using the function keys, alone and in combination with the shifting keys—Ctrl, Alt, and Shift—and by using combinations of shifting keys and alpha keys. Formatting and printing commands are entered from the Command Line, one of three nondocument lines at the top of the screen (the other two are the Prompt Line and the Ruler Line). In XW III, the F5 key is used to move the cursor from the document portion of the screen to the Command Line; F10 moves the cursor back to its original position in the document. Most of XW III's more than 125 editing commands can be entered from the Command Line as 2-letter "function calls"—commands that represent basic keyboard actions—as well as by using the function keys. Most formatting and printer commands likewise consist of two letters followed by different variables. Because they consist of 2-letter codes, XW III's formatting commands are shorter, simpler, and can be issued more quickly than FW II's. For example, *LM 10* sets the left margin ten columns from the left edge of the screen, *TY* <*filename*> sends a file to the printer. Longer commands can be abbreviated. For example, *KILTYPE* (for stopping the printer) can be issued as *KT*. XW III's macro capabilities allow users to alter which commands are attached to which keys and to at-

---

104. I noticed at least one mistake in the index. On index page 8, column 1, all the subtopics listed under "Force Fill (FF)" properly belong under the preceding listing "footnote commands."

105. The function key command to define a word is Alt-F4 and should be listed in red but instead is listed in black, which is the code for using F4 by itself, an action used to define a line.

tach new commands to keys to which XW III has attached no commands. Thus by using function keys and shifting keys, forty editing commands can be defined. XW III's formatting and printing commands, though numerous, are fairly easy to learn.

In the Normal Display Mode (which is the mode most commonly used for text entry), formatting commands are embedded in the text as small delta symbols that appear in intense video (these and paragraph markers can be suppressed by using the NM—no marker—command). When the cursor is placed on a delta, the formatting command that the delta represents is displayed on the Prompt Line. Conversely, by switching to the Expanded Display Mode, the contents of each delta are displayed between small double angle brackets (European quotation marks) and may be edited like regular text. Because deltas represent formatting codes, by erasing a delta users erase the codes those deltas represent. And because footnotes are represented by highlighted numbers, erasing a footnote number causes the entire footnote to be erased. This is a dangerous and potentially disastrous situation, since it only takes one incorrect keystroke to erase an entire footnote.

Error Handling. Although XW III's simple and quick command entry and speedy execution make it easy to save documents, the program does not contain automatic save or crash recovery features, and that is a liability. Exiting a document without saving it causes all changes made since last saving the document to be irretrievably lost. XW III allows users to undelete their last deletion. Fortunately, XW III is not easy to crash, and its error messages are clear.

Support. In the course of learning the program, I called XyQuest three times, once to learn how to get the program to display underlined, bold underlined, and bold reverse text properly on-screen with the HGC+ (something not covered in the XW III manual) and twice to quiz their technical support staff on XW III's foreign-language capabilities. My first call was returned within 15 minutes, and the second and third times I got through immediately. All three technicians were very knowledgeable, thorough, and patient; they stayed with me until I understood their answers. Unfortunately, the XyQuest technical support number is not toll-free.

Bibliography. Bill Breeze and Tony Iannotti, "XyWrite III," *Personal Publishing* (October 1986): 34–42; Rubin Rabinovitz, "XyWrite II Plus," *BYTE* (September 1985): 297–302; Craig L. Stark, "The Business of Words: Professional—XyWrite 2.0 Plus," *PC Magazine* (January 28, 1986): 173–74 (a review of XyWrite 2.0 Plus that is still quite helpful); Bernie Zilbergeld, "Xywrite is Fast But Difficult," *InfoWorld* (April 14, 1986): 41–42; Merv Adrian, "Major Word Processors Get Better," *PC Magazine* (May 26, 1987): 219–220; Hal Nieburg, "XyWrite III: The Taming of the Shrewd," *PC World* (August 1986): 224–29; Jordan J. Breslow, "Almost Perfect," *PC World* (July 1987): 224–25.

2.5.1.3 Nota Bene

- *BASIC PRODUCT INFORMATION*

Name of Program: Nota Bene™ (NB)
Company Name: Dragonfly Software, a Division of Equal Access Systems, Inc.
Address: 285 W. Broadway, Suite 500, New York, NY 10013; in the United Kingdom: Academic Division, Oxford University Press, Walton St., Oxford OX2 6DP, U.K., telephone: 44-865-56767, ext. 4163; in Israel: Daniel Boyarin, The Last Word, Hardus 8, Omer, Israel, telephone: 972-57-69994
Phone: (212) 334-0445
Technical Support: (718) 624-0127
Price: $495; $275 for graduate students; $346 with educational discount for 3-9 copies; $297 with educational discount for 10-19 copies
Version Tested: 2.0 (Beta version); current version is 2.01
Runs On: IBM PCs and compatibles

Memory Requirements: 256K, 384K if using auto hyphenation and text base features; 512K strongly recommended
Operating System Requirements: DOS 2.0 or greater
Disk Drive Requirements: 2
Copy Protected: No
Possible Backups: Unlimited
Hard Disk Compatible: Yes
Produces ASCII Files: Yes
Produces PostScript Files: Yes
Drives Laser Printers: Yes, LaserWriter, LaserJet, Canon LBP 8A, Blaser, Corona
Drives Typesetters: No
SideKick Compatible: Yes
Mnemonic Commands: Yes, for the most part
User Interface: Command-driven or menu-driven
Text Display: Auto word wrap, no on-screen justification
Screen Display Reformatting: Constant and automatic
Formatting Text for Printing: Continuously
Text Orientation: Document
Screen Mode: Text
WYSIWYG: Yes
Edit Files Larger Than Memory: Yes
Uses Function Keys: Yes
Key Template or Labels: Yes, around function keys and across top of keyboard
Product Includes: Disks, manual, key template, quick reference guide, tutorial booklet
Number of Disks: 4

• INSTRUCTIONAL MATERIALS/SOURCES

Manual: 900+ pages, three-ring binder, slipcase, typeset, tabbed, indexed
Tutorial: Yes, tutorial booklet
Quick Reference Card: No, but quick reference guide is included.
Demo Disk Available: No
On-Line Help: Yes
Pop-Up Command Menus: Yes
SIGs: No
Newsletters: "Dragonfly Wings," published by Dragonfly Software
Major Reviews: *PC World* (March 1986): 196–202; *Yale Review* 74 (1985): 615–40; *Yale Review* 75 (1986): 454–80; *Research in Word Processing Newsletter* 4 (1986): 9–11; *Computers and the Humanities* 20 (January-March 1986): 62–71; *Social Science Microcomputer Review* 3 (1985): 421–25; *Bits & Bytes Review* 1 (October 1986): 9–15; *PC Magazine* (July 1987): 43; *BYTE* (Summer 1987 Bonus Edition): 55–67, esp. 66–67.
Other Learning Aids: None

• MULTILINGUAL FEATURES

Video Cards Supported: MDA, CGA, EGA, HGC, HGC+, Quadvue, and other "standard" cards
Specify Different Fonts in Document: Yes
Print Different Fonts: Yes
Display Different Fonts On-Screen: Yes, but see qualifications below.
Foreign Fonts Included: NB comes preconfigured with different keyboard layouts for various Western European languages. A special foreign-language version of NB that works with Hebrew, Greek, Cyrillic, and other alphabets should be available by the time this book appears; I have seen and used a Beta version of this foreign-language version of NB. Six 512-character supplementary screen and printer font sets will be available: (1) Classical Languages (including Greek with all diacritical marks), (2) Biblical Studies (including vocalized Hebrew, Greek with all diacritics, German, and French), (3) European and Slavic Languages, (4) Transliterated Characters, (5) Hebrew (vocalized and transliterated), and (6) a Combined Version. Font sets cost $100 each for the first set and $80 per set thereafter, the Combined Version not included. Font sets will include extra documentation, extra help screens, and extra sort routines. Semitic fonts support right-to-left text entry and editing.
RAM-Based Character Generator: No, but the EGA and HGC+ have RAM-based character generators, and NB works with both of them.
Font Editor: No, but the HGC+ does.
Number Characters Per Font: 256, unless a special foreign-language version of NB is used.

Maximum Screen Fonts Per Document: 1, unless used with the EGA or HGC+. Release 1 of the special
font sets restricts users to two 256-character active fonts; Release 2 will support up to twelve 256-
character active fonts.
Mode Used to Display Nonstandard Characters: Text
Edit Right-to-Left: No, but the special foreign-language versions of NB that work with the EGA and
HGC+ do.
Display Entire ASCII Character Set: Yes

• SPECIAL FEATURES

Run DOS Commands from Program: Yes
Chain Files for Printing: Yes
Queue Files for Printing: Yes
Spelling Checker: Yes, approximately 100,000 words; can add 10,000 words.
Thesaurus: Yes, 15,000 root terms, approximately 220,000 words
Windows/Split-Screen: Yes, maximum of 9
Columns: Yes, maximum of 16
Footnotes: Yes
Bibliography: Yes
Table of Contexts: Yes
Indices: Yes
Keyboard Macros: Yes, text and commands
Text Retrieval System: Yes
Internal Programming Language: Yes
Other: Multiple file search, on-line reference manual, mailmerge, text-base

• SUPPORT ETC.

Warranty: Media only
Support: Phone, letter
Update Policy: A "reasonable fee" is charged.
Other Information: NB is the only computer program ever endorsed by the Modern Language Association
(see *PC Magazine* (July 23, 1985): 64 and (August 6, 1985): 59).

Introduction. Nota Bene™ (hereafter NB)—Latin for "mark well"—is an aptly
named program with a threefold pedigree. The program itself deftly combines extensively modified versions of XW III (see above) and FYI 3000 (a free-from, textual data
base—see below) with an incredible array of enhancements that make NB a distinct
entity of its own. XW III, as we learned above, traces its roots to the publishing industry; FYI 3000 is primarily designed for scientists, managers, and researchers.[106] The
third component in NB's pedigree, and the one that defines the program as a whole, is
its consistent academic orientation. NB has been custom designed and handcrafted by
academicians to meet the needs of professors, students, and professional writers who
want the utmost in control, flexibility, and power in one program. Not only is NB
greater than the sum of XW III and FYI 3000, it is significantly different from and
more powerful than either of those two programs taken alone or together. Like XW
III, NB has a command-driven user interface and a WYSIWYG screen display. Unlike
XW III but like FW II, NB can be command-driven *or* menu-driven.

Performance and Versatility. NB can do everything that XW III can do and do it
just as fast, but NB has more features and is more flexible than XW III. NB is an outstanding program for those who need power, speed, flexibility, and lots of features in a
package designed for composing, editing, and printing large, complex, and multilingual documents. NB, then, combines all of XW III's features, including that program's
extensive keyboard macro capabilities, internal programming language, and on-line
spell checker and thesaurus with a whole host of its own. Rather than relist all of XW

---

106. Zandre, "SHAPE," *PC Magazine* (June 12, 1984): 313.

III's features, I will list some of the additional features that NB offers. NB allows users to (1) produce a *multilevel* table of contents (up to five levels) in a variety of formats, (2) generate three separate user-specifiable lists (e.g., tables, figures, maps), (3) create a two-level bibliography of works cited in a document, (4) generate up to three separate indices of up to three levels each, (5) create indices automatically or conditionally from a user-specified list of terms, (6) use roman numerals, letters, daggers, asterisks, and so forth for numbering footnotes, endnotes, or pages, (7) have unnumbered notes, (8) have footnote numbering automatically restarted at the top of each page, (9) mix footnotes and endnotes in the same document, (10) have multiple levels of footnotes on the same page, (11) bidirectionally cross-reference footnotes, paragraphs, sections, outlines, and lists, (12) move the cursor in either direction by character, word, phrase, line, sentence, paragraph, page, and document, (13) delete in either direction by character, word, phrase, line, sentence, and paragraph, (14) transpose text by character, word, line, sentence, and paragraph, (15) edit footnotes, format deltas, and bibliography markers without entering the Expanded Display Mode, (16) sort directories by date, size, filename, and extension, (17) compare two files for similarities and differences, (18) display true line spacing (single, double, triple, etc.) on-screen, (19) access *context-sensitive* help screens, (20) set place markers in the text, (21) use menus to implement many formatting and print functions, and (22) create free-form text bases (textual data bases) that can be searched with the Boolean operators AND, NOT, OR, and XOR.

NB shares some, but not all, of XW III's limitations. Like XW III, NB does not support (1) viewing different portions of the same file in different windows and (2) *unlimited* levels when automatically numbering text sections (though the limit of ten should be enough for most users). NB supports over 40 different makes and models of printers.

The features that make NB a distinctive writing tool are its (1) multilingual abilities, (2) style sheets, and (3) text retrieval system.

NB's multilingual features are extensive. Version 2.0 of NB can display all 256 characters in the IBM ROM and has incorporated the European characters in the "extended" ASCII set into customized logical keyboards for German, French, Spanish, and other major Western European languages. These logical keyboards allow users to display Western European character sets correctly on-screen, as well as to print them on appropriate printers. If a keyboard is unsatisfactory, users may create their own or modify the appropriate table in NB's keyboard file. Combinations of shifting keys and accent keys are used to enter temporary accents, whose entry is followed by the letter to be accented, which results in the properly accented character from the extended character set being displayed.

By the time this book appears, a multilingual version of NB that allows users to display Greek, Hebrew, Cyrillic, and many other alphabets on-screen simultaneously, to print them, to edit right-to-left (as well as left-to-right), and to mix and display different fonts on-screen on the same line should be available. Because of their commitment to on-screen formatting and fast screen updating, this version of NB will work in text mode with the EGA card and in RamFont mode with the HGC+ (see above). EGA- and Hercules-based special-language versions of Nota Bene will cost approximately $100 more than the base price and will include screen fonts, printer fonts, extra documentation, extra help screens, and extra sort routines. The Hebrew character set will include vowels, and the Greek character set will include all diacritical marks.

NB comes preconfigured with six distinct style sheets—for example, the Modern Language Association (MLA), Chicago Manual of Style (CMS), American Psychological Association (APA)—that specify and control various formatting parameters, such as margins, block quotations, line spacing, paragraph format, note type and position, heading levels, and figure and table numbering on a global basis. Users can define their own style sheets on a paragraph-by-paragraph basis or globally for a document as a whole. Style sheets, which are stored as disk files, may be named, assigned to macro key combinations, attached anywhere in a document, and mixed in a document. FW II, Microsoft Word, and T^3 (see below)—three other word processing programs that use style sheets to define formatting parameters—do not provide *predefined* style sheets that conform to the dictates of the CMS, APA, MLA, and so forth.

NB's powerful text retrieval system allows users to create free-form data bases, which NB calls "text-bases." Text-bases can consist of any textual information, such as bibliographies, notes on articles and books, whole documents, and so forth. Each text-base must follow one of eight predefined formats, or users may create their own text-base format. One text-base format, for example, allows entries to be blocks of text up to 1,000 words or 6,000 characters long (whichever is less), with every word of each entry indexed, unless a stop-list is used to exclude certain words from the index. Text containing accented foreign characters may be indexed and retrieved. Text-bases may be accessed from within the word processor.

An unlimited number of separate text-bases may be created. In theory, on a floppy-based system, each text-base may contain up to 65,535 entries (blocks of text) and 65,535 unique keywords, which may be spread over as many as 256 360K disks, each of which may contain up to 100 files—25,600 files in all—as long as the index and vocabulary files fit on one diskette. In practice, however, when using the every-word-is-a-keyword approach, text-bases are usually limited to three to five 360K diskettes. Using a hard disk for the index files and for the text files of a text-base restricts that text-base to 1,800 files, which may be spread out over 18 subdirectories.

NB supports 4-operator Boolean searches of the text-base (AND, OR, XOR, NOT). Text-bases may be searched in an auto mode, which is menu-driven, or in a full control mode, which is command driven. Boolean operators may be combined in search commands. Search terms may be terminally truncated with "*," and up to 250 terms may be searched for simultaneously across different files and disks. Initial and medial truncation are not supported. When using terminal truncation, NB informs users of possible matches, and users may then choose to include or exclude terms. Hits, which consist of the blocks of text in which the search term(s) appears, may be displayed in various formats (e.g., whole block of text, first sentence only, first line only) and may be inserted into a document or placed in a window for review and then discarded, modified, or inserted into a document. Search terms may be entered on the Command Line of the word processor.[107]

NB also allows users to search any file, in any directory or subdirectory, on any drive, for character strings, which may consist of alpha or numeric characters or both. An assortment of wild cards may be used in the initial, medial, or terminal positions.

Documentation. NB's extremely comprehensive and well-indexed 900-page manual is a model of clarity, organization, and easy-to-understand discursive explanations. The effects of all commands are clearly described, and the effects of many commands are illustrated. It would be nice, however, if the result of *every* command was illustrated. The manual consistently anticipates questions, warns of incorrect syntax, and carefully guides the reader through the intricacies of the various features of the program. Fortunately, for such a complex program the manual contains an extensive and thorough index. And NB contains excellent, on-line, context-sensitive help (see below).

Ease of Use. Like FW II and XW III, NB is a program for power users; and like those programs, NB has a very steep learning curve. But because of its excellent documentation and elaborate, detailed, interactive help screens (many of which function as menus that allow various formatting and printing functions to be invoked), I

---

107. The terminology in this paragraph will be explained later in this chapter and in chapter 3.

found Nota Bene version 2.0 easy to learn and easy to use, even though it is complex and powerful.

NB has a WYSIWYG screen display and can be command-driven *or* menu-driven. Text attributes such as underline, bold, and bold underline are displayed on-screen as such. The operations of function keys and editing commands are virtually instantaneous, as is scrolling, deleting, and cursor movement.

NB's pull-down menus and help screens are without a doubt the best I have seen in *any* program. They are extensive, context-sensitive, hierarchically arranged, and interactive, making the program easy to use. They are not merely lists of commands but explanations and illustrations of NB's functions that are presented in an aesthetically attractive way, using multiple, nested windows and reverse and intense video. Many help screens display multiple levels of information about related topics, and some of the screens are interactive and allow formatting and printing functions to be invoked directly from menus. NB's menus and on-line help are so good, in fact, that I found I could use many—indeed most—of the program's features simply by using the pull-down menus and help screens, though the documentation and examples in the manual are invaluable for a thorough understanding of all the program's features.

The main Help Menu options are displayed by hitting F6, which lists up to twelve items across the space where the Ruler Line normally appears. The hierarchically arranged system of pull-down menus allows choices to be invoked by highlighting the desired menu item and hitting Return or by typing the first letter of the option name. Invoking a first-level option displays a second menu of suboptions, and sometimes the second menu allows various third-level menus to be selected. Invoking a particular suboption displays a help screen of information. That help screen may allow users to invoke yet another help screen or to implement a formatting or printing function. Especially helpful and functional is the main menu option *INFO*, which allows users to enter the name of a topic about which information is desired.

Editing commands are entered either by using the menus or by using the function keys, alone and in combination with the shifting keys—Shift, Alt and Ctrl—or by using combinations of shifting keys and alpha keys or directly from the Command Line. Formatting and printing commands are entered from the Command Line, one of three nondocument lines at the top of the screen (the other two are the Prompt Line and the Ruler Line), which is replaced by a list of menus when menus are called for. The F9 key is used to move the cursor from the document portion of the screen to the Command Line; F8 moves the cursor back to its original position in the document. NB has approximately 300 file-handling, editing, and formatting commands, most of which consist of two letter abbreviations that are entered from the Command Line. Entering *PN*, for example, inserts a page number command delta in a header or footer. *RM 72* sets the right margin to 72. Most formatting and printer commands likewise consist of two letters followed by different variables and are entered from the Command Line. Because they consist of 2-letter codes, NB's formatting and printing commands are short, simple, and can be issued quickly.

In the Normal Display Mode, formatting commands are embedded in the text as small delta symbols that appear in intense video. These and paragraph markers can be suppressed by issuing the NM—No Marker—command from the Command Line or by pressing Shift + F6. When the cursor is placed on a delta, the formatting command that the delta represents is displayed on the Prompt Line. Conversely, by switching to the Expanded Display Mode, the contents of each delta are displayed between small double-angle brackets (European quotation marks) and may be edited, searched for, and replaced like regular text.

Because in the Normal Display Mode footnotes are "hidden" from view and their places marked by highlighted footnote numbers, deleting a footnote number deletes the footnote it represents. Deleting one mark (the footnote number), then, will delete an entire footnote, no matter how long. This is a dangerous situation and one that should be corrected by making it impossible to erase footnote numbers (and hence footnotes) except by moving to the Command Line and issuing a specific "erase footnote" command.

Error Handling. Although NB's simple and quick command entry and speedy execution make it easy to save documents, the program does not contain automatic save or crash recovery features, and that is a liability. Thus if you exit a document without saving it, all changes made between your last save and the point of exit are irretrievably lost. At the beginning of the editing session, however, NB does make a backup copy of the document being edited, unless users turn this feature off. (As long as there is available disk space, it is strongly advisable to leave this feature on.) Thus in the event of a major disaster, users still have the backup copy of the document. And NB allows users to undelete their last deletion. Fortunately, NB is not easy to crash, and its error messages are clear. Dragonfly Software plans to add an autosave feature to a future version of NB.

Support. During the course of learning to use NB, I called Dragonfly Software several times. Each time my questions were knowledgeably and courteously answered. Once when an experimental printer driver for the NEC 7730 failed to work, one of the technicians was able to debug it while we were on the phone and to tell me how to fix my copy. He waited patiently while I printed a NB test file to make sure the problem had indeed been corrected. Unfortunately, the Dragonfly Software support number is not toll free.

Bibliography. Patrick W. Hamlett, "Nota Bene, Version 1.1," *Social Science Microcomputer Review* 3 (1985): 421–25; John J. Hughes, "Nota Bene: State-of-the-Art Academic Word Processing," *Bits & Bytes Review* 1 (October 1986): 9–15; Willard McCarty, "Nota Bene, An Academic Word Processing and Text Retrieval System for the IBM PC," *Computers and the Humanities* 20 (January-March 1986): 63–71; Edward Mendelson, "Word Processing: A Guide for the Perplexed," *Yale Review* 74 (1985): 615–40; "Word Processing: A Continuing Guide for the Perplexed," *Yale Review* 75 (1986): 454–80; Brian Pfaffenberger, "The Scholar's Software Library—Nota Bene," *Research in Word Processing Newsletter* 4 (January 1986): 9–11; Elizabeth Wallace, "Notable Nota Bene," *PC World* (March 1986): 196–202; Phillip Robinson, "Word Processors," *BYTE* (Summer 1987 Bonus Edition): 55–67, esp., 66–67; Edward Mendelson, "Nota Bene: Grade A Technical Scholarly Document Processor," *PC Magazine* (July 1987): 43.

2.5.1.4 PCT_EX and METAFONT

- *BASIC PRODUCT INFORMATION*

Name of Programs: PCT_EX™ and METAFONT
Company Name: Personal T_EX, Inc.
Address: 20 Sunnyside, Suite H, Mill Valley, CA 94941
Phone: (415) 388-8853
Technical Support: (415) 388-8853
Price: $249
Version Tested: Not able to test; current version is 1.50f.
Runs On: IBM PCs and compatibles
Memory Requirements: 512K
Operating System Requirements: DOS 2.0 or greater
Disk Drive Requirements: 2; hard disk with 3 free megabytes required
Copy Protected: No
Possible Backups: Unlimited
Hard Disk Compatible: Yes
Produces ASCII Files: No
Produces PostScript Files: Yes

Drives Laser Printers: Yes, LaserJet, LaserWriter, Cordata LP-300, QMS Lasergrafix 800 and 1200, and the Imagen 8/300, 12/300 and 24/300 Laser Printers
Drives Typesetters: Yes, APS-5 phototypesetter
SideKick Compatible: Depends on text editor or word processor used.
Mnemonic Commands: Depends on macros.
User Interface: Command-driven
Text Display: Not applicable
Screen Display Reformatting: Not applicable
Formatting Text for Printing: At print time
Text Orientation: Document
Screen Mode: Text
WYSIWYG: Only with the Preview graphics display driver.
Edit Files Larger Than Memory: Yes
Uses Function Keys: Yes
Key Template or Labels: No
Product Includes: Disks, *The PCTEX Manual*, *The LaTEX Users Guide*, TEX tutorial, and the following macro packages: PLAIN, VANILLA, AMS-TEX, and LaTEX.
Number of Disks: 13

- ## INSTRUCTIONAL MATERIALS/SOURCES

Manuals: *The PCTEX Manual* by Michael Spivak (248 pages), *The LaTEX Users Guide* by Leslie Lamport (256 pages)
Tutorial: Yes
Quick Reference Card: No
Demo Disk Available: No
On-Line Help: No
Pop-Up Command Menus: No
SIGs: TEX Users Group (TUG), % American Mathematical Society, P.O. Box 9506, Providence, RI 02940-9506; (401) 272-9500, ext. 232; annual fee of $25 includes subscription to "TUGboat."
Newsletters: "TUGboat," available from TUG
Major Reviews: BYTE (April 1986): 267–72; *Dr. Dobb's Journal* (September 1985): 80–91; *Personal Publishing* (September 1986): 30–33; Luther Sperberg, "For Technical Prose," *Pubish!* (June 1987): 65, 69–71; *Personal Publishing* (August 1987): 82–87.
Other Learning Aids: Donald E. Knuth's 5-volume "Computers and Typesetting" series, which begins with his *The TEXbook* (Addison-Wesley); *The Joy of TEX* by Michael Spivak. Registered users of PCTEX may gain access to Personal TEX's bulletin board, which includes a message area and downloadable files, by logging on at the following number and leaving a message that includes the serial number of their copy of the program: (415) 388-1708; baud rates: 300, 1,200, 2,400; protocols: none/8/1.

- ## MULTILINGUAL FEATURES

Video Cards Supported: MDA, CGA, EGA, HGC, and other "standard" cards
Specify Different Fonts in Document: Yes
Print Different Fonts: Yes
Display Different Fonts On-Screen: Not known
Foreign Fonts Included: Not known
RAM-Based Character Generator: No
Font Editor: Yes, METAFONT, which must be purchased separately.
Number Characters Per Font: 128 or 256
Maximum Screen Fonts Per Document: Not known, but up to 75 printer fonts may be specified per document.
Mode Used to Display Nonstandard Characters: Text; graphics if using the Preview graphics display driver.
Edit Right-to-Left: No
Display Entire ASCII Character Set: Depends on text editor or word processor.

- ## SPECIAL FEATURES

Run DOS Commands from Program: No
Chain Files for Printing: Not known
Queue Files for Printing: No
Spelling Checker: No

Thesaurus: No
Windows/Split-Screen: No
Columns: Yes
Footnotes: Yes
Bibliography: Yes
Table of Contexts: Yes
Indices: Yes
Keyboard Macros: Yes, text and commands
Text Retrieval System: No
Internal Programming Language: No
Other: Interfaces to PC Paintbrush, PC Palette, Fancy Font, and Fontrix are available for $50. The Preview graphics display driver is available for $175, the DVI previewer for $125, and the MAXview previewer for $125. Printer drivers are available for $95 to $275 each. pcMF, a font design program, is available for $195.

- *SUPPORT ETC.*

Warranty: Not known
Support: Phone, bulletin board, letter
Update Policy: Not known
Other Information: TEX requires 3 megabytes of hard disk space.

Introduction. TEX™ (pronounced "tech" as in *technical,* which this program definitely is) was created by Stanford University's Dr. Donald E. Knuth. TEX not a word processor but a powerful typesetting program/page-description language that works with files produced by text editors and word processors. The name TEX says a lot about this program; it was developed for creating technical books, "especially for books that contain a lot of mathematics."[108] As we will learn in the section below on "Scientifically Oriented Programs," the word processing needs of scientists and mathematicians and those of linguists and persons interested in multilingual word processing overlap to a great extent because of their common need to be freed from the shackles of predefined, small, inflexible character sets. Because it gives users complete control over the appearance of the printed page, TEX can be classified as a page-description language as well as a typesetting program.[109] Because it is frequently used to format files created with word processing programs and to print them on dot-matrix and laser printers, I am including this discussion of one microcomputer implementation of TEX in this section of this chapter, rather than later under some other heading.

TEX, which originated on mainframes, gives users an extraordinary—indeed an unprecedented—amount of flexibility over the format of printed output. Among its many features, TEX supports: (1) mixing typestyles and typefaces in a document, (2) sophisticated and accurate justification and (3) automatic hyphenation algorithms, (4) automatic kerning and (5) ligatures, (6) user-specified leading, (7) footnotes, (8) headers and footers, (9) multiple columns, and (10) working with up to seventy-five fonts per document. And it can (11) prepare indices and (12) tables of contents, as well as (13) drive typesetters.[110] And (14) primitive TEX commands can be used to create complex, custom typesetting commands.[111]

---

108. Knuth, *TEXbook,* v.

109. Other page- or document-description languages include PostScript (Adobe Systems), Interpress (Xerox Corporation), *troff* (Unix), and DDL (Document Description Language from Imagen).

110. Hoenig, "Typesetting," 30.

111. My review copy of TEX arrived too late to be reviewed for this edition of this book. The following remarks, then, are a description of one microcomputer implementation of TEX. I will not describe Addison-Wesley's MicroTEX since it is similar to PCTEX, though I will list the main facts about it.

Here's how TEX works. (1) Using word processors or text editors, users create pure ASCII files that include TEX formatting commands.[112] (2) Such ASCII files are then processed by the TEX program, which formats them according to the embedded TEX codes. That creates "device-independent files" (DVI) that are ready to be printed. (3) A TEX device driver is then used to translate the formatted DVI files for a particular output device and to print them on that device, using TEX fonts, in full graphics mode. Thus TEX is a post-processor that batch processes source files to create DVI output files. Because the DVI files are *device-independent*, the printed output looks the same (except for resolution), regardless of whether it is printed on an Epson FX-80 at 120 dpi, an HP LaserJet at 300 dpi, or an APS-5 phototypesetter at 1,200 dpi. Thus TEX DVI files are *transportable*, regardless of the computer and word processor used to create them. With the proper TEX device drivers, DVI files may be printed on *any* output device.

In addition to the two parts of the actual program, Knuth's 483-page *The TEXbook*, the first of a 5-volume series called "Computers and Typesetting," is required to fully understand and use any of the microcomputer implementations of TEX. Also recommended is Michael Spivak's *The Joy of TEX* (!).

Description. PCTEX version 1.50f is a complete implementation of Knuth's "final" version of his program, TEX82 version 2.0, and is written in Pascal.[113] Whatever TEX can do, PCTEX can do; the two programs are fully compatible. In fact, since the name TEX is a trademark of the American Mathematical Society (AMS), any implementation of the program that wishes to use the name TEX must be a *full* implementation of the program that creates files that are fully compatible with those created by TEX82. Thus for all practical purposes, PCTEX is synonymous with TEX.

TEX appears to be the most complex, flexible, powerful, difficult-to-learn, and totally command-driven program mentioned anywhere in this book. It is a full-bore professional typesetting program designed to satisfy the needs, wants, and dreams of the wildest and fussiest users. After studying Knuth's 483-page user's manual, *The TEXbook* (large pages and lots of very small print), I've decided that mastering Final-Word II, XyWrite III, or Nota Bene would be *child's play* compared to mastering TEX, whose commands and syntax can often result in complex and highly convoluted combinations of opaque formatting codes.

To give you an idea of TEX's precision and intricacy, consider the following. TEX allows users to express vertical and horizontal distances in terms of points, picas, inches, big points, centimeters, millimeters, didot points, cicero, and scaled points. That's flexibility. But here's precision. Internally, within the program, TEX translates those various units of measure into integer multiples of an infinitesimally small unit of measure called an *sp* (the wavelength of visible light is approximately 100 sp; 2^{30} sp = 18.892 feet),[114] which means that small rounding errors are invisible to the naked eye. And using such a small common unit of measure insures that TEX's printed results will not vary from computer to computer. That's consistency!

Fortunately, TEX's extremely powerful macro capabilities save it from being overwhelmingly complex. TEX works with macros written in ASCII and with macros that have been highly compiled and compressed into formatted (FMT) files, which execute much faster than ASCII macros. TEX's macros can execute long, complex sequences of formatting commands, load fonts, and specify predefined or user-defined formats, thus simplifying the task of using TEX. In those regards, TEX sounds a lot like FW II. PCTEX supports user-defined ASCII and FMT macros and includes the following

---

112. TEX includes a set of about 300 basic, or "primitive," formatting commands and about 600 macros, which simplify the job of issuing the proper formatting commands.

113. TEX82 is written in WEB, a Pascal-based documentation and algorithmic language.

114. Knuth, *The TEXbook*, 58.

large libraries of fully documented, predefined macros: PLAIN, VANILLA, AMS-TeX, and LaTeX.

Output device drivers for PCTeX must be purchased separately.

Each driver includes 236 TeX font files. I believe these are 128-characters fonts, though TeX can work with 256-character fonts. Additional fonts are available from other suppliers. For example, the Metafoundry (6565 Frantz Road, Dublin, Ohio 43017; (614) 764-6482) markets the MF Medley fonts, three sets of TeX fonts (22 printer and 22 preview fonts per set; each set costs $100/set) that are optimized for 180- and 240-dpi Epson and for 300-dpi laser printers. The Austin Code Works (11100 Leafwood Lane, Austin, TX 78750-3409; (512) 258-0785) markets the KST Fonts package ($30), which contains 139 fonts, including Hebrew, and the Roman Fonts package ($30), which contains 108 sizes and styles of roman characters (both packages for $50). The KST Fonts were created for 200-by-200 dpi devices, and the Roman Fonts for 300-by-300 dpi devices.

TeX can typeset documents with *any* fonts, including Hebrew and Greek; and METAFONT, a font creation language that is documented in Knuth's *The METAFONTbook* and in his *METAFONT: The Program*, allows knowledgeable users to design their own fonts for digital typesetting devices. Personal TeX markets pcMF, a microcomputer implementation of Knuth's font design program that includes a copy of his *The METAFONTbook*, for $195. Some of PCTeX's drivers convert DVI files to PostScript files. Additional drivers are available from ArborText, Inc., 416 Fourth St., P.O. Box 7993, Ann Arbor, MI 48107; (313) 996-3566.

Personal TeX sells three programs for previewing formatted TeX files before they are printed. These programs, which require one of the standard graphics boards, display TeX files in a WYSIWYG fashion on-screen at resolutions from 118 dpi to 300 dpi. The programs are (1) Preview (from ArborText): $175, (2) DVISCRN (from N^2 Computer Consultants): $125, and (3) MAXview (from Aurion Tecnología): $125. Preview has the most features. Personal TeX plans to market a front-end program (developed by Mike Spivak and the TeXMate Corporation 4151, S.W. Freeway, Houston, TX 77027; (713) 523-5700) that simplifies using TeX commands.

Printing from DVI files on dot-matrix printers is V-E-R-Y S-L-O-W because TeX performs full-page graphics dumps of DVI files to the printer. As you may have guessed, DVI files are a pixel-by-pixel specification of what each page in the printed document is to look like. Thus instead of operating printers in text mode, TeX operates printers in graphics mode, and that is a slow, memory-intensive process. For example, according to the PCTeX product catalog, the driver for the Epson FX or RX, printing at 240 dpi (quad mode), takes 10 to 20 minutes *per page*! The driver for the Epson LQ800, LQ1000, and LQ1500 takes 1 to 2 minutes to print a page at 180-dpi. Of course driver speeds are greatly influenced by page complexity, the type of microprocessor used, and the speed at which the microprocessor is operated.

There are four versions of TeX for the Macintosh: (1) TextSet (a TeX-to-PostScript device driver),[115] (2) Macintosh TeX by Kellerman and Smith,[116] (3) MacTeX, and (4) TeXTURES™. Each of these implementations includes TeX-to-PostScript file conversion utilities that automatically convert TeX files to PostScript files. MacTeX, a full implementation of TeX82 version 1.3, allows PostScript codes to be mixed with TeX codes and is designed to work with PostScript printers and fonts (drivers for the LaserWriter and Linotronic 300 are included). This program is menu-driven, has a built-in editor, supports the PLAIN and LaTeX macro sets, has a preview utility that gives a WYSIWYG display of a file before it is printed, and requires 1MB of memory. Addison-Wesley's TeXTURES supports windows, has an ASCII file-import utility and a WYSIWYG preview mode with up to 300 dpi resolution, and supports PostScript printers and fonts.

---

115. "TeX on the Mac," *A+ Magazine* (May 1985): 128.
116. Ibid.

MacTEX
Personal TEX, Inc.
20 Sunnyside, Suite H
Mill Valley, CA 94941
(415) 388-8853
List Price: $750 or

MacTEX
FTL Systems, Inc.
234 Eglinton Ave. E., Suite 205
Toronto, Ontario
Canada M4P 1K5
(416) 487-2142
List Price: $750 or

MacTEX
MENU
Customer Service Dept.
1520 S. College Ave.
Fort Collins, CO 80524
(303) 482-5000
List Price: $750

TEXTURES
Addsion-Wesley Publishing Co.
Route 128
Reading, MA 01867
(617) 944-3700, (617) 944-6795
List Price: $495

MENU also markets TEX CP/M Formatter, a CP/M-80 version (2.2, Digital Research, 8-inch diskettes) of TEX that requires 20K of memory and that costs $75. And TEX for the Amiga (512K, 2 drives) is available for $300 ($200 additional for QMS-Kiss and -Smartwriter driver with fonts) from

n^2 Computer Consultants
P.O. Box 2736
College Station, TX 77841

The following companies offer professional typeset output from TEX DVI files.

TEX Source
3333 W. Alabama, Suite 109
Houston, TX 77008
(713) 520-7206

ArborText, Inc.
416 Fourth St.
P.O. Box 7993
Ann Arbor, MI 48107
(313) 996-3566
Prices: $4 to $5.50 per page
Typesetter: Autologic APS-5

Computer Composition Corporation
1401 West Girard Ave.
Madison Heights, MI 48071
(313) 545-4330
Prices: $4.50 to $8 per page
Typeseter: Autologic APS-5

Aldine Press
12625 La Cresta Dr.
Los Altos Hills, CA 94022
(415) 948-2149

Alan Hoenig
17 Bay Ave.
Huntington, NY 11743
(516) 385-0736

Arthur Ogawa
5957 Shattuck Ave.
Oakland, CA 94609
(415) 653-4336

Amy Hendrickson
T$_E$XNOLOGY, Inc.
57 Longwood Ave.
Brookline, MA 02146
(617) 738-8029 or Amy@MIT__MC

Bibliography. Anon, "T$_E$X on the Mac," A+ 3 (May 1985): 128; R. W. Bemer, "Introduction to the T$_E$X Language," *Interface Age* 3 (August 1978): 144–47; Richard Fritzson, "TEX and METAFONT: New Directions in Typesetting," BYTE (June 1981): 374–76; Richard Furuta and Pierre A. MacKay, "Two TEX Implementations for the IBM PC," *Dr. Dobb's Journal* (September 1985): 80–91; Alan Hoenig, "Typesetting with T$_E$X," *Personal Publishing* (September 1986): 30–33; Richard Ilson, "Recent Research in Text Processing," *IEEE Transactions on Professional Communications* 5 (1980): 168–70; Donald E. Knuth, *Computer Modern Typefaces*, Reading, Mass.: Addison-Wesley Pub. Co., 1986; METAFONT: *The Program*, Reading, Mass.: Addison-Wesley Pub. Co., 1986; TEX & METAFONT: *New Directions in Typesetting*, Digital Press, 1979; TEX: *The Program*, Reading, Mass.: Addison-Wesley, 1986; *The METAFONTbook*, Reading, Mass.: Addison-Wesley, 1986; *The T$_E$Xbook*, Reading, Mass.: Addison-Wesley, 1986; Leslie Lamport, *LaT$_E$X User's Guide*, publication data not known (available from Personal T$_E$X, Inc.); Pierre A. MacKay, "T$_E$X for Arabic Script," in *Sixth International Conference on Computers and the Humanities*, eds. Sarah K. Burton and Douglas D. Short. Rockville: Computer Science Press, 1983, 391–400; "T$_E$X's Coming of Age," *PROTEXT I. Proceedings of the First International Conference on Text Processing Systems* (1984), 26–34; "Typesetting Problem Scripts," *BYTE* (February 1986): 201–2, 204; Michael Spivak, *The Joy of T$_E$X*, publication data not known (available from Personal T$_E$X, Inc.); Michale Swaine, "Knuth Makes Mathematical Typography an Art," *InfoWorld* (March 14, 1983): 25, 28; Hal R. Varian, "PCT$_E$X and MicroT$_E$X," BYTE (April 1986): 267–72; Alan Hoenig, "TeX for the Mac," *Personal Publishing* (August 1987): 82–87.

2.5.1.5 MicroT$_E$X

- BASIC PRODUCT INFORMATION

Name of Program: MicroT$_E$X
Company Name: Addison-Wesley Publishing Company
Address: Educational Media Systems Division, One Jacob Way, Reading, MA 01867
Phone: (617) 944-6795
Technical Support: (617) 944-6795
Price: $295
Version Tested: Not able to test; current version is 1.5A

Runs On: IBM PCs and compatibles
Memory Requirements: 512K
Operating System Requirements: DOS 2.0 or greater
Disk Drive Requirements: 2 floppies or a hard and a floppy; hard disk not required.
Copy Protected: No
Possible Backups: Unlimited
Hard Disk Compatible: Yes
Produces ASCII Files: No
Produces PostScript Files: Yes
Drives Laser Printers: Yes, LaserWriter, LaserJet Plus, QMS Lasergrafix, Imagen
Drives Typesetters: Yes, PostScript-compatible Linotype L100 and L300
SideKick Compatible: Depends on text editor or word processor used.
Mnemonic Commands: Depends on macros
User Interface: Command-driven
Text Display: Not applicable
Screen Display Reformatting: Not applicable
Formatting Text for Printing: At print time
Text Orientation: Document
Screen Mode: Text
WYSIWYG: Only with the Preview graphics display driver.
Edit Files Larger Than Memory: Yes
Uses Function Keys: Yes
Key Template or Labels: No
Product Includes: Program disks, manual, and *The TEXbook*
Number of Disks: 26: 4 for program, 12 for TEX Preview, 10 for laser printer drivers

- *INSTRUCTIONAL MATERIALS/SOURCES*

Manual: 56 pages
Tutorial: No
Quick Reference Card: No
Demo Disk Available: No
On-Line Help: No
Pop-Up Command Menus: No
SIGs: TEX Users Group (TUG), % American Mathematical Society, P.O. Box 9506, Providence, RI 02940-9506; (401) 272-9500, annual fee of $25 includes subscription to "TUGboat."
Newsletters: "TUGboat," available from TUG
Major Reviews: BYTE (April 1986): 267–72; *Dr. Dobb's Journal* (September 1985): 80–91
Other Learning Aids: Donald E. Knuth's 5-volume "Computers and Typesetting" series, which begins with his *The TEXbook* (Addison Wesley); *The Joy of TEX* by Michael Spivak.

- *MULTILINGUAL FEATURES*

Video Cards Supported: MDA, CGA, EGA, HGC, and other "standard" cards
Specify Different Fonts in Document: Yes
Print Different Fonts: Yes
Display Different Fonts On-Screen: Not known
Foreign Fonts Included: Not known
RAM-Based Character Generator: No
Font Editor: No
Number Characters Per Font: 128 or 256
Maximum Screen Fonts Per Document: Not known, but up to 100 printer fonts may be used per document.
Mode Used to Display Nonstandard Characters: Text; graphics if using the Preview graphics display driver.
Edit Right-to-Left: No
Display Entire ASCII Character Set: Depends on line editor or word processor.

- *SPECIAL FEATURES*

Run DOS Commands from Program: No
Chain Files for Printing: Not known
Queue Files for Printing: No
Spelling Checker: No

Thesaurus: No
Windows/Split-Screen: No
Columns: Yes
Footnotes: Yes
Bibliography: Yes
Table of Contexts: Yes
Indices: Yes
Keyboard Macros: Yes, text and commands
Text Retrieval System: No
Internal Programming Language: No
Other: T$_E$X Preview driver is available for $250. Printer drivers are available for $100 to $300. MicroT$_E$X is
written in C.

- *SUPPORT ETC.*

Warranty: 90 days, media only
Support: Not known
Update Policy: Not known
Other Information: None

2.5.1.6 Professional Writer's Package/AcademicFont

- *BASIC PRODUCT INFORMATION*

Name of Program: Professional Writer's Package/AcademicFont®
Company Name: University MicroComputers
Address: 623 Forest Ave., Suite E, Palo Alto, CA 94301
Phone: (415) 326-3114
Technical Support: (800) 782-4896
Price: $590
Version Tested: Not able to test
Runs On: IBM PCs and compatibles
Memory Requirements: 512K
Operating System Requirements: DOS 2.1 or greater
Disk Drive Requirements: 2
Copy Protected: No
Possible Backups: Unlimited
Hard Disk Compatible: Yes
Produces ASCII Files: Yes
Produces PostScript Files: No
Drives Laser Printers: Yes
Drives Typesetters: No
SideKick Compatible: Yes
Mnemonic Commands: Yes
User Interface: Command-driven
Text Display: Auto word wrap, on-screen justification when formatter run in separate window
Screen Display Reformatting: Constant and automatic
Formatting Text for Printing: At print time
Text Orientation: Document
Screen Mode: Text
WYSIWYG: No
Edit Files Larger Than Memory: Yes
Uses Function Keys: Yes
Key Template or Labels: Yes
Product Includes: Disks and three manual
Number of Disks: 6

- *INSTRUCTIONAL MATERIALS/SOURCES*

Manual: Two reference and one tutorial
Tutorial: 2 tutorials on disk, 6 tutorial lessons in manual

Quick Reference Card: Yes
Demo Disk Available: Yes (English only)
On-Line Help: Yes
Pop-Up Command Menus: No
SIGs: Yes
Newsletters: Yes, *Emerging Technology Newsletter* and *The University Microcomputer Newsletter*
Major Reviews: *PC Magazine* (March 19, 1985): 211–14.
Other Learning Aids: None

- MULTILINGUAL FEATURES

Video Cards Supported: MDA, CGA, EGA, HGC, and other "standard" cards
Specify Different Fonts in Document: Yes
Print Different Fonts: Yes
Display Different Fonts On-Screen: Yes
Foreign Fonts Included: Depends on ROM purchased. Greek (includes all diacritical marks), Coptic, Old Church Slavic, Cyrillic, Polish, Japanese (katakana), Romance-Germanic, and others are available. ROM chip not necessary with EGA or HGC+ cards.
RAM-Based Character Generator: No
Font Editor: No
Number Characters Per Font: 256
Maximum Screen Fonts Per Document: 2
Mode Used to Display Nonstandard Characters: Text
Edit Right-to-Left: No
Display Entire ASCII Character Set: Yes

- SPECIAL FEATURES

Run DOS Commands from Program: Yes
Chain Files for Printing: Yes
Queue Files for Printing: Yes
Spelling Checker: Yes, SPELLIX, a 66,000 word spelling checker
Thesaurus: No
Windows/Split-Screen: Yes, a maximum of 4
Columns: Yes
Footnotes: Yes
Bibliography: No
Table of Contexts: Yes
Indices: Yes, by using INDIX
Keyboard Macros: Yes, text and commands
Text Retrieval System: No
Internal Programming Language: No
Other: None

- SUPPORT ETC.

Warranty: Not known
Support: Not known
Update Policy: Not known
Other Information: None

AcademicFont® (hereafter AF) is the old name for a product that is now marketed by Emerging Technology as the Professional Writer's Package/Academic Font. AF is a version of EDIX + WORDIX, a pair of text editing and page formatting programs distributed by Emerging Technology Consultants of Boulder, Colorado (4760 Walnut St., Boulder, CO 80301; (800) 782-4896, (303) 447-9495), that includes INDIX and SPELLIX. Various multilingual versions of AF include Slavic, Classical Greek, Coptic-Greek, Logic-Greek, Romance-Germanic, Old Scandinavian, and the International Phonetic Alphabet. Multilingual versions of AF require either a special character

ROM chip or a video board like the EGA or HGC+ that accepts downloadable fonts. When used with a replacement ROM, multilingual versions of AF are restricted to 256 characters each. When used with the EGA or HGC+, multilingual versions of AF can work with up to 512 unique characters. AF's Greek ROM contains a full set of diacritical marks, which are entered by using a "dead-key" approach (see above).

Because I have not been able to obtain a review copy of this program, I refer the interested reader to the following review of EDIX, WORDIX, and INDIX: Dean Hannotte, "Put Your Text in Top Form," *PC Magazine* (March 19, 1985): 211–14. I have not been able to locate reviews of AF.

2.5.2 Business Oriented Programs

Well-known programs in this category include WordStar®, Spellbinder™, WordPerfect™, and Microsoft® Word. Because it has received the most consistently favorable and flattering reviews of any word processing program I know of, I am including a review of WordPerfect™ in this section, though in many ways it is not as powerful or suitable for academic and multilingual word processing as the programs we have already reviewed. It is, however, a superb, feature-laden program that works smoothly and is easy to use.

This section also includes a review of Microsoft® Word, many of whose features make it well-suited for academic and multilingual word processing. I am not including a review of or information about the venerable WordStar® (whose reviews are always quite mixed) because in my opinion it is not nearly as suitable for academic and multilingual word processing as programs we have already discussed.

2.5.2.1 *WordPerfect*

● BASIC PRODUCT INFORMATION
Name of Program: WordPerfect™
Company Name: Word Perfect Corporation
Address: 288 West Center St., Orem UT 84057
Phones: (800) 321-4566, (801) 225-5000 in Utah
Technical Support: (800) 321-5906, (801) 226-6800 in Utah, Mon. – Fri.: 7:00 A.M. – 6:00 P.M.
Price: $495; $125 with educational discount
Version Tested: 4.1 for the IBM PC/XT AT; latest version is 4.2.
Runs On: IBM PCs and compatibles, Apple IIe, gs; Macintosh version promised for 1987.
Memory Requirements: 256K
Operating System Requirements: DOS 2.0 or greater
Disk Drive Requirements: 2
Copy Protected: No
Possible Backups: Unlimited
Hard Disk Compatible: Yes
Produces ASCII Files: Yes
Produces PostScript Files: Yes
Drives Laser Printers: Yes, LaserJet, LaserJet Plus, LaserWriter, AST TurboLaser, Canon A1, and others
Drives Typesetters: No
SideKick Compatible: Yes
Mnemonic Commands: No
User Interface: Menu-driven (Function-Key driven)
Text Display: Auto word wrap, no on-screen justification
Screen Display Reformatting: Constant and automatic
Formatting Text for Printing: Continuously
Text Orientation: Document, but page breaks shown on-screen
Screen Mode: Text
WYSIWYG: Yes
Edit Files Larger Than Memory: Yes
Uses Function Keys: Yes

Key Template or Labels: Yes
Product Includes: Disks, manual, installation guide, key template, quick reference card
Number of Disks: 5

- ## INSTRUCTIONAL MATERIALS/SOURCES

Manual: 513 pages, three-ring binder, slipcase, typeset, tabbed, indexed
Tutorial: Yes, twelve lessons (146 pages) in manual and a special learning diskette
Quick Reference Card: Yes
Demo Disk Available: Yes, from WordPerfect User Group (see below)
On-Line Help: Yes
Pop-Up Command Menus: No
SIGs: WordPerfect User Group, 2812 St. Paul St., Baltimore, MD 21218
Newsletters: *The WordPerfectionist*, published by the WordPerfect Support Group, Wilkes Software Systems, Inc., P.O. Box 1577, Baltimore, MD 21203; telephone: (301) 889-7894.
Major Reviews: *InfoWorld* (November 4, 1985): 41–42; *PC Magazine* (January 28, 1986): 169–71; *PC World* (February 1987): 285–91; *InfoWorld* (February 2, 1987): 53–55; *PC Magazine* (May 26, 1987): 208–9, 214.
Other Learning Aids: See the bibliography at the end of this section, and write WordPerfect Corporation, Instructional Services (at the address above), and request their two sheets "Training Materials for WordPerfect."

- ## MULTILINGUAL FEATURES

Video Cards Supported: MDA, CGA, EGA, HGC, and other "standard" cards
Specify Different Fonts in Document: Yes
Print Different Fonts: Yes
Display Different Fonts On-Screen: No
Foreign Fonts Included: None per se, though the Roman 8 character set contains the characters for all Western European languages.
RAM-Based Character Generator: No
Font Editor: No
Number Characters Per Font: 256
Maximum Screen Fonts Per Document: 1
Mode Used to Display Nonstandard Characters: Text
Edit Right-to-Left: No
Display Entire ASCII Character Set: Yes

- ## SPECIAL FEATURES

Run DOS Commands from Program: Yes
Chain Files for Printing: No
Queue Files for Printing: Yes
Spelling Checker: Yes, over 115,000 words
Thesaurus: Yes, 10,000 key words, over 60,000 total words
Windows/Split-Screen: Yes, maximum of 2
Columns: Yes, maximum of 5 (maximum of 24 in version 4.2)
Footnotes: Yes
Bibliography: No
Table of Contexts: Yes
Indices: Yes
Keyboard Macros: Yes, text and commands
Text Retrieval System: No
Internal Programming Language: No
Other: Built-in 4-function math, mail merge, auto-hyphenation (4.2), and sort features. WordPerfect Corporation markets the WordPerfect Library—a RAM-resident, pop-up utility that contains six desktop accessories (calculator, calendar, notebook, macro editor, program editor, file manager) and a DOS shell—$129 (less with educational discount). WordPerfect Corporation also markets special-language versions of WordPerfect for IBM PCs and compatibles. French, German, Dutch, Spanish, Finish, Norwegian, Swedish, and Danish are available. A network version of WordPerfect is available for Novell NetWare, AST-PCnet, 3Com EtherSeries, and the IBM PC Network.

• *SUPPORT ETC.*

Warranty: 90 days, program and media
Support: Phone, letter
Update Policy: $35 to upgrade from version 4.1 to version 4.2; $60 to upgrade from previous versions.
Other Information: None

Introduction. With well over 600,000 registered users, WordPerfect™ (hereafter WP) is one of the most successful word processing programs ever created. Not only is the program available for IBM PCs, but versions also are available for the Apple IIe, c, and gs, and a Macintosh version is promised for late 1987. WP consistently receives rave reviews because it is extremely powerful, feature-laden, easy to learn and use, coherent, cleanly programmed, fast, and well documented. For many applications, especially for office and corporate use, WP may well be the best word processor available today. Many academicians use WP and are enthusiastic about it. In my opinion, however, for complex academic and for multilingual applications, WP is not as powerful, flexible, and useful as FW II, XW III, and Nota Bene™, as we will see below.

Performance and Versatility. WP's impressive array of features include the following. WP supports (1) four-function, on-screen math, (2) powerful macros, (3) automatic generation of indices, outlines, and tables of contents, including (in version 4.2) a concordance feature that will index all occurrences of a word without having to mark each occurrence, (4) split-screen editing, (5) three-level undeleting (a unique feature among word processors), (6) up to twenty-four side-by-side, snaking columns of text (in version 4.2), which are properly displayed on-screen during editing (very few word processors can do this), (7) wild-card and Boolean searches,[117] (8) a file-scanning option that allows users to view a file without leaving the file they are in, (9) a whole host of file-management options (e.g., rename, copy, delete, import, view), (10) a sort function that will sort lines, pages, or other user-specified units in alphabetical or numerical order, (11) a variety of merge functions that allow data from two or more different sources to be combined in a single document, (12) bidirectional cursor movement by character, word, line, end/beginning of line, page, screen, and document, (13) deletion by character, word, end of line, and page, (14) a GOTO command that allows the cursor to be moved by character, paragraph, or page and returned to the initial cursor position, (15) a REPEAT command that will repeat certain operations a user-specified number of times, (16) a wide assortment of block operations, (17) queuing documents for printing, (18) print spooling, (19) global and conditional case-insensitive search and replace, (20) almost 200 printers, (21) automatic file saving, (22) exiting to DOS and then returning to the same place in the same file, (23) on-line help, and (24) footnotes and endnotes. And WP (25) displays page breaks on-screen, (26) has a built-in, 115,000-word spelling checker, and (27) a built-in 10,000-word thesaurus that contains antonyms as well as synonyms. And version 4.2 of WP can (28) number text lines, (29) generate a table of authorities cited, (30) display nonprinting comments anywhere in a document, (31) index words from a predefined list, (32) automatically hyphenate,[118] and it (33) allows up to seven different sheet feeders to be defined.

As incredibly powerful, flexible, and feature-laden as it is, and despite its name, WP is not (yet) perfect. WP (1) restricts users to two windows, which may be full- or split-screen (XW III and NB allow nine windows; FW II allows six), (2) does not allow two parts of one file to be edited in two different windows (FW II does), (3) does not support wild cards in search-and-replace mode (FW II, XW III, and NB do), (4) sup-

---

117. A "Boolean search" allows logical operators such as AND, OR, and NOT to be used to link search terms.

118. WP uses a rule-based approach to hyphenation.

ports only one wild-card character when searching (unlike FW II, XW III, and NB), (5) cannot generate a table of contents or indices (as FW II, XW III, and NB can) or bibliography across multiple files (as XW III and NB can, though WP's file size is limited only by available disk space), (6) cannot link files for printing so that page and footnote numbering are automatically numbered sequentially across files (as FW II, XW III, and NB can), (7) does not have predefined style sheets that globally control major formatting parameters (as FW II and NB do), (8) cannot perform bidirectional cross referencing (as FW II, XW III and NB can), (9) cannot create bibliographies from entries scattered throughout a file or files (as NB can), (10) does not allow side-by-side or snaking columns to contain footnotes (as FW II, XW III and NB do, though WP's columns may contain endnotes), (11) does not allow side-by-side columns to be variably spaced, assigned styles, or straddle page breaks (as XW III and NB do), (12) does not provide predefined foreign-language keyboards (as NB does; even WP's foreign-language versions come with the same keyboard layout that their English-language version has), (13) does not allow the cursor to be moved bidirectionally by phrase, sentence, and paragraph (as NB does), though macros could be created to do these things, (14) cannot delete forwards and backwards to the beginning or end of a phrase, sentence, or paragraph (as NB can), though macros could be created to do these things, (15) cannot transpose by character, word, sentence, or paragraph (as NB can), (16) does not have *context-sensitive*, on-line help or hierarchically arranged help screens or interactive help screens that allow program functions to be invoked (as does NB), (17) does not allow users to set paragraph, section, and outline numbering in *any* user-specified formats (as XW III and NB do), (18) allows only seven levels in numbered paragraphs, sections, and outlines (XW III and NB allow ten; FW II allows an unlimited number), (19) restricts users to one index of two levels (NB and XW III allow three 2-level indices), (20) does not contain an internal programming language (XW III, NB, and FW II do), and (21) does not reformat as text is inserted (as FW II, XW III, and NB do), only when the cursor moves out of the region in which the text was inserted. And (22) WP's file-search command does not allow proximity searching or show the context of the match (as do XW III's and NB's). Although feature-laden, (23) WP is noticeably slower at almost everything—moving, copying, deleting, inserting, moving through files—than either XW III or NB and is not nearly as flexible and user-customizable as FW II, XW III, and NB. If WP is the luxury car of word processors—smooth, solid, safe, automated—then Nota Bene, XyWrite, and FinalWord are the custom-built race cars—fast, exciting, responsive, and fun.

WP is ill-suited for multilingual word processing. WP contains no predefined keyboards for special Western European symbols. To access the "extended" ASCII character set, users must assign extended characters to macros, using the Ctrl and Alt keys in combination with the alpha keys A-Z. Thus only 52 special characters may be mapped to macros and be active at any one time, though macro key assignments may be changed at any time. The actual process of assigning "extended" characters to a macro is awkward. After displaying the Ctrl/Alt key menu, which displays all available "extended" characters across the bottom of the screen, users must define a macro (Ctrl + A-Z or Alt + A-Z) and bind it to one of the "extended" characters by entering that character's decimal value (which is listed at the bottom of the screen).

Although WP can be used with the EGA card, and though a font utility like Duke University's LOADFONT (see below) can be used from within WP to load fonts into the EGA, WP offers no way to create *composite* characters from downloaded fonts because WP provides no facilities for defining a key as a dead key. Thus although a Greek font could be loaded into the EGA and used with WP, WP provides no means for entering a Greek character and then entering a diacritical mark so that the diacritical mark is displayed properly with the character.[119] In my opinion, for persons interested in using downloaded fonts to properly display composite characters on-screen, this is a *fatal* flaw in an otherwise outstanding program.

Documentation. In an industry where many user's manuals read as if they had been written as an afterthought by a fatigued programmer who thought in binary, WP's documentation is legendary for its clarity, comprehensiveness, usefulness, and readability. An easy-to-follow installation pamphlet walks users through the process of installing the program, and the manual itself contains a 146-page, 12-lesson learning section. The explanation of each of the main features of the program is accompanied by a vertical listing of the keys that are used to invoke the feature being described, a description of what each keystroke does, and a picture of the screen that shows the effect of the keystroke sequence. Additionally, this section of the manual contains frequent question-and-answer subsections that anticipate and answer questions users may have about certain features of the program. Although WP's manual is not perfect (the items in the special features section are not listed in alphabetical order; the index could be more extensive), it certainly sets a standard for other manuals.

The manual also contains a 152-page reference section that lists each of WP's commands alphabetically and explains them in more detail. Separate sections are included for the spelling/thesaurus, merge, math, and special features parts of the program.

In addition to a superb manual and installation pamphlet, WP includes a function-key template and on-line help. Both are useful, though WP's help screens are not in the same league with NB's (see above).

Ease of Use. WP is an amazingly easy program to use. Almost all editing, formatting, and printing commands are entered by using the function keys, alone and in combination with the shifting keys (Ctrl, Shift, and Alt). A handy, color-coded function-key template lists forty basic commands. Cursor key movements are assigned to the numeric keypad. WP allows users to assign frequently used commands and text strings to macros.

WP comes close to being true WYSIWYG. Version 4.2 shows right justification and headers and footers on-screen. Formatting codes are hidden, though they may be revealed (in version 4.2 revealed codes appear in intense video), searched and replaced, and edited. A Status Line at the bottom of the screen shows the document name, page number, and line and page position; and a Ruler Line can be displayed, if desired. Although WP is documented-oriented, page breaks are shown on-screen.

Error Handling. WP is one of the safest and most crash-proof programs on the market. Consider its list of safety features. (1) WP allows users to undelete their last *three* deletions, a unique feature among word processing programs. (2) WP automatically saves text to disk at user-specified intervals. (3) When an editing session begins, an optional feature automatically saves the original file by renaming it. And (4) error messages inform users of unformatted disks, open disk-drive doors, write-protect tabs, and other hazardous conditions.

Support. WP was so easy to learn and to use that I had no occasion to call Word Perfect's support line. Unlike many companies that sell word processing programs, Word Perfect Corporation has a toll-free number and almost 78 full-time support personnel! Registered users may receive unlimited, free support from the toll-free number as long as they own the program.

Bibliography. Eric Alderman and Lawrence J. Magid, *Advanced WordPerfect: Features & Techniques* (Berkeley: OSBORNE/McGraw-Hill, 1986); Vincent Alfieri, *Mastering WordPerfect* (Hasbrouck Heights, N.J.: Hayden Book Co., 1986); Deborah Beacham and Walton Beacham, *Using WordPerfect* (Indianapolis: Que Corporation, 1985—based on version 3.0 of the program); Ricardo Birmele, "WordPerfect," *BYTE*

---

119. Although the character-generator ROM chip on a display board could be changed and foreign-language characters in the new ROM displayed properly on-screen, as we learned above, that approach restricts users to a 256-character font.

(December 1984): 277–88 (a helpful review of a version of the program that antedates version 4.1); "WordPerfect 4.1," *BYTE* (September 1986): 311–12; Dineh M. Davis, *WordPerfect™ for the IBM PC* (New York: Holt, Rinehart and Winston/CBS College Publishing, 1985—based on version 3.0 of the program); Jordan Gold, *The Illustrated WordPerfect 4.1 Book* (Wordware Pub., 1986); Dawn Gordon, "The Business of Words: Professional—WordPerfect 4.1," *PC Magazine* (January 28, 1986): 169–71; Greg Harvey and Kay Y. Nelson, *WordPerfect Desktop Companion* (Berkeley: Sybex, 1987); Bill Howard, "WordPerfect Made Easy," *PC Magazine* (April 14, 1987): 221–22; Susan B. Kelly, *Mastering WordPerfect* (Berkeley: Sybex, 1986); Steven King, *WordPerfect: Macros, Desktop Publishing, File Management & Networking* (Weber Systems, 1986); Robert Krumm, *The Power Of WordPerfect, Version 4.2* (Management Information Inc., 1987); John Lombardi, "Heavy-Hitting Market Leader Improves a Bit With Update," *InfoWorld* (February 2, 1987): 53–55; Trish McClelland, *The Dynamics of WordPerfect* (Dow Jones-Irwin, 1985); Rhyder McClure, "Eight Ways to Improve WordPerfect," *PC Magazine* (April 14, 1987): 232–38, 245–46; Alan R. Neibauer, *WordPerfect Tips & Tricks* (Berkeley: Sybex, 1986); Stephen Robinett, *Advanced WordPerfect* (New York: Brady Communications, 1986); Daniel J. Rosenbaum, "Seventeen Ways to Learn WordPerfect," *PC Magazine* (April 14, 1987): 222–26, 231; "WordPerfect Meets LaserJet Plus," *PC World* (February 1987): 285–91; Leo J. Scanlon, *The WordPerfect Book* (Blue Ridge Summit, Penn.: TAB, 1986—covers Versions 4.0 & 4.1); Linda K. Schwartz and Patricia A. Menges, *How to Use WordPerfect* (FlipTrack, 1986); Charles O. Stewart III, *WordPerfect Tips, Tricks & Traps* (Indianapolis: Que Corporation, 1987); S. Wingrove, *Getting the Most from WordPerfect* (New York: McGraw-Hill, 1984); WordPerfect Corporation Staff, *WordPerfect: The McGraw-Hill College Version Set* (New York: McGraw-Hill, 1987); Bernie Zilbergeld, "WordPerfect 4.1: The Best Improved," *InfoWorld* (November 4, 1985): 41–42; S. Scott Zimmerman and Beverly B. Zimmerman, *Working with WordPerfect: A Complete Guide* (Glenview, Ill.: Scott, Forseman & Co., 1986); Terry Datz, "Present WordPerfect," *PC World* (October 1985): 196–201; Phillip Robinson, "Word Processors," *BYTE* (Summer 1987 Bonus Edition): 55–67, esp. 64–66; Jordan J. Breslow, "Almost Perfect," *PC World* (July 1987): 219–22.

2.5.2.2 Microsoft Word

- BASIC PRODUCT INFORMATION

Name of Program: Microsoft® Word
Company Name: Microsoft Corporation
Address: 16011 NE 36th Way, Box 97017, Redmond, WA 98073
Phone: (800) 426-9400, (206) 882-8080
Technical Support: (206) 882-8080
Price: $450
Version Tested: IBM, version 3.0
Runs On: IBM PC and compatibles; Macintosh
Memory Requirements: 256K
Operating System Requirements: DOS 2.0 or greater
Disk Drive Requirements: 2
Copy Protected: No
Possible Backups: Unlimited
Hard Disk Compatible: Yes
Produces ASCII Files: Yes
Produces PostScript Files: Yes
Drives Laser Printers: Yes, LaserWriter, Corona, DEC LN03, LaserJet, Xerox 2700, and others
Drives Typesetters: No, but when used with LinoWord (from Allied Linotronic), it can drive a non-PostScript Linotronic 100, and when used with Wordsetter (from Parallax), it can drive a PostScript-compatible Linotronic 100.
SideKick Compatible: Yes, with version 1.56A or later

Mnemonic Commands: No
User Interface: Menu-driven
Text Display: Auto word wrap, on-screen justification
Screen Display Reformatting: Constant and automatic
Formatting Text for Printing: Continuously
Text Orientation: Document
Screen Mode: Graphics or text
WYSIWYG: Yes
Edit Files Larger Than Memory: Yes
Uses Function Keys: Yes
Key Template or Labels: Yes
Product Includes: 2 manuals, printer booklet, disks, function-key command template, quick reference guide
Number of Disks: 6

• INSTRUCTIONAL MATERIALS/SOURCES

Manual: 2 manuals, 673 pages, three-ring binders, typeset, tabbed, indexed
Tutorial: Yes, disk-based
Quick Reference Card: Yes, as well as function key command template
Demo Disk Available: Yes, from retailers
On-Line Help: Yes
Pop-Up Command Menus: Yes
SIGs: Not known
Newsletters: Not known
Major Reviews: *InfoWorld* (June 2, 1986): 43–44; *PC Magazine* (January 1986): 148–50; *Publish!* (November/December 1986): 54–55; *BYTE* (October 1986): 261–63; *PC Magazine* (May 26, 1987): 201–2.
Other Learning Aids: Peter Rinearson, *Word Processing Power with Microsoft WORD*; Janet Rampa, *Getting Started with Microsoft WORD*; *Microsoft Word Made Easy*; *Microsoft Word Made Easy: Macintosh Edition*

• MULTILINGUAL FEATURES

Video Cards Supported: MDA, CGA, EGA, HGC, and other "standard" cards
Specify Different Fonts in Document: Yes
Print Different Fonts: Yes
Display Different Fonts On-Screen: No
Foreign Fonts Included: None
RAM-Based Character Generator: No
Font Editor: IBM: No; Macintosh: Yes
Number Characters Per Font: 256 (IBM)
Maximum Screen Fonts Per Document: 1 on IBM; unlimited on Macintosh
Mode Used to Display Nonstandard Characters: Graphics
Edit Right-to-Left: Yes
Display Entire ASCII Character Set: Yes

• SPECIAL FEATURES

Run DOS Commands from Program: Yes
Chain Files for Printing: Yes
Queue Files for Printing: Yes
Spelling Checker: Yes, over 80,000 words
Thesaurus: No
Windows/Split-Screen: Yes, maximum of 8
Columns: Yes, maximum of 10 per page
Footnotes: Yes
Bibliography: No
Table of Contexts: Yes
Indices: Yes
Keyboard Macros: Yes, text only
Text Retrieval System: No
Internal Programming Language: No
Other: Five-function math, built-in outliner, mail merge, sort function, mouse support; Microsoft markets a Macintosh version of Word. Microsoft Word supports the GENIUS VHR monitor (see above).

- *SUPPORT ETC.*

Warranty: Media: 90 days; mice: 1 year
Support: Phone, letter
Update Policy: Updates to version 3.0 cost $75.
Other Information: None

Introduction. Microsoft® Word (hereafter MW), produced by the company that created MS-DOS, is one of the most unusual professional word processing programs for IBMs and the Macintosh, combining in a graphics environment the best features of a powerful word processor with the flexibility of a page-definition and typesetting program. Other programs (e.g., FW II) support mice, but MW was designed with mice in mind (though every function can easily be invoked from the keyboard). Other programs, constrained by ROM-based character generation, struggle to present a WYSIWYG display; but MS, operating in graphics mode, can display different typestyles (e.g., italics, bold, small caps) and different fonts on-screen (on the Macintosh), as well as strikethrough, superscript, subscript, double underline, and so forth with a very high degree of correspondence to the printed product.[120] But MS may also be operated in text mode. And MS is well-known for its predefined style sheets, each of which allows users to specify 123 formatting parameters, and for its printer support (especially laser printers) and precise, highly controlled print output.

Performance and Versatility. MW comes with an impressive array of features. Among other things, MW supports (1) up to ten columns per page, (2) five-function math, (3) footnotes, (4) endnotes, (5) tables of contents of up to five levels each, (6) indices, (7) automatic paragraph numbering, (8) up to eight windows, (9) alphabetical and numerical sorting, (10) adjustable linespacing, (11) mail merge, (12) automatic hyphenation, (13) print queuing, and (14) executing DOS commands from within the program. MW includes (15) predefined, modifiable style sheets, (16) an automatic outlining utility, (17) a print-preview feature, and (18) a spelling checker whose functions are modeled after those of Oasis System's venerable The Word Plus (see below). MW allows users (19) to specify distances in points, inches, centimeters, lines, or 10- or 12-point spaces (but not in picas), and MW (20) displays accurate line, column, and page breaks on-screen. Version 3.1 will include (21) automatic line and column numbering.

But MS is not without its drawbacks in terms of versatility. For example, (1) its keyboard macros may only be used to assign formatting parameters and to label blocks of text; MS macros may not consist of editing or printing commands. And MS lacks some of the functions found in other programs such as (2) automatic saving while editing, (3) automatic generation of bibliographies, (4) an internal programming language, (5) bidirectional cross referencing, and (6) multilevel footnotes. And (7) documents must be repaginated for page breaks to display properly on-screen. Although version 3.0 of MS is faster than previous versions, (8) it is still noticeably slower in almost all functions than speed demons like XW III and NB.

Two of the most significant features that make MW a powerful writing tool for academicians are its style sheets and multilingual capabilities.

MW comes with predefined style sheets that may be modified, or users may create their own style sheets. As in FW II, MW's style sheets are sets of formatting macros. Each style sheet may specify up to 123 different formatting parameters. (That's a lot, but it would be nice if an unlimited number were allowed—as is the case with FW II.) One style sheet might be used for business letters, another for multicolumn newsletters, a third for journal articles, and so on. Style sheets, which are stored as text files, may be named, assigned to macro key combinations, and attached any place in a document. Multiple formats and style sheets may be mixed in a single document.

---

120. MW cannot display variations in font width and height and proportional spacing on-screen.

MW divides style sheet options into three main parts: (1) parameters that govern characters, (2) parameters that govern paragraphs, and (3) parameters that govern divisions of the text. Character parameters govern typestyle (normal, bold, italic, underlined), placement of text (superscripted, subscripted), the characters used in the hidden codes that govern indexing, and so forth. Paragraph parameters govern the formatting of paragraphs, footnotes, quotations, tables, headings, lists, titles, and so on. Division parameters govern page layout, front matter, appendices, indices, tables of contents, and other major divisions.

Unlike the Macintosh version, the IBM version of MW cannot display multiple fonts on-screen.[121] As I mentioned above, the HGC+ comes with a MW driver that allows MW to scroll up to four times faster than it normally does. The driver does not, however, allow MW to display multiple fonts on the IBM. By using font programs such as Fancy Word or SuperGreek or SuperHebrew (see below), however, the Macintosh version of MW can display multiple fonts on-screen and mix them on a single line.

Documentation. MW comes with two comprehensive, well-written, well-illustrated, easy-to-understand manuals—a user's manual and a reference manual—as well as a booklet about printers and fonts and a booklet about MW's outlining feature. Instructions and discussions are in black type; screen displays are in blue type. The index is adequate but incomplete. A quick reference card and a function-key command template are also included. And MW's disk-based tutorial and on-line help further facilitate learning (see below).

Ease of Use. Like the other programs we have reviewed so far, MW is intended for "power users." Unlike those programs, MW includes an amazingly thorough and well-thought-out disk-based tutorial that may be run alone or accessed *from within* MW. And MW includes extensive, context-sensitive, on-line help. MW's tutorial is the best I've seen for any program.

MW uses the last four lines of the screen as a window in which it displays a Command Line of menu options, a Message Line, and a Status Line (though by using the Options selection on MW's menu, the lower window may be closed and the entire screen used for editing). Pressing Esc moves the cursor to the Command Line. Like NB, MW uses a multilayered, or hierarchical, system of menus. Unlike NB, MW's menu selections are very opaque. I could use few of them without consulting the manual. And MW can only be menu-driven, a lamentable restriction that requires users to descend through hierarchies of choices to invoke almost every function. I said "almost" because some formatting functions may be invoked by using Alt-key combinations that bypass menus. Some of MW's cursor-movement commands involve using function keys, which seems counter-intuitive and takes a while to get used to (most programs use the function keys alone and in combination with the shifting keys to invoke commands, not to move the cursor). Last, but not least, is the fact that MW is noticeably slower at scrolling and rewriting the screen than XW III and NB, for example, though when used with the HGC+ (as I noted above), MW's speed increases twofold or more.

Error Handling. MW has an interesting single-level undelete feature that not only undeletes (even typeovers) but that also restores scrambled characters to their original sequence. Until closing an open file, MW saves editing changes in a temporary file, thereby preserving the original unchanged. Rebooting from within the program and exiting without saving causes MW to save the open file with a filename that has the extension .TMP. MW does not automatically save files during editing.

Support. I have had no occasion to call Microsoft and so cannot report on their support.

---

121. According to sources at Hercules Computer Technology, the engineers at Microsoft are *considering* designing an IBM version of MW that will take full advantage of the HGC+'s RamFont mode.

Bibliography. Diane Burns and S. Venit, "Word Takes Another Forward Stride," *PC Magazine* (June 25, 1985): 151–60 (a helpful review of version 2.0); John Dickinson, "Microsoft Word 3.0 Gets Better . . . ," *PC Magazine* (May 27, 1986): 52; Matthew Holtz, "The 3rd Word," *Publish!* (November/December 1986): 54–55; John Lombardi, "Faster, Feature-Rich Microsoft Word, 3.0," *InfoWorld* (June 2, 1986): 43–44; Bryan Pfaffenberger, *Dynamics of Microsoft Word: Apple Macintosh Edition* (Homewood, Ill.: Dow Jones-Irwin, 1986); *Dynamics of Microsoft Word: IBM Personal Computer Edition* (Homewood, Ill.: Dow Jones-Irwin, 1986); Janet Rampa, *Getting Started with Microsoft® WORD* (Bellevue, Wash.: Microsoft Press, 1984); Peter Rinearson, "Outlining With Style," *PC World* (October 1986): 300–9; *Word Processing Power with Microsoft® WORD* (Bellevue, Wash.: Microsoft Press, 1985); Steve Roth, "Making Pages with Word," *Personal Publishing* (February 1986): 38–41; "The Latest Word," *Personal Publishing* (May 1986): 36–41; Malcolm C. Rubel, "Microsoft Word Version 3.0," *BYTE* (October 1986): 261–63; Craig Stinson, "The Business of Words: Professional," *PC Magazine* (January 28, 1986): 148–50; Charles Seiter and Daniel Ben-Horin, "Insights on Microsoft Word," *Macworld* (March 1987): 183–87; Eric Aldermanm, "The Latest Word," *Macworld* (March 1987): 116–21; Burton L. Alperson, "And the Word Is Good," *PC World* (September 1985): 179–83; C. J. Weigand, "The Word on Word," *Personal Publishing* (August 1987): 24–35; Jeremy Joan Hewes, "The Latest Word," *Publish!* (July 1987): 64–67.

2.5.3 Scientifically Oriented Programs

This section includes a full review of one scientific word processing program and basic information about another. Although these programs are designed primarily to enable users to display complex scientific formulas on-screen and to print them on dot-matrix and laser printers, they are also capable of being used for multilingual word processing. These programs operate in graphics mode, are designed to display multiple fonts, include font editors, and allow users to switch among logical keyboards.

Other less powerful scientific word processing programs not included in this section are Hockney's Egg™,[122] WordMARC,[123] Tech/Word™,[124] TechWriter,[125] Spellbinder/Scientific,[126] and Volkswriter Scientific.[127] Reviews of all but the first two of those programs, as well as reviews of the programs discussed below, may be found in John Dickinson, "The Business of Words: Special Purpose," *PC Magazine* (February 25, 1986): 177–98. For reviews of WordMARC, see Merrily Shinyeda, "WordMARC: An Office Powerhouse," *PC World* (January 1985): 126–33, and Kaare Christian, "Scientific Word Processing," *PC Magazine* (May 28, 1985): 285–86. Lotus Development Corporation's Manuscript appeared too late to be included in this edition of this book. See the following articles for reviews of Manuscript: Robin Raskin and Kaare Christian, "Manuscript: A Technical Writer's Tool Kit," *PC Magazine* (April 14, 1987): 143–52; Jim Seymour, "Manuscript: Something Old, Something New," *PC Magazine* (February 10, 1987): 85, 87; Bill Machrone, "Manuscript Whips Large Documents Into Shape," *PC Magazine* (February 10, 1987): 33, 35; Daniel J. Rosenbaum, "For Technical Prose," *Publish!* (June 1987): 64, 66–68; Jordan J. Breslow, "Almost Perfect," *PC World* (July 1987): 222–23; Phillip Robinson, "Word

---

122. Peregrine Falcon Co., P.O. Box 2023, Mill Valley, CA 94942; (415) 331-8131; $495.
123. MARC Software International, Inc., 260 Sheridan Ave., Palo Alto, CA 94306; (415) 326-1971; $495.
124. Goldstein Software, 12520 Prosperity Dr., Suite 340, Silver Spring, MD 20910; (301) 622-9020; $350.
125. CMI Software, 1395 Main St., Waltham, MA 02154; (617) 899-7244; $595.
126. Lexisoft, Inc., P.O. Box 1378, Davis, CA 95617; (916) 758-3630; $695.
127. Lifetree Software, Inc., 411 Pacific St., Monterey, CA 93940; (408) 373-4718; $495.

Processors," *BYTE* (Summer 1987 Bonus Edition): 55–67, esp. 66; Eric Brown, "Building Manuscripts Block By Block," *PC World* (May 1987): 214-23.

2.5.3.1 T^3 Scientific Word Processing System

- ### BASIC PRODUCT INFORMATION

Name of Program: T^3™ Scientific Word Processing System
Company Name: TCI Software Research, Inc.
Address: 1190-B Foster Rd., Las Cruces, NM 88001
Phones: (800) 874-2383, (505) 522-4600
Technical Support: (800) 874-2383, (505) 522-4600
Price: $595; academic discount of 20% reduces price to $476.
Version Tested: 2.11
Runs On: IBM PCs and compatibles
Memory Requirements: 640K
Operating System Requirements: DOS 2.0 or greater
Disk Drive Requirements: 2; hard disk *highly recommended*
Copy Protected: No
Possible Backups: Unlimited
Hard Disk Compatible: Yes
Produces ASCII Files: Yes
Produces PostScript Files: Not yet, but PostScript drivers are promised for version 2.2.
Drives Laser Printers: Yes, Xerox 4045, Xerox 2700 (II), Talaris 810, QMS Smartwriter, QMS Lasergrafix 800, QMS Kiss, Canon A1 and A2, LaserJet, LaserJet Plus, and others
Drives Typesetters: No
SideKick Compatible: Yes, if proper screen driver is used.
Mnemonic Commands: No
User Interface: Menu-driven
Text Display: Auto word wrap, no on-screen justification
Screen Display Reformatting: Constant and automatic
Formatting Text for Printing: At print time
Text Orientation: Document
Screen Mode: Graphics
WYSIWYG: Yes
Edit Files Larger Than Memory: Yes
Uses Function Keys: Yes
Key Template or Labels: No, but keyboard maps for any program may be displayed from within the program and printed for reference.
Product Includes: Manual, disks, quick reference card, one printer driver
Number of Disks: 6; 8 or 9 for version 2.2

- ### INSTRUCTIONAL MATERIALS/SOURCES

Manual: 661 pages, three-ring binder, slipcase, typeset, tabbed, indexed
Tutorial: Yes, two disk-based tutorials and three tutorial chapters in the manual
Quick Reference Card: Yes
Demo Disk Available: Yes, $60, which includes all documentation and a full system that cannot save user-created text but that can print; a nonlaser printer driver of the customer's choice is included; price is applicable toward purchase price.
On-Line Help: No, but context-sensitive, on-line help is promised for version 2.2.
Pop-Up Command Menus: Yes
SIGs: No
Newsletters: Yes, "TCI Software Research Newsletter"
Major Reviews: *PC Magazine* (January 25, 1986): 190–92; *Notices of the American Mathematical Society* (January 1986); *Mathematical Intelligencer* (January 1986); *PC Products* (October 1985); *Computers and the Humanities* 20 (January-March 1986): 62–71.
Other Learning Aids: None

● *MULTILINGUAL FEATURES*

Video Cards Supported: CGA, EGA, HGC, and other "standard" graphics cards; T^3 requires a graphics card
Specify Different Fonts in Document: Yes
Print Different Fonts: Yes
Display Different Fonts On-Screen: Yes
Foreign Fonts Included: Cyrillic
RAM-Based Character Generator: Yes
Font Editor: Yes
Number Characters Per Font: 128
Maximum Screen Fonts Per Document: 8; version 2.2 allows up to 16 screen fonts per document.
Mode Used to Display Nonstandard Characters: Graphics
Edit Right-to-Left: No
Display Entire ASCII Character Set: Yes

● *SPECIAL FEATURES*

Run DOS Commands from Program: No
Chain Files for Printing: No
Queue Files for Printing: No
Spelling Checker: No; TCI recommends Microspell from Trigram Systems, which TCI sells at the discounted price of $110.
Thesaurus: No
Windows/Split-Screen: No
Columns: No
Footnotes: Yes
Bibliography: No
Table of Contexts: No
Indices: No
Keyboard Macros: Yes, text and commands
Text Retrieval System: No
Internal Programming Language: No
Other: See below for information about version 2.2.

● *SUPPORT ETC.*

Warranty: 90 days, media only
Support: Phone, letter
Update Policy: Upgraded printer drivers: $20 to $60; upgraded screen drivers: $20; update to version 2.2: $95
Other Information: Dot-matrix drivers: $60 each; laser drivers: $95 each; graphics font set: $100; sample printer-driver source code: $150; T^3 font-to-laser-printer font-converter source code: $150.

Introduction. $T^{3\text{™}}$ ("Tee cubed") is a powerful, flexible, professional, full-featured word processing program with multilingual capabilities that was created by several mathematicians at the University of New Mexico's Department of Mathematical Sciences for composing technical, scientific, and mathematical documents. T^3 is enormous in size and voracious in appetite: it requires about 1.5MB of disk space and 640K of memory. Like MW, T^3 operates in graphics mode; unlike MW, T^3 cannot operate in text mode. Like the Macintosh version of MW, T^3 can display different fonts simultaneously; unlike MW, T^3 comes with a font editor (which allows users to create new fonts) and supports downloading fonts from disk to RAM. And like MW, T^3 presents a WYSIWYG display that shows bold, italics, superscripts, strikeouts, and so forth. Also, like the IBM version of MW, T^3 cannot display changes in character size, right justification, or proportional spacing on-screen.

Performance and Versatility. T^3 includes many of the standard formatting features found in other professional word processing programs. It supports (1) macros, (2) footnotes, (3) automatic page formats, (4) multiple line headers and footers, (5) automatic

113

page numbering (Arabic or Roman numerals), and (6) has a useful GOTO command that works with pages, markers, and highlighted text. Version 2.2 of T^3, which should be available by the time this book is printed, will include (7) a spelling checker, (8) additional character sets (possibly including some fonts from the T_EX set), (9) mailing list capability, and (10) on-line help. It will support (11) up to eight logical keyboards, (12) additional key sequences, (13) a true insert mode that may be configured to be the default text entry mode, (14) multiple column printing, (15) automatic indexing, (16) automatic document saving during editing, (17) user customization of menus, (18) endnotes, (19) up to sixteen active 128-character fonts (i.e., 2,048 different characters), (20) characters as large as 160-by-160, (21) turning the Status Line off and using that space for text, (22) proportional spacing, (23) improved footnote numbering and printing, (24) support for PostScript printers, including the LaserWriter, (25) graphics import for PostScript printers, (26) reserving space for graphics, and more.

Unfortunately, T^3 does not support (1) endnotes, (2) multilevel footnotes, (3) bidirectional cross referencing, (4) the automatic generation of bibliographies and tables of contents, (5) windows, (6) running DOS commands from within the program, (7) chaining files for printing, (8) wild-card search and replace, (9) print preview, and it lacks (10) an undelete feature.

Like NB and MW, T^3 allows users to create style sheets, which in T^3 jargon are referred to as "shell documents." The use of shell documents in T^3 is mandatory (T^3 has no global default formatting settings), and when creating a new file, T^3 requires that an existing shell document be copied and renamed—one of T^3's several unusual but useful features. The idea of shell documents is useful because different custom shells (i.e., style sheets) may be created for a variety of purposes—personal letters, scholarly documents in different formats, or books. Because T^3 requires users to log on, different sign-on names can be assigned to different default shell documents.

T^3 does all its screen displays in graphics mode and thus is well-suited for multilingual word processing. T^3 allows up to eight 128-character fonts (1,024 different characters) to be used simultaneously in one document.[128] T^3's font editor allows users to edit existing screen and printer fonts and to create as many new screen and printer fonts as they wish in sizes that range up to 30-by-50. T^3 comes with (1) a standard IBM font, (2) an upper ASCII font, (3) an italics font, (4) a symbol font, (5) a Cyrillic font, (6) a script font, and (7) a second symbol font. Two logical keyboards may be active at one time, and other keyboards may be substituted as needed by selecting them from a menu listing.[129] The Alt key is used to toggle between keyboards. A menu item allows key assignments to be displayed on-screen. T^3 comes with over 900 mathematical, chemical, and other special characters already defined.

Documentation. T^3's manual is well-written and easy to understand, though T^3 is a complex program. About half of the manual is devoted to three extensive tutorials: (1) basic word processing, (2) scientific word processing, and (3) advanced formatting. Plenty of screen diagrams help to illustrate the discussions in the text. T^3's index is better than most. Unfortunately, there is no on-screen help, though the program does include a 9-by-7.5-inch quick reference card.

Ease of Use. T^3 describes its approach to word processing as "object oriented" and "mode free." *Object oriented* means that T^3's main menu requests users to select an object, which may be a document, keyboard, font, printer, or some other listing. *Object oriented* apparently contrasts with *function oriented*, that is, with main menus that display lists of functions to choose from, for example, "Edit Existing Document," "Create New Document." In addition to a clean, deductively and hierarchically arranged menu structure, the main advantage of this philosophy is that the common operations that apply to multiple objects may be invoked by keystrokes that are standardized across the system. In keeping with that philosophy, T^3 assigns each function

---

128. Version 2.2 will support sixteen 128-character fonts, i.e., 2,048 different characters.
129. Version 2.2 will allow eight logical keyboards to be active at one time.

key one value so that each function key implements the same type of function on each object it may be used with. *Mode free* is another T^3*ism* that also directly relates to the standardization of command-key usage. *Mode free* means that the effect of a key is not a function of what modality—insert or overwrite—the system is in; the keys used to issue commands in one mode are used to issue the same commands in other modes. The T^3 manual acknowledges that T^3 is not *really* modeless; no word processing system could be mode*less*, otherwise no text could be entered! Even a word processing system with one mode would have one *mode*. And any word processing system that allows users to insert *and* to overwrite text, as T^3 does, has *two* modes, semantics not withstanding.

T^3's cursor control and flexibility in deleting are among the best in the business. T^3's cursor can be moved in either direction by character, word, line, sentence, paragraph, screen, and document, and T^3 can delete in all those ways as well. All that is missing is the ability to move T^3's cursor by page, though T^3's helpful GOTO command allows the cursor to be moved to the beginning of any page, marker, or highlighted text. Depressing the right or left cursor keys and entering a character causes T^3 to move to the next occurrence of that character. The PgUp and PgDn keys move the cursor vertically, half line at a time, which allows accurate super- and subscripting. The Page Menu allows users to delete single or multiple pages. T^3 has disabled the repeating nature of all the keyboard keys. To make the cursor scroll horizontally or vertically requires depressing a cursor key and the 5 key on the keypad, which T^3 refers to as the "repeat key." This causes the cursor to move considerably faster than it normally does, which is a blessing in most cases but a curse when moving vertically through menu listings since it is hard to stop a fast moving cursor in the desired place. Fortunately, T^3 allows users to adjust the speed at which the "repeat key" causes the cursor to move, as well as to adjust the character delay and character repeat rates.

T^3 is menu-driven. Pop-up menus, function keys, and the keypad are used to issue commands. T^3 has made clever use of the difference between the keyboard's "make" and "break" codes. You may remember from our discussion of those topics in chapter 1 that the make code (the code a key transmits when it is depressed) is different from the break code (the code a key transmits when it is released). T^3's menus are activated when the proper key is depressed (that is, they are activated by the make code) but not displayed until the key is released (that is, when the break code is transmitted). Thus by holding down the key that activates a menu and then entering the proper selections from that undisplayed menu, users can bypass menu displays.

T^3's editing screen (T^3 calls it a "document revision screen") uses the top two lines as status lines that display the following information: (1) document name, (2) current page the cursor is on, (3) the names of the standard and alternate keyboards, (4) the position of the cursor, (5) the name of the line format, (6) the height in half-lines that superscripts may be, (7) the depth in half-lines that subscripts may be, and (8) spacing. The third to top line is a ruler line that displays margin and tab settings. T^3 uses the last line of the screen as a message line to display (1) error messages (see below), (2) the time, (3) whether the CPU is engaged or free, (4) whether the alternate keyboard, Caps Lock key, and Num Lock key are "locked," and (5) if a macro is being recorded. The remainder of the screen is used for text.

T^3's strangest characteristic is its default overwrite mode, which cannot be changed to default insert mode.[130] To insert characters instead of overwriting them, T^3 requires that an "insert point" be created by pressing the Insert key. Insert points are actual characters—thin vertical bars—to the right of which the cursor is "dropped down" and text is inserted. When the cursor is moved off the insert point, T^3 defaults back to the overwrite mode. An insert point remains visible in the text until a new insert point is created. *Insert point* is T^3 jargon for *insert mode* and is a way of semantically maintaining that T^3 is "mode free." Persons used to a inserting as a default mode may

---

130. Version 2.2 allows users to configure the program so that insert is default.

115

find overwriting and drop-down inserting difficult to get used to, especially since the only way to disable overwrite is to work with insert points. Fortunately, version 2.2 has a true insert mode that may be configured as T^3's default editing mode.

Error Handling. T^3 lacks an undelete function and does not automatically save files during editing.[131] T^3 has an Undo key that causes a file to be abandoned in the midst of editing and that loads the most recently saved version of an abandoned file into the editor. If the MESSAGE.TXT file is present and active in the system, error messages are displayed in the lower left corner of the screen or in a pop-up window. If the MESSAGE.TXT file is not present or active, error messages are displayed as numbers whose meaning must be looked up in T^3's ten pages of error messages.

Support. I have had no occasion to call TCI and so cannot report on their support.

Bibliography. John Dickinson, "The Business of Words: Special-Purpose—T^3 2.1," *PC Magazine* (January 25, 1986): 190–92; Willard McCarty, "T^3, A Multilingual Word Processing Package for the IBM PC," *Computers and the Humanities* 20 (January–March 1986): 62–71; *Mathematical Intelligencer* (January 1986); *Notices of the American Mathematical Society* (January 1986); *PC Products* (October 1985).

2.5.3.2 Brit Multitex

● *BASIC PRODUCT INFORMATION*

Name of Program: Brit Multitex
Company Name: Scientific Communications Corp.
Address: 2136 Locust St., Philadelphia, PA 19103
Phone: (215) 732-7978
Technical Support: (215) 732-7978
Price: $795
Version Tested: Not tested; latest version is 6.58
Runs On: IBM PCs and compatibles, Xenith Z100/Z120, Victor 9000, TI Professional, Tandy 2000
Memory Requirements: 256K
Operating System Requirements: DOS 2.0 or greater
Disk Drive Requirements: 2
Copy Protected: Yes, a special hardware key that plugs into a parallel or serial port is required and comes with the program.
Possible Backups: Unlimited
Hard Disk Compatible: Yes
Produces ASCII Files: No
Produces PostScript Files: No
Drives Laser Printers: Yes, CDS2300, Xerox 2700
Drives Typesetters: No
SideKick Compatible: No
Mnemonic Commands: Not known
User Interface: Menu-driven
Text Display: Auto word wrap, no on-screen justification
Screen Display Reformatting: Background, auto insert
Formatting Text for Printing: Continuously
Text Orientation: Document
Screen Mode: Graphics
WYSIWYG: Yes
Edit Files Larger Than Memory: No, full document is in memory.
Uses Function Keys: Yes
Key Template or Labels: Not known
Product Includes: Disks, manual
Number of Disks: Not known

---

131. Version 2.2 contains an automatic save-during-editing feature.

- INSTRUCTIONAL MATERIALS/SOURCES

Manual: Not able to see
Tutorial: Yes, in manual and on disk
Quick Reference Card: No
Demo Disk Available: Yes, $35; a demo disk that allows files to be saved and printed is available for $50. Prices count against purchase.
On-Line Help: Yes
Pop-Up Command Menus: Yes
SIGs: No
Newsletters: Not known
Major Reviews: *PC Magazine* (February 25, 1986): 185–87.
Other Learning Aids: None

- MULTILINGUAL FEATURES

Video Cards Supported: CGA, EGA, HGC, and other graphics cards
Specify Different Fonts in Document: Yes
Print Different Fonts: Yes
Display Different Fonts On-Screen: Yes
Foreign Fonts Included: Classical Greek (no diacritical marks), Cyrillic, Western European
RAM-Based Character Generator: Yes
Font Editor: Yes
Number Characters Per Font: Not known
Maximum Screen Fonts Per Document: 5, a maximum of 416 different characters per document
Mode Used to Display Nonstandard Characters: Graphics
Edit Right-to-Left: No
Display Entire ASCII Character Set: Yes

- SPECIAL FEATURES

Run DOS Commands from Program: Not known
Chain Files for Printing: Yes
Queue Files for Printing: Yes
Spelling Checker: No; Oasis System's The Word Plus is recommended.
Thesaurus: No
Windows/Split-Screen: No
Columns: No
Footnotes: Yes
Bibliography: No
Table of Contexts: No
Indices: No
Keyboard Macros: No; NewKey is recommended.
Text Retrieval System: No
Internal Programming Language: No
Other: Mail merge

- SUPPORT ETC.

Warranty: Not known
Support: Not known
Update Policy: Not known
Other Information: None

2.6 Dedicated Multilingual Programs

In this section we will examine a large number of programs that are designed expressly for multilingual word processing. Generally speaking, with some exceptions, these programs tend to have fewer features, to support fewer printers, to be less flexible and powerful, and to be considerably less expensive than the professional programs with multilingual features reviewed above.

2.6.1 Multiple Languages

2.6.1.1 *IBYCUS Scholarly Computer*

• *BASIC PRODUCT INFORMATION*

Name of Program: IBYCUS Scholarly Computer (ISC)
Company Name: IBYCUS Systems
Address: P.O. Box 1330, Los Altos, CA 94022
Phone: (213) 274-8765
Technical Support: (213) 274-8765
Price: $4,000
Version Tested: Beta version 2.0
Runs On: IBYCUS
Memory Requirements: None, the ISC's word processing program comes installed in ROM chips.
Operating System Requirements: The ISC has a proprietary operating system.
Disk Drive Requirements: None, the program is already in the computer.
Copy Protected: Not known
Possible Backups: Not applicable
Hard Disk Compatible: Yes
Produces ASCII Files: Not known
Produces PostScript Files: No
Drives Laser Printers: Yes, LaserJet, LaserJet Plus
Drives Typesetters: No
SideKick Compatible: No
Mnemonic Commands: Mostly
User Interface: Command-driven
Text Display: Auto word wrap, no on-screen justification
Screen Display Reformatting: Constant and automatic
Formatting Text for Printing: At print time
Text Orientation: Document
Screen Mode: Text
WYSIWYG: Mostly
Edit Files Larger Than Memory: Not known
Uses Function Keys: Yes
Key Template or Labels: No
Product Includes: Computer system, monitor, keyboard, CD-ROM drive, one microfloppy drive, and a variety of programs—some in ROM and some on a microfloppy diskette—and a manual.
Number of Disks: Not applicable

• *INSTRUCTIONAL MATERIALS/SOURCES*

Manual: Not able to see
Tutorial: No
Quick Reference Card: No
Demo Disk Available: Not applicable
On-Line Help: Yes
Pop-Up Command Menus: No
SIGs: None
Newsletters: No
Major Reviews: *Bits & Bytes Review*™ 1 (October 1986): 1–8.
Other Learning Aids: None

• *MULTILINGUAL FEATURES*

Video Cards Supported: The IBYCUS SC is a completely proprietary machine.

Specify Different Fonts in Document: Yes
Print Different Fonts: Yes
Display Different Fonts On-Screen: Yes
Foreign Fonts Included: Greek, Hebrew, Coptic
RAM-Based Character Generator: No, ROM-based
Font Editor: No
Number Characters Per Font: 2,048
Maximum Screen Fonts Per Document: 2
Mode Used to Display Nonstandard Characters: Text
Edit Right-to-Left: Yes
Display Entire ASCII Character Set: Not known

- *SPECIAL FEATURES*

Run DOS Commands from Program: No
Chain Files for Printing: No
Queue Files for Printing: No
Spelling Checker: No
Thesaurus: No
Windows/Split-Screen: Yes, maximum of 15
Columns: Not known
Footnotes: Yes
Bibliography: No
Table of Contexts: No
Indices: Not known
Keyboard Macros: No
Text Retrieval System: No
Internal Programming Language: No
Other: None

- *SUPPORT ETC.*

Warranty: Limited 1 year warranty
Support: Phone and letter
Update Policy: Free software updates for 1 year
Other Information: None

Introduction. The Ibycus Scholarly Computer (hereafter ISC) is a fast, flexible, and powerful special-purpose computer with multilingual word processing capabilities. Designed by David W. Packard for classicists and humanists who work with ancient texts, the multitasking ISC can (1) display up to 4,096 unique characters on-screen in a single document, (2) work with up to fifteen different windows, and (3) search texts at astonishingly high rates of speed for multiple character strings. The ISC (4) supports the latest CD-ROM and laser-printing technologies and (5) is designed to work with the TLG's data base of machine-readable ancient texts (see chapter 7).

Because at the time I am writing this book the ISC's word processing program is still evolving, rather than reviewing this program in the way I have done with other programs, I will describe the ISC as a system and include a discussion of its multilingual capabilities.

The ISC is a computer system that, among other things, is designed for multilingual word processing. It uses a ROM-based, text-mode approach to displaying characters on-screen. Those characters are stored in four 32K ROM chips that together hold a staggering 4,096 characters. Because the ISC allows composite characters to be created by superimposing two characters at the same screen location, the ISC makes it easy to create accented letters and to locate diacritical marks in their proper places. Presently, roman, Greek, Hebrew, and Coptic character sets (including all special Western European symbols and all vowels, breathing, and diacritical marks) are included with the ISC.

The Display. As we learned above, just as important as the number of unique characters that can be displayed simultaneously on-screen in a single document is the clarity with which those characters are displayed. The ISC creates characters that are 16-by-16 pixels in matrices that are 18-by-16 pixels. More precisely, ISC characters are 16 *half-pixels* wide; each pixel is one-eighth the width of the character. This means that the ISC can overlap pixels, thereby creating characters whose members have varying thicknesses, such as the characters in the ISC's Hebrew font. It also means that the ISC can create diagonal lines, such as acute and grave accents, that appear on-screen as straight lines, not as ragged, saw-toothed lines (as they do on lower resolution displays). And it means that the ISC's character matrix is twice as high as it is wide.

To understand just how high the ISC's screen resolution is, let's contrast it with the IBM PC's. As we have learned, the MDA works with 7-by-9 characters in 9-by-14 matrices, and the EGA, in the high-resolution graphics mode, works with 7-by-9 characters in 8-by-14 matrices. Thus the ISC's character density (character width by height) is 256, and the MDA's and EGA's are 63. The ISC packs much more detail into each character than do the IBM adapters. Not surprisingly, then, the ISC's characters are *noticeably* crisper—better defined—than those produced by an MDA or EGA card.

The ISC's Greek characters are slightly larger than those in the United Bible Society's Greek New Testament, and the ISC's Hebrew characters are about the same size as those in Kittel's *Biblia Hebraica*. The ISC clearly displays Greek characters with iota subscripts, breathing marks, and accents, even if one character has all those diacriticals and happens to line up under the descending member of a character on the line above. Reading vocalized Hebrew (or accented Greek) on the ISC is like reading a printed text. The Hebrew *shewa*, *hireq*, and *daghesh* are clearly visible from three feet away, as are diaresis and iota subscripts in Greek!

The ISC uses a 12-inch, black-on-white, ultrahigh resolution monitor that supports underlining, double underlining, overline at two heights, strike through, inverse video, and faint intensity. The monitor has a built-in, tilt-and-swivel base. The ISC's screen is 80 columns wide and 24 lines high, and the ISC has a horizontal resolution of 1,440 pixels (80 columns of 18-pixel-wide character matrices) and a vertical resolution of 384 pixels (24 lines of 16-pixel-tall character matrices).

Word Processing. Readers who are used to word processing programs with elaborate text editing and page formatting features will find the ISC Spartan. As of late 1986, the ISC does not support (1) search and replace, (2) keyboard macros, (3) automatic numbering and placement of footnotes, (4) automatic generation of indices and tables of contents, (5) style sheets, (6) multiple columns, and (7) automatic formatting of documents for printing, though it does support soft hyphens, soft page breaks, and has widow and orphan control. But don't despair! According to David Packard, a future version of the ISC's word processing program will (probably) support footnotes, dynamic pagination (with page breaks shown on-screen), keyboard macros, and more. Given the state-of-the-art character of other aspects of the ISC, I imagine that future versions of its word processing program will be quite flexible and powerful.

Ease of Use. The ISC's only mode for text input is overwrite. A character may be inserted in existing text by depressing the Insert Character key and then typing the desired character. Depressing the Insert Character key creates one blank space, which the inserted character overwrites. To insert a second character, the Insert Character key must be depressed again. The Insert Line key inserts a line of text into the midst of a paragraph. When the cursor is in the midst of a paragraph, pressing the − key (which is referred to as the Split Key) on the top row of the numeric keypad splits the line from the cursor to the right margin, moving that text down into a new line and thus creating an open space for text to be inserted into the midst of the paragraph. After using the Split Key, users may insert as many lines of text as they wish. As useful as that is, it is still not a true insert *mode* because it does not allow users to insert characters into the midst of a line of running text so that characters to the right of the cursor are pushed to the right. In my opinion the ISC would be an easier machine to use if it had a true insert mode.

The ISC uses the eight function keys on the top row of the keyboard for fonts and their attributes. Function keys 1-4 toggle the roman, Greek, Hebrew, and Coptic fonts. Function keys 5-8, in shifted and unshifted modes, toggle the following text attributes (called "display enhancements" by the ISC help screens): strike through, inverse video, faint video, underline, double underline, and overline. Attributes are active until canceled or toggled out of, and attributes may be combined. For example, text may be displayed in inverse video, struck through, and overlined.

All fonts may be mixed on a single line. When entering text in the roman, Greek, or Coptic fonts, the cursor moves to the right of the letters that are entered. When entering Hebrew characters, the cursor is stationary, and the text flows to its right. Any line of text on-screen can be "flipped" to a different font by placing the cursor on that line and pressing the function key of the desired font. The change affects text from the right of the cursor to the right margin.

When typing in the roman alphabet, diacritics are entered by using the Extended Character (EC) key in combination with one of ten alpha keys. Diacritics are entered with the cursor immediately to the right of the letters they go with and are properly displayed above or below those letters. (When entering diacritics in the midst of existing text, the cursor is placed under the letter to receive the mark.) For example, EC + *a* is acute, EC + *g* is grave, EC + *c* is circumflex, EC + *u* is umlaut, EC + *t* is tilde, and so forth.

When typing in Greek, breathing marks, accents, and other diacritics are entered immediately after the letters they go with and are properly displayed above the letters they modify. The Extended Character key is used only to enter a subscript dot (not an iota subscript). Eight nonalpha keys are used for diacritics. For example, / is acute, ? is circumflex, ' is smooth breathing, + is diaresis, and = is macron.

Although the roman and Greek fonts each contain a full set of uppercase letters, the Hebrew and Coptic fonts are lowercase only. When typing in Hebrew, vowels are entered immediately to the left of the letters they go under. The *daghesh* is entered by using the *b, g, d, k, p, t* keys in their shifted states. Quite logically, Hebrew vowels are bound to the *a, e, i, o,* and *u* keys in their shifted and unshifted states. For example, *segol* is entered by hitting *e, sere* by using *e* in its shifted state. Final forms of characters with special final forms are bound to the number keys on the top row of the keyboard. At this time, no accents are available in the Hebrew character set, though according to David Packard, Hebrew accents will be supported.

The ISC's cursor may be moved bidirectionally by character, word, screen, and document but not by sentence, end or beginning of line, paragraph, and page. The ISC can delete by character, line, and screen. The screen may be scrolled a line at a time or a screen at a time. All cursor and screen movements are virtually instantaneous.

Block moves are restricted to copying a section of text, which may be undeleted once, and to deleting a section of text. Continuously pressing Insert Line + Shift undeletes line after line of deleted text, and the Insert Character + Shift combination undeletes up to 256 of the most recently deleted characters.

Tabs and margins may be set for each window. Paragraphs must be reformatted manually. Word wrap may be enabled and disabled.

Documentation. At the time I am writing this book, there is no user's *manual* as such, though there is some printed documentation. The ISC has a useful pop-up help menu that provides on-line help about (1) function keys, (2) fonts, (3) accents and diacritical marks, (4) font attributes, (5) the floppy disk, and (6) searching. Additionally, by selecting "Function Key" from the help menu, help is available for nearly every key on the keyboard. When completed, the ISC's documentation will include a User's Guide and a Programmer's Guide.

At this point in its evolution, when compared to commercial word processing programs, the ISC's word processing capabilities are limited. And presently the ISC has no data base management program or communications program. At this time, then, the ISC is better suited for special-purpose use as a one-of-a-kind tool for studying ancient texts than it is for general-purpose computing.

Bibliography. John J. Hughes, "The Ibycus SC: A Multilingual Computer System for Scholars," *Bits & Bytes Review*™ 1 (October 1986): 1–8.

2.6.1.2 Proofwriter Graphics

● *BASIC PRODUCT INFORMATION*

Name of Program: Proofwriter™ Graphics
Company Name: Image Processing Systems
Address: 6409 Appalachian Way, P.O. Box 5016, Madison, WI 53705
Phone: (608) 233-5033
Technical Support: (608) 233-5033
Price: $425
Version Tested: 2.22 for CGA card
Runs On: IBM PCs and compatibles
Memory Requirements: 320K
Operating System Requirements: DOS 2.0 or greater
Disk Drive Requirements: 2
Copy Protected: Yes
Possible Backups: Comes with one backup disk
Hard Disk Compatible: Yes, may be installed once; may not be uninstalled
Produces ASCII Files: Yes
Produces PostScript Files: No
Drives Laser Printers: Yes, LaserJet, LaserJet Plus
Drives Typesetters: No
SideKick Compatible: Yes
Mnemonic Commands: No
User Interface: Command-driven and menu-driven
Text Display: Auto word wrap, no on-screen justification
Screen Display Reformatting: Constant and automatic
Formatting Text for Printing: At print time
Text Orientation: Document
Screen Mode: Graphics
WYSIWYG: No
Edit Files Larger Than Memory: No, see below
Uses Function Keys: Yes
Key Template or Labels: No
Product Includes: Manual, disks, quick reference card
Number of Disks: 6

● *INSTRUCTIONAL MATERIALS/SOURCES*

Manual: 274 pages, three-ring binder, tabbed, indexed, not typeset
Tutorial: Yes, on-screen and in manual (as Appendix G)
Quick Reference Card: Yes
Demo Disk Available: Yes, $5
On-Line Help: Yes
Pop-Up Command Menus: No
SIGs: None
Newsletters: No
Major Reviews: *PC Magazine* (February 25, 1986): 187–88.
Other Learning Aids: None

- ## *MULTILINGUAL FEATURES*

Video Cards Supported: CGA, EGA, HGC, and other graphics cards; Proofwriter Graphics requires a graphics card.
Specify Different Fonts in Document: Yes
Print Different Fonts: Yes
Display Different Fonts On-Screen: Yes
Foreign Fonts Included: Russian, Slavic, Classical Greek, European languages, and romanized versions of Arabic, Hebrew, Ugaritic, and Egyptian
RAM-Based Character Generator: Yes
Font Editor: Yes
Number Characters Per Font: 128
Maximum Screen Fonts Per Document: 2
Mode Used to Display Nonstandard Characters: Graphics
Edit Right-to-Left: No
Display Entire ASCII Character Set: Yes

- ## *SPECIAL FEATURES*

Run DOS Commands from Program: No
Chain Files for Printing: Yes
Queue Files for Printing: No
Spelling Checker: Yes, number of words not known
Thesaurus: No
Windows/Split-Screen: No
Columns: No
Footnotes: Yes
Bibliography: No
Table of Contexts: No
Indices: No
Keyboard Macros: No
Text Retrieval System: No
Internal Programming Language: No
Other: No

- ## *SUPPORT ETC.*

Warranty: Not known
Support: Phone, letter
Update Policy: Not known
Other Information: None

Introduction. Proofwriter™ Graphics (hereafter PG) is one of a family of three programs—Proofwriter Standard, Proofwriter International, and Proofwriter Graphics—marketed by Image Processing Systems. Proofwriter Standard ($250) uses a ROM-based character generator. Proofwriter International ($300) uses a ROM-based character generator and allows users to define up to twelve logical keyboards, though no more than 256 different characters may be displayed in one document (more, however, may be printed). Image Processing Systems sells scientific and foreign language PROMS ($125 each)[132] for the Standard and International versions of their program. PG comes in three configurations: for CGA boards ($425), for HGC cards ($425), and for the EGA ($475).

Performance and Versatility. As its name indicates, PG works in graphics mode and is designed to display nonstandard fonts. PG allows up to twelve logical keyboards to be defined per document, but only two 128-character fonts may be displayed in a document. One of these fonts must be the lower 128 ASCII characters; the other may be

---

132. A PROM is a Programmable Read-Only Memory chip.

defined by the user. Thus alternate fonts are restricted to the upper 128 ASCII positions—a severe limitation. PG comes with almost 2,000 different characters already defined in fonts that include Russian, Slavic, Classical Greek, Western European languages, and romanized versions of Arabic, Hebrew, Ugaritic and Egyptian. And PG includes (1) a font editor that allows characters to be designed in 8-by-8-pixel matrices, (2) a spell checker (PROOF), (3) a mail merge utility, and the program supports (4) footnotes, (5) endnotes, and (6) has a print preview feature.

Unfortunately, PG does not allow (1) windows, (2) text columns, (3) keyboard macros, (4) the automatic generation of indices or of (5) tables of contents. (6) Only one file at a time may be open. And (7) PG does not allow moving the cursor by sentence, paragraph, or page, (8) nor does it support deleting by paragraph, screen, or page.

Documentation. PG's manual is readable but poorly organized and indexed and contains some inaccuracies (see below). For example, the index for this multilingual word processing program contains no entry under *Font!* I had to read PG's information about character generation to learn how many characters may be in a PG font and how many fonts may be displayed in one document. The on-screen tutorial (which is identical to Appendix G in the manual) does not explain formatting commands. PG's on-line help, which may be displayed on-screen while users edit beneath it, consists of a half-screen summary of basic editing commands and function-key usage. The quick reference card is helpful but fails to define the Alt + F5 combination, which displays the help screen.

Ease of Use. PG is both menu- and command-driven. When possible, PG uses menus. Formatting commands, which are entered directly into a document, have the form "@X," where X is a variable, such as CT (for "center text"). @LL 65, for example, entered at the beginning of a document, would set the line length to a value of 65. PG's editor uses four modes for editing text and issuing commands: Command, Append, Insert, and Change. Command is used for issuing commands, though most editing commands also may be issued from within the Insert or Change modes. Append opens a blank new line within a paragraph (without creating a new paragraph) so that text may be inserted into the existing paragraph. Append is PG's default setting when beginning to edit a new document. (The manual incorrectly indicates (1-24) that Command is PG's general default setting, but that is true only when beginning to edit an already existing file.) Insert is used to enter text into the midst of a line of existing text; Append may not be used that way. But like Append, Insert may be used to enter text into the midst of a paragraph. *Change* is PG's name for the overwrite mode, which may be specified in PG's set-up file as the editor's default setting. (Insert may not be specified as the editor's default setting.)

PG handles files larger than memory in a unique and strange fashion. PG's text buffer can be no larger than 64K. After working to the end of a 64K section of a file, the F2 key (Load Next Segment of Text) must be depressed to load more of the document, or users must go to the end of the text (with the E command) and depress the PgDn key to load more text. If the F2 key is used, PG asks how many segments of text to load (a segment is 2,560 characters, just slightly more than two double-spaced pages of typed text). When the editor's memory contains more than 62,500 characters, PG writes to disk. After that occurs that section of text may not be edited until the cursor is returned to the beginning of the document and the PgUp key depressed. This is the "clunkiest," least automated way of swapping material in and out of memory I've ever seen!

Alt + F is used to toggle from the main font to the alternate font. PG allows users to define up to six "dead keys," which can represent diacritical marks. PROOF, PG's spell checker, simply lists words it does not recognize, without offering any suggestions about their correct spelling. Users may add words to the dictionary. PG, which is copy protected, can be installed once on a hard disk, but it cannot be uninstalled!

Error Handling. PG automatically saves text to disk every twenty minutes and whenever the text buffer holds more than 62,500 characters, whichever occurs first. The timed-save feature may be turned off but not modified. PG has an undelete feature that allows the last word, line, or sentence that was deleted to be restored. The program dumps users to DOS if they try to use the spelling checker without correctly informing PG of the location of the dictionary file.

Support. I have had no occasion to call Image Processing Systems and so I cannot comment on their support.

Bibliography. Craig Stinson, "The Business of Words: Special-Purpose—Proofwriter 2.27," *PC Magazine* (February 25, 1986): 187–88.

2.6.1.3 *Gutenberg Sr.*

• BASIC PRODUCT INFORMATION

Name of Program: Gutenberg® Sr.
Company Name: Gutenberg Software Ltd.
Address: 47 Lewiston Rd., Scarborough, Ontario M1P 1X8, Canada
Phone: (416) 757-3320
Technical Support: (416) 757-3320
Price: $360 (US), $460 (Canadian)
Version Tested: Not known, disks dated 1984
Runs On: Apple II+, Apple IIe, and Apple IIc
Memory Requirements: 64K
Operating System Requirements: Proprietary
Disk Drive Requirements: 1, but 2 are recommended
Copy Protected: Yes, program disk only
Possible Backups: 1 backup provided, unlimited copying of other disks
Hard Disk Compatible: No
Produces ASCII Files: No
Produces PostScript Files: No
Drives Laser Printers: No
Drives Typesetters: No
SideKick Compatible: No
Mnemonic Commands: Yes
User Interface: Command-driven
Text Display: Auto word wrap, no on-screen justification
Screen Display Reformatting: Constant and automatic
Formatting Text for Printing: At print time
Text Orientation: Document
Screen Mode: Graphics
WYSIWYG: No
Edit Files Larger Than Memory: Yes
Uses Function Keys: Not applicable
Key Template or Labels: No
Product Includes: Manual and disks
Number of Disks: 7

• INSTRUCTIONAL MATERIALS/SOURCES

Manual: 750 pages, hardback, typeset, indexed
Tutorial: Yes, in manual
Quick Reference Card: No
Demo Disk Available: No
On-Line Help: No
Pop-Up Command Menus: No
SIGs: Not known
Newsletters: Yes, from Gutenberg Software
Major Reviews: Moises Silva, "Gutenberg Sr.," in *The Book of Apple Software.*
Other Learning Aids: None

- *MULTILINGUAL FEATURES*

Video Cards Supported: Standard Apple cards (see below for a complete list); Apple 80-column card and Super Serial Card recommended.
Specify Different Fonts in Document: Yes
Print Different Fonts: Yes
Display Different Fonts On-Screen: Yes
Foreign Fonts Included: Greek (Classical and Koine), Russian, Ukrainian, phonetics, math/science, chemical rings, 39 roman fonts, 16 headline fonts; available fonts include: Hebrew (with vowels), Syriac, Coptic, Arabic, Cree
RAM-Based Character Generator: Yes
Font Editor: Yes
Number Characters Per Font: 94 per printer font, 212 per screen font
Maximum Screen Fonts Per Document: 1 that consists of two sets of 94 characters each, plus an additional 23 characters and the space code (maximum of 212 different characters); twenty-one 94-character fonts may be used in one document and printed (1,974 different characters); printer fonts contain 94 characters each.
Mode Used to Display Nonstandard Characters: Graphics
Edit Right-to-Left: Yes
Display Entire ASCII Character Set: Yes, but some of the extended ASCII characters have to be defined.

- *SPECIAL FEATURES*

Run DOS Commands from Program: No
Chain Files for Printing: Yes
Queue Files for Printing: No
Spelling Checker: No
Thesaurus: No
Windows/Split-Screen: Yes, maximum of 2
Columns: Yes, unrestricted, but not displayed on-screen.
Footnotes: Yes, maximum of 8 per page
Bibliography: No
Table of Contexts: No
Indices: No
Keyboard Macros: Yes, text and commands
Text Retrieval System: No
Internal Programming Language: No
Other: Mail merge, communication utility. Gutenberg Jr., a stripped down version of Gutenberg Sr., is available for US $91 and purchasers of this program may upgrade to Gutenberg Sr. for US $285.

- *SUPPORT ETC.*

Warranty: Not known
Support: Phone and letter
Update Policy: Free for minor updates
Other Information: None

Introduction. In may seem strange to include a review of a program that runs on Apple IIs, since these machines are so inherently weak and slow, but Gutenberg® Sr. (hereafter GS) turns Apple IIs into powerful multilingual word processors.[133] GS is an

---

133. One other Apple II multilingual word processing program worth mentioning is The Diplomat, from International Solutions, Inc., P.O. Box 2381, Saratoga, CA 95070; (408) 354-2988; $198 to $398, depending on options. This program requires changing the Apple II ROM to a bilingual ROM.

To speed things up, GS *probably* will work with (1) 16-bit add-in processor boards for the Apple IIs, (2) the Apple II gs (which uses a 16-bit 65C816 microprocessor), and with (3) emulation programs like II-in-a-Mac that allow Apple II programs to be run on Macintoshes.

Gutenberg Software recommends using GS with (1) an 80-column card, (2) an Apple Super Serial Card, (3) two disk drives, (4) a monochrome monitor, (5) a surge suppressor, and (6) an Apple Imagewriter.

amazing program not only because it is unarguably the most powerful word processor for the Apple II but also because it is one of the most powerful microcomputer word processors period! In flexibility, features, and power (but not speed), GS resembles FW II, XW III, Nota Bene, Microsoft Word, and T$_E$X. GS is a purely command-driven, highly complex, flexible program that is capable of printing intricate formulas and multiple character sets in almost any predefined or user-defined format. GS's formatting codes closely resemble those used by typesetters, which makes the program "well suited for input to front-end typesetting systems" (GS manual, 1). A quick glance at GS's 750-page, hardbound user's manual, which was typeset directly from GS text files, shows just what GS can do.

Performance and Versatility. GS works in either 40- or 80-column modes. For obvious reasons, an 80-column card is recommended.[134] GS operates either in low resolution mode with the resident Apple character set and character generator or in high resolution mode with the Gutenberg character sets and character generator. GS sports a long list of features that include: (1) split screen editing, (2) keyboard macros, (3) multiple fonts, (4) style sheets (GS calls them format files), (5) multiple columns,[135] (6) automatic numbering of text sections, (7) footnotes and endnotes, (8) wild-card search and replace, (9) multiple, simultaneous search and replace in either direction, (10) graphics in text, (11) a program (PAINT) for creating and editing graphics files, (12) automatic transliteration of Cyrillic names, (13) a utility that automatically converts GS text files to CP/M or Apple DOS 3.3 text files (and vice versa) and that can automatically translate "foreign" word processing commands in the input file into Gutenberg commands in the output file, and (14) a utility that counts characters, words, and paragraphs.

GS's limitations are as follows. GS (1) restricts users to eight footnotes per page, (2) has no preview mode for seeing what formatted text will look like before it is printed, (3) cannot display multiple columns on-screen, (4) restricts the active font to two 94-character sets, plus an additional 23 characters and the space code (a maximum of 212 unique characters), (5) cannot print multiple copies, (6) cannot print a range of pages, (7) restricts block operations on text (e.g., cut and paste) to a maximum of 3,750 characters (less than four double-spaced typed pages), (8) cannot delete by sentence or paragraph, and (9) cannot move the cursor by word, sentence, paragraph, to the end of a line, to a marker, to the top of the screen, or to a specified page or point in a file. Apparently, footnotes may be any length and are wrapped from page to page, though the manual does not address these two topics.

GS is adept at displaying nonstandard fonts, allows them to be mixed on the same line (up to twenty-one per line!), and prints them with proportional spacing. GS comes with many predefined fonts, among which are included Classical and Koine Greek (including all diacritical marks), phonetics, thirty-nine roman fonts, and sixteen headline fonts. Other available fonts include Hebrew (with vowels), Syriac, Coptic, Arabic, and Cree. And a font editor allows users to create their own characters. Characters for screen fonts are 7-by-12 pixels and are created in matrices of the same size. Characters for printer fonts can be up to 16-by-8 and are created in 16-by-9 matrices. Each GS screen font contains two sets of 94 characters, the space code, plus

---

GS supports the following printers: Apple Imagewriter, Apple DMP, C.Itoh Prowriter, NEC 8023, Epson MX-100 (and other Epsons), Gemini 10-X, and a number of impact printers. Only Apple's Imagewriter and DMP printers, however, can accept GS's downloadable fonts, and since Gutenberg prints everything in text mode, one of these printers is required to print nonstandard characters.

The following interface cards are supported: Apple Super Serial, Apple Parallel, Dumpling-64, Dumpling-GX, Epson, Grappler, Grappler+, Grappler/Serial, Microbuffer II, Microengineering, PKASO, Prometheus, Skyman-2001, and Quadram APIC.

134. The Apple II+ and IIe can only display 40 columns, unless an 80-column board is added.

135. Columns may be snaked and contain mixed fonts. Footnotes are printed under columns. Text in columns may be microspaced and justified. GS supports an unlimited number of columns.

an additional 23 characters (212 different characters). Only one screen font may be active at a time, though up to twenty-one 94-character fonts may be used in a document and properly printed. Although accents, breathing marks, and other diacritics are displayed on-screen to the right of the characters with which they are associated (trailing accents), they are printed in their correct positions. GS allows text to be entered right-to-left, though left-to-right and right-to-left directions may not be mixed on a line or within a paragraph but operate on paragraphs as a whole. Thus Semitic text entered within a line or paragraph of roman characters must be typed in backwards, and vice versa.

Documentation. GS comes with a typeset, bound manual that has obviously been created and produced with much pride and care. It is complex and long, though well-written and intelligible, and includes illuminating educational sections on the history of printing and typesetting, as well as on the design philosophy of Gutenberg Senior. By and large, the manual's indices are very thorough, and its table of contents is quite detailed. GS's manual contains a lengthy seven-chapter, 200-page, graded tutorial. But in a program as complex as GS, it is lamentable that the manual includes no summary of commands, that no quick reference card comes with the program, and that the program contains no on-line help or menus. And in a manual for a program that was, in part, designed to be compatible with phototypesetters, I find it amazing that no list of GS-compatible phototypesetters is provided. Apparently, to get GS to work with a typesetter requires using GS's GLOBAL command to translate all Gutenberg formatting and print commands to those any given typesetter understands. In other words, it requires recoding the entire document, though GLOBAL (a search and replace utility) can search for and replace multiple strings simultaneously (a highly unusual and quite useful feature). Search strings and replacement strings are restricted to nineteen characters each. Translation files (input files) are restricted to 12,000 characters, about 12K. Apparently, there is no limit to the number of strings that GLOBAL will accept as variables to search for and replace.

Ease of Use. Like Proofwriter, GS uses a number of modes to get the jobs of text entry, manipulation, and editing done. Text is created in Insert mode. To insert material into existing text, however, requires toggling out of Insert mode by using the Escape key, moving the cursor to the point where insertion is to begin, and then entering text (a form of drop-down inserting). Users must then toggle back into Insert mode by pressing *I* (moving the cursor over text erases it). To shift to "X-over" (overwrite) mode requires going through Command mode, which is awkward.

Although GS uses virtual memory architecture (which allows files that are larger than memory to be edited), the size of the program and the Apple II's small 64K memory restrict GS's text buffer to a measly 4K (about four double-spaced 8.5-inch-by-11-inch typed pages), which means that any global activity (e.g., search and replace, scrolling) is very slow because it requires frequent reading and writing of the disk.

GS allows split-screen editing. Two separate files or the same file may be edited in two separate windows. When one file is displayed in two windows, text may be edited in only one of the windows, though text may be copied from one window to the other.

GS uses format files, which are its equivalent of style sheets. GS comes with many predefined format files, and users may create their own. As the name suggests, format files specify on a global basis the formatting parameters that govern printed output. At print time, users specify which format file is to govern the formatting of the text file that is to be printed. Thus by specifying different format files, one text file may be printed in a variety of formats. Predefined format files include those for letters, resumés, multiple column text, envelopes, and labels.

Because GS's formatting codes closely resemble those used by typesetters, GS's codes are longer and more complex than those used with most other word processors. Normal indented paragraphs, for example, must each begin with the formatting macro

<P1>. Because GS's formatting terminology reflects that of typesetting, users must learn how to specify text to be quadleft (flushleft, ragged right), quadright (flushright, ragged left), and justified (flushleft and flushright). And because GS's command syntax is patterned after that used in typesetting, users must learn some pretty complex command sequences. Fortunately, however, most standard formatting commands are defined in macros that may be executed with a keystroke or two, and users may create their own formatting macros. GS has over 100 formatting commands, about twenty system (i.e., print) variables, about 180 user variables, and 255 user-definable commands.

Error Handling. GS automatically saves text to disk each time the 4K text buffer fills up (it has to in order to make room for more text), but it contains no undelete or undo feature.

Support. I have had no occasion to call Gutenberg Software and so cannot comment on their support.

Bibliography. Moises Silva, "Gutenberg Sr.," in Jeffrey Stanton and Mia McCroskey, eds., *The Book of Apple Software* (1986).

2.6.1.4 GRAMEDIT

- *BASIC PRODUCT INFORMATION*

Name of Program: GRAMEDIT Theological Word Processing System
Company Name: Project GRAMCORD
Address: The GRAMCORD Institute, 2065 Half Day Rd., Deerfield, IL 60030
Phone: (312) 223-3242 (Paul A. Miller)
Technical Support: (312) 223-3242
Price: Not yet established
Version Tested: Not able to test; current version is 1.2.
Runs On: NEC-APCs only
Memory Requirements: 128K
Operating System Requirements: CP/M-86
Disk Drive Requirements: 2
Copy Protected: No
Possible Backups: Unlimited
Hard Disk Compatible: Yes
Produces ASCII Files: Yes
Produces PostScript Files: No
Drives Laser Printers: No
Drives Typesetters: No, but GRAMTYPESET can produce text that is properly coded for typesetters; only the Varityper Comp/Edit is mentioned.
SideKick Compatible: No
Mnemonic Commands: Yes
User Interface: Command-driven
Text Display: Auto word wrap, on-screen justification
Screen Display Reformatting: Constant and automatic
Formatting Text for Printing: At print time
Text Orientation: Document
Screen Mode: Text
WYSIWYG: Yes, mostly
Edit Files Larger Than Memory: No
Uses Function Keys: Yes
Key Template or Labels: Yes
Product Includes: Manual, disks, key template
Number of Disks: 1

- *INSTRUCTIONAL MATERIALS/SOURCES*

Manual: 73 pages, computer printed, no tabs, no index
Tutorial: Yes, on-disk and in manual

Quick Reference Card: No
Demo Disk Available: Yes
On-Line Help: Yes
Pop-Up Command Menus: No
SIGs: None
Newsletters: No
Major Reviews: None
Other Learning Aids: None

- MULTILINGUAL FEATURES

Video Cards Supported: NEC-APC cards only
Specify Different Fonts in Document: Yes
Print Different Fonts: Yes
Display Different Fonts On-Screen: Yes
Foreign Fonts Included: Greek and Hebrew
RAM-Based Character Generator: Yes
Font Editor: Yes, for NEC-APC screen fonts and for Toshiba printer fonts, but these are "in-house" utilities
    and are not generally distributed with the program.
Number Characters Per Font: 256
Maximum Screen Fonts Per Document: 2
Mode Used to Display Nonstandard Characters: Text
Edit Right-to-Left: No
Display Entire ASCII Character Set: Yes

- SPECIAL FEATURES

Run DOS Commands from Program: No
Chain Files for Printing: Yes
Queue Files for Printing: No
Spelling Checker: Yes (GRAMSPELL), number of words not known
Thesaurus: No
Windows/Split-Screen: Yes
Columns: Yes
Footnotes: Yes
Bibliography: No
Table of Contexts: No
Indices: No
Keyboard Macros: Yes, text and commands
Text Retrieval System: No
Internal Programming Language: No
Other: Includes GRAMTYPSET, GRAMINSERT, and GRAMSPELL

- SUPPORT ETC.

Warranty: Not known
Support: Phone, letter
Update Policy: Free
Other Information: None

Introduction. GRAMEDIT (hereafter GE) is one of a set of programs (GRAMTYPSET, GRAMINSERT, and GRAMSPELL)[136] produced for persons in the field of biblical studies by Paul A. Miller of Project GRAMCORD. GE, which is designed for "theological" word processing and typesetting, is an enhanced and customized version of the OK Editor.[137] GE runs only on NEC-APC (Advanced Personal Computer) computers, which are 8086-compatible (5 MHz), CP/M-86 machines that

---

136. In chapter 7 we will discuss GRAMCORD, the grammatical concording program whose data base is the Greek New Testament.
137. The OK Editor is available from DFM Software, P.O. Box 288, Enfield NSW 2136, Australia.

were chosen because of their high resolution (640-by-475), large character matrices (8-by-19), large character size (8-by-16), and built-in support for bilingual word processing (see below). There are no plans to port the program to other computers, such as IBM. Because I have not been able to use the program, the following remarks are based on GE's manual and on discussions with Paul Miller.[138]

Performance and Versatility. GE's many features include: (1) allowing up to ten files to be open at once, (2) multilingual editing and printing, (3) on-screen display of character attributes (e.g., underlined letters are printed underlined, letters in reverse video are printed as italics, characters in intense video are printed in bold), (4) displaying Greek and English on-screen, (5) the ability to mix fonts on a single line or within a paragraph, (6) keyboard macros (GE refers to these as "log on/off" because they use a special dedicated key), (7) a repeat command that repeats the last command n-number of times (this only works with search commands and block insertions), (8) a utility to convert WordStar documents to GRAMEDIT.DOC files, (9) exceptionally accurate and attractive printing (on Toshiba printers) of Greek and Hebrew with all vowels and diacritical marks properly placed, (10) footnotes and endnotes, and (11) a print preview feature.

Unfortunately, however, GE lacks: (1) a proper undelete feature, (2) automatic save during editing, (3) split-screen editing, (4) search and replace, (5) automatic generation of indices and tables of contents, (6) support for laser printers or for any printers other than Toshiba dot-matrix printers, (7) the ability to move the cursor by sentence and paragraph, (8) the ability to move backward by word, (9) the ability to delete by word, sentence, paragraph, or page, and (10) a font editor. And (11) if the NEC-APC is equipped with only its standard 128K of memory, GE documents are limited to about 50K.[139]

GE's power lies more in its ability to display Greek on-screen and to print Greek and Hebrew than it does in its editing and formatting features, which are adequate but not elaborate.

GE works in text mode with ROM-based and RAM-based fonts. By issuing one system-level command before entering the editor, two special fonts (Greek and Hebrew) are downloaded to a Toshiba P1315 or P351,[140] and a Greek font is loaded into the NEC's RAM-based character generator.[141] The NEC, which has ROM-based *and* RAM-based character generators, allows GE to access its ROM-based resident font and the RAM-based Greek font and to display both in a single document.[142] Characters not available in the ROM-based font or in the RAM-based font may be created by overstrike, which GE refers to as concatenation.

Greek is displayed on-screen, but Hebrew is not. The Greek keyboard and character set are toggled by using the Alt key (see below). Diacritics are entered by using a "dead-key" approach. The cursor is placed over the letter or space immediately to the right of the character that is to receive the diacritical mark, the Function key is held down,[143] and the correct alpha key is used to enter the diacritical mark.[144] The result is a properly displayed composite character. "Free" diacritics, that is, diacritics that do not appear over a character (e.g., rough and smooth breathings and accents that ap-

138. It should be kept in mind that GE is much more of an *in-house*, "theological" word processing system for students and scholars at Trinity Evangelical Divinity School than it is a commercial product or a product designed for the scholarly community at large.

139. The NEC-APC can hold and address up to 512K of RAM.

140. GE only supports the Toshiba P1351, P351, and P321. The first two printers allow two character sets to be downloaded. The P321 requires a Font Kit ($100) and works with a special version of GE.

141. GE's fonts cannot be loaded from within the editor but must be loaded before entering it.

142. The NEC-APC includes a font editor.

143. Although NEC-APC's have only one key that is labelled "Function" key, they have twenty-two dual-mode, user-definable, unlabeled function keys across the top of the keyboard.

144. For entering diacritics, GE uses the Function key in combination with the *U, I, O, P, J, K, L, ;, M, .,* and / keys, which are referred to collectively as a "diacritic keypad."

pear before uppercased initial letters, the elision mark at the end of words) are entered by typing a Greek *delta*, placing the cursor over it, and entering the diacritic, a procedure that causes the delta to disappear but that leaves the proper diacritic on-screen. In the case of a word whose initial letter is uppercased, the letters of that word may then be entered.[145] Iota subscripts are entered by holding down the Function key and the Shift key and then depressing U. One hundred and twenty-five diacritics and combinations of diacritical marks may be entered by using this two-keystroke method. Symbols involving diaresis are entered from the Alt keyboard. Text critical symbols are represented on-screen by using symbols in the NEC's character-generator ROM and are printed properly by using one of GE's downloadable printer fonts.

Hebrew is entered left-to-right with the NEC's "brilliant" attribute (a combination of reverse video and highlight) invoked. The brilliant attribute serves three purposes: (1) it indicates on-screen that the brilliant text is transliterated Hebrew, (2) it functions as a printer code that causes the Toshiba to print the transliterated Hebrew characters as proper Hebrew characters, and (3) it instructs the printer to reverse the transliterated Hebrew words so that they print properly in a right-to-left fashion, fully justified. Hebrew vowels and diacritical marks are entered in transliterated form to the right of the letters with which they are associated. Hebrew, Greek, and English text may be mixed on the same line and still be fully justified when printed.

Documentation. I have only seen a preliminary form of GE's documentation. It is clearly written, easy to follow, and well organized. The discussion of GE's formatting commands (many of which are invoked by using ROM-based icons—special characters in the NEC's ROM) is sketchy, and sometimes commands that take arguments (i.e., variables) are explained without discussing the range of possible arguments. For example, I could find no list of the arguments that the MAN-ICON command can take, an icon that is used frequently in GE and that is frequently referred to in GE's instructional material.[146] GE has two on-line help screens (which are invoked with an Escape-Help key combination). One summarizes GE's file, area, movement, editing, and miscellaneous commands; the other displays a key to the major GE formatting icons. Use of the STATS key provides information about file buffers.

Ease of Use. GE is command-driven. Commands are issued from the command line, which is reached by using the Escape key (with the Graph1, Graph2,[147] and Alt keys toggled to their up positions). The top four lines of the upper right corner of the screen are a "control panel" that provide information about (1) date and time, (2) cursor line and column position, name of current file, which window the current file is in, (3) which keys are activated, what the current attributes are, how much memory is available, and (4) the command line. The top four lines of the upper left corner of the screen function as a keyboard template. They correlate physical keys with the active logical keyboard (i.e., active character set) and display the appropriate keyboard map. The remaining twenty-two lines of the NEC's twenty-six line screen are used for editing. The Alt key is used to shift from ROM-based keyboards to RAM-based keyboards, and the NEC's Help key is used to toggle between the shifted and unshifted versions of the current keyboard template. Each template represents either a set of ROM-based characters or a set of RAM-based characters. Thus templates may be thought of as character sets (or more properly as subsets of character sets). The ROM- and RAM-based character sets are divided into six templates each.

GE uses a number of other special keys for editing and formatting. Five special keys on the top of the keyboard are used to toggle into various video modes (e.g., underline, reverse video, intense video), which are toggled out of by using the Reset key. Since video modes affect printed output, using them is the same as entering formatting

---

145. Other Function key/alpha key combinations are used to enter other special symbols and characters.

146. The use of icons is undoubtedly easier to understand, however, if the instruction sheets are being read in conjunction with GE's on-screen tutorial.

147. The two Graph keys are special, dedicated keys on NEC-APC's.

commands. Seventeen other special keys are used alone and in combination with the Function key to invoke a broad range of editing activities, such as cursor and screen movement, deletion, and on-screen justification.

Up to ten files may be open at once, and these are kept in full-screen windows that are labeled A through J on the second line of the "control panel."

Print commands cannot be issued from within the editor. Text files are formatted for printing by issuing the proper command at the system level. Files formatted for printing can be loaded into the editor and viewed. Page breaks are displayed.

Error Handling. GE has no true undelete feature and does not automatically save files during editing.

Support. Since I was unable to review this program, I cannot comment on its support.

2.6.1.5 *Graphics Toolbox for Languages*

● *BASIC PRODUCT INFORMATION*

Name of Program: Graphics Toolbox for Languages
Company Name: Center for the Computer Analysis of Texts
Address: % Dr. John R. Abercrombie, Box 36 College Hall, University of Pennsylvania, Philadelphia, PA 19104
Phone: (215) 898-4917
Technical Support: (215) 898-4917
Price: $200 for codevelopers, $400 for University Site License
Version Tested: Not known
Runs On: IBM PCs and compatibles
Memory Requirements: 256K
Operating System Requirements: DOS 2.0 or greater
Disk Drive Requirements: 1
Copy Protected: No
Possible Backups: Unlimited
Hard Disk Compatible: Yes
Produces ASCII Files: Yes
Produces PostScript Files: No; but conversion to T_EX files has been done.
Drives Laser Printers: Yes, LaserJet, LaserJet Plus
Drives Typesetters: An interface to Oxford University Press's phototypesetter has been developed.
SideKick Compatible: No
Mnemonic Commands: Yes
User Interface: Command-driven
Text Display: Auto word wrap, no on-screen justification
Screen Display Reformatting: Constant and automatic
Formatting Text for Printing: At print time
Text Orientation: Page
Screen Mode: Graphics
WYSIWYG: Yes
Edit Files Larger Than Memory: Edit files as large as 500 pages.
Uses Function Keys: Yes
Key Template or Labels: No
Product Includes: Disk only
Number of Disks: 1

● *INSTRUCTIONAL MATERIALS/SOURCES*

Manual: Contained in printable disk files
Tutorial: No
Quick Reference Card: No
Demo Disk Available: No
On-Line Help: Yes
Pop-Up Command Menus: Yes
SIGs: No

Newsletters: No, but ONLINE NOTES is available (free) over BITNET. To subscribe, contact Dr. Abercrombie at JACKA@PENNDRLS or at the address above.
Major Reviews: Forthcoming in IBM's *Perspectives in Computing* (Spring 1987)
Other Learning Aids: None

- *MULTILINGUAL FEATURES*

Video Cards Supported: CGA, EGA, PGA (1987)
Specify Different Fonts in Document: Yes
Print Different Fonts: Yes
Display Different Fonts On-Screen: Yes
Foreign Fonts Included: Arabic/Persian, Cyrillic, Old Church Slavonic, Tamil, Armenian, Hebrew (pointed and unpointed), Greek/Coptic, Devanagari/Sanskrit, International Phonetic Alphabet, European languages, roman
RAM-Based Character Generator: No, characters are directly bit-mapped to the screen.
Font Editor: No
Number Characters Per Font: Up to 256 characters. In each font the lower 94 characters are the standard roman ones.
Maximum Screen Fonts Per Document: 4
Mode Used to Display Nonstandard Characters: Graphics
Edit Right-to-Left: Yes
Display Entire ASCII Character Set: Yes

- *SPECIAL FEATURES*

Run DOS Commands from Program: No
Chain Files for Printing: No
Queue Files for Printing: No
Spelling Checker: No
Thesaurus: No
Windows/Split-Screen: No
Columns: No
Footnotes: No
Bibliography: No
Table of Contexts: No
Indices: No, but support for automatic generation of indices is planned in a future version.
Keyboard Macros: No
Text Retrieval System: No
Internal Programming Language: No
Other: The GTL drives Tandberg tape recorders and video tape and video disc players through Ashton Inc.'s interface box connected to an RS-232C serial port. Eventually, the GTL will drive a CD-ROM player.

- *SUPPORT ETC.*

Warranty: Not known
Support: Phone and ONLINE NOTES (see above)
Update Policy: Free for one year
Other Information: John Hurd (University of Toronto) has developed a bidirectional file transfer program for use with the Graphics Toolbox for Languages and the Duke Language Toolkit (see below).

Introduction. The Graphics Toolbox for Languages (hereafter GTL) was written by Dr. John R. Abercrombie at the University of Pennsylvania for academic researchers who need a flexible, affordable way to display and print nonroman characters. The GTL contains (1) fonts for Arabic/Persian, Cyrillic, Devanagari/Sanskrit, Greek/Coptic, Hebrew (pointed and unpointed), Armenian, Tamil, the International Phoenetic Alphabet, European languages, and roman characters, (2) PENNWRITE, a rudimentary word processing program, (3) PENNPRINT, a graphics printing program, (4) SEEK, a search program, (5) TEACH, a computer-assisted language instruction program, (6) thirty all-purpose subroutines for handling the screen, for editing and for printing, (7) DRAW, a primitive MacPaint for the IBM PC, and (8) a manual contained in printable disk files. This is not a commercial program but an evolving set of tools for academicians and students at the University of Pennsylvania.

Performance and Versatility. PENNWRITE, the editing module of the GTL, is described as a research tool with "rudimentary" word processing capabilities that is primarily designed for (1) correcting optically scanned material, (2) literary research, and (3) adding "exotic" characters to already prepared ASCII text. PENNWRITE is partially patterned after PC-Write.[148] Although adequate for the purposes for which it was designed, PENNWRITE is not (yet) as powerful a text editor or page formatter as PC-Write. But like PC-Write, PENNWRITE is constantly being upgraded and improved. Presently, PENNWRITE's strengths are in searching texts that are already in machine-readable form, accessing user-prepared dictionaries, and in addressing peripheral equipment, such as video tape and video disc, for pictorial display.

PENNWRITE supports many important editing and formatting functions, including the automatic placement and numbering of footnotes. It also has a sophisticated search feature, SEEK (which is modeled after Ibycus's LEX—see chapter 7), that will simultaneously search for up to five strings, in any font, within user-defined contexts of up to three lines of text. Matches are displayed in boldface in user-defined contexts of from 9 to 24 lines. SEEK allows users to write hits to a new file for editing or printing and to index them. PENNWRITE's user-defined dictionary feature (not a spell checker) allows users to issue a look-up command that causes the program to look up whatever information has been bound to the form the cursor was on when the command was issued. This is similar to the notion of "hypertext" that we will discuss in chapter 7 in the subsection on the Harvard Classics Computer Project.

The GTL's capacity to work with both digitized and analog images opens exciting possibilities for papyrologists and art historians. Manuscripts scanned for CGA and EGA displays can be changed into ASCII text or manipulated in their own right. Pictorial images stored on video tape or video disc can be linked directly to ASCII texts, as has already been done for several projects in ancient and medieval studies at the University of Pennsylvania.

PENNWRITE writes bit-mapped graphics directly to video memory. It does not use ROM- or RAM-based characters; it operates entirely in the EGA's high-resolution graphics mode. Because it writes directly to video memory, it does not always use the standard video interrupt (10 hex) and related BIOS services (see chapter 1 on these topics). Thus PENNWRITE's approach to displaying nonstandard, or "exotic," characters is program-specific. The advantages of this approach are that (1) the size of characters, (2) the number of characters in a font, and (3) the number of different characters that PENNWRITE can display simultaneously are not limited by hardware, as they are in ROM- and RAM-based approaches to character display. The disadvantages of this approach are (1) the slower speed with which the screen is redrawn, (2) the fact that in terms of its editing, formatting, and printing features, PENNWRITE is not in the same league with programs such as Nota Bene, Microsoft Word, or Final-Word II, and (3) the fact that PENNWRITE's program-specific approach to displaying nonstandard characters cannot, by definition, be used with other application programs.

Because PENNWRITE defines characters as bit maps, it does not contain a font editor, though it does include a routine for defining images "on the fly." Any ASCII text editor may be used to design characters on X-Y coordinates, using lowercase Xs to specify character shape. PENNWRITE stores exotic characters as *vectors*, which express distance and direction (e.g., n-number of pixels on the X axis by n-number of

---

148. PC-Write is available from Quicksoft, 219 First Ave. N., #224, Seattle, WA 98109; (206) 282-0452. PC-Write is available for $10 (which covers the cost of the diskette, documentation, and postage) and has been reviewed in PC *Magazine* (October 15, 1985): 125–26 and in PC *Magazine* (January 28, 1986): 154–55.

pixels on the Y axis), not as rasters, which express pixel settings (i.e., which specific pixels on the screen are to be lit and which are not)—see above. To design a character for PENNWRITE requires specifying all its X and Y coordinates. Thus each PEN-NWRITE font file specifies all the X and Y coordinates—all the vectors—for every character in that font. But the microcomputer screens and video cards on which PEN-NWRITE runs write the screen as a raster (see the discussion earlier in this chapter); to form a character they need to know which specific pixels are to be lit and which are not to be lit. Thus to be displayed on conventional hardware, PENNWRITE's vector-designed characters must be translated into specific pixel settings that correspond to the X and Y coordinates used to define the characters. A special GTL program, CON-VERT.PAS, does that and stores the results in files called "output plot files."[149] Output plot files consist of "compiled" fonts. Each numerical value (i.e., pixel setting) in the output plot file specifies the X and Y coordinates of the pixel or pixels that form one of the strokes that the PLOT command draws to display a character on-screen. To redraw the screen as fast as possible, PENNWRITE writes directly to video memory, bypassing the ROM BIOS routines. PENNWRITE comes with approximately 10,000 different characters already defined in the fonts listed above.

PENNWRITE excels at displaying multilingual fonts on-screen (along with typestyles such as bold, italics, and underlined) and printing them. Up to four fonts may be in memory and active at the same time. Each font consists of up to 256 characters. In each font the lower 94 characters are the standard roman ones, and the remaining characters are exotic. Thus PENNWRITE can work with 648 different nonroman characters at a time.

PENNWRITE works with 9-by-16 characters that are created in 36-by-16 character matrices, which is the largest size character that standard dot-matrix printers can print in two passes of the print head. The large character matrix allows plenty of space for under- and overstrikes so that accents, breathing marks, vowels, and other diacritics may be displayed on-screen and printed in their proper positions. Using bit-mapped fonts and multiple striking allows PENNWRITE to store complete fonts in less space than would be required if a character generator were used. For example, multiple striking allows the complete Greek character set to be stored in 94 pixel-set-ting definitions, instead of the 512 separate characters that would be required if using a character generator. Thus although each font contains the roman character set, PEN-NWRITE's approach to character display allows plenty of room in each font for a complete set of exotic characters as well.

The GTL allows character sets to be downloaded to Epson FX80+ and Toshiba dot-matrix printers, as well as to LaserJet printers. On other Epson printers, however, PENNPRINT prints nonstandard characters in raster (i.e., graphics) mode, which is slower by a factor of ten or more than printing with downloadable fonts. Roman characters are printed by using the printer's built-in roman character set.

Documentation. The documentation for the program, which is contained in a printable disk file, is clearly written and quite adequate. In addition to programming tips and explanations of bit-mapped graphics, it contains helpful examples and summaries of commands and an index and glossary. PENNWRITE includes on-line help, which consists of five screens of information about editing commands and the keyboard templates for each font. ONLINE NOTES (on BITNET) updates users about the GTL and frequently contains new program listings in Turbo Pascal.

Ease of Use. PENNWRITE is a command-driven word processor that uses function keys and embedded commands. Function keys are used to display help files and to switch fonts. The Alt key is used in combination with mnemonically appropriate alpha keys to set typestyles such as italics, bold, and underlined, as well as to super-script or subscript characters on-screen and to implement other editing functions, such

---

149. Conversely, two programs, SHOW.COM and SHOW.PAS, can translate output plot files into ASCII files whose character designs can be studied and edited.

as searching, transposing letters, centering, deleting, and so forth. Embedded commands control spacing, placement of headers and footers, and page numbers.

PENNWRITE handles right-to-left text entry by changing from its default overwrite mode to pushover mode, so that the cursor remains stationary and text that is being entered flows to the right of the cursor.

A set of utility programs, the Penn-Duke Bridge Utilities, supports bidirectional file transfer between the Graphics Toolbox for Languages and the Duke Language Toolkit, since those two sets of programs create files with different formats. For more information, contact Dr. John R. Abercrombie (see above) or

> Dr. John C. Hurd
> Trinity College
> 6 Hoskin Ave.
> Toronto, Ontario
> Canada M4N 1V5
> (416) 485-2429.

Error Handling. PENNWRITE contains no undelete feature and does not automatically save files during editing.

Support. I have had no need to call the author of the program and so cannot comment on support.

2.6.1.6 *Duke Language Toolkit*

● *BASIC PRODUCT INFORMATION*

Name of Program: Duke Language Toolkit
Company Name: Duke University Computer Assisted Language Learning (DUCALL) Project
Address: Jeffrey William Gillette, Senior Programmer, Humanities Computing Facility, 104 Languages Bldg., Duke University, Durham, NC 27706
Phone: (919) 684-3637
Technical Support: (919) 684-3637
Price: Free to individuals and institutions (send $5 to cover the cost of the diskette and mailing), $10 if PC-Write is ordered (see below).
Version Tested: 2.10
Runs On: IBM PCs and compatibles
Memory Requirements: 256K
Operating System Requirements: DOS 2.0 or greater
Disk Drive Requirements: 1
Copy Protected: No
Possible Backups: Unlimited
Hard Disk Compatible: Yes
Produces ASCII Files: Yes, PC-Write, a word processing program that is distributed with the Duke Language Toolkit, does. The answers in the following categories refer to PC-Write as used with Duke's FED and LOADFONT.
Produces PostScript Files: No
Drives Laser Printers: Yes, LaserJet Plus
Drives Typesetters: No
SideKick Compatible: Not known
Mnemonic Commands: Yes
User Interface: Command-driven
Text Display: Auto word wrap, no on-screen justification
Screen Display Reformatting: Constant and automatic
Formatting Text for Printing: At print time
Text Orientation: Page
Screen Mode: Text
WYSIWYG: Yes
Edit Files Larger Than Memory: Not known
Uses Function Keys: Yes
Key Template or Labels: No

Product Includes: Disk
Number of Disks: 1, 2 if PC-Write is included

- INSTRUCTIONAL MATERIALS/SOURCES

Manual: On disk as printable file
Tutorial: No
Quick Reference Card: Yes (PC-Write)
Demo Disk Available: No
On-Line Help: Yes
Pop-Up Command Menus: Yes
SIGs: No
Newsletters: No
Major Reviews: CALICO *Journal* 3 (March 1986): 34–36.
Other Learning Aids: None

- MULTILINGUAL FEATURES

Video Cards Supported: EGA only
Specify Different Fonts in Document: Yes
Print Different Fonts: Yes
Display Different Fonts On-Screen: Yes
Foreign Fonts Included: Greek, Hebrew, Cyrillic, IBM extended ASCII
RAM-Based Character Generator: Yes
Font Editor: Yes
Number Characters Per Font: 256
Maximum Screen Fonts Per Document: 4, any 2 of which may be combined into an active font of 512
  characters.
Mode Used to Display Nonstandard Characters: Text
Edit Right-to-Left: No
Display Entire ASCII Character Set: Yes

- SPECIAL FEATURES

Run DOS Commands from Program: Yes
Chain Files for Printing: Yes
Queue Files for Printing: No
Spelling Checker: No
Thesaurus: No
Windows/Split-Screen: Yes, maximum of 2
Columns: No
Footnotes: Yes
Bibliography: No
Table of Contexts: No
Indices: No
Keyboard Macros: Yes
Text Retrieval System: No
Internal Programming Language: No
Other: The Duke Language Toolkit comes with PC-Write.

- SUPPORT ETC.

Warranty: Not known
Support: Letter, phone, and on BITNET % DYBBUK@TUCCVM or on UUCP % MCNC!DUKE!JWG
Update Policy: Not known
Other Information: Graphics Memory Expansion Card for EGA recommended.

Introduction. Like the GTL, the Duke Language Toolkit (hereafter DLT) is a set of related utilities—"tools"—that were created for designing and manipulating foreign language fonts. The DLT is not a word processor, but because it has been designed to work with PC-Write, which is distributed with it, and because the GTL and the DLT are similar and often compared to one another, I am including a review of the DLT here and not later in this chapter under "Font-and-Printer Utilities," though it would fit equally well in that category. The DLT has been developed as part of the larger Duke University Language Learning Project.

The DLT includes (1) FED, a generic font editor, (2) LOADFONT, an interactive, pop-up, memory-resident, menu-driven font utility for manipulating fonts, (3) Greek (with breathing and diacritical marks), Hebrew (consonantal), and Cyrillic sample fonts, (4) sample data files (the first two chapters of Matthew), (5) "filters" that convert fonts created with FED to pixel-setting files for use on the EGA and on the Toshiba P351, IBM Proprinter, and FX-80/85 series of printers, (6) special keyboard and printer files for use with PC-Write, and (7) PC-Write. This is not a commercial program but an evolving set of tools for academicians and students.

Performance and Versatility. The DLT differs from the GTL in several significant ways. The GTL is a graphics-mode program that directly bit-maps its characters to video memory. The DLT works with the EGA's RAM-based character generator in text mode and uses the standard video interrupt (10 hex) and BIOS for input and output. That means that the DLT's fonts are, by and large, compatible with other programs, such as WordPerfect and PC-Write, which also operate in text mode and use the standard video interrupt and BIOS routines. Screen fonts created with the DLT's font editor will only work on monochrome or Enhanced Color Displays (not on "regular" RGB color monitors) that are driven by an EGA card. Unlike the GTL, the DLT contains a generic font editor, FED, that allows users to create fonts with character sizes from 2-by-2 to 30-by-30. Thus users may create fonts that are the correct size for downloading to different dot-matrix printers, as well as fonts for the EGA (which the DLT operates in mode 7, the high-resolution—720-by-350—text mode). Screen fonts created with FED for the EGA must consist of 256 8-by-14 characters each.

LOADFONT is the DLT's interactive, menu-driven, memory-resident, pop-up utility for manipulating fonts—for changing from one font to another and for reconfiguring fonts. Depending on the EGA's memory configuration (see above), LOADFONT can store up to four 256-character fonts in memory, switch among them, and link any two of them to form one 512-character font, which is the maximum number of unique characters the EGA can work with at one time. LOADFONT also supports a 43-line screen display. When working with 256-character alternate fonts, LOADFONT translates the values of the active logical keyboard into values specified by the active font, so that pressing the *a* key on the physical keyboard, for example, causes the EGA character generator to display the value of the corresponding character in the active screen font (Greek *alpha*, for example). When working with 512-character fonts that are composed of two character sets of 256 characters each, the EGA displays a character from the alternative (second) character set when the character's intensity bit (in its attribute byte) is 1 (high intensity). Because LOADFONT is a memory-resident, pop-up utility, once it has been loaded into memory it permits users to change fonts from the DOS level or from within application programs that are using the EGA, thus permitting multilingual word processing (for example) with programs that are not specifically designed with that in mind (e.g., WordPerfect, but see my remarks above).

The DLT contains files that customize it to work with PC-Write. RULER.GRK and RULER.HEB, for example, are logical keyboards for Greek and Hebrew that are included with the DLT. PC-Write is able to display diacritical marks, supports multiple fonts, and allows the keyboard to be remapped. Using the DLT utilities with PC-Write (and an EGA card), then, permits multilingual editing and printing. PC-Write uses the back-quote key as an accent key, so that accents are entered after the letters they go with. Use of the accent key allows sophisticated multilingual keyboards to be created. Function keys are used to switch from font to font. By modifying PC-Write source code (which is supplied to every *registered* user of PC-Write,[150]) the DLT programmers have created an in-house Greek version of PC-Write with full support for diacritical marks, a Coptic keyboard that will automatically place diacritical marks over letters, and an Amharic keyboard that can automatically modify characters when their vowel is entered (all Amharic symbols represent a consonant-vowel combination). The DLT diskette contains a file (PATCH.ED) that works with DOS's DEBUG.COM to patch PC-Write's ED.EXE file so that the altered PC-Write can display the Greek diacritical marks.

Documentation. The DLT's documentation is contained in a 23-page, printable disk file. It is well organized, not too technical, and contains examples but no index. It includes instructions on using FED, LOADFONT, the EGA, and PC-Write.

Ease of Use. Both FED and LOADFONT are easy to use. LOADFONT is interactive and menu-driven. FED uses windows and function keys.

Error Handling. LOADFONT displays messages if users attempt to load more fonts than memory allows.

Support. I have had no occasion to call the support number and so cannot comment on this topic.

Bibliography. Jeffrey William Gillette, "The Duke Language Toolkit: Foreign Alphabets for the IBM PC," *CALICO Journal* 3 (March 1986): 34–36.

2.6.1.7 *Multi-Lingual Scribe*

* *BASIC PRODUCT INFORMATION*

Name of Program: Multi-Lingual Scribe™ (MLS)
Company Name: Gamma Productions, Inc.
Address: 710 Wilshire Blvd., #609, Santa Monica, CA 90401
Phone: (213) 394-8622
Technical Support: (213) 394-8622
Price: $350; $500 for laser printer version
Version Tested: 2.01, latest version is 2.9.
Runs On: IBM PCs and compatibles
Memory Requirements: 512K or 640K recommended
Operating System Requirements: DOS 2.0 or greater
Disk Drive Requirements: 1; hard drive recommended
Copy Protected: No
Possible Backups: Unlimited
Hard Disk Compatible: Yes
Produces ASCII Files: No
Produces PostScript Files: No
Drives Laser Printers: Yes, LaserJet Plus, with JLaser card—Cordata, Canon, LaserJet
Drives Typesetters: No, but typesetting support is offered through Avi Davidow, 753 Walker Ave., Oakland, CA 94610; (415) 834-9038.
SideKick Compatible: Yes
Mnemonic Commands: Yes
User Interface: Command-driven
Text Display: Auto word wrap, no on-screen justification
Screen Display Reformatting: Constant and automatic
Formatting Text for Printing: At print time
Text Orientation: Document
Screen Mode: Graphics
WYSIWYG: No
Edit Files Larger Than Memory: No
Uses Function Keys: Yes
Key Template or Labels: Yes
Product Includes: Disks, manual, pressure-sensitive, keyboard labels
Number of Disks: 3

---

150. To register costs $75.

- *INSTRUCTIONAL MATERIALS/SOURCES*

Manual: 154 pages, 3-ring binder, tabbed, indexed
Tutorial: Yes, in manual
Quick Reference Card: No, but the manual contains a summary of Command Key commands, Command Window commands, and Print Formatting commands.
Demo Disk Available: Yes, $15
On-Line Help: Yes
Pop-Up Command Menus: No
SIGs: No
Newsletters: Yes, from Gamma Productions, Inc.
Major Reviews: *The Hebrew Users' Group* Newsletter 2 (July-September 1986): 3–9.
Other Learning Aids: None

- *MULTILINGUAL FEATURES*

Video Cards Supported: CGA, EGA, HGC, HGC+, and other "standard" graphics cards; requires a graphics card; on the EGA, MLS runs in CGA (color graphics) mode.
Specify Different Fonts in Document: Yes
Print Different Fonts: Yes
Display Different Fonts On-Screen: Yes
Foreign Fonts Included: Greek, Hebrew, Cyrillic, Arabic, roman; version 3.0 will include Hindi and math fonts. Gamma Productions will create custom alphabets for $150 each.
RAM-Based Character Generator: Yes
Font Editor: Yes
Number Characters Per Font: Up to 243
Maximum Screen Fonts Per Document: 5
Mode Used to Display Nonstandard Characters: Graphics
Edit Right-to-Left: Yes
Display Entire ASCII Character Set: No

- *SPECIAL FEATURES*

Run DOS Commands from Program: No
Chain Files for Printing: Yes
Queue Files for Printing: No
Spelling Checker: No
Thesaurus: No
Windows/Split-Screen: No
Columns: Yes, in version 3.0.
Footnotes: Yes
Bibliography: No
Table of Contexts: No
Indices: No
Keyboard Macros: No
Text Retrieval System: No
Internal Programming Language: No
Other: Can import WordStar and ASCII files; output is compatible with FancyFont (see below).

- *SUPPORT ETC.*

Warranty: None
Support: Phone
Update Policy: $108 to version 3.0
Other Information: Laser printer support is $150

Introduction. Multi-Lingual Scribe™ (hereafter MLS) is a command-driven, multi-lingual word processing program that operates in graphics mode and that can display multiple character sets on-screen, complete with vowels, accents, and other diacritical marks in their proper places.

141

Performance and Versatility. MLS contains many of the standard text editing, page formatting, and printing features of the more powerful programs we have reviewed in this chapter. Although this review is based on version 2.01 of MLS, by the time this book is printed, version 3.0 should be available. Some of the features listed below will only be available in that version. Among other features, MLS supports (1) multilingual footnotes, (2) multiple fonts, (3) laser printers, (4) block moves, (5) headers and footers, (6) search and replace (works with all character sets, and can include or exclude accents), (7) super- and subscripts, (8) proportional spacing, (9) microspacing, (10) bidirectional word wrap, (11) on-screen displays of nonstandard fonts, a (12) print review feature, (13) composing and printing in up to sixteen different alphabets, and (14) vowels and accents. And MLS (15) comes with five fonts—roman, Cyrillic, Greek, Hebrew, and Arabic—and the appropriate vowels and accents for each, and (16) MLS can import WordStar files and ASCII files created by FinalWord, XyWrite, Multimate, Samna, and other word processing programs. MLS's character sets allow users to compose and print in twenty-five languages, including Modern and Classical Hebrew, Yiddish, Aramaic, Modern and Classical Greek, Arabic, Bulgarian, Russian, Serbian, Ukrainian, Spanish, German, French, Norwegian, Polish, Swedish, Welsh, Turkish, Dutch, Danish, English, Finnish, Icelandic, Italian, and so on. MLS includes (17) Font Editor™, a utility that allows users to modify fonts, create fonts, and rearrange key assignments. The Font Editor accepts characters scanned by a Canon IX-12 scanner.

Unfortunately, MLS does not support (1) windows, (2) automatic generation of tables of contents and (3) indices, (4) keyboard macros, (5) the EGA card in its high resolution modes, (6) cursor movement by line, paragraph, and page, and a (7) GOTO command. Because MLS operates in graphics mode, (8) it is noticeably slower than text-mode programs. Although earlier versions of MLS could not export ASCII files (and so those MLS files could not be spell checked), MLS Version 3.0 can export ASCII files.

Documentation. By and large, MLS's manual is clearly written, though, occasionally, it is obscure. Pressure-sensitive keyboard labels for Hebrew attach directly to the keys. The manual contains a summary of Command Key commands, Command Window commands, and Print Formatting commands, as well as several pages of keyboard maps. Limited but useful on-line help is available.

Ease of Use. MLS is a command-driven program that displays characters and typestyles correctly on-screen. MLS may be used in either 40- or 80-column modes. Although the 40-column mode reduces the amount of information displayed by half, it makes it easier to see small diacritical marks, such as Hebrew vowels. Fonts are switched by using function keys. Accents and other diacritical marks are also added with the function keys, and up to three sets of diacritical marks may be added to each character. Diacritical marks are entered immediately after the letters they are associated with, and MLS automatically places them on-screen in their proper places. Final Hebrew letters are produced by using the Alt key, and *dagesh* is inserted into Hebrew letters by using the Shift key. Although different size fonts may be displayed with MLS's print preview feature, they may not be displayed in different sizes on-screen during editing. MLS includes two different sizes of Hebrew characters. Arabic characters automatically change shape depending on their position in a word.

MLS allows multiple fonts within lines and paragraphs, as well as right-to-left text entry. Up to five different fonts may be mixed on a single line or paragraph, and up to thirty different fonts may be used in a single document. Switching from right-to-left to left-to-right text entry returns the cursor to the rightmost character, and vice versa.

The powerful font editor that comes with MLS allows users to modify existing fonts, to reassign keys, and to design custom fonts and accents. MLS comes with two Hebrew keyboard layouts—standard (like Israeli typewriters) and mnemonic—which are software selectable.

On screens with poor resolution (e.g., a color screen driven by a CGA card), diacritical marks may be omitted for the sake of legibility or a 40-column mode may be used or both. When used with a CGA card in an 80-column mode, the legibility of the MLS's characters is marginal, at best, and that is especially true of composite characters. With the HGC or HGC+, however, characters are displayed more legibly because of the higher resolution of those cards. Nevertheless, even with an HGC+, in the 80-column mode I found it very difficult to distinguish Hebrew characters, especially composite ones, unless I moved my face to within about 10 inches of the screen.

MLS comes with limited, but useful, on-line help. Especially useful are MLS's on-line keyboard, vowel, and accent maps, which may be displayed at any time in the midst of an editing session. With little effort, I quickly learned how to type in Hebrew and how to enter accents, letters with final forms, and letters that contain a *dagesh*.

Error Handling. MLS has no undelete feature and does not automatically save files during editing.

Support. I have had no occasion to call Gamma Productions and so cannot comment on their support.

Bibliography. Jack Love, "Multi-Lingual Scribe™," *The Hebrew Users' Group Newsletter* 2 (July-September 1986): 3–9.

2.6.1.8 ChiWriter—The Scholar's Edition

● *BASIC PRODUCT INFORMATION*

Name of Program: ChiWriter—The Scholar's Edition
Company Name: Paraclete Software
Address: 1000 E. 14th St., Suite 187, Plano, TX 75074
Phone: (214) 578-8185
Technical Support: (214) 578-8185
Price: $99.95; screen drivers for the HGC, HGC+, and EGA cards and printer drivers for 24-pin and laser printers are extra.
Version Tested: 2.15
Runs On: IBM PCs and compatibles
Memory Requirements: 256
Operating System Requirements: DOS 2.0 or greater
Disk Drive Requirements: 1
Copy Protected: No
Possible Backups: Unlimited
Hard Disk Compatible: Yes
Produces ASCII Files: Yes
Produces PostScript Files: No
Drives Laser Printers: Yes, LaserJet with J cartridge
Drives Typesetters: No
SideKick Compatible: Yes
Mnemonic Commands: Yes
User Interface: Command-driven or menu-driven
Text Display: Auto word wrap, no on-screen justification
Screen Display Reformatting: Constant and automatic
Formatting Text for Printing: At print time
Text Orientation: Document
Screen Mode: Graphics
WYSIWYG: Yes
Edit Files Larger Than Memory: No; with 640K maximum document length is approximately 100 pages.
Uses Function Keys: Yes
Key Template or Labels: No
Product Includes: Manual and disks
Number of Disks: 2

- *INSTRUCTIONAL MATERIALS/SOURCES*

Manual: 129 pages, 3-ring binder, indexed
Tutorial: Not on-line but included in separate file.
Quick Reference Card: No
Demo Disk Available: Yes
On-Line Help: Yes
Pop-Up Command Menus: Yes
SIGs: None
Newsletters: Occasionally from Paraclete Software
Major Reviews: None
Other Learning Aids: None

- *MULTILINGUAL FEATURES*

Video Cards Supported: CGA, HGC, HGC+, EGA, AT&T 6300, and other standard graphics cards
Specify Different Fonts in Document: Yes
Print Different Fonts: Yes, Greek and Hebrew
Display Different Fonts On-Screen: Yes
Foreign Fonts Included: 14 different character sets in 4 different alphabets: Roman, Western European and Scandinavian, Classical, Koine, and Modern Greek (with all diacritics), Classical and Modern Hebrew (with all vowels and diacritics)
RAM-Based Character Generator: No
Font Editor: Yes
Number Characters Per Font: 94
Maximum Screen Fonts Per Document: 20
Mode Used to Display Nonstandard Characters: Graphics
Edit Right-to-Left: Yes
Display Entire ASCII Character Set: Yes

- *SPECIAL FEATURES*

Run DOS Commands from Program: No
Chain Files for Printing: No
Queue Files for Printing: No
Spelling Checker: No
Thesaurus: No
Windows/Split-Screen: No
Columns: Yes
Footnotes: Yes
Bibliography: No
Table of Contexts: No
Indices: No
Keyboard Macros: Yes, text only
Text Retrieval System: No
Internal Programming Language: No
Other: No

- *SUPPORT ETC.*

Warranty: 30-day, limited, money-back guarantee
Support: Phone and letter
Update Policy: Not known
Other Information: None

ChiWriter—The Scholar's Edition (hereafter CW) is a remarkably flexible and reasonably priced, menu- or command-driven, multilingual word processing program that operates in graphics mode and that can display multiple character sets on-screen, complete with vowels, accents, and other diacritical marks in their proper places.

CW supports: (1) footnotes, (2) multiple screen fonts, (3) composite characters, (4) automatic document saving during editing at user-specified intervals, (5) columns, (6) on-line help, (7) text-only macros, (8) lines with overlapping super- and subscript levels, (9) displayable keyboard layouts, (10) a font editor, (11) unbreakable spaces, (12) block moves, (13) search and replace, (14) on-screen dynamic pagination, (15) decimal tabs, (16) proportional spacing, (17) headers and footers, (18) hanging indents, (19) microspacing, (20) page numbering, and more.

Fonts are bound to function keys. Font-key assignments may be changed, and keyboard templates that illustrate each logical keyboard may be displayed. Blocks of text in one font may be "flipped" to another font. Accents and other diacritical marks used to create composite characters may be entered in one of three ways. (1) Diacritics can be entered manually by moving the cursor up and over (or below) the letter that is to receive the diacritic and then typing the diacritic. (2) Composite characters can be designed with the font editor and assigned to single keys. (3) Diacritics can be assigned to macros that may, for example, be programmed to scroll up a line, back up a character, enter the diacritic, and return the cursor to its point of origin.

The high-resolution HGC/HGC+ screen fonts are 9-by-16, and the CGA screen fonts are 8-by-10. Nine-pin dot-matrix printer fonts are 16-by-24, 24-pin printer fonts are 24-by-30, and laser-printer fonts are 32-by-50. The manual does not specify the resolution of the EGA screen fonts.

CW can be menu- or command-driven. The last line on CW's editing screen contains menu items, which may be selected by highlighting them or by typing the first letter of an item's name. (Esc toggles the cursor in and out of the menu window.) Highlighting an item causes information about its function or a submenu to be displayed beneath it. Experienced users may bypass menus by using the Alt key in combination with the letter that designates the command they wish executed. A Hide command allows users to turn the menu off and thereby gain two more lines for editing. Some commands are issued directly with Ctrl + alpha key combinations. For example, Ctrl + K is the command given to begin defining a macro.

Because CW is a graphics-mode program, screen redrawing on my 8088, 4.77 MHz machine is sluggish, and I found it easy to fill up the type-ahead buffer. On AT-class machines and on 8088s with faster processors (e.g., a NEC V-20) and clock rates, this problem does not exist. A keyboard buffer program, KB.BUF, that is included with CW eliminates this problem on slow 8088s by increasing the size of the keyboard buffer.

CW comes configured so that spaces are represented on-screen by small raised dots—an annoying feature that may be turned off by editing the font file so that the dot symbol is no longer assigned to the Space Bar. Page breaks are displayed on-screen as dotted lines. The top line of the screen is used as a status line. CW produces Greek and Hebrew characters that are easy to read on a monochrome screen driven by an HGC+ card.

2.6.1.9 *PowerWriter*

• *BASIC PRODUCT INFORMATION*

Name of Program: PowerWriter
Company Name: None
Address: % Dr. Vern S. Poythress, Westminster Theological Seminary, P.O. Box 27009, Chestnut Hill, Philadelphia, PA 19118
Phone: (215) 887-5511 (seminary)
Technical Support: (215) 887-5511 (seminary)
Price: $50
Version Tested: 1.0
Runs On: IBM PCs and compatibles and Z-100 computers

Memory Requirements: 128K
Operating System Requirements: DOS 2.0 or greater
Disk Drive Requirements: 1
Copy Protected: No
Possible Backups: Unlimited
Hard Disk Compatible: Yes
Produces ASCII Files: Yes
Produces PostScript Files: No
Drives Laser Printers: Yes, LaserJet
Drives Typesetters: No
SideKick Compatible: Yes
Mnemonic Commands: Yes
User Interface: Command-driven or menu-driven
Text Display: Auto word wrap, no on-screen justification
Screen Display Reformatting: Constant and automatic
Formatting Text for Printing: At print time
Text Orientation: Document
Screen Mode: Text
WYSIWYG: No
Edit Files Larger Than Memory: No, maximum file size is approximately 50K.
Uses Function Keys: Yes
Key Template or Labels: No
Product Includes: Manual and disk
Number of Disks: 1

• INSTRUCTIONAL MATERIALS/SOURCES

Manual: 90 pages, stapled, no index (but excellent, detailed table of contents)
Tutorial: No
Quick Reference Card: No
Demo Disk Available: No
On-Line Help: No
Pop-Up Command Menus: No
SIGs: None
Newsletters: No
Major Reviews: None
Other Learning Aids: None

• MULTILINGUAL FEATURES

Video Cards Supported: MDA, HGC, HGC+, EGA and other standard cards that operate in text-mode
Specify Different Fonts in Document: Yes
Print Different Fonts: Yes, Greek and Hebrew
Display Different Fonts On-Screen: No
Foreign Fonts Included: None. A program like Lettrix (see below) or a downloadable printer font must be used to print in Greek, Hebrew, and other alphabets.
RAM-Based Character Generator: No
Font Editor: No
Number Characters Per Font: 224
Maximum Screen Fonts Per Document: 1; PW supports up to 10 printer fonts per document.
Mode Used to Display Nonstandard Characters: Text
Edit Right-to-Left: No
Display Entire ASCII Character Set: No

• SPECIAL FEATURES

Run DOS Commands from Program: Yes
Chain Files for Printing: No, but file size is limited only by disk size.
Queue Files for Printing: No
Spelling Checker: No
Thesaurus: No
Windows/Split-Screen: Yes, maximum of 9

Columns: Yes
Footnotes: Yes
Bibliography: No
Table of Contexts: Yes
Indices: Yes
Keyboard Macros: Yes, commands and text
Text Retrieval System: No
Internal Programming Language: No, but PW's macro capabilities include variables and conditional branching.
Other: Mail merge

- *SUPPORT ETC.*

Warranty: Media only
Support: Not known
Update Policy: $20 for future versions
Other Information: None

Introduction. PowerWriter (hereafter PW), which was written by Dr. Vern S. Poythress at Westminster Theological Seminary, is a text-mode program that allows users to code files so that they may be printed in different alphabets, including Greek and Hebrew. PW is an impressive program for several reasons. It is small (about 68K) and requires only 128K of memory, but it is flexible, powerful, full-featured, and highly customizable. PW is inexpensive ($50), yet includes many features lacking in more expensive programs. And it comes with a thorough, well-written manual.

Although available from the author at the address above, PW is not yet marketed on a commercial basis, though a commercial distributor is being sought.

Performance and Versatility. A number of features distinguish this innovative program. PW supports (1) automatic file backup at the start of editing, (2) on-line help, (3) footnotes, (4) endnotes, (5) up to nine windows, (6) specifying up to ten printer fonts in a single document, (7) microjustification, (8) true proportional spacing, (9) headers, (10) footers, (11) automatic page numbering, (12) case-sensitive and case-insensitive conditional and global search and replace, (13) macros for text and commands, (14) temporarily exiting the program to run DOS commands, (15) merge and mail merge, (16) automatically generated tables of contents, (17) automatically generated indices, (18) undeletion, (19) programmable function keys, (20) redefinable commands, (21) block moves (copy, move, delete), (22) stringing commands together (also known as "stacking" commands), (23) bidirectional cursor movement by character, word, end/beginning of line, line, screen, and document, (24) deletion by character, word, to end of line, paragraph, and document, (25) soft hyphens, (26) specifying numerical arguments (values) for cursor, block, and delete commands, (27) block moves with columns of text, (28) print preview, (29) widow and orphan control, (30) superscripts and subscripts, (31) character attributes such as italics, underlined, and bold, as well as (32) double-strike, (33) block quotes, (34) nonprinting notes within text, (35) changing print formats anywhere within a document, and (36) wild-card searches. And (37) PW may be menu- or command-driven.

Unfortunately, PW does not support (1) searching the on-line help file, which is only minimally context sensitive, (2) moving the cursor by phrase, sentence, paragraph, or page, (3) deleting by phrase, sentence, screen, or page, (4) automatic outlining of text sections, (5) bidirectional cross referencing, (6) virtual memory architecture (so that files larger than memory may be edited), (7) searching files for words and phrases, and (8) automatic save-during-editing. And (9) PW comes configured for only five printers, though a user-defined printer configuration option allows users to define undefined printers.

PW comes correctly configured to print Hebrew (complete with all vowels and major punctuation marks) and Greek (complete with all diacritical marks) on the five printers it supports (Diablo 630, NEC 7710/7720, NEC 2050, LaserJet, Epson MX-80), if those printers are properly equipped with Hebrew or Greek fonts or if a program such as Lettrix is used.[151] Two user-definable fonts allow other character sets to be defined and printed. Nonroman character strings are entered in roman characters after print format commands, which are preceded by a backslash. Hebrew must be entered backwards, left-to-right, since PW has no right-to-left text entry mode. Although the PW manual lists the character combinations that represent diacritical marks for Greek and Hebrew, it fails to explain whether diacriticals are typed before or after the letters they modify.

Documentation. PW comes with a well-written, 90-page, 8.5-inch-by-11-inch manual. Unfortunately, although the manual contains a detailed table of contents, it does not contain an index or a tutorial section. PW's manual is clear and comprehensive, though sometimes difficult to navigate. Creating new terminology such as *nook, hold, unhold,* and *dark* seems unnecessary.[152] PW includes an on-line help file, which is minimally context-sensitive and which can be scrolled through but not searched. Because it is in ASCII, users may modify the help file.

Ease of Use. PW is easy to learn and use. When installing the program, users are given the option of installing it for beginning, intermediate, or regular word processing users. Each successive level of installation makes more complex lists of command options available to the user.

PW operates in one of three modes: Edit, Command, and Do. The Do mode is used by the program when it executes a command, the Edit mode is used for editing, and the Command mode is used for issuing commands. Users toggle between the Command and Edit modes with F10. Any command may be canceled by using the Home key on the numeric keypad.

Function keys are used for many editing chores, such as deleting, undeleting, tabbing, reformatting the screen, inserting a soft hyphen, and so forth. In the edit mode, Ctrl + 7 displays: (1) the paragraph number the cursor is in, (2) the ASCII value of the character the cursor is on in the file, (3) the number of characters in the file before the cursor, (4) the number of characters in the file after the cursor, and (5) the amount of free memory left.

PW may be menu-driven or command-driven. The bottom portion of the screen is divided from the upper 20-line text area by a line. Beneath that line, the last four lines of the screen contain a 3-line menu area and below that a 1-line communication area. The menu area is used in two ways. When PW is in the Command mode, the menu area is used to display command options (much like Microsoft Word). When PW is in the Edit mode, the menu area is used to display editing options. Below the menu area, on the last line of the screen (the communication area), is the information area (on the far left), the command area (in the middle), and the message area (on the far right). The menu area may be switched off and three additional lines gained for editing. PW's Command Menu options are selected by entering the first letter of the option name. This often causes a second menu of options to be listed or requires a variable, such as a filename, to be entered. Execution of commands is lightning fast, as fast (or so it seems to me) as XyWrite III and Nota Bene.

PW's powerful macro capabilities support branching, two types of variables—integer and string (whose values may change during the course of execution)—and conditional statements. Each line of a macro may contain any sequence of commands that

---

151. PW's installation program allows users to define their own printer translation tables for other printers.

152. *Nook* is a synonym for *window, hold* is a synonym for the more common block-move term *copy, unhold* is a synonym for the more common block-move term *undelete,* and *dark* is a synonym for *bold.* Spellbinder also uses the terms *hold* and *unhold.*

are legal for PW. Although PW comes with over twenty predefined integer variables, users may define up to twenty-six additional ones.[153] Nine string variables come predefined with PW, and users may define up to ten more.[154] PW comes with predefined macros for (1) mail merge, (2) endnotes, (3) moving columns of text, (4) creating an index, and (5) merging texts.

PW's commands are all embedded in text, not hidden. Like T_EX (see above), most of PW's formatting and printing commands begin with the backslash character followed by an argument such as *i* (for "italic"), the text that is to be acted upon, and a closing delimiter.

Error Handling. PW does not have an automatic save-during-editing feature. Its undelete feature works only if more than 40 characters have been deleted. PW has an extensive list of error messages.

Support. I have had no occasion to call for support and so cannot comment on this topic.

2.6.1.10 *Alexander*

• *BASIC PRODUCT INFORMATION*

Name of Program: Alexander™
Company Name: Design Enterprises of San Francisco
Address: P.O. Box 14695, San Francisco, CA 94114; distributed by Gessler Publishing Co., Inc., 900 Broadway, New York, NY 10003-1291; (212) 673-3113
Phone: (415) 282-8813
Technical Support: Not known
Price: $245
Version Tested: Demo version
Runs On: IBM PCs and compatibles, AT&T PC 6300, Compaq, Leading Edge, Tandy 1000 and 2000, Zenith 158 and 171
Memory Requirements: 192K
Operating System Requirements: DOS 2.0 or greater
Disk Drive Requirements: 1
Copy Protected: No
Possible Backups: Unlimited
Hard Disk Compatible: Yes
Produces ASCII Files: Yes
Produces PostScript Files: No
Drives Laser Printers: Yes, LaserJet
Drives Typesetters: No, it but can produce files that are properly coded for Itek, AM Varityper, Compugraphic, Linotype (Mergenthaler), and for the Intergraphics typesetting service.
SideKick Compatible: No
Mnemonic Commands: No
User Interface: Menu-driven
Text Display: Auto word wrap, no on-screen justification
Screen Display Reformatting: Drop-down insert, auto reformat
Formatting Text for Printing: At print time
Text Orientation: Document
Screen Mode: Graphics
WYSIWYG: No
Edit Files Larger Than Memory: No
Uses Function Keys: Yes
Key Template or Labels: Yes, for Hebrew, Greek, and Cyrillic (Cyrillic is $20; Hebrew and Greek are $15 each).
Product Includes: Manual and disks
Number of Disks: 3

---

153. Integer variables are variables whose value is that of a non-negative integer.
154. String variables are variables whose value can be any string of up to 80 characters.

- ## INSTRUCTIONAL MATERIALS/SOURCES

Manual: 674 pages
Tutorial: Yes, on demo disk and in "Getting Started" manual
Quick Reference Card: No
Demo Disk Available: Yes, demo disk A (conversion from word processing to typesetting, includes typesetting manual): $20; demo disk B (multilingual word processing, math, music): $15; both demo disks: $25
On-Line Help: Yes
Pop-Up Command Menus: Yes
SIGs: Not known
Newsletters: The first issue of Design Enterprises' newsletter is scheduled for 1987.
Major Reviews: None
Other Learning Aids: None

- ## MULTILINGUAL FEATURES

Video Cards Supported: MDA, CGA, HGC+; support is planned for the EGA.
Specify Different Fonts in Document: Yes
Print Different Fonts: Yes
Display Different Fonts On-Screen: Yes
Foreign Fonts Included: Roman, Western European, Eastern European, Native American, African, Cyrillic, Greek, Hebrew (with vowels), International Phonic Alphabet, music composition, math/science symbols, molecular structures, electronic schematic symbols
RAM-Based Character Generator: Yes
Font Editor: Yes
Number Characters Per Font: 123
Maximum Screen Fonts Per Document: 3 (a total of 341 unique characters)
Mode Used to Display Nonstandard Characters: Graphics
Edit Right-to-Left: Yes
Display Entire ASCII Character Set: Yes

- ## SPECIAL FEATURES

Run DOS Commands from Program: No
Chain Files for Printing: Yes
Queue Files for Printing: No
Spelling Checker: No
Thesaurus: No
Windows/Split-Screen: No
Columns: No
Footnotes: Yes
Bibliography: No
Table of Contexts: No
Indices: No
Keyboard Macros: Yes, text and commands
Text Retrieval System: No
Internal Programming Language: No
Other: LaserJet character sets are available for $15, and characters sets for the Toshiba P321 and P351 are available for $15 each. Alexander works with light pens (FTG Data Systems) and mice (Logitech, Microsoft, and Mouse System's PC Mouse).

- ## SUPPORT ETC.

Warranty: None
Support: Phone and letter
Update Policy: Currently, no charge
Other Information: None

Introduction. Alexander™ (hereafter AL), named after Alexander the Great (because of his patronage of the humanities, arts, and sciences), is a menu-driven, graphics-mode multilingual word processing program that can code files for typesetting. Four things make AL distinctive: (1) it allows users to make menu selections and to perform editing tasks by using keyboard, mouse, or light pen, (2) it can display nonroman fonts, musical notes and symbols, math/science symbols, molecular structures, and electronic schematic symbols, (3) it can translate word processing codes into typesetting codes for a variety of typesetting machines—Itek, AM Varityper, Compugraphic, and Linotype (Mergenthaler), and (4) it allows word processing files that are coded for typesetting output to be proofed on a variety of dot-matrix, impact, and laser printers. (AL does not, however, drive typesetters.) Although AL's word processing functions are not as elaborate as those of many other programs we have reviewed, its marriage of word processing and typesetting features make it an attractive program.

Performance and Versatility. AL has many helpful features that include: (1) editing with keyboard, mouse, or light pen, (2) a communication program, (3) automatic conversion of AL files to files that are properly coded for typesetting, (4) left-to-right and right-to-left text entry, (5) multiple character sets, (6) a font generator, (7) support for up to thirty-eight macros (which are stored as text files and which may be edited), (8) search and replace for up to twenty phrases at a time, (9) on-line help (stored in text files that may be edited), (10) footnotes, (11) chaining files for printing, and (12) creating style sheets that may be stored and used with any document.

Unfortunately, AL does not support (1) windows, (2) columns, (3) indices, (4) tables of contents, and (5) it lacks an undelete feature. Its (6) file length is limited to 500 lines per file (500 lines of 65 characters each is about 32.5K, though AL permits lines up to 250 characters, i.e., 125K). Its (7) cursor cannot move by sentence, paragraph, or page (unless using a light pen or mouse), and it (8) cannot delete by word, sentence, paragraph, page, or document.

AL can display the lower 96 ASCII characters in the CGA ROM, 122 additional "extended characters," and 123 "graphics characters" per document, which is three fonts that total 341 unique characters.[155] Extended characters are roman letters with diacritical marks or nonroman characters. Graphics characters include music notes, scientific and mathematical symbols, molecular structures, and so forth. On the CGA card, the extended and graphics characters are retrieved from AL screen-font files. ASCII and extended characters may be used on the same line, and ASCII and graphics characters may be used on the same line. But because AL defines graphics characters as those that must maintain fixed horizontal and vertical relationships to one another, graphics characters may not be mixed on the same line with extended characters. Extended and graphics characters, however, may be mixed on the same page. AL allows users to switch between two logical keyboards. AL comes with an extensive array of foreign-language character sets, and AL's built-in font editor allows users to create their own fonts.

As a multilingual word processing program, AL is functional and acceptable. As a program for preparing a document (created with AL) for typesetting, AL is very useful. Using AL to prepare files created with word processors for typesetting requires converting the word processing codes to codes the typesetter understands.[156] Although this can be done manually, the margin for error is great. By using a series of menu-driven steps, AL automatically and globally translates word processing codes to typesetting codes. AL enables users to code for the following elements: chapter headings, main headings, subheadings, fixed page breaks, margins, indentation, hanging indents, line spacing, paragraph indents, centering, typestyle (e.g., bold, italic), nonroman characters, fonts, type size, line length, line spacing, and *any* feature available on a given typesetter, such as hyphenation, kerning, ligatures, superscripts and subscripts, and

---

155. Although AL works in text mode with the MDA, because the MDA uses a ROM-based approach to character generation, AL cannot be used for nonroman multilingual word processing with the MDA, though it can be used with that card to display and print the "extended" ASCII character set.

156. Unless the word processor can drive the typesetter.

Em- and En-spaces and dashes. Unfortunately, AL's automated translation of word processing codes to typesetting codes works only on documents prepared with AL.

AL uses two complimentary methods to combine Greek diacritical marks with the letters they modify: a dead-key approach and a floating-diacritic approach. Dead-key diacritics are formed by entering the diacritic followed by the letter it modifies. This results in the letter and diacritic being properly displayed as a single combined character on-screen and properly printed as such. Floating diacritics appear as separate characters on-screen, following the characters they modify. Floating diacritics are, however, properly printed with the letters they modify as single combined characters. AL uses the dead-key approach because there are more possible combined characters in Greek that the 122 text characters AL can support over and above the roman alphabet, and the dead-key approach reduces the number of diacritic-letter combinations to a manageable number. The dead-key approach also allows AL files to be printed as raster screen dumps on dot-matrix printers that print in graphics mode. And the floating-diacritic approach works well with printers that print in text mode.

Documentation. The documentation for AL is extensive, thorough, clear, and well-done. Most of the documentation fits into an 8.5-by-11-inch notebook. Three additional spiral-bound books—Getting Started, Control Program, and Character Generation—contain more information. When entering or editing text, on-line help is available. Help messages, which are displayed on the bottom three lines of the screen, really consist of simple equations, such as "Alt + such and such = so and so."

Ease of Use. AL is a totally menu-driven program that distinguishes text-entry and text-editing modes. AL's menu options may be selected by keystroke, mouse, or light pen. It is easy to use the menus because they are few and simple, though they force users to implement commands by descending through a hierarchy of questions and choices, rather than allowing users to issue commands directly. In text-entry and text-editing modes, hard new lines (which indicate paragraph breaks) begin with the extended-ASCII cloverleaf character, and all lines are numbered down the left of the screen (AL's editor is line-oriented). Twenty lines per screen may be used for text; three lines are reserved for help messages. Text entered in insert mode is not wrapped until the editor is switched back to overwrite mode.

Error Handling. Lamentably, AL has no undelete feature, does not automatically save text during editing, and makes no back-up file at the beginning of an editing session.

Support. I have had no occasion to call Design Enterprises of San Francisco for support and so cannot comment on this topic.

2.6.1.11 *Grafeas*

* BASIC PRODUCT INFORMATION

Name of Program: Grafeas™
Company Name: Apollon Engineering, Inc.
Address: P.O. Box 807, Columbia, MD 21044
Phones: (800) 822-3327 or (301) 596-0146
Technical Support: (800) 822-3327, (301) 596-0146
Price: $399
Version Tested: 2.10
Runs On: IBM PCs and compatibles
Memory Requirements: 512K
Operating System Requirements: DOS 2.0 or greater
Disk Drive Requirements: 2, hard disk required.
Copy Protected: Yes, using the SECOM printer-key system
Possible Backups: Unlimited
Hard Disk Compatible: Yes, hard disk required.
Produces ASCII Files: Yes

Produces PostScript Files: No
Drives Laser Printers: Yes, LaserJet, LaserJet Plus
Drives Typesetters: No
SideKick Compatible: No
Mnemonic Commands: Yes
User Interface: Command-driven
Text Display: Auto word wrap, on-screen justification
Screen Display Reformatting: Constant and automatic
Formatting Text for Printing: At print time
Text Orientation: Document
Screen Mode: Text or Graphics
WYSIWYG: Yes
Edit Files Larger Than Memory: No, but up to 2 megabytes of extended memory may be used.
Uses Function Keys: Yes
Key Template or Labels: Yes, key labels are provided for the 8 supported languages.
Product Includes: Manual and disks
Number of Disks: 2

- *INSTRUCTIONAL MATERIALS/SOURCES*

Manual: Not able to see.
Tutorial: In manual
Quick Reference Card: Not known
Demo Disk Available: Yes, $15 (applicable to purchase price).
On-Line Help: Yes
Pop-Up Command Menus: Yes
SIGs: None
Newsletters: None
Major Reviews: None
Other Learning Aids: None

- *MULTILINGUAL FEATURES*

Video Cards Supported: HGC, HGC+ (not in RamFont mode), EGA
Specify Different Fonts in Document: Yes
Print Different Fonts: Yes
Display Different Fonts On-Screen: Yes
Foreign Fonts Included: Greek (with all accents and diacritical marks), Hebrew (with all vowels), Western European, scientific
RAM-Based Character Generator: Yes
Font Editor: Yes
Number Characters Per Font: 256 in one font, 128 in each of two other fonts, maximum of 512 unique characters active at once
Maximum Screen Fonts Per Document: Maximum of 9 fonts (created from a total of 512 unique characters)
Mode Used to Display Nonstandard Characters: Graphics and EGA downloaded characters
Edit Right-to-Left: Yes
Display Entire ASCII Character Set: Yes

- *SPECIAL FEATURES*

Run DOS Commands from Program: Yes
Chain Files for Printing: No
Queue Files for Printing: No
Spelling Checker: No
Thesaurus: No
Windows/Split-Screen: Yes, maximum of 2 windows
Columns: Only with LaserJet Plus
Footnotes: Not automatically placed or numbered. Automatic placement and numbering of footnotes is promised for the next revision.
Bibliography: No
Table of Contexts: No
Indices: No

Keyboard Macros: No
Text Retrieval System: No
Internal Programming Language: No
Other: On-screen math, mail merge

● *SUPPORT ETC.*

Warranty: 30-day, full-money-back guarantee
Support: Phone
Update Policy: Not yet determined
Other Information: None

Introduction. Grafeas™ (hereafter GF), is the commercial name for the Bibliotech Multifont Word Processor, a full-featured, command-driven, multilingual word processing program that can operate in text or in graphics mode. I will describe the program as it operates in graphics mode.

Performance and Versatility. GF's many features include the following: (1) a WYSIWYG approach to word processing, (2) up to seven fonts per line and nine fonts per document, (3) split-screen editing, (4) Greek (with accents, breathing marks, and other diacritics) and Hebrew (with vowels), (5) mail merge, (6) super-and subscripts, (7) proportional spacing, (8) on-line help, (9) on-screen math, (10) a font editor, (11) case-sensitive and case-insensitive global and conditional search and replace, (12) wild-card characters in search and replace, (13) block moves, (14) right-to-left text entry, (15) standard file management commands, (16) issuing DOS commands from within the program, (17) on-line keyboard maps, (18) a GOTO command, (19) a sorting utility, (20) headers and footers, (21) files that may be scrolled through and searched for strings (without loading the file into memory), (22) graphics that may be merged with text for printing with the LaserJet and LaserJet Plus printers,[157] and (23) up to 18 files may be open at once.

Unfortunately, GF (1) is copy protected, (2) is not SideKick compatible, (3) does not have *context-sensitive* on-line help, (4) does not support footnotes (though support is promised in a future version), (5) does not allow files to be chained or queued, (6) does not support macros (though it is compatible with ProKey—see below), (7) does not produce PostScript files, (8) does not allow the same file to be edited in two different windows, (9) supports only two windows, (10) does not automatically save files during editing, (11) has no undelete feature, and (12) does not create indices. The inability of the program to handle footnotes may be considered a fatal flaw by many academic users.

By purchasing the Hebrew, Greek, or English (KJV) data bases from Apollon Engineering, users may display ranges of text from those data bases by using the appropriate commands.[158] *BIK* loads a user-specified portion of the KJV, *BIG* loads a user-specified portion of the Hebrew or Greek text (whichever is appropriate), and *BIB* loads both the English version of the user-specified text and its Greek or Hebrew counterpart. In graphics mode, Greek is displayed with accents and other diacritical marks, and Hebrew is displayed fully vocalized. Using a HGC+ (in graphics, not Ram-Font, mode) with an IBM monochrome screen, I found GF's Greek and Hebrew fonts easy to read, though the Greek *gamma* is rather strangely shaped. Vowels, accents, and other diacritical marks were quite legible. When printed on a LaserJet Plus, GF produces very pleasing and professional looking Greek and Hebrew.

---

157. The graphics information must be a raster dump of a graphics screen. Printer resolution can be specified at 75, 150, and 300 dpi. The horizontal and vertical location of the upper left-hand corner of the graphics image may be specified relative to the current cursor location or absolutely.

158. As of the first quarter of 1987, the data bases were not yet available. They will be sold for the cost of diskettes only as soon as approval from the data base creators is obtained.

In graphics mode, GF's multilingual features allow users to work with up to nine logical keyboards that are defined from a total of 512 unique characters.[159] Each of the nine logical keyboards is mapped to a part of the 512-character set. GF comes preconfigured with nine fonts: English, Graphic, German, French, Italian, Spanish, Greek, Hebrew, and Special. Keyboard assignments may be displayed at the bottom of the screen above the Command Line and left displayed while editing occurs above them. This is a useful feature that enables beginners to learn key assignments quickly. Unfortunately, font maps extend off the right edge of the screen, and I could find no on-line help that explained how to scroll the screen to the left to display what was off the right edge of the screen. Up to seven fonts may be mixed on a single line. Hebrew, or characters from any font, may be entered right-to-left. Key assignments may be edited and saved. When entering text right-to-left, the cursor moves to the left of the text that is being entered. When the cursor position is then reversed on the same line and text entered left-to-right, the new text overwrites the text that was entered right-to-left, unless the user remembers to toggle the insert text entry mode on. GF's default overwrite mode (see below) makes mixing right-to-left and left-to-right text entry on a single line troublesome and awkward.

GF supports a dead-key approach to entering diacritical marks in fonts 2 and 3 (whose default values are, respectively, Greek and Hebrew), so that when the diacritical mark is typed, the cursor does not advance and the next character combines with the diacritical mark to form a combined character.

Documentation. Documentation was not available at the time of this review.

Ease of Use. Although I could find no command that allowed me to exit the program (and I tried many), GF is easy to use (it turns out that *END* and *EN* are the commands for "exit"). The two on-line help screens list seventy-two 2-letter commands, which are invoked from the Command Line at the bottom of the screen. Although overwrite is the default text-entry mode, insert may be toggled. At line ends, however, when in insert mode, GF automatically reverts to overwrite, thus making it impossible to get in insert mode and stay there. That is disconcerting and frustrating for users who prefer insert mode. The only reason I could discover for this quirk is that in graphics mode, when entering text in insert mode, it is very easy to fill up the type-ahead buffer. I do now know why that happens. Auto word wrap and on-screen left-and-right justification are default settings; each may be disabled.

Error Handling. GF has no automatic save-during-editing or undelete features, though single lines can be undeleted.

Support. At the time of this writing, Apollon Engineering was not handling phone support.

2.6.1.12 *WorldWriter*

● *BASIC PRODUCT INFORMATION*

Name of Program: WorldWriter™
Company Name: Economic Insights
Address: 414 Hungerford Dr., Suite 216, Rockville, MD 20850
Phone: (301) 294-2660
Technical Support: (301) 294-2660
Price: Latin/Western European: $450; Greek/English: $595; Arabic: $995
Version Tested: Not able to test
Runs On: IBM PCs and compatibles
Memory Requirements: 128K, 192K if using TerM™
Operating System Requirements: DOS 2.0 or greater

---

159. This and the following remarks suggest that GF's multilingual capabilities were designed with the EGA in mind. GF includes a full-featured font editor/loader that works with the EGA.

Disk Drive Requirements: 2
Copy Protected: No
Possible Backups: Unlimited
Hard Disk Compatible: Yes
Produces ASCII Files: Yes
Produces PostScript Files: Not known
Drives Laser Printers: Yes, LaserJet, Corona
Drives Typesetters: No
SideKick Compatible: Not known
Mnemonic Commands: Yes
User Interface: Command-driven and menu-driven
Text Display: Auto word wrap, no on-screen justification
Screen Display Reformatting: Drop-down insert, manual reformatting
Formatting Text for Printing: At print time
Text Orientation: Document
Screen Mode: Text
WYSIWYG: No
Edit Files Larger Than Memory: Yes
Uses Function Keys: Yes
Key Template or Labels: Not known
Product Includes: Manual, disks, quick reference card
Number of Disks: 1

• INSTRUCTIONAL MATERIALS/SOURCES

Manual: Not able to see
Tutorial: Yes, in manual
Quick Reference Card: Yes
Demo Disk Available: Yes, $10
On-Line Help: Yes
Pop-Up Command Menus: Yes
SIGs: No
Newsletters: No
Major Reviews: None
Other Learning Aids: None

• MULTILINGUAL FEATURES

Video Cards Supported: MDA, CGA, HGC, Quadvue, and other "standard" cards
Specify Different Fonts in Document: Yes
Print Different Fonts: Yes
Display Different Fonts On-Screen: Yes
Foreign Fonts Included: Depends on configuration chosen; Roman/Western European, English/Greek, Arabic, and other versions are available.
RAM-Based Character Generator: No
Font Editor: No
Number Characters Per Font: 256
Maximum Screen Fonts Per Document: 1
Mode Used to Display Nonstandard Characters: Text
Edit Right-to-Left: No
Display Entire ASCII Character Set: No

• SPECIAL FEATURES

Run DOS Commands from Program: Not known
Chain Files for Printing: No
Queue Files for Printing: No
Spelling Checker: Yes, additional add-on option ($125)
Thesaurus: No
Windows/Split-Screen: No
Columns: No
Footnotes: No

Bibliography: No
Table of Contexts: No
Indices: No
Keyboard Macros: Yes, text only
Text Retrieval System: No
Internal Programming Language: No
Other: None

● *SUPPORT ETC.*

Warranty: Not known
Support: Not known
Update Policy: Not known
Other Information: WorldWriter is an enhanced version of Palantir™. A mail merge utility is included. TerM, a text retrieval system, is available for $200; a spell checker is available for $125; extended roman character sets are available for $75 each. The Greek and Arabic versions require the Quadvue card (see above).

Introduction. Like AcademicFont and GRAMEDIT, WorldWriter™ (hereafter WW) is a multilingual version of a nonmultilingual word processing program, in this case a program called Palantir™[160] that was created by Mike Griffin, who wrote Magic Wand, one of the original word processing programs for IBM PCs.[161] Like Academic-Font and GRAMEDIT, WW is basically a multilingual version of its parent.

Performance and Versatility. WW shares the strengths and weaknesses of Palantir. Like Palantir, WW features (1) virtual memory architecture, which allows files larger than memory to be edited, (2) menus, (3) twenty-five help screens, (4) wild-card search and replace, (5) multiple font changes within a document and mixing two fonts on the same line, (6) multiple-copy printing, (7) printing a range of pages, (8) proportional spacing, (9) global format controls, (10) mixing multiple formats in a single document, (11) headers and footers, (12) decimal tabs, (13) a page-break line, and (14) up to thirty-six text-only macros (which can each be 250 characters long). Unfortunately, WW does not support (1) windows, (2) indices, (3) text columns, (4) footnotes, (5) tables of contents, (6) chaining files for printing, (7) right-to-left editing, (8) automatic file saving during editing, (9) print preview, and (10) it restricts users to one 256-character font per document, a result of WW's ROM-based approach to character generation. Furthermore, (10) WW's cursor cannot be moved forward or backward by sentence or paragraph or backward by word, (11) WW cannot delete by sentence, paragraph, page, or document, and (12) WW's text buffer is only 20K, which results in lots of disk reading and writing.

Documentation. I was not able to see the users' manual. WW contains twenty-five help screens, which are chosen from a ten-item menu, and a quick reference card.

Ease of Use. WW is a menu-driven program that uses some commands to implement certain formatting features. The top line of the screen is the Status Line, and it indicates cursor position, typing mode (insert or overwrite), and commands that are in effect. The second from the top line is the Ruler Line, and it displays tab settings and the justification that has been chosen (normal, semi, full). The last line of the screen is the Message Line. Function keys are used to set text attributes (e.g., italics, bold), which are displayed correctly on-screen. Format codes are hidden but may be revealed.

---

160. Palantir is available from Designer Software, 3400 Montrose Blvd., Suite 718, Houston, TX 77006; (713) 520-8221; $450. For reviews of Palantir see C. Stuart Douglas, "The Wizardry of Palantir," *PC Magazine* (December 1983): 491-505; *Softalk for the IBM Personal Computer* (July 1983): 131–33; and Russell Letson, "Palantir and Volkswriter: Worth a Second Look," *Business Computer Systems* (July 1985): 97, 100–103.

161. Magic Wand was sold to IBM, who updated it and renamed it *PeachText*.

Error Handling. WW contains no undelete feature and does not automatically save files during editing.

Support. I have had no occasion to call for support and so cannot comment on this topic.

2.6.1.13 WordMill

- ● BASIC PRODUCT INFORMATION

Name of Program: WordMill®
Company Name: Omnigall Systems
Address: P.O. Box 50184, Palo Alto, CA 94303
Phones: (415) 493–0463, (415) 494-2757
Technical Support: (415) 493-0463, (415) 968-4909
Price: $475 (includes backup diskette); volume and institutional discounts available.
Version Reviewed: EH/3.1; current version is ML/4.18
Runs On: IBM PCs and compatibles
Memory Requirements: 256K, 320K when using WordMill with WordMilon (Hebrew-English dictionary)
Operating System Requirements: DOS 2.0 or greater; DOS 3.1 required to use WordMill on LANs.
Disk Drive Requirements: 2
Copy Protected: Yes
Possible Backups: Unlimited (though the license agreement restricts users to 1 backup copy); distribution diskette must be used as software "key" each time the program is loaded.
Hard Disk Compatible: Yes
Produces ASCII Files: Yes
Produces PostScript Files: No
Drives Laser Printers: Yes, which ones not known.
Drives Typesetters: No
SideKick Compatible: Yes
Mnemonic Commands: No
User Interface: Command-driven
Text Display: Auto word wrap, on-screen justification
Screen Display Reformatting: Constant and automatic
Formatting Text for Printing: At print time
Text Orientation: Document
Screen Mode: Text
WYSIWYG: Yes
Edit Files Larger Than Memory: Yes
Uses Function Keys: Yes
Key Template or Labels: Yes
Product Includes: Manual, diskettes, keyboard stickers and template
Number of Disks: 3

- ● INSTRUCTIONAL MATERIALS/SOURCES

Manual: Bilingual, 252 pages (126 pages each for English and for Hebrew), 8.5-by-11-inch, computer printed and photocopied, not indexed
Tutorial: No
Quick Reference Card: No
Demo Disk Available: No
On-Line Help: No
Pop-Up Command Menus: No
SIGs: No
Newsletters: No
Major Reviews: Not known
Other Learning Aids: None

- ● MULTILINGUAL FEATURES

Video Cards Supported: MDA, EGA, HGC, and compatible cards

Specify Different Fonts in Document: Yes
Print Different Fonts: Yes
Display Different Fonts On-Screen: Yes
Foreign Fonts Included: Hebrew (consonants only), Arabic, French, German, Spanish, English, scientific
RAM-Based Character Generator: Yes for EGA; ROM-based character chips are available.
Font Editor: No
Number Characters Per Font: 256
Maximum Screen Fonts Per Document: 1
Mode Used to Display Nonstandard Characters: Text
Edit Right-to-Left: Yes
Display Entire ASCII Character Set: No
Other: When used with the EGA and with printers that accept downloaded fonts, no hardware modifications are required for WordMill to display and print different alphabets. When used with other cards and with printers that do not accept downloaded fonts, WordMill requires users to replace the character ROM chip in the display adapter with a ROM chip that contains the normal and special characters that are to be displayed and to replace the printer's ROM chip with one that corresponds to the one placed in the display adapter. These ROM chips, as well as Hebrew-English print wheels for letter-quality printers, are available from Omnigal Systems.

● *SPECIAL FEATURES*

Run DOS Commands from Program: Yes
Chain Files for Printing: Yes
Queue Files for Printing: No; requires spooling program, hardware spooler, or LAN.
Spelling Checker: No
Thesaurus: No
Windows/Split-Screen: No
Columns: Yes, maximum of 256
Footnotes: No
Bibliography: No
Table of Contexts: No
Indices: No
Keyboard Macros: Yes, text only
Text Retrieval System: No
Internal Programming Language: No
Other: WordMill supports English and Hebrew help screens, bilingual search and replace, headers and footers, widow and orphan control, mail merge, cursor movement by character, word, line and page, a GOTO command, block moves, column moves, hyphenation, proportional spacing, microspacing, bidirectional word wrap, and print preview. WordMilon is a Hebrew-English dictionary. Built-in communication features allow WordMill to receive telex, to send and receive files from mainframes, to support LANs, and to function as a file server.

● *SUPPORT ETC.*

Warranty: None
Support: Phone
Update Policy: Not known
Other Information: Only Hebrew consonants are available.

2.6.1.14 *Vuwriter Arts*

● *BASIC PRODUCT INFORMATION*

Name of Program: Vuwriter Arts
Company Name: Vuman Computer Systems, Ltd.
Address: Enterprise House, Manchester Science Park, Lloyd St. N., Manchester M15 4EN, United Kingdom; distributed in the U.S.A. through CHAM, 1525-A Sparkman Dr., NW, Huntsville, AL 35816; (205) 830-2620.
Phone: 061-226-8311
Technical Support: 061-226-8311
Price: £95, £295, or £595, depending on printer driver

Version Tested: Not able to test
Runs On: IBM PCs and compatibles
Memory Requirements: 256K
Operating System Requirements: DOS 2.0 or greater
Disk Drive Requirements: 2
Copy Protected: No, but requires a hardware key to work.
Possible Backups: Unlimited
Hard Disk Compatible: Yes
Produces ASCII Files: Yes
Produces PostScript Files: Yes, £595 version only
Drives Laser Printers: Yes, LaserJet, LaserJet Plus, Canon LBP8, Canon LBP8-A2, LaserWriter, Kyocera
Drives Typesetters: No
SideKick Compatible: Yes, CGA version
Mnemonic Commands: Yes
User Interface: Menu-driven
Text Display: Auto word wrap, no on-screen justification
Screen Display Reformatting: Constant and automatic
Formatting Text for Printing: Not known
Text Orientation: Not known
Screen Mode: Graphics
WYSIWYG: Yes, mostly
Edit Files Larger Than Memory: No
Uses Function Keys: Yes
Key Template or Labels: No
Product Includes: Manual and disks
Number of Disks: 1 to 3, depending on version

• INSTRUCTIONAL MATERIALS/SOURCES

Manual: Not able to see
Tutorial: Not known
Quick Reference Card: Not known
Demo Disk Available: Yes
On-Line Help: Yes
Pop-Up Command Menus: No
SIGs: Not known
Newsletter: Yes, from Vuman Computer Systems, Ltd.
Major Reviews: *PC User* (August 1985).
Other Learning Aids: None

• MULTILINGUAL FEATURES

Video Cards Supported: CGA, HGC, EGA, and AST
Specify Different Fonts in Document: Yes
Print Different Fonts: Yes
Display Different Fonts On-Screen: Yes
Foreign Fonts Included: Greek (including all diacritical marks), European, Cyrillic, symbolic, italic, normal
RAM-Based Character Generator: Yes
Font Editor: Yes, known as Fontgen, available for £75
Number Characters Per Font: 128
Maximum Screen Fonts Per Document: 5
Mode Used to Display Nonstandard Characters: Graphics
Edit Right-to-Left: No
Display Entire ASCII Character Set: Yes

• SPECIAL FEATURES

Run DOS Commands from Program: No
Chain Files for Printing: No
Queue Files for Printing: Yes
Spelling Checker: Yes, available for £95; included with £595 version.
Thesaurus: No

Windows/Split-Screen: No
Columns: Yes, maximum of 2
Footnotes: No, but promised for 1987.
Bibliography: No
Table of Contexts: No
Indices: No
Keyboard Macros: Yes
Text Retrieval System: No
Internal Programming Language: No
Other: Vuwriter includes a mail merge utility; a font pack for Canon and Hewlett-Packard printers is available for £450.

- *SUPPORT ETC.*

Warranty: 12 months
Support: Not known
Update Policy: £50 per license
Other Information: None

2.6.2 Single Foreign Languages—Hebrew

Programs in this section are bilingual word processors that work with the roman alphabet and with either Hebrew or Arabic. Because (with only one or two exceptions) they are less powerful than programs we have already looked at that work with Hebrew and Arabic, only the basic facts will be provided for the following programs.

2.6.2.1 WorldMaster

- *BASIC PRODUCT INFORMATION*

Name of Program: WorldMaster™
Company Name: Ektron™ Systems, Inc.
Address: 194 Joralemon St., Brooklyn, NY 11201
Phone: (718) 625-7222
Technical Support: (718) 625-7222
Price: $495
Version Tested: Hebrew demo version 1.1
Runs On: IBM PCs and compatibles
Memory Requirements: 128K
Operating System Requirements: DOS 2.0 or greater
Disk Drive Requirements: 1
Copy Protected: Not known
Possible Backups: Not known
Hard Disk Compatible: Yes
Produces ASCII Files: Not known
Produces PostScript Files: Not known
Drives Laser Printers: Not known
Drives Typesetters: Not known
SideKick Compatible: Yes
Mnemonic Commands: Yes
User Interface: Command-driven and menu-driven
Text Display: Auto word wrap, no on-screen justification
Screen Display Reformatting: Constant and automatic
Formatting Text for Printing: At print time
Text Orientation: Document
Screen Mode: Graphics
WYSIWYG: No
Edit Files Larger Than Memory: No
Uses Function Keys: Yes
Key Template or Labels: Yes

Product Includes: Disks, manual, keyboard overlays, quick reference card
Number of Disks: 2

• INSTRUCTIONAL MATERIALS/SOURCES

Manual: Not able to see
Tutorial: Not known
Quick Reference Card: Yes
Demo Disk Available: Yes
On-Line Help: Yes
Pop-Up Command Menus: Yes
SIGs: No
Newsletters: No
Major Reviews: None
Other Learning Aids: None

• MULTILINGUAL FEATURES

Video Cards Supported: CGA
Specify Different Fonts in Document: Yes
Print Different Fonts: Yes
Display Different Fonts On-Screen: Yes
Foreign Fonts Included: Either Hebrew, Russian, French, German, or Spanish
RAM-Based Character Generator: No
Font Editor: No
Number Characters Per Font: 256
Maximum Screen Fonts Per Document: 2
Mode Used to Display Nonstandard Characters: Graphics
Edit Right-to-Left: Yes
Display Entire ASCII Character Set: Yes

• SPECIAL FEATURES

Run DOS Commands from Program: No
Chain Files for Printing: No
Queue Files for Printing: No
Spelling Checker: No
Thesaurus: No
Windows/Split-Screen: No
Columns: No
Footnotes: No
Bibliography: No
Table of Contexts: No
Indices: No
Keyboard Macros: No
Text Retrieval System: No
Internal Programming Language: No
Other: No

• SUPPORT ETC.

Warranty: Not known
Support: Not known
Update Policy: Not known
Other Information: INTEX Software Systems International, Ltd. (488 Madison Ave., New York, NY 10022; (212) 750-1140; INTEX SYSTEMS (U.K.) LTD., 6 Knolls Way, Clifton, Beds. SG17 5QZ, United Kingdom; (0462) 811817) markets a WorldMaster clone called INTEX. English/Hebrew, English/Arabic, and other bilingual versions of this program are available for $495 each.

2.6.2.2 Screenwriter II/Hebrew

- ### BASIC PRODUCT INFORMATION

Name of Program: Screenwriter II/Hebrew
Company Name: Davka Corporation
Address: 845 N. Michigan Ave., Suite 843, Chicago, IL 60611
Phones: (800) 621-8227, (312) 944-4070
Technical Support: (800) 621-8227, (312) 944-4070
Price: $250
Version Reviewed: 3.0
Runs On: Apple IIs
Memory Requirements: 48K
Operating System Requirements: Comes with Diversi-DOS
Disk Drive Requirements: 1
Copy Protected: No
Possible Backups: Unlimited
Hard Disk Compatible: Yes
Produces ASCII Files: Yes
Produces PostScript Files: No
Drives Laser Printers: No. Supports the Epson MX-80 and RX-80 (which require a special EPROM charac-
ter chip), Apple ImageWriter, and other dot-matrix printers, as well as certain daisy-wheel printers.
Drives Typesetters: No
SideKick Compatible: Not applicable
Mnemonic Commands: No
User Interface: Command-driven
Text Display: Auto word wrap, no on-screen justification
Screen Display Reformatting: Constant and automatic
Formatting Text for Printing: At print time
Text Orientation: Document
Screen Mode: Graphics
WYSIWYG: No
Edit Files Larger Than Memory: Yes
Uses Function Keys: Not applicable
Key Template or Labels: Yes
Product Includes: Manual, disks, quick reference card, keyboard stickers
Number of Disks: 4

- ### INSTRUCTIONAL MATERIALS/SOURCES

Manual: 321 pages, typeset, tabbed, indexed, 3-ring binder
Tutorial: Yes, in sheets that accompany manual and in manual.
Quick Reference Card: Yes
Demo Disk Available: No
On-Line Help: Yes
Pop-Up Command Menus: No
SIGs: None
Newsletters: None
Major Reviews: None
Other Learning Aids: None

- ### MULTILINGUAL FEATURES

Video Cards Supported: Standard Apple cards
Specify Different Fonts in Document: Yes
Print Different Fonts: Yes
Display Different Fonts On-Screen: Yes, Hebrew and upper-case English or upper- and lower-case English
and Hebrew, if the ROM chip set is used (see below).
Foreign Fonts Included: Hebrew (consonants only)
RAM-Based Character Generator: Yes
Font Editor: No
Number Characters Per Font: Not known

Maximum Screen Fonts Per Document: 2
Mode Used to Display Nonstandard Characters: Graphics
Edit Right-to-Left: Yes
Display Entire ASCII Character Set: No

- *SPECIAL FEATURES*

Run DOS Commands from Program: Yes
Chain Files for Printing: Yes
Queue Files for Printing: No
Spelling Checker: No
Thesaurus: No
Windows/Split-Screen: No
Columns: Yes
Footnotes: Yes
Bibliography: No
Table of Contexts: No
Indices: Yes
Keyboard Macros: Yes, text and commands
Text Retrieval System: No
Internal Programming Language: No
Other: This is a Hebrew version of Sierra On-Line's Screenwriter II that includes mail merge. By installing a set of ROM character chips in the Apple IIe (not II+ or IIc), Hebrew characters may displayed on-screen with English characters. This version of the program costs an *additional* $110.

- *SUPPORT ETC.*

Warranty: 30 days, media only
Support: Phone and letter
Update Policy: Not known
Other Information: None

2.6.2.3 MINCE Hebrew/English

- *BASIC PRODUCT INFORMATION*

Name of Program: MINCE™ Hebrew/English
Company Name: Davka Corporation
Address: 845 N. Michigan Ave., Suite 843, Chicago, IL 60611
Phones: (800) 621-8227, (312) 944-4070
Technical Support: (800) 621-8227, (312) 944-4070
Price: $370 for graphics version; $395 with ROM character chip for use in MDA; special vocalized version, which includes Greek, available for $425.
Version Reviewed: 2.0
Runs On: IBM PCs and compatibles
Memory Requirements: 128K
Operating System Requirements: DOS 2.0 or greater
Disk Drive Requirements: 1
Copy Protected: No
Possible Backups: Unlimited
Hard Disk Compatible: Yes
Produces ASCII Files: Yes
Produces PostScript Files: No
Drives Laser Printers: No
Drives Typesetters: No
SideKick Compatible: Yes
Mnemonic Commands: No
User Interface: Command-driven
Text Display: Auto word wrap, no on-screen justification
Screen Display Reformatting: Constant and automatic
Formatting Text for Printing: At print time

Text Orientation: Document
Screen Mode: Graphics
WYSIWYG: No
Edit Files Larger Than Memory: Yes
Uses Function Keys: Yes
Key Template or Labels: Yes
Product Includes: Manual, disk, keyboard stickers
Number of Disks: 1

- ● *INSTRUCTIONAL MATERIALS/SOURCES*

Manual: 100 pages, typeset, 3-ring binder, indexed
Tutorial: Yes, in manual
Quick Reference Card: No
Demo Disk Available: No
On-Line Help: Yes
Pop-Up Command Menus: No
SIGs: None
Newsletters: None
Major Reviews: None
Other Learning Aids: None

- ● *MULTILINGUAL FEATURES*

Video Cards Supported: CGA and compatibles (would not work with HGC+)
Specify Different Fonts in Document: Yes
Print Different Fonts: Yes
Display Different Fonts On-Screen: Yes
Foreign Fonts Included: Consonantal Hebrew only, unless a special vocalized version, which includes Greek, is purchased.
RAM-Based Character Generator: Yes
Font Editor: No
Number Characters Per Font: 256
Maximum Screen Fonts Per Document: 1
Mode Used to Display Nonstandard Characters: Graphics, unless a special text-mode version is purchased that includes a special ROM character-generator chip.
Edit Right-to-Left: Yes
Display Entire ASCII Character Set: Yes

- ● *SPECIAL FEATURES*

Run DOS Commands from Program: Yes
Chain Files for Printing: Yes
Queue Files for Printing: No
Spelling Checker: No
Thesaurus: No
Windows/Split-Screen: Yes, maximum of 2 windows
Columns: No
Footnotes: No
Bibliography: No
Table of Contexts: No
Indices: No
Keyboard Macros: Yes
Text Retrieval System: No
Internal Programming Language: No
Other: MINCE (a recursive acronym for MINCE Is Not Complete EMACS) is a subset of FinalWord II. Twelve files may be open at once. MINCE includes mail merge and undelete features, auto-save during edit, and running DOS commands from the within program.

- ● *SUPPORT ETC.*

Warranty: None

Support: Phone and letter
Update Policy: Not known
Other Information: None

2.6.2.4 KEDIT/Semitic

• BASIC PRODUCT INFORMATION

Name of Program: KEDIT/Semitic (2 products: commercial text editor called KEDIT plus freeware Semitic files)
Company Name: Mansfield Software Group, Inc.
Address: P.O. Box 532, Storrs, CT 06268
Phone: (203) 429-8402
Technical Support: (203) 429-8402
Price: KEDIT: $125; Semitic files are free.
Version Reviewed: 3.52 of KEDIT, version 1.0 of the Semitic files
Runs On: IBM PCs and compatibles (with EGA or compatible board and KEDIT 3.52)
Memory Requirements: 192K
Operating System Requirements: DOS 2.0 or greater
Disk Drive Requirements: 1
Copy Protected: No
Possible Backups: Unlimited
Hard Disk Compatible: Yes
Produces ASCII Files: Yes
Produces PostScript Files: No
Drives Laser Printers: No, KEDIT is an editor only and does not include formatting and printing capabilities.
Drives Typesetters: No
SideKick Compatible: Yes
Mnemonic Commands: Yes
User Interface: Command-driven
Text Display: Auto word wrap, no on-screen justification
Screen Display Reformatting: Constant and automatic
Formatting Text for Printing: Must use a separate formatter purchased from another company (e.g., ReadiWriter[162]).
Text Orientation: Depends on formatter
Screen Mode: Text or graphics
WYSIWYG: No
Edit Files Larger Than Memory: No
Uses Function Keys: Yes
Key Template or Labels: No
Product Includes: KEDIT manual, disk, quick reference card, Semitic files, and 9 pages of instruction for those files
Number of Disks: KEDIT: 1; Semitic 1

• INSTRUCTIONAL MATERIALS/SOURCES

Manual: KEDIT: 380 8.5-by-11-inch pages, laser printed, 3-ring binder, indexed, not tabbed; Semitic: nine 8.5-by-11-inch pages.
Tutorial: KEDIT: Yes, in manual; Semitic: No
Quick Reference Card: KEDIT: Yes; Semitic: No
Demo Disk Available: No
On-Line Help: No
Pop-Up Command Menus: No
SIGs: None
Newsletters: None
Major Reviews: None
Other Learning Aids: None

---

162. Available from ReadyWare Systems, Inc., P.O. Box 515, Portage, MI 49081; (616) 327-9172

- ## MULTILINGUAL FEATURES

Video Cards Supported: EGA and compatible cards. The Semitic fonts are designed to work with the EGA.
Specify Different Fonts in Document: Yes
Print Different Fonts: Yes
Display Different Fonts On-Screen: Yes, with the EGA card up to 512 unique characters may be displayed in a document.
Foreign Fonts Included: Hebrew (consonants only), Arabic
RAM-Based Character Generator: Yes, if the EGA card is used.
Font Editor: No
Number Characters Per Font: Not known
Maximum Screen Fonts Per Document: 1 active font of up to 512 unique characters with the EGA[163]
Mode Used to Display Nonstandard Characters: Text
Edit Right-to-Left: Yes
Display Entire ASCII Character Set: No

- ## SPECIAL FEATURES

Run DOS Commands from Program: Yes
Chain Files for Printing: Depends on formatter.
Queue Files for Printing: Depends on formatter.
Spelling Checker: No
Thesaurus: No
Windows/Split-Screen: Yes, maximum of 8
Columns: Depends on formatter.
Footnotes: Depends on formatter.
Bibliography: Depends on formatter.
Table of Contexts: Depends on formatter.
Indices: Depends on formatter.
Keyboard Macros: Yes, commands and text, if Personal REXX, Mansfield Software's macro program, is used with KEDIT.
Text Retrieval System: No
Internal Programming Language: No
Other: KEDIT is Mansfield Software's text editor; the Semitic fonts and programs are provided free of charge through Mansfield Software by another source.

- ## SUPPORT ETC.

Warranty: KEDIT: 3 months, program and media; Semitic files: none
Support: KEDIT: phone and letter; Semitic files: problems passed on to author with no guarantee of response.
Update Policy: Not known
Other Information: None

2.6.2.5 WordStar/Hebrew

- ## BASIC PRODUCT INFORMATION

Name of Program: WordStar/Hebrew
Company Name: Business Automation
Address: P.O. Box 39514 Ramat Aviv, Israel 61394
Phone: Not known
Technical Support: Not known
Price: $490

---

163. KEDIT/Semitic is a two-part package: (1) KEDIT, a general-purpose text editor, and (2) the Semitic files, which tailor KEDIT to work with Hebrew and Arabic characters. The Semitic files are distributed by the Mansfield Software Group under the authorization of a KEDIT customer who does not guarantee any support and who will stay anonymous. The Semitic files were developed at Princeton University with the Duke Language Toolkit.

Version Reviewed: Not reviewed.
Runs On: IBM PCs and compatibles, Apple IIs, TRS 80s, Kaypros, and Digitals
Memory Requirements: Not known
Operating System Requirements: Depends on computer system
Comment: This is a consonants-only Hebrew version of Micropro Corporation's WordStar 3.0 that uses replacement ROM character-chips.

2.6.2.6 Hebrew Writer

- *BASIC PRODUCT INFORMATION*

Name of Program: Hebrew Writer
Company Name: Davka Corporation
Address: 845 N. Michigan Ave., Suite 843, Chicago, IL 60611
Phones: (800) 621-8227, (312) 944-4070
Technical Support: (800) 621-8227, (312) 944-4070
Price: $75; $105 with Zoom Grafix Package
Version Reviewed: 1.7
Runs On: Apple IIs
Memory Requirements: 48K
Operating System Requirements: Apple DOS 3.3
Disk Drive Requirements: 1
Copy Protected: No
Possible Backups: Unlimited
Hard Disk Compatible: Yes
Produces ASCII Files: Not known
Produces PostScript Files: No
Drives Laser Printers: No, works with Epson MX-80 and with most dot-matrix printers that can operate in graphics mode.
Drives Typesetters: No
SideKick Compatible: Not applicable
Mnemonic Commands: No
User Interface: Command-driven
Text Display: Auto word wrap, no on-screen justification
Screen Display Reformatting: Constant and automatic
Formatting Text for Printing: At print time
Text Orientation: Page
Screen Mode: Graphics
WYSIWYG: Yes
Edit Files Larger Than Memory: No
Uses Function Keys: Not applicable
Key Template or Labels: Yes
Product Includes: Manual, disk, keyboard stickers
Number of Disks: 1

- *INSTRUCTIONAL MATERIALS/SOURCES*

Manual: 19 8.5-by-11-inch pages, photocopied, not indexed, stapled
Tutorial: Yes, in manual
Quick Reference Card: No
Demo Disk Available: No
On-Line Help: No
Pop-Up Command Menus: No
SIGs: None
Newsletters: None
Major Reviews: None
Other Learning Aids: None

- *MULTILINGUAL FEATURES*

Video Cards Supported: Standard Apple cards

Specify Different Fonts in Document: Yes
Print Different Fonts: Yes, using a separate screen output program, such as Phoenix Software's Zoom Grafix
Display Different Fonts On-Screen: Yes
Foreign Fonts Included: Hebrew (with and without vowels)
RAM-Based Character Generator: Yes
Font Editor: No
Number Characters Per Font: Not known
Maximum Screen Fonts Per Document: Not known
Mode Used to Display Nonstandard Characters: Graphics
Edit Right-to-Left: Yes
Display Entire ASCII Character Set: No

- *SPECIAL FEATURES*

Run DOS Commands from Program: No
Chain Files for Printing: No
Queue Files for Printing: No
Spelling Checker: No
Thesaurus: No
Windows/Split-Screen: No
Columns: No
Footnotes: No
Bibliography: No
Table of Contexts: No
Indices: No
Keyboard Macros: No
Text Retrieval System: No
Internal Programming Language: No
Other: This is a no-frills program that allows Hebrew to be displayed with and without vowels. Documents are restricted to about 14 pages.

- *SUPPORT ETC.*

Warranty: None
Support: Phone and letter
Update Policy: Not known
Other Information: None

2.6.2.7 Achbar/MouseWrite

- *BASIC PRODUCT INFORMATION*

Name of Program: Achbar/MouseWrite
Company Name: Davka Corporation
Address: 845 N. Michigan Ave., Suite 843, Chicago, IL 60611
Phones: (800) 621-8227, (312) 944-4070
Technical Support: (800) 621-8227, (312) 944-4070
Price: $249.95
Version Reviewed: 2.03
Runs On: Macintosh
Memory Requirements: 512K
Operating System Requirements: Macintosh
Disk Drive Requirements: 1
Copy Protected: Yes, distribution disk must be used as a software key.
Possible Backups: Unlimited
Hard Disk Compatible: Yes
Produces ASCII Files: Yes
Produces PostScript Files: Not known
Drives Laser Printers: Yes, which ones not known; 4 Hebrew laser fonts are available from Davka for $99.
Drives Typesetters: No
SideKick Compatible: No

Mnemonic Commands: Not applicable
User Interface: Menu-driven
Text Display: Graphics
Screen Display Reformatting: Constant and automatic
Formatting Text for Printing: Not known
Text Orientation: Not known
Screen Mode: Graphics
WYSIWYG: Yes
Edit Files Larger Than Memory: Not known
Uses Function Keys: Not applicable
Key Template or Labels: Yes
Product Includes: Manual, disk, keyboard stickers
Number of Disks: 1

- *INSTRUCTIONAL MATERIALS/SOURCES*

Manual: 35 8.5-by-11-inch pages, not tabbed, not indexed
Tutorial: No
Quick Reference Card: No
Demo Disk Available: No
On-Line Help: No
Pop-Up Command Menus: Yes
SIGs: None
Newsletters: None
Major Reviews: *MacWorld* (November 1986)
Other Learning Aids: None

- *MULTILINGUAL FEATURES*

Video Cards Supported: Not applicable
Specify Different Fonts in Document: Yes
Print Different Fonts: Yes
Display Different Fonts On-Screen: Yes

Foreign Fonts Included: Five consonants-only Hebrew fonts[164]
RAM-Based Character Generator: Yes
Font Editor: No
Number Characters Per Font: Not known
Maximum Screen Fonts Per Document: Not known
Mode Used to Display Nonstandard Characters: Graphics
Edit Right-to-Left: Yes
Display Entire ASCII Character Set: No

- *SPECIAL FEATURES*

Run DOS Commands from Program: No
Chain Files for Printing: No
Queue Files for Printing: No
Spelling Checker: No
Thesaurus: No
Windows/Split-Screen: No
Columns: No
Footnotes: No
Bibliography: No
Table of Contexts: No
Indices: No
Keyboard Macros: No
Text Retrieval System: No
Internal Programming Language: No
Other: Mail merge

---

164. By using SuperHebrew from Linguists' Software (see below), Achbar can display consonants and vowels. Davka also sells two vocalized Hebrew fonts ($25 for the pair).

- SUPPORT ETC.

Warranty: 90 days, media only
Support: Not known
Update Policy: Not known
Other Information: None

2.6.2.8 Hebrew II Plus

- BASIC PRODUCT INFORMATION

Name of Program: Hebrew II Plus
Company Name: Anthro Digital, Inc.
Address: P.O. Box 1385, 103 Bartlett Ave., Pittsfield, MA 01202
Phone: (413) 448-8278
Technical Support: (413) 448-8278
Price: $49.95
Version Reviewed: 4.0
Runs On: Apple IIs
Memory Requirements: 48K
Operating System Requirements: Apple DOS 3.3
Disk Drive Requirements: 1
Copy Protected: No
Possible Backups: Unlimited
Hard Disk Compatible: Not known
Produces ASCII Files: Not known
Produces PostScript Files: No
Drives Laser Printers: No
Drives Typesetters: No
SideKick Compatible: Not applicable
Mnemonic Commands: No
User Interface: Menu-driven
Text Display: Graphics
Screen Display Reformatting: Constant and automatic
Formatting Text for Printing: At print time
Text Orientation: Page
Screen Mode: Graphics
WYSIWYG: Yes
Edit Files Larger Than Memory: Not known
Uses Function Keys: Not applicable
Key Template or Labels: Yes
Product Includes: Disk, manual, keyboard stickers
Number of Disks: 1

- INSTRUCTIONAL MATERIALS/SOURCES

Manual: 9 8.5-by-11-inch pages, photocopied, not tabbed, not indexed
Tutorial: No
Quick Reference Card: No
Demo Disk Available: No
On-Line Help: No
Pop-Up Command Menus: Yes
SIGs: None
Newsletters: None
Major Reviews: None
Other Learning Aids: None

- MULTILINGUAL FEATURES

Video Cards Supported: Standard Apple cards
Specify Different Fonts in Document: Yes

Print Different Fonts: Yes
Display Different Fonts On-Screen: Yes
Foreign Fonts Included: Hebrew (with vowels)
RAM-Based Character Generator: Yes
Font Editor: No
Number Characters Per Font: Not known
Maximum Screen Fonts Per Document: Not known
Mode Used to Display Nonstandard Characters: Graphics
Edit Right-to-Left: Yes
Display Entire ASCII Character Set: No

- *SPECIAL FEATURES*

Run DOS Commands from Program: No
Chain Files for Printing: No
Queue Files for Printing: No
Spelling Checker: No
Thesaurus: No
Windows/Split-Screen: No
Columns: No
Footnotes: No
Bibliography: No
Table of Contexts: No
Indices: No
Keyboard Macros: No
Text Retrieval System: No
Internal Programming Language: No
Other: None

- *SUPPORT ETC.*

Warranty: None
Support: None
Update Policy: None
Other Information: None

2.6.3 Single Foreign Languages—Arabic

Some products already discussed in this chapter enable users to display and print Arabic.[165] Those products are (1) Multi-Lingual Scribe, (2) KEDIT/Semitic, (3) WorldWriter, (4) INTEX Software Systems (see above under WorldMaster™), (5) the Graphics Toolbox for Languages, (6) Gutenberg Sr., (7) the FonTableaux board and similar boards (e.g., the EGA) that accept downloaded character sets, and (8) various microcomputer implementations of TEX.

2.6.3.1 ARABRITE

- *BASIC PRODUCT INFORMATION*

Name of Program: ARABRITE
Company Name: Gulf Data, Inc.
Address: 9310 Deering Ave., Chatsworth, CA 91311
Phone: (818) 886-9898
Technical Support: (818) 998-0922
Price: $1,125 (without ARABDOS 2.0), $1,495 (with ARABDOS 2.0)
Version Reviewed: Not able to review.
Runs On: IBM PCs and compatibles

---

165. See Musa, "System," 288–93.

Memory Requirements: 256K
Operating System Requirements: DOS 2.0 or greater
Disk Drive Requirements: 2
Copy Protected: Not known
Possible Backups: Not known
Hard Disk Compatible: Yes
Produces ASCII Files: Not known
Produces PostScript Files: Not known
Drives Laser Printers: Not known
Drives Typesetters: No
SideKick Compatible: Not known
Mnemonic Commands: Not known
User Interface: Command-driven
Text Display: Auto word wrap, on-screen justification
Screen Display Reformatting: Constant and automatic
Formatting Text for Printing: At print time
Text Orientation: Document
Screen Mode: Not known
WYSIWYG: Yes, mostly
Edit Files Larger Than Memory: Not known
Uses Function Keys: Not known
Key Template or Labels: Yes
Product Includes: Disks, manual, special board (not required for all systems)
Number of Disks: Not known

- ## INSTRUCTIONAL MATERIALS/SOURCES

Manual: Not able to see.
Tutorial: Not known
Quick Reference Card: Not known
Demo Disk Available: No
On-Line Help: Yes
Pop-Up Command Menus: Yes
SIGs: None
Newsletters: None
Major Reviews: None
Other Learning Aids: None

- ## MULTILINGUAL FEATURES

Video Cards Supported: Not known
Specify Different Fonts in Document: Yes
Print Different Fonts: Yes
Display Different Fonts On-Screen: Yes
Foreign Fonts Included: Arabic
RAM-Based Character Generator: Not known
Font Editor: No
Number Characters Per Font: Not known
Maximum Screen Fonts Per Document: Not known
Mode Used to Display Nonstandard Characters: Not known
Edit Right-to-Left: Yes
Display Entire ASCII Character Set: Not known

- ## SPECIAL FEATURES

Run DOS Commands from Program: Not known
Chain Files for Printing: Not known
Queue Files for Printing: Not known
Spelling Checker: No
Thesaurus: No
Windows/Split-Screen: Yes, maximum of 2
Columns: Yes

Footnotes: No
Bibliography: No
Table of Contexts: No
Indices: No
Keyboard Macros: Yes, text only
Text Retrieval System: No
Internal Programming Language: No
Other: None

- *SUPPORT ETC.*

Warranty: Not known
Support: Not known
Update Policy: Not known
Other Information: None

2.6.3.2 AlKaatib

- *BASIC PRODUCT INFORMATION*

Name of Program: AlKaatib™
Company Name: Arabic Software Associates
Address: 240 E. Center St., Provo, UT 84601
Phone: (801) 377-4558
Technical Support: (801) 377-4558
Price: $99; laser font support is an additional $199.
Version Reviewed: Not able to review.
Runs On: Macintosh
Memory Requirements: Not known
Operating System Requirements: Macintosh
Disk Drive Requirements: 1
Copy Protected: Not known
Possible Backups: Not known
Hard Disk Compatible: Not known
Produces ASCII Files: Not known
Produces PostScript Files: Not known
Drives Laser Printers: Yes, LaserWriter; laser font support is $199.
Drives Typesetters: No
SideKick Compatible: Not applicable
Mnemonic Commands: Not applicable
User Interface: Menu-driven
Text Display: Graphics
Screen Display Reformatting: Constant and automatic
Formatting Text for Printing: At print time
Text Orientation: Not known
Screen Mode: Graphics
WYSIWYG: Yes
Edit Files Larger Than Memory: Not known
Uses Function Keys: Not applicable
Key Template or Labels: Yes, keyboard caps
Product Includes: Disk, manual, and keyboard caps
Number of Disks: Not known

- *INSTRUCTIONAL MATERIALS/SOURCES*

Manual: Not able to see.
Tutorial: Not known
Quick Reference Card: Not known
Demo Disk Available: Yes, $7
On-Line Help: Not known
Pop-Up Command Menus: Yes

SIGs: None
Newsletters: *Shubbaak AlKaatib*
Major Reviews: None
Other Learning Aids: None

• MULTILINGUAL FEATURES

Video Cards Supported: Not applicable
Specify Different Fonts in Document: Yes
Print Different Fonts: Yes
Display Different Fonts On-Screen: Yes
Foreign Fonts Included: Arabic (with vowels)
RAM-Based Character Generator: Yes
Font Editor: No
Number Characters Per Font: Not known
Maximum Screen Fonts Per Document: Not known
Mode Used to Display Nonstandard Characters: Graphics
Edit Right-to-Left: Yes
Display Entire ASCII Character Set: No

• SPECIAL FEATURES

Run DOS Commands from Program: No
Chain Files for Printing: No
Queue Files for Printing: No
Spelling Checker: No
Thesaurus: No
Windows/Split-Screen: No
Columns: No
Footnotes: No
Bibliography: No
Table of Contexts: No
Indices: No
Keyboard Macros: No
Text Retrieval System: No
Internal Programming Language: No
Other: Automatically forms ligatures and automatically determines the proper shapes of characters from their contexts.

• SUPPORT ETC.

Warranty: Not known
Support: Not known
Update Policy: Not known
Other Information: None

2.6.3.3 *Alifba-Word*

• BASIC PRODUCT INFORMATION

Name of Program: Alifba-Word
Company Name: Alis-Soft, Inc.
Address: 901 Tennessee St., San Francisco, CA 94107
Phone: (415) 285-4891
Technical Support: (415) 285-4891
Price: $1,290
Version Reviewed: Not able to review.
Runs On: IBM PCs and compatibles
Comments: This is a modified version of the Spellbinder word processing program that includes on-screen math, two-column printing, and automatic determination of character shape based on context.

| | PROGRAMS WITH MULTILINGUAL CAPABILITIES | | | | | | | | | | DEDICATED MULTILINGUAL PROGRAMS | | | | | | | | | | | | |
| | Academic | | | | | Business | | Scientific | | | Multiple Languages | | | | | | | | | | | | |
FEATURES	FW	XY	NB	PCT	AF	WP	MW	T³	BM	ISC	PG	GS	GE	GTL	DLT	MLS	CW	PW	AL	GF	WW	WM	VA
BASIC FACTS																							
Price	395	445	495	249	500	495	450	595	795	—	425	460	?	200	Free	350	100	50	245	399	450	475	£95
Runs On	I	I	I	I,M	I	I,M,A	I,A	I	I	—	I	A	CP	I	I	I	I	I	I	I	I	I	I
Memory (in K)	256	256	256	512	320	256	256	640	256	—	320	64	128	256	256	512	256	128	192	512	128	256	256
Disk Drives	2	1	2	2	2	2	2	2	2	—	2	1	2	1	1	1	1	1	1	2	2	2	2
User Interface	C,M	C	C,M	C	C	M	M	M	M	C	C,M	C	C	C	C	C,M	C,M	C,M	M	C,M	C	C	M
WYSIWYG	○	●	●	●	○	●	●	●	○	●	○	○	●	●	●	○	○	○	○	○	○	●	●
MULTILINGUAL FEATURES																							
Foreign Fonts Included	○	○	○	○	●	○	○	●	●	●	●	●	●	●	●	●	●	○	●	●	●	●	●
RAM-Based Character Generator	○	○	○	○	●	○	○	●	●	○	●	●	●	●	●	●	○	○	●	○	●	●	●
Font Editor	○	○	○	○	○	○	○	●	●	○	●	●	●	●	●	●	●	○	●	○	○	●	●
Characters/Font	256	256	256	256	256	256	256	128	?	2048	128	94	256	256	256	243	94	224	123	256	256	256	128
Maximum Screen Fonts/Document	1	1	2	2	2	1	1	16	5	2	2	21	2	4	4	5	20	1	3	9	1	1	5
Edit Right to Left	○	○	●	○	○	○	○	○	○	●	○	●	●	●	●	●	○	○	●	○	●	●	○
SPECIAL FEATURES																							
Windows	●	●	●	○	●	●	●	○	○	○	○	●	●	●	●	○	○	○	○	○	○	○	○
Columns	●	●	●	●	●	●	●	○	○	?	○	●	●	○	○	●	○	○	○	○	●	●	○
Footnotes	●	●	●	●	●	●	●	●	●	●	●	●	●	○	○	●	○	○	●	○	○	●	○
Bibliography	●	○	●	●	○	○	○	○	○	○	○	○	○	○	○	○	○	○	●	○	○	○	○
Table of Contents	●	●	●	●	●	●	○	●	○	○	○	○	○	○	○	○	○	○	○	○	○	○	○
Indices	●	●	●	●	●	●	●	○	○	?	○	○	○	○	○	○	○	○	○	○	○	○	○

Table 2.2: Word processor comparisons. I = IBM, A = Apple II, M = Macintosh, C = command-driven, M = menu-driven, CP = CP/M, FW = FinalWord II, XY = XyWrite III Plus, NB = Nota Bene, PCT = PCTEX, AF = AcademicFont, WP = WordPerfect 4.1, MW = Microsoft Word 3.0, T³ = T³, BM = Brit Multitex, ISC = Ibycus Scholarly Computer, PG = Proofwriter Graphics, GS = Gutenberg Sr., GE = GRAMEDIT, GTL = Graphics Toolbox for Languages, DLT = Duke Language Toolkit, MLS = Multi-Lingual-Scribe, CW = ChiWriter, PW = PowerWriter, AL = Alexander, GF = Grafeas, WW = WorldWriter, WM = WordMill, VA = VuWriter Arts.

2.7 Font and Printer Utilities

In this section we will look at three related categories of font and printer utilities: (1) font programs that use formatting codes and that include printer drivers, (2) font editors, and (3) font sets for various printers.

2.7.1 Print Processors

Several programs allow users to format and print text in a wide array of fonts (e.g., Greek and Hebrew) not normally included with word processing programs.[166] For lack of a better name, I will call these programs "print processors" or "printer processors" because they give users typographic control over word processing files. These programs were developed to provide letter quality results from inexpensive dot-matrix printers[167] and to give users greater control over fonts and typography.

Some print processors display information in a WYSIWYG graphics mode, allow users to enter, edit, and print text, and allow text and graphics to be mixed in a document. Thus this type of print processor functions as a rudimentary word processing or desktop publishing program,[168] though the fact that such programs are specially designed around typographic concerns causes them to be categorized as print processors.

Most print processors, however, display information in text mode, require that formatting codes be embedded into text prepared with a word processor or text editor, do not allow text to be entered or edited, and do not allow graphics and text to be mixed in a document.[169] Such print processors function as postprocessors; they translate coded text into the printed output specified by the codes; they replace the formatting and printing functions of word processing programs.[170] In addition to having different user interfaces, print processors differ in terms of the printers and the fonts (typestyles and type sizes) they support.

Some print processors are capable of controlling the print heads on certain dot-matrix printers, operated in graphics mode, in vertical increments as small as 1/216 of an inch and in horizontal increments as small as 1/120 of an inch. By making multiple passes over each line of text and by controlling the print head in such fine increments, print processors are able to create truly astonishing, high-resolution results from those printers, often producing copy that has a near-typeset look to it (at least it looks a *lot* better than regular dot-matrix output).

The main advantage of print processors is that they allow text to be printed in a wide variety of fonts. The main disadvantage of print processors is that they usurp the formatting and printing capabilities of word processing programs, which in many cases are more powerful than those offered by the print processors.[171] A second disadvantage of print processors is speed, or rather the lack of it! Because print processors generally use bit-mapped fonts and operate printers in graphics mode, sometimes making up to

---

166. Remember, a font is a specific size of a specific style of type.

167. Most of these programs now support laser printers.

168. See "Fontasy Revealed," *Personal Publishing* (February 1986): 32–35, on this topic.

169. Print processors that work this way are not a type of word processing program because they do not allow text to be entered, manipulated, and edited.

170. Some print processors (e.g., Fancy Word from SoftCraft—see below) have been designed to work *with*, not *in place of*, the formatting and printing functions of word processing programs.

171. Although print processors can produce remarkable results—allowing users to print in Greek, Hebrew, and other alphabets—they typically do not support footnotes, indices, bidirectional cross referencing, and other formatting and printing functions that scholars may need. An exception to this is Fancy Word, from SoftCraft, which works *with*, rather than *in place of*, Microsoft Word's formatting and printing functions.

six printing passes per line of text, some printers take up to fifteen minutes to print a single page!

Because I assume that most readers of this book are not going to abandon the formatting and printing functions of their word processing programs and may only occasionally need to use a print processor, I will only list the basic facts about these programs. For more information see Alfred Poor, "Printer Utilities," *PC Magazine* (September 17, 1985): 219–40.[172]

2.7.1.1 Fancy Font

- ### BASIC PRODUCT INFORMATION

Name of Program: Fancy Font
Company Name: SoftCraft, Inc.
Address: 11 N. Carroll St., Suite 500, Madison, WI 53703
Phones: (800) 351-0500, (608) 257-3300
Price: $180; $90 for business font pack; $180 for Laser Fonts version of Fancy Font; $30 for kern utility; $15 for Dispfont utility; $15 for Modfont utility; $200 for stand-alone advanced Font Editor using graphics/mouse; many, many fonts are available for $15 per disk.
Runs On: IBM PCs and compatibles and various CP/M systems (Kaypro, Apple, Osborne, and 8-inch CP/M)
Memory Requirements: MS/IBM-DOS: 192K; CP/M 2.2: 64K
Operating System Requirements: MS/IBM-DOS 2.0 or greater; CP/M 2.2
Disk Drive Requirements: 2
Copy Protected: No
Demo Disk Available: Yes, $10
Laser Printers Supported: LaserJet, LaserJet Plus, Canon LBP8-A1 and LBP8-A2
Dot-Matrix Printers Supported: Epson EX, RX, JX, LX, MX-80, MX (with Graftrax), LQ-1500, Toshiba P351, Okidata 2.1 (Plug 'n Play version), IBM Graphics, NEC P2, P3, CP2
Font Editor: Yes (included in basic package); the advanced and very sophisticated SoftCraft Font Editor is available for $200.
Fonts Included: 13 in various sizes, including Roman, Old English, Script, Sans Serif, Special, and the Hershey Character Database (approximately 1,600 characters from many alphabets and typestyles)
Greek and Hebrew Fonts Available: Greek (with all vowels and diacritical marks) and Hebrew (with vowels)
Type Sizes Supported: 4 to 72 points
Maximum Characters Per Font: 256
Maximum Fonts Per File: 99 Fancy Fonts and 99 normal printer fonts in IBM version 3.0 (due to be released in 1987), 10 Fancy Fonts and 10 normal printer fonts on CP/M systems
Screen Mode: Text
Print Mode: Graphics
Proportional Spacing: Yes
Micro-Justification: Yes
Allows Text To Be Entered and Edited: No
Allows Graphics and Text To Be Mixed: Yes (in version 3.0)
Can Show Line/Page Breaks: Yes, in print preview mode
Uses Embedded Formatting Codes: Yes
Works with Tall Tree System's J-Laser Board: Yes[173]

---

172. I am not including information about Printer Boss™ (Connecticut Software Systems Corp., 30 Wilson Ave., Rowayton, CT 06853; (800) 321-0409; $139) and Printworks (SoftStyle™, Hawaii Kai Office Bldg., Suite 205, 7192 Kalanianaole Hwy., Honolulu, HI 96825; (808) 396-6368; $69.95).

173. Tall Tree System's J-Laser board is a special memory board that allows laser printers driven by older Canon engines (e.g., LaserJet, Canon A1) to print a full page of graphics at 300 dpi. Contact Tall Tree Systems, 1120 San Antonio Rd., Palo Alto, CA 94303; (415) 964-1980, for more information.

Reviews: Richard H. Zander, "Fancy Printing with Fancy Font," *PC Magazine* (January 24, 1984): 299–305; Jim Chposky, "Software to Turn Plain Printers Into Typesetters," *LIST* (August 1984); Pat McKeague, "Fancy Font Typesetting Package," *InfoWorld* (May 2, 1983); Paul E. Hoffman, "Fancy Font," *BYTE* (October 1983); Bryan Pfaffenberger, "The Scholar's Software Library—Fancy Font 2," *Research in Word Processing Newsletter* 4 (March 1986): 11–14; Glenn Hart, "Harnessing the Laser Printer," *PC Magazine* (February 11, 1986): 214–15; "Fancy Word," *Personal Publishing* (October 1985): 40–41; Arnold M. Kuzmack, "Using Fancy Font for Hebrew and Yiddish," *The Hebrew Users' Group Newsletter* (Sept/Oct 1985): 1–5.

Other: SoftCraft's related product Fancy Word is designed to work with Microsoft Word. Fancy Word makes many more fonts available for Microsoft Word users and prints Word documents in greater resolution on dot-matrix printers than is otherwise possible. Fancy Word allows Microsoft Word users to use all of Word's features except double underline and Print Merge and does not require inserting special codes. Price: $140, includes about 25 fonts in various sizes.

2.7.1.2 *Lettrix*

● *BASIC PRODUCT INFORMATION*

Name of Program: Lettrix
Company Name: Hammerlab
Address: 5700 Arlington Ave., Riverdale, NY 10471
Phone: (800) 351-4500
Price: $98.50
Runs On: IBM PCs and compatibles
Memory Requirements: 128K
Operating System Requirements: DOS 2.0 or greater
Disk Drive Requirements: 1
Copy Protected: Yes
Demo Disk Available: No
Laser Printers Supported: None
Dot-Matrix Printers Supported: Epson FX, LX, JX, MX, RX, Okidata (IBM version) 84/92/93/192/193, Panasonic (any model), IBM Graphics and Proprinter
Font Editor: Yes
Fonts Included: 21 (Courier, Gothic, Orator, Prestige, Old English, Park Avenue, ABC Block, and others, including Hebrew—see below)
Greek and Hebrew Fonts Available: Yes, they are included. Greek has all vowels and diacritical marks but no iota subscript; Hebrew lacks vowels.
Type Sizes Supported: Depends on printer.
Maximum Characters Per Font: 256
Maximum Fonts Per File: 7
Screen Mode: Text
Print Mode: Graphics
Proportional Spacing: Yes
Micro-Justification: Yes
Allows Text To Be Entered and Edited: No
Allows Graphics and Text To Be Mixed: No
Can Show Line/Page Breaks: No
Uses Embedded Formatting Codes: Yes
Works with Tall Tree System's J-Laser Board: No
Reviews: Alan R. Miller, "Lettrix," *BYTE* (May 1986): 299–304.
Other: Lettrix is a pop-up, menu-driven, memory-resident utility. Lettrix intercepts characters sent to the printer from application programs and substitutes user-specified characters for them. Thus Lettrix neither replaces nor negates formatting commands.

2.7.1.3 *Fontasy*

● *BASIC PRODUCT INFORMATION*

Name of Program: Fontasy
Company Name: Prosoft

Address: 7248 Bellaire Ave., P.O. Box 560, N. Hollywood, CA 91603
Phone: (818) 765-4444
Price: $69.95; $24.95 per font disk (8-12 fonts per disk); $29.95 per clip art disk (100 pictures per disk)
Runs On: IBM PCs and compatibles
Memory Requirements: 256K (partial-page images), 448K (full-page images)
Operating System Requirements: DOS 2.0 or greater
Disk Drive Requirements: 1
Copy Protected: No
Demo Disk Available: No
Laser Printers Supported: LaserJet, LaserJet Plus, Ricoh Laser
Dot-Matrix Printers Supported: Epson FX, LX, RX, LQ-1500, IBM Proprinter, IBM Graphics, Toshiba
P351, P1340, P1351, Thinkjet, Microline 92, 92, 192, 193, Gemini 10X, 15X, Radio Shack DMP series
Font Editor: Yes
Fonts Included: 28
Greek and Hebrew Fonts Available: Yes, but both lack vowels, accents, and diacritical marks. Fontasy
operates left-to-right only.
Type Sizes Supported: 4–48 points on 9-pin dot matrix; most fonts are in one size only.
Maximum Characters Per Font: 94
Maximum Fonts Per File: Unlimited
Screen Mode: Graphics
Print Mode: Graphics
Proportional Spacing: Yes
Micro-Justification: Yes
Allows Text To Be Entered and Edited: Yes
Allows Graphics and Text To Be Mixed: Yes
Can Show Line/Page Breaks: Yes
Uses Embedded Formatting Codes: No
Works with Tall Tree System's J-Laser Board: No
Reviews: "Fontasy Revealed," *Personal Publishing* (February 1986): 32–35; "Fontastic Output on a Budget,"
PC Magazine (May 13, 1986): 341.
Other: Requires graphics board (MDA, CGA, or HGC). This is a WYSIWYG program that operates in
graphics mode and that supports kerning, sideways printing, mice, conditional hyphenation, columns,
and has on-line help and menus. Over 300 fonts and 600 pieces of clip art are available.

2.7.1.4 Fontrix

• BASIC PRODUCT INFORMATION

Name of Program: Fontrix™
Company Name: Data Transforms, Inc.
Address: 616 Washington St., Denver, CO 80203
Phone: (303) 832-1501
Price: IBM: $155; Apple: $95; $25 per Fontpak character set (10 or more fonts per set); Printrix (batch
typesetting program) is $165.
Runs On: IBM PCs and compatibles and on Apple IIs
Memory Requirements: IBM: 512K (for version 2.8); Apple: 48K
Operating System Requirements: IBM: DOS 2.0 or greater; Apple: DOS 3.3
Disk Drive Requirements: 1
Copy Protected: No
Demo Disk Available: No
Laser Printers Supported: IBM: LaserJet, LaserJet Plus, QuadLaser, Kyocera F1010; Apple: LaserJet,
Kyocera F1010, Laser Image 2000
Dot-Matrix Printers Supported: ImageWriter, Epson FX-80, FX-100, RX-80, MX-80, MX-100, LQ-1500,
NEC, Okidata, Toshiba, and over 60 others
Font Editor: Yes
Fonts Included: 11
Greek and Hebrew Fonts Available: Yes, but no vowels, accents, or diacritical marks are available.
Type Sizes Supported: IBM version: 3–24 points; Apple version: 3–12 points
Maximum Characters Per Font: 94
Maximum Fonts Per File: Unlimited
Screen Mode: Graphics
Print Mode: Graphics

Proportional Spacing: Yes
Micro-Justification: IBM: Yes (version 2.8); Apple: No
Allows Text To Be Entered and Edited: Yes
Allows Graphics and Text To Be Mixed: Yes
Can Show Line/Page Breaks: Line breaks yes, page breaks no
Uses Embedded Formatting Codes: IBM: Yes; Apple: No
Works with Tall Tree System's J-Laser Board: Yes
Reviews: Henry F. Beechhold, "Fontrix," *InfoWorld* (January 21, 1985): 41–43.
Other: Requires graphics board; menu-driven; help screens. Supports mice. Up to nine fonts in memory at one time. Supports up to three columns.

2.7.1.5 *LePrint 2.0*

- *BASIC PRODUCT INFORMATION*

Name of Program: LePrint™ 2.0
Company Name: LeBaugh Software Corp.
Address: 10824 Old Mill Rd., Suite 6, Omaha, NB 68154
Phones: (800) 532-2844, (402) 334-4820
Price: $175 with 5 typefaces; $325 with 16 typefaces; additional typefaces $19 each; $79 for laser support
Runs On: IBM PCs and compatibles
Memory Requirements: 384K
Operating System Requirements: DOS 2.0 or greater
Disk Drive Requirements: 1, hard disk recommended
Copy Protected: No
Demo Disk Available: No
Laser Printers Supported: LaserJet, LaserJet Plus, Canon LBP8-A1, Corona LP-300, TurboLaser, Quad-Laser, BLASER printers, several QMS laser printers, and others
Dot-Matrix Printers Supported: Epson MX-80 (with Graftrax), MX-100 (with Graftrax), RX-80, RX-100, FX-80, FX-100, FX-80+, FX-100+, FX-85, FX-185, LQ-1500, SQ-2000, IBM Graphics, NEC P2 Pinwriter and P3 Pinwriter, Toshiba P351, P1340, P1350, P1351
Font Editor: No
Fonts Included: 5 (Courier 10, Pica 10, Prestige Elite 12, Times Roman, Times Italic)
Greek and Hebrew Fonts Available: Greek with no accents or diacritical marks, no Hebrew; special characters for Western European languages included.
Type Sizes Supported: 4–72 points (and up to 10 inches)
Maximum Characters Per Font: 256
Maximum Fonts Per File: 150
Screen Mode: Text or graphics
Print Mode: Text or graphics
Proportional Spacing: Yes
Micro-Justification: Yes
Allows Text To Be Entered and Edited: No
Allows Graphics and Text To Be Mixed: Yes
Can Show Line/Page Breaks: Yes
Uses Embedded Formatting Codes: Yes
Works with Tall Tree System's J-Laser Board: Yes
Reviews: Charles Anderson, "Dot Matrix Typesetting With LePrint," *PC Magazine* (June 25, 1985): 303–4; "LePrint," *Personal Publishing* (October 1985): 36–37; "Printing With Style," *PC Products* (July 1986): 25–33.
Other: LePrint is specially designed to work with WordStar but will work with any ASCII text. Multiple copies and ranges of text may be printed. A graphics adapter is recommended and, if used, allows LePrint files to be previewed on-screen. LePrint supports pop-up menus and can draw boxes (with or without shading) and vertical and horizontal rules.

2.7.1.6 *Marvel Print*

- *BASIC PRODUCT INFORMATION*

Name of Program: Marvel Print™

181

Company Name: Marvel Software
Address: 1922 Avenue N, Brooklyn, NY 11230
Phones: (800) 622-4070, (800) 942-7317—Illinois only—(718) 336-2323
Price: $170, $95 with Character Set
Runs On: IBM PCs and compatibles, CP/M-80 systems
Memory Requirements: IBM: 64K, less for CP/M-80 systems
Operating System Requirements: IBM: DOS 2.0 or greater; CP/M: CP/M 2.2
Disk Drive Requirements: 1
Copy Protected: No
Demo Disk Available: Yes, $5
Laser Printers Supported: None
Dot-Matrix Printers Supported: Epson FX-80, FX-100, Okidata 92, 93, 84, 192, 193, Pacemark 2410, Toshiba P351
Font Editor: No
Fonts Included: 11
Greek and Hebrew Fonts Available: Yes, but without vowels, accents, or other diacritical marks; consonantal Arabic also available.
Type Sizes Supported: Depends on printer.
Maximum Characters Per Font: Depends on printer.
Maximum Fonts Per File: 8
Screen Mode: Text
Print Mode: Text
Proportional Spacing: Yes
Micro-Justification: Yes
Allows Text To Be Entered and Edited: No
Allows Graphics and Text To Be Mixed: No
Can Show Line/Page Breaks: No
Uses Embedded Formatting Codes: Yes
Works with Tall Tree System's J-Laser Board: Not known
Reviews: None
Other: Supports columns, backspacing (for creating compound characters, e.g., with diacritical marks), right-to-left printing of Hebrew and Arabic. Character Set package allows users to combine characters from predefined fonts into new fonts.

2.7.1.7 BIBLIO/STAR

- *BASIC PRODUCT INFORMATION*

Name of Program: BIBLIO/STAR™
Company Name: The Computer Linguist™
Address: P.O. Box 70742, Eugene, OR 97401
Phone: (503) 345-1494
Price: $195
Runs On: MS/IBM-DOS: IBM PCs and compatibles; CP/M-80: Kaypro, Osborne; Apple II with CP/M card
Memory Requirements: MS/IBM-DOS: 128K; CP/M: 64K
Operating System Requirements: MS/IBM-DOS 2.0 or greater; CP/M 2.2
Disk Drive Requirements: 1
Copy Protected: No
Demo Disk Available: No
Laser Printers Supported: LaserJet
Dot-Matrix Printers Supported: Epson FX-80, FX-100, MX, RX, LQ-1500, all Toshibas and Okidatas
Font Editor: Available at extra cost (price not known).
Fonts Included: 1 set of 94 characters
Greek and Hebrew Fonts Available: Hebrew (with vowels) and Greek (with accents and most diacritical marks)
Type Sizes Supported: Pica and Elite
Maximum Characters Per Font: 94
Maximum Fonts Per File: 2
Screen Mode: Text or graphics
Print Mode: Text or graphics, depending on printer
Proportional Spacing: Yes
Micro-Justification: Yes

Allows Text To Be Entered and Edited: Yes
Allows Graphics and Text To Be Mixed: No
Can Show Line/Page Breaks: Yes
Uses Embedded Formatting Codes: Yes
Works with Tall Tree System's J-Laser Board: Not known
Reviews: Jim Spickard, "It's Greek to Me!," *Profiles* (June 1985): 54–61; Jack Love, "Pangloss," *The Hebrew Users' Group Newsletter* (January-March 1986): 7–14.
Other: Among other helpful features, BIBLIO/STAR, which works only with WordStar (versions 3.0 and 3.3), allows Hebrew and Arabic to be entered right-to-left. Special character-generator ROMs are available for certain computers so that nonroman characters may be displayed on-screen. Alternatively, with compatible graphics cards (e.g., CGA), BIBLIO/STAR characters can be displayed properly on-screen. TECH/STAR, a related product ($195) that also works only with WordStar, produces up to 94 scientific and mathematical symbols on dot-matrix printers.

FEATURES	FF	LET	FON	FTR	LEP	MP	BS
Price	180	98	70	155	175	170	195
Runs On	I, C	I	I	I, A	I	I, C	I, C
Memory (in K)	192, 64	128	256	512, 48	384	64	128, 64
Demo Disk	●	○	○	○	○	●	○
Font Editor	●	●	●	●	○	○	●
No. Fonts Included	13	21	28	11	5	11	1
Greek	●	●	●	●	●	●	●
Hebrew	●	●	●	●	○	●	●
Type Sizes in Points	4-72	—	4-48	3-12	4-72	—	2
Max. Chars./Font	256	256	94	94	256	256	94
Max. Fonts/File	99	7	Unl.	Unl.	150	8	2
Screen Mode	T	T	G	G	T, G	T	T, G
Print Mode	G	G	G	G	T, G	T	T, G
Proportional Spacing	●	●	●	●	●	●	●
Micro-Justification	●	●	●	●, ○	●	●	●
Enter/Edit Text	○	○	●	●	○	○	●
Mix Text & Graphics	●	○	●	●	●	○	○
Show Line/Page Breaks	●	○	●	●	●	○	●
Uses Embedded Codes	●	●	○	●, ○	●	●	●
Works with J-Laser Board	●	○	○	●	●	○	?
Supports Laser Printers	●	○	●	●	●	○	●

Table 2.3: Comparison of print processors. I = IBM, C = CP/M, A = Apple, T = text, G = graphics, FF = Fancy Font, LET = Lettrix, FON = Fontasy, FTR = Fontrix, LEP = LePrint, MP = Marvel Print, BS = BIBLIO/STAR

2.7.2 Font Editors

In addition to the font editors that come with many of the print processors described above, several companies market stand-alone font editors that may be used to create screen fonts or printer fonts or both for IBM PCs, Macintoshes, CP/M machines, and for a whole host of printers. Font utilities that come with these

183

programs allow users to download fonts to appropriate dot-matrix and laser printers.[174] Unlike the print processors listed above, font editors do not replace the formatting and printing functions of word processors. Rather, they allow fonts to be downloaded into appropriate printers and used by word processing or other application programs.

The three main advantages of font editors are (1) flexibility, (2) speed, and (3) portability. Users may purchase fonts or create their own. Downloaded fonts allow dot-matrix printers to operate at much higher speeds than print processors do. And downloaded fonts may be used with any word processing or other application program, something that is not true with print processors. Furthermore, (4) this approach to displaying fonts does not weaken word processing programs by replacing their formatting and printing functions.

The main disadvantage of font editors is that they do not give users the precise control over printers that print processors do. Downloaded fonts can only be printed at the resolution a given application program's printer driver is capable of obtaining. Furthermore, although using a font editor to edit an existing font is not too difficult, creating a font from scratch takes some practice. To create a new character, for example, users must choose a keyboard character (i.e., *a*, 6, !) to represent the new character and then design the new character and save it. After that process has been carried out for all the characters that are to belong to the new font, the new font may be downloaded to an appropriate printer. As long as the downloaded font is resident in the printer, incoming character codes will be translated into the characters of the active printer font. If the active application program and printer allow different fonts to be used concurrently, then two or more fonts may be mixed in a document and printed correctly.

In addition to the products listed below, Macintosh users may wish to consult David H. Leserman, *MacFonts* (New York: McGraw-Hill, 1985) and William Kemp, "The Global Microcomputer: Multi-Lingual Word Processing with the Macintosh," *Research in Word Processing Newsletter* 4 (November 1986): 2–8.

2.7.2.1 Character Design Kit

- BASIC PRODUCT INFORMATION

Name of Program: Character Design Kit
Company Name: Woodsmith Software
Address: Rt. 3, Box 550A, Nashville, IN 47448
Phone: (812) 988-2137
Price: $44.50; $34.50 for Custom Character Set; $20 each for Greek and Hebrew fonts (apparently, no vowels, accents, or diacritical marks are available with these character sets).
Runs On: IBM PCs and compatibles
Memory Requirements: Not known
Operating System Requirements: DOS 2.0 or greater
Disk Drive Requirements: 1
Copy Protected: Not known
Laser Printers Supported: Not known
Dot-Matrix Printers Supported: Okidata 92, 93, 84 (with character set RAM), 2350, 2410, Star Micronics (Gemini 10X, 15X, Radix, Delta), Epson FX-80, FX-100
Reviews: Jim Spickard, "It's Greek to Me!," *Profiles* (June 1985): 54–61.
Other: None

---

174. See Hugh S. Jackson, "NEWFONT," *PC Magazine* (May 1, 1984): 133–42, for information about a BASIC program for creating a font editor.

2.7.2.2 *Language Kit*

- *BASIC PRODUCT INFORMATION*

Name of Program: Language Kit
Company Name: Woodsmith Software
Address: Rt. 3, Box 550A, Nashville, IN 47448
Phone: (812) 988-2137
Price: $54.50
Runs On: IBM PCs and compatibles
Memory Requirements: Not known
Operating System Requirements: DOS 2.0 or greater
Disk Drive Requirements: 1
Copy Protected: Not known
Laser Printers Supported: Not known
Dot-Matrix Printers Supported: Okidata 92, 93, 192, 193, 292, 293, Star Micronics SG, SR, SD, Gemini
    10X, 15X, Epson FX-80, FX-100, 85, 185, 286, JX80, LQ 800, 1000, 1500, IBM Proprinter, Panasonic
    1092, 1093
Reviews: None
Other: Requires HGC+ or Quadvue Card (see above)

2.7.2.3 *DigiCon Print Package*

- *BASIC PRODUCT INFORMATION*

Name of Program: DigiCon Print Package
Company Name: Digital Concepts, Inc.
Address: 4232 Northern Pike, Monroeville, PA 15146
Phone: (412) 856-1919
Price: $49.95
Runs On: IBM PCs and compatibles
Memory Requirements: 128K
Operating System Requirements: DOS 2.0 or greater
Disk Drive Requirements: 1
Copy Protected: No
Laser Printers Supported: None
Dot-Matrix Printers Supported: Epson, IBM Graphics, and compatibles
Reviews: None
Other: Sideways printing, on-line help, menus, prints "any character size," additional fonts available.

2.7.2.4 *Fontographer*

- *BASIC PRODUCT INFORMATION*

Name of Program: Fontographer
Company Name: Altsys Corp.
Address: 720 Avenue F, Suite 108, Plano, TX 75074
Phone: (214) 424-4888
Price: $395 (includes FONTastic™ font editor—see below)
Runs On: Macintosh 512, Plus, XL
Memory Requirements: 512K
Operating System Requirements: Macintosh
Disk Drive Requirements: 2 or hard disk
Copy Protected: Yes, but can be installed on hard disk.
Laser Printers Supported: LaserWriter, LaserWriter Plus, any PostScript compatible laser printer or output
    device
Dot-Matrix Printers Supported: None

Reviews: *Publish!* (September/October 1986): 66–68; *MacUser* (December 1985): 20; *Macazine* (May 1986): 45–51, 104; *MacUser* (June 1986—desktop publishing insert): 18–24; *The Macintosh Journal* (June/July 1986): 37–39; *Macazine* (August 1986): 89–90; *Personal Publishing* (July 1986): 31–34; *MacWorld* (July 1986): 142–44.

Special Features: Characters are defined with cubic Bezier curves and straight lines. Character outlines are defined with curve points, tangent points, and corner points. Characters may be rotated, flipped, scaled, slanted, cut, pasted, and copied. Inter-character spacing may be previewed and interactively adjusted on-screen. Kerning and zero-width characters are supported. Print samples may be seen at any time during font development. PostScript fonts and bit-mapped fonts may be generated automatically.

Other: Altsys claims that this is the only professional font editor available for the Macintosh. Fontographer creates laser fonts and bit maps to use on-screen. The package includes the FONTastic™ font editor, which can be used to edit the automatically generated bit-map fonts for dot-matrix printers—see below.

2.7.2.5 FONTastic

- ## BASIC PRODUCT INFORMATION

Name of Program: FONTastic™
Company Name: Altsys Corp.
Address: 720 Avenue F, Suite 108, Plano, TX 75074
Phone: (214) 424-4888
Price: $49.95
Runs On: Macintosh
Memory Requirements: 128K
Operating System Requirements: Macintosh
Disk Drive Requirements: 1
Copy Protected: No
Laser Printers Supported: LaserWriter
Dot-Matrix Printers Supported: ImageWriter
Reviews: *MacWorld* (December 1985): 96–100; *MacWorld* (February 1986): 126–31; *Macazine* (March 1986): 54–62; *A+* (December 1985): 191–93; *MacUser* (December 1985): 38.
Other: Supports scaling (independent control of horizontal and vertical scales), styling, cutting and pasting (including bilevel cut and paste), copying, editing with pencil, line, box and eraser, undo and revert, and creating characters from 0 to 254 points wide and from 1 to 127 points high with independent horizontal and vertical scale factors. The FONTastic™ Plus (512K, 2 drives, Macintosh 512, Plus, XL, $79.95) supports variable size fatbits, multiple simultaneous font editing, four levels of UNDO, a background editing plane, full character styling abilities (e.g., bold, italic), print samples available anytime during editing, zero-width and overlapping characters (important for creating foreign language characters and logos), kerning pairs and fractional character-width specification.

2.7.2.6 FontGen IV+

- ## BASIC PRODUCT INFORMATION

Name of Program: FontGen IV+
Company Name: VS Software, a division of VideoSoft, Inc.
Address: P.O. Box 6158, Little Rock, AR 72216
Phone: (501) 376-2083
Price: $250 (includes font editor, VS Tool Kit, and 2 fonts); $39.95 – $ 169.95 per additional font sets.
Runs On: IBM PCs and compatibles
Memory Requirements: 256K, 384K recommended
Operating System Requirements: DOS 2.0 or greater
Disk Drive Requirements: 2, hard disk recommended
Copy Protected: No (Yes outside of the U.S.A.)
Laser Printers Supported: LaserJet Plus, LaserJet 500 Plus, LaserJet Series II, Cordata LP-300 and 300X, Canon LBP8-A1 and A2, NCR 6416 Model 1 and 2, Oasys, Ricoh Laser Printers, other printers that emulate the HP+, LaserMaster, Kyocera, QuadLaser
Dot-Matrix Printers Supported: None
Reviews: Kim W. Bridges, "Special Characters," *Personal Publishing* (August 1986): 34–36; Marvin Bryan, "Learning to Drive," *Personal Publishing* (March 1987): 81–83.

Special Features: FontGen includes drivers for WordPerfect and for Microsoft Word. Built-in editing tools support line, circle, ellipse, spline, and box drawing, character centering, pixel inserting and deleting, copying, moving and deleting, outline filling, mirror imaging, character merging between fonts, enlarging, reducing, compressing, shearing, changing fixed-space fonts to proportionally-spaced fonts, and vice versa, adding and subtracting characters, expanding and compressing character height and width, landscape rotation, and "rubberbanding" all drawing and erase features. Characters are edited pixel-by-pixel at full-screen size. Supports mice.

Other: Over 1,000 proportional and fixed-space fonts are available, including fonts from the Compugraphic and International Typeface Corporation collections. Several Greek fonts (which do not include breathing marks, accents, iota subscripts, or other diacritical marks) and many fonts for Western European languages are available. FontGen has on-line help. A graphics card is not needed. FontGen supports the EGA, CGA, HGC, HGC+, and MDA.

2.7.2.7 Laser Fonts

- BASIC PRODUCT INFORMATION

Name of Program: Laser Fonts
Company Name: SoftCraft, Inc.
Address: 16 N. Carroll St., Suite 500, Madison, WI 53703
Phones: ((800) 351-0500, (608) 257-3300
Price: $180
Runs On: IBM PCs and compatibles
Memory Requirements: 128K
Operating System Requirements: DOS 2.0 or greater
Disk Drive Requirements: 2
Copy Protected: No
Laser Printers Supported: LaserJet Plus, Canon LBP8-A1, A2, NCR, and compatibles
Dot-Matrix Printers Supported: None
Reviews: None
Special Features: Laser Fonts downloads fonts for laser printers and automatically installs fonts for Microsoft Word, WordPerfect, WordStar 2000, Fancy Font, and Fancy Word. Comes with nine fonts, the 1,600-character Hershey Database, supports up to 128 characters per font, and can print up to 30-point characters on the LaserJet Plus and up to 14-point characters on the Canon laser printers.
Other: None

2.7.2.8 Better Letter Setter

- BASIC PRODUCT INFORMATION

Name of Program: Better Letter Setter
Company Name: Dr. LST: Software
Address: 545 33rd St., Richmond, CA 94804-1535
Phone: (415) 236-7415
Price: $25 to $50, depending on printer
Runs On: IBM PCs and compatibles and CP/M-80 (with Z-80 microprocessor) and 86 systems (5.25-inch, soft-sectored disks only)
Memory Requirements: 64K
Operating System Requirements: MS/IBM-DOS 1.0 or greater; CP/M 2.2 or 3.0
Disk Drive Requirements: 1
Copy Protected: No
Laser Printers Supported: None
Dot-Matrix Printers Supported: Epson LQ-1500, LQ-1000, LQ-800, FX-80, FX-100, FX-85, FX-185, FX-286, Toshiba P351, P1351, P1350, Okidata 92, 93, IBM Pro Printer, TI 855, 865, Gemini 10, 15, and others
Reviews: None
Other: Includes "starter library" of predefined fonts. A Greek font with all accents, breathing marks, and other characters is available for some versions. Proportionally spaced fonts may be designed. Program is menu-driven and supports flipping, inverting, leaning, shifting, using the cursor as pencil and eraser, copying, protecting and unprotecting, and deleting and undeleting.

2.7.2.9 LaserWorks

- ● *BASIC PRODUCT INFORMATION*

Name of Program: LaserWorks™
Company Name: EDO Communications
Address: 63 Arnold Way, West Hartford, CT 06119
Phone: (203) 233-5850
Price: $295
Runs On: Macintosh
Memory Requirements: Not known
Operating System Requirements: Macintosh
Disk Drive Requirements: 1
Copy Protected: Not known
Laser Printers Supported: LaserWriter, LaserWriter Plus
Dot-Matrix Printers Supported: None
Reviews: C. J. Weigand, "LaserWorks," *Personal Publishing* (August 1986): 38–40; *Publish!* (September/October 1986): 69.
Special Features: Supports input from digitizers, MacPaint™ and scanners, 360-degree rotation of characters, 360-degree slanting of characters, 150 control points per character, mirror, flip, italicize, adjust weights, and scaling. Creates PostScript fonts.
Other: Simpler, easier to use, less powerful, and less precise than Fontographer (see above).

2.7.2.10 The Signifier

- ● *BASIC PRODUCT INFORMATION*

Name of Program: The Signifier
Company Name: Institute for Research in Information and Scholarship (IRIS)
Address: IRIS, P.O. Box 1946, Brown University, Providence, RI 02912
Phone: Not known
Price: $20
Runs On: Macintosh
Memory Requirements: 128K
Operating System Requirements: Macintosh
Disk Drive Requirements: 1
Copy Protected: No
Laser Printers Supported: None
Dot-Matrix Printers Supported: ImageWriter
Reviews: *Wheels for the Mind* 1 (Fall 1985): 65–66.
Other: Includes Greek and neo-Cyrillic fonts.

2.7.2.11 Arizona I/O Enhancements

- ● *BASIC PRODUCT INFORMATION*

Name of Program: Arizona I/O Enhancements
Company Name: % Dr. Dan Brink
Address: Dept. of English, Arizona State University, Tempe, AZ 85287
Phone: (602) 965-3168
Price: Free
Runs On: IBM PCs and compatibles
Memory Requirements: 128K
Operating System Requirements: DOS 2.0 or greater
Disk Drive Requirements: 1
Copy Protected: No
Laser Printers Supported: None
Dot-Matrix Printers Supported: TI 855, Epson FX-80, Okidata 92

Reviews: None
Special Features: This is not a font editor but a series of independent interrupt routines that translate incoming codes and assign them different values before sending them to screen or printer, thereby making custom screen and printer fonts available. Supports right-to-left editing with WordStar 3.24.
Other: None

2.7.2.12 FED

• BASIC PRODUCT INFORMATION

Name of Program: FED
Company Name: FED is part of the Duke Language Toolkit
Address: % Jeffrey William Gillette, Humanities Computing Facility, 104 Languages Bldg., Duke University, Durham, NC 27706
Phone: (919) 684-3637
Price: Free
Runs On: IBM PCs and compatibles
Memory Requirements: 256K
Operating System Requirements: DOS 2.0 or greater
Disk Drive Requirements: 2
Copy Protected: No
Laser Printers Supported: LaserJet Plus
Dot-Matrix Printers Supported: Toshiba P351, IBM Pro Printer, Epson FX-80, FX-85
Reviews: None
Special Features: FED (and its companion utility LOADFONT) allow printer and screen fonts (up to 30-by-30 pixels) to be created, edited, loaded into memory, and downloaded into appropriate printers. FED is a generic, fully interactive, pop-up, memory-resident, menu-driven font editor that has a 43-line mode, that supports up to 512 characters per active font, and that allows up to four 256-character fonts to be in memory simultaneously.
Other: Requires EGA or clone.

2.7.2.13 ConoFonts

• BASIC PRODUCT INFORMATION

Name of Program: ConoFonts
Company Name: Conographic Corporation
Address: 17841 Fitch, Irvine, CA 92714
Phone: (714) 474-1188
Price: $70 for Manager, $125 per font package (4 different weights per package)
Runs On: IBM PCs and compatibles
Memory Requirements: 256K
Operating System Requirements: DOS 2.0 or greater
Disk Drive Requirements: 2
Copy Protected: No
Laser Printers Supported: LaserJet Plus, LaserJet 500 Plus
Dot-Matrix Printers Supported: None
Reviews: *Personal Publishing* (November 1986): 45.
Special Features: Sizes from 6 to 30 points. Menu-driven. The Manager allows users to edit and create fonts, to load fonts, and to change fonts for the application programs mentioned below.
Other: Supports Microsoft Word 2.0 or later, WordPerfect 4.1 or later, WordStar 2000 2.0 or later, Ventura Publisher, and the Lexisoft Spellbinder Publisher. Any application program that can use HP soft fonts can use ConoFonts. ConoVision 2800, a very-high-resolution graphics board, supports up to 2,880-by-1,024 resolution and doubles the output from any Canon CX engine up to 600-by-300 dpi.

2.7.2.14 supraFONT

• BASIC PRODUCT INFORMATION

Name of Program: supraFONT™
Company Name: Soft Evolutions, Inc.
Address: 484 Lake Park Ave., Suite 17, Oakland, CA 94610-2730
Phone: (415) 863-0691
Price: Not known
Runs On: IBM PCs and compatibles
Memory Requirements: Not known
Operating System Requirements: DOS 2.0 or greater
Disk Drive Requirements: Not known
Copy Protected: Not known
Laser Printers Supported: Not known
Dot-Matrix Printers Supported: Not known
Reviews: None
Special Features: Supports 12 256-character user-definable fonts. Character size is adjustable from 4-16 pixels high to 8-9 pixels wide.
Other: Requires HGC+ or Hercules InColor graphics card. This is a developing product that is not available at the time of this writing.

2.7.2.15 HOT LEAD

• BASIC PRODUCT INFORMATION

Name of Program: HOT LEAD™
Company Name: Janus Associates
Address: 94 Chestnut St., Boston, MA 02108
Phones: (617) 720-5085, (617) 354-1999
Price: $148
Runs On: IBM PCs and compatibles
Memory Requirements: 256K
Operating System Requirements: DOS 2.0 or greater
Disk Drive Requirements: 1
Copy Protected: Not known
Laser Printers Supported: LaserJet Plus, LaserJet 500 Plus, and compatibles
Dot-Matrix Printers Supported: None
Reviews: *PC Week* (April 7, 1987)
Special Features: Allows soft fonts to be downloaded in 17 different ways, including: double, halve, increase, decrease, invert, slant, and shade. Transformed fonts may be stored in files. Transformed fonts may be transformed a second and third time.
Other: None

2.7.3 Font Sets

Several companies market fonts for IBM PCs and for the Macintosh. See Marvin Bryan, "Learning to Drive," *Personal Publishing* (March 1987): 74–83 and Peter Neuhaus, "From Soft Fonts to Hard Copy," *PC World* (July 1986): 252–59, for helpful information on using downloaded printer fonts.

2.7.3.1 Linguists' Software

• BASIC PRODUCT INFORMATION

Company Name: Linguists' Software
Address: 106R Highland St., South Hamilton, MA 01982

Phone: (617) 468-3037
Computer Supported: Macintosh
Laser Printers Supported: LaserWriter, LaserWriter Plus; also supports Linotronic 100 and 300 phototypesetters.
Dot-Matrix Printers Supported: ImageWriter
Fonts Offered: Greek (all accents and diacritical marks), Hebrew (all vowels and diacritical marks and inscription fonts), Phoenician, Akkadian, Ugaritic, Arabic, Farsi, Cyrillic, Devanagari, Hieroglyphics, Sanskrit, Coptic, Korean, Kanji, Western European, International Phonetic Alphabet, Syriac, Nestorian, Jacobite, Estrangela, Ethiopic, TECH.
Price: $49.95 to $149.95, depending on font set; maximum of $79.95 for one language; maximum of $149.95 for laser font.
Copy Protected: No
Other: Each font includes all vowel, breathing, and diacritical marks, as appropriate. Each character set is supplied in a variety of sizes. All fonts work with MacWrite and with Microsoft Word.

2.7.3.2 SMK GreekKeys and Attika

● *BASIC PRODUCT INFORMATION*

Company Name: SMK GreekKeys
Address: 5760 S. Blackstone Ave., Chicago, IL 60637
Phone: (312) 947-9157
Computer Supported: Any Macintosh
Laser Printers Supported: LaserWriter and other PostScript laser printers and output devices
Dot-Matrix Printers Supported: ImageWriter, ImageWriter II, HP Inkjet
Fonts Offered: Classical, Koine, and Modern Greek, with all accents and diacritical marks (bound to 14 dead keys), scholarly marks and sigla, metrical symbols for Classical Greek poetry; two Greek fonts in 9, 10, 12, 18, 20, and 24 points; one roman font in two sizes.
Price: GreekKeys: $25; Attika: $40; both: $65; Site License: $100; European versions are more expensive.
Copy Protected: No
Other: All fonts work with MacWrite and Microsoft Word. Attika, a fully bit-mapped PostScript font, is automatically substituted for GreekKeys fonts without manual conversion. Attika can be printed in resolutions from 300 to 2,400 dpi, depending on the output device.

2.7.3.3 Allied Typographics

● *BASIC PRODUCT INFORMATION*

Company Name: Allotype Typographics
Address: 1600 Packard Rd., Suite 5, Ann Arbor, MI 48104
Phone: (313) 663-1989
Computer Supported: Macintosh
Laser Printers Supported: LaserWriter, LaserWriter Plus
Dot-Matrix Printers Supported: ImageWriter, ImageWriter II
Fonts Offered: Kadmos©, a complete Classical Greek PostScript font that runs directly from SMK GreekKeys (see above). Also available in Wayne State University's (WSU) Colophon (public-domain) keyboard arrangement (see below).
Price: $85
Copy Protected: No
Other: None

2.7.3.4 Colophon

● *BASIC PRODUCT INFORMATION*

Company Name: Wayne State University
Address: Documentation Librarian, Computing Services, Wayne State University, 5980 Cass Ave., Detroit, MI 48202
Phone: (313) 577-4762

Computer Supported: Macintosh
Laser Printers Supported: None
Dot-Matrix Printers Supported: ImageWriter, ImageWriter II
Fonts Offered: Colophon; comes in 5 screen sizes (10, 12, 18, 20, and 24 points)
Price: $5
Copy Protected: No
Other: None

2.7.3.5 NeoScribe International

- *BASIC PRODUCT INFORMATION*

Company Name: NeoScribe International
Address: P.O. Box 633, East Haven, CT 06512
Phone: (203) 467-9880
Computer Supported: Macintosh
Laser Printers Supported: LaserWriter, LaserWriter Plus, any PostScript printer
Dot-Matrix Printers Supported: None
Fonts Offered: Several, including a fully-pointed Hebrew font and Devanagari font for laser printers
Price: $55 to $125
Copy Protected: No
Other: Supports Linotronic 100/300 phototypesetter

2.7.3.6 ProofWriter TURBOFONTS

- *BASIC PRODUCT INFORMATION*

Name of Program: ProofWriter TURBOFONTS™
Company Name: Image Processing Software, Inc.
Address: 4414 Regent St., P.O. Box 5016, Madison, WI 53705
Phone: (608) 233-5033
Computer Supported: IBM and compatibles
Laser Printers Supported: LaserJet Plus, LaserJet Plus, Epson GQ-3,500
Dot-Matrix Printers Supported: Toshiba P1350, 1340, 351, 341, 321; Epson MX, RX, LX, JX, FX, LQ (800, 1,000, 1,500, 2,500), and many, many more
Fonts Offered: Classical Hebrew, Greek (Classical, Koine, and Modern), Scientific, Mathematics, Western European, Medieval English, Cyrillic, Slavic, Russian, romanized Arabic, Baltic languages, Sanskrit, Semitic and Ugaritic
Price: $149; $75 for optional character PROM; $175 for LaserJet Plus or Epson GQ-3,500
Copy Protected: Not known
Other: Works with EGA or HGC. Includes 20 character sets, over 1,000 characters, and supports up to 6 dead keys and 12 logical keyboards. Supports over 60 printers and 20 popular word processors, including WordPerfect, Microsoft Word, XyWrite III, PC-Write, and FinalWord II. Various fonts in PROMs (including Classical and Koine Greek and Classical Hebrew) are available for a variety of nongraphic display adapters. The TURBOFONTS DOWNLOADABLE LIBRARY for the LaserJet Plus and the Epson GQ-3,500 includes over 1,000 fixed-width, 10-point scientific, foreign-language, and business characters. The LIBRARY also includes one 10-point, 12-pitch English font. LaserJet requires J cartridge.

2.8 Stand-Alone Spelling, Thesaurus, and Style Programs

In this section we will look at a number of stand-alone spelling, thesaurus, and style programs. When used properly, these writing tools can be worth their weight in gold. Although this is a book about the use of computers in biblical and classical studies and not about software in general, no writer should be ignorant of the power and usefulness of the following programs.[175]

Spell programs check for incorrect spellings; they do not define words (they are not dictionary programs). Thesaurus programs display synonyms. And style programs flag different types of grammatical, punctuation, and word-usage mistakes, as well as draw attention to long and complex sentences.

2.8.1 Spelling Programs

Like a man with mud on his $500, hand-tailored suit, the most carefully constructed and beautifully written document can be spoiled by the presence of improperly spelled words. Misspellings in a document are signs of sloppiness, laziness, and ignorance. They are an embarrassment to the author and a stumbling block to the reader. Frequent misspellings may cause readers to question an author's competence—if an author cannot be trusted to get the little things correct, how can he be trusted to get the big things right?

Proofreading documents is tedious and time consuming, and all too frequently misspellings slip through undetected. Human beings are not machines, and for a variety of reasons, it is easy to overlook misspelled words. Fortunately, for persons who compose their documents with word processors, there is a simple, inexpensive, and (almost) infallible way to catch misspellings: use a spell-checking program.

Spell checkers operate in one of two basic ways. Batch-mode, stand-alone spell checkers check a file after it is completed, and interactive spell checkers check spelling as a file is created. Interactive spell checkers are memory-resident programs that may be set to autocorrect text as it is entered, or they can be "popped up" and used to spell check single words or blocks of words. Batch-mode spell checkers can check files created by a variety of word processors. Interactive spell checkers are usually (but not always) built in to particular word processing programs.

There are two basic types of spell checkers—brute-force and smart. "Brute-force" spell checkers scan documents, list all the unique words, sort the words alphabetically, and compare that list with their dictionaries. Unrecognized words are then listed alphabetically, and users are given the option of seeing those words in one or more lines of context, at which time they may (1) ignore the word for the remainder of the spell-checking session, (2) ignore the word for its current occurrence only, (3) add the word to a supplemental or special dictionary, (4) display possible correct spellings. After all the corrections have been specified, the spell checker makes the appropriate changes in the document. That way of spell checking can be thought of as a "brute-force" approach because it merely compares one list of words against another, lists the differences, and allows users to specify corrections. Brute-force spell checkers can only process documents in batch mode, that is, a whole document at a time. They cannot operate interactively, which means that they cannot operate concurrently with word processing and other application programs.

"Smart" spell checkers are smart for two reasons. First, many of them employ various forms of artificial intelligence to parse words; and second, they all catch and display spelling mistakes as they scan through documents, without alphabetizing and creating lists. Programs in this category (like Word Proof II, MicroSpell, and Jet:Spell™) spell check word-by-word, just as a human would. When they encounter a word that is not in their dictionaries and that does not match one of their parsing algorithms, they immediately flag it, and users are then given options for ignoring the word, adding it to a special dictionary, and so forth. Generally speaking, smart spell checkers are much faster than brute-force spell checkers and allow users to see more

---

175. As I indicated earlier, several of the word processing programs we have reviewed include spell checkers (which may be used interactively or in batch mode) and thesauri.

context. Furthermore, because they do not have to create a list of each file's unique words, smart spell checkers are able to spell check files of unlimited size. And unlike brute-force spell checkers, smart spell checkers allow changes to be made directly in the document being spell checked. Finally, some smart spell checkers allow users to perform rudimentary editing chores. Smart spell checkers operate in batch or interactive modes, depending on the program.

In addition to being "brute" or "smart," spell checkers differ in other ways. Some flag doubled words, such as *the the*. Some flag incorrect capitalization, such as *EVerest* and *denver* and *cOlOrADo*. Some spelling programs include a thesaurus. Some include a hyphenation utility. Most allow users to add words to a special user dictionary (or dictionaries). A few allow users to add words to and to delete words from their main dictionaries. Almost all of them allow users to look up single words that are not in files. And some support text-only macros, so that users may specify strings that the program automatically changes into other user-specified strings, for example, "tsr" into "terminate and stay resident."

Six of the most significant differences among spelling programs are (1) number of dictionary entries, (2) ratio of dictionary entries to dictionary size, (3) program size, (4) look-up speed, (5) memory requirements, and (6) "intelligence." Other differences include mode of operation—batch or interactive—number of words that can be added to the main dictionary or to user dictionaries, user interface, whether a program automatically and instantaneously displays suggestions for unrecognized words, and "bells and whistles." Most spell-checking programs work only with ASCII text files.

Generally speaking, the more entries a dictionary contains, the better, as long as the quality of words chosen to be in the dictionary is high. The ratio of the number of entries in a dictionary to its size reflects the degree to which the dictionary has been compressed. Generally speaking, the higher the degree of compression, the better. Dictionary and program size are usually concerns only for users whose machines do not include hard drives and who do not have an adequate amount of RAM. Because of the 640K memory barrier of current versions of DOS, the less memory a program requires the better. Look-up speed is primarily a function of the different look-up formulas each program uses and of whether or not a program loads its dictionary into memory.

"Intelligence" refers to how clever a program is at analyzing words and to how shrewd its guesses are when presented with a word it does not recognize. A spelling program's "intelligence" is manifested in three basic ways. (1) Some spelling programs are able to parse correctly spelled words that do not occur in their unparsed forms in the program's dictionaries into their stems and affixes and to recognize and accept valid stem/affix combinations. (2) Some spelling programs are able to parse unrecognized words whose stem/affix combinations are not recognized as valid and to display the parsing results on-screen for users to see, a feature that allows users to make educated guesses about the correctness of unrecognized terms. For example, MicroSpell's dictionary does not include *intraarterial* nor do MicroSpell's parsing algorithms recognize this as a valid stem/affix combination. MicroSpell parses *intraarterial* as *intra + arterial* and displays that result on-screen, thus allowing users to make an educated guess about the correctness of the word. (3) And some programs make better guesses at the correct spelling of unknown words than do other programs because they have been endowed with better rules—algorithms—for doing so.

In this subsection **Specify Drive, Pathname, and Subdirectory** indicates whether the program can access a file on a drive and in a subdirectory other than the drive and subdirectory where the program is located. **Total Program Size** refers to the combined size of the main program, its auxiliary programs, and its dictionary. **Add to Dictionary**, followed by a number, indicates the number of words users may add to the dictionary.[176] **Amount of Context Shown** refers to the amount of context that may be displayed in the document being spell checked when an unknown or misspelled word is encountered. **Global Correction** indicates whether a program can automatically fix all identical misspellings of a word after the first occurrence of that word has been corrected. **Automatic Insertion** indicates whether a program automatically inserts the correct spelling of a word or whether users must type the correct spelling into documents. Programs that automatically insert words save time. **Specify Delimiter Characters** indicates whether a program allows users to define certain characters or character combinations for it to ignore when spell checking (e.g., embedded formatting commands). If a spell checker cannot ignore formatting commands, it will stop at or flag every formatted word. **Word Count** indicates whether a program has a utility that counts words in a file. Word count utilities are helpful when documents or manuscripts must be kept to a certain size. **Automatic Hyphenation** indicates whether a program has a utility for automatically inserting soft hyphens into words. Soft hyphens (hyphens that indicate where a word *may*, not *must*, be broken at a line end) are crucial when printing text in columns and when typesetting. **Hyphenation Exception List** indicates whether a program allows users to construct a list of words that do not follow the hyphenation rules. Since no hyphenation algorithm is perfect, a hyphenation exception list allows users to "educate" the hyphenation program so that it does not incorrectly hyphenate exceptions to its rules. **Mark Words That Change Length** indicates whether a program can mark corrected words whose length is different from their misspelled versions. This feature is important for those whose word processing programs require paragraphs to be manually reformatted. And **Mode of Operation** indicates whether a program is *interactive* and spell checks in "real time" as text is entered or whether it checks a document all at once in *batch mode*. Most interactive spell-checking programs allow users to toggle in and out of the interactive, auto-check mode, and to spell check selected blocks of text.

Many of the spelling programs listed below have been reviewed in the *Bits & Bytes Review*™, Vol. 1, Nos. 5 & 6, April & May 1987. For additional information, see Jon Pepper, "Banish Typos with Spelling Checkers," *PC Magazine* (December 24, 1985): 199–213; Jon Edwards, "RAM-Resident Utilities," *BYTE* (Summer 1987 Bonus Edition): 103–18; Christopher O'Malley, "Going Beyond Word Processing," *Personal Computing* (December 1986): 113–21; "Word Processing Programs with Spelling Checkers for IBM, AT&T, COMPAQ and Other Compatible Personal Computers," *Software Digest Ratings Newsletter* 2 (January 1985): 1–76; F. Ladson Boyle, "Memory-Resident Spelling Checkers," *The Lawyer's PC* 4 (November 1, 1986): 8–11; Leslie Eiser, "I Luv To Rite: Spelling Checkers in the Writing Classroom," *Computer Classroom Learning* 7 (November/December 1986): 50–57; and Edward Mendelson, "Clonkers and Coolitude: Spelling Checkers Get Better," *PC Magazine* (October 13, 1987): 349–87.[177]

---

176. Only a very few of these programs allow users to add words to the main dictionary or to edit the main dictionary, which is usually stored in compressed form. Most of the programs, however, allow users to add words to an auxiliary dictionary or dictionaries.

177. For various reasons, I am not including reviews of (1) Spellix (Emerging Technology Consultants, Inc., 4760 Walnut St., Boulder, CO 80301; (303) 447-9495; $95), (2) Paperback Speller (Paperback Software International, 2612 Eighth St., Berkeley, CA 94710; (415) 644-2116; $39.95), (3) V-Spell (Compu View Products, Inc., 1955 Pauline Blvd., Ann Arbor, MI 48103; (313) 995-1299; $125), (4) The Speller (Hayden Software, 600 Suffolk St., Lowell, MA 01853; (800) 343-1218; $39.95), (5) G-Spell (Pico Publishing, P.O. Box 3266, Iowa City, IA 52244; (319) 354-5736; $9.95), (6) Whoops!™ (Cornucopia Software, Inc., P.O. Box 6111, Albany, CA 94706; (800) 343-2443, (415) 528-7000; $49.95), (7) PC Type Right™ (Xerox Corp., Xerox Square 10A, Rochester, NY 14644; (716) 423-1052; $199.95), (8) Strike™ and (9) the Resident Speller™ (both from S&K Technology, Inc., 4610 Spotted Oak Woods, San Antonio, TX 78249; (512) 492-3384; $29.95 and $99.95, respectively), and (10) Window's Spell (Palantir Software, 12777 Jones Rd., Suite 100, Houston, TX 77070; (713) 955-8880; $79.95).

2.8.1.1 The Word Plus

- BASIC PRODUCT INFORMATION

Name of Program: The Word Plus
Company Name: Oasis Systems/FTL
Address: 6160 Lusk Blvd., #C-206, San Diego, CA 92121
Phone: (619) 453-5711
Price: $120
Version Reviewed: IBM 1.21
Runs On: IBM PCs and compatibles and CP/M machines
Memory Requirements: 64K
Operating System Requirements: IBM: DOS 1.0 or greater; CP/M: 2.2
Disk Drive Requirements: 1
Copy Protected: No
Hard Disk Compatible: Yes
Specify Drive, Pathname, and Subdirectory: Drive only
Total Program Size: 185K
Size of Dictionary: 45,000 words
Add To Dictionary: Yes, number of words limited only by available disk space.
Mode of Operation: Batch
Amount of Context Shown: 1 line
Global Correction: Yes
Automatic Insertion: No
Specify Delimiter Characters: Yes
Mark Words That Change Length: Yes
Automatic Hyphenation: Yes (uses Donald Knuth's algorithm described in $T_{E}X$ and METAFONT—see above)
Hyphenation Exception List: Yes
Word Count: Yes
Word Processors Supported: Any word processor that produces ASCII text files
Reviews: Terry Tinsley Datz and F. Lloyd Datz, "The Word Plus," *Personal Computer Age* (January 1984): 100–101; Wayne Holder, "Software Tools for Writers," BYTE (July 1982): 138–63.
Special Features: LOOKUP (looks up words), ANAGRAM (finds anagrams of words), FIND (locates words, supports wild-card characters), WORDFREQ (word count), DICTSORT (alphabetizes any word list or ASCII file). Separate, specialized dictionaries may be created. Contains a search-and-replace feature.
Comments: A remarkably useful spell-checking program with many helpful auxiliary utility programs. The ability to create a secondary dictionary of unlimited size, as well as to create separate, specialized dictionaries, is especially helpful. Small main dictionary, skimpy amount of context, and "brute-force" approach to spell checking are drawbacks. HYPHEN inserts soft hyphens into documents in accordance with Knuth's algorithm as overridden by a user-modifiable exceptions dictionary that may be as large as (approximately) 75K. Users may specify the soft hyphen character to be inserted. HYPHEN is a very fast stand-alone utility that is worth its weight in gold for users who have no automatic hyphenation feature on their word processor or desktop publishing program and who print text in multiple columns or who typeset or who do both. Very few word processors have hyphenation features. The Word Plus is the only spelling program I know of that includes a hyphenation utility. Polyglot, the company that markets Jet:Spell™ (see below), also sells HY-PHEN, an excellent stand-alone hyphenation utility.
Warranty: Not known
Support: Phone and letter
Update Policy: Not known

2.8.1.2 Webster's NewWorld Spelling Checker

- BASIC PRODUCT INFORMATION

Name of Program: Webster's NewWorld Spelling Checker
Company Name: Simon & Schuster Software
Address: Gulf & Western Bldg., One Gulf + Western Plaza, New York, NY 10023
Phones: (800) 624-0023; (800) 624-0024 (NJ)
Technical Support: (201) 592-2900
Price: $59.95

Version Reviewed: IBM 1.3
Runs On: IBM PCs and compatibles and Apple IIs
Memory Requirements: IBM: 128K; Apple: 128K (64K for Apple+)
Operating System Requirements: IBM: DOS 2.0 or greater; Apple: ProDOS or DOS 3.3
Disk Drive Requirements: 1
Copy Protected: No
Hard Disk Compatible: Yes
Specify Drive, Pathname, and Subdirectory: Yes
Total Program Size: 207K
Size of Dictionary: 114,000 words
Add To Dictionary: Yes, an auxiliary dictionary can contain approximately 3,000 words. Users may create as many auxiliary dictionaries as they wish, but the program can only use one auxiliary dictionary at a time.
Mode of Operation: Batch
Amount of Context Shown: Up to 9 lines
Global Correction: Yes (may be toggled)
Automatic Insertion: Yes
Specify Delimiter Characters: Yes
Mark Words That Change Length: Yes
Automatic Hyphenation: No
Hyphenation Exception List: Not applicable
Word Count: Yes
Word Processors Supported: Bank Street Writer™, HomeWord™, PerfectWriter™, pfs®: Write, Textra®, Volkswriter®, Volkswriter Deluxe™, WordStar®, WordStar® 2000, XyWrite™, and any word processor that produces ASCII text files
Reviews: None
Special Features: The dictionary contains many computer terms and can be set to automatically suggest possible correct spellings. The program corrects transpositions, contractions, nonhyphenated words that should be hyphenated, repeated words (e.g., *the the*), abbreviations, run-on words, and phonetic misspellings. A look-up function allows browsing through the dictionary. The manual includes a "Writer's Guide to Punctuation and Manuscript Preparation," from *Webster's New World Dictionary*, Second College Edition.
Comments: Large dictionary and 9-line context are strengths. "Brute-force" approach to spell checking, a "clunky" interface, and the restriction of 3,000 additional words are drawbacks. Accepts British spellings without warning users. The Apple version requires an 80-column or extended 80-column card; the Apple II+ version requires a Videx Videoterm 80-column text card.
Other: Simon & Schuster also markets Webster's NewWorld Writer ($150), a fairly full-featured word processor with built-in thesaurus and spelling checker, and Webster's NewWorld On-Line Thesaurus ($69.95).
Warranty: 30 days, media only
Support: Phone and letter
Update Policy: Not Known

2.8.1.3 Electric Webster

● *BASIC PRODUCT INFORMATION*

Name of Program: Electric Webster
Company Name: Cornucopia Software, Inc.
Address: P.O. Box 6111, Albany, CA 94706
Phones: (800) 343-2432, (415) 524-8098
Price: $129.95 ($149.95 for TRS version; $129.95 for CP/M version)
Version Reviewed: IBM 2.0
Runs On: IBM PCs and compatibles, TRS-80 Models 1, III, or 4, and CP/M-80 systems
Memory Requirements: IBM: 64K
Operating System Requirements: IBM: DOS 1.10 or greater
Disk Drive Requirements: 1
Copy Protected: No
Hard Disk Compatible: Yes
Specify Drive, Pathname, and Subdirectory: Yes
Total Program Size: 200K (dictionary and program); grammar program is additional 76K.
Size of Dictionary: 50,000 words

Add To Dictionary: Yes, maximum number of words not known.
Mode of Operation: Batch
Amount of Context Shown: 4 to 10 lines
Global Correction: No
Automatic Insertion: Yes, if desired
Specify Delimiter Characters: No
Mark Words That Change Length: Yes
Automatic Hyphenation: Yes
Hyphenation Exception List: Yes
Word Count: Yes
Word Processors Supported: Any word processor that produces ASCII text files
Reviews: Dan Robinson, "Much More Than a Spelling Checker," *Creative Computing* (November 1983); Frank J. Derfler, "Electric Webster," *InfoWorld* (other bibliographical data not known); *Personal Publishing* (June 1986): 15; *Personal Publishing* (August 1986): 19.
Special Features: Cornucopia markets, Whoops! ($49.95), a real-time, interactive spell checker and thesaurus program, without the grammar and style programs that come with the Electric Webster.
Comments: The grammar program is a nice feature. The small dictionary, "brute-force" approach to spell checking, and "clunky" interface are drawbacks, as is the two-step process required to correct misspelled words. Users cannot see the display of suggested words while the spell-checker is running or spelling errors in context while the suggested words list is displayed.
Warranty: Not known
Support: Not known
Update Policy: Not known

2.8.1.4 MicroSpell

- ## BASIC PRODUCT INFORMATION

Name of Program: MicroSpell
Company Name: Trigram Systems
Address: 5840 Northumberland St., Pittsburgh, PA 15217
Phone: (412) 422-8976
Price: $69
Version Reviewed: Beta version 7.4
Runs On: IBM PCs and compatibles
Memory Requirements: 128K, 320K recommended
Operating System Requirements: DOS 2.0 or greater
Disk Drive Requirements: 2
Copy Protected: No
Hard Disk Compatible: Yes
Specify Drive, Pathname, and Subdirectory: Yes
Total Program Size: 236K
Size of Dictionary: 80,000 words
Add To Dictionary: Yes, up to 40,000 words may be added to the main dictionary, and an unlimited number of auxiliary dictionaries of unlimited size may be created.
Mode of Operation: Batch
Amount of Context Shown: 8 lines
Global Correction: No
Automatic Insertion: Yes
Specify Delimiter Characters: Yes
Mark Words That Change Length: Yes
Automatic Hyphenation: No
Hyphenation Exception List: Not applicable
Word Count: Yes
Word Processors Supported: WordPerfect™, PerfectWriter™, WordStar®, XyWrite™, Nota Bene™, Volkswriter®, PC-Write™, Chiwriter™, Hockney's Egg™, FinalWord™, EasyWriter™, Microsoft® Word, and any ASCII text files
Reviews: Glenn A. Hart, "A Spelling Checker with a Mind of Its Own," *PC Magazine* (October 16, 1984): 261–66.
Special Features: Corrects doubled words. Has look-up function with single and global wild-card characters.

Dictionary contains many geographical and computer terms. This is the spell checker T^3 recommends and the one that is incorporated into FinalWord II (see above).

Comments: This is the fastest, most useful, most "intelligent," and best MS-DOS spell-checking program available. Its long list of options allow it to be highly customized. MicroSpell includes an 8-line editor, a "learn mode," and can work with "correction pairs" (text-only macros). It automatically and instantaneously displays suggested spellings for words it does not recognize. The five-level undo feature is especially impressive and useful.

Warranty: 30-day, money-back guarantee
Support: Phone and letter
Update Policy: $10 to $25 to registered users

2.8.1.5 Jet:Spell

- ## BASIC PRODUCT INFORMATION

Name of Program: Jet:Spell™
Company Name: POLYGLOT, Inc.
Address: 2450 Central Ave., Suite P-4, Boulder, CO 80301-9947
Phone: (303) 449-7002
Price: $109.95; extra dictionaries are $59.95 each.
Version Reviewed: Beta version 3.02.
Runs On: IBM PCs and compatibles
Memory Requirements: 384K
Operating System Requirements: DOS 2.0 or greater
Disk Drive Requirements: 2
Copy Protected: No
Hard Disk Compatible: Yes
Specify Drive, Pathname, and Subdirectory: Yes
Total Program Size: 324K
Size of Dictionary: 130,000 to 2,000,000, depending on language
Add To Dictionary: Yes, up to nine user dictionaries of unlimited size may be created.
Mode of Operation: Batch
Amount of Context Shown: 9 lines
Global Correction: No
Automatic Insertion: Yes
Specify Delimiter Characters: Yes
Mark Words That Change Length: No
Automatic Hyphenation: No, but Polyglot markets HY-PHEN ($49.95 per language), an excellent hyphenation program that works with 13 different languages.
Hyphenation Exception List: HY-PHEN appears to include an exceptions list, which may not be added to or modified.
Word Count: Yes
Word Processors Supported: WordPerfect™ and ASCII text in files whose lines end in carriage returns/linefeeds
Reviews: Not known
Comments: Jet:Spell™ dictionaries are available for American English, British English, Danish, Dutch, French, German, Italian, Norwegian, Spanish, Swedish, and Québécois French. Jet:Spell checks for abbreviations, improper capitalization, compound words, incorrectly used apostrophes, and incorrect use of ordinal and cardinal numbers. Foreign-language user interfaces are available. The program spell checks by analyzing a dictionary that is morphologically coded by root, word type, grammatical exceptions, possible modifications, and possible suffixes. A demo disk is available for $10.
Warranty: 30 days, media only
Support: Phone and letter
Update Policy: $15 to $25

2.8.1.6 Mentor

- ## BASIC PRODUCT INFORMATION

Name of Program: Mentor™ (formerly MacLightning)
Company Name: Target Software, Inc.
Address: 14206 S.W. 136th St., Miami, FL 33186

Phones: (800) 622-5483, (305) 252-0892
Price: $99.95
Version Reviewed: Not able to review; scheduled to be released late 1987/early 1988.
Runs On: Macintoshes
Memory Requirements: 512K
Operating System Requirements: Macintosh
Disk Drive Requirements: 2
Copy Protected: No
Hard Disk Compatible: Yes
Specify Drive, Pathname, and Subdirectory: Not applicable
Total Program Size: Not known
Size of Dictionary: 140,000 words
Add To Dictionary: Yes, an unlimited number of words may be added.
Mode of Operation: Interactive or batch
Amount of Context Shown: Full-screen
Global Correction: Yes
Automatic Insertion: Yes
Specify Delimiter Characters: Not applicable
Mark Words That Change Length: No
Automatic Hyphenation: Yes
Hyphenation Exception List: No
Word Count: Yes
Reviews: Paul Saffo, "Augmented Dictionary Betters Mac Lightning," *InfoWorld* (September 22, 1986): 54–56; James Bierman and Eli Hollander, "Checking on a Few Spelling Checkers," *Semaphore SIGNAL* (May 30, 1986): 1–6; Walter C. Burns, "Letter-Perfect Documents," *Macworld* (July 1986): 102–7.
Special Features: Incorporates the entire *Merriam Webster 9th New Collegiate Dictionary*. Can perform phonetic dictionary searches. Works from within word processing or other application program (operates as a Desk Accessory). Words may be removed from the main dictionary.
Comments: Compatible with Switcher, MacWrite, MacPaint, Interlace, Microphone, Microsoft Word, and many other programs but not with MacDraw, MacDraft, or ThinkTank. When available, this program will offer the largest dictionary for the Macintosh. Does not check contractions, spacing, homonyms, or hyphenated words. Legal and medical dictionaries and a 45,000-word, Merriam Webster thesaurus are available from Target Software. Mentor Plus ($199.95) includes definitions.
Warranty: 90 days, media only
Support: Phone and letter
Update Policy: Free

2.8.1.7 Spellswell

- ## BASIC PRODUCT INFORMATION

Name of Program: Spellswell™
Company Name: Working Software, Inc.
Address: 321 Alvarado, Suite H, Monterey, CA 93740
Phones: (800) 331-4321; (800) 851-1986 (CA), (408) 375-2828
Price: $74.95
Version Reviewed: 2.0
Runs On: Macintoshes
Memory Requirements: 512K
Operating System Requirements: Macintosh
Disk Drive Requirements: 1
Copy Protected: No
Hard Disk Compatible: Yes
Specify Drive, Pathname, and Subdirectory: Not applicable
Total Program Size: 334K
Size of Dictionary: 93,000 words
Add To Dictionary: Yes, limited only by available disk space.
Mode of Operation: Batch
Amount of Context Shown: 6 lines
Global Correction: Yes
Automatic Insertion: Yes
Specify Delimiter Characters: Not applicable

Mark Words That Change Length: No
Automatic Hyphenation: No
Hyphenation Exception List: No
Word Count: Yes
Reviews: James Bierman and Eli Hollander, "Checking on a Few Spelling Checkers," *Semaphore SIGNAL* (May 30, 1986): 1–6; Walter C. Burns, "Letter-Perfect Documents," *Macworld* (July 1986): 102–7; Casey Green, "A Useful Spelling Checker for the Mac," *InfoWorld* (July 14, 1986): 53–54.
Special Features: Checks hyphenated words, contractions, possessives, abbreviations, homonyms, spacing, compatibility of suffixes and roots, doubled words, and the incorrect use of upper and lower case letters. Contains many proper nouns. Maintains capitalization when correcting. Users can delete words from dictionary, look up single words, and scroll through dictionary. Comes with homonym dictionary that can check U.S. postal state abbreviations. Promised future versions will allow foreign-language spell checking. No limit to size of document that can be checked.
Comments: Compatible with Microsoft® Word, MacWrite™, Jazz®, Switcher, MORE™, ThinkTank™, Acta™, and many other Macintosh programs. Includes 1,000 word homonym dictionary. A medical dictionary (40,000 words, $99.95) is available. Lookup™ ($49.95), a Desk Accessory, allows users to look up the spelling of any word from within any application program and supports wild-cards.
Warranty: 90 days, media only
Support: Phone and letter
Update Policy: $15

2.8.1.8 MacSpell+

- ## BASIC PRODUCT INFORMATION

Name of Program: MacSpell+
Company Name: Creighton Development, Inc.
Address: 16 Hughes, Suite C106, Irvine, CA 92718
Phone: (714) 472-0488
Price: $99
Version Reviewed: Not able to review.
Runs On: Macintoshes
Memory Requirements: 512K
Operating System Requirements: Macintosh
Disk Drive Requirements: 2
Copy Protected: No
Hard Disk Compatible: Yes
Specify Drive, Pathname, and Subdirectory: Not applicable
Total Program Size: 40K
Size of Dictionary: 75,000 words
Add To Dictionary: Yes, up to 2,500 additional words.
Mode of Operation: Interactive
Amount of Context Shown: 3 lines
Global Correction: Not known
Automatic Insertion: Yes
Specify Delimiter Characters: Not applicable
Mark Words That Change Length: No
Automatic Hyphenation: Yes
Hyphenation Exception List: Not known
Word Count: Yes
Reviews: Walter C. Burns, "Relief for Reckless Writers," *Macworld* (March 1986): 125, 30; *Computer Retail News* (November 4, 1985): 92–93.
Special Features: Includes thesaurus. Works from within word processing program as a Desk Accessory.
Comments: Works with Microsoft® Word, MacWrite™, and Microsoft® Works.
Warranty: 90 days
Support: Not known
Update Policy: Not known

2.8.1.9 Spelling Champion

● BASIC PRODUCT INFORMATION

Name of Program: Spelling Champion
Company Name: Champion Swiftware.
Address: 6617 Gettysburg Dr., Madison, WI 53705
Phone: (608) 833-1777
Price: $39.95
Version Reviewed: 2.2
Runs On: Any Macintosh
Memory Requirements: 128K
Operating System Requirements: Macintosh
Disk Drive Requirements: 1
Copy Protected: No
Hard Disk Compatible: Yes
Specify Drive, Pathname, and Subdirectory: Not applicable
Total Program Size: 213K
Size of Dictionary: 125,533 words (56,692 root words)
Add To Dictionary: Yes, up to 100,000 additional words
Mode of Operation: Batch
Amount of Context Shown: 8 lines
Global Correction: No
Automatic Insertion: Yes
Specify Delimiter Characters: Not applicable
Mark Words That Change Length: No
Automatic Hyphenation: No
Hyphenation Exception List: No
Word Count: No
Reviews: Not known
Special Features: Can add to or delete from main dictionary, exit spell checker and edit text, spell check
    any size document, and undo any changes made to a document or to the dictionary while spell checking
    a document. Supports mice.
Comments: Works with Microsoft® Word and with MacWrite™.
Warranty: Not known
Support: Not known
Update Policy: Not known

2.8.1.10 WorksPlus Spell

● BASIC PRODUCT INFORMATION

Name of Program: WorksPlus™ Spell
Company Name: Lundeen & Associates
Address: P.O. Box 30038, Oakland, CA 94604
Phone: (800) 233-6851
Price: $59.95
Version Reviewed: 1.0
Runs On: Macintoshes
Memory Requirements: 512K
Operating System Requirements: Macintosh
Disk Drive Requirements: 1
Copy Protected: No
Hard Disk Compatible: Yes
Specify Drive, Pathname, and Subdirectory: Not applicable
Total Program Size: 190K, 336K if using hyphenation dictionary.
Size of Dictionary: 73,000 words
Add To Dictionary: Yes, users may add to the main dictionary and to auxiliary dictionaries. Maximum num-
    ber of words limited only by available disk space.
Mode of Operation: Interactive or batch
Amount of Context Shown: 16 lines

Global Correction: No
Automatic Insertion: Yes
Specify Delimiter Characters: Not applicable
Mark Words That Change Length: No
Automatic Hyphenation: Yes
Hyphenation Exception List: Yes
Word Count: No
Reviews: Not known
Special Features: Users may add words to and delete words from the main dictionary. A "glossary," text-only macro feature allows users to define abbreviations that WorksPlus™ Spell replaces with their user-assigned definitions. The "glossary" function accepts up to 256 abbreviations each of which may be up to 255 characters long. An integrated hyphenation utility with user-definable exceptions dictionary is included.
Comments: WorksPlus™ Spell works only with Microsoft® Works.
Warranty: Not known
Support: Phone and letter
Update Policy: Not known

2.8.1.11 Thunder!

- ## BASIC PRODUCT INFORMATION

Name of Program: Thunder!™
Company Name: Batteries Included
Address: 30 Mural St., Richmond Hill, Ontario L4B 1B5, Canada
Phones: (416) 881-9941, (416) 881-9816
Price: $49.95
Version Reviewed: 1.1
Runs On: Macintoshes
Memory Requirements: 512K
Operating System Requirements: Macintosh
Disk Drive Requirements: 1
Copy Protected: No
Hard Disk Compatible: Yes
Specify Drive, Pathname, and Subdirectory: Not applicable
Total Program Size: 140K
Size of Dictionary: 50,000
Add To Dictionary: Yes, up to 2,000 words may be added to the main dictionary, and supplementary dictionaries may each hold 32K worth of words.
Mode of Operation: Interactive or batch
Amount of Context Shown: Full-screen
Global Correction: Yes
Automatic Insertion: Yes
Specify Delimiter Characters: Not applicable
Mark Words That Change Length: No
Automatic Hyphenation: No
Hyphenation Exception List: Not applicable
Word Count: Yes
Reviews: Not known
Special Features: Includes statistical utility that can analyze documents with the Gunning Fog or the Flesch readability indices. "Abbreviations Expander" allows users to create text-only macros and to instruct Thunder! to transform common misspellings into their proper spellings.
Comments: This is a fast and flexible program.
Warranty: 90 days, media *and program*
Support: Phone and letter
Update Policy: Not known

2.8.2 Thesaurus Programs

These memory-resident, real-time, interactive programs allow users to display synonyms from within application programs and to insert synonyms into text. Among other parameters, these programs differ in terms of (1) the number of unique words and phrases they recognize and can provide synonyms for, (2) the number of synonyms they "know," (3) how "sophisticated" and helpful their key words are, (4) how "sophisticated" and helpful their synonyms are, (5) whether they allow users to search for synonyms of synonyms, and (6) their interfaces.[178] Being able to search for synonyms of synonyms is called "synonym chaining."

Here's how these programs work. Placing the cursor on the word for which synonyms are desired and hitting the "hot key" combination that activates the synonym program causes a list of synonyms for the chosen word to be displayed in a window. Users then may (1) close the window without choosing a synonym, (2) use the cursor keys to highlight a synonym, which may then be directly substituted in the text for the original word, (3) look up a synonym of a synonym.

Number of Words/Phrases Recognized refers to the number of key words and phrases the program can recognize and provide synonyms for. **Number of Synonyms** refers to the total number of synonyms the program can provide for the key words and phrases it can recognize.

For more information see Charles Bermant, "Five Thesaurus Selections Synonymous with Success," *PC Magazine* (June 24, 1986): 42, 44; and Rubin Rabinovitz, "A Way with Words," *PC Magazine* (July 1987): 249–66.

2.8.2.1 *Webster's NewWorld On-Line Thesaurus*

• *BASIC PRODUCT INFORMATION*

Name of Program: Webster's NewWorld On-Line Thesaurus
Company Name: Simon & Schuster Software
Address: Gulf & Western Bldg., One Gulf + Western Plaza, New York, NY 10023
Phones: (800) 624-0023; (800) 624-0024 (NJ)
Technical Support: (201) 592-2900
Price: $69.95
Version Reviewed: 1.03
Runs On: IBM PCs and compatibles
Memory Requirements: 128K; 256K for PCjr
Operating System Requirements: DOS 2.0 or greater
Disk Drive Requirements: 2, hard disk recommended
Copy Protected: No
Hard Disk Compatible: Yes
Specify Drive, Pathname, and Subdirectory: Yes
Total Program Size: 436K
Number of Words/Phrases Recognized: 20,000
Number of Synonyms: 120,000 words (500,000 including derivatives)
Mode of Operation: Interactive
Automatic Insertion: Yes
Reviews: Tan A. Summers, "Synonym Finder Works Well Without Sacrificing on Speed," *InfoWorld* (November 10, 1986): 89–91; Rubin Rabinovitz, "A Way with Words," *PC Magazine* (July 1987): 254, 261.
Special Features: Can strip suffixes and prefixes to find roots of words and add the proper suffixes and prefixes to synonyms suggested by a root. Supports synonym chaining, scrolling through the dictionary, storing notes for potential words users may want to use, and an undo feature. Maintains inflection (e.g., number, construction, tense, case) and article/noun agreement. Locates synonyms for hyphenated words and for phrases. Can be installed for over 25 word processing programs and for many other popular application programs. Manual contains five very helpful appendices on synonyms and word usage.

---

178. As I noted earlier, some word processing programs, such as WordPerfect™ (see above), include a thesaurus.

Comments: This is an impressive and useful program with a vast repertoire of synonyms. Its ability to locate word roots and to suggest synonyms accordingly and its ability to strip and replace prefixes and suffixes are unique among this type of program. Locating synonyms for phrases also is a very useful feature. The size of its dictionary could be a drawback, and the program may be incompatible with other RAM-resident programs.

Other: Simon & Schuster also markets Webster's NewWorld Writer ($150), a fairly full-featured word processor with built-in thesaurus and spelling checker, and Webster's NewWorld Spelling Checker ($59.95).

Warranty: 30 days, media only
Support: Phone and letter
Update Policy: Not known

2.8.2.2 Word Finder

• BASIC PRODUCT INFORMATION

Name of Program: Word Finder™
Company Name: Microlytics, Inc.™
Address: 300 Main St., Suite 516, East Rochester, NY 14445
Phones: (800) 828-6293, (716) 377-0130
Price: $79.95
Version Reviewed: 2.2b
Runs On: IBM PCs and compatibles and Macintoshes
Memory Requirements: IBM: 128K
Operating System Requirements: IBM: DOS 2.0 or greater
Disk Drive Requirements: 2
Copy Protected: No
Hard Disk Compatible: Yes
Specify Drive, Pathname, and Subdirectory: Yes
Total Program Size: 325K (a 163K synonym file with 120,000 synonyms is provided for persons who wish to conserve disk space).
Number of Words/Phrases Recognized: 15,000
Number of Synonyms: 220,000
Mode of Operation: Interactive
Automatic Insertion: Yes
Reviews: *Personal Publishing* (October 1985): 42; Sharon L. Rufener, "Word Finder: Simple, Limited, Easy Thesaurus for Nonwriters," *InfoWorld* (November 4, 1985): 43; Jim Seymour, "Two Priceless, Overlooked Utility Programs," *PC Week* (June 24, 1986): 56; *Inside Word Management* 6 (February 1985): 1; David Obregon, "Word Finder: Shaping Those Elusive Thoughts," *PC Magazine* (October 15, 1985); *Computer Living* (November 1986): 14; *InfoWorld* (December 8, 1986): 68–69; Rubin Rabinovitz, "A Way with Words," *PC Magazine* (July 1987): 262, 266.
Special Features: May be installed for over two dozen word processing programs. Can display synonyms of synonyms. Has automatic root-word look-up feature. Approximately 15 synonyms per word are displayed. Compatible with terminate-and-stay-resident utilities such as SuperKey™, SideKick™, SmartKey™, ProKey™, etc.
Comments: This is a straightforward program with *lots* of synonyms.
Warranty: 30-day, money-back guarantee
Support: Phone and letter
Update Policy: $5 to $20

2.8.2.3 Webster's Electronic Thesaurus

• BASIC PRODUCT INFORMATION

Name of Program: Webster's Electronic Thesaurus
Company Name: Proximity®
Address: 3511 N.E. 22nd Ave., Fort Lauderdale, FL 33308
Phones: (800) 543-3511, (305) 566-3511
Price: $89.95
Version Reviewed: Not able to review.

Runs On: IBM PCs and compatibles
Memory Requirements: 96K of free RAM
Operating System Requirements: DOS 2.0 or greater
Disk Drive Requirements: 2
Copy Protected: No
Hard Disk Compatible: Yes
Specify Drive, Pathname, and Subdirectory: Yes
Total Program Size: 445K
Number of Words/Phrases Recognized: 40,000
Number of Synonyms: 470,000
Mode of Operation: Interactive
Automatic Insertion: Yes
Reviews: *PC Week* (August 4, 1987): 103.
Special Features: May be installed for over 30 word processing programs. Can display synonyms of synonyms. Maintains proper inflection (e.g., tense, number). Corrects misspelled words. This is the only thesaurus program that allows users to select synonyms based on shades of meaning. When a word in a document is highlighted, the program displays a list of various meanings for that word. Users select which shade of meaning they want synonyms for, and the program displays them.
Comments: This is a straightforward program with an enormous number of synonyms. Based on the Merriam-Webster *Webster's Collegiate Thesaurus*. May be uninstalled and memory regained.
Warranty: Media only
Support: Phone and letter
Update Policy: Free

2.8.3 Spelling-and-Thesaurus Programs

In this subsection we will look at several powerful spelling-and-thesaurus programs.

2.8.3.1 *Word Proof II*

- *BASIC PRODUCT INFORMATION*

Name of Program: Word Proof II
Company Name: IBM Personally Developed Software Division
Address: P.O. Box 3280, Wallingford, CT 06494
Phones: (800) 426-7279, (305) 998-2000
Price: $39.95
Version Reviewed: 1.00
Runs On: IBM PCs and compatibles
Memory Requirements: 128K
Operating System Requirements: DOS 2.0 or greater
Disk Drive Requirements: 1, 2 if using synonym function
Copy Protected: No
Hard Disk Compatible: Yes
Specify Drive, Pathname, and Subdirectory: Drive only
Total Program Size: 317K
Size of Dictionary: 125,000 words
Add To Dictionary: Yes, maximum of approximately 600 words.
Number of Words/Phrases Recognized: Not known
Number of Synonyms: Not known
Mode of Operation: Interactive or batch
Amount of Context Shown: Full-screen
Global Correction: No
Automatic Insertion: Yes
Specify Delimiter Characters: Yes
Mark Words That Change Length: No
Automatic Hyphenation: No
Hyphenation Exception List: Not applicable
Word Count: No
Reviews: Barry Owen, ed. "It's About Time," *PC Magazine* (November 26, 1985): 121–22.

Special Features: Includes full-screen editor, on-line help and menus, and anagram feature. Supports search and replace. Works with any ASCII text file. Spell check a single word, spell check starting at cursor, display synonyms. Star Proof Bridge ($14.95), available from IBM Personally Developed Software Division, converts WordStar files to ASCII, so they may be spell checked by Word Proof II.

Comments: This is a fast, feature-laden, inexpensive spell checker with a "natural," menu-driven interface. Its synonyms are usually quite helpful. Unlike many of the programs in this section, when its window with possible correct spellings or with synonyms pops up, it always pops up under the word in question, so that the word in its context is always visible. And like MicroSpell (see above), Word Proof II spell checks word by word, stopping when it comes to a word it does not recognize and allowing users to request possible correct spellings, to ignore the word, or to add the word to the supplemental dictionary. At any time during spell checking, users may exit the spelling mode and use Word Proof II to perform rudimentary word processing and editing chores on the file that was being spell checked and then return to the spell-checking mode. The most serious drawback to this program is the puny limitation of 600 additional words to the supplemental dictionary. The "manual" is a printable disk file.

Warranty: 90 days, media only
Support: Your local Authorized IBM Dealer
Update Policy: Not known

2.8.3.2 Turbo Lightning

- ## BASIC PRODUCT INFORMATION

Name of Program: Turbo Lightning™
Company Name: Borland International
Address: 4584 Scotts Valley Dr., Scotts Valley, CA 95066
Phones: (800) 255-8008, (800) 742-1133 (CA), (408) 438-8400
Price: $99.95
Version Reviewed: 1.0
Runs On: IBM PCs and compatibles
Memory Requirements: 128K
Operating System Requirements: DOS 2.0 or greater
Disk Drive Requirements: 2, hard disk recommended
Copy Protected: No
Hard Disk Compatible: Yes
Specify Drive, Pathname, and Subdirectory: Yes
Total Program Size: Maximum of 437K for hard disk configuration (including large 39K RAM dictionary), minimum of 343K for floppy systems (including small 16K RAM dictionary). Only 16,000 words can be in RAM at one time, unless Expanded Memory (EMS) is being used, in which case the entire 83,000 word dictionary may be placed in memory. Users must specify one of three different RAM-resident dictionaries to be used in auto-correct mode. The smallest dictionary is 16K (6,000 words) and the largest is 39K (16,000 words). The program requires a minimum of 84K of free RAM and a maximum of 104K.
Size of Dictionary: 83,000 words
Add To Dictionary: Yes, maximum of approximately 300 words.
Number of Words/Phrases Recognized: 5,000 words
Number of Synonyms: 50,000 words
Mode of Operation: Interactive
Amount of Context Shown: Full page
Global Correction: No
Automatic Insertion: Yes
Specify Delimiter Characters: No
Mark Words That Change Length: No
Automatic Hyphenation: No
Hyphenation Exception List: Not applicable
Word Count: No
Reviews: Ross Ramsey, "Turbo Lightning and Strike," *BYTE* (November 1986): 289–91; David L. Cipra, "Borland Is on Target With Turbo Lightning," *InfoWorld* (December 16, 1985): 33–34; "Lightning Strikes," *PC Magazine* (December 10, 1985): 113–18; "The Spark of Lightning," *PC Magazine* (December 10, 1985): 119–23; Ken Milburn, "Random Accessed," *PC World* (May 1986): 240–47; Rubin Rabinovitz, "A Way with Words," *PC Magazine* (July 1987): 252–54.

Special Features: Lightning's dictionary is the Random House Speller and Word List, and its synonym list is an abbreviated version of the Random House Thesaurus. Lightning's "look-up engine" has the ability to work with any compressed, alphabetized ASCII library file, which means that Lightning's potential applications extend far beyond those of a spell checker and thesaurus. The look-up engine could be used to access an encyclopedia, a list of quotations, and so forth. The program supports the Lotus/Intel/Microsoft Expanded Memory Specifications (EMS) and contains a large dictionary and thesaurus for hard disk users and smaller versions for floppy disk users.

Comments: The thesaurus is quite helpful, though it does not support synonym chaining and recognizes fewer root words and supplies fewer synonyms than some other programs. Synonyms are not grouped according to meaning. The spell checker is based on phonetic spellings and includes proper names, computer terms, and abbreviations. The spell checker can check a word at a time or a screen at a time but not a whole document at a time. Using the auto-correct spell check feature is frustrating since the largest dictionary that may be loaded into memory (without using EMS) is a paltry 16,000 words, which means that there will be lots of words it does not recognize and, consequently, lots of annoying "beeps." When used to proofread a word or screen, however, Lightning consults an 83,000 word dictionary. Pop-up windows sometimes cover the word being spell checked or for which synonyms are being offered.

Warranty: 60 days, media only

Support: Phone and letter

Update Policy: Not known

2.8.3.3 Random House Reference Set

● *BASIC PRODUCT INFORMATION*

Name of Program: Random House Reference Set

Company Name: Reference Software, Inc.

Address: 330 Townsend St., #135, San Francisco, CA 94107

Phones: (800) 872-9933, (415) 947-1000

Price: $89; $69 for thesaurus or dictionary alone

Version Reviewed: Not able to review.

Runs On: IBM PCs and compatibles

Memory Requirements: 128K

Operating System Requirements: DOS 2.0 or greater

Disk Drive Requirements: 2

Copy Protected: No

Hard Disk Compatible: Yes

Specify Drive, Pathname, and Subdirectory: Yes

Total Program Size: Not known. Dictionary file is 421K in size.

Size of Dictionary: 83,000 words

Add To Dictionary: Yes, maximum number of words not known.

Number of Words/Phrases Recognized: 30,000 words

Number of Synonyms: 300,000 words

Mode of Operation: Interactive or batch

Amount of Context Shown: Full-screen

Global Correction: No

Automatic Insertion: Yes

Specify Delimiter Characters: Not known

Mark Words That Change Length: No

Automatic Hyphenation: No

Hyphenation Exception List: Not applicable

Word Count: No

Reviews: Leon A. Wortman, "Dictionary and Speller Offer Power, Speed for Writers," *InfoWorld* (September 16, 1985); Leon A. Wortman, "Reference Set Version 2.02 Offers Many More Features," *InfoWorld* (April 21, 1986): 53–54; Ken Milburn, "Random Accessed," *PC World* (May 1986): 240–47; Rubin Rabinovitz, "A Way With Words," *PC Magazine* (July 1987): 251–52.

Special Features: Includes a macro feature that allows users to create and store text and commands. Up to nine 72-character macros may be created. Supplies antonyms. Can display DOS directory from within application programs, allows users to read files without exiting application programs, has wild-card look-up feature, and supports synonym chaining. Like Turbo Lightning, the Reference Set's generic look-up engine could be used to access other alphabetized, compressed, ASCII files, such as encyclopedia articles, quotations, and so forth. Supports Lotus/Intel/Microsoft Expanded Memory Specifications (EMS). Contains large dictionary and thesaurus for hard disk users and smaller versions for floppy disk users. Pop-up window does not cover word but allows it to be seen in context.

Comments: Contains the same dictionary and thesaurus as Turbo Lightning (see above). Has no auto-correct feature. The spell checker is based on phonetic spellings.

Warranty: Not known

Support: Not known

Update Policy: Not known

2.8.4 Style Programs

Style programs, also known as "style analyzers," flag grammatical, punctuation, and word-usage mistakes and suggest corrections. Before listing the salient facts about these programs, we need to pause and discuss the differences between *grammar* and *style* so that we will have a better understanding of what "style analyzers" can and cannot do—or rather how seriously we should take their criticisms and suggestions.

Generally speaking, *style* has to do with word usage, sentence length, and sentence structure. It is difficult, however, to give an exact definition of *style*, and it is even more difficult to formulate stylistic rules with which contemporary authorities all agree. Although general stylistic principles and guidelines exist, to a greater or lesser extent style is a matter of taste and preference, not of hard-and-fast, immutable rules. To a lesser but nevertheless real extent, *grammar*, too, is difficult to capture precisely in a set of rules. Grammatical conventions undergo subtle and sometimes not so subtle changes from era to era. Even within an era, punctuation, syntax, agreement of verb and subject, and other grammatical considerations can vary from culture to culture (e.g., British grammar versus American grammar) and from authority to authority within a culture (e.g., subtle differences between *The Chicago Manual of Style* and *Words Into Type*). William Zinsser, Theodore Bernstein, H. W. Fowler, William Safire, Strunk and White, William Follett, and other modern authorities do not agree on every grammatical or stylistic issue. In a given culture, except for new words (Is it compact *disk* or compact *disc*?), a word is spelled correctly or incorrectly. Disputes are easily settled by consulting a dictionary whose spellings are regarded as authoritative, something a computer program can be "taught" to do, as we have seen. Grammatical disputes, too, can be fairly easy to settle. As long as the parties to the dispute can agree on a common authority and set of rules, a computer program can be "taught" to look for violations of these rules, to mark infractions, and to suggest corrections.

But style is a different matter. It is not easy to write a computer program that accurately and judiciously advises users on matters of style.[179] Computer programs that check style do so by following rules that specify how words, phrases, and punctuation are to be used, what is grammatically acceptable and what is not, and what constitutes long and complex sentences. Style analyzers are rule-oriented programs. Although style programs "know" many rules, they cannot apply these rules sagaciously because they lack "intelligence." They (1) cannot discern the meaning of words and phrases or (2) understand the structural and semantic contexts in which words and phrases are

---

179. Most microcomputer style programs trace their lineage to Bell Labs' famous Writer's Workbench, a minicomputer-based cornucopia of over three dozen programs for proofreading (spelling, punctuation, capitalization, faulty phrases), style analysis (number of sentences, word and sentence length, sentence type, voice, nominalizations, and so forth), and parts-of-speech checking. The Writer's Workbench runs under UNIX. Currently, Writer's Workbench source or binary code is available for $800.

FEATURES	WP	NWS	EW	MS	JS	Men	SW	MS+	SC	WPS	TH	WPII	NWF	WF	WET	TL	RHR
Price	120	60	130	69	110	100	75	99	40	60	50	40	70	80	90	100	89
Runs On	I,C	I,A	I,T,C	I	I	M	M	M	M	M	M	I	I	I	I	I	I
Memory (in K)	64	128	64	128	384	512	512	512	128	512	512	128	128	128	96	128	128
Disk Drives	1	1	1	2	2	1	1	2	1	1	1	1	2	2	1	2	2
Program Size (in K)	185	207	200	236	324	350	334	40	213	190	140	317	436	325	400	437	421
Dictionary Size (in K)	45	114	50	80	130	80	93	75	125	73	50	125	—	—	—	83	83
Add to Dictionary	●	●	●	●	●	●	●	●	●	●	●	●	—	—	—	●	●
Root Words (in K)	—	—	—	—	—	—	—	—	—	—	—	—	20	15	40	5	30
Synonyms (in K)	—	—	—	—	—	—	—	—	—	—	—	—	120	220	470	50	300
Mode of Operation	B	B	B	B	B	I,B	B	I	B	I,B	I,B	B	I	I	I	I	I,B
Global Correction	●	●	○	○	○	○	●	○	○	○	●	○	—	—	—	○	○
Automatic Insertion	○	●	●	●	●	●	●	●	●	●	●	●	●	●	●	●	●
Delimiter Characters	●	●	○	●	●	—	—	—	—	—	—	●	—	—	—	○	?
Automatic Hyphenation	●	○	●	○	○	○	○	●	○	●	○	○	—	—	—	○	○
Hyphenation Exception List	●	○	●	○	○	○	○	?	○	●	○	○	—	—	—	○	○
Word Count	●	●	●	●	○	●	○	●	○	○	●	○	—	—	—	○	○
Lines of Context	1	9	10	8	9	Full	?	3	8	16	Full	Full	—	—	—	Full	Full

Table 2.4: Comparison of spelling and thesaurus programs. I = IBM, C = CP/M, A = Apple, T = TRS, B = Batch, I = Interactive, WP = The Word Plus, NWS = Webster's NewWorld Spelling Checker, EW = Electric Webster, MS = MicroSpell, JS = Jet:Spell, Men = Mentor, SW = Spellswell, MS+ = MacSpell+, SC = Spelling Champion, WPS = WorksPlus Spell, TH = Thunder!, WPII = Word Proof II, NWF = Webster's NewWorld On-Line Thesaurus, WF = Word Finder, WET = Webster's Electronic Thesaurus, TL = Turbo Lightning, RHR = Random House Reference Set.

used or (3) grasp the purpose of a piece of writing or (4) identify the audience to which the writing is directed or (5) understand a genre and its particular stylistic features. Thus style analyzers are unable to make accurate, context-sensitive judgments about the appropriateness of using a certain word or phrase in a particular context. All they can do is woodenly apply their rules to everything they are shown. Because of that, style analyzers do not allow for *personal* style, for deviations from the rules. And for every rule of style, of course, there are many situations in which it is not only permissible to break the rule but better to do so than to observe it.

Some people prefer William Faulkner, James Joyce, or e. e. cummings, but I doubt that any style program would. Other people prefer Ian Flemming or a Hemingway short story, and I suspect most style programs would, too! Here's why. Generally speaking, current shibboleths among style programs include (1) the passive voice, (2) lengthy sentences, (3) complex sentences, (4) fragmented sentences, (5) negative constructions, (6) long words, (7) sophisticated or little-used words, (8) superlatives, (9) clichés, (10) folksy, colloquial, and slang phrases, (11) wordy phrases, (12) split infinitives, (13) sentences that begin with a conjunction, (14) long paragraphs, (15) jargon, (16) redundancy, (17) vague words, and much more.

Those reservations notwithstanding, style programs have the potential to help inexperienced writers, overly technical writers, writers whose style is too complex for their audiences, and persons who do not know "the rules of style." For example, Writer's Workbench has been used at a number of universities and is reported to have improved the writing of both students and faculty.[180] Although less powerful than Writer's Workbench, after which many of them are patterned, the microcomputer style programs listed below can help to improve a person's writing. These programs work with ASCII text files, and the best of them allow users to edit the program's phrase dictionary or dictionaries and to add new phrases. All of the programs can be installed for a variety of word processors, and most of them are menu-driven and interactive.

For more information, see Robin Raskin, "The Quest for Style," *PC Magazine* (May 27, 1986): 189–207; A. Reed, "Anatomy of a Text Analysis Package," *Computer Languages* 9 (1984): 89–96; Steve Rosenthal, "Writing Utilities: PC Wordworking Tools Carve Their Niche Among Perfectionists," *PC Week* (April 8, 1986): 57–59; Deborah Kovacs, "Turning First Drafts Into Final Drafts," *Classroom Computer Learning* 7 (October 1986): 36–39; Joyce Kinkead, "Matching Software and Curriculum: A Description of Four Text-Analysis Programs," *Computers and Composition* 3 (August 1986): 33–35; David N. Dobrin, "Style Analyzers Once More," *Computers and Composition* 3 (August 1986): 22–32; and Barbara Lewis and Robert Lewis, "Do Style Checkers Work Work?," *PC World* (July 1987): 246–52.[181]

---

180. See Kathleen E. Kiefer and Charles R. Smith, "Textual Analysis with Computers: Tests of Bell Laboratories' Computer Software," *Research in the Teaching of English* 17 (October 1983): 201–14; Charles R. Smith, Kathleen E. Kiefer, and Patricia S. Gingrich, "Computers Come of Age in Writing Instruction," *Computers and the Humanities* 18 (1984): 215–24; Kathleen E. Kiefer and Charles R. Smith, "Improving Students' Revising and Editing: The Writer's Workbench System," in *The Computer in Composition Instruction,* ed. William Wresch (Urbana: National Council of Teachers of English, 1984), 65–82; Lorinda L. Cherry et al., "Computer Aids for Text Analysis," *Bell Laboratories Record* (May/June 1983): 10–16; William V. Van Pelt, "Another Approach to Using Writer's Workbench Programs: Small Class Applications," in *Sixth International Congress on Computers and the Humanities,* ed. Sarah K. Burton and Douglas D. Short (Rockville: Computer Science Press, 1983), 725–29; Charles R. Smith and Kathleen E. Kiefer, "Using the Writer's Workbench Programs at Colorado State University," in *Sixth International Congress on Computers and the Humanities,* ed. Sarah K. Burton and Douglas D. Short (Rockville: Computer Science Press, 1983), 672–84; Carol L. Raye, "Writer's Workbench System: Heralding a Revolution in Textual Analysis," in *Sixth International Congress on Computers and the Humanities,* ed. Sarah K. Burton and Douglas D. Short (Rockville: Computer Science Press, 1983), 569–72; cf. *PC Magazine* (May 27, 1986): 194.

181. Because it is not as powerful as the programs listed below, I am not including information about PC-Style (Buttonware, P.O. Box 5786, Bellevue, WA 98006; (206) 454-0479; $29.95).

2.8.4.1 Punctuation & Style

- BASIC PRODUCT INFORMATION

Name of Program: Punctuation & Style
Company Name: Oasis Systems/FTL
Address: 6160 Lusk Blvd., #C-206, San Diego, CA 92121
Phone: (619) 453-5711
Price: $125
Version Reviewed: IBM 1.21
Runs On: IBM PCs and compatibles and CP/M machines
Memory Requirements: 64K
Operating System Requirements: IBM: DOS 1.0 or greater; CP/M: 2.2
Disk Drive Requirements: 1
Copy Protected: No
Hard Disk Compatible: Yes
Specify Drive, Pathname, and Subdirectory: Drive only
Total Program Size: 48K
Marks Original or Backup Copy: Backup
Automatic Insertion: No
Amount of Context Shown: 1 to 4 lines
Global Correction: No
Specify Delimiter Characters: Yes

- GRAMMATICAL INFORMATION

Flags Mixed Cases: Yes
Flags Missing Capital Letter: Yes
Flags Faulty Punctuation: Yes
Flags Unbalanced Punctuation Pairs: Yes
Flags Faulty Spacing: Yes
Flags Faulty Punctuation in Abbreviations: Yes
Flags Doubled Words: Yes

- STYLISTIC INFORMATION

Size of Phrase Dictionary: 700+
Edit Phrase Dictionary: Yes
Add To Phrase Dictionary: Yes, maximum number of words limited only by available disk space.
Flags Negative Phrases: No
Flags Awkward Phrases: Yes
Flags Cliches: Yes
Flags Archaic Phrases: No
Flags Jargon: No
Flags Erroneous Phrases: Yes
Flags Folksy or Colloquial Phrases: Yes
Flags Vague or Ambiguous Phrases: Yes
Flags Overused Phrases: No
Flags Pompous Phrases: Yes
Flags Redundant Phrases: Yes
Flags Wordy Phrases: Yes
Flags Sexist and Other Offensive Phrases: No
Flags Incorrectly Used Verbs: No
Flags Incorrectly Used Pronouns: No
Flags Passive Voice: Yes
Flags Split Infinitives: No
Flags Legalese: No
Flags Long Sentences: No
Flags Complex Sentences: No
Flags Incomplete Sentences: No

Flags Sentences That Begin With *But*: No
Flags Long Paragraphs: No
Syllable Count: No
Word Count: No
Words-Per-Sentence Count: No
Sentence Count: No
Provides Readability Index: No

- *OTHER INFORMATION*

Warranty: None
Support: Phone and letter
Update Policy: Not known
Reviews: Terry Tinsley Datz and F. Lloyd Datz, "Punctuation + Style, StarIndex, and Updates," *Softalk* (February 1984): 81–86; Anne Wayman-Blick, "A Clash of Styles—What Two Packages Can—and Cannot—Do to Improve Your Writing," *Profiles* (June 1984): 59–66; Wayne Holder, "Software Tools for Writers," BYTE (July 1982): 138–63.
Special Features: The ability to edit and add to the phrase dictionary is quite useful.
Comments: The phrase portion of the program is based on the Writer's Workbench. The small amount of context shown can be frustrating, as is the fact that this program works in two passes: one pass to mark mistakes and a second to correct them.

2.8.4.2 Grammatik II

- *BASIC PRODUCT INFORMATION*

Name of Program: Grammatik II
Company Name: Reference Software, Inc.
Address: 330 Townsend St., #135, San Francisco, CA 94107
Phones: (800) 872-9933, (415) 947-1000
Price: $89
Version Reviewed: IBM 1.83
Runs On: IBM PCs and compatibles, CP/M machines
Memory Requirements: IBM: 128K
Operating System Requirements: IBM: DOS 2.0 or greater; CP/M: 2.2 or greater
Disk Drive Requirements: 1
Copy Protected: No
Hard Disk Compatible: Yes
Specify Drive, Pathname, and Subdirectory: Yes
Total Program Size: 63K
Marks Original or Backup Copy: User's choice
Automatic Insertion: No
Amount of Context Shown: 1 to 20 lines
Global Correction: No
Specify Delimiter Characters: Yes

- *GRAMMATICAL INFORMATION*

Flags Mixed Cases: Yes
Flags Missing Capital Letter: Yes
Flags Faulty Punctuation: Yes
Flags Unbalanced Punctuation Pairs: Yes
Flags Faulty Spacing: Yes
Flags Faulty Punctuation in Abbreviations: Yes
Flags Doubled Words: Yes

- *STYLISTIC INFORMATION*

Size of Phrase Dictionary: 1,000+
Edit Phrase Dictionary: Yes
Add To Phrase Dictionary: Yes, maximum number of words not known.

Flags Negative Phrases: No
Flags Awkward Phrases: Yes
Flags Cliches: Yes
Flags Archaic Phrases: Yes
Flags Jargon: Yes
Flags Erroneous Phrases: Yes
Flags Folksy or Colloquial Phrases: Yes
Flags Vague or Ambiguous Phrases: Yes
Flags Overused Phrases: Yes
Flags Pompous Phrases: Yes
Flags Redundant Phrases: Yes
Flags Wordy Phrases: Yes
Flags Sexist and Other Offensive Phrases: Yes
Flags Incorrectly Used Verbs: Some
Flags Incorrectly Used Pronouns: No
Flags Passive Voice: Yes
Flags Split Infinitives: Yes
Flags Legalese: No
Flags Long Sentences: Yes (longer than 14 words)
Flags Complex Sentences: No
Flags Incomplete Sentences: No
Flags Sentences That Begin With *But*: No
Flags Long Paragraphs: No
Syllable Count: No; incorporated into Flesch-Kincaid reading
Word Count: Yes
Words-Per-Sentence Count: Gives average
Sentence Count: Yes
Provides Readability Index: Yes; uses Flesch-Kincaid criteria.

- *OTHER INFORMATION*

Warranty: 90 days, media only
Support: Phone and letter
Update Policy: Not known
Reviews: Anne Wayman-Blick, "A Clash of Styles—What Two Packages Can—and Cannot—Do to Improve Your Writing," *Profiles* (June 1984): 59–66; Ernest E. Mau, "Grammatik II," *Online Today* (February 1987): 48–49; Barbara Lewis and Robert Lewis, "Do Style Checkers Work Work?," *PC World* (July 1987): 246–48.
Special Features: Users can add up to seven categories of words and/or phrases to be counted; detects some spelling errors; flags some terms that are trademarks.
Comments: This helpful program is hindered by its mark-now-correct-later, two-step approach; documents may not be corrected interactively. Can be installed for 14 different word processors.

2.8.4.3 *RightWriter*

- *BASIC PRODUCT INFORMATION*

Name of Program: RightWriter
Company Name: RightSoft, Inc.
Address: 2033 Wood St., Suite 218, Sarasota, FL 33577
Phone: (813) 952-9211
Price: $95; RightWords is available for $29.95 (allows words and phrases to be added to dictionary).
Version Reviewed: 2.1
Runs On: IBM PCs and compatibles
Memory Requirements: 256K
Operating System Requirements: DOS 1.1 or greater
Disk Drive Requirements: 2
Copy Protected: No
Hard Disk Compatible: Yes
Specify Drive, Pathname, and Subdirectory: Yes
Total Program Size: 229K
Marks Original or Backup Copy: Backup

Automatic Insertion: No
Amount of Context Shown: Whole page
Global Correction: No
Specify Delimiter Characters: No

- GRAMMATICAL INFORMATION

Flags Mixed Cases: Yes
Flags Missing Capital Letter: Yes
Flags Faulty Punctuation: Yes
Flags Unbalanced Punctuation Pairs: Yes
Flags Faulty Spacing: No
Flags Faulty Punctuation in Abbreviations: No
Flags Doubled Words: Yes

- STYLISTIC INFORMATION

Size of Phrase Dictionary: 45,000 words
Edit Phrase Dictionary: No
Add To Phrase Dictionary: No, but the utility RightWords allows users to add up to 100,000 words to the Uncommon Word List.
Flags Negative Phrases: Yes
Flags Awkward Phrases: Yes
Flags Cliches: Yes
Flags Archaic Phrases: Yes
Flags Jargon: Yes
Flags Erroneous Phrases: Yes
Flags Folksy or Colloquial Phrases: Yes
Flags Vague or Ambiguous Phrases: Yes
Flags Overused Phrases: Yes
Flags Pompous Phrases: Yes
Flags Redundant Phrases: Yes
Flags Wordy Phrases: Yes
Flags Sexist and Other Offensive Phrases: Yes
Flags Incorrectly Used Verbs: Yes
Flags Incorrectly Used Pronouns: Yes
Flags Passive Voice: Yes
Flags Split Infinitives: Yes
Flags Legalese: Yes
Flags Long Sentences: Yes (longer than 22 words)
Flags Complex Sentences: Yes
Flags Incomplete Sentences: Yes
Flags Sentences That Begin With *But*: Yes
Flags Long Paragraphs: Yes
Syllable Count: Yes
Word Count: Yes
Words-Per-Sentence Count: No
Sentence Count: Yes
Provides Readability Index: Yes

- OTHER INFORMATION

Warranty: 90 days, media only
Support: Phone and letter
Update Policy: Registered users may update to version 2.0 for $24.95.
Reviews: Helen A. Gordon, "Rightwriter," *DATABASE* (December 1985): 53–56; Bryan Pfaffenberger, "The Scholar's Library: Rightwriter 2.0," *Research in Word Processing Newsletter* 4 (April 1986): 27–31.
Special Features: RightWriter provides word counts, word-frequency lists, lists of uncommon words, an overall critique of writing styles, information about the grade level needed by readers to understand a document, the "strength level" of writing styles, a measure of the use of adjectives and adverbs, and recommendations about how to improve writing style. Unlike the other style analyzers we have ex-

amined (which operate interactively), RightWriter processes a document in a single batch-mode operation.

Comments: Readability level is calculated by using the Flesch-Kincaid formula, which is the U.S. Department of Defense's standard formula (DOD MIL-M-38784B). A document's Readability Index is equivalent to its Overall Reading Grade Level (ORGL). RightWriter uses 3,000 different rules. The ability to add to the Uncommon Word List is helpful, but the inability to add to the main dictionary—the phrase dictionary—(as you can with Punctuation & Style) is lamentable. RightWords includes seven special word lists (business, electrical and electronic, computer, navigation and communication, weapon systems control, shipboard electrical and mechanical, and aircraft), only one of which may be active at a time. Also lamentable is the lack of support for turning features off, such as the sentence-length or complex-sentence features.

2.8.4.4 Electric Webster

• *BASIC PRODUCT INFORMATION*

Name of Program: Electric Webster
Company Name: Cornucopia Software, Inc.
Address: P.O. Box 6111, Albany, CA 94706
Phones: (800) 343-2432, (415) 524-8098
Price: $129.95 ($149.95 for TRS version; $129.95 for CP/M version)
Version Reviewed: IBM 2.0
Runs On: IBM PCs and compatibles, TRS -80 Models 1, III, or 4, and CP/M-80 systems
Memory Requirements: 64K
Operating System Requirements: IBM: DOS 1.10 or greater
Disk Drive Requirements: 1
Copy Protected: No
Hard Disk Compatible: Yes
Specify Drive, Pathname, and Subdirectory: Yes
Total Program Size: 200K (dictionary and program); grammar program is additional 76K.
Marks Original or Backup Copy: Original
Automatic Insertion: Yes, if desired
Amount of Context Shown: 4 to 10 lines
Global Correction: No
Specify Delimiter Characters: No

• *GRAMMATICAL INFORMATION*

Flags Mixed Cases: No
Flags Missing Capital Letter: Yes
Flags Faulty Punctuation: Yes
Flags Unbalanced Punctuation Pairs: No
Flags Faulty Spacing: Yes
Flags Faulty Punctuation in Abbreviations: No
Flags Doubled Words: Yes

• *STYLISTIC INFORMATION*

Size of Phrase Dictionary: Not known
Edit Phrase Dictionary: Yes
Add To Phrase Dictionary: Yes
Flags Negative Phrases: Yes
Flags Awkward Phrases: No
Flags Cliches: Yes
Flags Archaic Phrases: Yes
Flags Jargon: No
Flags Erroneous Phrases: No
Flags Folksy or Colloquial Phrases: Yes
Flags Vague or Ambiguous Phrases: Yes
Flags Overused Phrases: No
Flags Pompous Phrases: No

Flags Redundant Phrases: No
Flags Wordy Phrases: No
Flags Sexist and Other Offensive Phrases: No
Flags Incorrectly Used Verbs: No
Flags Incorrectly Used Pronouns: No
Flags Passive Voice: Yes
Flags Split Infinitives: No
Flags Legalese: No
Flags Long Sentences: Yes (longer than 18 words; setting may be changed)
Flags Complex Sentences: Yes
Flags Incomplete Sentences: No
Flags Sentences That Begin With *But*: No
Flags Long Paragraphs: No
Syllable Count: No
Word Count: Yes
Words-Per-Sentence Count: Yes, gives average.
Sentence Count: No
Provides Readability Index: Yes

● *OTHER INFORMATION*

Warranty: Not known
Support: Not known
Update Policy: Not known
Reviews: Dan Robinson, "Much More Than a Spelling Checker," *Creative Computing* (November 1983); Frank J. Derfler, "Electric Webster," *InfoWorld* (other bibliographical data not known); *Personal Publishing* (June 1986): 15; *Personal Publishing* (August 1986): 19; Barbara Lewis and Robert Lewis, "Do Style Checkers Work Work?," *PC World* (July 1987): 248–51.
Special Features: None
Comments: As a grammar/style checker, Electric Webster is noticeably weaker than Punctuation & Style, Grammatik II, and RightWriter. As I noted above, it has a "clunky" interface.

2.8.4.5 *Thelma Thistleblossom*

● *BASIC PRODUCT INFORMATION*

Name of Program: Thelma Thistleblossom
Company Name: Timp Software
Address: P.O. Box 37, Orem, UT 84057
Phone: (801) 226-9865
Price: $90
Version Reviewed: 1.1
Runs On: IBM PCs and compatibles
Memory Requirements: 256K
Operating System Requirements: DOS 2.0 or greater
Disk Drive Requirements: 2
Copy Protected: No
Hard Disk Compatible: Yes
Specify Drive, Pathname, and Subdirectory: Yes
Total Program Size: 159K
Marks Original or Backup Copy: Original
Automatic Insertion: Yes
Amount of Context Shown: Full-screen
Global Correction: No
Specify Delimiter Characters: Automatically ignores codes in WordPerfect™ files.

● *GRAMMATICAL INFORMATION*

Flags Mixed Cases: No
Flags Missing Capital Letter: No
Flags Faulty Punctuation: Yes

Flags Unbalanced Punctuation Pairs: No
Flags Faulty Spacing: No
Flags Faulty Punctuation in Abbreviations: Yes
Flags Doubled Words: Yes

- ## STYLISTIC INFORMATION

Size of Phrase Dictionary: Not known
Edit Phrase Dictionary: No
Add To Phrase Dictionary: No
Flags Negative Phrases: No
Flags Awkward Phrases: Yes
Flags Cliches: Yes
Flags Archaic Phrases: No
Flags Jargon: No
Flags Erroneous Phrases: No
Flags Folksy or Colloquial Phrases: Yes
Flags Vague or Ambiguous Phrases: Yes
Flags Overused Phrases: Yes
Flags Pompous Phrases: No
Flags Redundant Phrases: Yes
Flags Wordy Phrases: Yes
Flags Sexist and Other Offensive Phrases: No
Flags Incorrectly Used Verbs: No
Flags Incorrectly Used Pronouns: No
Flags Passive Voice: No
Flags Split Infinitives: Yes
Flags Legalese: No
Flags Long Sentences: Yes
Flags Complex Sentences: No
Flags Incomplete Sentences: No
Flags Sentences That Begin With *But*: Yes
Flags Long Paragraphs: No
Syllable Count: No
Word Count: No
Words-Per-Sentence Count: Yes
Sentence Count: No
Provides Readability Index: Yes, four different scales (Flesch, Coleman, Kincaid, ARI)

- ## OTHER INFORMATION

Warranty: 15-day, money-back guarantee; 60 day warranty on media
Support: Phone and letter
Update Policy: Minimal cost
Reviews: None
Special Features: Interactive and menu-driven. Flags acronyms, words with incorrectly mixed lower- and upper-case letters, apostrophes, hyphenated words, phrases used three or more times, and doubled words.
Comments: This program is designed to work with WordPerfect™ files and with ordinary ASCII files. Version 1.2 will help locate changes in tense, passive constructions, nominalizations, and transitions.

2.8.4.6 MacProof

- ## BASIC PRODUCT INFORMATION

Name of Program: MacProof™
Company Name: Automated Language Processing Systems
Address: 295 Chipeta Way, P.O. Box 8719, Salt Lake City, UT 84108
Phones: (800) 354-5656, (801) 584-3000, (801) 375-0090
Price: $195
Version Reviewed: Not able to review; current version is 3.0.

Runs On: Macintoshes
Memory Requirements: 512K
Operating System Requirements: Macintosh
Disk Drive Requirements: 1
Copy Protected: No
Hard Disk Compatible: Yes
Specify Drive, Pathname, and Subdirectory: Not applicable
Total Program Size: Not known
Marks Original or Backup Copy: Original
Automatic Insertion: Yes
Amount of Context Shown: Full-screen
Global Correction: No
Specify Delimiter Characters: Not applicable

- GRAMMATICAL INFORMATION

Flags Mixed Cases: No
Flags Missing Capital Letter: Yes
Flags Faulty Punctuation: Yes
Flags Unbalanced Punctuation Pairs: Yes
Flags Faulty Spacing: No
Flags Faulty Punctuation in Abbreviations: No
Flags Doubled Words: Yes

- STYLISTIC INFORMATION

Size of Phrase Dictionary: Not known
Edit Phrase Dictionary: No
Add To Phrase Dictionary: Yes
Flags Negative Phrases: No
Flags Awkward Phrases: Yes
Flags Cliches: Yes
Flags Archaic Phrases: Yes
Flags Jargon: Yes
Flags Erroneous Phrases: Yes
Flags Folksy or Colloquial Phrases: Yes
Flags Vague or Ambiguous Phrases: Yes
Flags Overused Phrases: Yes
Flags Pompous Phrases: Yes
Flags Redundant Phrases: No
Flags Wordy Phrases: Yes
Flags Sexist and Other Offensive Phrases: Yes
Flags Incorrectly Used Verbs: Yes
Flags Incorrectly Used Pronouns: No
Flags Passive Voice: Not known
Flags Split Infinitives: Not known
Flags Legalese: No
Flags Long Sentences: No
Flags Complex Sentences: No
Flags Incomplete Sentences: No
Flags Sentences That Begin With *But*: Not known
Flags Long Paragraphs: No
Syllable Count: No
Word Count: Yes
Words-Per-Sentence Count: No
Sentence Count: Yes
Provides Readability Index: No

- OTHER INFORMATION

Warranty: Not known
Support: Phone and letter

Update Policy: Not known

Reviews: Cynthia Harriman, "English-Teacher-on-a-Disk," *Macworld* (March 1987): 151–52.

Special Features: Includes 93,000-word spell checker that identifies each word's grammatical category. A mulituser, networked version is available for $195 per node. Up to 15 Macintoshes may be networked via AppleTalk to a sixteenth Macintosh that functions as the server.

Comments: Version 3.0 functions as a Desk Accessory and so allows corrections to be made interactively from within the program.

2.9 Keyboard Macro Utilities

Keyboard macro utilities (also known as "keyboard enhancers" and as "macro programs") are handy, memory-resident programs that allow users to assign character strings, commands, or both to various two-key combinations.[182] Once a macro program has been loaded into memory, key assignments may be made and macros executed from within application programs. Hundreds and thousands of characters—whole pages and documents—may be assigned to a single two-key combination, as may complex sequences of word processing (or other) commands. Keyboard macro utilities can save countless keystrokes by allowing often-used phrases and commands to be entered with two-key combinations.[183] Some macro programs allow users to create pop-up, user-defined command menus, so that application programs may be run with user-created macros, which is a nice way to customize an application program.[184] Most macro programs, in fact, include sets of predefined macros for various popular application programs, such as Lotus 1-2-3™, dBase III™, VisiCalc™, WordStar®, Multiplan™, SuperCalc™, and so forth.

Here's how macro programs work. In chapter 1 we learned that the keyboard interrupt service routines are normally used to intercept and translate keyboard scan codes into ASCII codes and to store the results in the ROM-BIOS's 32-byte buffer, where they remain until a program removes them and sends them to video memory. Macro programs either substitute themselves for the service routines and do all the intercepting and translating of keyboard scan codes, or they work with the service routines and modify them as necessary. Thus macro programs are designed to take advantage of the difference between keyboard scan codes and the values those codes can be assigned before they are placed in the ROM-BIOS's buffer. Programs that use the first approach "steal" the interrupt by replacing the interrupt vector with vectors of their own that point into the macro programs. Programs that monitor and modify the interrupt's service routines attach themselves to its interrupt vector so that they can inspect every scan code for the special macro codes. Once they spot a special macro code, the programs intervene with routines that translate the code into the character string specified by the macro and place the results in the ROM-BIOS's buffer. XyWrite III and Nota Bene are examples of programs that steal the interrupt. Most keyboard macro programs, however, merely attach themselves to the interrupt's interrupt vector, whose routines they supplement with routines of their own.[185]

---

182. *Macro* refers to a single instruction that represents and executes multiple operations. *Memory-resident* refers to a program that stays in memory after it has been loaded and exited. Memory-resident programs are designed to be accessible from within application programs. Memory-resident programs are also known as "RAM-resident programs" and as "terminate-and-stay-resident programs" (TSR). Because of their memory-resident nature, some keyboard enhancers are incompatible with some application programs. Likewise, trying to work with two or more memory-resident programs concurrently (e.g., macro programs, print spoolers, desktop utility programs) may result in conflict and chaos.

183. Typically, one of the two keys is a shifting key and the other an alpha key.

184. The same trick also may be used to create complete menu-driven, macro-run, turnkey computer systems.

185. For more information on these topics, see chapter 1 and Charles Petzold, "Keyboard Macros and Redefinition," *PC Magazine* (June 24, 1986): 255–65, especially pages 255–58.

FEATURES	PS	GII	RW	EW	TT	MP
BASIC INFORMATION						
Price	125	89	95	130	90	195
Runs On	I, C	I	I	I, T	I	M
Memory (in K)	64	128	256	64	256	512
Disk Drives	1	1	2	1	2	1
Program Size (in K)	48	63	229	200	159	?
Automatic Insertion	O	O	O	●	●	●
No. of Lines of Context Shown	4	20	Full Scn.	10	Full Scn.	Full Scn.
GRAMMATICAL INFORMATION						
Flags Mixed Cases	●	●	●	O	O	O
Flags Missing Capital Letter	●	●	●	●	O	●
Flags Faulty Punctuation	●	●	●	●	●	●
Flags Faulty Spacing	●	●	O	●	O	O
Flags Unbalanced Punctuation Pairs	●	●	●	O	O	●
Flags Faulty Punct. in Abbreviations	●	●	O	O	●	O
Flags Doubled Words	●	●	●	●	●	●
STYLISTIC INFORMATION						
Size of Phrase Dictionary	700	900+	45,000	?	?	?
Edit Phrase Dictionary	●	●	O	●	O	O
Add to Phrase Dictionary	●	●	O	●	O	●
Flags Negative Phrases	O	O	●	●	O	O
Flags Awkward Phrases	●	●	●	O	●	●
Flags Clichés	●	●	●	●	●	●
Flags Archaic Phrases	O	●	●	●	O	●
Flags Jargon	O	●	●	O	O	●
Flags Erroneous Phrases	●	●	●	O	O	●
Flags Folksy or Colloquial Phrases	●	●	●	●	●	●
Flags Vague or Ambiguous Phrases	●	●	●	O	●	●
Flags Overused Phrases	O	●	●	O	●	●
Flags Pompous Phrases	●	●	●	O	O	●
Flags Redundant Phrases	●	●	●	O	●	O
Flags Wordy Phrases	●	●	●	O	●	●
Flags Sexist Phrases	O	●	●	O	O	●
Flags Incorrectly Used Verbs	O	●	●	O	O	●
Flags Incorrectly Used Pronouns	O	O	●	O	O	O
Flags Passive Voice	●	●	●	●	O	?
Flags Split Infinitives	O	●	●	O	●	?
Flags Legalese	O	O	●	O	O	O
Flags Long Sentences	O	●	●	●	●	O
Flags Complex Sentences	O	O	●	●	O	O
Flags Incomplete Sentences	O	O	●	O	O	O
Flags Sentences That Begin w/*But*	O	O	●	O	●	?
Flags Long Paragraphs	O	O	●	O	O	O
Syllable Count	O	O	●	O	O	O
Word Count	O	●	●	●	O	●
Word-Per-Sentence Count	O	●	O	●	●	O
Sentence Count	O	●	●	O	O	●
Readability Index	O	●	●	●	●	O

Table 2.5: Comparison of style programs. I = IBM, C = CP/M, T = TRS, M = Macintosh, PS = Punctuation & Style, GII = Grammatik II, RW = RightWriter, EW = Electric Webster, TT = Thelma Thistleblossom, MP = MacProof.

Separate sets of macros may be created for one application program or for separate application programs. Once created, macros may be stored on disk as files and read into memory as required. Macros may be created (defined), edited, and saved from within application programs by using a macro program's built-in macro editor or by using a macro program's ability to record keystrokes and assign them to key combinations. Most keyboard enhancers allow macros to be created with any ASCII text editor or word processing program. Other macro programs, such as SuperKey™, allow data from the screen to be captured and inserted into a specified macro, something that is useful for transporting information from program to program. And SmartKey II Plus™ allows users to define macros by recalling the last 64 keystrokes. When creating macros from within application programs by recording keystrokes, keyboard enhancers typically require that a "begin-definition" key sequence such as *Alt=* be used. The macro is then entered and followed by an "end-definition" key sequence such as *Alt−*. That method of creating macros allows them to be tested as they are created.

Among their many applications, keyboard enhancers enable users to assign the upper 128 ASCII characters to simple key combinations, to execute complex sequences of word processing (or other) commands with single two-key combinations, to enter short or long strings of characters, to reassign keys and redefine the keyboard, and to redefine application program commands. Not only do macro programs eliminate typing thousands of keystrokes, thus saving time, they also eliminate the tediousness of entering repetitive material and commands, thus reducing mistakes. Although some word processing programs (e.g., XyWrite III™, Nota Bene™, FinalWord II™, WordPerfect™) have extensive, built-in macro capabilities, keyboard enhancers allow macros to be used with a broad range of application programs and typically include bells and whistles not found on most word processing macro programs.

All of the keyboard programs listed below support the following functions: (1) verification before redefining an existing macro, (2) use of multiple directories, (3) pop-up editors for creating, reading, and writing macros from within application programs, (4) merging existing macro files, (5) displaying assigned macro titles, (6) displaying actual macros, (7) recording and echoing keystrokes, (8) variable- and fixed-length fields in macros, (9) separate macros for Shift with keypad numbers and Shift with top-row numbers, (10) user-created macro menus, (11) programmable playback delays, (12) a "skip-macro" key, (13) terminating a macro during execution, (14) listing all current macros, and (15) nested and recursive macros.

Most of the programs also (1) allow macros to be edited with any ASCII text editor (but RE/Call does not), (2) include textual descriptions of macros in the directory (but Newkey does not), (3) are compatible with ProKey files (but RE/Call is not), (4) allow a new macro to be defined within a macro (but RE/Call does not), (5) store macro files in ASCII (but RE/Call stores them in binary), (6) include expanded type-ahead buffers (but Keyworks and RE/Call do not), (7) can automatically blank the screen (but not RE/Call; KEYSWAP requires a macro to do so), (8) include a Dvorak keyboard setup (but not Keyworks and RE/Call), (9) allow the macro program's command keys to be reprogrammed (but not Newkey), (10) support text and graphics modes (but not Newkey), (11) allow extended characters to be redefined (but not ProKey), (12) allow macro menus to be displayed from within application programs (but not ProKey), (13) support help windows (but not ProKey), (14) support macro titles (but not RE/Call or KEYSWAP), (15) allow macros to be reassigned to different key combinations, (16) support variable speed playback (but not Keyworks), and (17) allow sound in macros (but ProKey and RE/Call do not).

For more information, see David Obregon, "Power Plays At Your Keyboard," *PC Magazine* (October 29, 1985): 167–75; John Walkenbach, "Keyboard Shortcuts," *PC Tech Journal* (October 1985): 131–44; Dan Swearingen, "In the Right Key," *PC Products* (October 1985): 33–49; Charles Petzold, "Keyboard Macros and Redefinition," *PC Magazine* (June 24, 1986): 255–65; and Jon Edwards, "RAM-Resient Utilities," *BYTE* (Summer 1987 Bonus Edition): 103–18.

2.9.1 ProKey 4.0

● *BASIC PRODUCT INFORMATION*

Name of Program: ProKey™ 4.0
Company Name: RoseSoft™, Inc.
Address: P.O. Box 45880, Seattle, WA 98145
Phone: (206) 282-0454
Price: $129.95
Version Reviewed: Revision 10
Runs On: IBM PCs and compatibles
Operating System Requirements: Any version of DOS
Disk Drive Requirements: 1
Copy Protected: No
Hard Disk Compatible: Yes
General Memory Requirements: 128K
RAM Occupied by Program: 40K
Additional Memory Required by Options: 1K for keyboard layout
Macro Memory Default Setting: 4K
Macro Memory Maximum Setting: 24K
Disk Space Needed for Help or Secondary Files: 9K
Type of Built-In Macro Editor: Up to 6 lines
Number of Nested Macros Permitted: Unlimited
Warns of Infinite Loops in Macros: Yes
User Verification To Overwrite Macro Files: No
User Verification To Overwrite Unsaved Macros in Memory: Yes
Access DOS Functions from within an Application Program: No
Allows SideKick to Be Accessed: No
Includes File Encryption Utility: No
Suspend Program: Yes
Uninstall Program from Memory: Yes
Memory Regained If Program Uninstalled: No
User Interface: Command-driven or menu-driven
Supports Mice: No
On-Line Help: Limited
Warranty: 90 days, media only
Support: Phone and letter
Update Policy: Nominal cost
Reviews: Stephen Manes, "A KEY MATCHUP: ProKey vs. SuperKey," *PC Magazine* (July 23, 1985): 27–38; Dara Pearlman, "Macro Dynamics for the PC," *PC Magazine* (May 14, 1986): 193–202; Corey Sandler, "Doing It Your Way With ProKey," *PC Magazine* (January 1983): 367–72; James F. Glass, "Name That Key!," *Personal Computer Age* (June 1983): 92–96; S. Sall, "Macros: Powerful Tools for Micro User," *PC Magazine* (May 1, 1984): 115–19; B. L. Aperson, "Macro Mastery," *PC World* (January 1984): 132–43.
Special Features: Macros may be named (up to 8 letters) and played back by entering the macro's name. Macros may be "guarded" so they cannot be overwritten. Automatic screen blackout feature. Can automatically include date in macros.
Comments: None

2.9.2 SuperKey

● *BASIC PRODUCT INFORMATION*

Name of Program: SuperKey™
Company Name: Borland International
Address: 4585 Scotts Valley Dr., Scotts Valley, CA 95066
Phones: (800) 255-8008, (800) 742-1133 (CA)

Price: $69.95
Version Reviewed: 1.0
Runs On: IBM PCs and compatibles
Operating System Requirements: DOS 2.0 or greater
Disk Drive Requirements: 1
Copy Protected: No
Hard Disk Compatible: Yes
General Memory Requirements: 128K
RAM Occupied by Program: 54K
Additional Memory Required by Options: 3K for DES encryption
Macro Memory Default Setting: 8K
Macro Memory Maximum Setting: 64K
Disk Space Needed for Help or Secondary Files: 37K
Type of Built-In Macro Editor: Full-screen
Number of Nested Macros Permitted: Unlimited
Warns of Infinite Loops in Macros: No
User Verification To Overwrite Macro Files: Yes
User Verification To Overwrite Unsaved Macros in Memory: Yes
Access DOS Functions from within an Application Program: Yes
Allows SideKick to Be Accessed: Yes
Includes File Encryption Utility: Yes, two, one of which is the U.S. Government's Data Encryption Standard (DES)
Suspend Program: Yes
Uninstall Program from Memory: Yes
Memory Regained If Program Uninstalled: Yes
User Interface: Command-driven or menu-driven
Supports Mice: Yes
On-Line Help: Yes, extensive
Warranty: 30 days, media only
Support: Phone and letter
Update Policy: Not known
Reviews: Stephen Manes, "A KEY MATCHUP: ProKey vs. SuperKey," *PC Magazine* (July 23, 1985): 27–38; Dara Pearlman, "Can SuperKey Soup Up Your Macros?," *PC Magazine* (October 1, 1986): 159–65; Rory J. O'Connor, "Superkey: A Rose By Any Other Name," *InfoWorld* (June 17, 1985): 40.
Special Features: Allows data from the screen to be assigned directly to a macro. Remembers the last 256 characters typed at DOS level and allows them to be displayed, edited, and executed. Automatic screen blackout feature. Allows keyboard to be password-protected. Can automatically include date and time in macros.
Comments: None

2.9.3 Newkey

- BASIC PRODUCT INFORMATION

Name of Program: Newkey
Company Name: FAB Software
Address: P.O. Box 336, Wayland, MA 01778
Phone: (617) 358-6357
Price: $27.45
Version Reviewed: Not able to review.
Runs On: IBM PCs and compatibles
Operating System Requirements: DOS 2.0 or greater
Disk Drive Requirements: 1
Copy Protected: No
Hard Disk Compatible: Yes
General Memory Requirements: 128K
RAM Occupied by Program: 50K + macro buffer
Additional Memory Required by Options: Not applicable
Macro Memory Default Setting: 1K
Macro Memory Maximum Setting: 64K
Disk Space Needed for Help or Secondary Files: None
Type of Built-In Macro Editor: Full

Number of Nested Macros Permitted: 8 levels
Warns of Infinite Loops in Macros: Yes
User Verification To Overwrite Macro Files: Yes
User Verification To Overwrite Unsaved Macros in Memory: Yes
Access DOS Functions from within an Application Program: No
Allows SideKick to Be Accessed: No
Includes File Encryption Utility: No
Suspend Program: Yes
Uninstall Program from Memory: Yes
Memory Regained If Program Uninstalled: Yes
User Interface: Command-driven or menu-driven
Supports Mice: No
On-Line Help: No
Warranty: 30-day, money-back guarantee
Support: Phone and letter
Update Policy: $15
Reviews: Dara Pearlman, "A Low-Budget Macro Handler," PC *Magazine* (October 1, 1985): 163.
Special Features: None
Comments: Newkey is a "shareware" product.

2.9.4 Keyworks

- *BASIC PRODUCT INFORMATION*

Name of Program: Keyworks™
Company Name: Alpha Software Corp.
Address: 30 B St., Burlington, MA 01830
Phone: (617) 229-2924
Price: $89.95
Version Reviewed: 1.1; latest version is 2.0
Runs On: IBM PCs and compatibles
Operating System Requirements: DOS 2.0 or greater
Disk Drive Requirements: 1
Copy Protected: No
Hard Disk Compatible: Yes
General Memory Requirements: 128K
RAM Occupied by Program: 64K to 105K
Additional Memory Required by Options: Not applicable
Macro Memory Default Setting: 5K (4,000 keystrokes, 150 macros)
Macro Memory Maximum Setting: 10K (9,500 keystrokes, 400 macros)
Disk Space Needed for Help or Secondary Files: 58K
Type of Built-In Macro Editor: Full-screen
Number of Nested Macros Permitted: 20 levels
Warns of Infinite Loops in Macros: Yes
User Verification To Overwrite Macro Files: Yes
User Verification To Overwrite Unsaved Macros in Memory: Yes
Access DOS Functions from within an Application Program: Yes
Allows SideKick to Be Accessed: Yes
Includes File Encryption Utility: Yes
Suspend Program: Yes
Uninstall Program from Memory: Yes
Memory Regained If Program Uninstalled: Yes
User Interface: Command-driven or menu-driven
Supports Mice: Yes
On-Line Help: No
Warranty: 30 days, media only
Support: Phone and letter
Update Policy: $23.95
Reviews: Harry Miller, "Transfer of Power," PC *World* (July 1985): 214–21; PC *Week* (June 18, 1985).
Special Features: Automatic screen blackout feature. Cut and paste from screen to printer, macro, or file.
"Keystroke Recall" stores last 300 keystrokes, thereby allowing after-the-fact macros to be created.
Comments: None

2.9.5 RE/Call

- *BASIC PRODUCT INFORMATION*

Name of Program: RE/Call™
Company Name: Yes Software, Inc.
Address: P.O. Box 91177, West Vancouver, B.C. V7V 3N6, Canada
Phone: (604) 922-6559
Price: $89.95
Version Reviewed: 1B
Runs On: IBM PCs and compatibles
Operating System Requirements: DOS 2.0 or greater
Disk Drive Requirements: 1
Copy Protected: No
Hard Disk Compatible: Yes
General Memory Requirements: 128K
RAM Occupied by Program: 24K
Additional Memory Required by Options: 5K for graphics option
Macro Memory Default Setting: 1K
Macro Memory Maximum Setting: 40K
Disk Space Needed for Help or Secondary Files: None
Type of Built-In Macro Editor: Single-line
Number of Nested Macros Permitted: Unlimited
Warns of Infinite Loops in Macros: No
User Verification To Overwrite Macro Files: No
User Verification To Overwrite Unsaved Macros in Memory: No
Access DOS Functions from within an Application Program: No
Allows SideKick to Be Accessed: Yes
Includes File Encryption Utility: No
Suspend Program: No (but individual macros may be turned off)
Uninstall Program from Memory: No
Memory Regained If Program Uninstalled: Not applicable
User Interface: Command-driven or menu-driven
Supports Mice: Yes
On-Line Help: Yes
Warranty: 90 days, media only
Support: Phone and letter
Update Policy: Not known
Reviews: Not known
Special Features: Has single-step mode for debugging macros. Can create menus for all macros and link menus in any order to provide a custom user interface.
Comments: None

2.9.6 SmartKey II Plus

- *BASIC PRODUCT INFORMATION*

Name of Program: SmartKey II Plus™
Company Name: Software Research Technologies, Inc.
Address: 2130 South Vermont Ave., Los Angeles, CA 90007-1654
Phones: (800) 824-5537, (213) 737-7663, (213) 653-9950
Price: $59.95
Version Reviewed: 5.1
Runs On: IBM PCs and compatibles
Operating System Requirements: DOS 2.0 or greater
Disk Drive Requirements: 1
Copy Protected: No
Hard Disk Compatible: Yes
General Memory Requirements: 128K
RAM Occupied by Program: 29K
Additional Memory Required by Options: 7K for help and user window

Macro Memory Default Setting: 0.09K
Macro Memory Maximum Setting: 60K
Disk Space Needed for Help or Secondary Files: 70K
Type of Built-In Macro Editor: Single-line to full-screen
Number of Nested Macros Permitted: 20 levels
Warns of Infinite Loops in Macros: Yes
User Verification To Overwrite Macro Files: Yes
User Verification To Overwrite Unsaved Macros in Memory: No
Access DOS Functions from within an Application Program: Yes
Allows SideKick to Be Accessed: Yes
Includes File Encryption Utility: Yes (as a separate tool)
Suspend Program: Yes
Uninstall Program from Memory: Yes
Memory Regained If Program Uninstalled: Yes
User Interface: Command-driven or menu-driven
Supports Mice: Yes
On-Line Help: Yes
Warranty: 90 days, media only
Support: Phone
Update Policy: $20
Reviews: Barry Owen, ed., "It's About Time," *PC Magazine* (November 26, 1985): 112–13.
Special Features: Automatic screen blackout feature. Can recall last 64 characters, assign them to a macro key combination, and edit them. Smart Print is a $29.95 add-on utility that allows printing from within application programs.
Comments: Also available for CP/M-80, CP/M-86, and DEC Rainbow.

2.9.7 KEYSWAP

- *BASIC PRODUCT INFORMATION*

Name of Program: KEYSWAP
Company Name: Maverick Software, Inc.
Address: 533 Main St., Suite 110, P.O. Box 998, Melrose, MA 02176
Phone: (617) 662-0856
Price: $99.95
Version Reviewed: 4.0
Runs On: IBM PCs and compatibles
Operating System Requirements: DOS 2.0 or greater
Disk Drive Requirements: 1
Copy Protected: No
Hard Disk Compatible: Yes
General Memory Requirements: 128K
RAM Occupied by Program: 18K
Additional Memory Required by Options: None
Macro Memory Default Setting: 10K
Macro Memory Maximum Setting: 64K
Disk Space Needed for Help or Secondary Files: None
Type of Built-In Macro Editor: Full-screen
Number of Nested Macros Permitted: 25 levels
Warns of Infinite Loops in Macros: Yes
User Verification To Overwrite Macro Files: Yes
User Verification To Overwrite Unsaved Macros in Memory: No
Access DOS Functions from within an Application Program: No
Allows SideKick to Be Accessed: Yes
Includes File Encryption Utility: No
Suspend Program: Yes
Uninstall Program from Memory: Yes
Memory Regained If Program Uninstalled: Yes
User Interface: Command-driven or menu-driven (user creates menus)
Supports Mice: No
On-Line Help: Yes, context-sensitive
Warranty: 90 days, media only

Support: Phone and letter
Update Policy: Registered customers automatically notified.
Reviews: Not known
Special Features: Can automatically include date and time in macros. Automatic screen blackout feature. Can define and control up to five windows. An entire screen may be saved and retrieved. Users may create custom help screens, macros that contain display-only text and user prompts, and delayed-execution macros. Supports memory partitioning, passwording, and macro grouping (turning sets of macros on and off with a single two-key combination). Allows DOS commands to be executed from within an application program.
Comments: None

FEATURES	PK	SK	NK	KW	RE	SK+	KS
Price	130	70	28	90	90	60	100
Runs On	I	I	I	I	I	I, C	I
General Memory Required (in K)	128	128	128	128	128	128	128
RAM Occupied By Program (in K)	40	54	50	64-105	24	29	18
Macro Memory Default Setting (in K)	4	8	1	5	1	.1	10
Macro Memory Max. Setting (in K)	24	64	64	10	40	60	64
Disk Space Req./Secondary Files (in K)	9	37	0	58	0	70	0
Type of Built-In Macro Editor	6 Lines	Full Scn.	Full Scn.	Full Scn.	1 Line	Full Scn.	Full Scn.
No. of Nested Macros Permitted	Unl.	Unl.	8 Levels	20 Levels	Unl.	20 Levels	25 Levels
Warns of Infinite Loops in Macros	●	○	●	●	○	●	●
User Verify/Overwrite Macro Files	○	●	●	●	○	●	●
User Verify/Overwrite Unsaved Macros	●	●	●	●	○	○	○
Access DOS from Application Prog.	○	●	○	●	○	●	○
File Encryption Utility	○	●	○	●	○	●	○
Suspend Program	●	●	●	●	○	●	●
Uninstall Program from Memory	●	●	●	●	○	●	●
Regain Memory If Uninstall Program	○	●	●	●	○	●	●
User Interface	CD,MD	CD,MD	CD,MD	CD,MD	CD,MD	CD,MD	CD,MD
Supports Mice	○	●	○	●	●	●	○
On-Line Help	●	●	○	○	●	●	●

Table 2.6: Comparison of keyboard enhancer programs. I = IBM, C = CP/M, CD = command-driven, M = menu-driven, PK = ProKey 4.0, SK = SuperKey, NK = Newkey, KW = Keyworks, RE = RE/Call, SK+ = SmartKey II Plus, KS = KEYSWAP

2.10 Bibliography and Sorting Programs

In various ways and to varying extents, programs in this category overlap conceptually and functionally with programs in the following category, "Text Retrieval Programs." "Bibliography Programs" are programs that are designed primarily for recording and managing bibliographical information.[186] They allow users to create, search, sort, and print bibliographical information in various formats. Bibliography programs, then, are a specialized form of file management, or data base management, program that is designed for bibliographical material. Bibliography programs free users from 3-by-5 cards, allow more bibliographical information per item to be included in that item's record than can fit on one 3-by-5 card, and allow the information to be

---

186. Bibliography programs are also referred to as "citation managers," "literature-retrieval systems," "bibliography generators," and "bibliographic file-management programs."

retrieved much faster, more thoroughly, and with greater flexibility than can be done manually with 3-by-5 cards. Bibliography programs also provide a convenient way for users to continue adding to their store of bibliographical information without worrying about filing 3-by-5 cards in their correct place and sequence. Although originally created for information professionals (such as librarians), these programs are quite useful for academicians, lawyers, and others who need to manage large bibliographies.

Like data base programs,[187] bibliography programs record information in fixed fields that are organized into records that are part of a file, or data base. A *field* is a unique category of information in a record, such as the author field, title field, or year-of-publication field. A *record* is the collection of all such fields for a particular entry, such as a book, journal article, or dissertation. A *file*, or data base, is the collection of all the records on a particular subject. The easiest way to understand these concepts is to think of 3-by-5 bibliography cards in card drawers in the card catalog at a library. Each card is a record that contains unique fields of information about a single entry. The collection of cards (records) is equivalent to a file. If cards are grouped by topics, then the card catalog can be seen as a set of files or as a set of data bases.

Some bibliography programs support multiple files, others only one. Among other parameters, bibliography programs differ in terms of maximum field length, maximum number of fields per record, maximum number of records per file, maximum record size, and in the ways they may be sorted and searched. Each program allows records to be printed, and each program includes rudimentary word processing capabilities.

With few exceptions, the categories used below for presenting information about bibliography programs should be self-explanatory. To **search** a data base—a file—is to look for all records where the search term(s) appears. To **sort** a data base is to rearrange all the records in the data base, or in a subset of it, in accordance with one of its fields, either in ascending or in descending order. Sorting does not rearrange the internal structure of records, that is, the sequence of fields in a record, only the sequence of the records in the data base.

"Sorting Programs" are programs that sort records into user-specified sequences, that rearrange (reformat) fields within records according to user-specified criteria, and that merge records into files (data bases) according to user specifications. Sorting programs require that the text to be sorted exist in records, which may be of fixed or variable length, and that records exist in files (data bases). Sorting programs, then, sort, merge, and reformat records.

Sorting programs have many practical applications. For example, sorting programs provide the fastest way I know of to alphabetize a list of bibliographical items, and in that capacity I have frequently used a sorting program to prepare some of the bibliographies in this book. Unlike bibliography programs, sorting programs do not allow records to be searched.[188]

"Text Retrieval Programs" are powerful, data base programs that operate on free-form text—text that has not been assigned to fields—and that allow users to locate, retrieve, and manipulate blocks of text by searching for keywords or for strings of words. Text retrieval programs differ from sorting and bibliography programs in that they locate but do not rearrange information.

---

187. Data base programs may be configured to function as bibliography programs. "High-end" data base programs (e.g., dBase III Plus, KnowledgeMan/2, Revelation, R:base System V) tend to be faster, more powerful, and more flexible than bibliography programs, but they also are far more complex, expensive, and difficult to learn and use. "Low-end" (e.g., PC-File III, Free Filer) and "middle-level" (e.g., PFS:Professional File) data base/filing programs also may be used for bibliographical purposes.

188. PCSort (IBM Entry Systems Division, P.O. Box 1328, Boca Raton, FL 33432; (800) 426-3333; $175) came to my attention too late to be included in this edition of this book. According to reviewers, PCSort is weaker and slower in almost every category and test than the three sorting programs about which I have included information.

Bernard Conrad Cole, BEYOND WORD PROCESSING: *Using Your Personal Computer As a Knowledge Processor* (New York: McGraw-Hill Book Co., 1985) provides useful introductions to and explanations of several of the programs (Notebook II, Citation, ZyINDEX, FYI 3000) I will discuss in this and the following section. Also see Timothy C. Weiskel, "Bibliographic Research and the Love of Learning," *Perspectives in Computing* 5 (Winter 1985): 12–21.[189]

2.10.1 Bibliography Programs

2.10.1.1 The Research Assistant 3.0

* BASIC PRODUCT INFORMATION

Name of Program: The Research Assistant 3.0
Company Name: Hi-Q Microware
Address: 16252 Northglen Place, Surrey, B.C. V3R 8MA, Canada
Phone: (604) 585-1629
Price: $70
Version Reviewed: 3.0
Runs On: IBM PCs and compatibles
Memory Requirements: 128K
Operating System Requirements: DOS 2.0 or greater
Disk Drive Requirements: 2
Copy Protected: No
Hard Disk Compatible: Yes
User Interface: Menu-driven
On-Line Help: Yes

* DATA ENTRY INFORMATION

Prompted Data Entry: Yes
Automatic Field Advance: Yes
Automatic Record Numbering: Yes
Other: None

* DATA BASE STRUCTURE

Maximum Characters Per Field: Not known
Maximum Fields Per Record: 10 (including abstract)
Maximum Record Length: 512 characters
Maximum Records Per File: 999
Maximum Files Per Data Base: Limited only by available disk space.
Author Field: Yes, 100 characters
Title Field: Yes, 160 characters
Publisher/Journal Field: Yes, 35 characters

---

189. Because of their high prices, I will not include information about FINDER (Finder Information Tools, Inc., 1422 Peachtree St., N.W., Suite 518, Atlanta, GA 30309; (404) 872-3488; $1,500) and IN-MAGIC (Inmagic, Inc., 238 Broadway, Cambridge, MA 02139; (617) 661-8124; $975 or $510 each for the second through the tenth copies or $828.75 for government, educational and nonprofit institutions). Martz-BIBLIOFILE™ (Martz Software Power Tools, Inc., 48 Hunter's Hill Circle, Amherst, MA 01002; (413) 256-0751; $250) came to my attention too late to be included in this edition of this book, as did Bookends Extended (Sensible Software, 210 S. Woodward #229, Birmingham, MI 48011; (313) 258-5566; $149.95; for Apple IIc and IIe), BIBLIOTEK (Scientific Software Products, Inc., 5726 Professional Circle, Suite 105, Indianapolis, IN 46241; (317) 244-6163; $95; for Apple IIs), and REF-11 (DG Systems, 322 Prospect Ave., Hartford, CT 06106; (203) 247-8500; list price: not known; for CP/M-80 systems, IBM PCs and compatibles, and DEC VAX/VMS).

Place of Publication Field: Yes (same as volume field).
Volume Field: Yes (same as place of publication field).
Date Field: Yes
Number of Pages Field: Yes
Accession Number Field: Yes, 8 characters
Call Number Field: Yes (Dewey or Library of Congress), 7 characters
Subject or Keyword Headings: Yes, 160 characters
User-Defined Fields: No
Obligatory Fields: Yes, 9
Abstracts: Yes, maximum of 1,280 characters per record (stored on disk in separate abstract file).
Other: None

- *SORT FEATURES*

Sort By Author: Yes
Sort By Title: Yes
Sort By Call Number: Yes
Sort By Accession Number: Yes
Sort By Date: Yes
Sort By Keywords: Yes
Other: None

- *SEARCH FEATURES*

All Fields Searchable: Yes
All Words in Field May Be Used As Search Terms: Yes
Specify Two or More Fields in Searches: Yes
Search Across Fields: Yes, when searches include abstract files.
Every Word a Keyword: Yes
Maximum Combined Length of Search Term(s): 50 characters
Search Terms Highlighted When Matches Displayed: Yes
Use Boolean ANDs: No
Use Boolean ORs: No
Use Boolean NOTs: No
Other: None

- *FILE AND RECORD MANAGEMENT*

Intersect Files: No
Merge Files: Yes
Modify File: Yes
Display Files: Yes
Delete Files: Yes
Copy Files: Yes
Export Files: Yes
Add Records: Yes
Delete Records: Yes
Modify Records: Yes
Display Records: Yes
List Records: Yes
Search Records: Yes
Transfer Records from Existing File to New File: Yes
Transfer Records from Existing File to Existing File: Yes
Print Records: Yes (supported printers not known)
Create ASCII Text Files of Records: Yes
Type of Reports Available: Bibliographies only, annotated bibliographies, indices

- *OTHER INFORMATION*

Warranty: Not known
Support: Phone and letter
Update Policy: Not known

Reviews: None
Special Features: Printable 56-page user's guide included on diskette; printed guide available for $15.
Comments: The Research Assistant is a straightforward, easy-to-use, reasonably-priced bibliography program.

2.10.1.2 Pro-Cite

• BASIC PRODUCT INFORMATION

Name of Program: Pro-Cite (formerly the Professional Bibliographic System)
Company Name: Personal Bibliographic Software, Inc.
Address: P.O. Box 4250, Ann Arbor, MI 48106
Phone: (313) 996-1580
Price: $395; Biblio-Link: $195
Version Reviewed: IBM
Runs On: IBM PCs and compatibles, OCLC M300 workstation, Macintosh
Memory Requirements: IBM: 128K
Operating System Requirements: IBM: DOS 2.0 or greater
Disk Drive Requirements: 1
Copy Protected: Yes
Hard Disk Compatible: Yes
User Interface: Menu-driven
On-Line Help: Yes

• DATA ENTRY INFORMATION

Prompted Data Entry: Yes
Automatic Field Advance: Yes
Automatic Record Numbering: Yes
Other: There are 22 document types for data entry, including two user-defined workforms. Document types include journal, monograph, report, newspaper, dissertation, music score, map, motion picture, and sound recording.

• DATA BASE STRUCTURE

Maximum Characters Per Field: 16
Maximum Fields Per Record: Varies
Maximum Record Length: 16K
Maximum Records Per File: 32,500 (using hard disk; 1,000 for floppies)
Maximum Files Per Data Base: 1
Author Field: Yes
Title Field: Yes
Publisher/Journal Field: Yes
Place of Publication Field: Yes
Volume Field: Yes
Date Field: Yes
Number of Pages Field: Yes
Accession Number Field: Yes
Call Number Field: Yes
Subject or Keyword Headings: Yes
User-Defined Fields: Yes, in user-defined workforms
Obligatory Fields: None; all fields are optional.
Abstracts: Yes, unlimited length
Other: Index field limited to 74 characters. Supports note field and extended character set.

• SORT FEATURES

Sort By Author: Yes
Sort By Title: Yes
Sort By Call Number: Yes
Sort By Accession Number: Yes

Sort By Date: Yes
Sort By Keywords: Yes
Other: Can sort by all fields, up to 3 levels deep

- ## SEARCH FEATURES

All Fields Searchable: Yes
All Words in Field May Be Used As Search Terms: Yes
Specify Two or More Fields in Searches: Yes
Search Across Fields: Yes
Every Word a Keyword: Yes
Maximum Combined Length of Search Term(s): 255 characters
Search Terms Highlighted When Matches Displayed: No
Use Boolean ANDs: Yes
Use Boolean ORs: Yes
Use Boolean NOTs: Yes
Other: Supports initial and terminal truncation; parentheses, greater than, and less than signs may be used in searches; full-text searching with unlimited keyword searching.

- ## FILE AND RECORD MANAGEMENT

Intersect Files: No
Merge Files: Yes
Modify File: Yes
Display Files: Yes
Delete Files: Yes
Copy Files: Yes
Export Files: Yes
Add Records: Yes
Delete Records: Yes
Modify Records: Yes
Display Records: Yes
List Records: Yes
Search Records: Yes
Transfer Records from Existing File to New File: Yes
Transfer Records from Existing File to Existing File: Yes
Print Records: Yes
Create ASCII Text Files of Records: Yes
Type of Reports Available: Various

- ## OTHER INFORMATION

Warranty: 30-day, money-back guarantee
Support: Phone and letter
Update Policy: $95 to upgrade to Pro-Cite.
Reviews: Audrey N. Grosch, "Personal Bibliographic System and Data Transfer System," *Collegiate Microcomputer* 2 (Winter 1984): 309–15; *Information Today* (November 1986): 17, 39; *Laboratory Computer Letter* (July 1986): 7; Deena Weinstein, "Pro-Cite 1.2," *Social Science Microcomputer Review* 5 (Summer 1987): 263–65; William Saffady, *Library Technology Review* (January-February 1987): 161–67; Michael D. Wesley, *Macuser* (February 1987): 61.
Special Features: Biblio-Link ($195) automatically transfers data from DIALOG, BRS, MEDLARS, OCLC, and RLIN into the proper Pro-Cite fields, format, and user-specified data base. Pro-Cite automatically deletes duplicate records, can create an index of any field, and supports customized bibliographical formats (the ANSI standard is the default setting). The Personal Bibliographic System is available for the Macintosh.
Comments: This is the most complex, powerful, and flexible of the bibliographical programs. It is best suited for information professionals and others with "serious" bibliographical needs.

2.10.1.3 Sapana: Cardfile

- ## BASIC PRODUCT INFORMATION

Name of Program: Sapana: Cardfile
Company Name: Sapana Micro Software
Address: 1305 South Rouse, Pittsburgh, KS 66762
Phone: (316) 231-5023
Price: $195
Version Reviewed: 1.03
Runs On: IBM PCs and compatibles
Memory Requirements: 128K
Operating System Requirements: DOS 2.0 or greater
Disk Drive Requirements: 1
Copy Protected: No
Hard Disk Compatible: Yes
User Interface: Menu-driven
On-Line Help: Yes

- ## DATA ENTRY INFORMATION

Prompted Data Entry: Yes
Automatic Field Advance: Yes
Automatic Record Numbering: Yes
Other: Repeating items in fields may be entered automatically without rekeying. There are 11 document types for data entry, including letters, bibliographical, products, notes, and books. Periodicals or other publications may be defined by up to 255 unique numerical codes and then searched by code numbers.

- ## DATA BASE STRUCTURE

Maximum Characters Per Field: 1,024 characters and 255 lines for text
Maximum Fields Per Record: 24 (default setting is 11)
Maximum Record Length: 4K
Maximum Records Per File: 32K
Maximum Files Per Data Base: 1
Author Field: Yes, 25 characters (can be changed).
Title Field: Yes, 60 characters (can be changed).
Publisher/Journal Field: Yes, journal field
Place of Publication Field: No (but may be added).
Volume Field: Yes, 12 characters
Date Field: Yes, 10 characters
Number of Pages Field: Yes, 12 characters
Accession Number Field: No (but may be added).
Call Number Field: No (but may be added).
Subject or Keyword Headings: Yes, three separate fields, 26 character combined maximum
User-Defined Fields: Yes, names and lengths of all fields (up to 24) may be changed.
Obligatory Fields: Yes, minimum of 6
Abstracts: Yes, maximum of 15,300 characters (255 60-character lines)
Other: None

- ## SORT FEATURES

Sort By Author: Yes
Sort By Title: Yes
Sort By Call Number: Yes
Sort By Accession Number: Yes
Sort By Date: Yes
Sort By Keywords: Yes
Other: Can sort on multiple fields.

- *SEARCH FEATURES*

All Fields Searchable: Yes
All Words in Field May Be Used As Search Terms: Yes
Specify Two or More Fields in Searches: Yes
Search Across Fields: Yes
Every Word a Keyword: Yes
Maximum Combined Length of Search Term(s): 1,920 characters (24 80-character words/phrases)
Search Terms Highlighted When Matches Displayed: No
Use Boolean ANDs: Yes
Use Boolean ORs: Yes
Use Boolean NOTs: No
Other: None

- *FILE AND RECORD MANAGEMENT*

Intersect Files: No
Merge Files: No
Modify File: Yes
Display Files: Yes
Delete Files: Yes
Copy Files: No
Export Files: Yes
Add Records: Yes
Delete Records: Yes
Modify Records: Yes
Display Records: Yes
List Records: Yes
Search Records: Yes
Transfer Records from Existing File to New File: No
Transfer Records from Existing File to Existing File: No
Print Records: Yes
Create ASCII Text Files of Records: Yes
Type of Reports Available: Various

- *OTHER INFORMATION*

Warranty: 30-day, money-back guarantee; free trial version available
Support: Phone and letter
Update Policy: $10
Reviews: *Business Software* 2 (November 1984): 67; *Computer Shopper* (November 1986): 127.
Special Features: Can automatically reformat records when output to printer. Selected fields only can be
    listed. Disk space is not reserved but used dynamically.
Comments: Not as easy to use as The Research Assistant.

2.10.1.4 BIBLIOG

- *BASIC PRODUCT INFORMATION*

Name of Program: BIBLIOG
Company Name: Micro-Dynamics of Texas
Address: P.O. Box 40691, Houston, TX 77240
Phone: (713) 896-9957
Price: $49.50
Version Reviewed: 1.00
Runs On: IBM PCs and compatibles
Memory Requirements: 192K
Operating System Requirements: DOS 2.0 or greater
Disk Drive Requirements: 1
Copy Protected: No
Hard Disk Compatible: Yes

User Interface: Menu-driven
On-Line Help: No

- ## DATA ENTRY INFORMATION

Prompted Data Entry: Yes
Automatic Field Advance: Yes
Automatic Record Numbering: No
Other: BIBLIOG is set up for journal article entries.

- ## DATA BASE STRUCTURE

Maximum Characters Per Field: Not known
Maximum Fields Per Record: Not known
Maximum Record Length: Not known
Maximum Records Per File: Not known
Maximum Files Per Data Base: Not known
Author Field: Yes, 26 characters
Title Field: Yes, 32 characters
Publisher/Journal Field: Yes, 26 characters
Place of Publication Field: No, but could be included in Miscellaneous field.
Volume Field: No, but could be included in Miscellaneous field.
Date Field: Yes, 8 characters
Number of Pages Field: No, but could be included in Miscellaneous field.
Accession Number Field: Yes, 5 characters
Call Number Field: No, but could be included in Miscellaneous field.
Subject or Keyword Headings: Yes, three separate fields, 60-character combined maximum.
User-Defined Fields: Yes, 1 field of 40 characters
Obligatory Fields: Yes, minimum not known.
Abstracts: Yes
Other: None

- ## SORT FEATURES

Sort By Author: Yes
Sort By Title: Yes
Sort By Call Number: No
Sort By Accession Number: No
Sort By Date: No
Sort By Keywords: Yes
Other: Sorting features available only as printer output options.

- ## SEARCH FEATURES

All Fields Searchable: Yes
All Words in Field May Be Used As Search Terms: Yes
Specify Two or More Fields in Searches: No
Search Across Fields: Yes
Every Word a Keyword: Yes
Maximum Combined Length of Search Term(s): Not known
Search Terms Highlighted When Matches Displayed: No
Use Boolean ANDs: No
Use Boolean ORs: No
Use Boolean NOTs: No
Other: None

- ## FILE AND RECORD MANAGEMENT

Intersect Files: No
Merge Files: No
Modify File: Yes

236

Display Files: Yes
Delete Files: Yes
Copy Files: Not known
Export Files: Not known
Add Records: Yes
Delete Records: Yes
Modify Records: Yes
Display Records: Yes
List Records: Yes
Search Records: Yes
Transfer Records from Existing File to New File: No
Transfer Records from Existing File to Existing File: No
Print Records: Yes
Create ASCII Text Files of Records: Not known
Type of Reports Available: Various

- *OTHER INFORMATION*

Warranty: 90 days, media only
Support: Phone and letter
Update Policy: Not known
Reviews: None
Special Features: None
Comments: None

2.10.1.5 Notebook II

- *BASIC PRODUCT INFORMATION*

Name of Program: Notebook II
Company Name: Pro/Tem Software, Inc.
Address: 814 Tolman Dr., Stanford, CA 94305
Phone: (415) 947-1000
Price: $189; Bibliography: $99; both: $264
Version Reviewed: 2.2
Runs On: IBM PCs and compatibles
Memory Requirements: 256K
Operating System Requirements: DOS 2.0 or greater
Disk Drive Requirements: 2
Copy Protected: No
Hard Disk Compatible: Yes
User Interface: Menu-driven
On-Line Help: Yes

- *DATA ENTRY INFORMATION*

Prompted Data Entry: Yes
Automatic Field Advance: Yes
Automatic Record Numbering: Yes
Other: None

- *DATA BASE STRUCTURE*

Maximum Characters Per Field: Up to 50,000
Maximum Fields Per Record: 50
Maximum Record Length: 50,000 characters
Maximum Records Per File: Limited only by available disk space.
Maximum Files Per Data Base: 1
Author Field: Yes
Title Field: Yes
Publisher/Journal Field: Yes

237

Place of Publication Field: Yes
Volume Field: Yes
Date Field: Yes
Number of Pages Field: Yes
Accession Number Field: Yes
Call Number Field: Yes
Subject or Keyword Headings: Yes
User-Defined Fields: Yes, all fields (maximum of 50) are user-definable.
Obligatory Fields: None
Abstracts: Up to 10 pages of text per record.
Other: Extended character set supported.

- *SORT FEATURES*

Sort By Author: Yes
Sort By Title: Yes
Sort By Call Number: Yes
Sort By Accession Number: Yes
Sort By Date: Yes
Sort By Keywords: Yes
Other: Can sort data base by the first 20 characters in any field.

- *SEARCH FEATURES*

All Fields Searchable: Yes
All Words in Field May Be Used As Search Terms: Yes
Specify Two or More Fields in Searches: Yes
Search Across Fields: Yes
Every Word a Keyword: Yes
Maximum Combined Length of Search Term(s): Not known
Search Terms Highlighted When Matches Displayed: No
Use Boolean ANDs: Yes
Use Boolean ORs: Yes
Use Boolean NOTs: Yes
Other: Supports less than, equal to or less than, greater than, equal to or greater than, begins with, does not begin with, contains, and excludes search delimiters.

- *FILE AND RECORD MANAGEMENT*

Intersect Files: No
Merge Files: Yes
Modify File: Yes
Display Files: Yes
Delete Files: Yes
Copy Files: No
Export Files: Yes
Add Records: Yes
Delete Records: Yes
Modify Records: Yes
Display Records: Yes
List Records: Yes
Search Records: Yes
Transfer Records from Existing File to New File: Yes
Transfer Records from Existing File to Existing File: No
Print Records: Yes
Create ASCII Text Files of Records: Yes
Type of Reports Available: Various

- *OTHER INFORMATION*

Warranty: 90 days, media *and program*
Support: Phone and letter

238

Update Policy: Not known

Reviews: Katherine S. Chiang et al., "Creating Bibliographies for Business Use," *PC Magazine* (November 12, 1986): 249–60; Lawrence Becker, "Notebook II: A Database Manager for Text," *Computers and the Humanities* 19 (January-March 1985): 53–56; Bryan Pfaffenberger, "The Scholar's Software Library: Notebook II," *Research in Word Processing Newsletter* 3 (November 1985): 10–13; Bryan Pfaffenberger, "The Researcher's Assistant," *PC Magazine* (January 24, 1984): 409–11.

Special Features: Bibliography is a utility that compares citations in a manuscript with a Notebook II data base and constructs a bibliography of all entries cited in the manuscript. Bibliography also can copy entries from Notebook into a manuscript's footnotes and replace the citations in the manuscript with numbers that correspond to their number in the bibliography.

Comments: Notebook II is powerful, very flexible, and easy to use. Of all the programs listed above, it supports the most characters per field, the most fields per record, and the most characters per record. Its Boolean search capabilities further enhance its attractiveness.

2.10.1.6 *Citation*

• BASIC PRODUCT INFORMATION

Name of Program: Citation
Company Name: Eagle Enterprises
Address: 2375 Bush St., San Francisco, CA 94115
Phone: (415) 346-1249
Price: $185
Version Reviewed: IBM 4.01
Runs On: IBM PCs and compatibles, CP/M systems
Memory Requirements: IBM: 128K; CP/M: 62K
Operating System Requirements: IBM: DOS 1.1 or greater; CP/M: 1.4 or 2.x
Disk Drive Requirements: 2
Copy Protected: No
Hard Disk Compatible: Yes
User Interface: Menu-driven
On-Line Help: Yes

• DATA ENTRY INFORMATION

Prompted Data Entry: Yes
Automatic Field Advance: Yes
Automatic Record Numbering: No
Other: None

• DATA BASE STRUCTURE

Maximum Characters Per Field: 80
Maximum Fields Per Record: 16
Maximum Record Length: Approximately 3,800 characters
Maximum Records Per File: Not known
Maximum Files Per Data Base: Limited only by available disk space
Author Field: Yes, 48
Title Field: Yes, 48
Publisher/Journal Field: Yes, 48
Place of Publication Field: No, but may be added.
Volume Field: Yes, 4
Date Field: Yes, 6
Number of Pages Field: Yes, 4
Accession Number Field: No, but may be added.
Call Number Field: No, but may be added.
Subject or Keyword Headings: Yes, maximum of 6 words (120 characters)
User-Defined Fields: Yes, up to the maximum of 16.
Obligatory Fields: Yes, minimum not known.
Abstracts: Yes, up to 2,400 characters (30 80-character lines).

Other: Up to 9 different user-designed screen formats (record formats) may be mixed in a file. Records from an external file may be loaded into a Citation data base.

• SORT FEATURES

Sort By Author: Yes
Sort By Title: Yes
Sort By Call Number: Yes
Sort By Accession Number: Yes
Sort By Date: Yes
Sort By Keywords: Yes, maximum of 6
Other: Can sort by all fields.

• SEARCH FEATURES

All Fields Searchable: Yes
All Words in Field May Be Used As Search Terms: Yes
Specify Two or More Fields in Searches: No
Search Across Fields: Yes, string search only
Every Word a Keyword: Yes
Maximum Combined Length of Search Term(s): 10 keywords
Search Terms Highlighted When Matches Displayed: No
Use Boolean ANDs: Yes
Use Boolean ORs: No
Use Boolean NOTs: Yes
Other: Supports wild-card searches. Can restrict searches to user-specified ranges.

• FILE AND RECORD MANAGEMENT

Intersect Files: No
Merge Files: Yes
Modify File: Yes
Display Files: Yes
Delete Files: No
Copy Files: No
Export Files: No
Add Records: Yes
Delete Records: Yes
Modify Records: Yes
Display Records: Yes
List Records: Yes
Search Records: Yes
Transfer Records from Existing File to New File: Yes
Transfer Records from Existing File to Existing File: No
Print Records: Yes
Create ASCII Text Files of Records: Yes
Type of Reports Available: Complete data base, keyword index, keyword list, multikeyword selection

• OTHER INFORMATION

Warranty: 12 months, media only
Support: Phone and letter
Update Policy: Not known
Reviews: Not known
Special Features: Includes integrated file recovery program that allows damaged files to be recreated.
Comments: Citation is a fast, flexible, and powerful program that supports user-defined fields, long abstracts, and mixing up to nine different user-defined record formats per data base.

2.10.1.7 Sequitur

- ● BASIC PRODUCT INFORMATION

Name of Program: Sequitur™
Company Name: Golemics, Inc.
Address: 2600 10th St., Berkeley, CA 94710
Phones: (415) 486-8347
Price: $79.95
Version Reviewed: Not able to review.
Runs On: IBM PCs and compatibles
Memory Requirements: 256K
Operating System Requirements: DOS 2.0 or greater
Disk Drive Requirements: 2
Copy Protected: No
Hard Disk Compatible: Yes
User Interface: Menu-driven
On-Line Help: Yes
Specify Drive, Pathname, and Subdirectory: Not known
Compatible with Local Area Networks (LANs): Not known
Other: Because Sequitur is a true relational data base, some of the categories used below are different from those used with the other programs in this subsection. Among other things, in a relational data base *any* two items may be related directly.

- ● DATA BASE STRUCTURE

Maximum Characters Per Field: 2,000
Maximum Characters Per Record: 2,000
Maximum Fields Per Record: 1,024 (including 975 user fields)
Maximum Fields Per File: 1,024 (including 975 user fields)
Maximum Records Per File: Unlimited
Maximum Fields Per Data Base: 1,024 (including 975 user fields)
Maximum File Size: 8 megabytes
Maximum Files Per Data Base: 255 (including 240 user files)
Maximum Data Base Size: 2.04 gigabytes
Maximum Data Bases Per System: Limited only by memory
Maximum Indices Per File: Unlimited
Works with ASCII Files: Yes
Works with Other Files: No

- ● DATA BASE MANIPULATION

Select Records: Yes
Add Records: Yes
Delete Records: Yes
Modify Records: Yes
Display Records: Yes
Sort Records: Yes
Combine Records (Union): Yes
Intersect Records: Yes
Show Unique Records: Yes
Show Duplicate Records: Yes
Remove Records: Yes
Rename Records: Yes
Show Difference Between Files: Yes
Join Files: Yes
Copy Files: Yes
Export Files: Yes
Transfer Files from One Data Base to Another: Yes
Use Boolean ANDs: Yes
Use Boolean ORs: Yes
Use Boolean NOTs: Yes

FEATURES	RA	PC	SC	BIB	NB	CIT	SEQ
BASIC FACTS							
Price	70	395	195	50	189	185	80
Runs On	I	I	I	I	I	I	I
Memory (in K)	128	128	128	192	256	128	256
Disk Drives	2	1	1	1	2	2	2
User Interface	MD	MD	MD	MD	MD	MD	MD
On-Line Help	●	●	●	○	●	●	●
DATA ENTRY							
Prompted Data Entry	●	●	●	●	●	●	—
Automatic Field Advance	●	●	●	●	●	●	—
Automatic Record Numbering	●	●	●	○	●	○	—
DATA BASE STRUCTURE							
Maximum Characters/Field	?	16	1,024	?	50,000	80	2,000
Maximum Fields/Record	10	Varies	24	?	50	16	1,024
Maximum Record Length	.5K	16K	4K	?	50K	4K	—
Maximum Records/File	999	32,500	32K	?	Unl.	?	Unl.
Maximum Files/Data Base	Unl.	1	1	?	1	Unl.	255
Author Field	●	●	●	●	●	●	—
Title Field	●	●	●	●	●	●	—
Publisher Field	●	●	●	●	●	●	—
Place of Publication Field	●	●	○	○	●	○	—
Volume Field	●	●	●	○	●	●	—
Date Field	●	●	●	●	●	●	—
Number of Pages Field	●	●	●	○	●	●	—
Accession Number Field	●	●	○	●	●	○	—
Call Number Field	●	●	○	○	●	○	—
Subject or Keyword Headings	●	●	●	●	●	●	—
User-Defined Fields	○	●	●	●	●	●	—
Obligatory Fields	9	0	6	●	0	●	—
Abstracts	●	●	●	●	●	●	—
SORT FEATURES							
Sort By Author	●	●	●	●	●	●	—
Sort By Title	●	●	●	●	●	●	—
Sort By Call Number	●	●	●	○	●	●	—
Sort By Accession Number	●	●	●	○	●	●	—
Sort By Date	●	●	●	○	●	●	—
Sort By Keywords	●	●	●	●	●	●	—

Use Parentheses: Yes
Mark/Save Matches to Create New File: Yes
Browse Bidirectionally Through Files Containing Hits: Yes
Print Records/Files: Yes
Type of Reports Available: Various
Other: Works with 5 data types (text, number, decimal, date, money)

FEATURES	RA	PC	SC	BIB	NB	CIT	SEQ
SEARCH FEATURES							
Search All Fields	●	●	●	●	●	●	—
All Words in Field Search Terms	●	●	●	●	●	●	—
Two or More Fields in Searches	●	●	●	○	●	○	—
Search Across Fields	●	●	●	●	●	●	—
Every Word Keyword	●	●	●	●	●	●	—
Max. Cmb. Lgth. Search Terms (Char.)	50	255	1,920	?	?	10 Wds.	—
Highlights Matches	●	○	○	○	○	○	—
Boolean ANDs	○	●	●	○	●	●	●
Boolean ORs	○	●	●	○	●	○	●
Boolean NOTs	○	●	○	○	●	●	●
FILE & RECORD MANAGEMENT							
Intersect Files	○	○	○	○	○	○	●
Merge Files	●	●	○	○	●	●	●
Modify Files	●	●	●	●	●	●	●
Display Files	●	●	●	●	●	●	●
Delete Files	●	●	●	●	●	○	●
Copy Files	●	●	○	?	○	○	●
Export Files	●	●	●	?	●	○	●
Add Records	●	●	●	●	●	●	●
Delete Records	●	●	●	●	●	●	●
Modify Records	●	●	●	●	●	●	●
Display Records	●	●	●	●	●	●	●
List Records	●	●	●	●	●	●	●
Search Records	●	●	●	●	●	●	●
Transfer Records - Existing to New File	●	●	○	○	●	●	●
Transfer Records - Exist. to Exist. File	●	●	○	○	○	○	●
Print Records	●	●	●	●	●	●	●
Create ASCII Files	●	●	●	?	●	●	●

Table 2.7: Comparison of bibliography programs. I = IBM, MD = menu-driven, RA = Research Assistant 3.0, PC = Pro-Cite, SC = Sapana: Cardfile, BIB = BIBLIOG, NB = Notebook II, CIT = Citation, SEQ = Sequitur.

- *OTHER INFORMATION*

Warranty: Not known
Support: Phone and letter. Phone support is $60/hr, 15 minute minimum.
Update Policy: Not known
Reviews: Not known
Special Features: Has built-in word processing functions, including form-letter and mailing-list capabilities.
Comments: This is the most powerful and flexible program listed in this subsection. Although it is not designed as a bibliography or sorting program, it certainly can be used as such.

2.10.2 Sorting Programs

2.10.2.1 Opt-Tech Sort

- BASIC PRODUCT INFORMATION

Name of Program: Opt-Tech Sort
Company Name: Opt-Tech Data Processing
Address: P.O. Box 678, Zephyr Cove, NV 98448
Phone: (702) 588-3737
Price: $149
Version Reviewed: 3.0L
Runs On: IBM PCs and compatibles
Memory Requirements: 64K
Operating System Requirements: DOS 2.0 or greater
Disk Drive Requirements: 1
Copy Protected: No
Hard Disk Compatible: Yes
User Interface: Command-driven or menu-driven
On-Line Help: Yes

- SORT/MERGE FEATURES

Maximum Record Length: Greater than 5K
Maximum Input Records: Limited only by available disk space.
Maximum Input Files: Unlimited
Maximum Keys/Fields for Comparing Records: 10
Positionally Defined Keys/Fields for Comparing Records: Yes
Comma-Delimited and Other Keys/Fields for Comparing Records: Yes
Use Boolean Operators in Record Comparison: Yes
Conditional Selection: Yes
Input Files ASCII, CR-Delimited: Yes
Input Files Other: Yes
Collating Sequence ASCII: Yes
Collating Sequence Other: Yes
User-Defined Collating Sequence: Yes
Include/Omit Records from Input: Yes, up to 10 control fields/keys may be specified.
Include/Omit Records from Output: Yes, up to 10 conditions may be specified.
Reformat Records on Output: Yes
Stand-Alone Driver: Yes
Linkable Module: Yes
Merging: Yes

- OTHER INFORMATION

Warranty: 90 days, media only
Support: Phone and letter
Update Policy: Not known
Reviews: Brad Stark, "Opt-Tech Sort: Blinding Pace, Budget Price," *PC Magazine* (March 11, 1986): 279–80.
Special Features: Can be called directly from IBM BASIC, BASICA, IBM Compiled BASIC (ver. 1 & 2), Microsoft Quick BASIC, GWBASIC, Better BASIC, CBASIC86, True BASIC, 8088 Assembler, COBOL, mbp COBOL, Microfocus COBOL, Realia COBOL, Ryan McFarland COBOL, IBM Professional Fortran, Lahey Fortran, Microsoft/IBM Fortran, Ryan McFarland Fortran, Borland Turbo Pascal, IBM (Microsoft) Pascal, D/R Pascal/MT+, D/R PL/I, Computer Innovations C86, Lattice C, Mark Williams C, Microsoft C (ver. 1 & 2), dBase II, and dBase III. Works with over a dozen different data types. Include/omit can be used with sort function or by itself to select records based on up to 10 conditions.

Comments: Opt-Tech Sort (OTS) is lightning fast. According to one reviewer, it is 5 times faster than dBase III's Sort function and 9 to 25 times faster than the DOS SORT routine. OTS can be used with dBase II and dBase III files. According to Opt-Tech Data Processing statistics, Opt-Tech Sort can sort a 1,000 record, 80K file in 9 seconds on an IBM PC-XT and in 5 seconds on an IBM PC-AT. The ability to use the include/omit output feature to select records based on up to 10 conditions allows Opt-Tech Sort to be used as a searching program. OTS sorts fixed and variable length records.

2.10.2.2 SuperSort II

• BASIC PRODUCT INFORMATION

Name of Program: SuperSort® II
Company Name: LifeStyle Software, Inc.
Address: 101 Lucas Valley Rd., Suite 110, San Rafael, CA 94903
Phone: (415) 459-0300
Price: $200
Version Reviewed: IBM: 2.06
Runs On: IBM PCs and compatibles; CP/M-80; CP/M-86
Memory Requirements: IBM: 72K
Operating System Requirements: IBM: DOS 2.0 or greater
Disk Drive Requirements: 1
Copy Protected: No
Hard Disk Compatible: Yes
User Interface: Command-driven or menu-driven
On-Line Help: No

• SORT/MERGE FEATURES

Maximum Record Length: 4K
Maximum Input Records: Up to 2 gigabytes per file
Maximum Input Files: 128
Maximum Keys/Fields for Comparing Records: 128
Positionally Defined Keys/Fields for Comparing Records: Yes
Comma-Delimited and Other Keys/Fields for Comparing Records: Yes
Use Boolean Operators in Record Comparison: Yes
Conditional Selection: Yes
Input Files ASCII, CR-Delimited: Yes
Input Files Other: Yes
Collating Sequence ASCII: Yes
Collating Sequence Other: Yes
User-Defined Collating Sequence: Yes
Include/Omit Records from Input: Yes, any number of conditional tests
Include/Omit Records from Output: No, but several special output formats/options are available.
Reformat Records on Output: No
Stand-Alone Driver: Yes
Linkable Module: No
Merging: Yes

• OTHER INFORMATION

Warranty: Not known
Support: Phone and letter
Update Policy: Not known
Reviews: Chris Terry, "Sorting Out Sorting Programs," *PC Magazine* (February 5, 1985): 50, 52.
Special Features: In sort/merge operations, users can specify ascending or descending sort order, collating sequence options, and data-type attributes for each of the 128 fields. Key data may be ASCII STRING text, ASCII NUMERIC, BCD (COBOL packed decimal), or BINARY. Multiple NUMERIC ASCII and BINARY data types are supported. Can sort files up to 4 gigabytes in size. Sorts dBase III and dBase III Plus files. Can convert dBase files to CR-delimited files, and vice versa. Runs on networks.

Comments: According to the manufacturer, SuperSort is up to 10 times faster than a BASIC bubble sort and can sort 1,376 100-character records in 1 minute on an 8088 machine. One reviewer described it as "the Cadillac of sort/merge utilities" and rated it as 6 to 22 times faster than the DOS SORT routine. Sorts fixed and variable length records.

2.10.2.3 COSORT

• BASIC PRODUCT INFORMATION

Name of Program: COSORT
Company Name: Information Resources, Inc.
Address: 70 Bourndale South, Box W, Manhasset, NY 11030
Phone: (516) 365-7629
Price: $200; 2 to 9 copies: $100 each; 10 or more copies: $75 each
Version Reviewed: IBM 4.2
Runs On: IBM PCs and compatibles, CP/M machines
Memory Requirements: IBM: 52K
Operating System Requirements: IBM: DOS 2.0 or greater; CP/M; CP/M-86; MP/M-86
Disk Drive Requirements: 1
Copy Protected: No
Hard Disk Compatible: Yes
User Interface: Command-driven or menu-driven
On-Line Help: No

• SORT/MERGE FEATURES

Maximum Record Length: 4K
Maximum Input Records: Unlimited
Maximum Input Files: Unlimited
Maximum Keys/Fields for Comparing Records: 255
Positionally Defined Keys/Fields for Comparing Records: Yes
Comma-Delimited and Other Keys/Fields for Comparing Records: Yes
Use Boolean Operators in Record Comparison: No
Conditional Selection: Yes
Input Files ASCII, CR-Delimited: Yes
Input Files Other: Yes
Collating Sequence ASCII: Yes
Collating Sequence Other: No
User-Defined Collating Sequence: No
Include/Omit Records from Input: Yes, any number of conditional tests
Include/Omit Records from Output: No
Reformat Records on Output: No
Stand-Alone Driver: Yes
Linkable Module: Yes
Merging: Yes

• OTHER INFORMATION

Warranty: Not known
Support: Phone and letter
Update Policy: Not known
Reviews: Chris Terry, "Sorting Out Sorting Programs," *PC Magazine* (February 5, 1985): 50, 52.
Special Features: Can be called directly from various versions and dialects of BASIC, COBOL, FORTRAN, and Pascal.
Comments: According to one reviewer, COSORT is 3 to 10 times faster than PCSORT and 5 to 22 times faster than the DOS SORT routine. Up to 255 sort keys are supported and each may specify ascending or descending order. Sorts fixed and variable length records.

FEATURES	OTS	SS	CS
BASIC FACTS			
Price	149	200	200
Runs On	I	I, C	I
Memory (in K)	64	72	52
Disk Drives	1	1	1
User Interface	CD, MD	CD, MD	CD, MD
On-Line Help	●	○	○
SORT/MERGE FEATURES			
Maximum Record Length	5K	4K	4K
Maximum Input Records	Unl.	2GB	Unl.
Maximum Input Files	Unl.	128	Unl.
Maximum Keys/Fields	10	128	255
Positionally Defined Keys	●	●	●
Comma-Delimited Keys	●	●	●
Boolean Operators	●	●	●
Conditional Selection	●	●	●
ASCII Input Files	●	●	●
Other Input Files	●	●	●
ASCII Collating Sequence	●	●	●
Other Collating Sequence	●	●	○
User-Defined Collating Sequence	●	●	○
Include/Omit Records from Input	●	●	●
Include/Omit Records from Output	●	○	○
Reformat Records on Output	●	○	○
Stand-Alone Driver	●	●	●
Linkable Module	●	○	●
Merging	●	●	●

Table 2.8: Comparison of sorting programs. I = IBM, CD = command-driven, MD = menu-driven, OTS = Opt-Tech Sort, SS = SuperSort II, CS = COSORT.

2.11 Text Retrieval Programs

We learned earlier that text retrieval programs are a type of data base program that operates on free-form text—text that has not been assigned to fields—and that they allow users to locate, retrieve, and manipulate blocks of text by searching for keywords or for strings of words. Because text retrieval programs do not require that data be entered in fields or identified by keywords or abstracts, they make it easy to maintain, search for, and retrieve information. And because of their power and flexibility, text retrieval programs make it easy to search vast quantities of material quickly, efficiently, and thoroughly, even if that material is scattered across a hard disk or several floppy disks.[190]

---

190. In this subsection, for various reasons, I will not review Total Recall (Packet Press, 14704 Seneca Castle Ct., Gaithersburg, MD 20878; (301) 762-7145; $39.50), KWIC-REF/1™ (Chen Information Systems, Inc., 1499 Bayshore Hwy., Suite 205, Burlingame, CA 94010; (415) 692-4358; $300), INSIGHT (Pearlsoft, 25195 S.W. Parkway, P.O. Box 638, Wilsonville, OR 97070; (503) 682-3636; $95), Office Correspondence Retrieval System—OCRS (IBM Entry Systems Division, P.O. Box 1328, Boca Raton, FL 33432; (800)

There are two basic types of text retrieval programs—concordance and text base—and they may be distinguished in terms of their ability to *concord*. Both types treat texts as free-form data bases that consist of words. Both types treat certain predefined text units (e.g., paragraph, verse) as records in the data base. With only a couple of exceptions, both types create indices of all the "non-noise" words in a text. Both types allow users to search texts with Boolean operators, wild-cards, and for words in user-specified sequences and proximities. And both types allow matches to be displayed on-screen, written to a file, or sent to a printer.

Concordance-type text retrieval programs concord words according to user-specified indexing, or sorting, sequences. This type of program allows users to search for words and word combinations, to display matches in user-specified contexts (including the context of the whole document), to sort words by frequency and suffix, and to display statistical information about word and distribution frequencies. Because text retrieval programs of this type create concordances that allow statistical information to be displayed, we may refer to them as "concordance programs," though as I have just explained, they do more than merely concord text. Concordance programs allow users to search, sort, and manipulate texts in ways that are difficult or impossible to do with printed concordances. The concordances created by this type of program are known as keyword-in-context (KWIC) concordances, and they may be used as tools for studying lexical, grammatical, morphological, and other linguistic features in a specified context of the concorded document or simply for locating words and word combinations. Examples of concordance programs include KWIC-MAGIC, KWIC-MERGE, micro-Watcon, the Micro-OCP, and WordCruncher®.

Text-base text retrieval programs allow users to search for words and word combinations and to display matches in the context of the record unit in which they occur (including the context of the whole document). This type of text retrieval program does not allow words to be sorted by frequency or suffix, or statistical information about word and distribution frequencies to be displayed.[191] For lack of better terminology, I have called this type of text retrieval program "text base," though concordance programs also, by definition, work with textual data bases. Examples of text base programs include ZyINDEX™, FYI-3000 Plus, 4-1-1, askSAM™, TextSearch, MICROARRAS, TEXTBANK®, and Sonar™.

Text retrieval programs allow users to search for combinations of terms such as "Jason AND (fleece w/2 golden) AND Argonauts OR Chiron NOT (Jason AND Lycophron)," a search that would be difficult but not impossible with a printed concordance. In that example, the AND operator commands the program to find only those records or lines of text that contain *Jason* and *fleece* and *golden* and *Argonauts*; it narrows the search. The proximity operator *w* and the argument 2 specify that *fleece* and *golden* must occur within two words of one another to count as matches, and so they too narrow the search. The OR operator broadens the search to include those records that contain *Chiron*. The NOT operator excludes those records that include *Jason* and *Lycophron*, since in this example we are looking for material about the Jason of mythology, the son of Aeson, not Jason the fourth-century tyrant of Pherae, the son of Lycophron. A concordance program would allow users to display statistical information about the frequency and distribution of each of those words.

Several of the categories used below require explaining. **WORM**, an acronym for "Write-Once, Read-Many," refers to a type of optical disk that users may record data on but that does not allow that data to be erased and recorded over. **Record Unit** refers to the text unit that the program treats as a record, that is, the text unit in terms of which indexing is carried out. ZyINDEX™, for example, considers each text file as a record, but FYI 3000 Plus treats paragraphs as records (it supports other record struc-

---

447-4700; $149), and Cross Reference Fastfiler (Sofdex International, Inc., P.O. Box 756, Camp Hill, PA 17011; (800) 345-1150, (717) 763-0707; $89.95).

191. MICROARRAS is an exception to these remarks.

tures as well). **Enter Comments for Each Record** refers to whether a program allows users to enter comments in the index file about each record that is indexed. Such comments could include information about the content of the record and where the file that contains it is stored. **Use Parentheses** refers to whether a program allows search terms to be placed in parentheses so that Boolean operators operate on all the terms within the parentheses. (See the example above that included *Jason* for an illustration of this.) **Nested Search Terms** refers to whether a program allows search constructions to use parentheses within parentheses. **Mark/Save Matches to Create New File** indicates whether a program allows users to mark and annotate matches in a user-defined context with comments and information about the filename and creation date, save those annotated matches and their contexts to a disk file, advance to the next match in the same or different file, and repeat the procedure. The term *truncation*, used in conjunction with wild-card searching, refers to a program's ability to search for all character strings that begin or end with the search term(s). When using such a program, entering "comp-" as a search term, for example, would locate all words that begin with the characters *comp*, such as *computer, computational, composition*, and so forth. Similarly, the truncated search term "-ion" would locate all words that ended with the characters *ion*. We discussed truncation earlier in this chapter when we discussed wild-card searching (under "Word Processing Terminology").

See the following articles for helpful reviews and comparisons of ZyINDEX™, FYI 3000, and 4-1-1: John Dickinson et al., "Lexical Electronic Filing," *PC Magazine* (August 20, 1985): 137–44; Phil Casella, "Tracking Electronic Paper," *InfoWorld* (May 6, 1985): 67–72; Bill Crider, "Every Word a Key," *PC World* (October 1985): 192–95; and Kathleen Melymuka, "Text-Retrieval Software," *PC Week* (February 1986): 57–59.

2.11.1 Text Base Programs

2.11.1.1 ZyINDEX

- *BASIC PRODUCT INFORMATION*

Name of Program: ZyINDEX™
Company Name: ZyLAB™ Corporation
Address: 233 East Erie St., Chicago, IL 60611
Phones: (800) 544-6339, (312) 642-2201
Price: $95 for Personal; $145 for Standard; $295 for Professional; $695 for Plus; ZyRECORDS ($95), an add-on product, allows users to define search ranges in terms of beginning and ending key words.
Version Reviewed: Professional, Release 2.10 batch J, current version is 2.20 batch C.[192]
Runs On: IBM PCs and compatibles
Memory Requirements: 256K
Operating System Requirements: DOS 2.0 or greater
Disk Drive Requirements: 2, hard disk recommended
Copy Protected: No
Hard Disk Compatible: Yes
User Interface: Menu-driven
On-Line Help: Yes
Specify Drive, Pathname, and Subdirectory: Yes

---

192. Personal, Standard, Professional, and Plus versions differ in terms of (1) price, (2) the maximum number of files per index, (3) the maximum number of unique words per index, (4) the "clean-up" program (not included with Personal and Standard versions), and (5) support for multiple indices on the same disk—not supported by the Personal and Standard versions. The Plus version includes ZyLIST, a utility that alphabetically lists all words in an index.

Compatible with Local Area Networks (LANs): Yes, Plus Version may be used with IBM Token Ring, Novell, and 3Com LANs, among others.

● INPUT AND INDEXING FEATURES

Index Text Stored in Files on Floppy Disks: Yes
Index Text Stored in Files on Hard Disks: Yes
Index Text Stored in Files on CD-ROMs: Yes, maximum of 20-megabyte section per index
Index Text Stored in Files on WORMs (Optical Disks): Yes, maximum of 20-megabyte section per index
Maximum Keywords (Non-Noise Words) Per File/Record: 65,000
Maximum Words Per File/Record: Approximately 100,000 (depends on number of noise words in file)
Maximum Full-Text Files Per Index: 500 (Standard), 5,000 (Professional), 15,000 (Plus)
Maximum Unique Words Per Index: Standard and Professional: 125,000, Plus: 500,000
Record Unit: File
Multiple Indices/Text Bases Per System: Unlimited
Auto Indexing: Yes
Display Index: No
Edit Index: Not manually, must use "clean-up" program (see below).
Enter Comments for Each Record: Yes
Display Comments for Each Record: Only by using a separate utility.
Works with ASCII Files: Yes
Works with WordStar Files: Yes
Works with WordPerfect Files: Yes
Works with Other Files: Yes, works with over 24 different word processing programs.

● SEARCH FEATURES/OPTIONS

Maximum Characters Per Search Term: 16
Maximum Combined Length of Search Term(s): 160 characters, including parentheses and Boolean operators
Search By Word: Yes
Search By Phrase: Yes
Search By Proximity: Yes, up to 30,000 words
Search By File Date: Yes
Search/Display Upper ASCII Characters: Yes
Search with Wild Cards: Yes, medial and terminal truncation, 2 wild-card characters: "?" for single characters and "*" for multiple characters.
Modify Search Request: Yes
Use Boolean ANDs: Yes
Use Boolean ORs: Yes
Use Boolean NOTs: Yes
Use Parentheses: Yes
Nested Search Terms: No
Can Edit Noise-Word List: Yes, maximum of 255 words, default is 134.
Search Terms Highlighted When Matches Displayed: Yes
Mark/Save Matches to Create New File: Yes, may copy any portions of text and append to output file.
Browse Bidirectionally Through Files Containing Hits: Yes
Browse Bidirectionally for Search Term(s): Yes
Other: None

● OUTPUT OPTIONS

Screen: Yes
Printer: Yes
Disk: Yes
Keywords Only: Yes
Keywords with Line: Yes
Keywords with Sentence: Yes
Keywords with Paragraph: Yes
Keywords with Record: Yes
Keywords with Whole Document: Yes
Other: All contexts for each hit must be marked manually.

- ## OTHER INFORMATION

Warranty: 90 days, media only
Support: Phone and letter
Update Policy: $35 to upgrade to Release 2.
Reviews: Barry Owen, ed., "It's About Time," *PC Magazine* (November 26, 1986): 110–25; Steve Rosenthal, "Creating Order from Chaos," *PC Magazine* (May 15, 1984): 325–28; Bill Crider, "Every Word a Key," *PC World* (October 1985): 192–95; John Dickinson, "Electronic Lexical Filing," *PC Magazine* (August 20, 1985): 137–44; Richard H. Zander, "Whipping Your Text Into SHAPE," *PC Magazine* (June 12, 1984): 305–18; Phil Casella, "Tracking Electronic Paper," *InfoWorld* (May 6, 1985): 67–72; Maurita Peterson Holland, "ZyINDEX: Full Text Retrieval Power," *ONLINE* (July 1985): 38–42; John A. Stibravy, "ZyINDEX—State-of-the-Art Text Management," *Research in Word Processing Newsletter* 3 (April 1985): 11–14.
Special Features: ZyINDEX has two indexing options: full-text and word-only. Word-only indexing indexes words in terms of the files in which they occur but not in terms of where they occur in those files. This feature allows more files to be indexed than with full-text indexing. The annotated copy-and-append feature is incredibly useful, as is the ability to search with Boolean and proximity operators and with two types of wild cards (single- and multiple-character). ZyINDEX's compatibility with text stored on CD-ROMs and on WORMs is a distinctive feature. A "clean-up" program deletes unnecessary information from indices.
Comments: The Plus version includes a multiuser license for up to five multiuser or networked workstations. Of all the commercially-available programs reviewed in this subsection, ZyINDEX is one of the most powerful, flexible, feature-laden, and useful. Support for initial truncation would make the program even more flexible and powerful, as would the ability to have matches in user-specified contexts automatically and conditionally written to disk files, as FYI 3000 Plus allows (see below).

2.11.1.2 FYI 3000 Plus

- ## BASIC PRODUCT INFORMATION

Name of Program: FYI 3000 Plus
Company Name: FYI, Inc.
Address: 4202 Spicewood Springs Rd., Suite 101, Austin, TX 78759
Phone: (512) 346-0134
Other: Software Marketing Associates, 4615 Bee Caves Rd., Austin, TX 78746; (512) 327-2882, is a major distributor of FYI 3000 Plus.
Price: $195; $174.95 with 10% educational discount
Version Reviewed: 3.14
Runs On: IBM PCs and compatibles
Memory Requirements: 128K; 384K if using Fast Indexer feature.
Operating System Requirements: DOS 2.0 or greater
Disk Drive Requirements: 2
Copy Protected: No
Hard Disk Compatible: Yes
User Interface: Menu-driven
On-Line Help: Yes
Specify Drive, Pathname, and Subdirectory: Yes
Compatible with Local Area Networks (LANs): Yes. FYI markets FYI-MCD, a mail/conference/data base program that supports 1,000 users (with up to 19 mail slots per user), 45 self-maintaining conferences (with up to 500 messages per conference), and 16 text bases of up to 65,000,000 words each that may be searched using FYI 3000 Plus's Boolean search features. FYI-MCD runs on IBM PCs and compatibles, requires 256K RAM, a hard disk, DOS 2.1 or greater, a serial port, and a Hayes-compatible 300- or 1,200-baud modem. FYI-MCD is an unusual, powerful, sophisticated conferencing and data base system. Price: $100 for FYI 3000 Plus owners; $295 otherwise (includes a copy of FYI 3000 Plus).

- ## INPUT AND INDEXING FEATURES

Index Text Stored in Files on Floppy Disks: Yes
Index Text Stored in Files on Hard Disks: Yes
Index Text Stored in Files on CD-ROMs: No
Index Text Stored in Files on WORMs (Optical Disks): Yes

Maximum Keywords (Non-Noise Words) Per File/Record: 7,000 characters/1,000 words

Maximum Words Per File/Record: Up to 2,000,000 if the record unit is defined using *C/*K/*E (see below), otherwise maximums not known (if using Fast Indexer with *C/*K/*E record format, maximum record size is 64,000, not 2,000,000, characters). Maximum words per data base is 65,000,000 (approximately 500 MB).

Maximum Full-Text Records Per Index: 65,000

Maximum Full-Text Files Per Index: Floppy systems: 25,500 files (100 on each of 255 disks); hard disk systems: 1,200 files (100 on each of 12 subdirectories)

Maximum Unique Words Per Index: 65,000

Record Unit: (1) Paragraph (every significant word is keyword), (2) *C/*E (every significant word between markers is keyword), or (3) *C/*K/*E (only words and phrases following *K are keywords)

Multiple Indices/Text Bases Per System: Yes

Auto Indexing: Yes

Display Index: Yes, on-screen, disk, or file; also can display words with specified character sequence or alphabetic range.

Edit Index: No

Enter Comments for Each Record: Yes

Display Comments for Each Record: Yes

Works with ASCII Files: Yes

Works with WordStar Files: Yes

Works with WordPerfect Files: Yes

Works with Other Files: Yes, a set-up file allows users to define end-of-paragraph markers for any word processing program.

• SEARCH FEATURES/OPTIONS

Maximum Characters Per Search Term: 64

Maximum Combined Length of Search Term(s): 250 keywords

Search By Word: Yes

Search By Phrase: No

Search By Proximity: No in every-word-is-keyword record format; Yes in specified-keyword format.

Search By File Date: No

Search/Display Upper ASCII Characters: No

Search with Wild Cards: Yes, terminal truncation only

Modify Search Request: No

Use Boolean ANDs: Yes

Use Boolean ORs: Yes

Use Boolean NOTs: Yes

Use Parentheses: Yes

Nested Search Terms: Yes

Can Edit Noise-Word List: Yes, size limited only by disk space.

Search Terms Highlighted When Matches Displayed: No

Mark/Save Matches to Create New File: Yes, but output unit must be whole record (entry), first sentence of paragraph (record), first screen line of record, or whole file—i.e., you cannot copy and append portions of text at will.

Browse Bidirectionally Through Files Containing Hits: Yes

Browse Bidirectionally for Search Term(s): Yes

Other: Supports Boolean XOR (exclusive or). If search term(s) not valid, program automatically displays the most similar terms from the index file—a very helpful feature.

• OUTPUT OPTIONS

Screen: Yes

Printer: Yes

Disk: Yes

Keywords Only: No

Keywords with Line: Yes

Keywords with Sentence: No, first sentence only

Keywords with Paragraph: Yes (since record is paragraph).

Keywords with Record: Yes

Keywords with Whole Document: No

Other: Automatically and conditionally allows matches in user-specified contexts to be written to disk files.

• OTHER INFORMATION

Warranty: Media only
Support: Phone, letter, On-line Users Club (see below)
Update Policy: Minimal cost or free
Reviews: Phil Casella, "Tracking Electronic Paper," *InfoWorld* (May 6, 1985): 67–72; John Dickinson, "Electronic Lexical Filing," *PC Magazine* (August 20, 1985): 137–44; Richard H. Zander, "Whipping Your Text Into SHAPE," *PC Magazine* (June 12, 1984): 305–18.
Special Features: Includes the FYI Sort Utility™, which can sort alphabetical or numerical information, format it, and print it. This is useful for alphabetizing indices and bibliographies. The Fast Indexer allows material to be indexed 6 to 10 times faster than before. The FYI 3000 Plus Online Users Club is a special conferencing and support system that runs on FYI-MCD (see above), that contains information about FYI 3000 Plus, and that supports E-mail (telephone: (512) 346-0135, logon as "GUEST").
Comments: This is a straightforward and powerful program for users who wish to search data that is in paragraph format (e.g., paragraphs in word processing files). Those who do not mind creating records by using special codes (*C/*E) also will find the program helpful. FYI 3000 Plus can automatically and conditionally write matches in user-specified contexts (typically the entire record) to disk files, which is an extremely useful feature. But FYI 3000 Plus is weakened by its inability to search by phrase, proximity, and file creation date, by the fact that matches are not highlighted, and by the fact that it does not support completely free-form copying and appending of text to disk files (as ZyINDEX does—see above). Support for medial and initial truncation would further strengthen the program. FYI 3000 Plus is the text base program that is included as part of Nota Bene™ (see above).

2.11.1.3 *4-1-1*

• BASIC PRODUCT INFORMATION

Name of Program: 4-1-1
Company Name: Summa Technologies, Inc.
Address: 919 Sir Francis Drake Blvd., Kentfield, CA 94904
Phone: (415) 459-4003
Price: $149
Version Reviewed: Not able to review.
Runs On: IBM PCs and compatibles
Memory Requirements: 256K
Operating System Requirements: DOS 2.0 or greater
Disk Drive Requirements: 2, hard disk required.
Copy Protected: No
Hard Disk Compatible: Yes, hard disk required.
User Interface: Menu-driven
On-Line Help: No
Specify Drive, Pathname, and Subdirectory: Yes
Compatible with Local Area Networks (LANs): Not known

• INPUT AND INDEXING FEATURES

Index Text Stored in Files on Floppy Disks: Yes
Index Text Stored in Files on Hard Disks: Yes
Index Text Stored in Files on CD-ROMs: No
Index Text Stored in Files on WORMs (Optical Disks): No
Maximum Keywords (Non-Noise Words) Per File/Record: Unlimited
Maximum Words Per File/Record: Unlimited
Maximum Full-Text Files Per Index: 1,000
Maximum Unique Words Per Index: Not known
Record Unit: File
Multiple Indices/Text Bases Per System: Yes
Auto Indexing: Yes
Display Index: Not known
Edit Index: Not known
Enter Comments for Each Record: Yes, a title of up to 40 characters
Display Comments for Each Record: Yes

Works with ASCII Files: Yes
Works with WordStar Files: Yes
Works with WordPerfect Files: No
Works with Other Files: YES

• SEARCH FEATURES/OPTIONS

Maximum Characters Per Search Term: 18
Maximum Combined Length of Search Term(s): 15 keywords + title + date
Search By Word: Yes
Search By Phrase: No
Search By Proximity: No
Search By File Date: Yes
Search/Display Upper ASCII Characters: No
Search with Wild Cards: Yes, 2 types, "*" and "?"
Modify Search Request: Yes
Use Boolean ANDs: Yes
Use Boolean ORs: Yes
Use Boolean NOTs: No
Use Parentheses: No
Nested Search Terms: No
Can Edit Noise-Word List: Yes
Search Terms Highlighted When Matches Displayed: No
Mark/Save Matches to Create New File: No
Browse Bidirectionally Through Files Containing Hits: Yes
Browse Bidirectionally for Search Term(s): No
Other: Automated or manual search-term entry.

• OUTPUT OPTIONS

Screen: Yes
Printer: Yes
Disk: Yes
Keywords Only: Not known
Keywords with Line: Not known
Keywords with Sentence: Not known
Keywords with Paragraph: Not known
Keywords with Record: Not known
Keywords with Whole Document: Not known
Other: None

• OTHER INFORMATION

Warranty: Not known
Support: Phone and letter
Update Policy: Not known
Reviews: Phil Casella, "Tracking Electronic Paper," *InfoWorld* (May 6, 1985): 67–72; John Dickinson, "Electronic Lexical Filing," *PC Magazine* (August 20, 1985): 137–44; Bill Crider, "Every Word a Key," *PC World* (October 1985): 192–95.
Special Features: Data encryption and file archiving.
Comments: None

2.11.1.4 askSAM Version 3

• BASIC PRODUCT INFORMATION

Name of Program: askSAM™ Version 3
Company Name: Seaside Software, Inc.
Address: 119 South Washington St., P.O. Box 31, Perry, FL 32347
Phone: (800) 327-5726, (904) 584-6590

Price: $200; demo copy available by mail for $15 or can be downloaded (free) from the askSam bulletin board at (904) 584-8287; mail merge available for $50.
Version Reviewed: 3.11
Runs On: IBM PCs and compatibles
Memory Requirements: 256K
Operating System Requirements: DOS 2.0 or greater
Disk Drive Requirements: 1
Copy Protected: No
Hard Disk Compatible: Yes
User Interface: Command-driven and menu-driven
On-Line Help: Yes
Specify Drive, Pathname, and Subdirectory: Yes
Compatible with Local Area Networks (LANs): Yes

- *INPUT AND INDEXING FEATURES*

Index Text Stored in Files on Floppy Disks: Yes
Index Text Stored in Files on Hard Disks: Yes
Index Text Stored in Files on CD-ROMs: No
Index Text Stored in Files on WORMs (Optical Disks): No
Maximum Keywords (Non-Noise Words) Per File/Record: 4 gigabytes is maximum file size.
Maximum Words Per File/Record: 1,600 bytes/characters per record (approximately 20 lines of 80-column text), though records may be linked to form logical documents of any length. The 1,600-byte restriction applies only to explicitly labelled fields. There is no 1,600-byte limitation for nonfield-specific, free-form text. In either case, physical files may be as large as available disk space.
Maximum Full-Text Files Per Index: Unlimited
Maximum Unique Words Per Index: Unlimited
Record Unit: Variable
Multiple Indices/Text Bases Per System: Yes
Auto Indexing: Yes
Display Index: Yes
Edit Index: Yes
Enter Comments for Each Record: Yes
Display Comments for Each Record: Yes
Works with ASCII Files: Yes
Works with WordStar Files: Yes, filter needed for non-document-mode WordStar files (see below).
Works with WordPerfect Files: Yes
Works with Other Files: Yes, though filters may be needed.

- *SEARCH FEATURES/OPTIONS*

Maximum Characters Per Search Term: 80 characters per query line
Maximum Combined Length of Search Term(s): Unlimited
Search By Word: Yes
Search By Phrase: Yes
Search By Proximity: Yes
Search By File Date: Yes
Search/Display Upper ASCII Characters: Yes
Search with Wild Cards: Yes
Modify Search Request: Yes
Use Boolean ANDs: Yes
Use Boolean ORs: Yes
Use Boolean NOTs: Yes
Use Parentheses: Yes
Nested Search Terms: Yes
Can Edit Noise-Word List: Not known
Search Terms Highlighted When Matches Displayed: Yes
Mark/Save Matches to Create New File: Yes
Browse Bidirectionally Through Files Containing Hits: Yes
Browse Bidirectionally for Search Term(s): Yes
Other: None

- ## OUTPUT OPTIONS

Screen: Yes
Printer: Yes
Disk: Yes
Keywords Only: Yes
Keywords with Line: Yes
Keywords with Sentence: No
Keywords with Paragraph: No
Keywords with Record: Yes
Keywords with Whole Document: No
Other: User-specifiable sort collating sequence

- ## OTHER INFORMATION

Warranty: None
Support: Phone, letter, bulletin board (904/584-8287)
Update Policy: $50 to upgrade to version 3; minor upgrades are free or minimal cost.
Reviews: *Collegiate Microcomputer* 4 (November 1986): 313–14; Vince Puglia, "askSam™," *PC Magazine* (November 25, 1986); *PC Magazine* (January 13, 1987); Steve King, *InfoWorld* (April 20, 1987): 59–62; *PC World* (July 1987): 245–46.
Special Features: Works with free-form data, data in fields, data in implied fields. Fields may be text, numbers, or dates. Field and data types may be mixed within the same file. Supports basic math operations on numerical fields, as well as the operations of average, sum, count, minimum and maximum values. Formal definition of fields not required. Fields are referenced by name, not location, and may be variable length. Fields may be up to 1,600 bytes in size. Files may be passworded and encrypted. Can append imported data to an existing, tagged file. Includes on-disk tutorial, built-in report generator, and automatic phone dialer. Supports up to four user-defined macros. Command files may be stored and executed later. Users may define translation tables for sorting foreign text. Automatic file-saving and screen blanking. Files may be color coded. IF . . . ELSE . . . END logical constructs may be used with any amount of nesting. Records may be time and date stamped. Includes full-screen editor that supports block moves and other word processing functions. Decimal precision to 13 places. Supports user-defined templates and overlays for data entry. Supports sequence-specific searching and proximity searching by number of words, number of lines, and number of sentences. A user-defined stop list of words to ignore when searching may be created. Text to be searched does not have to be indexed.
Comments: askSam is one of the most flexible (and perhaps the fastest) of the text-base programs listed in this section. The ability to define translation tables for sorting foreign text is especially useful, as is the fact that text does not have to be indexed to be searched. askSam does not support windows, multiple-file access, indexing, context-sensitive on-line help, and access to the DOS directory. Only one file may be open and active at a time. Filters for importing WordStar files are available on request. "Insert" is a utility for importing ASCII files, fixed-position files, comma-delimited files, and all versions of dBase files. Context sensitive help is promised for later in 1987.

2.11.1.5 Electra-Find

- ## BASIC PRODUCT INFORMATION

Name of Program: Electra-Find
Company Name: O'Neill Software
Address: 440 Davis Court, Suite 1822, San Francisco, CA 94111
Phone: (415) 398-2255
Price: $49; $299 for site license
Version Reviewed: 3.3
Runs On: IBM PCs and compatibles; CP/M-80 systems
Memory Requirements: IBM: 64K; CP/M: 64K
Operating System Requirements: IBM: DOS 2.0 or greater; CP/M: 2.2

Disk Drive Requirements: 1
Copy Protected: No
Hard Disk Compatible: Yes
User Interface: Command-driven or menu-driven

On-Line Help: Yes
Specify Drive, Pathname, and Subdirectory: Yes
Compatible with Local Area Networks (LANs): Yes

- *INPUT AND INDEXING FEATURES*

Index Text Stored in Files on Floppy Disks: Yes
Index Text Stored in Files on Hard Disks: Yes
Index Text Stored in Files on CD-ROMs: No
Index Text Stored in Files on WORMs (Optical Disks): No
Maximum Keywords (Non-Noise Words) Per File/Record: Unlimited
Maximum Words Per File/Record: Unlimited
Maximum Full-Text Files Per Index: Does not create indices.
Maximum Unique Words Per Index: Does not create indices.
Record Unit: User-defined, including word, line, sentence, paragraph, footnotes, material within quotation marks, fixed length records, and headers; any text between any delimiters.
Multiple Indices/Text Bases Per System: Not applicable
Auto Indexing: Not applicable
Display Index: Not applicable
Edit Index: Not applicable
Enter Comments for Each Record: Not applicable
Display Comments for Each Record: Displays file name and location of each retrieved item.
Works with ASCII Files: Yes
Works with WordStar Files: Yes
Works with WordPerfect Files: Yes
Works with Other Files: Yes, works with files created with any word processor.

- *SEARCH FEATURES/OPTIONS*

Maximum Characters Per Search Term: 64
Maximum Combined Length of Search Term(s): 40 items (words and/or phrases)
Search By Word: Yes
Search By Phrase: Yes
Search By Proximity: Yes
Search By File Date: No
Search/Display Upper ASCII Characters: Yes
Search with Wild Cards: Yes, initial, medial, and terminal positions
Modify Search Request: Yes
Use Boolean ANDs: Yes
Use Boolean ORs: Yes
Use Boolean NOTs: Yes
Use Parentheses: Yes
Nested Search Terms: Yes
Can Edit Noise-Word List: Not applicable
Search Terms Highlighted When Matches Displayed: Yes
Mark/Save Matches to Create New File: Yes, automatic output of matches in user-specified context to specified output file only.
Browse Bidirectionally Through Files Containing Hits: Forward only and only from beginning of file.
Browse Bidirectionally for Search Term(s): Yes
Other: Phonetic searching, case-sensitive and case-insensitive searches. Can search for punctuation, characters, and parts of words. Can automatically include file name and delete control characters in output. Unlike other programs in this subsection (except for askSAM Version 3), Electra-Find does not require indexing text that is to be searched. Maximum of 200 files of unlimited size may be searched at a time.

- *OUTPUT OPTIONS*

Screen: Yes
Printer: Yes
Disk: Yes
Keywords Only: Yes
Keywords with Line: Yes
Keywords with Sentence: Yes

Keywords with Paragraph: Yes
Keywords with Record: Yes
Keywords with Whole Document: Yes
Other: User may specify output context.

• OTHER INFORMATION

Warranty: 30-day, unconditional, money-back guarantee
Support: Phone and letter
Update Policy: Not known
Reviews: Glenn Hart, "Electra-Find: A Handy Way To Retrieve the Right Files," *PC Magazine* (May 13, 1986): 343–44.
Special Features: Can operate in background with multitasking environments such as TopView.
Comments: This is a fast, easy-to-use, efficient, and useful program, and the price is hard to argue with. It is the only program in this subsection that supports initial, medial, and terminal truncation. Electra-Find is much more sophisticated than the DOS "FIND" command and among other applications is an excellent replacement for it, especially since like FIND, Electra-Find can be invoked at the DOS level. By not using index files, Electra-Find saves disk space and initial set-up time but at the cost of requiring more time for searches than is required by programs that search fully indexed text. When searching short files or a small number of files, the increased time is not too noticeable. When searching long files or a large number of files, the increased time could be troublesome. O'Neill Software has developed a similar program called The Text Collector.

2.11.1.6 TextSearch

• BASIC PRODUCT INFORMATION

Name of Program: TextSearch (formerly FATRAS 3)
Company Name: LinguaTech International, Inc.
Address: 381 W. 2230 N., #360, Provo, UT 84604
Phone: (801) 373-8800; MCIMAIL (mailbox: LINGUATECH)
Price: $14 for program and documentation; $49 to become a registered user eligible for support and upgrade notices.
Version Reviewed: 3.0
Runs On: IBM PCs and compatibles
Memory Requirements: 256K
Operating System Requirements: DOS 2.0 or greater
Disk Drive Requirements: 2, hard disk recommended
Copy Protected: No
Hard Disk Compatible: Yes
User Interface: Command-driven
On-Line Help: Yes
Specify Drive, Pathname, and Subdirectory: Yes
Compatible with Local Area Networks (LANs): Not known

• INPUT AND INDEXING FEATURES

Index Text Stored in Files on Floppy Disks: Yes
Index Text Stored in Files on Hard Disks: Yes
Index Text Stored in Files on CD-ROMs: No
Index Text Stored in Files on WORMs (Optical Disks): No
Maximum Keywords (Non-Noise Words) Per File/Record: 200,000
Maximum Words Per File/Record: 200,000
Maximum Full-Text Files Per Index: 1.4 megabytes
Maximum Unique Words Per Index: 42,000
Record Unit: File
Multiple Indices/Text Bases Per System: Yes
Auto Indexing: Yes
Display Index: No
Edit Index: No
Enter Comments for Each Record: No

Display Comments for Each Record: No
Works with ASCII Files: Yes, and only with ASCII text.
Works with WordStar Files: Only if converted to ASCII.
Works with WordPerfect Files: Only in pure ASCII form.
Works with Other Files: No
Other: Maximum lines of text is 32,000 (approximately 200,000 words).

- ## SEARCH FEATURES/OPTIONS

Maximum Characters Per Search Term: 18
Maximum Combined Length of Search Term(s): 5 words
Search By Word: Yes
Search By Phrase: Yes
Search By Proximity: Yes
Search By File Date: No
Search/Display Upper ASCII Characters: Yes
Search with Wild Cards: No, but supports search by prefix and suffix.
Modify Search Request: No
Use Boolean ANDs: Yes
Use Boolean ORs: No
Use Boolean NOTs: No
Use Parentheses: No
Nested Search Terms: No
Can Edit Noise-Word List: Not applicable
Search Terms Highlighted When Matches Displayed: Yes, users have option.
Mark/Save Matches to Create New File: No
Browse Bidirectionally Through Files Containing Hits: No
Browse Bidirectionally for Search Term(s): No
Other: TextSearch displays the frequency of the occurrence of matches. Case-sensitive and case-insensitive searches (including accents) are supported. Can sort multiple-string searches by text order or by keywords. Matches are displayed with text line numbers. User defines alphabet used in searches; alphabets may be up to 31 letter classes long and include diacritics. The maximum number of matches TextSearch can display in a single search is 500. TextSearch can build a reference version of texts that includes line numbers, a word-frequency listing, and a reverse-alphabetical-order vocabulary listing.

- ## OUTPUT OPTIONS

Screen: Yes
Printer: No
Disk: Yes
Keywords Only: Yes
Keywords with Line: Yes
Keywords with Sentence: Yes
Keywords with Paragraph: Yes
Keywords with Record: Yes
Keywords with Whole Document: No
Other: None

- ## OTHER INFORMATION

Warranty: 30-day, money-back guarantee
Support: Phone and letter (registered users only)
Update Policy: $14 to upgrade to 3.1
Reviews: Not known
Special Features: Support for user-defined alphabets that may include accented characters sets this program apart from others in this subsection and is a feature common to some of the concordance programs described below. The ability to create word-frequency listings and a reverse-alphabetical-order vocabulary listing are helpful for statistical textual analysis.

259

Comments: Index files are 200% to 300% the size of input files. TextSearch is useful and affordable. Compared to ZyINDEX and FYI 3000 Plus, however, it is very slow in building indices, not as flexible in its search and output commands, and creates larger index files. Compared to Electra-Find, it is slow and not as flexible in its search and output commands. TextSearch is best suited for persons who need a text retrieval program that works with "extended" ASCII characters.

2.11.1.7 MICROARRAS

• BASIC PRODUCT INFORMATION

Name of Program: MICROARRAS
Company Name: % John B. Smith, Conceptual Tools, Inc.
Address: P.O. Box 247, Chapel Hill, NC 27514
Phone: (919) 967-2000
Price: Not known; IBM mainframe version costs $3,000 for a one-time academic site license.
Version Reviewed: Not able to review
Runs On: IBM PCs and compatibles, SUN workstations, VAX
Memory Requirements: Not known
Operating System Requirements: Not known
Disk Drive Requirements: Not known
Copy Protected: Not known
Hard Disk Compatible: Yes
User Interface: Not known
On-Line Help: Not known
Specify Drive, Pathname, and Subdirectory: Yes
Compatible with Local Area Networks (LANs): Yes, the program is designed for a distributed environment, though it also will work on single microcomputers.

• INPUT AND INDEXING FEATURES

Index Text Stored in Files on Floppy Disks: Yes
Index Text Stored in Files on Hard Disks: Yes
Index Text Stored in Files on CD-ROMs: Presumably
Index Text Stored in Files on WORMs (Optical Disks): Presumably
Maximum Keywords (Non-Noise Words) Per File/Record: Not known
Maximum Words Per File/Record: Not known
Maximum Full-Text Files Per Index: Not known
Maximum Unique Words Per Index: Not known
Record Unit: Not known
Multiple Indices/Text Bases Per System: Yes
Auto Indexing: Yes
Display Index: Not known
Edit Index: Not known
Enter Comments for Each Record: Presumably
Display Comments for Each Record: Presumably
Works with ASCII Files: Yes
Works with WordStar Files: Not known
Works with WordPerfect Files: Not known
Works with Other Files: Presumably

• SEARCH FEATURES/OPTIONS

Maximum Characters Per Search Term: Not known
Maximum Combined Length of Search Term(s): Not known
Search By Word: Yes
Search By Phrase: Yes
Search By Proximity: Presumably
Search By File Date: Not known
Search/Display Upper ASCII Characters: Not known
Search with Wild Cards: Yes
Modify Search Request: Not known

Use Boolean ANDs: Yes, in content search mode (see below).
Use Boolean ORs: Yes, in content search mode (see below).
Use Boolean NOTs: Yes, in content search mode (see below).
Use Parentheses: Not known, but presumably "Yes" (in content search mode—see below).
Nested Search Terms: Not known, but presumably "Yes" (in content search mode—see below).
Can Edit Noise-Word List: Not known
Search Terms Highlighted When Matches Displayed: Not known
Mark/Save Matches to Create New File: Yes
Browse Bidirectionally Through Files Containing Hits: Yes
Browse Bidirectionally for Search Term(s): Presumably
Other: Two basic types of searching are available. Text bases may be (1) searched for texts (i.e., by author, title, keyword, etc.), which is known as a bibliographic search, and (2) the content of those texts may be searched with Boolean operators, which is known as a content search. For text analysis purposes, in content searches MICROARRAS allows users to define three categories of word groups and to search the text in terms of any of those sets: (A) type lists (i.e., a specified set of word types, e.g., words that refer to computers), (B) token lists (i.e., sets of positions in the text that represent the occurrence of individual words, e.g., wherever *processor* refers to word processor, not central processing unit), and (C) recursive lists (i.e., sets of other categories). Thus MICROARRAS allows texts to be searched by word, by category, or both, with Boolean operators and user-specified ranges of text for each search term and category. The results of content searches can be searched and those results searched, etc. MICROARRAS can display text by logical divisions (volume, chapter, paragraph, sentence, word in sentence) and by physical divisions (page, line, word within line). Three types of lexical information are available: alphabetic sequence of words, character patterns, word frequency. Lexicons may be displayed by alphabetical range, and wild-cards may be used to display character patterns. Search constructions may be saved, reused, and used on different texts.

• OUTPUT OPTIONS

Screen: Yes
Printer: Yes
Disk: Yes
Keywords Only: No
Keywords with Line: Yes
Keywords with Sentence: Yes
Keywords with Paragraph: Yes
Keywords with Record: Yes
Keywords with Whole Document: Presumably
Other: User may specify output context.

• OTHER INFORMATION

Warranty: Not known
Support: Not known
Update Policy: Not known
Reviews: John B. Smith, "A New Environment for Literary Analysis," *Perspectives in Computing* 4 (Summer/Fall 1984): 20–31; John B. Smith, "ARRAS and Literary Criticism," in Bernard Derval and Michel Lenoble, eds., *La Critique Litteraire et L'Ordinateur* (Bibliotheque nationale du Quebec, 1985), 79–93.
Special Features: Supports an array of statistical and analytical features. Two types of statistical features: word-frequency (by term and by sets of terms) within a user-specified range of text and segmental measures (i.e., number of times one segmental unit occurs within another, e.g., number of words in sentence, number of sentences in paragraph). Ratios, distributions, and various types of lists, as well as bar graphs (e.g., the number of occurrences of a term or category per interval of text), may be computed and constructed. MICROARRAS recognizes scalars and vectors of both integers and reals. The ability to define sets and to search by sets is unique among programs in this subsection. MICROARRAS supports multiple-user interfaces that can be tailored for different applications and different groups of users.
Comments: MICROARRAS has the most sophisticated, flexible, and powerful search features by far of any program reviewed in this section. It is the only program reviewed in this section that offers true (and very powerful) analytical and statistical tools for studying text. MICROARRAS is a program designed for working with *large* text bases that contain multiple texts.

2.11.1.8 TEXTBANK

- ### BASIC PRODUCT INFORMATION

Name of Program: TEXTBANK®
Company Name: Group L Corp.
Address: 481 Carlisle Dr., Herndon, VA 22070
Phones: (800) 672-5300, (703) 471-0030
Price: $995
Version Reviewed: Not able to review.
Runs On: IBM PCs and compatibles
Memory Requirements: 640K
Operating System Requirements: DOS 2.0 or greater
Disk Drive Requirements: 2, one of which must be hard disk.
Copy Protected: No
Hard Disk Compatible: Yes
User Interface: Menu-driven
On-Line Help: Yes
Specify Drive, Pathname, and Subdirectory: Yes
Compatible with Local Area Networks (LANs): Yes, requires basic program ($995) and a minimum of 3 user's systems ($295 each).

- ### INPUT AND INDEXING FEATURES

Index Text Stored in Files on Floppy Disks: Yes
Index Text Stored in Files on Hard Disks: Yes
Index Text Stored in Files on CD-ROMs: Yes
Index Text Stored in Files on WORMs (Optical Disks): Yes
Maximum Keywords (Non-Noise Words) Per File/Record: Unlimited
Maximum Words Per File/Record: 20 megabytes
Maximum Full-Text Files Per Index: Not applicable
Maximum Unique Words Per Index: Unlimited
Record Unit: User-definable text "zones," i.e., line, sentence, paragraph, chapter
Multiple Indices/Text Bases Per System: Yes
Auto Indexing: Yes
Display Index: Yes
Edit Index: Not applicable
Enter Comments for Each Record: Not known
Display Comments for Each Record: Not known
Works with ASCII Files: Yes
Works with WordStar Files: No, must convert to ASCII.
Works with WordPerfect Files: No, must convert to ASCII.
Works with Other Files: No

- ### SEARCH FEATURES/OPTIONS

Maximum Characters Per Search Term: Unlimited
Maximum Combined Length of Search Term(s): Unlimited
Search By Word: Yes
Search By Phrase: Yes
Search By Proximity: Yes, by word, zone, and range
Search By File Date: No
Search/Display Upper ASCII Characters: Yes
Search with Wild Cards: Yes, supports initial, medial, and terminal truncation.
Modify Search Request: Yes
Use Boolean ANDs: Yes
Use Boolean ORs: Yes
Use Boolean NOTs: Yes
Use Parentheses: Yes
Nested Search Terms: Yes
Can Edit Noise-Word List: Yes, does not need stop-word list.
Search Terms Highlighted When Matches Displayed: Yes

Mark/Save Matches to Create New File: Yes
Browse Bidirectionally Through Files Containing Hits: Yes
Browse Bidirectionally for Search Term(s): Yes
Other: Can search with XOR (exclusive OR). Results of searches may be sorted. A macro command allows long search commands to be created, stored, and recalled.

- ## OUTPUT OPTIONS

Screen: Yes
Printer: Yes
Disk: Yes
Keywords Only: Not applicable
Keywords with Line: Not applicable
Keywords with Sentence: Not applicable
Keywords with Paragraph: Not applicable
Keywords with Record: Not applicable
Keywords with Whole Document: Not applicable
Other: None

- ## OTHER INFORMATION

Warranty: 90 days
Support: Phone and letter
Update Policy: Approximately once a year, cost not known
Reviews: *PC Week* (February 25, 1986); Ron Force, "Textbank/PC," *Library Software Review* 5 (May/June 1986): 196–99; Scott Mace, "Text System Updated for Search, Retrieval," *InfoWorld* (April 14, 1986): 56.
Special Features: User-definable text zones.
Comments: This program is reported to be more flexible and powerful than ZyINDEX.

2.11.1.9 Sonar

- ## BASIC PRODUCT INFORMATION

Name of Program: Sonar™
Company Name: Virginia Systems Software Services, Inc.
Address: 5509 West Bay Ct., Midlothian, VA 23113
Phone: (804) 739-3200
Price: $195
Version Reviewed: Not able to review; current version is 4.0.
Runs On: Macintoshes
Memory Requirements: 1MB
Operating System Requirements: Macintosh
Disk Drive Requirements: 2, hard disk recommended
Copy Protected: No
Hard Disk Compatible: Yes
User Interface: Menu-driven
On-Line Help: No
Specify Drive, Pathname, and Subdirectory: Not applicable
Compatible with Local Area Networks (LANs): Not known

- ## INPUT AND INDEXING FEATURES

Index Text Stored in Files on Floppy Disks: Yes
Index Text Stored in Files on Hard Disks: Yes
Index Text Stored in Files on CD-ROMs: No
Index Text Stored in Files on WORMs (Optical Disks): No
Maximum Keywords (Non-Noise Words) Per File/Record: 500K (approximately 166 pages) for first megabyte of RAM, 1.5MB per 1 MB RAM thereafter (approximately 500 additional pages)
Maximum Words Per File/Record: 500K
Maximum Full-Text Files Per Index: Unlimited (depends on primary and secondary memory).

FEATURES	ZY	FYI	411	SAM	EF	TS	MA	TB	SO
BASIC FEATURES									
Price	145	195	149	200	49	14	?	995	195
Runs On	I	I	I	I	I, C	I	I	I	M
Memory (in K)	256	128	256	256	64	256	?	640	1MB
Disk Drives	2	2	2	1	1	2	?	2	2
User Interface	MD	MD	MD	MD,CD	MD,CD	CD	?	MD	MD
On-Line Help	●	●	○	●	●	●	?	●	○
INPUT & INDEXING FEATURES									
Index Text on Floppies	●	●	●	●	●	●	●	●	●
Index Text on Hard Disks	●	●	●	●	●	●	●	●	●
Index Text on CD-ROMs	●	○	○	○	○	○	?	●	○
Index Texts on WORMs	●	●	○	○	○	○	?	●	○
Max. Keywords/Record (in K)	65	1	Unl.	4GB	Unl.	200	?	Unl.	500+
Max. Words/Record (in K)	100	2GB	Unl.	Unl.	Unl.	200	?	20MB	500
Max. Full-Text Files/Index (in K)	.5-15	25.5	1	Unl.	—	1.4MB	?	—	Unl.
Max. Unique Words/Index (in K)	125-500	65	?	Unl.	—	42	?	Unl.	Unl.
Record Unit	File	Para.	File	Variable	Usr-Def	File	?	Usr-Def	Para.
Multiple Indices/System	●	●	●	●	—	●	●	●	●
Auto Indexing	●	●	●	●	—	●	●	●	●
Display Index	○	●	?	●	—	○	?	●	●
Edit Index	○	○	?	●	—	○	?	—	○
Enter Comments on Records	●	●	●	●	—	○	?	?	○
ASCII Files	●	●	●	●	●	●	●	●	●

Maximum Unique Words Per Index: Unlimited
Record Unit: Paragraph
Multiple Indices/Text Bases Per System: Yes
Auto Indexing: Yes
Display Index: Yes
Edit Index: No
Enter Comments for Each Record: No
Display Comments for Each Record: No
Works with ASCII Files: Yes; works with text-only files.
Works with WordStar Files: Not applicable
Works with WordPerfect Files: Not yet (WordPerfect™ for the Macintosh has not been released at the time of this writing).
Works with Other Files: MacWrite™, Microsoft® Word, MORE™, WriteNow™

● *SEARCH FEATURES/OPTIONS*

Maximum Characters Per Search Term: 80
Maximum Combined Length of Search Term(s): 80
Search By Word: Yes
Search By Phrase: Yes
Search By Proximity: Yes
Search By File Date: No
Search/Display Upper ASCII Characters: Not applicable
Search with Wild Cards: No
Modify Search Request: No
Use Boolean ANDs: Yes

FEATURES	ZY	FYI	411	SAM	EF	TS	MA	TB	SO
SEARCH FEATURES/OPTIONS									
Max. Char./Search Term	16	64	18	80	64	18	?	Unl.	80
Max. Lgth. of Search Terms	160 Ch	250 Wd	15 Wd	Unl.	40 Wd	5 Wd	?	Unl.	80
Search by Word	●	●	●	●	●	●	●	●	●
Search by Phrase	●	○	○	●	●	●	●	●	●
Search by Proximity	●	—	○	●	●	●	?	●	●
Search by File Date	●	○	●	●	○	○	?	○	○
Search/Display Upper ASCII	●	○	○	●	●	●	?	●	—
Search with Wild Cards	●	●	●	●	●	○	●	●	○
Modify Search Request	●	○	●	●	●	○	?	●	●
Boolean ANDs	●	●	●	●	●	●	●	●	●
Boolean ORs	●	●	●	●	●	○	●	●	●
Boolean NOTs	●	●	○	●	●	○	●	●	○
Parentheses	●	●	○	●	●	○	?	●	●
Nest Search Terms	○	●	○	●	●	○	?	●	●
Edit Noise-Word List	●	●	●	?	—	—	?	●	○
Highlights Matches	●	○	○	●	●	●	?	●	●
Save Matches—New File	●	●	○	●	●	○	●	●	●
Brouse Bidirect. for Hits	●	●	●	●	●	○	●	●	●
Brouse Bidirect. for S. T	●	●	○	●	●	○	?	●	●
OUTPUT OPTIONS									
Screen	●	●	●	●	●	●	●	●	●
Printer	●	●	●	●	●	○	●	●	●
Disk	●	●	●	●	●	●	●	●	●
Keywords Only	●	○	?	●	●	●	○	—	●
Keywords with Line	●	●	?	●	●	●	●	—	○
Keywords with Sentence	●	○	?	○	●	●	●	—	○
Keywords with Paragraph	●	●	?	○	●	●	●	—	●
Keywords with Record	●	●	?	●	●	●	●	—	○
Keywords w/Whole Document	●	○	?	○	●	○	?	—	○

Table 2.9: Comparison of text retrieval programs. I = IBM, C = CP/M, M = Macintosh, MD = menu-driven, CD = comand-driven, ZY = ZyINDEX, FYI = FYI 3000 Plus, 411 = 4-1-1, SAM = askSAM, EF = Electra-Find, TS = TextSearch, MA = MICROARRAS, TB = TEXTBANK, SO = Sonar.

Use Boolean ORs: Yes
Use Boolean NOTs: No
Use Parentheses: Yes
Nested Search Terms: Yes
Can Edit Noise-Word List: Does not create noise-word list.
Search Terms Highlighted When Matches Displayed: Yes
Mark/Save Matches to Create New File: Yes; hits may be appended to Clipboard.
Browse Bidirectionally Through Files Containing Hits: Yes
Browse Bidirectionally for Search Term(s): Yes
Other: None

- OUTPUT OPTIONS

Screen: Yes
Printer: Yes
Disk: Yes
Keywords Only: Yes
Keywords with Line: No
Keywords with Sentence: No
Keywords with Paragraph: Yes
Keywords with Record: No
Keywords with Whole Document: No
Other: None

- OTHER INFORMATION

Warranty: Media and program
Support: Phone and letter
Update Policy: $30
Special Features: Sonar can automatically locate user-specified relations among search terms.
Comments: None

2.11.2 Concordance Programs

As I noted earlier in this section, concordance programs are programs that construct keyword-in-context (KWIC) concordances from free-form text according to specified indexing, or sorting, sequences. They are a specialized type of text-retrieval program. Generally speaking, the concordances they create are not used to locate words in the full text of the documents that were indexed. Instead, they are used as tools for studying lexical, grammatical, morphological, and other features in a specified context of the concorded document, a context that is usually only several lines long.

The following categories need to be defined. **Supports Morphologically Tagged Text** refers to whether a program allows morphological tags to be inserted into the text that is to be concorded. Morphological tags may reflect pure morphological values, morphosyntactic values, morphophonemic values, or semantic properties. A concorded, morphologically tagged text displays information below the word level. Tagged texts may be sorted by morphological category (**Sort By Morphological Categories**) so that a concordance that lists all nouns, all verbs, all suffixes, and so forth can be produced. **User-Definable Grammatical Categories** refers to whether a program allows users to define the grammatical categories, boundary characters, and left-boundary/right-boundary dependencies used in morphological tagging. **Supports Interlinear Glossing** refers to whether a program supports glosses—translations—on lines between text lines, so that the glosses on one line correspond sequentially to the nonglossed items of the preceding line. (A glossed text is like an interlinear translation.) **Include Interlinear Glosses in Concordance** refers to whether a program allows interlinear glosses to be included in the concordance. **Supports Free Glosses** refers to whether a program supports a nonconcorded translation line whose items (words) are not sequentially paired with those in the preceding line. **Supports Unanalyzed Text Lines** refers to whether a program supports lines of text that are not concorded. This feature is useful for retaining a nonmorphologically analyzed form of a text. **Supports Comment Lines** refers to whether a program supports nonconcorded, nongloss lines that may be used to insert comments about the concorded text. **User-Definable Alphabet** refers to whether a program allows users to define their own alphabets from the entire 256 ASCII values (on IBM PCs). **User-Definable Sorting Order** refers to whether a program allows users to define the order in which items will be sorted. **Reverse-Order Sorting** refers to whether a program allows items to be sorted in the reverse order of the default sort order, that is, sorted from right to left. Reverse-order sorting is useful for studying suffixes and may be used to sort Semitic (and other) right-to-left languages. **Reverse Indexing from Glosses to Text** refers to whether a program can create a reverse index from glosses to text items (i.e., from translations to the original). **Concord Numerals** refers to whether a program can concord numerals in a user-specified sequence. **Concord User-Specified Keywords Only** refers to whether a program allows users to concord only the items in a keyword list. **Exclude User-Specified Words from Concordance** refers to whether a program allows users to specify stop words that are to be excluded from the concordance, a feature that is useful for excluding word processing formatting codes and commands. And **Sort By Morphological Categories** refers to whether a program allows users to sort a tagged text by the grammatical categories used in tagging that text, an operation that is similar to sorting a data base by fields.

At the time this book was completed, the Micro-OCP (Oxford Concording Program)[193] and the Micro-Watcon,[194] both of which are microcomputer versions of mainframe programs, had not been released and so will not be reviewed. Neither will this section contain information about SATO (System d'analyse de texte par ordinateur) and its related programs DEREDEC and SAMATO,[195] since I do not have review copies of those programs and the information I have about them is scanty, and URICA (User Response Interactive Collation Assistant), a collation program that helps to determine variations between two texts.[196]

2.11.2.1 KWIC-MAGIC

- *BASIC PRODUCT INFORMATION*

Name of Program: KWIC-MAGIC (KeyWord In Context Morphologically Analyzed Glossed Item Concordance)
Company Name: Dr. LST: Software
Address: 545 33rd St., Richmond, CA 94804-1535
Phone: (415) 236-7415
Price: $75 (IBM version includes KWICSTAR, a complete WordStar-like editor that can work on the texts KWIC-MAGIC concords or on the concorded output).
Version Reviewed: IBM version 1.04
Runs On: IBM PCs and compatibles; Kaypro 2, 4, 10; Osborne Executive
Memory Requirements: IBM: 128K; 640K recommended; CP/M: 64K
Operating System Requirements: IBM: DOS 2.0 or greater
Disk Drive Requirements: 2
Copy Protected: No
Hard Disk Compatible: Yes, hard disk recommended.
User Interface: Menu-driven
On-Line Help: Some
Specify Drive, Pathname, and Subdirectory: Drive only
Compatible with Local Area Networks (LANs): No

- *INPUT AND CONCORDANCE CONSTRUCTION*

Index Text Stored in Files on Floppy Disks: Yes

---

193. % Anne Yates, Oxford Electronic Publishing, Oxford University Press, Walton St., Oxford OX2 6DP, United Kingdom; $450 (£300 + VAT).

194. % Philip H. Smith, Jr., Arts Computing Office, University of Waterloo, Waterloo, Ontario N2L 3G1; (519) 885-1211, ext. 3275; BITNET: Phil@Watdcs; price not known.

195. % Francois Daoust, Centre d'ATO, Université du Québec à Montreal A-1580, C.P. 8888, Succ. A Montreal Québec H3C 3P8, Canada; (514) 282-8256; $350.

196. % Dr. Robert L. Cannon or Dr. Robert L. Oakman, Dept. of Computer Science, University of South Carolina, Columbia, SC 29208; (803) 777-2840; Cannon's network address on UUCP is {ucbvax!ihnp4, psuvax1}!akgua!usceast!cannon; $50.

Index Text Stored in Files on Hard Disks: Yes
Index Text Stored in Files on CD-ROMs: No
Index Text Stored in Files on WORMs (Optical Disks): No
Input Text from Keyboard: Yes
Maximum Size of Input File(s): Approximately 500K
Maximum Lines of Text Per Input File: 9,000 (900 lines on CP/M version)
Maximum Line Length in Input File: 131 characters
Maximum Keyword Length: 32 characters
Minimum Keyword Length: 1 character
Maximum Entries Per Keyword: 32,676
Approximate Ratio of Free RAM to Text Concorded in Memory: 3:1
Maximum Ratio of Spill File(s) to Input File Size: 10:1
Approximate Ratio of Concordance File(s) to Input Files: 1:1
Supports Morphologically Tagged Text: Yes
User-Definable Grammatical Categories: Yes, maximum of 29
Supports Interlinear Glossing: Yes
Supports Free Glosses: Yes
Supports Unanalyzed Text Lines: Yes
Supports Comment Lines: Yes
Works with ASCII Files: Yes
Supports Extended ASCII Character Set: Yes

• SORTING FEATURES

User-Definable Alphabet: Yes
User-Definable Sorting Order: Yes
Reverse-Order Sorting: Yes
Reverse Indexing from Glosses to Text: Yes
Concord Numerals: Yes
Concord User-Specified Keywords Only: Yes, maximum of 25
Exclude User-Specified Words from Concordance: Yes, maximum of 25
Include Interlinear Glosses in Concordance: Yes, if desired
Sort By Morphological Categories: Yes
Sort with Wild Cards: No
Keywords Highlighted: Yes
Other: Color-coded display of line types

• OUTPUT OPTIONS

Screen: Yes
Printer: Yes
Disk: Yes
Maximum Keyword Context: 6 lines
Word-Frequency Information: Yes

• OTHER INFORMATION

Warranty: 60 days, media only
Support: Phone and letter
Update Policy: Not known
Reviews: None
Special Features: Reverse indexing from glosses to text, a completely flexible parsing grammar, and concording by morphological categories are distinctive features of KWIC-MAGIC.

Comments: This is an amazingly powerful and flexible concording program that supports up to 29 user-defined morphological categories (which may be concorded and searched by), that can sort in reverse order, and that can display keywords in a 1 to 6 line context. The full text of the concorded files can be displayed, with line numbers to the left of each line, and the entire concordance may be listed in order. Keywords are highlighted and Next/Previous single-letter commands allow users to move forward and backward through a concordance, one entry at a time. The program is completely menu driven and is very easy to set up and to use. A 15-item main menu at the top of the screen lists major options, and submenus list further options. In addition to including the main menu, part of the 3-line information area at the top of the screen includes a status area that informs users about the program's activities. When constructing a concordance, for example, the status area indicates the function (CONCORD-ING), the amount of free memory left, and the input file line number that is being concorded. The second and third items are constantly updated. Maximum input file size is limited by the amount of available free memory. After concording, KM places the entire input text in memory to create the concordance output. When the size of the input text exceeds the size that can be concorded in free memory (roughly 30% – 33% of the posted memory available when KM is running), KM creates large intermediate files that can temporarily grow to 1,000% of the size of the input files. Thus for concording large texts (e.g., 500K), a hard disk is needed. It is not clear if KM can work with boards that support the Lotus/Intel/Microsoft (LIM) Expanded Memory Specification (EMS).

2.11.2.2 KWICMERGE

- ### BASIC PRODUCT INFORMATION

Name of Program: KWICMERGE
Company Name: % Dr. John D. Turner
Address: Dept. of Classics, University of Nebraska-Lincoln, Lincoln NE 68588-0337
Phones: (402) 472-2460, (402) 472-5034; BITNET: CLAS056@UNLCDC3
Price: $20, $25 with source code; include formatted diskette with payment and order.
Version Reviewed: Not known
Runs On: IBM PCs and compatibles
Memory Requirements: 128K, but 640K highly recommended.
Operating System Requirements: DOS 2.0 or greater
Disk Drive Requirements: 1
Copy Protected: No
Hard Disk Compatible: Yes
User Interface: Menu-driven
On-Line Help: No
Specify Drive, Pathname, and Subdirectory: Yes
Compatible with Local Area Networks (LANs): Not known

- ### INPUT AND CONCORDANCE CONSTRUCTION

Index Text Stored in Files on Floppy Disks: Yes
Index Text Stored in Files on Hard Disks: Yes
Index Text Stored in Files on CD-ROMs: No
Index Text Stored in Files on WORMs (Optical Disks): No
Input Text from Keyboard: Yes
Maximum Size of Input File(s): Approximately 800K
Maximum Lines of Text Per Input File: 10,000 (with a 20MB hard disk)
Maximum Line Length in Input File: Unlimited
Maximum Keyword Length: Default = 24; may be adjusted.
Minimum Keyword Length: 1 character
Maximum Entries Per Keyword: Not known
Approximate Ratio of Free RAM to Text Concorded in Memory: 8:3
Maximum Ratio of Spill File(s) to Input File Size: 30:1
Approximate Ratio of Concordance File(s) to Input Files: 10:1
Supports Morphologically Tagged Text: No
User-Definable Grammatical Categories: Not applicable
Supports Interlinear Glossing: No
Supports Free Glosses: No
Supports Unanalyzed Text Lines: No
Supports Comment Lines: No

Works with ASCII Files: Yes
Supports Extended ASCII Character Set: Yes

- *SORTING FEATURES*

User-Definable Alphabet: Yes
User-Definable Sorting Order: Yes
Reverse-Order Sorting: No
Reverse Indexing from Glosses to Text: Not applicable
Concord Numerals: Yes
Concord User-Specified Keywords Only: Yes
Exclude User-Specified Words from Concordance: Yes, 2 stop options, one that excludes all 1- and 2-letter words and a second that allows users to specify a maximum of 25 stop words.
Include Interlinear Glosses in Concordance: Not applicable
Sort By Morphological Categories: Not applicable
Sort with Wild Cards: No
Keywords Highlighted: Yes
Other: Concords in one pass.

- *OUTPUT OPTIONS*

Screen: Yes
Printer: Yes
Disk: Yes
Maximum Keyword Context: 18 lines, 9 before and 9 after keyword line
Word-Frequency Information: Yes

- *OTHER INFORMATION*

Warranty: None
Support: Phone, letter, BITNET (CLASS056@UNLCDC3)
Update Policy: Not known
Reviews: None
Special Features: Program contains KWICKMERGE.COM and commented Turbo Pascal source code.
Comments: This is an extremely fast and straightforward concording program with few "bells and whistles."

2.11.2.3 WordCruncher

- *BASIC PRODUCT INFORMATION*

Name of Program: WordCruncher®, formerly known as BYU (Brigham Young University) Concordance Version 4.0
Company Name: Electronic Text Corp.
Address: 5600 North University Ave., Provo, UT 84604
Phone: (801) 226-0616
Price: $299; ViewETC®: $170; IndexETC®: $170; BYU Concordance™ upgrade to WordCruncher®: $50
Version Reviewed: 4.1
Runs On: IBM PCs and compatibles
Memory Requirements: 512K, 640K recommended
Operating System Requirements: DOS 2.1 or greater, preferably DOS 3.2
Disk Drive Requirements: 2, hard disk highly recommended.
Copy Protected: No
Hard Disk Compatible: Yes
User Interface: Menu-driven
On-Line Help: Yes, context-sensitive
Specify Drive, Pathname, and Subdirectory: Yes
Compatible with Local Area Networks (LANs): Yes

- ## INPUT AND CONCORDANCE CONSTRUCTION

Index Text Stored in Files on Floppy Disks: Yes
Index Text Stored in Files on Hard Disks: Yes
Index Text Stored in Files on CD-ROMs: Yes
Index Text Stored in Files on WORMs (Optical Disks): Yes
Input Text from Keyboard: No
Maximum Single Input File Size: 1 – 3 megabytes (depends on amount of memory and number of unique words)
Maximum Number of Files That May Be Linked In Any One Set: 50
Maximum Number of Sets That May Be Linked Together: Up to 4 gigabytes worth of text
Maximum Combined Size of Input File(s): 4 gigabytes
Maximum Keyword Length: 31 characters; words longer than 31 characters are truncated
Minimum Keyword Length: 1 character
Maximum Keyword Entries Per Nonlinked File: 13,000 – 15,000 (with 640K RAM); approximately 300,000 in a linked file
Approximate Ratio of Free RAM to Text Concorded in Memory: Not known
Approximate Ratio of Concordance File(s) to Input Files: Varies from 50% and up according to input file size and number of stop words.
Supports Morphologically Tagged Text: No
User-Definable Grammatical Categories: Not applicable
Supports Interlinear Glossing: No
Supports Free Glosses: No, but dictionary (see below) could contain glosses.
Supports Unanalyzed Text Lines: Not applicable
Supports Comment Lines: No, but thesaurus (see below) could contain comments.
Works with ASCII Files: Yes
Supports Extended ASCII Character Set: Yes

- ## SORTING FEATURES

User-Definable Alphabet: Yes, distribution disks include sample foreign-language sort tables; maximum of 256 characters in sort table.
User-Definable Sorting Order: Yes
Reverse-Order Sorting: No, but a reverse-order thesaurus could be created.
Reverse Indexing from Glosses to Text: Not applicable
Concord Numerals: Yes
Concord User-Specified Keywords Only: Yes
Exclude User-Specified Words from Concordance: Yes
Include Interlinear Glosses in Concordance: Not applicable
Sort By Morphological Categories: Not applicable
Sort with Wild Cards: Yes, initial and medial truncation supported.
Keywords Highlighted: Yes
Other: Sequence and proximity searching are supported, as are Boolean ANDs, ORs, NOTs and initial and medial truncation.

- ## OUTPUT OPTIONS

Screen: Yes
Printer: Yes
Disk: Yes
Maximum Keyword Context: 22 lines on-screen and 64K when printed
Word-Frequency Information: Yes, as well as distribution-frequency information.

- ## OTHER INFORMATION

Warranty: 30-day, full money-back guarantee
Support: Phone and letter
Update Policy: Not known
Reviews: *Bits & Bytes Review*™ 1 (February 1987): 1–8; *InfoWorld* (July 6, 1987): 50–51.

FEATURES	K-M	KM	WC
BASIC FEATURES			
Price	75	20	299
Runs On	I, C	I	I
Memory (in K)	128, 64	128	512
Disk Drives	2	1	2
User Inteface	MD	MD	MD
On-Line Help	●	○	●
INPUT & CONCORDANCE CONSTRUCTION			
Index Text on Floppies	●	●	●
Index Text on Hard Disks	●	●	●
Index Text on CD-ROMs	○	○	●
Index Text on WORMs	○	○	●
Index Text from Keyboard	●	●	○
Maximum Input File Size	500K	800K	1-3MB
Maximum Lines of Text Per Input File	9,000	10,000	—
Maximum Input File Line Length (in Char.)	131	Unl.	—
Maximum Keyword Length (in Char.)	32	24	31
Minimum Keyword Length (in Char.)	1	1	1
Maximum Entries Per Keyword	32,676	?	300,000
Ratio of RAM to Text Concorded in Memory	3:1	8:3	?
Maximum Ratio of Spill File to Input File	10:1	30:1	—
Supports Morphologically Tagged Text	●	○	○
User-Definable Grammatical Categories	29	—	—
Interlinear Glossing	●	○	○
Free Glosses	●	○	○
Unanalyzed Text Lines	●	○	—
Comment Lines	●	○	○
Extended ASCII Characters	●	●	●

Special Features: WordCruncher (WC) can work with Word Perfect Corporation's SHELL. WC displays information in windows, can produce KWICs, and allows the full text of indexed documents to be searched by word or word combinations (using Boolean ANDs, ORs, and NOTs, wild cards, and proximity and sequential searching) and to be displayed. WC allows text sections to be copied and appended to disk files or printed. Users may move from any occurrence of a keyword to the full text in which it occurs, scroll bidirectionally through that text, and then move back to the concordance mode. Users may look up specific references, scroll bidirectionally through a list of indexed words (which are displayed with their frequencies), and access dictionaries and thesauri.

FEATURES	K-M	KM	WC
SORTING FEATURES			
User-Definable Alphabet	●	●	●
User-Definable Sorting Order	●	●	●
Reverse-Order Sorting	●	○	○
Reverse Indexing from Glosses to Text	●	–	–
Concord Numerals	●	●	●
Concord User-Specified Keywords Only	●	●	●
Exclude User-Specified Words	●	●	●
Include Interlinear Glosses	●	–	–
Sort by Morphological Categories	●	–	–
Sort with Wild Cards	○	○	●
Highlight Keywords	●	●	●
OUTPUT OPTIONS			
Screen	●	●	●
Printer	●	●	●
Disk	●	●	●
Maximum Keyword Context (in Lines)	6	18	22
Word-Frequency Information	●	●	●

Table 2.10: Comparison of concording programs. I = IBM, C = CP/M, MD = menu-driven, K-M = KWIC-MAGIC, KM = KWICMERGE, WC = WordCruncher.

Comments: WC is the most powerful and feature-laden concording program mentioned in this book. It can create concordances from huge input files, and it allows the concorded texts to be searched by keyword and keyword combinations (using a variety of search techniques). It displays statistical information about the number of occurrences of each word and their frequency of distribution by type of work, specific work, and section in a specific work. Users may toggle from search mode to display mode to expanded mode. Having selected a keyword or keywords in search mode (the WC calls this "Select Word" mode), users may then display up to six 3-line references in the display mode (the WC calls this the "Reference List" mode). From there users may display any reference in its full-text context, which may be scrolled bidirectionally. Any group of keywords, 3-line matches, or section of full text may be printed or saved to a disk file. Text displayed on-screen can instantly be reformatted as paragraphs, sentences, or flipped and displayed right-to-left. By using a set-up file, text (such as Hebrew) may automatically be displayed right-to-left. WC supports the EGA and downloaded fonts. User created dictionaries and thesauri may be accessed from any mode. Unfortunately, such flexibility has a price. Files that are to be concorded must be stripped of all word processing codes and WC section codes inserted. (A section code demarcates different levels of text, e.g., section, chapter, paragraph). Fortunately, the WC has a utility that helps to automate section code insertion.

2.11.3 Related Text-Oriented Programs

In this subsection we will look at four text-oriented programs that are related to, but different from, text retrieval and concording programs. A fifth program, Guide, from Owl International (14218 NE 21st St., Bellevue, WA 98007; (206) 451-2286; $134.95), came to my attention too late to be included here. Guide is a first-generation hypertext system for Macintoshes and IBM PCs and compatibles (see chapter 7 for a discussion of *hypertext*).

2.11.3.1 Mercury

• BASIC PRODUCT INFORMATION

Name of Program: Mercury™
Company Name: LinguaTech International
Address: 381 West 2230 North, Suite 360, Provo, UT 84604
Phone: (801) 373-8800; MCI Mail: LINGUATECH
Price: $175
Version Reviewed: 1.1
Runs On: IBM PCs and compatibles
Memory Requirements: 145K of free RAM
Operating System Requirements: DOS 2.0 or greater
Disk Drive Requirements: 2
Copy Protected: No
Hard Disk Compatible: Yes
User Interface: Menu-driven
On-Line Help: Yes
Warranty: 30-day, money-back guarantee
Support: Phone and letter
Update Policy: Minor: $14; major: $39
Comments: Mercury is a memory-resident, glossary-and-dictionary program that allows users to attach information to keywords, to recall that information from within application programs, and to copy and paste data from Mercury into application programs. Files may contain up to 1 million entries. The head word or phrase for each entry may be up to 50 characters long and the data area for each entry may be up to 900 characters long and distributed among multiple fields. Mercury is useful for storing foreign-language definitions of source-language words and phrases. Mercury supports the "extended" ASCII character set, automatically alphabetizes entries, and works with most word processing programs. Text may be copied from Mercury and pasted into word processing files with a single keystroke. Various pre-compiled glossaries for a variety of subjects are available from LinguaTech for $15 each.

2.11.3.2 LBase

• BASIC PRODUCT INFORMATION

Name of Program: LBase
Company Name: Silver Mountain Software
Address: % Eisenbrauns, P.O. Box 275, Winona Lake, IN 46590
Phone: (219) 269-2011
Price: $345; $10 for a demo copy; $50 graduate student discount
Version Reviewed: 1.02A
Runs On: IBM PCs and compatibles
Memory Requirements: Text mode: 350K; graphics mode: 450K
Operating System Requirements: DOS 2.0 or greater
Disk Drive Requirements: 2, a hard disk is recommended.
Copy Protected: No
Hard Disk Compatible: Yes
User Interface: Menu-driven
On-Line Help: Yes
Warranty: 30 days, media only
Support: Phone and letter
Update Policy: Free for one year

274

Comments: LBase is a tree-structured text-base analysis and retrieval program. It does not use fixed fields or fixed record definitions but allows users to design and produce text bases for sorting and compiling linguistic data. Because LBase allows users to define the linguistic units with which they wish to work, it is compatible with all linguistic theories and may be used to define parsing structures that, among other things, include morphological, syntactic, and semantic categories. Up to 126 categories may be defined, and each category may have up to 253 distinct values, which may be single characters or strings. Strings may be up to 253 characters long, but if more that 19 string values and character groups are used for a given category, it is not possible to display the entire category on-screen. Categories may be defined recursively. LBase can import several machine-readable texts, including the BHS Old Testament and the Thesaurus Linguae Graecae texts (see chapter 7). With an appropriate graphics card, up to nine 256-character fonts may be active and right-to-left languages may be displayed properly. The maximum lexical concordance size is 32,767 entries. Wild-card and proximity searches are supported, as are stop lists and searching across multiple files. The BROWSER utility allows users to browse TLG or Hebrew text files, to display those files in Greek or Hebrew, not in their coded versions, and to GOTO any line number or reference division. BROWSER is included with LBase or may be purchased separately for $29.95. LBase includes an 18-minute, disk-based demonstration.

2.11.3.3 MTAS

- ## BASIC PRODUCT INFORMATION

Name of Program: MTAS (Microcomputer Text Analysis System)
Company Name: Centre for Computing in the Humanities
Address: Robarts Library, 14th Floor, 130 St. George St., Toronto, Ontario M5S 1A5, Canada
Phones: (416) 978-4238 (Ian Lancashire), (416) 978-5130 (Lidio Presutti); BITNET: Ian@UTorepas and Lidio@UToronto; UUCP: !utcs!ianne and !utcs!lidio
Price: $10 (and blank 5.25-inch diskette)
Version Reviewed: 1.2; current version is 1.3
Runs On: IBM PCs and compatibles
Memory Requirements: 256K
Operating System Requirements: DOS 2.0 or greater
Disk Drive Requirements: 1
Copy Protected: No
Hard Disk Compatible: Yes
User Interface: Menu-driven
On-Line Help: Yes
Warranty: Not known
Support: Phone and letter
Update Policy: Free by user request
Comments: MTAS is a set of text-analysis programs that allow users to construct word-frequency lists (by alphabetical order, reverse alphabetical order, and descending frequency), browse full texts, search texts with wild cards for keywords (restricted to strings within line boundaries), produce word-distribution bar graphs (histograms) and word-density plots. MTAS search options include global, case-insensitive, case-sensitive, words-only, and suppress matching diacritics. MTAS supports the "extended" ASCII character set and allows users to define the character set and the sort sequence. MTAS can do 2-level dictionary sorts of accented words. It supports the EGA and downloaded character sets. Maximum input text size for word-frequency program is 32,767 words. Turbo Pascal source code is available.

2.11.3.4 IT

- ## BASIC PRODUCT INFORMATION

Name of Program: IT (Interlinear Text)
Company Name: Summer Institute of Linguistics
Address: 7500 W. Camp Wisdom Rd., Dallas, TX 75236
Phones: (214) 298-3331
Price: $40; $25 for SIL members
Version Reviewed: 1.0
Runs On: IBM PCs and compatibles
Memory Requirements: Not known

Operating System Requirements: DOS 2.0 or greater
Disk Drive Requirements: 1
Copy Protected: No
Hard Disk Compatible: Yes
User Interface: Menu-driven
On-Line Help: No
Warranty: Not known
Support: Phone and letter
Update Policy: Free through version 1.2.
Comments: IT is a set of text analysis programs designed to help linguists develop interlinear annotations for a user-defined collection of textual dimensions. IT treats text as a sequence of text units, each of which contains a text line plus a multidimensional set of annotations provided by the analyst. IT allows users to define five fields, or dimensions, of information for a corpus: (1) the unit marker, (2) the baseline text, (3) aligning annotations, (4) freeform annotations, and (5) extraneous fields. Unit markers define text unit boundaries (e.g., word, line, sentence), thus allowing text units to be referenced within a corpus. The baseline text is the source text being annotated. Aligning annotations are annotations of the baseline text that are done on a word-by-word or a morpheme-by-morpheme basis. The first character of the annotation always aligns vertically with the first character of the word or morpheme in the baseline text that it annotates. Freeform annotations are annotations of the baseline text that refer to the text unit as a whole. Such annotations could include translations of the text, background information, explanations, and so forth. Any field marker that is not a unit marker, baseline text marker, aligning annotation marker, or a freeform annotation marker is an extraneous marker. Such markers could include high level divisions such as paragraph, chapter, section, and so forth. IT programs ignore extraneous fields. Once a text is annotated, a set of IT programs may be used to manipulate the different interlinear fields of information and the lexical database IT maintains.

2.12 Desktop Publishing and Typesetting

2.12.1 Introduction

Desktop publishing is one of the newest and fastest growing areas in the field of microcomputers. With increasing frequency, OEMs[197] and VARs[198] are announcing and bringing to market complete desktop publishing systems. Desktop publishing does not address a vertical market but is designed for any microcomputer user—businessman, scientist, scholar, student—who wishes to control page layout in documents that incorporate text and graphics. Because of its inherent usefulness for almost any page formatting and printing task, desktop publishing appeals to a broad audience that includes graphic designers at the *New York Times*, the *Wall Street Journal*, and *Newsweek*, as well as those whose publishing needs are more modest and less demanding. Because of the growing use of desktop publishing programs among businessmen, scientists, and scholars, it seems fitting to include a brief section on this topic. Indeed, as the cost of publishing skyrockets, many professionals are finding desktop publishing an acceptable, cost-effective way to produce near-typeset material and to prepare material for typesetting.

Desktop publishing is an area of technological development that includes hardware—laser printers, optical scanners, full-page, very-high-resolution monitors—and software—desktop publishing and graphics programs. In terms of price, performance, features, and flexibility, desktop publishing systems—the software and the hardware—lie somewhere between word processing programs and printers on the one hand and typesetting programs, page-composition systems, phototypesetters, and printing presses on the other. At the upper end of the spectrum, desktop publishing programs "blend" into expensive page-composition and typesetting programs that cost

---

197. Original Equipment Manufacturer.
198. Value-Added Resellers.

thousands of dollars. At the lower end of the spectrum, some programs advertised as desktop publishing programs are little more than print processors or graphics programs.

Many desktop publishing programs include output-device drivers for PostScript™ and other page description languages. A *page description*, or *page definition*, language is a device-independent set of rules (a programming language) that application programs may follow to describe the appearance of pages to output devices that include interpreters for the language.[199] Application programs specify pages in terms of series of procedures and parameters (rather than as sets of codes or as sets of bit maps) that are interpreted by the page description language (PDL) in the output device and then translated into the marks that appear on the page. (Output devices that work with PDLs include the appropriate page description software and controller.) By following the conventions of the PDL, an application program insures that its files can be printed or typeset at the maximum resolution any output device that can interpret the page description language is capable of. Because PDLs function as a common logical interface, they allow application programs and output devices to be standardized around a common set of protocols and conventions and so are device-independent languages.[200] Thus one PDL driver can operate a wide variety of output devices. Because PDLs treat text as a subset of graphics, they allow text and graphics to be combined in the input file and on the printed page. PDLs are transparent to users; PDL instructions are created by application programs and sent to output devices without user intervention.

All three of the PDLs (see below) use "outline," or "vector," printer fonts.[201] We learned earlier in this chapter that graphics-mode programs typically work with bitmapped printer fonts and that bit-mapped printer fonts consist of the actual pixel, or dot, sequences required to print each letter. Vector printer fonts, however, consist of descriptions of the path that the output device print head should follow to draw each character. Vector printer fonts consist of a "compact mathematical description of each character's outline. Before printing a character, PostScript™ [for example] converts the outline to the proper scale, orientation, and shading, and then generates a bit map that is converted into a pattern of dots on paper."[202] Because they consist of descriptions of how to draw characters, rather than of actual dot patterns for characters, vector printer fonts may easily be scaled up or down, rotated, changed into various styles and weights, shaded, and filled with any pattern an application program is capable of producing. Although bit-mapped printer fonts may be printed more quickly than vector fonts, bit-mapped fonts are more difficult to scale, rotate, and modify. For example, since bit-mapped printer fonts specify exact character sizes, shapes, and styles, to scale a bit-mapped font up or down requires creating a new bit map for each character in the new font; it requires creating a new bit-mapped font. Storing multiple bit-mapped fonts places great demands on the printer's memory.

PostScript™ (Adobe Systems)[203] is the PDL most widely supported by application

---

199. Presently, all three page description languages are interpreted, not compiled. Thus input files and translators can be smaller but the imaging time is increased over what it would be if the languages were compiled.

200. This frees program developers from having to worry about the details of output hardware.

201. PDLs typically work with bit-mapped screen fonts.

202. Ted Nace, "PostScript: Master of the Raster," *PC World* (August 1985): 260.

203. See Adobe Systems, *PostScript Language Tutorial and Cookbook* (Reading, Mass.: Addison Wesley Pub. Co., 1985); Adobe Systems, *PostScript Language Reference Manual* (Reading, Mass.: Addison Wesley Pub., Co., 1985); Ted Nace, "PostScript: Master of the Raster," *PC World* (August 1985): 257–62; Denis G. Pelli, "Programming in PostScript," *BYTE* (May 1987): 185–202; Steve Roth, "PostScript Typefaces," *Personal Publishing* (October 1986): 30–34; Ron Jeffries, "An Important PostScript," *PC Magazine* (September 17, 1985): 77–80; Robin Raskin, "Adobe Systems PostScript," *PC Magazine* (January 14, 1986): 108–9; James Cavuoto, "Digitized Fonts in PostScript," *Computer Graphics World* 8 (September 1985): 27–30; Richard Sprague, "The Language That Talks to Your Printer," *MacWorld* (February 1985): 106–15; Steve Rosenthal, "Shaping PostScript to Do Your Bidding," *A+* (July 1985): 61–66; "Text Presentation with

programs, laser printers, typesetters, and other output devices. Other PDLs include Interpress™ (Xerox Corp.)[204] and DDL™ (developed by Imagen Corp., adopted by Hewlett-Packard).[205] PDLs differ in terms of features, speed, graphics capabilities, and whether they address a document one page at a time or as a whole.[206] For helpful comparisons of PostScript, Interpress, and DDL, see Steve Rosenthal, "Putting Text and Graphics in Their Place," *PC Magazine* (February 10, 1987): 181–92; Jerry Mendelson, "Interpress and PostScript Compared," *Graphic Arts Monthly* 57 (September 1985): 90; R. Schneiderman, "Standards Battle Brews over Page-Description Language," *Systems & Software* (September 1985): 22, 24. Also see Karen Sorensen, "Page Description Languages Make Headlines," *InfoWorld* (May 12, 1986): 38, 40; Linda Bridges, "Competing Page-Description Languages Share Capabilities, Market Reputation," *PC Week* (September 9, 1986): 153, 156; and D. Murphy, "Adding Page Description Languages," *Computer Systems News* 221 (July 22, 1985): 26.

There is a large and rapidly growing body of literature on desktop publishing and related topics.[207] Listed below are some of the most recent and helpful books and articles.

Alsop, Stewart. "Desktop Publishing without HYPE." *PC Magazine* (February 10, 1987): 111–15.
_____. "Is Desktop Publishing Fit To Print?" *PC Magazine* (October 14, 1986): 117–18.
Bell, Norman T., and James W. Warner. "Desktop Publishing: A New Frontier for Instructional Technologists." *T.H.E. Journal* 14 (August 1986): 71–73.
Biel, Don. "A Page Maker Talks about Pagination." *Personal Publishing* (February 1986): 18–19.
Bove, Tony, and Cheryl Rhodes. "Camera-Ready?" *Publish!* (November/December 1986): 64–68.
Bove, Tony, Cheryl Rhodes, and Wes Thomas. *The Art of Desktop Publishing*. Bantam Computer Books, 1986.
Burns, Diane, and S. Venit. "Muscling in on the MAC: PC-Based Page Composition." *PC Magazine* (February 10, 1987): 119–56.
_____. "Page Design on the PC Screen." *PC Magazine* (December 10, 1985): 180–210.
_____. "Stacking Up to the MAC." *PC Magazine* (February 10, 1987): 159–72.
Carney, T. F. "Personal Publishing on Microcomputers." *Research in Word Processing Newsletter* 4 (April 1986): 2–11.
Cavuoto, James. *LaserPrint It!*. Reading, Mass.: Addison Wesley Pub. Co., 1986.
Celko, Joe. "The ABCs of H&J." *Personal Publishing* (August 1986): 18–21.
Coleman, Dale, and Arthur Naiman. *The Macintosh Bible*. Berkeley, Calif.: Goldstein and Blair, 1986.
Corr, Robert M. "Careful Selection of Components Key to Assembling PC Publishing System." *InfoWorld* (November 10, 1986): 47.
D'Acquisto, Dominic R. "Macintosh Publishing." *Personal Publishing* (November 1986): 32–36.
Davis, Frederic E., John Barry, and Michael Wiesenberg. *Desktop Publishing*. Homewood, Ill.: Dow Jones-Irwin, 1986.
Devlin, Joe. "Desktop Publishing Is Breaking the Print Barrier." *Computer Dealer* 9 (March 1986): 28–33.
Dvorak, John C. "Wysiwyg Mania." *PC Magazine* (October 14, 1986): 77.
Gantz, John. "Will Desktop Publishing Turn Out To Be a Mirage?" *InfoWorld* (February 16, 1987): 31.
Green, Michael. *Zen and the Art of the Macintosh: Discoveries on the Path to Computer Enlightenment*. Philadelphia, Penn.: Running Press Book Pub., 1986).
Grout, Bill, Irene Athanasopoulos, and Rebecca Kutlin. *Desktop Publishing from A to Z*. Berkeley: Osborne McGraw-Hill, 1986.
Holmes, Thom. "Make My Page!" *BYTE* (May 1987): 159–66.
Jantz, Richard. "Design Pros Take to the Desktop." *Publish!* (November/December 1986): 72–79.
Jenkins, Avery. "Desktop Publishing." *PC Week* (September, 9, 1986): 49–52.

Postscript," *A+* (August 1985): 73–77; "PostScript: The Medium and the Message," *A+* (September 1985): 81–84.

204. PostScript™ was developed by former members of the Interpress design team.

205. See Domonic R. D'Acquisto, "DDL: Standard #3?," *Personal Publishing* (October 1986): 62–63.

206. PostScript is page-oriented, Interpress and DDL are document-oriented.

207. There are several excellent newsletters and journals on desktop publishing: the *microPublishing Report*, *The Seybold Report on Desktop Publishing*, *Publish!*, and *Personal Publishing*.

Kleper, Michael L. *The Illustrated Handbook of Desktop Publishing and Typesetting*. Blue Ridge Summit, Penn.: TAB Books, 1987.

Knorr, Eric, and Robert Luhn. "Personal Publishing in Black and White." *PC World* (July 1986): 183–88.

Knuth, Donald E. *The T$_E$Xbook*. Reading, Mass.: Addison Wesley Pub. Co., 1986. Cf. Knuth's four other volumes in the series "Computers and Typesetting" (see above under "T$_E$X)."

Lem, Dean Phillip. *Graphics Master 3*. Los Angeles: Dean Lem Assoc., 1986.

Machrone, Bill. "Desktop Publishing: Fact or Fiction." *PC Magazine* (July 1986): 61.

Makuta, Daniel J., and William F. Lawrence. *The Complete Desktop Publisher*. Compute! Publications, 1986.

MicroPublishing Report. *Directory of Suppliers*. Redondo Beach, Calif.: MicroPublishing, 1986.

Nace, Ted. *LaserJet Unlimited*. Berkeley, Calif.: Peachpit Press, 1986.

_____. *Ventura Tips and Tricks*. Berkeley: Peachpit Press, 1987.

Rardin, Kevin. *Desktop Publishing on the Mac*. New York: Plume/Waite, 1986.

Ritvo, Ken, and Greg Kearsley. *Desktop Publishing*. La Jolla, Calif.: Park Row Press, 1986.

Roberts, Catherine. *Desktop Publishing & Beyond*. Havemeyer Books, 1987.

Rosenthal, Steve. "Printers for Publishing." *PC Week* (March 11, 1986): 53–55.

Roth, Steve. "A Roundup of Page Layout Programs." *Computer Dealer* 9 (March 1986): 40–45.

_____. "Publishing On IBMs." *Personal Publishing* (November 1986): 38–54.

_____. "Processing Copy." *Personal Publishing* (November 1986): 54–58.

_____. "Text into Type." *Personal Publishing* (December 1985): 20–35.

Sans, John C. *Handbook of Desktop Publishing*. Wordware Publications, 1987.

Seybold, John W. "The Desktop-Publishing Phenomenon." *BYTE* (May 1987): 149–54.

Sorensen, Karen. "Desktop Publishing Software." *InfoWorld* (January 5, 1987): 39–50.

_____. "Desktop Publishing Sparks New Services." *InfoWorld* (September, 1, 1986): 25–26.

Spiegelman, Marjorie. "Interior Design for Documents." *PC World* (March 1987): 178–85.

Steinke, Steve. "Desktop Publishing on the Macintosh." *Computerland Magazine* (November/December 1986): 46–49.

Strehlo, Kevin. *PageMaker: Desktop Publishing on the IBM PC & Compatibles*. Scott Foresman, 1987.

Ulick, Terry. "Page Makeup Software in Perspective: Macintosh's Big 3." *Personal Publishing* (February 1986): 26–31.

_____. "Pagination Explained." *Personal Publishing* (February 1986): 16–17.

_____. *Personal Publishing with the Macintosh*. Hasbrouch Heights, N.J.: Hayden Book Co., 1986.

Ulick, Terry, and Steve Roth. "Page Planning." *Personal Publishing* (November 1986): 60–68.

Webster, Bruce. "Publish and/or Perish." *BYTE* (May 1987): 279–90.

Wiley, Jack. *The Complete Guide to Desktop Publishing*. Solipaz Pub. Co., 1987.

This section includes a detailed review of one representative desktop publishing program and information about a number of others, as well as information about typesetting programs, typesetting services, and typesetting equipment. No attempt has been made to include information about every program and about every input and output device available for desktop publishing. Some of the books listed above attempt to provide such information.

2.12.2 Terminology

Desktop publishing can refer (1) to the system or type of technology used to create a document (the desktop publishing program, microcomputer, printer, and other hardware and software), (2) to the desktop publishing program itself, and (3) to the process of using such programs and equipment to produce documents. Desktop publishing programs run on Macintoshes and on IBM PCs and are often used in conjunction with PostScript-compatible laser printers, such as the Apple LaserWriter and LaserWriter Plus, to produce documents of "near-typeset" quality. Sometimes scanners—devices that digitize photographs and artwork so that it may be manipulated and incorporated with text—are used as auxiliary input devices.

Desktop, then, refers to the equipment used in desktop publishing—to the microcomputers, laser printers, and scanners that can sit on desktops—and contrasts with larger, more expensive, stand-alone publishing systems (such as dedicated page-composition systems, offset presses, and phototypesetters with dedicated front ends).

Publishing is used somewhat euphemistically to refer to the results produced with that equipment—to the "near-typeset-quality" output in which text and graphics may be mixed together so that the finished product has the appearance of having been produced on something fancier that a personal computer and laser printer. *Near-typeset quality* refers to the resolution of laser printers—typically 300 dpi—and contrasts with the 1,200- to 2,400-dpi resolution of phototypesetters. And, yes, there *is* a noticeable difference between documents printed from phototypeset copy and documents produced on a laser printer. Because phototypeset characters are darker and better defined, phototypeset text is blacker and easier to read than laser-printed text.

2.12.3 Desktop Publishing Programs

2.12.3.1 Ventura Publisher

- *BASIC PRODUCT INFORMATION*

Product Name: Xerox Desktop Publishing Series: Ventura Publisher™ Edition
Company Name & Address: Xerox Corporation, 101 Continental Blvd., El Segundo, CA 90245
Phones: (800) 822-8221, (800) 832-6979
List Price: $895
Runs On: IBM PCs and compatibles, Xerox 6065, Compaq Portable, Compaq Deskpro, Compaq Deskpro 286
Operating System Requirements: DOS 2.1 or greater
Memory Requirements: 512K, 640K recommended
Disk Drive Requirements: 2, 1 of which must be a hard disk
Copy Protected: No
Possible Backups: Unlimited
Supports Mice: Yes, mouse required
Printers Supported: PostScript™, LaserJet, LaserJet Plus, AST Turbo Laser, IBM Proprinter, Tall Tree Systems JLaser printer card and compatible printers (e.g., laser printers with Canon engines), Xerox 4020 Color Ink Jet printer, Xerox 4045 Laser printer, HP ThinkJet, Epson MX-80/FX-80/RX-80
Supports Scanners: Yes, Datacopy, Dest, Microtek, any scanner that can generate PC Paintbrush™ image files
Supports Full-Page Monitors: Yes
Video Cards Supported: HGC, HGC+, CGA, EGA, Micro Display Systems Genius VHR, Wyse 700, Xerox 6065 monitors; Moniterm and LaserView monitors also support the Ventura Publisher.
Page Description Languages Supported: PostScript, support for DDL and Interpress announced.
On-Line Help: No
On-Line Tutorial: No
User Interface: Mouse-driven with icons, drop-down menus, and dialog boxes
Interactive WYSIWYG: Yes
Maximum Pages Per File: Limited only by memory

- *TEXT FORMATTING FEATURES*

Word Processing Programs Supported: Microsoft® Word, MultiMate™, WordPerfect™, WordStar®, Xerox Writer™
Text Formatted in Word Processor: Yes
Converts Word Processor Formatting Codes: Yes
Imports ASCII Text: Yes
Imbeds Typographic Codes: Yes
Uses Style Sheets: Yes
Rule-Based Hyphenation: Yes
Dictionary-Based Hyphenation: No
Automatic Kerning: Yes
Leading Increments: Decimal
Tabs: Yes
Tab Leaders: Yes

Maximum Number of PostScript Typefaces: 8
Maximum Number of PostScript Type Styles: 8
Size Range in Points: 1 – 254
Size Increments in Points: 11 options

• GRAPHICS FEATURES

Graphics Software Supported: AutoCAD™, GEM Draw™, Mentor Graphics™, Lotus .PIC, Scans, Lotus 1-2-3™, PC Paintbrush™, PC Paint™, GEM Paint™, programs that support the DXF format
Maximum Number of Rules: 6
Rectangles: Yes
Rounded Corners: Yes
Circles & Ovals: Yes
Polygons: No
Maximum Number of Fill Patterns: 9 (color variable)
Free-Hand Options: No
Scaling: Yes
Cropping: Yes
Rotation: No
Undo: Yes

• LAYOUT FEATURES

View Full Page: Yes
View Facing Pages: Yes
Percentage Page Enlargement: 200
Automatic Column Guides: No
Adjust Column Widths: Yes
Maximum Number of Columns: 8
Automatic Page Numbering: Yes
Automatic Index Generation: Yes
Automatic Footnoting: Yes
Automatic Table of Contents: Yes
Text Wrap from Page to Page and Column to Column: Yes
Wraps Text Around Graphics: Yes, automatically
Automatic Vertical Justification: No
Snap-to-Grid: Yes
Headers & Footers: Yes
Creates Templates: Yes
Number of Ruler Measures: 3
Ruler Indicator: No

• EDITING FEATURES

Globally Edit Text: No
Globally Edit Typographic Codes: Yes
Globally Edit Paragraph Formats: Yes
Insert & Remove Pages: Yes
Move Pages: No
Move Columns: Yes
Undo: No

• SUPPORT ETC.

Warranty: 30 days, covers media and program performance
Support: Phone and letter
Update Policy: Free or for a fee
User's Group: Ventura Publishers User's Group, 675 Jarvis Dr., Morgan Hill, CA 95037; telephone: (408) 778-1125

Major Reviews: John J. Hughes, "The Ventura Publisher—Desktop Publishing's New Heavyweight," *Bits &*
Bytes Review 1 (January 1987): 1–11; Ted Nace, "Ventura: Complete Desktop Publishing," *PC World*
(March 1987): 198–209; "Basic Business Reports with Ventura Publisher," *PC World* (June 1987):
265–73; Ted Nace and Janet Bein, "Ventura Tips and Tricks," *Publish!* (April 1987): 70–73; Steve
Roth, "Ventura: A New 1-2-3," *Personal Publishing* (December 1986): 26–39; Diane Burns and S.
Venit, "Muscling in on the MAC: PC-Based Page Composition," *PC Magazine* (February 10, 1987):
119–56, esp. 150–56; Karen Sorensen, "Xerox Buys Rights to Page Program," *InfoWorld* (April 14,
1986): 5; Ken Freeze, "Desktop Publishing on the PC Has Finally Arrived," *InfoWorld* (March 2, 1987):
45–48; Danny Goodman, "Taking a Page from the Pros," *PC World* (July 1986): 244–51; Jesse Berst
and James Cavuoto, "Tips for Tagging," *Personal Publishing* (August 1987): 58–65.

The Xerox Desktop Publishing Series Ventura Publisher Edition (hereafter Ventura Publisher™ or VP) is a professional page layout system that allows users (1) to combine text from word processors with line art generated by graphics programs such as AutoCAD™, Lotus 1-2-3™, GEM Draw™, and PC Paintbrush™, images digitized with a scanner (e.g., Microtek, Dest) and converted to the GEM or PC Paintbrush file formats, and graphics generated with VP's drawing package, (2) to format text and images, and (3) to output the results on devices ranging from dot-matrix and laser printers to phototypesetters. Throughout this review, *picture* and *pictures* will be used generically to refer to line art, digitized images, and graphics, that is, to all nontext material.

The VP was developed by Ventura Software of Morgan Hill, California, and the exclusive, worldwide marketing rights licensed to the Xerox Corporation—hence the product's lengthy "official" name. The VP is one of the two or three heavyweights of desktop publishing programs in the under $1,000 category. PageMaker™, which runs on Macintoshes and on IBMs, and Ready,Set,Go!™ 3, which runs on Macintoshes, are the VP's chief rivals. In its price category, in terms of features and flexibility, the VP is the most powerful desktop publishing program currently available for working with long documents. Future versions of the VP are promised that (1) will run under Microsoft Windows, (2) support foreign languages, and (3) include drivers for devices that support Interpress™ and DDL™.

Like Macintosh-based desktop publishing programs, the Ventura Publisher is a WYSIWYG program. Unlike many of the Macintosh desktop publishing programs, the VP can handle book-length documents, even documents over 5,000 pages long. Unlike programs such as PageMaker™, which formats documents interactively, page-by-page, treating each page as a discrete entity, the VP formats documents globally, in batch mode, treating the pages in a document as part of a unified whole, an approach that makes it much easier to produce long, uniformly formatted documents. Although it is ideally suited for producing long, complex, standardized documents like books, manuals, and reports, the VP is able to handle shorter, layout-intensive jobs—newsletters, flyers, brochures, and forms—just as easily, though perhaps not quite as easily as PageMaker™.

The VP is no lightweight. It comes with eleven disks and requires at least 512K of RAM and from 1 to 3 megabytes of hard disk space (depending on the printer and fonts installed); 640K of RAM is required for producing documents longer than twenty pages. Maximum document size depends on the version of DOS, screen driver, width table, number of paragraphs, number of tabs, and number of frames per document. Although it runs well on an XT, the VP runs faster on an AT. It will not run at all without a mouse (almost any mouse will do) and a graphics card (see above) because it operates under a run-time version of Digital Research's GEM (Graphics Environment Manager) operating environment, which includes bit-mapped graphics, mouse support, drop-down menus, icons, and scroll bars. In addition to the standard graphics cards, the VP also supports the following oversize, very-high-resolution monitors: (1) Micro Display Systems Genius VHR, (2) Wyse 700, and (3) Xerox 6065 full-page display. Additionally, the (4) Moniterm and (5) LaserView oversize, very-high-resolution monitors support the VP.

Performance and Versatility. The VP supports an amazing number of features and functions that include: (1) up to eight columns per page or frame, (2) columns of unequal width and indent, (3) automatic column balance, (4) specifying gutter width between columns, (5) automatic word wrap, (6) vertical rules between columns, plus two vertical rules per frame, (7) up to three ruling lines of different widths above, below, and around each frame, (8) portrait or landscape formats (set globally for entire file/chapter), (9) up to eight different colors per text/ruling line, (10) multiple, noncontiguous articles per document, (11) formatting up to 150K files with 640K RAM (up to 30K files with 512K RAM), (12) chaining up to 64 files for printing so that numbering is contiguous and the same style sheet used for each file, (13) displaying two facing pages or one full page, (14) displaying documents at 100% or enlarged to 200%, (15) user-modifiable style sheets (twenty-one are supplied on disk and illustrated and explained in the manual; more may be created), (16) automatic, separate headers (up to two lines each) for even and odd pages, (17) automatic, separate footers for even and odd pages, (18) automatic section heads in headers and footers, (19) automatic figure and page numbering, (20) page numbering in Arabic numbers, upper or lower case roman numerals, upper or lower case letters, or alphabetic (e.g., One, Two), (21) page counter from 1 to 9999, (22) automatic footnote placement and numbering, (23) footnote numbering with numbers or symbols, (24) automatic section numbering (up to eight levels), (25) importing any ASCII text file, (26) importing text files from Microsoft® Word, MultiMate™, WordPerfect™, WordStar®, and Xerox Writer™, (27) allowing text from different word processors to be mixed in the same document, (28) insert/delete text at any point, (29) block moves (delete, cut, copy, paste), (30) dynamic, real-time, on-screen reformatting with justification, hyphenation, and proportional spacing during editing, (31) changing letters or groups of words to bold, italic, bold italic, small caps, strikethrough, subscript, superscript, underline, all lower case, all upper case, all initial caps, and any available font, (32) accepting digitized images generated by GEM Draw™, GEM Graph™, GEM Paint™, Lotus 1-2-3™, Symphony™, Mentor Graphics™ CAD, PC Paintbrush™, and from Microtek, Dest, and Datacopy scanners (any scanner that can generate PC Paintbrush image files), and CAD DXF files, (33) resizing, cropping, scaling, and stretching images, (34) running text around irregular pictures, (35) captions for pictures, figures, tables, rules, (36) built-in line graphics capability for creating lines, boxes, circles, and caption boxes, (37) single or double sided printing, starting on left or right side, (38) printing on 8.5-by-5.5-inch paper up to 11-by-17-inch paper, (39) printing A4 and B5 size pages, (40) collating and printing order control, (41) printing all, current, or selected pages, (42) chaining chapters for printing, (43) automatic generation of tables of contents, (44) automatic generation of indices, (45) up to five printers installed simultaneously, (46) drop-down menus, (47) icon-based, mouse-selected menu options, (48) selecting and moving text and pictures with mouse, (49) rulers and column guides, (50) automatic hyphenation with overriding exceptions and user dictionaries, (51) kerning, (52) built-in text editor for entering and editing text, (53) specifying measurements in inches, centimeters, picas (approximately 1/6 inch), points (1/12 pica), and fractional points, (54) separate, variable widow and orphan controls, (55) executing DOS file operation commands from within the program, (56) adding additional fonts, and (57) hanging indents.

The recently released version 1.1 adds the following features in the areas of typography, file importation, printer support, and interactive page-composition: (1) a second hyphenation algorithm for US English that hyphenates more completely, (2) hyphenation algorithms for UK English, French, Spanish, and Italian, (3) support for using two hyphenation algorithms simultaneously on properly tagged text, (4) support for importing coded XyWrite files and files in DCA format (e.g., OfficeWriter™, DisplayWrite™, Volkswriter™ 3, Samna™, some IBM mainframe files), (5) support for importing Macintosh PICT and PAINT graphics files, Microsoft vector clipboard files, and

VideoShow, HPGL, CGM, and PostScript graphics files (version 1.1 of the VP can read files from over 500 different graphics programs), (6) automatic, user-selectable kerning that can be turned on or off at the tag level, (7) support for cropping line art, (8) support for installing new items without having to reinstall the entire program, (9) support for extended and expanded memory, (10) support for virtual-memory architecture (version 1.1 can work 500K-long files and supports up to 128 linked chapters/files), (11) support for binding, or anchoring, pictures to text, (12) microjustification, (13) the ability to avoid reloading fonts every time a document is printed, (14) an easier way to use the Symbol font, (15) support for tracking (making letter spacing relative to font size), (16) successive hyphenation control (specifying the number of lines in a row that can end with hyphens), (17) typographic spaces (i.e., thin, thick, M, and N), (18) tracking rulers (ruler cursors track the mouse cursor), (19) easier, interactive multicolumn layouts for newsletters, magazines, and short page-layout jobs, (20) support for the Cordata laser printer, as well as support for Interpress™ and DDL™ devices, (21) support for double underlines and overscore, and (22) more control over loose lines, dropped capitals, indenting, outdenting, and more. Support for Microsoft Windows also is due sometime in 1987, and a German hyphenation algorithm is being developed.

In many ways, then, the VP is like a super-flexible word processing program with advanced formatting and graphics-handling capabilities.

User Interface. The VP is icon- and menu-driven; Macintosh users will feel right at home. The mouse is used to select one of the four basic modes: (1) Frame, (2) Tag, (3) Text, and (4) Draw. The Frame Mode is used to draw frames on a page into which text and graphics will be inserted. Frames may be selected, altered, and moved. The Tag Mode is used to select and tag paragraphs with existing tags, to create new tags, and to delete unwanted tags. The Text Mode is used to edit text, to copy, delete, cut, and paste, to change fonts and attributes, and so forth. The Draw Mode is used to draw lines, circles, boxes, and boxed text.

Modes are selected by clicking the mouse cursor on one of the four Mode Icons on the left side of the screen; additional options are chosen by selecting from one of the nine drop-down menus that run across the top of the screen. Those menus are Desk, File, Edit, View, Page, Frame, Paragraph, Graphic, and Options. Drop-down menus drop down when the cursor is placed on the menu name. They remain "dropped down" until a selection is made by highlighting an item and clicking the mouse, until another drop-down menu is selected, or until the mouse cursor is placed in a nonmenu area or in a nonhighlighted menu area and the mouse button clicked. Pull-down menus, however, such as are used on many Macintosh programs, must be "grabbed" with a mouse and pulled down to display their items. Pull-down menus disappear when the mouse button is released. Drop-down menus are easier to work with since the mouse button does not have to be held down to open the menu and to keep it open.

The Mode Icons are displayed above the Assignment List, which runs down the left side of the screen and which displays status indicators and the options available for the selected mode. The far left rectangular area of the screen that displays the Mode Icons and Assignment List is know as the Side Bar.

The shape of the mouse cursor changes to reflect the active mode. The cursor keys are active only in Text Mode, though PgUp and PgDn work in all modes. Home and End are used to move to the first and last page of a document. Pages are scrolled right, left, up, and down by using the mouse with horizontal and vertical scroll bars. A GOTO selection on the Page Menu allows users to specify the page to which they wish to go.

In each mode, drop-down menus are used to select options. Once a mode and menu item have been selected, a dialog box appears on-screen. *Dialog boxes* list the set of choices for each menu item. Features in dialog boxes are chosen with the mouse.

Variables that must be specified numerically (such as spacing, for example) are entered from the keyboard. Dialog boxes pop up in the middle of the screen. A number of keyboard shortcuts may be used to select options and circumvent menus. Ctrl + W, for example, functions as a toggle to hide and reveal the Side Bar, Ctrl + B renumbers a document, Ctrl + E gives an enlarged view of a document.

Users may list the root and subdirectories and change the active drive from within the program.

Ease of Use. Although it comes on eleven disks, the VP is easy to load. Self-explanatory menus lead users through the process. Many of the disks are not used since they contain drivers and character width tables for different printers and fonts.

The VP can work with files that are larger than memory, as well as with extended and expanded memory. To speed up overall program operation, the VP can be run on RAM disks that are 1.3 megabytes or larger and that begin after the 640K system RAM. Thus to run the VP on a RAM disk requires a minimum of 2 megabytes of RAM.

Although it contains no on-line help, because I worked through each of the six exercises in the excellent disk- and manual-based tutorials, I found the VP very easy to use. Its mouse-driven interface, well thought-out icons, clear menus, and self-explanatory dialog boxes make the program as intuitive as I can image a program of this complexity and power being.

To load and format a document, users (1) select the Frame Icon to activate a frame, (2) select a file by using the drop-down File Menu, and (3) select a style sheet by using the File Menu. Step (2) requires selecting an item from the File Menu, making choices in a dialog box, and then selecting a file from a list. Step (3) requires selecting an item from the File Menu and selecting a style sheet from a list. The selected file can be tagged, or its tags may be modified by selecting the Paragraph Icon (i.e., Tag Mode), which lists the active tags. In this mode, clicking the mouse on a paragraph highlights it. After highlighting a paragraph, clicking the mouse on an item in the Tag List causes the highlighted paragraph to be formatted in accordance with the selected tag. In the Tag Mode, to highlight several paragraphs, users must depress and hold the Shift key and then click the mouse on each paragraph that is to be highlighted. Text cannot be highlighted in this mode by "swiping" the mouse cursor over it, as it can be in the Text Mode.

To copy or delete text, pictures, or frames, users select Text Mode, Draw Mode, or Frame Mode. Next, the "object" that is to be copied or deleted—the text, picture, or frame—must be selected by highlighting it with the mouse cursor. This places the object on one of three "clipboards," depending on the type of object it is. Finally, the desired function—copying or deleting—is selected from the Edit Menu. (The Delete key may be used to delete objects.) Objects that have been copied or deleted may be undeleted—*pasted* in VP jargon—by placing the cursor in the desired position and then selecting the Paste option on the Edit Menu or by using the Insert key.

To change type style, users select the Text Mode. Next, the text whose style is to be changed is highlighted with the mouse, which may be "swiped" across the text. Finally, a text style (e.g., italic, bold, superscript) is selected from the Text Mode's Assignment List.

Horizontal and vertical rulers, whose units may be specified in inches, centimeters, and picas (but not in points) may be displayed across the top and down the left size of the screen to aid in page layout. In Enlarged and Reduced view modes, the actual spacing of the units of measure on rulers is relative to the mode. Thus the Enlarged mode causes inch measurements to be greater than inches, and the Reduced mode causes them to be smaller than inches.

The View Menu allows users to select Normal, Reduced, Facing, and Enlarged view modes. On a standard 12-inch monochrome monitor, Reduced and Facing modes reduce the text to an unreadable size. Thus in these two modes, on monitors that size, text and pictures should be "greeked," a feature that allows the program to rewrite the screen much faster (see below). On 12-inch monochrome monitors in the Normal mode, in some type sizes and page formats, it is impossible to display all the text from left to right on a page without hiding the Side Bar. (The Side Bar displays the Mode Icons and active Assignment List and is used for changing modes and working with selections from the drop-down menus.) That is a nuisance. It would be nice if users could control the percentage that text was reduced in Reduced mode. The best solution to these problems is to use the VP with an oversize (e.g., 15- or 19-inch) very-high-resolution monitor that can display more text than a standard 12-inch monitor.

In Normal, Reduced, and Facing-Pages modes, full pages of text are displayed on 19-inch monitors. In Enlarged mode, less than a full page of text is displayed. A Page Counter near the bottom of the Side Bar displays page numbers and page orientation (left or right).

Style Sheets and Templates. At the heart of the VP's flexibility and power are style sheets and page templates. In the VP page templates are distinguished from style sheets, but because template specifications are style-sheet specific, template settings are bound to style sheets. Every document called to screen must be assigned a style sheet (and thus a page template). A document may be assigned only one style sheet at a time, but documents that have been assigned different style sheets may be chained together and printed. Once assigned, style sheets (and their page templates) are automatically stored with documents and put into effect when the documents are called to screen.

A style sheet causes a document to be displayed on-screen in accordance with the specifications in the style sheet. The VP comes with twenty-one predefined style sheets that may be edited, and users may create custom style sheets from scratch. Predefined style sheets are included for various kinds of publications, such as books, brochures, invoices, product listings, newsletters, magazines, directories, press releases, proposals, reports, tables, and technical documents.

A style sheet is a discrete file that specifies page layout settings (e.g., margin and column settings, ruling widths), and typographic attributes (e.g., typeface, type style, type size) globally, on a paragraph-by-paragraph basis. Style sheets are used to specify (1) fonts (a unique combination of typeface, type size, type style, and type weight, e.g., Helvetica 12 point bold), (2) text alignment within column, (3) hyphenation and justification, (4) first line indent/outdent, (5) line-to-line spacing, (6) paragraph spacing, (7) temporary margins, (8) page, line, and column breaks, (9) large first letter of paragraph, (10) automatic bullets, (11) tabs (up to 16 horizontal tabs per paragraph; left, center, right, or decimal point aligned; with leaders and adjustable leader spacing), (12) vertical tabs, (13) horizontal rules (up to three ruling lines of different thicknesses and spacing; above, below, around text; up to eight textures and colors; text within ruling lines allowed), (14) margins, (15) columns, (16) portrait or landscape mode, (17) paper size, (18) widows and orphans, and (19) automatic section numbering.

Because style sheets act globally on a document, they make it possible (1) to format a document quickly, (2) to format and print different documents or sections of the same document uniformly, regardless of which word processors those documents or sections of documents were produced on, and (3) to format a document differently by using a different style sheet. Desktop publishing programs that require each page to be formatted individually lack that kind of speed, consistency, and flexibility; they make it difficult to format a document quickly and uniformly and to change a document's formatting on a global basis. Because predefined style sheets may be edited and because new style sheets may be created, users are able to format and print documents exactly as they wish them to appear. Any changes made to a style sheet by changing the paragraph, page layout, widow and orphan, or frame settings are immediately reflected on-screen, because the VP's extremely fast assembly-language formatter dynamically reformats documents to reflect the active style sheet. New style sheets may be created simply by saving the new settings, with or without overwriting the original style-sheet file.

Although style sheets act on files globally, the information in style sheets is specified at the paragraph level by using tags. *Tag* refers to the typographic attributes or layout settings specified for a particular paragraph. Tags specify fonts, alignment (justification, hyphenation, spacing, indentation), levels of headings, spacing (above, below, inter-line, inter-paragraph), whether an item is to be included in the table of contents or in the index or both, special effects (items marked by bullets, large first letters in a paragraph), tabs, ruler lines, and so forth. Thus tags include specifications for characters and paragraph formats. A document's distinct collection of tags, then, is its style sheet.

Tags and tag names may be created by users, assigned values, edited, and saved. Tags may be bound to function keys to speed up entry. Because tags act on a document globally, modifying the value of a tag at one place in a document changes its value everywhere else it occurs in the document. When headers, footers, captions, section numbers, table of contents and index entries, and boxed text are created, tags known as "generated tags" are automatically created. Although the initial, or default, attributes of these tags are taken from the "body text" tag, the attributes of generated tags may be edited just like those of other tags. Up to 64 different tags may be defined per style sheet. When inserted into paragraphs, tag names are invisible, though the tag takes effect and the paragraph is immediately reformatted according to the text attributes associated with the tag.

Just as style sheets specify all the typographic attributes and page layout settings for a document, page templates specify all the placement and individual frame attribute information for a document. A *frame* is any rectangular box used to hold text or pictures; it is the VP's primitive category for, or basic element of, page layout. Thus the imaginary box that underlies a page of text is a frame, as are portions of a page that consist of pictures, boxed text, and so forth. A page template, then, consists of one or more frames that specify where text and pictures are to be placed in a document. Templates define areas of pages, and style sheets specify how the content of those areas is to be formatted.

Although some page-composition systems and some word processing programs like Microsoft® Word (MW), FinalWord™ II (FW II), and T^3™ use style sheets, the VP is the first desktop publishing or word processing program for any microcomputer to *combine* style sheets and page templates. Unlike the style sheets used by MW or by FW II, for example, the VP's style sheets are "invisible"; a whole style sheet cannot be displayed on-screen or printed. There are several disadvantages to this. (1) VP style sheets cannot be edited the way ASCII or word processing files can but may be changed only by going through a series of menus for each of the items on a sheet. (2) Users are not able to see all of a document's specifications in a single place, and so it is difficult to picture what an entire document will look like. (3) Users are not able to compare the specifications for one document with those of another. MW and FW II, by contrast, allow users to see, edit, and print entire style sheets because they treat style sheets as ordinary text files. A utility that would convert style sheets to an ASCII file that could be edited and printed would be most helpful.

Frames. As we just learned, text and images are imported into the VP into templates called frames, which on-screen consist of rectangular areas that are demarcated by dashes. The active frame—the one into which a particular image or piece of text or graphics is to be imported— is identified on-screen by small, black, surrounding broken lines. The dashes that demarcate frames may be turned off by using the Options Menu. In a document with no pictures or boxed text, there will be one frame type, a full-page frame. In a document that has text and pictures, there will be frames for text and frames for pictures. Every type of "item" in a document must be placed somewhere, and that somewhere must be defined as a frame before items may be placed in a document. Frames can only contain four types of items, or data—text, line art, graphics, and images—and the VP keeps track of the type of data in each frame. Just as a parent might tell a child "A place for everything and everything in its place," so the VP requires that there be a place for every "item" and that every item be in its place. The program knows what types of items are in what places.

A template's initial frame is a full-page frame called an "underlying page," within which, or "on top" of which, other frames are defined. The underlying page may be thought of as the basic document area, as the area that defines the document's default layout styles and values. Anything defined on a document's underlying page is reflected on all subsequent pages of that document. Thus it is in terms of the underlying page that headers, footers, footnotes, primary margins, columns, rules, and other documentwide layout features are defined. Additional frames may be nonrepeating or repeating. Repeating frames are duplicated exactly—ruling lines, background, and contents—on every right, every left, or on every right and left page and may contain text or pictures. Up to six different repeating frames may be defined per document.

All frames may be defined with attributes such as columns, rules, margins, and different fill patterns, and frames may be sized and scaled. The position, width, and height (i.e., depth) of frames may be specified and changed, and columns within frames may be balanced automatically so that they are of equal depth. Adjusting the size of a frame and its inner margins determines the size of its contents. Line art can be stretched horizontally and vertically to fill a frame or stretched proportionally so that its aspect ratio is correct, but line art cannot be cropped. Bit-mapped graphics images may be stretched to fill a frame or scaled to be smaller or larger than a frame. When made larger than a frame, graphics images may be moved around over the frame and cropped. Because the VP knows the type of contents of each frame—text, graphics, images, line art—it automatically attaches caption frames to frames that contain non-text material. The contents of caption frames can be specified, edited, and saved. When a frame is placed over existing text, the text automatically wraps around the frame, a powerful feature found on only a couple of other desktop publishing programs (e.g., Ready,Set,Go!™ 3).

Integration. One of the cleverest aspects of the VP is the way it integrates text and pictures produced in many different file formats into a seamless whole, without requiring users to convert source files from one format to another.

The VP allows text created with a variety word of processors to be imported. Although the VP allows users to key text directly into the program, text that is to be formatted and printed with the VP may be created and formatted with any word processor or program that can create ASCII files (such as Nota Bene™, XyWrite™, Final-Word™, PerfectWriter™). If Microsoft® Word, MultiMate™, WordPerfect™, WordStar®, or Xerox Writer™ files are used, the VP recognizes and automatically implements their codes for bold, underlined, subscript, superscript, strikethrough, soft hyphens, and nonbreaking spaces. (The VP does not allow users to define new word processors.) Additionally, users may insert VP codes and tags into word processing files so that when those files are imported, VP implements the codes and tags. For example, an <I> inserted into a word processing file turns italic on when that file is read by VP. Similarly, any tag defined in a VP style sheet and used in a word processing file is implemented when that file is read by VP. For example, inserting the tag and variable "@SECTION = The Ventura Publisher At Work" in a word processing file would cause the VP to implement the style sheet tag known as SECTION and all the formatting specifications associated with it when it reads the file. (The variable in that example is "The Ventura Publisher at Work"; tags are inserted into text files by prefacing the tags with the @ symbol.) Thus users have the choice of creating plain text files with a word processor and using the VP to do the formatting chores of attaching tags and specifying text attributes (i.e., fonts and attributes such as bold, italic, superscripted), or users may specify text attributes and attach tags with their word processing programs (and let VP implement those tags and format the text automatically in accordance with a style sheet). Users who do not mind coding and tagging text as they create it may do so, and users who do mind may wait until they import their text into the VP and then format it. The first type of user would probably include those who are used to inserting formatting codes into text and who are used to a non-WYSIWYG display. The second type of user would probably include those who are used to formatting text interactively and who are used to a WYSIWYG display. The VP saves text files with all the codes and tags in place, regardless of whether the codes and tags were inserted in the text file to begin with or inserted with the VP. Thus to preserve an unmarked copy of an original file, users should save it under a different name or extension, or on a different drive or disk, before reading it into the VP.

Not only can the VP import text created by word processors, it also can import line art generated by graphics programs and images digitized with scanners or created with paint programs, either or both of which can be referred to as *pictures*. Line art may be imported from files created with AutoCAD™, GEM Draw™, GEM Graph™, Lotus 1-2-3™, and Mentor Graphics™. Because line art is stored in a mathematically defined fashion (as vectors and objects), the mathematical expressions that define any piece of line art are recomputed for any output device, so that line art is printed at the highest resolution the active output device can produce. Images may be imported from any scanner, from GEM Paint, and from PC Paintbrush. Because scanned images are stored as simple bit maps, not as mathematical expressions that can be recomputed, scanned images can only be printed at the resolution at which they were scanned, regardless of the maximum resolution a given output device can produce.[208] Images also can be imported into the VP from any program that can output files in any of the following formats: GEM, Lotus (PIC), AutoCAD (SLD), or PC Paintbrush (PCX). Additionally, the VP comes with a utility that can convert files in AutoCAD DXF format to the GEM format.

The VP also includes a built-in drawing package that allows users to draw lines, circles, squares, and round-edge squares. These shapes can be filled with different colors and shades. The VP's drawing package allows users to create call-out boxes, forms, and tables, to place additional ruling lines anywhere on a page, and to create additional graphic effects. Graphics created with VP will print at the maximum resolution an output device is capable of producing. All graphics created with the VP are attached to a frame and so move with the frame when it is moved and are deleted when the frame is deleted.

The drawing package also supports boxed text, that is, text that is placed in a box, which can be moved anywhere on a page. Text typed in a boxed-text environment is formatted according to the "boxed text" tag. The ability to work with boxed text is *unique* among desktop publishing programs.

Two graphics-related options, Send to Back and Bring to Front, allow users to alter the sequence of overlapping frames that contain graphics material, something that can be useful in tables and callouts. Send to Back places the uppermost graphic frame at the bottom of the overlapping graphics frames; Bring to Front places the bottommost graphic frame on top of all other graphics frames. Another graphics-related option, Grid Snap, allows users to define an invisible grid of intersecting lines in the X and Y axes of the active frame so that frames that contain pictures are automatically attached to intersecting points on the grid. The Grid Snap feature forces graphics to line up with one another and is useful for aligning forms, tables, and adjacent boxes. Grid Snap dimensions may be specified in inches, centimeters, picas, and points to within 0.001 inch. A related feature, the Line Snap option, forces frames to line up with the inter-line spacing of the underlying page, thus vertically justifying text lines and the

---

208. Scanned images require a lot of disk space. Images scanned at 300 dpi require 1 bit per horizontal and 1 bit per vertical unit of resolution per amount of scanned area. Thus an 8.5-by-11-inch page scanned at 300 dpi would require $300 \times 300 \times 8.5 \times 11$ bits, 8,415,000 bits, over 1 megabyte of disk space.

tops and bottoms of boxes (frames). This is a useful feature for making sure that graphics, headings, and multicolumn copy that wraps around boxes all line up correctly. Line Snap, then, is most useful in a multicolumn environment that contains multiple frames. Because the VP does not allow graphics frames to be tied to specific sections of text, however, graphics can be separated from the text with which it belongs (if that text is added to, for example), and this is a weakness.

The Line Attributes Menu allows users to change the thickness, color, and end style of the line placed around each graphic, and the Fill Attributes Menu allows users to change the color and background of each graphic. Seven different colors and seven different fill patterns, plus hollow and solid, are available as fill attributes, and either colors or patterns may be set to opaque or transparent. Opaque and transparent are used for overlapping graphics. If Opaque is selected for the uppermost graphic, it completely blocks the portion of any graphic beneath it. If Transparent is selected for the top graphic and if the fill pattern is anything other than the color black, the graphics below will show through the graphics on top.

Text and graphics may be "greeked," that is, depicted by lines that show where text and graphics will go on pages. "Greeking" text and graphics dramatically speeds up the time required to redraw a full screen. Users can specify what sizes of text are to be "greeked," thus leaving some text displayed as text.

The VP does not merge text and picture source files into one formatted document file, as PageMaker™ does. Instead, the VP stores information about its documents as sets of pointers that indicate which source files and style sheets are to be used to create the documents. More precisely, documents stored in the VP consist of a pointer to a style sheet and a list of the chapter files that make up the document. The chapter files are listed in the order in which they are to be printed and contain the pointers to the actual text and picture files. When the VP is told to create a document, it finds all the appropriate files, wherever it has been told they are on the hard disk, and it recreates the document, hyphenating, justifying, and formatting it in accordance with the source file's tags and style sheet.

The main advantage of this scheme is that it saves space by not creating a merged file from all the source files, thereby duplicating them. The main disadvantage of the scheme is that if users move or delete one of the source files without "telling" the VP that the file has been deleted or moved, the VP may be unable to locate it to build a document.

Typographics. The VP includes four screen fonts and four corresponding printer fonts for each printer and typesetter it supports, thus providing uniformity among those four fonts from device to device. The fonts are (1) Times, (2) Courier, (3) Helvetica, and (4) Symbol. (The VP provides these fonts for non-PostScript printers that do not include them.) Screen fonts may be displayed only in the four predefined typefaces and only in sizes and styles defined for the default printer. Although the VP allows users to create new fonts, it does not allow typefaces other than the four predefined ones to be displayed on-screen. Users can, however, buy additional screen fonts from third-party vendors (e.g., Adobe screen fonts for the LaserWriter Plus from the Ventura User's Group) and then edit the VP's ASSIGN.SYS file, which lists available screen fonts, so that the new screen fonts are added to the list of available fonts. Unfortunately, fonts may not be stretched, rotated, or scaled to any size; users may work only with the sizes (and styles) of fonts installed for the active printer.

Different typefaces, sizes, and styles may be mixed on a single line or in a single paragraph. The Symbol Font includes all the lower and upper case Greek characters but no accents, breathing, or diacritical marks; it does not include the digamma, but it does include a final sigma.

To display the typeface, style, and size of any text, users must change to Text Mode, highlight the text in question, chose the Set Font button on the Side Bar, and then read the information that appears in the font dialog box. That seems unnecessarily complex, and a simpler way of displaying typographic information would be helpful.

Within the parameters of what a given printer supports, any combination of new typefaces and sizes may be added to the VP by creating new width tables with a utility provided for that purpose. To allow users to install new fonts, the VP provides installation routines for all the printers it supports. Thus new fonts may be used but only after converting them and creating width tables by using the special VP utility.

To reformat the screen quickly, the VP stores character width tables in memory. But the amount of memory used for storing those tables directly decreases the amount of memory available for creating documents. Thus only the tables that are needed for a particular job should be stored in memory. Because width tables can be installed and uninstalled, it is possible to install a width table for a phototypesetter and then print page proofs on a dot-matrix or laser printer. Although this results in incorrect word spacing, text is justified and all line, column, and page breaks are properly shown.

The VP does not allow fonts in graphics input files to be mapped to the screen fonts used by the VP. Thus when imported into the VP, the characters in a graphics file may not properly match those in the VP's screen fonts. For example, though it runs under GEM, the VP uses different printer drivers and screen fonts than GEM uses, which means that type in graphics files created with GEM Draw™ behaves unpredictably when imported into the VP.

The VP supports automatic kerning and allows kerning distances may be specified in points, centimeters, and inches. (Kerning refers to increasing or decreasing the space between characters for aesthetic purposes.) Users may define kerning-pair tables so that character pairs are kerned automatically. Leading—the distance from baseline to baseline—can be set with tags on a paragraph-by-paragraph basis in decimal increments (e.g., points, picas, inches, centimeters) and can be varied between paragraphs and from paragraph to paragraph but not between the lines within a paragraph. In other words, extra leading cannot be added between the lines of a paragraph but must remain constant in each paragraph. More sophisticated programs allow users to insert extra leading wherever desired. For justified text, the VP allows users to specify a minimum space width between words as a percentage of the normal space width, and that width is calculated and shown in EMs (a unit of measurement equivalent to the width of M in the active font). It does not allow users to specify a maximum space width between words that is greater than the normal space width. Although the VP supports microjustification—inserting microspaces between letters as well as between words—it does not support vertical justification—inserting extra leading between lines to insure equal page depth (i.e., height).

Hyphenation. The VP works with discretionary and soft hyphens. The VP inserts "soft" hyphens automatically, according to a logical algorithm, each time it loads a file, unless the hyphenation feature has been turned off. Additionally, users may insert "discretionary" hyphenation points in words. When a file is closed, the soft hyphens are not saved with it, though user-inserted discretionary hyphens are. Text files may be imported with user-inserted hyphens in place.

Soft and discretionary hyphens aid in justification, especially when using narrow columns. Because of the irregularity of English, all hyphenation algorithms (formulas) are less than 100% accurate. To compensate for this, the VP allows the hyphenation algorithm to be overridden by an exceptions dictionary—a list of exceptions to the algorithm—that is included with the program. Hyphenation algorithms often fail to insert as many hyphenation points as are possible. To compensate for that, the VP allows the hyphenation algorithm and exceptions dictionary to be overridden by a user dictionary, a user-created list of words and their discretionary hyphenation points. Creating a user dictionary gives the user complete control over the hyphenation of the words in that dictionary. Thus, in the final analysis, the VP's hyphenating capabilities are only as good as its exceptions and user dictionaries.

A more accurate and complete, though slower, way to hyphenate is to use a dictionary-based method, one that includes all the possible hyphenation points for a large number of words, an approach used by higher priced page-composition and typesetting systems, as well as by some desktop publishing programs, such as PageMaker/PC, which hyphenates according to the 110,000-word Houghton-Mifflin dictionary. In a program that is already as large as the VP, it is lamentable that users are not given the option of using a dictionary-based approach to hyphenating.

As noted earlier, the VP includes hyphenation algorithms for US English, UK English, French, Spanish, and Italian, any two of which may be used concurrently on properly tagged text. The VP also supports successive hyphenation control, that is, specifying the number of lines in a row that can end with a hyphen.

Word Processing. Although the VP has rudimentary text entry and block move features, it is not a complete word processor. For example, (1) it does not have a search and replace function (Ready,Set,Go!™ 3 does); (2) it does not allow the cursor to be moved bidirectionally by word, phrase, line, sentence, paragraph, page, or screen; and (3) it does not support multiple windows or (4) macros (Ready,Set,Go!™ 3 supports both (3) and (4)). The VP's word processing functions are designed for making minor corrections and changes in text that has been prepared with a word processing program and for preparing very short documents, not for creating long documents. When entering text on an XT-class machine, it is easy to overtype the keyboard buffer because the VP hyphenates, justifies, and formats text as it is entered and frequently rewrites the screen. (Turning hyphenation off did not help to alleviate this problem.) Because it does not support windows, two documents cannot be open simultaneously so that material in one can be copied into the other.

The procedure for using foreign language characters, symbols, and typesetting characters in the Courier, Helvetica, and Times fonts is awkward: users must hold the Alt key down and enter the ASCII values of those characters and symbols to cause them to display on-screen. Alt + 189, for example, produces ©, the symbol for Copyright. Alt + 169 and Alt + 170 produce proper opening and closing double quotes. Alt + 197 produces an M-dash. Surely a faster, simpler, and more elegant method for entering such characters can be devised. When the Symbol font is the active font, Greek characters and symbols may be entered directly from the keyboard in the Edit Mode, but the VP does not include an on-screen or written template that specifies key assignments; users must experiment to discover the correlation between keys and characters in this font.[209]

Entering footnotes takes several steps and involves using several menus. First, footnotes must be enabled by using the Footnote Settings option on the Page Menu. Second, the Text Editing function must be chosen. Third, the cursor must be placed in the text at the place where the footnote is to appear. Fourth, the Insert Footnote option on the Edit Menu must be selected. This causes a footnote number to appear in the text at that point and a footnote window to appear at the bottom of the page. Fifth, users must scroll to (or PgDn to) the bottom of the page to the footnote window, which contains the following text: "TEXT OF FOOTNOTE." Sixth, users must delete that text. Seventh, users must type the text of the footnote into the footnote window. And then users must scroll back to the place in the text where they left off typing. Surely such an involved procedure could be simplified. Given the complexity of that procedure, the simplest way to deal with footnotes is to code footnotes in the word processing input file so that the VP automatically formats them correctly. The code to use is < $F*text of footnote* >.

---

209. These problems have been addressed by Corel Systems Corporation (1600 Carling Ave., Ottowa, Ontario, Canada K1Z 7M4; (613) 728-8200). According to Corel System's Gary Cartwright, Corel is a VAR of VP, and part of the value they add consists of help screens for almost every one of the VP's features, including short cuts for entering symbols and typesetting characters, such as the ones just discussed. Corel sells their enhanced version of the VP for the standard retail price.

The VP can automatically format up to a half-page of footnotes per text page. Footnotes that take up more than a half-page must be entered manually. The VP cannot wrap long footnotes from page to page and will simply truncate footnotes that are too long!

Printing. The VP works with laser printers and phototypesetters that support PostScript, with Canon-engine laser printers running with Tall Tree Systems' J-Laser card, and with several other types of printers. Among the supported printers are the Apple Laserwriter and Laserwriter Plus, the HP LaserJet and LaserJet Plus, the AST TurboLaser, the IBM Proprinter, the Xerox 4020 Color Ink Jet printer, the Xerox 4045 Laser printer, the HP ThinkJet, and the Epson MX-80/FX-80/RX-80. Unfortunately, dot-matrix support is limited to Epson printers. The popular Toshiba 9- and 24-pin dot matrix printers, for example, are not supported. The VP can work with a maximum of eight PostScript typefaces and eight PostScript type styles and can print text in type sizes from 1 to 254 points in 1-point increments.

When printing on the HP LaserJet (which has a measly 59K RAM), the VP's maximum graphics resolution is a coarse 75 dpi. On this printer, text may be output at 300-dpi only with the HP 92286F font cartridge. The HP LaserJet Plus allows 40% of a page to be printed with 300-dpi graphics.

Every time the print command is given, the VP automatically downloads the proper fonts. Thus if a document is printed several times, the fonts must be downloaded each time the document is printed. It would be far less time consuming if fonts could be downloaded and left resident in the printer.

Documentation. The VP's Reference Guide, Training Guide, and Quick Reference Guide are models of clarity and thoroughness. They are well written, helpfully illustrated, and amply indexed. Although the VP can drive phototypesetters, these manuals were produced from laser-printed originals.

The Reference Manual is careful to define new terms. When introducing an option, the manual always (1) describes the option, (2) discusses its application, and (3) explains how to use it—in that order. A judicious mixture of bold type, headings, and screen illustrations help to distinguish items and to make important points stand out. After chapters on installation, the user interface, and the program's four basic modes, the manual has a 170-page chapter that explains in detail all the drop-down menus and each of their options and functions. Two subsequent chapters are devoted to the advanced layout topics of pictures and style sheets. Twelve appendices cover topics such as installation, common problems and error messages, word processors supported, character sets, printer information, glossary, the utilities disk, style sheets, and so forth. Although pin and cabling information is provided for printers, no such information is provided for typesetters. The appendix on style sheets includes illustrations, descriptions, and specifications for each of the twenty-one style sheets that are included on-disk, which makes it easy to get a good idea of how a document will look when formatted with a particular style sheet. Tab dividers between chapters would make this manual easier to use.

The thorough and easy-to-use Training Guide, which contains many helpful illustrations of different screens, is designed to be used with a set of example files that are installed with the VP. After mastering the VP, the example files can be deleted and an additional 256K of disk space freed up. A couple of hours spent working through the six exercises in the 126-page Training Guide enabled me to run the program accurately and with confidence.

Support. I had no occasion to call the Xerox Ventura Publisher support number. Xerox has a reputation for providing excellent support for its products. A Ventura Publishers User's Group has been formed at Ventura Software in Morgan Hill, California.

Summary. The VP is a powerful, flexible, sophisticated program that is easy to learn and easy to use. It is ideally suited for producing long, complex, standardized

293

documents like books, manuals, and reports. Because it is document oriented, works with style sheets and templates, and can accept coded and tagged files from a variety of word processors, the VP could be a perfect addition to an office, department, or business where several persons use different word processors to produce material that needs to be printed in standardized formats. Additionally, editors of journals and books that contain material created by various authors could dramatically reduce production costs, speed up production time, and ensure a uniform style and layout by using the VP to format material for phototypesetting.

2.12.3.2 PageMaker

- **BASIC PRODUCT INFORMATION**

Product Name: PageMaker™
Company Name & Address: Aldus Corp., 411 First Ave., South, #200, Seattle, WA 98104
Phone: (206) 622-5500
List Price: $695 for the IBM, $495 for the Macintosh
Runs On: IBM PCs and Macintoshes
Operating System Requirements: IBM: DOS 3.2 recommended, Microsoft® Windows required
Memory Requirements: IBM: 512K, 640K recommended; Macintosh: 512K
Disk Drive Requirements: IBM version: 2, 1 of which must be a hard disk; Macintosh version: 1.
Copy Protected: No
Possible Backups: Unlimited
Supports Mice: Yes, use mandatory
Printers Supported: PostScript, LaserJet Plus (IBM version only)
Supports Scanners: Yes
Supports Full-Page Monitors: Yes
Video Cards Supported: IBM version: HGC, HGC+, EGA
Page Description Languages Supported: PostScript, DDL
On-Line Help: Yes
On-Line Tutorial: Yes
User Interface: Menu-driven
Interactive WYSIWYG: Yes
Maximum Pages Per File: 128

- **TEXT FORMATTING FEATURES**

Word Processing Programs Supported: Macintosh version: MacWrite™, Microsoft® Word, Microsoft® Works; IBM version: Microsoft® Word, MultiMate™, WordPerfect™, WordStar®, XyWrite™
Text Formatted in Word Processor: Yes
Converts Word Processor Formatting Codes: Yes
Imports ASCII Text: Yes
Imbeds Typographic Codes: No
Uses Style Sheets: No
Rule-Based Hyphenation: No
Dictionary-Based Hyphenation: Macintosh version: No; IBM version: Yes
Automatic Kerning: Macintosh version: No; IBM version: Yes
Leading Increments: Macintosh version: integer; IBM version half-point
Tabs: Yes
Tab Leaders: Macintosh version: No; IBM version: Yes
Maximum Number of PostScript Typefaces: Unlimited
Maximum Number of PostScript Type Styles: Macintosh version: 8; IBM version: 5
Size Range in Points: 4 – 127
Size Increments in Points: Integers

• GRAPHICS FEATURES

Graphics Software Supported: AutoCAD™ (IBM version only), Windows Draw™, Lotus .PIC (IBM version only), Scans, PC Paintbrush™ (IBM version only, PC Paint™ (IBM version only), Windows Paint™, MacPaint™ (Macintosh version only), MacDraw™ (Macintosh version only), MacDraft™ (Macintosh version only)
Maximum Number of Rules: Macintosh version: 16; IBM version: 18
Rectangles: Yes
Rounded Corners: Yes
Circles & Ovals: Yes
Polygons: No
Maximum Number of Fill Patterns: Macintosh version: 16; IBM version: 17
Free-Hand Options: No
Scaling: Yes
Cropping: Yes
Rotation: No
Undo: Yes

• LAYOUT FEATURES

View Full Page: Yes
View Facing Pages: Yes
Percentage Page Enlargement: 200
Automatic Column Guides: Yes
Adjust Column Widths: Yes
Maximum Number of Columns: Macintosh version: 8; IBM version: 20
Automatic Page Numbering: Yes
Automatic Index Generation: No
Automatic Footnoting: No
Automatic Table of Contents: No
Text Wrap from Page to Page and Column to Column: Yes
Wraps Text Around Graphics: Manual
Automatic Vertical Justification: No
Snap-to-Grid: Yes
Headers & Footers: Yes
Creates Templates: Yes
Number of Ruler Measures: Macintosh version: 3; IBM version: 4
Ruler Indicator: Yes

• EDITING FEATURES

Globally Edit Text: No
Globally Edit Typographic Codes: No
Globally Edit Paragraph Formats: No
Insert & Remove Pages: Yes
Move Pages: No
Move Columns: Yes
Undo: Yes

• SUPPORT ETC.

Warranty: Not known
Support: Phone and letter
Update Policy: Not known

Major Reviews: Diane Burns and S. Venit, "Muscling in on the MAC: PC-Based Page Composition," *PC Magazine* (February 10, 1987): 119–56, esp. 143–50; Keith Thompson, "Pagemaker Remains Chief Page Composer," *InfoWorld* (June 9, 1986): 39–41; "Macintosh Layout Package Remarkably Fast, Powerful," *InfoWorld* (June 8, 1987): 50–52; Karen Sorensen, "Pagemaker for PC Among New Publishing Products," *InfoWorld* (September 1, 1986): 1, 8; Danny Goodman, "Taking a Page from the Pros," *PC World* (July 1986): 244–51; Peter E. Dyson, "Aldus' PC Pagemaker: Defending Its Title," *The Seybold Report on Desktop Publishing* (March 9, 1987): 3–14; Terry Ulick, "PC PageMaker Arrives," *Personal Publishing* (March 1987): 30–43; Jim Heid, "Pagemaker In a Big Blue Suit," *Publish!* (March 1987): 71–78; *Library Technology News* (January-February 1987): 155–60; *InfoWorld* (June 8, 1987): 50–52; *Personal Computing* (July 1987): 155–56.

2.12.3.3 *Harvard Professional Publisher*

- ### BASIC PRODUCT INFORMATION

Product Name: Harvard Professional Publisher™
Company Name & Address: Software Publishing Corp., 1901 Landings Dr., Mountain View, CA 94039
Phone: (415) 962-8910
List Price: $695
Runs On: IBM PCs and compatibles
Operating System Requirements: DOS 2.1 or greater
Memory Requirements: 640K
Disk Drive Requirements: 2, 1 of which must be a hard disk.
Copy Protected: No
Possible Backups: Unlimited
Supports Mice: Yes, use optional
Printers Supported: PostScript™, LaserJet Plus
Supports Scanners: Yes
Supports Full-Page Monitors: No
Video Cards Supported: HGC, HGC+, EGA
Page Description Languages Supported: PostScript™
On-Line Help: Yes
On-Line Tutorial: Yes
User Interface: Menu-driven
Interactive WYSIWYG: Yes
Maximum Pages Per File: 999

- ### TEXT FORMATTING FEATURES

Word Processing Programs Supported: Microsoft® Word, Samna™, WordStar®
Text Formatted in Word Processor: Yes
Converts Word Processor Formatting Codes: No
Imports ASCII Text: Yes
Imbeds Typographic Codes: Yes
Uses Style Sheets: Yes
Rule-Based Hyphenation: No
Dictionary-Based Hyphenation: Yes
Automatic Kerning: Yes
Leading Increments: Integer
Tabs: No
Tab Leaders: No
Maximum Number of PostScript Typefaces: Unlimited
Maximum Number of PostScript Type Styles: 4
Size Range in Points: 6 – 72
Size Increments in Points: 11 options

- ### GRAPHICS FEATURES

Graphics Software Supported: Lotus .PIC, Scans, PC Paintbrush™, PC Paint™, Windows Paint™
Maximum Number of Rules: 8
Rectangles: Yes

Rounded Corners: Yes
Circles & Ovals: Yes
Polygons: No
Maximum Number of Fill Patterns: 11
Free-Hand Options: No
Scaling: Yes
Cropping: No
Rotation: No
Undo: No

- *LAYOUT FEATURES*

View Full Page: Yes
View Facing Pages: No
Percentage Page Enlargement: 150
Automatic Column Guides: Yes
Adjust Column Widths: Yes, 6 settings available
Maximum Number of Columns: 6
Automatic Page Numbering: Yes
Automatic Index Generation: No
Automatic Footnoting: No
Automatic Table of Contents: No
Text Wrap from Page to Page and Column to Column: Yes
Wraps Text Around Graphics: Yes, automatically
Automatic Vertical Justification: No
Snap-to-Grid: Yes
Headers & Footers: Yes
Creates Templates: Yes
Number of Ruler Measures: 2
Ruler Indicator: Yes

- *EDITING FEATURES*

Globally Edit Text: No
Globally Edit Typographic Codes: Yes
Globally Edit Paragraph Formats: Yes
Insert & Remove Pages: No
Move Pages: Yes
Move Columns: No
Undo: No

- *SUPPORT ETC.*

Warranty: Not known
Support: Phone and letter
Update Policy: Not known
Other: See below under Superpage II.
Major Reviews: Diane Burns and S. Venit, "Muscling in on the MAC: PC-Based Page Composition," *PC Magazine* (February 10, 1987): 119–56, esp. 140–43; Richard Jantz, "Ivy League Publishing," *PC World* (July 1987): 229–31; *InfoWorld* (April 20, 1987): 49–54.

2.12.3.4 PFS:ClickArt Personal Publisher

- *BASIC PRODUCT INFORMATION*

Product Name: PFS:ClickArt Personal Publisher™
Company Name & Address: Software Publishing Corp., 1901 Landings Dr., Mountain View, CA 94039
Phone: (415) 962-8910
List Price: $185
Runs On: IBM PCs and compatibles
Operating System Requirements: DOS 2.0 or greater

Memory Requirements: 512K
Disk Drive Requirements: 2
Copy Protected: No
Possible Backups: Unlimited
Supports Mice: Yes, use optional
Printers Supported: PostScript™, LaserJet Plus
Supports Scanners: No
Supports Full-Page Monitors: No
Video Cards Supported: HGC, HGC+, CGA, EGA
Page Description Languages Supported: PostScript™
On-Line Help: Yes
On-Line Tutorial: No
User Interface: Menu-driven
Interactive WYSIWYG: Yes
Maximum Pages Per File: 5K per imported file, 99 per document

• TEXT FORMATTING FEATURES

Word Processing Programs Supported: None
Text Formatted in Word Processor: No
Converts Word Processor Formatting Codes: No
Imports ASCII Text: Yes
Imbeds Typographic Codes: No
Uses Style Sheets: No
Rule-Based Hyphenation: No
Dictionary-Based Hyphenation: No
Automatic Kerning: No
Leading Increments: Integer
Tabs: No
Tab Leaders: No
Maximum Number of PostScript Typefaces: 14
Maximum Number of PostScript Type Styles: 3
Size Range in Points: 10 – 48
Size Increments in Points: 9 options

• GRAPHICS FEATURES

Graphics Software Supported: Mentor Graphics™, Lotus .PIC, PC Paintbrush™, PC Paint™, MacPaint™
Maximum Number of Rules: 4
Rectangles: Yes
Rounded Corners: Yes
Circles & Ovals: Yes
Polygons: No
Maximum Number of Fill Patterns: 0
Free-Hand Options: Yes
Scaling: Yes
Cropping: Yes
Rotation: Yes
Undo: No

• LAYOUT FEATURES

View Full Page: Yes
View Facing Pages: No
Percentage Page Enlargement: 100
Automatic Column Guides: No
Adjust Column Widths: Yes
Maximum Number of Columns: 4
Automatic Page Numbering: No
Automatic Index Generation: No
Automatic Footnoting: No
Automatic Table of Contents: No

Text Wrap from Page to Page and Column to Column: No
Wraps Text Around Graphics: Yes, automatically
Automatic Vertical Justification: No
Snap-to-Grid: No
Headers & Footers: No
Creates Templates: No
Number of Ruler Measures: 1
Ruler Indicator: No

- *EDITING FEATURES*

Globally Edit Text: No
Globally Edit Typographic Codes: No
Globally Edit Paragraph Formats: No
Insert & Remove Pages: Yes
Move Pages: No
Move Columns: Yes
Undo: No

- *SUPPORT ETC.*

Warranty: Not known
Support: Phone and letter
Update Policy: Not known
Major Reviews: Diane Burns and S. Venit, "Muscling in on the MAC: PC-Based Page Composition," *PC Magazine* (February 10, 1987): 119–56, esp. 126–32; Terry Ulick, "Personal Publisher," *Personal Publishing* (September 1986): 20–28; Ken Freeze, "MS-DOS World Gets Page Layout Program," *InfoWorld* (June 23, 1986): 33–34.

2.12.3.5 *FrontPage*

- *BASIC PRODUCT INFORMATION*

Product Name: FrontPage™
Company Name & Address: Studio Software Corp., 17862-C Fitch St., Irvine, CA 92714
Phone: (714) 474-0131
List Price: $695; FrontPage Plus: $1,295; Front Page to Type: $1,495
Runs On: IBM PCs and compatibles
Operating System Requirements: DOS 2.0 or greater
Memory Requirements: 512K
Disk Drive Requirements: 2, 1 of which must be a hard disk.
Copy Protected: No
Possible Backups: Unlimited
Supports Mice: Yes, use optional
Printers Supported: PostScript™, LaserJet Plus, AST TurboLaser
Supports Scanners: Yes
Supports Full-Page Monitors: Yes
Video Cards Supported: HGC, HGC+, CGA, EGA
Page Description Languages Supported: PostScript™, DDL™
On-Line Help: Yes
On-Line Tutorial: Yes
User Interface: Menu-driven
Interactive WYSIWYG: Yes
Maximum Pages Per File: 8 pages per "board," number of boards limited only by disk space.

- *TEXT FORMATTING FEATURES*

Word Processing Programs Supported: DisplayWrite™, MultiMate™, WordPerfect™, WordStar®, XyWrite™
Text Formatted in Word Processor: Yes
Converts Word Processor Formatting Codes: Yes

Imports ASCII Text: Yes
Imbeds Typographic Codes: Yes
Uses Style Sheets: Yes
Rule-Based Hyphenation: Yes
Dictionary-Based Hyphenation: Yes
Automatic Kerning: Yes
Leading Increments: Decimal
Tabs: Yes
Tab Leaders: Yes
Maximum Number of PostScript Typefaces: Unlimited
Maximum Number of PostScript Type Styles: 4
Size Range in Points: 4 – 254
Size Increments in Points: Decimal

- **GRAPHICS FEATURES**

Graphics Software Supported: AutoCAD™, Mentor Graphics™, Lotus .PIC
Maximum Number of Rules: Unlimited
Rectangles: Yes
Rounded Corners: Yes
Circles & Ovals: Yes
Polygons: Yes
Maximum Number of Fill Patterns: 34
Free-Hand Options: No
Scaling: Yes
Cropping: No
Rotation: No
Undo: No

- **LAYOUT FEATURES**

View Full Page: Yes
View Facing Pages: Yes
Percentage Page Enlargement: 10,000
Automatic Column Guides: No
Adjust Column Widths: Yes
Maximum Number of Columns: Unlimited
Automatic Page Numbering: No
Automatic Index Generation: No
Automatic Footnoting: No
Automatic Table of Contents: No
Text Wrap from Page to Page and Column to Column: Yes
Wraps Text Around Graphics: Yes, automatically
Automatic Vertical Justification: Yes
Snap-to-Grid: Yes
Headers & Footers: No
Creates Templates: Yes
Number of Ruler Measures: 4
Ruler Indicator: Yes

- **EDITING FEATURES**

Globally Edit Text: No
Globally Edit Typographic Codes: Yes
Globally Edit Paragraph Formats: Yes
Insert & Remove Pages: Yes
Move Pages: No
Move Columns: Yes
Undo: No

300

- ## SUPPORT ETC.

Warranty: Not known
Support: Phone and letter
Update Policy: Not known
Major Reviews: Diane Burns and S. Venit, "Muscling in on the MAC: PC-Based Page Composition," *PC Magazine* (February 10, 1987): 119–56, esp. 132–40

2.12.3.6 Ready, Set, Go!

- ## BASIC PRODUCT INFORMATION

Product Name: Ready, Set, Go!™ 4.0
Company Name & Address: Letraset USA, 40 Eisenhower Dr., Paramus, NJ 07653
Phones: (800) 631-1603, (201) 845-6100
List Price: $495
Runs On: Macintoshes
Operating System Requirements: Macintosh operating system
Memory Requirements: 512K
Disk Drive Requirements: 1 (two 400K or one 800K drives)
Copy Protected: No
Possible Backups: Unlimited
Supports Mice: Yes
Printers Supported: PostScript™
Supports Scanners: Yes
Supports Full-Page Monitors: Yes
Video Cards Supported: Not applicable
Page Description Languages Supported: PostScript™
On-Line Help: No
On-Line Tutorial: No
User Interface: Menu-driven
Interactive WYSIWYG: Yes
Maximum Pages Per File: Limited only by memory

- ## TEXT FORMATTING FEATURES

Word Processing Programs Supported: MacWrite™, Microsoft® Word
Text Formatted in Word Processor: Yes
Converts Word Processor Formatting Codes: Yes
Imports ASCII Text: Yes
Imbeds Typographic Codes: No
Uses Style Sheets: Yes
Rule-Based Hyphenation: Yes
Dictionary-Based Hyphenation: No
Automatic Kerning: Yes
Leading Increments: Integer
Tabs: Yes
Tab Leaders: Yes
Maximum Number of PostScript Typefaces: Varies with device
Maximum Number of PostScript Type Styles: 200
Size Range in Points: 1 – 255
Size Increments in Points: Yes

- ## GRAPHICS FEATURES

Graphics Software Supported: MacPaint™, PICT files
Maximum Number of Rules: Unlimited
Rectangles: Yes
Rounded Corners: Yes
Circles & Ovals: Yes

Polygons: No
Maximum Number of Fill Patterns: 39
Free-Hand Options: No
Scaling: Yes
Cropping: Yes
Rotation: No
Undo: Yes

- *LAYOUT FEATURES*

View Full Page: Yes
View Facing Pages: Yes
Percentage Page Enlargement: 200
Automatic Column Guides: Yes
Adjust Column Widths: Yes
Maximum Number of Columns: Unlimited
Automatic Page Numbering: Yes
Automatic Index Generation: No
Automatic Footnoting: No
Automatic Table of Contents: No
Text Wrap from Page to Page and Column to Column: Yes
Wraps Text Around Graphics: Yes
Automatic Vertical Justification: No
Snap-to-Grid: Yes
Headers & Footers: Yes
Creates Templates: Yes
Number of Ruler Measures: 4
Ruler Indicator: Yes

- *EDITING FEATURES*

Globally Edit Text: Yes
Globally Edit Typographic Codes: Yes
Globally Edit Paragraph Formats: Yes
Insert & Remove Pages: Yes
Move Pages: Yes
Move Columns: Yes
Undo: Not known

- *SUPPORT ETC.*

Warranty: 90 days, media only
Support: Phone and letter
Update Policy: Not known
Major Reviews: *Cider Press* (January/February 1987): 10; *Computer Buying Guide* (1987), 182–83; John Stachlewski, *Macworld*—Australian (February 1987): 78–83; *Personal Publishing* (March 1987): 64–68; *Publish!* (April 1987): 64–68.

For various reasons, less information will be provided for the following programs.

2.12.3.7 Ragtime 2.0

- *BASIC PRODUCT INFORMATION*

Product Name: Ragtime™ 2.0
Company Name & Address: Orange Micro, Inc., 1400 N. Lakeview Ave., Anaheim, CA 92807
Phone: (714) 779-2772
List Price: $395
Runs On: Macintoshes

Operating System Requirements: Macintosh operating system
Memory Requirements: 512K
Disk Drive Requirements: 1 (800K)
Copy Protected: No
Possible Backups: Unlimited
Supports Mice: Yes
Printers Supported: PostScript™, ImageWriter, ImageWriter II
Supports Scanners: Yes
Supports Full-Page Monitors: Yes
Video Cards Supported: Not applicable
Page Description Languages Supported: PostScript™
On-Line Help: No
On-Line Tutorial: No
User Interface: Menu-driven
Interactive WYSIWYG: Yes
Maximum Pages Per File: 350

- TEXT FORMATTING FEATURES

Word Processing Programs Supported: MacWrite™, Microsoft® Word; Ragtime includes a word processor.
Text Formatted in Word Processor: Yes
Converts Word Processor Formatting Codes: Yes, Microsoft® Word, MacWrite™
Imports ASCII Text: Yes
Uses Style Sheets: No
Automatic Hyphenation: Yes, rule-based
Automatic Kerning: No
Leading Control: Yes

- GRAPHICS FEATURES

Graphics Software Supported: MacPaint™, MacDraw™, MacDraft™, PICT-formatted files
Maximum Number of Fill Patterns: 40
Size Graphic Elements: Yes

- LAYOUT FEATURES

View Full Page: Yes
View Facing Pages: No
Percentage Page Enlargement: 100
Automatic Page Numbering: No
Automatic Index Generation: No
Automatic Footnoting: No
Automatic Table of Contents: No
Text Wrap from Page to Page and Column to Column: Yes
Wraps Text Around Graphics: No
Headers & Footers: Yes
Creates Templates: Yes

- EDITING FEATURES

Globally Edit Text: Yes
Insert & Remove Pages: Yes
Move Pages: Yes
Move Columns: Yes

- SUPPORT ETC.

Warranty: 1 year, media only
Support: Phone and letter
Update Policy: Free
Major Reviews: C. J. Weigand, "Ragtime," *Personal Publishing* (November 1986): 70–76.

2.12.3.8 MacPublisher II

- #### BASIC PRODUCT INFORMATION

Product Name: MacPublisher™ II
Company Name & Address: Boston Software, 1260 Boylston St., Boston, MA 02215
Phone: (617) 267-4747
List Price: $195
Runs On: Macintoshes
Operating System Requirements: Macintosh operating system
Memory Requirements: 512K
Disk Drive Requirements: 1
Copy Protected: Yes
Possible Backups: Not known
Supports Mice: Yes
Printers Supported: PostScript™, ImageWriter
Supports Scanners: Yes
Supports Full-Page Monitors: Yes
Video Cards Supported: Not applicable
Page Description Languages Supported: PostScript™
On-Line Help: Yes
On-Line Tutorial: Yes
User Interface: Menu-driven
Interactive WYSIWYG: Yes
Maximum Pages Per File: 96

- #### TEXT FORMATTING FEATURES

Word Processing Programs Supported: MacWrite™, Microsoft® Word
Text Formatted in Word Processor: No
Converts Word Processor Formatting Codes: No
Imports ASCII Text: Yes
Uses Style Sheets: Yes
Automatic Hyphenation: No
Automatic Kerning: Yes
Leading Control: Yes

- #### GRAPHICS FEATURES

Graphics Software Supported: Not known
Maximum Number of Fill Patterns: 99
Size Graphic Elements: Yes

- #### LAYOUT FEATURES

View Full Page: Yes
View Facing Pages: Yes
Percentage Page Enlargement: 900
Automatic Page Numbering: Yes
Automatic Index Generation: No
Automatic Footnoting: No
Automatic Table of Contents: Yes
Text Wrap from Page to Page and Column to Column: Yes
Wraps Text Around Graphics: No
Headers & Footers: Yes

- #### EDITING FEATURES

Globally Edit Text: No

304

Insert & Remove Pages: Yes
Move Pages: No
Move Columns: No

- *SUPPORT ETC.*

Warranty: Not known
Support: Phone and letter
Update Policy: Not known
Major Reviews: "MacPublisher II," *Personal Publishing* (August 1986): 42–44.

2.12.3.9 PS Compose

- *BASIC PRODUCT INFORMATION*

Product Name: PS Compose™
Company Name & Address: PS Publishing, Inc., 290 Green St., Suite 1, San Francisco, CA 94133
Phone: (415) 433-4698
List Price: $800
Runs On: Macintoshes
Operating System Requirements: Macintosh operating system
Memory Requirements: 512K
Disk Drive Requirements: 1
Copy Protected: No
Possible Backups: Unlimited
Supports Mice: Yes
Printers Supported: PostScript™
Supports Scanners: Yes
Supports Full-Page Monitors: Yes
Video Cards Supported: Not applicable
Page Description Languages Supported: PostScript™
On-Line Help: Yes
On-Line Tutorial: No
User Interface: Menu-driven
Interactive WYSIWYG: Yes
Maximum Pages Per File: 200

- *TEXT FORMATTING FEATURES*

Word Processing Programs Supported: None
Text Formatted in Word Processor: Yes
Converts Word Processor Formatting Codes: Yes, MacWrite™, Microsoft® Word
Imports ASCII Text: Yes
Uses Style Sheets: Yes
Automatic Hyphenation: Yes, dictionary-based
Automatic Kerning: Yes
Leading Control: Yes

- *GRAPHICS FEATURES*

Graphics Software Supported: All Macintosh-compatible programs, e.g., MacPaint™, MacDraw™
Maximum Number of Fill Patterns: No limit to number of shades.
Size Graphic Elements: Yes

- *LAYOUT FEATURES*

View Full Page: Yes
View Facing Pages: No
Percentage Page Enlargement: 100
Automatic Page Numbering: Yes

Automatic Index Generation: No
Automatic Footnoting: No
Automatic Table of Contents: No
Text Wrap from Page to Page and Column to Column: Yes
Wraps Text Around Graphics: Yes
Headers & Footers: Yes

• EDITING FEATURES

Globally Edit Text: Yes
Insert & Remove Pages: Yes
Move Pages: Yes
Move Columns: Yes

• SUPPORT ETC.

Warranty: 90 days, media only
Support: Phone and letter
Update Policy: Not known
Major Reviews: None

2.12.3.10 *Quark Express*

• BASIC PRODUCT INFORMATION

Product Name: Quark Express™
Company Name & Address: Quark, 2525 W. Evans, Suite 220, Denver, CO 80219
Phones: (800) 543-7711, (303) 934-2211, (303) 934-0784
List Price: $699
Runs On: Macintoshes
Operating System Requirements: Macintosh operating system
Memory Requirements: 512K
Disk Drive Requirements: 1
Copy Protected: Yes
Possible Backups: 3
Supports Mice: Yes
Printers Supported: PostScript™, ImageWriter, ImageWriter II
Supports Scanners: Yes
Supports Full-Page Monitors: Yes
Video Cards Supported: Not applicable
Page Description Languages Supported: PostScript™
On-Line Help: Yes
On-Line Tutorial: Yes
User Interface: Menu-driven
Interactive WYSIWYG: Yes
Maximum Pages Per File: Limited only by disk

• TEXT FORMATTING FEATURES

Word Processing Programs Supported: MacWrite™, Microsoft® Word, Microsoft® Works
Text Formatted in Word Processor: Yes
Converts Word Processor Formatting Codes: Yes, MacWrite™, Microsoft® Word, Microsoft® Works
Imports ASCII Text: Yes
Uses Style Sheets: No
Automatic Hyphenation: Yes, rule-based
Automatic Kerning: Yes
Leading Control: Yes

- ## GRAPHICS FEATURES

Graphics Software Supported: MacDraw™, MacPaint™, FullPaint™, PICT files, EPSF files, TIFF files
Maximum Number of Fill Patterns: 0
Size Graphic Elements: Yes

- ## LAYOUT FEATURES

View Full Page: Yes
View Facing Pages: Yes
Percentage Page Enlargement: 200
Automatic Page Numbering: Yes
Automatic Index Generation: No
Automatic Footnoting: Yes
Automatic Table of Contents: No
Text Wrap from Page to Page and Column to Column: Yes
Wraps Text Around Graphics: Yes
Headers & Footers: Yes

- ## EDITING FEATURES

Globally Edit Text: Yes
Insert & Remove Pages: Yes
Move Pages: Yes
Move Columns: Yes

- ## SUPPORT ETC.

Warranty: Not known
Support: Phone and letter
Update Policy: Free for first 90 days after purchase
Major Reviews: Domonic R. D'Acquisto, "XPressive Pages," *Personal Publishing* (July 1987): 24–36; Joost Romeu, "A Star Is Born," *The MACazine* (August 1987): 34–37; Fred Terry, "Desktop Publishing Round Two," *The MACazine* (August 1987): 25–29; Mike Krell, "XPress," *Macworld* (August 1987): 148–50.

2.12.3.11 Scoop

- ## BASIC PRODUCT INFORMATION

Product Name: Scoop™
Company Name & Address: Target Software, Inc., 14206 S.W. 136th St., Miami, FL 33186
Phones: (800) 622-5483, (305) 252-0892
List Price: $495
Runs On: Macintoshes
Operating System Requirements: Macintosh operating system
Memory Requirements: 1MB
Disk Drive Requirements: 1
Copy Protected: No
Possible Backups: Unlimited
Supports Mice: Yes
Printers Supported: PostScript™
Supports Scanners: Yes
Supports Full-Page Monitors: Yes
Video Cards Supported: Not applicable
Page Description Languages Supported: PostScript™
On-Line Help: Yes
On-Line Tutorial: Yes
User Interface: Menu-driven
Interactive WYSIWYG: Yes

307

Maximum Pages Per File: 128

- *TEXT FORMATTING FEATURES*

Word Processing Programs Supported: MacWrite™, Microsoft® Word
Text Formatted in Word Processor: Yes
Converts Word Processor Formatting Codes: Yes
Imports ASCII Text: Yes
Uses Style Sheets: Yes
Automatic Hyphenation: Yes, dictionary-based (Merriam-Webster®)
Automatic Kerning: Yes
Leading Control: Yes

- *GRAPHICS FEATURES*

Graphics Software Supported: MacPaint™, FullPaint™, SuperPaint™, MacDraw™, PICT files
Maximum Number of Fill Patterns: 38
Size Graphic Elements: Yes

- *LAYOUT FEATURES*

View Full Page: Yes
View Facing Pages: Yes
Percentage Page Enlargement: 800
Automatic Page Numbering: Yes
Automatic Index Generation: Yes
Automatic Footnoting: Yes
Automatic Table of Contents: Yes
Text Wrap from Page to Page and Column to Column: Yes
Wraps Text Around Graphics: Yes
Headers & Footers: Yes

- *EDITING FEATURES*

Globally Edit Text: Yes
Insert & Remove Pages: Yes
Move Pages: Yes
Move Columns: Yes

- *SUPPORT ETC.*

Warranty: 90 days, media only
Support: Phone and letter; 6 months toll-free support, $10/month thereafter
Update Policy: Not known
Major Reviews: None

2.12.3.12 FormEasy

- *BASIC PRODUCT INFORMATION*

Product Name: FormEasy™
Company Name & Address: Graphics Development International, 41 Calafia Court, San Rafael, CA
  94903
Phone: (415) 382-6600
List Price: $495
Runs On: IBM PCs and compatibles
Operating System Requirements: DOS 2.0 or greater
Memory Requirements: 256K (512K for Cordata)
Disk Drive Requirements: 2; hard disk required for Cordata.
Copy Protected: No

Possible Backups: Unlimited
Supports Mice: Yes
Printers Supported: LaserJet, LaserJet Plus, PostScript™
Supports Scanners: Yes
Supports Full-Page Monitors: No
Video Cards Supported: HGC, HGC+, CGA, EGA
Page Description Languages Supported: None
On-Line Help: Yes
On-Line Tutorial: Yes
User Interface: Menu-driven
Interactive WYSIWYG: Yes
Maximum Pages Per File: 20

- *TEXT FORMATTING FEATURES*

Word Processing Programs Supported: WordStar
Text Formatted in Word Processor: Includes its own word processor.
Converts Word Processor Formatting Codes: Yes, WordStar®
Imports ASCII Text: Yes
Uses Style Sheets: Yes
Automatic Hyphenation: Yes
Automatic Kerning: No
Leading Control: Yes

- *GRAPHICS FEATURES*

Graphics Software Supported: Lotus™, PICT, PC Paintbrush™
Maximum Number of Fill Patterns: 200
Size Graphic Elements: Yes

- *LAYOUT FEATURES*

View Full Page: Yes
View Facing Pages: No
Percentage Page Enlargement: 90
Automatic Page Numbering: Yes
Automatic Index Generation: No
Automatic Footnoting: No
Automatic Table of Contents: No
Text Wrap from Page to Page and Column to Column: Yes
Wraps Text Around Graphics: No
Headers & Footers: Yes

- *EDITING FEATURES*

Globally Edit Text: Yes
Insert & Remove Pages: Yes
Move Pages: Yes
Move Columns: Yes

- *SUPPORT ETC.*

Warranty: 30-day, money-back guarantee, media and functionality
Support: Phone and letter
Update Policy: Free upgrades for first 90 days after purchase.
Major Reviews: Not known

2.12.3.13 PagePerfect

- BASIC PRODUCT INFORMATION

Product Name: PagePerfect™
Company Name & Address: International Microcomputer Software, Inc., 1299 Fourth St., San Rafael, CA 94901
Phone: (415) 454-7101
List Price: $595
Runs On: IBM PCs and compatibles
Operating System Requirements: DOS 2.0 or greater
Memory Requirements: 640K
Disk Drive Requirements: 2, one of which must be a hard disk.
Copy Protected: No
Possible Backups: Unlimited
Supports Mice: Yes
Printers Supported: LaserJet, LaserJet Plus, LaserWriter, LaserWriter Plus, PostScript™
Supports Scanners: Yes
Supports Full-Page Monitors: No
Video Cards Supported: EGA
Page Description Languages Supported: PostScript™, DDL™
On-Line Help: Yes
On-Line Tutorial: Yes
User Interface: Menu-driven
Interactive WYSIWYG: Yes
Maximum Pages Per File: Limited only be disk space.

- TEXT FORMATTING FEATURES

Word Processing Programs Supported: Microsoft® Word, WordStar®, MultiMate™, Samna™, WordPerfect™
Text Formatted in Word Processor: Yes
Converts Word Processor Formatting Codes: Yes, WordStar®, WordPerfect™, Microsoft® Word, MultiMate™
Imports ASCII Text: Yes
Uses Style Sheets: Yes
Automatic Hyphenation: Yes, dictionary-based (Houghton Mifflin)
Automatic Kerning: Yes
Leading Control: Yes

- GRAPHICS FEATURES

Graphics Software Supported: Dr. Halo™
Maximum Number of Fill Patterns: 12
Size Graphic Elements: Yes

- LAYOUT FEATURES

View Full Page: Yes
View Facing Pages: Yes
Percentage Page Enlargement: 600
Automatic Page Numbering: Yes
Automatic Index Generation: Yes
Automatic Footnoting: No
Automatic Table of Contents: No
Text Wrap from Page to Page and Column to Column: Yes
Wraps Text Around Graphics: Yes
Headers & Footers: Yes

- ## EDITING FEATURES

Globally Edit Text: Yes
Insert & Remove Pages: Yes
Move Pages: Yes
Move Columns: Yes

- ## SUPPORT ETC.

Warranty: 45 days
Support: Phone and letter, 45 days toll-free support
Update Policy: Not known
Major Reviews: Not known

2.12.3.14 The Office Publisher

- ## BASIC PRODUCT INFORMATION

Product Name: The Office Publisher™
Company Name & Address: Laser Friendly, Inc., 930 Benecia Ave., Sunnyvale, CA 94086
Phone: (408) 730-1921
List Price: $995
Runs On: IBM PCs and compatibles
Operating System Requirements: DOS 2.0 or greater
Memory Requirements: 512K
Disk Drive Requirements: 2, one of which must be a hard disk.
Copy Protected: No
Possible Backups: Unlimited
Supports Mice: Yes
Printers Supported: PostScript™, LaserJet Plus
Supports Scanners: Yes
Supports Full-Page Monitors: Yes
Video Cards Supported: HGC, HGC+, CGA, EGA
Page Description Languages Supported: PostScript™, DDL™, Interpress™
On-Line Help: Yes
On-Line Tutorial: No
User Interface: Menu-driven
Interactive WYSIWYG: Yes
Maximum Pages Per File: Limited only by disk space.

- ## TEXT FORMATTING FEATURES

Word Processing Programs Supported: DisplayWrite™, Microsoft® Word, WordPerfect™, WordStar®,
MultiMate™, Samna™, XyWrite™
Text Formatted in Word Processor: Yes
Converts Word Processor Formatting Codes: Yes
Imports ASCII Text: Yes
Uses Style Sheets: Yes
Automatic Hyphenation: Yes, rule- and dictionary-based (Merriam-Webster®)
Automatic Kerning: Yes
Leading Control: Yes

- ## GRAPHICS FEATURES

Graphics Software Supported: Dr. Halo™, PICT
Maximum Number of Fill Patterns: Not known
Size Graphic Elements: Yes

311

- ## *LAYOUT FEATURES*

View Full Page: Yes
View Facing Pages: No
Percentage Page Enlargement: 999
Automatic Page Numbering: Yes
Automatic Index Generation: Yes
Automatic Footnoting: Yes
Automatic Table of Contents: Yes
Text Wrap from Page to Page and Column to Column: Yes
Wraps Text Around Graphics: Yes
Headers & Footers: Yes

- ## *EDITING FEATURES*

Globally Edit Text: Yes
Insert & Remove Pages: Yes
Move Pages: Yes
Move Columns: Yes

- ## *SUPPORT ETC.*

Warranty: Not known
Support: Phone and letter
Update Policy: Not known
Major Reviews: None

2.12.3.15 Spellbinder Desktop Publisher

- ## *BASIC PRODUCT INFORMATION*

Product Name: Spellbinder Desktop Publisher™
Company Name & Address: Lexisoft, Inc., P.O. Box 1950, Davis, CA 95617
Phone: (916) 758-3630
List Price: $695
Runs On: IBM PCs and compatibles
Operating System Requirements: DOS 2.0 or greater
Memory Requirements: 256K
Disk Drive Requirements: 2
Copy Protected: No
Possible Backups: Unlimited
Supports Mice: No
Printers Supported: PostScript™, LaserJet Plus, Cordata 300
Supports Scanners: Yes
Supports Full-Page Monitors: No
Video Cards Supported: HGC, HGC+, CGA, EGA
Page Description Languages Supported: PostScript™
On-Line Help: Yes
On-Line Tutorial: No
User Interface: Command-driven
Interactive WYSIWYG: No
Maximum Pages Per File: Limited only by disk space.

- ## *TEXT FORMATTING FEATURES*

Word Processing Programs Supported: None
Text Formatted in Word Processor: Yes
Converts Word Processor Formatting Codes: Not applicable
Imports ASCII Text: Yes
Uses Style Sheets: Yes

Automatic Hyphenation: Yes
Automatic Kerning: Yes
Leading Control: Yes

● *GRAPHICS FEATURES*

Graphics Software Supported: Dr. Halo™, PICT, IMG
Maximum Number of Fill Patterns: 100
Size Graphic Elements: Yes

● *LAYOUT FEATURES*

View Full Page: Yes
View Facing Pages: No
Percentage Page Enlargement: 256
Automatic Page Numbering: Yes
Automatic Index Generation: No
Automatic Footnoting: Yes
Automatic Table of Contents: No
Text Wrap from Page to Page and Column to Column: Yes
Wraps Text Around Graphics: Yes
Headers & Footers: Yes

● *EDITING FEATURES*

Globally Edit Text: Yes
Insert & Remove Pages: Yes
Move Pages: Yes
Move Columns: Not known

● *SUPPORT ETC.*

Warranty: Not known
Support: Phone and letter
Update Policy: Not known
Major Reviews: Not known

2.12.3.16 Halo DPE

● *BASIC PRODUCT INFORMATION*

Product Name: Halo DPE™
Company Name & Address: Media Cybernetics, Inc., 8484 Georgia Ave., Suite 200, Silver Spring, MD 20910
Phone: (301) 495-3305
List Price: $195
Runs On: IBM PCs and compatibles
Operating System Requirements: DOS 2.0 or greater
Memory Requirements: 512K
Disk Drive Requirements: 2
Copy Protected: No
Possible Backups: Unlimited
Supports Mice: Yes
Printers Supported: Canon- and Ricoh-based printers
Supports Scanners: Yes
Supports Full-Page Monitors: Yes
Video Cards Supported: HGC, HGC+, CGA, EGA, PGA
Page Description Languages Supported: None
On-Line Help: No
On-Line Tutorial: No

User Interface: Menu-driven
Interactive WYSIWYG: Yes
Maximum Pages Per File: Limited only by disk space.

• TEXT FORMATTING FEATURES

Word Processing Programs Supported: WordPerfect™
Text Formatted in Word Processor: Yes
Converts Word Processor Formatting Codes: Yes, WordPerfect™, most major word processors
Imports ASCII Text: Yes
Uses Style Sheets: No
Automatic Hyphenation: No
Automatic Kerning: No
Leading Control: No

• GRAPHICS FEATURES

Graphics Software Supported: Can "grab" any graphics image and output it in GEM, Windows, or Halo
    format.
Maximum Number of Fill Patterns: 56
Size Graphic Elements: Yes

• LAYOUT FEATURES

View Full Page: Yes
View Facing Pages: No
Percentage Page Enlargement: 800
Automatic Page Numbering: No
Automatic Index Generation: No
Automatic Footnoting: No
Automatic Table of Contents: No
Text Wrap from Page to Page and Column to Column: No
Wraps Text Around Graphics: No
Headers & Footers: No

• EDITING FEATURES

Globally Edit Text: No
Insert & Remove Pages: Yes
Move Pages: Yes
Move Columns: Yes

• SUPPORT ETC.

Warranty: 90 days, media only
Support: Phone and letter
Update Policy: $50 to $60
Major Reviews: Winn L. Rosch, "Rockwell Finds 'Dr. Halo' Has the Right Stuff," *PC Week* (July 9, 1985);
    "PC Graphics Packages Spell Mainframe Relief," *PC Week* (July 9, 1985).

2.12.3.17 First Impression

• BASIC PRODUCT INFORMATION

Product Name: First Impression™
Company Name & Address: Megahaus Corp., 6215 Ferris Square, San Diego, CA 92121
Phone: (619) 450-1230
List Price: $895
Runs On: IBM PCs and compatibles
Operating System Requirements: DOS 2.0 or greater

Memory Requirements: 640K
Disk Drive Requirements: 2, one of which must be a hard disk.
Copy Protected: No
Possible Backups: Unlimited
Supports Mice: Yes
Printers Supported: PostScript™, LaserJet Plus
Supports Scanners: Yes
Supports Full-Page Monitors: Yes
Video Cards Supported: HGC, HGC+, CGA, EGA
Page Description Languages Supported: PostScript™
On-Line Help: Yes
On-Line Tutorial: No
User Interface: Menu-driven
Interactive WYSIWYG: Yes
Maximum Pages Per File: Limited only by disk space.

- ## TEXT FORMATTING FEATURES

Word Processing Programs Supported: MultiMate™, WordStar®, Samna™, WordPerfect™, DisplayWrite™, Microsoft® Word, DCA format
Text Formatted in Word Processor: Yes
Converts Word Processor Formatting Codes: Yes
Imports ASCII Text: Yes
Uses Style Sheets: Yes
Automatic Hyphenation: Yes, rule-based
Automatic Kerning: Yes
Leading Control: Yes

- ## GRAPHICS FEATURES

Graphics Software Supported: AutoCAD™
Maximum Number of Fill Patterns: 10
Size Graphic Elements: Yes

- ## LAYOUT FEATURES

View Full Page: Yes
View Facing Pages: Yes
Percentage Page Enlargement: 200
Automatic Page Numbering: Yes
Automatic Index Generation: Yes
Automatic Footnoting: Yes
Automatic Table of Contents: Yes
Text Wrap from Page to Page and Column to Column: Yes
Wraps Text Around Graphics: Yes
Headers & Footers: Yes

- ## EDITING FEATURES

Globally Edit Text: Yes
Insert & Remove Pages: Yes
Move Pages: Yes
Move Columns: Yes

- ## SUPPORT ETC.

Warranty: Not known
Support: Phone and letter
Update Policy: Not known
Major Reviews: Not known

2.12.3.18 Pagewriter

- ● *BASIC PRODUCT INFORMATION*

Product Name: Pagewriter™
Company Name & Address: The 'Puter Group, 1717 North Beltline Hwy., Madison, WI 53713
Phone: (608) 273-1803
List Price: $495
Runs On: IBM PCs and compatibles
Operating System Requirements: DOS 2.0 or greater
Memory Requirements: 640K
Disk Drive Requirements: 2
Copy Protected: Yes, uses key disk; unprotected version available.
Possible Backups: Unlimited
Supports Mice: No
Printers Supported: PostScript™, LaserJet Plus, LaserWriter, LaserWriter Plus
Supports Scanners: Yes
Supports Full-Page Monitors: Yes
Video Cards Supported: CGA
Page Description Languages Supported: PostScript™
On-Line Help: No
On-Line Tutorial: Yes
User Interface: Menu-driven
Interactive WYSIWYG: Yes
Maximum Pages Per File: 100

- ● *TEXT FORMATTING FEATURES*

Word Processing Programs Supported: None
Text Formatted in Word Processor: Yes
Converts Word Processor Formatting Codes: Yes
Imports ASCII Text: Yes
Uses Style Sheets: No
Automatic Hyphenation: Yes
Automatic Kerning: Yes
Leading Control: Yes

- ● *GRAPHICS FEATURES*

Graphics Software Supported: PC Paintbrush™
Maximum Number of Fill Patterns: 100
Size Graphic Elements: No

- ● *LAYOUT FEATURES*

View Full Page: Yes
View Facing Pages: Yes
Percentage Page Enlargement: 300
Automatic Page Numbering: No
Automatic Index Generation: No
Automatic Footnoting: No
Automatic Table of Contents: No
Text Wrap from Page to Page and Column to Column: Column to column only
Wraps Text Around Graphics: No
Headers & Footers: Yes

- ● *EDITING FEATURES*

Globally Edit Text: Yes
Insert & Remove Pages: No
Move Pages: No

Move Columns: Yes

● *SUPPORT ETC.*

Warranty: 30-day, money-back guarantee
Support: Phone and letter
Update Policy: $25
Major Reviews: *PC Publishing* (March 1987); *Personal Publishing* (February 1987).

2.12.3.19 *Pagework*

● *BASIC PRODUCT INFORMATION*

Product Name: Pagework™
Company Name & Address: Pansophic Graphics Systems, Inc., 1825 Q Street N.W., Washington, DC 20009
Phone: (202) 232-7733
List Price: $1,500 to $1,900 depending on graphics card
Runs On: IBM PCs and compatibles
Operating System Requirements: DOS 2.0 or greater
Memory Requirements: 512K
Disk Drive Requirements: 2
Copy Protected: Yes, uses key disk
Possible Backups: Unlimited
Supports Mice: Yes
Printers Supported: PostScript™
Supports Scanners: Yes
Supports Full-Page Monitors: Yes
Video Cards Supported: HGC, HGC+, CGA, EGA, PGA
Page Description Languages Supported: PostScript™
On-Line Help: Yes
On-Line Tutorial: No
User Interface: Menu-driven
Interactive WYSIWYG: Yes
Maximum Pages Per File: Limited only by memory.

● *TEXT FORMATTING FEATURES*

Word Processing Programs Supported: None
Text Formatted in Word Processor: No
Converts Word Processor Formatting Codes: No
Imports ASCII Text: Yes
Uses Style Sheets: No
Automatic Hyphenation: No
Automatic Kerning: No
Leading Control: Yes

● *GRAPHICS FEATURES*

Graphics Software Supported: AutoCAD™
Maximum Number of Fill Patterns: Unlimited
Size Graphic Elements: Yes

● *LAYOUT FEATURES*

View Full Page: Yes
View Facing Pages: No
Percentage Page Enlargement: 500
Automatic Page Numbering: No
Automatic Index Generation: No

Automatic Footnoting: No
Automatic Table of Contents: No
Text Wrap from Page to Page and Column to Column: Yes
Wraps Text Around Graphics: Yes
Headers & Footers: Yes

- *EDITING FEATURES*

Globally Edit Text: No
Insert & Remove Pages: No
Move Pages: No
Move Columns: No

- *SUPPORT ETC.*

Warranty: Not known
Support: Phone and letter
Update Policy: Free for first year after purchase.
Major Reviews: Not known

2.12.3.20 Pagebuilder

- *BASIC PRODUCT INFORMATION*

Product Name: Pagebuilder™
Company Name & Address: White Sciences, Inc., 2 West Almeda, Tempe, AZ 85282
Phone: (602) 967-8257
List Price: $495
Runs On: IBM PCs and compatibles
Operating System Requirements: DOS 2.0 or greater
Memory Requirements: 384K
Disk Drive Requirements: 2, one of which must be a hard disk.
Copy Protected: No
Possible Backups: Unlimited
Supports Mice: Yes
Printers Supported: Requires J-Laser card; supports Canon CX, SX, Ricoh 4080E, and 4080I laser engines.
Supports Scanners: Yes
Supports Full-Page Monitors: Yes
Video Cards Supported: HGC, HGC+, EGA
Page Description Languages Supported: None
On-Line Help: Yes
On-Line Tutorial: Yes
User Interface: Menu-driven
Interactive WYSIWYG: Yes
Maximum Pages Per File: Limited only by disk space.

- *TEXT FORMATTING FEATURES*

Word Processing Programs Supported: Not known
Text Formatted in Word Processor: Yes
Converts Word Processor Formatting Codes: Yes
Imports ASCII Text: Yes
Uses Style Sheets: Yes
Automatic Hyphenation: No
Automatic Kerning: Yes
Leading Control: No

- **GRAPHICS FEATURES**

Graphics Software Supported: DXF, PCX files, AutoCAD™, VersaCAD™, PC Paintbrush™, Dr. Halo™, most paint programs
Maximum Number of Fill Patterns: Unlimited
Size Graphic Elements: No

- **LAYOUT FEATURES**

View Full Page: Yes
View Facing Pages: Yes
Percentage Page Enlargement: Unlimited
Automatic Page Numbering: Yes
Automatic Index Generation: No
Automatic Footnoting: No
Automatic Table of Contents: No
Text Wrap from Page to Page and Column to Column: Yes
Wraps Text Around Graphics: Yes
Headers & Footers: Limited

- **EDITING FEATURES**

Globally Edit Text: No
Insert & Remove Pages: Yes
Move Pages: Yes
Move Columns: Yes

- **SUPPORT ETC.**

Warranty: 90 days, media only
Support: Phone and letter
Update Policy: 10% of software cost
Major Reviews: *Computer Graphics World* (March 1987): 113–18.

2.12.4 Typesetting Programs

By *typesetting programs* I am referring to microcomputer-based programs that allow users to enter, manipulate, format, and typeset text (and graphics) on digital typesetters, to programs that (among other things) include drivers for specific typesetters.[210] Although typesetting programs are the next step up from the most powerful desktop publishing programs, typesetting programs are more complex, less user friendly, and include features designed specifically for composing pages for digital typesetters. Because of their specialized application, limited market, and many features, typesetting programs are much more expensive than desktop publishing programs. Microcomputer typesetting programs, however, tend to be considerably less expensive than traditional typesetting programs that run on dedicated, brand-and-program-specific hardware under proprietary operating systems.

I am including this section on typesetting programs because many businesses, institutions, departments, and individuals are discovering that they can save time, cut costs, and exercise more control over the quality of their documents by doing their own typesetting.

---

210. Sometimes these programs are divided into "typesetting front-end" and "page-composition" programs. The former category is used for code-based programs that do not support WYSIWYG editing and/or preview modes and the later category for those programs that do. Front-end programs simplify the process of coding texts for typesetting by allowing codes to be chosen from menus. Page-composition programs are more complex and give users a greater degree of control over page design and layout.

FEATURES	VP	PMₙ	PMₘ	HPP	CA	FP	RSG	RT	MP	PSC	QE	SC	FE	PP	OP	SB	HAL	FI	PWR	PW	PB
BASIC FACTS																					
Price	895	695	495	695	185	695	495	395	195	800	595	495	495	595	995	695	195	895	495	1500+	495
Runs On	I	I	M	I	I	I	M	M	M	M	M	M	I	I	I	I	I	I	I	I	I
Memory (in K)	512	512	512	640	512	512	512	512	512	512	512	1MB	256	640	512	256	512	640	640	512	384
Disk Drives	2	2	1	2	2	2	1	1	1	1	1	1	2	2	2	2	2	2	2	2	2
Supports Mice	●	●	●	●	●	●	●	●	●	●	●	●	●	●	●	○	●	●	○	●	●
Supports Scanners	●	●	●	●	○	●	●	●	●	●	●	●	●	●	●	○	●	●	●	●	●
Supports Full-Page Monitors	●	●	●	○	○	●	○	●	●	●	●	●	○	○	●	●	○	●	●	●	●
Supports PostScript	●	●	●	●	●	●	○	●	●	●	●	○	○	●	●	●	○	●	●	●	○
On-Line Help	○	●	●	●	●	●	○	○	●	●	●	●	●	○	●	○	○	●	○	●	●
User Interface	MD	MD	MD	MD	MD	MD	MD	MD	MD	MD	MD	MD	MD	MD	MD	CD	MD	MD	MD	MD	MD
Interactive WYSIWYG	●	●	●	●	●	●	●	●	●	●	●	●	●	●	●	○	●	●	●	●	●
Maximum Pages Per File	Unl.	128	128	999	99	Unl.	Unl.	350	96	1,000	200	Unl.	128	20	Unl.	Unl.	Unl.	Unl.	Unl.	100	Unl.
TEXT FORMATTING FEATURES																					
Text Formatted in Word Processor	●	●	●	●	○	●	○	●	●	●	●	●	○	●	●	●	●	●	●	○	●
Converts W P Formatting Codes	●	●	●	○	○	●	●	●	●	●	●	●	○	●	●	−	○	○	○	○	●
Imports ASCII Text	●	●	●	●	○	●	●	●	●	●	●	●	○	●	●	●	●	●	●	●	●
Uses Style Sheets	●	○	○	●	○	●	○	○	●	○	○	●	○	○	○	●	○	○	○	○	●
Rule-Based Hyphenation	●	○	○	●	○	●	○	○	○	●	●	○	○	●	●	●	○	●	●	○	○
Dictionary-Based Hyphenation	○	●	●	●	○	○	○	○	○	○	○	○	○	○	○	○	○	○	○	○	○
Automatic Kerning	●	●	○	●	○	●	○	●	●	●	●	●	○	○	●	○	○	●	●	○	●

Table 2.11: Comparison of desktop publishing programs. I = IBM, M = Macintosh, MD = menu-driven, CD = command-driven, VP = Ventura Publisher, PMₙ = PageMaker (IBM), PMₘ = PageMaker (Macintosh), HPP = Harvard Professional Publisher, CA = PFS: ClickArt Personal Publisher, FP = Front Page, RSG = Ready, Set, Go!, RT = Ragtime, MP = MacPublisher II, PSC = PS Compose, QE = Quark Express, SC = Scoop, FE = Form Easy, PP = PagePerfect, OP = The Office Publisher, SB = Spellbinder Desktop Publisher, HAL = Halo DPE, FI = First Impression, PWR = Pagewriter, PW = Pagework, PB = Pagebuilder.

FEATURES	VP	PM₁	PMₘ	HPP	CA	FP	RSG	RT	MP	PSC	QE	SC	FE	PP	OP	SB	HAL	FI	PWR	PW	PB
LAYOUT FEATURES																					
View Full Page	●	●	●	●	●	●	●	●	●	●	●	●	●	●	●	●	●	●	●	●	●
View Facing Pages	●	●	●	○	○	●	●	○	●	○	●	●	●	●	●	○	○	●	○	○	●
Percentage Page Enlargement	200	200	200	150	100	10K	200	100	900	100	200	800	90	600	999	256	800	200	300	500	Unl.
Automatic Column Guides	○	●	●	●	○	○	●	●	●	●	●	●	●	●	●	○	○	●	●	●	●
Adjust Column Widths	●	●	●	●	●	●	●	●	●	●	●	●	●	●	●	●	●	●	●	●	●
Maximum Number Columns	8	20	8	6	4	Unl.	Unl.	Unl.	6	Unl.	10	Unl.	Unl.	Unl.	99	8	Unl.	10	Unl.	Unl.	Unl.
Automatic Page Numbering	●	●	●	●	●	●	●	●	●	●	●	●	●	●	●	●	●	●	●	●	●
Automatic Index Generation	●	○	○	○	○	○	○	○	○	●	●	●	○	○	●	○	●	●	○	○	○
Automatic Footnoting	●	○	○	○	○	○	○	○	○	●	●	●	○	○	●	○	●	●	○	○	○
Automatic Table of Contents	●	○	○	○	○	●	○	○	●	●	●	●	○	●	●	○	●	●	○	○	●
Text Wrap Page/Page & Col./Col.	●	●	●	●	●	●	●	●	●	●	●	●	●	●	●	●	●	●	●	●	●
Wraps Text Around Graphics	●	●	●	●	●	●	●	○	●	●	●	●	○	○	○	○	○	●	○	○	○
Automatic Vertical Justification	○	○	○	○	○	●	○	○	●	●	●	●	●	●	●	○	●	●	○	○	●
Snap-to-Grid	●	●	●	●	●	●	●	●	●	●	●	●	●	●	●	●	●	●	●	●	●
Headers & Footers	●	●	●	●	○	●	●	●	●	●	●	●	●	●	●	●	○	●	●	●	●
EDITING FEATURES																					
Globally Edit Text	○	○	○	●	○	○	●	●	○	●	●	●	●	●	●	●	●	●	○	○	○
Insert & Remove Pages	○	○	●	●	●	●	●	●	●	●	●	●	●	●	●	●	●	●	●	●	●
Move Pages	○	○	○	○	○	●	○	●	○	●	●	●	●	●	●	●	●	●	○	○	●
Move Columns	●	●	●	○	○	●	●	●	○	●	●	●	●	●	●	●	●	●	○	○	●

Table 2.11: Comparison of desktop publishing programs. I = IBM, M = Macintosh, MD = menu-driven, CD = command-driven, VP = Ventura Publisher, PM₁ = PageMaker (IBM), PMₘ = PageMaker (Macintosh), HPP = Harvard Professional Publisher, CA = PFS: ClickArt Personal Publisher, FP = Front Page, RSG = Ready, Set, Go!, RT = Ragtime, MP = MacPublisher II, PSC = PS Compose, QE = Quark Express, SC = Scoop, FE = Form Easy, PP = PagePerfect, OP = The Office Publisher, SB = Spellbinder Desktop Publisher, HAL = Halo DPE, FI = First Impression, PWR = Pagewriter, PW = Pagework, PB = Pagebuilder.

321

Rather than review typesetting programs, I will include a brief bibliography and the basic facts about several of the most powerful programs. The following books and articles provide in-depth information for the interested reader.

Burns, Diane, and S. Venit. "Page Design on the PC Screen." *PC Magazine* (December 10, 1985): 180–210.
———. "PCs and Typesetters." *PC Magazine* (December 10, 1985): 194–202.
———. "Word Into Type." *PC Magazine* (December 10, 1985): 180–82.
Felici, James, and Ted Nace. "Typesetting Point by Point." *PC World* (July 1986): 170–81.
Jantz, Richard. "Step Up to Linotronic Typesetting." *Publish!* (March 1987): 65–70.
Labuz, Ronald. *How to Typeset from a Word Processor: An Interfacing Guide.* New York: Bowker, 1984.
Lem, Dean Phillip, and James O. Cremeans. *Type Processing: The Word Processing/Typesetting Connection.* Dean Lem Associates, Inc., P.O. Box 25920, Los Angeles, CA 90025.
McSherry, James E. *Computer Typesetting: A Guide for Authors, Editors, and Publishers.* Arlington, Va.: Open-Door Press, 1984.
Packard, David W. "Can Scholars Publish Their Own Works?" *Scholarly Publishing* (October 1973): 65–74.
Seybold, John W. *The World of Digital Typesetting.* Media, Penn.: Seybold Publications, 1984.
Ulick, Terry. "Typesetting for Writers." *PC Magazine* (March 19, 1985): 329–30.

2.12.4.1 *Superpage II*

- ## BASIC PRODUCT INFORMATION

Product Name: Superpage II™
Company Name & Address: Bestinfo Inc., Rosetree Corporate Center, 1400 N. Providence Rd., Suite 117, Media PA 19063
Phone: (215) 891-6500
List Price: $7,000
Related Programs: Harvard Professional Publisher, Typedit™, Typesat™
Runs On: IBM PCs and compatibles
Operating System Requirements: DOS 2.0 or greater
Memory Requirements: 640K
Disk Drive Requirements: 2, one of which must be a hard disk with at least 10 free megabytes
Video Cards Supported: HGC, HGC+, Viking™ monitor
Copy Protected: Yes
Possible Backups: Not known
Supports Mice: Yes, mouse recommended
Page Description Languages Supported: PostScript™
Typesetters Supported: Linotype, Compugraphic, and Autologic in slave mode; AM Varityper, Compugraphic, and Itek in direct-entry mode; can generate code for Atex, Penta, CCI, AKI, and Quadex front-end systems.
Printers Supported: IBM Graphics, Epson FX-80, LaserJet, LaserJet Plus, QMS, Imagen, Xerox 2700
User Interface: Menu-driven
Interactive WYSIWYG: Yes
Code-Based: Yes
Other: Supports headers, footers, vertical justification, 80 features per style sheet, 999 pages per document, documents up to 16MB, unlimited number of fonts per page, up to 60,000 characters per page, font sizes from .5 to 127 points in half-point increments, positive and negative leading in half-point increments, unlimited kerning pairs, adjustable word and letter spacing, up to 40 columns per page, 93,000 word hyphenation dictionary—user-expandable—with logic-based hyphenation for words not in dictionary, user-specifiable number of consecutive lines that may end with hyphens, interactive pagination, widow and orphan control, built-in tools for line graphics, importing graphics.
Major Reviews: Diane Burns and S. Venit, "Page Design on the PC Screen," *PC Magazine* (December 10, 1985): 204–10, especially 209–10; "Bestinfo's Superpage II—Beyond Desktop Publishing," *PC Magazine* (February 10, 1987): 174–78.

2.12.4.2 Deskset

● *BASIC PRODUCT INFORMATION*

Product Name: Deskset™
Company Name & Address: G. O. Graphics, 18 Ray Ave., Burlington, MA 01830
Phones: (800) 237-5588, (617) 229-8900
List Price: $995; optional program to drive typesetters is extra.
Related Programs: Horizon Series Composition Management Software
Runs On: IBM PCs and compatibles
Operating System Requirements: DOS 2.0 or greater
Memory Requirements: 512K
Disk Drive Requirements: 2, one of which must be a hard disk.
Video Cards Supported: EGA, HGC, HGC+, Wyse WY-700, Genius VHR
Copy Protected: Yes
Possible Backups: Not known
Supports Mice: Yes, recommended
Page Description Languages Supported: PostScript™
Typesetters Supported: Linotype, Compugraphic
Printers Supported: LaserWriter, LaserWriter Plus, other PostScript™ printers
User Interface: Menu-driven
Interactive WYSIWYG: No
Code-Based: Yes
Other: Primarily intended for use with PostScript™ laser printers. This is *not* a document processor and does
  not support automatic running headers and footers, page breaks, footnotes, and so forth. It does support
  up to 256 kerning pairs, microspacing, adjustable spacebands, adjustable character width tables, macros,
  a preview screen, translating word processing commands into typesetting commands, reverse leading,
  automatic and floating tabs, graphics import, running text around graphics, an unlimited number of
  fonts per line in 248 sizes ranging from 4 to 127.5 points in half-point increments, variable forward and
  backward font slanting, font condensation and expansion.
Major Reviews: Kevin Lippert, "Desktop Typesetting," *Personal Publishing* (March 1987): 88–94; Bill
  Crider, "Typeset Like a Pro," *Publish!* (March 1987): 50–53.

2.12.4.3 MagnaType

● *BASIC PRODUCT INFORMATION*

Product Name: MagnaType™
Company Name & Address: Magna Computer Systems Inc., 14724 Ventura Blvd., Sherman Oaks, CA
  91403
Phone: (818) 986-9233
List Price: $8,500 with typesetter drivers; $5,250 with laser printer drivers only
Related Programs: MagnaWord, MagNet
Runs On: IBM PC-XT, AT and compatibles
Operating System Requirements: DOS 2.0 or greater
Memory Requirements: 512K
Disk Drive Requirements: 2, one of which must be a hard disk.
Video Cards Supported: EGA, CGA, HGC, HGC+, PGA
Copy Protected: Yes (hardware "lock")
Possible Backups: Yes, number not known
Supports Mice: No
Page Description Languages Supported: PostScript™
Typesetters Supported: Linotype, Compugraphic, Autologic, AM Varityper, Tegra, Monotype
Printers Supported: PostScript™ laser printers
User Interface: Menu-driven
Interactive WYSIWYG: No, but supports a passive preview mode.
Code-Based: Yes

323

Other: Supports up to 1,500 automatic kerning pairs per font, four levels of white-space adjustment, up to 40 columns, five methods for hyphenation, hyphenating in six foreign languages, multitasking, widow and orphan control, vertical and horizontal rules, automatic page numbering, vertical justification of single- and multiple-column pages, unlimited fonts per page, and formatting macros. Text globally controlled by predefined or user-defined style sheets. Built-in text editor. Automatically runs text around graphics. Compatible with most RAM-resident MS-DOS programs.

Major Reviews: Diane Burns and S. Venit, "Page Design on the PC Screen," *PC Magazine* (December 10, 1985): 204–10, especially 205–6; James Felici and Walter Omstead, "MagnaType: The Personal Typographer," *PC World* (July 1986): 202–10.

2.12.4.4 DO-IT

- ● *BASIC PRODUCT INFORMATION*

Product Name: DO-IT™
Company Name & Address: Study Soft, 17862-C Fitch, Irvine, CA 99714
Phone: (714) 559-0117
List Price: $2,495
Related Programs: None
Runs On: IBM PCs and compatibles
Operating System Requirements: DOS 2.0 or greater
Memory Requirements: 512K, 640K recommended
Disk Drive Requirements: 2, one of which must be a hard disk.
Video Cards Supported: HGC, HGC+, CGA, EGA
Copy Protected: Not known
Possible Backups: Not known
Supports Mice: Yes
Page Description Languages Supported: PostScript™
Typesetters Supported: Linotype, Alphatype, AM Varityper, Autologic, Compugraphic
Printers Supported: PostScript™ printers
User Interface: Menu-driven
Interactive WYSIWYG: Yes
Code-Based: Not known
Other: Math coprocessor required.
Major Reviews: Diane Burns and S. Venit, "Page Design on the PC Screen," *PC Magazine* (December 10, 1985): 204–10, especially 208–9.

2.12.4.5 ScenicWriter

- ● *BASIC PRODUCT INFORMATION*

Product Name: ScenicWriter™
Company Name & Address: ScenicSoft, Inc., 12314 Scenic Dr., Edmonds, WA 98020
Phone: (206) 776-7760
List Price: $995
Related Programs: None
Runs On: IBM PCs and compatibles
Operating System Requirements: DOS 2.0 or greater
Memory Requirements: 384K
Disk Drive Requirements: 2, one of which must be a hard disk.
Video Cards Supported: Not known
Copy Protected: No
Possible Backups: Unlimited
Supports Mice: No
Page Description Languages Supported: PostScript™
Typesetters Supported: PostScript™, AM Varityper, Linotype
Printers Supported: LaserWriter, LaserWriter Plus, LaserJet, LaserJet Plus
User Interface: Menu-driven
Interactive WYSIWYG: Yes
Code-Based: Yes

Other: Supports automatic indices, footnotes, tables of contents, and cross references, multiple columns, variable justification, headers and footers, tabs, proportional spacing, condensed, and expanded text, baseline shifts, unlimited mixing of fonts, macros, undelete function, many editing features.
Major Reviews: Diane Burns and S. Venit, "Page Design on the PC Screen," *PC Magazine* (December 10, 1985): 204–10, especially 205.

2.12.4.6 DeskSet Design

- ### BASIC PRODUCT INFORMATION

Product Name: DeskSet Design
Company Name & Address: G. O. Graphics, 18 Ray Ave., Burlington, MA 01830
Phones: (800) 237-5588, (617) 229-8900
List Price: $1,995 (Varityper), $1,445 (Compugraphic) including board
Related Programs: None
Runs On: IBM PCs and compatibles
Operating System Requirements: DOS 2.0 or greater
Memory Requirements: 640K
Disk Drive Requirements: 2, one of which must be a hard disk.
Video Cards Supported: CGA, EGA, HGC, HGC+
Copy Protected: Yes
Possible Backups: Yes, number not known
Supports Mice: Yes
Page Description Languages Supported: None
Typesetters Supported: Compugraphic 8000 series, AM Varityper Comp/Set and Comp/Edit
Printers Supported: Canon-engine CX printers, J-Laser board
User Interface: Menu-driven
Interactive WYSIWYG: Yes
Code-Based: Yes
Other: Allows word processing files to be coded for typesetting and then translated into formats compatible with typesetters.
Major Reviews: Diane Burns and S. Venit, "Page Design on the PC Screen," *PC Magazine* (December 10, 1985): 204–10, especially 206.

2.12.4.7 ULTIMATE Professional Publishing System

- ### BASIC PRODUCT INFORMATION

Product Name: ULTIMATE Professional Publishing System
Company Name & Address: Composition Technologies 1000, Inc., 505 Dorchester Blvd. West, Suite 1000, Montreal, Québec H2Z 1A8, Canada
Phone: (514) 875-7586
List Price: $10,000
Related Programs: None
Runs On: IBM PC-ATs and compatibles
Operating System Requirements: DOS 3.2
Memory Requirements: 640K, Intel AboveBoard (or compatible) with 1MB extended memory and 256K expanded memory (LIM EMS)
Disk Drive Requirements: 2, one of which must be a 30-megabyte hard disk.
Video Cards Supported: HGC, HGC+
Copy Protected: Yes
Possible Backups: Unlimited
Supports Mice: No
Page Description Languages Supported: PostScript™
Typesetters Supported: Linotron 202s, Linotronic 100, 202, 300, Compugraphic 8000 series and 9600, AM Varityper, Autologic, Monotype, PostScript™
Printers Supported: PostScript™
User Interface: Command-driven
Interactive WYSIWYG: No, but supports semi-interactive WYSIWYG editing mode and WYSIWYG preview mode.

Code-Based: Yes

Other: Supports 250,000-word, user-expandable hyphenation dictionary and logic-based hyphenation, multiple-language hyphenation dictionaries, multisector kerning (kerns any combination of letters), pairs kerning, 4-track character spacing, 32 horizontal and 32 vertical coordinate markers, rules, boxes, borders, filling, vertical justification, style sheets, multiple tab definition, footnotes, up to six columns per page, and a file importation utility. Includes built-in spell checker and editor.

Major Reviews: None

FEATURES	SP	DS	MT	DI	SW	DSD	UL
Price	7,000	995	8,500	2,495	995	1,445	10,000
Runs On	I	I	I	I	I	I	I
Memory (in K)	640	512	512	512	384	640	640+
Disk Drives	2	2	2	2	2	2	2
Supports Mice	●	●	○	●	○	●	○
Supports PostScript	●	●	●	●	●	○	●
Supports Compugraphic	●	●	●	●	○	●	●
Supports Linotype	●	●	●	●	●	○	●
Supports Autologic	●	○	●	●	○	○	●
Supports Varityper	●	○	○	●	○	●	●
User Interface	MD	MD	MD	MD	MD	MD	CD
Interactive WYSIWYG	●	○	○	●	●	●	○
Code-Based	●	●	●	?	●	●	●

Table 2.12: Comparison of typesetting programs. I = IBM, MD = menu-driven, CD = command-driven, SP = SuperPage II, DS = Deskset, MT = Magna Type, DI = DO-IT, SW = SenicWriter, DSD = DeskSet Design, UL = ULTIMATE Professional Publishing System

2.12.5 Typesetting Services

In lieu of typesetting your own documents, there are a number of services that will do it for you from files you prepare with your word processor. Some of these services require users to insert special typesetting codes in manuscripts that are to be typeset, others typeset directly from coded word processing files.

For more information, see Jeff Frane, "Typeset-Perfect Prose," *PC Magazine* (April 3, 1984): 269–71; Susan Wolbarst, "A PC In The Type Shop: Better Than Dedicated," *PC Magazine* (January 24, 1984): 215–16, 221; Betsy Simnacher, "The Typesetter Connection," *PC Magazine* (April 17, 1984): 309–12, 317; George R. Beinhorn, "Galleys By Phone," *Publish!* (September/October 1986): 56–61; Odvard Egil Dyrli, "Self-Service Publishing," *Publish!* (September/October 1986): 40–43.

2.12.5.1 Intergraphics

Company Name & Address: Intergraphics, Inc., 106 S. Columbus St., Alexandria, VA 22314
Phones: (800) 368-3342, (703) 683-9414
Prices: $2 per 1,000 characters; $5 minimum
Membership Fee: Yes, $25
Method of Payment: MasterCard®, VISA®, American Express®
Method of Communicating Files: Floppy disk or modem
Turnaround Time: 24 to 48 hours
Type of Files Accepted: ASCII
Special Coding Required: Yes
Manual/Style Sheet Available: Yes, $18 for special 220 page guide book
Typefaces Available: Over 200 Merganthaler typefaces

Point Sizes Available: 1 – 72
Other: Optional preview program available.

2.12.5.2 Typeline

Company Name & Address: Typeline, 170 State St., Teaneck, NJ 07666
Phone: (201) 836-2300
Prices: $2.50 per 1,000 characters for regular, non-PostScript; $8 per page for PostScript™ service; $5 minimum
Membership Fee: No
Method of Payment: Account, VISA®, MasterCard®, American Express®, C.O.D.
Method of Communicating Files: Floppy disk or modem
Turnaround Time: 24 hours
Type of Files Accepted: PostScript™ or ASCII
Special Coding Required: No for PostScript™ files, Yes if non-PostScript files are sent
Manual/Style Sheet Available: Yes
Typefaces Available: PostScript™ (approximately 50), ITC
Point Sizes Available: 5 – 72 in half-point increments
Other: None

2.12.5.3 Laser Printing Services

Company Name & Address: Laser Printing Services, 26058 W. 12 Mile Rd., Southfield, MI 48034
Phone: (313) 356-1004
Prices: $8 per page
Membership Fee: None
Method of Payment: Personal and company checks, VISA®, MasterCard®, American Express®, money orders, account
Method of Communicating Files: Floppy disk or modem
Turnaround Time: 24 hours
Type of Files Accepted: This typesetting service accepts files (including PostScript™ files) from a number of application programs for the Macintosh and IBM PC—PageMaker™, Microsoft® Word, Excel™, WordStar®, Lotus 1-2-3™—and typesets directly from those files.
Special Coding Required: No
Manual/Style Sheet Available: Yes
Typefaces Available: PostScript™ (approximately 50)
Point Sizes Available: 1 – 100
Other: None

2.12.5.4 MacTypeNet

Company Name & Address: MacTypeNet™, P.O. Box 52188, Livonia, MI 48152-0188
Phone: (313) 477-2733
Prices: $8 per page (at 1,270 dpi)
Membership Fee: Yes, $25
Method of Payment: Corporate accounts, P.O., VISA®, MasterCard®
Method of Communicating Files: Floppy disk or modem
Turnaround Time: 24 hours
Type of Files Accepted: PostScript™
Special Coding Required: No
Manual/Style Sheet Available: Yes
Typefaces Available: PostScript™ (approximately 150)
Point Sizes Available: 1 – 500
Other: None

2.12.5.5 Sprintout

Company Name & Address: Typesetting Service Corp., Brennan Bldg., 50 Clifford St., Providence, RI 02903
Phones: (401) 421-2264, (800) 777-8973 (modem)
Prices: $5.50 to $10 per page depending on quantity (at 1,270 dpi) plus $1 to $2 per file input charge for PostScript™ files and $2 to $4 per file input charge for non-PostScript files. $1/page surcharge for longer pages. No additional charge for input or for graphics.
Membership Fee: Yes, $60
Method of Payment: VISA®, MasterCard®, American Express®
Method of Communicating Files: Floppy or modem
Turnaround Time: 24 hours
Type of Files Accepted: PostScript™; non-PostScript application files
Special Coding Required: No for PostScript™ and files from most desktop publishing programs
Manual/Style Sheet Available: Not known
Typefaces Available: PostScript™ (more than 150)
Point Sizes Available: 4 – 127
Other: None

2.12.5.6 Aptos Typography

Company Name & Address: Aptos Typography, P.O. Box 910, Aptos, CA 95001
Phone: (408) 688-7474
Prices: $5.97 to $8.96 per page
Membership Fee: No
Method of Payment: Checks only
Method of Communicating Files: Floppy disk or modem
Turnaround Time: 24 to 72 hours
Type of Files Accepted: PostScript™
Special Coding Required: No
Manual/Style Sheet Available: No
Typefaces Available: PostScript™ (more than 200)
Point Sizes Available: 4 – 127
Other: None

FEATURES	IG	TL	LPS	MTN	SO	MTC
Price Per 1,000 Characters (in $)	2	2.50	8/page	8/page	5.5/page	6/page
Membership Fee (in $)	25	0	0	25	60	0
Charge Cards	V,M,A	V,M,A	V,M,A	V,M	V,M,A	0
Send Text on Floppy Disks	●	●	●	●	●	●
Send Text via Modem	●	●	●	●	●	●
24-Hour Turnaround	●	●	●	●	●	●
Accepts ASCII Files	●	●	●	○	●	○
Accepts PostScript Files	○	●	●	●	●	●
Special Coding Required	●	●	○	○	●	○
Manual/Style Sheet	●	●	●	●	○	○
No. of Typefaces Available	200	50	50	150+	150+	200+
Point Sizes Available	1—72	5—72	1—100	1—500	4—127	4—127

Table 2.13: Comparison of typesetting services. V = VISA®, MC = MasterCard®, A = American Express®, IG = Intergraphics, TL = Typeline, LPS = Laser Printing Services, MTN = MacTypeNet, SO = Sprintout, MTC = Mac Typesetting Club

2.12.6 Typesetting Equipment

Here is a list of some of the major typesetters. Earlier in this chapter I defined *digital phototypesetter* as any computer-driven typesetting machine that stores text, graphics, and fonts in digital form and that uses a laser beam or other imaging technology to create images on photographic film that must be processed with a developer. Manufacturers of typesetters that can handle graphics often call their machines "raster image processors" (RIPs) or "page image processors" (PIPs) or "imagesetters," instead of typesetters. (You'll notice that *image* is the common denominator in those three terms.) *Image* is used to indicate that the machines in question do more than electronically set type (words); they can also set graphics. In this context, then, *image* is used to include both *text* and *graphics*. In fact, any output device that creates text-and-graphic images as rasters of dots—bit maps—may be thought of as a RIP, regardless of the medium on which it outputs its images.[211] To allow text and graphics to be mixed together and set electronically (or otherwise), these machines (like PDLs) treat text as a subset of graphics and translate all text and graphics into bit maps. Not all of the typesetters listed below are RIPs in the narrow sense of allowing text and graphics to be mixed.

2.12.6.1 APS-6 Laser Imager with APS-55/800 Page Image Processor

Product Name: APS-6 Laser Imager with APS-55/800 Page Image Processor
Company Name & Address: Autologic, Inc., 1050 Rancho Conejo Blvd., Newbury Park, CA 91320
Phone: (805) 498-9611
Imaging Technique: Laser
PostScript-Compatible Models: No
Maximum Resolution: Up to 1,446 dpi
Maximum Number On-Line Fonts: Up to 1,000 with APS-55/800 Page Image Processor serving as a front-end data file converter
Typefaces Available: 1,000
Type Sizes Supported: 3 – 227 points
Character Rotation: 360 degrees in 0.25-degree increments
Condense/Expand: Complete scaling available
Maximum Line Length: 80 picas
Maximum Page Depth: 24 inches
Maximum Galley Length: 350 feet
Maximum Reverse Feed/Lead: 24 inches
Leading Increments: 1/10 point
Electronic Slant: ± 1 – 45 degrees in 0.25-degree increments
Baseline Jump: Not known
Mirror Imaging: Yes
Rules: Unlimited
Speed: Up to 15 ipm
Output Material: RC paper, film, plate
Input Cassette: 200 feet
CPU: Not known
Memory: 4MB
Options: Not known
Other: When used with the APS-55/500 or the APS-55/800 Page Image Processors, the APS-6 laser Imager can produce tinted, mirrored, and reversed images and rounded corners.
Price Range: $18,500 – $72,500

---

211. Technically it could be argued that any device that outputs images as a raster of dots is a RIP, whether or not such an output device is capable of handling graphics.

2.12.6.2 Varityper 6700 Series

Product Name: Varityper 6700 Series
Company Name & Address: Varityper, 11 Mount Pleasant Ave., East Hanover NJ 07936
Phone: (201) 887-8000
Imaging Technique: CRT
PostScript-Compatible Models: No
Maximum Resolution: 2,602 dpi
Maximum Number On-Line Fonts: Up to 700 with 20MB hard disk
Typefaces Available: Varityper, ITC (over 1,200 fonts)
Type Sizes Supported: 4 – 85 points
Character Rotation: Not available
Condense/Expand: From 2 to 99 points depending on size and character design in 1/36-point increments
Maximum Line Length: 70 picas
Maximum Page Depth: Unlimited
Maximum Galley Length: 150 feet
Maximum Reverse Feed/Lead: 24 inches
Leading Increments: 1/36 point
Electronic Slant: ± 1 – 45 degrees in 1 degree increments
Baseline Jump: 0.25-point increments
Mirror Imaging: Yes
Rules: Unlimited
Speed: Up to 400 lpm depending on model and resolution
Output Material: S paper, RC paper, film in standard widths from 3 to 12 inches
Input Cassette: 150 feet
CPU: None; operates as slave.
Memory: 512K, 1,024K optional
Options: Not known
Price Range: $18,000 – $24,000

2.12.6.3 Compugraphic MCS 8000 Series

Product Name: Compugraphic® MCS™ 8000 Series
Company Name & Address: Compugraphic Corp., 200 Ballardvale St., Wilmington, MA 01887
Phone: (617) 658-5600
Imaging Technique: CRT
PostScript-Compatible Models: Yes, 9600 Series
Maximum Resolution: 2,600 dpi
Maximum Number On-Line Fonts: 16 (8400), 500 when using 500-Font Option, 32- and 116-Font Options also available.
Typefaces Available: 1,700
Type Sizes Supported: 5 – 72 points in half-point increments
Character Rotation: Not available
Condense/Expand: Yes, from 5 to 72 points in half-point increments
Maximum Line Length: 70 picas
Maximum Page Depth: Unlimited
Maximum Galley Length: 20 feet
Maximum Reverse Feed/Lead: 14 inches
Leading Increments: 0 to 999 points in 0.25-point increments
Electronic Slant: ± 31 degrees in 1 degree increments
Baseline Jump: 1/10 point increments
Mirror Imaging: Yes
Rules: Unlimited
Speed: 8000: 50 lpm; 8400: 150 – 250 lpm
Output Material: RC paper, S paper, film, in 3-, 4-, 6-, 8-, and 10-inch widths
Input Cassette: 150 feet
CPU: Not known
Memory: Not known
Options: Various font options, High-Sped Option (increases throughput speed), H&J Controller, Multiport Serial Interface
Price Range: $14,950 (8000) – $50,000 (8600)

2.12.6.4 *Linotronic Series 100 and Series 200*

Product Name: Linotronic™ Series 100 and Series 200
Company Name & Address: Linotype Company, A Division of Allied-Signal, 425 Oser Ave., Hauppauge, NY 11788
Phone: (516) 434-2000
Imaging Technique: Laser
PostScript-Compatible Models: Yes
Maximum Resolution: 2,540 dpi on Linotronic™ 300
Maximum Number On-Line Fonts: 24 in Linotronic™ 300 font RAM plus disk capacity
Typefaces Available: Mergenthaler
Type Sizes Supported: 1 – 186 points in 1/10 point increments
Character Rotation: 360 degrees in 1/10 point increments
Condense/Expand: Characters may be expanded up to 500% of original set width and condensed up to 50% of original set width in 1% increments.
Maximum Line Length: 72 picas
Maximum Page Depth: 154.8 picas (composed page)
Maximum Galley Length: 98 feet
Maximum Reverse Feed/Lead: 154 picas
Leading Increments: 1/10 point
Electronic Slant: ± 1 – 45 degrees in 1 degree increments
Baseline Jump: 1/10 point increments
Mirror Imaging: Yes
Rules: Limited only by setting format of 72 × 165.8 picas
Speed: Up to 255 lpm depending on operating mode
Output Material: RC paper, S paper, film, in 4-, 6-, 8-, 10-, or 12-inch widths
Input Cassette: Maximum of 196 feet by 12 inches
CPU: Motorola 68000
Memory: 1.5MB
Options: Graphics input port, tints and patterns generator, PostScript™ processor
Price Range: $29,950 – $59,000

2.12.6.5 *Genesis XM*

Product Name: Genesis™ XM
Company Name & Address: Tegra, Inc., Middlesex Technology Center, 900 Middlesex Turnpike, Billerica, MA 01821
Phone: (617) 663-7435
Imaging Technique: Laser
PostScript-Compatible Models: No
Maximum Resolution: 1,000 dpi on plain paper, 2,000 dpi on RC paper
Maximum Number On-Line Fonts: Up to 300 with optional 20MB hard disk
Typefaces Available: Bitstream™, ITC
Type Sizes Supported: 4.5 – 127 points
Character Rotation: 360 degrees in 90 degree increments
Condense/Expand: Yes
Maximum Line Length: 65 picas
Maximum Page Depth: Unlimited
Maximum Galley Length: 6 feet
Maximum Reverse Feed/Lead: Not applicable; sets images as a raster.
Leading Increments: 1/8 point
Electronic Slant: Yes
Baseline Jump: Yes
Mirror Imaging: Yes
Rules: Unlimited, 0.25 point minimum
Speed: 1,500 lpm without XM option, 215 lpm with XM option
Output Material: Plain paper, S paper, RC paper, film, plate
Input Cassette: 100 feet
CPU: Not known
Memory: Not known
Options: Emulators for Linotron 202, Compugraphic 8400 and 8600
Price: $37,500 – $61,000

FEATURES	APS-6	VT 6700	CG 8000	LT 100,200	GS XM
Imaging Technique	Laser	CRT	CRT	Laser	Laser
PostScript Compatible Models	○	○	●	●	○
Maximum Resolution (in DPI)	1,446	2,602	2,600	2,540	1,000
Maximum Number On-Line Fonts	1,000	700	500	24	300
Number Available Typefaces	1,000	1200+	1,700	?	?
Type Sizes Supported (in Points)	3—227	4—85	5—72	1—186	4.5—127
Character Rotation	360°	○	○	360°	360°
Condense/Expand	●	●	●	●	●
Maximum Line Length (in Picas)	80	70	70	72	65
Maximum Page Depth (in Inches)	24	Unl.	14	25⅔	Unl.
Maximum Reverse Feed/Lead (in Inches)	24	24	14	25⅔	—
Leading Increments (in Points)	1/10	1/36	1/4	1/10	1/8
Electronic Slant	1—45°	1—45°	1—31°	1—45°	●
Mirror Imaging	●	●	●	●	●
Maximum Number of Rules	Unl.	Unl.	Unl.	Unl.	?
Speed	15 ipm	400 lpm	100 lpm	255 lpm	1,500 lpm
Output on RC Paper	●	●	●	●	●
Output on Film	●	●	●	●	●
Output on Plate	●	○	○	○	●
Price Range (in Thousands of $)	18.5—72.5	18—24	15—50	29.95—59	37.5—61

Table 2.14: Comparison of typesetting equipment. ipm = inches per minute, lpm = lines per minute, APS = APS-6 Laser Imager with APS-55/800 Page Image Processor, VT 6700 = Varityper 6700 Series, CG 8000 = Compugraphic MCS 8000 Series, LT 100, 200 = Linotronic Series 100 and Series 200, GS XM = Genesis XM

Bibliographical Resources

The following publications provide information about the types of programs reviewed in this chapter. Addresses and phones numbers are those of the circulation/subscription offices.

A+
% Subscription Services
P.O. Box 56493
Boulder, CO 80321-6493
(800) 525-0643, (303) 477-9330 (Canada)
Monthly, magazine, $24.97/year. Popular reviews and news of
        products for the Apple II family of microcomputers.

Bits & Bytes Review™
% Bits and Bytes Computer Resources
623 Iowa Ave.
Whitefish, MT 59937
(406) 862-7280
9 times a year, newsletter, $40/year (students), $55/year
        (faculty), $70/year (institutions); Canadian and
        international subscriptions higher. Moderately
        technical, in-depth reviews of hardware and
        software for IBM PCs and Macintoshes. News and
        information about academic computing.

BYTE
% McGraw-Hill, Inc.
One Phoenix Mill Lane
Peterborough, NH 03458
(603) 924-9281
Monthly, magazine, $22/year. Technical reviews of
        microcomputer hardware, software, and
        programming languages for microcomputers;
        industry news.

The Hebrew Users' Group Newsletter
% Berkeley Hillel Foundation
2736 Bancroft Way
Berkeley, CA 94704
(415) 845-7793
Quarterly, newsletter, $7.50/year (North America), $10/year
        (outside North America). News and brief reviews of
        products for Hebrew/English word processing,
        desktop publishing, and related topics.

InfoWorld
% InfoWorld
P.O. Box 5994
Pasadena, CA 91107
(818) 577-7233
Weekly, tabloid, free to qualified individuals, $100/year
        otherwise. IBM PC and Macintosh product reviews.
        Up-to-the-minute news coverage and industry
        analysis. An excellent news source.

The Macintosh Buyer's Guide
℅ Redgate Communications Corp.
660 Beachland Blvd.
Vero Beach, FL 32963
(305) 231-96904
5 times per year, catalog, $14/year. Comprehensive listing of
hardware and software for Macintoshes. Very useful.

Macintosh Today
℅ Macintosh Today
P.O. Box 5456
Pasadena, CA 91107-9896
(415) 978-3370
Biweekly, tabloid, free to qualified individuals, $125/year
otherwise. Macintosh product reviews. Up-to-the-
minute news coverage and industry analysis. An
excellent news source.

MacUser
℅ Subscription Services
P.O. Box 56986
Boulder, CO 80321-6986
(800) 525-0643, (303) 477-9330 (Canada)
Monthly, $27/year, magazine. Reviews and news of Macintosh
products. Less technical than *Macworld*.™

MacWEEK™
℅ MacWEEK, Inc.
525 Brannan St.
San Francisco, CA 94107
(415) 882-7370
Weekly, tabloid, free to qualified individuals. Macintosh
product reviews. Up-to-the-minute news coverage
and industry analysis.

Macworld™
℅ Subscription Services
P.O. Box 54529
Boulder, CO 80322-4529
(800) 525-0643
Monthly, magazine, $29.90/year. Moderately technical reviews
of hardware and software for Macintoshes. The best
magazine about Macintoshes.

microPublishing Report
℅ Micro Publishing
2004 Curtis Ave., #A
Redondo Beach, CA 90278
(213) 376-5724
Monthly, newsletter, $175/year. Reviews of microcomputer
products for desktop publishing, page layout, and
typesetting; industry news.

Microsoft® Systems Journal
℅ Circulation Dept.
Microsoft Systems Journal
P.O. Box 1903
Marion, OH 44305
(800) 533-6625, (800) 633-3157 (OH)
Bimonthly, magazine, $50/year. Technical reviews and
information about software, hardware, and
programming languages pertaining to Microsoft®
operating systems and programs.

nibble® Mac®
% MicroSPARC, Inc.
52 Domino Dr.
Concord, MA 01742
(617) 371-1660
Bimonthly, magazine, $27.95/year. Reviews of products for
    Macintoshes.

PC Magazine
% Subscription Services
P.O. Box 2443
Boulder, CO 80322
(800) 525-0643, (303) 477-9330 (Canada)
22 issues/year, magazine, $39.97/year. Reviews of IBM PC
    hardware and software; industry news. Frequent
    multi-product, comparative-type reviews. The best
    magazine about IBM PCs.

PC Tech Journal
% Subscription Services
P.O. Box 2698
Boulder, CO 80321
(800) 525-0643, (303) 447-9330 (Canada)
13 issues/year, magazine, $29.97/year. Technical reviews of
    IBM PC hardware, software, and programming
    languages.

PC Week
% Ziff-Davis Pub. Co.
One Park Ave.
New York, NY 10016
(212) 503-5444
Weekly, tabloid, free to qualified individuals. IBM PC product
    reviews. Up-to-the-minute news coverage and
    industry analysis.

PC World
% Subscription Services
P.O. Box 55029
Boulder, CO 80322-5029
(800) 642-9606
Monthly, magazine, $29.90/year. Reviews of IBM PC hardware
    and software. Less technical than *PC Magazine* and
    PC Tech Journal.

Personal Publishing
% The Renegade Co.
P.O. Box 390
Itasca, IL 60143
(312) 250-8900
Monthly, magazine, $30/year. Reviews of desktop publishing
    products for IBM PCs and Macintoshes. The best
    specialized source of information on this topic.

Profiles
% PROFILES Subscriptions
P.O. Box 2889
Del Mar, CA 92014
(619) 481-4353
Monthly, magazine, $25/year. Reviews of hardware and
    software for Kaypro computers. Reviews of CP/M
    software.

Publish!
% Subscription Services
P.O. Box 55400
Boulder, CO 80322
(800) 222-2990, (303) 447-9330 (CO)
Monthly, magazine, $39.90/year. Reviews of desktop
        publishing products for IBM PCs and Macintoshes.

Research in Word Processing Newsletter
% South Dakota School of Mines and Technology
Rapid City, SD 57701-3995
(605) 394-2481
9 times a year, newsletter, $15 (US), $21 (Canada), $27
        (foreign). Brief reviews of word processing and
        related programs.

The Seybold Report on Desktop Publishing
% Seybold Publications
P.O. Box 644
Media, PA 19063
(215) 565-2480
Monthly, newsletter, $192/year. Reviews of microcomputer
        products for desktop publishing; industry news.

Tugboat
% TEX Users Group
P.O. Box 9506
Providence, RI 02940
No listed number
3 times a year, journal, $30 (North America), $40 (outside
        North America). Technical reviews of TEX
        products, including TEX, METAFONT, program
        listings, macros, and news. This is the TEX Users
        Group Newsletter.

TypeWorld®
% TypeWorld Publications
P.O. Box 170
35 Pelham Rd.
Salem, NH 03079
(603) 898-2822
Biweekly, tabloid, $25/year. Reviews and industry news of
        typesetting products.

Wheels for the Mind
% Apple Computer, Inc.
Wheels for the Mind 23L
P.O. Box 810
Cupertino, CA 95015
(408) 973-2222
Quarterly, journal, $12/year. Comprehensive information
        about the ways Macintoshes are being used in the
        academic environment, including information
        about software, development kits, programming
        languages, university projects, and more.

Bibliography

Note: This selected bibliography does not contain single-program reviews. To locate articles on specific programs, readers should turn to the review of the program and look under the heading marked **Major Reviews** or **Reviews**.

Adrian, Merv. "Major Word Processors Get Better." *PC Magazine* (May 26, 1987): 199–233.

Alsop, Stewart. "Desktop Publishing without HYPE." *PC Magazine* (February 10, 1987): 111–15.

_____. "The Enhanced Graphics Standard Comes of Age." *PC Magazine* (August 1986): 141–43.

_____. "Is Desktop Publishing Fit To Print?" *PC Magazine* (October 14, 1986): 117–18.

Anderson, Lloyd. "Multi-Lingual Word Processing Systems: Desirable Features from a Linguist's Point of View." *Newsletter for Asian and Middle Eastern Languages on Computer* 1 (January 1985): 28–30.

Bagnall, Roger S. *Word Processing for the Classicist.* American Philological Association, Committee on Education, Educational Papers 2, 1985.

Becker, Joseph D. "Multilingual Word Processing." *Scientific American* 251 (1984): 96–107.

Bell, Norman T., and James W. Warner. "Desktop Publishing: A New Frontier for Instructional Technologists." *T.H.E. Journal* 14 (August 1986): 71–73.

Bermant, Charles. "Five Thesaurus Selections Synonymous with Success." *PC Magazine* (June 24, 1986): 42, 44.

Bernard, Josef. "HP's New LaserJet Printer." *Computers and Electronics* (July 1984): 36–87.

Biel, Don. "A Page Maker Talks about Pagination." *Personal Publishing* (February 1986): 18–19.

Bonoma, Thomas V. "The Word on Word Processors." *Microcomputing* (November 1984): 86–99.

Boudrot, Thomas E. *Byte-Sized Activities: The Generic Word Processing Book.* Glenview, Ill.: Scott, Foresman, & Co., 1985.

Bove, Tony, and Cheryl Rhodes. "Camera-Ready?" *Publish!* (November/December 1986): 64–68.

Bove, Tony, Cheryl Rhodes, and Wes Thomas. *The Art of Desktop Publishing.* Bantam Computer Books, 1986.

Boyle, F. Ladson. "Memory-Resident Spelling Checkers." *The Lawyer's PC* 4 (November 1, 1986): 8–11.

Brown, Eric. "Building Manuscripts Block By Block." *PC World* (May 1987): 214–23.

_____. "Word Processing and the Three Bears." *PC World* (December 1985): 193–201.

Burke, James. *Connections.* Boston: Little, Brown and Co., 1979.

Burns, Diane, and S. Venit. "Desktop Publishing: If the Term Fits." *PC Magazine* (October 13, 1987): 159–68.

_____. "Desktop Publishing: Outfitting Your System." *PC Magazine* (October 13, 1987): 179–82.

_____. "Gaining on the Mac." *PC Magazine* (October 13, 1987): 137–57.

_____. "Laser Printers at the Cutting Edge." *PC Magazine* (December 10, 1985): 184–92.

_____. "Muscling in on the MAC: PC-Based Page Composition." *PC Magazine* (February 10, 1987): 119–56.

_____. "Page Design on the PC Screen." *PC Magazine* (December 10, 1985): 180–210.

_____. "PC Desktop Publishing Comes of Age." *PC Magazine* (October 13, 1987): 92–132.

_____. "PCs and Typesetters." *PC Magazine* (December 10, 1985): 194–202.

_____. "PC vs. Mac: An Unfair Match?" *PC Magazine* (July 23, 1985): 110–31.

_____. "Stacking Up to the MAC." *PC Magazine* (February 10, 1987): 159–72.

_____. "Word Into Type." *PC Magazine* (December 10, 1985): 180–82.

Carney, T. F. "Personal Publishing on Microcomputers." *Research in Word Processing Newsletter* 4 (April 1986): 2–11.

Caruso, Denise. "New Ways to Outline Your Ideas." *Personal Computing* (September 1986): 79–83.

Casella, Phil. "Tracking Electronic Paper." *InfoWorld* (May 6, 1985): 67–72.

Cavuoto, James. *LaserPrint It!.* Reading, Mass.: Addison Wesley Pub. Co., 1986.

Celko, Joe. "The ABCs of H&J." *Personal Publishing* (August 1986): 18–21.

Christian, Kaare. "Lasers Get Graphic." *PC Magazine* (September 17, 1985): 211–14.

_____. "Scientific Word Processing." *PC Magazine* (May 28, 1985): 285–86.

Cockerham, John T. "The EGA Spectrum. Part 1." *PC Tech Journal* (October 1986): 80–86.

_____. "The EGA Spectrum. Part 2." *PC Tech Journal* (November 1986): 147–63.

Cole, Bernard Conrad. *Beyond Word Processing*. New York: McGraw-Hill, 1985.

Coleman, Dale, and Arthur Naiman. *The Macintosh Bible*. Berkeley, Calif.: Goldstein and Blair, 1986.

Conkey, Don, and Sharyn Conkey. "A Printer Shopping List." *PC World* (November 1985): 133–43.

Corr, Robert M. "Careful Selection of Components Key to Assembling PC Publishing System." *InfoWorld* (November 10, 1986): 47.

Cowart, Robert. "Key Tronic." *PC Magazine* (July 9, 1985): 162–70.

Crawford, Chris. "The Macintosh Plus." *BYTE* (November 1986): 247–51.

Crider, Bill. "Every Word a Key." *PC World* (October 1985): 192–95.

D'Acquisto, Dominic R. "Macintosh Publishing." *Personal Publishing* (November 1986): 32–36.

Datz, Terry Tinsley. "Word Processing Tips." *PC Magazine* (May 1985): 240–47.

Datz, Terry Tinsley, and F. Lloyd Datz. "The Processed Word." *Softalk* (August 1983): 49–53.

Davis, Frederic E., John Barry, and Michael Wiesenberg. *Desktop Publishing*. Homewood, Ill.: Dow Jones-Irwin, 1986.

DeLoach, Allen. "Custom Characters." *PC Tech Journal* (October 1985): 45.

Derval, Bernard, and Michel Lenoble, eds. *La Critique Litteraire et L'Ordinateur*. Québec: Derval and Lenoble, 1985.

Devlin, Joe. "Desktop Publishing Is Breaking the Print Barrier." *Computer Dealer* 9 (March 1986): 28–33.

Dickinson, John. "Connecting the Dots." *PC Magazine* (November 27, 1984): 260–70.

_____. "Dot Matrix Printer Character Building." *PC Magazine* (November 27, 1984): 134–260.

_____. "Editor's Choice." *PC Magazine* (September 17, 1985): 194–98.

_____. "Getting Graphics to Speak ASCII." *PC Magazine* (September 17, 1985): 243–45.

_____. "Laser Printers." *PC Magazine* (September 17, 1985): 208–9.

_____. "Printer Guide." *PC Magazine* (September 17, 1985): 183–93.

_____. "Printers." *PC Magazine* (September 17, 1985): 92–180.

Dickinson, John, et al. "The Business of Words: Corporate, Professional, Personal." *PC Magazine* (January 1986): 93–251.

_____. "The Business of Words: Outlines." *PC Magazine* (March 25, 1986): 199–220.

_____. "The Business of Words: Special Purpose." *PC Magazine* (February 25, 1986): 177–214.

_____. "Lexical Electronic Filing." *PC Magazine* (August 20, 1985): 137–44.

Dobrin, David N. "Style Analyzers Once More." *Computers and Composition* 3 (August 1986): 22–32.

Duncan, Ray. "Graphics on the IBM Monochrome Display." *PC Tech Journal* (March 1984): 142–53.

Dvorak, John C. "Wysiwyg Mania." *PC Magazine* (October 14, 1986): 77.

Edwards, Jon. "RAM-Resident Utilities." *BYTE* (Summer 1987 Bonus Edition): 103–18.

Eiser, Leslie. "I Luv To Rite: Spelling Checkers in the Writing Classroom." *Computer Classroom Learning* 7 (November/December 1986): 50–57.

Felici, James, and Ted Nace. "Typesetting Point by Point." *PC World* (July 1986): 170–81.

Fluegelman, Andrew, and Jeremy Joan Hewes. *Writing in the Computer Age: Word Processing Skills and Style for Every Writer*. New York: Anchor, 1983.

Foster, Edward. "Outlining: A New Way of Thinking." *Personal Computing* (May 1985): 74–83.

_____. "Word Processing." *InfoWorld* (January 12, 1987): 35–43.

Gallagher, Brian. *Microcomputer Word Processing Programs: An Evaluation and Critique*. New York: Instructional Resource Center of CUNY, 1985.

Gantz, John. "Will Desktop Publishing Turn Out To Be a Mirage?" *InfoWorld* (February 16, 1987): 31.

Gardner, Michael. "A Streamlined LaserJet." *PC World* (August 1987): 229–33.

Gibson, Steve. "Understanding the Mysterious Role Software Device Drivers Play in Our Industry." *InfoWorld* (October 20, 1986): 59.

Good, Phillip. *Choosing a Word Processor*. Mattawan, Mich.: Information Research, 1982.

Green, Michael. *Zen and the Art of the Macintosh: Discoveries on the Path to Computer Enlightenment*. Philadelphia: Running Press Book Pub., 1986.

Grout, Bill, Irene Athanasopoulos, and Rebecca Kutlin. *Desktop Publishing from A to Z*. Berkeley: Osborne McGraw-Hill, 1986.

Harriman, Cynthia W. "MacCharlie Shown Promise But Needs Some Refinements." *InfoWorld* (September 16, 1985): 48, 50.

_____. "Mac Plus Makes Clear Difference." *InfoWorld* (April 14, 1986): 52–53.

Hart, Glenn A. "Harnessing the Laser Printer." *PC Magazine* (February 11, 1986): 205–15.

_____. "IBM Sets a New Standard." *PC Magazine* (December 25, 1984): 171–78.

Hart, Glen A., and Jim Forney. "Adapted for the Screen." *PC Magazine* (February 19, 1985): 116–82.

Harts, Bill. "The Little Engine That Could." *PC Magazine* (September 17, 1985): 210–11.

_____. "The Ricoh Laser Engine." *PC Magazine* (November 11, 1986): 353–56.

Harts, Bill, and John Dickinson. "Picking a Winner." *PC Magazine* (November 27, 1984): 130–32.

Heid, Jim. "Laserjet or Laserwriter?" *Publish!* (September/October 1986): 34–40.

Hershey, William. "Idea Processors." *BYTE* (June 1985): 337–50.

Hession, William, and Malcom Rubel. *Performance Guide to Word Processing Software*. New York: McGraw-Hill, 1985.

Holmes, Thom. "Make My Page!" *BYTE* (May 1987): 159–66.

Information Research, *Word Processing Comparison Tables*. Mattawan, Mich.: Information Research, 1985.

Hewitt, Helen-Jo Jakusz. "Computers, Bibliography, and Foreign Language Typography." *CHum* 19 (April–June 1985): 89–95.

Hockey, Susan. "Input and Output of Non-Standard Character Sets." *ALLC Bull.* (Summer 1973): 32–37.

Hoffmann, Thomas V. "Graphic Enhancement." *PC Tech Journal* (April 1985): 58–77.

Hughes, John J. "Four Stand-Alone, MS-DOS Spelling Programs." *Bits & Bytes Review*™ 1 (April 1987): 1–17.

Jantz, Richard. "Design Pros Take to the Desktop." *Publish!* (November/December 1986): 72–79.

_____. "Step Up to Linotronic Typesetting." *Publish!* (March 1987): 65–70.

Jenkins, Avery. "Desktop Publishing." *PC Week* (September 9, 1986): 49–52.

Kemp, William. "The Global Microcomputer: Multi-Lingual Word Processing with the Macintosh." *Research in Word Processing Newsletter* 4 (November 1986): 2–8.

Kinkead, Joyce. "Matching Software and Curriculum: A Description of Four Text-Analysis Programs." *Computers and Composition* 3 (August 1986): 33–35.

Kleper, Michael L. *The Illustrated Handbook of Desktop Publishing and Typesetting*. Blue Ridge Summit, Penn.: TAB Books, 1987.

Knorr, Eric. "Display Intelligence." *PC World* (February 1987): 198–209.

Knorr, Eric, and Karl Koessel. "Seven Up on EGA." *PC World* (August 1986): 210–19.

Knorr, Eric, and Robert Luhn. "Personal Publishing in Black and White." *PC World* (July 1986): 183–88.

Knuth, Donald E. *The T$_E$Xbook*. Reading, Mass.: Addison Wesley Pub. Co., 1986. Cf. Knuth's four other volumes in the series "Computers and Typesetting" (see above under "T$_E$X.")

Kovacs, Deborah. "Turning First Drafts Into Final Drafts." *Classroom Computer Learning* 7 (October 1986): 36–39.

Labuz, Ronald. *How to Typeset from a Word Processor: An Interfacing Guide*. New York: Bowker, 1984.

Lawrence, John Shelton. *The Electronic Scholar: A Resource Guide to Academic Microcomputing*. Norwood, N.J.: Ablex Pub. Corp., 1984.

Lem, Dean Phillip. *Graphics Master 3*. Los Angeles: Dean Lem Assoc., 1986.

Lem, Dean Phillip, and James O. Cremeans. *Type Processing: The Word Processing/Typesetting Connection*. Dean Lem Associates, Inc., P.O. Box 25920, Los Angeles, CA 90025.

Leserman, David H. *MacFonts*. New York: McGraw-Hill, 1985.

Lewis, Barbara, and Robert Lewis. "Do Style Checkers Work Work?" *PC World* (July 1987): 246–52.

McGovern, Edmond. *Word Processing: A Writer's Guide*. Exeter: Globefield Press, 1985.

McKenzie, Alan T., ed. *A Grin on the Interface: Word Processing for the Academic Humanist*. New York: The Modern Language Association of America, 1984.

McSherry, James E. *Computer Typesetting: A Guide for Authors, Editors, and Publishers*. Arlington, Va.: Open-Door Press, 1984.

McWilliams, Peter A. *The Word Processing Book*. Garden City, N.Y.: Doubleday, 1984.

Machrone, Bill. "Desktop Publishing: Fact or Fiction." *PC Magazine* (July 1986): 61.

_____. "Manuscript Whips Large Documents Into Shape." *PC Magazine* (February 10, 1987): 33, 35.

_____. "Waiting for WYSIWYG." *PC Magazine* (August 20, 1985): 59–61.

Machrone, Bill, and John Dickinson. "A Hard Look at Hard Copy." *PC Magazine* (November 27, 1984): 116–23.

Makuta, Daniel J., and William F. Lawrence. *The Complete Desktop Publisher*. Greensboro, N.C.: Compute! Publications, 1986.

Marshak, R. *Word Processing Software for the IBM PC*. New York: McGraw Hill, 1985.

Martin, Janette. "Laser Printers." *PC World* (September 1984): 83–91.

_____. "New Dimensions in Word Processing." *PC Magazine* (January 1985): 42–51.

Martinez, Thomas E., ed. *Collected Essays on the Written Word and the Word Processor*. Villanova, Penn.: Villanova Press, 1984.

Meilach, Dona Z. *Before You Buy Word Processing Software*. New York: Crown, 1984.

Melymuka, Kathleen. "Text-Retrieval Software." *PC Week* (February 1986): 57–59.

Mendelson, Edward. "Clonkers and Coolitude: Spelling Checkers Get Better." *PC Magazine* (October 13, 1987): 349–87

_____. "Word Processing: A Continuing Guide for the Perplexed." *The Yale Review* 75 (1986): 454–80.

_____. "Word Processing: A Guide for the Perplexed." *The Yale Review* 74 (1985): 615–40.

MicroPublishing Report. *Directory of Suppliers.* Redondo Beach, Calif.: MicroPublishing, 1986.

Miller, Michael J. "Mac Plus: Not Perfect, But It Fixes Some Faults." *InfoWorld* (January 20, 1986): 30.

Mohammadioun, Said. "Waiting for Quality Word Processing." *PC Magazine* (January 22, 1985): 85.

Musa, F. A. "A System for Processing Bilingual Arabic/English Text." *Journal of the Society for Information Science* 37 (September 1986): 288–93.

Nace, Ted. *LaserJet Unlimited.* Berkeley, Calif.: Peachpit Press, 1986.

_____. *Ventura Tips and Tricks.* Berkeley: Peachpit Press, 1987.

Noble, David F., and Virginia Noble. *Improve Your Writing with Word Processing.* Indianapolis: Que Corporation, 1984.

Norton, Peter. "Choosing Character Sets with EGA." *PC Magazine* (November 26, 1985): 79–84.

_____. "Display Screen Issues, *PC Magazine* (July 1986): 73–75.

_____. *Inside the IBM PC. Access to Advanced Features and Programming.* Bowie, Md.: Robert J. Brady Co., 1983.

_____. *Inside the IBM PC. Access to Advanced Features and Programming.* Revised and Enlarged. New York: Robert J. Brady Co., 1986.

_____. *Programmer's Guide to the IBM PC.* Bellevue, Wash.: Microsoft Press, 1985.

_____. "The Vagaries of WYSIWYG." *PC Magazine* (September 3, 1985): 83–85.

O'Brien, Bill. "Pluses for Your HP Laserjet." *PC Magazine* (April 28, 1987): 161–73.

O'Malley, Christopher. "Going Beyond Word Processing." *Personal Computing* (December 1985): 113–21.

_____. "Word Processing Programs with Spelling Checkers for IBM, AT&T, COMPAQ and Other Compatible Personal Computers." *Software Digest Ratings Newsletter* 2 (January 1985): 1–76.

O'Shea, John B. "Document-Oriented Vs. Page-Oriented Word Processors." *PC Week* (July 16, 1985): 73–74.

Obregon, David. "Power Plays At Your Keyboard." *PC Magazine* (October 29, 1985): 167–75.

Packard, David W. "Can Scholars Publish Their Own Works?" *Scholarly Publishing* (October 1973): 65–74.

Pappas, Chris H., and William H. Murray. "EGA Times 12." *BYTE* (January 1987): 313–18.

Pearlman, Dara. "A Footnote to Word Processing." *PC Magazine* (August 20, 1985): 177–80.

Pepper, Jon. "Banish Typos with Spelling Checkers." *PC Magazine* (December 24, 1985): 199–213.

Petzold, Charles. "Achieving The Standard: 12 EGA Boards." *PC Magazine* (August 1986): 145–82.

_____. "The EGA Standard: Monitors That Measure Up." *PC Magazine* (March 25, 1986): 109–19.

_____. "Exploring the EGA, Part 1." *PC Magazine* (August 1986): 367–84.

_____. "Exploring the EGA, Part 2." *PC Magazine* (September 16, 1986): 287–313.

_____. "Keyboard Macros and Redefinition." *PC Magazine* (June 24, 1986): 255–65.

_____. "New Hercules Card Bridges World of Text, Graphics." *PC Magazine* (August 1986): 51–52.

Petzold, Charles, and Winn L. Rosch. "Four-Figure Video." *PC Magazine* (May 26, 1987): 235–74.

Pfaffenberger, Bryan. *The College Students Personal Computing Handbook.* Berkeley: Sybex, 1984.

_____. *Macintosh for College Students.* Berkeley: Sybex, 1984.

_____. *The Scholars Personal Computing Handbook: A Practical Guide.* Boston: Little, Brown and Co., 1986.

_____. "A Typology of Word-Processing Programs." *Research in Word Processing Newsletter* 4 (February 1986): 2–15.

Poor, Alfred. "Advanced Tech Print: Speeding Ahead." *PC Magazine* (November 27, 1984): 392–99.

_____. "Laser Tag." *PC Magazine* (July 1987): 269–86.

_____. "MacCharlie Bridges the Gap." *PC Magazine* (November 26, 1985): 179–84.

_____. "Printer Utilities." *PC Magazine* (September 17, 1985): 219–40.

Poor, Alfred, and Bill Machrone. "Laser Printer Technology." *PC Magazine* (April 28, 1987): 123–45.

Posa, Thomas. "This Keyboard Is a Ball." *InfoWorld* (May 13, 1985): 56.

Price, Anne Jamison. "A Survey of Computer Use in Projects Sponsored by the National Endowment for the Humanities." Washington: The Office of Scholarly Communication and Technology, 1986.

Rabinovitz, Rubin. "A Way with Words." *PC Magazine* (July 1987): 249–66.

Ranney, Elizabeth. "Apple Planning 'Open' Mac." *InfoWorld* (January 20, 1986): 1, 8.

Rardin, Kevin. *Desktop Publishing on the Mac.* New York: Plume/Waite, 1986.

Raskin, Robin. "More Power for the Money." *PC Magazine* (February 24, 1987): 127–73.

_____. "The Quest for Style." *PC Magazine* (May 27, 1986): 189–207.

Raskin, Robin, and Kaare Christian. "Manuscript: A Technical Writer's Tool Kit." *PC Magazine* (April 14, 1987): 143–52.

Reed, A. "Anatomy of a Text Analysis Package." *Computer Languages* 9 (1984): 89–96.

Ritvo, Ken, and Greg Kearsley. *Desktop Publishing.* La Jolla, Calif.: Park Row Press, 1986.

Roberts, Catherine. *Desktop Publishing & Beyond.* Greenwich, Conn.:Havemeyer Books, 1987.

Rosch, Winn L. "New Looks for Replacement Keyboards." *PC Magazine* (January 14, 1986): 203–20.

_____. "A Superset of Graphics Standards." *PC Magazine* (December 24, 1985): 147–58.

Rosenthal, Steve. "Electro-Optical Printers: Beyond the Cutting Edge." *PC Magazine* (September 17, 1985): 214–16.
_____. "How PC Printers Make Their Mark." *PC Magazine* (November 27, 1984): 124–29.
_____. "Printers for Publishing." *PC Week* (March 11, 1986): 53–55.
_____. "Writing Utilities: PC Wordworking Tools Carve Their Niche Among Perfectionists." *PC Week* (April 8, 1986): 57–59.
Roth, Steve. "Getting Wyse." *Personal Publishing* (June 1986): 38, 41.
_____. "J-Laser Printing." *Personal Publishing* (October 1986): 46–50.
_____. "Publishing On IBMs." *Personal Publishing* (November 1986): 38–54.
_____. "Processing Copy." *Personal Publishing* (November 1986): 54–58.
_____. "A Roundup of Page Layout Programs." *Computer Dealer* 9 (March 1986): 40–45.
_____. "Text into Type." *Personal Publishing* (December 1985): 20–35.
Sachs, Jonathan. "Up on the Big Screen." *PC Magazine* (May 1984): 122–33.
Sandler, Corey. "Key Tronic's Soft Touch." *PC Magazine* (January 1983): 347–50.
Sans, John C. *Handbook of Desktop Publishing.* Plano, Tex.: Wordware Publications, 1987.
Sargent, Murray, and Richard L. Shoemaker. *The IBM Personal Computer from the Inside Out.* Reading, Mass.: Addison-Wesley Pub. Co., 1984.
Seidman, Arthur H., and Ivan Flores, eds. *The Handbook of Computers and Computing.* New York: Van Nostrand Reinhold Co., 1984.
Seybold, John W. "The Desktop-Publishing Phenomenon." *BYTE* (May 1987): 149–54.
_____. *The World of Digital Typesetting.* Media, Penn.: Seybold Publications, 1984.
Seymour, Jim. "Manuscript: Something Old, Something New." *PC Magazine* (February 10, 1987): 85, 87.
_____. "The New Challenger in the Word Processing Wars." *PC Magazine* (December 10, 1985): 91–94.
Shinyeda, Merrily. "Word Processing: The Deciding Factors." *PC Magazine* (March 1985): 52–57.
Skiba, Gary. "Color Printers Add to Your Palette." *PC Magazine* (November 27, 1984): 356–91.
Software Digest™. *The Ratings Book™: IBM PC Word Processing Programs.* Wynnewood, Penn.: Software Digest, Inc., 1984.
Sorensen, Karen. "Desktop Publishing Software." *InfoWorld* (January 5, 1987): 39–50.
_____. "Desktop Publishing Sparks New Services." *InfoWorld* (September 1, 1986): 25–26.
Sorensen, Karen, et al. "Dot-Matrix Printers." *InfoWorld* (July 28, 1986): 29–43.
Spiegelman, Marjorie. "Interior Design for Documents." *PC World* (March 1987): 178–85.
Stallings, Stephanie. "The Business of Words: Outliners." *PC Magazine* (March 25, 1986): 199–220.
Steinke, Steve. "Desktop Publishing on the Macintosh." *Computerland Magazine* (November/December 1986): 46–49.
Stone, M. David. "Fully Formed Print: The Wheel Thing." *PC Magazine* (November 27, 1984): 270–348.
_____. "Making a Good Impression." *PC Magazine* (November 27, 1984): 348–54.
Strehlo, Kevin. *PageMaker: Desktop Publishing on the IBM PC & Compatibles.* Glenview, Ill.: Scott, Foresman, & Co, 1987.
Swearingen, Dan. "In the Right Key." *PC Products* (October 1985): 33–49.
Teichman, Milton. "What College Freshman Say About Word Processing." *Perspectives in Computing* 5 (1985): 43–48.
Terry, Chris. "Sorting Out Sorting Programs." *PC Magazine* (February 5, 1985): 50, 52.
Ulick, Terry. "The HP LaserJet Plus." *Personal Publishing* (October 1986): 52–61.
_____. "Page Makeup Software in Perspective: Macintosh's Big 3." *Personal Publishing* (February 1986): 26–31.
_____. "Pagination Explained." *Personal Publishing* (February 1986): 16–17.
_____. *Personal Publishing with the Macintosh.* Hasbrouck Heights, N.J.: Hayden Book Co., 1986.
_____. "Typesetting for Writers." *PC Magazine* (March 19, 1985): 329–30.
Ulick, Terry, and Steve Roth. "Page Planning." *Personal Publishing* (November 1986): 60–68.
University of Toronto Computing Services. *Academic's Guide to Microcomputer Systems.* Toronto: University of Toronto, 1985.
Van Dam, Andries. "Computer Software for Graphics." *Scientific American* 251 (1984): 146–59.
Vaughn, Susan. "The State of the Art in Word Processing." *ABA Journal* 71 (1985): 84–88.
Wadlow, Tom. "The Hercules Graphics Card." *BYTE* (December 1983): 343–56.
Waith, Mitchell, and Julie Arca. *Word Processing Primer.* Peterborough, N.H.: BYTE/McGraw-Hill, 1982.
Waldrop, Heidi. "Composing Prose with WANDAH." *PC Magazine* (April 3, 1984): 161–64.
Walkenbach, John. "Downloading: Building Your Own Characters." *PC Magazine* (May 1, 1984): 145–51.
_____. "Keyboard Shortcuts." *PC Tech Journal* (October 1985): 131–44.
Webster, Bruce. "Publish and/or Perish." *BYTE* (May 1987): 279–90.

Weiskel, Timothy C. "Bibliographic Research and the Love of Learning." *Perspectives in Computing* 5 (Winter 1985): 12–21.

Wiley, Jack. *The Complete Guide to Desktop Publishing.* Lodi, Calif.: Solipaz Pub. Co., 1987.

Williams, Gregg, and Tom Thompson. "The Apple Macintosh II." BYTE (April 1987): 85–106.

Wilton, Richard. "Programming the Enhanced Graphics Adapter." BYTE (1986 Special Issue): 209–20.

_____. "RAM-Loadable Character Sets for the IBM PC." BYTE (1986 Extra Edition): 197–208.

Winograd, Terry. "Computer Software for Working with Language." *Scientific American* 251 (1984): 131–45.

Wiswell, Phil. "Word Processing: The Latest Word." *PC Magazine* (August 20, 1985): 110–34.

Zander, Richard H. "Whipping Your Text Into SHAPE." *PC Magazine* (June 12, 1984): 305–18.

Zinsser, William. *Writing with a Word Processor.* New York: Harper, 1983.

Chapter 3

Bible Concordance Programs

Not only was the Teacher wise, but
Also he imparted knowledge to the people.
He pondered and searched out and set in
Order many proverbs. The Teacher
Searched to find just the right words,
And what he wrote was upright and true.
Ecclesiastes 12:9-10

3.1 Introduction

Anyone who has used a printed concordance knows how frustrating and slow finding "just the right words" can be. For example, try finding all the places where *God, righteous,* and *judge* occur within three verses of one another, and you will see what I mean. The invention of the printing press in the fifteenth century and the versification of the New Testament in the sixteenth[1] made it possible to construct and accurately reproduce concordances that would refer to the biblical text in a standardized way. But the task of making a concordance by hand is an arduous one that is fraught with the possibility of error. Robert Young's *Analytical Concordance to the Holy Bible*, first published in 1879, contains about 311,000 biblical citations from the Authorized Version (KJV) that are subdivided under the Hebrew and Greek words used to translate the keyword[2] in the citation. Think of the work involved in constructing such a concordance. Young had to prepare an individual slip of paper for each word, decide how much context to retain, write the word in its context on the slip of paper, and then index those slips alphabetically, first by keyword and then by the Hebrew and Greek words the keyword translated. The printer then had to typeset those slips in their proper sequence, making as few spelling and other mistakes as possible.

Today concordances to the Bible and to other literary works can be prepared accurately, quickly, and automatically by computers. As we learned in chapter 1 (and as we saw illustrated by the text retrieval programs in chapter 2), computers can perform many logical operations. They can search "to find just the right words." They can build lists of words and sort those lists. And they can do all of those operations

---

1. The famous Parisian printer Robert Stephanus (Estienne) divided the text of the New Testament into verses, and the versification of his fourth printed edition of the Greek New Testament (1551) is the one we still use today. The versification of the Old Testament that we use can be traced back to the Masoretic family of Ben Asher, who versified the Masoretic Text (the Hebrew Old Testament) around A.D. 900.

2. Keywords are the English words that serve as entry words in a concordance.

quickly, accurately, and tirelessly. Computers, then, are particularly well-suited to searching for words in large textual data bases, constructing concordances from those texts, and sorting the entries alphabetically or otherwise. The programs reviewed in this chapter, however, are not designed to produce complete concordances to the Bible but to allow users to perform customized concording operations, "to find just the right words."

In this chapter I will evaluate software packages that combine machine-readable versions of English translations of the Bible with text retrieval programs that allow that text to be concorded. Machine-readable versions of the Hebrew Bible (the Masoretic Text), the Greek Old Testament (the Septuagint—LXX), and the Greek New Testament will be discussed in chapter 7. A machine-readable text (MRT) is any text that exists on media that can be read by a computer.[3] These programs, which vary in complexity and degree of sophistication from package to package, typically allow users to perform concording, word processing, and printing operations. On the one hand, names such as THE WORD processor, SCRIPTURE SCANNER, compu-BIBLE,™ Bible Search, WORDsearch,™ and COMPUTER BIBLE indicate that this type of software allows users to scan, concord, manipulate, and print the biblical text. On the other hand, these names suggest a degree of uncertainty about the generic label that is most appropriate for this software. For lack of a better name, I will refer to these programs as "Bible concordance programs" since their primary function is to allow users to create custom indices by concording the biblical text.

Although most of the Bible concordance programs include word processing and printing functions, it is their concording capabilities that make them distinctive and helpful for studying the Bible. Take away the word processing and printing features from the software we are examining in this chapter, and useful programs still remain for studying the Bible. Take away their ability to concord text, and all that is left are MRTs with no programs for manipulating the text in ways that bring new information to light. Thus in evaluating these programs, I will focus on their concording capabilities.

The software we will review in this chapter can be divided into three categories: (1) concordance programs that work with nonindexed MRTs of the Bible, (2) concordance programs that work with indexed MRTs of the Bible, and (3) MRTs of the Bible that do not include concordance programs. Programs in the first category must search through ranges of text sequentially to build indices, a process that can take quite a while if a large range (such as the whole Bible) is specified. Programs in the second category include precompiled indices of every word in the Bible and so can instantly provide comprehensive lists of words and phrases. The data base for this type of program is larger than that for the first type and requires a hard disk. Software in category three consists of little more than machine-readable versions of the Bible with no programs for manipulating that data. Such software is useful for those who already have a generic text retrieval or concordance program, such as WordCruncher™ or one of the other text retrieval programs listed in chapter 2.

Before we review Bible concordance programs, it might be helpful to create a "wish list" of features an *ideal* Bible concordance program might include and then use this list as a standard against which to judge the strengths and weaknesses of each program. The following list does *not* take into account the special text-retrieval needs of biblical scholars. On that topic, see chapter 7.

Generally speaking, an ideal concordance program would be as fast and flexible as possible in its abilities to (1) create indices, (2) display the results on-screen, and (3) manipulate indices. The faster and more flexible a program, the greater its power and usefulness. Specifically, an ideal concordance program might support the following features. (A few of these features pertain to programs that work with indexed texts.

---

3. Unless otherwise stated, all the programs in this chapter were reviewed on a 5.25-inch floppy-disk drive of an 8088 IBM PC-XT running under DOS 2.1 at 4.77 MHz.

Terms not explained in chapter 2 will be defined in the course of evaluating programs in this chapter.)[4]

- *Searching/Indexing Features*

The Boolean operators AND, OR, XOR, and NOT,
Nested Boolean operators,
User-specifiable default Boolean operators,
Mixed Boolean operators,
Long, multiple search-term constructions with expressed operators,
Multiple, simultaneous index creation,
Indices at least as large as the total number of verses in the Bible (31,102),
Initial, medial, and terminal truncation of search terms,
Single and global wild-card characters,
Pattern-matching for word and phrase fragments,
Case-sensitive and case-insensitive searches,
Punctuation-sensitive and punctuation-insensitive searches,
Proximity searches specified by character, word, sentence, verse, paragraph, chapter, or book,
Sequence-specific searches,
Exact-phrase searches,
User-specifiable, noncontiguous search ranges,
Statistical information about word usage as search terms are entered,
Warning users when search terms do not occur in the specified range,
Matching search terms across verse and chapter boundaries,
Restricting search-term matches to verses,
Restricting search-term matches to chapters,
Search term selection from alphabetized, exhaustive, word-frequency list,
Automatic saving of search constructions with indices,
User comments—header information—in indices.

- *Display/Print Features*

Display search construction—terms, operators, range—when creating index,
Dynamic update of the following concording operations: name of index being created, search term being indexed, operation being performed, location of hits by book, chapter, and verse, cumulative number of hits, cumulative time required to perform function, and time remaining to complete entire concording operation,
Suppressing on-screen display of intermediate results of concording operations,
Display and print indices as verse references only,
Display and print indices as verse references and text,
Display indices a user-specified number of entries at a time,
Display and print "hits" in a user-specifiable context of N-number of words, lines, sentences, verses, or paragraphs,
Jump directly from "hits" to full-text context and back,
Page bidirectionally through index a user-specified number of entries at a time,
Jump to beginning/end of index,
Automatically scroll indices a user-specified number of entries at a time, in either direction, at user-controlled scroll rate,
Highlight search terms in indices,
Display and print word-frequency information,
Display and print distribution-frequency information,
Display any range of the biblical text beside index entries,
Print noncontiguous, user-selected ranges of indices or of the biblical text,
Scan (read) the biblical text,
Go directly to any book, chapter, or verse in the Bible,
Page bidirectionally through the biblical text a user-specifiable number of characters, words, sentences, verses, chapters, or books at a time,
Jump to the beginning/end of the current chapter and book,
Search the biblical text for words and word combinations without creating an index,

---

4. The program that comes the closest to fulfilling this "wish list" is WordCruncher™ (see chapter 2), a generic concording program reviewed in the *Bits & Bytes Review*™ 1 (February 1987): 1–8.

Automatically scroll through the biblical text a user-specified number of words, verses, sentences, chapters, or books at a time, in either direction, at user-controlled scroll rate,
Insert biblical references only or references and text into a word processing file,
Multiple, dynamic, user-adjustable, user-definable windows for displaying verse references, index entries, biblical text, notes, and other information,
Cut and paste between windows,
Allow users to install as much or as little of the data base as they wish,
Allow users to display two or more English translations side by side in parallel columns that can be scrolled simultaneously or singly.

- *Index Manipulation*

Combine two or more indices (the equivalent of a Boolean OR operation),
Intersect two or more indices (the equivalent of a Boolean AND operation),
Show the difference between two indices (the equivalent of a Boolean NOT operation),
Edit indices by adding or eliminating verses.

- *Lexical and Other*

On-line theological dictionary,
On-line historical/archaeological dictionary,
On-line explanatory notes,
On-line commentary,
On-line atlas,
On-line, precompiled, topical cross references,
On-line Hebrew, Aramaic, and Greek lexicons,
Use transliterated Hebrew, Aramaic, and Greek search terms in all the ways English search terms can be used,
Concord from Hebrew, Aramaic, and Greek terms to their English glosses (translations),
Concord from English glosses to the underlying Hebrew, Aramaic, and Greek terms.

3.2 Nonindexed Bible Concordance Programs

In this section we will examine six Bible concordance programs that work with nonindexed data bases.

3.2.1 THE WORD processor

- *BASIC PRODUCT INFORMATION*

Name of Program: THE WORD processor
Company Name: Bible Research Systems
Address: 2013 Wells Branch Parkway, Suite 304, Austin, TX 78728
Phone: (512) 251-7541
Price: $199.95
Version Tested: 3.0, demo disk, NIV text, IBM version
Runs On: 16 different computers, including Macintosh, Apple II+, IIe, IIc, IBM PCs and compatibles, Compaq and other MS-DOS machines, TRS-80 Models II, III, and 4, Kaypro and other CP/M machines, and Commodore 64
Memory Requirements: Macintosh: 512K; Apple: 48K; IBM: 64K (with DOS 2.0, 128K), XT and other 8088s: 128K; TRS-80 Model II: 64K, Models III and 4: 48K; Kaypro and other Z80s: 64K; Commodore: 64K
Operating System Requirements: IBM: DOS 2.0 or greater
Disk Drive Requirements: Macintosh: 1; Apple: 1; IBM: 1; other 8088s: 2; TRS-80: 2; Kaypro: 2; other Z80s: 1; Commodore: 1
Supports Color Monitors: Yes
Uses Sound: Yes
Number of Text Disks: Between 6 and 8, depending on the machine
Number of Program Disks: 1

Boolean Operator	Search Term	Venn Diagram	Search Term	Explanation

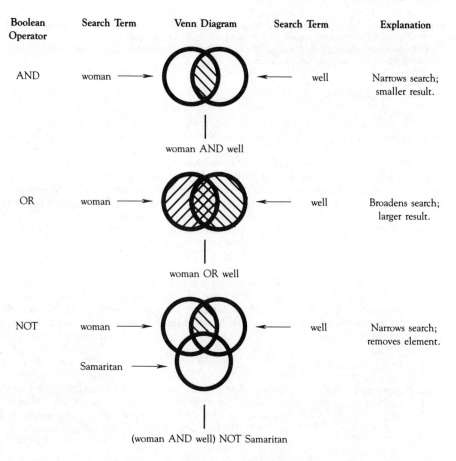

AND — woman → ← well — Narrows search; smaller result.

woman AND well

OR — woman → ← well — Broadens search; larger result.

woman OR well

NOT — woman → ← well — Narrows search; removes element.

Samaritan →

(woman AND well) NOT Samaritan

Figure 3.1: Venn diagrams of Boolean operators.

Size of Program Files: 53K (not including BASIC.COM—about 16K in size—which users must supply)
Size of Help Files: 14K
Size of Text Files: 1.8MB
Text Files in ASCII: No
Produces ASCII Output Files: No, but the ASCII Utility (included with TWP) can convert TWP output to ASCII text.
Search String Limitations: 255 characters
Maximum Number of Entries per Index: 53,040
Type of Disks Used: Flippy and double-sided
Texts Available: KJV, NIV
Product Includes: Program disk, text disks, user's manual, 3-ring binder
Manual: 46 pages, book-size, computer-printed, stapled, 5 appendices, indexed
Demo Disk Available: Yes, no cost
Copy Protected: No
Hard Disk Compatible: Yes
Menu-Driven: Yes
On-line Help: Yes
Tutorial: Chapter 2 in manual
Warranty: Money-back guarantee
Support: Phone—(512) 835-7981—and letter
Update Policy: Updates to version 3.1 are $100.

Related Products: TOPICS ($49.95); PEOPLE ($49.95); THE GREEK Transliterator ($199.95); THE HEBREW Transliterator ($249.95); PERSONAL COMMENTARY ($49.95)
Other Information: Reviewed in *Newsweek* (April 5, 1982): 53; *Softalk* (May 1982); *InfoWorld* 4 (Dec. 27, 1982): 19–21; *Popular Computing* 2 (February 1983): 128–32.

3.2.1.1 Introduction

THE WORD processor, first introduced in 1982, was created by Kent Ochel and Bert Brown. The KJV was chosen as their first text because it was popular, not copyrighted, had not changed in 400 years, and was available in a highly proofed form as an IBM 370 tape that had been used to typeset the KJV. The KJV consists of 36 million bits (4.5 megabytes) of information and about 14,000 unique words, which are used a total of approximately 789,000 times. By employing sophisticated compression techniques, Brown and Ochel were able to reduce the KJV's 4.5 megabytes to about 1.8 megabytes. Today THE WORD processor may be purchased in KJV and NIV versions. Of all the Bible concordance programs reviewed in this chapter, TWP runs under the most operating systems and has the most auxiliary programs available for it.

Because THE WORD processor (hereafter TWP) uses BASIC for all user input and output, it is easy to modify I/O parameters (the manual contains instructions for doing this); and because its search routines are written in Assembler, TWP's searches are fast. For example, using Boolean OR logic, TWP concorded forty references to *woman, husband, well,* and *friend* in the Gospel of John in 2 minutes and 30 seconds. And using the same range and logic, TWP concorded fifteen search terms and built a 465-verse index in 7 minutes and 20 seconds. Doing that by hand would take at least an hour.

Although brief (46 pages), TWP's manual is well-written, well-organized, clear, and helpful. Its brevity and directness reflect TWP's clean, uncluttered user interface. Eight pages are devoted to a tutorial that provides a hands-on introduction to all of TWP's main features, and five appendices provide information about the abbreviations used for the books of the Bible, how to modify I/O and other parameters, and using the TOPICS, PEOPLE, and ASCII Utility products. Thankfully, the manual is indexed.

3.2.1.2 Description

User Interface. TWP is a menu-driven program that operates in one of two main modes—Scan and Index—though these are not identified as such in TWP's user manual but are referred to as the Display Scripture Text and the Work with Indices options. I will refer to these as "modes," however, to maintain a continuity of terminology between this and the other programs we will examine in this chapter.[5] In the Scan Mode, TWP can scroll through a preselected range of text or scan that range for user-specified character strings. In the Index Mode, TWP concords through the preselected range and constructs an index based on the character strings it was told to search for. In either mode, the words of Jesus are highlighted in reverse video, and Scripture is properly displayed in upper- and lower-case letters.

The main menu on the IBM version of TWP lists nine options that are invoked by using the IBM function keys. F1 is Display Help Instructions; F2 is Set Range; F3 is Set Control Options; F4 is Display Scripture Text; F5 is Print Comments; F6 is Print Scripture Text; F7 is Work with Indices; F8 is End This Session; and F9 is ASCII Utility. In certain modes the last line of the screen displays submenu prompts that

---

5. I will use *Scan Mode* and *Scripture Mode* as synonyms and *Index Mode* and *Concordance Mode* as synonyms in this chapter.

specify available options. Esc is used to back up through menus. TWP's help screens are clear, concise, and useful.

The main menu selection Set Control Options (F3) is used to configure TWP for the screen, printer, and disk parameters of a particular system. The Print Comments option (F5) directs up to 4,096 characters to the printer at any time, and the Print Scripture Text option (F6) prints the Scripture in the specified range. The Set Range option (F2) is used to set the range of the text that is to be scanned, displayed, or indexed.

Search Logic. TWP supports Boolean AND/OR logic when scanning or concording, though ANDs and ORs may not be mixed in a single concording operation. For example, if the range is the Pentateuch, and if the search strings are "stone," "rock," and "tree," TWP will create an index that contains every reference to *stone* OR *rock* OR *tree* or an index that includes only those verses where *stone* AND *rock* AND *tree* occur together, but it cannot build an index of verses that contain (*stone* AND *rock*) OR *tree*. To do that, TWP would have to create an index of *stone* AND *rock* verses and a second index of *tree* verses and then merge the two indices by combining them (see below). AND and OR searches are neither sequence- nor case-specific. For example, "WoMaN, husBANd, WELL, friend" will find the same verses as "well, husband, woman, friend." Search strings may be up to 255 characters long and consist of words, phrases, or a mixture of the two. Exact-phrase searches are supported.

TWP also supports the use of initial, medial, and terminal truncation in the Scan and Index Modes.[6] "Stone" finds *stone*. "Stone =" finds *stone* only if it is followed by a blank. "Stone=" finds any word that begins with *stone*. "=Stone" finds any word that ends with *stone*. "=Stone =" finds any word that ends with *stone* and a blank. "=Stone=" finds any word that contains *stone*. And "=l==e=" finds any string that began with *l* followed by any two characters and then an *e*, for example, *life*, *children*, *fullness*, and *translated*.

Scan Mode. The Display Scripture Text option (F4) is used to scroll through and to scan the selected range of text for user-specified search strings. Scrolling through the text is the electronic equivalent of paging through the Bible. When scrolling, TWP can display and advance the text a verse or a page at a time, and function keys may be used to move to the top or bottom of the range. When scanning for search strings, TWP highlights all the text that qualifies as a match and allows users to move through the text bidirectionally. The Display Scripture Text option may also be used to go directly to a specified verse and to print text from the search range. Since there are multiple data disks, TWP prompts users when it is time to change diskettes.

Index Mode. The Work with Indices option (F7) will create an index within the range of text that has been specified with the Set Range option. An index may hold up to 53,040 entries, and users can set the upper limit of entries an index will accept. After an index has been created, users have the option of saving the search construction used to create it. When an index is displayed, hits are highlighted.

When concording, TWP displays the range and chapter in the range it is currently searching and the number of hits it has located. (A "hit" is any string of characters that matches the search construction; hits are also referred to as "matches.") After an index is created, it is displayed as a list of verses. Submenu options allow users to view each reference as a single verse or in context,[7] to scroll up or down from the reference, and to insert and delete references and save indices to disk. When displaying a reference in context, TWP displays the hit as the uppermost verse on the screen, with

---

6. As we learned in chapter 2, a truncator is a kind of wild-card character that allows users to specify some portion of a search string without having to specify the entire string. Truncators allow variations in word length and spelling. The truncated part of a string can be anything.

7. The Set Control Options (F3 on the main menu) is used (among other things) to specify whether TWP displays text a verse or a screen at a time in the Scan and Index Modes.

subsequent verses in the range following (unless TWP has been configured to display single verses only), but it does not highlight the verse or its first letter.

By using the Merge Indices function (item F5 in the Work with Indices submenu), indices may be combined or intersected. Combining two indices simply adds their contents together, which is equivalent to using a Boolean OR; it creates an index that is as large as the sum of the two source indices. For example, combining an index of *bush* with an index of *stone*, *rock*, and *tree* would create an index that contained every reference to *stone*, *rock*, *tree*, and *bush*. Intersecting two indices creates an index that contains only those verses that are common to each of the source indices, which is equivalent to using a Boolean AND; it creates an index that is smaller than the sum of the two source indices. Intersecting the *stone*, *rock*, *tree* and the *bush* indices, for example, would create an index that contained only those verses where *stone*, *rock*, *tree*, and *bush* occurred together in the same verse.[8] The Display or Modify an Index option (item F4 on the Work with Indices submenu) is used to review an index and to modify it by deleting or inserting items. Indices can be displayed as verse references only or as verses in context. When an index verse is displayed, it appears at the top of the screen (with subsequent verses in the selected range following it), and the words in the verse that match the search construction are highlighted. Users may scroll bidirectionally throughout the range from the verse that contains the hit. The Merge Indices and Delete an Index options are used to perform the functions their names suggest.

Other. Included with TWP is the ASCII Utility, a program that converts TWP index and data files into ASCII files, which can then be used with word processing programs.

Bible Research Systems produces a family of products that relate to and that enhance TWP. TOPICS is a set of cross references to over 200 biblical topics, and PEOPLE is a set of cross references to more than 140 of the most frequently mentioned biblical personalities. THE GREEK Transliterator is a complete text of the KJV New Testament that includes Strong's reference numbers and a Greek lexicon, as well as pertinent information about each Greek word. THE GREEK Transliterator can display (1) any verse in the NT, (2) the Strong's reference number for each word, (3) a transliterated form of the Greek word that underlies each English word (giving the definition, root, and derivation of the former), and it can (4) locate NT occurrences of Greek words and display their English translations. And THE GREEK Transliterator can perform the inverse of that procedure: it can (5) trace an English word through the NT and show the Greek words that underlie each of the English word's occurrences. Finally, THE GREEK Transliterator can (6) create indices based on NT Greek word usage. THE HEBREW Transliterator, the counterpart of THE GREEK Transliterator, is a complete text of the KJV Old Testament that includes Strong's reference numbers and a Hebrew lexicon, as well as pertinent information about each Hebrew word. The PERSONAL COMMENTARY allows users to annotate each verse. A planned CHRONOLOGICAL BIBLE will allow users to display the biblical text in chronological order.

3.2.1.3 Evaluation

TWP meets many of our criteria for an ideal concordance program. It supports (1) Boolean AND/OR logic in Scan and Index Modes and (2) when manipulating indices, (3) search strings of up to 255 characters, (4) simultaneous multiple word and phrase searches (thus facilitating topical Bible study), (5) indices as large as 53,040 entries, (6) initial, medial, and terminal truncation (which function as wild cards) in the Scan and Index Modes, (7) exact-phrase searches, (8) user-specified search ranges, and a (9)

---

8. Combining and intersecting will not work in the Scan Mode because scanning does not create indices that can be combined or intersected.

GOTO command. TWP displays (10) the range when scanning or concording and (11) dynamically updates the current location of the program's concording activities. (12) Hits are highlighted in the Scan Mode and may be (13) saved to disk, (14) printed, (15) inserted into documents prepared with word processing programs, and (16) scrolled bidirectionally in the Scan and Index Modes. TWP allows indices to be (17) combined, (18) intersected, and (19) edited. (20) Indices and text may be scanned for matches. And (21) TWP is one of the few Bible concordance program that offers versions (THE GREEK Transliterator, THE HEBREW Transliterator) that display information about Greek and Hebrew words. (22) On-line help is included.

As useful as it is, TWP suffers from the following shortcomings. TWP does not support (1) Boolean XOR and NOT operators in the Scan and Index modes, (2) nested operators, (3) mixed operators, (4) case-sensitive, (5) proximity, and (6) sequence-specific searches, (7) nonsequential search ranges, (8) displaying the difference between indices, or (9) windows. When intersecting indices, (10) verse boundaries arbitrarily and artificially restrict the field in which TWP looks for search strings, an almost universal problem among Bible concordance programs.

3.2.2 The SCRIPTURE SCANNER

- *BASIC PRODUCT INFORMATION*

Name of Program: The SCRIPTURE SCANNER
Company Name: Omega Software
Address: P.O. Box 355, Round Rock, TX 8680-0355
Phone: (512) 255-9569
Price: Old Testament: $159.95, New Testament: $159.95, Entire Bible: $249.95; Copyrighted Testaments: $174.95 each, Entire Bible: $274.95; KJV and NKJV or TLB: $379.95; KJV, NKJV, and TLB: $489.95
Version Tested: 1.20F, full program, KJV text
Runs On: IBM PCs and compatibles, Compaq
Memory Requirements: 128K, 192K recommended for hard disk use.
Operating System Requirements: DOS 2.0 or greater
Disk Drive Requirements: 1
Supports Color Monitors: Yes
Uses Sound: Yes
Number of Text Disks: 7
Number of Program Disks: 1
Size of Program Files: 105K
Size of Help Files: 18K
Size of Text Files: 2MB
Text Files in ASCII: No
Produces ASCII Output Files: No, but SS output can be converted to ASCII text; see below under *Description.*
Search String Limitations: 10 entries, each up to 60 characters long (i.e., a maximum of 600 characters)
Maximum Number of Entries per Index: 3,000 (7,000+ possible with 192K or more of memory)
Type of Disks Used: Flippy
Texts Available: KJV, NKJV, Today's Living Bible (TLB)
Product Includes: Program disk, text disks, quick reference card, list of corrections, user's manual, 3-ring binder, slipcase
Manual: 110 pages, book-size, typeset, 6 appendices, not indexed
Demo Disk Available: Yes, KJV, $15 with abbreviated manual, $5 without manual
Copy Protected: No
Hard Disk Compatible: Yes
Menu-Driven: Yes
On-line Help: Yes
Tutorial: Yes, chapter 3 in manual
Warranty: Limited to replacing defective diskettes
Support: Phone—(512) 255-9569—and letter
Update Policy: Notification of errors in software for one year from date of purchase
Related Products: None
Other Information: None

3.2.2.1 Introduction

The SCRIPTURE SCANNER, first released in 1984, was created by Michael L. Brandes, James W. Collins, W. David Jenkins, and T. Vick Livingston. SCRIPTURE SCANNER (hereafter SS), which is available in KJV, NKJV, and Living Bible versions, has compressed the text of those translations to about 2.0 megabytes each. Among other files, the program disk contains SSOPT.OPT, an ASCII text file that is designed to be modified with a text editor or word processing program to configure SS for a particular computer system. Using Boolean OR logic, SS concorded thirty-seven instances of *woman, husband, well,* and *friend* in the Gospel of John in 2 minutes and 36 seconds, just 6 seconds slower than TWP. And using the same range and logic, SS concorded 367 references to ten words in 5 minutes and 20 seconds.

SS's 110-page manual is well-written, well-organized, clear, and helpful. Its length and number of subdivisions reflects SS's somewhat complex user interface. Chapter 3—thirty pages—contains a tutorial that provides a hands-on introduction to all of SS's main features. Six appendices provide information about SS's commands, the abbreviations used for each book of the Bible, the content of each data disk, system options and problems, using SS with a hard disk, and error messages. Unhappily, there is no index, though the two-page table of contents can substitute for one. The inclusion of a "Quick Reference Card" is unique with this type of software and a feature SS's competitors would do well to imitate.

3.2.2.2 Description

User Interface. SCRIPTURE SCANNER's introductory routine greets users with the program's logo, displays the text of Psalm 100:4, and plays one of several tunes, such as "Rise Up, O Men of God," "Onward Christian Soldiers," or the Doxology. Fortunately, users may bypass this time-consuming and somewhat annoying procedure by hitting any key. Like TWP, SS is a menu-driven program, and its main menu is displayed on-screen in two horizontal windows. The upper window contains a list of all the books of the Bible, divided into OT and NT groups and displayed under traditional headings, such as Pentateuch, Major Prophets, and Paul's Epistles. The lower window consists of four lines: (1) the Status Line, which provides status information about the current program, (2) the Message Line, which displays program messages and prompts, (3) the Command Line, which displays the commands users may choose from, and (4) the Function Line, which lists the IBM function keys 1–8 and their uses. These eight function keys are used in each of SS's major modes of operation. F1, the Help key, brings up one or more screenfuls of information about whatever mode the program is in at the time, and although such on-line help is always available, it is not always as helpful as one might wish. F2, the Print Verse key, prints the current verse, which is usually the one at the top of the screen. F3, the Menu key, moves the program to the previous menu, as does pressing the Escape key. F4, the Exit key, causes SS to exit to DOS, with an option to save any changes made to an index or file. F5, the Range key, is used to set a range of text for SS to work with, and that range is displayed on the Message Line. F6, the Reference key, is used in the Scripture and Concordance Modes to specify a reference for SS to locate and in the Word Processing Mode to insert a reference or text into a document. F7, the Disk key, changes the letter of the drive that contains the text files. F8, the Text key, is used only in the Concordance Mode to display the text of a reference. Esc is used to exit any operation at any time and to back up through menus.

SS operates in one of four main modes—Scripture, Concordance, Word Processing, and Odds and Ends—and those modes are selected from the main-menu Command Line. The Odds and Ends Mode contains three options that are used in the other three main modes. Its Print Option is used to specify certain basic printer parameters, such as paper length and margins, its Word Processing Option to set parameters that govern how text will be displayed on-screen and inserted into documents that are being edited, and its Screen Option to set screen parameters. Using the fourth option, the Bible Print Function, users can specify and print a range of text. Like TWP, SS displays and prints verses in upper- and lower-case letters, though the program can be configured to display and print all text in upper-case letters only.

Search Logic. SS can scan for or concord up to ten words or phrases at a time, though no word or phrase may exceed sixty characters, including spaces and punctuation. Thus it is possible to search for multiple strings that add up to as many as 600 characters. SS joins separate search strings by an implied Boolean OR, so that a search for "woman" and "well" would find all occurrences of each term within the specified range. Unlike TWP, SS does not support Boolean ANDs when scanning or concording. All SS searches are case-sensitive. Thus, for example, "WoMaN, husBANd, WELL, friend" would locate a different set of references than "woman, husband, well, friend."

SS supports initial, medial, and terminal truncation when scanning and concording. The symbol "__" represents a space and is used in the following ways. "Stone__" finds words that end with *stone*. "__Stone" finds words that begin with *stone*. "Stone" finds words that contain *stone*. And "__stone__" only finds *stone*. In addition to truncation, SS also supports the unlimited use of "?" as a single-character wild-card that may be used in the initial, medial, and terminal positions. For example, "?ight" finds *might, right, light*; "Je?" finds *Jew, Jews, Jesus, Jericho*; and "w?ll" finds *wall, well, will*, and so forth.

The Scripture Mode. This mode is used to display and scan text and can be used to print any portion of the Bible, from a verse to a book. There are four main options in this mode. (1) The Display Option is used to display text in the preselected range, a screenful at a time, and to scroll up and down the range of text. A submenu GOTO option allows users to go to specific verses. (2) The Scan Option is used to search for strings of text. SS highlights the word or phrase it is scanning for and displays the verse in which it is found at the top of the screen, followed by the rest of the verses from that point on in the range. Scrolling forward from the hit is supported, but unlike TWP (which supports bidirectional scrolling), SS does not allow scrolling backward when using the scan function. This makes it impossible to display more than nine verses before the hit—if the Odds and Ends menu has been used to specify a nine-verse context (see below). (3) The Browse Option is used to scroll through the text and to adjust the scroll speed from a snail's pace to one fast enough for the swiftest speed reader. (4) The Window Function splits the screen into two vertical windows of equal size. A range can be specified for each window, so that SS could display the text of Genesis in one window and the text of the Gospel of Matthew in the other. The Window Function supports bidirectional scrolling and going to specific verses, but it does not support scanning, using an index to search through the range, or printing. Windows, then, may only be used for reading text.

The Concordance Mode. This mode is used to create indices. The same logic and limitations used to formulate searches in the Scripture Mode are used to formulate searches in the Concordance Mode. An index may contain up to 3,000 entries (7,000 if 192K RAM is present). Each index may be titled.

As SS creates an index, it displays the search terms and range and dynamically displays the number of the chapter being searched, the number of the verse being inserted into the index, and the total number of verses in the index. An index's name, size, and title are displayed on-screen when it is displayed. SS keeps no record of the search construction used to create indices. When an index is complete, SS displays a list of the entries in the index, as well as its name, title, size, and the length of time required to create it. After using the Create Option to construct an index, the Edit Option may be used to display the index or to revise it by deleting, inserting, and changing references. A Sort Option sorts a modified index, placing each entry in its proper biblical order. References may be displayed with or without context, which can be set in the Odds and Ends Mode to include from zero to nine verses on each side of each verse in an index. The F8 Text key is used to initiate the display of an index's entries. Index entries are not highlighted when displayed, and if the Context Option has been selected, users must remember how many verses SS was instructed to display before each hit and then count down that many verses from the top of the screen to locate the match—a clumsy procedure. If the Context Option has not been selected, an index entry appears as the first verse at the top of the screen. As is true when scanning for verses in the Scripture Mode, the Concordance Mode only supports forward scrolling, unlike TWP, which offers bidirectional scrolling. The Merge Option is used to combine all the entries in each of two files into a new index (the equivalent of a Boolean OR) or to create an index that is the intersection of the two source files and so contains only those entries the two files have in common (the equivalent of a Boolean AND).

The Word Processing Mode. This mode is used to perform rudimentary word processing functions, such as creating, updating, copying, deleting, or printing documents. The Scan and Insert function takes ASCII or other source files (e.g., a WordStar® file) created with word processing programs and reads into them the text of any Scripture references or range of references specified in the source files with the "%%" code, which must be placed before and after the references SS is to insert. For example, if a source file contained "%%John1:1–2:1%%," SS's scan and insert function would take the source file, insert all of those verses from the Gospel of John into it, and produce an output file (whose name would have been specified in advance) that consisted of the source file with the inserted verses. Output files created in this way consist of pure ASCII text that can be transported back to a word processing program for further editing and manipulation. The size of source and output files is limited only by disk space. In approximately 2 minutes the scan and insert function inserted the entire Gospel of John into a file I created with my word processor.[9] By using SS's scan and insert function, all of SS's non-ASCII text files could be translated into standard ASCII files. Alternatively, in the Word Processing Mode, users can insert a specified range of text into a file that may be manipulated with SS's word processing functions or with those of another word processing program. Up to a whole book of the Bible may be inserted with a single keystroke, and more than one book may be inserted in a single file. File size is limited only by disk space. Since the original text has been compressed by about 45%, uncompressing it by this or by the preceding procedure expands it by a factor of about 2.2.

3.2.2.3 Evaluation

SS meets many of our criteria for an ideal concordance program. SS supports (1) Boolean AND/OR logic when manipulating indices, (2) search strings of up to 600 characters, (3) indices as large as 7,000 entries,[10] (4) simultaneous multiple word and phrase searches (thus facilitating topical Bible study), (5) initial, medial, and terminal truncation, (6) wild-card search characters, (7) case-sensitive searches, (8) user-specified search ranges, (9) windows, and (10) a GOTO command. SS displays (11) the range when scanning and concording, and dynamically updates (12) the current location of the program's concording activities, the (13) location and (14) number of index

---

9. I did this on a RAM disk. It would take longer to do on a hard disk and far longer on a floppy disk.

10. Of the more than 14,000 unique words in an English translation of the Bible, only the top twenty (e.g., *the, and, an, of*) occur more than 7,000 times.

entries, and (15) the size, (16) name, and (17) title of indices, as well as the (18) time required and (19) range used to construct them. Users may (20) specify the amount of context to include when displaying hits in the Concordance Mode. Hits are (21) highlighted in the Scripture Mode, and may be (22) saved to disk, (23) sent to a printer, (24) inserted into documents prepared with word processing programs, and (25) scrolled bidirectionally in the Scripture Mode. (26) SS allows indices and the text to be scanned for matches. (27) On-line help is included.

SS's shortcomings are as follows. SS does not support (1) Boolean ANDs, NOTs, and XORs in the Scripture and Concordance Modes, (2) nested operators, (3) mixed operators, (4) proximity, (5) sequence-specific, and (6) exact-phrase searches, (7) nonsequential search ranges, (8) bidirectional scrolling in the Concordance Mode or when using the scan function in the Scripture Mode, or (9) highlighting hits in the Concordance Mode. When intersecting indices, (10) verse boundaries arbitrarily and artificially restrict the field in which SS looks for matches. And SS does not (11) keep a record of the search construction used to concord indices. Also, (12) SS sometimes leaves material from the previous screen at the top and bottom of a new screen, thus distracting users with irrelevant clutter. This occurs, for example, every time SS first displays a verse in an index. And sometimes (13) SS fails to reveal needed menus, as is the case when displaying verses with the edit feature in the Concordance Mode. In this situation the top line of the screen still contains information from the previous screen (see the preceding criticism), but the bottom line, which should display the submenu for this mode, is blank. This means that users must remember the options in this submenu and how to invoke them or else consult the manual, Quick Reference Card, or on-line help.

3.2.3 compuBIBLE

- *BASIC PRODUCT INFORMATION*

Name of Program: compuBIBLE™
Company Name: NASSCO (National Software Systems Co.)
Address: P.O. Box 5660, Borger, TX 79008-5660
Phones: (800) 262-7726, (806) 274-6674
Price: $249
Version Tested: 1.1, full program, KJV text
Runs On: IBM PCs and compatibles
Memory Requirements: 192K
Operating System Requirements: DOS 2.0 or greater
Disk Drive Requirements: 2
Supports Color Monitors: Yes
Uses Sound: Yes
Number of Text Disks: 8
Number of Program Disks: 1
Size of Program Files: 209K (including overlays)
Size of Help Files: 38K
Size of Text Files: 2.7MB
Text Files in ASCII: No
Produces ASCII Output Files: No, but CB output can be converted to ASCII text; see below under *Description.*
Search String Limitations: 25 strings of up to 60 characters each (a maximum of 1,500 characters)
Maximum Number of Entries per Index: No limit, though no index may exceed the maximum number of verses in the Bible—31,102.
Type of Disks Used: Double-sided, double-density
Text Available: KJV, NIV, ASV
Product Includes: Program disk, text disks, user's manual, 3-ring binder, slipcase
Manual: 104 pages, book-size, computer-printed, 2 appendices, not indexed
Demo Disk Available: Yes, $10
Copy Protected: No

Hard Disk Compatible: Yes
Menu-Driven: Yes
On-line Help: Yes
Tutorial: Yes, chapter 2 in manual
Warranty: 90 day limited warranty covers materials and workmanship
Support: Phone—(800) 262-7724, (806) 274-6674—and letter
Update Policy: Minor updates are free; major updates available at minimal cost.
Related Products: Strong's Hebrew-Greek Dictionaries
Other Information: None

3.2.3.1 Introduction

CompuBIBLE™, first released in 1985, was created by Delmer Hightower and programmer Chris Epps. Currently, compuBIBLE™ (hereafter CB) offers the KJV, NIV, and ASV texts, which it has compressed to about 2.7 megabytes each. Extensive options allow users to customize CB to fit particular computer systems. These options include specifying screen types (monochrome or color), drives (floppy, hard, or RAM), and printers. CB is quite a bit larger than TWP and SS for three reasons. (1) CB has eight extensive overlays—screens of menus and information—that take up more than 120K. These overlays help give CB its power and sophistication, but they increase its size. (2) CB's help file is almost 40K in size, and its three executable (EXE) files add up to over 80K. And unlike TWP and SS, (3) CB includes 60,000 characters (plus white space) in the form of "{ }," where the words within the brackets do not directly translate an underlying Hebrew or Greek word but were supplied by the translators to make their translation more readable.[11]

CB is *very fast*. For example, using Boolean OR logic, CB built a thirty-three reference index of *woman, husband, well*, and *friend* in the Gospel of John in 1 minute and 20 seconds, a task that took TWP and SS about 2 minutes and 30 seconds each.[12] Generalizing on the basis of that test suggests that CB is almost twice as fast as TWP and SS and more than 25% faster than Bible Search (see below). In 4 minutes and 45 seconds, using OR logic and searching the Gospel of John, CB concorded twenty-five different terms and created five indices that contained a total of 719 verses. That's impressive speed and power, to say the least.

CB's 104-page manual is well-written, well-organized, clear, detailed, and helpful, though not without fault (see below). Its lengthy but logically organized table of contents reflects CB's complex but logical user interface. Chapter 2—six pages—is a brief tutorial that provides a hands-on introduction to SS's fundamental concording, editing, and printing features. Two appendices provide information about abbreviations used for the books of the Bible and about error messages. Sadly, for a program of this complexity, there is no index, though the six-page table of contents is sufficiently detailed to substitute for one.

3.2.3.2 Description

User Interface. Like TWP and SS, CB is a menu-driven program. Its YES/NO questions usually have a default value that is displayed in brackets (e.g., [YES]/NO), so that hitting Return invokes that value and expedites the process of using menus and prompts to operate the program. CB's Lotus-like main menu is divided horizontally into five major sections. The top line displays the name "compuBIBLE" and lists the version being used, the serial number of the program disk, and informs users that this is

---

11. Altogether, CB's data and program files take up about 3.1 megabytes of disk space.

12. According to NASSCO, version 1.2 of CB can build that same index in 52 seconds on a 4.77-MHz, 8088 machine, and with the program's screen-update function turned off, CB can do that in 42 seconds.

the main menu level. The next line of information is a list of seven options, most of which are different modes in which CB can be operated.[13] Using the left and right cursor keys to highlight the name of a mode displays a brief help line that lists the mode's main functions. The Concordance Mode is used to create topical indices, the Edit Mode to edit indices, and the Print Mode to set various formatting parameters that govern the printing of indices. The Scripture Mode is used to read, scan, and print Scripture. The Utilities Mode inserts Scripture into a document created with word processors, converts indices created with TWP or SS into the compuBIBLE™ format, and allows users to install word processors other than those CB explicitly supports. The Index Management Mode is used to copy and delete indices, and the Options Mode sets the screen, drives, and printer parameters. The middle portion of the main menu contains copyright notices, and the date and time. The last line of the main menu lists six function keys and their use.

Like TWP and SS, CB makes extensive use of the IBM function keys. On the IBM version of compuBIBLE™, the F1 key is the Help key and provides information about CB in general and about the program's current mode. As the 40K size of CB's help file indicates, an amazing amount of useful information is on-line. Additionally, CB provides brief help lines under every highlighted item in any menu. The F2 key displays a Directory of indices on the program drive. The F3, or Print, key sends verses or a directory of indices to the printer. The F4 key is the Display key and displays current information about the index that is being constructed, about the parameters that have been set, and about the current index. The F5, or Top, key moves the cursor to the top of the range in the Scripture Mode and to the top of the index in the Edit Mode. The F6, or Bottom, key moves the cursor to the bottom of the range in the Scripture Mode and to the bottom of the index in the Edit Mode. Like the QUIT command in each menu, the Escape key returns CB to the previous menu level.

In each mode, CB uses the top six lines and the last line of the screen for the following purposes. Line 1 gives the name of the program, or mode, CB is in. Line 2 provides the menu items for that mode. Line 3 is the menu help line and contains information about each menu item. Line 4 is the message prompt line where error messages, prompts, and information about current activity are displayed. Line 5 is the query line where users answer questions the program asks. Line 6, the status line, displays information about the current range, current index, location of Scripture, and so forth. The last line of the screen displays the function key definitions, which do not change, though some keys are inoperative in some modes. The top right corner of the screen is often used to display messages (such as "SEARCH" and "WAIT") in blinking, reverse video.

Search Logic and the Concordance Mode. The Concordance Mode is used to create indices. Its submenu includes the following options: Create, Option, Range, Analysis, and Search. CB can create up to five indices simultaneously, each of which may contain up to five words or phrases, and each word or phrase may be up to sixty characters in length (i.e., a maximum of 1,500 characters).

CB supports Boolean AND/OR logic in the Concordance Mode. By default, separate search strings are joined with an implied OR, unless one of CB's two Boolean operators is used. CB uses the "*" sign for a Boolean AND and the "|" sign for a Boolean OR, and CB allows ANDs and ORs to be mixed in the same search construction and index. Using symbols for Boolean operators and allowing the operators to be mixed in the same search places CB's search features ahead of those of most other Bible concordance programs. CB's Boolean operators are used in conjunction with its pattern-matching feature. A pattern consists of strings of text (whole or partial words or phrases) joined with "*" or with "|." Although these Boolean operators may not be mixed on the same line of a search construction, they may be used on different lines

---

13. The CB manual also refers to these modes as "programs" and as "sections."

when constructing a single index. Thus one line of search terms could be joined by "*" and another by "|."[14]

Boolean "*" searches (i.e., AND) are sequence-specific but not exact-phrase searches. Any number of words may intervene (within the context of a verse) between the two search strings, and the order of the strings *is* significant. For example, to locate New Testament verses that include *prayer, faith,* and *sick* (James 5:15), the search construction should be "prayer * faith * sick." Or, for example, if the range is set to Matthew's gospel, "women * far off" will locate Matthew 27:55, but "far off * women" will not. "Son * man" will locate thirty-one references in Matthew to "Son of Man," but "man * son" yields only two references (Matt. 7:9; 21:28), neither of which is to "Son of Man." Boolean "|" searches (i.e., OR) are neither sequence-specific nor exact-phrase searches. Any number of words may intervene (within the context of a verse) between the two search strings, whose order is *not* significant. Thus "|" is used in searches to locate words or phrases in *any* order. "Son | man," then, will locate "Son of Man," as well as the inverted order "man . . . son" in Matthew 7:9 and 21:28.

Boolean ANDs and ORs may be mixed in the following way when pattern-matching. Using the Gospel of John as the range and "in | beginning" and "was * God" as search strings entered on separate lines in a single index, for example, CB located all the verses in John where "was . . . God," "in . . . beginning," and "beginning . . . in" occur, listing twice in the index those verses that contain both patterns (e.g., John 1:1).

CB also supports the use of initial, medial, and terminal wild-card *characters* ("?" represents any character, "!" represents alpha-characters only, and "#" represents any digit), though this is an undocumented feature of the program. Wild-card characters and pattern-matching may be used together. Thus "in | begi? | ?ord" correctly located John 1:1. CB's ability to combine wild-cards and pattern-matching in searches places its search features ahead of those of most of the programs reviewed in this chapter. Searching with Boolean pattern-matching symbols is more specific than searching with wild-card characters.

The Concordance Mode *submenu* is used to set text ranges that are to be scanned to create indices, to analyze the English used in search constructions to make certain that it conforms to the English of the version being used, to delete the information in the current active index so that new information may be entered, to clear all information from all five indices, and to specify the following search options: Speed Search, Define, Preview, Case, and Whole. Speed Search is the fastest way of searching but does not support the Preview, Case, and Whole options. Define supports searching for incomplete words but is slower than Speed Search. Preview highlights matches as they are found and allows users to decide on a case-by-case basis whether to place matches in an index. Preview may be used with the Case and Whole options but is much slower than Speed Search. Case matches words regardless of the way upper- and lower-case letters have been used in search constructions. Whole locates exact, literal matches of search constructions.

The Search submenu option is used to start a cocording operation. As CB creates an index or indices, it displays a window with the name and number of the indices it is creating, the range being concorded, the concording options selected, the number of entries found, the current chapter and verse, and the message "SEARCH" in blinking, reverse video. CB does not inform users which verses are being inserted into indices (unless the Preview option has been specified) or the terms it is searching for. When indices are completed, an alarm sounds. An alarm also sounds on floppy disk versions to notify users to change disks, a useful feature not found on TWP or SS. Indices may contain an unlimited number of entries, but since there are 31,102 verses in

---

14. When using CB's pattern-matching search logic, be sure *not* to use the Concordance Mode submenu option Whole, something version 1.0 of the manual fails to mention.

the KJV, no index will contain more entries than that. CB does not indicate how long concording operations take.

The Edit Mode. This mode is used to edit indices, to display their contents, to sort, save, delete, and rename indices, and to insert additional references in indices. When displaying index verses in this mode, verses are displayed in context (usually as the third verse from the top of the screen, with four or five verses following), and the entire verse that contains the hit is highlighted. The Edit Mode does not support scrolling, unlike SS, which supports forward scrolling through indices in the Concordance Mode, and TWP, which supports bidirectional scrolling through indices in the Index Mode. This limitation, however, is offset by the fact that unlike TWP and SS, CB allows users to load an index in the Scripture Mode, display the hits, and scroll bidirectionally (see below). CB's Edit Mode also supports a GOTO function that allows users to go to a selected verse. And the Edit Mode allows users to create indices by specifying the references they should contain. CB allows the original index and an edited version of it to be saved and supports undeleting references, moving references, and editing index titles. Finally, CB *automatically* saves a copy of each search construction, and allows this information to be displayed in the Edit Mode. When displaying text, like TWP and SS, CB uses upper- and lower-case letters correctly.

The Print Mode. This mode is used to set formatting parameters that govern the printing of indices. By setting the proper parameters, users can print either the text of the verses in an index, the book and reference numbers of those verses, or the verse references in column form with space left for notes. Index names and titles may be printed with indices. Other settings govern common printing parameters, such as pagination, pausing between pages, spacing, justification, and so forth, though this brief description hardly does justice to CB's wide range of powerful and flexible Print Mode features.

The Scripture Mode. This mode is used to browse bidirectionally through a selected range. In this mode, an index may be loaded into memory and all its references displayed in context. Index entries are highlighted by a left-hand margin pointer, and the book, chapter, and verse they appear in are displayed in a window near the top of the screen, thus making hits impossible to miss. Only one index may be in memory at a time. Like TWP and SS, CB's Scripture Mode supports a GOTO function that allows users to go directly to a particular verse. The Scripture Mode also may be used to create an index from an existing one or to create an index from scratch by inserting verse references. Furthermore, in this mode verses may be transferred from one index to another, and the screen may be split into two vertical windows of equal size, each of which may contain the same or a different range of text through which users may scroll bidirectionally. Although switching windows sometimes takes a few seconds, *all* CB functions are available when using windows, something that is not true of most other programs reviewed in this chapter. Because only one index may be in memory at a time, both windows may be used to scan different parts of the same index, though each window may not contain a separate index. A command called MATCH can scan for one (and only one) word at a time in this mode. Using MATCH is similar to scanning in TWP's Scan Mode, though unlike TWP, CB does not support Boolean AND/OR logic when MATCHing since MATCHes are limited to single words. Matches, or hits, are highlighted in reverse video. The NEXT command instructs CB to locate the next match in a memory-resident index.

The Utilities Mode. This mode is used to insert Scripture verses into an ASCII file prepared with a word processor. The insert command for this may have the forms "//BIBLEBOOK n:n//, //BIBLEBOOK n:n-n//, //BIBLEBOOK n:n-//, //BIBLEBOOK n://," or "//BIBLEBOOK n:n-n:n//," where n:n represents chapter and verse numbers. CB can insert more than one chapter at a time into a document, though 1,024 verses appears to be the most it can insert per command. By using this procedure, CB can convert all of its text files to ASCII files, though that can be done more easily by using

CB's "print to disk" default option in the Print Mode. The Utilities Mode also may be used to convert indices prepared by THE WORD processor and by SCRIPTURE SCANNER to compuBIBLE™ format. A utility command called DIVIDE is used to divide large, difficult-to-manage indices into smaller ones that are easier to handle. The Utilities Mode is also used to install word processors CB does not explicitly support.[15]

Index Management Mode. The penultimate main mode, Index Management, is used to copy, delete, transfer, rename, unmark, and merge indices. The LOG command displays the drives indices are located on and allows users to change the logged drive. Like TWP and SS, CB merges either by combining all the references in two indices (the equivalent of a Boolean OR) or by intersecting the references in two indices, so that only the references the indices have in common are preserved (the equivalent of a Boolean AND). CB cannot combine or intersect indices that contain more than 1,500 references each.

The Options Mode. This mode is used to tailor CB for specific computer systems. Users may specify screen type, default program drive, default data-disk drive, and printer type. CB supports fourteen different printers (most of them dot matrix), from eight manufacturers. A printer program enables users to install printers that are not explicitly supported.

3.2.3.3 Evaluation

CB is easily the most impressive of the nonindexed Bible concordance programs for many reasons, and it has the best user interface of any program reviewed in this chapter. It is very fast, quite flexible, and cleanly programmed. It meets many of our criteria for an ideal concordance program. CB supports (1) Boolean AND and OR operators when concording text and manipulating indices, (2) mixed operators, (3) initial, medial, and terminal truncation, (4) wild-card characters, (5) case-sensitive, (6) sequence-specific, and (7) exact-phrase searches, (8) search constructions of up to 1,500 characters, (9) indices of unlimited length, (10) simultaneously creating multiple indices (thus facilitating topical Bible study), (11) pattern-matching, (12) user-specified search ranges, (13) windows, and (14) a GOTO command. CB displays (15) the range when scanning and concording, and (16) dynamically updates the current location of the program's concording activities and the location of hits, as well as providing a running total of index entries. Hits are (17) highlighted in the Edit Mode and may be (18) saved to disk, (19) printed, (20) inserted into files prepared with word processing programs, and (21) scrolled bidirectionally. Indices may be (22) combined, (23) intersected, and (24) edited. (25) Indices and the text may be scanned for matches. And (26) CB has the most impressive breadth and depth of on-line help of any of the Bible concordance programs, as well as the (27) most detailed manual and the (28) most powerful printing features.

For all its strengths, CB suffers from the following shortcomings. CB does not support (1) Boolean XORs and NOTs, (2) nested operators, (3) mixing operators on the same line of a search, (4) proximity searches, (5) searching nonsequential ranges, or (6) showing the difference between indices. And (7) verse boundaries arbitrarily and artificially restrict the field in which TWP looks for search strings.

---

15. CB explicitly supports EasyWriter™, the Leading Edge Word Processor™, VolksWriter®, Word-Perfect™, WordStar®, and WordVision™. CB will work with any word processor that produces standard ASCII files.

3.2.4 Bible Search

● *BASIC PRODUCT INFORMATION*

Name of Program: Bible Search
Company Name: Scripture Software
Address: P.O. Box 531131, Orlando, FL 32853
Phone: (305) 896-4264
Price: $225
Version Tested: 1.4, demo disk, KJV text, TRS-80 Model III version
Runs On: TRS-80, Models I, III, and 4 (in Model III mode)
Memory Requirements: 48K
Operating System Requirements: Not known
Disk Drive Requirements: 2, at least one of which must be a 40-track drive
Supports Color Monitors: No
Uses Sound: No
Number of Text Disks: 8
Number of Program Disks: 1 (contains a stripped-down version of LDOS); program contained on one of text disks in some versions.
Size of Program Files: 33K
Size of Help Files: No help files available
Size of Text Files: 2.2MB
Text Files in ASCII: No
Produces ASCII Output Files: Yes
Search String Limitations: 10 words or phrases
Maximum Number of Entries per Index: 320 entries
Type of Disks Used: Flippy
Text Available: KJV
Product Includes: Program disk, text disks, user's manual
Manual: 45 pages, letter-quality computer printout, 3 appendices, indexed
Demo Disk Available: Yes, $6
Copy Protected: No
Hard Disk Compatible: Yes
Menu-Driven: Yes
On-line Help: No
Tutorial: Yes
Warranty: No
Support: Phone and letter
Update Policy: Minimum fee for registered users
Related Products: None
Other Information: Reviewed in *CCUA News* (Mar/Apr, 1985): 8–10; CP/M and MS-DOS versions planned.

3.2.4.1 Introduction

Bible Search (hereafter BibS), created by Thomas L. Cook, is a menu-driven, KJV-based Bible concordance program that runs on TRS-80 microcomputers. Smal-LDOS, a subset of the LDOS 5.1.4 operating system, is used because it is faster and more flexible than TRSDOS and provides complete file compatibility between TRS-80 Models I, III, and 4. Because of the Model 4's higher clock rate, BibS runs the fastest on that machine.[16] BibS is fast. Using Boolean OR logic, BibS took only in 1 minute and 46 seconds to construct an index of the forty-two places in the Gospel of John where it found a reference to *woman*, *husband*, *well*, and *friend*, making it the second-fastest program that works with nonindexed text.[17] CB completed this task in 1 minute and 20 seconds, and TWP and SS each took about 2 minutes and 30 seconds. BibS, then, is roughly 25% slower than CB and 25% faster than TWP and SS.

---

16. The Model 4 runs at 4 MHz and the Model III at 2 MHz.
17. I ran this test from a floppy drive in a TRS-80 Model 4-D with 64K.

BibS's 45-page manual is well-written, well-organized, clear, and helpful. Its brevity and simplicity reflect BibS's simple and friendly user interface. Four pages are devoted to a brief, hands-on tutorial that introduces BibS's basic features. Four appendices provide information about resources for Bible study, hermeneutics, and the abbreviations used for the books of the Bible. Four pages of indices make this manual very easy to use.

3.2.4.2 Description

User Interface. BibS's main menu has four options: Text Scanning, Reference Study, Change Parameters, and Exit. Text Scanning is used to read or search through a selected range of text, Reference Study is used to manipulate indices generated with Text Scanning, and Change Parameters is used to customize the screen, print, and file specifications to match a particular system. BibS includes in angle brackets (< >) those portions of the text that are italicized in printed editions of the Bible (places where the KJV translators supplied words that are implied by but that do not actually correspond to the Hebrew and Greek texts). Scripture is correctly displayed in upper- and lower-case letters.

Search Logic and the Scan Mode. The Text Scanning mode's submenu items include Save Text (Y/N) and Select by Subject or Select All (S/A). If the Save Text feature is selected, BibS prompts users to specify a passage or range of text, which it then locates and reads into memory, either directly or as a result of its index-building operation (see below). Once the text is loaded into memory, users may page through it bidirectionally. BibS loaded the Gospel of John into memory in 2 minutes and 30 seconds, displaying the text on-screen as it did so. If more text is found than will fit into memory, however, BibS stops. The Save Text feature, then, is best used when the amount of text BibS has been commanded to read into memory will fit. Selecting Select All causes BibS to read through a range of text, and selecting Select by Subject causes BibS to concord through a range of text.

BibS can search for up to ten words or phrases at a time. Search terms are entered on the same line, separated by a slash, for example, "woman/husband/well/friend." BibS's default setting causes it to join two or more words with an implied Boolean OR, but that value can be changed to an implied AND by using one of the Change Parameters submenu options. ANDs and ORs cannot be mixed in a search. BibS searches for subjects on a literal character-by-character basis. BibS supports initial, medial, and terminal truncation by using spaces. For example, "just" not preceded or followed by a space causes BibS to find every word that contains that string, that is, *justify, justification, justifier, just, unjust,* and so forth. "Just" preceded but not followed by a space causes BibS to locate only those words that begin with *just.* "Just" preceded and followed by a space causes BibS to locate *just* and no other word (an exact match). And "just" followed but not preceded by a space causes BibS to locate all words that end with *just,* for example, *unjust.* Leading and trailing punctuation must be taken into consideration when constructing searches.

After search terms have been entered, BibS prompts users for the search range. Nonsequential ranges may be searched. Range values include book, chapter, and verse levels. For example, BibS will accept "ROM-COL, MAT, GEN" (book level), "ROM 1:,3:,5:" (chapter level), and "ROM 5:1–6:8" (verse level) as valid ranges, and these range types may be mixed. As it builds an index, BibS displays the number of the chapter and verse it is searching, as well as the *complete text* of each hit, which it saves to memory. BibS does not, however, display the range being searched, the number of entries an index contains, the size of indices, or the time required to create them. Nor does BibS provide a way to display search constructions, though it does allow indices to be given file names and saved to disk. Indices are limited to 320 entries. When the 320-entry mark is reached, BibS continues to scan to the end of the range, displaying any hits with the message "OVER 320 REFERENCES." No hit after the 320 mark, however, is saved.

Index Mode. The Reference Study main menu option is used to study the indices constructed with the Text Scanning option. Indices may be loaded and displayed as a list of references, as single verses only, or as verses in context. BibS supports bidirectional scrolling in the Context mode. When viewing verses in context, BibS does not highlight hits but displays them approximately in the middle of the screen. As with the other programs we have reviewed, references may be added to or deleted from indices. Indices also may be flagged, unflagged, combined and printed. Unhappily, however, indices may not be intersected.

3.2.4.3 Evaluation

BibS meets several of our criteria for an ideal concordance program. BibS supports (1) Boolean AND/OR logic when compiling indices, (2) simultaneous multiple word searches (thus facilitating topical Bible study), (3) initial, medial, and terminal truncation, (4) exact-phrase searches, and (5) nonsequential search ranges. BibS displays (6) the number of the chapter being scanned and (7) the location and complete text of hits. Hits may be (8) saved to disk, (9) printed, and (10) scrolled bidirectionally.

But BibS suffers from a number of significant shortcomings. BibS does not support (1) indices that contain more than 320 verses, (2) long search strings (10 words is the limit), (3) combining, intersecting, and showing the difference between indices, (4) Boolean XORs and NOTs, (5) nested operators, (6) mixed operators, (7) wild-cards, (8) case-sensitive, (9) proximity, and (10) sequence-specific searches, (11) windows, (12) a GOTO command, (13) a word processing interface, (14) displaying the search range and construction, or (15) scanning the text and indices for matches. When concording, BibS does not (16) dynamically display the number of entries indices contain, (17) their size, or (18) the search constructions used to create them. BibS does not (19) highlight hits. (20) No on-line help is available.

Because they are considerably less powerful than TWP, SS, CB, and BibS, or because they do not contain the complete text of the Bible, only the basic facts will be given about the following nonindexed Bible concordance programs.

3.2.5 BIBLE-ON-DISK

* *BASIC PRODUCT INFORMATION*

Name of Program: BIBLE-ON-DISK
Company Name: Logos Information Systems
Address: 333 Cobalt Way, Suite 107, Sunnyvale, CA 94086
Phone: (408) 737-9127
Price: $129.95: New Testament, Psalms, Proverbs; $99.95: New Testament; $39.95: Psalms, Proverbs
Version Tested: 1.73, demo disk, KJV text, IBM version
Runs On: IBM PCs and compatibles
Memory Requirements: 128K
Operating System Requirements: Not known
Disk Drive Requirements: 1
Supports Color Monitors: Yes
Uses Sound: No
Number of Text Disks: 6 (Only the New Testament, Psalms, and Proverbs are currently available.)
Number of Program Disks: Programs included on text disks.
Size of Program Files: 106K
Size of Help Files: 730 bytes

Size of Text Files: 1.1MB (New Testament only)
Text Files in ASCII: Yes
Produces ASCII Output Files: Yes
Search String Limitations: Single word or phrase, up to 1,000 characters
Maximum Number of Entries per Index: Does not produce indices, though users may redirect output to files.
Type of Disks Used: Double-sided, double-density; single-sided disks available.
Text Available: KJV
Product Includes: 6 disks and user's guide
Manual: 14 pages, not indexed
Demo Disk Available: Yes, $10
Copy Protected: No
Hard Disk Compatible: Yes
Menu-Driven: Yes
On-line Help: Yes
Tutorial: Yes, in manual
Warranty: 90 days on media
Support: Limited
Update Policy: $10 in exchange for master disks
Related Products: None
Other Information: Searches are restricted to looking up single words, phrases, or specific locations in the text. Boolean operators, wild-card characters, truncation, and index manipulation are not supported. BIBLE-ON-DISK does not create indices per se, though results of searches can be redirected to a file. Printing from within the program is supported. All text is straight, uncompressed ASCII. Italicized words are in curly brackets ({ }), words of Jesus are in square brackets ([ ]), and poetry and OT quotations are in angle brackets (< >). BIBLE-ON-DISK can be menu-driven or command-driven. When using a color monitor, the words of Jesus appear on-screen in red. A Living Bible version of BIBLE-ON-DISK is being prepared. BIBLE-ON-DISK is fast. In 35 seconds it located and wrote to a file over 150 references in the Gospel of John to *Jesus*, and in 55 seconds it wrote to a file the complete text of every verse in John that contains *Jesus*.

3.2.6 COMPUTER BIBLE

● *BASIC PRODUCT INFORMATION*

Name of Program: COMPUTER BIBLE™
Company Name: Computer Bibles International, Inc.™
Address: Invercauld Park, Rt. #12, Greenville, SC 29609
Phone: (803) 242-9254
Price: $99.50
Version Tested: 1.0, full program, GNB text, IBM version; current version is 1.21.
Runs On: IBM PCs and compatibles
Memory Requirements: 128K
Operating System Requirements: Not known
Disk Drive Requirements: 1
Supports Color Monitors: No (only in black-and-white mode)
Uses Sound: No
Number of Text Disks: 2 (Only the New Testament is available.)
Number of Program Disks: Programs included on text disks.
Size of Program Files: 65K
Size of Help Files: 2 screens of information
Size of Text Files: 600K
Text Files in ASCII: No
Produces ASCII Output Files: No
Search String Limitations: Single word
Maximum Number of Entries per Index: Does not produce indices.
Type of Disks Used: Double-sided, double-density
Text Available: Good News Bible New Testament
Product Includes: 2 disks and user's notes
Manual: 11 photocopied pages, not indexed
Demo Disk Available: Yes $5
Copy Protected: No

Hard Disk Compatible: Yes
Menu-Driven: Yes
On-line Help: Yes
Tutorial: Yes, in manual
Warranty: Media only
Support: Available corrections to program and data provided on request.
Update Policy: $5 to correct bugs
Related Products: None
Other Information: Searches are restricted to looking up single words or specific locations in the text. The COMPUTER BIBLE does not create indices or support wild-card searches, though it permits ten references to be flagged and supports printing from within the program. GNB subject headings are included with the text but are not distinguished from it. Computer Bibles International plans to market on twenty floppy diskettes three complete English translations of the Bible, as well as *Biblia Hebraica Stuttgartensia*[5] (a critical edition of the Hebrew Old Testament) and an unspecified version of the Greek New Testament. Full MRTs of the KJV and Good News Bible are promised.

3.3 Indexed Bible Concordance Programs

Seven Bible concordance programs use indexed versions of the biblical text. Because these programs contain indices of every word in the Bible, they do not search sequentially through the text when concording; they go directly to existing indices. Therefore they are extremely fast—far faster than nonindexed Bible concordance programs. For example, indexed Bible concordance programs typically are ready to display every occurrence of any word in the Bible in under 3 seconds. Indexed Bible concordance programs are larger than their nonindexed counterparts, since their data bases include precompiled indices to all the words in the Bible, and require a hard disk.

Indexed Bible concordance programs are "second-generation" programs. Unfortunately, all seven of them came to my attention too late to be given full reviews in this edition of this book. The brevity of the following remarks, however, should not be taken as a reflection of the power, speed, and flexibility of these programs.

Although it is not available for review at this time, Zondervan Publishing House is developing a "third-generation" indexed English/Greek Bible concordance program, using the NIV text. This as yet unnamed and unpriced program, which should be available sometime in 1988, exists in Alpha form and will run on IBM PCs and compatibles under DOS 2.0 or greater and will require at least 128K RAM and a 10 megabyte hard disk. Combined, the text and programs are between 4 and 5 megabytes in size. Text files are compressed but may be output to disk as plain ASCII. The program is not copy protected, contains on-line help, and is menu-driven. Color monitors will be supported, as will IBM's Enhanced Graphics Adapter (EGA), the Hercules Graphics Card (HGC), and the Hercules Graphics Card Plus (HGC+). The EGA and Hercules cards will allow Greek characters to be displayed properly on-screen. An unspecified set of printers will be supported and Greek fonts provided for them. According to company spokesman Mark Hunt, Zondervan's program will support the following features: (1) Boolean ANDs, ORs, and NOTs in search constructions, (2) nested constructions, (3) long search strings, (4) indices of unlimited size, (5) wild-card searches, (6) fragment searches, (7) proximity searching by phrase, verse, paragraph, and chapter, (8) exact-phrase searches, (9) noncontiguous search ranges, (10) saving search constructions with indices, (11) attaching user comments to indices, (12) dynamic updating of search term, matches, time, and location, (13) displaying results as verse references only, (14) displaying results as verses and text, (15) bidirectional scrolling through indices and text, (16) highlighted search terms, (17) scanning text for matches, (18) a GOTO command, (19) a word processing interface, (20) up to 29 user-adjustable/definable windows, (21) on-line, user-provided, explanatory notes, (22) on-line help, (23) transliterated Greek (Hebrew and Aramaic will be offered later),

(24) concording from Greek (concording from Hebrew and Aramaic will be supported later), and (25) editing search results.

3.3.1 The Powerful Word

- *BASIC PRODUCT INFORMATION*

Name of Program: The Powerful Word
Company Name: Hatley Computer Services
Address: Route 20, Box 2016, Springfield, MO 65803
Phone: (417) 833-0629
Price: $149
Version Tested: 2.2
Runs On: IBM PCs and compatibles; Wang PC
Memory Requirements: 512K
Operating System Requirements: DOS 2.0 or greater
Disk Drive Requirements: 2, one of which must be a hard disk
Supports Color Monitors: Yes
Uses Sound: No
Number of Text Disks: 10
Number of Program Disks: 1
Size of Program Files: 330K
Size of Help Files: Not applicable
Size of Text Files: Approximately 3.2MB, including index files
Text Files in ASCII: No
Produces ASCII Output Files: Yes
Search String Limitations: 480 characters
Maximum Number of Entries per Index: 31,102
Type of Disks Used: Double-sided, double-density
Text Available: KJV
Product Includes: Program disks, text disks, user's manual, shell feature
Manual: 51 pages, not indexed, but detailed table of contents can serve as index.
Demo Disk Available: Yes, $5
Copy Protected: Yes
Hard Disk Compatible: Yes
Menu-Driven: Yes; some functions are command-driven.
On-line Help: No
Tutorial: No
Warranty: 90 days, media only
Support: Phone and letter
Update Policy: Available at nominal cost; maximum of $25.
Related Products: None
Other Information: Major new release planned for late 1987.

3.3.1.1 Introduction

The Powerful Word (hereafter TPW), created during 1985–1986 by Dewey Hatley, is an indexed version of the KJV that has one of the best combinations of features, flexibility, speed, and power of all the Bible concordance programs reviewed in this chapter. Only compuBIBLE's and EveryWord's search features rival those of TPW. TPW is more expensive than GodSpeed™ but less expensive than ComWord 1 and EveryWord™ (see below). TPW is far more powerful than GodSpeed™ and ComWord 1 and has search features not found in EveryWord™. At $149, TPW is not just a bargain, it's a steal.

TPW is fast. On an 8-MHz 8086 machine, using a 65-millisecond hard drive, it located all the instances of *woman, husband, well,* and *friend* in the Gospel of John in 4 seconds, and it located *all* the instances of those words in the entire Bible in *less* than 4 seconds (searching a restricted range of text requires an extra operation not required when searching the whole Bible).

3.3.1.2 Description

TPW is menu- and command-driven, and because it is a powerful program, its menus have more options than those of less powerful programs. Most of TPW's menu functions may be chosen by using the numeric keypad keys (toggled into their numeric mode).

TPW's main menu has four options: (1) Use the Concordance, (2) Access Text via Menu, (3) Access Text via Command Line, and (4) Define System Printer. Selecting Use the Concordance displays a submenu with seven options: (1) Build New Index from Scratch, (2) Edit Index, (3) Print Index, (4) Build New Index from Existing One, (5) Delete Index, (6) Display Concordance, and (7) Return to Main Menu.

When using the Build New Index option, TPW supports Boolean ANDs, ORs, XORs, and NOTs and allows users to specify which operator is the default operator in multi-word searches. (A default operator is one that does not have to be entered in the search string; spaces between words in multi-word searches function as the default operator.) Only TPW and EveryWord™ (see below) support the NOT operator in concording operations; only TPW supports the XOR operator and allows users to specify default operators.[18] Search strings may be up to 480 characters long, indices may contain up to 31,102 entries, and Boolean operators may be mixed and inserted directly into search constructions, so that "Moses aa Aaron nn Miriam" is a valid search construction. (*Aa* and *nn* are the AND and NOT operators respectively.) Support for the four major operators, for mixing them on the same line in search constructions, and for entering them as part of constructions are all unique to TPW. Unfortunately, however, TPW does not allow Boolean operators to be nested. For example, "(Moses aa (Aaron oo Miriam)) nn (Egypt oo Pharaoh)" is not a valid search construction. Except for a few terms that refer to deity, search terms are not case-specific. Intervening punctuation is ignored in searches. Sequence-specific and exact-phrase searches are not supported.

Search constructions are entered at the top of the screen on six lines, below which are listed the search options. As each term is entered and the Space Bar pressed, TPW instantly displays the number of times the term occurs and in how many verses it occurs in the selected range. If the term does not occur, the program instantly informs users of that fact, thus enabling them to avoid running searches for nonexistent words. No other program reviewed in this chapter displays statistical information about word usage as search terms are entered or at that time informs users if the term does not appear in the selected range. This is a very helpful and desirable feature.

TPW supports initial, medial, and terminal truncation in the following manner. Entering "pray >" as a search term causes TPW to display a numbered list of all the words in the Bible that begin with *pray* (terminal truncation). Users may then specify by number or by contiguous range of numbers the words they wish included in a search, and those words are highlighted in the list and added automatically to the search construction. That operation may be repeated until all the desired terms have been chosen, thus making it possible to add noncontiguous sets of terms to the search construction. An All option allows users to select the entire list. Initial and medial truncation are handled in a similar manner. By selecting truncated terms from a numbered list, users are able to include in search constructions only those words they wish included in an index. Although this way of supporting truncation requires the additional step of selecting words from a list (or of selecting the entire list), it allows searches to be more specific.

---

18. EveryWord™ and WORDsearch™ (see below) support the NOT operator when manipulating indices.

TPW also supports wild-card searches. "?" represents any single character and may be used in the initial, medial, and terminal positions. Thus "m?n," "?re," "ma?," and "a??e" are valid search constructions. Wild-cards may be used with truncation, with Boolean operators, and in proximity searches. TPW does not support a global wild-card character (e.g., "*").

Searches may be restricted to a particular chapter or range of chapters in a book or books. Books are numbered sequentially (1–66) and selected from a Book Selection Menu in the same way that words in truncated word lists are selected. Noncontiguous ranges of text may be searched.

TPW supports multi-word proximity searches that locate matches across verse and chapter boundaries. Only TPW and Wordworker (see below) support this feature; all other Bible concordance programs are "verse-bound" and can locate matches only if the search terms occur in the same verse. TPW allows users to specify a range of verses in which a search term or terms must appear. Acceptable values are 1 to 999. Thus users may search for instances where one or more terms occur within from 1 to 999 verses of one another. Boolean operators and proximity operators may be used together. Thus "Abraham oo+25 Isaac" causes TPW to create an index of all the verses where either *Abraham* or *Isaac* or both appear, regardless of whether those terms are in the same verse or -chapter, as long as they occur within twenty-five verses of one another.

Unless instructed otherwise, TPW dynamically displays the intermediate results of concording operations on-screen. Users are told what Boolean operation is being performed on which search term, how many verses containing the word have been found in the specified range, and how long it took to find all the verses that contained the term. Placing an "&" anywhere in a search string speeds up the search by suppressing the on-screen display of intermediate results. Indices may be saved under user-assigned file names. TPW automatically saves the current index in a file called LAST INDEX, which is overwritten by each successive index. Search constructions are automatically saved with indices.

In the Display Concordance Mode, an exhaustive, alphabetized frequency list of every word in the Bible may be displayed in a 3-column-wide format and paged through bidirectionally a screenful at a time. Users may select search terms directly from this list, as they can from lists of truncated words (see above). And users may specify alphabetical ranges of terms to be displayed. In this mode, initial, medial, and terminal truncation and wild cards are supported. This makes it easy to see words that begin with, contain, or end with user-specified character strings. Displaying the concordance allows users to check the spelling of words and to discover related terms.

Once an index has been created, users may edit the search construction used to create it, but they may not add or delete verses to the index. Indices may be printed, deleted, and their search constructions used to build new indices. Regardless of their user-assigned names, all indices that have been saved are numbered. To edit an index or to use an existing index to create a new one, users select an index from the Index Listing Screen by entering the index's number. Once an index is selected, the search terms and search commands used to create the index are displayed. Users may modify those terms and commands and then create a modified index. Once created, if the new index is not saved, the old index will not be overwritten as it will be if the new index is saved under the same file name as the old index. A modified index may be saved under a new name, thus preserving the original index. Indices may be printed to screen, to disk, or sent to a printer. TPW can export indices and ranges of verses to user-specified text files as plain ASCII text. References only or references and the text of the references may be printed. Ranges of verses may be selected and printed.

Once an index has been created, hits may be displayed singly or in context in the Index Window of the Reference Display Screen. (This window occupies the left half of the screen.) In each verse, all terms that count as matches are highlighted. When using the full window display option, hits are displayed at the top of the Index Window with context verses following, and users may scroll bidirectionally on either side of the hit, as far as they wish to, a line or windowful of text at a time by using the PgUp, PgDn, and cursor keys. Hits that occur in context verses are highlighted. Alternatively, users may move bidirectionally through hits one at a time or five at a time and jump directly to the first or last entry in an index. Additionally, TPW supports a bidirectional auto-scroll feature (with user-adjustable scroll rate) that automatically scrolls index references. The Context Window (which occupies the right half of the Reference Display Screen) is used to display any range of verses. Verses in this window may be scrolled bidirectionally one at a time or a windowful at a time, and users may jump to the first or last verse in the chapter and book that is being displayed. Search terms that appear in verses in this window are highlighted. A pop-up, command-line, GOTO option in this window allows users to go to any book, chapter, and verse. Users may switch from the Index to the Context Window with a single keystroke. Using the Print Index Mode, users may print any verse or range of verses from the Context Window or any index entry or range of index entries from the Index Window. Using TPW's print function, users may print a verses-only version of an index to screen, save it in a file, or send it to the printer.

In addition to creating custom indices, TPW has a two-window Text Mode Display Screen that allows users to display two different ranges of verses simultaneously. Verses may be displayed one at a time or a windowful at a time. In this mode, users may scroll text bidirectionally by line, window, and verse, jump five verses at a time, go directly to the beginning and end of a chapter or book, and switch windows with a single keystroke. This mode also supports auto-scroll, print, and GOTO features. TPW includes a shell that allows users to exit the program with a single keystroke, run application programs or DOS commands, and return to TPW without reloading it.

3.3.1.3 Evaluation

TPW is the most powerful indexed Bible concordance program and one of the most impressive of all the programs reviewed in this chapter. It meets many of our criteria for an ideal Bible concordance program. TPW supports (1) the explicit use of Boolean ANDs, ORs, XORs, and NOTs in search constructions, (2) mixed operators, (3) initial, medial, and terminal truncation, (4) wild cards, (5) proximity searches, (6) nonsequential search ranges, (7) user-specified search ranges, (8) search strings of up to 480 characters, (9) indices as large as 31,102 entries, (10) noncontiguous search ranges, (11) windows, (12) a GOTO function, (13) proximity searches that locate matches across verse and chapter boundaries, and (14) multiple word searches. TPW dynamically displays information about (15) the logical operation, number of hits, and time required to complete concording operations. (16) Context verses may be displayed with indices, and (17) TPW includes an auto-scroll feature. TPW (18) displays statistical information about word usage as search terms are entered and (19) informs users if search terms do not occur in the specified range (thus enabling users to avoid running searches for nonexistent words). (20) Hits are highlighted, and (21) index entries and context verses may be displayed singly or a windowful at a time.

As powerful as it is, TPW suffers from the following shortcomings. TPW does not support (1) nested operators, (2) case-sensitive, (3) sequence-specific, and (4) exact-phrase searches, (5) intersecting and combining indices and displaying the difference between indices, (6) editing the contents of indices, (7) displaying the range when concording, (8) displaying the search construction when concording, or (9) scanning text and indices for matches. (10) No on-line help is available.

3.3.2 EveryWord Scripture Study System

● *BASIC PRODUCT INFORMATION*

Name of Program: EveryWord™ Scripture Study System
Company Name: Echo Solutions, Inc.
Address: P.O. Box 7271 University Station, Provo, UT 84602
Phone: (801) 226-7800
Price: $379
Version Tested: 1.2
Runs On: IBM PCs and compatibles
Memory Requirements: 640K
Operating System Requirements: DOS 2.0 or greater
Disk Drive Requirements: 2, one of which must be a hard drive.
Supports Color Monitors: Yes
Uses Sound: No
Number of Text Disks: 8
Number of Program Disks: 1
Size of Program Files: 207.8K
Size of Help Files: 3K
Size of Text Files: Approximately 3MB
Text Files in ASCII: No
Produces ASCII Output Files: Yes
Search String Limitations: 255 characters
Maximum Number of Entries per Index: 2,000
Type of Disks Used: Single-sided
Text Available: KJV
Product Includes: Disks, manual, WordPerfect™ Junior and Shell, keyboard template
Manual: 73 pages for EW, 164 pages for WordPerfect™ Jr., 3-ring, typeset, slipcase, appendices, glossary, indexed
Demo Disk Available: Yes, $15
Copy Protected: No
Hard Disk Compatible: Yes
Menu-Driven: Yes
On-line Help: Yes
Tutorial: Yes, in manual
Warranty: 60 days, media only
Support: Phone and letter
Update Policy: Available at special price to registered users.
Other Information: According to company spokesman Bill Woahn, version 2.0 will support exact-phrase and proximity searches.

3.3.2.1 Introduction

EveryWord™, created during 1985–1986 by Dave Sorensen and Jay Ekstrom, is an indexed KJV Bible concordance program with impressive text retrieval features. EveryWord™ (hereafter EW) includes a copy of WordPerfect™ Junior and of WordPerfect Corporation's Shell and runs under the Shell, either with WordPerfect™ Junior or with WordPerfect™.[19] The Shell's clipboard feature allows EW to output indices and text to WordPerfect™ Junior, where that output may be edited and inserted in documents, and to switch back and forth from one program to the other without exiting either program. WordPerfect™ Junior also allows users to perform a full range of word processing functions.

EW is extremely fast. Using the demo disk on a floppy drive, EW located all twenty-three references to *woman*, *husband*, *well*, and *friend* in the Gospel of Matthew

---

19. EW cannot be in memory concurrently with WordPerfect™, though it can be with WordPerfect™ Junior.

in under 2 seconds. And EW located 968 references to ten different words in Matthew in less than 11 seconds.

3.3.2.2 Description

EW is a menu-driven program that displays information in overlapping windows. Function keys and single-word commands are used to operate some of EW's features. Esc is used to backup from window to window. Two help screens display lists of all commands, key assignments, and abbreviations of Bible books, and there are one or two context-sensitive help screens for program functions. EW's main screen is used to enter search constructions, which may be up to 255 characters long. Indices may contain up to 2,000 entries. Search constructions that produce more that 2,000 entries may not be displayed on-screen or saved to an index but may be sent to a disk file or printer.

After entering a search construction, EW responds almost instantly by listing in parentheses the number of matches, for example, "(45)." Hitting return or F2 opens a window that lists hits in biblical order by book, chapter, and verse. Cursor and page-control keys may be used to scroll the list and highlight selections. Hitting Return causes the highlighted entry to be displayed in a 12-line-high window that overlaps the previous window. Using the grey "−" and "+" keys on the numeric keypad causes the previous or next match to be displayed. Search terms are highlighted. Unfortunately, only one match may be displayed at a time.

Once an index entry is displayed, using the up and down cursor keys displays the preceding and succeeding context verses, one at a time. The currently selected context verse is indicated by an asterisk that appears in intense-video to its left, and the verse reference also appears in intense video. Up to twelve lines of context verses may be displayed concurrently. The up-cursor and PgUp keys can be used to fill the 12-line window with verses, as can the down-cursor key. When using the PgDn key, however, only one context verse at a time may be displayed in the window. Index entries and context verses are displayed in the same 12-line window and may be interspersed. Because EW uses overlapping windows, only the information in the uppermost window is visible. Thus users may not display an index in one window, context verses in another, and an alphabetized frequency list in a third.

EW supports the explicit use of the AND, OR, and NOT operators in search constructions. Nested operators are supported through menu selection; they may not be typed in along with search terms. Thus "woman AND well NOT husband" is a valid construction, but users may not type in "(woman AND well) NOT husband" or "((woman AND husband) OR friend) NOT well," for example, and have EW accept those as valid constructions. Spaces in multi-word constructions function as default ANDs, a value that cannot be changed. Successive searches that begin with an operator append the result of the new search to the index created by the previous search. Thus appending "AND Matthew" to an index created by "Jesus" creates a new index that contains all the verses that include *Jesus* and *Matthew*. *And*, *or*, and *not* may be searched for by prefixing them with a single apostrophe (e.g., *'or*).

Entering the command INDEX at the command level causes EW to display an alphabetized frequency list of every word in the Bible. Users may scroll this list with the cursor and page-control keys and highlight terms. Alternatively, at the command level users may enter the FIND command followed by a word, and EW will display that word and its frequency. Frequency is measured by the number of verses in which a term appears, not by the number of times a term is used in the Bible. Once a highlighted term has been selected with Return, a small menu pops up that allows the selected term to be inserted in a search construction with no operator preceding the term or with the AND, OR, or NOT operator preceding the term. Because this operation can be repeated for each term in a search construction, multiple terms may be nested in complex ways in a single construction. In my opinion, it would be far easier and faster to allow users to formulate a search directly with parentheses, rather that requiring the use of a word index and menus to do so.

EW supports two types of wild cards—global ("*") and single ("?")—that may be used to truncate search terms initially, medially, and terminally. For example, entering "lov*" at the command level locates all words that begin with *lov*, that is *love* and *loveth*, and entering "lov?" locates *love*—two examples of terminal truncation. Entering "*ove" causes EW to locate all words that end with *ove*, that is, *above*, *dove*, *move*, and *remove*—an example of initial truncation. The construction "m?n" causes EW to locate all three-letter words that begin with *m* and end with *n*, that is, *man* and *men*—an example of medial truncation. Entering "*odl*" causes EW to locate all words that contain *odl* anywhere in the word, such as *godly* and *goodly*—another example of medial truncation. Entering ??? causes EW to locate all three-letter words; entering ????????????? causes EW to locate all fifteen-letter words (e.g., *notwithstanding*). Entering "*" causes EW to locate every word in the Bible. The two wild-card characters may be used with the FIND command (see above) to list truncated words. For example, "FIND *ing" causes EW to list all the words in the Bible that end with *ing*. This is a useful feature since (as discussed above) search terms may be selected directly from a list of words displayed by using FIND.

All search constructions are saved in the "stack" and may be displayed in a window by pressing F8, the stack key. Constructions are displayed with parentheses (if any). Long constructions disappear off the right side of the window, and there is no way to display the missing portion of those constructions. The most recent search construction is displayed first. The stack may be scrolled with the cursor and page-control keys and a highlighted search construction selected with Return. Once a highlighted search construction has been selected, a small "logical operator" window pops up. This window allows the selected construction to be appended to the most recent construction (the one displayed at the top of the stack's window) in one of several ways: as is (i.e., with no operator preceding the search construction) or preceded by AND, OR, or NOT. Once a selection has been made from the "logical operator" window, hitting Return creates an index from the two indices that were selected (i.e., the most recent index and the one selected from the stack and modified in the "logical operator" window). The Undo key (F10) deletes the most recent search construction from the stack, and the command RESET (issued at the command level) clears all search constructions from the stack. The stack's memory buffer can hold fifty indices. After forty-nine searches, a message informs users that there is room for only one more search/index.

The stack has two main functions. It serves as a list of indices from which users may select an index for viewing, and it allows indices to be combined, intersected, and the difference between two indices to be shown. EW and WORDsearch™ (see below) are the only two programs reviewed in this chapter that allow that last operation. For example, if the current index is "father OR mother" and another index is "father," then selecting the "father" index from the stack and the NOT operator from the logical operator window and pressing Return would create an index that contained all the verses in the Bible that include *mother* but not *father*. (The same result could have been achieved by entering "mother NOT father" as a search construction.) EW's ability to show the difference between two indices is a powerful feature that could be helpful when manipulating complex indices.

At the command-line level, entering VERSE followed by a book abbreviation and a chapter and verse number causes EW to go directly to any verse in the Bible. Once a verse is displayed, the cursor and page-control keys may be used to scroll through the text in the manner described above.

EW allows users to save indices and to output text and indices to the Shell's Clipboard, to a printer, or to a disk file under a user-assigned or default filename. The search construction used to create an index is automatically included with the entries

372

when the index is output to a printer or disk file. Indices may be output as full text or as references only. Sets of words that exceed EW's limit of 2,000 index entries and that therefore may not be displayed on-screen may be sent to a file or output device.

3.3.2.3 Evaluation

EW meets many of our criteria for an ideal concordance program. It supports (1) Boolean ANDs, ORs, and NOTs in search constructions, (2) nested operators, (3) mixed operators, (4) wild-cards, (5) initial, medial, and terminal truncation, (6) windows, (7) a GOTO feature, (8) manipulating indices with the AND, OR, and NOT operators, (9) search strings of up to 255 characters, and (10) indices as large as 2,000 entries. (11) Hits are highlighted, and (12) hits and context verses may be scrolled bi-directionally. EW includes (13) WordPerfect™ Junior and the WordPerfect Corporation's Shell, so that EW's indices may easily be edited and comments added to them. A (14) FIND feature allows users to display word frequency information. (15) On-line help is available.

EW's shortcomings are as follows. EW does not support (1) Boolean XORs, (2) case-sensitive, (3) proximity, (4) sequence specific, and (5) exact-phrase searches, (6) nonsequential search ranges, (7) scanning text a screenful at a time, (8) displaying more than one index entry at a time, or (9) scanning text and indices for matches. (10) Verse boundaries arbitrarily restrict matches to search terms that occur in the same verse. Users may not (11) specify search ranges, and (12) noncontiguous ranges of text may not be searched. (13) Only one window may be visible at a time, and EW does (14) not dynamically update the results of concording operations. (15) It would be nice if users were given the *option* of running EW under WordPerfect's Shell, rather than being required to do so. According to company spokesman Bill Woahn, version 2.0 will support exact-phrase and proximity searches.

3.3.3 WORDsearch

• *BASIC PRODUCT INFORMATION*

Name of Program: WORDsearch™
Company Name: WORDworks Software Architects
Address: 5014 Lakeview Drive, Austin, TX 78732
Phones: (800) 888-9898, (512) 266-9898
Price: $189.95
Version Tested: Beta test version 0.04
Runs On: IBM PCs and compatibles
Memory Requirements: 256K, 320K recommended
Operating System Requirements: DOS 2.0 or greater
Disk Drive Requirements: 2, one of which must be a hard disk
Supports Color Monitors: Yes
Uses Sound: No
Number of Text Disks: 6
Number of Program Disks: 1
Size of Program Files: 90K
Size of Help Files: 110K
Size of Text Files: Approximately 2.5MB, including index files
Text Files in ASCII: No
Produces ASCII Output Files: Yes
Search String Limitations: 30 characters
Maximum Number of Entries per Index: Unlimited
Type of Disks Used: Double-sided, double-density
Text Available: NIV
Product Includes: Program disk, text disks, user's manual
Manual: 25 pages, not indexed

Demo Disk Available: Yes, $5
Copy Protected: No
Hard Disk Compatible: Yes
Menu-Driven: Yes
On-line Help: Yes, context-sensitive
Tutorial: Yes, in manual
Warranty: 90 days, media only
Support: Phone and letter
Update Policy: Minor updates will be $5.
Related Products: None
Other Information: None

3.3.3.1 Introduction

WORDsearch™ (hereafter WS), created in 1987 by W. James Sneeringer, is an indexed version of the NIV.

Because WS does not support Boolean operators in search constructions, it was not possible to see how fast it could concord the instances of *woman, husband, well,* and *friend* in the Gospel of John in one pass. When concording single words, WS is quite fast, typically finding all occurrences of any word in under 3 seconds. Thus, concording one word at a time, WS could locate all the references to *woman, husband, well,* and *friend* in the Gospel of John in under 15 seconds. Phrase searches take longer, since WS must compare the verses in the individual indices to determine which ones contain all the search terms in their proper order. Constructing an index of all the verses in the Bible in which *son of man* occurs took WS 1 minute and 12 seconds, but it required only 29 seconds to construct an index that contained all the references to *Kingdom of God.*

3.3.3.2 Description

WS is fully menu driven and uses the function keys exclusively to implement commands. The bottom five lines of the screen list the function keys and their assignments, which change from mode to mode. Esc may be used to back up through menus. Of all the indexed Bible concordance programs, WS has the best on-line help.

Search constructions, which are entered in a small 1-line window, are limited to single words or phrases that may not exceed 30 characters. All WS phrase searches are exact and sequence-specific. Boolean logic is supported by allowing multiple searches for one word or phrase at a time to be run and the results of each search combined with (i.e., a Boolean OR), intersected with (i.e., a Boolean AND), or subtracted from (i.e., a Boolean NOT) those of a previous search. Multiple searches may be run in this manner and the results saved in a single index.

A global wild-card operator is supported ("*") but may only be used in the terminal position. Thus "ma*" is a valid search construction but "*an" and "m*n" are not. Proximity and case-sensitive searches are not supported nor are noncontiguous search ranges, though users may restrict searches to specific books of the Bible. Matches are restricted to verses. The range and search construction are displayed when concording, and when performing a phrase search, WS dynamically updates the screen to inform users which biblical books, chapters, and verses it is searching.

Once WS has created an index, users may add and remove references, display the full text of references on-screen, insert, modify, and remove notes, print notes and Scripture, and save the index. Indices are kept in user-named "reference lists," and reference lists are divided into sections. Each section may contain a user-definable list of Scripture references (an index) or user notes. Reference lists may contain up to twenty sections each, and each section is numbered. The grey "+" and "−" keys on the numeric keypad are used to move back and forth between sections. Thus users may create one reference list that contains many indices and sets of user notes, a nice feature that facilitates topical studies.

Indices are displayed as 4-column-wide lists of verse references that may be scrolled using the cursor and page-control keys. When terms appear in consecutive verses, WS displays that fact, so that a search for *Lord* in Genesis, for example, causes WS to display Gen. 2:4-5, Gen. 2:7-9, and so forth—a distinctive feature among Bible concordance programs. Placing the cursor on a verse and hitting the Show Full Verse function key causes WS to display that verse at the top of the screen followed by a screenful of the verses that follow in the index. Thus verses containing hits may be displayed a screenful at a time. PgDn and PgUp are used to scroll hits a screenful at a time, and Ctrl + Home displays the first verse in an index and Ctrl + End the last. On monochrome monitors, matches are highlighted in inverse video. Context verses may be displayed for any match by placing the cursor on a verse containing a hit and pressing the Show Context function key. This causes WS to display the verse containing the match at the top of the screen followed by a screenful of context verses. (Hits that occur in context verses are highlighted.) Context verses are displayed in regular video and verses containing matches in intense video, thus making it easy to visually distinguish the two types. Users may scroll bidirectionally through hits and context verses, and hits and context verses may be inserted into sections in reference lists. Users have the option of displaying the NIV text with or without textual notes, a unique feature among Bible concordance programs. When context verses or verses containing hits are displayed, users may add context verses to a reference list or delete verses containing hits.

An Undo feature allows users to undo their last action. Pressing Undo twice restores the last action.

3.3.3.3 Evaluation

WS meets a number of our criteria for an ideal Bible concordance program. WS supports (1) terminal truncation (a wild-card feature), (2) on-line help, (3) sequence-specific and (4) exact-phrase searches, (5) displaying the range when concording, (6) displaying the search construction when concording phrases, (7) displaying a full screen of hits at a time, (8) displaying a full screen of context verses at a time, and (9) manipulating indices with Boolean ANDs, ORs, and NOTs. (10) Hits are highlighted. (11) WS's very useful "reference list" feature allows users to create and store multiple indices and user notes under a single filename.

WS's shortcomings are as follows. WS does not support (1) the Boolean XOR operator, (2) nested operators, (3) mixed operators, (4) long search strings (the limit is 30 characters—though multiple searches may be run when creating a single index), (5) initial and medial truncation, (6) case-sensitive and (7) proximity searches, (8) nonsequential search ranges, (9) a GOTO feature, (10) scanning text and indices for matches, or (11) multiple windows. (12) Verse boundaries arbitrarily restrict matches to search terms that occur in the same verse.

3.3.4 GodSpeed

● *BASIC PRODUCT INFORMATION*

Name of Program: GodSpeed™
Company Name: Kingdom Age Software
Address: Texas and East Coast Distributor: Paraclete Computers & Software, 1000 E. 14th St., Suite 187, Plano, TX 75074; West Coast Distributor: Jones Computing Systems, P.O. Box 5505, Carson, CA 90749

Phones: Paraclete Computers: (214) 578-8185, BBS/Data line: (214) 422-2387; Jones Computing: (213) 538-1995, BBS/Data line: (213) 324-8454
Price: Whole Bible: $100; New Testament: $27; Gospels: free
Version Tested: Gospels, version 1.0
Runs On: IBM PCs and compatibles, Compaq, Atari Gospel version available.
Memory Requirements: 256K
Operating System Requirements: DOS 2.1 or greater
Disk Drive Requirements: Whole Bible: 2, one of which must be a hard disk; New Testament: 2
Supports Color Monitors: Yes
Uses Sound: No
Number of Text Disks: Whole Bible: 7; New Testament: 2; Gospels: 1
Number of Program Disks: 1
Size of Program Files: 120K
Size of Help Files: 2K
Size of Text Files: 2.2MB
Text Files in ASCII: No
Produces ASCII Output Files: Yes
Search String Limitations: 79 characters; may be merged indefinitely.
Maximum Number of Entries per Index: Not applicable
Type of Disks Used: Double-sided, double-density
Text Available: KJV
Product Includes: Disks and manual
Manual: 24 pages, book-size, typeset, glossary, not indexed
Demo Disk Available: Yes, free version of Gospels
Copy Protected: No
Hard Disk Compatible: Yes
Menu-Driven: No, except help menu
On-line Help: Yes, whole Bible package only
Tutorial: No
Warranty: 90 days, media only
Support: Phone and letter
Update Policy: Free for one year by mail or on BBS for registered users.
Related Products: Hebrew and Greek concordances are promised for 1987.
Other Information: None.

3.3.4.1 Introduction

GodSpeed™, created in 1986 by Bryan Moore, is an extremely compact and fast indexed Bible concordance program. By using multiple compression techniques, the indexed biblical text has been reduced to about 2.2 megabytes, which is considerably smaller than the text files of The Powerful Word, EveryWord™, and even of a nonindexed text such as compuBIBLE™. When installed on a hard disk, a GS batch file merges all the files on the seven GS data disks—the entire indexed text of the KJV—into one large data file. GodSpeed™ (hereafter GS) can locate any verse or word in the Bible in under 3 seconds.

Run on an 8-MHz system from a 65-millisecond, 62-megabyte hard disk, GS located all the references in the entire Bible to *woman, husband, well,* and *friend* in approximately 2.5 seconds. Run on a 4.77-MHz, 8088 system from a floppy drive, GS located those search terms (in the Gospels) in approximately 15 seconds. Neither figure includes the time it took to key in the separate search terms. GS does not support Boolean ORs, and its unchangeable default operator in multi-word searches is an AND. GS does not create indices that can be saved. Thus *woman, husband, well,* and *friend* had to be searched for one term at a time, with each successive search overwriting the results of the previous one. Those searches, then, did not produce one index of all the verses in the Bible (or the Gospels) where the search terms appear.

3.3.4.2 Description

GS's interface and its concording, word processing, and printing functions are the least developed of all the Bible concordance programs, which is one reason its program files are so small (120K). GS does not use menus or create indices. Neither does it support truncation, sequence-specific, wild-card, proximity, case-sensitive, and exact-phrase searches. It does not allow text to be scrolled backwards, and it does not support the cursor and page-control keys. Currently, the only way to print references from within the program is with the DOS PrintScreen utility. Alternately, users may direct output to a file and print the file after exiting the program.

Words of Christ and general titles to the Psalms are included in curly braces ({}). On color monitors, GS may be configured to display the words of Christ in red and to omit the braces. English words that are not translations of underlying Hebrew or Greek words but that have been supplied by the translators for the sake of clarity and proper English are included in square brackets ([]).

GS is a one-mode program. Text is displayed and searches are conducted from the same screen. Any verse in the Bible may be displayed by entering a 3-letter book abbreviation followed by a chapter and verse reference. Users may scroll forward through the biblical text from that point but not backward. Entering a keyword or keywords at the top of the screen causes a whole screenful of matches to be displayed with keywords underlined in intense video. Keywords are joined with a default Boolean AND, which may not be changed. A word frequency and distribution message at the top of the screen states how many times a search term occurs and in how many verses. Searches may be started from the beginning of any book of the Bible by prefixing the search term(s) with the three-letter abbreviation for the book from which the search is to begin. Although GS displays hits faster than any program reviewed in this chapter, once hits are displayed, users may not scroll backwards, display any context verses, or save hits to an index or disk file. Hits are scrolled forward a screenful at a time with the Return key. Help screens provide information about search instructions and book abbreviations.

GS supports an explicit AND operator, which intersects the current set of hits with the members of the set defined by the word or phrase that follows the operator. For example (using the demo disk, which contains only the text of the Gospels), having created a set of all the verses that include the words *Kingdom*, *of*, and *God* in the Gospels, the command "&righteousness" would intersect that set with the set of all the verses that include *righteousness* and then display Matthew 6:33, the one verse in the Gospels where *Kingdom of God* and *righteousness* occur.

3.3.4.3 Evaluation

In its present incarnation, GS is a rudimentary Bible concordance program whose main strength is its great speed. It allows lightening-fast random access to any verse or set of words in the Bible. And GS can intersect two sets of verses faster than any program reviewed in this chapter.

Unfortunately, GS does not support (1) Boolean OR, NOT, and XOR operators, (2) nested operators, (3) mixed operators, (4) initial, medial, and terminal truncation, (5) wild-cards, (6) case-sensitive, (7) proximity, (8) sequence-specific, and (9) exact-phrase searches, (10) nonsequential search ranges, (11) windows, (12) bidirectional scrolling of text, (13) creating indices that may be saved, scrolled, and manipulated, (14) a word processor interface, (15) menus, (16) on-line help, (17) displaying context verses, or (18) a print function. And (19) verse boundaries arbitrarily restrict matches to search terms that occur in the same verse.

According to company spokesman Bryan Moore, GodSpeed™ release 2 is due sometime in the fourth quarter of 1987 and is expected to support (1) the AND, OR, XOR, and NOT Boolean operators, (2) exact-phrase searches, (3) wild-cards, (4) truncation, (5) proximity searching by verse, paragraph, and chapter, (6) noncontiguous search ranges, (7) the normal use of the cursor keys, and (8) a split-screen mode. According to Mr. Moore, future versions of GS will include (1) a shell feature for accessing GodSpeed™ from word processing and other application programs, (2) an interface to The Scholar's Edition of the ChiWriter word processor (see chapter 2) that will allow users to call and run GodSpeed™ from within ChiWriter and to send GodSpeed™ output to ChiWriter's screen, (3) enhanced commands, file management, and print capabilities, and (4) Strong's Hebrew and Greek lexicons (at additional cost). (5) Atari and Macintosh versions are promised.

3.3.5 ComWord 1

- *BASIC PRODUCT INFORMATION*

Name of Program: ComWord 1
Company Name: Word of God Communication
Address: 68 Long Court, Suite 1B, Thousand Oaks, CA 91360
Phones: (800) 523-7578, (805) 495-4441
Price: $695
Version Tested: Not able to test.
Runs On: IBM PCs and compatibles; Atari 520ST
Memory Requirements: 512K
Operating System Requirements: DOS 2.1 or greater
Disk Drive Requirements: 2, one of which must be a hard disk
Supports Color Monitors: Yes
Uses Sound: Not known
Number of Text Disks: Not known
Number of Program Disks: Not known
Size of Program Files: Not known
Size of Help Files: Not known
Size of Text Files: 8MB
Text Files in ASCII: Yes
Produces ASCII Output Files: Yes
Search String Limitations: 4 words
Maximum Number of Entries per Index: Not known
Type of Disks Used: Double-sided, double-density
Text Available: KJV
Product Includes: Disks and manual
Manual: Not able to see.
Demo Disk Available: Yes, $10
Copy Protected: Not known
Hard Disk Compatible: Yes
Menu-Driven: Yes
On-line Help: Yes
Tutorial: Yes
Warranty: Not known
Support: Phone and letter
Update Policy: Not known
Related Products: None

Other Information: ComWord 1 includes an uncompressed version of the KJV and the complete *Strong's Exhaustive Concordance*, including its Hebrew and Greek dictionaries. This program supports multiple word searches, a word processor interface, printer functions, and user-adjustable windows. A passage of the KJV text can be displayed in one window, a selection from Strong's *Concordance* in a second, and a portion of Strong's Greek and Hebrew dictionaries in a third. Searches may be restricted to user-specified, noncontiguous ranges. All the words in Strong's *Concordance* can be listed alphabetically without frequency information. Multiple keyword searches are supported. The AND operator may be used to join up to four words, but the OR and NOT operators, wild-cards, sequence-specific, case-specific, punctuation-specific, and proximity searches are not supported.

3.3.6 Wordworker: The Accelerated New Testament

- ● *BASIC PRODUCT INFORMATION*

Name of Program: Wordworker: The Accelerated New Testament
Company Name: The Way International
Address: P.O. Box 328, 19100 East Shelby Rd., New Knoxville, OH 45871
Phone: (419) 753-2523
Price: This is a shareware program; $45 with manual.
Version Tested: 1.05
Runs On: IBM PCs and compatibles
Memory Requirements: 256K
Operating System Requirements: DOS 2.0 or greater
Disk Drive Requirements: 2
Supports Color Monitors: Yes
Uses Sound: Yes
Number of Text Disks: 1
Number of Program Disks: 1
Size of Program Files: 303K
Size of Help Files: 7K
Size of Text Files: 362.3K
Text Files in ASCII: No
Produces ASCII Output Files: Yes
Search String Limitations: 10 words
Maximum Number of Entries per Index: Not applicable
Type of Disks Used: Double-sided, double density
Text Available: KJV
Product Includes: Disk and manual
Manual: 24 pages, not indexed
Demo Disk Available: No
Copy Protected: No
Hard Disk Compatible: Yes
Menu-Driven: Yes
On-line Help: Yes
Tutorial: No
Warranty: 30 days, media only
Support: Phone and letter
Update Policy: Minimal cost to registered users
Related Products: Version 2.0 will include the Old Testament.
Other Information: This menu-driven program supports Boolean ANDs and ORs and proximity searching across verse and chapter boundaries. It does not build indices. Hits may be highlighted in reverse video or displayed in blinking video. Verses are cross referenced to 14,800 passages in the Way International research publications.[20] A memory-resident option for use with word processors is included. With more than 256K, this option allows users to cut and paste verses from Wordworker into word processing files. All the 6,063 unique words in the KJV New Testament text can be listed alphabetically with frequency information, and a GOTO function allows users to go directly to any word and select it as a search term. Run from a floppy drive on an 8088, 4.77-MHz system, Wordworker will locate the first verse of a search in under 2 seconds.

---

20. The Way International is a nonorthodox Christian sect whose publications—to which Wordworker cross references New Testament verses—reflect their theology.

3.3.7 KJV on DIALOG—File 297

- *BASIC PRODUCT INFORMATION*

Name of Program: KJV on DIALOG
Company Name: DIALOG® Information Retrieval Service
Address: 3460 Hillview Ave., Palo Alto, CA 94304
Phones: (800) 334-2564, (415) 858-3810
Price: $0.40 per minute ($24 per hour); $0.10 per full record printed; there are no TYPE or DISPLAY charges.
Size of Text Files: 36,600 records
Produces ASCII Output Files: Yes
Search String Limitations: Not known
Maximum Number of Entries per Index: Not known
Text Available: KJV
Menu-Driven: No
On-line Help: Yes
Other Information: DIALOG® Information Retrieval Service, vendor of the world's largest set (over 300) of commercially-available, on-line, bibliographical and full-text data bases, has the most powerful search lexicon, syntax, and grammar of any on-line service. (DIALOG will be discussed in some detail in chapter 5). DIALOG File 297, the 1769 version of the KJV (other revisions of the KJV, originally published in 1611, occurred in 1629, 1638, and 1672), is made available on DIALOG by the Thomas Nelson Publishing Company. DIALOG search features include Boolean and proximity operators, sequence-specific searches, nested operators, multi-word searches, and more. Users may restrict matches in proximity searches to verses or to chapters. Searches may be restricted to either testament. A GOTO feature allows users to go directly to any book, chapter, and verse in the Bible. Entries are cascaded so that entire chapters may be retrieved in one step. Output options are (1) DIALOG Accession Number, (2) full record, and (3) biblical citation.

3.4 Text-Only Bible Packages

The following entries provide relevant information about machine-readable texts of the Bible. This software comes with a textual data base that consist of some or all of the Bible, and several of the packages include rudimentary search programs.

3.4.1 COMPUTER NEW TESTAMENT

- *BASIC PRODUCT INFORMATION*

Name of Program: COMPUTER NEW TESTAMENT
Company Name: The Spiritual Source
Address: 24 Carol Avenue, Manorville, NY 11949
Phone: (516) 878-1523
Price: $25 if you provide 20 disks, $65 if they provide the disks.
Version Tested: Not able to test.
Runs On: Commodore 64
Memory Requirements: 64K
Operating System Requirements: Not known
Disk Drive Requirements: 1
Supports Color Monitors: Yes
Uses Sound: No
Number of Text Disks: 20; only the New Testament is available.
Text Available: KJV
Copy Protected: No
Warranty: Not known
Support: Phone and letter
Other Information: Includes rudimentary programs; when using a color monitor the words of Jesus appear on-screen in red.

3.4.2 INTERNATIONAL BIBLE SOCIETY TEXT

- *BASIC PRODUCT INFORMATION*

Name of Program: INTERNATIONAL BIBLE SOCIETY TEXT
Company Name: The International Bible Society
Address: 144 Tices Lane, East Brunswick, NJ 08816
Phone: (201) 238-5454
Price: $50
Version Tested: Not able to test.
Runs On: Apple II series
Memory Requirements: Not known
Operating System Requirements: Not known
Disk Drive Requirements: 1
Supports Color Monitors: Yes
Uses Sound: No
Number of Text Disks: 8
Text Available: NIV
Copy Protected: No
Warranty: Not known
Support: Phone and letter
Other Information: Versions for the Commodore 64, IBM PCs, Kaypro, and TRS Models 1000, 1200, and 2000 are planned.

3.4.3 VERSE BY VERSE

- *BASIC PRODUCT INFORMATION*

Name of Program: Verse by Verse
Company Name: G.R.A.P.E. (Gospel Resources and Program Exchange)
Address: P.O. Box 576, Keyport, WA 98345
Phone: No listed number
Price: $5 per disk
Version Tested: Not able to test.
Runs On: Apple II series
Memory Requirements: 48K
Operating System Requirements: Not known
Disk Drive Requirements: 1
Supports Color Monitors: Yes
Uses Sound: No
Number of Text Disks: Several (Only the New Testament is available.)
Text Available: KJV
Copy Protected: No
Warranty: Media only
Support: Minimal to none
Other Information: Comes with rudimentary program to manipulate the text; will not work with PRODOS.

3.4.4 MacBible

- *BASIC PRODUCT INFORMATION*

Name of Program: MacBible™
Company Name: Encycloware™
Address: 715 Washington St., Ayden, NC 28513
Phone: (919) 746-3589
Price: $169
Version Tested: Not able to test.
Runs On: Macintoshes, Apple IIs, IBM PCs, Commodore
Memory Requirements: 128K
Operating System Requirements: Not known

Disk Drive Requirements: 1
Supports Color Monitors: Not applicable
Uses Sound: Not known
Number of Text Disks: 25
Text Available: KJV, NIV
Copy Protected: No
Warranty: Not known
Support: Phone and letter
Other Information: Macintosh version uses search features of MacWrite™ and Microsoft® Word and contains overlays for those two programs. MacBible files appear to those two word processors as ordinary text files.

3.4.5 MacConcord

● *BASIC PRODUCT INFORMATION*

Name of Program: MacConcord
Company Name: Medina Software
Address: P.O. Box 1917, Longwood, FL 32750-1917
Phone: (305) 281-1557
Price: $42.95
Version Tested: Not able to test.
Runs On: Macintoshes
Memory Requirements: 128K
Operating System Requirements: Macintosh operating system
Disk Drive Requirements: 1
Supports Color Monitors: Not applicable
Uses Sound: Not known
Number of Text Disks: 2
Text Available: KJV New Testament
Copy Protected: No
Warranty: One free update
Support: Phone and letter
Other Information: This is a series of MacWrite™ documents that contain a library of more than 10,000 topical cross references from the KJV New Testament.

3.4.6 MacScripture

● *BASIC PRODUCT INFORMATION*

Name of Program: MacScripture™
Company Name: Medina Software
Address: P.O. Box 1917, Longwood, FL 32750-1917
Phone: (305) 281-1557
Price: $119.95: KJV Old Testament; $39.95: KJV New Testament; $140 for both testaments
Version Tested: Not able to test.
Runs On: Macintoshes
Memory Requirements: 128K
Operating System Requirements: Macintosh operating system
Disk Drive Requirements: 1
Supports Color Monitors: Not applicable
Uses Sound: Not known
Number of Text Disks: Old Testament: 13; New Testament: 4
Text Available: KJV
Copy Protected: No
Warranty: Not known
Support: Phone and letter
Other Information: These text disks are designed to be used with MacWrite™.

3.4.7 New Testament Concordance

- *BASIC PRODUCT INFORMATION*

Name of Program: New Testament Concordance
Company Name: Midwest Software
Address: P.O. Box 214, Farmington, MI 48024
Phones: (800) 422-0095, (313) 477-0897
Price: $49.50
Version Tested: Not able to test.
Runs On: Apple IIs, Commodore 64
Memory Requirements: Not known
Operating System Requirements: Not known
Disk Drive Requirements: 1
Supports Color Monitors: Yes
Uses Sound: Not known
Number of Text Disks: 3
Text Available: KJV New Testament
Copy Protected: No
Warranty: Not known
Support: Phone and letter
Other Information: This package includes a program that allows users to locate verse references for any New Testament word and to display the text of the verses. Users may specify the number of context verses before and after the word they are searching for. Supports multiple word searches and allows the results of searches to be combined. Verses may be displayed, printed, and written to disk. Menu-driven; words of Christ display in reverse video.

FEATURES	TWP	SS	CB	BibS	TPW	EW	WS	GS	CW	WW
BASIC FACTS										
Price	200	250	250	225	150	380	190	100	700	45
Runs On	I,A,M	I,	I	T	I	I	I	I	I	I
Memory (in K)	64 (I)	128	192	48	512	640	256	256	512	256
Disk Drives	1	1	2	2	2	2	2	2	2	2
Program Size (in K)	53	105	209	33	330	207	90	120	?	303
Text Size (in MB)	1.8	2	2.7	2.2	3.2	3	2.5	2.2	8	.3
Available Texts	K,N	K,J,L	K,N,A	K	K	K	N	K	K	K
User-Interface	M	M	M	M	M	M	M	C	M, C	M
On-Line Help	●	●	●	○	●	○	●	●	●	●
SEARCHING/INDEXING FEATURES										
Boolean AND	●	○	●	●	●	●	○	●	●	●
Boolean OR	●	●	●	●	●	●	○	○	○	●
Boolean XOR	○	○	○	○	●	○	○	○	○	○
Boolean NOT	○	○	○	○	●	●	○	○	○	○
Nested Operators	○	○	○	○	○	●	○	○	○	○
Mixed Operators	○	○	●	○	●	●	○	○	○	○
Initial Truncation	●	●	●	●	●	●	○	○	○	○
Medial Truncation	●	●	●	●	●	●	○	○	○	○
Terminal Truncation	●	●	●	●	●	●	●	○	○	○
Wild Cards	●	●	●	○	●	●	●	○	○	○
Case-Sensitive	○	●	●	○	○	○	○	○	○	○
Proximity	○	○	○	○	○	○	○	○	○	●
Sequence-Specific	○	○	●	○	○	○	●	○	○	○
Exact-Phrase	●	○	●	●	○	○	●	○	○	○
Nonsequential Ranges	○	○	○	●	●	○	○	○	●	○
Verse-Bound	●	●	●	●	○	●	●	●	●	○
Max. Search String (in Chars)	255	600	1,500	10 wd	480	255	30	79	4 wd	10 wd
Maxium Index Entries (in K)	53	7	Unl.	.3	31	2	Unl.	—	?	—
DISPLAY/PRINT FEATURES										
Search Construction	●	●	●	○	●	●	●	○	○	○
Range	●	●	●	○	○	○	●	○	○	●
Dynamic Updating	●	●	●	●	●	○	●	○	○	○
Index Hits Highlighted	●	○	●	○	●	●	●	●	●	●
Verse References Only	●	●	●	●	●	●	●	○	○	○
References & Text	●	●	●	●	●	●	●	●	●	●
Context Verses	●	●	●	●	●	●	●	○	○	○
Scroll Index Bidirectionally	●	○	●	●	●	●	●	○	●	●
Scroll Text Bidirectionally	●	●	●	●	●	●	●	○	●	●
GOTO	●	●	●	○	●	●	○	●	●	●
Scan Text/Indices for Matches	●	●	●	○	○	○	○	○	○	○
Multiple Display Windows	○	●	●	○	●	○	○	○	○	○
Word Processing Interface	●	●	●	○	○	●	○	○	●	●
Print Function	●	●	●	●	●	●	●	○	●	○
INDEX MANIPULATION										
Combine (OR)	●	●	●	○	○	●	●	○	○	○
Intersect (AND)	●	●	●	○	○	●	●	○	○	○
Show Difference (NOT)	○	○	○	○	○	●	●	○	○	○
Edit	●	●	●	●	●	●	○	○	●	○

Table 3.1: Comparison of Bible concordance programs. I = IBM, A = Apple, M = Macintosh, T = TRS 80, K = KJV, N = NIV, J = New KJV, L = Today's Living Bible, A = ASV, M = menu-driven, C = command-driven, TWP = THE WORD processor, SS = Scripture Scanner, CB = compuBIBLE, BibS = Bible Search, TPW = The Powerful Word, EW = EveryWord, WS = WORDsearch, GS = GodSpeed, CW = ComWord 1, WW = Wordworker.

Chapter 4

Computer-Assisted Language Learning

They have been at a great feast of languages,
and stolen the scraps.
William Shakespeare[1]

4.1 Introduction

The formal acquisition of a foreign language is one of a student's most tedious academic experiences. Although most colleges and universities offer linguistic feasts, students often prefer scraps. In this diet-conscious age, serious eating seems out of the question! Since the mid 1960s, language teachers have increasingly turned to computer-assisted language learning (CALL)—also known as computer-assisted language instruction (CALI)—in an effort to make their linguistic feasts more appealing, palatable, and easier to digest. As more and more colleges follow the lead of MIT,[2] and of Drexel,[3] Stanford,[4] Carnegie-Mellon,[5] and Brown universities,[6] increasing numbers of incoming students will be required to purchase microcomputers, and a growing number of faculty members will have the purchase of microcomputers subsidized for them by their institutions. With over 600 CALL programs available for at least sixteen languages,[7] it is only a matter of time before all foreign language instruction at the college and postgraduate level is supplemented by computer-assisted instruction.

CALL is a subcategory of CAI—computer-aided instruction—which is also known as CAL, computer-aided learning. There are large bodies of literature about CAL and CALL. Although most of the articles in the latter category have to do with modern languages, such as French, German, Spanish, English, and Russian, the principles and techniques used to supplement the teaching of those languages with CALL also apply to unspoken, "dead" languages, such as Sumerian, Egyptian, Classical (biblical) Hebrew, Classical and Hellenistic (Koine) Greek, and Latin.

In this chapter we will examine the advantages of CALL, describe how CALL has been used in college-level Sumerian, Egyptian, Hebrew, Greek, and Latin courses, touch briefly on an important CALL project at Duke University, and review a number of commercial microcomputer CALL programs for Hebrew and Latin.

---

1. William Shakespeare (1564–1616), *Love's Labour's Lost* (1594–1595), V, i, 39.
2. Brann, "MIT," 269–79.
3. Mace, "Drexel," 24–28.
4. Littman, "Computing," 266–74.
5. Freeman, "Chemistry," 192–97.
6. Ibid.
7. Bergheim and Chin, "Computers," 30.

4.2 Advantages of CALL

Traditionally, "dead" languages are taught with grammars, workbooks, and auxiliary vocabulary lists and handouts. Class time is devoted to grammar and vocabulary drills, quizzes and exams, reviewing homework, and recitation and reading. Students memorize lists of vocabulary words, grammatical rules, and examples. To those procedures teachers of modern languages add the use of tape recorders to enable students to learn to speak the languages correctly. Whether taught inductively, deductively, or otherwise, learning a "dead" language is usually an experience in tedium for student and teacher alike. Teaching a child to speak his or her mother tongue is one thing, teaching college or graduate students to read Hebrew, Greek, or Latin is another! Although CALL is not a panacea for all language-learning problems, it can remove some of the tedium from learning a foreign language and produce better results than are otherwise possible.

CALL not only supplements and enhances traditional modes of language instruction, it also creates unique, individualized learning experiences that cannot be duplicated in the classroom and that result in a better knowledge of a language. Numerous studies have consistently shown that compared to traditional modes of instruction, CALL (1) increases reading and writing scores, (2) decreases the time required to learn a language, and produces better (3) writing skills, (4) sound discrimination, and (5) retention.

CALL is an effective teaching tool that has several advantages over traditional modes of instruction. (1) CALL allows teachers to combine instructional media in creative ways. Using computer-driven optical disks and tape recorders, for example, teachers can combine still and motion color pictures, color graphics, text, sound, music, and speech to create more interesting, appealing, and challenging learning experiences.[8] Books, vocabulary lists, and workbooks, however, are restricted to communicating with still visual images, such as words, graphs, photographs, and tables. Tape recorders can be used in conjunction with books, but the visual information in the book and the auditory information on the tape cannot be integrated as dynamically from a presentational point of view as is possible with computers and optical disks. Auditory reinforcement is important when learning *any* language, and only computers are able to display text and to "speak" words at the same time.[9]

(2) CALL is interactive and allows students to work alone, at their own pace, in a structured environment. A good CALL program permits students to control the pace of learning, the number of repetitions of an item, the sequence of presentation, and whether or not clues and help are given. CALL programs can allow students to choose whether material will be presented linearly (like a book or tape recorder), randomly, and with the easiest items first or last. CALL programs can randomly reask missed questions. When used interactively, CALL is superior to traditional rote drills. Books and tape recorders do not lend themselves to interactive learning.

(3) CALL provides instant feedback to students and allows instructors to monitor student progress. Instant feedback reinforces and encourages learning. Mistakes can

---

8. CALICO (see below under "Bibliographical Resources") distributes an "Interactive Videodisk Study Guide" that explains videodiscs, discusses their uses in CALL, and lists bibliographical references for further reading.

9. There are three ways that computers can "speak." (1) Audio synthesis uses a mechanical larynx to make sounds that simulate human speech, but the results are quite poor. (2) Voice digitation begins with a speaker whose words are sampled hundreds or thousands of times a second and then recorded as digitized bits (this is the technology that is used for digital music recordings), and the quality of the result is superb. Unfortunately, the high sampling rates necessary for acceptable voice reproduction require large amounts of memory. (3) Computers can control analog devices, such as tape recorders and optical or compact disks. For individualized instruction, however, *each* computer must be coupled with a recorder or disk player, and these devices are expensive. See Ariew, "Materials," 43–47.

be trapped as they occur, diagnosed, and help provided. Scores and progress reports can be displayed. Control programs can monitor how much time each student spends on each lesson and on each problem in each lesson, which problems each student missed, what past lessons each student has reviewed, and so forth.

As attractive as CALL may sound, however, many CALL programs suffer from the following weaknesses.[10] (1) Program design is often deficient, and (2) the techniques of discovery learning and problem solving are infrequently employed. Many CALL programs are (3) trivial and (4) fragmented, instead of being integrated internally and externally with other programs and texts. Often (5) the lesson content is inadequate, and (6) the documentation and (7) format of CALL programs difficult for students to use. Foreign characters are (8) displayed in various ways, and (9) many programs lack portability from one computer system to another.

4.3 College-Level CALL Programs

In this section we will look briefly at several college-level CALL programs for teaching Sumerian, Egyptian, Hebrew, Greek, and Latin. For more information about the programs that were developed at the University of Minnesota (i.e., the Sumerian, Egyptian, first and second Greek programs, and the first Latin program), contact the following persons.

For all of the Minnesota CALL programs contact:

Dr. Peter C. Patton, Director
Minnesota Supercomputer Institute
1200 Washington Ave. South
Minneapolis, MN 55415
(612) 624-1588.

For the Greek and Latin CALL programs contact:

Dr. Gerald Erickson
Department of Classics
309 Folwell Hall
9 Pleasant Street S.E.
University of Minnesota
Minneapolis, MN 55455
(612) 625-2026.

4.3.1 Sumerian

In their article "Sumerian: An Experiment in CAI Language Learning,"[11] William R. Brookman, Geri Hockfield, and Peter C. Patton describe the CALL program they developed for teaching Sumerian at the University of Minnesota. Sumerian is the world's oldest and longest-used written language (from the fourth millennium B.C. until the first century B.C.). Because it is a nonalphabetic, agglutinative language that is written in cuneiform logograms, Sumerian presented some interesting graphics problems for the programmers. The Sumerian language was preserved by the Babylonians and Assyrians, who wrote in Akkadian using triangular-pointed reed styli on wet clay tablets to produce wedge-shaped cuneiform characters.

Sumerian contains 600 characters that are used in two distinct ways. Some are used as syllables and others as signs that have a root meaning. Characters used as signs—word graphemes—are known as logograms, and this is the basic nature of

---

10. See Baker, "State," 6–10, 27.
11. Patton and Holoien, *Computing*, 235–51.

Sumerian. An individual logogram can have several shades of meaning, all related to the root meaning of the sign. The Sumerians created words in two ways. On the one hand, because an agglutinative language is one that combines separate, optional meaning elements to create single words, the Sumerians combined logograms—individual signs with fixed meanings—to make words. On the other hand, characters used as syllables—syllable graphemes—could be combined with other syllable graphemes to form words.[12] One of the main challenges for the programmers, then, was to figure out how to display the odd-shaped cuneiform characters on-screen.

The Sumerian program was written for Control Data Corporation's PLATO instructional system,[13] and is patterned after the methodology used by Professor Tom B. Jones (former University of Minnesota Regents Professor) in his ancient history seminar to analyze Sumerian economic documents from the Ur III period.[14] Thus the course that was developed introduces students to the Sumerian language as it is exhibited in economic documents. "The course," the authors state, "was designed to enable a true beginner, without prior knowledge of cuneiform signs or Sumerian grammar, to work with actual ancient texts."[15] The course consists of an introduction, texts, a sign list, a dictionary, and Help Lessons. Each lesson consists of an economic document that students must transliterate and then translate. The sign list is a nine-page display of all the cuneiform signs used in the course, and this list functions as an index to the dictionary. Each sign is matched with a reference number from Labat's *Manuel d'epigraphie akkadienne*.[16] By using the reference numbers, students may access dictionary entries. There are about 400 entries, and each entry includes the cuneiform sign and all its possible translations and meanings. Students may jump to a dictionary entry from any part of the program and then return to the point of origin. Similarly, the Help Lessons, which cover personal names, place names, the names of gods, month formulas, year formulas, a map, and a bibliography of the course, may be accessed from any point in the program.

4.3.2 Egyptian

In their article "A Computer-Based Course in Ancient Egyptian Hieroglyphics,"[17] Kenneth W. Decker, O. J. Schaden, Peter C. Patton, and Kellen C. Thornton describe the CALL program they developed for teaching Ancient (Middle) Egyptian at the University of Minnesota. Like Sumerian, Ancient Egyptian is a nonalphabetic, logographic language. Unlike the wedge-shaped characters of Sumerian, however, Ancient Egyptian logograms are pictorial, and so cannot be built up from lines and wedges, as Sumerian logograms can, but must be drawn as pictures. Like the Sumerian CALL program, the Ancient Egyptian program uses the PLATO system.

Unlike the Sumerian CALL course, which emphasizes reading texts, the Egyptian CALL course employs an audiovisual approach and emphasizes grammar. In this course students are exposed to three types of exercises. First, they are required to transliterate and to translate common phrases and sentences. Second, they must answer multiple choice questions. And third, they build phrases by adding to or by replacing words or phrases in preceding phrases.

---

12. See Mulhern et al., "Lexicography," and Sparley et al., "Lexicon," for more information on the Sumerian language and on computer-aided Sumerian lexicography.

13. See Robert Hart's article "Language Study and the PLATO System" for a through discussion of PLATO as it existed in 1981.

14. See T. B. Jones and J. W. Snyder, *Sumerian Economic Texts from the Third Ur Dynasty* (Westport, Conn.: Greenwood Press, 1974).

15. Patton and Holoien, *Computing*, 237.

16. René Labat, *Manual d'epigraphie akkadienne* (Paris: Librairei Orientaliste Paul Geuthner, S.A., 1976).

17. Patton and Holoien, *Computing*, 253–62.

4.3.3 Hebrew

In their article "Teaching Hebrew with the Aid of Computers: The Illinois Program,"[18] Peter Cole, Robert Lebowitz, and Robert Hart describe the CALL program they developed for teaching Modern Hebrew at the University of Illinois. Because Modern Hebrew is explicitly based on Classical Hebrew and shares many of the characteristics of that language, we will now examine the Cole-Lebowitz-Hart program. Since 1973, the authors have used the PLATO system to develop an extensive program of individualized computer-based instruction in Modern Hebrew, which they have used to supplement classroom instruction. In addition to the CALL program, the authors have written three textbooks and developed audio tapes. The textbooks and accompanying computer programs teach grammar in a graded, systematic way. Graded and controlled vocabulary instruction, extensive oral and written exercises, and an emphasis on Hebrew as it is actually spoken today characterize this course.

The programs and textbooks are designed to lead students from colloquial to literary Hebrew. Students learn through a wide variety of oral and written exercises, including chain and transformation drills. Hebrew is entered right to left and properly displayed on-screen. Lessons are menu-driven, and the system includes grammar exercises and grammatical aids, Hebrew word games, a bulletin board, mail, and on-line help. Grammatical exercises require students to complete one unit before moving to the next, though at any time students may review completed grammar units. Review drills on Hebrew verb conjugations and Hebrew number names are available. A dictionary lesson permits students to look up English equivalents of Hebrew words (and vice versa) and to see examples of word usage in sentence-long contexts. Students, instructors, and programmers may communicate by electronic mail.

Word games consist of Hangman, Wordwar, Talkomatic, and crossword puzzles. Hangman gives students a finite number of chances to guess a hidden word. In Wordwar students compete to be the first to correctly type a list of misspelled Hebrew words. Talkomatic allows up to five students to conference in Hebrew by typing messages that simultaneously appear on each participant's screen. The content of the crossword puzzles reflects the current week's vocabulary.

The authors are considering developing a series of computer-assisted lessons in Classical Hebrew.

For more information about the Cole-Lebowitz-Hart Hebrew program, contact the authors at the following address.

Dr. Robert Lebowitz or Dr. Robert Hart
The Language Learning Laboratory
G 70 Foreign Languages Bldg.
707 S. Mathews Ave.
University of Illinois at Urbana
Urbana, IL 61801
(217) 333-1719

4.3.4 Classical and Koine Greek

In this section we will look at three computer-assisted Greek programs.

(1) Dale V. Gear's article "A Small-Computer CAI Course in Classical Greek"[19] describes the CALL program that he, George Gonzalez, Meg Tarbet, and Paul Sonkowsky developed for teaching introductory-level Classical Greek at the University of Minnesota. Unlike the other three programs we have discussed, to minimize ex-

---

18. *Computers and the Humanities* 18 (1984): 87–99.
19. Patton and Holoien, *Computing*, 263–78.

penses, this program does not run on the PLATO system (which requires special, costly terminals) or use TUTOR (PLATO's special authoring language).[20] Gear and his colleagues created their program by translating a PLATO program (Classical Greek—written by Professor Gerald Erickson and Michael Kunin) into Pascal and then configuring it to run on Terak microcomputers.[21]

The microcomputer-based program for Classical Greek that resulted from that effort can format and display text in roman and Greek characters and switch character sets in midline. The program also branches to different instructional areas, drills students randomly or sequentially, and provides help, hints, and answers. This program includes no reading exercises but concentrates on grammar.

The Classical Greek program for Terak microcomputers is available on floppy disks for $450. Interested parties should contact Dr. Erickson or Dr. Patton at the addresses listed above.

(2) Gear and his colleagues also have transferred a PLATO-based Koine Greek CALL program to Terak microcomputers.[22] The Koine program is coordinated with J. Gresham Machen's *New Testament Greek for Beginners*.[23] This program, which from a design point of view closely resembles Gear's Classical Greek program, is available on floppy disks for $450. Interested parties should contact Dr. Erickson or Dr. Patton at the addresses listed above.

(3) John C. Hurd's article "Psychological Considerations in CAI and the 'Greek Tutor,' a Language Instruction Package"[24] discusses the psychological considerations of using CAI and then describes his CALL program, the Greek Tutor. Written in APL, the Greek Tutor (hereafter GT) is an inductive approach to language learning for elementary Greek students and is based on the Gospel of John. This interactive program can simultaneously display roman and Greek characters on-screen, offers various types of timed drills, analyzes mistakes, and has on-line help.

The GT is composed of six main parts, or files. (1) A 1.5-megabyte dictionary file contains every word in the Greek NT, coded in such a way that the GT can inflect any form. (2) A fully parsed version of the Gospel of John includes basic morphological forms for each word. (3) Another file provides general information about using the GT, about Greek grammar, and about difficulties and peculiarities of the Greek text. (4) An index of all the forms in the Gospel of John can be used like an analytical lexicon to parse any form in John. (5) A diary file is used to record each student's work. (6) The "restart file" contains information about each student—name, grades, and so forth. Because the GT can inflect any form in the Greek NT and parse any form in John, it functions as a limited grammar, dictionary, and analytical lexicon.

The Greek Tutor's main commands include INFLECT, IDENTIFY, DICTIONARY, DEFINITION, EXPLODE, COMMENT, MESSAGES, and MAILBOX. Each command may be entered by using its first two or three letters. To inflect a form and create its paradigm, at the ")" prompt a student types "INFLECT" (INF) followed either by the number of the word for which a paradigm is desired (each word in each verse is numbered) or by the lexical form of the word (typed in Greek). The GT responds by providing the word's (1) orthographic form, (2) lexical form (lemma), (3) principal parts, (4) English definition(s), (5) parsing, and (6) complete paradigm. Item 6 is optional. The GT asks users if a paradigm should be printed and if the information should be saved to a file. Verbs may be inflected by choosing a verb and specifying a tense and voice (that actually occur in NT usage) and a mood. All paradigms may be

---

20. The program is written in Pascal, because Pascal has flexible data structures, supports modular programming, is widely available, and is portable from one computer system to another.

21. I have been unsuccessful in locating information about the PLATO-based programs in Classical and Koine (see below) Greek.

22. Patton and Holoien, *Computing*, 273.

23. New York: The Macmillan Co., 1923.

24. In Parunak, ed., *Computer Tools for Ancient Texts* (Winona Lake, Ind.: Eisenbrauns, forthcoming).

saved in files. To display a paradigm in a file, at the ")" prompt students type "PRINT" followed by the paradigm number. Typing "PRINT" with no number at the ")" prompt displays a numbered list of what a student has on file.

To parse a form, at the ")" prompt students type "IDENTIFY" (ID) followed by the number(s) of the word(s) to be parsed. The GT responds by giving the (1) class, (2) part of speech, and (3) appropriate identification of the word. When parsing verbs, for example, the GT displays their (1) class, (2) part of speech, (3) tense (aspect), (4) voice, (5) mood, and (6) lexical form. By using the DICTIONARY (DIC) command, students may display the lexical form of a word before parsing it. When used with verbs, the DIC command results in a list of principal parts.

DEFINITION (DEF) displays words in Greek, the numbers of the vocabulary cards they are listed on (Dr. Hurd supplies these cards for his students), and their English definitions. EXPLODE (EXP) divides words into their morphological components. COMMENT allows students to send messages to the professor, and MESSAGES allows the professor to read those messages. MAILBOX allows all users to send and receive electronic mail.

Dr. Hurd plans to add a concordance function to the GT and to include the rest of the grammatically analyzed NT in its data base. Although the GT currently runs only on mainframes, Dr. Hurd is working on transferring it to microcomputers.

For more information about the Greek Tutor, contact Dr. Hurd at the following address.

Dr. John C. Hurd
Trinity College
6 Hoskin Ave.
University of Toronto
Toronto, Ontario M5S 1H8
Canada
(416) 978-3056

Also worth mentioning in this section is David W. Packard's article "Teaching Ancient Greek (with the Help of a Computer),"[25] which describes CALL techniques for teaching Classical Greek. Although most of his remarks about hardware are out of date (the microcomputer as we know it had not been invented in 1974), Packard's article is rich in its understanding of *how* computers can and should be used most effectively to assist in teaching Greek and other languages.

4.3.5 Latin

In this section we will examine three noncommercial, computer-assisted Latin programs, and in the section below ("Microcomputer CALL Courses") we will examine three major CALL Latin programs that may be purchased for microcomputers, as well as a number of other commercial Latin programs for microcomputers. Like the Latin programs we are about to discuss, the commercial microcomputer Latin CALL programs could be used in introductory Latin courses at the secondary and college levels.

(1) In their article "A Latin Course on a Small Computer,"[26] George Vellios, Gerald M. Erickson, and Rosanne Gulino describe the CALL program they developed at the University of Minnesota for teaching Latin on Terak microcomputers. Syntactical and morphological functions are presented in the order of their importance, and drills are coordinated with a written text that explains grammar and mor-

---

25. *ALLC Bull.* 3 (1975): 45–51.
26. Patton and Holoien, *Computing*, 279–86.

phology. Remedial aids make up for individual differences in students' abilities. Reading exercises stress comprehension.

The Latin noun system is introduced a case at a time, followed by the verb system, which also is presented in a step-by-step fashion, so that students progressively acquire a knowledge of its various moods, voices, and tenses. If a student's score calls for remedial work, the program automatically branches to remedial drills. Hints to correct answers are available.

(2) Richard T. Scanlon's article "Computer-Assisted Instruction in Latin"[27] describes an introductory Latin program—subsequently known as *Index of Beginning Latin Lessons*—that uses the PLATO system. The forty lessons of this highly interactive, fully menu-driven program follow the order in which materials are presented in Frederick Wheelock's text, *Latin: An Introductory Course* (Harper & Row). Scanlon's lessons are composed of original materials and may be used independently or together as a whole course. Each lesson follows the same pattern—vocabulary, morphology, translation, self-test—and requires approximately 80 minutes to complete. According to Scanlon, "The program assumes that the grammar is either explained or studied prior to each lesson and that narrative reading is done in the classroom."

Vocabulary sections contain twenty words each, and vocabulary is presented randomly from Latin to English. Missed words are reasked. Morphology sections each consist of four sets of twenty-question drills that require Latin-to-English, English-to-Latin, and Latin-to-Latin responses. Translation sections each contain fifteen Latin sentences that must be translated into English and five English sentences that must be translated into Latin. Self-test sections quiz students randomly on material from the first three parts of a lesson and display running scores at the top of the screen. After each test, the program displays the score and analyzes student performance in each of the three lesson areas. Scanlon's program is available as part of the PLATO Subscription Courseware offerings under the title *Index of Beginning Latin Lessons*.[28]

(3) A second Scanlon Latin program, *Index of Latin Composition Lessons*, also is available as part of the PLATO Subscription Courseware offerings. This program is a complete review of Latin grammar and syntax through the medium of prose composition (English to Latin). This highly interactive, fully menu-driven program consists of thirty-one composition lessons, each of which has four parts—form drills, composition, vocabulary, and a self-test. Each lesson requires about 60 minutes to complete. Seven lessons are designed as cumulative practice tests. Each lesson contains an explanation of the forms and structures being reviewed.

I am impressed by the thoroughness of *Index of Beginning Latin Lessons* and *Index of Latin Composition Lessons*. Each program would be quite helpful to beginning students of Latin and for review purposes.

4.4 The Duke MicroCALIS Program

All readers interested in CALL should be aware of Duke University's ambitious humanities computing project—Computerization of Language Oriented Enterprises (COLOE)—which began in the early 1980s. One of the many tools produced by this project is CALIS (Computer Assisted Language Instructional System), a generic foreign-language authoring system, which is now available as MicroCALIS for IBM PCs and compatible machines. Using CALIS and MicroCALIS, scholars at Duke have created CALL programs for teaching Russian, Chinese, Modern Greek, Arabic, Am-

---

27. *Foreign Language Annals* 13 (1980): 53–55.

28. For more information on PLATO and PLATO Subscription Courseware offerings, contact Control Data Publishing, Inc., 3111 Sibley Memorial Dr., Eagan, MN 55121 or Control Data Corp., 8100 34th Ave. S, P.O. Box O, Minneapolis, MN 55440; (800) 345-9903, (800) 233-8908, (612) 375-8111.

haric, Swahili, French, German, and a number of other foreign languages. Plans are underway to use CALIS to create a CALL program for Hellenistic Greek.

According to information supplied by Duke University, MicroCALIS is a "CAI environment designed to emphasize transportability, adaptability, and flexibility." Using MicroCALIS, teachers can easily design CALL programs for the foreign language(s) they teach. MicroCALIS runs on different combinations of hardware and operating systems and allows for "the modular incorporation of advanced technologies (e.g., digitized audio, videodiscs, alternative input devices)" in program creation.

The MicroCALIS demonstration disk that I reviewed is superb. It is cleanly programmed, menu-driven, highly interactive, and has a very logical user interface. The bottom line on the screen is a status line that lists the special functions assigned to the IBM function keys. Keys F1, F2, F3, and F4 are used to generate compound letters (i.e., letters with accents and diacritical marks). By typing the appropriate letter and hitting the proper function key, the specified accent or diacritical mark is automatically added to the letter. F5 moves users to the next question in the drill. F9 displays directions, and F10 is used to review earlier questions or answers or both. (F6–F8 are not used.) The Escape key is used to exit the program. Various types of questions are randomly asked, friendly remarks (in the language being studied) are displayed at the bottom of the screen for correct and incorrect answers, and the program keeps track of the number of correct answers users gave on their first, second, and third tries and displays this information in graph form when lessons have been completed.

For more information about MicroCALIS or a free copy of the program, contact either of the following two persons. Be sure to include a properly formatted diskette and a self-addressed, stamped disk mailer if requesting the program.

Jeffrey William Gillette
Senior Programmer
Humanities Computing Facility
104 Languages Bldg.
Duke University
Durham, NC 27706
(919) 684-3637

Prof. Frank L. Borchardt
Department of Germanic Language and Literature
Duke University
Durham, NC 27706
(919) 684-3836

4.5 Microcomputer CALL Programs

Many CALL programs for popular microcomputers are available for learning Hebrew and Latin (none, alas, for Classical or Hellenistic Greek!), and in this section I will briefly evaluate a number of them. It will quickly become apparent that the Davka Corporation specializes in Hebrew language programs. Interested readers should write for their "HEBREW LANGUAGE Software Catalog." Unlike the Hebrew programs, each of the three major Latin programs (DISCO, LATIN SKILLS, SCIO) is designed to be used in semester-long courses.

4.5.1 Hebrew Programs

4.5.1.1 *Divide and Conquer*

• *BASIC PRODUCT INFORMATION*

Name of Program: Divide and Conquer
Company Name: Davka Corporation
Address: 845 North Michigan Ave., Suite 843, Chicago, IL 60611
Phones: (800) 621-8227, (312) 944-4070
Price: $34.95
Version Tested: 1.4
Runs On: Apple II series
Memory Requirements: 48K
Disk Drive Requirements: 1
Supports Color Monitors: Yes
Uses Sound: No
Number of Disks: 1
Product Includes: Disk and instructions
Manual: None
Copy Protected: Yes
Hard Disk Compatible: Yes
Menu-Driven: Yes
On-Line Help: No
Tutorial: No
Warranty: 30 days, media only; after 30 days, $5 replacement fee
Support: Phone and letter
Update Policy: Reduced cost ($10) for major updates
Related Products: Divide and Conquer II (see next entry)
Other Information: None
Comments: Divide and Conquer is a menu-driven program that teaches students to divide nouns and verbs into their prefixes, suffixes, and stems. Once successfully divided, words must be translated. Other drills use multiple choice and matching questions. Hebrew words are vocalized. The current word must be correctly divided before students may move to the next word. Some mistakes ara analyzed. The on-screen Hebrew letters are large and easy to read, and the menu-driven interface facilitates learning and use. All the nominal and verbal prefixes and suffixes are covered, and the straightforward drills make learning interesting and easy. This is a helpful program for beginners.

4.5.1.2 *Divide and Conquer II*

• *BASIC PRODUCT INFORMATION*

Name of Program: Divide and Conquer II One-On-One
Company Name: Davka Corporation
Address: 845 North Michigan Ave., Suite 843, Chicago, IL 60611
Phones: (800) 621-8227, (312) 944-4070
Price: $34.95
Version Tested: 1.2
Runs On: Apple II series
Memory Requirements: 48K
Disk Drive Requirements: 1
Supports Color Monitors: Yes
Uses Sound: No
Number of Disks: 1
Product Includes: Disk and instructions
Manual: None
Copy Protected: Yes

Hard Disk Compatible: Yes
Menu-Driven: Yes
On-Line Help: No
Tutorial: No
Warranty: 30 days, media only; after 30 days, $5 replacement fee
Support: Phone and letter
Update Policy: Reduced cost ($10) for major updates
Related Products: Divide and Conquer (see previous entry)
Other Information: None
Comments: This sequel to Divide and Conquer allows teachers and students to create their own vocabulary files. Letters and vowels are entered right-to-left. Users may enter (1) two correct answers for each part of a word, (2) the response the program is to give for wrong answers, (3) the translation of the word, (4) hints, and (5) a code word for the word. Up to nine parts of a word may be defined. Two testing modes quiz students by asking them to divide and translate words or by asking them to do so within a time limit set by a user or by a teacher. The number of successfully divided and translated words is displayed at the end of the session, thereby allowing teachers to maintain a record of student scores. Like the preceding program, Divide and Conquer II displays vocalized words and is an excellent tool for learning Hebrew.

4.5.1.3 *Dynamic Hebrew Dictionary*

• *BASIC PRODUCT INFORMATION*

Name of Program: Dynamic Hebrew Dictionary
Company Name: Davka Corporation
Address: 845 North Michigan Ave., Suite 843, Chicago, IL 60611
Phones: (800) 621-8227, (312) 944-4070
Price: $50
Version Tested: 2.1
Runs On: Apple II series
Memory Requirements: 48K
Disk Drive Requirements: 1
Supports Color Monitors: Yes
Uses Sound: No
Number of Disks: 2 flippy disks
Product Includes: Disks and instructions
Manual: None
Copy Protected: Yes
Hard Disk Compatible: Yes
Menu-Driven: Yes
On-Line Help: No
Tutorial: No
Warranty: 30 days, media only; after 30 days, $5 replacement fee
Support: Phone and letter
Update Policy: Reduced cost ($10) for major updates
Related Products: See the other Davka software in this section.
Other Information: Demo disk available for $15; price deductible from purchase of set.
Comments: The Dynamic Hebrew Dictionary teaches basic Hebrew vocabulary. Several hundred vocalized Hebrew nouns are divided into twenty-two categories that often reflect modern objects. Each word may be studied individually or as part of a unit of related words. Each entry is illustrated in color and appears on-screen with Hebrew and English equivalents. Students are able to choose one of two multiple choice methods of testing: matching Hebrew words with pictures of objects, or vice versa. Each answer is graded, and students are given cumulative scores at the end of each lesson. Unfortunately, users may not add new vocabulary words to the program. Although the program's vocabulary is more oriented toward Modern Hebrew, there is no reason in principle that Davka could not issue a version that taught vocabulary that was more suited to the needs of biblical students. Ideally, the program should allow users or teachers to delete and add vocabulary words. The Hebrew letters and the accompanying graphics representations of objects are quite legible.

4.5.1.4 Hebrew Phrasebook

- BASIC PRODUCT INFORMATION

Name of Program: Hebrew Phrasebook
Company Name: Davka Corporation
Address: 845 North Michigan Ave., Suite 843, Chicago, IL 60611
Phones: (800) 621-8227, (312) 944-4070
Price: $34.95
Version Tested: 1.1
Runs On: Apple II series
Memory Requirements: 48K
Disk Drive Requirements: 1
Supports Color Monitors: Yes
Uses Sound: Yes, cassette tape
Number of Disks: 1 flippy disk
Product Includes: Disk and instructions
Manual: None
Copy Protected: Yes
Hard Disk Compatible: Yes
Menu-Driven: Yes
On-Line Help: No
Tutorial: No
Warranty: 30 days, media only; after 30 days, $5 replacement fee
Support: Phone and letter
Update Policy: Reduced cost ($10) for major updates
Related Products: See the other Davka software in this section.
Other Information: None
Comment: This program is accompanied by a tape in "authentic Israeli-accented Hebrew" and contains 271 commonly used Hebrew phrases and expressions, most of which are illustrated on-screen by colorful pictures. There are twenty lessons, and all Hebrew words appear with vowels, translations, and transliterations. The program also includes tests. Because it instructs at the phrase level, this program can be beneficial to students of Classical Hebrew, though it was designed to help students learn Modern Hebrew.

4.5.1.5 Chumash Compu-Flash Cards

- BASIC PRODUCT INFORMATION

Name of Program: Chumash Compu-Flash Cards
Company Name: Davka Corporation
Address: 845 North Michigan Ave., Suite 843, Chicago, IL 60611
Phones: (800) 621-8227, (312) 944-4070
Price: $20 per set; complete set of five: $75
Version Tested: 1.0
Runs On: Apple II series
Memory Requirements: 48K
Disk Drive Requirements: 1
Supports Color Monitors: Yes
Uses Sound: No
Number of Disks: 1 per set
Product Includes: Disk and instructions
Manual: No
Copy Protected: No
Hard Disk Compatible: Yes
Menu-Driven: Yes
On-Line Help: Yes
Tutorial: No
Warranty: 30 days, media only; after 30 days, $5 replacement fee
Support: Phone and letter
Update Policy: Reduced cost ($10) for major updates

Related Products: See the other Davka software in this section.
Other Information: Complete set of 5 disks is available for $75.
Comment: This vocabulary program focuses on words from the *Chumash*, or Pentateuch. There is a separate vocabulary disk for each of the Five Books of Moses. Vowels are used. Words are grouped into six sets of thirty words each, and each word is displayed in Hebrew, identified by book, chapter, and verse, and its English meaning given. Students may review words before testing. Incorrect answers are automatically corrected, and subsequent sets of words contain words from previous sets. A record (which may be displayed anytime during the quiz) is kept of student scores. Beginning students of Hebrew could profit greatly from this program.

4.5.1.6 *Compu-Dikduk*

- BASIC PRODUCT INFORMATION

Name of Program: Compu-Dikduk
Company Name: Davka Corporation
Address: 845 North Michigan Ave., Suite 843, Chicago, IL 60611
Phones: (800) 621-8227, (312) 944-4070
Price: $25
Version Tested: 1.1
Runs On: Apple II series, Atari
Memory Requirements: Apple: 48K; Atari: 48K
Disk Drive Requirements: 1
Supports Color Monitors: Yes
Uses Sound: No
Number of Disks: 1
Product Includes: Disk and instructions
Manual: No
Copy Protected: No
Hard Disk Compatible: Yes
Menu-Driven: Yes
On-Line Help: Yes
Tutorial: No
Warranty: 30 days, media only; after 30 days, $5 replacement fee
Support: Phone and letter
Update Policy: Reduced cost ($10) for major updates
Related Products: See the other Davka software in this section.
Other Information: None
Comment: This three-part, drill-and-review program teaches Hebrew grammar. Students are drilled on prefixes and suffixes, present and future tenses, and on noun declension. Questions are multiple choice, and students may not proceed until the correct answer has been given. For elementary Hebrew students.

4.5.1.7 *Ulpan Davka*

- BASIC PRODUCT INFORMATION

Name of Program: Ulpan Davka
Company Name: Davka Corporation
Address: 845 North Michigan Ave., Suite 843, Chicago, IL 60611
Phones: (800) 621-8227, (312) 944-4070
Price: $39.95; supplementary disks $14.95 each
Version Tested: Not able to test.
Runs On: Apple II series
Memory Requirements: 48K
Disk Drive Requirements: 1
Supports Color Monitors: Yes
Uses Sound: No
Number of Disks: 1
Product Includes: Disk and instructions

Manual: No
Copy Protected: Yes
Hard Disk Compatible: Yes
Menu-Driven: Yes
On-Line Help: No
Tutorial: No
Warranty: 30 days, media only; after 30 days, $5 replacement fee
Support: Phone and letter
Update Policy: Reduced cost ($10) for major updates
Related Products: See the other Davka software in this section.
Other Information: None
Comment: In many ways, this is Davka's most interesting language program. In Israel the *Ulpan* is a special
school where new immigrants receive a "crash course" in Modern Hebrew. Focusing on vocabulary,
Davka's basic Ulpan module contains 1,000 Modern Hebrew words and phrases in a flashcard format
that allows users to study them with or without vowels, transliteration, and translation. A quiz section
tests users' knowledge of vocabulary. The program's built-in editor, which allows users to create their
own computer-based Hebrew vocabulary flashcards (complete with vowels, transliteration, and translation) makes this program potentially valuable for students of biblical Hebrew. Several of this program's
six supplementary diskettes may interest readers of this book. Mishnaic and Talmudic Terms contains
several hundred of the most widely used Talmudic words and phrases in the *Mishna* and *Talmud*.
Chumash Vocabulary (see above) contains vocabulary from the Pentateuch. And Hebrew Verb Conjugations contains examples from all seven major verb forms.

4.5.1.8 The Creative Hebrew Quizzer

- ● *BASIC PRODUCT INFORMATION*

Name of Program: The Creative Hebrew Quizzer
Company Name: Davka Corporation
Address: 845 North Michigan Ave., Suite 843, Chicago, IL 60611
Phones: (800) 621-8227, (312) 944-4070
Price: $39.95
Version Tested: 2.1
Runs On: Apple II series
Memory Requirements: 48K
Disk Drive Requirements: 1
Supports Color Monitors: Yes
Uses Sound: No
Number of Disks: 1
Product Includes: Disk and instructions
Manual: None
Copy Protected: No
Hard Disk Compatible: Yes
Menu-Driven: Yes
On-Line Help: No
Tutorial: No
Warranty: 30 days, media only; after 30 days, $5 replacement fee
Support: Phone and letter
Update Policy: Reduced cost ($10) for major updates
Related Products: See the other Davka software in this section.
Other Information: None
Comment: This program allows users to create and print questions in unpointed Hebrew, English, or a mix-
ture of the two. Two quiz formats allow teachers to quiz single students or an entire class, and teachers
may create multiple-choice questions (up to four choices per question) with hints. The Creative Hebrew
Quizzer supports the following Epson printers: MX-70, 80, 100 (with GrafTrax), RX series, and FX
series.

4.5.1.9 *Learning to Read Hebrew*

- *BASIC PRODUCT INFORMATION*

Name of Program: Learning to Read Hebrew
Company Name: Davka Corporation
Address: 845 North Michigan Ave., Suite 843, Chicago, IL 60611
PhoneS: (800) 621-8227, (312) 944-4070
Price: $50, with sound tape $75
Version Tested: 4.1
Runs On: Apple II series, Commodore 64
Memory Requirements: Apple: 48K; Commodore: 64K
Disk Drive Requirements: 1
Supports Color Monitors: Yes
Uses Sound: Yes, cassette tape
Number of Disks: 1
Product Includes: Disk and instructions
Manual: No
Copy Protected: Yes
Hard Disk Compatible: Yes
Menu-Driven: Yes
On-Line Help: Yes
Tutorial: No
Warranty: 30 days, media only; after 30 days, $5 replacement fee
Support: Phone and letter
Update Policy: Reduced cost ($10) for major updates
Related Products: $25 for sound tape; see the other Davka software in this section.
Other Information: None
Comment: This program consists of fourteen units for teaching beginning students to read vocalized Hebrew. An optional sound tape teaches Sephardic pronunciation, and quizzes and review materials are used for reinforcment.

4.5.1.10 *Hebrew Super-Pilot*

- *BASIC PRODUCT INFORMATION*

Name of Program: Hebrew Super-Pilot
Company Name: Davka Corporation
Address: 845 North Michigan Ave., Suite 843, Chicago, IL 60611
Phones: (800) 621-8227, (312) 944-4070
Price: $340
Version Tested: Not able to test.
Runs On: Apple II series
Memory Requirements: 64K
Disk Drive Requirements: 2 to create programs; 1 drive is sufficient to run programs.
Supports Color Monitors: Yes
Uses Sound: Yes
Number of Disks: 7 (3 Hebrew and 4 English)
Product Includes: Disk and instructions
Manual: Yes
Copy Protected: No
Hard Disk Compatible: Yes
Menu-Driven: Yes
On-Line Help: No
Tutorial: Yes
Warranty: 30 days, media only; after 30 days, $5 replacement fee
Support: Phone and letter
Update Policy: Reduced cost for major updates
Related Products: See the other Davka software in this section.
Other Information: Includes English version of Super-Pilot.

Comment: This program includes English and Hebrew versions of Apple's authoring language, Super-Pilot, and allows users to create their own computer lessons, complete with sound, music, and color graphics. Manuals and tutorials are included, and English and Hebrew may by combined in the same lesson. According to Davka, "Super-Pilot was developed in Israel, and is used extensively in the Israeli school system." Although the Hebrew version does not come with ready-made vowels, the flexibility of Super-Pilot allows users to create a vowel set.

4.5.1.11 The Best of Davka

Beginning students of Classical Hebrew who own an Apple II computer and who wish to use it to supplement their Hebrew instruction would do well to purchase the following programs from Davka.

> Divide and Conquer
> Divide and Conquer II
> Chumash Compu-Flash Cards
> Compu-Dikduk
> Ulpan Davka with Hebrew Verb Conjugations

These programs offer drills on vocabulary, word divisions, and parsing. Divide and Conquer II allows users to create their own Hebrew word lists, and Ulpan Davka allows them to create their own vocabulary flashcards. Students with some programming knowledge could use Hebrew Super-Pilot to write their own CALL Hebrew lessons, complete with sound, music, and color graphics.

4.5.1.12 Hebrew Parsing Guide

* *BASIC PRODUCT INFORMATION*

Name of Program: Hebrew Parsing Guide
Company Name: % Dr. Lloyd M. Barré
Address: 12445 Damasco Ct., San Diego, CA 92128
Phone: (619) 485-5281
Price: $20
Version Tested: 1.5, IBM version
Runs On: IBM PC; CP/M version available
Memory Requirements: 128K
Disk Drive Requirements: 1
Supports Color Monitors: Yes
Uses Sound: No
Number of Disks: 1
Product Includes: Disk only
Manual: None
Copy Protected: No
Hard Disk Compatible: Yes
Menu-Driven: Yes
On-Line Help: No
Tutorial: No
Warranty: No
Support: None
Update Policy: None
Related Products: QuickParse (see below)
Other Information: Requires Microsoft BASIC to run.

The Hebrew Parsing Guide (HPG) is an easy-to-use, menu-driven program that partially parses Hebrew verbs. Instructions are included in a brief READ.ME file. HPG runs under Microsoft BASIC.

All answers to menu prompts must be given in upper-case letters. The first menu asks, "Does the form have a verbal prefix (Y/N)?" Users respond "Y" (for *yes*) or "N" (for *no*), and then a second menu appears. If the answer to the first prompt was "Y," then the second prompt asks, "WHAT IS THE PREFIX?," and users must choose from a list of prefixes that are displayed. A new menu appears, and the third prompt then asks, "To what class does the VOWEL under the prefix belong?," to which users must reply "A," "I," "U," or "S" (for *shewa*). Subsequent questions depend on the response given to the preceding question. When the program has parsed the verb, it displays the answer and beeps. Typing any character returns the program to the main screen. Entering "P" displays a menu of paradigm options. Users may select any paradigm of the strong verb, and Parse will display the perfect, imperfect, imperative, participle, and both infinitives of that paradigm. Entering "X" allows users to exit the program from any point.

The Hebrew Parsing Guide is quite helpful, though it has a few drawbacks. (1) Sometimes the HPG concludes with an indeterminate answer. For example, when parsing *yabdil* (from the root *bdl*, "separate, distinguish"), the HPG responds, "The form is HIPHIL IMPERFECT or a QAL IMPERFECT (1st Gutteral-3rd He) or QAL IMPERFECT (Hollow-middle yod)" (the correct answer is HIPHIL IMPERFECT). Although partial parsing makes it easier to analyze a form, it is disappointing that the program does not completely parse all words. (2) Sometimes verbal prefixes do not have vowels under them, and users must answer the question "To which class does the vowel under the prefix belong?" in terms of the vowel associated with the first radical of the root. The word *under* in the question can be misleading. (3) The program is not as specific as it could be because it does not parse suffixes. For example, the program may parse a form as QAL IMPERFECT, but it would be more helpful if, for example, users were told that the form is SECOND MASCULINE SINGULAR QAL IMPERFECT.

The Hebrew Parsing Guide is a unique and excellent tool for the beginning Hebrew student or for the former student of Hebrew who needs to review. It shows what can be done to take some of the drudgery out of learning to parse verbs.

4.5.1.13 QuickParse

- BASIC PRODUCT INFORMATION

Name of Program: QuickParse
Company Name: % Dr. Lloyd M. Barré
Address: 12445 Damasco Ct., San Diego, CA 92128
Phone: (619) 485-5281
Price: $25
Version Tested: 1.0, IBM version
Runs On: IBM PCs and compatibles
Memory Requirements: 128K
Disk Drive Requirements: 1
Supports Color Monitors: Yes
Uses Sound: No
Number of Disks: 1
Product Includes: Disk only
Manual: None
Copy Protected: No
Hard Disk Compatible: Yes
Menu-Driven: Yes
On-Line Help: No
Tutorial: No
Warranty: No
Support: None
Update Policy: None

FEATURES	DC	DC2	DHD	HP	CCC	CD	UD	CHQ	LRH	HSP	HPG	QP	HOL
BASIC FACTS													
Price	35	35	50	35	20	25	40	40	50	340	20	25	60
Runs On	A	A	A	A	A	A, At	A	A	A, C	A	I, C	I	I
Memory (in K)	48	48	48	48	48	48	48	48	48	64	128	128	?
Disk Drives	1	1	1	1	1	1	1	1	1	2	1	1	1
User Interface	MD	MD	MD	MD	MD	MD	MD	MD	MD	MD	MD	MD	MD
CONTENT COMPONENTS													
Vocabulary	○	●	●	●	●	○	●	—	●	—	○	○	●
Grammatical Terminology	○	○	○	○	○	●	○	—	○	—	○	○	○
Morphology	●	●	○	○	○	●	○	—	○	—	●	●	○
Syntax	○	○	○	○	○	●	○	—	○	—	○	○	○
Translation Skills	○	○	○	●	○	○	○	—	●	—	○	○	○
History/Culture	○	○	○	○	○	○	○	—	○	—	○	○	○
Etymology/Derivation	○	○	○	○	○	○	○	—	○	—	○	○	○

Table 4.1: Comparison of microcomputer Hebrew language programs. A = Apple, At = Atari, I = IBM, C = CP/M, MD = menu-driven, DC = Divide & Conquer, DC2 = Divide & Conquer II, DHD = Dynamic Hebrew Dictionary, HP = Hebrew Phrasebook, CCC = Chumash Compu-Flash Cards, CD = Compu-Dikduk, UD = Ulpan Davka, CHQ = Creative Hebrew Quizzer, LRH = Learning to Read Hebrew, HSP = Hebrew Super-Pilot, HPG = Hebrew Parsing Guide, QP = Quick Parse, HOL = Hebrew On-Line!

FEATURES	DC	DC2	DHD	HP	CCC	CD	UD	CHQ	LRH	HSP	HPG	QP	HOL
PART OF SPEECH													
Noun	●	●	●	●	●	●	●	–	●	–	○	○	●
Pronoun	○	●	●	●	●	○	●	–	●	–	○	○	●
Adjective	○	○	●	●	●	○	●	–	●	–	○	○	●
Verb	●	●	●	●	●	●	●	–	●	–	●	●	●
Other	○	○	○	●	○	○	●	–	●	–	○	○	○
PROGRAM CHARACTERISTICS													
Color	●	●	●	●	●	●	●	●	●	●	●	●	●
Graphics	○	○	○	●	○	○	○	○	○	●	○	○	●
Sound	○	○	○	●	○	○	●	○	●	●	○	○	○
Scoring	●	●	●	●	●	●	●	●	●	●	●	●	○
Record	●	○	●	●	●	○	○	●	●	●	○	○	○
Printer	○	○	○	○	○	○	●	●	○	?	○	○	○
Editor	○	●	○	○	○	○	○	○	○	●	○	○	○
Help	●	●	○	○	○	○	○	●	○	●	○	○	○
Hints	○	●	○	○	○	○	○	○	○	●	○	○	○
Gamelike	○	○	○	○	○	○	○	○	○	●	○	○	○

Table 4.1: Comparison of microcomputer Hebrew language programs. A = Apple, At = Atari, I = IBM, C = CP/M, MD = menu-driven, DC = Divide & Conquer, DC2 = Divide & Conquer II, DHD = Dynamic Hebrew Dictionary, HP = Hebrew Phrasebook, CCC = Chumash Compu-Flash Cards, CD = Compu-Dikduk, UD = Ulpan Davka, CHQ = Creative Hebrew Quizzer, LRH = Learning to Read Hebrew, HSP = Hebrew Super-Pilot, HPG = Hebrew Parsing Guide, QP = Quick Parse, HOL = Hebrew On-Line!

Related Products: Hebrew Parsing Guide (see above)
Other Information: Requires Microsoft BASIC to run.
Comment: QuickParse parses Hebrew verbs without teaching users parsing procedures. It is menu-driven and uses function keys. Like Parse, QuickParse allows users to display paradigms of the strong verb in any measure.

4.5.1.14 *Hebrew On-Line!*

● *BASIC PRODUCT INFORMATION*

Name of Program: Hebrew On-Line!
Company Name: Hebrew On-Line!
Address: P.O. Box 96, Staunton, VA 24401
Phone: Not known
Price: $59.95
Version Tested: Not able to test.
Runs On: IBM PCs and compatibles; requires graphics adapter.
Memory Requirements: Not known
Disk Drive Requirements: 1
Supports Color Monitors: Yes
Uses Sound: Not known
Number of Disks: 1
Product Includes: Disk and manual
Manual: Not able to see.
Copy Protected: No
Hard Disk Compatible: Yes
Menu-Driven: Yes
On-Line Help: Not known
Tutorial: Not known
Warranty: Not known
Support: Not known
Update Policy: Not known
Related Products: None
Other Information: None
Comment: Hebrew On-Line! is a menu-driven Hebrew vocabulary program that properly displays vocalized Hebrew on-screen and that will print vocalized Hebrew on a graphics printer. All Hebrew words (except proper names), their English equivalents, and their Strong's reference numbers are on one disk. Users may enter a Hebrew term, and the program will display the English meaning of the term. Or users may enter an English term, and the program will display all the Hebrew words with that English translation. Hebrew words may be looked up by using their Strong's number. Hebrew On-Line! includes vocabulary drills on all nouns and verbs that occur more than fifty times in the Hebrew Bible. Verbal roots and derivatives are matched and displayed.

4.5.2 Latin Programs

Readers interested in any of the following Latin programs are encouraged to purchase Robert B. Latousek, Jr.'s excellent "Survey of Latin Instructional Software for the Microcomputer," which is available from

American Classical League
Teaching Materials and Resource Center
Miami University
Oxford, OH 45056
(513) 529-4116.

Mr. Latousek's 23-page publication includes critical reviews, helpful discussions and evaluations, and comparative analyses and charts of many of the Latin programs discussed below. Most of these programs are available from the American Classical League.

4.5.2.1 DISCO

● *BASIC PRODUCT INFORMATION*

Name of Program: DISCO
Company Name: DISCO
Address: % Latin Department, John Burroughs School, 755 S. Price Rd., St. Louis, MO 63124 or % Judy Rubenstein, 7394 Westmoreland Dr., St. Louis, MO 63130
Phones: (314) 993-4040 (school), (314) 863-3834 (Rubenstein)
Price: $30 per disk with a decreasing cost per disk; $125 for all 9 disks; $350 Site License; $25 per set discount for multiple sets; $25 per notebook
Version Tested: 1.1
Runs On: Apple II series and IBM PCs with Quadlink board.[29]
Memory Requirements: 48K
Disk Drive Requirements: 1
Supports Color Monitors: Yes
Uses Sound: No
Number of Disks: 9
Product Includes: Disks, manual, and *Permanent Latin Notebook*
Manual: Yes
Copy Protected: No
Hard Disk Compatible: Yes
Menu-Driven: Yes
On-Line Help: No
Tutorial: No
Warranty: Not known
Support: Call or write Ms. Rubenstein.
Update Policy: No charge if user pays postage.
Related Products: None
Other Information: Will customize if reasonable.

DISCO, which in Latin means "I learn, I get to know," is an interactive, menu-driven program designed to help students of Latin master morphology, vocabulary, and syntax. The DISCO package includes *The Permanent Latin Notebook* (37 lessons, 99 pages). The standard vocabulary is Anderson and Groten, *Latin: A Course for Scholars and Colleges*; specific vocabularies are available on request.

Disk one consists of drills on indicative verb conjugations (including drills on principal parts, tense, and voice) and allows students to select the tense and voice used in drills. All DISCO programs allow students to escape from drills at any time and to check and correct their work before DISCO reads it.

Disk two drills students on the indicative and subjunctive moods of irregular verbs and allows them to select the irregular verb and principal part(s) they wish to practice on.

Disk three contains drills on the number, gender, case, and degree of adjectives, and on noun declensions. DISCO selects adjectives at random, or users may specify the gender, number, case, and degree to be tested on. Students select the noun declension for DISCO to use. The MENU for IRREGULAR NOUNS lists *os, bos, caro, senex, sus,* and *vis.*

Disk four drills students on vocabulary by parts of speech. DISCO vocabulary files may be used, or students may create their own vocabulary files (DISCO contains a menu-driven utility for doing this). DISCO drills students on English meanings of Latin words, and vice versa. Verb practice requires students to supply each verb's principal parts and translation. Noun drills ask for the genitive, gender, and translation.

---

29. Quadlink boards are coprocessing boards that allow IBM PCs to run many programs written for Apple IIs. Contact Quadram Corp., 4355 International Blvd., Norcross, GA 30093; (404) 923-6666; $495.

Drills on prepositions require students to provide the case and translation. Students may be prompted several times to supply English meanings for Latin words with multiple meanings.

Disk five contains drills on *unus nauta*, regular adjectives, and relative pronouns. This disk's look-up function allows students to look up the meaning of Latin words.

Disk six allows students to look up conjugations and declensions. Students enter the verb to be conjugated or the noun to be declined, and DISCO automatically conjugates or declines the form. Because all declensions except irregular nouns are programmed generically, users could type in a non-Latin word and DISCO would decline it. And where not indicated to the contrary, DISCO will conjugate non-Latin words.

Disk seven is a game that drills students on adjective and noun agreement. The menu allows users to select (1) first, second, and third declension nouns, (2) fourth declension nouns, or (3) fifth declension nouns. The adjectives used are first, second, and third declension. After a noun declension is chosen, DISCO randomly chooses the nouns, adjectives, cases, and numbers to use. Gender, of course, is determined by the noun.

Disk eight consists of drills on deponent verbs. These drills are similar to those on disk one. (I have no information about disk nine.)

All user input must be in upper case letters when using DISCO. Typing 99 at any menu prompt returns the program to the main menu. DISCO has detailed error messages, such as "STEM ERROR 2ND PERSON SINGULAR" and "TENSE ERROR 3RD PERSON PLURAL," and after each error message users are given the opportunity to try again. Some exercises will not allow users to proceed until the correct answer is given. At the end of drills, DISCO displays a score, which represents the percentage of correct answers given on the first attempt.

The Permanent Latin Notebook, which consists of paradigms, rules, drills, and brief explanations, is designed to be used with DISCO and a grammar by beginning students of Latin. DISCO and *The Permanent Latin Notebook* should prove helpful to all first year students of Latin, as well as to students who wish to refresh their basic Latin skills.

4.5.2.2 LATIN SKILLS

- *BASIC PRODUCT INFORMATION*

Name of Program: LATIN SKILLS
Company Name: University of Delaware
Address: % Office of Computer-Based Instruction, Willard Hall Educational Bldg., University of Delaware, Newark, DE 19716
Phone: (302) 451-8161
Price: $395 for first package; $295 for second package; $245 for third package; $195 for each additional package; $89 for individual programs; $20 for a light pen (optional); $15 per back-up disk ($75 for a complete package); $15 for a demonstration disk
Version Tested: 1.1
Runs On: Apple II series and IBM PC with Quadlink board
Memory Requirements: 48K
Disk Drive Requirements: 1
Supports Color Monitors: Yes
Uses Sound: No
Number of Disks: 5
Product Includes: Disks and manual
Manual: 34 pages, three-ring binder, not indexed
Copy Protected: Yes
Hard Disk Compatible: No
Menu-Driven: Yes
On-Line Help: Yes
Tutorial: No

Warranty: 90 days, media only
Support: Phone and letter
Update Policy: No plans for future updates
Related Products: None
Other Information: Use of light pen is optional.

LATIN SKILLS was produced by the Office of Computer-Based Instruction at the University of Delaware. It is designed to supplement the first year of college Latin or the first two years of high school Latin. LATIN SKILLS is a comprehensive, menu-driven program that comes in five versions, each of which is configured to complement one of the following five Latin textbooks: (1) Wheelock's *Latin: An Introductory Course* (Harper & Row), (2) Jenny's *First/Second Year Latin* (Allyn & Bacon), (3) Ullman's *Latin for Americans* (Macmillan), (4) Goldman's and Nyenhuis's *Latin via Ovid* (Wayne State University Press), or (5) *Ecce Romani*, rev. ed. (Longman). The five LATIN SKILLS disks are designed to supplement Latin instruction in three areas: morphology, sentence translation, and contextual parsing. The disks contain 40 hours of materials. LATIN SKILLS was developed over a period of six years at the University of Delaware as PLATO courseware.

Disk one, THE VERB FACTORY, uses diagnostic quizzes to drill students on verb morphology. Its fifteen sections cover all the regular verb forms, and each section requires 15–40 minutes to complete (4–7 hours in all). Students enter Latin verb forms in response to English verb phrases, and sophisticated diagnostic help directs users toward the correct answer. The program analyzes answers part-by-part (that is, bare stem, tense/mood sign, personal ending), and as soon as it spots an error, it stops and gives a hint. By using help menus, students can assemble the correct mood, voice, tense, number, and person of verbal forms, thereby seeing how forms are constructed. A feature called "verb scan" immediately parses user input so that users may see how it differs from the requested form.

Disk two, CURSUS HONORUM, drills students on verb morphology by requiring them to recognize and produce inflected forms. Students may choose from all regular forms and be drilled in a gamelike format. The time involved is open ended and varies from 5 minutes and up per session (about 5 hours in all).

Disk three, MARE NOSTRUM, drills students on noun and adjective morphology by requiring them to recognize and produce the proper forms. The program covers all regular nouns and adjectives, including comparatives and superlatives, but students determine which declensions and cases are to be used. Exercise time is open ended, varying from 15 minutes and up per session (about 3 hours in all).

Disk four, TRANSLAT, drills students on Latin sentence translation. Translation skills are developed by synthesizing lexical and grammatical data. Students may request the program to provide the lexical form, the lexical meaning, the grammatical form, and explain the syntax of every word in each sentence that is to be translated. Unsuccessful attempts at translation are analyzed with the aid of eight symbols that designate translation errors, such as an extra character, a wrong character, inverted letters, or a missing word. Its seventeen sections require about 30 minutes each to complete (about 9 hours in all).

Disk five, ARTIFEX VERBORUM, requires students to analyze Latin words in context. Skill in understanding Latin sentence structure is developed by contextually identifying and parsing each part of speech. The twenty-one sections of this program require about 45 minutes each to complete (about 18 hours in all).

In addition to offering textbook-specific versions, each of LATIN SKILL's five programs has variable skill levels. For example, beginning students may use MARE NOSTRUM with only one declension and two cases, while more advanced students may use it with all declensions, all cases, and comparative and superlative forms. LATIN SKILLS also provides intelligent feedback, or help, for partially correct answers. VERB FACTORY, for example, might give the following message: "The stem and tense mood sign are correct, but the personal ending is wrong." Such intelligent feedback guides students toward correct answers. Furthermore, LATIN SKILLS can act as a generative grammar; it can inflect parts of speech. If users provide the principle parts of a regular verb, for example, LATIN SKILLS can conjugate the verb. A technique known as "invisible review" is another of LATIN SKILLS's strengths. If a student misses a form, such as *mittemini*, LATIN SKILLS does not give *mittemini* for review but will show a similar verb in the same grammatical form, for example, *vincemini*. The item is not repeated, but the concept is. Finally, LATIN SKILLS provides a full range of helps. Each program allows students to select an appropriate skill level, to obtain hints or explanations, and to move about from display to display.

The documentation, design, and implementation of LATIN SKILLS are excellent from didactic and educational points of view. The flexibility, depth, and breadth of this series of programs and the creative and analytical hints and helps clearly make LATIN SKILLS the best choice of the three commercial microcomputer CALL Latin programs.

4.5.2.3 SCIO

- *BASIC PRODUCT INFORMATION*

Name of Program: SCIO
Company Name: % Dr. Peg Kershenbaum
Address: Department of Classics, Brooklyn College, The City University of New York (CUNY), Beaford
   Ave. & Campus Rd., Brooklyn, NY 11210
Phone: (212) 780-5191
Price: $500
Version Tested: Not known
Runs On: IBM PC
Memory Requirements: 128K
Disk Drive Requirements: 1
Supports Color Monitors: Yes
Uses Sound: Yes
Number of Disks: 2
Product Includes: Disk and instructions
Manual: No
Copy Protected: No
Hard Disk Compatible: Yes
Menu-Driven: Yes
On-Line Help: No
Tutorial: No
Warranty: Not known
Support: Phone and letter
Update Policy: Free for one year
Related Products: None
Other Information: Peg Kershenbaum, "Latin: Requiescat in PC," *Collegiate Microcomputer* 5 (May 1987):
   139–47.

SCIO, which in Latin means "I know, I understand, I have knowledge of,"[30] is an interactive, menu-driven program designed to help students of Latin master morphology, vocabulary, and syntax. SCIO is flexible and uses computer-generated files of suffixes to build and check words. Subroutines create the parts of speech on which students are drilled, check user input, and correct the placement of macrons. Dr. Kershenbaum is using an expanded version of the main program module in her Latin

---

30. SCIO also is an acronym for Shoemaker Computerized Instruction Office.

classes to provide the grammatical knowledge necessary for students to parse Cicero's *First Catilinarian*.

SCIO consists of two programs, SCION and SCIOV. SCION is the noun and adjective program, and SCIOV is the verb program. When SCIO displays its logo, users are given the option of having a song, "Gaudeamus Igitur," played. Users are then prompted for their names, which are used to record the dates that drills were taken and the scores that were made. Exiting SCIO causes the score and date to be recorded in a record file that may be displayed and printed.

SCION has four menu levels. First, users must choose one of six vocabulary levels, which include the five declensions and an option called "no restrictions." Each successive level contains material from the previous levels. Second, users must choose one of two parts of speech: nouns or adjectives. Third, users must choose from one or more of the five declensions and the i-stem. Finally, users must choose what kind of drill SCION is to use. SCION offers English-to-Latin and Latin-to-English vocabulary drills, and the drill submenu allows users to review declensions and case uses and to create drills. Macrons, which are represented by a "*" after the vowel that is to be lengthened, must be used where appropriate.

SCIO always prompts users. Correct answers are rewarded with a word of congratulation in Latin and with a high-pitched sound from the speaker, and incorrect answers are rewarded with an appropriate Latin word and with a low-pitched sound from the speaker. All drills (1) display the words students are to be drilled on, (2) drill randomly, (3) reask missed questions, and (4) provide correct answers. After each drill, SCIO gives students their score. At the prompt, users may exit from a drill by typing "r" followed by a carriage return.

SCIOV has four menu levels. First, users must choose to include or to exclude examples of subjunctives, passive forms, and verbs from the perfect system. Second, users must choose to be drilled on verbs or to exit the program. Third, users must choose from one or more of the four conjugations and the i-stem. And finally, users must choose one of eight verb drills, which include English-to-Latin exercises, sentence, and synopsis drills. This submenu also allows users to choose an analysis of the Latin verb, to see a synopsis of the verb, and to review verbs.

SCIO is a sound and useful program that should appeal to all beginning students of Latin. It is well-designed, easy to operate, and thorough. Its screen displays are attractive and easy to read. Although SCIO usually works smoothly, on several occasions I was dumped from the program when I gave an incorrect answer. Because SCIO is menu-driven, being dumped from the program means that users must descend through the hierarchy of menus to return to the drills. SCIO's sentence drills are grammatically correct, though the sentences are often nonsensical because they are constructed randomly from word lists.

SCIO has several other shortcomings as well, though these are being addressed by the programmers. (1) Sometimes SCIO displays abstract and proper nouns in the plural. (2) SCIO *seems* to select some words more frequently than others. (3) The number of adjectives is limited, and (4) SCIO only uses active verbs.

4.5.2.4 Latin Certamen Practice

The following Latin programs came to my attention too late to be reviewed. The information provided below includes the basic facts about each program.

• *BASIC PRODUCT INFORMATION*

Name of Program: Latin Certamen Practice
Company Name: Tessera, Inc.
Address: % Langley Webber, P.O. Box 522, Bedford, VA 24523

Phones: (703) 586-0624 (home)
Price: $45
Version Tested: Not able to test.
Runs On: Apple II/e or c, TRS-80 Model III/4
Memory Requirements: Apple: 64K; TRS-80: 48K
Disk Drive Requirements: 1
Supports Color Monitors: Yes
Uses Sound: Not known
Number of Disks: 4
Product Includes: Disks and instructions
Manual: None
Copy Protected: No
Hard Disk Compatible: Not known
Menu-Driven: Yes
On-Line Help: No
Tutorial: No
Warranty: Media only
Support: Phone and letter
Update Policy: Not known
Related Products: (1) Latin Certamen Practice: Subject Review Question Libraries—300 Certamen questions on each of four disks ($15/disk), for Apple II series and TRS-80 Model III/4; (2) Latin Certamen Practice: Book Review Questions—300 Certamen questions on Ovid's *Metamorphoses* ($15), for Apple II series; (3) Additional Latin Certamen Practice Drills—300 questions on each of five disks: *Metamorphoses*, *Aeneid*, Roman History, Roman Culture, Greek and Roman Mythology ($15/disk), all for Apple II series except *Metamorphoses*, which is for the TRS-80 Model III/4; (4) Upper Level Latin Certamen Practice Subject Review Questions for Apple—300 additional questions for upper-level drills ($15); and (5) Comprehensive Questions of Readings ($15), (6) Grammatical Structures from the Readings ($15), and (7) Rules and Syntax Review. *(5), (6)* and *(7)* are discussed below under the Jenny's First Year Latin program.
Other Information: None.
Comments: In Latin *certamen* means "contest," and the Latin Certamen Practice program uses a contestlike format to ask students "Certamen and book review questions with varying time limits." Certamen questions cover Latin grammar, mythology, culture, history, and literature. Answers are by word or phrase. A Teacher's Update Disk allows teachers to edit existing questions and answers and to add new ones. Teachers may include up to eight correct answers per question. The package also includes a Latin Certamen Practice Disk and two Certamen Questions Library disks.

4.5.2.5 Latin Verb Forms

• BASIC PRODUCT INFORMATION

Name of Program: Latin Verb Forms
Company Name: Tessera, Inc.
Address: % Langley Webber, P.O. Box 522, Bedford, VA 24523
Phones: (703) 586-0624 (home)
Price: $75
Version Tested: Not able to test.
Runs On: Apple II/e or c
Memory Requirements: 64K
Disk Drive Requirements: 1
Supports Color Monitors: Yes
Uses Sound: Not known
Number of Disks: 3
Product Includes: Disks and instructions
Manual: None
Copy Protected: No
Hard Disk Compatible: Not known
Menu-Driven: Yes
On-Line Help: Yes
Tutorial: No
Warranty: Media only
Support: Phone and letter

Update Policy: Not known
Related Products: (1) Latin Verb Forms: Participle Test Disk—used with Latin Verb Forms; asks students for the declension of Latin participles; can request any participle form of the 400 verbs on the Latin Verb Forms Dictionary disk. (2) Latin Certamen Practice for Jenny's First Year Latin Verb Test disk (see below).
Other Information: None.
Comments: This dictionary-based program quizzes students on Latin verb forms. Using the Teacher's Update Disk, the teacher may create tests from the 200 verb forms and 400 verbs on the Verb Dictionary Disk. After two misses, the program analyzes the incorrect answers and displays verb formation rules and correct answers. Tests and test results may be printed. INcludes The Latin Verb Forms Test Disk.

4.5.2.6 Latin Nouns, Adjectives, and Adverbs

* *BASIC PRODUCT INFORMATION*

Name of Program: Latin Nouns, Adjectives, and Adverbs
Company Name: Tessera, Inc.
Address: % Langley Webber, P.O. Box 522, Bedford, VA 24523
Phones: (703) 586-0624 (home)
Price: $90
Version Tested: Not able to test.
Runs On: Apple II/e or c
Memory Requirements: 64K
Disk Drive Requirements: 1
Supports Color Monitors: Yes
Uses Sound: Not known
Number of Disks: 3
Product Includes: Disks and instructions
Manual: None
Copy Protected: No
Hard Disk Compatible: Not known
Menu-Driven: Yes
On-Line Help: No
Tutorial: No
Warranty: Media only
Support: Phone and letter
Update Policy: Not known
Related Products: Latin Certamen Practice for Jenny's First Year Latin Noun Test disk (see below)
Other Information: None
Comments: This dictionary-based program, which is similar in format to the Latin Verb Forms program discussed above, drills students on the declension of Latin nouns and adjectives. The endings and stems of incorrect forms are analyzed, and the program provides help about these two topics. The program checks agreement between nouns and adjectives, pronouns, the formation of the comparative and superlative, and the formation of the three degrees of adverbs. The Noun-Adjective Dictionary disk contains 400 nouns and 200 adjectives. The program can be used for vocabulary review, and it allows exercises and the results of student tests to be printed.

4.5.2.7 Latin Certamen Practice for Jenny's First Year Latin

* *BASIC PRODUCT INFORMATION*

Name of Program: Latin Certamen Practice for Jenny's First Year Latin
Company Name: Tessera, Inc.
Address: % Langley Webber, P.O. Box 522, Bedford, VA 24523
Phones: (703) 586-0624 (home)
Price: $15 to $60, depending on module
Version Tested: Not able to test.
Runs On: Apple II/e or c
Memory Requirements: 64K
Disk Drive Requirements: 1

Supports Color Monitors: Yes
Uses Sound: Not known
Number of Disks: 5 modules, 13 disks in all
Product Includes: Disks and instructions
Manual: None
Copy Protected: Not known
Hard Disk Compatible: Not known
Menu-Driven: Yes
On-Line Help: No
Tutorial: No
Warranty: Media only
Support: Phone and letter
Update Policy: Not known
Related Products: Not known
Other Information: None
Comments: This is a series of drills and tests on Jenny's *First/Second Year Latin* (see above). The complete program contains five modules. (1) Verb Test ($60) consists of six disks that cover verb forms lesson by lesson. This module requires the Latin Verb Forms master disk (see above) to run. (2) Noun Test ($50) consists of four disks that cover the declension of nouns and adjectives, degrees of adjectives and adverbs, and agreement. This module requires the Latin Nouns, Adjectives, and Adverbs program (see above) to run. (3) Comprehensive Questions of Readings ($15), (4) Grammatical Structures from the Readings ($15), and (5) Rules and Syntax Review ($15) each consist of one disk and require the Latin Certamen Practice master system (see above) to run.

4.5.2.8 Latin Vocabulary Testing System for the Cambridge Latin Course

● BASIC PRODUCT INFORMATION

Name of Program: Latin Vocabulary Testing System for the Cambridge Latin Course, also known as Computatus
Company Name: Educom
Address: % Christopher or Janet Turner, Route 1, Thornton, Ontario, Canada L0L 2N0
Phone: (705) 456-6531
Price: $35 per module
Version Tested: Not able to test.
Runs On: Apple II/e or c, Commodore 64, Commodore Pet
Memory Requirements: Apple: 48K; Commodores: 48K
Disk Drive Requirements: 1
Supports Color Monitors: Yes
Uses Sound: Yes
Number of Disks: 1
Product Includes: Disk, instructions, and manual
Manual: Yes
Copy Protected: No
Hard Disk Compatible: Yes, on Apples
Menu-Driven: Yes
On-Line Help: No
Tutorial: No
Warranty: Media only
Support: Phone and letter
Update Policy: Not known
Related Products: Derivatus Computatus
Other Information: None
Comments: This Latin-to-English vocabulary program allows teachers to choose which of the eight principal parts of speech students will be tested on and keeps a record of their scores. Two alternate English translations per Latin word are included. The program contains vocabulary from Units I, II, and III of the Cambridge Latin Course.

4.5.2.9 *Derivatus Computatus*

- *BASIC PRODUCT INFORMATION*

Name of Program: Derivatus Computatus
Company Name: Educom, % Christopher or Janet Turner
Address: Route 1, Thornton, Ontario, Canada L0L 2N0
Phone: (705) 456-6531
Price: $55 (Canadian)
Version Tested: Not able to test.
Runs On: Apple II/e or c
Memory Requirements: 48K
Disk Drive Requirements: 1
Supports Color Monitors: Yes
Uses Sound: Yes
Number of Disks: 2
Product Includes: Disk, instructions, and manual
Manual: Yes
Copy Protected: No
Hard Disk Compatible: Yes
Menu-Driven: Yes
On-Line Help: No
Tutorial: No
Warranty: Media only
Support: Phone and letter
Update Policy: Not known
Related Products: Latin Vocabulary Testing System for the Cambridge Latin Course
Other Information: This program, which is only available from the authors at the address above, consists of eleven different vocabulary drills. One Latin-to-English program drills users on numbers, another on Roman numerals, a third on cardinal numbers, a fourth and fifth on terms associated with family relationships, a sixth on the derivation of English words from Latin words, a seventh on prefixes and suffixes, an eighth on nouns and adjectives (Latin to English, or vice versa), a ninth on forty verb stems (eight derivatives per stem), a tenth on completing sentences, and the eleventh program is a review quiz on a mixture of (multiple choice) questions from all the other programs. All of these programs save student's scores to disk and allow the scores to be printed. After one wrong guess, each program provides a clue. An answer is scored as incorrect only on the second wrong guess.

4.5.2.10 *Latin Flash Drill*

- *BASIC PRODUCT INFORMATION*

Name of Program: Latin Flash Drill
Company Name: Centaur Systems, Ltd.
Address: P.O. Box 3220, Madison, WI 53704
Phone: Not known
Price: $95
Version Tested: IBM version
Runs On: Apple IIe (with 80-column card) and c; IBM PCs
Memory Requirements: Apple: 64K; IBM: 64K
Disk Drive Requirements: 1
Supports Color Monitors: Yes
Uses Sound: No
Number of Disks: Apple: 2; IBM: 1
Product Includes: Disk and manual
Manual: 36 pages, not indexed
Copy Protected: No
Hard Disk Compatible: Yes
Menu-Driven: Yes
On-Line Help: Yes
Tutorial: No
Warranty: 12 months, media only

413

Chapter 4 *Computer-Assisted Language Learning*

Support: Letter
Update Policy: Not known
Related Products: None
Other Information: None
Comments: None
Comments: This is a drill-and-practice program that concentrates on the paradigm charts of Latin forms and endings. Paradigm-chart drills cover the four major parts of speech (nouns, verbs, pronouns, adjectives). Noun and adjective drills are chosen by declension (including "i-stem" nouns and irregular adjectives); verb drills are chosen by tense, voice, conjugation (including third "i-stem"), and mood (indicative or subjunctive). Pronoun drills cover the full forms of eight major pronouns. Sample, elementary-level vocabulary words are used (for all except pronoun drills) and presented in a dictionary format along with their English translations. On-line hints are available.

4.5.2.11 Latin Grammar Computerized-I

* *BASIC PRODUCT INFORMATION*

Name of Program: Latin Grammar Computerized-I
Company Name: Lingo Fun, Inc.
Address: P.O. Box 486, Westerville, OH 43081
Phone: (614) 882-8258
Price: $49.95; $150 for Site License
Version Tested: 1.1
Runs On: Apple II series
Memory Requirements: 48K
Disk Drive Requirements: 1
Supports Color Monitors: Yes
Uses Sound: Yes
Number of Disks: 1
Product Includes: Disk and instruction sheets
Manual: 2 pages of instructions
Copy Protected: Yes
Hard Disk Compatible: Yes
Menu-Driven: Yes
On-Line Help: No
Tutorial: No
Warranty: Not known
Support: Phone and letter
Update Policy: Not known
Related Products: Quo Modo Dicis?, Latin Idiom Master (see below)
Other Information: None
Comments: This program contains twenty review-and-practice lessons covering most of the grammatical forms for nouns, adjectives, pronouns, and verbs.

4.5.2.12 Latin Idiom Master

* *BASIC PRODUCT INFORMATION*

Name of Program: Latin Idiom Master
Company Name: Lingo Fun, Inc.
Address: P.O. Box 486, Westerville, OH 43081
Phone: (614) 882-8258
Price: $49.95; $150 for Site License
Version Tested: 1.1
Runs On: Apple II series
Memory Requirements: 48K
Disk Drive Requirements: 1
Supports Color Monitors: Yes
Uses Sound: Yes
Number of Disks: 1

Product Includes: Disk and instruction sheets
Manual: 12 pages of instructions
Copy Protected: Yes
Hard Disk Compatible: Yes
Menu-Driven: Yes
On-Line Help: No
Tutorial: No
Warranty: Not known
Support: Phone and letter
Update Policy: Not known
Related Products: Quo Modo Dicis? (see below), Latin Grammar Computerized-I (see above)
Other Information: None
Comments: Ten 10-sentence exercises test users on various Latin idioms, for example, expressions of time and place, the dative used with adjectives, and expressions of measure.

4.5.2.13 Quo Modis Dicis?

● *BASIC PRODUCT INFORMATION*

Name of Program: Quo Modis Dicis?
Company Name: Lingo Fun, Inc.
Address: P.O. Box 486, Westerville, OH 43081
Phone: (614) 882-8258
Price: $49.95; $150 for Site License
Version Tested: 1.1
Runs On: Apple II series
Memory Requirements: 48K
Disk Drive Requirements: 1
Supports Color Monitors: Yes
Uses Sound: Yes
Number of Disks: 1
Product Includes: Disk and instruction sheets
Manual: 18 pages of instructions
Copy Protected: Yes
Hard Disk Compatible: Yes
Menu-Driven: Yes
On-Line Help: No
Tutorial: No
Warranty: Not known
Support: Phone and letter
Update Policy: Not known
Related Products: Latin Idiom Master, Latin Grammar Computerized-I (see above)
Other Information: None
Comments: This program, whose name means "How do you say?," contains thirty 10-sentence sets. Each sentence focuses on a specific grammatical point. Latin-to-English and English-to-Latin quizzes are supported.

4.5.2.14 Introduction to Latin Vocabulary I

● *BASIC PRODUCT INFORMATION*

Name of Program: Introduction to Latin Vocabulary I
Company Name: Gessler Educational Software
Address: 900 Broadway, New York, NY 10003-1291
Phone: (212) 673-3113
Price: $32.95 or $59.95 for this and the next program
Version Tested: 1.0
Runs On: Apple II series
Memory Requirements: 48K
Disk Drive Requirements: 1

Supports Color Monitors: Yes
Uses Sound: Yes
Number of Disks: 1
Product Includes: Disk
Manual: Does not include manual.
Copy Protected: No
Hard Disk Compatible: No
Menu-Driven: Yes
On-Line Help: No
Tutorial: No
Warranty: 90 days, media only
Support: Phone and letter
Update Policy: $9.95
Related Products: Introduction to Latin Vocabulary II
Other Information: None
Comments: This program drills users on vocabulary. Eight sections of from 20 to 112 words per section cover many everyday words. Familiar Latin cognates, Roman numerals, derivatives, the macron, and other types of terms and topics are included. Multiple choice and one-word formats are supported, as are English-to Latin and Latin-to English drills.

4.5.2.15 *Introduction to Latin Vocabulary II*

● *BASIC PRODUCT INFORMATION*

Name of Program: Introduction to Latin Vocabulary II
Company Name: Gessler Educational Software
Address: 900 Broadway, New York, NY 10003-1291
Phone: (212) 673-3113
Price: $32.95 or $59.95 for this and the previous program
Version Tested: 1.0
Runs On: Apple II series
Memory Requirements: 48K
Disk Drive Requirements: 1
Supports Color Monitors: Yes
Uses Sound: Yes
Number of Disks: 1
Product Includes: Disk
Manual: Does not include manual.
Copy Protected: No
Hard Disk Compatible: No
Menu-Driven: Yes
On-Line Help: No
Tutorial: No
Warranty: 90 days, media only
Support: Phone and letter
Update Policy: $9.95
Related Products: Introduction to Latin Vocabulary I
Other Information: None
Comments: This program drills users on vocabulary. Eight sections of from 20 to 112 words per section cover many everyday words. Medical, mathematical, and household terms are included, as are terms from Roman life and verbs. Multiple choice and one-word formats are supported, as are English-to Latin and Latin-to English drills.

4.5.2.16 *On Target*

● *BASIC PRODUCT INFORMATION*

Name of Program: On Target
Company Name: Langenscheidt Languageware
Address: 46-35 54th Rd., Maspeth, NY 11378

Phone: (718) 784-0055
Price: Cost not known.
Version Tested: 1.0
Runs On: Apple II series
Memory Requirements: 48K
Disk Drive Requirements: 1
Supports Color Monitors: Yes
Uses Sound: Yes
Number of Disks: 1
Product Includes: Disk, manual, and vocabulary list
Manual: 32 pages, not indexed
Copy Protected: No
Hard Disk Compatible: No
Menu-Driven: Yes
On-Line Help: No
Tutorial: No
Warranty: 90 days, media only
Support: Phone and letter
Update Policy: None
Related Products: Vocabulary on the Attack
Other Information: None
Comments: On Target is a game-based, 750-word, Latin vocabulary drill program.

4.5.2.17 Vocabulary on the Attack

- *BASIC PRODUCT INFORMATION*

Name of Program: Vocabulary on the Attack
Company Name: Langenscheidt Languageware
Address: 46-35 54th Rd., Maspeth, NY 11378
Phone: (718) 784-0055
Price: Cost not known.
Version Tested: 1.0
Runs On: Apple II series
Memory Requirements: 48K
Disk Drive Requirements: 1
Supports Color Monitors: Yes
Uses Sound: Yes
Number of Disks: 1
Product Includes: Disk, manual, and vocabulary list
Manual: 32 pages, not indexed
Copy Protected: No
Hard Disk Compatible: No
Menu-Driven: Yes
On-Line Help: No
Tutorial: No
Warranty: 90 days, media only
Support: Phone and letter
Update Policy: None
Related Products: On Target
Other Information: None
Comments: Vocabulary on the Attack is a game-based, 750-word, Latin vocabulary drill program.

4.5.2.18 Latin Exercises

- *BASIC PRODUCT INFORMATION*

Name of Program: Latin Exercises
Company Name: International Film Bureau, Inc.
Address: 332 South Michigan Ave., Chicago, IL 60604-4382

FEATURES	VF	MN	CH	AV	TR	VA	OT	QM	IM	C	SC	LF	IL	LE	LH	DI	DC	LV	LN	CE	LT
BASIC FACTS																					
Price	395	–	–	–	–	?	?	50	50	50	500	95	33	150	30	125	55	75	90	15+	35
Runs On	A	A	A	A	A	A	A	A	A	A	I	A,I	A	A	A	A	A	A	A	A	A,C
Memory (in K)	48	48	48	48	48	48	48	48	48	48	128	64	48	48	48	48	48	64	64	64	48
Disk Drives	1	1	1	1	1	1	1	1	1	1	1	1	1	1	1	1	1	1	1	1	1
User Interface	MD	MD	MD	MD	MD	MD	MD	MD	MD	MD	MD	MD	MD	MD	MD	MD	MD	MD	MD	MD	MD
TEXTBOOK COMPATABILITY																					
Any Text	○	○	○	○	○	●	●	●	●	●	●	●	●	○	●	●	○	●	●	●	○
Jenney	●	●	●	●	●	○	○	○	○	○	○	○	○	●	○	●	○	●	●	●	○
Wheelock	●	●	●	●	●	○	○	○	○	○	○	○	○	○	○	○	○	●	●	○	○
Ullman	●	●	●	●	●	○	○	○	○	○	○	○	○	○	○	○	○	○	○	○	○
Goldman	●	●	●	○	○	○	○	○	○	○	○	○	○	○	○	○	●	○	○	●	○
Cambridge	●	●	○	○	○	○	○	○	○	○	○	○	○	○	○	○	●	○	○	○	●
Ecc. Rom.	●	○	○	○	○	○	○	○	○	○	○	○	○	○	○	○	○	○	○	○	○
Other	○	○	○	○	○	○	○	○	○	○	○	○	○	○	○	●	○	○	○	○	○
CONTENT COMPONENTS																					
Vocabulary	○	○	○	○	○	●	●	●	●	●	●	○	●	●	●	○	●	○	○	●	●
Grammatical Terminology	○	●	●	○	○	○	○	○	●	●	○	○	○	●	○	●	○	○	○	●	○
Morphology	●	●	●	●	●	○	○	●	●	●	○	○	○	●	○	●	●	●	●	●	○
Syntax	○	○	○	○	○	○	○	●	●	●	●	○	○	●	●	○	○	○	○	●	○
Translation Skills	●	○	○	○	○	○	○	●	●	●	●	○	○	●	●	○	○	○	●	●	○
History/Culture	○	○	○	○	○	○	○	○	○	○	○	○	●	○	●	○	○	○	○	●	○
Etymology/Derivation	○	○	○	○	○	○	○	○	○	○	○	○	●	○	○	○	○	○	○	●	○

Table 4.2: This table is based on one created by Robert B. Latousek, Jr. and is used with permission. Comparison of microcomputer Latin language programs. A = Apple, I = IBM, C = Commodore Pet, MD = menu-driven, VF = Verb Factory, MN = Mare Nostrum, CH = Cursus Honorum, AV = Artifex Verborum, TR = Translat, VA = Vocabulary on the Attack, OT = On Target, QM = Quo Modis Dices?, IM = Latin Idiom Master, LC = Latin Certamen Practice, SC = SCIO, LF = Latin Flash Drill, IL = Introduction to Latin Vocabulary, LE = LE = Latin Exercises, LH = Latin Hangman, DI = DISCO, DC = Derivatus Computatus, LV = Latin Verb Forms, LN = Latin Nouns, Adjectives, and Adverbs, CE = Latin Certamen Practice for Jenny's First Year Latin, LT = Latin Vocabulary Testing System for the Cambridge Latin Course.

FEATURES	VF	MN	CH	AV	TR	VA	OT	QM	IM	LC	SC	LF	IL	LE	LH	DI	DC	LV	LN	CE	LT
PART OF SPEECH																					
Noun	○	●	○	●	●	●	●	●	●	●	●	●	●	●	●	●	●	○	●	●	●
Pronoun	●	○	○	●	●	○	●	●	●	●	○	●	○	○	●	●	○	○	○	●	○
Adjective	○	●	○	●	●	●	●	●	●	●	●	●	●	●	●	●	●	○	●	●	●
Verb	●	○	●	●	●	●	●	●	●	●	●	●	●	○	●	○	●	●	○	●	●
Other	○	○	○	●	●	○	●	●	●	○	○	○	○	○	○	○	○	○	○	●	●
PROGRAM CHARACTERISTICS																					
Color	○	●	○	○	○	○	●	○	○	○	●	○	○	○	○	○	○	○	○	○	●
Graphics	●	●	○	○	○	●	●	●	●	●	○	○	○	○	○	○	○	○	○	○	○
Sound	○	○	○	○	●	○	○	○	○	○	○	○	○	○	○	○	●	○	○	○	●
Scoring	●	●	●	●	●	●	●	●	●	●	●	○	●	○	○	○	●	●	●	●	●
Record	○	○	○	○	●	○	○	○	●	○	○	○	●	○	○	○	●	○	○	●	○
Printer	○	○	○	○	●	○	○	○	○	○	○	○	●	○	○	○	○	○	○	●	○
Editor	○	○	○	○	●	○	○	○	○	●	●	●	○	○	○	○	○	○	●	○	○
Help	●	○	○	○	●	●	●	○	○	●	●	●	●	●	●	○	○	○	○	●	○
Hints	●	○	○	○	○	○	○	○	○	○	○	●	●	●	○	○	○	○	○	○	○
Gamelike	○	●	●	○	○	○	●	●	●	○	○	○	○	○	●	○	●	○	○	○	○

Table 4.2: This table is based on one created by Robert B. Latousek, Jr. and is used with permission. Comparison of microcomputer Latin language programs. A = Apple, I = IBM, C = Commodore Pet, MD = menu-driven, VF = Verb Factory, MN = Mare Nostrum, CH = Cursus Honorum, AV = Artifex Verborum, TR = Translat, VA = Vocabulary on the Attack, OT = On Target, QM = Quo Modis Dicis?, IM = Latin Idiom Master, LC = Latin Certamen Practice, SC = SCIO, LF = Latin Flash Drill, IL = Introduction to Latin Vocabulary, LE = Latin Exercises, LH = Latin Hangman, DI = DISCO, DC = Derivatus Computatus, LV = Latin Verb Forms, LN = Latin Nouns, Adjectives, and Adverbs, CE = Latin Certamen Practice for Jenny's First Year Latin, LT = Latin Vocabulary Testing System for the Cambridge Latin Course.

Phone: (312) 427-4545
Price: $150
Version Tested: 1.0
Runs On: Apple II series
Memory Requirements: 48K
Disk Drive Requirements: 1
Supports Color Monitors: Yes
Uses Sound: Yes
Number of Disks: 1
Product Includes: 4 disks and Teacher's Guide
Manual: Does not include manual.
Copy Protected: No
Hard Disk Compatible: No
Menu-Driven: Yes
On-Line Help: No
Tutorial: No
Warranty: Media only
Support: Phone and letter
Update Policy: None
Related Products: None
Other Information: None
Comments: This is a series of 60 individual programs that provide drills for the 60 lessons in Allyn and Bacon's *First Year Latin.*

4.5.2.19 Latin Hangman

- *BASIC PRODUCT INFORMATION*

Name of Program: Latin Hangman
Company Name: George Earl Software
Address: 1302 S. General McMullan, San Antonio, TX 78237
Phone: (512) 434-3681
Price: $29.95
Version Tested: Not able to test.
Runs On: Apple II series
Memory Requirements: 48K
Disk Drive Requirements: 1
Supports Color Monitors: Yes
Uses Sound: Not known
Number of Disks: 1
Product Includes: Disk only
Manual: None
Copy Protected: No
Hard Disk Compatible: No
Menu-Driven: Yes
On-Line Help: No
Tutorial: No
Warranty: None
Support: None
Update Policy: None
Related Products: French, German, Russian, and Spanish Hangman
Other Information: None
Comments: Latin Hangman is a Latin drill program that uses the game of hangman to quiz users on vocabulary and translation. Side one contains nine groups of fifty words each and twelve groups of twenty-five sentences each. Students may preview material without being drilled on it and may choose to translate from Latin to English or from English to Latin. Four incorrect answers cause a creature to appear, at which point the correct answer is given. After each drill, Latin Hangman displays the score. Macrons appear in their proper places. The material on side two is similar to that on side one. Latin Hangman seems helpful, straightforward, and well done.

4.5.3 Language Tutor

- *BASIC PRODUCT INFORMATION*

Name of Program: Language Tutor
Company Name: Telion Software
Address: P.O. Box 1464, La Mirada, CA 90637-1464
Phone: (213) 946-1015
Price: $49.95
Version Tested: 1.0
Runs On: IBM PC, CP/M machines
Memory Requirements: 64K
Disk Drive Requirements: 1
Supports Color Monitors: Yes
Uses Sound: Yes
Number of Disks: 1
Product Includes: Disk and instructions on disk
Manual: None
Copy Protected: No
Hard Disk Compatible: Yes
Menu-Driven: Yes
On-Line Help: No
Tutorial: No
Warranty: 30-day, money-back guarantee
Support: Not known
Update Policy: Half-price on all updates
Related Products: Memory (see below)
Other Information: None

Language Tutor allows users to create as many separate files of vocabulary words and definitions as disk space allows. The program (1) can test by asking words in consecutive order or randomly, (2) will retest users on missed words, (3) will place missed words in a separate file, and (4) will keep track of the score. Because Language Tutor has a search feature that allows users to locate words by vocabulary entry or by definition, the program can function as an on-line dictionary. Other features of Language Tutor allow users to create vocabulary files, display and edit vocabulary data, switch from one vocabulary file to another, and associate vocabulary words with other words. Language Tutor gives users an unlimited number of chances to answer questions correctly. After users answer "No" to the prompt "Want to guess again?," the program displays the correct answer, which users must enter before proceeding to the next question.

Because it is menu-driven, Language Tutor is extremely easy to use, and because it is a general-purpose vocabulary program, Language Tutor is suited to many languages. Unfortunately, however, in the interests of portability and cost, Language Tutor only supports the standard 128 ASCII characters. On the IBM version of Language Tutor, though, users can hold down the Alt key and type in the numerical ASCII value for any of the upper 128 characters, and Language Tutor will accept that input and display it correctly.[31] Thus with a little patience and experimentation, users of the IBM version of Language Tutor can correctly display letters with umlauts, cedillas, circumflexes, acute and grave accents, as well as certain Greek letters. This is a clumsy and by no means perfect solution to displaying diacritical marks, accented characters, and some Greek letters, but it is better than not being able to display them at all.

Language Tutor is a well-designed and useful program that can facilitate vocabulary learning. Because users define the content of vocabulary files and because

---

31. IBM users will find a list of all 256 ASCII characters and their codes in Appendix G of the 2d ed. of the BASIC manual by Microsoft (1982) that comes with IBM machines.

421

the program is so flexible, Language Tutor can be adapted to many vocabulary needs. By defining a string of text in terms of its reference, Language Tutor can be used to memorize Bible verses or passages from any document, though Telion Software markets another product, Memory, that is specifically designed for that application. When used to memorize strings of text, Language Tutor limits users to about 125 characters (approximately one and a half lines of text) per entry.

Bibliographical Resources

The following publications provide information about the types of programs reviewed in this chapter. Addresses and phones numbers are those of the circulation/subscription offices.

The ACH Newsletter
% Association for Computers and the Humanities
% Dr. Harry W. Lincoln
Dept. of Music
State University of New York (SUNY)
Binghamton, NY 13901
(607) 777-2436, (607) 777-2592
Quarterly, newsletter, $15/year.

CALICO Journal
% 3078 JKHB
Brigham Young University
Provo, UT 84602
(801) 378-6533
Quarterly, journal, individuals: $30 (US), $40 (Canada), $45 (outside North America); institutions: $60 (US), $70 (Canada), $75 (outside North America); corporations: $120 (US), $130 (Canada), $135 (outside North America). Articles on CALL in higher education.

Centre for Information on Language Teaching and Research (CILT)
% Regent's College
Inner Circle, Regent's Park
London NW1 4NS
United Kingdom
01-486-8221/2/3/4
Free catalog of CALL publications.

Collegiate Microcomputer
% Rose-Hulman Institute of Technology
Terre Haute, IN 47803
(812) 877-1511
Quarterly, journal, $28/year (US), $36/year (elsewhere). Articles on the use of microcomputers in higher education.

Computers and the Humanities
% Paradigm Press
P.O. Box 1057
Osprey, FL 33559
(813) 922-7666
Quarterly, journal, $89/year. Articles on the use of computers in higher education.

Computing and the Classics
% Dr. Joseph Tebben, Classics Dept.
The Ohio State University
University Dr.
Newark, OH 43055
(614) 366-9338
Quarterly, newsletter, free.

Journal of Computer Assisted Learning
% Blackwell Scientific Publications Ltd.
P.O. Box 88
Oxford OX2 8EL
United Kingdom
(011-44) 865-240-201
Three times a year, journal, $18/year. Articles on CAL.

Journal of Educational Computing Research
% Baywood Publishing Co., Inc.
120 Marine St.
Farmingdale, NY 11735
(516) 249-2464, (516) 293-7130
Quarterly, journal, $85/year.

Literary and Linguistic Computing
% Journal Subscription Department
Oxford University Press
Walton St.
Oxford OX2 6DP
United Kingdom
(865) 512-201; from North America dial direct (011-44)
        865-512-201
Quarterly, journal, £24/year (institutions), £12/year (in-
        dividuals), $45/year (institutions), $22.50/year (in-
        dividuals). Incorporates the *ALLC Bulletin* and
        ALLC Journal.

Newsletter for Asian and Middle Eastern Languages on Computer
% Bear River Systems
P.O. Box 1021
Berkeley, CA 94701
(415) 644-1738
Frequency not known, newsletter, $10/year.

Studies in Language Learning
% Language Learning Laboratory
G70 Foreign Languages Bldg.
707 S. Mathews Ave.
University of Illinois at Urbana-Champaign
Urbana, IL 61801
(217) 333-9776
Semiannually, journal, $10/issue.

Wheels for the Mind
% Apple Computer, Inc.
Wheels for the Mind 23L
P.O. Box 810
Cupertino, CA 95015
(408) 973-2222
Quarterly, journal, $12/year. Comprehensive information
        about the ways Macintoshes are being used in the
        academic environment, including information
        about CALL.

Bibliography

Adams, Anthony, and Esmor Jones. *Teaching Humanities in the Microelectronic Age*. Milton Keynes, England: Open University Press, 1983.

Adams, E. N. "The Use of CAI in Foreign Language Instruction." IBM Research Report RC 2377. Yorktown Heights, N.Y.: October 30, 1968.

Ahmad, Khurshid, et al. *Computers, Language Learning, and Language Teaching*. New York: Cambridge University Press, 1985.

Allen, John R. "Current Trends in Computer-Assisted Instruction." *CHum* 7 (September 1972): 47–55.

Anon. "Classroom Bits (Curriculum, videocassettes, teaching Greek and Latin)." *Classroom Computer News* 2 (May/June 1982): 52–54.

Anon. "Computer-Based Language Learning. Specialized Bibliography 32." CILT. January 1984. Available from Centre for Information on Language Teaching and Research, Regent's College, Inner Circle, Regent's Park, London, United Kingdom NW1 4NS.

Anon. "Computers in the Groves of Academe." *T.H.E. Journal* 10 (1982): 80–81.

Anon. "Specialized Bibliography B32, Computer-Based Language Learning." CILT, October 1982. Code: SB B32. Available from CILT/British Council Language Teaching Library, 20 Carlton House Terrace, London SW1Y 5AP, United Kingdom.

Ariew, Robert. "Computer-Assisted Foreign Language Materials: Advantages and Limitations." *CALICO Journal* 2 (1984): 43–47.

Atkinson, Richard C., and H. A. Wilson. *Computer-Assisted Instruction: A Book of Readings*. New York: Academic Press, 1969.

Avner, R. A. "How to Produce Ineffective CAI Material." *Educational Technology* 14 (1974): 26–27.

Bacon, Gary. "A PC for the Teacher." *PC World* (July 1984): 292–99.

Baker, Robert L. "Foreign-Language Software: The State of the Art or Pick A Card, Any (Flash) Card." *CALICO Journal* 2 (1984): 6–10, 27.

Berger, Harvey. "An IBM First for Secondary Schools." *PC Magazine* (April 3, 1984): 165–70.

Bergheim, Kim, and Kathy Chin. "Computers in Classrooms." *InfoWorld* (September 10, 1984): 28–37.

Blake, Robert, and Bruce Duncan. "CALL for the Macintosh." *CALICO Journal* 3 (1985): 11–15.

Borello, Enrico, and Mario Italiani. "CAI Techniques in Linguistics." In *Computing in the Humanities*. Edited by Richard W. Bailey, 39–40. New York: North-Holland Pub. Co., 1982.

Brookman, William R., Geri Hockfield, and Peter C. Patton. "Sumerian: An Experiment in CAI Language Learning." In *Computing in the Humanities*. Edited by Peter C. Patton and Renee A. Holoien, 235–52. Lexington, Mass.: D.C. Heath and Co., 1981.

Burling, Robbins. "A Proposal for Computer-Assisted Instruction in Vocabulary." *System* 11 (1983): 181–90.

Butler, Christopher. *Computers in Linguistics*. Oxford: Basil Blackwell Ltd., 1985.

Carev-Maruna, Tatjana. "Dialectical Aspects of the Application of the Microcomputer in the Teaching of Foreign Languages." In *Sixth International Conference on Computers and the Humanities*. Edited by Sarah K. Burton and Douglas D. Short, 51–69. Rockville: Computer Science Press, 1983.

Chapelle, Carol, and Joan Jamieson. "Authoring Systems for Courseware Development: What Should Beginners Look For?" *CALICO Journal* 3 (1986): 14–19.

Choi, Soo-Young. "Application of Component Display Theory in Designing and Developing CALI." *CALICO Journal* 3 (1986): 40–45.

Cole, Peter, Robert Lebowitz, and Robert Hart. "A Computer-Assisted Program for the Teaching of Modern Hebrew." In *Studies in Language Learning* 3 (1981): 74–91.

_____. "Teaching Hebrew with the Aid of Computers: The Illinois Program." *CHum* 18 (1984): 87–99.

Culley, Gerald R. "A Computer-Aided Study of Confusion in Latin Morphology." In *Linguistics and Literacy*. Edited by William Frawley, 239–54. New York: Plenum, 1982.

_____. "Computer-Assisted Instruction and Latin: Beyond Flashcards." *Classical World* 72 (1978–9): 393–401.

_____. "A Computer Supplement to Individualize the Latin Course." In *Proceedings of the 1st National Conference on Individualized Instruction in Foreign Languages*, 121–24. Ohio State University, 1979.

_____. "Individualized Latin at Delaware: A Progress Report," in *Proceedings of the 2nd National Conference on Individualized Instruction in Foreign Languages*. Ohio State University, 1980, 75–79.

_____. *Teaching the Classics with Computers*. APA Committee on Educational Services Educational Papers 1, 1984. Available from the Teaching Materials and Resource Center, American Classical League, Miami University, Oxford, OH 45056.

_____. "When PLATO Knows Latin: Benefits of Letting the Computer Inflect the Forms," in *Proceedings of the Association for the Development of Computer-Based Instructional Systems*. Washington, D.C., 1980, 237–40.

Davis, G., and J. J. Higgins. *Computers, Language and Language Learning*. Centre for Information on Language Teaching and Research, 1982. CILT Information Guide 22: Code IG22. Available from Baker Book Services, Little Mead, Alford Road, Cranleigh, Surrey, United Kingdom GU6 8NU.

Decker, Kenneth W. "A Computer-Aided Course in Ancient Egyptian." Unpublished master's thesis, Center for Ancient Studies, University of Minnesota, 1980.

Decker, Kenneth W., et al. "A Computer-Based Course in Ancient Egyptian Hieroglyphics." In *Computing in the Humanities*. Edited by Peter C. Patton and Renee A. Holoien, 253–62. Lexington, Mass.: D.C. Heath and Co., 1981.

_____. "A PLATO Course for Egyptian Hieroglyphics." Technical Report 79003. University of Minnesota, University Computer Center, September 1979.

Dick, Walter, and Raymond Lalta. "Comparative Effects of Ability and Presentation Mode in Computer-Assisted Instruction and Programmed Instruction." *AV Communication Review* 18 (1970): 33–45.

Evans, James E. "Instructional Computing in the Liberal Arts: the Lawrence Experiment." *T.H.E. Journal* 11 (1984): 98–103.

Fisher, Francis D. "Computer-Assisted Education: What's Not Happening?" *Journal of Computer-Based Instruction* 9 (1982): 19–27.

Gale, Larrie E. "Montevidisco: An Anecdotal History of an Interactive Videodisk." *CALICO Journal* 1 (1983): 42–46.

Gear, Dale V. "A Small-Computer CAI Course in Classical Greek." In *Computing in the Humanities*. Edited by Peter C. Patton and Renee A. Holoien, 263–78. Lexington, Mass.: D.C. Heath and Co., 1981.

Geens, Dirk. "Computer-Driven Teaching of Foreign Languages." In *Computing in the Humanities*. Edited by Richard W. Bailey, 41–46. New York: North-Holland Pub. Co., 1982.

Hart, Robert. "Language Study and the PLATO System." *Studies in Language Learning* 3 (1981): 1–24.

Helliwell, John. "A Victory for Computer Literacy at Waterloo." *PC Magazine* (April 2, 1985): 205–9

Hetherington, Norris S. "Computers in the Humanities." *PC Magazine* (September 4, 1984): 87.

Higgins, John. "Can Computers Teach?" *CALICO Journal* 1 (1983): 4–6.

_____. "Computer-Assisted Language Learning." *Language Learning* 16 (1983): 579–83.

_____. "The State of the Art: Computer-Assisted Language Learning." *Medium* 9 (1984): 15–21.

Higgins, John, and Tim Johns. *Computers in Language Learning*. Reading, Mass.: Addison-Wesley, 1984.

Hildebrandt, Darlene Myers. *Computer Based Education: Handbook and Overview*. Terre Haute, Ind.: Rose-Hulman Institute of Technology, 1986.

Hope, Geoffrey R. *Using Computers in Teaching Foreign Languages*. Orlando, Fla.: Harcourt, Brace, Jovanovich, 1985.

Information Systems Consultants, Inc. *Videodisk and Optical Disk Technologies and Their Applications in Libraries: A Report to the Council on Library Resources*. Washington: D.C.: Council on Library Resources, Inc., 1985.

Ireland, Stanley. "The Computer and Its Role in Classical Research." *Greece and Rome* 23 (1976): 40–54.

Jorgensen, Peter A. "Versatility in the Design of Foreign Language Computer-Assisted Instruction." *Die Unterrichtspraxis* 17 (1984): 104–8.

Kramsch, Claire, Douglas Morgenstern, and Janet H. Murray. " An Overview of the MIT Athena Language Learning Project." *CALICO Journal* 2 (1985): 31–34.

Kossuth, Karen C. "Using the Adventure Formats for CALI." *CALICO Journal* 3 (1985): 13–17.

Lange, Dale L., Richard Raschio, and Paul Wieser. "An Information Processing Model for Computer-Assisted Instruction for Foreign Language Reading." *CALICO Journal* 3 (1985): 31–37.

Larson, Jerry W., ed. *Planning and Using Language Learning Centers*. Volume 1, CALICO Monograph Series. Provo, 1986.

Last, Rex W. "Computer-Assisted Language Learning: A Growth Area in Humanities Computing." *ALLC Bull.* 11 (1983): 83–86.

_____. *Language Teaching and the Microcomputer*. Oxford: Basil Blackwell, 1984.

Latousek, Robert B. Jr. *Survey of Latin Instructional Software for the Microcomputer*. Available from the Teaching Materials and Resource Center, American Classical League, Miami University, Oxford, OH 45056.

Lee, Alfred. "Higher Education." *InfoWorld* (October 8, 1984): 7.

Littman, Jonathan. "Computing the Classics." *PC World* 1 (1984): 266–74.

McDermott, Brian. "The Online Schoolhouse." *Link-Up* (September 1984): 16–20.

Mace, Scott. "Drexel U. Meets the Macintosh." *InfoWorld* (June 4, 1984): 24–28.

Moore, James, and Jack Nelson. "A Program to Teach Logic." *CHum* 8 (September-November 1974): 278.

Mulhern, John F., Steven R. Sparley, and Peter C. Patton. "Computer Aids to Sumerian Lexicography." In *Computing in the Humanities*. Edited by Peter C. Patton and Renee A, Holoien, 53–83. Lexington, Mass.: D.C. Heath and Co., 1981.

Nancarrow, P. H. "Processing of Ancient Egyptian Hieroglyphic Texts by Computer." In *Computing in the Humanities*. Edited by Richard W. Bailey, 175–84. New York: North-Holland Pub. Co., 1982.

Olsen, Solveig, ed. *Computer-Aided Instruction in the Humanities*. New York: Modern Language Association, 1986.

Otto, Frank. "CALICO Enters a New Era." *CALICO Journal* 3 (1986): 14–15, 47.

Otto, Sue K., and James P. Pusak. "Stringing Us Along: Programming for Foreign Language CAI." *CALICO Journal* 1 (1983): 26–33.

Packard, D. W. "Teaching Ancient Greek (with the Help of a Computer)." *ALLC Bull.* 3 (1975): 45–51.

Parker, Wayne. "Interactive Video: Calling the Shots." *PC World* (October 1984): 99–108.

Parunak, H. Van Dyke, ed., *Computer Tools for Ancient Texts*. Winona Lake, Ind.: Eisenbrauns, forthcoming.

Patton, Peter C., William R. Brookman, and Geri Hockfield. "Computer-Aided Instruction in Reading Sumerian Cuneiform Economic Texts." UCC Report 79004. University of Minnesota, November 1979.

Patton, Peter C., and Renee A. Holoien, eds., *Computing in the Humanities*. Lexington, Mass.: D.C. Heath and Co., 1981.

Patton, Peter C., and William C. Roos. "Introduction to Computing in the Humanities." In *Computing in the Humanities*. Edited by Peter C. Patton and Renee A. Holoien, 1–13. Lexington, Mass.: D.C. Heath and Co., 1981.

Pearlman, Dara. "A School Without Walls." *PC Magazine* (April 16, 1985): 225–30.

Phillips, Martin K. "Approaches to the Design of Software Language Teaching." *CALICO Journal* 3 (1986): 36–48.

Putnam, Constance E. "Foreign Language Instruction Technology: The State of the Art." In *Sixth International Conference on Computers and the Humanities*. Edited by Sarah K. Burton and Douglas D. Short, 533–44. Rockville: Computer Science Press, 1983.

Ragsdale, R. G. ed., *Programming Projects Across the Curriculum*. Toronto: The Ontario Institute for Studies in Education, 1977.

Ratliff, John B. III. "Producing Foreign Language Study Materials on the Xerox Star." *CALICO Journal* 3 (1986): 21–48.

Sanders, Ruth H. "PILOT, SNOBOL, and LOGO as Computing Tools for Foreign-Language Instruction." *CALICO Journal* 3 (1985): 41–47.

Scanlan, Richard. "A Computer-Assisted Instruction Course in Vocabulary Building Through Latin and Greek Roots." *Foreign Language Annals* 9 (1976): 579–83.

_____. "Computer-Assisted Instruction in Latin." *Foreign Language Annals* 13 (1980): 53–55.

_____. "Computer-Assisted Instruction in Latin and in English Vocabulary Development." *Studies in Language Learning* 3 (1981): 113–22.

Selzer, R. A. "Computer-Assisted Instruction—What It Can and Cannot Do." *American Psychologist* 26 (1971): 373–77.

Skow, John. "In Hanover: SAS and Synclavers (Dartmouth Computer Courses in the Humanities)." *Time* 114 (September 24, 1979): 9–11.

Solorzano, Lucia. "Computers on Campus: The Good News, Bad News." *U.S. News & World Report* (October 7, 1985): 60–61

Sparley, S. R., J. F. Mulhern, and P. C. Patton. "Methods in Computer-Aided Sumerian Lexicography: An Approach to Building a Lexicon." In *Computer Tools for Ancient Texts*. Edited by H. Van Dyke Parunak. Winona Lake, Ind.: Eisenbrauns, forthcoming.

Sparley, S. R., D. D. Reisman, and P. C. Patton. "A Computerized Lexicon of the Sumerian Emesal Dialect." *ALLC Bull.* 7 (1979): 283–94.

Suppe, Frederick. "Logic, Computers, and Humanity: A New Course." *Teaching Philosophy* 1 (Spring 1976): 259–321.

Underwood, John H. *Linguistics, Computers, and the Language Teacher*. Rowley, Mass.: Newbury House, 1984.

Vellios, George, Gerald M. Erickson, and Rosanne Gulino. "A Latin Course on a Small Computer." In *Computing in the Humanities*. Edited by Peter C. Patton and Renee A. Holoien, 279–86. Lexington, Mass.: D.C. Heath and Co., 1981.

Waite, S. V. F. "Computers and Classical Literature: 1970–1971." *CHum* 6 (1971–72): 31–34.

_____. "Computers and Classical Literature: 1971–1972." *CHum* 7 (1972–73): 99–104.

_____. "Computer-Supplemented Latin Instruction at Dartmouth College." *CHum* 4 (1970): 313–14.

Waldrop, Heidi. "Waking Up to Computer Education." *PC Magazine* (March 20, 1984): 301-9.

Waldrop, M. Mitchell. "Personal Computers on Campus." *Scholarly Communication Reprint* 3 (1985): 1-7.

Weible, David H. "The Foreign Language Teacher as Courseware Author." *CALICO Journal* 1 (1983): 62-64.

Widmann, R. L. "Trends in Computer Applications to Literature." *CHum* 9 (1975): 231-35.

Wyatt, David H., ed. *Computer-Assisted Language Instruction*. New York: Pergamon Press, 1984.

———. "Three Major Approaches to Developing Computer-Assisted Language Learning Materials for Microcomputers." *CALICO Journal* 1 (1983): 34-38.

Chapter 5

Communicating and On-Line Services

The new electronic interdependence
Recreates the world in the image of a global village.
Marshall Herbert McLuhan[1]

5.1 Introduction

The electronic recreation of the world has not yet occurred, but since McLuhan wrote *The Medium is the Massage* (1967)—before the microcomputer and telecommunication revolutions—significant steps have been taken toward the fulfillment of his vision. Imagine being able to sit at your computer in Washington, London, Sydney, Geneva, Tokyo, or anywhere there is a telephone and having nearly instant access to billions of words of information on tens of thousands of different topics in thousands of on-line data bases. Everything from *The Encyclopedia Britannica* to *Books in Print*, from the entire Library of Congress card catalog to the American Theological Library Association's *Religion Index*, and from *U.S. News & World Report* to *The Wall Street Journal* is no more than a computer phone call away! This electronic cornucopia of knowledge is stored on over 3,000 on-line data bases that can serve the information needs of anyone, anywhere, anytime.[2] So sophisticated have communication techniques become that it is now possible to use a mobile telephone and portable computer to access a properly equipped host computer, to have one computer automatically dial other computers at preselected times and upload and download files, and to send electronic mail from one computer to another computer anywhere in the world. The world is not and may never be a global village as McLuhan envisioned it, but the explosion of telecommunication and computer technology and the proliferation and diversification of on-line services are making it possible to access and share information in ways that formerly were impossible.

In this chapter we will see how (1) information utilities, (2) encyclopedic data bases, (3) on-line educational services, (4) academic networks, (5) special microcomputer information services and data bases, (6) electronic bulletin boards, and (7) "front-end" programs help to make this wealth of knowledge available to us.

We will look at three information *utilities*—CompuServe®, The Source®, and DELPHI™—and we will examine four information *services*—DIALOG® Information Retrieval Service, Knowledge Index℠, BRS Search Service, and BRS After Dark™—all

---

1. Marshall Herbert McLuhan (1911–1980), *The Medium is the Massage* (1967).
2. According to Glossbrenner (*Communications*, 4), on-line data bases have increased 600% in the past five years and are growing at a rate of 35% a year.

of which are encyclopedic, bibliographical data bases.[3] We will also discuss NewsNet, an on-line news service, and The Electronic University™, an on-line educational service. And we will examine BITNET and ScholarNet, two academic networks, as well as *PC Magazine*'s on-line interactive reader service and BIX—*BYTE* magazine's on-line information service. This chapter also includes information about two bulletin board services.

5.2 Terminology

Before proceeding we need to define several technical terms. *On-line service* is a broad generic term that refers to computer-based (1) communication, (2) information, and (3) personal services that are accessible by computer through telecommunication networks. *Communication services* include electronic mail, bulletin boards, discussion forums, and file uploading and downloading. *Information services* provide information about various topics, including news, weather, sports, business, investing, industry, computers, chemistry, aviation, engineering, real estate, education, law, medicine, and theology. *Personal services* include games, home shopping and banking, stock brokerage, and airline rates, schedules, and booking. On-line services that offer all three—communication, information, and personal services—are called *information utilities* or *videotex services*. *Information utility* refers to the content of what such a service offers and *videotex* to the form in which that information is displayed: text on a video (TV or CRT) screen. Unlike television, however, on-line services are *interactive*. Users query and the system responds. By issuing the proper commands, users control the system, causing it to provide the desired service or information. Like department stores, information utilities offer a wide variety of services and information from which to choose.

Other terms include *data base, data bank, record, file,* and *field.* A *data bank* is a somewhat loosely organized collection of data, much like a library full of books. A *data base,* or *file,* is a highly-structured, tightly-organized collection of data (often in bibliographical or abstract form), much like a specialized reference book. The data in most data bases is organized into self-contained logical units called *records,* and each record consists of *fields* of information about the particular entry. A file card in a library card catalog is an example of a record that contains fields of information about the entry (a book), and the card catalog is an example of a data base. As the two analogies I have just given suggest, the information in a data bank is often accessed through a data base, just as the books in a library (the data bank) are accessed through a card catalog (the data base). Often, however, *data bank* and *data base* are used interchangeably, and frequently *data base* is used to refer to any collection of information. And to complicate matters even more, *data base* is sometimes used collectively to refer to a group of separate files (data bases) and sometimes in the singular to refer to particular files in a collection, as in "DIALOG is a data base that contains over 300 separate data bases." Most data bases are compiled by independent producers and marketed through on-line vendors, just as department stores market merchandise produced by various manufacturers.

---

3. We will not examine SDC® Orbit®, an encyclopedic bibliographical data base, because it does not contain files of interest to readers of this book that are not already contained in DIALOG or BRS, and we will not examine NEXIS®, Mead Data Central's on-line data base that contains the full text of dozens of magazines, journals, newspapers, and newsletters, because of its prohibitive cost for the average user. See Glossbrenner, *Communications,* 409–11, for information on SDC/Orbit. Nor will we examine GEnie, the General Electric Network for Information Exchange, a relatively new information utility. For information about GEnie, contact General Electric Information Services Co., 401 North Washington St., Rockville, MD 20850; (800) 638-8369 (data), (800) 638-9636 (voice), ext. 21.

AN 266872. (RI). 8506.
AU GUNDRY-ROBERT-H.
TI GRACE, WORKS, AND STAYING SAVED IN PAUL
(REPLY TO E P SANDERS, PAUL AND PALES-
TINIAN JUDAISM, PAUL, THE LAW AND
JEWISH PEOPLE).
SO BIBLICA. 66 NO 1,1–38 1985.
YR 85.
LG EN.
DE PAUL-SAINT-APOSTLE: THEOLOGY: GRACE.
PAUL-SAINT-APOSTLE: THEOLOGY:
SOTERIOLOGY. CHRISTIANITY-AND-
JUDAISM: 0030–600. LAW-AND-GOSPEL.
PALESTINE. SALVATION. GOOD-WORKS-
THEOLOGY. SANDERS-E-P.
AB BIBLICAL CITATIONS: PHIL 3:2–11; ROM
4:2–4;9:30–10:13;7:7–25; DEUT 27:26.

Figure 5.1: Sample BRS After Dark record from Religion Index

Encyclopedic data bases are on-line information services that contain many diverse data bases, or files, that cover a broad range of subject matter, and *bibliographical data bases* are files whose records consist of fields of bibliographical information. *Encyclopedic*, then, refers to the scope of the data base and *bibliographical* to its content and to the form in which its information is arranged.

Figure 5.1 is a sample record from a bibliographical data base, *AN* stands for accession number, *AU* for author, *TI* for title, *SO* for source, *YR* for year of publication, *LG* for language in which the article is written, *DE* for descriptor words applied to the article, and *AB* for abstract.

As the name suggests, a *bulletin board service* (BBS), or *computer bulletin board service* (CBBS), is a computerized version of a physical bulletin board. These BBSs are used for posting and reading messages, uploading and downloading files, conferencing, sending electronic mail, and reading about topics of special interest.

A *special interest group*, or *SIG*, is an electronic version of a discussion group. Most information utilities and many BBSs have numerous SIGs, whose topics range from the esoteric to the erotic. *Network* is used to refer to (1) telecommunication networks (i.e., telephone, telex, or data networks)—the communication links between the host computer and users' terminals or computers—and to (2) organized groups of computer users who are interested in the same topic and who communicate and share information electronically or otherwise. The second sense of *network* is virtually synonymous with *SIG*. A group of computer users who are interested in a common topic may form a network, or SIG, on an information utility or BBS. In this chapter, I will use *telecommunication network* to refer to dedicated data networks, not to telephone systems.

The bibliography at the end of the chapter lists numerous articles and books that provide extensive information about—and helpful hints and instructions for using—the major on-line services. The summaries of basic facts about each service often include helpful bibliographical references. Because the information industry, like Heraclitus's river, is in a *constant* state of flux, some of the information in the older bibliographical references is dated. Alfred Glossbrenner, *The Complete Handbook of Personal Computer Communications: Everything You Need To Go Online with the World* (1985), is the single most helpful and up-to-date publication about telecommunicating. Glossbrenner's book, the "Bible" of the on-line information industry, is a cornucopia of clear and usable information, instructions, examples, and tips about telecommunicating in general and about every major on-line system in particular.

431

5.3 Telecommunicating

Before we plunge into the world of on-line services, let's take a moment to see how a personal computer in a small Rocky Mountain town in northwestern Montana can command millions of dollars worth of computers and software in Palo Alto, California (DIALOG Information Services, Inc.), Columbus, Ohio (CompuServe), or McLean, Virginia (The Source), to do its bidding. What is telecommunicating, and how does it work?

5.3.1 Telecommunication Networks

Telecommunicating refers to any form of electromagnetic communication between humans or machines. The electromagnetic medium may consist of telephone, telex, or data lines, fiber optics cables, or microwaves and related devices such as communication satellites.

My computer in Montana can call DIALOG's computers in California in two different ways. My computer can make a direct-dial call using the telephone system, or my computer can use one of the several telecommunication networks. In metropolitan areas with populations of 50,000 or more, telecommunication networks usually have local numbers. Because my community is smaller than that, my computer has to dial a telecommunication network number in a near-by town. Once my computer is successfully connected to the telecommunication network, I am prompted to specify the on-line service with which I wish to be connected. As this point in the communication process, the telecommunication network acts like an operator: it receives my call, asks with whom I wish to speak, and connects me with the proper party. Once that connection is established, however, the role of the telecommunication network changes into that of an interpreter or translator. My computer "talks" to the network's computers who "talk" to the on-line service's computers, and the on-line service's computers "talk" to my computer through the network's computers. Fortunately, however, the intermediary role of the network's computers is transparent; I am unaware that additional computers are involved in the communication process.

Telecommunication networks are also referred to as *packet-switching networks* because of the type of communication technology they use. Networks package all data into identically-sized packets before electronically addressing each packet and sending it to its proper on-line destination. If there is not enough data to fill up a packet, networks add "filler" to the packet to make it the proper (i.e., standard) size before sending it to the on-line service's computers. The switching part of the term *packet-switching network* refers to the fact that a network's computers switch data between themselves and the on-line service's computers by using the best available route. Because of the incredible speed at which packet-switching networks transmit data (56,000 bits per second, i.e., 56,000 baud, which is about 5,600 characters of information per second—approximately three pages), I am unaware that part of my computer's "conversation" with DIALOG's computers is routed from Montana to Dallas to Palo Alto and another part through Chicago and yet another part through Memphis. Telecommunication networks combine leased telephone lines, special dedicated data lines, and satellite and microwave systems to provide better quality connections that allow fast transmission rates. Readers interested in a more technical explanation of packet-switching networks, modems, and related topics should consult the bibliography at the end of this chapter.

Although telecommunication networks are not free, their rates are far lower than direct-dial long distance calls. For example, an hour-long direct-dial long distance call from my home in Montana to DIALOG Information Services' computers in Palo Alto, California, during the Day Rate period (8 A.M. to 5 P.M.) currently would cost

$17.97. Two of the major telecommunication networks (see below) charge a flat rate of $11 per hour for the same service, regardless of the point of access, and DIALOG has its own network, Dialnet, that is available in many large metropolitan areas for $8 an hour.

The three major telecommunication networks in North America are TYMNET, Telenet, and DataPac (in Canada only).[4] All major on-line services are served by one or more networks, as are most metropolitan areas with populations above 50,000. Some of the larger on-line services (e.g., DIALOG, CompuServe, The Source) have created their own networks to improve the quality of communications with their systems and to reduce users' on-line communication costs.

5.3.2 Serial Cards and Modems

Two pieces of hardware—a serial card and a modem—are required to communicate on-line, as well as communication software, a computer, and a phone line. A *serial card*, also known as a *communication card* or *comm card*, converts a computer's parallel flow of data into a one-bit-at-a-time, single file, serial flow of electronic information that can be sent over telephone lines. A *modem* modulates, or changes, the frequency of a computer's inaudible, electronic, digital signals into audible, analog signals so that they may be transmitted over telephone or data lines. Sometimes serial cards and modems are integrated into single cards that plug into a computer's mother board.

To understand the need for serial cards and modems, we must remember two things that we discussed in chapter 1. First, we must remember that *true* 16-bit computers, for example, transmit all sixteen bits of data—two bytes—simultaneously, in parallel, within the machine and over its external data bus. When communicating with peripheral devices (e.g., monitors and printers), a 16-bit computer simultaneously transmits sixteen bits of information because the ports that connect the computer's external data bus to the peripheral devices are sixteen bits wide; sixteen or more wires connect each port with the device it serves. Second, we must remember what *digital* and *binary* mean. Computers perceive everything as sets of binary numbers that are physically represented as series of high and low voltages. A 1 bit consists of a high voltage that falls within a narrowly specified range, and a 0 bit consists of a low voltage that falls within an equally narrow range. Computers, then, communicate (1) 8 or 16 (or more) bits of information at a time as (2) distinct combinations of precise voltage levels.

Telephone technology, however, uses significantly different principles of communication to which computers must *adapt* if they are to communicate over the telephone system. Although computers transmit data in parallel as precisely defined electrical voltages, the telephone system requires data to be transmitted serially and audibly. No matter how sophisticated a *telecommunication* network's technology, users access those networks over *telephone* lines. Thus when telecommunicating, telephone technology imposes limitations on the ways computers can telecommunicate.

The telephone system and its equipment were designed to allow parties to communicate by using the sound of the human voice. Telephone equipment responds to the audible, fluctuating, nondiscrete frequencies and amplitude—strength—of human speech. Because computers are designed to communicate by means of narrowly defined discrete voltage levels—not sound—telephone technology is inherently unsuitable for communication between computers. The two devices that solve those problems are the modem and the serial card. A *modem* is an electronic device that converts a computer's electrical signals into audible, voice-frequency signals that can be transmitted over telephone lines and that performs the inverse operation on the receiving end of

---

4. The Customer Service numbers of the two U.S. networks are: Telenet: (800) 336-0437, (703) 689-6300 (in Alaska and Hawaii); TYMNET: (800) 336-0149.

the connection. A modem, then, takes a computer's output, which consists of series of high and low voltages, and changes those voltages into audible signals that fall within the frequency range of the human voice. That transformation is called *modulation.* The reverse operation—transforming incoming voice-frequency signals into the proper series of high and low voltages—is known as *demodulation.* Because they modulate and demodulate signal frequencies, these devices are called *modems.* A modem, then, transforms (i.e., modulates) binary, electrical, digital signals into analogous audio signals, and vice versa. The sound that can be heard for a second or so when a modem initially establishes a connection with another modem is called the *carrier signal* (because it is used to carry data from one computer to another), and it is that signal that a modem creates and modulates to transmit data.

A device known as a serial card solves the problem of communication channels. Voice communication between two parties using the telephone system requires only one channel, or line, but computers are designed to communicate with the outside world over eight, sixteen, or more channels at once. A *serial card,* which is a special printed circuit board that fits into one of the expansion slots on the mother board of many computers, solves that incompatibility problem by changing the parallel flow of bits from a computer's external data bus into a serial flow of bits that can be sent over a telephone line one bit at a time—hence the name *serial card.*[5]

Baud[6] is a unit that measures the rate of data flow (the transmission rate) from one computer or communication device to another, just as miles-per-hour and kilometers-per-hour are measures of speed. For all practical purposes (this is a simplified explanation), a computer's baud rate is synonymous with the number of bits per second (bps) it can transmit or receive. A 300-baud modem transmits and receives at 300 bps, which is equivalent to 30 characters per second (cps). A 1,200-baud modem communicates four times that fast, or at the rate of 120 cps. 2,400-baud modems run at 240 cps. These transmission rates do not take into account the overhead incurred by error-checking protocols (see below) and on-line system response time. Thirty, 120, and 240 cps, then, are ideal rates. A 300-baud modem is quite slow; 1,200-baud modems are the de facto standard for serious on-line use, and 2,400-baud modems are tomorrow's standard. Although some on-line services charge more for 1,200 and 2,400 than for 300 baud use, and though 300/1,200-baud modems are more expensive than 300-baud modems, over the long run the faster modems will save on telecommunication charges, and their speed certainly makes them more pleasant to use. Readers should be advised, however, that though industry standards exist for 300- and 1,200-baud modems, this is not yet the case for 2,400-baud modems. Until such standards are agreed upon, 1,200-baud modems are a safer buy.[7]

5.3.3 Protocols

In chapter 1 we learned that computers are mindless machines that have a rule for everything and that do everything by the rules. Just as diplomats and fussy negotiators demand that clearly specified, well-defined rules—protocols—govern all interaction between two parties, so computers require that strictly defined protocols be observed when communicating with all external devices. In this context, then, *protocol* refers to the set of parameters that govern communication between any two devices, such as

---

5. The microchip on the serial card that performs this important conversion is called a UART—Universal Asynchronous Receiver-Transmitter.

6. *Baud* comes from J. M. E. Baudot (1845–1903), the Frenchman who invented the Baudot telegraph code (ca. 1880). Originally, *baud* was used to describe the transmission capabilities of a telegraph facility in terms of the number of signal events that facility was capable of per second. In that context, *baud* referred to the number of times the state of a telegraph line changed per second.

7. See Wilcox, "Safe," 249–59.

computer and printer, computer and monitor, and computer and computer. Computer-to-computer communication protocols include conventions that govern the start bit, the data bits, the parity bit, the stop bit, duplex, carriage returns, line feeds, answerback, and so on—terms we will discuss below. Thus to communicate properly, two computers must observe the protocols that govern each of those parameters.

Here's how some of the more important protocols work. Computers telecommunicate with one another serially, bit-by-bit, character-by-character. To communicate successfully, computers must speak the same language; they must use the same codes to represent letters, numbers, and other characters. The common language used in telecommunicating is called ASCII—the American Standard Code for Information Interchange. Technically speaking, each of the 128 standard ASCII characters—which include all lower and upper case letters, and all numerals, punctuation signs, and control characters[8]—is seven bits long, though the eight bits in a byte make possible 256 distinct values.[9] In telecommunication terminology, those seven bits are called the *data bits*. If all eight bits are used to represent characters, then those eight bits are the data bits. The eighth bit can be used to shift into the "high codes," the "extended ASCII" character set, or it may be used as a parity bit (see below), but it may not be used both ways. Regardless of how the eighth bit is used, computers always add a start bit to the beginning of each character being transmitted and a stop bit to the end of each character, thereby using *ten* bits per character to telecommunicate.[10]

The start, stop, and parity bits function in the following ways. To distinguish incoming characters, computers must know where the bits that make up each character begin and end. Otherwise, incoming data would appear as a meaningless jumble of 0s and 1s. When telecommunicating, every character begins with a start bit, which is always 0, and ends with a stop bit, which is always 1. Therefore every time a new string of bits is received, the initial 0, or start bit, signals the beginning of the character, and the receiving computer knows that the next seven or eight bits (depending on the protocol) are the data bits, that the ninth bit is the parity bit (if that is part of the protocol), and that the tenth bit is the stop bit. Each stop bit signals the end of a character. Without start and stop bits, the computer would be hopelessly confused, just as humans would be if we tried to read books without spaces between words or if we tried to receive Morse Code from a sender who did not pause between letters.

The form of communication we have just described is termed *asynchronous* because the rate of transmission may vary. In asynchronous communication the transmission rate does not have to be synchronized because start and stop bits are used to signal the beginning and ending of characters. *Synchronous* communication, however, requires an uninterrupted, precisely timed flow of data so that the receiving computer can know where characters begin and end. Most microcomputers telecommunicate asynchronously, though some manufacturers are now offering modems that can transmit data asynchronously and synchronously through a standard communication port.[11]

When telecommunicating, the eighth bit may be used as a *parity* bit to try and catch mistakes in transmission. There are three types of parity—odd, even, and none—and they work in the following ways. If the protocol specifies that the parity is

---

8. Control characters are nonprinting characters that control various communication functions, such as starting and stopping scrolling.

9. The eighth bit is often used to shift to the upper 128 positions, the "high codes" or "extended ASCII" character set, that an 8-bit word makes possible. The eighth bit is called the "high bit" because it adds 128 to the value of the preceding seven bits, thereby shifting to the high codes. Thus on an IBM PC, for example, the lower 128 characters (the "low codes") in the character generator ROM chip on the display adapter board are the standard 128 ASCII characters, but the upper 128 characters in that chip, the "extended ASCII" characters, have been given special values by IBM. There is no standardization of the upper 128 characters that 8-bit words make possible.

10. That is why a 300-baud modem, for example, transmits thirty characters per second—it takes ten bits to transmit each character.

11. E.g., Hayes Microcomputer Products, Inc.'s Smartmodem 2,400B and IBM's 5841 1,200 bps Modem.

even (the most common protocol), then the sending computer adds the numerical values of the seven data bits to see if they add up to an odd or an even number. If they add up to an odd number, then the computer gives the parity bit a value of 1 so that the protocol (which requires an even parity) may be observed. The receiving computer (which is observing the same protocol) likewise performs an arithmetic check on the numerical value of the seven data bits and the parity bit to make sure that they add up to an even value. If they do, then the character is accepted. If they do not, then depending on the software, the receiving computer may ask the sending computer to retransmit the character. If the numerical value of the seven data bits had been even, the sending computer would have set the parity bit to 0, and the receiving computer would have recognized even parity, the agreed upon protocol.

Parity checking is based on the assumption that it is more likely for one bit to be garbled during transmission than for two bits to be transformed into their opposites. If only one bit is garbled, then the parity will be incorrect, and the receiving computer can ask that the character be retransmitted. If two bits have been changed into their opposite values, the parity will appear correct to the receiving computer, even though a mistake in transmission has occurred. Parity checking is not perfect, but it is better than nothing. Once the receiving computer has performed its parity check and found that it meets the protocol, it strips off the eighth bit and discards it. Odd parity works the same way that even parity does, and no parity means that all eight bits are being used as data bits and that parity checking is not being performed. Various error-checking protocols used when transmitting files work much like parity-checking protocols. Error-checking protocols have names such as "XMODEM," "Kermit," "MNP," and "BLAST."

Another important protocol is the *X-ON/X-OFF* convention. These are the signals two computers use to indicate when they are ready to send and receive data. Like the other protocols we have discussed, this protocol is set with communication software. If you know how to start and stop screen scrolling on one of the on-line services, you will have learned the codes for X-ON and X-OFF. Control-S stops screen scrolling and is the code for X-OFF. It commands the host computer to stop sending data until you signal otherwise. Control-Q commands the host computer to resume transmitting and is the code for X-ON.

Finally, telecommunication protocols usually specify *full-duplex* or *half-duplex* and *call* or *answer* mode. *Half-duplex* means that a device can send or receive but not do both simultaneously, which is like talking on a CB radio. *Full-duplex* means that a device can send and receive simultaneously, which is like talking on the telephone. Full-duplex is faster than half-duplex because the receiving computer does not have to be queried by the transmitting computer after each transmission to see if it is permissible to transmit more data. When using full-duplex, the transmitting computer is *constantly* sending out "Is it OK to send?" signals, and the receiving computer is *constantly* sending out "It's OK to send!" signals. To communicate successfully, the two computers must agree that one of them will be in the *call* mode (also known as the *originate*, or *send*, mode) and that the other one will be in the *answer* mode (also known as the *receive* mode). When calling an on-line service, the computer that originates the call will be in the call mode and the on-line computer in the answer mode.

5.4 Information Utilities

Like a department store, an information utility consists of many separate information departments, each broken down into different areas. The men's clothing department in a department store, for example, might devote one area to slacks, another to shirts, and another to suits. Just as one department store might have more departments, more areas in a department, and more selections in an area than another department store, so information utilities differ in terms of the number and types of departments, the areas within departments, and the depth of coverage in an area.

There are three major and many minor information utilities in the United States. The three major ones are The Dow Jones News/Retrieval Service (DJN/R), CompuServe Information Service (CIS), and The Source. Because the DJN/R is primarily (though not exclusively) a financial information service, we will not cover it in this book, though anyone who needs financial information that is reliable, current, and comprehensive should consider it.[12] In this section we will look at CompuServe and The Source, as well as at DELPHI, a smaller, though very interesting, service. Please keep in mind that we will only look at a *small fraction* of what these information utilities have to offer.

5.4.1 CompuServe

- ● *BASIC INFORMATION*

Name of Service: CompuServe®
Name of Company: CompuServe Information Service, Inc.
Address: 5000 Arlington Center Blvd., P.O. Box 20212, Columbus, OH 43220
Business Phones: (800) 848-8199, (614) 457-8600
Customer Service Phones: (800) 848-8990, (614) 457-8650
Subscription Cost: $39.95 for Compuserve Information Service (CIS), which includes $25 worth of free connect time; $39.95 and $10.00 monthly minimum for Executive Service Option (ESO), which includes $25 worth of free connect time, additional data bases and services, augmented on-line storage facilities, and discounts on many CompuServe products.
Literature Included with Subscription: Manual and subscription to *Online Today* magazine[13]
Manual: 171 pages, hardback, spiral-bound, indexed, 6 reference cards, system configuration diagram.
Related Publications: Charles Bowen and David Peyton, *How to Get the Most Out of CompuServe*; chapter 7 in Glossbrenner, *Communications*.
Connect Times: 24 hours/day, 365 days/year
Hourly Rates: 300 baud = $6/hour, 1,200 and 2,400 baud = $12.50/hour
Monthly Minimum: CIS: none; ESO: $10
Telecommunication Networks: Telenet, TYMNET, DataPac (Canada), CompuServe Network Services (CNS)
Telecommunication Surcharge: From contiguous U.S.: Telenet and TYMNET: $10/hour for Prime/Daytime hours (8 A.M. - 6 P.M.), $2/hour for Standard/Evening hours (6 P.M. - 8 A.M.). CNS: $0.25/hour. Higher telecommunication surcharges for access from Canada, Alaska, Hawaii, and Puerto Rico.
On-line Storage Charges: First 128K free (192K for ESO members); each additional 64K costs $4/week.
Billing Options: VISA®, MasterCard®, American Express®, CHECKFREE® (electronic funds withdrawal)
Telecommunication Protocols: 300, 1,200, 2,400 baud, 7-bit ASCII even parity (or 8-bit ASCII no parity), 1 stop bit, full duplex, asynchronous
Other: There is an hourly surcharge for some services.

With more than 375,000 members—an estimated 37.5% of the almost 1,000,000 members of on-line information services—CompuServe®, a subsidiary of H&R Block, is the largest and most popular of the information utilities.[14] CompuServe's growth is nothing short of phenomenal. From 15,000 members in January of 1982, CompuServe grew to over 250,000 members by January of 1986 (1,600% in four years) and is adding between 4,000 and 7,000 new members to the system each month! CompuServe runs on forty custom-designed DEC mainframes and has over fifty gigabytes (50,000,000,000 bytes) of on-line information in 400 data bases. And through the

---

12. See chapter 10 in Glossbrenner, *Communications*.
13. Also available on-line in an electronic version.
14. Dow Jones News/Retrieval Service runs a close second.

IQuest gateway, CompuServe provides access to an additional 700 data bases on other on-line services.

Like all popular on-line services, CompuServe is menu-driven, but its GO command allows knowledgeable users to move directly to any offering in the system without having to proceed step by step through the hierarchy of menus. On-line help is available by typing GO HELP. Using the FIND command followed by a topic name results in a custom menu (an index) that lists the appropriate CompuServe services and "quick reference words" (see below). For example, issuing FIND RELIGION resulted in this response.

> 1 IQuest [IQUEST]
> 2 Religion Forum [RELIGION]

Typing GO QUICK provides a list of the almost 300 words that can be used with the GO command, and GO TOPIC or GO INDEX lists over 700 topics and their "quick reference words." Keying GO RATES at any "!" prompt results in detailed information about CompuServe's rate structure, and GO TOUR sends users on a tour of the CompuServe system. To find the CompuServe and Network numbers in your area, type GO PHONE or GO PHONES, and follow the prompts.

CompuServe's main, or TOP, menu looks like this.

> CompuServe TOP
> 1 Subscriber Assistance
> 2 Find a Topic
> 3 Communications/Bulletin Bds.
> 4 News/Weather/Sports
> 5 Travel
> 6 The Electronic MALL/Shopping
> 7 Money Matters/Markets
> 8 Entertainment/Games
> 9 Home/Health/Family
> 10 Reference/Education
> 11 Computers/Technology
> 12 Business/Other Interests

CompuServe contains many outstanding features, services, and data bases, only a few of which can be mentioned here. Selecting Reference/Education (item 10 on the main-menu) causes CompuServe to display the following submenu.

> CompuServe REFERENCE
> REFERENCE
> 1 IQuest
> 2 Academic Am. Encyclopedia ($)[15]
> 3 Government Information
> 4 Demographics
> 5 Other Reference Sources
> EDUCATION
> 6 Services for Educators
> 7 Services for the Handicapped
> 8 Services for Students/Parents
> 9 Educational Games
> 10 Educational Forums

Selecting item 2 from this submenu connects users to the on-line electronic version of Grolier's Academic American Encyclopedia (AAE). This 10-million word reference work, which contains over 30,000 articles on a wide range of topics, is updated quarterly, making it the most current on-line encyclopedia available. Over 40%

---

15. The "$" symbol indicates that there is a charge for the use of the service.

of the articles contain bibliographies, and an extensive set of cross references makes it easy to find related topics. The AAE is easy to search, and its excellent, well-written articles provide a wealth of information. With the proper communication software, the text of articles can be captured to disk or memory for off-line editing, viewing, and printing. Key GO ENCYCLOPEDIA at the "!" prompt to go directly to the AAE. To gain unlimited use of the encyclopedia for a specified period of time, one of the following subscription options must be selected: (1) one year for $49.95, (2) six months for $29.95, or (3) one month for $7.50. For the $400 to $500 that a printed encyclopedia costs, the on-line AAE could be used for many years, and users would never read an out of date article. So successful has the on-line AAE been that Grolier has released a full-version CD-ROM edition that retails for $199.[16]

In addition to the AAE, CompuServe has more than 100 SIGs, which are also called Forums. Choosing Communications/Bulletin Bds. (item 3 on the Main Menu) displays the following submenu.

```
COMMUNICATIONS/BULLETIN BOARDS
1 EasyPlex Electronic Mail
2 CB Simulator
3 Forums (SIGs)
4 National Bulletin Board
5 Directory of Subscribers
6 Ask Customer Service
7 CB Society
8 Access (Public File Area)
9 The Convention Center (tm)
```

Choosing item 3 from this submenu takes users to CompuServe's Forum area, as does entering GO FORUM at any "!" prompt. The number and breadth of the Forums make them one of CompuServe's most distinctive features. Forums provide a way for user groups to seek advice and to share information on topics of common interest by offering messaging and bulletin board facilities, real-time conferencing, and files and data bases. Users may read, upload, and download files from Forum data bases. Chapter 5 of the *CompuServe Information Service Users Guide* (which is included with the $39.95 subscription price) contains a summary of Forum commands.

In the Forum section, CompuServe offers the Religion Forum, which is run by Drs. Donald and Lindajo McKim, professors at the University of Dubuque Theological Seminary in Iowa. There are three ways to get to this forum: (1) key GO RELIGION at any "!" prompt, (2) choose item 3 (Communications/Bulletin Bds.) from the Main Menu and proceed from there, or (3) choose item 9 (Home/Health/Family) on the Main Menu and proceed from there. As of October 1987, over 600 people from across America were listed as members of this Forum; and their interests, which are listed online, cover every imaginable topic and then some: Catholicism, evangelical Christianity, Buddhism, Judaism, the influence of Wittgenstein on modern theology, astrology, near-death experiences, church history, pentecostalism, phenomenology, process theology, John Calvin, Christology, the New Testament, liturgy, pastoral care, gnosticism, New Age cults, witchcraft, sermon outlines, apologetics, Bible study, Greek and Hebrew, historical and systematic theology, and English Puritanism, to name but a few. In this Forum, bulletins, which are divided into ten categories that cover broad areas of interest—World Religions, Christianity, Judaism, Eastern Religions, and so forth—may be posted and read. As of October 1987, over 73,000 messages had been posted since this forum began. Each Monday night the Religion Forum holds a realtime, on-line conference that begins at 9 P.M. (Eastern Standard Time).

CompuServe includes 400 on-line data bases. Through the menu-driven IQuest gateway service, CompuServe offers its users access to an additional 700 bibliographic

---

16. See Langdell, "Grolier," and Foster "Grolier."

and full-text data bases from vendors such as DIALOG, BRS, NewsNet, SDC, VuText, Pergamon, QUESTEL, ADP Network Services, and several others. When searching bibliographic data bases, users are shown up to ten hits per search. When searching full-text data bases, users are shown up to fifteen titles per search, one of which may be chosen for reading at no extra cost. There is a $7 per search surcharge for this service.

Another useful feature is CompuServe's EasyPlex Electronic Mail. Begin with item 3, Communications/Bulletin Bds., on the Main Menu and proceed from there, or key GO MAIL or GO EASY or GO EASYPLEX at any "!" prompt. This service allows users to maintain an address book and to send messages as long as 8K (8,000 characters—about four double-spaced typed pages). Two line editors make composition easy, and electronic mail is sent to another CompuServe user's mailbox within minutes.

Last but by no means least, CompuServe allows users to send ("upload") and receive ("download") files, a particularly useful feature found on most information utilities and BBSs. Suppose that you have written a document or program that you wish a friend to read and critique. You can upload the file that contains the document or program to an information utility or BBS, and your friend can download it, read or run it, enter suggestions, upload it, and you can download it to see what he or she had to say. As long as the document was ASCII text, it would not matter that it had been written on an Macintosh and that your friend has an IBM, even though Macintoshes and IBMs are incompatible in a number of ways.[17] Uploading and downloading, then, allows files to be transferred between computers with incompatible operating systems.

CompuServe offers *thousands* of free, downloadable, microcomputer public-domain programs. Included in this vast assortment of on-line software are many useful and interesting programs for Macintoshes, Apples, IBMs, Commodores, TRS-80s, and other computers. Menus allow searching through the public-domain area by programs, categories of programs, programs for particular computers, and so forth. When downloading, CompuServe supports the following file-transfer, error-checking protocols: XMODEM, CompuServe 'B,' CompuServe 'A,' and DC2/DC4. To upload or download files or to access CompuServe's public-domain software, key GO ACCESS at any "!" prompt, and proceed from there. Many excellent public domain and shareware programs also may be found in the data library sections of CompuServe's forums.

5.4.2 The Source

• *BASIC INFORMATION*

Name of Service: The Source®
Name of Company: Source Telecomputing Corporation
Address: 1616 Anderson Road, McLean, VA 22102
Business Phones: (800) 336-3366, (703) 734-7500
Customer Service Phones: (800) 336-3330, (703) 821-8888
Subscription Cost: $49.95, includes no free time.
Literature Included with Subscription: Manual, subscription to *SourceWorld* (a monthly newsletter), Source Member Directory, and Command Guide.
Manual: 269 pages, three-ring binder, slip case, indexed
Related Publications: Charles Bowen and David Peyton, *How to Get the Most Out of The Source*; chapters 8 and 15 in Glossbrenner, *Communications*.
Connect Times: 24 hours/day, 365 days/year
Hourly Rates: Prime/Daytime (7 A.M. to 6 P.M., Mon.–Fri.): 300 baud = $21.60/hour, 1,200 baud = $25.80/hour, 2,400 baud = $27.60/hour; Non-Prime (6 P.M. to 7 A.M., Mon.–Fri., weekends and holidays): 300 baud = $8.40/hour, 1,200 baud = $10.80/hour, 2,400 baud = $12/hour. IN WATS =

---

17. Of course, a program written for an IBM will not run on an Macintosh, and vice versa.

$15/hour. All times are local (daylight savings) times. Higher hourly rates from Canada, Alaska, and Hawaii.

Monthly Minimum: $10/month; $95/year

Telecommunication Networks: Telenet, Sourcenet, IN WATS

Telecommunication Surcharge: Included in Hourly Rates (see above).[18]

On-line Storage Charges: From $0.05 to $0.50 per record per month (a record is 2,048 characters), depending on volume.

Billing Options: VISA®, MasterCard®, American Express®, Discover®, CHECKFREE® (electronic funds withdrawal)

Telecommunication Protocols: 300, 1,200, 2,400 baud, 8-bit ASCII, no parity, 1 stop bit, full duplex, asynchronous

Other: There is an hourly surcharge for some services. The Source may be accessed via Telenet from forty-six countries outside the North American continent.

Though much smaller in membership (approximately 70,000 as of early 1986),[19] The Source®, which is owned by The Reader's Digest Association, is CompuServe's main rival and an excellent information utility that offers over 800 features and programs. The Source runs on fifteen Prime 750 minicomputers and has over seven gigabytes (7,000,000,000 bytes) of on-line information in a multitude of data bases. Like other popular on-line services, The Source is menu-driven, but by issuing the appropriate command at the system-level —> prompt, knowledgeable users can move directly to any offering without having to proceed step by step through the hierarchy of menus. On-line help is available by typing HELP. Typing HELP SERVICES displays a list of over 100 services and their command names, and HELP COMMANDS displays The Source's commands. HELP RATES displays detailed information about The Source's rate structure. To find the Network numbers in your area for accessing The Source, type ACCESS at any —> prompt, and for an introductory tutorial to The Source, enter LEARN.

The Source's introductory menu looks like this.

```
WELCOME TO THE SOURCE
1 Tutorial and Intro. < INTRO > **FREE**
2 Menu of Services < MENU >
3 Member Information < INFO > **FREE**
4 Today From The Source < TODAY >
```

Choosing item 2 of that menu displays the following *main* menu.

```
MENU OF SERVICES < MENU >
1 Today From The Source < TODAY >
2 News, Weather and Sports < NEWS >
3 Business and Investing < BUSINESS >
4 Communication Services < COMM >
5 Special Interest Groups < SIGS >
6 Professional Exchanges < EXCHANGES >
7 Personal Computing < PC >
8 Travel Services < TRAVEL >
9 Education, Shopping and Games < HOME >
10 Member Information < INFO > **FREE**
```

One of The Source's most distinctive features is the PARTI, or PARTICIPATE, service, a computerized conferencing system similar to, though more flexible than,

---

18. The Source's hourly rates may seem higher than CompuServe's, but *unlike* CompuServe, The Source *includes* telecommunication network charges in its hourly rate pricing structure, thus making the actual hourly on-line cost of using The Source slightly *less* expensive, in many cases, than using CompuServe.

19. The Source Telecomputing Corporation no longer gives out these figures.

CompuServe's Forums. PARTI permits users to start conferences about any topic they choose and to join conferences that already exist. PARTI has its own command structure and is discussed at length in chapter 15 of Glossbrenner, *Personal Computer Communications*. The number of conferences on The Source fluctuates (I have counted as many as 200). PARTI conference topics have ranged from Robots and Nuclear War to Organized Religions and Electronic Love (whatever that means!). Other topics have included Abortion, Christian Marriage, Christology, Church, Comparative Religions, Conscience, Death and Dying, Eastern Catholics, Jesus, Philosophy, Pilgrimage, Scriptures, Secular Music, and Vatican II. To access this service directly, type PARTI at the — > prompt and select *12* "Philosophy and Religion."

The Source's Personal Computing section (item 7 on the Main Menu or key PC 1 at the command level) contains a PC Member Publishing service (key PUBLIC 1 DIRECT at any — > prompt), where individuals may publish magazines, catalogs, newsletters, and related items. Of the sixteen PUBLIC selections, one that should interest readers of this book is a publication called *Religion-Online* (PUBLIC 52), an electronic religious newsletter published weekly by the Lutheran Church in America's (LCA) Office for Communications. Its editors are Charles Austin, formerly a religion reporter for the *New York Times*, the *Bergen Record* (Hackensack, New Jersey), and an editor at Religious News Service, and Kris Lee, a film and video producer and consultant on electronic media. Both are Lutheran clergy on the staff of the LCA's Office for Communications. *Religion-Online* includes news about religion, media, computers, modern technology, ethics, church software, computer books of a religious nature, and other topics related to computers and religion. SourceMail for *Religion-Online* should be addressed to BCF060.

Like CompuServe, The Source also includes Grolier's Academic American Encyclopedia (key ENC at any — > prompt, or choose item 9, Education, Shopping, and Games, from the Main Menu), which is available for $7.50 a month or $29.50 for six months of unlimited use, almost exactly what CompuServe charges.

And The Source provides services for sending electronic mail and for uploading and downloading files. SourceMail, in fact, is one of the most sophisticated electronic mail services available. HELP MAIL OVERVIEW provides on-line general information about SourceMail, which also can be accessed by keying MAIL or by choosing item 4 (Communication Services) from the Main Menu. For information about uploading and downloading files, use either the RCV or the FILETRAN programs, and key HELP RCV and HELP FILETRAN to provide on-line instructions.

5.4.3 DELPHI

- *BASIC INFORMATION*

Name of Service: DELPHI™
Name of Company: General Videotex Corporation
Address: 3 Blackstone Street, Cambridge, MA 02139
Business Phones: (800) 544-4005, (617) 491-3393
Customer Service Phones: (800) 544-4005, (617) 491-3393
Subscription Cost: $49.95, which includes two free hours of evening connect time.
Literature Included with Subscription: Manual, system-summary card, command card
Manual: 163 pages, three-ring binder, indexed
Related Publications: Chapter 9 in Glossbrenner, *Communications*
Connect Times: 24 hours/day, 365 days/year
Hourly Rates: Prime/Daytime (7 A.M. to 6 P.M., Mon.–Fri.): $17.40/hour; Standard/Evening (6 P.M. to 7 A.M., Mon.–Sun., holidays): $7.20/hour. All times are local (daylight savings) times. No telecommunication surcharge for 1,200 baud. Higher hourly rates from Canada, Alaska, Bermuda, Puerto Rico, and Hawaii.
Monthly Minimum: No
Telecommunication Networks: TYMNET, Telenet, DataPac (Canada)
Telecommunication Surcharge: No

On-Line Storage Charges: First 25K free; each additional 1K $0.16/month.
Billing Options: VISA®, MasterCard®, American Express®, direct billing ($3.50/month direct billing fee)
Telecommunication Protocols: 300, 1,200, 2,400 baud, 8-bit ASCII, no parity, 1 stop bit, full duplex, no auto-linefeed or carriage-return linefeed, enable X-ON/X-OFF or handshaking, asynchronous
Other: Hourly rates higher in Canada. There is a surcharge for some services.

DELPHI™, the third largest information utility (over 40,000 members as of January 1987),[20] is marketed by General Videotex Corporation and runs on a DEC VAX 750 and a DEC VAX 785. Although offering fewer services than CompuServe and The Source, because of its many stimulating intellectual resources, DELPHI may rightly be called "the thinking man's information utility." Before highlighting some of DELPHI's distinctive features, it is worthwhile to note four important economic facts about this system. DELPHI (1) does not charge extra for 1,200 and 2,400 baud, (2) has no telecommunication surcharges, (3) has no monthly minimum fee, and (4) offers extremely reasonable hourly rates. Furthermore, DELPHI has fast response time, excellent system software, and offers some of the most popular services found on CompuServe and The Source, as well as some they do not. Keying HELP followed by a topic name provides information on that service, and typing "?" at any level of the system provides information about that level. DELPHI's Main Menu looks like this.

```
MAIN Menu:
Business & Finance
News-Weather-Sports
Conference
People on DELPHI
DELPHI Mail
Travel
Entertainment
Workspace
Groups and Clubs
Library
Using DELPHI
HELP
Magazines & Books
EXIT
Merchants' Row
```

DELPHI's innovative features can be captured in the phrase "one stop information shopping." Like CompuServe, DELPHI offers a "front-end," or "gateway," service that allows users to access the services of other on-line vendors. DELPHI's front-end feature includes the ability to send electronic mail to members of The Source and CompuServe (the reverse procedure does not yet exist), to use Western Union's EasyLink electronic mail, without paying $25 a month for that service, and to access DIALOG Information Service's enormous set of data bases at the standard DIALOG on-line search rates. DELPHI also contains the Kussmaul Encyclopedia (named after J. Wesley Kussmaul, the founder of General Videotex Corporation), an on-line version of the *Cadillac Modern Encyclopedia*.

Of special interest to readers of this book is DELPHI's Theological Network, which may be reached by choosing the Groups and Clubs selection from DELPHI's Main Menu. The Theological Network (a SIG), which is run by Nancy Johnson (DELPHI name: NJOHNSON), exists to further the education of the religious community and to promote greater understanding among Christian denominations and Bible-based theistic religions. Every Sunday night at 10:00 P.M. (Eastern Standard Time), the

---

20. The General Videotex Corporation no longer gives out these figures.

Theological Network holds on-line, real-time conferences. The Theological Network's main offerings are as follows.

> Theological Network Menu:
> Announcements
> Set Preferences
> Conference
> Shopping Service
> Databases
> Topic Descriptions
> Entry Log
> Who's Here
> Forum (Messages)
> Workspace
> MAIL (Electronic)
> Help
> Member Directory
> Exit
> Poll

The Network's data bases, which change from time to time, currently offer the following choices.

> Databases Available Menu:
> Thesis Library
> Studies in Judaism
> Meditation & Spirituality
> Early Church Fathers
> Gandhian Studies
> New Testament Studies
> Programs for the Clergy
> Hebrew Bible Studies
> Talk to Vendors
> Religious Concepts
> Book Reviews
> Members Lounge
> Sig Newsletter

The New Testament Studies data base, for example, currently contains a lecture (with responses from DELPHI members) by Paul D. Hanson, a professor of theology at Harvard Divinity School, on "The Apocalyptic Consciousness"[21] and an article, "The Beginnings of Fundamentalism." Past discussions and topics in the Theological Network have included apocalypticism, Christology, early Christian fathers, Ignatius of Antioch, cults and utopias, abortion, Christian sex education for teens, rape, Jewish-Christian relations, Pauline studies, spirituality, community, Buddhism, biblical criticism, and New Age cults. The SIG Newsletter is the DELPHI edition of *Church News International*, which is also available on NewsNet (see below).

5.5 Encyclopedic Data Bases

If an information utility is like a department store, an encyclopedic data base is like a specialty shop. Just as some specialty shops are larger and better equipped than others, so encyclopedic data bases differ in terms of the number and subject matter of the files they contain, as well as in terms of the ease and power with which those files

---

21. See his *The Dawn of Apocalyptic. The Historical and Sociological Roots of Jewish Apocalyptic Eschatology*. Rev. ed. Philadelphia: Fortress Press, 1979, and Paul D. Hanson, ed. *Visionaries and Their Apocalypses*. Philadelphia: Fortress Press, 1983.

may be accessed. The files in most encyclopedic data bases consist of bibliographical records about articles and books, though some files and some encyclopedic data bases offer documents in full-text form. Information utilities offer a broad array of services about many areas of interest; encyclopedic data bases offer information about printed documents.

In this section we will look at the four largest encyclopedic data bases. Some of the files in each of these services may be found in one or more of the information utilities or in other encyclopedic data bases. The prices information utilities charge for using such files are usually lower than the prices the encyclopedic data bases charge. For example, to use Grolier's Academic American Encyclopedia (AAE) on BRS After Dark costs $14/hour, on Knowledge Index $24/hour, on DJN/R $36/hour, and on BRS $45/hour. CompuServe and The Source, however, offer *unlimited use* of the AAE for $7.50 per month, $29.95 for six months, and (on CompuServe only) $49.95 a year.[22] It pays to shop around! Readers interested in learning more about saving money when using data bases should consult Glossbrenner, *Communications,* and Matthew Lesko, "Low-Cost On-Line Databases," *BYTE* (October 1984): 167–73.

Samuel Johnson said, "Knowledge is of two kinds. We know a subject ourselves, or we know where we can find information on it."[23] In this day and age, it is difficult to control the bibliographical information about a subject, much less to know a subject with the sort of thoroughness that was possible when Dr. Johnson wrote to Lord Chesterfield in the eighteenth century. But as Dr. Johnson stated, knowing where to find information on a subject *is* a kind of knowledge and one that on-line services and bibliographical data bases provide in abundance.

Because they are command-driven, highly interactive, use sophisticated search logic, and are designed for professional researchers, these data bases allow users to search in extremely refined and specific ways. But such sophistication comes at a price; searching these data bases can be intimidating for those with no training. In lieu of (or in addition to) formal training, several companies offer special menu-driven, "front-end" software interfaces that help users formulate searches off-line, communicate with encyclopedic data base services, conduct searches of specific files, and download and print results.

The information utilities we discussed above—CompuServe, The Source, and DELPHI—offer a moderate amount of information about many topics (as well as provide services like banking, conferencing, and electronic mail), but the encyclopedic data base vendors offer much more information on a far broader range of topics (and some offer services like electronic mail and conferencing, too). As Glossbrenner contrasts them, the utilities offer breadth of information, and the encyclopedics offer depth of information.[24] Data bases are created by "information providers" (IPs) and marketed through on-line vendors such as DIALOG and BRS. Thus it is not at all uncommon to find the same data bases on several services.

To give you an idea of the phenomenal growth in the on-line data base industry, consider the statistics in Table 5.1.[25]

In seven years the number of data bases has increased by more than 700%, the number of data base producers by almost the same amount, and the number of on-line services by almost 800%. Furthermore, as of January 1986, thirty-five "gateways" transparently provided users with access to one or more on-line services. Many files (data bases) are available in the area of humanities/social sciences, and many more will be available in the future.

Although using the on-line services we are about to discuss is still primarily the prerogative of reference librarians, professional researchers, and other information

---

22. The CompuServe prices do not include telecommunication surcharges.
23. Letter to Lord Chesterfield, April 18, 1775.
24. Glossbrenner, *Communications,* 393.
25. These statistics are taken from the *Directory of Online Databases* 7 (January 1986): v.

Dir. Issue	No. Data Bases	No. Producers	No. On-Line Services
1979/80	400	221	59
1980/81	600	340	93
1981/82	965	512	170
1982/83	1350	718	213
1983/84	1878	927	272
1984/85	2453	1189	362
1986	2901	1379	454

Table 5.1: On-line data base industry statistics 1979–1986.

specialists, more and more individuals and academicians are attending training sessions to learn how to use the services for themselves. After understanding the speed, power, flexibility, variety, and scope of the on-line bibliographical services, performing bibliographical-type searches manually seems as time and cost effective—not to mention as boring and loaded with potential pitfalls—as riding a bus from New York to Los Angeles. If a plane is available, why not fly? Once a person has learned to use an on-line bibliographical service to search through hundreds of thousands of bibliographical entries in a matter of *seconds*, there is no turning back to doing such searches manually.

In the following discussions, please keep in mind that we will only look at a *small fraction* of what the encyclopedic data bases have to offer.

5.5.1 DIALOG Information Retrieval Service

- *BASIC INFORMATION*

Name of Service: DIALOG® Information Retrieval Service
Name of Company: DIALOG Information Services, Inc.
Addresses: In the U.S.A.: 3460 Hillview Ave., Palo Alto, CA 94304; in Canada: % Micromedia Ltd./DIALOG, 158 Pearl St., Toronto, Ontario M5H 1L3, Canada; in the United Kingdom and Europe: % DIALOG Information Retrieval Service, P.O. Box 188, Oxford OX1 5AX, United Kingdom.; in Germany: DIALOG Information Services, Inc., Tizianweg 2, 4010 Hilden, West Germany; in Japan: Kinokuniya Company Ltd., ASK Information Retrieval Services Dept., Village 101 Bldg., 1–7 Sakuragaoka-machi, Shibuyu-ku, Tokyo, 150, Japan (KIN); in Korea: Data Communications Corporation of Korea (DACOM), The Business Office, 12th Floor, Korea Stock Exchange Bldg., 1–116 Yeoeido-Dong, Yeongdungpo-Ku, Seoul, Korea; in Australia: Insearch Ltd./DIALOG, P.O. Box K16, Haymarket NSW 20000, Australia; in Mexico: Asesores Especializados en Information y Documentation, S.C., AEID/DIALOG, 2a Cerrada de Romero de Terreros 49A, Colonia del Valle, 03100 Mexico D.F.
Business Phones: In the U.S.A.: (800) 334-2564, (415) 858-3810 (call collect in CA); in Canada: (800) 387-2689, (416) 593-5211 (in Toronto); in the United Kingdom and Europe: (0865) 730275 (Learned Information Ltd., Oxford, U.K.); in Germany: 02103-69904; in Japan: (03) 463-4391; in Korea: 783-5201, 5/783-6471; in Australia: (02) 212-2867; in Mexico: 543-7207, 543-9069
Customer Service Phones: (800) 334-2564, (415) 858-3810 (U.S.A. numbers)
Subscription Cost: Standard service is available for free and includes up to $100 for system use during first 30 days after initial logon (credit covers DIALOG on-line connect time only); $25 annual password fee (billed each September).
Literature Included with Subscription: None; manuals must be purchased separately. *Chronolog*, a monthly newsletter, is free to all registered DIALOG users (also available on-line as File 410, $15/hour).

446

Manual: The *Guide to DIALOG Searching*—3 volumes, in three 2-inch, 3-ring, notebook-size binders—is available for $50 + $5 shipping and handling (North America and elsewhere by surface mail); $75 foreign airmail.

Related Publications: "Pocket Guide to DIALOG Version 2" (up to 5 copies are free; additional copies are $0.75 each); "Database Catalog" ($2); "DIALOG Database Chart" (up to 5 copies free; additional copies $0.75 each); "Database Chapters" ($6 each). See "DIALOG Publications Catalog" for additional listings and for more information. Also see chapter 16 of Glossbrenner, *Communications*.

Connect Times: 24/hours a day, 365 days/year, midnight Sat. to noon Sun. (Eastern Standard Time)

Hourly Rates: Varies by data base from $25/hour to $300/hour.

Monthly Minimum: No

Telecommunication Networks: TYMNET, Telenet, Dialnet, IN WATS

Telecommunication Surcharge: Dialnet $8/hour; TYMNET, Telenet: $11/hour

On-Line Storage Charges: Yes, see DIALOG literature under "Search*Save."

Billing Options: Direct billing only

Telecommunication Protocols: 300, 1,200, 2,400 baud, 8-bit ASCII, no parity, 1 stop bit (or 7 data bits, 1 start bit, 1 stop bit, 1 parity bit), answerback off, no auto-linefeed or carriage-return linefeed, asynchronous. If using telecommunication networks: even or no parity, full duplex, enable X-ON/X-OFF. If using direct dial: half duplex, disable X-ON/X-OFF.

Other: No surcharge for 1,200 and 2,400 baud.

5.5.1.1 Introduction

DIALOG® Information Retrieval Service, a subsidiary of the Lockheed Corporation, is the "granddaddy" of on-line encyclopedic data bases. With more than 300 individual files that contain 120 million records in over 400 gigabytes (400,000,000,000 bytes) of on-line information, DIALOG is indisputably the largest on-line data base in the world. DIALOG was started in 1963 as the Lockheed Corporation's in-house information retrieval system. In 1969 DIALOG began to be used by NASA as a computerized documentation system for the United State's space program, with subsequent contracts coming from the U.S. Atomic Energy Commission and the U.S. Office of Education. DIALOG, whose name comes from the highly interactive command language used for searching the data base, became a commercial system in 1972. According to company spokeswoman Paula Dowell, as of September 1987, DIALOG is using one dual-sided National Advanced Systems (NAS) 9080 and two National Advanced Systems XL60 mainframes, which collectively are capable of processing 80 million instructions per second (MIPS). Hooked up to these computers (which are among the largest made) are several hundred high-capacity hard-disk drives.

In addition to including abstracts from over 100,000 different journals, the DIALOG data bases contain abstracts of dissertations, research and conference reports, patents, government documents, books, pamphlets, corporate financial reports, and the full text of various magazines (e.g., *Time*, *Life*, *Fortune*, *Sports Illustrated*, *People*, *U.S. News & World Report*, *Forbes*, *American Banker*) and two on-line electronic encyclopedias (*Academic American Encyclopedia* and *Everyman's Encyclopedia*).

5.5.1.2 Becoming a User

It costs nothing to receive a DIALOG user number and password, there is no monthly minimum, and DIALOG levies no surcharge for 1,200- and 2,400-baud service, though there is an annual $25 password fee (billed each September). Furthermore, in many cities DIALOG's own Dialnet network is available at the very reasonable rate of $8 per hour. Without the *Guide to DIALOG Searching* and some formal training, however, it is almost impossible for a novice to use the system. In my opinion, though the *Guide* alone may be sufficient for experienced on-line data base users, attending a training seminar is mandatory if one wishes to use DIALOG efficiently and without a great deal of frustration. The information-packed three-volume *Guide* costs $50 (plus

$5 for shipping and handling), and training seminars, which are held monthly throughout the United States and the world, cost $125 for a whole-day session and $55 for a half-day session. In the United States alone, DIALOG holds approximately 300 separate training seminars *per month* in cities of all sizes—from New York City and Chicago to Little Rock, Arkansas, and Shawnee Mission, Kansas—and according to company spokeswoman Paula Dowell, in 1986 DIALOG held 20,000 training seminars worldwide. DIALOG Information Service is *serious* about information retrieval! And so are the system's users. In 1986 DIALOG's 80,000 members (located in over fifty countries) logged on to the system 5.5 million times, an average of 68.75 logons per user.

Several years ago, I attended two DIALOG seminars in Billings, Montana. The instructor from Palo Alto was knowledgeable, helpful, and professional, and the instructional materials were excellent and covered all the fundamental aspects of searching. Within a few hours of starting the basic seminar, the instructor had our class making successful searches on DIALOG, using the portable terminals she brought with her for that purpose. The advanced seminar introduced us to more sophisticated search strategies and like the basic seminar included a lot of "hands-on" time that we spent running searches on DIALOG's computers in Palo Alto. In addition to the basic and advanced seminars, DIALOG also provides seminars for using specific data bases.

To provide users with an inexpensive way to practice using the system and to practice formulating search strategies, each month DIALOG selects a file and gives every registered user up to one half hour of free connect time in that file. But that's not all. DIALOG also has twenty-five ONTAP™ (ONline Training And Practice) files that contain a selection of records from a diverse set of data bases and that are available for $15 per connect hour—an extremely reasonable rate. ONTAP files allow users to practice search strategies in different data bases.

5.5.1.3 The Guide

The three-volume *Guide* consists of a volume of "Bluesheets" that describe each data base, a volume that holds issues of *Chronolog*, DIALOG's monthly newsletter (also available on-line as File 410, $15/hour), and a volume that explains DIALOG's search terms and syntax. The cost of the *Guide* also includes a copy of the "Database Catalog," which lists the data bases alphabetically and briefly describes each one. Additionally, the free "Pocket Guide to DIALOG Version 2" is a valuable summary of all the key commands and procedures.

5.5.1.4 Search Logic

Using DIALOG is like flying a jet fighter: the system is fast, accurate, complex, and powerful. Using it correctly, a knowledgeable person can quickly score direct hits. Just as describing a jet plane's specifications and performance parameters would require many pages, so it would require more space than we have to describe the entire DIALOG system and all of DIALOG's commands. In this subsection, then, I will only touch on the basic aspects of DIALOG searching.

DIALOG is a command-driven system that supports free-text searches and searching with descriptors. A *descriptor* is a member of a carefully chosen set of terms called a *controlled vocabulary* that is used by data base creators as consistently as possible to describe the contents of the records in the data bases they create. A descriptor is sometimes referred to as an *identifier*, though, technically speaking, an identifier is not chosen from a controlled vocabulary list but is assigned by the indexer. *Free-text searching* refers to searching without using descriptors or identifiers, even though they may be available.

DIALOG supports Boolean ANDs, ORs, and NOTs, which may be mixed and nested in the same search construction. For example, "SELECT (Jones AND Smith AND (Williams OR Turner)) OR (Howard AND Tucker) NOT (John OR James OR Fred)" is a valid construction. Search constructions may include up to 240 characters. Initial, medial, and terminal truncation are supported, as are proximity and sequence-specific searches. Users may specify the search range and search by fields. For example, "SELECT Europe?(2N)History" would command DIALOG to locate all instances in a particular file where any word beginning with *Europe* occurs within two words of *History*, in any order (*2W* would have required the search terms to occur within two words of each other in the order listed). Fields vary from file to file but usually include abstract, descriptor, full descriptor, identifier, full identifier, title, note, and section heading. For example, "SELECT Europe?(2N)History/ti" would restrict the search to those instances in a particular file where any word beginning with *Europe* occurs within two words of *History* (in any order) in the title field of records in the data base. Additional fields include author, company name, corporate source, document type, journal name, language, publication year, and update. Range searching is used to indicate a range of sequential entries to be retrieved in a logical OR relationship. For example, "SELECT PY=1982:1985" would restrict a particular search to items published between 1982 and 1985 (*PY* means "publication year"). Hits are listed in sequentially numbered sets, and each set specifies the number of hits it contains. Sets may be manipulated with the AND, OR, and NOT operators. Those are the main commands, though DIALOG supports dozens of others.

A simple DIALOG search and its results are illustrated in Figure 5.2. In that search, *b* means "begin" and *190* is the file in which the search is to take place; *ss* means "select steps" and is the search command that instructs the system to create separately numbered sets of hits; *w* means "with" and is the adjacency operator that requires the second search term to follow the first with no intervening words;[26] *ti* restricts the search to the title field of articles; and *t* means "type" and is the command for displaying the results of a search on-screen. The "?" is the DIALOG system prompt.

After logging on to the system, performing that simple search and displaying the results on-screen took less than 2 minutes and cost under $2.

5.5.1.5 Other Information

Help. DIALOG's on-line help for basic commands may be accessed by typing "EX-PLAIN xxx" or "? xxx" where *xxx* is the name of the command for which an explanation is desired. "?EXPLAIN" lists all the commands that DIALOG will explain on-line.

Data Base Chapters. Data base chapters, which are available for $6 each and which vary between 20 and 30 pages, provide extensive information about using and searching individual data bases and include many examples of sample searches, as well as lists of search aids, such as available indices.

Thesauri. Many DIALOG data bases include on-line thesauri that work like printed thesauri to help researchers locate terms that are related to or synonymous with other terms. This greatly facilitates accurate searching.

Display Formats. Up to eight different formats may be selected to display and print hits. When using the proper communication software, all information displayed on-screen may be captured to disk or memory and manipulated and printed. Alternatively, hits may be printed on DIALOG's printer and mailed to users. A small fee is

---

26. Stop words—nonindexed words such as *and, or, the*—may intervene.

?b 190
File 190:RELIGION INDEX — 1949–1985/OCT
Copr. Amer. Theological Library Assoc.
Set Items Description
ss Covenant(w)Practice/ti
S1 418 COVENANT/TI
S2 455 PRACTICE/TI
S3 1 COVENANT(W)PRACTICE/TI
?t 3/5/1
3/5/1
0041160
215227
HEBREWS 9:15FF AND GALATIANS 3:15FF: A STUDY
         IN COVENANT PRACTICE AND PROCE-
         DURE
HUGHES, JOHN J
NOV TEST, 21, 27–96, JA 1979
THE INTERPRETATION AND TRANSLATION OF
         DIATHEKE IN HEB 9:15 FF. AND GAL 3:15 FF.
         HAS BEEN NOT ONLY GREATLY DEBATED
         AND IMPORTANT IN ITS OWN RIGHT BUT
         ALSO OF NO LITTLE IMPORTANCE FOR UN-
         DERSTANDING THE RELATIONSHIP BE-
         TWEEN THE THEOLOGY OF THE EARLY
         CHURCH AND THE COVENANT MOTIF IN
         THE OT AND LATER JUDAISM. A SUBSTAN-
         TIAL AMOUNT OF CONFUSION STILL PER-
         SISTS. NOT ONLY ARE CERTAIN FALSE AS-
         SUMPTIONS ABOUT GREEK AND ROMAN
         LEGAL PRACTICE STILL COMMONLY
         FOUND IN THE NT LITERATURE ON THESE
         TWO PERICOPAE BUT NT SCHOLARS HAVE
         OVERLOOKED THE POTENTIAL IMPOR-
         TANCE FOR UNDERSTANDING THESE
         PERICOPAE OFFERED BY THE MANY OT
         STUDIES WHICH HAVE INVESTIGATED THE
         NATURE AND THE RELATIONSHIP BE-
         TWEEN COVENANT POLICY AND PRAXIS IN
         ISRAEL WITH THAT OF HER ANE NEIGH-
         BORS. THIS ARTICLE DEMONSTRATES NOT
         MERELY THE POSSIBILITY OF INTERPRET-
         ING DIATHEKE AS "COVENANT", NOR
         EVEN THE PROBABILITY OF SUCH AN IN-
         TERPRETATION, BUT RATHER THE NECES-
         SITY FOR SO UNDERSTANDING THIS
         WORD, TO DEMONSTRATE THE IMPOS-
         SIBILITY OF INTERPRETING DIATHEKE TO
         MEAN EITHER "WILL", "TESTAMENT",
         "DISPOSITION" OR "COVENANT OF
         GRANT" IN THESE TWO CASES. (ED EX-
         CERPT).
Descriptors: BIBLE (NT)- HEBREWS; BIBLE (NT)-
         GALATIANS; COVENANTS (THEOLOGY);
         GREEK LANGUAGE—TERMS—DIATHEKAI,
         DIATHEKE; JEWISH LAW; ROMAN LAW;
         WILLS

Figure 5.2: Sample DIALOG search and record from File 190, Religion Index.

charged for displaying the number of hits in a search; a higher fee is charged for displaying individual hits on-screen. Typically, bibliographical information may be displayed in the following formats.

> 1 DIALOG Accession Number
> 2 Full record except abstract
> 3 Bibliographic citation
> 4 Abstract and title
> 5 Full record
> 6 Title
> 7 Bibliographic citation and abstract
> 8 Title and indexing

Ordering Documents. DIALORDER™ allows users to order the full text of bibliographical citations on-line from more than 100 information suppliers across North America and throughout the world. "Yellowsheets" that come with the *Guide* list each information supplier and explain the scope of the service, delivery options, and charges and terms. Most information suppliers offer overnight service. Using DIALORDER is not cheap, but if no less expensive way of retrieving a necessary document is available and if time is important, the service can be invaluable. A representative DIALORDER cost is $10 for the first 10 pages of documentation and $0.20 per page thereafter, including first-class postage in North America.

SDI Service. DIALOG's SDI (Selective Dissemination of Information) Service, which is similar to NewsNet's NewsFlash® (see below), allows users to construct searches and have them run automatically in user-specified data bases each time those data bases are updated. Hits are printed in user-specified formats and mailed.

DIALMAIL. DIALMAIL℠ allows users to send and receive electronic mail to other DIALOG users and to join or create a conference or bulletin board.

DIALINDEX. DIALINDEX™ (File 411) is the on-line information directory to DIALOG data bases and contains all the indices from all the data base files. DIALINDEX allows users to scan up to 100 files at once for search terms and to see the postings (hits) and their frequencies. Actual searches, however, must be run in the appropriate data bases. DIALINDEX, then, allows users to search the indexed terms for each DIALOG file.

5.5.1.6 Selected Data Bases

DIALOG contains the world's most comprehensive set of on-line bibliographical data bases. Particular data bases that may be of interest to readers of this book include the following. (The prices listed are for hourly connect rates only and do not include telecommunication charges. Starred items ("*") are available on Knowledge Index for $24/hour. These prices were correct as of October 1987.)

> *Academic American Encyclopedia/File 180 ($45/hour)
> Bible (King James Version)/File 297 ($24/hour)
> Book Review Index/File 137 ($48/hour)
> *Books in Print/File 470 ($65/hour)
> Business Software Database™/ File 256 ($90/hour)
> Chronolog® Newsletter/File 410 ($15/hour)
> Compendex®/File 8 ($108/hour)
> *Computer Database™/File 275 ($96/hour)
> Dissertation Abstracts Online/File 35 ($72/hour)
> *ERIC (Educational Resources Information Center)/File 1
>   ($30/hour)
> Everyman's Encyclopedia/File 182 ($42/hour)
> GPO Monthly Catalog/File 66 ($35/hour)
> *GPO Publications Reference File/File 166 ($35/hour)

Information Science Abstracts/File 202 ($70/hour)
LC Marc/Files 426, 427 ($45/hour)
*Legal Resource Index™/File 150 ($90/hour)
Linguistics and Language Behavior Abstracts (LLBA)/File 36
    ($66/hour)
Magazine ASAP™/File 647 ($87/hour)
*Magazine Index™/File 47 ($84/hour)
*MENU™—The International Software Database™ (ISD)/File
    232 ($60/hour)
*Microcomputer Index™/File 233 ($45/hour)
Microcomputer Software & Hardware Guide/File 278
    ($60/hour)
MLA Bibliography/File 71 ($66/hour)
*National Newspaper Index™/File 11 1 ($84/hour)
Newsearch™/File 211 ($120/hour)
*Peterson's College Database/File 214 ($54/hour)
Philosopher's Index/File 57 ($55/hour)
PsycALERT/File 140 ($55/hour)
*PsycINFO/File 11 ($55/hour)
Religion Index/File 190 ($48/hour)
REMARC/Files 421, 422, 423, 424, 425 ($85/hour)
Social Scisearch®/File 7 ($99/hour)
Sociological Abstracts/File 37 ($60/hour)

Several of those files merit a brief explanation. We have already discussed the Academic American Encyclopedia (see above under "CompuServe"). Books in Print and Dissertation Abstracts Online are the electronic versions of their printed counterparts. *Everyman's Encyclopedia* is the on-line version of the published 12-volume set (6th ed) of the same name, which contains 50,000 records on a broad range of topics, including 13,500 biographies of famous people. Compendex® (the on-line version of the *Engineering Index*), Computer Database™, MENU™, Microcomputer Software and Hardware Guide, and the Microcomputer Index™ contain much information about hardware and software for mini and microcomputers and collectively abstract over 5,000 journals and other publications. The MLA Bibliography corresponds to the printed annual bibliography of the Modern Language Association called the *MLA International Bibliography of Books and Articles on the Modern Languages and Literatures.* Philosopher's Index, produced by the Philosophy Documentation Center at Bowling Green State University, corresponds to the printed publication of the same name and provides comprehensive coverage of U.S. journal articles and books published since 1940 and coverage of major philosophy journals published in the Western World since 1967. Over 270 journals are indexed.

Religion Index, which is produced by the American Theological Library Association (ATLA), is the on-line version of the following hardcopy indices: *Index to Religious Periodical Literature (Vols. 1–4, 12), Religion Index One (RIO), Religion Index Two (RIT), Religion Index Two: Festschriften,* and numerous selected bibliographies. The 358,000 records in the Religion Index represent periodical articles, Festschriften, conference proceedings, other collected works, and book reviews in the fields of religion, theology, biblical studies, and related areas such as anthropology, archaeology, social history, sociology, psychology, philosophy, music, and literature. Abstracts are provided for about half of the periodical articles. Over 380 journals are indexed and many more are scanned for relevant articles. Approximately 60% of the material indexed is in English, the remaining 40% is in German, French, Scandinavian, Italian, and Spanish. Over 350 multi-authored books or collections are indexed annually, and the data base is updated on a monthly basis.

5.5.2 Knowledge Index

- ## BASIC INFORMATION

Name of Service: Knowledge Index^{SM}
Name of Company: DIALOG Information Services, Inc.
Addresses: In the U.S.A.: 3460 Hillview Ave., Palo Alto, CA 94304; in Canada: % Micromedia Ltd./DIALOG, 158 Pearl St., Toronto, Ontario M5H 1L3, Canada; in the United Kingdom and Europe: % DIALOG Information Retrieval Service, P.O. Box 188, Oxford OX1 5AX, United Kingdom.; in Germany: DIALOG Information Services, Inc., Tizianweg 2, 4010 Hilden, West Germany; in Japan: Kinokuniya Company Ltd., ASK Information Retrieval Services Dept., Village 101 Bldg., 1–7 Sakuragaoka-machi, Shibuyu-ku, Tokyo, 150, Japan (KIN); in Korea: Data Communications Corporation of Korea (DACOM), The Business Office, 12th Floor, Korea Stock Exchange Bldg., 1–116 Yeoeido-Dong, Yeongdungpo-Ku, Seoul, Korea; in Australia: Insearch Ltd./DIALOG, P.O. Box K16, Haymarket NSW 20000, Australia; in Mexico: Asesores Especializados en Information y Documentation, S.C., AEID/DIALOG, 2a Cerrada de Romero de Terreros 49A, Colonia del Valle, 03100 Mexico D.F.
Business Phones: In the U.S.A.: (800) 334-2564, (415) 858-3810 (call collect in CA); in Canada: (800) 387-2689, (416) 593-5211 (in Toronto); in the United Kingdom and Europe: (0865) 730275 (Learned Information Ltd., Oxford, U.K.); in Germany: 02103-69904; in Japan: (03) 463-4391; in Korea: 783-5201, 5/783-6471; in Australia: (02) 212-2867; in Mexico: 543-7207, 543-9069
Customer Service Phones: (800) 334-2564, (415) 858-3810 (U.S.A. numbers)
Subscription Cost: $35; includes two free hours of connect time worth $48.
Literature Included with Subscription: Manual, subscription to *Knowledge Index News* (a quarterly newsletter), and a system summary card.
Manual: 110 pages, three-ring binder, indexed, additional 100+ pages of data base summaries.
Related Publications: Chapter 17 of Glossbrenner, *Communications*.
Connect Times: Mon.–Th.: 6 P.M. to 5 A.M.; Fri.: 6 P.M. to midnight; Sat: 8 A.M. to midnight; Sun.: 3 P.M. to 5 A.M. All times are local (daylight savings) times.
Hourly Rates: $24/hour flat rate for on-line searching, $12/hour for DIALMAIL^{SM} (messages, conferences, bulletin boards).
Monthly Minimum: No
Telecommunication Networks: TYMNET, Telenet, Dialnet, IN WATS
Telecommunication Surcharge: No
On-Line Storage Charges: $0.005 per page (1,024 characters) per night for messages. Conference and bulletin board host charge is $0.25 per night.
Billing Options: VISA®, MasterCard®, American Express®
Telecommunication Protocols: 300, 1,200, 2,400 baud, 8-bit ASCII, no parity, 1 stop bit (or 7 data bits, 1 start bit, 1 stop bit, 1 parity bit), answerback off, no auto-linefeed or carriage-return linefeed, asynchronous. If using telecommunication networks: even or no parity, full duplex, enable X-ON/X-OFF. If using direct dial: half duplex, disable X-ON/X-OFF.
Other: There is a charge of $0.25 per page and a per-time $7.25 service charge for obtaining full-text photocopies of documents and articles.

DIALOG's Knowledge Index^{SM} is everyman's version of its parent, DIALOG Information Services, the original, best, and largest of the encyclopedic data bases. DIALOG and Knowledge Index differ in seven ways. (1) DIALOG is available 24 hours a day during the week, but Knowledge Index can be accessed only in the evenings, except for Saturday and Sunday. (2) DIALOG costs vary from $15 to $300 per on-line hour, depending on the file,[27] but Knowledge Index charges a flat rate of $24/hour for on-line searching. (3) DIALOG charges for most of the records typed (i.e., displayed on-screen), but Knowledge Index does not. (4) DIALOG contains over 300 data bases, but Knowledge Index contains only sixty-five. (5) DIALOG sends account statements that are due on receipt, but the cost of using Knowledge Index is charged to users' credit cards. (6) DIALOG's search commands are more powerful and flexible than those used with Knowledge Index, though Knowledge Index is easier to

---

27. Very few data bases on DIALOG are as inexpensive as $15 hour. Most DIALOG files cost from $50 to $100 per on-line hour.

use than DIALOG. (7) DIALOG allows searchers to make off-line prints (using DIALOG's printer) of the bibliographical records in its data bases, and to have those prints mailed. Knowledge Index does not offer such a service, though users may order photocopies of the *full text* of articles from KI.

Knowledge Index (KI) is a command-driven system that incorporates many of the flexible search features that make DIALOG so powerful. KI supports Boolean ANDs, ORs, and NOTs, initial, medial, and terminal truncation, descriptors, free-text searches, and searching by fields. Short, medium, and long formats may be used to display the results of searches, and full-text copies of documents may be ordered on-line. KI also offers on-line help for any command, and users may request KI to display search costs and monthly costs.

Knowledge Index is a very economical way to use some of the best bibliographical data bases available. In the following list, abbreviations after the "/" mark are KI's codes for the data bases. Included in Knowledge Index's inventory of files are:

> Academic American Encyclopedia/REFR1
> Books in Print/BOOK1
> Computer Database/COMP4
> ERIC (Educational Resources Information Center)/EDUC1
> GPO Publications Reference File/GOVE1
> Legal Resource Index™/LEGA1
> Magazine Index/MAGA1
> MENU™—The International Software Database/COMP2
> Microcomputer Index/COMP3
> National Newspaper Index/NEWS2
> NEWSEARCH™/NEWS1
> Peterson's College Database/EDUC2
> Psycinfo/PSYC1,

as well as files on medicine, pharmacology, engineering, and other major fields of knowledge. When searched properly, KI's files allow users to retrieve a wealth of bibliographical and full-text information.

5.5.3 BRS Information Technologies

● *BASIC INFORMATION*

Name of Service: BRS Search Service
Name of Company: BRS Information Technologies
Address: 555 East Lancaster Ave., 4th Floor, St. Davids, PA 19087
Business Phones: (800) 468-0908, (215) 254-0233
Customer Service Phones: (800) 345-4277, (800) 553-5566 (NY)
Subscription Cost: Open Access Plan (pay as you go): $75 annually, not credited toward regular use.
Literature Included with Subscription: Subscription to BRS *Bulletin*, a bimonthly newsletter, which is also available on-line as BULL ($35/hour total connect hour cost).
Manual: *BRS/SEARCH System User's Manual*, $35, 168 pages, 3-ring binder, indexed.
Related Publications: Individual guides to each data base are available for $5 each. Also see chapter 16 in Glossbrenner, *Communications*.
Connect Times: Mon.–Sun.: 6 A.M. to 4 A.M., 365 days/year. All times are Eastern Standard Times.
Hourly Rates: Open Access Plan: $25/hour connect rate; up to $90/hour data base royalty fee, depending on data base.
Monthly Minimum: No
Telecommunication Networks: Telenet, TYMNET, DataPac (Canada), direct dial
Telecommunication Surcharge: $9/hour
On-Line Storage Charges: Not applicable
Billing Options: VISA®, MasterCard®, American Express®, direct bill
Telecommunication Protocols: 300, 1,200, 2,400 baud, 8-bit ASCII, no parity, 1 stop bit, full or half duplex (or 7 data bits, 1 stop bit, even parity, full or half duplex), asynchronous
Other: No surcharge for 1,200 and 2,400 baud; command- or menu-driven.

5.5.3.1 Introduction

BRS Information Technologies (BRS), which was founded in 1976, is similar to DIALOG, though with "only" 125 data bases BRS is less than half DIALOG's size. Unlike DIALOG, BRS's Search Service can be command-driven or menu-driven. Also unlike DIALOG, which has two cost components (an hourly data base fee and a telecommunication fee), BRS has three components to its cost structure: (1) a BRS hourly connect rate, (2) a telecommunication rate, and (3) data base royalty fees. Thus though BRS data base fees are lower than DIALOG's, by charging an hourly connect rate, BRS effectively increases the cost per hour of using each data base. For example, using an Open Access account to search a data base that costs $90 per hour actually would cost users $115 per hour, when BRS's connect rates ($25/hour) are added in, as well as an additional $9 per hour for telecommunication surcharges, thus increasing the price to $124 per hour. Like DIALOG, BRS's search logic is complex, and attending a training seminar is recommended (full-day: $95, half-day: $55).

5.5.3.2 Search Logic

Like DIALOG, BRS is a highly interactive system that supports free-text searches and searching with descriptors. BRS offers full support of the three major Boolean operators, which may be mixed and nested in the same search construction. Multiple terms may be searched for. Initial and terminal truncation are supported, and searches may be restricted by proximity and range.

5.5.3.3 Other Information

Like DIALOG, BRS allows users to print records on-line and have them mailed. And like DIALOG, BRS has a Selective Dissemination of Information feature. A BRS feature called CROSS is similar to DIALOG's DIALINDEX. And like DIALOG, BRS users may order the full text of articles and dissertations while on-line, though currently BRS has only one vendor who provides this service (University Microfilms of Ann Arbor, Michigan).

5.5.3.4 Selected Data Bases

Particular data bases that may be of interest to readers of this book include the following. (The prices listed are for total connect hourly rates—connect time + data base royalties—and do not include telecommunication charges. Starred items ("*") are available on BRS After Dark for the second hourly price listed in parentheses. Abbreviations after the "/" sign are the BRS codes for the files. BRS After Dark rates include connect time, telecommunications, and data base royalties. All prices were current as of October 1987.)

*Academic American Encyclopedia/AAED ($45/hour, $14/hour)
*Arts and Humanities Search/AHCI ($42.50/hour, $25.50/hour)
Associations' Publications in Print/APIP ($65/hour)
*Books in Print/BBIP ($65/hour, $16/hour)
Booksinfo/BOOK ($40/hour)
Compendex/COMP ($80/hour)

*Dissertation Abstracts Online/DISS ($59/hour, $18/hour)
*Educational Resources Information Center/ERIC ($25/hour, $8/hour)
*Educational Testing Service's Test Collection/ETST ($50/hour, $20/hour)
*Exceptional Child Education Resources/ECER ($35/hour, $13/hour)
*Family Resources/NCFR ($50/hour, $23/hour)
*Knowledge Industry Publications Database/KIPD ($50/hour, $17/hour)
*Language and Language Behavior Abstracts/LLBA ($50/hour, $22/hour)
*Legal Resource Index™/LAWS ($92.50/hour, $22/hour)
*Magazine Index/MAGS ($88/hour, $18/hour)
*National College Databank™/PETE ($45/hour, $18/hour)
*National Newspaper Index/NOOZ ($88/hour, $18/hour)
*Online Microcomputer Software Guide and Directory/SOFT ($65/hour, $22/hour)
*PyscINFO/PSYC ($40, $16.30/hour)
*Religion Index/RELI ($40/hour, $15/hour)
*Resources in Computer Education/RICE ($35/hour, $13/hour)
*Social Scisearch/SSCI ($50, $33/hour)
*Social Scisearch—Backfile/SSCB ($85, $33/hour)
*Sociological Abstracts/SOCA ($50/hour, $32/hour)

5.5.4 BRS After Dark

- *BASIC INFORMATION*

Name of Service: BRS After Dark™
Name of Company: BRS Information Technologies
Address: 555 East Lancaster Ave., 4th Floor, St. Davids, PA 19807
Business Phones: (800) 468-0908, (215) 254-0233
Customer Service Phones: (800) 345-4277, (800) 553-5566 (NY)
Subscription Cost: $75, includes no free time.
Literature Included with Subscription: Manual
Manual: 92 pages, three-ring binder, not indexed.
Related Publications: Chapter 17 in Glossbrenner, *Communications*.
Connect Times: Mon.–Fri.: 6 P.M. to 4 A.M.; Sat.: 6 A.M. to 4 A.M.; Sun.: 6 A.M. to 2 P.M. and 7 P.M. to 4 A.M. All times are Eastern Standard Times.
Hourly Rates: $8/hour to $48/hour, depending on data base.
Monthly Minimum: $12/month; $144/year
Telecommunication Networks: Telenet, TYMNET, DataPac (Canada)
Telecommunication Surcharge: None within U.S.A.; $6/hour in Canada
On-Line Storage Charges: Not applicable
Billing Options: VISA®, MasterCard®, American Express®
Telecommunication Protocols: 300, 1,200, 2,400 baud, 8-bit ASCII, no parity, 1 stop bit, full or half duplex (or 7 data bits, 1 stop bit, even parity, full or half duplex), asynchronous
Other: Some data bases add a $0.10 per citation surcharge. BRS has added a new, related service, BRS/BRKTHRU™ (see Glossbrenner, *Communications*, 425–26).

Like Knowledge Index, BRS After Dark™ is the child of a larger on-line bibliographical data base service—BRS Information Technologies—and like Knowledge Index, BRS After Dark is a diminutive copy of its progenitor. Currently, BRS After Dark offers over seventy-five data bases in five areas: (1) science and medicine, (2) business and finance, (3) reference, (4) education, and (5) social science and the humanities.

Many of BRS After Dark's files are identical with those offered on Knowledge Index, and often After Dark's on-line search fees are lower than KI's. But hourly rates are not the only part of the financial equation in on-line searching. It costs $144 a year in monthly fees just to belong to BRS After Dark, but Knowledge Index has no monthly minimum. There are other significant similarities and differences between the two systems. Unlike KI, After Dark is a menu-driven system, though experienced users can stack several commands on one line and thus bypass multiple menus. Like KI, After Dark supports Boolean ANDs, ORs, and NOTs and truncation, and allows users to search with descriptors, to perform free-text searches, to restrict searches by fields, and to display results in three different formats (short, medium, and long). Unlike KI, After Dark does not allow users to order copies of documents on-line, and After Dark will not display search costs or monthly costs. After Dark's ability to search by fields is more refined than KI's because After Dark allows searches to be restricted by date, author, language, title, and name-of-publication fields, whereas in most KI data bases, only the author and name-of-journal fields can be specified. After Dark includes on-line help.

The following BRS After Dark files may be of interest to readers of this book. (Abbreviations after the "/" sign are the After Dark codes for the files. These files are listed under several main headings in BRS—Reference Databases, Education Databases, and Social Science and Humanities Databases. All prices were current as of October 1987.)

Academic American Encyclopedia/AAED ($14/hour)
Arts and Humanities Search/AHCI ($25.50/hour)
Books in Print/BBIP ($16/hour)
Dissertation Abstracts/DISS ($18/hour)
Educational Resources Information Center/ERIC ($8/hour)
Educational Testing Service's Test Collection/TESF ($18/hour)
Exceptional Child Education Resources/ECER ($13/hour)
Family Resources/NCFR ($33/hour)
Knowledge Industry Publications Database/KIPD ($17/hour)
Language and Language Behavior Abstracts/LLBA ($22/hour)
Legal Resource Index™/LAWS ($22/hour)
Magazine Index/MAGS ($18/hour)
National College Databank™/PETE ($18/hour)
National Newspaper Index/NOOZ ($18/hour)
Online Microcomputer Software Guide and Directory/SOFT
    ($22/hour)
PyscINFO/PSYC ($16.30/hour)
Religion Index ($15/hour)
Resources in Computer Education/RICE ($13/hour)
Social Scisearch/SSCI ($33/hour)
Social Scisearch—Backfile/SSCB ($33/hour)
Sociological Abstracts/SOCA ($22/hour)

5.6 Bibliographical Data Base Resources

The following publications provide information about on-line data bases and front-end programs. Addresses and phones numbers are those of the circulation/subscription offices.

Database®
Bimonthly, journal, $78/year (organization), $39/year (in-
     dividual).
% Online, Inc.
11 Tannery Lane
Weston, CT 06883
(203) 227-8466

Database Directory
Book, $120.
% Knowledge Industry Publications, Inc.
701 Winchester Ave.
White Plains, NY 10604
(914) 328-9157

The Data Base Informer
Monthly, newsletter, $78/year.
% *Information USA*
Computer Data Service
12400 Beall Mt. Road
Potomac, MD 20854
(301) 983-8220

Database Update
Monthly, newsletter, $197/year.
% 10076 Boca Raton Blvd.
Boca Raton, FL 33433
(800) 662-2444

Datapro Directory of On-Line Services
Book (two 3-ring binders, updated monthly), $479/year.
% Datapro Research Corporation
1805 Underwood Blvd.
Delran, NJ 08075
(609) 764-0100, (800) 257-9406

Directory of Online Databases
Quarterly, $95.
% Cuadra/Elsevier
52 Vanderbilt Ave.
New York, NY 10017
(212) 916-1180

Document Retrieval. Sources and Services. 3d ed (1985)
Edited by Katherine T. Alvord
Book, $60.
% The Information Store
140 Second St.
San Francisco, CA 94105
(415) 543-4636

EDUCOM Networking
Quarterly, newsletter, free.
BITNET Communications
P.O. Box 364
Princeton, NJ 08540
(609) 734-1915

EM World
Monthly, newsletter, $149/year.
% 8701 Georgia Ave., Suite 800
Silver Spring, MD 20910

Encyclopedia of Information Systems and Services
% Gale Research Company
Book Tower
1249 Washington Blvd.
Detroit, MI 48226

Guide to Online Databases
Book, $69.
% Newsletter Management
10076 Boca Entrada Blvd.
Boca Raton, FL 33433
(305) 483-2600

Inc Magazine's Databasics: Your Guide to Online Business In-
formation
Book, $24.95 (hardback), $16.95 (paperback).
Doran Howitt and Marvin I. Weinberger
% Garland Publishing, Inc.
136 Madison Ave.
New York, NY 10016
(212) 686-7492

Information Sources
The Annual Directory of the Information Industry Association
(IIA)
% 316 Pennsylvania Ave., SE, Suite 400
Washington, DC 20003
(202) 544-1969

Information Today
Monthly, tabloid, $18/year.
% Learned Information, Inc.
143 Old Marlton Pike
Medford, NJ 08055
(609) 654-6266

Micro Communications
Magazine, free to information professionals; $22/year other-
wise.
% Miller Freeman Publications
500 Howard St.
San Francisco, CA 94105

Modem Notes
Monthly, newsletter, $36/year.
% Cache Data Products, Inc.
2921 South Brentwood Blvd.
St. Louis, MO 63144

North American Online Directory
Book, $75.
% R. R. Bowker Company
P.O. Box 1807
Ann Arbor, MI 48106
(800) 521-8110

OMNI Online Database Directory—1986
Edited by Owen Davies and Mike Edelhart
Book, $14.95.
% Collier Books
MacMillan Publishing Co.
866 Third Avenue
New York, NY 10222
(212) 702-2000

ONLINE®
Bimonthly, journal, $78/year (organization), $39/year (in-
    dividual).
% Online, Inc.
11 Tannery Lane
Weston, CT 06883
(203) 227-8466

VideoPrint
Bimonthly, newsletter, $270/year.
% International Resource Development, Inc.
6 Prowitt St.
Norwalk, CT 06855
(203) 866-7800

VIEWTEXT
Monthly, newsletter, $197/year.
% Phillips Publishing, Inc.
7315 Wisconsin Ave.
Bethesda, MD 20814
(301) 986-0666, (800) 227-1617

5.7 Data Base "Front-End" Programs

In this section we will briefly examine several "front-end" programs. *Front-end* programs are a special type of menu-driven software designed to make using complex data bases like DIALOG and BRS easy for novices and untrained users and to allow experienced users and information professionals to search multiple on-line services without having to learn several command languages. These sophisticated communication programs are also known as *gateway*, or *search-assistance* programs,[28] and they include built-in searching capabilities. They allow users to formulate search constructions while off-line, automatically dial a selected data base, log on, run searches, and save the results to memory or disk. Because they are menu-driven, front-end programs spare users from learning complex sets of commands, data base structures, and so forth. Nevertheless, users must learn how to use wild-cards, truncation, and other search techniques. Although front-end programs greatly simplify on-line searching, they do not eliminate the need to learn basic search techniques. And although gateway software can assist novice and occasional data base users, as well as seasoned professionals, nothing can fully replace formal training, learning a system's commands, and becoming familiar with the data bases that will be searched.

Generally speaking, front-end programs offer ease of use by sacrificing power and flexibility. They provide a friendly, menu-driven interface by eliminating interactive, command-driven searching.

---

28. Gateway software is, of course, different from gateway services.

In the information included about each product, **Auto-Dial & Logon** means that a program can automatically call and log on to an on-line system. **Off-Line Query Preparation** means that a program allows users to formulate searches off-line and have them run when on-line. **Dumb Communications Capability** means that a program is able to function as an ordinary communications program, allowing users to connect to various on-line sources. **Select Data Base** means that a program can automatically select a user-specified data base. Tom Badgett "Search Software: Directory Assistance," *PC Magazine* (May 12, 1987): 263–73 provides helpful, comparative reviews of Pro-Search, Sci-Mate Searcher, and the Search Helper.

5.7.1 Pro-Search

● *BASIC PRODUCT INFORMATION*

Name of Program: Pro-Search™
Name of Company: Personal Bibliographic Software
Address: P.O. Box 4250, Ann Arbor, MI 48106
Business Phone: (313) 996-1580
Customer Service Phone: (313) 996-1580
Price: $495
Version Tested: IBM, full program, version 1.03
Runs On: IBM PCs and compatibles, TI
Modem: Any modem
Baud Rates: 300, 1,200, 2,400
Memory Requirements: 256K
Operating System: DOS 2.0 or later
Disk Drive Requirements: 2
Supports Color Monitors: Yes
Uses Sound: No
Number of Disks: 6 (including 4 category disks, a system disk, and a backup system disk)
Produces ASCII Output Files: Yes
On-Line Service(s) Supported: DIALOG, BRS
Auto-Dial & Logon: Yes
Off-Line Query Preparation: Yes
Downloading: Yes
Dumb Communications Capability: No
Select Data Base: Yes
Prepare Search Statement: Yes
Search String Limitations: Those of DIALOG, BRS
Product Includes: Disks, manual, keyboard overlay for IBM function keys
Manual: 200 pages, typeset, 3-ring binder, slip case, indexed
Demo Disk Available: Yes, $19.95. Includes manual and program; program will operate for three hours on-line.
Copy Protected: No
Hard Disk Compatible: Yes
User Interface: Menu-driven
On-Line Help: Yes
Tutorial: Yes
Warranty: 90 days, media only; $25 to replace damaged system disk
Update Policy: $100 to upgrade from In-Search to Pro-Search; $25 to upgrade from one version of Pro-Search to another.
Other: Pro-Search comes with a backup system disk.

Pro-Search™ is a professional search program that works with BRS and DIALOG data bases. Help screens are well done and useful, and the program contains extensive explanations of commands, DIALOG and BRS search options, and related information. Pro-Search is flexible, powerful, and thorough.

Pro-Search has divided all the DIALOG and BRS data bases into four main categories: (1) business, government, news, (2) engineering, mathematics, physical sciences, (3) arts, education, social sciences, and (4) biology and medicine. Each of Pro-Search's four "category disks" contains all the pertinent information about the data bases in one of those four categories. Once users have selected a particular data base (see below), the key facts about that data base may be accessed by using the F6, DATA SHEET, key. Each data sheet contains the following information: (1) file description, (2) subject coverage, (3) sources used to construct the data base, (4) file data, (5) the origin of the data base, (6) the file format—displayed as a sample record, (7) what the basic index includes, and (8) custom format options. Because new data bases are constantly added to DIALOG and BRS, and because data base prices and formats are subject to change, Pro-Search's data base information must be updated periodically for an additional fee.

The user interface employs the metaphor of bibliographical cards to simplify choosing data bases. After choosing one of the four data base categories, which are displayed in a window, the cursor moves to a window that displays the subject areas covered by the files in the selected category. After selecting a subject area, the files for that subject are displayed in a third window as overlapping bibliographical cards. (Those three windows are open simultaneously and are interactive.) The title of the first card (i.e., data base) is highlighted, and users may move backward and forward through cards with the cursor keys. The highlighted card is always the foremost card and includes a brief description of the file, its size (i.e., number of records), when it was created, how frequently it is updated, the hourly on-line rate, and the cost per off-line print. Files are selected with Return.

After a file has been selected, Pro-Search displays a "Search Keywords and Phrases" screen, which is used for entering search terms. A knowledge of DIALOG or BRS search strategy is necessary to operate the program at this point, but Pro-Search's excellent tutorials, explanations, and examples make it easy to learn what to do. After formulating a search, hitting the PHONE key (F5) causes the program to dial a previously specified network number, log on to DIALOG or BRS, attach to the user-specified data base, and run the search construction. Hits are displayed as numbered sets of search terms, and users have the option of searching interactively, of displaying records, of capturing records to memory, disk, or printer, of ordering the full text of documents, and so forth.

5.7.2 Sci-Mate

- *BASIC PRODUCT INFORMATION*

Name of Program: Sci-Mate® Searcher
Name of Company: ISI®—Institute for Scientific Information®
Addresses: In the U.S.A.: 3501 Market Street, Philadelphia, PA 19104; in Europe and the United Kingdom: ISI, 132 High Street, Uxbridge, Middlesex UB8 1DP, United Kingdom
Business Phones: In the U.S.A.: (800) 523-4092, (215) 386-0100; in Europe and the United Kingdom: 44-895-70016
Customer Service Phones: (800) 523-4092, (215) 386-0100 (U.S.A. numbers)
Price: $150
Version Tested: 2.0
Runs On: IBM PCs and compatibles, Z-80 microcomputer running CP/M-80
Modem: Any modem
Baud Rates: 300, 1,200, 2,400
Memory Requirements: 256K
Operating System: DOS or CP/M-80
Disk Drive Requirements: 2
Supports Color Monitors: Yes
Uses Sound: No

Number of Disks: 1
Produces ASCII Output Files: Yes
On-Line Service(s) Supported: BRS, DIALOG, NLM,[29] ORBIT, QUESTEL
Auto-Dial & Logon: Yes
Off-Line Query Preparation: Yes
Downloading: Yes
Dumb Communications Capability: Yes
Select Data Base: No
Prepare Search Statement: Yes
Search String Limitations: Those of on-line system.
Product Includes: Disk, manual
Manual: 234 pages, typeset, tabbed, 3-ring binder, indexed
Demo Disk Available: Not known
Copy Protected: No
Hard Disk Compatible: Yes
User Interface: Menu-driven
On-Line Help: Yes
Tutorial: Yes
Warranty: 60 days, media only
Update Policy: ISI may update products from time to time, but user must purchase update.
Other: ISI also markets two related programs: The Manager ($295, for information management) and The Editor ($195, for bibliographic formatting)

The Sci-Mate® System consists of three menu-driven programs: the Searcher, the Manager, and the Editor. The Searcher allows users to formulate and execute searches on hundreds of data bases on several large on-line services and to download results. The Manager, which is like a data base management system, allows users to store, organize, retrieve, and manipulate information that has been downloaded from data bases with the Searcher, as well as to add text to that material. The Manager can sort up to 32,767 records using six sorting keys for each of six fields. The Editor, which is an auxiliary tool for word processing, helps users prepare bibliographies in different formats and format bibliographical entries that have been downloaded with the Searcher.

This is a complex, elaborate, extremely flexible system designed for professional searchers. Numerous menu options on the INSTALL program allow Sci-Mate to be customized in a variety of ways that specify modems, communication ports, keyboard and disk drive assignments, video characteristics, word processing controls, and more. The installation manual alone is 124 pages long! The Searcher is fully menu-driven, though it does not use the visual metaphor of bibliographical cards, as Pro-Search does. The Searcher's menus are visually simple but very thorough. Pro-Search has more polish and "pizazz," is easier to use, and seems to rewrite the screen faster than Sci-Mate, though Sci-Mate and its three inter-related modules have more depth and flexibility.[30]

The Searcher manual contains in-depth tutorials for BRS, DIALOG, NBLM, ORBIT, and QUESTEL.[31] Like Pro-Search, the Searcher allows users to formulate searches off-line, which are then run automatically after the Searcher has called and logged on to the specified data base. Unlike Pro-Search, the Searcher uses "generic" search terms that are automatically translated into those that are appropriate for the selected on-line service, a feature that makes it easy for searchers to use several on-line systems without having to learn separate command languages, syntax, and search

---

29. National Library of Medicine.

30. Pro-Search works with Pro-Cite (see chapter 2) so that results of searches may automatically be downloaded into Pro-Cite in user-specified formats, though the older version of Pro-Search that I have does not support that function.

31. QUESTEL is a French on-line service that is marketed through Télésystèmes Questel, Départment Ingénierie de l'Information, 83–85 Boulevard Vincent Auriol, F-75013 Paris, France, telephone: 331-582-6464.

strategies. Once connected to an on-line system, the Searcher may be used in menu-or command-driven modes. When menu-driven, the Searcher greatly simplifies searching, but by breaking down every search decision into its elementary parts, the program tends to fragment the process of formulating searches. On the one hand, the Searcher's menu-driven mode is designed so that users do not need to know much, if anything, about a particular system's search vocabulary and syntax. On the other hand, Pro-Search teaches users the fundamental search vocabulary and syntax of DIALOG and BRS. Therefore (in my opinion), Pro-Search's approach to searching results in more knowledgeable searches, in a higher level of interaction between searcher and system, and in faster searches (since users do not have to make every decision by using menus).

5.7.3 Searchware

• *BASIC PRODUCT INFORMATION*

Name of Program: Searchware
Name of Company: Searchware, Inc.
Address: 22458 Ventura Blvd., Suite E, Woodland Hills, CA 91364
Business Phone: (818) 992-4325
Customer Service Phone: (818) 992-4325
Price: $290 for first disk, $100 for each additional disk
Version Tested: IBM
Runs On: IBM PCs and compatibles Apple II series
Modem: Any modem
Baud Rates: 300, 1,200, 2,400
Memory Requirements: 128K
Operating System: DOS
Disk Drive Requirements: 1
Supports Color Monitors: Yes
Uses Sound: Yes
Number of Disks: Up to 54
Produces ASCII Output Files: Yes
On-Line Service(s) Supported: DIALOG
Auto-Dial & Logon: Yes
Off-Line Query Preparation: Yes
Downloading: Yes
Dumb Communications Capability: No
Select Data Base: Yes
Prepare Search Statement: Yes
Search String Limitations: Those of DIALOG.
Product Includes: Disk(s) and manual
Manual: 103 pages, photocopied, tabbed, 3-ring binder, not indexed
Demo Disk Available: Yes, $15
Copy Protected: No
Hard Disk Compatible: Yes
User Interface: Menu-driven
On-Line Help: No
Tutorial: Yes
Warranty: None specified
Update Policy: None specified
Other: None

Searchware's approach to searching is subject-specific. Fifty-four different programs allow users to search specific subject areas in the DIALOG data bases. Users must purchase separate disks for each subject area they wish to search. Like Pro-Search and the Searcher, Searchware allows users to formulate searches off-line and run them when on-line. Searchware will automatically dial, log on, run a search, save the results, log off, and break the connection. Unlike Pro-Search and the Searcher, Searchware allow users to search only those DIALOG data bases and subject areas that are included on the Searchware subject disks.

Searchware is menu-driven and allows users to formulate searches in three ways. Level I allows novice searchers to construct searches without knowing anything about DIALOG. Users enter key terms and follow menu prompts, and Searchware supplies the search commands and syntax. Level II supports an extended set of search commands, such as EXPAND, SELECT, SELECT STEPS, COMBINE, TYPE, that are explained in chapter 10 of the manual (which users must read and understand before attempting to formulate a Level II search), and users provide the search syntax. A Level III search allows users to construct and implement searches in a command-driven mode, with no help from Searchware. As the manual correctly notes, this type of search offers the most flexibility but requires users to master DIALOG commands and syntax, which are briefly explained and illustrated in chapter 10 of Searchware's manual. The manual also contains practice problems and descriptions of the data bases in the subject areas Searchware supports.

The Searchware company offers a gateway service to DIALOG. Billing is on a monthly basis, and there is no monthly minimum.

Searchware is easier to use than Pro-Search and the Searcher. Because users must purchase separate disks for each subject area, however, using Searchware to search several subjects can be expensive. Searchware is best suited for users who plan to restrict their searches to a few subject areas.

5.7.4 Dialoglink

- *BASIC PRODUCT INFORMATION*

Name of Program: Dialoglink™
Name of Company: DIALOG Information Retrieval Service
Addresses: In the U.S.A.: 3460 Hillview Ave., Palo Alto, CA 94304; in Canada: % Micromedia Ltd./DIALOG, 158 Pearl St., Toronto, Ontario M5H 1L3, Canada; in the United Kingdom and Europe: % DIALOG Information Retrieval Service, P.O. Box 188, Oxford OX1 5AX, United Kingdom.; in Germany: DIALOG Information Services, Inc., Tizianweg 2, 4010 Hilden, West Germany; in Japan: Kinokuniya Company Ltd., ASK Information Retrieval Services Dept., Village 101 Bldg., 1–7 Sakuragaoka-machi, Shibuyu-ku, Tokyo, 150, Japan (KIN); in Korea: Data Communications Corporation of Korea (DACOM), The Business Office, 12th Floor, Korea Stock Exchange Bldg., 1–116 Yeoeido-Dong, Yeongdungpo-Ku, Seoul, Korea; in Australia: Insearch Ltd./DIALOG, P.O. Box K16, Haymarket NSW 20000, Australia; in Mexico: Asesores Especializados en Information y Documentation, S.C., AEID/DIALOG, 2a Cerrada de Romero de Terreros 49A, Colonia del Valle, 03100 Mexico D.F.
Business Phones: In the U.S.A.: (800) 334-2564, (415) 858-3810 (call collect in CA); in Canada: (800) 387-2689, (416) 593-5211 (in Toronto); in the United Kingdom and Europe: (0865) 730275 (Learned Information Ltd., Oxford, U.K.); in Germany: 02103-69904; in Japan: (03) 463-4391; in Korea: 783-5201, 5/783-6471; in Australia: (02) 212-2867; in Mexico: 543-7207, 543-9069
Customer Service Phones: (800) 334-2564, (415) 858-3810 (U.S.A. numbers)
Price: $149 (Communications Manager and Account Manager), $125 (Communications Manager), $45 (Account Manager)
Version Tested: 1.1
Runs On: IBM PCs and compatibles
Modem: Hayes Smartmodem 300, 1,200, 1,200B, or 2,400 and 10 other modems; any acoustic modem
Baud Rates: 300, 1,200, 2,400
Memory Requirements: 256K
Operating System: DOS 2.0 or greater
Disk Drive Requirements: 2
Supports Color Monitors: Yes
Uses Sound: No
Number of Disks: 2
Produces ASCII Output Files: Yes
On-Line Service(s) Supported: DIALOG, Knowledge Index

Auto-Dial & Logon: Yes
Off-Line Query Preparation: Yes
Downloading: Yes
Dumb Communications Capability: Yes
Select Data Base: Yes
Prepare Search Statement: Yes
Search String Limitations: Those of DIALOG and Knowledge Index.
Product Includes: Disks and manual
Manual: 93 pages, printed, 3-ring binder, indexed
Demo Disk Available: Yes, $15. Includes Communications Manager, Account Manager and 2 hours on the system, for which users pay prevailing rates.
Copy Protected: No
Hard Disk Compatible: Yes
User Interface: Menu-driven
On-Line Help: Yes
Tutorial: Yes
Warranty: 30 days, media and program
Update Policy: Not known
Other: None

The Dialog*link* System is a feature-loaded front-end program from DIALOG Information Retrieval Service for searching DIALOG data bases. Dialog*link* consists of two main programs: the Communications Manager and the Account Manager. The Communications Manager allows searches to be prepared off-line, automatically dials selected telecommunications networks, logs on to specified DIALOG services (e.g., DIALOG, DIALMAIL℠, Knowledge Index), and runs the search construction. Like other gateway programs, Dialog*link* is menu-driven and allows users to download search results to disk or printer. Context-sensitive help screens are available in all program modes. Unlike some front-end programs, Dialog*link* requires users to know DIALOG commands and syntax.

IBM function keys may be used as macro keys. Up to forty characters may be bound to each key. Macros may be sent to DIALOG when on-line or to a type-ahead buffer while off-line. Dialog*link* supports search constructions of up to 250 80-character lines (i.e., 20,000 characters).

The Account Manager enables users to track DIALOG on-line costs and can generate reports that specify usage and cost by data base, searcher, charge code, and client name for each session or on a daily or monthly basis.

5.7.5 PC/NET-LINK

- *BASIC PRODUCT INFORMATION*

Name of Program: PC/NET-LINK™
Name of Company: Sterling Federal Systems, Inc.
Address: 6011 Executive Blvd., Rockville, MD 20852
Business Phones: (800) 638-6595, (301) 770-3000
Customer Service Phone: (800) 638-6595
Price: $500 (with Telios™—see below), $400 (without Telios)
Version Tested: Not tested
Runs On: IBM PCs and compatibles
Modem: Hayes Smartmodem or compatibles
Baud Rates: 300, 1,200, 2,400
Memory Requirements: 128K
Operating System: DOS 2.0 or greater
Disk Drive Requirements: 1 floppy and 1 hard disk
Supports Color Monitors: Yes
Uses Sound: No
Number of Disks: Not known

Produces ASCII Output Files: Yes
On-Line Service(s) Supported: BRS, DIALOG, DJN/R, LEXIS/NEXIS, Net-Search, NewsNet, NLM, OCLC, ORBIT, QUESTEL, RLIN, WESTLAW
Auto-Dial & Logon: Yes
Off-Line Query Preparation: Yes
Downloading: Yes
Dumb Communications Capability: Yes
Select Data Base: Yes
Prepare Search Statement: No
Search String Limitations: Those of on-line system.
Product Includes: Disks and manual
Manual: Not able to see.
Demo Disk Available: No, but an on-line remote demo is available to interested parties. For more information, contact the company at the address and telephone number above.
Copy Protected: Yes
Hard Disk Compatible: Yes
User Interface: Menu-driven
On-Line Help: Yes
Tutorial: Yes
Warranty: Not known
Update Policy: User maintainable
Other: The program and data files require 1 megabyte of disk space. PC/NET-LINK works only with Telios, a communication program. The PC/NET-LINK user manual may be purchased for $30.

Like the Searcher, this powerful, menu-driven program is designed for information professionals and experienced users of on-line data bases. Although PC/NET-LINK™ supports more on-line services than any other front-end system, it does not help users prepare search constructions. Users must understand the search vocabulary and syntax of the systems they intend to search. Help screens, however, provide information about each system's basic commands. PC/NET-LINK automatically logs on to data bases. The program may be customized by editing data base descriptions, menus, menu options, search commands, and so forth. No other gateway program allows that type of user customization.

PC/NET-LINK is programmed in dBase II and supports multiple passwords. Multiple logon procedures for various data bases can be stored under each password. Thus in a networked environment, multiple user accounts could each be passworded. Like other gateway programs, PC/NET-LINK allows searches to be formulated off-line. The program will automatically dial a specified service, log on, run the search construction, save the results, log off, and break the connection.

PC/NET-LINK works with Telios, a powerful communication program, which may be used in a stand-alone mode.

5.7.6 Searchmaster

- *BASIC PRODUCT INFORMATION*

Name of Program: Searchmaster
Name of Company: SDC Information Services
Address: 2500 Colorado Ave., Santa Monica, CA 90406
Business Phone: (213) 453-6194
Customer Service Phone: (213) 453-6194
Price: $229
Version Tested: Not tested
Runs On: IBM PCs and compatibles
Modem: Hayes Smartmodem or compatible
Baud Rates: 300, 1,200, 2,400
Memory Requirements: 256K
Operating System: DOS

Disk Drive Requirements: 1
Supports Color Monitors: Yes
Uses Sound: No
Number of Disks: 1
Produces ASCII Output Files: Yes
On-Line Service(s) Supported: BRS, DIALOG, NLM, ORBIT
Auto-Dial & Logon: Yes
Off-Line Query Preparation: Yes
Downloading: Yes
Dumb Communications Capability: No
Select Data Base: No
Prepare Search Statement: Yes
Search String Limitations: Those of on-line system.
Product Includes: Disk(s) and manual
Manual: Not able to see.
Demo Disk Available: No
Copy Protected: No
Hard Disk Compatible: Yes
User Interface: Menu-driven
On-Line Help: Yes
Tutorial: No
Warranty: No
Update Policy: $25
Other: None

Like the Searcher and PC/NET-LINK, Searchmaster is designed for experienced searchers. This program does not assist users in creating search constructions or in locating data bases.

5.7.7 Conclusion

Readers with strong interests in on-line information retrieval should attend a training session for the service they plan to use, study the appropriate user manuals, and run actual searches in practice files or otherwise. The training, knowledge, and experience gained by doing that will prove invaluable in constructing accurate, effective searches. Although gateway programs are useful and help shield users from needing to master a system's search vocabulary and syntax, there is no substitute for knowing how a system works. Searching an on-line system interactively in a command-driven mode is far more interesting and satisfying that using a menu-driven front-end program to prepare searches off-line that the program automatically executes.

5.8 Electronic News

In this section we will look at NewsNet, one of several on-line services that specialize in news. Electronic news services allow their members to read hundreds of specialized newsletters and major newspapers, to receive wire service information, and to create special files that automatically "clip" news items that fall into user-specified categories.

5.8.1 NewsNet

● *BASIC INFORMATION*

Name of Service: NewsNet
Name of Company: NewsNet, Inc.

Address: 945 Haverford Road, Bryn Mawr, PA 19010
Business Phones: (800) 345-1301, (215) 527-8030
Customer Service Phones: (800) 345-1301, (215) 527-8030
Subscription Cost: $120/year, $75/6 months, $15/month. 12 and 6 month subscription rates include $60 free connect time. Monthly subscriptions include $30 free connect time.
Literature Included with Subscription: Two-part pocket guide, subscription to *The NewsNet Action Letter* (a monthly newsletter), mini-guide, and quick reference card.
Manual: 144 pages, indexed
Related Publications: Chapter 12 in Glossbrenner, *Communications.*
Connect Times: 24 hour/day, 365 days/year
Hourly Rates: $60/hour to $252/hour, depending on data base.
Monthly Minimum: $15/month; $120/year
Telecommunication Networks: TYMNET, Telenet, direct-dial
Telecommunication Surcharge: No
On-Line Storage Charges: No
Billing Options: VISA®, MasterCard®, American Express®, CHECKFREE® (electronic funds withdrawal).
Telecommunication Protocols: 300, 1,200, 2,400 baud, 7-bit ASCII, even parity, 1 or 2 stop bits, full duplex, enable X-ON/X-OFF, asynchronous.
Other: The $60/hour basic rate ($18/hour after 8 P.M.) for 300 and 1,200 baud covers use of all system features except reading articles. When reading articles, the $60/hour rate is dropped and users are charged the read rate of the article being read. These rates vary at 300 and 1,200 baud from $60/hour to $252/hour depending on the data base.

NewsNet is to on-line news what DJN/R is to on-line financial information: fast, accurate, comprehensive, and useful. NewsNet offers instant on-line access to full-text versions of over 330 newsletters and news services that are divided into thirty-eight categories that cover everything from aerospace to taxation. NewsNet is menu-driven and offers on-line help. Users can search for keywords or phrases, scan headlines, and read the full text of an article or newsletter. The AND, OR, and NOT operators are supported and may be mixed in the same search construction. Exact-phrase and proximity searches are supported, as are searches using parentheses (though not nested parentheses) and initial, medial, and terminal truncation. Single searches may cover up to three specific services (data bases), up to three of the thirty-eight industry groups, or up to a combination of three services and groups. Search fields may be narrowed by using the EXCLUDE delimiter to exclude services and groups. Specifying a date range also narrows searches.

NewsNet allows users to create special NewsFlash™ accounts. A NewsFlash account allows users to formulate search constructions that are automatically run each time user-specified data bases are updated. Users are automatically notified of hits, and there is no charge for storing hits on-line, though each hit placed in a NewsFlash file costs $0.50. NewsFlash, then, functions as an automated news clipping service. Over 2,000 news items are added to NewsNet each day.

NewsNet's Social Sciences category (SS) should interest readers of this book. SS contains the full-text versions of the following newsletters and services. (The prices listed below are for the nonvalidated read rates—the rates for users who do not subscribe to the printed versions of the newsletters—and the abbreviations after the "/" sign are NewsNet's codes for the newsletters. All prices were correct as of October 1987.)

ChurchNews International/SS05 ($108/hour)
RNS Daily News Reports/SS07 ($132/hour)
United Methodist Information/SS06 ($60/hour)
Lutheran News Service/SS11 ($60/hour)

ChurchNews International (which is also available on DELPHI) monitors religion worldwide, and includes news, background articles, alerts, features, and information about resources. It covers all major denominations. *RNS Daily News Reports* provides comprehensive coverage of significant religious developments in the United States and abroad, and of the interaction of religion and society. United Methodist Information offers news, human interest features, and a United Methodist Church resource listing. I have no information about the Lutheran News Service.

In addition to those newsletters and services, readers also may be interested in the following NewsNet selections. (Prices quoted are for nonvalidated read rates, and the abbreviations after the "/" sign are NewsNet's codes for the newsletters. All prices were correct as of October 1987.)

> College Press Service/ED01 ($60/hour)
> Computer Book Review/EC27 ($84/hour)
> The Computer Cookbook/EC10E ($84/hour)
> Data Base Informer/EC32 ($60/hour)
> Electronic Information Report/PB07 ($132/hour)
> Kirkus Book Reviews/PB27 ($60/hour)
> P. C. Letter/EC57 ($108/hour)
> Telecommunications Reports/TE11 ($204/hour)
> Telecommuting Report/EC54 ($108/hour)
> Optical Information Systems Update/EC51 ($84/hour)
> Online Product News/TE27 ($60/hour)
> Viewdata/Videotex Report/PB09 ($132/hour)
> Worldwide Videotex Update/PB08 ($84/hour)

5.9 Networks

In this section we will briefly examine BITNET and ScholarNet, two networks designed for academicians, information specialists, and education professionals. These networks support electronic mail, file transfer, conferencing, and SIGs.

There are two basic types of networks, host-to-host and terminal-to-host. A host-to-host network consists of computers that are physically connected to one another by shared telecommunication lines. TYMNET, Telenet, and DataPac, for example, are all host-to-host networks. A terminal-to-host network consists of host computers that may be accessed over the telephone system in a dial-up manner by remote terminals (e.g., a personal computer). EDUNET, CompuServe, The Source, and DELPHI, for example, are all terminal-to-host networks. In computer jargon, any host computer in a network is known as a *node*, which simply means that it is a connection point or exchange (like a telephone exchange) in a communications network. A computer, or node, that connects two or more host-to-host networks (or on-line services) is known as a *gateway*. To function as a gateway, a computer must be able to translate the protocols of one network (or service) into those of another network (or service), and vice versa, so that information that has been formatted for transmission on one network meets the protocols of the second network and so may successfully be switched from one network to another.

Some networks are referred to as *physical networks* and some as *logical networks*. A *logical network* is an inter-related group of machines and (sometimes) terminals that use the networking facilities—the telecommunication lines and, perhaps, telecommunication software—of a physical network to communicate with one another. A *physical network* is one in which all the machines are physically connected by telecommunication lines. Thus a physical network can only be a host-to-host network, but a logical network can be either host-to-host or host-to-terminal.

BITNET is a host-to-host, physical Network. ScholarNet is a host-to-terminal, logical network that uses TYMNET's communication facilities and DELPHI as the host computer.

5.9.1 BITNET

BITNET is an academic and research network that began in 1981 and that links over 1,500 computers—including almost 500 in Europe (EARN), Canada (NetNorth), and the Far East—at more than 425 academic institutions in approximately 20 countries. The BITNET Executive Committee is responsible for network policies and services associated with running the network. Historically represented by the larger central sites, the BITNET Executive Committee has converted to an elected body chosen from BITNET Site Directors. EDUCOM operates the BITNET Information Center (BIC) (funded by an IBM grant) to provide user services and administrative support. BIC and the BITNET Executive Committee codify network policies and procedures.

BITNET is an acronym for *Because It's Time NETwork*. BITNET users may share information by means of real-time messages and electronic mail, transfer of documents, programs, and other data, and access to the BITNET file-server machine (formerly known as BITSERVE, now known as NICSERVE—see below) and its associated data services. BITNET provides a flexible, world-wide network that allows users to communicate in a variety of ways. BITNET is financially self-sustaining; each node pays for the data it forwards; no bills are sent to individual users. Any college, university, or other institution of higher learning may join BITNET by leasing a telephone line that supports 9,600 baud, by providing two 9,600-baud modems, and by promising to serve as a node for at least one additional BITNET member.

BITNET is command-driven. With a little help, communicating on BITNET is easy. User identification codes ("userid" in BITNET parlance) and user node codes ("nodeid") are used when sending mail and files. The communication form is "userid@nodeid." To send a message to me, for example, a BITNET user would enter "XB.J24@Stanford" (my userid on the Stanford computer is "XB.J24" and the Stanford nodeid is simply "Stanford"). Using BITNET as a gateway to communicate with someone on another network involves more complicated procedures and protocols, which, unfortunately, are frequently changed. Information about these procedures and protocols is available in a file called "Bitnet Gateway." A second file, "Bitnet Gates," contains related information.[32]

Figure 5.3 lists some of the networks BITNET users may access.

As you can see from that list, BITNET provides access to a worldwide system of networks. For more information on-line, contact NICSERVE@BITNIC or send a message to INFO@BITNIC.

Computers in the BITNET system are connected by leased lines that support 9,600-baud. BITNET is a "store-and-forward" system, which means that a transmission from one BITNET node is received by an intermediate node and transmitted to its final destination subject to resource and line utilization. Transmission is usually instantaneous, however, and BITNET notifies users on-line of the status, routing, location, and delivery of transmissions. Although most university users access BITNET through their institutional computer mail system (and so must learn that computer's commands for telecommunicating), BITNET itself uses IBM's Remote Spooling Communications Subsystem (RSCS)—or a system that emulates the RSCS system—as its communication software.

NICSERVE, the BITNET Network Information Center's file server that is accessible from all BITNET nodes, provides on-line help, a BITNET news service, a user directory that includes user identification codes, a general directory of installation codes, a list of BITNET sites and computers, and information on conferences,

---

32. To receive the file "Bitnet Gateway," when on-line type "NICSERVE SENDME BITNET GATEWAY," and the file will be sent to your BITNET address. Similarly, typing "NICSERVE SENDME BITNET GATES" will cause NICSERVE to send that file. Depending on the operating system being used, some BITNET nodes require a different form of those commands.

ARPANET (Advanced Research Project Agency Network)
BERKELEY.EDU (University of California at Berkeley Campus
    Mail Network)
CALTECH (aka CIT—*California* Institute of *Technology*
    LAN)
CDN (Canadian University Research Network)
CHUNET (Swiss University Network)
CMU.EDU (Carnegie Mellon University LAN)
COLUMBIA.EDU (Columbia University LAN)
CSNET (Computer Science Research Networks)
DFN (German National Network)
EARN (European Academic Research Network)
IL (Israel Network)
MAILNET (EDUCOM's Commercial University Network)
MLNET (University of Western Ontario LAN)
OZ (soon to become OZ.AU—Australian University Network)
SUNET (Swedish University Network)
UK (United Kingdom University/Research Network, aka
    JANET—Joint Academic Network)
UNINETT (Norwegian University Network)
UUCP (Unix-to-Unix Communications Package—the Unix
    Network)
UWO (University of Western Ontario LAN)
WISC.EDU (University of Wisconsin LAN)
WUSTL (Washington University LAN)

Figure 5.3: Some networks accessible from BITNET.

software, and special facilities available at BITNET member sites. The NICSERVE user directory may be searched by key words, institution name, and nodeid. Other NICSERVE files about using BITNET and NICSERVE may be listed by issuing "NIC-SERVE SENDME NICSERVE INDEX" (or a similar form of that command) and may be searched in various ways. NICSERVE supports truncation and Boolean operators.

A list of BITNET sites, available RSCS emulation software, procedures for connecting to BITNET, general membership categories, a membership application form, a free newsletter (*EDUCOM Networking*—see below under "Bibliographical Resources"), and other information is available from EDUCOM (or on-line by requesting the appropriate files). Individuals not affiliated with institutions that have a BITNET node may find it possible to open accounts on university computers that do. Contact EDUCOM at the following address to determine the nearest BITNET node, and then contact that institution's computer service or information technology service for information about establishing an account.

EDUCOM
BITNET Network Information Center
P.O. Box 364
Carter and Rosedale Roads
Princeton, NJ 08540
(609) 734-1915, (609) 734-1878

5.9.2 ScholarNet

ScholarNet, a network for scholars in the humanities and social sciences, was started in 1985/1986 and is composed of two separate networks, PoliNet and

HumaNet, that run on DELPHI (see above).[33] ScholarNet is menu-driven and links scholars and professionals in over 65 countries around the world. ScholarNet supports on-line newsletter publishing, electronic mail, conferencing, and file distribution and serves as a gateway to DIALOG and DELPHI.

ScholarNet is hosted by the School of Humanities and Social Sciences at North Carolina State University at Raleigh (NCSU) and directed by Dr. Richard W. Slatta, Associate Professor of History at NCSU at Raleigh.[34] ScholarNet is owned by North Carolina State University. PoliNet, whose director is Dr. Michael L. Vasu (Associate Professor of Political Science at NCSU),[35] HumaNet, whose director is Dr. Walter Meyers (Professor of English at NCSU), and ScholarNet are sponsored by the Brooks-Cole Publishing Company of Monterey, California, and distributed by the General Videotex Corporation of Cambridge, Massachusetts.

PoliNet was created for students and professionals in the areas of political science, public administration, and criminal justice; and HumaNet was created for students and scholars in the areas of history, philosophy, religion, and English. PoliNet offers the following newsletters on-line.

> *Public Policy*
> *Public Administration/Public Management*
> *Intergovernmental Relations/State and Local Government*
> *Computer Applications*
> *Methodology*
> *SPSS Newsletter*
> *ICPSR Newsletter*

HumaNet is scheduled to offer the following newsletters.

> *SCOPE*, including a full index
> *ScholarNews*[36]
> *Online English Composition*

Currently, only PoliNet is available. A one-time PoliNet membership fee (which includes access to DELPHI, DIALOG, and HumaNet and electronic mail access to The Source and CompuServe) is $29.95 for individuals and $100 for academic departments. PoliNet costs $9.50 per hour during off hours and $18.50 per hour during prime time. Like DELPHI, PoliNet supports 300, 1,200, and 2,400 baud, does not charge extra for the higher baud rates, and is available during the same hours that DELPHI is available. PoliNet users pay for TYMNET at the prevailing DELPHI rates.

To subscribe to PoliNet, call DELPHI at (800) 544-4005 and have a major credit card ready (MasterCard®, VISA®, American Express®) or write:

> DELPHI
> % General Videotex Corp.
> 3 Blackstone St.
> Cambridge, MA 01239

Assistants at DELPHI can provide the TYMNET numbers closest to you. For further information contact:

---

33. ScholarNet is a logical, host-to-terminal network that uses TYMNET's telecommunication nodes and lines and DELPHI's computers as the host machines.

34. P.O. Box 8101, NCSU, Raleigh, NC 27695-8101; (919) 737-7908.

35. P.O. Box 8101, NCSU, Raleigh, NC 27695-8101; (919) 737-2481, (919) 737-3067.

36. In addition to being available on-line, ScholarNews, the newsletter of ScholarNet, is mailed to ScholarNet users.

Dr. Michael L. Vasu
SSRIC Laboratory
P.O. Box 8101
NCSU
Raleigh, NC 27695-8101
(919) 737-3791, (919) 737-3067
(919) 737-7908 (Richard Slatta).

Though cheerful and well-intentioned, the DELPHI assistants frequently dissemi-
nate confused information about PoliNet, especially about PoliNet's logon procedures.
To save potential user's some frustration, keep these simple logon steps in mind. (1)
Connect to TYMNET. (2) When prompted for a service, respond "DELPHI." (3)
When prompted for a username, give the username provided when you subscribed to
PoliNet. (4) When prompted for a password, give the PoliNet password issued when
you subscribed. DELPHI members who wish to use PoliNet must purchase a separate
PoliNet membership. Members of both services should not use their DELPHI
password since doing so logs them on to DELPHI, and PoliNet is not accessible from
that service.

5.10 On-Line Educational Services

In this section we will look at The Electronic University Network™, an on-line
educational service that offers a variety of courses in a broad array of subject areas.

5.10.1 The Electronic University Network

- *BASIC INFORMATION*

Name of Service: The Electronic University Network™
Name of Company: CompuLearning, Inc.
Address: 1150 Sansome St., San Francisco, CA 94111
Business Phones: (800) 225-3276, (415) 956-7177
Customer Service Phones: (800) 642-4888, (415) 956-7177
Subscription Cost: $200 one-time fee
Tuition Costs: From $195 for noncredit courses to $652 for courses leading to an MBA.
Literature Included with Subscription: User's guide and course listings; communication software for BRS
   AfterDark also is included.
Manual: 58 pages, three-ring binder, not indexed.
Related Publications: The appropriate articles by Bergheim, Darling, Moss, Pearlman, Smith, and Stahr in
   the bibliography at the end of this chapter.
Connect Times: 24 hours/day, 365 days/year
Hourly Rates: $8.40/hour to $45/hour, depending on data base.
Monthly Minimum: $18/month; $216/year
Telecommunication Networks: Telenet, TYMNET
Telecommunication Surcharge: No
On-Line Storage Charges: Not applicable.
Billing Options: VISA®, MasterCard®, American Express®
Telecommunication Protocols: 300, 1,200 baud; other parameters set automatically by special communica-
   tion software.
Other: CompuLearning sells 300-baud modems for Apple IIs for $29 and for IBM PCs for $129. For more in-
   formation about the Electronic University, see Donna Osgood, "The Electronic University Network,"
   BYTE (March 1986): 171–76.

The Electronic University Network™ (EUN) was started in 1983 by Ron Gordon,
former president of Atari before Warner Communications acquired the company and
inventor of the Hand-Held Computer and Pocket Language Translator. Currently,

EUN has over 17,000 students enrolled in approximately 120 courses for college credit, self-improvement, and business and professional skills. EUN also offers an on-line electronic library that provides access to more that 8 million records in over sixty BRS data bases (see above), tutoring programs for children, and counselling services. Approximately 20 participating colleges and universities offer direct credit for individual courses taken through EUN,[37] and three institutions of higher learning offer full degrees for courses taken through EUN.[38] When enough course work has been completed, those institutions (not EUN) issue the appropriate degrees.

Anyone with an Apple II or IBM PC computer with at least 64K of memory and telecommunication capabilities may become a student of the EUN. For a modest charge (see above), CompuLearning will sell students one of their special 300-baud modems, which completely automate all telecommunication protocols. Special menu-driven CompuLearning communication software (included in the subscription cost) reduces on-line exchanges of information to single keystrokes and must be used when accessing the system. Students enroll in courses on-line. Textbooks, the course disk, and other materials are shipped via UPS within 24 hours.

All EUN courses are highly interactive, menu-driven, offer on-line help and hints, and make use of excellent graphics and sound. Courses cover everything from Classical Music/Grand Opera, Speed Reading, and Data Base Management to College Composition, Literary Analysis, and Introduction to Microeconomics. Typical courses are ten to twelve lessons long. Course "lectures" and lessons are on the course disk. Approximately one-half of a course's lessons require students to write and electronically transmit assignments or progress reports to an instructor. Instructors (most of whom are accredited university professors) typically respond via electronic mail within 24 to 48 hours. Instructors may specify "office hours," during which students can hold real-time, on-line, "conversations" with them. Examinations in courses taken for credit are given by the accrediting institution and proctored at a library or university near the student. The EUN frequently offers special system-wide lectures and seminars.

Currently, through various colleges and universities, the EUN offers the following degree programs: (1) an associate degree in the arts, (2) bachelor's degrees in business administration and the arts, and (3) a master's of business administration (MBA) degree. Additionally, EUN students who wish to receive course credit from a college or university are advised how to do so, though students are responsible for making the necessary arrangements with the appropriate institutions of higher learning. The EUN also offers a broad assortment of College Level Examination Program (CLEP)® preparatory courses and American College Testing/Proficiency Examinations Program (ACT/PEP) courses. Currently, approximately 1,800 institutions accept CLEP and ACT PEP scores toward the fulfillment of degree requirements.

The three major advantages of electronic education are flexibility, speed, and cost. No matter where they live, students may take courses through the EUN and work at their own pace at times that best suit their schedules. Thus many people who for a variety of reasons could never take college-level courses are able to do so through the EUN. And by avoiding transportation and on-campus costs, students save money.

Although the EUN does not offer many courses in the humanities, it allows educational and professional organizations to use its system to offer courses on-line, thus making it possible for humanities courses to be offered by interested institutions. Here, then, is a golden opportunity for humanities professors to make history!

---

37. Including Boston University, Oklahoma State University, and the University of Southern California.

38. Thomas Edison College, the Regents Degree Program of the University of the State of New York, and the John F. Kennedy University.

5.11 BIX and PC-IRS

In this section we will look at two specialized, on-line information services that are sponsored by two major microcomputer magazines.

5.11.1 BIX—BYTE Information Exchange

* *BASIC INFORMATION*

Name of Service: BIX—BYTE Information Exchange
Name of Company: BYTE, Inc.
Address: One Phoenix Mill Lane, Peterborough, NH 03458
Business Phone: (603) 924-9281
Customer Service Phones: (800) 227-2983, (603) 924-7681
BBS Phone (Data Line): (617) 861-9764, TYMNET (see below)
Subscription Cost: $25
Literature Included with Subscription: User's manual
Manual: 24 pages, printed; includes glossary and summary of commands.
Related Publications: BYTE magazine
Connect Times: 24hours/day, 365 days/year
Hourly Rates: $9/hour: 6 P.M. to 7 A.M., weekends & holidays; $12/hour: 7 A.M. to 6 P.M. (all times are local times)
Monthly Minimum: No
Telecommunication Networks: TYMNET, BYTEnet
Telecommunication Surcharge: $2/hour: 6 P.M. to 7 A.M.; $6/hour: 7 A.M. to 6 P.M. (all times are local times)
On-Line Storage Charges: No
Billing Options: VISA®, MasterCard®
Telecommunication Protocols: 300, 1,200 baud, 8-bit ASCII, no parity, 1 stop bit, full or half duplex (or 7 data bits, 1 stop bit, even parity, full or half duplex), asynchronous.
Other: On-Line help is available.

BYTE, whose readership is approximately 400,000, is the world's leading high-technology microcomputer magazine. Each monthly issue is approximately 500-pages long and is packed with useful information and in-depth articles. BYTE's readers are among the world's most knowledgeable microcomputer users. BIX—BYTE Information Exchange—is BYTE's sophisticated, electronic information exchange—not just another BBS—that allows users to join SIGs, upload and download programs and files, and send electronic mail. SIGs cover computers, chips, programming languages, operating systems, application programs, semiconductor technologies, microcomputer graphics, artificial intelligence, telecommunications, and much more. BIX can be an extremely valuable source of information about microcomputers.

To reach BIX via TYMNET, call TYMNET's 24-hour, toll-free, customer-service number (800) 336-0149 to learn your local TYMNET number, or use the following BYTEnet number: (617) 861-9764, and then proceed as follows. (1) Call your local TYMNET number (or the BYTEnet number) and log on. (2) When prompted for a "terminal identifier," type "A." (3) When asked to log on, enter "BIX." You will then be connected to the BIX computer. (4) At the next prompt, enter "BIX." Now you are on-line with BIX and will be prompted for your name. (5) Respond by entering "NEW," since this will be your first time on the system. That will take you to a special section where you will enter the information you need to register as a BIX user, including the number of your credit card. After registering, BIX will give you a tutorial on how to use the system. (At any prompt, typing "HELP" or "?" followed by a carriage return will list available commands.)

5.11.2 PC-IRS—*PC Magazine's* Interactive Reader Service

- *BASIC INFORMATION*

Name of Service: *PC Magazine's* Interactive Reader Service
Name of Company: PC Magazine, Inc.
Address: One Park Ave., New York, NY 10016
Business Phone (Voice Line): (212) 503-5255
BBS Phones (Data Lines): (212) 696-0360, (415) 598-9100
Subscription Cost: Data base is free.
Literature Included with Subscription: Not applicable
Manual: None
Related Publications: *PC Magazine*
Connect Times: 24 hours/day, 365 days/year
Hourly Rates: Not applicable
Monthly Minimum: No
Telecommunication Networks: None, direct dial only.
Telecommunication Surcharge: Prevailing long distance rates
On-Line Storage Charges: Not applicable
Billing Options: Not applicable
Telecommunication Protocols: 300, 1,200 baud, 8-bit ASCII, no parity, 1 stop bit, full duplex, asynchronous; supports XMODEM file-transfer protocol.
Other: Although this data base supports twelve or more phone lines through the one number listed above, they are often all in use. This is a very popular on-line service.

Unlike BIX, PC Magazine's menu-driven Interactive Reader Service (IRS) is a noninteractive, download-only data base that allows readers (and others) to download information and public-domain programs that are discussed and listed in *PC Magazine*, the premièr magazine about IBM PC computers. Although it is legal to download programs for personal use, all programs and materials on this bulletin board are copyrighted by the Ziff-Davis Publishing Company and so may not be commercially distributed, sold, or uploaded to another BBS.

For IBM PC users, this BBS is a dream come true. For the price of a phone call, the IRS BBS allows users to download a multitude of very useful programs that are not commercially available. The Main Menu, illustrated in Figure 5.4, provides an idea of the types of programs this system offers.

PC Magazine's Interactive Reader Service MAIN MENU
A. End the Interactive Reader Service Session / Hang Up
B. Leave Comments for SYSOP or subscribe to PC Magazine
C. Download Programming utility .COM files via XMODEM
D. Download Programming utility .ASM files via ASCII
E. Download Programming utility .BAS files (via ASCII)
F. Download PC Magazine Indices & User Groups via
    XMODEM
G. Download PC Magazine Indices & User Groups via ASCII
H. Download Power User, U2U, & other files via XMODEM
I. Download Power User, U2U, & other files via ASCII
J. Explanation of Ascii/Xmodem downloads (for beginners)
K. Descriptions of Program Listings.
L. Descriptions of Indices.
M. Descriptions of Other Available Files.

Figure 5.4: Interactive Reader Service's Main Menu.

5.12 Bulletin Board Services

Computer bulletin board services (BBS) are more than computerized versions of physical bulletin boards; they are "mini online services."[39] BBSs allow users to send and receive electronic mail, post and read messages, upload and download files, read about topics of special interest, form SIGs, hold conferences, and run programs. Most BBSs are menu-driven and provide on-line help. Literally thousands of free public-domain programs of every imaginable sort for all major brands of personal computers may be downloaded from BBSs. That fact alone makes bulletin boards worth serious investigation![40]

There are over 1,000 BBSs in North America, and almost everyone of them is free. Because most of them are run by individuals whose purpose is to provide a place where information can be exchanged electronically, the range of subjects covered is as broad as the tastes and interests of the hundreds of "sysops" (system operators) who operate the boards and the thousands of people who use them. Because they provide an inexpensive way for people to communicate and share information electronically, Glossbrenner says that BBSs "may be seen as one of the most significant results of the personal computer revolution,"[41] and he calls BBSs the "underground that has the potential to revolutionize personal communications."[42]

BBSs run on personal computers—Apples, Commodores, IBMs, TIs, TRS-80s, and so forth. Special BBS software is available. In addition to a personal computer and BBS software (which you can download for free from another BBS!), all you need to become the sysop of a BBS is a serial card, autoanswer modem, and phone line. See Glossbrenner, *Communications*, chapter 20, for more information.

5.12.1 BBS Directories

The following publications and on-line resources provide information about BBSs. Addresses and phones numbers are those of the circulation/subscription offices.

The BBS Sourcebook
$12.95. Verified numbers and descriptions of over 1,000 BBSs
        in North America.
% S & M Data Services
P.O. Box 1453
Bolingbrook, IL 60439-7453
(312) 739-5532

Bulletin Board Directory of North America (Christopher Fisher)
Quarterly, $14/year, $5.95 single issue. A state-by-state listing
        of over 750 BBSs.
% BBS Directory
P.O. Box 4150 Beach Station
Vero Beach, FL 32964-4150

---

39. Glossbrenner, *Communications*, 4.

40. See Alfred Glossbrenner *How To Get Free Software* and Bertram Gader and Manuel V. Nodar, *Free Software for the IBM PC* (over 600 free programs for IBM PCs).

41. Glossbrenner, *Communications*, 481.

42. Ibid., 480.

Bulletin Board Systems™
Newsletter, 8 times a year, $26.50/year. Up-to-date information
      about North American BBSs.
℅ Meckler Publishing
11 Ferry Lane West
Westport, CT 06990
(203) 226-6967

The Computer Phone Book™ (Mike Cane)
$18.95. Over 600 international, national, regional, and local
      BBSs, arranged by type and location; detailed
      description of each system's offerings.
℅ New American Library
1633 Broadway
New York, NY 10019

Hooking In: The Underground Computer Bulletin Board Workbook
      and Guide (Tom Beeston and Tom Tucker)
$14.95. Hundreds of BBS numbers and main menus.
℅ Computerfood Press
P.O. Box 608
Oracle, AZ 85623

Also check the bulletin boards and SIGS on CompuServe and The Source, and check the PARTI section on The Source. Also, many BBSs post lists and numbers of other BBSs.

5.12.2 Humanities and Religious Bulletin Boards

There are several humanities computer bulletin boards and a host of religious ones. In this section I will list the basic facts about one BBS from each of those categories.

5.12.2.1 Duke Humanities Bulletin Board

- *BASIC INFORMATION*

BBS Name: Duke Humanities Bulletin Board
Location: Humanities Computing Facility, 104 Languages Bldg., Duke University, Durham, NC 27706
Data Line: (919) 684-3169
Voice Line: (919) 684-3637
Electronic Address: DYBBUK@TUCCVM
Sysop: Don Mullen
Baud: 300, 1,200
Connect Times: 365 days/year, 5 P.M. to 8 A.M. and all day Saturday and Sunday
System Software: Not known
Telecommunication Protocols: 8 data bits, no parity
Supports Downloading: Yes
Supports Uploading: Not known
File Transfer Protocols: Not known
Supports E-Mail: No
Supports Conferences: Yes
Password Required: No
Special Features: Public domain and specialized software for computing in the humanities may be
    downloaded (e.g., the Duke Language Toolkit, MicroCALIS). Discussion forums for computing in the
    humanities are offered.
Other: There is no subscription fee or per session charge.

5.12.2.2 The Ministry Bulletin Board Service

● *BASIC INFORMATION*

BBS Name: The Ministry Bulletin Board Service
Location: Paraclete Computers & Software, 1000 E. 14th St., Suite 187, Plano, TX 75074
Data Line: (214) 422-2387, (214) 423-6705
Voice Line: (214) 578-8185
Sysop: Charlie Thrall
Baud: 300, 1,200, 2,400
Connect Times: 24 hours/day, 365 days/year
System Software: PCBoard 11.8/D
Telecommunication Protocols: 8 data bits, 1 stop bit, no parity
Supports Downloading: Yes
Supports Uploading: Yes
File Transfer Protocols: X- and Y- modem
Supports E-Mail: Yes
Supports Conferences: Yes
Password Required: Yes
Special Features: This full-featured BBS includes conferences on computer hardware and software, theology, philosophy, Christian education, languages, missions, the Bible, leadership issues, and more. "Doors" allow users to run various programs, such as GodSpeed™ (see chapter 3). The entire compressed text of the KJV may be downloaded, along with a program for uncompressing the text. The file CHRISTBBS.ARC in the downloads section includes an up-to-date list of other Christian BBSs. The first electronic weekly computer magazine, *InfoMat*, which includes reviews and news of computer products, as well as classified ads, is available on-line. This BBS provides technical assistance, and users may send and receive E-mail, post and read messages, and participate in conferences.
Other: Three subscription levels, free to $5/year.

5.12.2.3 Christian Computer Users Association

This is not a bulletin board but a Christian publication that, among other things, frequently provides information about religious bulletin boards and software.

● *BASIC INFORMATION*

Name: Christian Computer Users Association (CCUA)
Address: P.O. Box 7344, Grand Rapids, MI 49510-7344
Phone: (616) 241-0368
President or Director: Douglas Vos
Name of Publication: *Christian Computer News* (CCN)
Frequency of Publication: Bimonthly
Cost: $20/year

Bibliography

Ackerman, Katherine. "Rent-A-Researcher." *Link-Up*. (December 1985): 14–15.

Adams, Arthur L. "Planning Search Strategies for Maximum Retrieval from Bibliographic Databases." *Online Review* 3 (December 1979): 373–79.

Anderman, Ardis. "Searching for Online Information: A Primer." *Link-Up* (January 1985): 24–25.

Badgett, Tom. "On-line Databases: Dialing for Data." *PC Magazine* (May 12, 1987): 238–58.

_____. "Search Software: Directory Assistance." *PC Magazine* (May 12, 1987): 263–73.

Battin, Patricia. "The Electronic Library: A Vision of the Future." *EDUCOM Bulletin* (Summer 1984): 1–7.

Beeston, Tom, and Tom Tucker. *Hooking In: The Underground Computer Bulletin Board Workbook and Guide*. Oracle, Ariz.: Computerfood Press, 1985.

Bergheim, Kim. "College Courses via Computer." *InfoWorld* (October 1, 1984): 14.

Bottomly, Kirk. "CompuServe Means Business." *PC World* (December 1984): 56–63.

Bowen, Charles. "Online News: All That's Fit to Print and More." *Online Today* (January 1986): 18–21.

Bowen, Charles, and David Peyton, *How to Get the Most Out of CompuServe*. New York: Bantam Books, 1984.

_____. *How to Get the Most Out of The Source*. New York: Bantam Books, 1985.

Brown, Eric. "Fear and Lurking on CB Simulator." *PC World* (January 1984): 182–91.

Budd, John. "The Uses of Online Bibliographic Searching in Literary Research." In *Sixth International Conference on Computers and the Humanities*. Edited by Sarah K. Burton and Douglas D. Short, 39–46. Rockville: Computer Science Press, 1983.

Callahan, Kirkwood M. "Social Science Research in the Information Age: Online Databases for Social Sciences." *Social Science Microcomputer Review* 3 (1985): 28–44.

Calvo, Melissa. "On-Line Services." *InfoWorld* (November 3, 1986): 36–42.

Cambron, Jim. *The First Primer of Microcomputer Telecommunications*. Blue Summit, Penn.: TAB, 1984.

Cane, Mike. *The Computer Phone Book™*. New York: The New American Library, Inc., 1986.

Cook, William J. "No More Telephone Tag." *PC Magazine* (October 16, 1984): 377–80.

Darling, Sharon. "The Electronic University." *Compute!* (September 1985): 30–36.

Deighton, Suzan, John Gurnsey, and Janet Tomlinson. *Computers and Information Processing World Index*. Phoenix, Az.: Oryx Press, 1985.

Derfler, Frank J., Jr. "The Async Link." *PC Magazine* (January 22, 1985): 131–37.

_____. "Data by Satellite." *PC Magazine* (January 22, 1985): 140–43.

Eisenstein, Paul A. "Those Surprising Surcharges." *Link-Up* (July 1984): 30–31.

Fenichel, Carol H., and Thomas H. Hogan. *Online Searching: A Primer*. 2d ed. Medford, N.J.: Learned Information, Inc., 1985.

Ferrarini, Elizabeth M. *Infomania: The Guide to Essential Electronic Services*. Boston: Houghton Mifflin, 1985.

Fisher, Christopher. *Bulletin Board Directory of North America*. Vero Beach, Fla.: BBS Directory, 1984.

Foster, Edward. "Grolier Puts Works on CD-ROM." *InfoWorld*. (July 29, 1985): 22.

Friedman, Bernard. "A 22-Hour Library Card." *PC Magazine* (December 11, 1984): 375–77.

Fuchs, Ira H. "BITNET—Because It's Time." *Perspectives in Computing* 3 (1983): 16–27.

Gader, Bertram, and Manuel V. Nodar. *Free Software for the IBM PC*. New York: Warner Books, 1984.

Garfield, Eugene. "The Integrated *Sci-Mate* Software System." *Current Comments* 38 (September 23, 1985): 3–10.

Gerrie, Brenda. *Online Information Systems: Use and Operating Characteristics, Limitations and Design Alternatives*. Arlington, Va.: Information Research Press, 1983.

Gilreath, Charles L. *Computerized Literature Searching: Research Strategies and Databases*. Boulder, Colo.: Westview Press, 1984.

Glossbrenner, Alfred. *The Complete Handbook of Personal Computer Communications*. 2d ed. New York: St. Martin's Press, 1985.

_____. *How To Get Free Software*. New York: St. Martin's Press, 1984.

_____. "Looking It Up on Knowledge Index." *PC Magazine* (July 24, 1984): 369–72.

_____. "On-Line College." *PC Magazine* (October 30, 1984): 297–99.

_____. "Tricks of the On-Line Trade." *PC Magazine* (October 16, 1984): 177–92.

_____. "XMODEM: A Standard is Born." *PC Magazine* (April 17, 1984): 451–52.

Goldstein, Kevin. "Strategist Modems and the UART of Chatter." *Softalk* (October 1983): 24–28.

Goodman, Danny. "First Time On Line." *PC World* (January 1986): 135–40.

Gordon, Helen A. et al. "Databank Directory." *ONLINE* 9 (September 1985): 99–108.

Hannotte, Dean. "Telecommunications: The Net Effect." *PC Magazine* (September 3, 1985): 253–55.

Hansen, Augie. "Communicating from Within." *PC Tech Journal* (September 1985): 60–77.

———. "Electronic Messaging." *PC Tech Journal* (February 1985): 141–49.

———. "Kermit." *PC Tech Journal* (January 1985): 110–23.

Hansen, Carol. *The Microcomputer User's Guide to Information Online*. Hayden Book Co., 1984.

Harris, Mark. "On-Line Network News." *PC Magazine* (October 16, 1984): 143–45.

Harstad, Carl L. "The Online Database Comes of Age." *Link-Up* (June 1984): 20–22.

Hart, Glenn A. "The PC-Telephone Connection." *PC Magazine* (March 5, 1985): 133–45.

Hart, Robert. "Language Study and the PLATO System." *Studies in Language Learning* 3 (1981): 1–24.

Harts, Bill. "Bisync Comes of Age." *PC Magazine* (January 22, 1985): 149–53.

Hawkins, Donald T., and Louie M. Levy. "Front End Software for Online Database Searching. Part 1: Definitions, System Features, and Evaluation." *ONLINE* 9 (1986): 30–37.

———. "Front End Software for Online Database Searching. Part 2: The Marketplace." *ONLINE* 10:1 (1986): 33–40.

———. "Front End Software for Online Database Searching. Part 3: Product Selection, Chart, and Bibliography." *ONLINE* 10:3 (1986): 49–58.

Helliwell, John. "On-Line with Smart Modems & Software." *PC Magazine* (October 16, 1984): 118–25.

Hewes, Jeremy Joan. "Dialog: the Ultimate On-Line Library." *PC World* 1:6 (1983): 74–88.

———. "Gateway to On-Line Services." *PC World* (May 1985): 149–56.

Hewes, Jeremy Joan, and Eric Brown. "Fast is Not Enough." *PC World* (December 1985): 258–69.

Hoffman, David. "Across the Boards." *PC Magazine* (June 11, 1985): 311–13.

Hook, Sara Anne. "BRS/BRKTHRU: A Happy Medium." *ONLINE* 10 (1986): 97–101.

Howell, Frank M., and G. David Garson. "Professional Networking in the Social Sciences: Creating SocNet and PoliNet." *Social Science Microcomputer Review* 3 (1985): 85–92.

Howitt, Doran. "On-Line Access is Simplified." *InfoWorld* (January 21, 1985): 32–33.

———. "The Source Keeps Trying." *InfoWorld* (November 5, 1984): 59–64.

Howitt, Doran, and Marvin Weinberger, *Databasics: Your Guide to Online Business Information*. New York: Garland Publishing, Inc., 1985.

Ide, Nancy M. "Computer Networks." *ACH Newsletter* 7 (1985): 1–2.

Jennings, D. "Linking Europe's Academics." *Intermedia* 12 (1984): 53.

Johnson, Christopher. "One Year Later: PC Magazine's Interactive Reader Service." *PC Magazine* (July 1986): 251–63.

Jordan, Larry. "The Communicators." *PC World* (May 1985): 277–81.

———. "A Host of Hosts." *PC World* (February 1984): 132–43.

———. "In Box Out Box." *PC World* (June 1984): 132–38.

———. "Modems in the Fast Lane." *PC World* (July 1984): 103–7.

———. "The Modem Market." *PC World* (November 1983): 88–97.

———. "What Makes Modems Run?" *PC World* (November 1983): 54–66.

———. "What Makes Modems Run?" *PC World* (May 1985): 267–74.

Kariya, Scott. "When the Mini Plays Host." *PC Magazine* (January 22, 1985): 145–48.

Karten, Howard A. "In Search of a Significant Dialog." *PC Magazine* (August 21, 1984): 265–70.

———. "Packet Switching Puts You in Touch." *PC Magazine* (March 20, 1984): 161–68.

———. "Telex Changes with the Times." *PC Magazine* (April 3, 1984): 393–96.

Kenner, Hugh. "Computers, Libraries, Scholars." *Scholarly Communication* 4 (Spring 1986): 1, 6–8.

Kenny-Sloan, Linda. "CompuServe SIGs and their Data Libraries." *ONLINE* 10 (1986): 104–8.

Kieffer, Tom, and Terry Hansen. *Get Connected: A Guide to Telecommunications*. Culver City, Calif.: Ashton-Tate, 1984.

Knox, Douglas R., and Marjorie M. K. Hlava. "Effective Search Strategies." *Online Review* 3 (June 1979): 148–52.

Kolner, Stuart J. "The IBM PC as an Online Search Machine." *ONLINE* 10:4 (1986): 32–36.

Krasnoff, Barbara. "Databases: Believe It or Not." *PC Magazine* (October 16, 1984): 127–30.

———. "In Touch with the Outside World." *PC Magazine* (September 3, 1985): 153–60.

———. "Public E-Mail: Person-to-Person." *PC Magazine* (May 12, 1987): 276–91.

———. "RCA Enters the E-Mail Fray." *PC Magazine* (February 11, 1986): 171–78.

Lambert, Steve. *Online. A Guide to America's Leading Information Services*. Bellevue, Wash.: Microsoft Press, 1985.

Langdell, James. "Grolier Electronic Unleashes Its Knowledge on a Compact ROM Disk." *PC Magazine* (October 15, 1985): 51.

Lesko, Matthew. "Low-Cost On-Line Databases." *BYTE* (October 1984): 167–73.

Lewis, Sasha. *Plugging In: The Microcomputerist's Guide to Telecommunications*. Radnor, Penn.: Chilton Book Co., 1985.

Lisanti, Suzana. "The On-Line Search." *BYTE* (December 1984): 215–30.

Lloyd, A. "EARN: Europe's Academic Network." *Abacus* 1 (1984): 102–3.

Lomio, J. Paul. "The High Cost of NEXIS and What A Searcher Can Do About It." *ONLINE* 9 (September 1985): 54–56.

Look, Hugh E., ed. *An Introduction to Electronic Publishing: A Snapshot of the Early 1980s.* Medford, N.J.: Learned Information, Inc., 1983.

McCarthy, Michael, and Doran Howitt. "10,000 BPS Modem 'Breakthrough'." *InfoWorld* (July 22, 1985): 15–16.

McCredie, John W. "BITNET's Changing Role in Higher Education." *Educom* 19 (1984): 2–5, 11.

_____. "Gateways among Academic Computer Networks." *Cause/Effect* 7 (1984): 32–36.

McDermott, Brian. "Computer Crusaders." *Link-Up* (July 1984): 16–20.

McMullen, John, and Barbara McMullen. "2,400-bps Modems Arrive; Price Differs." *InfoWorld* (August 12, 1985): 44–46.

Mace, Scott. "On-line Data at Off-line Prices." *InfoWorld* (April 8, 1985): 36.

Magid, Lawrence J. "Battle of the Networks: The Source Versus CompuServe." *PC Magazine* (January 1983): 181–92.

Meeks, Brock N. "The Greening of Information." *Link-Up* (January 1986): 20, 22.

Miller, Tim. "Lexis, Nexis, and PCs." *PC Magazine* (October 16, 1984): 149–52.

Moss, Carol M. "The Electronic University." *Link-Up* (September 1984): 22–23.

Newlin, Barbara. *Answers On-Line: Your Guide to Informational Databases.* Berkeley: OSBORNE/McGraw-Hill, 1985.

_____. "On-Line Search Strategies." *PC World* (May 1985): 226–33.

Nichols, Tom. "The BBS Survival Kit." *Link-Up* (April 1986): 10.

O'Leary, Mick. "DELPHI: Letting the Users Run the Show." *ONLINE* 9 (1985): 118–23.

_____. "Gateway Software to the Information Stars." *PC Magazine* (August 20, 1985): 181–88.

Olmsted, Marcia. "Dialog Version 2/Questel Plus: A Comparison. Part I." *ONLINE* 10:1 (1986): 26–29.

_____. "Dialog Version 2/Questel Plus: A Comparison. Part II: Search Commands and Features." *ONLINE* 10:2 (1986): 31–35.

_____. "Dialog Version 2/Questel Plus: A Comparison. Part III: Accessing and Treating the Results." *ONLINE* 10:3 (1986): 68–72.

Osgood, Donna. "The Electronic University Network." *BYTE* (March 1986): 171–76.

Pearlman, Dara. "A School Without Walls." *PC Magazine* (April 16, 1985): 225–30.

Picard, Don. "Inside CompuServe." *Link-Up* (January 1985): 7–11.

Pisciotta, Henry. "Database Searching with Gateway Software." *Art. Doc.* 4 (1985): 3–5.

Plotnik, Art. "OCLC for You—and ME?!" *American Libraries* 7 (1976): 258–75.

Porter, Martin. "Oxford Goes On-Line." *PC Magazine* (February 19, 1985): 233–38.

Powers, Jack. "Modems: The Inside Story." *PC World* (April 1984): 80–85.

_____. "Putting Your PC on the Line." *PC World* 1 (1982): 142–49.

Quint, Barbara. "Menlo Corporation's Pro-Search: Review of a Software Search Aid." *ONLINE* 10:1 (1986): 17–25.

Robl, Ernest. "Of Muses & Modems." *Link-Up* (November 1984): 24–29.

Rosch, Winn L. "Good Things Come in Black Boxes." *PC Magazine* (September 3, 1985): 125–28.

Rosenberg, Victor. "Library Automation Reaches Out to the PC." *PC Magazine* (November 1983): 509–12.

Rubis, Dan. "An Outside Line for Your PC." *PC Magazine* (December 25, 1984): 141–60.

Schneider, Mary. "Going Online for the 'Food of the Soul'." *Link-Up* (September 1984): 27–28.

Schwaderer, W. David. "Communications Concepts." *PC World* (April 1984): 184–94.

Scott, Byron T. "Teaching Videotex." *Online Today* (September 1985): 12–16.

Sherblom, John. "BITNET: Inter-University Computer Network." *Journal Surv. English* 111 (1985): 57–70.

Silveria, Terry C., and Sanjiva K. Nath. *Buyer's Guide to Modems and Communications Software.* Blue Summit, Penn.: TAB Books, 1985.

Simnacher, Betsy. "The BBS in the Sky." *Link-Up* (September 1984): 38–41.

_____. "Bulletin Boards for Better Business." *Link-Up* (June 1984): 32–35.

_____. "Will the Real Online Communications Market Please Stand Up?" *Link-Up* (November 1984): 18–19.

Siwolop, Sana. "Touching All the Data Bases." *Discover* (March 1983): 68–71.

Smith, Wayne R. "Electronic College." *PC Magazine* (June 12, 1984): 359–61.

Stahr, Lisa B. "The Electronic University." *PC World* (January 1984): 246–49.

_____. "Supercommunicators Expand Frontiers." *InfoWorld* (April 8, 1985): 29–33.

Stone, M. David. "Asynchronous Communications. Shopping for Software." *PC Magazine* (October 28, 1986): 126–201.

_____. "Can We Talk? A Modem Primer." *PC Magazine* (May 15, 1984): 435–38.

_____. "E-Mail for the Well Connected Office." *PC Magazine* (September 3, 1985): 137–52.

_____. "Fastlink: Communicating at 10,000 BPS and Up." *PC Magazine* (December 10, 1985): 251–57.

_____. *Getting On-Line: A Guide to Accessing Computer Information Services.* Englewood Cliffs, N.J.: Prentice-Hall, 1984.

_____. "Getting On-Line with Your PC." *PC Magazine* (July 1986): 285–98.

_____. "Getting Started in Communications." *PC Magazine* (March 11, 1986): 315–18.

_____. "Modems Take to the Airwaves." *PC Magazine* (January 14, 1986): 184–93.

_____. "Picking the Proper Protocol." *PC Magazine* (July 11, 1985): 355, 360.

_____. "Posting A Message On-Line." *PC Magazine* (October 16, 1984): 165–73.

_____. "The Smartest Modem of Them All." *PC Magazine* (September 3, 1985): 130–34.

_____. "Taking Notice of Bulletin Boards." *PC Magazine* (April 30, 1985): 261–62.

_____. "Whizzzzzz . . . Here Come the 2400-Baud Modems." *PC Magazine* (September 18, 1984): 51.

Stoner, Don. *Compute!'s Personal Telecomputing.* Greensboro, N.C.: Compute! Publications, Inc., 1984.

Stork, Ronald F. *The BBS Sourcebook.* Bolingbrook, Ill.: S & M Data Services, 1985.

Sturtz, Larry, and Jeff Williams. *Using Computer Information Systems.* Indianapolis, Ind.: Howard W. Sams & Co., Inc., 1985

Taylor, Jared. "On-Line House Calls." *PC Magazine* (October 16, 1984): 135–38.

Teitelbaum, H. H., and Donald T. Hawkins. "Database Subject Index." *ONLINE* 2 (April 1978): 16–21.

Waldrop, M. Mitchell. "Personal Computers on Campus." *Science* (April 26, 1985): 1–7.

Wilcox, Art. "Safe at Any Speed?" *PC World* (May 1986): 249–59.

Witt, Michael. "An Introduction to Layered Protocols." *BYTE* (September 1983): 385–98.

Yalonis, Chris, and Anthony Padgett. "Tapping Into On-Line Data Bases." *PC World* (May 1985): 120–26.

Chapter 6

Archaeological Programs

Intruder in the Dust
William Faulkner[1]

6.1 Introduction

As archaeologists carefully sift through layer after layer of dust and dig through stratum after stratum of dirt, they laboriously record various types of facts about the location and attributes of each artifact they find. Using that information, archaeologists create social, cultural, and economic models of the people who produced the artifacts. Constructing such models requires large amounts of data, which means that great numbers of artifacts must be unearthed, recorded, organized, and compared. And the longer the chronological period covered by the model, the greater the amount of data required for its construction.[2]

Before computers, managing, manipulating, and analyzing such massive amounts of information was tedious, taxing, and time-consuming. Computers have simplified the task of data base management, speeded up the process of analysis, and opened up new ways of looking at data. Not only are computers being used to analyze data brought in from the field, portable computers are joining archaeologists at the actual sites of digs as a new type of intruder in the dust.[3]

6.2 Computers and Data Base Management

Data base programs allow archaeologists to enter, retrieve, manipulate, and analyze information in systematic ways. When archaeologists unearth artifacts, they record two types of information about each object: a three-dimensional description of its provenance (location) and information about its attributes. Facts about an item's attributes may include its size, shape, color, weight, design, material type, and apparent function. Each piece of information about an object may be entered in a separate field in the artifact's record in the data base, which itself consists of the collection of all such records.

Using the proper programs, users may query and manipulate a data base to organize its data in ways that help answer questions about a site's history and about the social, political, economic, religious, and cultural activities of the people who inhabited it.

---

1. William Faulkner (1897–1962), title of novel (1948).
2. Tate, "Minnesota," 205.
3. Cf. Arndt, *System*.

For example, an archaeologist might query a data base with the equivalent of "What are the locations of every piece of red pottery that has a snake motif and that is located at level five within two meters of all charred bone fragments?" Trying to sort through thousands of hand written records to find the answer to such a question would be tedious and time-consuming. A computer can do it in a matter of seconds.

Chenall[4] and Wilcock[5] discuss in some detail the issues of data categories, data coding, file structure, and other topics related to creating and maintaining an archaeological data base. James F. Strange's article, "Recent Computer Applications in Ancient Near Eastern Archaeology,"[6] discusses seven data bases that have been developed specifically for Ancient Near Eastern archaeology. According to Sylvia W. Gaines, as of 1981 European archaeologists had established thirty-three computerized data banks in seventeen countries.[7] She mentions four archaeological data banks in the United States,[8] though that is probably an incomplete listing.[9]

6.3 Computers and Data Base Analysis

Having an enormous data base and making sense out of the data it contains are two different things. In addition to conventional data base programs, archaeologists and computer scientists have developed special statistical and analytical programs for studying archaeological data. The following subsections briefly describe the various specialized techniques embodied in some of those programs.[10]

6.3.1 Cluster Analysis

Cluster analysis is a collection of methods for grouping set members on the basis of their characteristics. Archaeologists may use cluster analysis, for example, to classify squares (the smallest excavated plot) "by comparing their artifact distributions by material."[11] According to Strange, this method of analysis has been successful, though interpreting the significance of the results is often problematic.[12]

6.3.2 Seriation

Seriation is a technique used to establish relative chronologies for sites or groups of objects that have "no continuous stratigraphic relationship."[13] Seriation is the ordering of artifacts "in their presumed chronological sequence through the observance of their relative frequencies"[14] in an attempt to eliminate chronological ambiguity. When using seriation to determine the chronology of different sites in a region, archaeologists choose specific artifactual categories and compute their relative frequencies among the various sites. Two main assumptions underlie seriation: within a

---

4. Chenall, "Data Bank," 1–8.

5. Wilcock, "Information," 9–14.

6. Strange, *Answers*, 129–46.

7. Gaines, "Data Banks," 223–26.

8. Gaines, *Applications*, viii.

9. Cf. Strange, "Applications," 138.

10. For more information see Whallon, "Survey," 29–45, and Kelly-Buccellati and Elster, "Statistics," 195–211.

11. Strange, "Applications," 140.

12. Ibid.

13. Kelly-Buccellati and Elster," Statistics," 195.

14. Ibid.

geographical region, "sites with similar frequency distributions are contemporary,"[15] and styles of artifacts are replaced through time and space.[16] The latter assumption means that a type begins in one geographical location, grows in popularity there, and spreads to other locations. Sites most removed from the original site receive the item last. "The relative popularity of the class is usually shown by computing the percentage of each type at each site and plotting this on a graph."[17] One type recedes in popularity as another replaces it. Kelly-Buccellati and Elster use a cemetery as an example of a site where the stratification of artifacts does not indicate the relative chronology of the graves and where seriation would probably be a fruitful technique to employ. There are a number of different techniques[18] and algorithms used in seriation.[19]

6.3.3 Classification and Scaling

Classification and scaling are part of a cluster of analytical procedures that are closely related to and that shade into seriation, factor analysis, and multidimensional scaling. According to Whallon, "In almost every case [of cluster analysis] archaeologists are borrowing from and experimenting with the almost limitless range of methods and computer algorithms produced in other fields."[20]

Classification refers to arranging artifacts by categories, or type. *Scaling* refers to creating spatial analogs of an artifact's spatial or nonspatial characteristics. Both techniques help archaeologists structure data. Whallon's article[21] describes different ways in which computers have been used for classification and scaling.

6.3.4 Simulation (Modeling)

Simulation, or *modeling*, is the technique by which archaeological data are analyzed in terms of systems and systems theory. As Whallon notes,

> As archaeological explanation becomes more a matter of defining the relevant variables involved in any given phenomenon or process and of specifying the systemic interrelationships among those variables, simulation provides a new and unique means to experimentally recreate the proposed explanatory system and to test its behavior under an entire range of possible situations. The techniques and procedures of computer simulation so closely parallel the current thinking and processes of model-building of many archaeologists that the lateness and limits of their application are surprising.[22]

One of the most important books on this topic is *Simulations in Archaeology*, edited by J. A. Sabloff.[23] Vicky A. Walsh's article "Computer Simulation Methodology for Archaeology"[24] and her article with Holly J. Morris, "CATO: A Computer

---

15. Ibid.
16. Ibid., 199.
17. Ibid.
18. Ibid., 196–200.
19. Whallon, "Survey," 31–32.
20. Ibid., 33.
21. Ibid., 32–35.
22. Ibid., 38.
23. Albuquerque: University of New Mexico Press, 1981.
24. Bailey, *Computing*, 163–74.

Simulation of a Roman Wine and Oil Plantation,"[25] explain and illustrate how computer simulation can help archaeologists study systems, which Walsh defines as complex units of interconnecting attributes.[26] By isolating a system from its context and learning how it operates, archaeologists can better understand how the system relates to its context in the world.

6.3.5 Graphics

Sometime during the 1970s, archaeologists began to use computers to create graphic representations of archaeological data. Graphic representations of data enable archaeologists to display and analyze facts in creative and helpful ways. Charles W. McNett, Jr.'s article, "Computer Graphics in the Analysis of Archaeological Data," illustrates some of the uses of computer graphics in archaeology and discusses techniques such as scattergrams, backplots, and block routines.[27]

A *scattergram* plots data in two dimensions on a standard set of X-Y coordinates. Using a scattergram routine, the distribution of artifacts can be displayed graphically and output to a printer. It is difficult to change the angle of view on many scattergram routines, however, and "most . . . scattergram routines will not allow the use of special symbols for different classes of data so that it is difficult to locate, much less interpret, two or more classes of artifacts in the same plot."[28]

BACKPLOT is a special-purpose two-dimensional graphics routine that allows archaeologists to adjust the angle of view and to identify artifacts by serial numbers or by symbols. It can output data to a printer.

BLOCK is a three-dimensional program that allows archaeologists to view data from any angle. BLOCK can output data to a plotter in the form of a three-dimensional drawing.

According to a paper presented by Virginia R. Badler and Norman I. Badler at the 1986 AAR/SBL convention in Atlanta, recent technological advances in field-portable, 3-D digitizers now make "direct, on-site recording of site geometry and findspots . . . almost a reality."[29] The Badlers mention the Science Accessories Corporation's Sonic Digitizer (SD) as one such device. The SD, which works in a 5- to 10-foot cube and which costs $7,500 (plus $250 for IBM-PC software), uses sound waves to measure and map the location of objects and stores this information on diskette. Such 3-D measuring/mapping devices have the potential of speeding data collection by eliminating the need for measuring the location of artifacts.

In their article, the Badlers also discuss the direct 3-D digitization of artifact shape and size (i.e., photogrammetric data acquisition). They discuss a program called DRAWPOT, which works with a Polhemus 3-D digitizer, and which is able to build 3-D models of objects.

6.4 Microcomputers in Field Applications

In his doctoral dissertation for the University of Minnesota,[30] Dr. Alden A. Arndt, Jr. discusses the characteristics of archaeological data and presents a design for a microcomputer that can be used in the field to record and analyze data. Dr. Arndt's

---

25. Patton and Holoien, *Computing*, 181–96.

26. Walsh, "Simulation," 163.

27. Gaines, *Applications*, 90–99.

28. McNett, "Graphics," 94.

29. Badler and Badler, "Directions in 3-D Computer Graphics: Applications in Archaeology," 4.

30. June 1984, prepared under the direction of Professors Peter C. Patton, W. D. E. Coulson, Tom B. Jones, G. E. Gibbon, and G. R. Rapp, Jr.

dissertation discusses the hardware and software that he designed and contains two BASIC listings: "Field Recorder Software Listing" and "Base Station Software Listing."

Since Dr. Arndt began his project in 1980, many companies have begun to market truly portable "briefcase," or "laptop," computers, some of which are sophisticated enough to meet the needs of archaeologists in the field and rugged enough to withstand the harsh conditions found there. Among those companies are Hewlett-Packard, GRiD Systems, Zenith, NEC, IBM, and Data General. GRiD makes an especially rugged and powerful IBM-compatible laptop.[31] Most laptop computers can be run on batteries.

6.5 Bibliographical Resources

The following publications provide information about computers and archaeology. Addresses and phones numbers are those of the circulation/subscription offices.

Newsletter of Computer Archaeology
Newsletter, $6/year (US), $7/year (outside the US)
% Sylvia W. Gaines, Editor
Department of Anthropology
Arizona State University
Tempe, AZ 85287
(602) 965-7516

Archaeological Computing Newsletter
% Department of Computing
North Staffordshire Polytechnic
Blackheath Lane
Stafford ST18 0AD
United Kingdom

---

31. Contact GRiD Systems, 2535 Garcia Ave., Mountain View CA 94043; (415) 961-4800. Because of their ruggedness (among other reasons), GRiD laptops have been chosen for field use by the U.S. military.

Bibliography

Arndt, Alden A. Jr. A *Microprocessor Computer System for Field Capture of Archaeological Data*. Unpublished University of Minnesota Ph.D. dissertation, June 1984.

Arndt, A. A., and W. D. E. Coulson. "The Development of a Field Computer for Archaeological Use at Naukratis in Egypt." *Biblical Archaeology*. Forthcoming.

Arnold, J. B. III. "Archaeological Applications of Computer Graphics." In *Advances in Archaeological Method and Theory*, vol. 5. Edited by M. B. Schiffer, 179–216. New York: Academic Press, 1982.

Badler, Norman I., and Virginia R. Badler. "Directions in 3-D Computer Graphics: Applications in Archaeology." Unpublished paper delivered November 23, 1986, at the AAR/SBL meeting in Atlanta, Georgia.

————. "Interaction with a Color Computer Graphics Systems for Archaeological Sites." *Computer Graphics* 1 (October 1978): 12–18.

Buccellati, Giorgio, and Oliver Rouault. "Digital Plotting of Archaeological Floor Plans." *CARNES* 1 (September 1983): 3–40.

Buckland, P. "An Experiment in the Use of a Computer for On-Site Recording of Finds." *Science and Archaeology* 9 (1973): 22–24.

Coulson, William D. E., and Albert Leonard. "Investigations at Naukratis and Environs 1980 and 1981." *American Journal of Archaeology* 86 (1982): 361–80.

Doran, James. *Mathematics and Computers in Archaeology*. Cambridge, Mass.: Harvard University Press, 1975.

————. "Systems Theory, Computer Simulations and Archaeology." *World Archaeology* 1 (1969): 289–98.

Gaines, Sylvia, W. "Computer Use at an Archaeological Field Location." *American Antiquity* 39 (1974): 454–62.

————. "Computerized Data Bases in Archaeology: The European Situation." *Computers and the Humanities* 15 (1981): 223–26.

————., ed. *Data Bank Applications in Archaeology*. Tuscon, Ariz.: University of Arizona Press, 1981.

Galloway, P. "An Introduction to Archaeological Computing: Some Problems and Methods." *Humanistische Data* (1977): 15–20.

Kelly-Buccellati, Marilyn, and Ernestine S. Elster. "Statistics in Archaeology and its Application to Ancient Near Eastern Data." *Orientalia* NS 42 (1973): 195–211.

Klieger, Douglas M. *Computer Use for Social Sciences*. Allyn, 1983.

Lehman, R. S. *Computer Simulations and Modeling*. Hillsdale, N.J.: Lawrence Erlbaum Associates, 1977.

McNally, S. J., and V. A. Walsh. "A Computer-Assisted Artifact Cataloging System." *Journal of Field Archaeology*. Date not known.

Morris, Holly J., and Vicky A. Walsh. "CATO: A Computer Simulation of a Roman Wine and Oil Plantation." In *Computing in the Humanities*. Edited by Peter C. Patton and Renee A. Holoien, 181–96. Lexington, Mass.: D.C. Heath & Co., 1981.

Sabloff, J. A., ed. *Simulations in Archaeology*. Albuquerque, N.M.: University of New Mexico Press, 1981.

Strange, James F. "Recent Computer Applications in Ancient Near Eastern Archaeology." In *The Answers Lie Below: Essays in Honor of Lawrence Edmund Toombs*. 129–46. Lanham: University Press of America, 1984.

————. "Using the Microcomputer in the Field: The Case of the Merion Excavation Project." *Newsletter of the ASOR* 4 (1981): 8–11.

Tate, Ruth. "Minnesota Archaeological-Survey Data Base." In *Computing in the Humanities*. Edited by Peter C. Patton and Renee A. Holoien, 205–14. Lexington, Mass.: D.C. Heath & Co., 1981.

Walsh, V. "Computer-Aided Instruction in Archaeology." In *Computing in the Humanities*. Edited by Peter C. Patton and Renee A. Holoien, 215–29. Lexington, Mass.: D.C. Heath & Co., 1981.

————. "Computer Simulation Methodology for Archaeology." In *Computing in the Humanities*. Edited by Richard W. Bailey, 163–74. New York: North-Holland Pub. Co., 1982.

Whallon, R. "The Computer in Archaeology: A Critical Survey." *Computers and the Humanities* 7 (1972): 29–45.

Wilcock, J. D. "An Experiment in the Use of a Computer for On-Site Records." *Science and Archaeology* 9 (1973): 22–25.

Chapter 7

Machine-Readable Ancient Texts, Text Archives, and Related Projects

I am not so lost in lexicography
As to forget that words are the
Daughters of earth, and that
Things are the sons of heaven.
Samuel Johnson[1]

7.1 Introduction

Not long after humanists discovered computers, they began to adapt and use programming languages with colorful names, such as SNOBOL,[2] SPITBOL,[3] SNAP,[4] and SCAN,[5] and to create programs with even stranger names, such as EYEBALL,[6] OCCULT,[7] and PROVIDE,[8] to enable them to manipulate and study literary texts. They also started to establish large textual data bases and data banks. Soon biblical and classical scholars, following the lead of their humanist colleagues, began to develop elaborately coded, or "tagged," versions of the Masoretic Text, the Septuagint, and the Greek New Testament and to create textual data banks, such as the Thesaurus Linguae Graecae Project, which we will discuss later in this chapter.

It is not the purpose of this chapter to provide a history of all the various projects that have produced or that are in the process of producing "tagged" versions of classical, biblical, or religious texts or that are establishing textual data bases, though such a history would be interesting. Many biblical and classical scholars have labored in numerous projects around the world to create the fantastic electronic tools and resources we will discuss in this chapter, and they certainly deserve a wise and judicious historian to chronicle the contribution each has made. Although that history will have to wait, special mention should be made of the pioneering work of J. Arthur Baird and his The Computer Bible (see below under Andersen-Forbes), of the SBL

---

1. (1709–1784), Preface to his *Dictionary* (1755).
2. StriNg-Oriented SymBOlic Language. See Griswold, *SNOBOL4*; Hockey, *SNOBOL*; Gimpel, "Processing," 175–86.
3. The fast version of SNOBOL4.
4. See Barnett, "SNAP," and Housden, "SNAP."
5. See Brown, "SCAN."
6. See Ross, "EYEBALL," and Ross and Rasche, "EYEBALL."
7. See Petty and Gibson, *Project OCCULT*.
8. See Swigger, "PROVIDE."

Computer Assisted Research Group, and of David W. Packard. Both Baird and the SBL group did much to stimulate and foster the use of computers in the field of biblical studies,[9] as did Packard in the field of classical studies.[10]

Neither will this chapter devote space to a description of the ways computers are being used in the field of textual criticism[11] and to create concordances.[12] Nor will I elaborate on the use of computers in the humanities in general. On this topic, the interested reader should consult the books listed in the accompanying footnote, which survey the various ways humanists have used and are using computers.[13] Especially helpful in that regard are Susan Hockey, *A Guide to Computer Applications in the Humanities*, Robert L. Oakman, *Computer Methods for Literary Research*, and John R. Abercrombie, *Computer Programs for Literary Analysis*—a primer that discusses and lists various programs (written in BASIC, Pascal, and IBYX) that are designed for literary analysis.[14]

In this chapter we will examine the fruits of the scholarly labors of biblical scholars, classicists, and linguists who have produced computer tools and resources for the study of ancient texts. We will discuss individual machine-readable texts, text archives, specialized programs for manipulating tagged, machine-readable texts, and university-centered projects that are creating computer-based tools for text-oriented humanistic studies.

Also related to our interests in this chapter are several products discussed or described in chapter 2. David Packard's Ibycus Scholarly Computer and the WordCruncher® text-retrieval system, for example, are two of several such products, and both of them have been reviewed in detail in the *Bits & Bytes Review*™.[15]

Scholars interested in learning more about computer-assisted biblical-studies projects, most of which are discussed in this chapter, may wish to purchase *Bible and*

---

9. Kenneth Grayston, "Computers and the New Testament," *NTS* 17 (1971): 477–80, contains interesting historical information about some of the early pioneers in this field, the beginnings of the SBL Computer Assisted Research Group, and the beginnings of The Computer Bible.

10. See Levenson, "Crunching," and Glazebrook, "Classics."

11. See Burch, "Textual Criticism"; Dearing, "Textual Criticism," "Textual Analysis," "Determining Variations"; Weitzman, "Computer"; Epp, "Textual Criticism"; Fischer, "Textual Criticism," "Computer"; Mulken, "Text Variants"; Ott, "Textual Criticism"; Zarri, "Textual Criticism," "Automated Textual Criticism"; Froger, "La critique des textes," "Electronic Machine"; Griffith, "Numerical Taxonomy," "Numerical Analysis"; Mullen, "Text Variants."

12. See Burton, "Concordance," "The Fifties," "The Early Sixties," "Process, Programs, Products," "Machine Decisions," "Review"; Busa, "Index Thomisticus"; Oakman, "Computerized Collation," "Concordances"; Cabaniss, "Text Collation"; Devine, "Computer-Generated Concordances"; Dixon, "Concordances"; Howard-Hill, *Literary Concordances*; Ingram, "Concordances"; Koubourlis, "Concordance"; Parrish, "Concordance-Making," "Problems"; Parunak, "Prolegomena"; Preston and Coleman, "Considerations"; Raben, "Death"; Smith, "GENEDEX," 50–53.

13. See Pierson, *Computers*; Bowles, *Computers*; Burke, *Computers*; Wisbey, *Computer*; Aitken, *Computer*; Zampolli and Calzolari, *Linguistica Mathematica*; Mitchell, *Computers*; Jones, *Computer*; Lusignan and North, *Computing*; Zampolli and Calzolari, *Linguistics*; Ager et al., *Advances*; Malachi, *Proceedings*; Allen and Petofi, *Aspects*; Hockey, *Guide*; Oakman, *Methods*; Raben and Marks, *Data Bases*; Patton and Holoien, *Computing*; Bailey, *Computing*; Burton and Short, *Conference*; Allen, *Computers*; Abercrombie, *Programs*; Widemann, "Computers," "Recent Scholarship," "Trends."

14. E.g., index, frequency, concordance, text criticism, searching, parsing, and morphological analysis programs. This book, which contains many helpful programming hints, techniques, and general-purpose subroutines, as well as actual examples of programs in various computer languages, may be purchased with the programs on a 5.25-inch floppy disk. Contact: The University of Pennsylvania Press, Blockley Hall, 13th Floor, 418 Service Dr., Philadelphia, PA 19104; (215) 898-6261; book only: $14.95; book and disk: $26.50.

15. The Ibycus Scholarly Computer was reviewed in *Bits & Bytes Review*™ 1 (October 1986): 1–8, and the WordCruncher® text-retrieval system in *Bits & Bytes Review*™ 1 (February 1987): 1–8.

Computer: The Text (Proceedings of the First International Colloquium),[16] a collection of over three dozen papers from the conference held September 2-4, 1985, in Louvain-la-Neuve (Belgium). The papers in that book describe the state-of-the-art in computer-assisted biblical studies—broadly understood—as of 1985. Several of the descriptions of projects in this chapter are based on prepublication versions of material in that book; other descriptions are based on more recent material. With only a few exceptions, each section in this chapter has been carefully proofread and corrected by the person(s) whose work it describes.

7.2 A Matter of Words

Before we proceed, we must define a number of terms. What is a "machine-readable text"? How are they produced? What is "tagging"? How is a tagged, machine-readable, textual data base structured, or organized? What are tagged, machine-readable texts useful for?

7.2.1 Machine-Readable Texts

A machine-readable text (MRT) is a text that exists on media that can be read by a computer. Such media are magnetic (tape, hard disks, floppy disks) or optical (CD-ROMs, WORMs). Broadly speaking, any text that can be displayed on a computer screen is a MRT.

7.2.2 How They Are Produced

Written or printed texts may be converted into MRTs in several ways, including keying and scanning. To "key" the Hebrew Bible into a computer, for example, would require typing the entire Old Testament on disks. If a machine with a standard ROM character generator were used (see chapter 2), the Hebrew would be entered and displayed in a transliterated form, using alphanumeric characters to represent the vowels, cantillation signs, and other diacritical marks. Alternatively, a Hebrew ROM character generator would allow the text to be entered and displayed in Hebrew, as would working in graphics-mode. Although keying is tedious and time-consuming, because optical scanners cannot yet "read" pointed Hebrew text, it is the process that has been used by several projects to produce MRTs of the Old Testament. Generally speaking, however, with characters that are not as complicated as vocalized Hebrew, using an optical character recognizer (OCR) to create MRTs from printed texts is much faster and more accurate than keying.[17]

OCRs are electronic machines—not unlike photocopiers in size, appearance, and function—that automatically read alphanumeric characters from written or printed material and write the corresponding (ASCII or other) coded values of those symbols to disk. For a helpful review of nine scanners, see Tom Stanton, Diane Burns, and S. Venit, "Page-To-Disk Technology: Nine State-of-the-Art Scanners," *PC Magazine* (September 30, 1986): 128–77.[18] In ideal circumstances the most sophisticated OCRs can be configured to read a variety of type and print styles in all sorts of roman and nonroman (e.g., Greek, Hebrew, Coptic) alphabets, as well as handwritten material.

---

16. Paris-Geneva: Champion-Slatkine, 1986; available from the Association International Bible et Informatique, 13 rue de la Bruyère, B-5974 Opprebais, Belgium, telephone: (32) 10-88-8262; from North America dial direct: 011-32-10-88-8262.

17. The text files that OCRs create can be used with a wide range of text-manipulation programs.

18. Also see Greitzer, "Scanning,"; Shea, "Peripherals"; Nagy, "Digitizers"; Stewart, "Machines"; Stanton, "Peripheral Vision," "Kurzweil 4000"; Stanton and Stark, "OCRs"; Rosenthal, "Scanners."

The best OCRs automatically feed, scan, and digitize printed material at maximum rates of 100 to 300 pages per hour, with error ratings as low as 1 per 300,000 characters[19]—about ten to thirty times faster and 100 times more accurate than the best typist.[20] The most sophisticated OCRs are manufactured by Kurzweil Computer Products, and they cost approximately $36,500,[21] though there are a number of companies that sell less sophisticated machines in the $500 to $11,000 range.[22] The Kurzweil scanners are often referred to as KDEMs—Kurzweil Data Entry Machines—though the only scanner currently marketed by Kurzweil Computer Products is called the "Kurzweil 4000."

For more information on Kurzweil products, contact the company at the following address.

> Kurzweil Computer Products, Inc.
> 185 Albany St.
> Cambridge, MA 02139
> (617) 864-4700

Less expensive OCRs are available from the following companies.

> CompuScan PCS 230
> CompuScan, Inc.
> 81 Two Bridges Rd., Bldg. 2
> Fairfield, NJ 07006
> (201) 575-0500
> List Price: $5,695

> Personal Scanner 2000
> Electronic Information Technology, Inc.
> 373 Rt. 46
> West Fairfield, NJ 07006
> (201) 227-1447
> List Price: $2,995

> Datacopy 730
> Datacopy Corp.
> 1215 Terra Bella Ave.
> Mountain View, CA 94043
> (415) 965-7900
> List Price: $3,950

> Microtek MS-300A
> Microtek Lab, Inc.
> 16901 S. Western Ave.
> Gardena, CA 90247
> (213 321-2121
> List Price: $2,500

---

19. Actual rates vary according to machine, typeface, condition and complexity of document, and other factors. It is usually necessary to edit scanned material to correct mistakes, especially if the material contains nonroman characters.

20. Shea, "Peripherals," 46; Stanton and Stark, "OCRs," 116–17. According to Stanton and Stark (ibid., 116), most mid-range OCRs ($6,000–$11,000) scan at an average rate of 120 pages per hour. Because it uses a pattern-recognition rather than a template-matching approach to scanning, the Kurzweil 4000 (see below) is more versatile and powerful, though slower, than many scanners. It operates at a speed of 30 characters per second (i.e., about a typewritten page a minute, or 60 or so pages an hour, on the average) in the production mode (see Stanton, "Kurzweil 4000").

21. See Stanton, "Kurzweil 4000," and Galloway, "Kurzweil Data Entry Machine," for reviews of this state-of-the-art optical scanner. Cf. "Kurzweil"; "Scanner Debuts"; Hockey, "Computing," "Input and Output"; and Oakman, *Methods*, 12–40, for in-depth discussions of text input and output.

22. See Stanton and Stark, "OCRs," and Shea, "Peripherals," 53, for more information.

SpectraFAX 200
SpectraFAX Corp.
2000 Palm St. South
Naples, FL 33962
(813) 775-2737
List Price: $3,995

Dest PC Scan
DEST Corporation
1201 Cadillac Ct.
Milpitas, CA 95035
(408) 946-7100
List Price: $2,785

eSCAN
Tecmar, Inc.
6225 Cochran Rd.
Solon, OH 44139
(216) 349-0600
List Price: $2,495

Canon IX-12
Canon USA
One Canon Plaza
Lake Success, NY 11042-9979
(516) 488-6700
List Price: $1,685

Compound Document Processor
Palantir Corp.
2500 Augustine Dr.
Santa Clara, CA 95054
(408) 986-8006
List Price: $39,500

Professor M. A. Pollatschek, a colleague of Professor Y. T. Radday (see below under CASTLOTS) and a consultant for statistical data processing, has developed an OCR called "Elijah's Cave Reader" that is designed to scan consonantal, unpointed Hebrew text. Contact:

Prof. M. A. Pollatschek
Technion—Israel Institute of Technology
Haifa 32 000
Israel
(04) 38-8228; from North America: (011) 972-4-38-8228.

Several academic institutions will scan typed and printed texts. Dartmouth College's KIEWIT Computation Center will scan roman characters only for $1.50 per page (printed or typed, single or double-spaced) and a minimum per-time set-up charge of $10. Contact:

Warren Belding or Heather LaCasse
% KIEWIT Computation Center
Dartmouth College
Hanover, NH 03755
(603) 646-2643.

The University of Pennsylvania's Center for Computer Analysis of Texts (CCAT) will scan printed or typed material for approximately $1 per 400 words (an average

495

printed page or about two double-spaced typed pages). CCAT scans roman and non-roman characters, including Greek, Coptic, Armenian, and Hebrew/Yiddish. Contact:

Dr. John R. Abercrombie
Center for Computer Analysis of Texts
Box 36 College Hall
University of Pennsylvania
Philadelphia, PA 19104
(215) 898-5217.

The Oxford University Computing Service (OUCS) will scan printed and typed materials, in roman and nonroman characters (including Greek, Coptic, Hebrew, and Cyrillic), for the following hourly rates: £10 for Oxford and UK external universities, £20 for foreign universities, £27 for commercial work, and £20 for commercial concession. Contact:

KDEM Service
Oxford University Computing Service
13 Banbury Road
Oxford OX2 6NN
United Kingdom
(0865) 273214; from North America dial direct:
    011-44-865-273214
Electronic Mail: ARTSDATA@VAX2.OXFORD.AC.UK.

According to Dr. Peter B. Batke, Department of Germanic Languages and Literature, Duke University, scholars and students from outside the university may use Duke's KDEM (located in the department just mentioned). According to Dr. Batke, it takes "about 15 minutes" to be shown how to operate the machine. Contact:

Dr. Peter B. Batke
Duke University
Department of Germanic Languages and Literature
104 Language Bldg.
Durham, NC 27706
(919) 684-3836.

7.2.3 Tagging

Tagging is the process of attaching descriptive codes to words. Those codes, or *tags*, may consist of any information—textual, morphological, syntactical, or semantic—that is to be associated with a particular word or form. For example, *gegraptai* in Mark 1:2 might be assigned the following tags: (1) perfect passive, third person singular, (2) from *grapho*, (3) a derivative of *graph-* that may be found in (4) Mark, (5) chapter 1, (6) verse 2, (7) as word 2, (8) in the UBS3 version of the Greek New Testament. Tags allow texts to be searched and concorded in complex and creative ways, as we will learn below.

Tagged texts are usually stored in data base formats, not as continuous, freely flowing text (as are documents in word processing files). In an actual data base, the tags in the preceding example might be grouped into types and expressed in an abbreviated form that could look like this: "*gegraptai* [Vpp3s] [*grapho, graph-*] [Mk, 1, 2, 2] [UBS3]." The number and type of tags assigned to words in a MRT may be quite extensive and elaborate. (LBase, a program mentioned in chapter 2, allows users to create their own tagging scheme for MRTs.)

496

7.2.4 Data Base Structures

There are several fundamental types of data base structures—relational, hierarchical, and network[23]—that differ in the ways they organize and manipulate data. The data bases we will examine in this chapter, however, are *textual* (or bibliographical) data bases and so do not fall into any of those categories. Although there is some similarity between the way most of the following data bases organize their files and the way files are structured in a relational data base, the data bases described below do not support the use of relational operators such as JOIN, PROJECT, and SELECT, and so are not true relational data bases.[24]

The information in the data bases we are about to examine is structured in unordered flat files that consist of two-dimensional sets of intersecting rows and columns that can be arranged in any order (hence *unordered* in "unordered flat file"). The intersection of each row and column is called a *cell*. A *column* is all the data, or cells, on the same vertical line, and a *row* is all the data, or cells, on the same horizontal line. Each column represents a different fixed field, or domain, of information, and each cell of each row contains the specific datum that belongs in the field it is under. Each row, then, gives one set of specific values for the fields, or domains, and such a set of values is known as a *tuple*. A *tuple*, then, is a specific example of a particular relationship that is defined by a concrete set of values assigned to one set of fixed fields. In the example from Mark 1:2 above, the relation was part-of-speech (*gegraptai*), and the fields included book, chapter, verse, word number, inflection, lemma, and so forth. "Part-of-speech" is the name of the relation, and the specific set of values for the different fields (e.g., person, number, gender, root) is the tuple, or example, of the relation.

7.2.5 Using a Textual Data Base

Tagged textual data bases are extremely powerful tools. Depending on the type and level of tagging in such a data base, researchers may study (1) graphical words and (2) orthographical considerations, (3) lexical words and (4) their morphological analysis, (5) textual variants and (6) their collation, and (7) syntax, (8) grammar, and (9) semantics. Because biblical texts are a closed, relatively small corpus, data bases in which every graphical word is tagged have been created for the Masoretic Text, the Septuagint, and the Greek New Testament. And as we will see later in this chapter, many data banks of untagged MRTs, such as the TLG Project (60 million words of Greek text from Homer—ca. 750 B.C.—to A.D. 600), the Responsa Project (over 50 million words of Jewish religious texts), and projects working with the Documentary Papyri, Greek Inscriptions, and other bodies of ancient literature, are now available.

Exhaustive, complete, tagged versions of the biblical texts allow them to be studied more accurately and powerfully and in ways that are not otherwise possible. For example, computers can quickly locate *every* occurrence of *any* tagged orthographical, morphological, lexical, syntactical, or grammatical construction, in any range of text, and arrange and display that information in different formats—a task that otherwise would be impossible. The texts of different versions and translations can easily be compared on any biblical passage, and translation tendencies and patterns of change between and among texts can be analyzed and studied. Complex syntactical phenomena can be investigated, and more refined, more accurate grammars constructed. Not only are computers powerful tools that can assist in many traditional

---

23. See Flores, *Architecture*; Aho et al., *Structures and Algorithms*; Gonnet, *Algorithms and Data Structures*; Mehlhorn, *Structures and Algorithms*.

24. See Parunak, "Data Base Design for Biblical Texts," for a theoretical description of a relational data base model for biblical texts; cf. Cercone and Goebel, "Data Bases" (and its extensive bibliography) and Porch, "Devices."

types of textual and linguistic studies, they also open up new ways of analyzing and studying texts.

7.3 Machine-Readable Versions of the Masoretic Text

In this section we will examine the results of computer projects from around the world that have produced MRTs of the Masoretic Text. Each tagged version of the Masoretic Text (or of any text) has a distinctive design that reflects the linguistic philosophy and goals of its creators, and so is better suited for some research purposes than for others.[25] My concern in this section, however, is to describe the programs and data bases and to explain what they are designed to do, not to evaluate them.

The order in which we will examine the following programs and data bases indicates nothing about their chronological relationships or relative values. In some cases, scholars have provided brief histories and explanations of their work, which I have edited and incorporated in my remarks. Because some scholars provided more information than others, some of the following sections are longer and more complete than others. The relative lengths of the following discussions, however, is not meant to reflect the relative values of the different projects.[26]

7.3.1 Andersen and Forbes

• *BASIC DATA BASE INFORMATION*

Key Person(s): Francis I. Andersen (University of Queensland), A. Dean Forbes (Hewlett-Packard Laboratories, Palo Alto, California)
Location of Project: Queensland, Australia
Project Address: Department of Studies in Religion, University of Queensland, St. Lucia, Queensland, Australia 4067
Telephones: (07) 377-3985; from North America dial direct: 011-61-07-377-3985
Date Project Began: 1970
Date Project Completed: 1979 (MRT), 1980 (dictionary)
Sources of Funding: The National Endowment for the Humanities of the United States of America, Australian Research Grants Commission
Primary Purpose of Project: To create a fully lemmatized, fully parsed, linguistic dictionary of the entire vocabulary of the Hebrew Bible to facilitate the scientific study of Hebrew grammar.
Textual Authority: L (Leningrad Codex B 19ᵃ)
Machine-Readable Text Includes: Full orthographic details
Vocalized: Yes
Cantillated: Only *maqqep, paseq, silluq,* and *'tnah*
Type of Tagging: Morphological and syntactical
Level of Tagging: 70 tags are used to describe all the distinctions that are made for 32 "families" (parts of speech), which consist of stems and their obligatory prefixes and suffixes. In addition to identifying the "family" to which each entry belongs, each item's parsing vector is used to specify number, gender, person, state, stem, and voice. Tags parse vocabulary items by specifying morphological identity and syntactic potential.
Scope of Tagging: The entire Masoretic Text, as represented by L
Type of Text Files: Not known
Programming Language: Not known
Output Options: Screen, tape, print; transliterated, vocalized, coded text or vocalized Hebrew text. *Ketib* and *qere* may be switched on and off.
Availability of Tapes or Disks: Not available
Cost of Tapes or Disks: Not applicable

---

25. Linguistic questions of a general, introductory nature are discussed in John Lyons, *Introduction to Theoretical Linguistics* (Cambridge: Cambridge University Press, 1968).

26. Most of the projects discussed below are continually being refined and improved. In this section, all Hebrew will be given in transliterated form.

Key Bibliographical References: "Problems in Taxonomy and Lemmatization," 37–50; "A Machine-Readable Hebrew Dictionary," vols. 6, 9, 10, 14, and 14a in The Computer Bible Series.[27] Also see Andersen, *The Verbless Clause in the Hebrew Pentateuch*, and Andersen, *The Sentence in Biblical Hebrew*.

7.3.1.1 Introduction

The material in this section is based on and partially extracted from a prepublication copy of "Problems in Taxonomy and Lemmatization."[28] Since 1970 Francis I. Andersen and A. Dean Forbes have worked as a team to produce a fully lemmatized, fully parsed, linguistic dictionary of the entire vocabulary of the Hebrew Bible to facilitate the scientific study of Hebrew grammar.[29] Although the following description focuses on the creation of the machine-readable Hebrew text and dictionary, it should be kept in mind that the Andersen-Forbes data base is a tool for studying Hebrew grammar *in general*. Although Andersen's earlier work (e.g., *Clause* and *Sentence*) was influenced by tagmemic theory,[30] and though to a limited extent he and Forbes now follow descriptivist models, both Andersen and Forbes consider themselves eclectic and uncommitted in their approach to grammar; they are not members of a particular linguistic school.[31]

Andersen's and Forbes's MRT is one of only four *complete* MRTs of the Masoretic Text. The other three have been produced by Gérard Weil (see below under CATAB), Parunak and Whitaker (the Michigan-Claremont Old Testament, see below under MPCABS), and Poswick (see below under CIB). The MRTs used by Mikrah Research Systems's COMPU-BIBLE and COMPUCORD, the Global Jewish Database, and CATSS (see below) are proofed (also known as "verified"), improved versions of the Michigan-Claremont Old Testament, as is part of the OTIK's data base of machine-readable Hebrew texts (see below).

7.3.1.2 The Text

In preparing their machine-readable version of the Masoretic Text (MT), Andersen and Forbes decided to follow L, the Leningrad Codex B 19ᵃ, as scrupulously as possible and to transcribe consonants, vowels, and four of the major cantillation marks (*maqqep, paseq, silluq,* and *'tnah*) with a one-to-one code that allows them to be

---

27. The Computer Bible Project, begun in the early 1970s under the leadership of Dr. J. Arthur Baird (who with David Noel Freedman is the editor of each volume), is published by Biblical Research Associates (The College of Wooster, Wooster, Ohio 44691; (216) 263-2470) and consists of a series of specialized concordances on many of the books of the Bible. These KWIC (key-word-in-context) concordances differ in the type and amount of linguistic information they associate with each word. Generally speaking, they contain morphological, grammatical, and syntactical information about every entry, as well as (where appropriate) information about each word's form, source, redaction, audience, and so forth. Because contributors to The Computer Bible have different linguistic philosophies, have used different codes, and have tagged, organized, and displayed their texts in different ways, the volumes vary in their suitability for specific research purposes. See Baird, "Biblical Research Associates"; Gil, "Computer Bible"; and Talstra, "Exegesis."

28. *Bible and Computer*, 37–50. Similar, though less recent, information can be found in Andersen and Forbes, *Ruth and Jonah*, 3–49, though that information does not explain the current capabilities of their programs and data base.

29. They completed their machine-readable version of the Masoretic Text in 1979 and their linguistic dictionary in 1980.

30. On tagmemic theory see, for example, Andersen, *Clause*, esp. 25–27; Pike, "On Tagmemes," "Guide," *Coordination, Language, Linguistic Concepts, Tagmemics*; Longacre, "Insights," "Tagma to Tagmeme," "String Constituent Analysis," *Grammar Discovery, Discourse*; Pike and Pike *Analysis, Text and Tagmeme*; Brend and Pike, *Tagmemics*; Ballard et al., *Deep and Surface Grammar*; Waterhouse, *Tagmemics*; Cook, *Tagmemic Analysis*; Costello, *Change*.

31. See Lyons, *Introduction*, for an explanation of these terms.

regenerated into pointed Hebrew script. Because the *defective* and *plene* spelling of certain vowels provides information about the history of Hebrew spelling that can be important in helping to date sections of the Hebrew Bible,[32] special symbols are used to represent the five diagraphs that can result from using *yod* and *waw* as *matres lectionis*. *Qames gadol* and *qames hatup*, however, are not distinguished in the transcription. The orthographic word is the transcriptional unit and is defined as a string of syllables with a spacer (space, hyphen, or other punctuation) before and after it.

A typical transcribed line might look like this:)%LEY'H@ WA'Y. IT. %N YHWH L'@H. H%R̂@YON WA'T. %LED B. %N=. The termination of each verse is marked with a "=," a "+" (when it ends a chapter), or an "X" (when it ends a book).

The Leningrad Codex was not adopted because its claims are beyond dispute but because it presently enjoys more prestige than other manuscripts and has been used as the basis for several modern critical editions, including the *Biblia Hebraica Stuttgartensia* (BHS), which has replaced Kittel's third edition (BH³).[33]

The schedule of *ketib/qere* variants, as found in BHS, was preserved. Each variant is individually labeled in the data base, along with information about which variant is a *ketib/qere* of which manuscript. The *ketib* was transcribed as consonants only and the *qere* as fully pointed. The *ketib* and the *qere* can be switched on and off as desired.

7.3.1.3 The Vocabulary

Orthographic words are not the most appropriate unit for studying grammar because many of them are complex constructions whose constituents may be identified as members of the basic vocabulary. Rather than working with primitive morphemes (the ultimate constituents of orthographic words), which would have been extremely complex and in many types of situations prone to ambiguity,[34] Andersen and Forbes followed a different path. They dissected prefixes and suffixes from complex verbs and nouns but left as whole constructions those stems that have obligatory affixes (prefixes or suffixes). They did not isolate roots and stem-forming morphemes, though they did leave intact the noun inflections of number and gender and the verb inflections of number, gender, and person. Thus they demarcated vocabulary items that have grammatical functions on the higher levels of syntax.[35]

By following that technique, Andersen and Forbes isolated various types of text "segments," which represent an inventory of the lexical-grammatical vocabulary of the language. Some segments are whole words, but words with one or more optional affixes are analyzed as two or more segments. For example, QOL ("voice") is one segment, HAQ.OL ("the voice") is two segments, and W.B:QOLO ("and with his voice") is four segments.

7.3.1.4 Parsing

In their analysis of the text, Andersen and Forbes created a parsing vector for each vocabulary item, since some items are not words in the orthographic sense. A "parsing vector," which is a coded description of each item's grammatical features, contains up to six elements: (1) family (see below), (2) number (singular, dual, plural, collective,

---

32. See Andersen and Forbes, "Orthography and Text Transmission" and *Spelling in the Hebrew Bible*.

33. Andersen and Forbes corrected several typographical errors in the BHS edition of L by consulting the facsimile of L.

34. See Andersen and Forbes, *Ruth and Jonah*, 15–20.

35. See ibid., 14–26, for an explanation and justification of the way they divided orthographic words into segments for linguistic analysis.

distributive), (3) gender (masculine, feminine, common), (4) person (first, second, third), (5) state (normal, definite, pausal, construct, suffixed), (6) stem (of verbs), and (7) voice (active, middle, passive). Since "state" is distinguished only for nouns and "person" is distinguished only for verbs and pronouns, these two parsing vector features share the same field in the Andersen-Forbes data base, thereby reducing the number of vector items, or fields, to six.

The intrinsic semantic and linguistic features that a lexical item, or "segment," manifests in each of its textual occurrences (i.e., the formal-structural features) are parsed as a gloss (translation value). Intrinsic semantic meanings belong to systemic categories such as number, gender, person, and so forth, and are provided for in Hebrew morphology by the forms of inflections of verbs and nouns. A noun, for example, must have gender and number, just as it is obligatory for all finite verbs to have number, gender, and person. The Hebrew verb system also manifests a set of formal contrasts that correspond to mood-tense-aspect-transitivity-voice distinctions, in various combinations, and that are categorized according to stem type.

Andersen and Forbes developed a taxonomic system for the entire Hebrew vocabulary that divides words into sets called "families," which closely parallel conventional parts of speech. There are three fundamental "orders" of families: verbals (including infinitives and participles), substantives (which include nouns, pronouns, and verbal nouns), and particles (which include conjunctions, prepositions, modals, interrogatives, negatives, and adverbs). Altogether, there are 32 taxonomic families in the Andersen-Forbes system: 12 families of verbals, 8 families of substantives, and 12 families of particles. Seventy alphanumeric symbols are used to tag all the distinctions that are made in the taxonomic category *family*.

The hierarchical arrangement that Andersen and Forbes created permits lexical items to be described and categorized on a gradient that ranges from formal-grammatical distinctions that focus on morphology and syntax to lexical-semantic distinctions that focus on meaning and use. Thus Andersen and Forbes believe that lexical *form* and lexical *function* both must be used to adequately describe and categorize language, a philosophy not shared by some of the other scholars who have created MRTs of the Hebrew Bible (see below). Andersen and Forbes believe that morphological, lexicographical, syntactical, and semantic categories must all be used to construct a taxonomy that does justice to the language.[36] For some families (e.g., prepositions), the taxonomy has moved so far into the lexicon that some individual lexical items have been made into a distinct family. Thus the hierarchy has a different shape in some places than in others. Although some semantic distinctions have been made among proper nouns, other nouns and all verbs have not yet been submitted to semantic analysis and classification. Andersen and Forbes plan to do that in the future.

7.3.1.5 Lemmatizing

After machine coding the text and parsing its words, the next logical step in creating the linguistic dictionary was to lemmatize all the parsed lexical information. *Lem-*

---

36. In other words, unlike many of their colleagues (see below), Andersen and Forbes do not restrict themselves to an analysis of the forms of words (morphology) and their combinations (syntax) to try to understand their function in the language as a whole (grammar), nor do they simply analyze the function of words to try to construct a grammar. Their approach is more holistic and incorporates both linguistic forms and linguistic functions as categories used to understand grammar. As Andersen says in a different, though related, context: "The descriptive language model used in this study is holistic rather than analytical. It highlights grammatical relationships within a unified construction rather than the isolated functions of the individual constituents. . . . While the tagmemic model utilizes certain identification procedures found also in immediate constituent analysis, it offers more flexibility, especially in doing justice to the hierarchical features of grammatical structure and to the functional equivalence of forms on different levels of structure, thus breaking the morphology-versus-syntax deadlock" *Clause*, 25–26.

matization refers to the task of collating all related words according to their underlying stems or roots into conventional paradigms and then alphabetizing the results. To lemmatize a language is to sort its words by root across inflections. Once the words in the data base had been lemmatized, sorting the data base by vectors creates sets of identically parsed items. For example, sorting by the vector NPMS creates the set of all items that have the stem form of a masculine plural noun. Alphabetizing those items would scatter them; their common vector gathers them together. In all, 1,023 different vectors are used to sort vocabulary into grammatically distinct sets. Each of those 1,023 vectors, then, describes a distinctly parsed linguistic set whose members are grammatically the same. Those sets range in size. Some vectors label only one item (e.g., the pausal form of the *hiphil* feminine singular participle), but other vectors label large sets (e.g., normal masculine singular nouns = 2,552). Members of the same set tend to have similar orthographical shapes that correspond to their morphological identity, and that shape is often related to the root in a regular way.

Those regularities provided Andersen and Forbes with a basis for creating rules for extracting the root of each word. That was important because the root of a word is the key to its lemmatization.[37] Each set of items with the same parsing vector, then, was analyzed by rules that correspond to the specific patterns of derivation from the root found in that set.

Hebrew has two very different morphological systems, one for nouns and another for verbs. Although many nouns and verbs have the same root in common, the modes of derivation are quite different. Because the verb system is highly ordered and regular, it is best to group all cognate verbs, including infinitives and participles, under their common root. But to group all nouns that share an apparently common root under one lexical entry is artificial and often speculative. Therefore Andersen and Forbes listed nouns by stem consonants, instead of by roots.[38] They followed a descriptive-orthographic, rather than a historical-etymological, approach to lexical ordering.

After finding a root or stem for every lexical item, each of the 1,023 parsing vector sets was rearranged in a sequence that corresponds to the following paradigmatic ordering: verbs precede nouns with matching roots; verbs follow the traditional order of *qal* perfect third singular masculine active to *hitpa'el*; finite verbs (perfect, imperfect, cohortative, imperative) precede verbal nouns.

Finally, each root of each item in each parsing vector was collated and arranged into one comprehensive alphabetical listing, so that all the paradigms for each root are listed with it in the correct sequence. The result of that effort is a fully lemmatized, fully parsed, linguistic dictionary of the entire vocabulary of the Hebrew Bible. "Looking up" any entry provides an exhaustive listing of the paradigms for that root.

7.3.1.6 The Dictionary

The linguistic dictionary contains 41,731 differently parsed forms, or "types," that are described by the 1,023 different parsing vectors. As we saw above, the parsing vectors contain *grammatical information* about an item's family (part of speech), stem-type, voice, number, gender, person (pronouns and finite verbs), and state (nouns). But the linguistic dictionary provides nongrammatical information about each entry, too. In addition to the (1) grammatical information provided by the parsing vectors, the dic-

---

37. From a descriptive point of view, the root of a Hebrew word is a (usually discontinuous) consonantal morpheme common to all the items in a paradigm. In practice, due to the existence of "weak" roots, two or more alloroots may be evident in one paradigm (or set of cognate paradigms) generated from "the same" root. One of those alloforms then has to be selected as the prime form of all the others.

38. Organizing words by etymological roots is exemplified in the concordance of Mandelkern and in the lexicon of Brown, Driver, and Briggs. Ordering verbs by roots and nouns by stems is exemplified in the concordance of Even-Shoshan and in the lexicon of Koehler and Baumgartner.

			PARSING VECTOR		
LEM	LEX	ROOT	S V F N G P	SEGMENT	GLOSS
01075	000	)HB	G A S S M 3	)@HAB	he loved
01075	005	)HB	G A S S M 3	)@H%B	he loved
01075	010	)HB	G A S S M 3	)"H%B	he loved
01075	015	)HB	G A S S F 3	)@H"B@H	she loved
01075	020	)HB	G A S S F 3	)"H%BAT	she loved
01075	025	)HB	G A S S M 2	)@HAB:T.@	thou(m) didst love
01075	030	)HB	G A S S M 2	)"HAB:T.@	thou(m) didst love
01075	035	)HB	G A S S M 2	)"HAB:T.	thou(m) didst love
01075	040	)HB	G A S S F 2	)@HAB:T.:	thou(f) didst love
01075	045	)HB	G A S S C 1	)@HAB:T.|	I loved
01075	050	)HB	G A S S C 1	)@H@B:T.|	I loved
01075	055	)HB	G A S S C 1	)"HAB:T.|	I loved
01075	060	)HB	G A S P C 3	)@H"B*	they loved
01075	065	)HB	G A S P C 3	)"H%B*	they loved
01075	070	)HB	G A S P M 2	)"HAB:T.EM	you(m) loved
01076	000	)HB	G A / S M 3	WA')"H%B	he will love
01076	005	)HB	G A / S M 2	W:')@HAB:T.@	thou(m) shalt love
01076	010	)HB	G A / P M 2	WA')"HAB:T.EM	you(m) will love
01080	000	)HB	G A V S M 3	YE)#HAB	he will love
01080	005	)HB	G A V S M 3	YE)#H@B	he will love
01080	010	)HB	G A V S M 2	T.E)#HAB	thou(m) shalt love
01080	015	)HB	G A V S M 2	T.E)#H@B	thou(m) shalt love
01080	020	)HB	G A V S C 1	)%H@B	I will love
01080	025	)HB	G A V S C 1	)_HAB	I will love
01080	030	)HB	G A V P M 2	T.E)#H@B*	you(m) will love
01080	035	)HB	G A V P M 2	T.E.)#H@B*N	you(m) will love

Figure 7.1: A sample from the Andersen-Forbes data base of some of the inflected forms of the lemma)HB ("love"). G = *qal* stem, A = active voice, V = imperfect, S = suffixed conjugation (i.e., perfect), S = singular, P = plural, M = masculine, F = feminine, C = common. Here is an explanation of the items in the first row (the first tuple). The lemma number of)HB is 01075, the position of the example—)@HAB—in its paradigm is 000, and the root is)HB ("love"). In the Parsing Vector—SVFNGP—the stem type is "G" for *Grund*, that is, *qal*, the voice is "A" for active, the form is "S" because it belongs to a suffixed conjugation (the perfect), a second "S" indicates that the number is singular, the "M" denotes the masculine gender, and the "3" the third person. And the segment of text is)@HAB, whose gloss is "he loved."

tionary (2) gives each entry an English gloss (translation value), (3) provides information about the use or nonuse of *dagesh* with the initial consonant of each form,[39] (4) identifies each paradigm by means of its lead item, using symbols that correspond as closely as possible to the symbols used for the major grammatical families, (5) assigns each entry a lemma number and a (6) lexicon number to facilitate sorting and rearrang-

---

39. The use or nonuse of *dagesh* with the initial consonant of a form constitutes the commonest minimal difference between pairs of segments that in all other respects must be deemed "the same."

BK	CH	VR	PO	L	R	Z	S	V	F	N	G	P	ROOT	SEGMENT	D	GLOSS	LEM	LEX
GE	37	28	18	H	J	N				H	S	M	N YWSP	YOS%P		Yosep	10492	0
GE	37	28	19	H	J	N	p	l					L	L		' to	13166	6
GE	37	28	20	H	J	N				0			H	A		' the	6036	2
GE	37	28	21	H	J	N				E	P	M	a Y$M( )	Y.I$:M:(%)L|M		Ishmaelite	11762	200
GE	37	28	22	H	J	N	p	]					B	B.:		' in	2520	0
GE	37	28	23	H	J	N				#	P	M	N (&R	(E&:R|M		twenty	21746	0
GE	37	28	24	H	J	N				N	S	M	P KSP	K.@SEP		silver	12732	304
GE	37	28	25	H	E	N		J	w				W	WA		' and then	6654	6
GE	37	28	26	H	E	N	H	A		P	M	3 B)	Y.@B	)*		they(m) did bring	2542	12538
GE	37	28	27	H	E	N	p	e					)WT	)ET		— nota acc.	600	0
GE	37	28	28	H	E	N				H	S	M	N YWSP	YOS%P		Yosep	10492	0
GE	37	28	29	H	E	N	L	—	L	S	F	P M/BYM	MI/:R@Y:M@H	=	Egypt	15766	10

Figure 7.2: A sample of a configuration of the Andersen-Forbes data base that sequentially lists the biblical text with pertinent information attached to each word. BK = book, CH = chapter, VR = verse, PO = position, L = language, R = source, Z = genre (as indicated by form criticism), S = stem type, V = voice, F = family (i.e., part of speech), N = normal, G = gender, P = person, ROOT = root, SEGMENT = segment of text, D = delimiter, GLOSS = English gloss, LEM = lemma number, LEX = lexicon, or paradigm, number. Here is an explanation of the items in the first row (the first tuple). The book is Genesis, the chapter 37, the verse 18, the position of the word in the verse is 18, the language is Hebrew, the source is J (Jehovah, or Yahweh), the genre is narrative, there is no stem type, nouns do not have voice so none is specified, the family is proper noun, the number is singular, the gender masculine, the person is none, the root is YWSP, the segmemnt is YOS%P, there is no delimiter, the gloss is "Joseph," the lemma number is 10492, and because the form is the lead entry in the lemmatization, it is numbered 0.

ing sequences,[40] (7) states as a numerical value how many times the lexical item appears in the Hebrew Bible, and (8) lists the first occurrence of the item in the Old Testament. Thus the dictionary contains a wide range of grammatical, lexical, and lexicographical information about each entry.

The usefulness of such a dictionary is multifold. It is possible, for example, to select any subset of the vocabulary as defined by any feature, by any value or values, or by any combination of features and values. Thus all masculine singular nouns can be segregated, or a person could easily and quickly locate all *qal* passive participles for study.

But the greatest usefulness of the dictionary is when it is used in conjunction with the machine-readable text. Information in the dictionary can be "attached" to the text and the result reformatted for study. In its fullest reformatted range, such a version of the text might have up to twenty-three distinct pieces of information associated with it: (1) segment, (2) delimiter, (3) book, (4) chapter, (5) verse, (6) position in verse, (7) status of reading, (8) language, (9) source, (10) genre, (11) stem-type, (12) voice, (13)

---

40. All entries with the same lemma number constitute one paradigm. The lexicon, or paradigm, number gives the sequence of all the members of the same paradigm.

family, (14) number, (15) gender, (16) person, (17) state, (18) root, (19) gloss, (20) lemma number, (21) paradigm position number, (22) *dagesh* or *raphe*, and (23) symbol of paradigm type (noun, verb, etc.).

7.3.2 OTIK—Old Testament in the Computer

● *BASIC DATA BASE INFORMATION*

Key Person(s): Eep Talstra, Ferenc Postma
Location of Project: Free University, Amsterdam
Project Address: Vrije Universiteit, Werkgroep Informatica, Faculteit der Godgeleerdheid, 1081 HV Amsterdam, De Boelelaan 1105, The Netherlands
Telephones: 548-5448, 548-2653; from North America dial direct: 011-31-548-5448 or 548-2653
Date Project Began: 1977 (Werkgroep Informatica), 1979 (OTIK)
Date Project Completed: Not yet complete.
Sources of Funding: Research Stimulating Fund of the Free University of Amsterdam (B.R.O.), the Netherlands Organization for the Advancement of Pure Research (Z.W.O.)
Primary Purpose of Project: To create a machine-readable text of the entire Hebrew Bible that is fully tagged at the morphological, lexical, and grammatical levels to facilitate the scientific study of Hebrew grammar.
Textual Authority: BHS
Machine-Readable Text Includes: Consonantal text only
Vocalized: No
Cantillated: No
Type of Tagging: Morphological, lexical, grammatical
Level of Tagging: 12 tags used for morphological tagging; number of lexical and grammatical tags not known.
Scope of Tagging: 60% of the Old Testament has been morphologically coded, and the Book of Deuteronomy has been fully coded at the morphological, lexical, and syntactical levels.
Type of Text Files: DISPLAY
Programming Language: Pascal (for application programs)
Output Options: Screen, tape, print; transliterated, coded, consonantal text or consonantal Hebrew text
Availability of Tapes or Disks: Tapes available to projects that cooperate with OTIK in the areas of research and publishing.
Cost of Tapes or Disks: Not applicable
Key Bibliographical References: Talstra, "An Hierarchically Structured Data Base of Biblical Hebrew Texts," 335–49; *Deuterojesaja, Exodus, II Kon., Tritio-Isaiah, Amos.*

7.3.2.1 Introduction

The material in this section is based on (and partially extracted from) "The Werkgroep Informatica," an unpublished report (February 1985) written by Dr. Eep Talstra, an Old Testament scholar at the Free University of Amsterdam. The OTIK, the Old Testament in the Computer, is one of the projects of the Werkgroep Informatica, a special computer-research group that was founded in 1977 and that is composed of members of the Faculty of Theology at the Free University. This group includes biblical scholars, dogmaticians, sociologists of religion, and church historians—all of whom use some kind of data base, many of which are textual. Dr. Talstra began to create a small, experimental, textual data base and programs in 1977 and was joined in 1979 by Dr. Ferenc Postma, an Old Testament colleague at the Free University, who then began work on the OTIK project.[41] When completed, the OTIK will be a complete MRT of the Hebrew Bible in which all words are tagged at the morphological, lexical, and grammatical levels.

---

41. Drs. Talstra and Postma have been assisted in the OTIK project by Mrs. H. A. van Zwet (encoding Hebrew text—1979, 1980), Mr. G. J. Roebersen (plotting Hebrew text—1980), and Mr. A. Steenbeek (an experienced Pascal programmer of the C.W.I.—1980 to the present).

The grammatical approach that Talstra and Postma have implemented in their tagging has been closely informed by W. Schneider's *Grammatik des biblischen Hebräisch*,[42] by the work of P. M. K. Morris (which we will discuss below), and by the work of the Continental structuralists W. Richter[43] and H. Schweizer.[44] Like Andersen and Forbes, Talstra and Postma tend to be linguistic descriptivists, and like the Andersen-Forbes data base, the OTIK data base is intended to be a tool for studying Hebrew grammar more scientifically.

7.3.2.2 The Text

Talstra and Postma are using BHS as their textual authority. They have coded and keyed some of the Masoretic Text themselves (e.g., the Book of Deuteronomy) and are using a set of conversion programs to morphologically tag the Michigan-Claremont Old Testament (see below) to complete their data base. The Michigan-Claremont Old Testament, a complete, transliterated, untagged, vocalized, cantillated MRT of the Hebrew Bible, follows BHS.[45] A typical transcribed word in the OTIK data base might look like this: CM< or HXQJM or L<FWT and its vocalized version might look like this: !!CM<[or H-XQ/JM or L-!!<F)HW[T/.

7.3.2.3 The Vocabulary

Like Anderson and Forbes, Talstra and Postma are not coding at the level of orthographic words because orthographic words are not the most appropriate unit for studying grammar. Unlike Anderson and Forbes, who tagged at the level of text "segments" (see above), eschewed tagging primitive morphemes, and used morphological, lexical, syntactical, and semantic categories to create their taxonomy of Hebrew, Talstra and Postma are coding words solely according to their morpheme structure. Marking morphemes, they believe, provides information that is sufficient for a program to organize material about lexemes and about the grammatical functions of words, though the decision to tag morphemes means that only three parts of speech are identified—nouns, verbs, and "other" words. Those parts of speech are divided into fourteen grammatical classes. Thus Talstra and Postma "try to define words and functions formally and textual-linguistically by means of verbs and nouns as given."[46] By way of contrast, Anderson and Forbes identified 32 taxonomic families, that is, parts of speech, that they divided into three fundamental orders of families: verbals, substantives, and particles. Unlike Andersen and Forbes, Talstra and Postma believe that a *purely formal* analysis of morphology and syntax is the key to determining a language's grammar, that is, the way various sized linguistic units function separately and in combination.

In accordance with their grammatical mentors, Talstra and Postma have adopted a hierarchically arranged approach to tagging the vocabulary and are adding lexical tags, as well as morphological ones. For example, at the morphological level TXT is tagged as a noun, but at the lexical level it is tagged as a preposition. A morphological analysis would include TXT as a noun and a lexical analysis as a preposition. A third

---

42. See Schneider, *Grammatik*. See Talstra's two-part review of Schneider's grammar: "Text Grammar and Hebrew Bible. I and II."

43. See Richter, *Grundlagen*.

44. See Schweizer, *Grammatik*. On structuralism, see Pettit, *Structuralism*; Abraham and Kiefer, *Structural Semantics*; Saumjan, *Principles*; Apresjan, *Principles*; Coseriu and Geckeler, *Trends*; Lepschy, *Survey*; Taylor, *Theory*; Robey, *Structuralism*; Harris, *Linguistics*; Malmberg, *Linguistics*.

45. Talstra and Postma have not yet included the vocalization of the Michigan-Claremont Old Testament in their data base.

46. Talstra, "Exegesis," 127.

level of tagging adds grammatical information about clauses and the hierarchical relationships that exist between and among them.

Thus at a primary level, Talstra and Postma are isolating distinct morphemes in the text. At a secondary level, they are providing lexical information about words. And at a tertiary level, they are providing grammatical information beyond the word level—information about clauses and the hierarchical relationships that exist between and among them. Each successive level builds on the information provided by the preceding level(s), without modifying or destroying that information. Thus in addition to being able to provide various types of lexical information, the OTIK can locate and display syntactical constructions that are similar or identical.

7.3.2.4 Parsing

In their analysis of morphemes, Talstra and Postma use various symbols to tag different morphological features of each orthographic word. Although the literature that I have does not provide a complete listing and explanation of all the tags, the following examples (taken from the tagging in Deuteronomy 4:1) illustrate the technique. In the example CM< : !!CM<[, "!" marks the beginning and ending of the preformative, and "[" marks the beginning of the verbal ending. Because no character, such as J or T, stands between the paired "!" signs, the program analyzes the construction as a zero morpheme. The verbal ending "[" also is a zero morpheme. Because no morpheme indicating a verbal stem is present, the program will analyze the two zero morphemes and the construction as a verb, qal, imperative, second masculine, whose lexeme is CM<, that is, shm'. In the example HXQJM : H-XQ/JM, "-" is placed between two words that appear as one on the surface of the text, and "/" marks the beginning of the nominal ending. Those two tags are sufficient to allow the program to isolate the lexeme XQ and to parse it as a masculine plural noun that is based on the morpheme -JM. And in the example L<FWT : L-!!<F)HW[T/, the "/" marks the beginning of a nominal ending, which is a zero nominal morpheme, "[T" indicates a verbal morpheme, and the "!!" indicates a zero preformative morpheme. On the basis of that information, the program parses this construction as an infinitive construct. The code)HW follows the form)XY, where X is the paradigmatic character and Y is the actually realized character—a code used when a character has been deleted or substituted. This allows the program to retain and produce information about the lexeme and its orthographic realization.

To have a more convenient and consistent method for tagging untagged texts, a set of programs was developed to create a dictionary that contains all the words that are already tagged. By consulting the dictionary, the program can automatically tag new words whose corresponding forms appear in the dictionary.[47] The program places unknown and ambiguous words in a separate list for manual coding.

7.3.2.5 The Programs

The OTIK programs are now in their third generation. Results of applying the first generation of programs were published in *Deuterojesaja*, and results of applying the second generation were published in "The Use of *ken* in Biblical Hebrew." The results of the third and current version of the program have been published in *Exodus*, which is part of the series *Instrumenta Biblica* (produced in cooperation with the

---

47. See Price, "Algorithm," for an explanation of an algorithm that performs an automatic morphological analysis of Modern Hebrew (also see below under WCP). Also see Boot, "Design," for an explanation of how a program can automatically place syntactical tags in literary texts. And see Brooks and Zahavy, "Form Analysis," 113–34; cf. Oomen, *Analyse*; Jones and Wilks, *Parsing*; Winograd, "Software" and *Language*.

I Coded Text	II Part of Speech	III Phrase	IV Clause	V Sentence/Text
W-	6 (conj.)	.	.	.
<TH	4 (adv.)	64	.	.
JFR>L//	3 (prop.noun)	3	64-3	+1:103
!!CM<[	1 (verb)	1	.	
>L	5 (prep.).	.	.	
H-	0 (art.)	.	.	
XQ/JM	2 (noun)	502	.	
W-	6	6	.	
>L	5	.	.	
H-	0	.	.	
MCPV/JM	2	502	1-502-6-502	-1:103 +1:16 +3:703
>CR	6	6	.	
>NKJ	7 (pron.pers.)	7	.	
MJJLMD[/	1	1	.	
>T+KM	5 +sfx.	5	6-7-1-5	-1:16 +1:162
L-	5	.	.	
!!<FH[T/ *	1	51	51	-1:162
LM<N	6	6		
!T!XJH[W *	1	1	6-1	-3:703

Figure 7.3: A simplified example of a file from the OTIK data base, using part of Deuteronomy 4:1.

scholars at the abbey at Maredsous, Belgium—see below under CIB).[48] This third version of the program can list various types of lexical and grammatical information in different formats. For example, the program can: (1) list lines or verses that contain any specified verbal ending (e.g., -WN), (2) list alternate surface realizations of lexemes and morphemes (e.g., the nominal ending -M for -JM), (3) list lexemes and combinations of lexemes in variable contexts (e.g., CMR and <FH) in a line, a verse, a range of N-number of words, or a range of N-number of lines, (4) list combinations of lexical and grammatical information, (e.g., K+ >CR +perf.+KN +imperf.), where the person and number of the verbs are identical or where the verbal lexemes are identical. The results can be displayed as a simple list of textual references or as a listing of the texts themselves. If users choose the second option, the texts may be displayed in the order of their references or concorded to display the lexical items that occur in each con-

---

48. Talstra and Postma (and the Werkgroep Informatica) cooperate with the CIB, CATSS (see below), and with the KTHA (Katholieke Theologische Hogeschool Amsterdam). Two series of printed studies and tools are being produced by the Werkgroep Informatica, in cooperation with other scholars and projects. Brepols Publishers is publishing the series *Instrumenta Biblica*, of which *Exodus* is the first volume; and the Free University Press is publishing the series *Applicatio*, of which *II Kon.* (1983) is the first volume, *Amos* (1984) the second, and *Tritio-Isaiah* the fourth.

struction. Examples of these options, and of the grammatical instructions the program expects, can be found in Part I of *Instrumenta Biblica 1* (see above). Further information about the programs may be found in Talstra's article "Exegesis," 127–28.

Since 1983, Talstra and Postma have been working on programs that provide grammatical information beyond the word level—information about the relationships between and among clauses. This new set of programs first parses word groups and phrases to decide which words belong in a group. Then the program decides which groups constitute a clause. Finally, the program decides which relationship or hierarchy exists between clauses in a text. In five steps, by using different sets of grammatical rules that are valid for each step, the program: (1) begins with the coded text, (2) uses morphological and lexical information to identify each part of speech, (3) uses morpho-syntactical rules to form word groups (phrases),[49] (4) uses a set of combinatory rules for word groups to identify clauses,[50] and (5) uses another program to identify the type and level of clause connections. The program identifies three different sets of connections: formal relationships (e.g., second part of a clause separated from the first part by an embedded clause), asyndetic relationships (e.g., imperfect followed by perfect), and conjunction-dependent relationships (e.g., imperfect followed by *waw* and the perfect). The results of step five can be displayed graphically, so that the phrases and clauses are identified by book, chapter, and verse in such a way that each word of each phrase is displayed in its coded lexical form, or in its true orthographic form, as unpointed Hebrew, and so that each clausal connection is tagged with a numerical code that specifies the type of connection found. The program uses "–" to draw horizontal lines and "!" to draw vertical lines to display the connections graphically. Search routines allow users to find and display a wide variety of information from hierarchically arranged text files.

7.3.3 CASTLOTS—Radday and Shore

● *BASIC DATA BASE INFORMATION*

Key Person(s): Yehuda T. Radday, Haim Shore
Location of Project: Haifa, Israel
Project Address: Technion—Israel Institute of Technology, Department of General Studies, Haifa 32 000, Israel
Telephones: 29-2111; from North America dial direct: 011-972-29-2111
Date Project Began: The late 1960s
Date Project Completed: Not yet complete.
Sources of Funding: Technion, the Israel Academy of Sciences and Humanities
Primary Purpose of Project: To study the linguistic questions of the composition and authorship of biblical books by means of statistically analyzing their machine-readable versions.
Textual Authority: *The Letteris Bible* = The British and Foreign Bible Society Text of M. L. Letteris (1852, reprint 1952)[51]
Machine-Readable Text Includes: Not known
Vocalized?: No
Cantillated?: No
Type of Tagging: Morphological, lexical, grammatical
Level of Tagging: Not known
Scope of Tagging: Genesis, Exodus, Judges, Haggai, Zechariah, Malachi, Ruth, Esther, Lamentations, Song of Songs, Ecclesiastes, Genesis
Type of Text Files: EBCDIC
Programming Language: PL/1
Output Options: Screen, tape, print; consonantal Hebrew text only
Availability of Tapes or Disks: Tapes or diskettes of all tagged books are available; programs are not available.

---

49. See Talstra, "Definition," for an explanation of how this is done.
50. Ibid.
51. See Radday, "Isaiah," 68, n. 12, for an explanation about why this text was chosen.

Cost of Tapes or Disks: $10 per 1,000 words. Genesis, for example, is about 20,000 words, and Haggai is about 1,200 words. Postage and cost of tape are extra.

Key Bibliographical References: Volumes 2, 4, 11, 16, 18 in The Computer Bible Series; *Isaiah and the Computer, The Unity of Isaiah*, "The Unity of Zechariah," "The Book of Judges," and *Genesis—A Computer-Assisted Authorship Study in Statistical Linguistics*

7.3.3.1 Introduction

The material in this section is based on (and partially extracted from) an unpublished report (early 1985) provided by Dr. Yehuda T. Radday. Unlike the preceding two projects, Dr. Radday and his colleagues and associates[52] are not engaged in constructing an elaborately tagged version of the text of the entire Hebrew Bible. Their primary interests are not morphology, lexicography, and grammar but questions of composition and authorship, which they investigate by using computers to statistically analyze various Old Testament books. Their interests, then, are more literary than linguistic, as the acronym CASTLOTS (Computer-Assisted STatistical Linguistic Old Testament Studies) suggests; and their approach focuses on the formal aspects of the text, not on its contents. Dr. Radday was one of the first scholars to use a computer to study the biblical text.[53] Because of his interests in composition and authorship and his controversial conclusions, Radday's work has received more publicity in the popular press than most of the other projects described in this chapter.[54]

Dr. Radday first used a computer to study the Hebrew Bible in the late 1960s when he analyzed the text of the prophet Isaiah. Using twenty-nine criteria of "language behavior" (such as sentence length, syllabification, vocabulary richness, and eccentricity—which are outside of the conscious control of an author), Radday was surprised when the results of his computer-assisted study strongly indicated that Isaiah was the work of three authors. Cautiously and judiciously, however, he concluded his "Preliminary Report" by asserting that his results were "no more than probabilities" and that the Book of Isaiah "may yet have been written by one man."[55] Beginning with that study of Isaiah, all of Radday's linguistic analyses of biblical books have resulted in the publication of analytical, KWIC concordances in The Computer Bible Series that is published by Biblical Research Associates (see above under Andersen and Forbes, and see the bibliography below).

In an article published in 1975,[56] Radday and Wickmann applied the same types of statistical linguistic analyses to the Book of Zechariah that earlier had been applied to the Book of Isaiah, and concluded that Zechariah 1–9 probably forms a unity, as do chapters 11–14, but that the latter set of chapters probably were not written by the author who wrote the first set of chapters.

Similarly, in an article published in 1977,[57] on the basis of a computer-assisted statistical analysis of the text of the Book of Judges, Radday and Talmon concluded

---

52. Dr. Haim Shore (statistician at the Israel Institute of Productivity, lecturer on statistics at Bar-Ilan University, Ramat-Gan), Prof. Moshe A. Pollatschek (specialist in computer techniques and professor at Technion), and (formerly) Dr. Dieter Wickmann (mathematician at the Technische Hochschule, Aachen, West Germany).

53. Gérard Weil in France, and Peter M. K. Morris and Edward B. James in Great Britain, were probably the first scholars to engage in computer-assisted investigation of the Hebrew Bible (see below); Radday was the first to study the Old Testament *statistically* with the aid of a computer.

54. E.g., "The Isaiah Enigma," *Newsweek* 82 (July 16, 1973): 77; "By One Hand?," *Time* 118 (December 7, 1981): 99. In the field of computer-assisted studies of the Bible in general and of the New Testament in particular, the Reverend Andrew Q. Morton has received the most extensive coverage in the popular press (see below).

55. Radday, "Isaiah," 73; ibid., 65–73; "Tests," 319–24; *Isaiah* (1972); *Isaiah* (1973).

56. Radday, "Zechariah," 30–55.

57. Radday, "Judges Examined," 469–99.

that Judges 1–12 was most probably the work of one author, though the Samson Cycle was penned by another.[58]

Next Radday and Pollatschek analyzed the books of Haggai and Malachi and concluded, on the grounds of word usage, that Haggai is a unity but that last chapter of Malachi[59] is heterogeneous with the first two chapters.[60] He and his colleagues also analyzed Ruth, Ecclesiastes, the Song of Solomon, Esther, and Lamentations. In the latter, their inquiries supported the view that the chapters are arranged chronologically.

The results of Radday's most recent computer-assisted investigation of authorship on the basis of statistical linguistics are different. Using the same fundamental techniques previously employed to analyze other biblical books, but this time on the basis of fifty-six criteria of "language behavior" (such as word length, use of the definite article, use of conjunctive and consecutive *waw*, and the frequencies of transitions between word categories), Radday and his team examined the Book of Genesis and found the three-source Documentary Hypothesis wanting. Radday explains the distinct nature of the alleged P passages on the basis of their formal content, and Shore showed, with the aid of sophisticated statistical analysis, that the difference in word usage between the words of the narrator and those of his *dramatis personae* is by far greater (and statistically significant) than the stylistic variation sensed by the critical school between J, E, and P.[61] Here, then, Radday's approach, which had previously supported the critical view of the heterogeneity of certain biblical books, now supported the traditional view of the homogeneity of at least one of them. Radday and his team are now analyzing Exodus and will continue to work their way through the Pentateuch.

7.3.3.2 The Text

Because their interests are primarily literary and not linguistic, Radday and his colleagues are not concerned to follow a modern critical text, such as BHS. The minor variations between BHS and *The Letteris Bible*, for example, would not significantly affect the results of Radday's work. Unfortunately, the literature contains no example of Radday's coded text on which his statistical analyses are based, and so it is impossible to provide an example.

7.3.3.3 The Vocabulary

Although the literature does not provide a list of the tags Radday employs, he does say that every word of each text he has analyzed has been tagged in "minute detail" at the levels of grammar, word category, syntax, semantic group, lemma, prefix, suffix, length in terms of syllables and phonemes, and more. Rather than code in such a way that programs can be written to assist with lexical and grammatical studies (as Andersen and Forbes, and as Talstra and Postma do), it appears that Radday has coded formal criteria that are designed to assist in identifying what he calls a writer's *language behavior*, his linguistic fingerprints, as it were. Although he eschews *style* because of its polyvalent nature, Radday uses *language behavior* in a roughly equivalent way. Radday's tags (or codes) function to help identify a writer's style. To qualify as a tag, a linguistic feature must: (1) not be prescribed by grammar or syntax, (2) be quantifiable

---

58. Radday believes that the "main body" of Judges (chs. 3:7–12), the Samson Cycle (chs. 13–16), and the two "appendices" (chs. 17–21) were probably written by different authors.

59. The last chapter in the Hebrew text includes what is designated as Malachi 4:1-6 in most modern translations.

60. See Radday and Pollatschek, "Richness," 333–46.

61. See Radday et al., "Genesis," 467–81; Radday et al., *Genesis*.

(i.e., countable), (3) be beyond the author's conscious control, and (4) not be content- or genre-bound. Only then, Radday argues, do we have a set of criteria that reflect what cannot be changed at will or imitated. (See above for some of the tags Radday uses.)

7.3.3.4 Programs

The programs that Shore and Radday use are highly technical *statistical* ones, such as UNIVARIATE, MULTIVARIATE, FACTOR, DISCRIMINANT, CLUSTER and RELIABILITY ANALYSES, and SSA1. The interested reader is directed to the various articles and books listed in the bibliography for explanations of those programs and for justifications of their use in literary analysis.[62]

7.3.4 Morris and James

- *BASIC DATA BASE INFORMATION*

Key Person(s): The Reverend Canon Peter M. K. Morris; Edward B. James
Location of Project: Dyfed, Wales, and London
Project Address: The Reverend Canon Peter M. K. Morris, Saint Davids University College, Department of Theology, Lampeter, Dyfed SA48 7ED, United Kingdom
Telephones: Lampeter (0570) 422-351; from North America dial direct: 011-44-570-422-351
Date Project Began: 1964
Date Project Completed: Not yet complete.
Sources of Funding: Saint Davids University College
Primary Purpose of Project: To create a machine-readable version of the Pentateuch to study the literary problems of composition and authorship by means of statistical analyses and, if successful, to continue with further sections of the Hebrew Bible.
Textual Authorities: Pentateuch: N. H. Snaith (BFBS, London, 1958), Former Prophets: BHS
Machine-Readable Text Includes: Consonantal text
Vocalized?: Only long vowels included
Cantillated?: No
Type of Tagging: Morphological
Level of Tagging: Morphological
Scope of Tagging: Pentateuch and Former Prophets
Type of Text Files: EBCDIC; ASCII available
Programming Language: FORTRAN
Output Options: Screen, tape, print; transliterated, coded, consonantal text only
Availability of Tapes or Disks: Tapes, 8-inch and 5.25-inch, MS-DOS diskettes are available; text-analysis programs are available for scholarly purposes.
Cost of Tapes or Disks: Time and materials
Key Bibliographical References: Volumes 8 and 17 in *The Computer Bible*

---

62. Readers not familiar with statistical linguistics may profit from the following books and articles. See Weil et al., "Le Livre d'Isaie"; Weil and Chenique, "Prolegomenes"; Adams and Rencher, "Critical View"; Adams, "Selection"; Drake, "Questions"; Damerau, "Frequencies"; Hirschman et al., "Word Class Formation"; Kemp, "Observations," "Aspects"; Leed, *Literary Style*; Bee, "Statistical Methods"; Zampolli and Calzolari, *Computational and Mathematical Linguistics*; Pool, "Computer"; Salton and Wong, "Words and Phrases"; Hays, "Computational Linguistics"; Beatie, "Measurement"; Thompson, "Statistics I, II, III, IV, V, VI"; Herdan, "Controversial Results"; McKinnon and Webster, "Method"; Wickmann, "Disputed Authorship"; Wyatt, "Function Word Distribution"; Mey, "Computational Linguistics"; Andersen, "Style and Authorship"; Culik, "Basic Problems"; Anshen, *Statistics*; Clayton, *Introduction to Statistics*; Hatch and Farhady, *Research Design*; Brainerd, *Weighing Evidence*; Yule, *Statistical Study*; Gladkij and Mel'cuk, *Elements*; Hockett, *Language*; Manna, *Introduction*; Wall, *Introduction*; Pike, *On Describing Languages*; Partee, *Mathematical Fundamentals*; Gross, *Mathematical Models*; Herdan, *Quantitative Linguistics*; Cercone, *Computational Linguistics*; Dolozel and Bailey, *Statistics and Style*.

7.3.4.1 *Introduction*

In 1963 in Oxford, Dr. Peter Morris heard a lecture by Andrew Q. Morton (see below) about the latter's computer-assisted analysis of the composition and authorship of the Pauline Epistles. That lecture prompted Dr. Morris to contact Edward James in October of 1964 and to collaborate with him on a computer-assisted investigation of the composition and authorship of various portions of the Pentateuch and Former Prophets. By 1965 they had devised a system for coding machine-readable texts, and by late 1971 the (more-or-less) final versions of their programs and coded Pentateuchal text were ready. (Morris did the coding and James wrote the programs.) Like Radday, Morris and James are interested in investigating the literary questions of composition and authorship; unlike Radday, they are interested in using their MRT for grammatical analysis, too.

7.3.4.2 *The Text*

N. H. Snaith's 1958 edition was used for the Pentateuch (with consultation of BH³). BHS was used for the Former Prophets. The unit of transcription was the orthographic word, and only consonants and long vowels are coded. *Dagesh* is not coded; *maqqeph* is denoted by a hyphen and *soph pasuq* by a stop. A typical transcribed line might look like this: B)R'JIT(1 BR'/411 EH 'T H)JM(3 W) 'T H)'RC(1.

7.3.4.3 *The Vocabulary*

Unlike Andersen and Forbes, and Talstra and Postma, Morris and James tagged their text at the morphological level only. For example, "the king" (*hamelek*) is H)MLK(1. Tags are used to indicate nouns and adjectives, the inseparable prepositions, numerals, and the person, tense, and suffix of all verbs, as well as participles. Proper nouns are not tagged (e.g., YSR'L is "Israel"), and neither are particles, adverbs, and prepositions, unless used as substantives. Identical codes are used for nouns and adjectives; they are not distinguished. The accusatives of all nouns and participles are tagged. All instances of *ketib/qere* have been preserved, *qere* following *ketib*, as in *+)BKH/421 **+)BKH/921, that is, *ketib*: "and he wept," *qere*: "and they wept." *Nun energicum* and nunnation are tagged. All homonyms are distinguished. Full information about the complete system of tags may be found on pages 1–14 of Morris and James, *A Critical Word Book of the Pentateuch* (The Computer Bible, vol. 17).

7.3.4.4 *Parsing*

The Morris-James morphological codes are similar to those of Talstra and Postma. In the example above —H)MLK(1— "H)" is the code for the definite article, "MLK" is the consonantal form of *melek*, "(" indicates that *melek* is a noun or an adjective, and "1" indicates the absolute state. Similarly, "and it came to pass" (*wayyehi*) is coded as +)HYH/421, where "+)" represents a *waw* consecutive, "HYH" represents the stem *hayah*, "/" indicates that the word is a verb, "4" indicates that it is third masculine singular, "2" imperfect, and "1" *qal*. Technical accuracy is not always necessary; the verb in the previous example is a jussive form, not merely a simple imperfect. The phrase "in his house" (*bebhetho*) is coded as B)BYT(14, where "B)" represents the inseparable preposition *b*, "BYT" represents a noun (*bayith*, in the absolute form), "(" indicates that the word is a noun, "1" that it is singular, and "4" that it is the third masculine singular suffix. Because Morris does not actually mark morphemes but replaces them by figures (e.g., 421) that are indicators of the grammatical function(s) of the word, the surface structure of his version of the text is changed, so that research is not possible below the level of lexemes. Morris's text, then, does not record the actual form of the orthographic words of the Masoretic Text; it records the root letters of the MT's words, to which are affixed coded symbols. Thus Morris's text is a coded, grammatical *interpretation* of the original text.

7.3.4.5 The Programs

Although the literature contains no detailed description of the programs used, like Radday, Morris and James are interested in investigating the literary questions of composition and authorship by means of studying stylistic criteria, such as sentence length and the frequency of words (e.g., *waw* consecutive, the definite article, the inseparable prepositions). They can sort their data base by grammatical types (e.g., verbs, nouns, *waw* consecutives), by subtypes (e.g., *piel*, *qal*), or by affixes (e.g., nominal or verbal suffixes or prefixed prepositions). Their tagging, then, makes it possible to obtain listings of syntactical and morphological features.

The only specific statistical technique Morris and James mention is CUMULATIVE SUM PLOTS, which are graphs that indicate by change of slope a change in the frequency of the presence of any feature.

7.3.5 CATAB—Weil

- *BASIC DATA BASE INFORMATION*

Key Person(s): Gérard E. Weil
Location of Project: Villeurbanne, France
Project Address: Université Jean-Moulin—Lyon III, 43 boulevard du 11 Novembre 1918, 69622 VILLEURBANNE Cedex, France
Telephones: (7) 893-7437; from North America dial direct: 011-33-7-893-7437
Date Project Began: 1963
Date Project Completed: 1977 (for tagging L)
Sources of Funding: CNRS (Centre National de la Recherche Scientifique); Ministère de l'Education nationale, Crédits Recherches et Crédits Conseil scientifique de l'Université Jean-Moulin (Lyon III); Conseil régional, Crédits Investissements et Fonctionnement dans le cadre du Programme pluri-annuel des Sciences humaines; Agence de l'Informatique (Agence Nationale) pour les développements technologiques dont profitent les recherches bibliques; Agence Nationale de la Valorisation de la Recherche pour les développements technologiques dont profitent les recherches bibliques
Primary Purpose of Project: To create a fully vocalized, fully cantillated, machine-readable text of the entire Hebrew Bible and to use that data base and its accompanying programs to study Hebrew and Aramaic philology, morphology, syntax, grammar, discourse structure, questions of authorship, and the Masorah, Masoretic vocabulary, and cantillation of the text, statistically and otherwise.
Textual Authorities: L (Leningrad Codex B 19ᵃ), A (Aleppo Codex), B (Or. 4445, London Pentateuch), C (Cairo Codex of the Prophets), Targum Onkelos (Sperber text)
Machine-Readable Text Includes: Full orthographic details, based on the actual manuscripts themselves, not on editions
Vocalized?: Yes, fully
Cantillated?: Yes, fully
Type of Tagging: Morphological, lexical, semantic
Level of Tagging: Paleographic, orthographic, morphological, and lexical
Scope of Tagging: The entire Masoretic Text of B 19ᵃ
Type of Text Files: EBCDIC, ASCII
Programming Languages: PL/1, Pascal, C, FORTRAN
Output Options: Screen, tape, diskettes, print; transliterated or Hebrew text, complete with vowels and cantillation marks
Availability of Tapes or Disks: CATAB shares material with scholars and institutions by formal arrangement only.

Cost of Tapes or Disks: BASE DE DONNEES BIBLIQUES EN HEBREU MASSORETIQUE (BDBHM)—Biblical Data Base of Hebrew Masoretic Texts—is available at cost (media and time) to qualified research centers by contract with CATAB; tape: 1,600 bpi; diskettes: Apple II series; BDBHM is approximately 21 megabytes.

Key Bibliographical References: Weil, "Massorah, Massoretes, et Ordinateurs," 351–61; CNRS ERA 758 (subsequently 1071) CATAB *Rapport Scientifique et Technique* (1984–1985), (1982–1984), (1980–1982), (1981–1982), (1978–1980), (1978–1979); "Le Livre d'Isaie"; "Section Biblique"; the various volumes in the CNRS CATAB *Documentation de la Bible* series

7.3.5.1 Introduction

Gérard E. Weil was the first scholar (1963) to use a computer to study the text of the Hebrew Bible. Because of his strong research interests in cantillation, in linguistic statistics about the Masoretic Text, and in the Masorah itself, it would not be inaccurate to describe him as a modern-day, computerized Masorete.[63]

CATAB®, the Centre d'Analyse et de Traitement Automatique de la Bible et des Traditions Ecrites (of which Gérard E. Weil is the founder and director) is the result of the working union of the Section Biblique de l'IRHT (Institut de Recherche et d'Histoire des Textes),[64] located in Paris, and the Département Sémitique of the CRAL (Centre de Recherches et d'Applications Linguistiques), located in Nancy. CATAB, whose physical headquarters are in Villeurbanne, operates under the auspices of the CNRS (Centre National de la Recherche Scientifique) as UA 1071 (UA stands for Unité Associée).[65] At its creation as ERA 758 du CNRS, CATAB was given two precise missions: (1) to continue to pursue the research that the Section Biblique de l'IRHT (LP du CNRS) had been carrying out on biblical manuscripts, on the history of the transmission of the Bible, and on the exegesis of the biblical text and (2) to con-

---

63. The Masoretes, a group of scholars who were active from about A.D. 500 to A.D. 1000, continued the textual work of the scribes. As Hebrew died out as a spoken language, the Masoretes developed a system of accents, symbols, and textual notations, which they entered under, within, and above the letters of the words of the consonantal text, as well as in its margins, to definitively fix its form, pronunciation, and meaning. The text that resulted from that activity subsequently became known as the Masoretic Text (MT). In addition to placing diacritical marks in the text, the Masoretes compiled detailed statistics about each book of the Hebrew Bible. They counted the number of letters, words, and verses of each book, established their midpoints, and made notations about stylistic differences among the books. The Masoretes also created the system of *ketib/qere* readings. Statistical information about each book that was placed at its end is known as the *Masorah finalis*. That, along with similar notes made by the Masoretes in the side (the *Masorah parva*) and top and bottom margins of the text (the *Masorah magna*) were printed together as the *Masorah*. The three Masoretic schools (Palestinian, Babylonian, and Tiberian) used three sets of diacritical marks. The system of the school at Tiberias, established about A.D. 900 by the famous Masoretic scholars Ben Asher and Ben Naphtali, dominated and later was "canonized" by the rabbinical authorities.

Apparently, in using diacritical marks to fix the form, pronunciation, and meaning of the text, the Masoretes were guided by the cantillation, or oral recitation and chanting, of Scripture as that was performed in the synagogues. The cantillation of the Hebrew Bible, which antedated the Masoretes by centuries—going back, perhaps, to the time of Ezra in the fourth century B.C.—had been preserved in various forms in the synagogues of the Masoretes' day. According to one source, the "Cantillation of scripture was governed by grammatical rules, syntactic analysis, and the interpretation of the text" (IDB, 3.297). The Masoretic system of cantillation can be understood as a very sophisticated combination of punctuation signs and accent marks that, along with the vowels the Masoretes added to the text, helped to fix the text's form, pronunciation, and meaning. Thus by studying the diacritical marks of the Masoretes—including the system of cantillation—scholars can formulate hypotheses about the traditional oral pronunciation of the text, which in turn can help them understand its meaning (traditionally understood). The study of the text's cantillation, then, has as its goal the exegetical concern of understanding the text's meaning.

64. See below under IRHT.

65. In the following presentation, I will only describe the work of CATAB UA 1071 du CNRS in the field of the computer-assisted study of Semitic texts. The acronym CATAB also stands for Centre d'Analyse et de Traitement Automatique des Bases de Données, an indication that the work of CATAB extends into areas outside of our sphere of interest (e.g., Chinese character generators).

tinue to pursue the research that the Département Sémitique du CRAL (LA 68 du CNRS) had been pursuing on the automatic analysis of the biblical text and on the idea of interactive, multilingual computer terminals.

As the acronym CATAB indicates and as the next several sections will explain, the scope of the work at CATAB includes, but goes beyond, studying the Masoretic Text per se. I have included CATAB in this section on Machine-Readable Versions of the Masoretic Text, however, because CATAB is noted for its machine-readable version of the MT and because CATAB's work predominantly focuses on studying this text and related topics.

7.3.5.2 The Masoretic Text

There are several broad, interrelated areas in which CATAB is carrying out its twofold mission. CATAB researches the Masoretic Bible. This research has resulted in: (1) the publication of *Biblia Hebraica Stuttgartensia* (begun in 1961 and published in 1979), a new critical edition of B 19ª, (2) the publication of critical editions of the *Masorah Gedolah* (four volumes of commentaries) and the *Masorah Parva*, (3) the creation of the *Catalogue Général des Manuscrits de la Bible Hébraique et Araméenne, dans les collections Publiques et Privées* (see the following section), (4) the macrophotography of manuscripts, (5) the acquisition of microfilms of texts, (6) the publication of biblical commentaries from the Middle Ages, and (7) the publication of other works related to the study of the Masoretic Bible.

7.3.5.3 Bibliographical Data Banks

Furthermore, CATAB has established several data bases and data banks that relate to its areas of interest and investigation. These include the following.

> BANQUE DE DONNEES BIBLIOGRAPHIQUES
> BASE DE DONNEES DOCUMENTAIRES
> BASE DE DONNEES TEXTUELLES DE LA BIBLE
> BASE DE DONNEES BIBLIQUES EN HEBREU MAS-
>   SORETIQUE
> BANQUE DE DONNEES TEXTUELLES

The BANQUE DE DONNEES BIBLIOGRAPHIQUES—Bibliographical Data Bank—catalogs the various collections of literary and historical manuscripts in the world. CATAB has contacted over 10,000 institutions throughout the world, and this data bank contains information about public and private collections of Hebrew and Aramaic manuscripts of the Bible, as well as information about manuscripts in other languages.[66] The data bank contains facts about the actual manuscripts, not about facsimiles or MRTs of those manuscripts.

The BASE DE DONNEES DOCUMENTAIRES—Documentary Data Base—runs under CP/M on Televideo 806/800A microcomputers and includes the following data bases: (1) BIBFILM contains information about CATAB's collection of the photographic facsimiles of Hebrew and Aramaic manuscripts of the Bible, including bibliographical, historical, and documentary information about each manuscript. (2) MANUSCRITS contains information about Hebrew and Aramaic biblical manuscripts in public and private collections, including information about each manuscript's date, location, paleography, codicology, philology, and so forth.

---

66. See the CATAB publications in the series *Répertoire Général des Bibliothèques, Collections, Dépôts de Manuscrits et Archives dans le Monde*, edited by G. E. Weil, M. Frinot, M. C. Duchenne, and R. Roung, as listed in the CNRS publication *Rapport Scientifique et Technique* (1978–1980), ERA 758 CATAB, 1*.

MANUSCRITS is closely related to the following four data bases. (3) SCRIBES includes information about the names and origin of the scribes who copied Hebrew manuscripts (biblical or otherwise), as well as information about the place and date the manuscripts (extant as well as missing) were copied and the catalogs they are listed in. (4) POSSESSEURS includes the names of the patrons of letters and of others who have possessed extant or lost Hebrew and Aramaic manuscripts—biblical or otherwise. (5) CATALOGUE includes information about catalogues and collections of Hebrew and Aramaic manuscripts of the Bible. And (6) RETRODOC contains information about biblical linguistics, paleography, codicology, philology, and the Masoretes—but not about exegesis or the history of religions—that have appeared in various journals.

The BASE DE DONNEES TEXTUELLES DE LA BIBLE—Data Base of Biblical Texts—contains CATAB's four major MRTs of the Hebrew Bible, each of which is the machine-readable form of a major manuscript itself, not of a printed edition of the manuscript. These MRTs are (1) A (the Aleppo Codex, located in Jerusalem), (2) B (Or. 4445, the London Pentateuch, located in the British Museum), (3) C (the Cairo Codex of the Prophets, located in the Qaraite Synagogue in Cairo), and (4) L (the Leningrad Codex B 19ª, located in the Russian Public Library in Leningrad).

The BASE DE DONNEES BIBLIQUES EN HEBREU MASSORETIQUE (BDBHM)—Biblical Data Base of Hebrew Masoretic Texts—includes the BASE DE DONNEES TEXTUELLES DE LA BIBLE, as well as CATAB's machine-readable version of the Aramaic text of (the Babylonian) Targum Onkelos on the Pentateuch (based on A. Sperber's critical edition).[67]

The BANQUE DE DONNEES TEXTUELLES—Data Bank of Texts—consists of three main indices (nouns, verbs, and particles) that help researchers statistically analyze texts.[68]

7.3.5.4 Computer-Assisted Study of the Biblical Texts

Machine-Readable Semitic Texts. Like the Andersen-Forbes MRT of L, but unlike the other MRTs we have discussed so far in this chapter, CATAB's MRTs are based on facsimiles of the actual manuscripts themselves, not on critical editions produced from those manuscripts (e.g., BH, BHS). The actual orthographic form of each manuscript has been coded, including all superlinear, linear, and sublinear signs. Thus CATAB's MRTs contain every feature of each manuscript, including *dagesh, raphe,* all cantillation marks, and all *ketib/qere.*[69]

Concordance Automatique de la Bible. The BANQUE DE DONNEES TEXTUELLES (see above) contains the important CONCORDANCE AUTOMATIQUE DE LA BIBLE, which is used for the statistical study of lexical and grammatical aspects of the text. The concordance, which displays information in tabular, statistical form, is produced by MATYMOT (a concording program), which arranges words alphabetically, according to their semantic affinity, in grammatical categories that are larger than traditional parts of speech. MATYMOT is able to perform the following operations: (1) lemmatize nouns,[70] adjectives, verbs, and participles, (2) create statistical lists, arranged by book and category, that indicate the total number of occurrences of the grammatical type that the category defines (e.g., ordinal numbers, divine names), the total number of different forms that make up the total number of occurrences, and

---

67. *The Bible in Aramaic,* 5 vols. (Leiden: E. J. Brill, 1959–1973).

68. See Weil, "Analyse Automatique," 55–96; Weil and Serfaty, "Le Livre d'Isaie," 1–86; and Weil and Chenique, "Proligomènes," 344–66. For more details and for examples of the ways in which Weil uses statistical linguistics to analyze texts.

69. See Weil, "Section Biblique et Massorétique," 115–33, for an explanation of how the coding was done and of the different codes that are used for consonants, vowels, and cantillation marks.

70. Nouns are subdivided into various categories, such as numbers, divine names, and ethnic names.

the total number of lemmata that underlie the total number of forms, and (3) provide statistical lists by category and book of the occurrences of articles, definite and indefinite particles, *waw* conjunctives, the use of *he* as an interrogative, and *waw* conversives.

Displaying the Texts. There are three ways to display CATAB's MRTs: (1) in an 80 × 10 column format known as TEMUNAH—this is the format used for manually entering corrections into the textual data base, (2) in a sequential, variable-length format (defined by the length of each verse) known as GELILAH—this is the format used by all the programs that automatically analyze the text, and (3) in a special format known as HADPAS that allows the text to be phototypeset. Additionally, CATAB has developed a special bit-mapped graphics screen known as CATAB/CALLIGRAPHE® 44, which we discussed briefly in chapter 2. This screen, which was designed specifically to display nonroman characters (Cyrillic, Slavic, Armenian, Greek, Hebrew, Coptic, Syriac, Arabic, Chinese, etc.), is plug-compatible with any mainframe, minicomputer, or microcomputer that has an RS-232C interface (a standard type of asynchronous—serial—communications adapter). According to Professor Weil,[71] the CATAB/CALLIGRAPHE® 44 screen is not dependent on any particular operating system but is fully portable from one system and computer to another.

The Cantillation of the Text. CATAB's statistical analysis of various levels of the text has resulted in the publication of the series called the *Documentation de la Bible*, which consists of five concordances on the cantillation of the Masoretic Text and one on the Aramaic text (see the bibliography at the end of this chapter). Each of these volumes follows the same format: (1) a complete concordance of nodal accents by verse, with references to verses that have the same cantillation structure grouped together, (2) a complete concordance of nodal accents in *atnah* clauses, and (3) a complete concordance of nodal accents in *silluq* clauses.

According to Weil, the Masoretic chains of cantillation are mathematically governed, following "very rigid rules of production and succession," and have nothing to do with a musical system. Instead, they constitute a precise, rule-governed reading system that enables the reader "to give to his sentence an accent of meaning which is linked to the traditional reading." Weil bases these conclusions on his study of chains of signs, such as *me'ayela, darban* or *hamza,* and the *merkha' kephulah,* and the *tiphha, zaqeph-gadol, paseq, munah, reviya, legarmeh,* and *tevir.*

The Main Programs. Weil and his associates at CATAB have developed the following programs for studying various aspects of texts. SEMUT-23, the main program, works with the coded MRTs, analyzing them paleographically, orthographically, and morphologically. SEMUT-23 can test the validity of (1) consonants, (2) vowels, and (3) cantillation marks. It can provide statistical information on (4) the length of words, (5) the number and (6) types of syllables, (7) the correspondence of words to consonants and of (8) words to vowels. It is able to analyze and list (9) definite articles and (10) definite, (11) indefinite, and (12) interrogative particles. It can separate and list (13) *waw* conjunctives and (14) *waw* consecutives. It is able to analyze and display (15) the parts of speech and (16) prefixed morphemes and (17) the types of words with which they are constructed. It can (18) establish algorithms for analyzing the chains of cantillation and (19) concord the cantillation of the chains of nodal accents, using the *atnah* and the *silluq,* at the verse and clause level, as well as (20) display the chains of the complete nodal and subordinate cantillation marks throughout the Hebrew Bible. It is able to (21) verify the validity of the morphological analysis of words with their graphic form and vocalization, (22) create indices of the parts of speech, and (23) show the distribution of nouns, verbs, and particles at the verse, chapter, and book levels. And it can (24) create indices of those elements in such a way that similar sequences of elements can be concorded and displayed together.

---

71. Private letter, dated November 25, 1985.

MATYMOT, a concording-type program, performs different types of morphological analyses of the text. MATYMOT (1) divides the text into sections and concords each word according to its first consonant (separating and retaining prefixes) in a context of from 1 to 15 words before and after the concorded word and includes with each concorded word up to 650 characters of information about the word's morphological and grammatical status. MATYMOT (2) analyzes words as graphical units and as different parts of speech at the verse, chapter, and book levels, (3) provides statistics about the frequency of occurrence of each part of speech at the chapter and book level, (4) establishes indicators that can be used for morphological analysis (such as the length of words), (5) provides the Aramaic equivalent of each word, and creates the following types of indices: (6) an alphabetical index of words, (7) a reverse word index, (8) an index of articles, (9) an index of interrogative particles, (10) an index of *waw* consecutives and of (11) *waw* conversives, and (12) an index of the inseparable prepositions (*b, k, l,* as well as *m*).

Other, less well-discussed CATAB programs include the PROGRAMME D'ECLATEMENT, which works with MATYMOT and which indexes verbs, nouns, particles, and proper nouns to facilitate the study of their lemmatization, as well as composite nouns, metaphors, Hebraisms, divine names, names of deities, anthropomorphisms, names for the temple of God, and so forth. The CHAINE DE VERBES is a program that lemmatizes verbs by chapter and by verse and that tags words with the following information: time, mood, aspect, person, gender, number, special mood (imperative, cohortative, jussive, operative), absolute or construct state, contracted or apocopated, transitive, intransitive or stative, poetic or emphatic, plene or defective, presence of a *maqqeph, ketib/qere,* presence of a *waw,* presence of a prefixed interrogative or relative article, and type of preposition.

CATAB and Microcomputers. Some of CATAB's programs and data bases run on microcomputers. As we learned earlier, the BASE DE DONNEES DOCUMENTAIRES runs under CP/M on Televideo 806/800A microcomputers. CATAB microcomputer programs that will run under UNIX include: (1) a communications program, cleverly known as JANUS, that permits micros to communicate with other micros or with mainframes, (2) a program (CALENDER) that calculates dates in different calendrical systems—Julian, Gregorian, and Hebrew (using different Hebrew dating systems, e.g., Temple Era, Seleucid Era), (3) a series of programs for linguistic research that can automatically lemmatize and morphologically analyze Semitic texts, (4) an indexing program that can also create a table of contents, (5) a Semitic character generator that can display all the Hebrew and Aramaic consonants, vowels, and cantillation marks, (6) a Semitic text editor, and (7) a Ugaritic character generator and text editor that can display Ugaritic texts in true cuneiform or in a transliterated fashion (presumably on the CALLIGRAPHE® 44 bit-mapped graphics screen).

7.3.6 CIB—Poswick

- *BASIC DATA BASE INFORMATION*

Key Person(s): Fr. R.-Ferdinand Poswick, OSB
Location of Project: Benedictine abbey of Maredsous in Denée, Belgium
Project Address: Centre : Informatique et Bible, Maredsous, B-5198 Denée, Belgium, or Mr. Paul Maskens, Promotion Biblique et Informatique, A.S.B.L., 13 rue de la Bruyère, B-5974 Opprebais, Belgium, telephone: (32) 10-88-8262; from North America dial direct: 011-32-10-88-8262
Telephones: (32) 82-69-9647; from North America dial direct: 011-32-82-69-9647
Date Project Began: 1975
Date Project Completed: Not yet complete.
Sources of Funding: l'Abbaye de Maredsous, Association Sans But Lucratif (ASBL) Promotion Biblique et Informatique

Primary Purpose of Project: To publish (in print or electronically) the *Concordantia Polyglotta* (5 volumes, 1,200 pages per volume)—an exhaustive, comparative, analytical, multilingual index of the primary biblical texts (Masoretic, Septuagint, Greek New Testament), selected Latin, French, and English translations (Vulgate, *La Bible de Jerusalem*, La Sainte Bible, Maredsous ed. and the 1975 Scofield text of Louis Segond's 1944 ed., TOB [Alliance Biblique Universelle's 1977 French translation], RSV [3 versions]), and all the Hebrew manuscripts of the Book of Ben Sira.

Textual Authorities: Hebrew: BHS; LXX: Rahlfs; NT: UBS3

Machine-Readable Texts Include: Fully vocalized and cantillated text; all punctuation; all additional diacritical marks; all *ketib/qere* for the MT.

Vocalized: Yes (for Hebrew Bible)

Cantillated: Yes (for Hebrew Bible)

Type of Tagging: Lexical and morphological

Level of Tagging: Lexical and morphological

Scope of Tagging: See *Centre : Informatique et Bible*, 16.

Type of Text Files: EBCDIC, ASCII

Programming Languages: COBOL, Assembler, BASIC

Output Options: Screen, tape, diskettes, print; original characters or transliteration

Availability of Tapes or Disks: Materials available to qualified institutions by special arrangement; otherwise, the CIB's MRTs are accessible only through custom CIB programming and CIB-run searches using existing programs. See *Centre : Informatique et Bible*, 175, for a list of services and prices. Output is available in printed form or on 9-track tapes (800, 1,600, and 6,250 bpi) and various types of diskettes. A limited textual data base and accompanying programs are available for microcomputers (also see below and under COMPU-BIBLE and COMPUCORD).

Cost of Tapes or Disks: Not applicable

Key Bibliographical References: *Centre : Informatique et Bible*. Three times a year the Promotion Biblique et Informatique publishes a newsletter, *INTERFACE*, that provides news of the work at the CIB.

7.3.6.1 Introduction

The information in this subsection is based on the publication *Centre : Informatique et Bible*.[72] The primary goal of the CIB (Centre : Informatique et Bible), which is directed by Fr. R.-Ferdinand Poswick, is to produce the *Concordantia Polyglotta*, an exhaustive, comparative, analytical, multilingual index of the primary biblical texts (Masoretic,[73] Septuagint,[74] Greek New Testament[75]), selected Latin,[76] French,[77] and English translations,[78] and all the Hebrew manuscripts of the Book of Ben Sira.[79] When finished, the *Concordantia Polyglotta* will be a completely cross-referenced, parallel concordance of the various texts and translations and will display the translation correspondences among the different versions. Just as the Hatch and Redpath concordance to the LXX shows the underlying word in the MT, and just as Young's concordance indicates the Hebrew and Greek words that underlie the English translation values of the KJV, so the *Concordantia Polyglotta*, in a vastly more complex and sophisticated manner, will reveal the lexical correspondences among twelve versions.

---

72. Brepols Publishers, 1981. In addition to providing detailed information about each of the texts in the data bank (12–51), this book includes an extensive and helpful bibliography ("A Bibliography of Bible and Computer," 87–155) that is divided into nineteen sections.

73. BHS.

74. Ralphs.

75. UBS2 and UBS3.

76. *Biblia Sacra Iuxta Vulgatam Versionem*, ed. R. Weber, B. Fischer, J. Gribomont, H. F. D. Sparks, and W. Thiele. 2 vols. (Stuttgart: Württembergische Bibelanstalt, 1969, 1977).

77. *La Bible de Jerusalem*, new ed. (Paris: Editions du Cerf, 1973); *La Sainte Bible*, Maredsous ed. (Paris: Turnhout, 1970); *La Sainte Bible*, trans. Louis Segond (Geneva, Paris, Marseille, 1944); *Traduction Oecumenique de la Bible* (Paris: Alliance Biblique Universelle, 1979).

78. *Revised Standard Version*, as published in *The Layman's Parallel Bible* (Grand Rapids: Zondervan Publishing House, 1973); *The Holy Bible, Revised Standard Version* (Collins, 1973); the RSV text of 1971, with revisions.

79. *The Book of Ben Sira*, ed. Z. Ben-Hayyim (Jerusalem: The Academy of the Hebrew Language and the Shrine of the Book, 1973).

The completed *Concordantia Polyglotta*, which will be published electronically or conventionally, is expected to consist of five 1,200-page volumes. Each text is approximately 850,000 words long.

The CIB data base that is being used to construct the *Concordantia Polyglotta* includes eight texts (Masoretic, Septuagint, Greek New Testament, RSV, and four French translations)—about 6,800,000 words in all. Additionally, the data base includes: (1) a lemmatized version of manuscript Sinai Arab 72 (A.D. 897), an unpublished Arabic manuscript of the Gospels from Saint Catherine's Monastery, (2) the fragmentary Old Syriac version of the Gospels (two manuscripts: Curetonianus—fifth century A.D.—and Sinaiticus—fourth to fifth century A.D.), (3) a bibliographical data base of Septuagint manuscripts, with a summary of the date, location, and contents of each, and (4) several other files that I will mention below.

Because of its important work with the Masoretic Text (it has developed one of the four complete MRTs of the Hebrew Bible), I am including the CIB in this section on "Machine-Readable Versions of the Masoretic Text," instead of under "Machine-Readable Text Archives and Data Banks."

The CIB, which is located in the Benedictine abbey at Maredsous, traces its roots to 1972, when Fr. R.-F. Poswick and Fr. E. de Borchgrave came to the assistance of Fr. Georges Passelecq. Since 1958 Passelecq had been working on an alphabetical index to all the themes of the Bible. After compiling over 135,000 references on index cards, his task appeared more and more impossible. By retyping the information on the index cards onto punched cards and by using computers to process that information, in 1974 Poswick and de Borchgrave were able to help Passelecq publish a 1,214-page book that includes 9,000 entries to 150,000 biblical citations.[80] Subsequently, in 1975, in cooperation with the publishers Editions Brepols–IGP, S.A., Poswick and de Borchgrave formed the CIB, which consists of ten persons under Poswick's direction. In 1980 the Promotion Biblique et Informatique ASBL (Association Sans But Lucratif, i.e., nonprofit organization) was founded to develop public relations and commercial prospects for the CIB's work.[81] And in 1982 the CIB created the Association International Bible et Informatique (AIBI) to organize international meetings about computer-assisted biblical research—the first of which was the International Colloquium "Bible and Computer: the Text," which was held in Louvain-la Neuve (Belgium) in September 1985—and to communicate with groups whose aims are similar to those of the CIB's. Associations related to the CIB include:

Association Francaise Bible et Informatique Multimedia
106 rue du Bac
75007 Paris
France[82]
No listed number

American Bible Systems, Inc.
% Development Direction, Inc.
Garden City Executive Offices
1539 Franklin Ave.
Mineola, NY 11501
(516) 747-0100

---

80. G. Passelecq and F. Poswick, *Table Pastorale de la Bible. Index analytique et analogique* (Paris: Lethielleux, 1974).

81. Promotion Biblique et Informatique publishes a newsletter, *INTERFACE*, that reports on the work of the CIB.

82. See *INTERFACE* (Spring 1984): 4.

7.3.6.2 The Texts

Each word in each text in the CIB data base is treated as a record with an expandable number of fields. The fields include the following information: book, chapter, and verse numbers, and a number that represents the word's position in the verse. A vertical listing of records provides the information just mentioned, as well as data included in other fields, such as the word and the context in which the word occurs. All elements required for typographical composition are encoded—accents, cantillation, and other diacritical marks such as punctuation. In other words, all the orthographic details of each text are preserved. A coded section of CIB's Masoretic Text might look like this: B*:+R&''W.2IT B*=R=10'' '':;L2OH.3IM ''&1T H__+W*=MA2I.M V:+''&1T+H=+''=,R;Y.

7.3.6.3 Tagging

The publication *Centre : Informatique et Bible* includes a chart on page 16 that indicates at what levels each of the texts in the data base are tagged. Tags for the MT include: (1) root, (2) *ketib/qere*, (3) suffix gender, (4) suffix number, (5) state, (6) grammatical class, (7) voice, (8) time, (9) person, (10) case function, (11) gender, (12) number, (13) homographs, (14) proper names, (15) personal names, (16) ordinal numbers, (17) cardinal numbers, (18) comparative, (19) superlative, (20) lemma, and (21) *maqqeph*.

7.3.6.4 Lemmatization

The language of each text is lemmatized in accordance with its grammatical traditions. Each word is given a number and alphabetized within its proper lemma, and the lemmata are alphabetized and assigned numbers. By using a previously compiled form-lemma dictionary, about two-thirds of the Hebrew, Greek, and English texts can be lemmatized automatically. One French text was manually lemmatized, and the form-lemma dictionary (about 30,000 forms and 14,000 lemmata) that resulted served as the basis for the automatic lemmatization of other French texts. Homographs, homonyms, and synonyms are analyzed manually. Information about lemmata is added to each word's file. Identical record formats and complementary codes allow texts in different languages to be treated simultaneously. A corrected, lemmatized file may be used to print a partial or complete reconstruction of the original text (to which subtitles and footnotes may be added) that is suitable for phototypesetting.

7.3.6.5 Tools

The basic tools that the CIB is in the process of producing include frequency lists, reference tables, indices, and concordances. Specifically, the CIB now has: (1) an exhaustive concordance of the four machine-readable French translations, (2) a selective French concordance, (3) a lexicon of Greek forms with analysis, (4) a dictionary of the Masoretic Text with analysis, (5) a Greek concordance, (6) a concordance to BHS, and (7) a concordance to Ben Sira. While working toward the production of the *Concordantia Polyglotta*, the CIB has produced *La Bible de Maredsous* (Brepols, 1978), *Traduction Oecumenique de la Bible*, 3 volumes (Paris, 1979), *Concordance de la Bible de Jerusalem* (Paris: Brepols, 1982), and *A Concordance of the Apocrypha/Deuterocanonical*

Books of the Revised Standard Version (Grand Rapids: Eerdmans, 1983), among other works.[83]

More advanced tools will result from syntactic, linguistic, semantic, and content analysis of the texts. The CIB plans to publish an exhaustive, comparative, analytical concordance that will compare eight versions of the Bible.[84] Each word in a text will be displayed with the corresponding words from the seven other texts. The correlation of terms will be done automatically by reducing each word to its underlying lemma and aligning its lemma in one language with its corresponding lemmata in the other languages.[85] The Masoretic Text already has been aligned with the RSV. The alignment of the eight texts will form a data base from which numerous tools will be extracted by means of different programs.

7.3.6.6 DEBORA

As the CIB pursues its long-term goal of publishing the *Concordantia Polyglotta*, it is involved in related projects to develop and make available scholarly tools for textual study. In 1983–1984 the CIB began to diversify its research and development activities, which are now integrated under the name DEBORAH.[86] DEBORA consists of: (1) DEBORA-BIBLE, a data base of the eight machine-readable biblical texts mentioned above, (2) DEBORA-MICROBIBLE, biblical materials for microcomputers,[87] (3) DEBORA-DOCUMENTATION, services for theological libraries, and (4) DEBORA-PEPP (Paluch European Pastoral Programs)—services for certain Christian communities.

DEBORA-DOCUMENTATION has six goals. (1) Establish a network of microcomputers in libraries to standardize and facilitate the exchange, purchase, and creation of bibliographical records and the retrieval and loan of documents.[88] (2) Market in microfiche form the card catalogs of the specialized holdings of theological libraries.[89] (3) Create custom cards for card catalogs. (4) Consult with libraries on library automation. (5) Conduct seminars on using computers in library documentation. (6) Publish a book about on-line access to religious documents.[90]

---

83. For those publications, the CIB has developed Hebrew, Greek, Syriac, and Arabic printer fonts for an IBM-3800 laser printer.

84. This is a preliminary form of the CIB's goal of publishing the *Concordantia Polyglotta*.

85. Each word's record is 1,039 characters long: 9 characters are used for its identification number, and 103 characters are used for each of the ten versions (10 × 103 = 1,030 characters) to specify fields such as reference, lemma, and analysis.

86. See Judges 4:4–5:32. Documentation et Etudes Bibliques par Ordinateurs et Reseaux Automatises. DEBORA's address is the same as the CIB's.

87. Currently, only the Apple IIe is supported; support for IBM PCs is promised.

88. This sounds very similar to the American OCLC. See "OCLC for You—and ME?! A Humanized Anatomy for Beginners," *American Libraries* 7 (May 1976): 258–75 (includes a helpful bibliography on OCLC).

89. The following microfiches are available (all prices are subscription prices; each microfiche—105mm × 148mm—contains 1,870 frames): (1) Bibliothéque Maredsolienne—4,500 frames that include all the publications made in various fields by the monks of the abbey at Maredsous, $6, (2) Eikon—2,500 frames about iconography from Prof. Voordeckers's library at Gent, $7, (3) Lemmens Institut of Leuven—33,000 frames about religious music, $31, (4) Nationale Raad voor Gezinspastoraal of Brugge—24,000 titles about family pastoral, $29, and (5) the Seminary at the University of Gent—4,500 frames about Byzantine studies, $14.

90. See Michel Gilles, *Le Livre Religieux dans les Systems Informatises* (Denée: Centre : Informatique et Bible, 1985). This book provides basic facts and descriptions (primarily but not exclusively) about selected European library networks, data bases, on-line vendors, and communication programs that provide access to or information about religious works. A newsletter, *DEBORA-DOC. INFORMATION*, is published monthly.

Currently, DEBORA-MICROBIBLE consists of the MRT of *La Bible de Jerusalem*, and five programs. The programs include (1) a main program (written in BASIC) that is used by the other four programs, (2) a program for displaying the text by chapter, verse, or both, (3) a program for researching the text by lemma, (4) a mini-lexicon, and (5) a program that provides statistical information about the text. The text-display program—*(2)*—displays two verses at a time and supports bidirectional scrolling. The lemma-research program—*(3)*—searches for lemmata and lists the results by frequency and location. The program can search for several lemmata simultaneously. Searches may be restricted to a book, chapter, or group of chapters. Lemmata may be displayed in context. In effect, then, this is a concording program. The mini-lexicon program—*(4)*—includes over 200 entries and allows users to display words and their definitions. The statistical-information program—*(5)*—displays classifications, percentages, various tables, and so forth. Information displayed by programs 2–5 can be printed. Currently, only the text of the Gospels is available and only for the Apple IIe. DEBORA-MICROBIBLE is programmed in Applesoft BASIC and comes on eleven 5.25-inch, double-sided diskettes for $215.[91]

CIB plans to make the whole *La Bible de Jerusalem* New Testament text available for IBM PCs and subsequently for CP/M machines. Eventually, DEBORA-MICROBIBLE will include machine-readable versions of the Hebrew, Greek, and Latin texts of the Bible (displayed in the original characters), a parallel version of the synoptic Gospels, and programs that allow users to perform sophisticated grammatical and stylistic searches.

7.3.6.7 Additional Data Base Items

In addition to the biblical texts, translations, and Septuagint manuscripts, the CIB's data base includes comparative lists of the proper names in BHS, RSV, and TOB, (2) a list that compares the proper names in A. Chouraqui's translation of the Bible with those in *La Bible de Jerusalem*, (3) a pastoral table of the Bible, (4) an electronic encyclopedia that includes a dictionary of the Bible and of Christianity, Judaism, and Islam (4,200 entries, 4,000,000 characters, about 4 megabytes),[92] and (5) a machine-readable version of A. Chouraqui's ten-volume *Commentaires chrétiens à l'Univers de la Bible* (Paris, 1984–1985). CIB has plans to add (6) a second encyclopedia of the Bible and (7) a bibliographical and documentary data base.

7.3.7 MPCABS—Parunak

- *BASIC DATA BASE INFORMATION*

Key Person(s): H. Van Dyke Parunak, Richard E. Whitaker
Location of Project: Ann Arbor, Michigan
Project Address: Formerly: the University of Michigan at Ann Arbor; currently: % Dr. H. Van Dyke Parunak, 1027 Ferdon Rd., Ann Arbor, MI 48104
Telephone: (313) 996-1384 (Parunak/home)
Date Project Began: 1980
Date Project Completed: 1982
Sources of Funding: The Michigan Project for Computer-Assisted Biblical Studies, the University of Michigan Computing Center, the University of Michigan Society of Fellows, the David and Lucile Packard Foundation

---

91. Unfortunately, I was not able to review this program and compare it with the concording programs in chapter 3.

92. This dictionary and two texts of the French Bible (Maredsous, TOB) are available through the TELETEL-MINITEL French VIDEOTEX network from Compagnie Générale de Télématique, Bordeaux, France; 33-136—31515/DEXTEL.

Primary Purpose of Project: To stimulate the use of computers in biblical studies in general, in part by producing a MRT of the MT.
Textual Authority: BHS
Machine-Readable Text Includes: Full orthographic details, including open and close paragraph marks, versification, and all *ketib/qere*
Vocalized: Yes
Cantillated: Yes
Type of Tagging: Not tagged
Level of Tagging: Not applicable
Scope of Tagging: Not applicable
Type of Text Files: EBCDIC, ASCII
Programming Languages: Assembler, Pascal
Output Options: Screen, tape, print; Hebrew characters or transliteration
Availability of Tapes or Disks: Formerly, tapes were available in 9-track, IBM standard, OS label, user-specified block and density. The Michigan-Claremont Old Testament is now available on tape and 5.25 MS-DOS diskettes through Dr. Richard E. Whitaker and CATSS/CCAT (see below).
Cost of Tapes or Disks: Time and material
Key Bibliographical References: "Code Manual for the Michigan Old Testament."

7.3.7.1 Introduction

The MPCABS (Michigan Project for Computer-Assisted Biblical Studies), which began in 1980 under the directorship of Dr. H. Van Dyke Parunak, is now inactive. In its brief history, this project was instrumental in creating a machine-readable version of the BHS edition of the MT, formerly known as the Michigan Old Testament and currently known as the Michigan-Claremont Old Testament, that has subsequently been corrected and used in several other projects (see below).

The Michigan-Claremont Old Testament, which was offered as a public-domain text on 9-track tape for $50 a reel in an unproofed form, is now being used in improved, proofed versions by several projects, including OTIK (see above), CATSS, COMPU-BIBLE,[93] COMPUCORD, and the Global Jewish Database (see below). In addition to the Michigan-Claremont Old Testament, the MPCABS archive of MRTs includes (or included) the Analytical Greek New Testament (see below), the GRAMCORD data base (see below), the Ugaritic corpus of Richard E. Whitaker[94] (see below), the Morris and James Pentateuch (see above), several of Radday's texts (see above), and Parunak's Ezekiel and Proverbs. According to Dr. Parunak,[95] the Michigan-Claremont Old Testament is available on tape from

> Dr. Richard E. Whitaker
> 300 Broadway
> Pella, IA 50219
> (515) 628-4360.

The Michigan-Claremont Old Testament also is available on MS-DOS, 5.25-inch diskettes from CATSS/CCAT (see below).

7.3.7.2 The Text

An example of a coded portion of the Michigan-Claremont Old Testament (Ruth 4:4) looks like this: 4 WA/):ANI63Y)FMA61R:T.IY)EG:LE94H)FZ:N/:KF74 L"/)MO81R 14Q:N"H. The thoroughness of the coding allows the text to be per-

---

93. COMPU-BIBLE should not be confused with NASSCO's compuBIBLE, the concording program discussed in chapter 3.

94. This is the machine-readable form of the text of Richard E. Whitaker, *A Concordance of the Ugaritic Literature* (Cambridge: Harvard University Press, 1972).

95. Private letter from Dr. Parunak, dated September 3, 1984.

HEBREW	(and VOCALIZATION)		GREEK	(and ACCENTS)
alef	)		alpha	A
bet	B		beta	B
gimel	G		gamma	G
daleth	D		delta	D
hay	H		epsilon	E
waw	W		digamma	V
zayin	Z		zeta	Z
heth	X		eta	H
tet	+		theta	Q
yod	Y		iota	I
kaf	K		kappa	K
lamed	L		lamda	L
mem	M		mu	M
nun	N		nu	N
samek	S		ksi	C
ayin	(		omicron	O
pe	P		pi	P
tsade	C		rho	R
qof	Q		sigma (all)	S
resh	R		final	J
sin	&		tau	T
shin	$		upsilon	U
sin/shin	#		phi	F
taw	T		chi	X
			psi	Y
			omega	W

pathah	A		smooth breathing	)
hireq	I		rough breathing	(
segol	e		iota subscript	|
tsere	E		acute accent	/
holam	O		grave accent	\
qibbuts	u		circumflex accent	=
shureq	U		capital letter	*
shewa	:		midpoint punctuation	:
hateph-	:		diaeresis	+
patah	2		question mark	;
qametz	1		period	.
segol	3		subscript dot	?
dagesh	.			

Figure 7.4: MPCABS and TLG coding schema.

fectly reproduced in Hebrew, complete with all vowels, cantillation marks, and in a versified form. The final form of Parunak's code has now become (more or less) the standard for all subsequent coding of the Hebrew text (see Figure 7.4).

7.3.7.3 Kepple's Programs

Although Parunak had developed, or was in the process of developing, several interesting and helpful programs for manipulating and studying the Michigan-Claremont Old Testament[96] before the MPCABS became inactive, these are no longer available. Other persons, however, are developing programs to display and manipulate the Michigan-Claremont Old Testament.

The Reverend Mr. Daniel Kepple has written programs (in Turbo Pascal for IBM PCs) to help the WCP (see below) proofread and morphologically tag (i.e., parse) the Michigan-Claremont Old Testament. Additionally, he has developed a program that can convert any text coded in the Michigan-Claremont format to pointed Hebrew and display it on-screen. He has also created Greek and Hebrew character sets for the Malibu Dual Mode 200 printer.[97] These character sets, which are patterned after the one used in BH, are available in EPROMs or on disk. Mr. Kepple also has designed a proportionally spaced Hebrew font, complete with all vowels and cantillation marks. For more information contact:

> Rev. Daniel H. Kepple
> R.D. #2, Box 205
> New Alexandria, PA 15670
> (412) 836-0226 (home), (412) 668-2834 (work).

7.3.8 WCP—Westminster Computer Project

- *BASIC DATA BASE INFORMATION*

Key Person(s): J. Alan Groves
Location of Project: Philadelphia, Pennsylvania
Project Address: Westminster Computer Project, Westminster Theological Seminary, P.O. Box 27009, Chestnut Hill, Philadelphia, PA 19118
Telephones: (215) 887-5511 (WTS), (215) 887-3891 (home)
Date Project Began: 1983
Date Project Completed: Not yet complete.
Sources of Funding: The National Endowment for the Humanities of the United States of America, as a sub-contract to CATSS
Primary Purpose of Project: To provide an accurate, verified version of the Michigan-Claremont Old Testament and of Richard E. Whitaker's morphological analysis of that text; to provide software for searching and manipulating the text; to research Hebrew morphology, syntax, and semantic issues.
Textual Authority: The Michigan-Claremont Old Testament, corrected by the CATSS and WCP teams, cross-checked twice against the CIB text, checked by Richard E. Whitaker; to be checked one more time against IRCOL's proofed version of the Michigan-Claremont Old Testament (see below).
Machine-Readable Text Includes: Complete vocalized and cantillated text; book, chapter, and verse numbers; all open and close paragraph marks; all *ketib/qere*; textual variants
Vocalized: Yes
Cantillated: Yes
Type of Tagging: Premorphological, morphological, lexical, and syntactical[98]
Level of Tagging: Premorphological, morphological, lexical, and syntactical

---

96. E.g., DYNACORD, a dynamic concording package that combines the features of GRAMCORD with linguistic density plots. Parunak had adapted the GRAMCORD programs to work with the Michigan-Claremont Old Testament.

97. I do not know what other printers Kepple supports.

98. Lexical and syntactical tagging will be added to the text in the future.

Scope of Tagging: Future plans call for tagging the entire MT including variants.
Type of Text Files: ASCII; EBCDIC available
Programming Languages: Turbo Pascal, DEC Pascal
Output Options: Screen, tape, disk, print; transliterated or fully vocalized text; fully cantillated text to be available.
Availability of Tapes or Disks: Tape: 600-foot, 1,600-bpi for a variety of mainframe and minicomputers; diskettes: 14 DSDD available for IBM PC/MS-DOS machines.
Cost of Tapes or Disks: Tape: approximately $30; diskettes: approximately $70.[99]
Key Bibliographical References: See below under CATSS.

7.3.8.1 Introduction

The Westminster Computer Project (WCP), directed by J. Alan Groves, is subcontracted to the CATSS Project (see below). The primary goal of the WCP is to provide the CATSS Project (see below) with an accurate, verified version of the Michigan-Claremont Old Testament and of the morphological analysis done on that text by Dr. Richard E. Whitaker. Among other things, the CATSS staff will use the proofed, morphologically tagged version of the Michigan-Claremont Old Testament to verify and expand the aligned parallel Hebrew-Septuagint texts. Additionally, CATSS/WCP plans to make available to the scholarly community the morphologically tagged Michigan-Claremont Old Testament and software for manipulating it. Presently, only the proofed, vocalized and cantillated but *untagged* MRT of BHS is available.[100]

7.3.8.2 Text and Tagging

The Michigan-Claremont Old Testament was machine-compared against CIB's MRT of the MT (see above). Differences were flagged, and, where appropriate, the Michigan-Claremont Old Testament was corrected. After two machine-comparisons, the result was sent to Dr. Whitaker for a third check against his most recent proofed version of the Michigan-Claremont Old Testament. That procedure has produced a highly accurate, machine-readable version of BHS. According to Professor Groves, this is the only time that independently coded versions of BHS have been cross-checked against one another. The proofed CATSS/WCP version of the Michigan-Claremont Old testament is to be cross-checked once more, this time against IRCOL's independently proofed version of the Michigan-Claremont Old Testament (see below under the Global Jewish Database Project).

The WCP is using the output of a package of programs known as HEBMORPH, written in IBYX by Dr. Whitaker, which automatically parses and tags Hebrew words at the morphological level. After these morphological tags have been proofed, the WCP plans to tag the text lexically and syntactically. Professor Michael Fox at the University of Wisconsin is coding Semitic variants to the text.

The fully vocalized and cantillated text is approximately 3.3 megabytes (when stored in variable-length records, or 5–6 megabytes if stored in 80-byte fixed-length records). The uncantillated text is approximately 2.7 megabytes. The fully cantillated, vocalized, morphologically tagged data base is expected to be 13–15 megabytes.

---

99. These are prices for the nonmorphologically analyzed data base only.
100. Readers interested in purchasing copies of this text should contact CATSS/CCAT (see below).

7.3.8.3 *Programs*

Programs are being developed through WCP and CATSS to permit the tagged and untagged data bases to be searched and manipulated in sophisticated ways. Hebrew can be displayed on-screen on IBM PCs and compatibles equipped with graphics cards (see chapter 2). Plans for syntactical and lexical programming are underway at WCP.

7.3.9 COMPU-BIBLE

- *BASIC PRODUCT INFORMATION*

Key Person(s): Ronnie Benun
Location of Project: Brooklyn, New York
Project Address: Mikrah Computer Research Systems, 583 Kings Hwy., Brooklyn, NY 11223
Telephone: (718) 375-2505
Date Project Began: 1984
Date Project Completed: 1986
Sources of Funding: Privately produced
Description: A microcomputer system that allows users to concord and edit the consonantal text of the Hebrew Bible.
Textual Authorities: The Michigan-Claremont Old Testament and CIB's text
Machine-Readable Text Includes: Complete consonantal text; book, chapter, and verse numbers; all open and close paragraph marks; all *ketib/qere*; textual variants
Vocalized: No
Cantillated: No
Type of Tagging: Not tagged
Level of Tagging: Not applicable
Scope of Tagging: Not applicable
Programming Languages: Assembler, (compiled) BASIC
Output Options: Screen, disk, print; transliterated or consonantal text
Price: $1,000
Version Tested: Not able to test.
Runs On: IBM PC, XT, AT, and compatibles, using DOS 2.0 or higher
Memory Requirements: 128K for COMPU-BIBLE, 192K for MIKRAH-EDIT
Disk Drive Requirements: 2
Supports Color Monitors: Yes
Uses Sound: Yes
Number of Text Disks: 7
Number of Program Disks: 2
Size of Program Files: Not known
Size of Help Files: Not known
Size of Text Files: Not known
Text Files in ASCII: No
Produces ASCII Output Files: Yes
Search String Limitations: 20 words
Maximum Number of Entries per Index: Not known
Product Includes: Hebrew character generator chip for monochrome and color graphics adapters, Hebrew keyboard template, 9 diskettes, documentation
Manual: Not able to see.
Demo Disk Available: No
Copy Protected: No
Hard Disk Compatible: Yes
Special Hard Disk Version: No
Menu-Driven: Yes
On-line Help: Yes
Tutorial: Not known
Warranty: Media only
Support: Free phone support
Update Policy: Corrections and revisions to text and current programs updated for nominal fee.
Related Products: COMPUCORD System (see below)
Key Bibliographical References: None

Other Information: COMPUCORD (see below) includes COMPU-BIBLE.

7.3.9.1 Introduction

COMPU-BIBLE (hereafter CB),[101] created by Ronnie Benun of Mikrah Computer Research Systems, is one of four complete versions of the Hebrew Bible currently available for microcomputers. COMPUCORD, also from Mikrah Computer Research Systems, is the second (see below); the CATSS/WCP MRT of the Michigan-Claremont MT, which is available from CATSS/CCAT (see below), is the third; and The MacHebrew Old Testament, which is available from Linguists' Software (see below), is the fourth. COMPU-BIBLE is an untagged, consonantal-only text that is based on the Michigan-Claremont and CIB MRTs (see above) and that comes with a concording program. COMPUCORD is a tagged, fully vocalized and cantillated text that is also based on the Michigan-Claremont and CIB texts and that comes with a powerful concording program. The CATSS/WCP MRT is presently available only as an untagged, fully vocalized and cantillated text that comes with no text-retrieval programs. COMPU-BIBLE, COMPUCORD, and the CATSS/WCP MRT are MS-DOS compatible. The fourth complete MRT of the MT is The MacHebrew Old Testament from Linguists' Software.[102] This is an untagged, fully vocalized and cantillated version of the Michigan-Claremont text of BHS as edited and corrected by CATSS/WCP. The MacHebrew Old Testament is Macintosh-compatible and is available in MacWrite™ and Microsoft® Word formats. Like the CATSS/WCP MRT, The MacHebrew Old Testament does not come with programs for manipulating the text. (See below for more information.)

Because it uses a Hebrew character generator chip, CB displays Hebrew characters on monochrome or color screens. Because the character generator chip includes the English alphabet, commands are entered and messages are displayed in English. A program called LOADFONT is used to download the Mikrah Hebrew character set to suitable dot matrix printers. The literature does not indicate what printers are supported, though I believe Epsons are. Although the CB data base is 1.9 megabytes and ideally needs a hard disk, it can be used without one.

7.3.9.2 The Programs

There are three basic CB programs: (1) SCAN-TEX, (2) SNAP-TEX, and (3) GEMAT-TEX. SCAN-TEX is a sophisticated concordance program that supports lexical, exact-phrase, and sequence-specific searches, as well as truncation. The literature does not indicate what Boolean operators CB supports or what SCAN-TEX's search limitations are. SCAN-TEX can display hits with or without providing a count. Information about the number of hits can be inserted in the text either as a subtotal or a running total. SCAN-TEX dynamically updates the screen during concording operations and provides information about the number of hits, including subtotals by book and a cumulative total. SCAN-TEX can simultaneously concord up to twenty terms. Output may be directed to screen, printer, or file, and SCAN-TEX automatically downloads the Hebrew character set to printers.

SNAP-TEX allows users to create files that contain any portion of the text and to analyze that material with SCAN-TEX or GEMAT-TEX. In effect, then, SNAP-TEX allows users to specify search ranges. The results of using SNAP-TEX may be directed to screen, printer, or file.

---

101. COMPU-BIBLE should not be confused with NASSCO's compuBIBLE, the concording program discussed in chapter 3.

102. Linguists' Software, 106R Highland St., S. Hamilton, MA 01982; (617) 468-3037; $99.95.

GEMAT-TEX can display the numerical value of any Hebrew word. It displays an individual word total, a running total, and a grand total. Users may search for single or multiple numerical values. Hits are referenced by book, chapter, and verse. Output may be directed to screen, printer, or file.

7.3.9.3 The Editor

CB also includes a powerful, bilingual (Hebrew/English), full-screen editor and program processor, MIKRAH-EDIT. The editor supports: (1) mixing Hebrew and English in the same text and line, (2) right-to-left and left-to-right text entry, (3) files of unlimited size, (4) lines as long as 239 characters, (5) wrap and nonwrap modes, (6) split screen editing, (7) on-line help, (8) block moves, (9) an automatic label processor for BASIC (this eliminates the need to type line numbers), (10) an undelete feature, (11) up to ten markers, (12) one-key move to marker, last change, last block, or window, (13) directory sorts, (14) macros as long as 239 characters, (15) automatic capitalization for BASIC, COBOL, and Assembler, and (16) conditional and global search and replace. Additionally, the program allows users to (17) rename, remove, and erase files, (18) change, create, and remove directories from within the editor, and (19) merge and append text from another file. And MIKRAH-EDIT includes (20) a user-programmable batch file generation feature for compile and assemble.

7.3.10 COMPUCORD System

- **BASIC PRODUCT INFORMATION**

Key Person: Ronnie Benun
Location of Project: Brooklyn, New York
Project Address: Mikrah Computer Research Systems, 583 Kings Hwy., Brooklyn, NY 11223
Telephone: (718) 375-2505
Date Project Began: 1984
Date Project Completed: 1986
Sources of Funding: Privately produced
Description: A powerful microcomputer system that allows users to concord the vocalized and cantillated text of the Hebrew Bible morphologically, lexically, and grammatically; can provide statistical information.
Textual Authorities: The Michigan-Claremont Old Testament and CIB's text
Machine-Readable Text Includes: Completely vocalized and cantillated text; book, chapter, and verse numbers; all open and close paragraph marks; all *ketib/qere*; no textual variants
Vocalized: Yes
Cantillated: Yes
Type of Tagging: Morphological, lexical, grammatical
Level of Tagging: Morphological, lexical, grammatical
Scope of Tagging: The entire Masoretic Text of BHS
Programming Languages: Assembler, (compiled) BASIC
Output Options: Screen, disk, and printer; transliterated or consonantal text
Price: $1,500, $750 with educational discount
Version Tested: Not able to test.
Runs On: IBM PC, XT, AT, and compatibles, using DOS 2.0 or higher
Memory Requirements: 256K
Disk Drive Requirements: Hard disk required.
Supports Color Monitors: Yes
Uses Sound: Yes
Number of Text Disks: Approximately thirty-five 1.2MB disks
Number of Program Disks: One 1.2MB disk
Size of Program Files: 450 kilobytes
Size of Help Files: Not known
Size of Text Files: Approximately 37.5 megabytes; Statistics Module is an additional 8 megabytes.
Text Files in ASCII: No

Produces ASCII Output Files: Yes
Search String Limitations: 42 flagged lemmata or 42 roots or 1,008 individually flagged lemmata and/or roots divided among 14 groups (each of the 14 groups may contain twenty-four 3-word entries)
Maximum Number of Entries per Index: Limited only by disk space.
Type of Disks Used: Floppy; 1.2MB disks used unless 360K disks requested
Product Includes: Hebrew character generator chip for monochrome and/or color graphics adapter, Hebrew keyboard templates, thirty-six 1.2MB diskettes, documentation
Manual: Approximately 100 pages, 3-ring binder, appendices
Demo Disk Available: No
Copy Protected: No
Hard Disk Compatible: Yes
Special Hard Disk Version: Yes, COMPUCORD can be purchased on a 60-megabyte Priam hard disk (30-millisecond average access time).
Menu-Driven: Yes
On-line Help: Yes
Tutorial: Yes, in the manual
Warranty: Media only
Support: Free phone support
Update Policy: Corrections and revisions to text and current programs updated for nominal fee.
Related Products: COMPU-BIBLE (see above), Statistics Module (see below)
Key Bibliographical References: None
Other Information: COMPU-BIBLE (see above) is included with COMPUCORD.

7.3.10.1 Introduction

COMPUCORD is a powerful concording program that allows users to perform sophisticated and complex morphological, lexical, grammatical, and statistical studies of the Hebrew Bible. COMPUCORD runs on properly equipped IBM PC-compatibles. Like the text of COMPU-BIBLE (see above), COMPUCORD's text is a proofed version of the Michigan-Claremont Old Testament and the full CIB text. Unlike COMPU-BIBLE's text, COMPUCORD's text is fully vocalized, cantillated, and tagged. Consonants are displayed in Hebrew letters; vowels and cantillation are displayed in a coded form. Both programs use a Hebrew/English character generator chip to display the consonantal text of the Hebrew Bible on monochrome or color screens, and both programs concord the text of the Hebrew Old Testament and allow the results to be displayed and printed. COMPUCORD, however, works with a fully tagged text and is a vastly more powerful program that can perform far more complex searches than COMPU-BIBLE. COMPUCORD has been designed for the scholarly study of the text of the Hebrew Bible. COMPUCORD comes with COMPU-BIBLE and MIKRAH-EDIT.

The analysis and tagging of COMPUCORD's text was made with the help of the following tools:

S. Brown, S. R. Driver, and C. A. Briggs
Hebrew and English Lexicon of the OT
Oxford: Clarendon Press, 1906

A. Even-Shoshan, ed.
A New Concordance of the Bible
Ridgefield, 1982

L. Köhler and W. Baumgartner
Hebraisches und aramaisches Lexicon zum AT
Leiden: E. J. Brill, 1948–1953; supp. 1958; 3d ed. 1967–)

G. Lisowsky
Konkordanz zum hebraisches AT
Stuttgart: Württembergische Bibelanstalt, 1958

S. Mandelkern
Veteris Testamenti Concordantiae
Graz, 1937

E. Vogt. ed.
Lexicon Linguae Aramaicae Veteris Testamenti
Rome: Pontifical Biblical Institute, 1971

Zorell
Lexicon Hebraicum Veteris Testamenti, 1955

COMPUCORD is enormous. The programs take up 450 kilobytes of disk space, and the data base 37.5 megabytes. If purchased with the Statistics Module (not priced at this time, see below), an additional 8 megabytes of space is needed, thus bringing the total to approximately 46 megabytes. With or without the Statistics Module, COMPUCORD is one of the largest—and most powerful—programs reviewed in this book.

COMPUCORD may be purchased on a 60-megabyte Priam hard disk (30-millisecond average access time). Users who purchase COMPUCORD in this format also receive the program on thirty-six 1.2 megabyte, 5.25-inch floppies, unless 360-kilobyte disks are requested.[103] COMPUCORD runs on IBM PCs, XTs, ATs, and compatible machines, such as the Compaq 286. According to Mr. Benun, using a 3 megabyte RAM disk and an 8-MHz IBM PC-AT with a 30-millisecond, 60-megabyte Priam hard disk, COMPUCORD can search the entire Pentateuch in 14 seconds. Although that is not as fast as the indexed Bible concordance programs discussed in chapter 3, COMPUCORD's data base is much larger, far more elaborate, and includes a great deal more information than those data bases do.

Because COMPUCORD is such a powerful tool for the scholarly study of the Hebrew Bible, and because it is the only such tool available for microcomputers, we will now discuss it in some detail. To facilitate the discussion, I have included a number of printouts of various COMPUCORD screens.

7.3.10.2 Description

User Interface. COMPUCORD is fully menu-driven and makes extensive use of the IBM function keys. In each program mode, at the bottom of the screen below the windows, a command line lists a summary of commands. On-line help is available in the Scan Mode (see below). Esc is used to back up through menus. Up to five windows are used to display various fields of information.

COMPUCORD operates in one of two main modes, Scan or View. Roughly speaking, the Scan Mode is equivalent to the Concordance Mode of the concordance programs discussed in chapter 3 and the View Mode to their Scripture Mode. The View Mode is used to browse through a range of text, search for strings, go directly to a passage, and so forth. The Scan Mode is used to create indices in accordance with user-specified search constructions.

COMPUCORD MAIN MENU
Esc
End the current session
F1 Scan Menu
F2 Directory of Scan Files
F3 View the Tanach
F4 Change Parameters

---

103. I.e., approximately 105 360-K diskettes!

Tagging. The text is fully tagged at the morphological, lexical, and grammatical levels, and the following information is available for each word.

1. Book, chapter, verse
2. Word number in verse
3. Relative word number in the Hebrew Bible
4. Punctuation—*petuhah, setumah, passeq*
5. Consonantal form of the word
6. Complete form of the word (vowels and cantillation displayed in code)
7. Root/lemma
8. Consonantal form of the lemma
9. Complete form of the lemma (vowels and cantillation displayed in code)
10. Homographic number of the lemma (indicates homographic lemmata; gives the different meanings)
11. English glosses of the lemma (up to three per word, based on RSV and/or BDB)
12. Homographic number of the English gloss (indicates two or more English glosses for same Hebrew lemma)
13. Additional information on lemma—13 items in all, including attestation, frequency, form, and homographic information
14. Flags Window information—15 categories of information, including *ketib/qere*, state, grammatical number, proper noun
15. Homographic Information Window—5 categories of information
16. Word Category-Gender-Conjugation Window—60 items in all, including: prefix, suffix, part of speech, grammatical number, gender, conjugation, and more
17. Number Window (numerical value of simple and compound numbers)

Additional information is available on lemmata, homographs, and numbers.

The View Mode. The View Mode is used to perform three basic operations: (1) scan a user-specified range of text by word, lemma, or root, (2) view words, lemmata, and roots in the context of the verses in which they occur, and (3) display morphological and lexical information about any word in the text.

Here's how the View Mode works. To scan, view, or display information about the text, users select the View the Tanach (Hebrew Bible) option on the Main Menu. This causes five windows to open. Users then specify a biblical book to scan or view. A GOTO feature allows users to go directly to a specified verse.

```
Relative: 265811                15 8 אסתר                Word: 1
.--------------------------------------------------------------------.
| Complete Word:          '28_כ=:*ד:ר=מ+*ו  Consonantal Word:    ומרדכי |
|====================================================================|
|    ומרדכי יצא מלפני המלך בלבוש מלכות תכלת וחור ועטרת זהב גדולה ותכריך בוץ |
|                   וארגמן והעיר שושן צהלה ושמחה                       |
|                                                                     |
|                                                                     |
|=========================================v==========================|
| Homographic Information:    ‖Word Category-Gender-Conjugation:‖      |
|                             ‖ Prefix: Ambig. Not Subst./Adj. ‖      |
|                             ‖ Prefix:                        ‖      |
|                             ‖ Prefix:                        ‖ Simple Nbr |
|                             ‖   Word: Substantive            ‖    0 |
|                             ‖         Masculine              ‖      |
|                             ‖ Suffix:                        ‖ Whole Nbr |
|                             ‖                                ‖    0 |
'-----------------------------‖--------------------------------‖------'
1:MORDECAI

        [F1]=View Lexicon   [F2]=Search Concord   [F8]=View Context

        [G]=Go to Book      [S]=Set a Marker      [M]=Go to Marker
        [L]=Lexicon Window  [E]=English Window     [F]=Flags Window
```

Figure 7.5: COMPUCORD View Mode displaying sample entire verse.

COMPUCORD highlights the first word of the selected book, chapter, or verse and displays the following information (see Figure 7.5). Above the uppermost window, COMPUCORD displays the relative word number (i.e., word position in the Hebrew Bible), book name (in Hebrew), chapter and verse numbers, and the word number in the verse. The uppermost horizontal window lists the complete (pointed and cantillated) word and its consonantal form.

```
Relative: 265811                15 8 אסתר                Word: 1
.--------------------------------------------------------------------.
| Complete Word:          '28_כ=:*ד:ר=מ+*ו  Consonantal Word:    ומרדכי |
|====================================================================|
|    1:                   6: Prefixed           11:                  |
|    2:                   7:                     12:                  |
|    3: Proper Noun       8:                     13:                  |
|    4:                   9:                     14:                  |
|    5: Singular         10:                     15:                  |
|=========================================v==========================|
| Homographic Information:    ‖Word Category-Gender-Conjugation:‖      |
|                             ‖ Prefix: Ambig. Not Subst./Adj. ‖      |
|                             ‖ Prefix:                        ‖      |
|                             ‖ Prefix:                        ‖ Simple Nbr |
|                             ‖   Word: Substantive            ‖    0 |
|                             ‖         Masculine              ‖      |
|                             ‖ Suffix:                        ‖ Whole Nbr |
|                             ‖                                ‖    0 |
'-----------------------------‖--------------------------------‖------'
1:MORDECAI

        [F1]=View Lexicon   [F2]=Search Concord   [F8]=View Context

        [G]=Go to Book      [S]=Set a Marker      [M]=Go to Marker
        [L]=Lexicon Window  [E]=English Window     [F]=Flags Window
```

Figure 7.6: COMPUCORD View Mode displaying Flags Window.

The next to top horizontal window is used alternatively to display the entire verse (with the word on which the cursor rests highlighted) and as the Flags Window (in which case up to fifteen facts about the word's grammatical number, prefixes, suffixes, *ketib/qere*, and so forth are displayed). Figure 7.6 shows what the screen looks like when the Flags Window is displayed.

535

```
Relative: 265811                  15 8 אסתר                  Word: 1
.--------------------------------------------------------------------------.
| Complete Word:          '28_כ=:*ד:ו=מ+*ו  Consonantal Word:        ומרדכי |
|==========================================================================|
|    1:                  6: Prefixed             11:                        |
|    2:                  7:                       12:                        |
|    3: Proper Noun      8:                       13:                        |
|    4:                  9:                       14:                        |
|    5: Singular        10:                       15:                        |
|==========================================================================|
||Lemma:           ',_כ=:*ד:ו=מ |        מרדכי  Root:                        ||
||                                                          Freq:      60||
||                                            נתובים        Persons:       2||
||1:MORDECAI                        Substantive            Proper Noun    ||
||                                                                         ||
||                                                                         ||
||                                                                         ||
||                                                                         ||
|==========================================================================|
```

```
     [F1]=View Lexicon    [F2]=Search Concord   [F8]=View Context

     [G]=Go to Book       [S]=Set a Marker      [M]=Go to Marker
     [L]=Lexicon Window   [E]=English Window    [F]=Flags Window
```

Figure 7.7: COMPUCORD View Mode displaying Lexicon Window.

Users may toggle between that window's two functions. The lower horizontal portion of the display is divided into three windows. The left window (the Homographic Window) lists homographic information, the middle bottom window (the Word Category-Gender-Conjugation Window) includes information about parts of speech, gender, and conjugation, and the right lower window (the Number Window) includes information about the numerical value of simple and compound numbers. A word's English gloss is displayed below the bottom row of three windows. The entire lower horizontal portion of the display (the three windows just described) may be toggled and used as the Lexicon Window (see Figure 7.7). The Lexicon Window displays a word's root, complete and consonantal forms, frequency (total occurrences of the lemma in the OT), gloss, part of speech, and so forth. The information displayed in those windows provides a complete parsing of the highlighted word. Words are parsed instantaneously when selected with the cursor in the View Mode.

```
Relative: 265811                  15 8 אסתר                  Word: 1
.--------------------------------------------------------------------------.
| Complete Word:          '28_כ=:*ד:ו=מ+*ו  Consonantal Word:        ומרדכי |
|==========================================================================|
| ומרדכי יצא מלפני המלך בלבוש מלכות תכלת וחור ועטרת זהב גדולה ותכריך בוץ |
|            וארגמן והעיר שושן צהלה ושמחה                                   |
|                                                                          |
|                                                                          |
|==========================================================================|
||Lemma:           ',_כ=:*ד:ו=מ |        מרדכי  Root:                        ||
||                                                          Freq:      60||
||                                            נתובים        Persons:       2||
||1:MORDECAI                        Substantive            Proper Noun    ||
||                                                                         ||
||                                                                         ||
||                                                                         ||
|==========================================================================|
```

```
     [F1]=View Lexicon    [F2]=Search Concord   [F8]=View Context

     [G]=Go to Book       [S]=Set a Marker      [M]=Go to Marker
     [L]=Lexicon Window   [E]=English Window    [F]=Flags Window
```

Figure 7.8: COMPUCORD View Mode displaying sample Full Verse over Lexicon Window.

Users may close the Flags Window and leave the Lexicon Window open, so that the complete verse is displayed in the main upper window and the lexical information about that verse in the lower window. When that is done, the screen looks like Figure 7.8.

Verses may be displayed in eighteen lines of context, with the user-specified verse first. Book names and chapter and verse numbers are displayed to the right of each verse. Users may scroll bidirectionally by word, verse, chapter, book, and volume (the four volumes are Pentateuch, Early Prophets, Later Prophets, and Scripture).

The View Mode allows users to save any text that is displayed on-screen, to translate from Hebrew to English (using the first English translation listed in the lexicon for each word), and to switch from one language to the other. The View Mode also allows users to have the program create a Hebrew/English translation of the uppermost verse on the screen.

In the View Mode, COMPUCORD allows users to search for lemmata, roots, words, or English glosses. When searching for glosses, if an exact match is not found, COMPUCORD displays the closest match.[104] Users may specify an English word and COMPUCORD will locate the closest matching Hebrew lemma. All searches in the View Mode are interactive. When searching for matches, users may move bidirectionally by hits in chapters, books, and volumes.

The View Mode also allows users to view the lexicon entries on either side of the current (highlighted) lemma and to move in either direction to a different lemma. When the Lexicon Scrolling Window has been opened on the top half of the screen, the following information about the highlighted word is displayed from left to right in vertical columns: root, complete lemma, consonantal lemma, and English translation. The Lexicon Scrolling Window may be used with the Lexicon Window below it (see Figure 7.9), or the Lexicon Window can be closed, in which case the Lexicon Scrolling Window occupies the whole screen, except for the command line. Users may alter the order in which the entries in the Lexicon Scrolling Window are arranged and displayed. Items may be displayed by concordance, lemma, root, or English translation. The concordance sequence displays the lexicon entries as they might be found in Mandelkern's *Veteris Testamenti Concordantiae*, the lemma sequence displays them as an alphabetized sequence of consonantal lemmata, the root sequence as an alphabetized sequence of roots, and the English sequence as an alphabetized list of English glosses.

```
 Root            Complete Lemma           Lemma   English Translation
                  מ=ר:ד*:=כ_,י            מרדכי   1:MORDECAI
 רדף               מֹר:ד*=,ף              מרדף    1:PERSECUTION
 מרר                 מ=ר%=,ה               מרה    1:BITTERNESS  2:BITTER
 מרה               1 מ=ר=,ה             1 מרה    1:REBEL 2     2:REBELLIOUS  3:
                   2 מ=ר=,ה             2 מרה    1:MARAH
 רוד                מ=ר,ו*ד               מרוד   1:BITTERNESS  2:HOMELESS
                    מ&ר,ו%ז               מרוז   1:MEROZ
 מרח              מ=ר,ו%<_<ח             מרוח   1:CRUSHED
╔═══════════════════════════════════════════════════════════════════════╗
║Lemma:            מ=ר:ד*:=כ_,י           מרדכי  Root:                    ║
║                                                       Freq:          60║
║                                      כתובים           Persons:        2║
║1:MORDECAI                       Substantive           Proper Noun      ║
║                                                                       ║
║                                                                       ║
║                                                                       ║
╚═══════════════════════════════════════════════════════════════════════╝

      [F1]=View Concordance   [F2]=Search Lexicon   [F3]=Change Sequence

                              [L]=Lexicon Window
```

Figure 7.9: COMPUCORD View Mode displaying sample Lexicon Scrolling Window over Lexicon Window.

104. COMPUCORD has a feature that helps users locate a lemma's correct spelling.

Search Logic and the Scan Mode. The Scan Mode is used to concord the text in complex morphological, lexical, and grammatical ways that create indices that may be edited, saved to disk, and printed. COMPUCORD is easily the most flexible, sophisticated, and powerful concording program discussed in this book. Like some of the concording programs reviewed in chapter 3, COMPUCORD concords preindexed text. The text in COMPUCORD's data base has been indexed by lemma, root, gloss, and in other ways. COMPUCORD's literature describes concording by lemma, root, and morphological form and makes little mention of concording grammatical constructions. Because COMPUCORD's data base includes sixty types of grammatical tags, however, it may be searched for grammatical constructions.

The Scan Menu displays the following options, each of which helps to define and restrict concording operations in different ways.

> Esc
> Return to Main Menu
> F1 Lemma Range
> F2 Lemma Following Lemma
> F3 Lemma Consonantal Range
> F4 Lemma Consonantal Following
> F5 Morphological Match
> F7 Format the Scan Results
> F8 Merge the Scan Results

When creating indices, COMPUCORD concords any user-specified range of text (including nonsequential ranges) across punctuation, verse, and chapter boundaries, but not across book and volume boundaries. All five of the scan options we are about to discuss can be restricted by using flags that will be discussed below in the "Scan Mode Input" section.

The Scan Mode is used to perform five basic concording operations (Scan Menu items F1–F5 above): (1) concord by consonantal lemma (the Lemma Range scan—see below), (2) concord by a key lemma in a group of lemmata (the Lemma Following Lemma scan—see below), (3) concord by morphological form of a consonantal lemma (the Lemma Consonantal Range scan—see below), (4) concord by a key morphological form of a lemma in a group of lemmata (the Lemma Consonantal Following scan—see below), and (5) concord by morphologically specified words (the Morphological Match option—see below). The Scan Mode also allows users to edit, format, merge, and print indices. Only the combine operation is available when merging indices.

Concording by Lemma. The Lemma Range scan is used in the following ways to concord a user-specified range of text by lemma, root, or a combination of the two. When concording by lemma, searches may be restricted to (1) a single lemma, (2) a two-lemma phrase where the lemmata are separated only by conjunctions and inseparable prepositions (i.e., Boolean AND logic), (3) a three-lemma phrase where the lemmata are separated only by conjunctions and inseparable propositions (i.e., Boolean AND logic), (4) a three-lemma phrase where the middle lemma is a wild card (i.e., Boolean AND logic), and (5) a group of lemmata, an occurrence of any one of which is accepted (i.e., Boolean OR logic). Scan options (2), (3), and (4) are sequence-specific; only lemmata that match the sequence of the lemmata in the search construction count as matches. Option (5), which treats multiple lemmata as a single group, searches for up to twenty-four lemmata simultaneously. Scan options (2), (3), and (4) are similar to compuBIBLE's pattern matching search feature (see chapter 3).

COMPUCORD also can concord by root. Root searches may be restricted to (1) single roots, (2) a sequence-specific, two-root phrase, (3) a sequence-specific, three-root phrase, and (4) a sequence-specific, two-root phrase with the middle root a wild card. All four variations count an occurrence of any of the lemmata listed under a root in COMPUCORD's index files as a match.

When performing a Lemma Range scan for two or more terms, the on-screen order of the search terms may change as the search begins. To speed up concording operations, COMPUCORD automatically makes the lemma with the fewest occurrences the key lemma, unless this "Sort Feature" is turned off. For example, if the search terms are the lemmata *bryt* ("covenant") and *(olm* ("everlasting"), and if the range is 0 verses and the whole OT is searched, enabling the Sort Feature (its default setting is Yes) causes COMPUCORD to make *bryt*, which occurs 284 times in the OT, the key lemma, instead of *(olm*, which occurs 439 times. Thus when constructing the index, COMPUCORD looks up the 284 verses where *bryt* occurs to see if they include *(olm*. Otherwise the program would have to look up the 439 verses where *(olm* occurs to see if they include *bryt*. Searching 155 fewer occurrences by making *bryt* the key lemma speeds up this search by about 35%.

Concording by Key Lemma. The Lemma Following Lemma scan is a sequence-specific way of structuring a search that makes the lead lemma in a group of lemmata the key lemma in the search, so that COMPUCORD will list as hits only those instances where the key lemma precedes the other lemmata, which may occur in any order. For example, if the search string is "Abraham, Isaac, Jacob," COMPUCORD will list as hits "Abraham . . . Jacob . . . Isaac" and "Abraham . . . Isaac . . . Jacob" but not "Isaac . . . Abraham . . . Jacob" or "Jacob . . . Isaac . . . Abraham."

All other search parameters and options discussed above under Lemma Range Scan apply to Lemma Following Lemma scans.

Concording by a Morphologically Defined Lemma. The Lemma Consonantal Range scan is an exact-phrase search technique that allows users to restrict searches to the morphological forms of consonantal lemmata. All other search parameters and options discussed above under Lemma Range scan apply to Lemma Consonantal Range scans.

Concording by a Key, Morphologically Defined Lemma. The Lemma Consonantal Following scan combines the sequence-specific and exact-phrase search features of the two previous scan options and restricts searches to strings that begin with a specific, morphologically defined lemma. All other search parameters and options discussed above under Lemma Range Scan apply to Lemma Consonantal Following scans.

Concording by Morphological Categories. The Morphological Match option supports truncation and wild-card searches. Search terms are not restricted to lemma, root, or group. Search terms may be qualified morphologically, lexically, and grammatically by using various combinations of flags from the Flags Window, Homographic Window, and Word Category-Gender Conjugation Window (see below). Morphological Match supports initial and terminal (but not medial) truncation. The "*" sign functions as a global wild-card character, and "?" functions as a single wild-card character. Among other uses, Morphological Match allows users to concord complete grammatical categories, such as all forms of all verbs that are *hiphil* or all *qal* active participles.

Scan Mode Input. In this section we will discuss the ways that searches may be constructed using the five scan options discussed above. We will proceed by discussing the various windows that COMPUCORD uses in the Scan Mode for user input.

The Scan Mode uses two main windows for user input, the Lexicon Scrolling Window at the top of the screen and the Scan Entry Window below it (see Figure 7.10). The Lexicon Scrolling Window is used to display roots, complete lemmata, consonantal lemmata, and English translations that may be used as search terms.

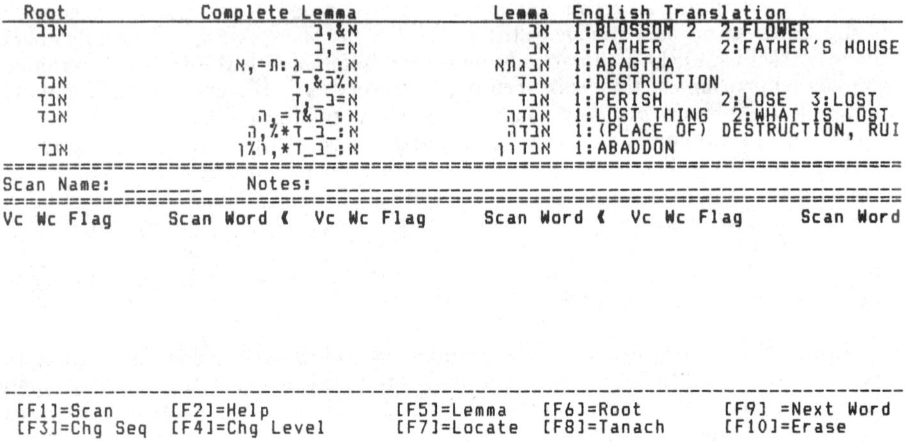

```
Root            Complete Lemma            Lemma  English Translation
 אבד                   אבְ,&ן               אב    1:BLOSSOM 2  2:FLOWER
                        אבְ,=ן               אב    1:FATHER       2:FATHER'S HOUSE
              אבַ,=ןבַ,: אבְ,_: ן                 אבגתא  1:ABAGTHA
 אבד                   אבְ,&בַ%ן              אבד   1:DESTRUCTION
 אבד                   אבְ,_בַ=ן              אבד   1:PERISH        2:LOSE   3:LOST
 אבד                   אבַ,=בַ&בַ,: ן              אבדה  1:LOST THING  2:WHAT IS LOST
                        אבַ,%*בַ_בַ,: ן             אבדן  1:(PLACE OF) DESTRUCTION, RUI
 אבד                   אבַ%בַ,*בַ_בַ,: ן          אבדון  1:ABADDON
=====================================================================================
Scan Name: _____    Notes: _____
=====================================================================================
Vc Wc Flag   Scan Word 《 Vc Wc Flag   Scan Word 《 Vc Wc Flag      Scan Word
```

```
----------------------------------------------------------------------------
[F1]=Scan     [F2]=Help            [F5]=Lemma   [F6]=Root      [F9] =Next Word
[F3]=Chg Seq  [F4]=Chg Level       [F7]=Locate  [F8]=Tanach    [F10]=Erase
```

Figure 7.10: COMPUCORD Scan Mode displaying sample Lexicon Scrolling Window over Scan Entry Window.

The Scan Entry Window is used to enter the lemmata and roots—the search terms—for which COMPUCORD is to construct indices. Both windows are open simultaneously and are interactive. Entering a lemma or root in the Scan Entry Window causes that lemma or root to appear in highlighted form in the Lexicon Scrolling Window. Below the highlighted lemma or root are listed the seven lemmata in the lexicon that follow it. These lemmata are listed in concordance sequence and with the corresponding roots, complete lemmata, and English glosses displayed (see Figure 7.10). Users may scroll the lemmata in the Lexicon Scrolling Window and select lemmata or roots as search terms by "picking them up" and moving them to the Scan Entry Window.

Between the Lexicon Scrolling Window and the Scan Entry Window is a small horizontal window that serves three functions. (1) It allows users to name the index COMPUCORD is about to create (up to seven characters may be used).[105] (2) It allows users to enter optional notes that describe the search. Notes may be entered in English, Hebrew, or both and may be up to sixty characters long.[106] (3) This window is used to enter the following three search string parameters: Books, Match, and Range. *Range* and *books* are used rather strangely in this context, as we will see.

Books is used to set the range of text COMPUCORD is to scan to create an index, an operation most other concording programs refer to as setting the "range." As I mentioned earlier, every book has a number (listed in Appendix A of the user's manual), and the search range may consist of nonsequential portions of text. To search all of book 1 (Genesis) chapter 1 and book 3 (Leviticus) chapter 4 verse 1 through book 3 chapter 5 verse 7 and all of book 6 (Joshua), users would enter "1.1,3.4–3.5.7,6."

Match is used to specify the number of search terms in a set that must occur within a specified proximity of words, verses, or chapters to count as hits (see below on "Range").[107] The Match option allows users to instruct COMPUCORD to accept as

---

105. Previously created indices are loaded by typing their names. Cursor keys are used to scroll index names.

106. COMPUCORD automatically saves all search constructions, automatically displays them on-screen, and automatically prints them with indices. Thus it is not necessary to enter notes to describe an index, though it is wise to do so.

107. COMPUCORD uses *range* to mean "proximity."

legitimate hits the occurrence of a certain number of the members of a set within the specified proximity. The default setting for Match is zero, which means that all members of the set must occur within the specified proximity. The values for Match are 0–9. For example, if the search terms are "Miriam, Moses, Aaron" (unflagged proper names), if the proximity is a single verse (see below under "Range"), if the whole OT is searched, and if the Match value is zero, COMPUCORD will locate five verses in the OT that include all three members of the set. But if the Match value is changed to two, COMPUCORD will locate 144 verses that include two (or more) of the members of the set within the specified proximity. A Match value of one causes all members of the set to be counted, thereby effectively disabling the proximity ("Range") number (see below).

Range is used to specify the proximity in which multiple search terms must occur to count as matches. *Range* is used to specify the distance on either side of the first search term as N-number of words, verses, or chapters (not books or volumes). A range value of zero verses requires COMPUCORD to count as matches only those search terms that occur in the same verse, and this is the default setting. A range of zero chapters requires COMPUCORD to count as matches search terms that occur in the same chapter. A range of zero words is not logically possible since by definition more than one lemma cannot be found in the same word. A range value of fifty words, for example, causes COMPUCORD to count as matches those search terms that occur within fifty words on either side of the first search term. Range values are 0 to 9,999.

COMPUCORD allows each of the four major lemma scan options (F1–F4—see above) to be restricted by defining (1) up to three flags from the fifteen listed in the Flags Window (e.g., *ketib/qere*, state, grammatical number, proper noun, presence or absence of prefix, etc.), (2) one flag from the twenty-nine Word Category Codes (e.g., grammatical part of speech, grammatical number), and (3) one flag from the thirty-one Gender and Verbal Conjugation Codes (e.g., gender, verbal conjugation)—up to five flags per search construction. Users need not worry about memorizing flags. The F2, or Help, key, displays flags and their codes.

Here's how flag-restricted searches are constructed. A search for the lemma *byt* ("house") could be restricted by flagging the search string with the masculine, third person suffix. That would cause COMPUCORD to build an index that included only those instances where *byt* occurs with a masculine, third person suffix. Similarly, *hlk* ("go," "walk") could be flagged with a *hiphil* flag, so that COMPUCORD built an index that included only those instances where *hlk* occurs in the *hiphil*.

As we learned above, in the four major lemma scan options (F1–F4), there are three types of search terms: lemma, group, and root. Up to fourteen lines of search terms may be specified per search, and each line may contain up to three flagged lemmata, three roots, or a group of up to twenty-four individually flagged 3-word entries (lemmata and/or roots). Thus COMPUCORD can simultaneously concord 42 lemmata or 42 roots or 14 groups that may contain twenty-four 3-word entries each (i.e., 1,008 terms)! When concording groups, COMPUCORD concords each group as a single entry, treating the lemmata that define the group not as phrases but as individual members of the set that defines the group. Lemmata and roots are entered in Hebrew, right to left. *Qere* are automatically excluded from all searches unless users specify otherwise.

```
Scan Name: SAMPLE      Notes: Sample Morphological Match
                       Books: 1-39
r-----------------------------------------------------------------------------1
|                         Consonantal Word:                                   |
|=============================================================================|
|   1: Qere Excluded       6: Prefix Allowed      11: Aramaic Allowed         |
|   2: Allow Any State     7: Allow Postpos Article 12: Allow Compound Numbers |
|   3: Allow Proper Noun   8: Allow Com Proper Name 13: Allow Last Numbers     |
|   4: Atnah Allowed       9: Maqqef Allowed      14: Allow Discontinuous Nbr  |
|   5: All Persons        10:                      15: Numbers Allowed         |
|=============================================================================|
| Homographic Information: ||Word Category-Gender-Conjugation:|| Group Nbr    |
| Lemma Homograph is Allowed ||  Prefix:                       ||         1   |
| Homograph Proper Noun Allowed ||  Prefix:                    ||             |
| Various Categories Allowed ||  Prefix:                        || Simple Nbr |
| Two Distinct Lemmatta Allowed ||  Word:                       ||         0   |
| Form Homograph is Allowed ||                                  ||             |
|                          ||  Suffix:                         || Whole Nbr  |
|                          ||                                   ||         0   |
L-----------------------------||-----------------------------------||----------J


                        Press [F1] to Begin Scan
```

Figure 7.11: COMPUCORD Scan Mode displaying sample Morphological Match screen.

The Morphological Match scan option allows users to flag a word by using (1) as many of the flags in the Flags Window, (2) Word Category Codes, and (3) Gender and Verbal Conjugation Codes as appropriate, as well as to use appropriate flags from the (4) Homographic Information and (5) Numbers Windows. Figure 7.11 shows what the screen looks like when a Morphological Match search is being constructed.

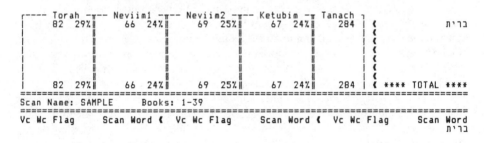

```
r---- Torah -ᵧ-- Neviim1 -ᵧ-- Neviim2 -ᵧ-- Ketubim -ᵧ Tanach ᵧ
|   82   29%||   66   24%||   69   25%||   67   24%||   284   | <                בדית
|           ||           ||           ||           ||         | <
|           ||           ||           ||           ||         | <
|           ||           ||           ||           ||         | <
|           ||           ||           ||           ||         | <
|           ||           ||           ||           ||         | <
|   82   29%||   66   24%||   69   25%||   67   24%||   284   | < **** TOTAL ****
=================================================================================
Scan Name: SAMPLE      Books: 1-39
=================================================================================
Vc Wc Flag      Scan Word <  Vc Wc Flag      Scan Word <  Vc Wc Flag      Scan Word
                                                                               בדית
```

```
-------------------------------------------------------------------------------
     Press:   [ENTER]=Format   [Esc]=Menu   [F1]=Restart
```

Figure 7.12: COMPUCORD Scan Mode displaying sample Progress Update Window.

The Progress Update Window. As COMPUCORD constructs an index (or indices), it dynamically displays information in the Progress Update Window (see Figure 7.12). The Progress Update Window, which replaces the Lexicon Scrolling Window, is divided into five sections, one for each of the four divisions of the Hebrew Bible and one for total counts. When concording with a Lemma Range scan, COMPUCORD uses those windows and the Parameters Line below them and dynamically displays the following information: the (1) book, (2) chapter, and (3) verse in which hits occur, (4) the number of hits by volume, and (5) the percent of occurrences of hits by volume (based on the parameters of the search) in relation to the number of occurrences of hits in one or more other volumes.[108] Because it takes processor time to update the Progress Update Window, users may speed up concording operations by turning this feature off.

```
Scan Name: ESTHER      Notes: Occurences Of אמרה And מהרדכי In 1 Verse
                       Books: 1-39              Match: 0  Range:  0  Verses
Selection: Words       Options:
===================================================================================
                           87&*ח:0;א        אמרה      7   2      אמרה
                        י01^Vכ=:*ד:ד=מ       מהרדכי    7   2
                          76&*ח:0;א         אמרה     10   2
                        י01^Vכ=:*ד:ד=מ       מהרדכי   10   2
                          6י^Vכ=:*ד:ד=מ      מהרדכי   11   2
                          76&*ח:0;א         אמרה     11   2
                          74&*ח:0;א         אמרה     15   2
                        י09^Vכ=:*ד:ד=מ       מהרדכי   15   2
                          87&*ח:0;א         אמרה     15   2
                          75&*ח:0;א         אמרה     20   2
                        י3=כ=:*ד:ד=מ         מהרדכי   20   2
                        8י^Vכ=:*ד:ד=מ        מהרדכי   20   2
                          74&*ח:0;א         אמרה     20   2
                        י6^Vכ=:*ד:ד=מ+:ל     למהרדכי  22   2
                          74&*ח:0;א+:ל      לאמרה    22   2
                          701&*ח:0;א         אמרה     22   2
                        י,=כ=:*ד:ד=מ         מהרדכי   22   2
-----------------------------------------------------------------------------------
F1=Print Text      F2=Save to File    F5=Movement      F6=Color Chg   .F9= Translate
F3=Chg Sequence    F4=Chg Language    F7=Delete Word   F8=Context     F10=Totals
```

Figure 7.13: COMPUCORD Scan Mode displaying sample portion of index in Format Window.

Display Options. Once COMPUCORD has created an index (or indices), the results may be displayed on-screen in the Format Window, which shows the following information: scan name, notes, and the Books, Match, and Range scan parameters (see Figure 7.13). The Format Window may be used to display an index in three different ways. (1) Indices may be displayed by search terms (words). In that case, COM-PUCORD lists the book, chapter, verse, consonantal form, and complete form of the search term for each occurrence. Users may scroll this listing. (2) Indices may be displayed as the verses in which search terms appear. In that case, COMPUCORD highlights hits and displays the book, chapter, and verse in which each hit appears. Users may scroll these listings. (3) Indices may be displayed in terms of the following numerical information: subtotal of the number of hits by volume, book, chapter, word forms, lemma, and group; subtotal of each lemma found; and total of all the lemmata found. That kind of information is extremely useful for purposes of statistical analysis.

The Format Menu allows indices to be edited, saved to disk, and formatted and printed. The contents of indices may be rearranged, saved to disk, and printed in the following sequences: book/chapter/verse, lemma, alphabetical order of hits, or group. Furthermore, indices may be printed in Hebrew or English. When printing indices, COMPUCORD automatically prints the search construction at the top of the index, as well as an index's name, notes, book value, range value, and date of creation. An index may be printed as a list of words (the default setting) or as hits in verses. Either way, COMPUCORD lists the book, chapter, and verse of each hit. And either way, COMPUCORD can intersperse Hebrew with English glosses. When printing hits in the context of verses, COMPUCORD automatically prints hits in bold-faced type, unless this feature has been turned off. In either printing format, COMPUCORD can print three types of totals—subtotals of hits by book, totals by volume, and the grand total of hits in the whole Hebrew Bible. These totals may be printed at the end of the index or interspersed after each chapter, book, and volume.

---

108. Pressing the Escape key at anytime during the concording operation stops the program. Pressing F1 restarts it, pressing Esc again returns the program to the previous menu, and pressing Enter formats the results of the concording operation up to the point where it was stopped.

On color monitors, up to five different colors can be used to distinguish five different lemmata on-screen. And by using the Epson JX color printer, hits can be printed in up to five different colors. By the time this book is released, COMPUCORD should be able to print indices in *fully vocalized* form, using the actual Hebrew vowel signs, not codes, though I do not know if COMPUCORD is yet able to display vocalized Hebrew on-screen. Currently, COMPUCORD supports the Epson FX and JX printers, though support for more dot matrix and laser printers, including the Toshiba P351 (see chapter 2), has been promised.

Statistics Module. The Statistics Module, which at this time is not yet priced, consists of two programs: STATISTICS and FREQUENCY DEVIATION. STATISTICS displays the following statistics about roots, lemmata, and morphological forms. It displays the number of occurrences of those items by (1) book, volume, and in the whole Hebrew Bible. It provides (2) English glosses, and for each word the program gives its (3) state, (4) grammatical number, and (5) other information, using the flags listed in the Flags Window and in the Word Category-Gender-Conjugation Window (see above). It also gives a count of the total number of (6) words, (7) different lemmata, (8) different lexical entries, and (9) different roots—all by book, volume, and in the Hebrew Bible as a whole. STATISTICS also provides (10) the percentages (ratios) of the occurrences of roots, lemmata, words, and flags by book, volume, and in the Hebrew Bible as a whole, and the program can (11) display on-screen and print bar graphs (39 bars) that represent those percentages.

FREQUENCY DEVIATION is a program that performs segment analysis of frequency deviation based on fixed or calculated standards. Here's how the program works. Users (1) select a range of text (by book, chapter, and verse) from which lemmata, roots, words, or letters of the alphabet will be chosen for statistical analysis. This range of text is known as the *segment.* Users then (2) pick a range of text (the whole Hebrew Bible, or one or more volumes and/or books) as a standard, or frame of reference. This range functions as a norm against which the frequency of the occurrence of terms in the segment is measured. Finally, users (3) specify the lemmata, roots, words, or letters of the alphabet that are to be counted in the segment and compared against the frequency of their occurrence in the standard. Based on the frequency of the occurrence of a chosen item in the standard, the program informs users what the expected frequency of its occurrence in the segment is and how much the actual frequency of that form's occurrence in the segment deviated from its expected frequency. In other words, this program compares the frequency of the occurrence of a form in one range of text with the frequency of its occurrence in another and shows the difference between the two as a percentage of deviation of the occurrences of the form in the segment from its occurrences in the standard. If the frequency of the occurrence of word X in the standard is ten times per book, and if word X only occurs five times per book in the segment, then the deviation of the frequency of the occurrence of X in the segment from its frequency of occurrence in the standard is 0.5.

Fixed standards are the whole Hebrew Bible, each volume, and each book. A calculated standard can be created by mixing volumes and/or books. Users have the option of specifying a percentage of deviation as a cutoff point, thereby requiring the program to display only those instances where the occurrence of a form deviated N% or more ("N" is a user-specified number) from its norm.

FREQUENCY DEVIATION can work with two segments of text at a time, comparing A with the standard, B with the standard, A and B together with the standard, and A with B. This is a powerful program that is quite useful for statistical analysis.

7.3.10.3 Evaluation

Of all the programs and projects that work with the text of the Hebrew Bible (or with any text, for that matter!), COMPUCORD stands out in several ways. First, it is commercially available and runs on microcomputers, which means that it can be used by many institutions and individuals, not just by a small handful of people. Second, it is fully menu-driven, which means that it is easy to use. Third, its ability to perform a wide range of morphological, lexical, grammatical, and statistical analyses of the text and to edit, rearrange, format, and print the results in ways that appear extremely "user friendly" make it powerful and distinctive.

COMPUCORD meets almost all of the criteria of an ideal concording program (see chapter 3). COMPUCORD supports (1) Boolean ANDs and ORs, (2) extremely long search strings (1,008 words), (3) multiple-term, (4) pattern-matching, (5) exact-phrase, (6) proximity, (7) sequence-specific, and (8) punctuation-specific searches, (9) indices of unlimited size, (10) initial and terminal truncation, (11) global and single wild cards, (12) nonsequential search ranges, (13) bidirectional scrolling in either program mode, (14) windows, (15) a GOTO function, and (16) statistical information. COMPUCORD (17) can search across verse and chapter boundaries, (18) automatically saves search strategies, (19) displays the search construction when scanning, concording, or working with indices, (20) dynamically updates the screen to reflect the results of searches, (21) highlights search terms on-screen and when printing, and (22) allows indices to be edited, (23) combined, and (24) printed.

Unfortunately, as incredibly powerful and flexible as it is, COMPUCORD does not support (1) scanning for or concording vocalized forms, (2) intersecting indices, (3) the explicit use of Boolean operators, (4) Boolean NOTs and XORs, (5) medial truncation, (6) suppressing cantillation codes, and (7) displaying two indices or ranges of text simultaneously. Furthermore, (8) COMPUCORD cannot display vocalized Hebrew on-screen.

7.4 Other Projects with Ancient Semitic Texts

In this section I will mention a number of projects, exclusive of large data banks, that are working with machine-readable versions of various Semitic texts. In the interests of comprehensiveness, I have included brief descriptions of several projects about which I have been unsuccessful in obtaining first-hand information. I hope to report more fully on them in the next edition of this book. Several projects included below might just as logically have been included later in this chapter under "Machine-Readable Text Archives and Data Banks" (e.g., Princeton's DSS project, the Cairo Geniza project), though they seem to fit equally well here.

7.4.1 EBAF

Dr. P. Refoule of the Ecole Biblique et Archeologique (EBAF) is reported to be using a machine-readable version of the (BHS) consonantal text of the Megilloth (i.e., the "scrolls"—Song of Songs, Ruth, Lamentations, Ecclesiastes, and Esther) and programs written in BASIC to research the numerical codes of the Masoretic Text by counting letters, words, verbs, open and close marks, and so forth. Text files and programs are Commodore-64 compatible. For more information, contact:

Dr. P. Refoule
Ecole Biblique
P.O. Box 19053
Jerusalem, Israel
(02) 282-213; from North America dial direct:
011-972-02-282-213.

7.4.2 Concordance to Targum Pseudo-Jonathan

Drs. John C. Hurd, E. G. Clark, and W. Aufrecht have created a machine-readable text of Targum Pseudo-Jonathan to the Pentateuch and a concordance thereof.[109] (In chapter 4 I discussed Dr. Hurd's CALL program, the Greek Tutor.) For more information, contact:

> Prof. John C. Hurd
> Trinity College
> 6 Hoskin Ave.
> University of Toronto
> Toronto, Ontario M5S 1H8
> Canada
> (416) 978-3056.

7.4.3 Greek and Hebrew Morphological Analysis

Dr. Raymond Martin and his colleagues are grammatically analyzing manually correlated machine-readable versions of the Masoretic Text and the Septuagint (in transcription)[110] to produce descriptive lexica of Septuagint books,[111] syntactical concordances of the correlated Greek and Hebrew texts,[112] and to determine additional syntactical criteria of translation Greek. Thus the work of Martin and his colleagues is quite similar to that of the CATSS project (see below). So far, Dr. Martin and his associates have completed the grammatical analysis of Baruch, the Epistle of Jeremiah (see The Computer Bible, vol. 12), and Ruth. They are in the process of finalizing Obadiah and Daniel and have begun work on Ezra, Ezekiel, Jeremiah, the Testament of the Twelve Patriarchs, and 1 Maccabees. For more information about this project, contact:

> Dr. Raymond Martin
> Wartburg Theological Seminary
> 33 Wartburg Place
> Dubuque, IA 52001
> (319) 556-8151.

7.4.4 Midrash Tanhuma

Dr. Alan Segal is engaged in a computer-assisted study of the Midrash Tanhuma. For more information, contact:

> Dr. Alan Segal
> Columbia University
> 219c Milbank Hall
> New York, NY 10027
> (212) 280-5419.

---

109. E. G. Clarke et al., *Targum Pseudo-Jonathan of the Pentateuch: Text and Concordance*. Hoboken, N.J.: KTAV Publishing House, 1984.

110. This project began in 1973 in conjunction with the late Sister Mary Kenneth at Clark College, was developed and expanded with the assistance of Dr. Peter C. Patton at the University of Minnesota, and in 1984 was transferred to the University of Dubuque Computer Center.

111. Dr. Gary Chamberlin of the University of Dubuque Theological Seminary is currently at work on a *Lexicon of the Greek of Obadiah*.

112. Dr. Martin and Dr. Sylvio Scorza of Northwestern College in Orange City, Iowa, are working on these.

7.4.5 Syriac Concordance

Dr. Johan Cook at the University of Stellenbosch, under the auspices of the International Organization for the Study of the Old Testament (IOSOT), is developing a computer-based Syriac concordance that will complement the Peshitta Institute's forthcoming *Vetus Testamentum Syriac*. See his "The Development of a Base for the Peshitta Version of the Old Testament," *Bible and Computer : The Text*, 165–77. For further information, contact:

Dr. Johann Cook
Department of Semitic Languages
University of Stellenbosch
Stellenbosch 7600
Republic of South Africa
77511 (University), 73156 (Semitic Languages); from North America dial direct: 011-27-2231-77511, 73156.

7.4.6 CAL—Comprehensive Aramaic Lexicon

This project, under the joint editorship of Drs. Joseph A. Fitzmyer, Delbert R. Hillers, and Stephen A. Kaufman, has completed its planning phase and is entering into the preparation of a comprehensive Aramaic lexicon for all branches of that language—inscriptions, Biblical Aramaic, Syriac, and so forth. Some Aramaic texts already exist in machine-readable form—Michael Sokoloff's machine-readable Jewish Palestinian texts (done at Bar-Ilan), some Biblical Aramaic texts of Richard E. Whitaker's, and E. G. Clarke's tape of Targum Pseudo-Jonathan, and some of these will be incorporated into the CAL data base. Dr. Hillers has entered a substantial portion of Palmyrene Aramaic, and Professors Ben-Hayyim (see below under HDP) and Tal have almost completed a machine-readable version of Samaritan Aramaic texts.

In addition to creating a comprehensive Aramaic lexicon, the CAL project plans to produce scholarly editions of Aramaic texts in machine-readable and printed forms.

For more information about the CAL project (which is expected to take about 15 years to complete) and to receive complementary copies of the *Newsletter of the Comprehensive Aramaic Lexicon Project*, contact:

Editors, CAL
The Johns Hopkins University
Dept. of Near Eastern Studies
Gilman Hall, Room 128
Charles and 34th Streets
Baltimore, MD 21218
(301) 338-7499 (Department), (301) 338-7496 (Hillers).

7.4.7 Sumerian Dictionary

Dr. David I. Owen of Cornell University is part of a worldwide group of scholars who are involved in creating a machine-readable dictionary for Sumerian documents from the third millennium B.C. Scholars from the universities of Berlin, Freiburg, Heidelberg, and Cornell, under the directorship of Prof. Giovanni Pettinato of the University of Rome, are overseeing data entry and coding of the vast body of Sumerian and Eblaite documents (tablets) that have come down from the third millennium. For more information contact:

David I. Owen
Dept. of Near Eastern Studies
Cornell University
Rockefeller Hall
Ithaca, NY 14853.

7.4.8 Dictionary of Modern Hebrew

Dr. Jonathan Paradise is reported to be creating a microcomputer-based, machine-readable dictionary of Modern Hebrew. For more information, contact:

Dr. Jonathan Paradise
178 Klaber Court, Room 180
320 16th Ave., SE
University of Minnesota
Minneapolis, MN 55455
(612) 373-5722.

7.4.9 Princeton DSS Project

Princeton Theological Seminary and Princeton University Press, under the directorship of Dr. James Charlesworth, are preparing to publish new transcriptions, photographs, and annotated translations of all the nonbiblical Dead Sea Scrolls. The production of a machine-readable version of the *nonbiblical* scrolls will be an offshoot of this project.[113] The machine-readable version of the nonbiblical scrolls is expected to be available on tape and for IBM PCs and Ibycus machines. For more information contact Dr. Whitaker (see above) or:

Princeton University Press
41 William St.
Princeton, NJ 08540
(609) 452-4896.

7.4.10 Cairo Geniza Project

Dr. Mark R. Cohen of Princeton University is involved in helping to prepare a machine-readable data base of the entire corpus, both published and unpublished, from the Cairo Geniza.[114] For more information contact:

Mark R. Cohen
Dept. of Near Eastern Studies
Princeton University
Princeton, NJ 08540.

7.4.11 Amorite

Ignace J. Gelb has published several items about his computer-assisted study of Amorite. See Ignace J. Gelb, "Computer-Aided Analysis of Amorite," *Journal of Cuneiform Studies* 34 (1982): 1–18; "Computer-Aided Analysis of Amorite," *JSS* 26

---

113. According to Dr. Richard E. Whitaker (see above), the Claremont Institute for Antiquity and Christianity is considering putting the *biblical* Dead Sea Scrolls in machine-readable form.

114. A "geniza" is a burial place in a synagogue for "sacred refuse," such as the discarded pages of sacred writings.

(1981): 277–80; and *Computer-Aided Analysis of Amorite*, Assyriological Studies 21 (Chicago: The Oriental Institute, 1980).

7.4.12 Projekt: Informatik + Bibel

Prof. Dr. Harald Schweizer is creating a MRT of the MT to use for text-critical, grammatical, syntactical, and statistical studies. He is working with CATAB's MRT of the OT (see above) and is using CATAB's special graphics terminal, CALLIGRAPHE® 44. See his "Elektronische Datenverarbeitung und Textinterpretation," *Computer and Bible : The Text*, 297–310. For more information, contact:

> Prof. Dr. Harald Schweizer
> Projekt: Informatik + Bibel
> Katholisch-theologisches Seminar
> Universität Tübingen
> Leibermeisterstrasse 12
> D-7400, Tübingen, 1
> West Germany
> (07071) 295-248; from North America dial direct:
> 011-70-71-295-248.

7.4.13 Hamburg Alttestamentliches Seminar

Prof. Dr. Reinhard Wonneberger is developing a MRT of BHS and software to publish theological texts that include Greek and Hebrew quotations and biblical citations. See his "Überlegungen zu einer maschinenlesbaren Neuausgabe der Biblia Hebraica Stuttgartensia," *Bible and Computer : The Text*, 363–79. For more information, contact:

> Prof. Dr. Reinhard Wonneberger
> Alttestamentliches Seminar
> Universität Hamburg
> 13 Sedanstrasse 19
> 2 Hamburg
> West Germany
> (040) 4123; from North America dial direct: 011-49-40-4123.

7.5 Machine-Readable Versions of the Septuagint

7.5.1 CATSS

- *BASIC DATA BASE INFORMATION*

Key Person(s): Robert A. Kraft, Emanuel Tov
Location of Project: Philadelphia and Jerusalem
Project Address: % Dr. Robert A. Kraft, Department of Religious Studies, Box 36 College Hall, University of Pennsylvania, Philadelphia, PA 19104-6303
Telephone: (215) 898-5827
Date Project Began: 1978/1981
Date Project Completed: Not yet complete.
Sources of Funding: The Research Tools Division of the National Endowment for the Humanities of the United States of America, the David and Lucile Packard Foundation, the Vira L. Heinz Fund of the Pittsburgh Foundation, the Research Foundation at the University of Pennsylvania, the University of Pennsylvania, the Israel Academy of Sciences and Humanities, and the Hebrew University

Primary Purpose of Project: To create a fully tagged and aligned, machine-readable data base of the Septuagint and the Masoretic Text, complete with all significant variants, that can be used to create scholarly tools for all aspects of Septuagintal studies—text-critical, lexical, grammatical, translational, conceptual, and bibliographical.

Textual Authority: LXX: Rahlfs from TLG (modified to the Göttingen edition where the latter exists); MT: BHS from MPCABS (collated with the texts of COMPU-BIBLE/COMPUCORD and CIB and proofed by the WCP)

Machine-Readable Text Includes: Hebrew text, vocalized, with analysis; LXX text, with accents, breathings, diacritical marks, and analysis

Vocalized: Yes (Hebrew text)

Cantillated: Yes (Hebrew text)

Diacritical Marks: Yes (Greek text)

Type of Tagging: Morphological, lexical, syntactical

Level of Tagging: Morphological, lexical, syntactical

Scope of Tagging: The entire MT and LXX, including LXX variants

Type of Text Files: EBCDIC, ASCII

Programming Languages: IBYX, Pascal, Turbo Pascal, C, Assembler, DEC BASIC-Plus

Output Options: Screen, tape, diskettes, print; transliterated, coded text or Greek and Hebrew text

Availability of Tapes or Disks: 9-track 6,250 and 1,600-bpi tapes will be available at cost to qualified parties through the University of Pennsylvania's CCAT (see below) and through Oxford University's OUCS (see below). Floppy disk formats for certain microcomputers also will be supported; diskettes for the IBM PC are currently available. *Portions* of the data base will also be made available in various formats.

Cost of Tapes or Disks: About $50 per 2,400-foot tape.[115] See below under CCAT for more information.

Key Bibliographical References: "Prospectus: Computer Assisted Tools for Septuagint Studies," *A Computerized Data Base for Septuagint Studies—The Parallel Aligned Text of the Greek and Hebrew Bible*; Kraft and Tov, "Computer Assisted Tools for Septuagint Studies," *BIOSCS* 14 (1981): 22–40.

Other: See above under WCP.

7.5.1.1 Introduction

The information in this subsection is based on materials provided by Dr. Robert A. Kraft and on published articles. CATSS (Computer-Assisted Tools for Septuagint Studies), directed by Drs. Robert A. Kraft (Codirector, University of Pennsylvania) and Emanuel Tov (Codirector, The Hebrew University, Jerusalem), is sponsored by the IOSCS (International Organization for Septuagint and Cognate Studies) under the auspices of the SBL and is primarily funded by the NEH Research Tools: Reference Materials Program. Planning and research for the CATSS project began in 1978; the project formally commenced in 1981. Drs. John R. Abercrombie, William Adler, David Packard (see below), Richard E. Whitaker (see above), and Stephen V. F. Waite (see below) have been closely involved in different ways and at various times as consultants.[116]

Septuagint (LXX) is the name conventionally used to refer to the corpus of ancient Greek translations of Hebrew scriptural works that was made by Greek-speaking Jews in Alexandria and elsewhere during a period of several centuries, beginning around the middle of the third century B.C.[117] Careful study of the LXX material can yield much valuable information about (1) the translation techniques that were employed, (2) the state of the Greek language during that period, especially in Egypt, (3) the cultural and intellectual settings of the translators, and (4) the Hebrew and Aramaic sources (i.e., the *Vorlagen*) behind the LXX.[118] Because the LXX embodies the Scrip-

---

115. Two 1,600-bpi tapes (over 170 320-K floppies!) will be required to hold the completed data base, which is estimated to be about 55 megabytes.

116. A partial history of the CATSS project can be found in Kraft and Tov, "Computer Assisted Tools for Septuagint Studies," *BIOSCS* 14 (1981): 22–40.

117. See *IDB* 4.273 and *IDB* Supp. Vol., 807–15. The standard introductory works are H. B. Swete, *Introduction to The Old Testament in Greek*, 2nd ed. (Cambridge: The University Press, 1914) and Sidney Jellicoe, *The Septuagint and Modern Study* (Oxford: The University Press, 1968).

118. See *IDB* Supp. Vol., 807–8; Kraft, "Prospectus," 4–5.

tures of the early Greek-speaking Jews and Christians, because it is strongly reflected in many early Greek citations of the Jewish Scriptures in the NT and elsewhere, and because it is the most famous and influential translation of the Hebrew Bible,[119] Christians and Jews alike have always had a strong scholarly interest in studying this text.

CATSS's primary goal is to create a flexible, multipurpose data base for Septuagintal studies that will allow users to study the LXX itself, the LXX in relation to the MT, and the LXX in relation to other versions and literatures. This data base will include (1) a morphologically analyzed, machine-readable version of Rahlfs's text of the LXX (i.e., the TLG machine-readable version, modified to the Göttingen edition where the latter exists), (2) a morphologically analyzed, machine-readable version of the Greek textual variants as published in the best critical apparatuses (Göttingen and Cambridge, see below), (3) a morphologically analyzed, machine-readable version of the MT (BHS—see above under WCP), and (4) the parallel alignment in vertical columns of the Greek and Hebrew texts.

With the aid of this data base, it will be possible to create the following types of tools, in printed and electronic form, for studying the LXX: (1) Greek-Hebrew and Hebrew-Greek concordances (including all Greek variants), (2) an analytical lexicon to the LXX (text with morphological analysis of each word), (3) a lexicon of the Greek materials (including variants),[120] (4) a grammar of LXX Greek, (5) critical editions of Greek books for which no suitable editions now exist (e.g., Samuel-Kings), and it will be possible to (6) investigate the translation techniques and conjectured Hebrew sources (*Vorlagen*) of the various LXX texts.

BK,	CH,	V,	ITEM,	SUBVARIANT,	COMMENTS
RT	03	05	(0100)	+ <KAI 18	{pr type reading with
RT	03	05	(0200)	eipen	KAI/DE variation
RT	03	05	(0301)	de] > 18	in MS 18}
RT	03	05	(0401)	Routh] > (˜)OA__OL(˜)	{possible transposition}
RT	03	05	(0500)	pros	
RT	03	05	(0601)	autên]	
RT	03	05	(0602)	:autê b__	{alternative readings}
RT	03	05	(0603)	:auton o*	
RT	03	05	(0700)	+ Routh (˜)OA__OL(˜)	{balances earlier "(˜)"}
RT	03	05	(0800)	Panta	
RT	03	05	(0901)	,] > (B-M)	{punctuation difference}
RT	03	05	(1000)	hosa	
RT	03	05	(1101)	ean ABacfkxb2]	{base text attestation}

Figure 7.14: Annotated sample of CATSS Greek variant text and notations from Ruth 3:5.

7.5.1.2 The Text and Tagging

CATSS acquired a machine-readable tape of the Rahlfs's *editio minor* of the LXX[121] from the TLG (Thesaurus Linguae Graecae) Project in Irvine, California (see below), a

---

119. See Kraft, "Prospectus," 2.

120. Although scholars have long had a concordance to the LXX—E. Hatch and H. A. Redpath, *A Concordance to the Septuagint and Other Greek Versions of the Old Testament*, 2 vols. (Oxford: Clarendon Press, 1897–1906. Supplement—1906; reprinted by Graz, 1954)—there is no comprehensive lexicon to this most important of biblical translations. Dr. Tov is the editor-designate for the Septuagint Lexicon Project.

121. A. Rahlfs, *Septuaginta*, 2 vols. (Stuttgart: Württembergische Bibelanstalt, 1935).

copy of the Michigan-Claremont Old Testament tape (see above), and a copy of CIB's MT (see above). CATSS has also made limited use of the Andersen-Forbes tape of 2 Kings (see above) and of some of the CATAB text (see above). The Michigan-Claremont Old Testament has been used as the starting point for CATSS's MT, and TLG's MRT of Rahlfs text has been used as CATSS's starting point for their LXX. The MRT of Rahlfs will gradually be changed as the textual variants from the Göttingen Septuagint are entered.[122] Where the Göttingen edition is not available, the variants are entered from the "Larger Cambridge Septuagint."[123] The variants to the Book of Ruth have been keyed in and fully verified; others are being entered with a KDEM (see above) at the University of Pennsylvania (previously also entered at the Oxford University Computing Service). As I mentioned above in the section on the WCP, Semitic variants to the MT are being coded by Dr. Michael Fox at the University of Wisconsin.

LOCATION,				TEXT FORM,	MORPH ANALYSIS,	DICT. FORM
RT	01	01	01	KAI\	C	KAI/
RT	01	01	02	E)GE/NETO	VBI AMI3S	GI/GNOMAI
RT	01	01	03	E)N	P	E)N
RT	01	01	04	TW=|	RA DSN	O(
RT	01	01	05	KRI/NEIN	VI PAN	KRI/NW
RT	01	01	06	TOU\S	RA APM	O(
RT	01	01	07	KRITA\S	N1M APM	KRITH/S
RT	01	01	08	KAI\	C	KAI/
RT	01	01	09	E)GE/NETO	VBI AMI3S	GI/GNOMAI
RT	01	01	10	LIMO\S	N2 NSM	LIMO/S
RT	01	01	11	E)N	P	E)N
RT	01	01	12	TH=|	RA DSF	O(
RT	01	01	13	GH=|,	N1 DSF	GH=

Figure 7.15: Sample of CATSS morphologically analyzed text from Ruth 1:1.

The Greek text has been tagged at the textual, morphological, and syntactical levels (see Figures 7.14 and 7.15).[124] This includes information about person, number, tense, mode, and type for verbs, and case, number, gender, and declension for nouns. Thus every word has been tagged according to its part of speech and lexical form. And as we learned earlier, the WCP team is verifying the morphologically tagged version of the Michigan-Claremont Old Testament prepared by Dr. Richard E. Whitaker's programs.

Figure 7.16 is a sample from Ruth of the kind of KWIC concordance that can be produced from the data bank. Figure 7.16 shows the morphological data of a text form, its lemma, its location, and a brief context. For purposes of analysis, the context could be expanded to any size. This type of concordance is superior to Hatch and Redpath because users may define the formats in which concordances are to be displayed and can access, sort, and concord the information in a variety of ways. For example, information could be sorted according to fields, such as textual form, lemma, or parsing.

---

122. 12 vols. thus far, Göttingen: Vandenhoeck & Ruprecht, 1931–.

123. A. E. Brooke and N. McLean, *The Old Testament in Greek*, 9 vols. (Cambridge: The University Press, 1906–1940). The Göttingen text is an eclectic text that attempts to preserve the best attested reading, whatever its source; the Cambridge edition is a "diplomatic" edition based on codex Vaticanus.

124. See Lippi, "Use," 48–62, for more details.

MORPH,	LOCATION,			CONTEXT
A)GRO/S				
N2 A S M	RT	01	02	EI)S A)GRO\N *MWAB
N2 A S M	RT	02	02	EI)S A)GRO\N KAI\
N2 A S M	RT	02	09	TO\N A)GRO/N, OU(=
N2 A S M	RT	04	05	TO\N A)GRO\N E)K
N2 G S M	RT	01	06	E)C A)GROU= *MWAB,
N2 G S M	RT	01	22	E)C A)GROU= *MWAB:
N2 G S M	RT	02	03	TOU= A)GROU= *BOOS
N2 G S M	RT	02	06	E)C A)GROU= *MWAB
N2 G S M	RT	04	03	TOU= A)GROU=, H(/
N2 G S M	RT	04	03	E)C A)GROU= *MWAB,
N2 D S M	RT	01	01	E)N A)GRW=| *MWAB,
N2 D S M	RT	01	06	E)N A)GRW=| *MWAB

Figure 7.16: Sample of CATSS KWIC concordance.

The fully accented and marked, transliterated Greek text is more than 5 megabytes in size.[125] Because there are about 600,000 words of textual variants to the LXX (requiring about 13.5 megabytes),[126] the full morphologically analyzed Greek text, including variants, is expected to be about 40 megabytes.[127] The unvocalized Hebrew text is about 1.2 megabytes,[128] the fully vocalized, morphologically analyzed Hebrew text about 5 megabytes,[129] and the aligned Greek-Hebrew text about 20 megabytes (if stored in an uncompressed form). Thus the combined size of the various elements in the projected CATSS data base could be as much as 84 megabytes, but when duplicated material is eliminated and appropriate data-management techniques applied, CATSS researchers anticipate that the data base will require just over 50 megabytes.

By using special Ibycus computers (see below), CATSS researchers are able to display texts in Greek, Hebrew, Coptic, and English and to print them on appropriate dot matrix and laser printers.

7.5.1.3 The Programs

The CATSS literature lists many different programs, existing or planned. Some of these programs run on an IBM mainframe, for example, David Packard's MORPH program (which automatically analyzes Greek words) and the Oxford Concordance Package (OCP, which can produce custom concordances from coded, morphologically analyzed text).[130] Others run on Ibycus minicomputers and microcomputers,[131] either

---

125. Some sections (e.g., Joshua, Judges, Tobit, Daniel) are present in two Greek forms in the TLG version of Rahlfs, and CATSS plans to condense and reformat such materials.

126. The size of the Greek variant text includes some variant readings from different versions, as well as information about textual witnesses (i.e., attestation) and punctuation.

127. Because the morphologically analyzed Greek text includes (1) text, (2) location, (3) parsing, and (4) lemmatization, it is about four times as long as the Greek text itself.

128. The vocalized text is considerably longer, and with cantillation included, longer still; see above under WCP.

129. For the same reasons as cited above for the LXX text, this file increases the basic text size of the MT by a factor of four.

130. A version of the OCP for IBM PCs and compatibles is soon to be released.

131. See the *Bits & Bytes Review*™ 1 (October 1986): 1–8 for a detailed review of the Ibycus Scholarly Computer.

as system programs, such as LEX, a program that performs rapid string searches, or as special project programs, including (1) PAPFRG, a program that attempts to identify small papyrus fragments, (2) VAR, a program that analyzes the variations between textual witnesses (e.g., quantitative variations, substitutions, transpositions, and variant spellings), (3) FAM, a program that analyzes and groups manuscripts according to significant patterns of agreement, (4) CONCORD, a program that organizes words according to lemmata, (5) and ALIGN (also known as PARTXT), a program that compares Hebrew and Greek texts and determines the extent of their similarities and differences. Those are but a few of the CATSS programs. We will now look at LEX, MORPH, and ALIGN, three of the main programs, in some detail.[132]

Written in HP Assembler by Packard for Ibycus machines, LEX supports Boolean ANDs and ORs and allows users to search by syllable, word, combinations of syllables, combinations of words, and by combinations of key words. It displays hits in inverse video with three lines of context, all in Greek, if requested, and it can search for nonconsecutive strings. LEX is extremely fast. According to Kraft, on the Ibycus Scholarly Computer (ISC) LEX can search the entire LXX in about 35 seconds.

Because the TLG tape of the LXX is not tagged, CATSS is using MORPH, an IBM assembly language program (written by Packard)[133] that parses each word and gives its lemma.[134] MORPH, which was originally designed to help beginning Greek students, reads through the text sequentially and performs the following operations on each word. MORPH looks up the word in the first of three dictionary files, a dictionary of indeclinable forms (e.g., prepositions, adverbs, particles, and highly irregular forms), where half of the words in the text are usually found. If the word is found there, MORPH tags the word according to the information contained about that form in the file. If the word is not listed in the dictionary of indeclinable forms, MORPH begins to apply Greek morphological rules, much as a beginning Greek student would do. MORPH strips the last letter from the word and tries to locate that letter in the second dictionary file, the dictionary of possible endings. If successful, MORPH strips the next letter from the word, adds it to the first (in the proper order), and reconsults the list. This process is continued until a suitable match is found. At that point, MORPH looks up what remains of the original word in the third dictionary file, the dictionary of stems.[135] If it is able to match the stem of the word with a stem in the dictionary and if the ending of the word is compatible with the stem in the dictionary, then MORPH suggests a possible analysis, which is output as four fields of information: (1) text word, (2) word type, (3) parsing, and (4) lemma.[136]

Forms that are given special treatment include (1) contracted forms, (2) third declension nouns, (3) irregularly augmented verbs, and (4) reduplicated perfect stems. Although MORPH can reconstruct ellided forms, crasis is difficult for it to recognize. In cases of ambiguous analysis, MORPH makes the most likely choice and alerts users to the situation.

Because all three dictionaries are loaded into memory and hence are "RAM resident," MORPH is fast (Adler and Hockey report that MORPH can parse and lem-

---

132. See Kraft, "Prospectus," 6–9, for more details.

133. Packard has translated the Assembler version of MORPH into IBYX for the ISC. According to CATSS's 1983 renewal proposal to the NEH (p. 17 of the subsection titled "Computer Aspects of the Proposal"), IBYX is an extremely fast, Pascal-like language that Packard developed to run on the Hewlett-Packard-based Ibycus minicomputer (which he developed for analyzing classical texts), and like Pascal, IBYX is a highly structured language that supports procedures, has strong string handling functions, and flexible input-output and file handling abilities.

134. See Hockey, *Guide*, 102–3; Packard, "Analysis"; Adler, "Analysis"; Abercrombie, *Programs*, 139–57.

135. The stem dictionary contains three fields: (1) stem, (2) stem type, and (3) lexical (dictionary) form.

136. For CATSS purposes, lemmata have been adapted, by and large, to the lexical forms in Hatch and Redpath where there are differences from Liddell and Scott or from Bauer, Arndt, and Gingrich. See Adler, "Analysis," 7–10.

matize about 2,000 words a second!), though the RAM-resident nature of the program's files means that dictionary size is restricted by memory. By updating the dictionaries to reflect the vocabulary of the LXX, the CATSS researchers have been able to make MORPH analyze 85–95% of the words in the LXX. All of MORPH's output and parsings are verified through a series of IBYX programs and then individually by hand.

LOCATION		HEBREW TEXT	GREEK TEXT
1	1	W/YHY	KAI\ E)GE/NETO
1	1	B/YMY	E)N- - -
1	1	$P+	TW=| KRI/NEIN
1	1	H/$P+YM	TOU\S KRITA\S
1	1	W/YHY	KAI\ E)GE/NETO
1	1	R(B	LIMO\S
1	1	B/)RC	E)N TH=| GH=|
1	1	W/YLK	KAI\ E)POREU/QH
1	1	)Y$	A)NH\R
1	1	M/BYT LXM	A)PO\ BAIQLEEM
1	1	YHWDH	TH=S IOUDA
1	1	L/GWR	TOU= PAROIKH=SAI
1	1	B/&DY	E)N A)GRW=|

Figure 7.17: Sample of CATSS aligned text of Ruth 1:1, using the Hebrew morphological unit as the key.

MORPH is being used to analyze all of the Rahlfs text and all variant readings. This will allow the CATSS researchers to produce a comprehensive concordance of the LXX that combines the Hebrew text, Greek text, and all significant variants in a parallel fashion, and that provides morphological analysis and lemmatization. Among other research applications, such an "electronic concordance" should be of great benefit to students of LXX lexicography and translation techniques. Using this tool, a student could, for example, easily study morphological and lexicographical features in one family of manuscripts or in one section of a translation.

WORD	BK,	CH,	V,	ITEM	SUBVARIANT
W/YHY	RT	01	01	(0101)	kai] > OL
	RT	01	01	(0200)	egeneto
	RT	01	01	(0300)	+ post [meta] OA
	RT	01	01	(0400)	+ hoc [tauta] OA
B/YMY	RT	01	01	(0500)	en
	RT	01	01	(0600)	+ tais AMNdefhijkmpqrstuvyb2˜ OA(codd)
	RT	01	01	(0700)	+ hêmerais AMNdefhijkmpqrstuvyb2˜ OA (codd) OE OL ([in diebus)
	RT	01	01	(0800)	+ <en A
	RT	01	01	(0901)	tô] > q OA(codd)
	RT	01	01	(0902)	: tou MNdefhijkmprstuvyb2˜ OA(ed) OE

Figure 7.18: Sample of merged CATSS texts with the full file of variants of a portion of Ruth 1:1.

The third main CATSS program, ALIGN, aligns the consonantal Hebrew and the Greek texts vertically, in parallel, so that formal equivalences between them can be studied to try to determine the relationship between the LXX and the MT (see Figure 7.17).[137] Thus ALIGN helps to identify Hebrew elements that are equivalent to or that stand in the place of their counterparts in the LXX.[138] To do that, ALIGN treats the LXX as a translation of the MT, though in the case of certain OT books (e.g., Jeremiah) that does not appear to be true.[139] Although formatted vertically, the result of ALIGN (known as column "a") is like a sophisticated interlinear Greek-English or Hebrew-English Bible, only in this case it is Hebrew and Greek that are paralleled. ALIGN, then, produces a text that consists of "the full set of *formal equivalents* of all elements of the two texts, as if the LXX were a mechanical translation from the MT."[140] After the automatic alignment is made, it is verified and corrected by hand (at the Hebrew University in Jerusalem) and a second Hebrew column ("b") is added where it seems probable that the Greek represents a Hebrew *Vorlage* that differs from the MT.

In his article "The Use of a Computerized Data Base for Septuagint Research: The Greek-Hebrew Parallel Alignment," Tov points out four major ways that the data can be extracted from the CATSS data base. (1) The data base can be searched by word, word pattern, word combinations (in the MT, LXX, or both), using LEX, the OCP, or similar programs. (2) All types of indices and concordances can be constructed. (3) Sophisticated morphological studies can be performed at various levels. (4) And any aspect of translation technique on which information is included can be located and analyzed.

7.6 Machine-Readable Versions of the Greek NT

7.6.1 Project GRAMCORD

- *BASIC PRODUCT INFORMATION*

Key Person: Paul A. Miller, Director
Location of Project: Deerfield, Illinois
Project Address: Project GRAMCORD, Trinity Evangelical Divinity School (TEDS), 2065 Half Day Road, Deerfield, IL 60015
Telephones: (312) 945-8800 (TEDS), (312) 223-3242 (office/home)
Date Project Began: 1976
Date Project Completed: 1979/1984
Sources of Funding: Trinity Evangelical Divinity School; The Edwin, Frederick, and Walter Beinecke Memorial Fund of the Sperry and Hutchinson Foundation; The Arthur R. Metz Foundation; The William and Jenny Curry Distinguished Scholar Program; The Foundation for Biblical Research
Primary Purpose of Project: To create a comprehensive, microcomputer-based research system for studying the Greek New Testament by creating programs that will concord morphologically or positionally dependent grammatical constructions using a morphologically and syntactically tagged, machine-readable version of the Greek New Testament, as well as programs for multilingual word processing, typesetting, and so forth.
Textual Authority: Nestle-Aland 26th Edition

---

137. See Tov, "Data Base," 36–47, and Abercrombie, "Alignment," 125–39, for full details. ALIGN was written by Abercrombie in DEC BASIC-Plus and then translated into IBYX and improved.

138. Tov, "Data Base," 41.

139. The fact that scholars do not know to what extent the present eclectic text of the LXX represents the original translation further complicates the issue, though the margin for error in the Rahlfs and Göttingen reconstructions is probably small.

140. Tov, "Data Base," 37, emphasis his. Abercrombie's article "Computer Assisted Alignment of the Greek and Hebrew Biblical Texts—Programming Background" explains how the different parts of the programs that are used to create the parallel texts work.

Machine-Readable Text Includes: The complete Greek New Testament (Nestle-Aland 26th ed.), distributed in uppercase letters only, with punctuation marks (no accents, breathing, or other diacritical marks) and morphological and syntactical tags. A fully accented version with all diacritical marks is used in-house at TEDS and may be available for the general public in the near future.

Type of Tagging: Morphological and syntactical

Level of Tagging: Morphological and syntactical

Scope of Tagging: The entire Greek New Testament

Programming Language: Turbo Pascal

Output Options: Screen, tape, disk, print; transliterated text; Greek text can be displayed on NEC-APC microcomputers.

Price: GRAMCORD is licensed to institutions for $500 per year. Individuals interested in purchasing the program should contact the Director at the address listed above.

Version Tested: Full version, IBM PC-XT

Runs On: IBM PCs and compatibles, NEC-APCs, CP/M-86 8-inch machines, and the DEC Rainbow MS-DOS 96TPI format

Memory Requirements: 128K

Supports Color Monitors: Yes

Uses Sound: Yes

Number of Text Disks: 8 (includes programs)

Number of Program Disks: See above

Size of Program Files: 113 kilobytes

Size of Help Files: None

Size of Text Files: 2.3 megabytes

Text Files in ASCII: No.

Produces ASCII Output Files: Yes

Search String Limitations: 7 construct definitions (10 elements per definition), 52 END statements, 30 repetitions of a part of speech per command file

Maximum Number of Entries Per Index: Limited only by disk space.

Product Includes: Diskettes and manual

Manual: 115 pages, 3-ring binder, 7 appendices, no index

Demo Disk Available: Yes, a set of GRAMCORD DEMO DISKETTES is available for IBM-DOS/MS-DOS, DEC Rainbow MS-DOS, and NEC-APC (CP/M) 8-inch microcomputers for $10.

Copy Protected: No

Hard Disk Compatible: Yes

Special Hard Disk Version: Yes

Menu-Driven: No

On-line Help: No

Tutorial: No

Warranty: Media only

Support: Free phone support

Update Policy: Not known

Availability of Tapes or Disks: GRAMCORD is available on 9-track, 1,600-bpi, ASCII, IBM unlabeled-format tape for a variety of mainframe and minicomputers and on 5.25-inch floppies for a variety of microcomputers.

Key Bibliographical References: "Project Gramcord: A Report," "Project Gramcord: Grammatical Analysis," "Project Gramcord Update" (available from the address listed above)

Other Information: A GRAMCORD INQUIRER'S PACKET is available for $5. The GRAMCORD staff will perform searches for interested parties; billing is on a per-search basis. Contact Project GRAMCORD for more information.

7.6.1.1 Introduction

Project GRAMCORD (GRAMmatical ConCORDance) consists of a morphologically and syntactically tagged, machine-readable version of the Greek New Testament and several programs that manipulate that data base, especially the main program, GRAMCORD, which concords grammatical constructions. (In chapter 2, we discussed GRAMEDIT, a multi-lingual word processing program that is a companion program to GRAMCORD.) To study word meanings, students consult concordances, looks up some or all of the instances of a word, and draw conclusions about its meaning(s). The written result of studying the usage of all the words in a given language is a lexicon. To study grammatical constructions, students consult grammars, which usually list several examples of each construction. By consulting several grammars about a particular construction, students may be able to locate many, but usually not all, of its occurrences. GRAMCORD is a powerful, flexible tool that allows users to locate *all* instances of *any* morphologically or positionally defined (i.e., positionally dependent) grammatical construction within any range of user-specified New Testament text. Thus GRAMCORD does for the study of syntax what a traditional concordance does for the study of word meanings.

Project GRAMCORD began in 1976 as an idea of Dr. James A. Boyer, who was then Chairman of the Department of New Testament and Greek at Grace Theological Seminary. By 1979, Professor Paul A. Miller—then a student at Indiana University, now Director of Project GRAMCORD at Trinity Evangelical Divinity School—had completed the first data base and first version of the program. Between 1979 and 1984, Project GRAMCORD was refined, new programs added (see below), and microcomputer versions made available.[141] Currently, the program runs on a wide variety of mainframe, mini, and microcomputers. Historically, Project GRAMCORD had one of the first complete, grammatically-tagged, machine-readable versions of the Greek New Testament. And GRAMCORD was the first program for concording syntactical constructions in the Greek New Testament and the first complete data base and program for manipulating an ancient text on microcomputers.

GRAMCORD comes with a user guide (115 pages, three-ring binder, 7 appendices, not indexed) that contains detailed explanations and illustrations of GRAMCORD's extensive features. The IBM PC version of the GRAMCORD data base and programs comes on eight 5.25-inch floppy diskettes and occupies about 2.4 megabytes of disk space (data base = 2.3MB, programs = 113KB). A GRAMCORD INQUIRER'S PACKET is available for $5 and a set of GRAMCORD DEMO DISKETTES for $10 (see above).

GRAMCORD can be used to study any morphologically or positionally defined grammatical construction at the phrase, clause, or sentence level. Using GRAMCORD, for example, it is possible to examine a whole category or class of grammatical objects in the New Testament, such as all future participles, all genitive absolutes, all first-class conditions (*ei* + indicative mood), or all the uses of *ev* with present and aorist infinitives (i.e., articular infinitives). Since *ev* occurs 2,767 times in the New Testament, using GRAMCORD to select the examples of articular infinitives that occur with *ev* is much faster than trying to perform such a study manually by looking up all 2,767 occurrences of that preposition! Alternatively, users may specify a range of text to be concorded. In addition to its ability to concord whole classes of grammatical objects, GRAMCORD can easily concord parts of speech, simple inflections, words, and complex grammatical constructions. GRAMCORD is an extremely flexible and powerful program.

As we will see, GRAMCORD's command-driven user interface is complex, but logical. After a few hours with the user's guide and some trial and error (and perhaps some help from an experienced user), the average student can begin to use GRAMCORD successfully. At Trinity Evangelical Divinity School, GRAMCORD has been incorporated into the language curriculum. All advanced Greek students are required to use GRAMCORD to study specific grammatical constructions about which they must write term papers. Among other institutions, GRAMCORD has been licensed to Cambridge University, Wheaton College, Westmont College, Grace Theological Seminary, the Wycliffe Bible Translators, and the American Bible Society.

---

141. This process of refinement and expansion is still going on.

7.6.1.2 The Text and Tagging

Project GRAMCORD uses the text of the Nestle-Aland 26th Edition (= UBS3) of the Greek New Testament.[142] Only words and punctuation marks in the main text are included in distributed versions of the GRAMCORD data base (though the in-house version contains all the vowels and diacritical marks),[143] and only variants significant enough to be included in the main text are included in the data base. Such words, which are included in square brackets—[. . .]—in the Nestle-Aland text, are included in angle brackets—<. . .>—in the GRAMCORD data base, because some of the early machines—mid 1970s—on which GRAMCORD initially ran (e.g., CDC mainframes) did not have full character sets. Text is displayed in upper-case, transliterated characters on all computer screens, except on NEC-APCs, which allow it to be displayed in Greek (including all diacritical marks).[144]

In the Project GRAMCORD data base, all verbs are completely parsed, and all nouns, adjectives, pronouns, and participles have been tagged for gender, number, and case. Additionally, pronouns have been assigned functional classifications, and prepositions, adverbs, conjunctions, and particles have been functionally identified. The majority of GRAMCORD's tags, then, are morphological. By and large, function tags are limited to noninflected parts of speech (e.g., adverbs, conjugations). Only verbs, pronouns, and prepositions are lemmatized.

```
OUTWS adverb
X GAR conjunction CX
JGAPJSEN verb 3SAAI from AGAPAW
O article MSN
QEOS noun MSN
TON article MSA
KOSMON noun MSA

,,,,,
WSTE conjunction SR
TON article MSA
UION noun MSA
TON article MSA
MONOGENJ adjective MSAX
EDWKEN verb 3SAAI from DIDWMI

,,,,,
INA conjunction SF
PAS adjective MSNX
O article MSN
PISTEUWN verb PAPMSN from PISTEUW
EIS preposition A from EIS
AUTON pronoun P3MSA from AUTOS
MJ particle N
APOLJTAI verb 3 SAMS from APOLLUMI
ALL conjunction CV
ECJ verb 3SPAS from ECW
ZWJN noun FSA
AIWNION adjective FSAX
. . . .
```

Figure 7.19: Sample of tagging in GRAMCORD data base.

---

142. As funding permits, GRAMCORD plans to add the Septuagint, Josephus, Philo, Polybius, and other extrabiblical Greek material to the data base.

143. Copyright restrictions on the UBS3 text have kept the Project GRAMCORD data base from being distributed with vowels and diacritical marks, though this restriction may change.

144. As we noted in chapter 2 under the discussion of GRAMEDIT, the NEC-APC uses larger character matrices and has a higher resolution than many microcomputers.

By using GRAMDIR, users may locate any text in the data base and display its tagging.[145] Figure 7.19 shows the tagging for John 3:16.

7.6.1.3 The Programs

GRAMCORD is the main program. As its name suggests, GRAMCORD concords any grammatical construction that is morphologically or positionally determined. On a floppy drive of a 4.77-MHz, IBM PC-XT, GRAMCORD took 2 minutes and 42 seconds to concord the thirty-six occurrences of the Greek words for *woman*, *husband*, *well*, and *friend* in John—about twice as long as it took compuBIBLE (see chapter 3).

GRAMCORD works by consulting a command file that specifies the exact grammatical construction users wish to concord. Each command file consists of from one to eight construct definitions.[146] Although construct definitions may be unrelated, it is more common for them to specify variations of a common grammatical construction. Each construct definition may contain up to five elements:

> Title Section (optional)
> Target Section (required)
> END statement (required)
> Option Section (optional)
> XSTOP statement (required)

All contexts that contain the construct definitions specified in the command file appear together in the final concordance that GRAMCORD produces, each identified in terms of the construct definition that caused it to be selected. GRAMCORD prefaces each concordance with a listing of the command file that produced it. With the exception of the Title Section, all characters in the command file must be in upper case letters. Various factors that limit command file size are listed at the beginning of each GRAMCORD execution.

```
TITLE 1 * A STUDY OF INFINITIVE VERBS CLASSIFIED
          BY VOICE *
TITLE 2 * Active voice *
VERB/***AN***.
END.
XSTOP.
TITLE 3 * Middle voice *
VERB/***MN***.
END.
XSTOP.
TITLE 4 * Passive voice *
VERB/***PN***.
END.
XSTOP.
```

Figure 7.20: Sample of simple GRAMCORD command file that contains three related, though distinct, grammatical constructs.

---

145. A copy of *A Grammatical Directory to the Greek New Testament*, a hardcopy version of the tagged GRAMCORD data base, may be obtained from Project GRAMCORD.

146. The number of construct definitions possible in one command file varies and depends on the host computer. On the IBM-PC version of GRAMCORD, up to seven construct definitions per command file are possible.

The optional Title Section of the command file contains information that specifies the construct definition's purpose but that is ignored by GRAMCORD. In some GRAMCORD installations, information in the Title Section is essential for the production of computer-generated histograms.

The mandatory Target Section follows the Title Section in the command file. The Target Section contains target definitions that consist of a grammatical class, a "/" character, a number of grammatical data fields, and (in some cases) an optional lemma.[147] Each target definition corresponds to at least one element of the grammatical construction that is being concorded. Grammatical classes consist of the traditional categories: adjective, adverb, article, conjunction, improper and proper preposition, interjection, noun, particle, pronoun, and verb. Each grammatical characteristic of each grammatical class occupies a fixed position. For example, ADJECTIVE/MPAC means "adjective—masculine, plural, accusative, comparative." When specifying the grammatical characteristics of an adjective, then, the characteristics *must* be specified in the following order: gender, number, case, degree. A "*" can be used as a wild-card character for one or all of the obligatory slots in the construction. Thus ADJECTIVE/*S** would mean "adjective of a singular number." That target definition would ask GRAMCORD to concord *all* singular adjectives, regardless of their gender, case, or degree. The GRAMCORD user's guide specifies the data fields and their order for each grammatical class and states which slots in the data fields may be represented by the "*" wild-card character. The "*" character is also used when a particular data field is not applicable to a particular target definition. For example, VERB/**AAN*** asks GRAMCORD to locate all aorist active infinitives. The first two "*" symbols are used because infinitives do not have person and number, and the last three "*" symbols are used because infinitives do not have the participial properties of gender, number, and case.

The obligatory End Statement marks the end of the target section.

The Option Section of the command file gives GRAMCORD much of its flexibility and power. This section allows users to restrict the construct definition, and it contains general directions for the format of the final output. *Option statements*, are best understood by understanding the difference between a *target* and an *element*. As stated previously, each target definition corresponds to at least one element of the grammatical construction that is being concorded. A *target*, then, defines one or more elements of a grammatical construction. An *element*, however, is a part of a grammatical construction that is manifested by one word in a given context. Each element described by the construct definition, then, will correspond with one and only one word in each entry in the concordance that GRAMCORD builds. With one exception, option statements refer primarily to elements, not to targets.[148] When an option statement restricts, or delimits, a construct statement, it does so by referring to an element in the construct, not to the target definition.

Option statements are divided into global and local options. Global options (which affect all constructs) include DISPLAYWIDTH, DOUBLESPACE, REFERENCEONLY, SETWINDOW, PLOTIT, STATISTICSONLY, and BOOKS. Local options (which are specific to a particular construct definition) include CONTEXTFIELD, SITUATION, OKPUNCTUATION, SPECWORD, -SPECWORD, SPECDATA, -SPECDATA, SPECLEMMA, -SPECLEMMA, PLACEMENT, SUBPLACEMENT, SAMEWORD, -SAMEWORD, AGREEMENT, -AGREEMENT, SAMELEMMA, -SAMELEMMA, SUBCONTEXTFIELD, INTERWORD, -INTERWORD, INTERDATA, -INTERDATA, -PREWORD, -PREDATA, -POSTWORD,

---

147. GRAMCORD lemmatizes four grammatical classes: verbs, pronouns, prepositions, and improper prepositions.

148. The exception is the option statement SITUATION, which is used to avoid writing a construct definition that contains two (or more) target definitions that refer to the same element in the grammatical construction. (Target definitions in each construct definition must be mutually exclusive.)

and -POSTDATA. All of these option statements are defined and explained in the user's guide.[149]

Although we cannot discuss all of GRAMCORD's option statements, certain ones deserve to be mentioned. SETWINDOW allows users to specify the amount of context that is to be included around hits. The form is SETWINDOW:10,15., where the two numbers specify the number of words in the concordance entry that will appear before the first element and after the last element in the construction. PLOTIT causes GRAMCORD to produce a histogram plot data file. BOOKS allows users to specify the range of New Testament text that GRAMCORD will search.[150] CONTEXTFIELD allows users to specify the number of words in a construction, from the first to the last element inclusive. By using CONTEXTFIELD, users can command GRAMCORD to accept intervening words in a grammatical construction. The form CONTEXTFIELD:15., for example, commands GRAMCORD to accept fifteen words in a construction, from the first to the last element inclusive. OKPUNCTUATION commands GRAMCORD to ignore minor punctuation (commas and dashes) that interrupts the elements in a grammatical construct. OKPUNCTUATION does not ignore major stops (period, question mark = semicolon, and high point = colon), however, and so GRAMCORD's constructions are always terminated by a full stop.[151] Unlike the concording programs we reviewed in chapter 3, GRAMCORD can concord across verse boundaries, as long as those boundaries are not marked by major stops. SPECWORD supports exact-word searches. For example, the construct definition

```
NOUN/MS*.
END.
SITUATION:2/1,1.
SPECWORD:1(IJSOUS,IJSOU,IJSOUN)
SPECWORD:2(CHRIST-)
XSTOP.
```

instructs GRAMCORD to build a concordance of all masculine singular nouns that begin with one of the three instances of the first SPECWORD and that end with the second SPECWORD. The option -SPECWORD is the equivalent of the NOT operator; it commands GRAMCORD not to count as hits those terms that follow the -SPECWORD command.

Just as SPECWORD and -SPECWORD help to define words that are related to single elements of a construction, so SPECDATA and -SPECDATA help to define data that are related to single elements of a construction, and SPECLEMMA and -SPECLEMMA help to define lemmata that are related to single elements of a construction. In addition to being able to define single elements by using those option statements, GRAMCORD provides a set of option statements that can be used to define the *position* of single elements in a construct definition. Those options include PLACEMENT and SUBPLACEMENT. Thus GRAMCORD supports sequence-specific searches.

GRAMCORD also includes options that define *relationships* between *pairs* of elements. At the word level they include SAMEWORD and -SAMEWORD; at the data level they include AGREEMENT and -AGREEMENT; at the lemma level they in-

---

149. The GRAMCORD users guide lists and explains all (1) target definition classes and codes, (2) option statements, (3) grammatical classes in the data base, and (4) ambiguous grammatical situations and varying opinions.

150. Some installations of GRAMCORD use STARTBOOK and STOPBOOK to invoke this option statement.

151. Therefore GRAMCORD cannot analyze the text past the sentence level, i.e., at the level of paragraph or discourse, though plans exist for tagging the data base so that high-level discourse analysis can be performed.

clude SAMELEMMA and -SAMELEMMA; and there is a proximity-related option called SUBCONTEXTFIELD.

Phenomena (words or phrases) that are allowed or disallowed to intervene between elements of a construct definition are specified by the INTERWORD(S), -INTER-WORD(S), INTERDATA, and -INTERDATA option statements. Phenomena that precede the construct definition, and that may affect it, are dealt with by using the -PREWORD and -PREDATA statements, and phenomena subsequent to the construct definition that may affect it are dealt with by using the -POSTWORD and -POSTDATA statements.

The obligatory XSTOP statement terminates the construct definition.

Other programs closely related to GRAMCORD include (1) GRAMPROOF, a program that checks the syntax of GRAMCORD command files before they are executed, (2) GRAMGREEK, a program that converts concordance files into Greek, so that they may be displayed or printed in Greek, (3) GRAMDIR, a program that allows users to view the tagged data base a verse at a time, and (4) GRAMVIEW, a windowing utility that allows users to divide the screen into several[152] independent windows that may be used for displaying different portions of the text or for scanning a concordance file created by GRAMCORD.

Programs less directly related to GRAMCORD include (5) GRAMEDIT, the word processing program discussed in chapter 3, (6) GRAMPAGE, a formatting program, (7) GRAMPRNT, a printer-driver for the Toshiba 1351 and P351 dot-matrix printers, (8) GRAMINSRT, a program that automatically inserts citations from the biblical text into files created with GRAMEDIT, (9) GRAMINDEX, a program that can create multilingual indices, (10) GRAMSPELL, a spell-checking program, and (11) GRAMTYPESET, which converts the codes in GRAMEDIT files to typesetting codes.

7.6.1.4 *Future Plans*

Project GRAMCORD hopes to create additional microcomputer-based theological research tools, such as a lexicon, grammar, and multi-lingual bibliographic and data base management systems. Project GRAMCORD's ultimate goal is to create a comprehensive, microcomputer-based research system for studying the Greek New Testament.

Dr. D. A. Carson (Professor of New Testament at Trinity Evangelical Divinity School) and Professor Paul A. Miller are using GRAMCORD to produce *A Syntactical Concordance to the Greek New Testament* (approximately 1,600 pages; to be published in late 1987 by the University of Chicago Press). Where possible, each entry will be keyed to *A Greek Grammar of the New Testament*[153] and cross referenced to other Greek grammars. There will be hundreds of main syntactical entries, with thousands of subentries. Each entry will be tagged with a numbered tag. Target items under the key word for each concordance entry will be printed in italicized Greek, and histograms (bar graphs depicting frequency per 1,000 words of text) will be included for high frequency constructions. Variants will be discussed and bibliographical references provided. This work will be more than just a concordance; it will also function as an advanced grammar. Figure 7.22, a sample page from that forthcoming publication, was created with GRAMCORD, GRAMEDIT, and GRAMTYPESET.

---

152. The literature does not specify the maximum number of windows.

153. F. Blass and A. Debrunner, a translation and revision of the 9th-10th German edition by Robert W. Funk, ed. Chicago: The University of Chicago Press, 1961.

The following is a prepublication excerpt from A Syntactical Concordance to the Greek New Testament *by D. A. Carson and Paul A. Miller with James L. Boyer (The University of Chicago Press). It has been prepared and typeset on the GRAMEDIT theological word-processing/typesetting system at Trinity Evangelical Divinity School.*

/130(3).**
Indefinite Subject: Active Voice, Introducing Quotation

10	quotation from Scripture
20	quotation not from Scripture
1	strictly impersonal verb, or subject vague
2	subject *may* be inferred from the context

11	Ac	13:35	διότι καὶ ἐν ἑτέρῳ λέγει· οὐ δώσεις τὸν ὅσιόν σου ἰδεῖν διαφθοράν.
11	Rm	9:25	ὡς καὶ ἐν τῷ 'Ωσηὲ λέγει· καλέσω τὸν οὐ λαόν μου λαόν μου
11	1C	6:16	ἔσονται γάρ, φησίν, οἱ δύο εἰς σάρκα μίαν.
12*		9: 9	οὐ κημώσεις βοῦν ἀλοῶντα. μὴ τῶν βοῶν μέλει τῷ θεῷ 10 ἢ δι' ἡμᾶς πάντως λέγει;
11		15:27	πάντα γὰρ ὑπέταξεν ὑπὸ τοὺς πόδας αὐτοῦ. ὅταν δὲ εἴπῃ ὅτι πάντα ὑποτέτακται
21*	2C	10:10	ὅτι αἱ ἐπιστολαὶ μέν, φησίν, βαρεῖαι καὶ ἰσχυραί *(v.l. φασίν)*
11	Gl	3:16	οὐ λέγει· καὶ τοῖς σπέρμασιν
11	Eph	4: 8	διὸ λέγει· ἀναβὰς εἰς ὕψος ᾐχμαλώτευσεν αἰχμαλωσίαν
21*		5:14	διὸ λέγει· ἔγειρε, ὁ καθεύδων
21*	1Th	5: 3	ὅταν λέγωσιν· εἰρήνη καὶ ἀσφάλεια
12	Hb	4: 4	εἴρηκεν γάρ που περὶ τῆς ἑβδόμης οὕτως· καὶ κατέπαυσεν ὁ θεός
12		4: 8	εἰ γὰρ αὐτοὺς 'Ιησοῦς κατέπαυσεν, οὐκ ἂν περὶ ἄλλης ἐλάλει μετὰ ταῦτα ἡμέρας.
12		5: 6	καθὼς καὶ ἐν ἑτέρῳ λέγει· σὺ ἱερεὺς εἰς τὸν αἰῶνα κατὰ τὴν τάξιν Μελχισέδεκ
11		8: 5	ὅρα γάρ φησιν, ποιήσεις πάντα κατὰ τὸν τύπον τὸν δειχθέντα σοι

Notes: Again, some grammarians would rule out of the "indefinite subject" category every verb that introduces a quotation from Scripture, believing that ὁ θεός or ἡ γραφή or the like is presupposed (cf. Notes on/130(1).***), as the specification of the subject is common enough (e.g. Rm 9:17, which is therefore absent from this list). That would leave only the entries at 2C 10:10 and 1Th 5:3. But others prefer to include those introductions to a quotation from Scripture that leave it quite unclear exactly what the subject is (tag 1). This forces us to make difficult decisions about how "unclear" the subject is. Many examples are excluded because the broader context is specific (e.g. ὁ θεός, Lk 1:70; 2C 6:2; Hb 1:5,6,7,13); but a few remain uncertain (tag 2; e.g. 1C 9:10: Is the inferred subject ὁ θεός [cf. τῷ θεῷ in 9:9] or ὁ νόμος [cf. 9:8]?). Very difficult is an entry like Eph 5:14, where the standard λέγει appears even though what is cited is not Scripture. Less ambiguous, and therefore excluded from this list, are instances where the quotation itself shows that it is God who is directly speaking (e.g. Ac 13:34; Rm 9:15; 10:21; 1C 6:2).

Refs: Winer-M 735; Rob.392, cf. 1027-28; Moule 29; BDF 130(3); Mlt.-T.293; Rehkopf 130(3).

Figure 7.21: Sample page from *A Syntactical Concordance to the Greek New Testament.*

7.6.2 Analytical Greek New Testament

- *BASIC DATA BASE INFORMATION*

Key Person(s): Timothy and Barbara Friberg
Location of Project: Dallas, Texas
Project Address: Analytical Greek New Testament Project, Translation Department, International Linguistics Center, 7500 West Camp Wisdom Road, Dallas, TX 75236
Telephone: (214) 298-3331
Date Project Began: 1977
Date Project Completed: 1982
Sources of Funding: University of Minnesota Computer Center
Primary Purpose of Project: To study discourse structure in the Greek New Testament by constructing a morphologically and syntactically tagged version of the text.
Textual Authority: UBS3
Machine-Readable Text Includes: The complete Greek New Testament, with punctuation marks (with or without accents, breathing, and other diacritical marks—two versions are available) and morphological and syntactical tags
Type of Tagging: Morphological and syntactical
Level of Tagging: Morphological and syntactical
Scope of Tagging: The entire Greek New Testament
Type of Text Files: ASCII or EBCDIC
Programming Language: Pascal and Assembler
Output Options: Screen, tape, disk, and printer; transliterated text and/or tags only
Availability of Tapes or Disks: (1) 9-track unlabeled tape (blocked to user's specifications) in ASCII or EBCDIC, (2) 5.25-inch diskettes for MS-DOS machines and for Apple II-compatible drives with the UCSD P-System, (3) 3.50-inch diskettes for Apple Macintosh and Lisa drives and for the Hewlett Packard HP 150, (4) other formats available on request. Tapes and diskettes are available through the American Bible Society/United Bible Societies, % Harold Scanlin, 1865 Broadway, New York, NY 10023; (212) 581-7400.
Cost of Tapes or Disks: Not known
Key Bibliographical References: "Computer-Assisted Analysis of the Greek New Testament Text," *Analytical Greek New Testament*

7.6.2.1 Introduction

The Analytical Greek New Testament was created by Timothy and Barbara Friberg at the University of Minnesota as part of Dr. Timothy Friberg's work for his Ph.D. in linguistics. Microcomputer versions of this morphologically and syntactically tagged, machine-readable version of the Greek New Testament are available at a modest cost from the American Bible Society/United Bible Societies, though unlike the Project GRAMCORD materials, the Friberg text is only a data base; no programs come with it.

Following in the theoretical footsteps of John Beekman of the Wycliffe Bible Translators,[154] the Fribergs (who now work as linguists and Bible translators in Indonesia with the Wycliffe Bible Translators' Summer Institute of Linguistics) tagged the Greek New Testament to promote and facilitate its discourse analysis. As we learned earlier in this chapter, some scholars have statistically analyzed vocabulary to make judgments about the authorship of various biblical books (e.g., Radday). According to the Fribergs, that approach to discourse analysis focuses on the frequency and distribution of lexical items (content words and function words) and ignores the relationship between genre and discourse. According to the Fribergs, because many words are discourse-governed, without understanding which discourse structures reflect which genres, the significance of the presence or absence of specific lexical

---

154. See John Beekman and John Callow, *Translating the Word of God* (Grand Rapids: Zondervan Publishing House, 1974) and *The Semantic Structure of Written Communication* (Dallas: Summer Institute of Linguistics, date not known).

items in a given discourse cannot be determined.[155] Word frequency may be a function of discourse, which is partially controlled by features of a language and partially controlled by an author. According to the Fribergs, the statistical approach to discourse analysis also suffers by failing to pay adequate attention to grammatical and syntactical issues.

Other scholars have used literary criticism to analyze discourse by studying semantic issues such as themes, focus, setting, participants, introduction, and climax,[156] but studies that follow this approach are not compelling because they are not exhaustive in their analysis of the phenomena. The approach shared by Beekman and the Fribergs combines syntactical and semantic analysis with a careful study of the lexical inventory of New Testament Greek and the insights of modern linguistics, especially into the topic of the universals of discourse. To enable those interested in discourse analysis to easily obtain the grammatical information they need about lexical items in the text of the Greek New Testament, the Fribergs tagged each word of that text morphologically and, where appropriate, syntactically, in a way that is consistent with Beekman's approach to discourse analysis.[157] Thus the Fribergs' grammatical analysis of the text reflects discourse-level considerations. They have created a tool for discourse analysis.

7.6.2.2 The Text and Tagging

The Friberg text consists of a machine-readable version of the UBS3 text and a morphological (and sometimes syntactical) tag for each word.[158] The following grammatical categories are tagged: noun, verb, adjective, determiner (i.e., definite article), preposition, conjunction, and particle. All words in those categories are morphologically tagged. All nouns, for example, are tagged by case, gender, person, and number; all verbs are tagged in terms of mood, tense, voice, case, gender, person, and number. Thus the *form* of all words is specified in the data base. Some words also have been given tags that specify their *function*. In those cases, a small square box is used to separate the grammatical form X from its function as grammatical form Y. All tags are given in upper case letters. Although the system of tagging is quite straightforward and usually transparent, it can also be quite complex. Fortunately, the UBS3 Greek text with the Fribergs' analysis placed beneath the words in an interlinear fashion is available from Baker Book House as the *Analytical Greek New Testament* (see Figure 7.23). That work describes the tags (xiii–xvi) and explains them in detail (797–854). The transliterated version of the text and tags of Matthew 1:1 from the accented, machine-readable version of the Friberg text looks like this:[159] 1.1 *BI/BLOJ <N-NF-S> GENE/SEWJ <N-GF-S> *)IHSOU= <N-GM-S> *XRISTOU= <N-GM-S> UI(OU= <N-GM-S> *DAVI!D <N-GM-S> UI(OU= <N-GM-S> *ABRAA/M <N-GM-S>. The unaccented version looks like this: 1.1 BIBLIOS (N-NF-S) GENESEWS (N-GF-S) IHSOU (N-GM-S) XRISTOU (N-GM-S) MT01.01> !UIOU (N-GM-S) DAUID (N-GM-S) !UIOU (N-GM-S) ABRAAM (N-GM-S). MT01.01. In the accented version, "*" indicates capital letters, "/" stands for an acute accent, the delimiters "< ...>" bracket the tag, ")" indicates a smooth breathing, "=" stands for a circumflex, and "(" represents a rough breathing. The tags are decoded as follows: (1) N-NF-S means "noun: nominative, feminine, singular," (2) N-GF-S means "noun: genitive, feminine, singular," and (3) N-GM-S means "noun:

---

155. Friberg and Friberg, "Text," 19.

156. Ibid., 18.

157. Ibid., 19.

158. The analysis represents the work of a dozen or so people.

159. I have changed the Fribergs' backslash to a "!," since none of the character sets available to me for typesetting includes a backslash!

genitive, masculine, singular." Hyphens ("-") function as place holders for unused slots in the tag order; they are dropped off at the end of tags. A complex tag like ABR[]APDGM-S&ABR for (OU= means "relative adverb (ABR) functioning as ([]) a demonstrative pronoun (genitive, masculine, singular—APDGM-S) and (&) as a relative adverb (ABR)." Some semantic phenomena implied but not specified by the grammatical structure of the text are marked by tags in accordance with word-level, sentence-level, and discourse-level considerations.[160] Thus in Matthew 10:38 KAI! (O!S OU) LAMBA/NEI . . . OU)K)E/STIN MOU)A/CIOS, the Fribergs analyze "(O!S" as APRNM-S[]APDNM-S&APRNM-S, that is, as a relative pronoun (nominative, masculine, singular) functioning as a demonstrative pronoun (nominative, masculine, singular—an antecedent implied by the grammar, by the "surface structure" of the text) and as a relative pronoun (nominative, masculine, singular). Thus they paraphrase "That one [supplied antecedent] who [relative] does not take (his cross) . . . is not worthy of me."[161]

ΚΑΤΑ ΙΩΑΝΝΗΝ

1.1 Ἐν ἀρχῇ ἦν ὁ λόγος, καὶ ὁ λόγος ἦν πρὸς τὸν
PD N-DF-S VIIA--ZS DNMS N-NM-S CC DNMS N-NM-S VIIA--ZS PA DAMS

θεόν, καὶ θεὸς ἦν ὁ λόγος. 1.2 οὗτος ἦν ἐν ἀρχῇ πρὸς τὸν
N-AM-S CC N-NM-S VIIA--ZS DNMS N-NM-S APDNM-S VIIA--ZS PD N-DF-S PA DAMS

θεόν. 1.3 πάντα δι᾽ αὐτοῦ ἐγένετο, καὶ χωρὶς αὐτοῦ ἐγένετο οὐδὲ
N-AM-S AP-NN-P PG NPGMZS VIAD--ZS CC PG NPGMZS VIAD--ZS AB

ἕν. ὃ γέγονεν 1.4 ἐν αὐτῷ ζωὴ ἦν,
APCNN-S APRNN-S□APDNN-S&APRNN-S†APRNN-S VIRA--ZS PD NPDMZS N-NF-S VIIA--ZS

καὶ ἡ ζωὴ ἦν τὸ φῶς τῶν ἀνθρώπων· 1.5 καὶ τὸ φῶς ἐν
CC DNFS N-NF-S VIIA--ZS DNNS N-NN-S DGMP N-GM-P CC DNNS N-NN-S PD

τῇ σκοτίᾳ φαίνει, καὶ ἡ σκοτία αὐτὸ οὐ κατέλαβεν.
DDFS N-DF-S VIPA--ZS CC DNFS N-NF-S NPANZS AB VIAA--ZS

Figure 7.22: Sample of tagged text from Analytical Greek New Testament.

7.6.2.3 Future Publications

The Fribergs and Baker Book House are working on five additional volumes that are based on the Friberg text. All four concordance volumes in this series are being prepared under the joint editorship of the Fribergs and Philip S. Clapp, and the lexicon volume is being prepared under the joint editorship of the Fribergs and Neva F. Miller. The next two volumes scheduled for publication are to be called *Analytical Concordance of the Greek New Testament: Lexical Focus*. These volumes will consist of the printed equivalent of the combined concordance of the whole Greek New Testament. Each lexical item will be listed in context according to its lemma and followed by the Fribergs' tags. It will be a tagged, key-word-in-context (KWIC) concordance.

---

160. See Friberg and Friberg, *Analytical Greek New Testament*, 799–801, 821–27. On the skewed nature of the relationship between syntax and semantics, see ibid., 799–801, and Friberg and Friberg, "Text," 21.

161. Ibid., 821.

All instances of a word will be grouped together, not listed in their canonical order, and arranged by conjugation or inflection.

The third and fourth volumes scheduled for publication are to be called *Analytical Concordance of the Greek New Testament: Grammatical Focus*. These volumes will consist of the printed equivalent of the whole Greek New Testament, with each grammatical form listed in context according to the Fribergs' tags. All instances of each form will be grouped together, not listed in their canonical order, and arranged by conjugation or inflection. Thus, for example, every instance of verbs that are aorist active indicative third person singular will be grouped together, regardless of the form of their lexical manifestation in the text.

The final volume in the series is to be called *Analytical Lexicon of New Testament Greek*. It will consist of alphabetized lexical items, followed by their tags, lemma, contextualized English gloss, and selected New Testament reference(s). Thus in its final form, the Fribergs' work on the Greek New Testament will consist of six volumes in a three-part series (text and tags, analytical concordances, analytical lexicon). According to the Fribergs, all the material in all six volumes will be available through the American Bible Society/United Bible Societies on tape (and, hopefully, on disk).

7.7 Other Projects with the New Testament

In this section I will mention several projects, exclusive of large data banks, that are working with machine-readable versions of the New Testament. In the interests of comprehensiveness, I have included brief descriptions of projects about which I have been unsuccessful in obtaining first-hand information. I hope to report more fully on them in the next edition of this book.

7.7.1 Institut Catholique

Professor Georges Wierusz Kowalski is developing ways to use computers to make traditional historical-critical methods of exegesis more precise. See his "Nouvelles analyses et nouveaux fonctionnements du texte dans un environment informatisé," *Bible and Computer : The Text*, 215–34. For more information contact:

> Prof. G. Kowalski
> Institut Catholique
> 61 rue Madame
> 75006 Paris
> France
> (1) 42-227-002; from North America dial direct:
>   011-33-14-222-7002

7.7.2 Institut für Neutestamentliche Textforschung

The Institut für Neutestamentliche Textforschung at Münster, under the directorship of Kurt Aland, is in the process of preparing a computer-based concordance to the Greek New Testament. For more information, see H. Bachmann and W. A. Slaby, *Computer-Konkordanz zum Novum Testamentum Graece* (Berlin-New York, 1980) and K. Aland, H. Bachmann, and W. A. Slaby,*Vollstaendige Konkordanz zum Griechischen Neuen Testament, Band II: Spezialubersichten* (Berlin-New York, 1978) or contact:

Institut für Neutestamentliche Textforschung
University of Münster Westfalischen
Wilhelms-Universität
Münster
Westfalen
West Germany

7.7.3 A. Q. Morton

Professor Andrew Q. Morton, of course, is not a project but a person, and a controversial one at that! Beginning in 1960, he was, I believe, the first person to use computers to analyze the Greek New Testament, in this case the Pauline Epistles.[162] Professor Morton is best known for his "stylometric" approach to studying authorship. By analyzing the frequency with which common words like *kai, de, einai, ev, ho,* and *ego* occur, the position of words, the pairing of words, sentence length, and other easily quantifiable variables, Morton believes he is able to reach decisive and scientific conclusions about style (hence *style* in "stylometrics").

Using those stylometric techniques, in 1975 Professor Morton and his colleague Sidney Michaelson garnered some rather sensational attention in the British press when the stylometric evidence they provided was used in the Old Bailey to convince the jury that Steve Raymond—accused among other things of having murdered his dentist (a charge that was later dropped)—did not make some of the statements attributed to him by the police, whom the defendant claimed were trying to frame him.[163] In academic circles, however, Morton is better known for persistently arguing that his stylometric approach to authorship has "proved" that Paul wrote only five[164] of the fourteen epistles traditionally ascribed to him and that the other nine Pauline Epistles were written by at least five different authors. That and other conclusions about the authorship of New Testament books have made Professor Morton a controversial figure, to say the least. Readers interested in learning more about Professor Morton's stylometric techniques and about the ways his work has been criticized should consult the bibliography at the end of this chapter.

7.7.4 ACP—Aramaic Computer Project

The Aramaic Computer Project (ACP), which is sponsored by The Way International, has produced a computer-based analytical concordance to the Syriac (i.e., Peshitta) version of the New Testament, published in 1985 by the American Christian Press as *The Concordance to the Peshitta Version.* The data base also has been used to create a bilingual Syriac-English/English-Syriac dictionary that was published in 1985 by the American Christian Press as the *English Dictionary Supplement to the Concordance to the Peshitta Version.*

The data base can be searched for occurrences of English and Syriac words, phrases, or grammatical constructions. Syriac search terms are highlighted and displayed in their Syriac context. English search terms are treated in a similar fashion. English words and phrases may be compared to their Syriac counterparts, and vice versa. The data base programs also can display the root, lemma, and parsing of every word in the Syriac text. At present, the data base is not ready for distribution.

The ACP plans to add the texts of the Old Syriac versions of the Gospels to the data base to make comparative textual work possible and to "tie together" Greek and

---

162. Morton, "Annals," 197.

163. Ibid., 199. In Professor Morton's own words, "He [the freed man] went on to bigger things and now holds the native record of stealing two million pounds from London airport," ibid.; cf. Oakman, *Methods,* 143–46.

164. Romans, 1 and 2 Corinthians, Galatians, and Philemon.

Syriac "fields of meaning" in an attempt to investigate translational and scribal tendencies.[165]

For more information, contact:

> Mrs. Bernita Jess, Project Director
> Aramaic Computer Project
> The Way International
> P.O. Box 328
> New Knoxville, OH 45871
> (419) 753-2523.

7.7.5 Syriac Research Center

The Syriac Research Center, under the directorship of Dr. Dale A. Johnson, has created machine-readable versions of approximately forty Peshitta manuscripts. These MRTs are available on 5.25-inch diskettes for Apple IIs. The MRTs consists of a critical text, variants from other Peshitta texts, and some newly discovered lectionary texts. The center is located at Zion Christian College, and funding is supplied in part by the Society for Biblical Manuscripts on Microfilm and Computer. For more information contact:

> Dr. Dale A. Johnson
> Zion Christian College
> 1209 Minor Rd.
> Kelso, WA 98626
> (206) 577-0620.

7.8 Machine-Readable Text Archives and Data Banks

A "text archive" of machine-readable texts is similar to a library, except that the MRTs in the archive are stored on tapes, diskettes, CD-ROMs, or WORMs, not in printed form, though of course the contents of the magnetic and optical media may be printed. Text archives are a form of data bank, and in this section I will use the terms interchangeably.

There are well over a dozen major text archives in the world (the OUCS Text Archive "shortlist" lists fifteen—see below) for languages as diverse as Arabic and Icelandic. In this section we will discuss those archives that contain MRTs of biblical, classical, Semitic, Hellenistic, and Ancient Near Eastern texts, documents, and inscriptions.

7.8.1 HDP—Historical Dictionary

- *BASIC DATA BASE INFORMATION*

Name of Project: Historical Dictionary Project of the Hebrew Language
Key Person(s): Zev Ben-Hayyim
Location of Project: Jerusalem
Project Address: The Academy of the Hebrew Language, Giv'at Ram, P.O. Box 3449, Jerusalem 91 034, Israel
Telephones: (02) 632-242; from North America dial direct: 011-972-02-632-242
Date Project Began: 1959
Date Project Completed: Not yet complete.
Sources of Funding: Academy of the Hebrew Language

---

165. From a private letter from Joseph A. Wise, former Project Director, dated January 8, 1986.

Scope: All words in the Hebrew language from all historical periods
Size: Projected: 25 million quotations; current: 8.6 million quotations (5 million fully lemmatized)
Computer System: CDC Cyber 180
Available on Tape: No
Available on Diskettes: No
Output Options: Tape, diskette, print, microfiche
Custom Searches: Not known
On-line Access Through Networks: BITNET
Costs/Price: Not applicable
Key Bibliographical References: "The Historical Dictionary of the Hebrew Language—Specimen Pamphlet. The Root "B.""
Other: None

7.8.1.1 Introduction

Most of the information in this subsection is taken from a brief report provided by The Academy of the Hebrew Language ("The Historical Dictionary of the Hebrew Language"). The Historical Dictionary Project (HDP), which began in 1959, is a research project of The Academy of the Hebrew Language and is directed by Professor Zev Ben-Hayyim (the editor of the dictionary) and a council of members from The Academy. The goal of the HDP is to publish a comprehensive, scholarly Historical Dictionary of the Hebrew Language (HDHL). The HDHL will include every vocabulary word from every historic and stylistic strata of the Hebrew language, in all its periods, as those words appear in the sources.[166] The result of the HDP will be something like *The Oxford English Dictionary* (1878–1928, Supp. 1972–1986), now in 16 volumes, only much larger and more comprehensive. Words will be arranged according to roots, verbs by mode (*binyan*), and nouns by pattern (*mishqal*). Thus the HDP will function both as a *historical dictionary* and as a *historical concordance* of the Hebrew language (see below).

The HDHL will make available the entire history of every word in the Hebrew language and will show each word's (1) source, (2) origin, (3) derivation, (4) meanings, (5) uses, (6) phrases in which it appears during the various periods in the life of the language, (7) its various forms (spelling, vocalization, and grammar), and (8) the frequency of its appearance in the different periods. "Each account of the history of a word appearing in the Historical Dictionary will be supported by a long list of extracts from Hebrew literature over the generations, arranged in chronological order."[167] When completed, the HDHL data base will contain well over 25 million quotations from various literary sources that cover a period of almost 3,000 years. So far, over 8.6 million quotations have been processed.

7.8.1.2 Sources

The Ancient Literature Section of the HDP currently deals with works that date from the end of the biblical period (200 B.C.) to the end of the period of the Geonim (A.D. 1050) and is subdivided into five subperiods. The oldest manuscripts for each work are examined, and the single best manuscript in which a given work is preserved is chosen as the basis for analyzing that work. That manuscript then serves as the source for constructing a concordance to the text in question. This process is repeated for every work the HDP analyzes. The analysis of manuscripts for all the sources of the Hebrew language will result in a more precise knowledge of its vocabulary and the

---

166. For full details of the HDP's sources, manuscripts, editions, dates, etc., see *Sefer ha-Meqorot* ("Book of Sources"), 2nd ed. (Jerusalem, 1970).

167. "The Historical Dictionary of the Hebrew Language," 15.

meaning of its words and their uses in the various linguistic strata throughout the generations.

All the works dating from 200 B.C. to A.D. 300 have been analyzed and concordances created. These works include Ben Sira, the nonbiblical Dead Sea Scrolls, the Mishna, the Tosephta, and the Halakic Midrashim (Sifra, Sifre to Numbers and Deuteronomy, Sifre Zuta, Mekilta de R. Ishmael, Mekilta de R. Simeon b. Yohai, Seder Olam Rabba)—about 830,000 words in all. Computers were used to construct and print the concordances (88 volumes—68 of concordances, 13 of lexicological lists, 7 of texts). This wealth of information—840,000 quotations, a complete, philologically checked "Text and Concordance" of all extant Hebrew sources from 200 B.C. up to and including the Tannaitic Period—is now available on microfiche for $250. Ben Sira is available in book form.[168]

Work is progressing on the literature that dates from A.D. 300–1050. The HDP researchers estimate the total number of words in that body of literature to be about 5 million. The works in this period include (1) the Talmud and the Midrash—about 2.6 million words (the Jerusalem Talmud, the Babylonian Talmud, and the Haggadic Midrashim—Midrash Rabba, Midrash Tanchuma, Pesiqta de Rav Kahana, Pesiqta Rabbati, Avoth de Rabbi Nathan, Derekh Eretz Zuta, Eliyahu Rabba, etc.), (2) Karaitic Literature—about 500,000 words, (3) Geonic Literature—about 1.1 million words, (4) Piyyut (liturgical poetry)—about 600,000 words, and (5) Masoretic Literature and Grammar—about 100,000 words. Currently, the HDP researchers are concentrating on the Talmud, the Midrash, the Karaitic literature, and the Piyyut.

The Modern Literature Section deals with works that were published during the period A.D. 1750 to the present. These works include literary writings (poetry and prose), rabbinic literature, newspapers, scientific books, periodicals, and so forth.

The HDP hopes to open a section to process texts from the period A.D. 1050–1750 but has not yet been able to do so.

7.8.1.3 The Process

Using the best manuscripts available, researchers at the HDP translate the *full* texts of *all* the extant sources of each period into machine-readable form. That information serves as an archive from which the compilers of the dictionary draw.[169] The archives are divided into two main files, a lexicographical index and a lexicological index.

The lexicographical index is a comprehensive list of lemmata, alphabetically arranged. Under each lemma, quotations are listed in chronological order according to source. Each quotation shows the word in context, lists its source, the date of the manuscript from which it was taken, and may include alternative readings.

The lexicological index lists lemmata according to their frequency and structure. Verbs are listed according to their root groupings, conjugations, and tenses; nouns are listed according to their "structure-patterns" and declensions.

The Academy publication "The Historical Dictionary of the Hebrew Language—Specimen Pamphlet: The Root "B," which illustrates the method the dictionary will follow, is available from The Academy for $10. From over 11,000 quotations, the HDP researchers chose 1,400 to illustrate the 102 lemmata this root takes. Each lemma is documented with a large number of quotations that are arranged chronologically.

---

168. *The Book of Ben-Sira: Text, Concordance and an Analysis of the Vocabulary* (Jerusalem: The Academy of the Hebrew Language, 1973).

169. The archives will be larger than the dictionary itself.

7.8.1.4 *Other Activities*

With the assistance of IBM "Israel," The Academy also is using its computers to prepare an index of Modern Hebrew terms, as codified by The Academy (since 1953) and by its predecessor, The Hebrew Language Council, from 1890 to the present period. This Index includes 80,000 Hebrew terms and their English equivalents. French and German equivalents are to be added.

7.8.2 GJD/RP—Global Jewish Database

● *BASIC DATA BASE INFORMATION*

Name of Project: Global Jewish Database/Responsa Project
Key Person(s): Yaacov Choueka
Location of Project: Ramat-Gan, Israel
Project Address: Bar-Ilan University, The Center for Computers and Jewish Heritage/Institute for Information Retrieval and Computational Linguistics, The Aliza and Menachem Begin Bldg., Ramat Gan 52 100, Israel
Telephones: (03) 718-411, (03) 718-343; from North America dial direct: 011-972-3-718-411 or 718-343
Date Project Began: 1967
Date Project Completed: Not yet complete.
Sources of Funding: The Weizman Institute of Science, Israel, Bar-Ilan University, Israel; a special endowment fund set up in Chicago by friends of Bar-Ilan University and managed by Thomas A. Klutznick; The National Endowment for the Humanities of the United States of America; The National Bureau of Standards of the United States of America; The National Academy of Science of the State of Israel; IBM Israel
Scope: Jewish biblical, rabbinical, legal, cultural, and historical literature from all periods
Size: Projected: over 3,000 volumes, 750 million words of text; current: 250 volumes, 50 million words[170]
Computer System: IBM 3081
Available on Tape: Yes; contact project directly.
Available on Diskettes: No
Output Options: Screen, tape, print; consonantal Hebrew text only
Custom Searches: Yes
On-line Access Through Networks: Yes, see below.
Costs/Price: Not known
Key Bibliographical References: *The Responsa Project: What, How, and Why: 1976#1981;* "Computerized Full-Text Retrieval Systems and Research in the Humanities: The Responsa Project"; Yaacov Choueka et al., "The Responsa Project: Computerization of Traditional Jewish Case Law," in B. Erez, ed., *Legal and Legislative Information Processing* (Greenwood Press, 1980), 261–86. Readers interested in receiving printed information about the work of the Bar-Ilan Center for Computers and Jewish Heritage should direct correspondence to the address above and ask for the free color pamphlet "Giving Wisdom to the Wise."
Other: None

7.8.2.1 *Introduction*

The following information is based on Yaacov Choueka's *The Responsa Project: What, How, and Why: 1976#1981,* on his "Computerized Full-Text Retrieval Systems and Research in the Humanities: The Responsa Project," and on various materials he provided. As the titles of the two articles mentioned in the previous sentence indicate, this project was formerly known as The Responsa Project (RP). In 1983 the RP became part of a larger project, the Global Jewish Database (GJD). In this section I will discuss the RP part of the GJD.

The Responsa Project was conceived by Aviezri Fraenkel in 1965–1966, begun in 1967, headed by Fraenkel until 1975, when it was formally incorporated into Bar-Ilan

---

170. These figures are only for the Responsa part of the Global Jewish Database.

University's Institute for Information Retrieval and Computational Linguistics (IRCOL)[171]—under the directorship of computer scientist Yaacov Choueka—and made part of the Global Jewish Database project in 1983. The RP consists of research, development, applications, service, and dissemination activities in the fields of (1) legal information retrieval, (2) computational linguistics, (3) text processing, and (4) Jewish studies.

The goals of the RP are (1) to develop and maintain a full-text retrieval system for the most important Hebrew works of Jewish culture and heritage, (2) to establish a service center for processing searches and queries of this data base, (3) to conduct basic research in information retrieval and computational linguistics, and (4) to develop and implement research programs in Jewish studies, using the data base and the project's tools.

7.8.2.2 The Data Base

The Responsa literature includes over half a million rabbinical "questions and answers"[172] in some 3,000 volumes, written mainly in Hebrew and Aramaic[173] over thirteen centuries[174] by about 1,800 different authors from approximately thirty countries.[175] It covers a widely ranging assortment of practical and legal topics. Over the centuries, individuals and communities around the world have posed questions to leading Rabbis whose answers—the Responsa—are interpretations and applications of Talmudic law and so have the status of legal decisions that become valuable precedents for further Jewish law. Responsa, then, are Judaic case laws and so are predominantly halakhic in nature.

Although most of the Responsa are of a practical and legal nature, the literature also covers history, economics, philosophy, religion, sociology, linguistics, musicology, folklore, and so forth. Thus the Responsa provide a unique window through which to view the rich patterns of the worldwide fabric of Jewish life during the past thirteen centuries.

Typical questions found in the Responsa—or that recently have been directed to it—include: "When is the exact moment of death?" "May an orthodox Jewish doctor send a patient to another doctor to receive treatment the Jewish doctor is prohibited by Jewish law from administering?" "May a Jewish criminal claim asylum in Israel?"[176] "What dietary standards must a kosher hotel keeper maintain for Gentile guests?"[177] "At what hour does the Sabbath begin for people travelling at supersonic speeds?"[178] "May a robot be a member of a *minyan*—the traditional ten-member Jewish prayer group?"[179] "If one Siamese twin is dying, may his life be taken to save the life of the

---

171. Bar-Ilan University has a special emphasis on Judaic and humanities research. IRCOL's basic role is to provide an academic and administrative framework for the GJD, RP, and related research and development activities.

172. E.g., *She'elot u'Tshuvot*.

173. Responsa also sometimes contain phrases and expressions in Arabic, Ladino, Persian, German, English, and Yiddish.

174. I.e., from the eighth century A.D. to the present.

175. E.g., Spain, Germany, Algiers, Syria, Yemen, Iraq, France, Austria, Poland, Israel, Italy, Russia, Galizia, Switzerland, Egypt, Turkey, Hungary, Lithuania, Syria, Czechoslovakia, Holland, Ireland, and Greece.

176. Responsa answer: Yes.

177. Responsa answer: Serve the Gentile guest kosher food.

178. Respona answer: the computer was stumped by this question!

179. Responsa answer: No, because an android—or golem—is not human and therefore is not responsible for its actions or obligated to obey the commandments.

other twin?"[180] "Is artificial insemination permissible for orthodox Jews?"[181] "May the only witness to the death of a man marry that man's widow?"[182] Other topics on which the RP data base has been searched include adolescent suicide, genetic engineering, tax collection, public funding, and embryo transplants. A special Responsa program can automatically translate Gentile dates to Jewish ones, and vice versa, as well as give the dates and week days of all holy days and the appropriate portion of the Torah that is to be read on each Sabbath.[183]

Before the inception of the RP, there was no global index to the vast body of Responsa literature, and the printed texts were scattered throughout the world—many of them inaccessible to rabbinical scholars. The RP was established to correct those two problems by making the Responsa literature accessible to scholars in full-text form in a way that allows it to be searched thoroughly and accurately. The Global Jewish Database extends those goals by making a broader spectrum of Jewish biblical, historical, and cultural literature available on-line. Currently, the RP has stored almost 250 Responsa collections,[184] consisting of about 47,000 individual responsa, in a data bank that contains over 50 million words—about 280 megabytes (assuming 5.6 bytes of storage per word—see below). Choueka estimates that the number of individual responsa may be as high as 750,000 and the number of words of text as high as 750 million.[185] Storing all the texts of all the Responsa, then, would require over 4 gigabytes.[186] By late 1987 the Responsa data base should contain 56 million words—313 megabytes—from 262 volumes, written by 120 authors, from 28 different countries, over a period of thirteen centuries.

The Global Jewish Database also contains the entire Hebrew Bible (fully vocalized and cantillated),[187] the Babylonian Talmud (with Rashi commentary), Midrashic literature, Maimonides Code, and more. IRCOL's master plan calls for making available in the GJD in full-text, machine-readable form all the basic works of Jewish culture, that is, the Mishna, Midrashic literature, Jewish law, philosophical literature, Modern Hebrew literature, and a complete computerized concordance of the Palestinian dialect of the Aramaic language. According to Professor Choueka,[188] IRCOL plans to add the following works to the GJD in 1986/1987: (1) the Mishna, with the commentaries of Bartenura, Tosafot Yom Tov, and Yachin U'Boaz, (2) the Palestinian Talmud (Venice 1523 edition), (3) commentaries on the Hebrew Bible by Rashi, Radak, Ibn Ezra, Ralbag, and Metzudot, (4) eight works of Tannaic and Amoraic literature—Tosefta, Mekilta de R. Ishmael, Mekilta de R. Simon b. Yohai, Sifra, Sifre, Sifre Zuta, Midrash Tannaim LeSefer Devarim, Avot de Rabbi Nathan, (5) fourteen more collections of Responsa, (6) seven more halakic works, and (7) ten works of the Yalkutim literature. Including the Responsa data base, the present size of the GJD is over 60 million words, or about 336 megabytes. By late 1987, the GJD should contain over 77 million words—more than 430 megabytes—from 473 volumes and works.

---

180. Responsa answer: No, because the dying twin is a person, and you may not hasten the death of a person, even to save the other twin.

181. Responsa answer: Yes, if performed with the husband's semen by a reputable physician.

182. Responsa answer: No, though his report about the death of the man may be trusted.

183. The Chronology-History Research Institute (77 Second Ave., Rossie, IA 51356; (712) 262-3334) markets the Ancient Calendar Conversion Program for $795. This program, which runs on IBM PCs and Apple IIs, converts dates among the Gregorian, Hebrew, Seleucid, Julian, and Egyptian calendrical systems and displays information about new moons, Jubilee years, Sabbath days, Sabbath years, and the priestly cycle.

184. According to Choueka, Schreiber, and Slae, there are about 3,000 printed collections of Responsa.

185. Choueka, "Systems," 154.

186. Ibid., assuming 5.6 bytes per word.

187. This is the Michigan Old Testament as corrected and edited by the Faculty of Jewish Studies at Bar-Ilan, under the direction of Menachem Cohen.

188. Private correspondence, dated January 17, 1986.

7.8.2.3 The Programs

The searching program supports (1) word, (2) exact-phrase, and (3) proximity searches, (4) Boolean and (5) metric operators, (6) initial, medial, and terminal truncation, (7) wild cards, and (8) searching by reference (citation). The (9) search range may be restricted to user-specified books. Hits are displayed on-screen in a KWIC format. The context in which hits are displayed may be expanded, and users may scroll through the full text bidirectionally on either side of each hit. The KWIC can be conditional, redundant lines may be omitted, and references can be labeled automatically in the form generally in use by halakhic scholars.

The searching program supports index manipulation. KWIC lines may be sorted chronologically, by key words, by the number of different retrieval conditions satisfied by the hit, or by the type of retrieval conditions satisfied by the hit. A compact list of references can be displayed and printed with the KWIC output in all its different sorting parameters.[189]

KEDMA, a powerful parsing program, provides full, accurate, automatic, on-line morphological analysis of any Hebrew word. KEDMA also can locate all linguistically correct variants of a given stem in a given text, as well as decline nouns and conjugate verbs. Because Hebrew is a highly inflected language with a small number of roots,[190] special algorithms were developed to inflect lemmata automatically, that is, to conjugate verbs and to decline nouns. This feature of the system allows users to search automatically for all the different forms of key words. To illustrate this in English, a search for "to watch" could be constructed to include all the verbal forms of the lemma *watch* (e.g., *watched, will watch, watching*) in its different tenses, voices, persons, and aspects. Or specific morphological forms may be searched for, for example all the occurrences of "watched" (past tense). Because some configurations have over 20,000 different forms,[191] this feature of the RP's program is indispensable for thorough searching.[192]

The RP is fast and accurate. In one test where leading Rabbis were pitted against the machine, the computer found 98% of all relevant references, the Rabbis 78%. The computer, of course, was much faster than the Rabbis and provided a printout of all references.

---

189. The RP uses four files. A (1) text file, which consists of the running text of the Responsa literature, is used only for displaying and for printing the KWIC results of a search. The (2) dictionary file consists of one record for each word in the text. Each record contains the word, its number of occurrences in the data base, the number of different documents in which it appears, and a pointer to a corresponding record in the (3) index file, which lists every occurrence of each word in chronological order. Information about author code, book code, document number, paragraph number, sentence number in the paragraph, word number in the sentence, and references to any grammatical flags by which the linguistic components of a word are marked are included in its record in the index file. The last file (4) is a collection of tables and lists, including linguistic files, that are used in search programs. See Choueka, "Systems," 160.

190. A comprehensive dictionary of Modern Hebrew, for example, contains only about 35,000 entries (including 3,500 international loan words, such as "bank" and "symphony") that are derived from 3,000–5,000 distinct roots, but the total number of different Hebrew words (i.e., a lexically correct, meaningful, inflected root) is about 100 million. See ibid., 162.

191. A Hebrew noun or adjective can appear in several thousand different forms, because it can be singular, plural, or dual; masculine or feminine; or construct state. To any of those forms, ten possessive pronouns may be suffixed and about 100 prepositions may be prefixed. And there may be combinations, such as "and from my house." Hebrew verbal forms can be even more complex. A verb may be conjugated in up to seven modes (*binyanim*), four tenses, and twelve persons, to which prepositions can be prefixed and causative pronouns suffixed, making 20,000 variants of a single lemma possible. See ibid., 162–63.

192. To make it possible to search for all the inflected forms of a word, the RP programmers constructed grammatical algorithms and applied them to a coded Hebrew dictionary to produce an exhaustive thesaurus of all Hebrew words (without prepositions), to which was added a complete record of lexical and morphological information about every word in the thesaurus. A special algorithm was written to handle prepositions. See above.

According to Professor Choueka,[193] the IRCOL data base management and full-text retrieval software I have just described may be used with any data base that contains Hebrew text. And recently, this software has been adapted to English-text data bases. Pending funding, IRCOL plans to add English translations of basic Jewish works, original works in English, and reference works in English (e.g., *The Encyclopedia Judaica*) to the Global Jewish Database.

7.8.2.4 RP/GJD Services

Several additional services and activities of the Bar-Ilan Center for Computers and Jewish Heritage should be noted.

On-line Access and Searches. Remote terminals are being set up at different locations in Israel and elsewhere so that interested parties may query IRCOL's data bases. Anyone in the world with a properly equipped IBM-PC-compatible microcomputer, IRCOL's special communication software that emulates an IBM 3270, and access to a telecommunication network may now use these data bases. Contact IRCOL for further details. Alternatively, IRCOL will conduct searches of the Responsa data base for modest charges. The North American center for the RP, which has a copy of the RP data base and which will conduct searches for interested parties, may be contacted at the following address.

> The Institute for Computers in Jewish Life
> ℅ Rabbi Alan B. Rosenbaum
> Responsa Project Coordinator
> 845 N. Michigan Ave., Suite 843
> Chicago, IL 60611
> (312) 787-7856

Jewish Law Service. In 1981 the Knesset (Israel's parliament) ruled that Israeli lawyers could cite precedents from Jewish law and that such case law is admissible as evidence in court. As a result, lawyers and justices from Israel's Supreme, District, and Lower Courts regularly consult the RP for legal precedents, and RP citations are often included in written decisions. To assist in the process of locating appropriate case-law citations in the Responsa literature, IRCOL has established the Jewish Law Service for the Courtroom Lawyer (JLS), with partial funding by the Israel Bar Association.

Videodisc. IRCOL is working on a pilot project to develop a pictorial data base that uses videodisc technology.

Educational Units. Two educational units—"Honesty in Business" and "Lost and Found"—are available in Hebrew and English versions for Apple IIs. Each unit is accompanied by a videotape in Hebrew (with English subtitles).

Selected Readings. IRCOL offers the following Selected Readings in Halakah and problems of modern society: (1) medical malpractice, (2) environmental protection and ecology, (3) gerontology, (4) the relationship of man to other living creatures, and (5) *Hevra Kadisha* (Burial Society) in the Jewish Community.

7.8.3 TLG—Thesaurus Linguae Graecae

● *BASIC DATA BASE INFORMATION*

Name of Project: Thesaurus Linguae Graecae Project
Key Person(s): Theodore F. Brunner
Location of Project: Irvine, California
Project Address: University of California at Irvine, Irvine CA 92717

---

193. Private correspondence, dated January 17, 1986.

Telephone: (714) 856-7031
Date Project Began: 1972
Date Project Completed: Not yet complete.
Sources of Funding: Dr. Marianne McDonald, The National Endowment for the Humanities of the United States of America, the Andrew W. Mellon Foundation, the David and Lucile Packard Foundation, the American Philological Association, and numerous other individuals, foundations, and institutions
Scope: All extant Greek literature from Homer (ca. 750 B.C.) through A.D. 600—almost 3,000 authors
Size: Projected: approximately 62 million words of Greek text; current: 56,306,232 words (as of January 1986)
Computer System: Ibycus
Available on Tape: Yes, text to date occupies eight 2,400-foot, 6250-bpi tapes.
Available on Diskettes: No, but a CD-ROM disk that contains the entire data base soon will be generally available (see below).
Output Options: Screen, tape, print
Custom Searches: Yes; a modest fee may be charged.
On-line Access Through Networks: No
Costs/Price: The entire data base or tapes of individual authors may be purchased; contact the project for further information.
Key Bibliographical References: *Thesaurus Linguae Graecae Newsletter*; K. A. Squitier, "The TLG Canon: Genesis of an Encyclopedic Data Base," in Bernard Frischer, ed. *Papers of the UCLA Conference on Classics and Computing* (Los Angeles, July 19–20, 1986) = *Favonius Supp. Vol. 1* (1987): 15–20.
Other: TLG Publications, Inc. publishes a number of concordances and indices of ancient Greek works in book and microfiche form.

The staff of the TLG Project, under the directorship of Theodore F. Brunner, after more than a decade of work, has almost completed transforming approximately 62 million words of Greek text from nearly 3,000 authors—all extant Greek literature from Homer (ca. 750 B.C.) through A.D. 600—into machine-readable form. At this time, over 32 million of those words have been proofed and corrected. Using the best scholarly versions available, each text is keypunched twice (in Manila, The Philippines), the results transferred to tape, the tape checked by a program designed to locate mistakes, and the results of that operation manually proofread. The contents of the data bank, listed by author and work, can be found in the *Thesaurus Linguae Graecae Canon of Greek Authors and Works*, which is available from Oxford University Press (1985).

Material is available in tape and CD-ROM formats. Presently, ten 2,400-foot tapes or one 4.75-inch, half-gigabyte CD-ROM are required to hold the portion of the data base that has been verified and corrected. The data base is available in Beta Format, a coding scheme developed by David Packard. Using Ibycus (or other properly equipped) computers, Beta-Formatted TLG texts can be displayed on-screen in Greek, complete with all diacritical marks.[194] (Because of the variety of operating systems and disk formats in use by microcomputers, the TLG Project does not disseminate materials on floppy disks.) The TLG offers an experimental CD-ROM, which may be read by appropriately equipped microcomputers and which contains the portion of the data base that had been proofed by late 1985. The complete data base will be offered on CD-ROMs as soon as all proofreading is completed.[195] The TLG's experimental CD-ROM is one of two. The Isocrates Project (see below), in conjunction with the Harvard Classics Computer Project (also see below), under license to the TLG Project, has developed a second TLG CD-ROM, which includes indices.

The TLG's experimental CD-ROM also includes (1) all Greek documentary papyri that were available from the Duke Data Bank of Documentary Papyri in late 1985

---

194. See the *Bits & Bytes Review*™ 1 (October 1986): 1–8 for a review of the Ibycus Scholarly Computer that includes pictures of portions of the TLG data base.

195. The whole data base should fit on one CD-ROM. Parties interested in developing software to work with the TLG CD-ROM should contact the TLG Project for full technical documentation. The TLG Project anticipates charging approximately $500 per CD-ROM disk, which would cover materials, labor, and license fees (this is an unofficial price at this time).

(DDBDP—see below), (2) a number of Latin texts (supplied by David Packard), (3) some Hebrew materials (supplied by Richard E. Whitaker—see above), (4) some Coptic materials (supplied by the Claremont Institute for Antiquity and Christianity),[196] (5) various Greek epigraphical materials (supplied by the Princeton Institute for Advanced Study and by the University of North Carolina—see below), and, on a different disk, (6) word indices to various TLG texts (prepared by the Harvard University Classics Department—see below).

The TLG Project is affiliated or works closely with the following projects: (1) the Duke Data Bank of Documentary Papyri (see below), (2) the Cornell Center for the Computerization of Greek Inscriptions (see below), (3) the Princeton Institute for Advanced Study Epigraphic Project (see below), (4) Claremont's Institute for Antiquity and Christianity, (5) the Bavarian Academy of Sciences Thesaurus Linguae Latinae Project, and (6) CATSS/CCAT (see above and below).

Various programs developed for Ibycus computers (see above under CATSS), as well as other programs, may be used to manipulate the TLG texts, create key-word-in-context concordances, and so forth. The Harvard Classics Computer Project (HCCP)—see below—has created indices of many words in the TLG corpus, along with exact citations of each indexed word. William Johnson is helping the TLG create a statistical index that lists the number of times forms occur in each work. Both sets of indices allow users to search indexed texts, rather than having to scan sequentially through the entire data bank to build indices from scratch. When used in conjunction with the proper programs, the TLG data base should prove invaluable for a broad spectrum of research purposes—etymology, morphology, lexicography, and grammar, to name but a few.

7.8.4 DDBDP—Duke Data Bank of Documentary Papyri

- *BASIC DATA BASE INFORMATION*

Name of Project: Duke Data Bank of Documentary Papyri
Key Person(s): William H. Willis, John Oates (codirectors), Louise P. Smith (project supervisor)
Location of Project: Durham, North Carolina
Project Address: Duke University, Room 201B, Perkins Library, P.O. Box 4762 Duke Station, Durham, NC 27706
Telephone: (919) 684-5753
Date Project Began: 1983
Date Project Completed: Not yet complete.
Sources of Funding: The David and Lucile Packard Foundation, The National Endowment for the Humanities of the United States of America, Duke University
Scope: All published Greek and Latin documentary papyri and ostraca.
Size: Projected: approximately 6,000,000 words of Greek text from between 30,000 and 35,000 published papyri; current: 1,250,000 words in 10,500 documents.
Computer System: Ibycus
Available on Tape: Yes, 1,600-bpi, ASCII or EBCDIC, fixed or variable record block
Available on Diskettes: Perhaps in the future
Output Options: Screen, tape, print
Custom Searches: Yes
On-line Access Through Networks: No
Costs/Price: Materials and postage
Key Bibliographical References: None
Other: When completed, the DDBDP will be incorporated into the TLG data bank.

---

196. Using funds provided by the David and Lucile Packard Foundation, Richard E. Whitaker oversaw the coding of the entire Nag Hammadi Coptic library at the IAC in 1981–1982 and with David Packard designed a Coptic alphabet that can be displayed on Ibycus computers.

The Duke Data Bank of Documentary Papyri Project (DDBDP), under the codirectorship of William H. Willis and John Oates, is in the process of converting approximately 6,000,000 words of Greek and Latin texts from documentary papyri into machine-readable form. These texts, which are defined as texts "written on papyrus, parchment, ostraca, wooden or waxed tablets," cover the period from the fourth century B.C. to the eighth century A.D. in published form, these 30,000–35,000 texts occupy 400 volumes (including 20 volumes of ostraca).[197] As of November 1986, 122 volumes (ca. 1,000,000 words) of the 131 volumes in Phase I (papyri published since 1966) of the project had been entered, as had twenty-six of the 130 volumes in Phase II (220,000 words) and two of the 92 in Phase III (50,000 words). Sixty-nine volumes had been proofed and corrected.[198]

Unlike the TLG Project's procedure for converting texts to machine-readable form, the DDBDP texts are being keyed in Greek directly into an Ibycus minicomputer.[199] A special program then converts those texts into Beta Format so that they work with LEX, the superfast Ibycus search program we discussed above under CATSS. Next, a printout is made in Greek and that material sent to the proofreaders at the University of Michigan, who work under the supervision of Prof. Ludwig Koenen and Dr. Randall Stewart.

Students of Koine (Hellenistic) Greek will especially profit from having access to all the documentary papyri in machine-readable form. Like the TLG data bank, when used in conjunction with the proper programs, the DDBDP will prove invaluable for an equally broad spectrum of research purposes.

7.8.5 CCCGI—Computerization of Greek Inscriptions

- *BASIC DATA BASE INFORMATION*

Name of Project: Cornell Center for the Computerization of Greek Inscriptions
Key Person(s): Kevin Clinton, Director; Nancy Cooper and John Mansfield, Managers
Location of Project: Ithaca, New York
Project Address: Cornell University, Department of Classics, Goldwin Smith Hall, Ithaca, NY 14853-3201
Telephones: (607) 255-3354, (607) 255-8259
Date Project Began: 1985
Date Project Completed: Not yet complete.
Sources of Funding: The David and Lucile Packard Foundation
Scope: All Attic inscriptions not already in machine-readable form (see below under DBAGI)
Size: Projected: over 14,000 inscriptions (in Phase I of the project); current: 9,000 inscriptions
Computer System: Ibycus Scholarly Computer
Available on Tape: No
Available on Diskettes: Yes
Output Options: Screen, diskettes, print
Custom Searches: Projected
On-line Access Through Networks: No
Costs/Price: Not known
Key Bibliographical References: None
Other: See below under DBAGI and IASEP.

This and the next two projects we will discuss are working to convert all ancient Greek inscriptions to machine-readable form. The Cornell Center for the Computerization of Greek Inscriptions (CCCGI) is an independent project that is entering

---

197. There may be as many as 100,000 unpublished documentary papyri.

198. Phase II will cover papyri published from 1924–1966, and Phase III will cover papyri published from 1890–1924.

199. Documentary papyri have been published since 1813 in as many as 250 different typefaces, a fact that precludes optical scanning as a practical means of data entry.

Attic inscriptions not entered by William C. West in the Data Bank for Ancient Greek Inscriptions (DBAGI) at Chapel Hill. (The CCCGI data base will incorporate the DBAGI inscriptions.) The Princeton Institute for Advanced Study Epigraphic Project (IASEP) is entering the Ionian inscriptions.[200] The CATSS CD-ROM Project hopes to incorporate these materials in its first CD-ROM (see below).

The CCCGI Project is converting to machine-readable form the inscriptions listed in the Attic volumes of *Inscriptiones Graecae* (IG) that have not been entered into an Ibycus computer elsewhere. Following that, the CCCGI Project will enter Attic texts that do not appear in or that supersede those in *IG*.

Unlike the TLG Project and the DDBDP Project, the CCCGI Project is using a Kurzweil optical scanner for text entry (though initially texts were entered by hand). The CCCGI Project uses an Ibycus Scholarly Computer. The Greek texts of the inscriptions published in *IG* are scanned and the Greek characters converted to Beta Format. All Attic texts published in *IG* are being entered, even those that have been outdated by later versions. In this respect CCCGI's approach is different from DBAGI's (see next entry). The Attic inscriptions in *IG* that have been converted to machine-readable form by William C. West (DBAGI) are being included and reformatted to conform to the CCCGI format.

In addition to the text, the record for each inscription includes the following fields of information: (1) reference number, (2) publication, (3) type of marble, (4) height, (5) width, (6) thickness, (7) number of columns, (8) number of faces, (9) *stoichos* dimensions, (10) number of *stoichoi*, (11) *editio priceps*, (12) finding place, (13) original location, (14) current location, including inventory number, (15) location of photograph, and (16) checklist number. Eventually, all of this information will be coordinated with the machine-readable texts in such a way that users may, for example, construct an index of all the inscriptions on white marble that date from 360 to 320 B.C. and that include the word *theatron*.

As of October 1986, the CCCGI Project had entered IG I^3 292–362 and IG II^2 1,322–6,500, 7,000–9,000. IG II^2 1–448, donated by William C. West, have been reformatted and again proofread, and are also included.

7.8.6 DBAGI—Ancient Greek Inscriptions

- *BASIC DATA BASE INFORMATION*

Name of Project: Data Bank for Ancient Greek Inscriptions
Key Person(s): William C. West
Location of Project: Chapel Hill, North Carolina
Project Address: University of North Carolina at Chapel Hill, Department of Classics, 212 Murphey Hall (030A), Chapel Hill, NC 27514
Telephone: (919) 962-7191
Date Project Began: 1983
Date Project Completed: 1984
Sources of Funding: Not known
Scope: All Athenian public decrees from the sixth century to 318 B.C.
Size: 784 inscriptions
Computer System: Ibycus
Available on Tape: Yes
Available on Diskettes: Not known

---

200. The revision of James H. Moulton's and George Milligan's *The Vocabulary of the Greek New Testament* (1930) that is being undertaken in Australia at Macquarie University by Drs. Edwin A. Judge and Greg H. R. Horsley (School of History, Macquarie University, North Ride, NSW, Australia 2113, telephone: (2) 88-88000, from North America dial direct: 011-61-288-88000) may make use of the epigraphical materials compiled by CCCGI, DBAGI, and IASEP. According to Dr. D. A. Carson (Trinity Evangelical Divinity School), there is a potential tie-in between the work of Judge and Horsley and Project GRAMCORD—see above.

Output Options: Screen, tape, print
Custom Searches: Yes
On-line Access Through Networks: No
Costs/Price: Nominal
Key Bibliographical References: William C. West, "A Data Bank for Ancient Greek Inscriptions: Athenian Decrees to 318 B.C." Forthcoming in *Proceedings of the International Conference on Data Bases in the Humanities and Social Science 1985* (Paradigm Press).
Other: See above under CCCGI and below under IASEP.

The Data Bank for Ancient Greek Inscriptions (DBAGI) contains the machine-readable form of 784 inscriptions of ancient Athenian public decrees that date from the sixth century B.C. to 318 B.C. The MRTs are based on the printed versions of the inscriptions found in (*IG*), *Supplementum Epigraphicum Graecae* (*SEG*), and the *Bulletin Epigraphique*.

Texts have been entered in Beta Format, and the project uses an Ibycus computer. The texts from 403 B.C. and later are lemmatized, and each inscription is tagged with technical information. By using LEX, the data bank may be searched for words, phrases, patterns, formulae, and so forth.

William C. West is sharing DBAGI's machine-readable versions of Attic inscriptions that are listed in *IG* with Cornell's CCCGI Project (see above). Unlike the CCCGI texts, DBAGI includes only the updated versions of the *IG* editions.

7.8.7 IASEP—Epigraphic Project

● *BASIC DATA BASE INFORMATION*

Name of Project: Institute for Advanced Study Epigraphic Project
Key Person(s): Donald F. McCabe
Location of Project: Princeton, New Jersey
Project Address: The Institute for Advanced Study, School of Historical Study, Princeton University, Princeton, NJ 08544
Telephone: (609) 734-8000
Date Project Began: 1983
Date Project Completed: Not yet complete.
Sources of Funding: The David and Lucile Packard Foundation
Scope: All Greek and Latin inscriptions of the eastern Roman Empire and the inscriptions of Ionia
Size: Not known
Computer System: Ibycus
Available on Tape: Yes
Available on Diskettes: No
Output Options: Screen, tape, print
Custom Searches: Not known
On-line Access Through Networks: No
Costs/Price: Not known
Key Bibliographical References: None
Other: See above under CCCGI and DBAGI.

The Institute for Advanced Study Epigraphic Project (IASEP) is an independent project that is working to produce machine-readable texts of all Greek inscriptions. This data base will become part of the TLG data base.[201] IASEP is focusing on the Ionian inscriptions and on Greek and Latin inscriptions from the eastern part of the Roman Empire. Like the CCCGI Project, the IASEP began text entry by keying but converted to a Kurzweil scanner. The IASEP uses an Ibycus minicomputer.

---

201. The CCAT plans to include this material in their first CD-ROM; see below.

So far, the inscriptions from Miletus, Didyma, Teos, Teichioussa, Lepsia, Leros, Patmos, Colophon, Notion, Chios, Erythrai, and elsewhere have been converted to machine-readable form.

7.8.8 DHDB—Duke Humanities Data Base

- *BASIC DATA BASE INFORMATION*

Name of Project: Duke Humanities Data Base
Key Person(s): Peter B. Batke
Location of Project: Durham, North Carolina
Project Address: Duke University, German Dept., Durham, NC 27706
Telephone: (919) 684-3836
Date Project Began: 1982/1983
Date Project Completed: Not yet complete.
Sources of Funding: Presumably the same as for the COLOE Project (see below)
Scope: Not known
Size: Projected: not known; current: not known
Computer System: See below under COLOE
Available on Tape: Not known
Available on Diskettes: Not known
Output Options: Screen, tape, disk, print
Custom Searches: Not known
On-line Access Through Networks: Not known
Costs/Price: Not known
Key Bibliographical References: None
Other: None

The Duke Humanities Data Base (DHDB) is being created with assistance from IBM. The DHDB provides a number of MRTs—including the Gospels in Greek and primary material from church history—and is developing an interface between those MRTs and mainframe-based research tools such as ARRAS and OCP. (As we learned in chapter 2, ARRAS—Archive Retrieval and Analysis System—and the OCP—Oxford Concordance Program—are two of several text analysis systems designed especially for humanists.) Among other things, then, this project will allow humanists to use powerful mainframe tools to study machine-readable texts.

7.8.9 OUCS—Oxford University Computing Service

- *BASIC DATA BASE INFORMATION*

Name of Service: Oxford University Computing Service
Key Person(s): Susan M. Hockey, Lou Burnard
Location of Project: Oxford, England
Project Address: 13 Banbury Rd., Oxford OX2 6NN, United Kingdom
Telephones: (0865) 273238 (text archive), (0865) 273275 (OCP and LaserComp); from North America dial direct: 011-44-865-273238 (text archive), 011-44-865-273275 (OCP and LaserComp); electronic mail: OCP@VAX2.OXFORD.AC.UK
Date Project Began: 1976
Date Project Completed: Ongoing
Sources of Funding: Oxford University, the United Kingdom Computer Board
Scope: Ancient and modern texts in nearly three-dozen languages
Size: Hundreds of individual works are available on tape.
Computer System: VAX, ICL 2988
Available on Tape: Yes
Available on Diskettes: By special request
Output Options: Screen, tape, and print
Custom Searches: Not applicable

On-line Access Through Networks: Yes, the Text Archive Shortlist of data bank titles is on-line, texts may be up or downloaded on-line (order forms are required to download any text), and electronic mail sent and received. Networks include JANET, ARPANET, BITNET, USENET, CSNET, MAILNET, and others. If using JANET to send electronic mail to OUCS, use this address: ARCHIVE@U-K.AC.OX.VAX3. The ARPANET address is ARCHIVE%UK.AC.OX.VAX3@UCL-CS.ARPA

Costs/Price: Per tape: £15 for academic institutions within Europe, £25 for non-European academic institutions, £5 additional charge per tape, and £10 surcharge if payment is made in currencies other than sterling

Key Bibliographical References: None

Other: The Text Archive Shortlist and information about OUCS's Lasercomp, KDEM, and other services are available free of charge to interested parties from the address above.

The Oxford University Computing Service (OUCS) Text Archive began in 1976 in an effort to preserve, catalog, and make available in machine-readable form a variety of texts. The scope of the archive is global. Texts in languages as diverse as English, Arabic, Gallic, and Khotanese are included, as well as a broad range of authors. In the English section of the archive, for example, one can find everything from Milton's *Paradise Lost* and Melville's *Moby Dick* to Bob Dylan's *Tarantula* and John Le Carré's *The Spy Who Came in from the Cold*, not to mention works by Shakespeare, Shelly, Keats, Pound, and dozens of others. Many Greek texts are listed, including some TLG texts, as well as some Greek, Hebrew, and Aramaic biblical texts (see below). Additionally, many Classical and Medieval Latin texts are available in machine-readable form. All texts held at the Literary and Linguistic Computing Centre in Cambridge, England, are listed in the OUCS Text Archive catalog, which is available from the address above. This publication also contains a list of the names and addresses of other major text archives throughout the world. Texts prepared at Oxford are usually edited to a common standard that is compatible with the Oxford Concordance Program (see below). Eventually, the entire CATSS data base (see above) will be available from OUCS.

OUCS offers the following machine-readable partial or whole texts of the Hebrew Bible: (1) Job (Targum), (2) the Pentateuch (Morris/James), (3) Psalms (Targum), and (4) the complete Old Testament. The Targum of Job and the Targum of the Psalms are each under 512 kilobytes and both are available to parties who are not registered at Oxford. The Pentateuch, which is between 512 kilobytes and 1 megabyte, also is available to parties who are not registered at Oxford, as is the complete MRT of the Hebrew Bible, which is between 1 and 2 megabytes in size. These texts are available only on 600-foot tapes and are normally supplied in the following format: 9-track, 1,600-bpi, fixed-length records, EBCDIC, though some adjustment of these parameters can be made. A 600-foot tape, which holds between 5 and 15 megabytes (depending on the format), costs £15 for academic institutions within Great Britain and Europe and £25 for non-European academic institutions. Additionally, there is a £5 charge per text ordered and a £10 additional charge if payment is made in currencies other than sterling.

OUCS offers the following machine-readable partial or whole Septuagintal texts: (1) the CATSS morphologically analyzed LXX Pentateuch, (2) the TLG LXX, and (3) volumes 3 and 13 of the Cambridge LXX. The morphologically analyzed LXX Pentateuch, which is between 512 kilobytes and 1 megabyte in size, is available to parties who are not registered at Oxford. The TLG LXX, which is between 512 kilobytes and 1 megabyte in size, is available to parties not registered at Oxford only from its depositor, the TLG Project. This text is based on the ninth edition of Rahlfs text. Volumes 3 and 13 of the Cambridge LXX, which are between 1 and 2 megabytes in size, are restricted in their availability and may be obtained only with the explicit permission of their depositor, Oxford University.

OUCS offers a machine-readable version of the Greek New Testament and one of the Gospels. The New Testament text, which is between 2 and 5 megabytes in size, is available to persons not registered at Oxford only through that text's depositor, the TLG Project. This text is based on the second edition of the UBS text. The text of the Gospels, which is less than 512 kilobytes in size, is available to parties who are not registered at Oxford.

OUCS sells the Oxford Concordance Program (OCP) on a 600-foot, 9-track, 1,600-bpi, EBCDIC or ASCII tape for £100 (plus postage and packing fees). This general-purpose program, written in ANSI FORTRAN, is machine-independent and will run on mainframes manufactured by IBM, CDC, Digital, ICL, Univac, Burroughs, Honeywell, Prime, and others. The OCP makes word counts, concordances, and indices from texts in a wide variety of languages and alphabets. This flexible program can be used for morphological analysis, textual criticism, stylistic analysis, and to construct dictionaries. The OCP is able to output text in the following formats: (1) word list with frequency, (2) index with references, (3) concordance with context, references, and frequencies, and (4) statistics (cumulative vocabulary frequencies and type/token ratio). Version 2 of OCP, written in Fortran77, will be released in 1987. This complete rewrite of the program is much faster and supports the same features as the old version. A microcomputer version of the OCP for IBM PCs and compatibles with at least 512K and a hard drive is scheduled to be released in 1987/1988 from Oxford University Press.

Inquiries about the mainframe version of the OCP should be sent to the OUCS address above or via electronic mail % ISSUE@VAX2.OXFORD.AC.UK. Inquiries about the microcomputer version of the OCP should be sent to:

Oxford Electronic Publishing
Oxford University Press
Walton St.
Oxford OX2 6DP
United Kingdom
(0865)-56767; from North America: 011-44-865-56767.

OUCS also will scan printed or typed material on their KDEM (see above at the beginning of this chapter), and will typeset materials using a Monotype Lasercomp digital phototypesetter, which is able to handle nonroman character sets, such as cursive and block Hebrew characters, Greek, Cyrillic, Arabic, Syriac, Coptic, Urdu, Devanagari, Armenian, and others, using a wide variety of fonts. The typesetting system will accept scanned text or machine-readable text prepared with a word processor. Text created with word processors must be coded to be typeset. The LASERCHECK Users Manual, available from OUCS for £8 plus £2.50 postage, lists the typesetting codes and explains how to use them. (A program, LASERCHECK, translates those codes into the codes actually used by the Lasercomp machine.) Material may be output as camera-ready, phototypeset copy on RC paper or as proof-quality, laser-printed copy on plain paper. The Lasercomp system and OUCS's wide range of experience in using it to typeset nonroman and exotic character sets makes possible the low-cost publication of otherwise prohibitively expensive academic works. Upon approval, remote users may upload text to the phototypesetter via JANET (see above), or tapes may be mailed to OUCS. All local (Oxford) inquiries about this service should be addressed to OUCS % the Internal Lasercomp Advisor and all external ones to OUCS % the External Lasercomp Advisor.

7.8.10 CCAT—Center for Computer Analysis of Texts

● BASIC DATA BASE INFORMATION

Name of Service: Center for Computer Analysis of Texts
Key Person(s): John R. Abercrombie

Location of Project: Philadelphia, Pennsylvania
Project Address: University of Pennsylvania, P.O. Box 36 College Hall, Philadelphia, PA 19104-6303
Telephone: (215) 898-4917
Date Project Began: 1985
Date Project Completed: Ongoing
Sources of Funding: The David and Lucile Packard Foundation, IBM Advanced Education Project Grant
Scope: Various biblical and nonbiblical texts in a variety of languages and alphabets
Size: Not known
Computer System: IBM and Ibycus
Available on Tape: Yes
Available on Diskettes: Yes, including IBM PCs and compatible machines
Output Options: Screen, tape, disk, CD-ROM, or print
Custom Searches: As appropriate
On-line Access Through Networks: No
Costs/Price: Time and materials
Key Bibliographical References: CCAT's newsletter, "Online Notes," is available at no cost via BITNET.
Other: Abercrombie may be reached via BITNET at this address: JACKA@PENNDRLS

The University of Pennsylvania's Center for Computer Analysis of Texts (CCAT), which officially began in 1985 with Dr. John R. Abercrombie as coordinator, offers three basic services. (1) CCAT will scan printed or typed text on their KDEM (see above at the beginning of this chapter). (2) CCAT stores MRTs created at the University of Pennsylvania and elsewhere and makes these available at cost on standard 9-track, 1,600-bpi tapes. Some MRTs (e.g., those from the CATSS project) will be available on floppy disks for IBM PCs and other microcomputers. MRTs include texts in Coptic, Greek, Hebrew, Yiddish, Spanish, French, and other languages. Eventually, CCAT will make the entire CATSS data base of MRTs available when that project is complete (see above); OUCS will also distribute the CATSS material. (3) John R. Abercrombie, CCAT's director, has developed a set of programs geared to the needs of scholars working with nonroman alphabets, and these programs are available at cost from CCAT. The programs include (A) the Graphics Toolbox for Languages (GTL—reviewed in chapter 2), a set of word processing routines (written in Turbo Pascal) for displaying, editing, and printing Arabic, Cyrillic, Devanagari, Greek, Coptic, Hebrew (pointed and unpointed), and European characters, and international phonetics (see below), including transcription schema for hieroglyphics, Sumerian, and Akkadian; (B) IBYTALK, a program for transferring files between Ibycus and IBM-PC computers; (C) IBYSPELL, an Ibycus-compatible spelling checker for texts in various languages, including scanned texts; and (D) TEXTCLEAN, an interactive editing program for text input by KDEM or keyboard. Additionally, CCAT is committed to producing a series of CD-ROMs containing public domain texts and related materials. Furthermore, CCAT is participating in the development at the University of Pennsylvania of The Language Analysis Project (computer-assisted text linguistics research) and a Proficiency-Based Arabic Syllabus that uses CAI techniques.

CCAT offers downloadable fonts for the LaserJet at cost ($100 per individual copy, $200 for University License). These fonts include Greek, Hebrew, Coptic, Phoenician, Armenian, Cyrillic, and international phonetics. The price includes the fonts, a font editor, and a program for downloading the fonts to LaserJets.

Presently, CCAT offers the following biblical materials on 5.25-inch, MS-DOS diskettes:

Hebrew Bible, Michigan-Claremont, full BHS text (10
    disks)—$45
Greek Jewish Scriptures (LXX), TLG Rahlfs edition (15
    disks)—$55
Greek New Testament, TKG UBS2 edition (4 disks)—$33
Hebrew Bible + Septuagint + Greek New Testament—$107
Hebrew Bible + Septuagint—$94
Septuagint + Greek New Testament—$69
Revised Standard Version with Apocrypha (18 disks)—$67
King James Version (18 disks)—$67
Update cost per disk—$2.

And CCAT offers the following biblical materials on 2,400-foot, 9-track, 1,600-bpi tape @ $40 per tape.

Hebrew Bible
Revised Standard Version
King James Version
CATSS Morphological Analysis of Septuagint
CATSS Aligned Hebrew and Greek Biblical Texts
CATSS Septuagint with Variants
Septuagint and Greek New Testament.

The first CATSS CD-ROM is expected to contain (1) Biblical (and related) texts and tools, (2) Greek materials not in the TLG literary corpus, and texts in (3) Latin, (4) Coptic, (5) Arabic, (6) Sanskrit, (7) Old English, (8) Modern English, (9) French, (10) Danish, and (11) Italian. Biblical materials will include the Masoretic text (Michigan-Claremont), Septuagint, Greek New Testament (UBS2), Tagged Greek New Testament (UBS3), Latin Vulgate, and more. Greek materials will include the Documentary Papyri from the Duke Documentary Papyri Project (DDBDP—see above), the Oxyrhynchos Papyri, Inscriptions from the Cornell Center for the Computerization of Greek Inscriptions project (CCCGI—see above) and from Princeton's Institute for Advanced Study Epigraphic Project (IASEP—see above), and more. Coptic materials will consist of the E. J. Brill edition of the Nag Hammadi library (encoded at Claremont). A complete (proposed) table of contents for the CD-ROM is available from CATSS at the address above.

CCAT's newsletter, ONLINE NOTES, is available at no cost via BITNET. Contact CATSS for further information.

7.8.11 Linguists' Software

- *BASIC PRODUCT INFORMATION*

Name of Company: Linguists' Software
Key Person(s): Philip B. Payne
Address: 106R Highland St., South Hamilton, MA 01982
Telephone: (617) 468-3037
Products: SuperGreek New Testament, SuperGreek Old Testament, MacHebrew Old Testament
Price: $99.95 each
Computers Supported: Macintosh
Printers Supported: LaserWriter, LaserWriter Plus, ImageWriter
Word Processing Programs Supported: MacWrite™ 1.05, Microsoft® Word 3.0
Number of Disks: SuperGreek New Testament: three 400-K disks; SuperGreek Old Testament: nine 800-K disks; MacHebrew Old Testament: number of disks not known.
Related Products: TLG > SuperGreek Converter and Text Editor: $79.95. This utility converts TLG codes into Macintosh-compatible codes and formats the text for reading. Includes the text editor Edit and a transfer window for transferring text to Microsoft Word. A separate program, SuperGreek ($79.95) or LaserGreek ($99.95) is required to display TLG texts on-screen in Greek.
Warranty: Not known

Linguists' Software is neither a data base nor a text archive but a company that markets a multitude of excellent nonroman fonts (see chapter 2) and machine-readable versions of the UBS3 Greek New Testament, Rahlfs Septuagint, and the BHS Old Testament for Macintoshes. The three MRTs include all accents and diacritical marks. The UBS Greek New Testament is licensed from the United Bible Societies, the Rahlfs edition of the Septuagint is licensed from Deutsche Bibelgesellschaft, and the BHS Old Testament is derived from the Michigan-Claremont/CATSS version of BHS and is "Deutsche Bibelgesellschaft authorized."

Another company, Seek and Find, offers The MacGreek New Testament (using Linguists' Software's SuperGreek font) for Macintoshes. Contact:

> Noel McRae
> Seek and Find
> 2857 Rose Valley Loop
> Kelso, WA 98626
> (206) 425-6495
> $50 (two 800-K disks)

7.8.12 RIMRTH—Rutgers Inventory of MRTs

- *BASIC DATA BASE INFORMATION*

Name of Project: Rutgers Inventory of Machine-Readable Texts in the Humanities
Key Person(s): Marianne I. Gaunt
Location of Project: New Brunswick, New Jersey
Project Address: Rutgers University Libraries, Alexander Library, New Brunswick, NJ 08903
Telephone: (201) 932-7505
Date Project Began: 1982
Date Project Completed: Not yet complete.
Sources of Funding: Council on Library Resources, the Andrew W. Mellon Foundation
Scope: All humanistic texts in machine-readable form
Size: Projected: not known; current: approximately 400 records now on-line
Computer System: AMDAHL (RLIN's computer at Stanford)
Available on Tape: Not known
Available on Diskettes: Not known
Output Options: Screen or print
Custom Searches: Not known
On-line Access Through Networks: Yes, through RLIN (Research Libraries Information Network)
Costs/Price: On-line costs only
Key Bibliographical References: Marianne I. Gaunt, "Rutgers Inventory of Machine-Readable Texts in the Humanities," in Robert F. Allen, ed., *Data Bases in the Humanities*, 283–90.
Other: Data base to be available on microfiche.

The Rutgers Inventory of Machine-Readable Texts in the Humanities Project (RIMRTH), which began in 1982 under the directorship of Ms. Marianne I. Gaunt, is to be a worldwide inventory of all machine-readable texts in the humanities. Texts being cataloged come from the fields of religion, literature, language, music, history, art, and philosophy. Information about each text is stored in a data base (using the MARC-MRDF format) and made available on-line through the RLIN network. That information will include various facts from the following types of categories.

> Contact person
> Bibliographical information about the text on which the MRT
> is based
> Bibliographical information about the MRT Formats in which
> the MRT is available
> Codes, tags, and other documentary facts about the MRT
> Hardware and software compatibility

The data base format will make it possible to locate MRTs by author name, compiler name, subject word, subject phrase, title word, title phrase, genre, and so forth. The RLIN data bases support searching by Boolean operators, truncation, and searching across fields. Institutions and individuals that do not have access to libraries that are members of the Research Libraries Group (RLG) may establish dial-up RLIN accounts by contacting RLG at the following address.

> The Research Libraries Group, Inc.
> Jordan Quadrangle
> Stanford, CA 94305
> (415) 328-0920

Alternatively, readers may go through Rutgers University Library or use a microfiche equivalent of the RIMRTH data base.

7.8.13 Stellenbosch Data Base

- *BASIC DATA BASE INFORMATION*

Name of Project: Stellenbosch Data Base
Key Person(s): Walter T. Claassen
Location of Project: Stellenbosch, South Africa
Project Address: Department of Semitic Languages, University of Stellenbosch, Stellenbosch 7600, Republic of South Africa
Telephones: 77511 (University), 73156 (Semitic Languages); from North America dial direct: 011-27-2231-77511 or 73156
Date Project Began: Not known
Date Project Completed: Not yet complete.
Sources of Funding: Not known
Scope: All relevant articles and books in the fields of Ancient Near Eastern and Old Testament studies
Size: Not known
Computer System: Microcomputer, specific type not known
Available on Tape: No
Available on Diskettes: Yes
Output Options: Screen, diskette, print
Custom Searches: Not known
On-line Access Through Networks: No
Costs/Price: Not known
Key Bibliographical References: Walter T. Claassen, "Spectrum of Data Base Needs in Ancient Near Eastern and Old Testament Studies," in Robert F. Allen, ed., *Data Bases in the Humanities*, 145–49; "A Research Unit for Computer Applications to the Language and Text of the Old Testament," *Journal of Northwest Semitic Languages* 13 (1987): 11–21; "Data Base Structured for an Interactive Microcomputer System for the Study of Biblical Hebrew," *Bible and Computer : The Text*, 143–54.
Other: Claassen and the Department of Semitic Languages also are experimenting with microcomputer-based CALL Hebrew courses.

Dr. Walter T. Claassen and the Department of Semitic Languages at the University of Stellenbosch are working on a bibliographical data base for Ancient Near Eastern and Old Testament studies. A single record structure and two data types (bibliographical and object-related) will be used. *Object-related data types* refers to references in the data base to pictures, illustrations, and related "objects." Each data type will be accessed from a single thesaurus.

7.8.14 The Leiden Armenian Database

● *BASIC DATA BASE INFORMATION*

Name of Project: The Leiden Armenian Database
Key Person(s): M. E. Stone and J. J. S. Weitenberg
Location of Project: Leiden and Jerusalem
Project Address: % Dr. Stone, P.O. Box 16174, Jerusalem 91161, Israel
Telephone: Not known
Date Project Began: 1983
Date Project Completed: Not yet complete.
Sources of Funding: Leiden University, Netherlands Organization of Pure and Associated Research Applications Programs
Scope: "A large data base" of Classical Armenian texts
Size: Not known
Computer Systems: IBM mainframe, IBM PCs, Apple IIs
Available on Tape: Yes
Available on Diskettes: No
Output Options: Screen, tape, and print
Custom Searches: Yes
On-line Access Through Networks: No
Costs/Price: Not known
Key Bibliographical References: M. E. Stone, "Computer Implementation of Armenian," *Bible and Computer : The Text*, 323–34.
Other: None

Together with Dr. J. J. S. Weitenberg (Department of Comparative Linguistics, University of Leiden, Leiden, The Netherlands; telephone: (2) 412906), Dr. M. E. Stone has been using a KDEM to create a data base of machine-readable Classical Armenian biblical and nonbiblical texts. To date, Deuteronomy, 4 Ezra, the Works of Ephraem Syrus, and other materials have been included. Seven- and 8-bit coding systems for Armenian have been developed for use on IBM mainframes, as have logical keyboards and other software.

The data base is kept in Leiden. System analysis and hardware development for Apple IIs and IBM PCs is done under Dr. Stone in Jerusalem.

7.8.15 BIBP—Patristic Bibliographical Information

● *BASIC DATA BASE INFORMATION*

Name of Project: Bibliographical Information Bank in Patristics
Key Person(s): R.-Michel Roberge
Location of Project: Québec, Canada
Project Address: Université Laval, Cité Universitaire, Québec G1K 7P4, Québec, Canada
Telephones: (418) 656-5828, (418) 656-3576, (418) 656-3616
Date Project Began: 1975
Date Project Completed: Not yet complete.
Sources of Funding: Université Laval
Scope: All relevant articles and books in the field of Patristics
Size: 15,000 documents from 250 journals
Computer System: IBM 4381
Available on Tape: Not known
Available on Diskettes: Yes
Output Options: Screen and print
Custom Searches: Not known
On-line Access Through Networks: Planned
Costs/Price: Not known
Key Bibliographical References: R.-Michel Roberge and Gilles Deschatelets, "Bibliographic Information Bank in Patristics—BIBP," in Robert F. Allen, ed., *Data Bases in the Humanities*, 254–57.

Other: None

The Bibliographical Information Bank in Patristics (BIBP) plans to create a data bank that catalogs all relevant articles and books in the field of Patristics, including literature from the following fifteen subdisciplines, as that literature bears on the interests of the Patristic researcher: (1) archaeology, (2) iconography, (3) epigraphy, (4) papyrology, (5) codicology, (6) the history of Christianity, (7) the history of theology, (8) the history of the councils, (9) the history of liturgy, (10) the history of spirituality, (11) the history of monasticism, (12) the history of biblical exegesis, (13) hagiography, (14) philology, and (15) the history of philosophy. Each document will be indexed under one or more of those categories, thus making it possible to search the data base by category. By using carefully defined and empirically based sets of primary and secondary descriptors (indexing terms), the data base creators hope to make it possible to study the development of scholarly interest in specific topics. Because of the large number of very specific descriptors, it is not unusual for a thirty-page article to be tagged with as many as fifteen different descriptors. The thesaurus (the normalized list of descriptors) that is being developed will greatly facilitate searching the data base.

The data base creators plan to make the BIBP available on-line through a commercial vendor, when the data base is complete.

7.8.16 CDMB—Manuscrits de la Bible

- *BASIC DATA BASE INFORMATION*

Name of Project: Centre de Documentation sur les Manuscrits de la Bible
Key Person(s): Christian Amphoux
Location of Project: Montpellier, France
Project Address: 13, Rue Louis Perrier, 34000 Montpellier, France
Telephones: (67) 927-990; from North America dial direct: 011-33-67-927-990
Date Project Began: 1984
Date Project Completed: Not yet complete.
Sources of Funding: CNRS
Scope: Various texts and translations of the New Testament, in a dozen languages, dating from the second to the sixteenth century
Size: Projected: 30,000 texts; current: not known
Computer System: Not known
Available on Tape: Not known
Available on Diskettes: Not known
Output Options: Screen and print
Custom Searches: Not known
On-line Access Through Networks: Not known
Costs/Price: Not known
Key Bibliographical References: None
Other: None

The Centre de Documentation sur les Manuscrits de la Bible (CDMB), which operates under the auspices of the Centre National de la Recherche Scientifique (CNRS), is located in the Centre Universitaire Protestant de Montpellier and is under the direction of Mr. Christian Amphoux. The CDMB's primary task is to create a data base of various New Testament manuscripts—texts and translations—written in a dozen different languages, from the second to the sixteenth centuries (and some more recently). When complete, the researchers at the CDMB estimate that the data base will contain 30,000 texts in a dozen languages.

Initially, the CDMB data base will not contain the full texts of the manuscripts but only information about those texts. Later, the full text of the manuscripts will be made available in machine-readable form. The data base is to include information about (and eventually the full text of) Greek, Syriac, Coptic, Aramaic, Georgian, Ethiopic, Syro-Palestinian, and Arabic biblical texts and translations. The ultimate goal of the CDMB is the creation of a "grand" critical edition of the New Testament. The CDMB is using the data base of the Institut de Recherche et d'Histoire des Textes (IRHT—see below) to create its data base.

7.8.17 IRHT—Recherche et d'Histoire des Textes

- *BASIC DATA BASE INFORMATION*

Name of Project: Institut de Recherche et d'Histoire des Textes
Key Person(s): Christine Pellistrandi
Location of Project: Paris
Project Address: 40, avenue d'Iéna, 75116, Paris, France
Telephones: (1) 47-236-104; from North America dial direct: 011-33-14-723-6104
Date Project Began: 1975
Date Project Completed: Not yet complete.
Sources of Funding: CNRS
Scope: Medieval manuscripts in various languages, dating from the eighth to the fifteenth century, the majority of which consist of biblical and theological texts
Size: Over 50,000 microfilms, not all of which are theological in nature
Computer System: IBM 3270
Available on Tape: No
Available on Diskettes: No
Output Options: Screen and print
Custom Searches: Not known, but presumably so
On-line Access Through Networks: Yes, any international network (e.g., BITNET, TYMNET, DataPac, Euronet, Transpac)
Costs/Price: Not known
Key Bibliographical References: Marie-Josèphe Baud, Agnès Guillaumoint, and Jean-Luc Minel, "A Medieval Manuscript Database," in Robert F. Allen, ed., *Data Bases in the Humanities*, 22–29.
Other: None

The Institut de Recherche et d'Histoire des Textes (IRHT), which was created in 1937 and which operates under the auspices of the CNRS (Centre National de la Recherche Scientifique), is located in Paris and employs over a hundred people in fourteen different sections, one of which is the "section d'informatique." Within that section, Christine Pellistrandi is one of the key persons who works with biblical and theological texts. The IRHT's primary task is to create a microfilm library of medieval manuscripts that date from the eighth to the fifteenth century. Texts and translations in Latin, Medieval French, Arabic, Greek, and Hebrew are part of the IRHT's collection of approximately 50,000 microfilms,[202] the majority of which are biblical texts or theological works.

Although the texts are on microfilm, the IRHT workers have created a data base (known as MEDIUM) that lists and describes the various microfilms, so that locating the texts is automated. Texts may be located by number, author, translator, commentators, title, words in the title, and by general or specific nomenclature about the work in question. This interactive, multiuser data base can be accessed through any of the main international telecommunication networks (see above). Once on-line with the data base, users interact with MEDIUM through a series of menus.

---

202. Each microfilm represents one manuscript, but a medieval manuscript may contain several texts.

7.8.18 Greek and Latin MRTs

- *BASIC DATA BASE INFORMATION*

Name of Project: APA Repository of Greek and Latin Texts in Machine-Readable Form
Key Person(s): Stephen V. F. Waite
Location of Project: Hanover, New Hampshire
Project Address: LOGOI Systems, 27 School St., Hanover, NH 03755
Telephone: (603) 643-3065
Date Project Began: July 1969
Date Project Completed: Not yet complete.
Sources of Funding: None
Scope: Selected Greek and Latin authors
Size: Over 100 Greek and Latin works from approximately 50 authors
Computer System: Ibycus
Available on Tape: Yes, 9-track, 1,600-bpi, no labels, no block or record headers, fixed-length blocks of 4,000 characters, fixed-length logical records of 80 characters, ASCII or EBCDIC; tapes may also be formatted in other ways if appropriate information is supplied.
Available on Diskettes: Not known
Output Options: Screen, tape, and print
Custom Searches: No
On-line Access Through Networks: No
Costs/Price: Materials and a copying fee of $0.00075 per line of text as it is stored in the computer
Key Bibliographical References: None
Other: None

The MRTs in the American Philological Association's Repository of Greek and Latin Texts in Machine-Readable Form formerly were part of Dartmouth's Project LIBRI (Literary Information Bases for Research and Instruction), which came to an end when Dr. Waite left Dartmouth College. These texts have been available from Dr. Waite at the address above. According to Dr. Waite, the corpus is now in a state of transition to a new location and probably to another computer system. For more information, contact Dr. Waite, or contact:

> The American Philological Association
> 617 Hamilton Hall
> Columbia University
> New York, NY 10027
> (212) 280-4051.

According to a 1985 issue of the APA *Newsletter*, Dr. Joseph Solodow, supported by a grant from the David and Lucile Packard Foundation, has been appointed (from July 1, 1985) Visiting Research Scholar at Yale University for the purpose of producing a Canon of Latin texts that will serve as the basis for a Latin Data Bank that would be similar to the TLG Project's data bank. See Joseph B. Solodow, "The Canon of Texts for a Latin Data Bank," in Bernard Frischer, ed. *Papers of the UCLA Conference on Classics and Computing* (Los Angeles, July 19–20, 1986) = *Favonius Supp. Vol.* 1 (1987): 25–24. For more information contact:

> Dr. Joseph Solodow
> Classics Department
> Yale University
> Box 1967 Yale Station
> New Haven, CT 06520
> (203) 432-0987.

593

Classicists also may find Roger S. Bagnall, ed., *Research Tools for the Classics* (Chico, Calif.: Scholars Press, 1980) to be a helpful (though somewhat dated) overview of how (some) classicists hope and plan to use computers as research tools.

7.8.19 RIM—Royal Inscriptions of Mesopotamia

• *BASIC DATA BASE INFORMATION*

Name of Project: Royal Inscriptions of Mesopotamia Project
Key Person(s): A. Kirk Grayson, Director, R. F. G. Sweet, Editor-in-Chief, and others
Location of Project: Toronto, Ontario
Project Address: Dept. of Near Eastern Studies, University of Toronto, Toronto, Ontario, Canada
Telephone: Not known
Date Project Began: 1983 (?)
Date Project Completed: Not yet complete. Anticipated date of completion is 2001.
Sources of Funding: Social Sciences and Humanities Research Council of Canada, the University of Toronto
Scope: All the Sumerian and Akkadian inscriptions of the ancient kings of Mesopotamia from the 3ed millennium B.C. to the late first millennium B.C.
Size: In published form, the inscriptions will fill twenty volumes.
Computer System: Sperry ITs
Available on Tape: Not known
Available on Diskettes: Not known
Output Options: Not known
Custom Searches: Not known
On-line Access Through Networks: No
Costs/Price: Not known
Key Bibliographical References: L. D. Levine, "The Royal Inscriptions of Mesopotamia and the Computer," *Annual Review of the RIM Project* 1 (1983): 19–20.
Other: None

The Royal Inscriptions of Mesopotamia Project (RIM) is creating a data base of all the Sumerian and Akkadian inscriptions of the ancient kings of Mesopotamia (Sumer, Babylonia, and Assyria) from the 3ed millennium B.C. to the late first millennium B.C. This information will be edited and published in twenty volumes through the University of Toronto Press.

7.8.20 CNA—Neo-Assyrian Text Corpus

• *BASIC DATA BASE INFORMATION*

Name of Project: Neo-Assyrian Text Corpus Project
Key Person(s): Simo Parpola, Director
Location of Project: Helsinki, Finland
Project Address: CNA Project, Dept. of Asian and African Studies, Fabianinkatu 24 A 226, SF-00100 Helsinki, Finland
Telephone: Not known
Date Project Began: January 1986
Date Project Completed: Not yet complete. Anticipated date of completion is 1991.
Sources of Funding: The Academy of Finland, Deutsche Orient-Gesellschaft, the Consiglio Nationale delle Ricerche, the Olivetti Corporation
Scope: The entire Neo-Assyrian text material, including the royal archives of Nineveh.
Size: Not known
Computer System: Not known
Available on Tape: Not known
Available on Diskettes: Not known
Output Options: Not known
Custom Searches: Not known

On-line Access Through Networks: No
Costs/Price: Not known
Key Bibliographical References: Simo Parpola, "The Neo-Assyrian Text Corpus Project of the University of Helsinki," *Akkadica* 49 (September/October 1986): 20–23.
Other: None

The Neo-Assyrian Text Corpus Project (CNA—Corpus Neo-Assyrian) is creating a data base of all Neo-Assyrian texts, including the royal archives of Nineveh. This material will be published in printed form by the Helsinki University Press as a series of text editions entitled *State Archives of Assyria* (SAA), a periodical entitled the *State Archives of Assyria Bulletin* (SAAB), and a monograph series entitled *Corpus of Neo-Assyrian Studies* (CNAS).

7.8.21 CAM—Mesopotamian Materials

- *BASIC DATA BASE INFORMATION*

Name of Project: Computer-Aided Analysis of Mesopotamian Materials
Key Person(s): Giorgio Buccellati, Editor *Cybernetica Mesopotamica*
Location of Project: No central location
Project Address: % Undena Publications, P.O. Box 97, Malibu, CA 90265
Telephone: (818) 366-1744
Date Project Began: 1967/1968
Date Project Completed: Not yet complete.
Sources of Funding: Not known
Scope: This is a diversified project; see below.
Size: Not applicable
Computer System: Various
Available on Tape: Not known
Available on Diskettes: Some material is.
Output Options: Not known
Custom Searches: Not known
On-line Access Through Networks: No
Costs/Price: Not known
Key Bibliographical References: Giorgio Buccellati, "The Old Babylonian Linguistic Analysis Project," in A. Zampolli and N. Calzolari, eds., *Computational and Mathematical Linguistics*, 383–404; Olivier Rouault, "Elements pour un logiciel assyriologique," *CARNES* 1 (June 1984): 1–81.
Other: None

The Computer-Aided Analysis of Mesopotamian Materials (CAM) is a generic title for a collection of computer-assisted research projects and data bases related by their common interest in Mesopotamian studies. Various scholars are involved in different projects. The range of interests represented by CAM includes computer-assisted archaeology, Middle Assyrian Laws, Akkadian cuneiform texts from Babylon and Mari, Ebla and Ugarit, Assur, Nuzi, and other sites, morphological analysis of Akkadian, and other topics. CAM is the official channel for creating machine-readable versions of the Ebla materials (see above under "Sumerian Dictionary"). A data base of Middle Assyrian materials has been created.

Some material (for example, the Terqa data bases, the Middle Assyrian Laws) is available in an ASCII-coded form on 5.25-inch diskettes for IBM PCs. Contact Undena Publications for more information.

7.8.22 LIMC—Index of Classical Iconography

● *BASIC DATA BASE INFORMATION*

Name of Project: Computer Index of Classical Iconography
Key Person(s): Jocelyn Penny Small, Director
Location of Project: New Brunswick, New Jersey
Project Address: U.S. Center Lexicon Iconographicum Mythologiae Classicae, Rutgers University, New Brunswick, NJ 08903
Telephone: (201) 932-7404
Date Project Began: Not known
Date Project Completed: Not yet complete.
Sources of Funding: The Research Tools Division of the National Endowment for the Humanities of the United States of America
Scope: All classical iconography from 800 B.C. to A.D. 400
Size: Not known
Computer System: IBM PC-ATs
Available on Tape: Not known
Available on Diskettes: Not known
Output Options: Not known
Custom Searches: Not known
On-line Access Through Networks: No
Costs/Price: Not known
Key Bibliographical References: Jocelyn Penny Small, "Computer Index of Classical Iconography," 1–10 (unpublished).
Other: None

The Lexicon Iconographicum Mythologiae Classicae (LIMC) project, which involves scholars from thirty-five countries, is creating a pictorial dictionary of classical iconography. The U.S. Center is creating a machine-readable data base from 7,500 cards and photographs, which will serve as the raw material for the project. Three volumes of a projected eight have been published. The project's central headquarters is in Basel, Switzerland.

7.8.23 Project Rhetor

● *BASIC DATA BASE INFORMATION*

Name of Project: Project Rhetor
Key Person(s): James J. Murphy, Director, Kevin P. Roddy, Staff Research Associate
Location of Project: Davis, California
Project Address: Rhetoric Dept., University of California at Davis, Davis, CA 95616
Telephones: (916) 752-0813 (Murphy), (916) 752-8241 (Roddy)
Date Project Began: 1975
Date Project Completed: Not yet complete.
Sources of Funding: The Research Tools Division of the National Endowment for the Humanities of the United States of America
Scope: All rhetorical works from the fifth century B.C. to A.D. 1914, approximately 5,000 authors and 15,000–18,000 works in twelve languages
Size: Current: 1 megabyte; projected: 12 megabytes
Computer System: PDP 11/70, VAX 11/750
Available on Tape: Yes, 9-track, 1,600-bpi, ASCII
Available on Diskettes: No
Output Options: Tape and print
Custom Searches: Not known
On-line Access Through Networks: No
Costs/Price: Not known

Key Bibliographical References: Kevin P. Roddy, "Project Rhetor: An Encyclopedia in the History of Rhetoric," in Sara K. Burton and Douglas D. Short, eds., *Sixth International Conference on Computers and the Humanities*, 579–87; Ann Gunion, "A Computer-Aided Dictionary of Classical Rhetoricians and Works of Rhetoric," in Bernard Frischer, ed. *Papers of the UCLA Conference on Classics and Computing* (Los Angeles, July 19–20, 1986) = *Favonius Supp. Vol.* 1 (1987): 99–100.
Other: None

Project Rhetor, which is now largely inactive pending further funding, hopes to create a data base of annotated bibliographical information about all rhetorical works from the fifth century B.C. to A.D. 1914—approximately 5,000 authors and 15,000–18,000 works in twelve languages—to serve as the basis for a comprehensive history of rhetoric. The data base will include an encyclopedia-type entry for each rhetorician and his works. Approximately 1 megabyte of data has been entered to date.

7.9 Related Projects

In this section we will examine several large-scale, university-centered projects whose goals, broadly speaking, are to integrate the use of computers into research and teaching in the humanities. Of the many universities and colleges that have begun projects to encourage the use of computer-assisted research and teaching in the humanities,[203] I have chosen several that in one way or another are developing tools for multilingual word processing and for studying biblical and classical texts.

We have already discussed the University of Pennsylvania's CCAT Project, which is developing a set of tools for CALL, computer-assisted textual analysis, and multilingual word processing, and which will scan texts and store and disseminate them in machine-readable form. CCAT supports the IBM range of microcomputers and much of their programming is done in Turbo Pascal.

7.9.1 COLOE

- *BASIC PROJECT INFORMATION*

Name of Project: COLOE—Computerization of Language Oriented Enterprises
Key Person(s): Frank L. Borchardt, Peter B. Batke, Jeffrey William Gillette
Location of Project: Durham, North Carolina
Project Address: Duke University, German Dept., Durham, NC 27706
Telephone: (919) 684-3886 (all three men)
Date Project Began: 1982/1983
Date Project Completed: Not yet complete.
Sources of Funding: Duke Endowment Fund, Trent Foundation, IBM
Scope: Multilingual CALL-authoring software, multilingual word processing software, KDEM scanning, Humanities Data Base of MRTs
Computers Supported: IBM PCs, Ibycus
Programming Language(s): Not known
Programs Available: Duke Language Toolkit, MicroCALIS, DUKEFONT
Available on Tape: No
Available on Diskettes: Yes
Costs/Price: Free if user provides two formatted disks and stamped, self-addressed disk mailer.
Key Bibliographical References: *Perspectives in Computing* 5 (1985): 49.
Other: Duke Language Toolkit requires IBM Enhanced Graphics Adapter (EGA).

---

203. See the beginning of chapter 4, where I mention several institutions that are "computerizing" their educational programs in various ways.

The name of this project, Computerization of Language Oriented Enterprises (COLOE), accurately summarizes its scope and goals: to "computerize" learning and teaching a broad spectrum of foreign languages, to develop a multilingual word processing system, to use a KDEM to enter text into machine-readable form, and to establish a data base for texts in machine-readable form. We have already discussed Duke's Humanities Data Base (see above in this chapter), and in chapter 2 we discussed MicroCALIS, its language-authoring system, the Duke Language Toolkit (DLT), and FED, the DLT's font program. COLOE supports IBM PCs. The Duke Language Toolkit requires IBM's Enhanced Graphics Adapter.

7.9.2 HCCP—Harvard Classics Computer Project

- *BASIC PROJECT INFORMATION*

Name of Project: Harvard Classics Computer Project
Key Person(s): Gregory Crane
Location of Project: Cambridge, Massachusetts
Project Address: Classics Dept., Boylston Hall 319, Harvard University, Cambridge, MA 02138
Telephones: (617) 495-1926 (Crane), (617) 495-4027 (Classics)
Date Project Began: 1983
Date Project Completed: Ongoing
Sources of Funding: Harvard University, IBM, and other sources
Scope: No narrowly defined goals
Computers Supported: Macintosh, VAX 11/780
Programming Language(s): C
Programs Available: Several are being developed in cooperation with other institutions; see below.
Available on Tape: Not known
Available on Diskettes: Not yet
Costs/Price: Not known
Key Bibliographical References: Gregory Crane, "Clay Balls and Compact Disks: Some Political and Economic Problems of the New Storage Media," in Bernard Frischer, ed. *Papers of the UCLA Conference on Classics and Computing* (Los Angeles, July 19–20, 1986) = *Favonius Supp. Vol.* 1 (1987): 1–6.
Other: The APA *Macintosh Users' Group News* 1985 (available from J. S. Rusten at the Boylston Hall address above for $2) contains some information about the use of Macintoshes at Harvard.

Unlike the CCAT and COLOE projects, which support IBM PCs, the Harvard Classics Computer Project (HCCP) supports only Macintosh microcomputers. That commitment reflects Harvard's broader, campus-wide commitment to the Macintosh.[204] The main goals of the HCCP are to support (1) multi-lingual word processing and (2) using the TLG data base. The HCCP has adapted Macintoshes to serve as remote terminals for manipulating the TLG data base, which is run under UNIX on a VAX 11/780 that is owned by Harvard's Division of Applied Sciences. Indexing and searching programs have been developed. Using a special version of Macterminal (a Macintosh communications package) that has been endowed with Greek fonts from SMK GreekKeys (see chapter 2), users are able to display the results of TLG searches in fully accented Greek, download the results to disk, and manipulate them with a word processor. Formatted text can be printed in Greek and English on Apple LaserWriters using Kadmos®, a complete Classical Greek PostScript® font (see chapter 2), or on a Mergenthaler typesetter that also supports PostScript, if genuine camera-ready copy is desired. When appropriate CD-ROM readers and Apple UNIX (A/UX) are available,

---

204. Many of the faculty at Harvard use Macintoshes at home and as remote terminals to the University Network. Several thousand Macintoshes have been sold to students and faculty. Over forty Macintoshes (which are networked into the campus system) are available in the Science Center for student use. Specialized Macintosh courseware has been developed for a broad spectrum of courses. All microcomputer support available to students is geared toward the Macintosh.

and when the TLG Project finalizes the format of its "production-version" CD-ROM, the HCCP will make the TLG data base available on a CD-ROM and adapt its UNIX-based search programs to run Macintoshes.

The HCCP is involved in several cooperative projects with other institutions. (1) The HCCP is working with Professor George Walsh at the University of Chicago to develop bibliographical data base software for classical literature. This program will run under UNIX on mainframe and minicomputers and under other operating systems on microcomputers like the Macintosh.

(2) With IBM funding, the HCCP has undertaken a joint project with Brown University's Institute for Research in Information and Scholarship to explore the potential of CD-ROM technology by creating a compact disk that will be used to test software recently developed at MIT's Media Lab (see below under Isocrates).

(3) Harvard, UCLA, and the University of California at Berkeley are jointly involved in creating programs (collectively referred to as the Berkeley Morphology Package—BMP) that will generate and parse fully accented Greek noun and verb forms, check Greek spelling, allow users to create their own personal lexicons, and permit the TLG data base to be searched by lemmata. Because it can generate all Greek noun and verb forms, the BMP is a valuable research tool for searching the TLG data base.

(4) Dr. Crane of the HCCP and Dr. V. Judson Harward of Boston University's Remote Sensing Lab have joined forces in an enterprise known as the Perseus Project to convert important Greek texts that are not in machine-readable form into machine-readable form, along with their English translations. The Perseus data base will contain these texts, as well as various types of graphics images, such as digitized landsat images, maps, and renditions of archaeological artifacts. The Perseus data base is to be made available on CD-ROMs that may be used with 68020 Macintoshes and Guide, the hypertext program mentioned in chapter 2 (see below).

(5) Using an equipment grant from the Xerox Corporation, the HCCP is working with the Computer Science Department and the Medical School to develop a windowing, cross-referencing, multi-path text environment with a menu-driven, mouse-operated interface that links multiple documents and allows users to "jump" from link to link and display linked passages simultaneously—an environment referred to by Brown University's IRIS center as *hypertext*.[205] Someone reading a Greek text, for example, could use a pull-down menu to open a window that displayed lexical information about a particular word, open another window that displayed an on-line concordance, open a third window to see the text's critical apparatus, open a fourth window to see a translation, and so on. The Harvard Medical School already has a prototype of such a hypertext environment running on Macintoshes.

For more information about hypertext, see the articles in the preceding footnote or contact IRIS at the address below.

Owl International (mentioned in chapter 2), markets Guide, a hypertext program for Macintoshes and IBMs. For more information contact:

Owl International
14218 NE 21st St.
Bellevue, WA 98007
(206) 747-3203.

---

205. For more information about hypertext, see Waldrop, "Personal Computers on Campus," 438–44; Bunnell, "Hypervisons," 21–30; Young, "Hypermedia"; Shipp et al., "Networks of Scholar's Workstations in a University Community," 1–15; and Yankelovich et al., "Reading and Writing the Electronic Book," 15–30.

7.9.3 Isocrates Project

- *BASIC DATA BASE INFORMATION*

Name of Project: Isocrates Project
Key Person(s): Paul Kahn
Location of Project: Brown University
Project Address: Institute for Research in Information Scholarship, Brown University, Box 1946, Providence, RI 02912
Telephone: (401) 863-2001
Date Project Began: 1985
Date Project Completed: 1987
Sources of Funding: IBM Academic Information Systems, the David and Lucile Packard Foundation
Scope: Creation of an indexed CD-ROM of Classical Greek literature
Size: Not applicable
Computer System: IBM PC-RT
Available on Tape: No
Available on Diskettes: Available in CD-ROM format.
Output Options: Screen, printed, disk
Custom Searches: Yes, the CD-ROM includes a search program.
On-line Access Through Networks: No
Costs/Price: Not known
Key Bibliographical References: Paul Kahn, "Isocrates Project: Final Report," *IRIS Technical Report* 87–2.
Other: See above under HCCP; "A Description of Isocrates: All of Greek Literature on a CD-ROM," in Bernard Frischer, ed. *Papers of the UCLA Conference on Classics and Computing* (Los Angeles, July 19–20, 1986) = *Favonius Supp. Vol.* 1 (1987): 27–50.

The Isocrates Project has developed application and system software that allows users to access a data base of Classical Greek literature on a CD-ROM. The data base is a subset of the TLG's data base (see above) and has been mastered as "The TLG Pilot CD-ROM #B For Experimental Purposes." The Isocrates CD-ROM includes indices to the TLG texts that were prepared with software supplied by the HCCP. Thus, presently, there are two experimental TLG CD-ROMs, the one created by the TLG Project (#A) and the one created by the Isocrates Project (#B). Reportedly, the TLG Project is in the process of finalizing the format for their "production" CD-ROM.

The Isocrates Project's CD-ROM is designed to be used on the IRIS version of a "scholarly workstation"—an IBM PC-RT running under the AIX operating system. The Isocrates Project adapted the searching and indexing programs developed by the HCCP (see above) to run on the RT under AIX. The HCCP programs allow users to search for words, sets of words, and phrases and to cut and paste material from the CD-ROM into various word processing programs.

The Isocrates Project's interests and accomplishments included more than the creation of a CD-ROM and the adaptation of the HCCP searching and indexing programs. The Isocrates Project also was interested in integrating the search and retrieval capabilities of the HCCP programs with a publication-quality document-preparation system. Readers interested in a full history of the Isocrates Project and its technological achievements should write IRIS at the address above and request a copy of Paul Kahn, "Isocrates Project: Final Report," *IRIS Technical Report* 87–2.

7.9.4 ETP—Exegetical Toolkit

- *BASIC PROJECT INFORMATION*

Name of Project: Exegetical Toolkit Project
Key Person(s): Jon M. Boring, Project Director, Robin C. Cover, Functional Design Director, Assistant Professor of Semitics and Old Testament

Location of Project: Dallas, Texas
Project Address: Dallas Theological Seminary, 3909 Swiss Ave., Dallas, TX 75204
Telephone: (214) 824-3094
Date Project Began: May 1987
Date Project Completed: Not yet complete.
Sources of Funding: Not known
Scope: The ETP will create a hypertext, CD-ROM-based exegetical toolkit for studying the Bible.
Computers Supported: IBM PCs and Macintoshes will be supported.
Programming Language(s): Not known
Programs Available: None yet.
Available on Tape: No
Available on Diskettes: No
Costs/Price: The price of Version One is expected to be approximately $300.
Key Bibliographical References: None
Other: None

Although the Exegetical Toolkit Project (ETP) is still in the planning stages, its ambitious goals and subject matter make it worthy of mentioning. (The ETP developers anticipate a late 1988 release for Version One.) The ETP, which will be produced in several stages, will be a CD-ROM-based, hypertext product designed for the lay and scholarly study of the Bible. The data base will consist of a series of linked texts (a "linked exegetical library") that may be displayed in windows and searched with Boolean logic. The AND, OR, XOR, and NOT operators will be supported. These texts will consist of (1) ancient versions (with English translations where possible), (2) modern versions, (3) lexica, (4) grammars, (5) Bible dictionaries and encyclopedias, and (6) commentaries. The design specifications call for almost six dozen different works to be included in the data base. These texts and tools will provide information about translation, morphology, parsing, grammar, historical and cultural backgrounds, and interpretation. The ETP is committed to theological breadth and will include a variety of universally recognized standard critical texts, translations, and reference tools.

The hypertext retrieval program will allow users to conceptually link multiple items in the data base and follow user-selected paths from one text or tool to another, as illustrated earlier when discussing the HCCP's plans for developing a hypertext program. Users will be able to move through the data base and collect information about a word, phrase, passage, or theme from a variety of resources and to perform concordance searches.

Programming for the ETP will be done in cooperation with Owl International, the company that developed Guide, the hypertext program mentioned above under the HCCP. Initially, the program will run on IBM PCs under Microsoft® Windows 2.0. Support for Macintoshes is anticipated. The program will be developed and disseminated in stages, with each successive stage adding more texts to the data base and features to the program. The ETP should be a powerful and useful tool for biblical studies.

7.9.5 Addresses of Other Computer Projects in the Humanities

The date after the project name is the date the project was founded.

Humanities Computing/1982
% Dr. Dan Brink
Director Department of English
Arizona State University
Tempe, AZ 85287
(602) 965-3168
BITNET: ATDXB@ASUACAD

Center for Computer Applications in the Humanities/1983
% Dr. Scott Locicero, Codirector
Dept. of History
or % Dr. Gary Palmer, Codirector
Dept. of Anthropology
University of Nevada at Las Vegas
Las Vegas, NV 89154
(702) 739-3793

Text Processing Center/1984
% Dr. Fritz Grupe, Director
University of Nevada at Reno
Reno, NV 89557
(702) 784-1110

Humanities and Arts Computing Center, DW-10/1985
% Dr. Leroy Searle, Director
or % Dr. Stacy Waters, Research Coordinator
The University of Washington
Seattle, WA 98195
(206) 543-4218 (Center), (206) 543-1488 (Searle), (206)
        543-5370 (Waters)

Centre for Computing in the Humanities/1985
% Dr. Ian Lancashire
Faculty of Arts and Science
University of Toronto
Wilson Hall, New College
40 Willcocks St.
Toronto, Ontario M5S 1A1
Canada
(416) 978-6487
BITNET: IANL@UTORONTO

Bibliographical Resources

The Bibliographical Resources listed at the end of chapter 4 often contain articles and information about topics covered in this chapter. In addition to those resources, the following newsletters and journals frequently offer helpful information. Addresses and phones numbers are those of the circulation/subscription offices.

APA Newsletter
℅ Dr. Roger S. Bagnall, Editor
American Philological Association
617 Hamilton Hall
Columbia University
New York, NY 10027
(212) 280-4051
Quarterly, newsletter, $10 to $40, depending on salary.

Computing in the Humanities
℅ Dr. Linda Iroff
Cornell University
College of Arts and Sciences
237 Goldwin Smith Hall
Ithaca, NY 14853-3201
(607) 256-7343
Newsletter, about every other month, free.

EDUCOM Networking
℅ BITNET Communications
P.O. Box 364
Princeton, NJ 08540
(609) 734-1915
Quarterly, newsletter, free.

Penn Printout
℅ Ms. Edda B. Katz, Editor
Computing Resource Center.
1202 Blockley Hall
University of Pennsylvania
Philadelphia, PA 19104-6021
(215) 898-1780
Ten times a year, newsletter, free.

Perspectives in Computing
℅ IBM Corporation
44 South Broadway
White Plains, NY 10561
(914) 686-5585
Quarterly, journal, free.

SCOPE
℅ Paradigm Press
P.O. Box 45069
Sarasota, FL 34277-4069
(813) 922-7666
Bimonthly, newsletter, $52/year.

Window on the Humanities
% Center for Computer Applications in the Humanities
University of Nevada at Las Vegas
Las Vegas, NV 89154
(702) 739-3793
Newsletter, free.

Bibliography

Abercrombie, John R. "Computer Assisted Alignment of the Greek and Hebrew Biblical Texts—Programming Background." *Textus* 11 (1984): 125–39.

_____. *Computer Programs for Literary Analysis*. Philadelphia: University of Pennsylvania Press, 1984.

Abercrombie, J. R. W. Adler, R. A. Kraft, and Emanuel Tov. *Computer Assisted Tools for Septuagint Studies: Ruth*. CATSS 1. SCS Series, Scholars Press/SBL-IOSCS, 1986.

Abraham, Samuel, and Ferenc Kiefer. *Theory of Structural Semantics*. Vol. 49 of *Janua Linguarum* series minor. The Hague: Mouton, 1966.

Adams, L. La Mar. "Selection of Appropriate Methods for Style Analysis in Relation to the Isaiah Problem." *HCLB* 7 (1973): 73–88.

Adams, L. La Mar, and Alvin C. Rencher. "The Popular Critical View of the Isaiah Problem in Light of Statistical Style Analysis." *CSHVB* 4 (1973): 149–57.

Addyman, A. M. "A Language for Literary Data Processing: I—The Choice of a Language." *ALLC Bull.* 4 (1976): 146–51.

_____. "A Language for Literary Data Processing: II—Simple ALGOL68." *ALLC Bull.* 4 (1976): 238–44.

_____. "A Language for Literary Data Processing: III—String Processing in ALGOL68." *ALLC Bull.* 5 (1977): 46–51.

_____. "A Language for Literary Data Processing: IV—ALGOL68 Exposed." *ALLC Bull.* 5 (1977): 119–25.

Adler, William. "Computer Assisted Morphological Analysis of the Septuagint." *Textus* 11 (1984): 1–16.

Ager, D. E., F. E. Knowles, and Joan Smith, eds. *Advances in Computer-Aided Literary and Linguistic Research*. Birmingham: University of Aston Press, 1979.

Aho, Alfred V., John E. Hopcroft, and Jeffrey D. Ullman. *Data Structures and Algorithms*. Reading, Mass.: Addison-Wesley Pub. Co., 1983.

Aitken, A. J., R. W. Bailey, and N. Hamilton-Smith, eds. *The Computer and Literary Studies*. Edinburgh: Edinburgh University Press, 1973.

Aland, K., H. Bachmann, and W. A. Slaby. *Vollstaendige Konkordanz zum Griechischen Neun Testament, Band II: Spezialubersichten*. Berlin-New York, 1978.

Allen, Robert F., ed. *Data Bases in the Humanities and Social Sciences*. Osprey, Fla.: Paradigm Press, 1985.

Allen, S. and J. S. Petofi, eds. *Aspects of Automated Text Processing*. Vol. 17 of *Papers in Textlinguistics*. Hamburg: Buske, 1979.

Allwright, Christine. "FISHER: A String-Handling Package." *CHum* 10 (1976): 297–98.

Andersen, Francis I. "Orthography and Text Transmission." *TEXT* 2 (1984).

_____. *The Sentence in Biblical Hebrew*. *Janua Linguarum* series practica no. 231. The Hague: Mouton, 1974.

_____. "Style and Authorship." *Tyndale Paper* 21 (1976): 1–44.

_____. *The Verbless Clause in the Hebrew Pentateuch*. JBL Monograph Series, vol. 14. Nashville: Abingdon Press, 1970.

Andersen, Francis I., and A. Dean Forbes. *Eight Minor Prophets: A Linguistic Concordance*. The Computer Bible, vol. 10. Edited by J. Arthur Baird and David Noel Freedman. Wooster, Ohio: Biblical Research Associates, Inc., 1976.

_____. *Jeremiah: A Linguistic Concordance: I. Grammatical Vocabulary and Proper Nouns*. The Computer Bible, vol. 14. Edited by J. Arthur Baird and David Noel Freedman. Wooster, Ohio: Biblical Research Associates, Inc., 1978.

_____. *Jeremiah: A Linguistic Concordance: II. Nouns and Verbs*. The Computer Bible, vol. 14a. Edited by J. Arthur Baird and David Noel Freedman. Wooster, Ohio: Biblical Research Associates, Inc., 1978.

_____. "The Language of the Pentateuch." In *Computer Tools for Ancient Texts*. Edited by H. Van Dyke Parunak. Winona Lake, Ind.: Eisenbrauns. Forthcoming.

_____. *A Linguistic Concordance of Ruth and Jonah: Hebrew Vocabulary and Idiom*. The Computer Bible, vol. 9. Edited by J. Arthur Baird and David Noel Freedman. Wooster, Ohio: Biblical Research Associates, Inc., 1976.

_____. "Problems in Taxonomy and Lemmatization." In *Bible and Computer : The Text*, 37–50. Paris-Geneva: Champion-Slatkine, 1986.

_____. " 'Prose Particle' Counts of the Hebrew Bible." In *The Word of the Lord Shall Go Forth: Essays in Honor of David Noel Freedman in Celebration of His Sixtieth Birthday*. Edited by Carol L. Myers and M. P. O'Connor. Winona Lake, Ind.: Eisenbrauns, 1983.

_____. *Spelling in the Hebrew Bible*. Mitchell Dahood Memorial Lectures. Rome: Biblical Institute Press, 1986.

_____. *A Synoptic Concordance to Hosea, Amos, Micah.* The Computer Bible, vol. 6. Edited by J. Arthur Baird and David Noel Freedman. Wooster, Ohio: Biblical Research Associates, Inc. 1972.

Anon. "Bible Study by Computer." *Language Monthly* 5 (February 1984): 17.

_____. "By One Hand?" *Time* 118 (Dec. 7, 1981): 99.

_____. "The Computerized Word." *Newsweek* (April 11, 1977): 61.

_____. "8-Bit Prozessor Bietet 32-Bit-Architektur." *Elektronik* 32 (Jan. 14, 1983): 43–46.

_____. "The Historical Dictionary of the Hebrew Language." *World Union of Jewish Studies Newsletter* 3 (1971): 5–8.

_____. "The Isaiah Enigma." *Newsweek* 82 (July 16, 1973): 77.

_____. "Jewish Institute Imparts Religious Law with Computers." *Softalk* (February 1983): 229.

_____. "Judaic Case Law Is Gathered Into a 'Data Bank' in Chicago." *The New York Times* (May 4, 1982).

_____. "Kurzweil 4000 Scanner Debuts." *Computerworld* 18 (Feb. 13, 1984): 99, 104.

_____. "Kurzweil Scanning and Processing System." *Program* 18 (1984): 95–97.

_____. "Synopsis of the Historical Dictionary of the Hebrew Language." The Academy of the Hebrew Language, 1977. (In Hebrew)

Anshen, Frank. *Statistics for Linguists.* Rowley, Mass.: Newbury House, 1978.

Apresjan, Ju. D. *Principles and Methods of Contemporary Structural Linguistics.* Translated by Dina B. Crockett. Vol. 144 of *Janua Linguarum* series minor. The Hague: Mouton, 1973.

Association Internationale Bible et Informatique. *Bible et Informatique (Bible and Computer).* Proceedings of the First International Colloquium. Paris-Geneva: Champion-Slatkine, 1986. = *Traveau de Linguistique Quantitative* 37.

Bachmann, H., and W. A. Slaby. *Computer-Konkordanz zum Novum Testamentum Graece.* Berlin-New York, 1980.

Bagnall, Roger S., ed. *Research Tools for the Classics.* Chico, Calif.: Scholars Press, 1980.

Bailey, W., ed. *Computing in the Humanities.* Amsterdam: North-Holland Pub. Co., 1982.

Baird, J. Arthur. "Biblical Research Associates (and the Computer)." *CSR Bull.* 3 (1972): 29–31.

_____. "Content Analysis and the Computer: A Case-Study in the Application of the Scientific Method to Biblical Research." *JBL* 95 (1976): 255–76.

_____. "Content Analysis, Computers and the Scientific Method in Biblical Studies." *Perspectives in Religious Studies* 4 (1977): 112–40.

Ballard, D. Lee, Robert J. Conrad, and Robert E. Longacre. *More on the Deep and Surface Grammar of Interclausal Relations.* Norman, Okla.: SIL Press, 1971.

Barnett, Michael P. "SNAP—A Programming Language for Humanists." *CHum* 4 (1970): 225–40.

Barth, A. J. "Designing with the 68008 Microprocessor." *Electronics and Wireless World* 90.1578 (March 1984): 66–68.

_____. "Designing with the 68008 Microprocessor." *Electronics and Wireless World* 90.1579 (April 1984): 30–33.

Bastiaens, J., W. Beuken, and F. Postma. *Tritio-Isaiah.* Applicatio 4. Amsterdam, 1984.

Beals, Gary D. "Extending Microprocessor Architectures." *BYTE* (May 1985): 185–98.

Beatie, Bruce A. "Measurement and the Study of Literature." *CHum* 13 (1979): 185–94.

Beaud, Marie-Josèphe, Agnès Guillaumoint, and Jean-Luc Minel. "A Medieval Manuscript Database." In *Data Bases in the Humanities and Social Sciences.* Edited by Robert F. Allen, 22–29. Osprey, Fla.: Paradigm Press, 1985.

Bee, Ronald E. "The Use of Statistical Methods in Old Testament Studies." *VT* 23 (1973): 257–72.

Beekman, John, and John Callow. *The Semantic Structure of Written Communication.* Dallas: SIL Press. Forthcoming.

_____. *Translating the Word of God.* Grand Rapids: Zondervan Publishing House, 1974.

Ben-Hayyim, Z., ed. "The Historical Dictionary of the Hebrew Language—Specimen Pamphlet. The Root "B." *Lesonenu* 46 (1982): 165–267.

Berkowitz, Luci, and Karl A. Squitier. *Thesaurus Linguae Graecae CANON Of GREEK AUTHORS AND WORKS.* 2d ed. New York: Oxford University Press, 1986.

Berry-Rogghe, G. L. M. "COCOA: A Word Count and Concordance Generator." *ALLC Bull.* 1 (1973): 29–31.

_____. *COCOA Technical Manual.* Radnor, Penn,: Chilton, Didcot: Atlas Computer Laboratory, 1973.

Boot, M. "An Experimental Design for Automated Syntactic Encoding of Natural Language Texts." *ALLC Bull.* 5 (1977): 237–48.

Borchgrave, E., and R.-F. Poswick. "Computer Work for Literary Production. A Particular Application for Biblical Studies." In *Proceedings of the International Computing Symposium 1977.* Edited by E. Morlet and D. Ribbens, 253–59. New York: North-Holland Pub. Co., 1977.

Borden, George A., and James J. Watts. "A Computerized Language Analysis System." *CHum* 5 (1971): 129–41.

Bowles, E. A., ed. *Computers in Humanistic Research. Readings and Perspectives.* Englewood Cliffs: N.J.: Prentice-Hall, 1967.

Boyer, James A. "Project Gramcord: A Report." *Grace Theological Journal* 1 (1980): 97–99.

Brainerd, Barron. *Weighing Evidence in Language and Literature: A Statistical Approach.* Toronto: University of Toronto Press, 1975.

Bratley, Paul, Serge Lusignan, and Francine Oullette. "JEUDEMO, A Package for Scholars in the Humanities." *SIGLASH Newsletter* 7 (June 1974): 15–19.

_____. "JEUDEMO: A Text-Handling System." In *Computers in the Humanities.* Edited by J. L. Mitchell, 234–49. Edinburgh: Edinburgh University Press, 1974.

Brend, Ruth M., and Kenneth L. Pike, eds. *Tagmemics: Theoretical Discussion Trends in Linguistics.* Vol. 2 of *Studies and Monographs.* The Hague: Mouton, 1976.

Brooks, Roger, and Tzvee Zahavy. "Form Analysis of Mishnaic Sentences." In *Computing in the Humanities.* Edited by Peter C. Patton and Renee A. Holoien, 113–34. Lexington, Mass.: D.C. Heath & Co., 1981.

Brown, P. J. "SCAN: A Simple Conversational Programming Language for Text Analysis." *CHum* 6 (1972): 223–27.

Buccellati, Giorgio. "The Old Babylonian Linguistic Analysis Project: Goals Procedures and First Results." In *Computational and Mathematical Linguistics.* Edited by A. Zampolli and N. Calzolari, 383–404. Florence: Leo S. Olschki, 1977, 1980.

Bunnell, David. "Hypervisions." *Macworld* (March 1987): 21–30.

Burch, J. "The Use of a Computer in New Testament Textual Criticism." *Restoration Quarterly* 8 (1965): 119–25.

Burke, E., ed. *Computers in Humanistic Research.* Englewood Cliffs, N.J.: Prentice-Hall, 1967.

Burton, Delores M. "Automated Concordances and Word Indices: Machine Decisions and Editorial Revisions." *CHum* 16 (1982): 195–218.

_____. "Automated Concordances and Word Indices: The Early Sixties and the Early Centers." *CHum* 15 (1981): 83–100.

_____. "Automated Concordances and Word Indices: The Fifties." *CHum* 15 (1981): 1–14.

_____. "Automated Concordances and Word Indices: The Process, the Programs, and the Products." *CHum* 15 (1981): 139–54.

_____. "Review of Robert Busa's 'Index Thomisticus Sancti Thomae Operum Omnium Indices et Concordantiae'." *CHum* 18 (1984): 109–20.

_____. "Some Uses of a Grammatical Concordance." *CHum* 2 (1968): 145–54.

Burton, Sara K., and Douglas D. Short, eds. *Sixth International Conference on Computers and the Humanities.* Rockville, Md.: Computer Science Press, 1983.

Busa, R. "The Annals of Humanities Computing: The Index Thomisticus." *CHum* 14 (1980): 83–90.

Cabaniss, Margaret Scanlon. "Using the Computer for Text Collation." *CSHVB* 3 (1970): 1–33.

Carter, H. S. "New Testament Studies: 7. Criticism by Computer." *Hibert Journal* 63 (1964–65): 42–44.

Cercone, Nick, and Randy Goebel. "Data Bases and Knowledge Representation for Literary and Linguistic Studies." *CHum* 17 (1983): 121–37.

Cercone, N. J., ed. *Computational Linguistics,* vol. 5 of *International Series in Modern Applied Mathematics and Computer Science.* Oxford: Pergamon, 1983.

Choueka, Yaacov. "Computerized Full-Text Retrieval Systems and Research in the Humanities: The Responsa Project." *CHum* 14 (1980): 153–69 (contains a helpful bibliography).

_____. "The Responsa Project—Aims and Activities." *CAMDAP* 7 (1977): 35–42.

_____. *The Responsa Project: What, How, and Why: 1976#1981.* Ramat Gan, Israel: Institute for Information Retrieval and Computational Linguistics, 1981.

Choueka, Yaacov, T. Klein, and E. Neuwitz. "Automatic Retrieval of Frequent Idiomatic and Collocational Expressions in a Large Corpus." *ALLC Jour.* 4 (1983): 34–38.

Choueka, Yaacov et al. "The Responsa Project: Computerization of Traditional Jewish Case Law." In *Legal and Legislative Information Processing.* Edited by B. Erez, 261–86. Greenwood Press, 1980.

Cignoni, L., and C. Peters, eds. *Computers in Literary and Linguistic Research.* Proceedings of the Seventh International Symposium of the Association for Literary and Linguistic Computing, Pisa (1982). Agnano Pisano: Giardini, 1983.

Claassen, Walter T. "Data Base Structured for an Interactive Microcomputer system for the Study of Biblical Hebrew." In *Bible and Computer : The Text,* 143–54. Paris-Geneva: Champion-Slatkine, 1986.

_____. "A Research Unit for Computer Applications to the Language and Text of the Old Testament." *Journal of Northwest Semitic Languages* 13 (1987): 11–21.

_____. "Spectrum of Data Base Needs in Ancient Near Eastern and Old Testament Studies." In *Data Bases in the Humanities and Social Sciences*. Edited by Robert F. Allen, 145–49. Osprey, Fla.: Paradigm Press, 1985.

Clarke, E. G., et al. *Targum Pseudo-Jonathan of the Pentateuch: Text and Concordance*. Hoboken, N.J.: KTAV Publishing House, 1984.

Clayton, J. *Introduction to Statistics: A Linguistic Approach*, 2d ed. Hurd Comm., 1984.

Cook, Johann. "The Development of a Base for the Peshitta Version of the old Testament." In *Bible and Computer : The Text*, 165–77. Paris-Geneva: Champion-Slatkine, 1986.

Cook, Walter A. *Introduction to Tagmemic Analysis*. Georgetown: Georgetown University Press, 1978.

Coseriu, Eugenio, and Horst Geckeler. *Trends in Structural Semantics*. Vol. 58 of *Tübinger Beitrage zür Linguistik*. Benjamins North America, 1981.

Costello, John R. *Syntactic Change and Syntactic Reconstruction: A Tagmemic Approach*. Norman, Okla.: SIL Press, 1983.

Crane, Gregory. "Clay Balls and Compact Disks: Some Political and Economic Problems of the New Storage Media." In *Papers of the UCLA Conference on Classics and Computing* (Los Angeles, July 19–20, 1986). = *Favonius Supp. Vol.* 1 (1987): 1–6.

Crennell, Kathleen M. "How To Use COCOA to Produce Indexes (To Both Books and Subroutine Libraries)." *ALLC Bull.* 3 (1975): 190–96.

Culik, K. "Basic Problems in the Mathematical Theory of Languages." *Linguistics* 115 (1973): 5–41.

Damerau, J. Fred. "The Use of Function Word Frequencies as Indicators of Style." *CHum* 9 (1975): 271–80.

Dearing, Vinton A. "Computer-Aided Textual Criticism: the Greek Text of the Gospels Before the Tenth Century." *ALLC Bull.* 7 (1979): 276–82.

_____. "Determining Variations (in the Greek N.T. Text) by Computer." In *SBL, 1974 Seminar Papers*, vol. 2. Cambridge, Mass.: SBL, 1974, 14–35.

_____. "Textual Analysis: A Consideration of Some Questions Raised by M. P. Weitzman." *VT* 29 (1979): 355–59.

Derval, Bernard, and Michel Lenoble, eds. *La critique litteraire et l'ordinateur (Literary Criticism and the Computer)*. Montreal: Derval & Lenoble, 3390 rue Limoges, St-Laurent, Quebec H4K 1Y1, 1986.

Devine, Joseph G. "Computer-Generated Concordances and Related Techniques in the Study of Theology." In *Computers in Humanistic Research*. Edited by E. A. Bowles, 170–78. Englewood Cliffs, N.J.: Prentice-Hall, 1967.

Dixon, J. E. G. "Concordances KWIC and Complete: An Appraisal." *ALLC Bull.* 6 (1978): 28–33.

Dolozel, Lubomir, and Richard W. Bailey, eds. *Statistics and Style*. New York: American Elsevier, 1969.

Drake, Bryan. "Unanswered Questions in Computerized Literary Analysis." *JBL* 91 (1972): 241–42.

Epp, Eldon J. "The Twentieth Century Interlude in New Testament Textual Criticism." *JBL* 93 (1974): 386–414.

Eshbaugh, Howard. "Biblical Criticism and the Computer." *Perspective* 13 (1972): 34–58.

Farina, Luciano F. "LDMS: A Linguistic Data Management System." *CHum* 17 (1983): 99–119.

Farringdon, Michael G. "POP-2 As a Programming Language for Literary Research." In *The Computer in Literary and Linguistic Research*. Edited by R. A. Wisbey, 271–79. Cambridge: Cambridge University Press, 1971.

Fischer, Bonifatius. "Computer und der Text des Neuen Testamentes." *Studia Evangelica* 6 (1973): 109–21.

_____. "The Use of Computers in New Testament Studies, with Special Reference to Textual Criticism." *JTS* 21 (1970): 297–308.

Flores, Ivan. *Data Base Architecture*. New York: Van Nostrand Reinhold Co., 1981.

Fraenkel, A. S., D. Raab, and E. Spitz. "Semi-Automatic Construction of Semantic Concordances." *CHum* 13 (1979): 283–88.

Friberg, Barbara, and Timothy Friberg. *Analytical Greek New Testament*. Grand Rapids: Baker Book House, 1981.

_____. "A Computer-Assisted Analysis of the Greek New Testament." In *Computing in the Humanities*. Edited by Peter C. Patton and Renee A. Holoien, 15–51. Lexington, Mass.: D.C. Heath & Co., 1981.

Friedman, Thomas L. "Computer Digests Talmud to Help Rabbis." *The New York Times* 134 (Nov. 24, 1984): 1, 7. Reprinted as "Computer Aids Rabbis With Talmud, Jewish Law." *International Herald Tribune* (Dec. 4, 1984).

Froger, Jacques. "La critique des textes et l'ordinateur." *Vigiliae Christianae* 24 (1970): 210–17.

_____. "The Electronic Machine at the Service of Humanistic Studies." *Diogenes* 52 (1965): 104–42.

Galloway, Patricia. "Hardware Review: The Kurzweil Data Entry Machine (KDEM)." *CHum* 15 (1981): 183–85.

Gaunt, Marianne I. "Rutgers Inventory of Machine-Readable Texts in the Humanities." In *Data Bases in the Humanities and Social Sciences*. Edited by Robert F. Allen, 283–90. Osprey, Fla.: Paradigm Press, 1985.

Gelb, Ignace J. *Computer-Aided Analysis of Amorite.* Assyriological Studies 21. Chicago: The Oriental Institute, 1980.

_____. "Computer-Aided Analysis of Amorite." *JCS* 34 (1982): 1–18.

_____. "Computer-Aided Analysis of Amorite." *JSS* 26 (1981): 277–80.

Genes, P., D. Meers, and B. Wells. "XEDIT—An Extended Interactive Text Editor." Minneapolis: University of Minnesota Computer Center, 1978.

Gil, J. "The Computer Bible." *Beth Mikra* 17 (1970): 373–75, 78.

Gilles, Michel. *Le Livre Religieux dans les Systems Informatises.* Maredsous: CIB, 1985.

Gimpel, James F. *Algorithms in SNOBOL4.* New York: John Wiley and Sons, 1976.

_____. "Processing Strings in SNOBOL4: Some Elegant Examples of This Language's Pattern-Matching Capabilities." *BYTE* (February 1986): 175–86.

Gladkij, Aleksej V., and Igor A. Mel'cuk. *Elements of Mathematical Linguistics.* Vol. 110 of *Janua Linguarum* series maior. The Hague: Mouton, 1983.

Glazebrook, Rebeckah R. " 'Saving' Literary Classics with Software." *Hardcopy* (July 1984): 59–64.

Glinert-Cole, Susan. "Vroom! Performance Benchmarks for the PC/AT." *PC Tech Journal* (December 1984): 108–10.

Gonnet, G. H. *Handbook of Algorithms and Data Structures.* Reading, Mass.: Addison-Wesley Pub. Co., 1984.

Grayston, Kenneth. "Computers and the New Testament." *NTS* 17 (1971): 477–80.

Greitzer, John. "Scanning the Horizon." *Publish!* (September/October 1986): 45–51.

Griffith, John G. "The Interrelations of Some Primary MSS of the Gospels in the Light of Numerical Analysis." *Studia Evangelica* 6 (1973): 221–38. = *TU* 112.

_____. "Numerical Taxonomy and Some Primary Manuscripts of the Gospels." *JTS* 20 (1969): 389–406.

Griswold, Ralph E. "The ICON Programming Language. An Alternative to SNOBOL4 for Computing in the Humanities." In *Computing in the Humanities.* Edited by W. Bailey, 7–17. Amsterdam: North-Holland Pub. Co., 1982.

Griswold, R. E., and M. T. Griswold. *A SNOBOL4 Primer.* Englewood Cliffs, N.J.: Prentice-Hall, 1973.

_____. *String and List Processing in SNOBOL4.* New York: John Wiley and Sons, 1975.

Gross, Maurice. *Mathematical Models in Linguistics.* Englewood Cliffs, N.J.: Prentice-Hall, 1972.

Gunion, Ann. "A Computer-Aided Dictionary of Classical Rhetoricians." In *Papers of the UCLA Conference on Classics and Computing* (Los Angeles, July 19–20, 1986). = *Favonius Supp. Vol.* 1 (1987): 99–110.

Harris, Zellig S. *Structural Linguistics.* Chicago: University of Chicago Press, 1960.

Harward, Jud. "TLG-QUEL: A Prototype for an Interactive Query Language for Using the TLG Database." In *Papers of the UCLA Conference on Classics and Computing* (Los Angeles, July 19–20, 1986). = *Favonius Supp. Vol.* 1 (1987): 57–64.

Hatch, Evelyn, and Hossein Farhady. *Research Design and Statistics for Applied Linguistics.* Rowley, Mass.: Newbury House, 1982.

Hays, David G. "Computational Linguistics and the Humanist." *CHum* 10 (1976): 265–74.

Herdan, G. "About Some Controversial Results of the Quantitative Method in Linguistics." *Zeitschrift für romanische Philologie* 85 (1969): 376–84.

_____. *Quantitative Linguistics.* Hamden, Conn.: Shoe String, 1964.

_____. "Scholarship and the Computer." *London Quarterly and Holborn Review* 34 (1965): 208–17.

Hirschman, L., R. Grishman, and N. Sager. "Grammatically-Based Automatic Word Class Formation." *IPM* 11 (1975): 39–57.

Hoban, Phoebe. "Church on a Chip: Artificial Intelligence." *OMNI* 6 (June 1984): 40–41.

Hockey, Susan M. "Computing in the Humanities at Oxford." *CAMDAP* 11 (1982): 8–16.

_____. *A Guide to Computer Applications in the Humanities.* Baltimore: The Johns Hopkins University Press, 1980.

_____. "Input and Output of Non-Standard Character Sets." *ALLC Bull.* 1 (1973): 32–37.

_____. *SNOBOL Programming for the Humanities.* New York: Oxford University Press, 1987.

Holoien, R. A., and E. E. Inman. "TAGEDIT User Reference Manual." UCC Technical Report. Minneapolis: University of Minnesota, 1985.

Hotchkiss, R. L., and S. K. Graffunder. "GENCORD: A Concordance Program." Minneapolis: University of Minnesota Computer Center, 1977.

Housden, Richard J. W. "Further Thoughts on SNAP." *CHum* 7 (1973): 407–12.

Howard-Hill, T. H. *Literary Concordances: A Complete Handbook for the Preparation of Manual and Computer Concordances.* Oxford: Pergamon, 1979.

Iker, H. P. "SELECT: A Computer Program to Identify Associationally Rich Words for Content Analysis. I. Statistical Results." *CHum* 8 (1974): 313–19.

_____. "SELECT: A Computer Program to Identify Associationally Rich Words for Content Analysis. II. Substantive Results." *CHum* 9 (1975): 3–12.

Iker, Howard P., and Robert H. Klein. "WORDS: A Computer System for the Analysis of Content." *Behavior Research Methods and Instrumentation* 6 (1974): 430–38.

Ingram, W. "Concordances in the Seventies." *CHum* 8 (1974): 273–77.

Inman, Eric E. "TAGEDIT: A Computer Tool for Literary and Linguistic Research." In *Computing in the Humanities*. Edited by Peter C. Patton and Renee A. Holoien, 145–54. Lexington, Mass.: D.C. Heath & Co., 1981.

_____. "TAGEDIT—An Interactive Pattern Matching Program." Minneapolis: University of Minnesota Computer Center, 1980.

Johnson, P. F. "The Use of Statistics in the Analysis of the Characteristics of Pauline Writing." *NTS* 20 (1973): 92–100.

Jones, Alan, and R. F. Churchhouse, eds. *The Computer in Literary and Linguistic Studies.* 3d ed. Cardiff: University of Wales Press, 1976.

Jones, K. Sparck, and Y. Wilks. *Automatic Natural Language Parsing.* Somerset, N.J.: John Wiley and Sons, Inc., 1985.

Kemp, Kenneth W. "Aspects of the Statistical Analysis and Effective Use of Linguistic Data." *ALLC Bull.* 4 (1976): 14–22.

_____. "Personal Observations on the Use of Statistical Methods in Quantitative Linguistics." In *The Computer in Literary and linguistic Studies*. Edited by Alan Jones and R. F. Churchhouse, 59–77. Cardiff: University of Wales Press, 1976.

Kahn, Paul. "A Description of Isocrates: All of Greek Literature on a CD-ROM." In *Papers of the UCLA Conference on Classics and Computing* (Los Angeles, July 19–20, 1986). = *Favonius Supp.* Vol. 1 (1987): 27–50.

_____. "Isocrates Project: Final Report." *IRIS Technical Report* 87–2.

Kenny, A. *The Computation of Style.* Oxford: Pergamon, 1982.

Knapp, Thomas R. "The Rev. Mr. Morton and St. Paul." *Dublin Review* 510 (1966): 354–57.

Knox, T. M. "The Computer and the New Testament." *SEA* 28 (1963): 111–16.

Koubourlis, D. J. "From a Word-Form Concordance to a Dictionary-Form Concordance." In *Computers in the Humanities*. Edited by J. L. Mitchell, 225–33. Edinburgh: Edinburgh University Press, 1974.

Kowalski, Georges W. "Nouvelles analyses et nouveaux fonctinnements du texte dans un environnement informatisé." In *Bible and Computer : The Text*, 215–34. Paris-Geneva: Champion-Slatkine, 1986.

Kraft, Robert A. "Computer Treatment of Septuagint Greek Textual Variants." In *Computer Tools for Ancient Texts*. Edited by H. Van Dyke Parunak. Winona Lake, Ind.: Eisenbrauns. Forthcoming.

_____. "Lexicon Project: Progress Report." *BIOSCS* 12 (1979): 14–16.

_____. "Prospectus: Computer Assisted Tools for Septuagint Studies." Philadelphia: CATSS, 1983 (distributed on request).

Kraft, Robert A., and Emanuel Tov. "Computer Assisted Tools for Septuagint Studies (CATSS)." *BIOSCS* 14 (1981): 22–40.

_____. *Ruth.* CATSS 1 = Septuagint and Cognate Studies 20. Atlanta: Scholars Press, 1986.

Larson, Richard. "SNOBOL4." *PC Tech Journal* (January 1985): 32–43.

Leed, Jacob., ed. *The Computer and Literary Style.* Kent, Ohio: Kent State University Press, 1966.

Lepschy, Giuilio C. *A Survey of Structural Linguistics*, 2d ed. Oxford: Basil Blackwell, 1984.

Levenson, Thomas. "Crunching the Classics." *Discover* (February 1984): 80–81.

Levine, L. D. "The Royal Inscriptions of Mesopotamia and the Computer." *Annual Review of the RIM Project* 1 (1983): 19–20.

Lindsey, C. H. "ALGOL68 with Fewer Tears." *Computer Journal* 15 (1972): 172–88.

Lippi, Paul. "The Use of the Computerized Data Base for the Study of the Septuagint Revisions." *BIOSCS* 17 (1984): 48–62.

Longacre, Robert E. "From Tagma to Tagmeme in Biblical Hebrew." In *A. William Cameron Townsend en el vigesimoquinto del Instituto Linguistico de Verano.* Mexico: D.F., 1961.

_____. *Grammar Discovery Procedures.* Vol. 33 of *Janua Linguarum* series minor. The Hague: Mouton, 1964.

_____. *The Grammar of Discourse.* Plenum Pub., 1983.

_____. "Some Fundamental Insights of Tagmemics." *Language* 41 (1965): 65–76.

_____. "String Constituent Analysis." *Language* 36 (1960): 63–68.

Lovik, Gordon H. "The IBM PC and the NT Join Hands." *Calvary Up-Date* 8 (Spring 1984): 1–2.

Lusignan, Serge, and John S. North, eds. *Computing in the Humanities.* Waterloo: University of Waterloo Press, 1977.

Lyons, John. *Introduction to Theoretical Linguistics.* Cambridge: Cambridge University Press, 1968.

McCarty, et al. *Academic's Guide to Microcomputer Systems.* Toronto: University of Toronto Computing Services, 1985.

Malachi, Zvi, ed. *Proceedings of the International Conference on Literary and Linguistic Computing. April 22#27, 1979.* Tel-Aviv University: The Katz Research Institute for Hebrew Literature, 1979.

Malmberg, B. *Structural Linguistics and Human Communication.* Vol. 2 of *Kommunikation und Kybernetik in Einzeldarstellungen.* New York: Springer-Verlag, 1976.

Manna, Zohar. *Introduction to Mathematical Theory of Computation.* New York: McGraw-Hill, 1974.

McKinnon, Alastair, and Roger Webster. "A Method of 'Author' Identification." In *Computers in Literary and Linguistic Research.* Edited by R. A. Wisbey, 65–74. Cambridge: Cambridge University Press, 1971.

Mehlhorn, Kurt. *Data Structures and Algorithms 3: Multi-dimensional Searching and Computational Geometry.* New York: Springer-Verlag, 1984.

Meunier, Jean-Guy, Stanislas Rolland, and Francois Daoust. "A System for Text and Content Analysis." *CHum* 10 (1976): 281–86.

Mey, Jacob L. "Computational Linguistics and the Study of Linguistic Performance." *CHum* 6 (1972): 131–36.

Michaelson, S., and A. Q. Morton. "Last Words: A Test of Authorship for Greek Writers." *NTS* 18 (1971): 192–208.

_____. "Things Ain't What They Used to Be: A Study of Chronological Change in a Greek Writer." In *The Computer in Literary and Linguistic Studies.* Edited by Alan Jones and R. F. Churchhouse, 78–84. Cardiff: University of Wales Press, 1976.

Miller, Paul A. "Applications in Computational Linguistics." In *Proceedings of the Fifth Annual Conference on Academic Computing Applications.* Bloomington, Ind.: University of Indiana Press, 1979.

_____. "Project GRAMCORD—A Grammatical Concordance Package Program for the Greek New Testament." In *Proceedings of the Third Biennial Conference on Computing in Indiana.* Bloomington, Ind.: Association for Computing Machinery, 1978.

_____. "Project Gramcord: Grammatical Analysis and Grammatical Concording of the Greek New Testament." In *Computer Tools for Ancient Texts.* Edited by H. Van Dyke Parunak. Winona Lake, Ind.: Eisenbrauns. Forthcoming.

Mitchell, J. L., ed. *Computers in the Humanities.* Edinburgh: Edinburgh University Press, 1974.

Moberg, Thomas, ed. *Data Bases in the Humanities and Social Sciences.* Osprey, Fla.: Paradigm Press, 1986.

Morris, P. M. K. "Brief Account of Computer Work on Old Testament." *HCLB* 1 (1969): 28–30.

_____. "Computers and the Hebrew Old Testament." Unpublished paper. 1972.

_____. "Computers and the Old Testament—Recent Analyses and Development." Unpublished paper. 1969.

Morris, P. M. K., and Edward B. James. "Computers and the Old Testament: A Progress Report." *ExpT* 79 (1968): 211–14.

_____. *A Critical Word Book of Leviticus, Numbers, Deuteronomy.* The Computer Bible, vol. 8. Edited by J. Arthur Baird and David Noel Freedman. Wooster, Ohio: Biblical Research Associates, Inc., 1975.

_____. *A Critical Word Book of the Pentateuch.* The Computer Bible, vol. 17. Edited by J. Arthur Baird and David Noel Freedman. Wooster, Ohio: Biblical Research Associates, Inc., 1980.

Morton, A. Q. "The Annals of Computing: The Greek New Testament." *CHum* 14 (1980): 197–99.

_____. "The Authorship of Greek Prose." *JRSS* 138 (1965): 169–233.

_____. "The Authorship of the Pauline Corpus." In *The New Testament in Historical and Contemporary Perspective.* Edited by H. Anderson and W. Barclay, 209–35. Oxford: Blackwell, 1965.

_____. *Literary Detection: How to Prove Authorship and Fraud in Literature and Documents.* New York: Charles Scribner's Sons, 1978.

_____. "The New Stylometry: A One-Word Test of Authorship for Greek Writers." *Classical Quarterly* N.S. 22 (1972): 89–102.

_____. "The Spaces in Between: A Multiple Test of Authorship for Greek Writers." *RELO Review* 1 (1972): 23–77.

Morton, A. Q., and Michael Levison. "The Computer in Literary Studies." In *Information Processing 1968.* Edited by A. J. H. Morrell, 1072–80. Amsterdam: North Holland, 1969.

_____. "Literary Uses of the Computer." *New Scientist* 39 (1968): 340–42.

_____. "Some Indicators of Authorship in Greek Prose." In *The Computer and Literary Style.* Edited by Jacob Leed, 141–79. Kent, Ohio: Kent State University Press, 1966.

Morton, A. Q., and J. McLeman. *Christianity and the Computer.* London: Hodder and Stoughton, 1964.

_____. *Paul, the Man and the Myth: A Study in the Authorship of Greek Prose.* London, 1966.

Morton, Andrew, Q., and Alan D. Winspear. *It's Greek with the Computer.* Montreal: Harvest House, 1971.

Mullen, Karen A. "Using the Computer to Identify Differences among Text Variants." *CHum* 5 (1970–1971): 193–201.

611

Nagy, G. "Optical Scanning Digitizers." *Computer* 16 (May 1983): 13–24.

Niebor, M. C. "The Statistical Analysis of A. Q. Morton and the Authenticity of the Pauline Epistles." *CTJ* 5 (1970): 64–80.

Oakman, R. L. *Computer Methods for Literary Research.* Rev. ed. Athens, Ga.: University of Georgia Press, 1984.

———. "Concordances from Computers: A Review Article." In *Proof: The Yearbook of American Bibliographical and Textual Studies.* 3d ed. Edited J. Katz, 411–26. Columbia, S.C.: University of South Carolina Press, 1973.

———. "The Present State of Computerized Collation: A Review Article." *Proof* 2 (1972): 335–48.

Oomen, Ursula. *Automatische Syntaktische Analyze.* Vol. 76 of *Janua Linguarum* series minor. The Hague: Mouton, 1968.

Ott, W. "Computer Applications in Textual Criticism." In *The Computer and Literary Studies.* Edited by A. J. Aitken, R. W. Bailey, and N. Hamilton-Smith, 199–223. Edinburgh: Edinburgh University Press, 1973.

Packard, David W. "Computer-Assisted Morphological Analysis of Ancient Greek." In *Computational and Mathematical Linguistics: Proceedings of the International Conference on Computational Linguistics, Pisa 1973.* Vol. 2, *Linguistica* 37. Edited by A. Zampolli and N. Calzolari, 343–56. Florence: Leo S. Olschki, 1980.

———. "A Greek Computer at Chapel Hill." *RELO* Review 4 (1975): 7–10.

Parpola, Simo. "The Neo-Assyrian Text Corpus Project of the University of Helsinki." *Akkadica* 49 (September/October 1986): 20–23.

Parrish, S. M. "Concordance-Making by Computer: Its Past, Future, Techniques and Applications." *Brockport Proceedings*, 16–33.

———. "Problems in the Making of Computer Concordances." *Studies in Bibliography* 15 (1962): 1–14.

Partee, Barbara H. *Mathematical Fundamentals of Linguistics.* Greylock Publishers, 1976.

Parunak, H. Van Dyke. "Code Manual for the Michigan Old Testament." Research Memorandum UM82–1, University of Michigan (Ann Arbor, March 1982).

———. "Data Base Design for Biblical Texts." In *Computing in the Humanities.* Edited by W. Bailey, 149–61. Amsterdam: North-Holland Pub. Co., 1982.

———. "Prolegomena to Pictorial Concordances." *CHum* 15 (1981): 15–36.

———. "Surveying Semantic Fields by Computer." Research Memorandum UM81–21, University of Michigan (Ann Arbor, October 1981).

———. "Text File Formats for the Michigan Bible and Computer Project." Research Memorandum UM80–7, University of Michigan (Ann Arbor, June 1981).

Patton, Peter C., and Renee A. Holoien, eds. *Computing in the Humanities.* Lexington, Mass.: D.C. Heath & Co., 1981.

Pellistrandi, C. "Présentation de MEDIUM: base de données sur le manuscrit médiéval." In *Bible and Computer : The Text*, 275–85. Paris-Geneva: Champion-Slatkine, 1986.

Pettit, Philip. *The Concept of Structuralism: A Critical Analysis.* University of California Press, 1975.

Petty, George R., and William M. Gibson. *Project OCCULT: The Ordered Computer Collation of Unprepared Literary Text.* New York University Press, 1970.

Pierson, G. W., ed. *Computers for the Humanities?* New Haven: Yale University Press, 1955.

Pike, Evelyn G. *Coordination and Implications for Roots and Stems of Sentence and Clause.* Vol. 1 of *PDR Press Publications in Tagmemics.* Atlantic Highlands, N.J.: Humanities Press, 1974.

Pike, Kenneth L. "A Guide to Publications Related to Tagmemic Theory." In *Current Trends in Linguistics*, vol. 3. Edited by Thomas A. Sebok, 365–94. The Hague: Mouton, 1966.

———. *Language in Relation to a Unified Theory of the Structure of Human Behavior.* The Hague: Mouton, 1967.

———. *Linguistic Concepts: An Introduction to Tagmemics.* Bison, Neb.: University of Nebraska Press, 1982.

———. *On Describing Languages.* Vol. 2 of *PDR Press Publications in Taqmemics.* Humanities, 1975.

———. "On tagmemes neé grammemes." *International Journal of American Linguistics* 24 (1958): 273–78.

———. *Tagmemics, Discourse and Verbal Art.* Vol. 3 of *Michigan Studies in the Humanities.* Michigan Slavic Publications, 1981.

Pike, K. L., and E. G. Pike. *Grammatical Analysis.* Rev. ed. Vol. 53 of *Publications in Linguistics and Related Fields.* Norman, Okla.: SIL Press, 1982.

———. *Text and Tagmeme.* Northwood, N.J.: Ablex Pub., 1983.

Plotnik, Art. "OCLC for You—and ME?! A Humanized Anatomy for Beginners." *American Libraries* 7 (May 1976): 258–75.

Pool, Eric. "The Computer in Determining Stemmatic Relationships." *CHum* 8 (1974): 207–16.

Porch, Ann. "An Overview of Devices for Preparing Large Natural Language Data Bases." *CSHVB* 4 (1973): 81–89.

Porter, M. F. "Designing a Programming Language for Use in Literary Studies." In *Computers in Literary and Linguistic Research.* Edited by R. A. Wisbey, 259–69. Cambridge: Cambridge University Press, 1971.

Porter, Stanley E. "The Adjectival Attributive Genitive in the New Testament: A Grammatical Study." *Trinity Journal* 4 NS(1983): 3–17.

Poswick, R.-Ferdinand. *Centre: Informatique et Bible. Bible Data Bank List of Data and Services.* Brepols Publishers, 1981.

Preston, M. J., and S. S. Coleman. "Some Considerations Concerning Encoding and Concording Texts." *CHum* 12 (1978): 1–12.

Price, James D. "An Algorithm for Analyzing Hebrew Words." *CSHVB* 2 (1969): 137–65.

Prieditis, Armand E. "Introduction to Research Design Using TAGEDIT." Minneapolis: University of Minnesota Computer Center, 1983.

Raben, Joseph. "The Death of the Handmade Concordance." *Scholarly Publishing* 1 (1969): 61–69.

―――. *The Electronic Scholars Resource Guide.* Oryx Press, 1987.

Raben, Joseph, and Gregory A. Marks, eds. *Data Bases in the Humanities and the Social Sciences.* Amsterdam: North-Holland, 1981.

Radday, Yehuda T. *An Analytical Linguistic Concordance of the Book of Isaiah.* The Computer Bible, vol. 2. Edited by J. Arthur Baird and David Noel Freedman. Wooster, Ohio: Biblical Research Associates, Inc., 1971.

―――. *An Analytical, Linguistic Key-Word-In-Context Concordance to Esther, Ruth, Canticles, Ecclesiastes and Lamentations.* The Computer Bible, vol. 16. Edited by J. Arthur Baird and David Noel Freedman. Wooster, Ohio: Biblical Research Associates, Inc., 1978.

―――. *An Analytical, Linguistic Key-Word-In-Context Concordance to the Book of Genesis.* The Computer Bible, vol. 18. Edited by J. Arthur Baird and David Noel Freedman. Wooster, Ohio: Biblical Research Associates, Inc., 1980.

―――. *An Analytical, Linguistic Key-Word-In-Context Concordance to the Book of Judges.* The Computer Bible, vol. 11. Edited by J. Arthur Baird and David Noel Freedman. Wooster, Ohio: Biblical Research Associates, Inc., 1977.

―――. *An Analytical, Linguistic Key-Word-In-Context Concordance to the Books of Haggai, Zechariah and Malachi.* The Computer Bible, vol. 4. Edited by J. Arthur Baird and David Noel Freedman. Wooster, Ohio: Biblical Research Associates, Inc., 1972.

―――. "A Computer Bible—a Survey and Desiderata." *HCLB* 13 (1978): 92–99.

―――. "The Homogeneity of Genesis." In *Proceedings of the International Congress for Literary Computing, Liege 1981, L.A.S.L.A.* Liege, 796–803.

―――. *Isaiah and the Computer.* Hildesheim: H. A. Gerstenberg Verlag, 1972.

―――. "Isaiah and the Computer: A Preliminary Report." *CHum* 5 (1970): 65–73.

―――. "Two Computerized Statistical-Linguistic Tests Concerning the Unity of Isaiah." *JBL* 89 (1970): 319–24.

―――. *The Unity of Isaiah in the Light of Statistical Linguistics.* Hildesheim: H. A. Gerstenberg Verlag, 1973.

―――. "The Unity of Zechariah Examined in the Light of Statistical Linguistics." *ZAW* 87 (1975): 30–55.

Radday, Yehuda T., and M. Pollatschek. "Frequency Profiles and the Five Scrolls." *Revue* 2 (1978): 1–35.

―――. "Vocabulary Richness—A Key to the Structure of Lamentations." In *Computer Tools for Ancient Texts.* Edited by H. Van Dyke Parunak. Winona Lake, Ind.: Eisenbrauns. Forthcoming.

―――. "Vocabulary Richness and Concentration in Hebrew Biblical Literature." *ALLC Bull.* 8 (1980): 217–31.

―――. "Vocabulary Richness in Post-Exilic Prophetic Books." *ZAW* 92 (1980): 333–46.

Radday, Yehuda. T., and H. Shore. "The Definite Article: A Type and/or Author-Specifying Discriminant in the Hebrew Bible." *ALLC Bull.* 4 (1976): 23–31.

―――. "An Inquiry into the Homogeneity of the Book of Judges by means of Discriminant Analysis." *Linguistica Biblica* 41/42 (1977): 21–36.

Radday, Yehuda T., et al. "The Book of Judges Examined by Statistical Linguistics." *Biblica* 58 (1977): 469–99.

―――. *Genesis. An Authorship Study in Computer-Assisted Statistical Linguistics.* Analecta Biblica 103. Rome: Biblical Institute Press, 1985.

―――. "Genesis, Wellhausen and the Computer." *ZAW* 94 (1982): 467–82.

Raskin, Jeffrey F. "FLOW: A Teaching Language for Computer Programming in the Humanities." *CHum* 8 (1974): 231–37.

Richter, W. *Grundlagen einer althebraischen Grammatik. B. Die Beschreibungsebenen, III. Der Satz (Satztheorie).* ATSAT 13. St. Otilien, 1980.

Roberge, R.-M., and G. Deschatelets. "Bibliographic Information Bank in Patristics—BIBP." In *Data Bases in the Humanities and Social Sciences*. Edited by Robert F. Allen, 252–57. Osprey, Fla.: Paradigm Press, 1985.

Robey, David, ed. *Structuralism: An Introduction—Wolfson College Lectures 1972*. Oxford: Oxford University Press, 1973.

Roddy, Kevin P. "Project Rhetor: An Encyclopedia in the History of Rhetoric." In Sara K. Burton and Douglas D. Short, eds., 579–87. *Sixth International Conference on Computers and the Humanities*. Rockville, Md.: Computer Science Press, 1983.

Rosenthal, Steve. "Scanners at a Glance." *PC Magazine* (July 9, 1985): 129–33.

Ross, Donald, Jr. "EYEBALL and the Analysis of Literary Style." In *Computing in the Humanities*. Edited by Peter C. Patton and Renee A. Holoien, 85–103. Lexington, Mass.: D.C. Heath & Co., 1981.

Ross, Donald, Jr., and Robert H. Rasche. "EYEBALL: A Computer Program for the Description of Style." *CHum* 6 (1972): 213–21.

Rosslyn, Wendy. "COCOA as a Tool for the Analysis of Poetry." *ALLC Bull.* 3 (1975): 15–18.

Rouault, Oliver. "Elements pour un logiciel assyriologique." *CARNES* 1 (June 1984): 1–81.

Rudall, B. H. "A Command Language for Text Processing." In *Computers in Literary and Linguistic Research*. Edited by R. A. Wisbey, 281–89. Cambridge: Cambridge University Press, 1971.

———. *Syntax and Semantics of PROTEXT—A Text Processing Language*. University College of North Wales Computing Laboratory Publication, 1969.

Salton, G., and A. Wong. "On the Role of Words and Phrases in Automatic Text Analysis." *CHum* 10 (1976): 69–87.

Saumjan, S. K. *Principles of Structural Linguistics*. Translated by James Miller. The Hague: Mouton, 1971.

Schippers, Reinier. "Paul and the Computer." *Christianity Today* 9 (1964): 223–25.

Schneider, Wolfgang. *Grammatik des biblischen Hebräisch*. München: Claudius Verlag, 1983–1985.

Schweizer, H. "Elektronische Datenverarbeitung und Textinterpretation." In *Bible and Computer : The Text*, 297–310. Paris-Geneva: Champion-Slatkine, 1986.

———. *Metaforische Grammatik. Wege zur Integration von Grammatik und Textinterpretation in der Exegese*. ASAT 15. St. Otilien, 1981.

Sedelow, Walter A., Jr., and Sally Y. Sedelow, ed. *Computers in Language Research 2*. Berlin: Mouton, 1983.

Sedgewick, Robert. *Algorithms*. Reading, Mass.: Addison-Wesley, 1983.

Sequitier, K. A. "The TLG Canon: Genesis of an Encyclopedic Data Base." In *Papers of the UCLA Conference on Classics and Computing* (Los Angeles, July 19–20, 1986). = *Favonius Supp. Vol.* 1 (1987): 15–20.

Shea, Ellen. "Peripherals on the Paper Trail." *Tools of Automation* (July 1983): 44–54.

Shipp, William S. "Networks of Scholar's Workstations in a University Community." *COMPCON* (1983): 1–15.

Sillery, Bob. "Scholars with Computers Dig Into the Classics." *Personal Computing* (December 1985): 29–30.

Solodow, Joseph B. "The Canon of Texts for a Latin Data Bank." In *Papers of the UCLA Conference on Classics and Computing* (Los Angeles, July 19–20, 1986). = *Favonius Supp. Vol.* 1 (1987): 21–24.

Smith, J. M. "Studying Literature with a Computer: Report of the Presentation by Rev. A. Q. Morton at Datafair 73, 3." *ALLC Bull.* 1 (1973): 46–47.

Smith, John B. "A New Environment for Literary Analysis." *Perspectives in Computing* 4 (1984): 20–32.

Smith, Romaine O., Jr. "GENEDEX: GENeral InDEXer of Words with Content." *CSHVB* 3 (1970): 50–53.

Spero, Samuel W., and Menachem Slae. " 'Computing' Jewish Law." *Jewish Life* (Fall 1976): 51–57.

Spurrier, John H. "Run a 68008–Based 1-Board Computer on the STD Bus." *EDN* 30 (1985): 247–52.

Stanton, Tom. "The Kurzweil 4000: A State of the Art Reader." *PC Magazine* (July 9, 1985): 110–14.

———. "Peripheral Vision: A Guide to Optical Character Readers." *PC Magazine* (July 9, 1985): 105–8.

Stanton, Tom, Diane Burns, and S. Venit. "Page-To-Disk Technology: Nine State-of-the-Art Scanners." *PC Magazine* (September 30, 1986): 128–77.

Stanton, Tom, and Craig Stark. "Mid-Range OCRs." *PC Magazine* (July 9, 1985): 116–27.

Stewart, Doug. "Machines That Read." *Digital Review* (December 1984): 53–58.

Stone, Michael E. "Computer Implementation of Armenian." In *Bible and Computer : The Text*, 323–34. Paris-Geneva: Champion-Slatkine, 1986.

Swigger, Boyd K. "PROVIDE—A Preliminary Program for Text Analysis." *SIGLASH Newsletter* 6 (1973): 1–3.

Talstra, Eep. "Context and Part of Speech. Concordance Production from a Textgrammatical Database." In *Hebrew Computational Linguistics*. Forthcoming.

———. "Exegesis and the Computer Science: Questions for the Text and Questions for the Computer." *Bibliotheca Orientalis* 37 (1980): 121–28.

614

_____. "An Hierarchically Structured Data Base of Biblical Hebrew Texts: The Relationship of Grammar and Encoding." In *Bible and Computer : The Text*, 335–49. Paris-Geneva: Champion-Slatkine, 1986.

_____. "Is Saul ook onder de profeten? De komputer in het theologisch onderzoek." *Geref. Theol. Tijdschrift* 79 (1979): 24–36.

_____. "Text Grammar and Hebrew Bible. I: Elements of a Theory." *Bibliotheca Orientalis* 35 (1978): 169–74.

_____. "Text Grammar and Hebrew Bible. II: Syntax and Semantics." *Bibliotheca Orientalis* 39 (1982): 26–38.

_____. "Towards a Distributional Definition of Clauses in Classical Hebrew: A Computer-Assisted Description of Clauses and Clause Types in Deut. 4, 3–8." Originally published as "Vrije Universiteit Working Papers in Linguistics, No. 12." Amsterdam, 1984. *Biblica* (1985).

_____. *II Kon. 3. Etuden zur Textgrammatik.* Applicatio 1. Amsterdam, 1983.

_____. "The Use of *ken* in Biblical Hebrew. A Case Study in Automatic Text Processing." *OTS* 21 (1981): 228–39.

Talstra, Eep., F. Postma, and H. A. van Zwet. *Deuterojesasa. Proeve van automatische tekstverwerking ten dienste van de exegese.* Amsterdam, 1980, 2d rev. ed. 1981.

Talstra, Eep, F. Postma, and M. Vervenne. *Exodus. Materials in Automatic Text Processing.* Instrumenta Biblica 1. 2 parts. Amsterdam: Turnhout, 1983.

Taylor, Talbot J. *Linguistic Theory and Structural Stylistics.* Vol. 2 of *Language and Communication Library.* Pergamon, 1981.

Thompson, N. D. "Literary Statistics I: On The Small Print of Statistics." *ALLC Bull.* 1 (1973): 10–14.

_____. "Literary Statistics II: On Probability Distributions." *ALLC Bull.* 2 (1974): 10–15.

_____. "Literary Statistics III: On Estimation." *ALLC Bull.* 2 (1974): 42–47.

_____. "Literary Statistics IV: Hypothesis Testing." *ALLC Bull.* 2 (1974): 55–61.

_____. "Literary Statistics V: On Correlation and Regression." *ALLC Bull.* 3 (1975): 29–35.

_____. "Literary Statistics VI: On the Future of Literary Statistics." *ALLC Bull.* 3 (1975): 166–71.

Tov, Emanuel. "Computer Assisted Alignment of the Greek and Hebrew Equivalents of the Masoretic Text and the Septuagint." In *La Septuaginta en la Investigation Contemporanea (V Congreso de la IOSCS).* Edited by N. Fernandez Marcos, 221–42. Madrid, 1985.

_____. *A Computerized Data Base for Septuagint Studies—The Parallel Aligned Text of the Greek and Hebrew Bible.* CATSS 2 = JNSL Supplementary Series 1. Stellenbosch, 1986.

_____. "The Use of a Computerized Data Base for Septuagint Research: The Greek-Hebrew Parallel Alignment." *BIOSCS* 17 (1984): 36–47.

Tov, Emanuel, and J. Cook. "A Computerized Database for the Qumran Biblical Scrolls." *JNSL* 12 (1984): 169–74.

Tov, Emanuel, and B. G. Wright. "Computer Assisted Study of the Criteria for Assessing the Literalness of Translation Units in the LXX." *Textus* 12 (1985): 149–87.

Valentine, S. H. "Comparative Notes on ALGOL68 and PL/I." *Computer Journal* 17 (1974): 325–31.

van der Wal, A. J. O. *Amos. A Classified Bibliography.* Amsterdam, 1981 (Dutch edition), 1983.

_____. *Amos. Concordance and Lexical Surveys.* Applicatio 2. Amsterdam, 1984.

_____. *Planten uit de Bijbel. Een systematische Literatuurlijst.* Amsterdam, 1980, 1981.

Wake, William C. "Numbers, Paul and Rational Dissent." *Faith and Freedom* 37 (1984): 2–15.

_____. "Sentence Length Distribution of Greek Authors." *JRSS* 120A(1951): 331–46.

Waldrop, M. Mitchell. "Personal Computers on Campus." *Science* 228 (April 26, 1985): 438–44.

Wall, Robert. *Introduction to Mathematical Linguistics.* Englewood Cliffs, N.J.: Prentice-Hall, 1972.

Waterhouse, Viola G. *The History and Development of Tagmemics.* Vol. 16 of *Janua Linguarum* series critica. The Hague: Mouton, 1974.

Weil, G. E. "Analyze automatique de la Bible hebraique et de la paraphrase arameenne. Consideration sur les notions de corpus, banque des donneés et validation des methodes d'analyse." In *Analyze et validation dans l'etude des donneés textuelles.* Edited by M. Borrillo and J. Virbel, 239–63. Paris: CNRS, 1977.

_____. "Analyze Automatique Quantifieé en Critique Textuelle Biblique. Limite des Analyses Statistiques." In *Proceedings of the International Conference on Literary and Linguistic Computing.* Edited by Zvi Malachi, 55–96. Tel-Aviv University, 1979.

_____. "Bible Hebraique et Targum Arameen: Traitment automatique et etude quantitative." *Informatique et Philologie* (1974): 5–39.

_____. "Massorah, Massorètes, et ordinateurs: Les sources textuelles et les recherches automatisées." In *Bible and Computer : The Text*, 351–61. Paris-Geneva: Champion-Slatkine, 1986.

_____. "Section Biblique et Massoretique. Methodologie de la Codification des Textes semitiques Servant aux Recherchges de Linguistique Quantitative sur Ordinateur." *IRHT Bull.* 13 (1964–1965): 115–33.

Weil, G. E., and F. Chenique. "Prolegomenes a l'utilisation des methodes de statistique linguistique pour l'etude historique et philologique de la Bible hebraique et de ses paraphrases." *VT* 14 (1964): 344–66.

Weil, G. E., P. Riviere, and M. Serfaty. *La Cantilation des Ouvrages Bibliques en Arameen.* CNRS: Paris-Nancy, 1983.

———. *Les Cantilations des Derniers Prophetes.* CNRS: Paris-Nancy, 1982.

———. *Les Cantilations des Livres Poetiques.* CNRS: Paris-Nancy, 198?.

———. *Les Cantilations des Premiers Prophetes.* CNRS: Paris-Nancy, 1981.

———. *Concordance de la Cantilation du Pentateuque et des Cinq Megillot.* CNRS: Paris-Nancy, 1978.

Weil, G. E., A. Salem, and M. Serfaty. "Le Livre d'Isaie et l'Analyse Critique des Sources Textuelles." *Revue* 2 (1976): 1–86.

Weitzman, M. P. "Computer Simulation of the Development of Manuscript Traditions." *ALLC Bull.* 10 (1982): 55–59.

West, William C. "A Data Bank for Ancient Greek Inscriptions: Athenian Decrees to 318 B.C." In *Proceedings of the International Conference on Data Bases in the Humanities and Social Science 1985.* Paradigm Press. Forthcoming.

Wickmann, D. "On Disputed Authorship, Statistically." *ALLC Bull.* 4 (1976) 32–41.

Widemann, R. L. "Computers and Literary Scholarship." *CHum* 6 (1971): 3–14.

———. "Recent Scholarship in Literary and Linguistic Studies." *CHum* 7 (1972): 3–27.

———. "Trends in Computer Applications to Literature." *CHum* 9 (1975): 231–35.

Winograd, Terry. "Computer Software for Working with Language." *Scientific American* 25 (1984): 131–45.

———. *Language as a Cognitive Process.* Reading, Mass.: Addison-Wesley Pub. Co., 1983.

Wirth, Niklaus. *Algorithms and Data Structures.* Englewood Cliffs, N.J.: Prentice-Hall, 1986.

Wisbey, R. A., ed. *Computers in Literary and Linguistic Research.* Cambridge: Cambridge University Press, 1971.

Wonneberger, Reinhard. "Überlegungen zu einer Maschinenlesbaren Neuausgabe der Biblia Hebraica Stuttgartensia." In *Bible and Computer : The Text,* 363–79. Paris-Geneva: Champion-Slatkine, 1986.

Wright, B. G. "A Note on Statistical Analysis of Septuagintal Syntax." *JBL* 104 (1985): 111–14.

Wyatt, James L. "Can Function Word Distribution Indicate Authorship?" *Siglash Newsletter* 13 (June 1980): 3–13.

Yankelovich, Nicole, Norman Meyrowitz, and Andries van Dam. "Reading and Writing the Electronic Book." *COMPUTER* (October 1985): 15–30.

Young, Jeffrey S. "Hypermedia." *Macworld* (March 1986).

Yule, G. Udny. *Statistical Study of Literary Vocabulary.* Repr. of 1944 ed. Hamden, Conn.: Shoe String, 1968.

Zampolli A., and N. Calzolari, eds. *Computational and Mathematical Linguistics.* Vols. 36 and 37 of *Linguistica.* Florence: Leo S. Olschki, 1977, 1980.

———. *Linguistica Mathematica e Calcolatori.* Florence: Leo S. Olschki, 1973.

Zarri, Gian Piero. "A Computer Model for Textual Criticism." In *The Computer in Literary and Linguistic Studies.* Edited by Alan Jones and R. F. Churchhouse, 133–55. Cardiff: The University of Wales Press, 1976.

———. "Some Experiments on Automated Textual Criticism." *ALLC Bull.* 5 (1977): 266–90.

Trademarks

Academic Font is a trademark of Emerging Technology Consultants.
Alexander is a trademark of Design Enterprises of San Francisco.
AlKaatib is a trademark of Arabic Software Association.
Apple is a registered trademark of Apple Computer, Inc.
AppleTalk and Apple II are trademarks of Apple Computer, Inc.
askSAM is a trademark of Seaside Software, Inc.
AutoCAD is a trademark of Autodesk, Inc.
Bank Street Writer is a trademark of Broderbund Software, Inc.
Bits & Bytes Review is a trademark of Bits and Bytes Computer Resources.
BOB is a trademark of the Emulex Corporation.
BRS After Dark and BRS/BRKTHRU are trademarks of BRS Information Technology.
Bulletin Board Systems is a trademark of Meckler Publishing Co.
BYU Concordance is a trademark of Electronic Text Corporation.
Canon is a registered trademark of Canon, Inc.
CATAB/CALLIGRAPHE 44 is a registered trademark of Centre d'Analyse et de Traitment Automatique
  de la Bible et des Traditions Ecrites .
Classical Greek Postscript is a registered trademark of Allotype Typographics.
CLEP is a registered trademark of College Level Examination Programs.
Commodore is a registered trademark of Commodore Business Machines, Inc.
COMPAQ is a trademark of Compaq Computer Corporation.
compuBIBLE is a trademark of NASSCO.
Compugraphic is a registered trademark of Compugraphic Corporation .
CompuServe is a registered trademark of CompuServe Corporation.
COMPUTER BIBLE is a trademark of Computer Bibles International, Inc.
Computer Database is a trademark of Information Access Co.
The Computer Phone Book is a trademark of Mike Cane.
Cordata LP-300 is a trademark of Cordata.
CP/M and CP/M-86 are trademarks of Digital Research, Inc.
Crosstalk is a trademark of Microstuf.
dBase III is a registered trademark of Ashton-Tate.
DDL is a trademark of Imagen Corporation.
DELPHI is a trademark of General Videotex Corporation.
Deskset is a trademark of G.O. Graphics.
Diablo is a registered trademark of Diablo Systems, Inc.
DIALINDEX is a trademark of DIALOG Information Services, Inc.
DIALMAIL is a servicemark of DIALOG Information Services, Inc.
DIALOG is a registered trademark of DIALOG Information Services, Inc.
Dialoglink is a trademark of DIALOG Information Services, Inc.
DIALORDER is a servicemark of DIALOG Information Services, Inc.
DisplayWrite 2 is a trademark of International Business Machines.
DJN/R is a trademark of Dow Jones, Inc.
DO-IT is a trademark of Study Soft.
Dr. Halo is a trademark of Media Cybernetics.
DVISCRN is a trademark of N2 Computer Consultants.
EasyWriter II is a registered trademark of Computer Associates International.
ELECTREON is a trademark of The Fontableaux Group.
The Electronic University is a trademark of CompuLearning, Inc.
EMULEX is a trademark of the Emulex Corporation.
Epson is a registered trademark of Epson America, Inc.

Trademarks

Ethernet is a registered trademark of the Xerox Corporation.
EveryWord is a trademark of Every Word, Inc.
Excel is a trademark of Excel System Corporation.
FinalWord II is a trademark of Mark of the Unicorn.
First Impression is a trademark of Megahaus Corporation.
FlickerFree is a trademark of Gibson Research Corporation.
FonTableux is a trademark of The FonTableux Group.
FONTastic is a trademark of Altsys Corporation.
Font Editor is a trademark of Gamma Products, Inc.
FontGen is a trademark of VideoSoft.
FontMan is a trademark of Hercules Computer Technology.
Fontrix is a trademark of Data Transforms, Inc.
FormEasy is a trademark of Graphics Development International.
Framework is a registered trademark of Ashton-Tate.
Free Filer is a trademark of Telion Software.
FrontPage is a trademark of Studio Software Corporation.
FullPaint is a trademark of Ann Arbor Softworks, Inc.
FYI Sort Utility is a trademark of FYI, Inc.
GEM is a trademark of Digital Research, Inc.
Genesis is a trademark of Tegra, Inc.
GodSpeed is a trademark of Kingdom Age Software.
Grafeas is a trademark of Apollon Engineering.
GRiD is a trademark of Grid System Corporation.
Gutenberg Sr. is a trademark of Gutenberg Software.
Halo DPE is a trademark of Media Cybernetics.
Harvard Professional Publisher is a trademark of Software Publishing Co.
Hercules is a trademark of Hercules Computer Technology.
Hockney's Egg is a trademark of Peregrine Falcon Co.
HomeWord is a trademark of Sierra On-Line, Inc.
HOT LEAD is a trademark of Janus Associates.
IBM and PC are registered trademarks of International Business Machines, Inc. PC/XT and PC/AT are
    trademarks of International Business Machines, Inc.
Imagen is a registered trademark of Imagen Corporation.
Imagewriter is a trademark of Apple Computer, Inc.
imPRESS is a trademark of Imagen Systems.
InfoMerge is a trademark of Mark of the Unicorn.
In-Search is a trademark of Personal Bibliographic Software.
Intel is a registered trademark and 8085, 8086, 8088 are trademarks of Intel Corporation.
Interleaf is a trademark of Interleaf, Inc.
Interpress is a trademark of the Xerox Corporation.
ISI is a registered trademark of the Institute for Scientific Information.
Jazz is a trademark of Lotus Development Corporation .
Jet:Spell is a trademark of POLYGLOT, Inc.
Kadmos is a registered trademark of Allotype Typographics.
Keytronic is a registered trademark of Keytronic Corporation.
Keyworks is a trademark of Alpha Software Corporation.
Knowledge Index is a servicemark of DIALOG Information Services, Inc.
KnowledgeMan/2 is a registered trademark of Micro Data Base Systems, Inc.
KWIC-REF/1 is a trademark of Chen Information Systems.
LazerJet and LazerJet Plus are trademarks of Hewlett-Packard Co.
LazerView is a trademark of Sigma Designs, Inc.
LazerWorks is a trademark of EDO Communications.
LazerWriter is a trademark of Apple Computer, Inc.
Legal Resource Index is a trademark of Information Access Co.
LePrint is a trademark of Le Baugh Software Corporation.
Lettrix is a trademark of Hammer Laboratory Corporation.
Lexis is a trademark of Mead Data Control.
Lifetree is a trademark of Lifetree Software, Inc.
Linotronic is a trademark of Linotype Co.
LinoWord is a trademark of Allied Linotype.

Lookup is a trademark of Working Software, Inc.

Lotus is a registered trademark of Lotus Development Corporation .

MacBible is a trademark of Encycloware.

MacCharlie is a trademark of Dayna Communications.

MacDraft is a trademark of Innovative Data Design, Inc.

MacDraw, MacPaint and MacWrite are trademarks of Apple Computer, Inc.

Macintosh is a trademark of McIntosh Laboratory, Inc. and is used with express permission of its owner. It is licensed to Apple Computer, Inc.

MacProof is a trademark of Automated Language Processing Systems.

MacPublisher II is a trademark of Boston Software.

MacScripture is a trademark of Medina Software.

MacTerminal is a trademark of Apple Computer, Inc.

Magazine ASAP, Magazine Index, National Newspaper Index, and Newsearch are trademarks of Information Access Co.

MagnaType is a registered trademark of Magna Computer Systems, Inc.

Management Contents is a registered trademark of Information Access Co.

Manuscript is a trademark of Lotus Development Corporation.

Martz-BIBLIOFILE is a trademark of Martz Software Power Tools, Inc.

MarvelPrint is a trademark of Marvel Software.

MCI Mail is a registered trademark of MCI Communication Corporation.

Mega Screen Plus is a trademark of Micro Graphic Images.

Mentor is a trademark of Target Software, Inc.

.MENU is a trademark of International Software Database, which is a trademark of International Software Database Corporation.

Mercury is a trademark of LinguaTech International.

Microcomputer Index is a trademark of Database Services.

Microlytics is a trademark of Microlytics, Inc.

Microsoft is a registered trademark of Microsoft Corporation.

Microspell is a trademark of Trigram Systems.

MINCE is a trademark of Davka Corporation.

Mouse Systems is a registered trademark of Mouse Systems Corporation.

Multifont is a trademark of Hash-Tech.

Multi-lingual Scribe is a trademark of Gamma Productions.

Multimate is a registered trademark of Multimate International, Inc.

Multiplan is a registered trademark of Microsoft Corporation.

NewsFlash is a registered trademark of NewsNet.

NEXIS is a registered trademark of Mead Data Central, Inc.

Nota Bene is a trademark of Dragonfly Software.

The Office Publisher is a trademark of Laser Friendly, Inc.

OfficeWriter is a trademark of Office Solutions, Inc.

1-2-3 is a registered trademark of Lotus Development Corporation.

ONTAP is a trademark of DIALOG Information Services, Inc.

Pagebuilder is a trademark of White Sciences, Inc.

Pagemaker is a trademark of Aldus Corporation.

PagePerfect is a trademark of International Microcomputer Software, Inc.

PagePlanner is a trademark of Page Planner Systems.

Pagework is a trademark of West End Film, Inc.

Pagewriter is a trademark of The 'Puter Group.

Palantir is a registered trademark of Palantir Software.

PC-File III is a trademark of Buttonware, Inc.

PC MacBridge is a trademark of Tangent Technologies.

PC/NET LINK is a trademark of Sterling Federal Systems, Inc.

PC Paint is a trademark of Mouse Systems Corporation.

PC Paintbrush is a trademark of IMSI.

PC Palette is a trademark of International Business Machines.

PC-Talk is a registered trademark of Headlands Press, Inc.

PC Type Right is a trademark of the Xerox Corporation.

PC-Write is a trademark of Quicksoft.

PeachText is a trademark of Peachtree Software.

Perfect Writer is a trademark of Perfect Software, Inc.

Trademarks

Persyst is a trademark of the Emulex Corporation.
pfs is a registered trademark of Software Publishing Corporation.
PFS:ClickArt Personal Publisher is a trademark of Software Publishing Corporation .
Postscript is a trademark of Adobe Systems, Inc.
Preview is a trademark of Arbor Text.
Printer Boss is a trademark of Connecticut Software Systems Corporation.
ProKey is a trademark of Rosesoft, Inc.
Proofreader and Grammatik are trademarks of Aspen Software.
Proofwriter TURBOFONTS is a trademark of Image Processing Systems.
Pro-Search is a trademark of Personal Bibliographic Software.
PS Compose is a trademark of PS Publishing, Inc.
QMS Lasergrafixis a trademark of QMS, Inc.
Quadscreen is a registered trademark of Quadram Corporation.
Quadvue is a trademark of Quadram Corporation.
Quark Express is a trademark of Quark.
Ragtime is a trademark of Orange Micro, Inc.
RamFont is a trademark of Hercules Computer Technology.
R:base is a registered trademark of Microrim, Inc.
Ready, Set, Go! is a trademark of Manhattan Graphics Corporation.
RE/Call is a trademark of Yes Software, Inc.
Resident Speller is a trademark of S & K Technology, Inc.
Revelation is a registered trademark of Cosmos.
Rosesoft is a trademark of Rosesoft, Inc.
SAMNA Word III is a trademark of Samna Corporation.
Scenic Writer is a trademark of Scenic Computer Systems.
Sci-Mate is a registered trademark of ISI.
SCRIBE is a trademark of Professional Business Systems, Inc.
Scoop is a trademark of Target Software, Inc.
Sequitur is a trademark of Golemics, Inc.
Sidekick is a trademark of Borland International.
SmartKey II Plus is a trademark of Software Research Technologies, Inc.
Social Scisearch is a registered trademark of the Institute for Scientific Information.
SoftSet is a trademark of the Emulex Corporation.
Sonar is a trademark of Virginia Systems Software Services, Inc.
The Source and Sourcemail are trademarks of The Source Telecomputing Corporation.
Spellbinder Desktop Publisher is a trademark of Lexisoft, Inc.
Strike is a trademark of S & K Technology, Inc.
SuperCalc is a trademark of Sorcim Corporation.
Superpage II is a trademark of Bestinfo, Inc.
SuperPaint is a trademark of Silicon Beach Software, Inc.
SuperSort II is a trademark of Lifestyle Software, Inc.
Superswell is a trademark of Working Software, Inc.
Suprafont is a trademark of Soft Evolutions.
Switcher is a trademark of Apple Computer, Inc.
Symphony is a registered trademark of Lotus Development Corporation.
T3 is a trademark of Triad Computing Software Research.
Taxan is a trademark of Taxan Corporation.
Tech/Word is a trademark of Goldstein Software.
Telenet is a registered trademark of Telenet Communications.
Telios is a trademark of Genasys Corporation.
TerM is a trademark of Economic Insights .
TEX and PC TEX are trademarks of the American Mathematical Society.
TEXTBANK is a registered trademark of Group L. Corporation.
TEXTRA is a registered trademark of Ann Arbor Software.
ThinkTank is a trademark of Living Videotext, Inc.
Thunder! is a trademark of Batteries Included.
ThunderScan is a trademark of Thunderware, Inc.
Trade and Industry Index is a trademark of Information Access Co.
TRS-80 Model II, TRS-80 Model III, are registered trademarks of Tandy Corporation.
TURBOFONTS is a trademark of Image Processing Software.

Turbo Lightning is a trademark of Borland International.
II-in-a-Mac is a trademark of Computer Applications, Inc.
Tymnet is a registered trademark of McDonnell Douglas Information Systems Group.
UNIX is a registered trademark of AT&T Bell Laboratories.
Ventura Publisher is a trademark of the Xerox Corporation.
VisiCalc is a trademark of Visicorp.
VolksWriter is a registered trademark of Lifetree Software, Inc.
VolksWriter Deluxe is a trademark of Lifetree Software, Inc.
Wang is a registered trademark of Wang Laboratories, Inc.
Whoops! is a trademark of Cornucopia Software, Inc.
WordCruncher is a registered trademark of Electronic Text Corporation.
WordFinder is a trademark of Microlytics Inc.
WordMill is a trademark of Omnigall Systems.
WordPerfect is a registered trademark of Satellite Software International.
WordStar is a registered trademark of MicroPro International, Inc.
WorksPlus is a trademark of Lundeen and Associates.
WorldMaster is a trademark of Ektron Corporation.
WorldWriter is a trademark of Economic Insights.
WriteNow is a trademark of T/Maker.
Xerox is a registered trademark of the Xerox Corporation.
XyWrite is a trademark of XyQuest Corporation.
ZyINDEX is a trademark of ZyLAB Corporation.
ZyLAB is a trademark of ZyLAB Corporation.

Glossary

Absolute Address—The combination of segment and offset addresses in segmented memory addressing.

Add-In Card—Any card (printed circuit board) that may be added to a computer.

Address—A specific location in memory.

Address Bus—An external data path used by the processor to address memory.

Algorithm—A method, rule, or procedure for solving a problem.

Alphanumeric Character—Any character of the alphabet, any numeral.

Application Program—Any program that performs a task related to the world outside of the computer, e.g., word processing, data base management, communication.

Arithmetic-Logic Unit—(ALU) The device in the processor that performs logical and arithmetical operations.

ASCII—American Standard Code for Information Interchange; the common 8-bit information code used in computer communications. The 128 standard ASCII characters include all upper- and lower-case letters and all numerals, punctuation signs, and control characters.

Assembler—A program that converts assembly language instructions into machine code.

Assembly Language—A low-level programming language one step removed from machine code.

Baud—A unit used to measure the rate at which data is transmitted from one device to another.

Baud Rate—The number of bits per second (bps) at which a device can communicate.

Bibliographic Data Base—A data base whose records consist of fields of bibliographical information.

Binary Number—Any combination of the 0s and 1s used in the binary, or base-2, number system.

Bit—A binary digit; a 0 or a 1 in the binary number system.

Bit-Mapped Graphics—A type of video memory mapping in which each pixel is represented in video memory by one or more bits.

Board—Any printed circuit board (card), that contains memory chips or logic chips or both.

Boolean Logic—The system of algebraic logic developed by George Boole. Boolean logic allows all propositions to be expressed algebraically.

Boolean Operator—The logical ANDs, ORs, and NOTs used in circuit design and information retrieval. Operators operate on operands, which may be propositions, sets, or binary numbers.

Boot Record—A small program that loads a computer's operating system.

Buffer—Any memory used to hold data temporarily.

Bus—Any type of circuit, or data path, that allows different parts of the computer to communicate with each other and with external devices.

Byte—A set of 8 bits; the minimal meaningful unit of information to a computer.

Card—See *Board*.

Cell—A single location in memory; the intersection of a row and column in a flat-file data base.

Central Processing Unit—(CPU) The main processor or microprocessor that controls a computer system. The CPU consists of four logically and physically distinct parts: the arithmetic-logic unit, the control unit, the registers, and the internal data bus. On microcomputers these parts are integrated in a single logic chip, e.g., an Intel 80286, a Motorola 68020.

Chaining—Connecting files for printing so that page, footnote, and outline numbers are continuous across the chained files.

Character Generator—A ROM chip on the display adapter that contains the dot patterns for ASCII characters.

Character Set—The set of characters in a font or character generator.

Chip—An integrated circuit. The two basic types of chips are logic chips and memory chips. Logic chips perform logical operations on data; memory chips store the data on which the logic chips operate.

Clock Chip—A chip that generates timing frequencies that enable the CPU to synchronize data flow and program execution.

Clock Cycle—The time required to change the state of a computer's registers.

Code—Any instruction that causes a computer to perform an operation.

Command-Driven—A type of program interface in which functions are invoked by typing commands.

Command Processor—A system-level program that processes internal and external commands.

Communication Card—See *Serial Card*.

Compiler—A program that translates the instructions in high-level languages (e.g., C, Fortran) into machine code that may be turned into an executable program by a link editor.

Computer—A programmable, automatic, electronic, general-purpose, logic machine.

Control Character—Any nonprinting character used to control output devices.

Control Unit—(CU) The part of the CPU that receives, interprets, and oversees the execution of all instructions. The CU consists of registers, counters, and other components required to control the movement of information between memory, the ALU, and other parts of the computer. Also known as an execution unit (EU).

Controlled Vocabulary—A fixed set of terms used to describe the contents of records in a data base.

Coprocessor—Any logic chip that assists the CPU in its tasks, e.g., a numeric coprocessor.

Data—The information on which a program operates.

Data Bank—A collection of data about a common subject or subjects.

Data Base—An organized collection of data (often in bibliographical or abstract form) about a particular subject; the files in such a collection.

Data Bus—Two types: internal and external. The internal data bus connects the components within the processor. The external data bus is used to transmit data from memory to the processor.

Dead Key—A key that allows two characters to be entered in the same position on the screen.

Descriptor—A member of a carefully chosen set of terms (a controlled vocabulary) used to describe the contents of records in a data base.

Desktop Publishing System—A combination of hardware and software capable of integrating text and graphics and outputting the results on laser printers and phototypesetters.

Device Driver—A program that controls an output device, e.g., a printer, a monitor. Each type and brand of output device requires a separate driver.

Device Handler—A system-level program that handles the requests of input/output devices.

Document-Oriented—An application program orientation that treats text as a continuous stream of information.

Driver—See *Device Driver*.

Escape Code—A nonprinting control code that begins with the Esc character (decimal 27) and that instructs printers to alter their print functions in a specified way.

Execution Unit—See *Control Unit*.

External Interrupt—A signal, sent to the processor by a piece of hardware or software, requesting the processor to run a routine specified by the interrupt.

External Data Bus—See *Data Bus*.

Field—A unique category of information in a record, e.g., the author field, title field, or year-of-publication field in a bibliographic record.

File—The collection of records in a data base; a synonym for *data base*; any collection of information.

File Allocation Table—(FAT) A table that lists the location and status of a disk's data sectors.

Firmware—Software (programs) that reside in ROM chips.

Flag—A special type of register that stores the results of operations to provide feedback to the control unit.

Font—A set of same-sized characters of various typestyles that are unified by belonging to one typeface.

Format—The procedure that organizes disks into logical units called sectors, in which data may be stored.

Front-End Program—Special software for formulating executing, storing, manipulating, and printing the results of on-line searches.

Front-End Service—A telecommunication service that allows users to access the services of other on-line vendors. Also known as a gateway service.

Full-Duplex—A communications mode in which data may be sent and received simultaneously.

Gateway Service—See *Front-End Service*.

Half-Duplex—A communications mode in which data may be sent or received but not simultaneously.

Hardware—A computer's physical components, e.g., disk drives, keyboard, screen, and modem.

Hardware Interrupt—A type of external interrupt where a piece of hardware requests the processor to run a specified routine.

Hex or Hexadecimal—The base-8 numbering system used by programmers for numbering addresses in a computer's memory.

High Level Language—Any programming language that more closely resembles a natural language than machine language, e.g., C, Pascal.

Hit—Any string of characters that matches a search construction; a match.

Identifier—A term assigned by an indexer to describe the contents of records in a data base.

Information Utility—An on-line service that offers communication, information, and personal services. Also known as videotex service, a reference to the form in which the on-line information is displayed: text on a video (TV or CRT) screen.

Input/Output Device—A device that sends signals to or that receives signals from a computer. Keyboards, mice, and light pens are input devices; screens, printers, and plotters are output devices.

Instruction—A step that contains the code for a single operation in a program.

Instruction Cycle—The execution of one complete program instruction, which usually requires several clock cycles. Also known as a machine cycle.

Instruction Set—The set of operations a given processor can perform; a list of the codes for those operations and their addressing schemes.

Integrated Circuit—A single chip on which multiple circuits are integrated.

Interface—The mode and manner in which users interact with programs. The two basic types of interfaces are command-driven and menu-driven.

Internal Data Bus—See *Data Bus*.

Interpreter—A program that translates the instructions in high-level languages (e.g., FORTH, APL, LOGO, BASIC) into machine code as the program is executed, one instruction at a time.

626

Interrupt—An interruption of the processor by hardware, software, or a logical condition in the processor.

Interrupt Service Routine—One of a set of system-level routines used to service the requests of interrupting devices.

Interrupt Vector—An address of an interrupt service routine. See *Vector*.

Interrupt Vector Table—A table that lists the addresses of interrupt service routines.

Kerning—Increasing or decreasing the space between characters for aesthetic purposes.

Logic Chip—See *Chip*.

Logic Circuit—A combination of logic gates (on a logic chip) that perform arithmetical or other operations.

Logic Gate—A part of a logic circuit that performs one Boolean operation (e.g., AND, OR, NOT); consists of one output channel whose state is determined by one or more input channels.

Logical Interrupt—An internal interrupt generated by the processor.

Logical Operator—The Boolean ANDs, ORs, and NOTs that may be used in search constructions.

Low-Level Language—Any programming language that more closely resembles machine language than human language, e.g., assembly language.

Machine Code—The strings of 1s and 0s that computers actually read and that are physically represented in computers by high and low voltage states.

Machine Cycle—See *Instruction Cycle*.

Machine-Readable Text—Any text that exists on media that can be read by a computer.

Macro—A single instruction that represents and executes multiple instructions.

Main Memory—Random-access memory (RAM); memory from which instructions are executed. Located on RAM chips on the system board or on add-in cards. Also known as read-write memory and as primary memory.

Match—See *Hit*.

Memory Chip—See *Chip*.

Memory-Mapped Display—An addressing technique in which the computer and screen share addressable memory, so that changing the contents of video memory changes what is displayed on-screen. Each address in video memory corresponds to a specific screen location.

Menu—An on-screen list of program commands or functions that is used to operate a program.

Menu-Driven—A type of program interface in which functions are invoked by selecting from menus.

Micro Processing Unit—(MPU) See *Central Processing Unit*.

Microjustification—Adding space in fractional units between characters and words to justify text.

Glossary

Microprocessor—See *Central Processing Unit.*

Modem—A communication device that modulates the frequency of the computer's in-audible, electronic, digital signals into audible, analog signals that may be transmitted over the telephone system and that performs the inverse of that operation on the receiving end of a communication transaction.

Mother Board—The large printed circuit board, which usually includes expansion slots, on which are located a microcomputer's main logic and memory chips and other circuitry. Also known as the system board.

Mouse—A button-loaded, hand-sized input device for moving the cursor and selecting menu items.

Multiprocessing—The simultaneous execution of two or more instructions; requires two or more processing units.

Multitasking—The concurrent execution of two or more programs that share a single processing unit.

Nibble—A 4-bit word; half a byte.

Node—A host computer that functions as a connection point or exchange in a communication network.

Object Code—Machine-language code produced by a compiler or assembler.

Operating System—A hierarchically arranged set of complimentary, modular programs designed to handle the needs of input/output devices and to perform basic file-management services.

Operation Code—The codes that instruct a computer to perform distinct operations. Also known as op-codes.

Page Description Language—A set of device-independent rules (a programming language) that application programs may use to describe the appearance of pages to output devices that include interpreters for the language. Also known as page definition language.

Page-Oriented—An application program orientation that treats text as a linked series of discrete pages.

Parallel—A way of transmitting or operating on eight or more bits of data at a time.

Peripheral Device—Any input/output device that is not physically part of the computer per se and so is peripheral to its operation, e.g., a disk drive, the keyboard.

Pixel—"Picture element." The smallest addressable segment on a raster line.

Port—An interface between a computer and the outside world through which data may pass bidirectionally to and from input/output devices.

Primary Memory—See *Main Memory.*

Prime Number—Any whole number that can only be divided evenly by one and by itself.

Procedure—A program within a program; a part of a program that performs some specific task; a subroutine.

Processor—See *Central Processing Unit.*

Program—Logically arranged, fixed series of instructions that are designed to achieve particular objectives or applications.

Programming Language—Any language that may be used to write programs for computers.

Protocol—The set of parameters that govern communication between any two devices, e.g., computer and printer, computer and monitor, computer and computer.

Random Access Memory—(RAM) See *Main Memory.*

Raster—The set of invisible parallel lines that are continuously generated by the monitor's scanning electron beam.

Read-Only Memory—(ROM) Memory that exists in chips that may be read from but not written to. The information in ROM chips is nonvolatile, unerasable, and immediately available at all times. ROM chips may contain operating-system routines or application programs.

Register—A special type of memory cell where the processor can temporarily store the intermediate results of operations.

Secondary Memory—Disk storage.

Serial—A way of transmitting or operating on data one bit at a time.

Serial Card—A communication card that converts a computer's parallel flow of data into a one-bit-at-a-time, serial data stream that may be sent over telephone lines. Also known as a communication card.

Sieve of Eratosthenes—A method for finding prime numbers developed by an Alexandrian mathematician under whom Archimedes studied.

Software—The system, application, and utility programs run on computers; any computer program.

Source Code—The code produced by programmers that must be assembled, compiled, or interpreted before it may be executed.

Stack—A portion of memory used by processors for record keeping.

String—Any combination of symbols, e.g., letters, numerals, or other signs.

Subroutine—See *Procedure.*

System Board—See *Mother Board.*

System Program—See *Operating System.*

Tuple—A specific example of a particular relationship defined by a concrete set of values assigned to one set of fixed fields.

User Interface—See *Interface.*

Vector—A memory address that holds another memory address; a pointer to another memory location.

Video Memory—Random-access memory used to store data to be displayed on-screen. In microcomputers video memory is located in RAM chips on video card(s).

Videotex Service—See *Information Utility.*

Virtual Memory—A programming technique that allows secondary memory to be used as primary memory, thus giving the appearance of more main memory.

Word Length—The number of bytes or bits a computer can operate on at one time.

Index of Proper Names

Index of Topics

Syriac Concordance, 547. *See also* Ancient semitic text projects.
Syriac Research Center, 570. *See also* New Testament projects.
T3, 112–16
TEACH, 593
Telecommunicating, 432–36. *See also* Communicating and on-line services.
  protocols, 434–36
  serial cards and modems, 433–34
  telecommunication networks, 432–33
Telecommunication networks, 432–33. *See also* Communicating and on-line services.
TEXTBANK, 262–63
Text base programs, 249–66
  askSAM Version 3, 254–56
  Electra-Find, 256–58
  4-1-1, 253–54
  FYI 3000 Plus, 251–53
  MICROARRAS, 260–61
  Sonar, 263
  TEXTBANK, 262–63
  TextSearch, 258–60
  ZyINDEX, 249–51
Text-only Bible packages, 380–83
  COMPUTER NEW TESTAMENT, 380
  INTERNATIONAL BIBLE SOCIETY TEXT, 381
  MacBible, 381–82
  MacConcord, 382
  MacScripture, 382
  New Testament Concordance, 383
  VERSE BY VERSE, 381
Text-oriented programs, 273–76
  IT, 275–76
  LBase, 274–75
  Mercury, 274
  MTAS, 275
TextSearch, 258–60
Thelma Thistleblossom, 217–18
Thesaurus Linguae Graecae Project, 577–79
Thesaurus programs, 203–6
  Webster's Electronic Thesaurus, 205–6
  Webster's NewWorld On-Line Thesaurus, 204–5
  WordFinder, 205
Thunder!, 203
TLG Project, 577–79
TOPICS, 350
Toshiba P351–Mode 2, 67–68
Turbo Lightning, 207–8
Typesetting equipment, 328–32
  APS-6 Laser Imager with APS-55/800 Page Image Processor, 329
  Compugraphic MCS 8000 Series, 330
  Genesis XM, 331
  Linotronic Series 100 and Series 200, 330–31
  Varityper 6700 Series, 329–30
Typesetting programs, 319–26
  Deskset, 322–23

  DeskSet Design, 325
  DO-IT, 324
  Magna Type, 323
  ScenicWriter, 324
  Superpage II, 322
  ULTIMATE Professional Publishing System, 325
Typesetting services, 326–28
  Intergraphics, 326
  Laser Printing Services, 327
  MacTypeNet, 327
  Mac Typesetting Club, 328
  Sprintout, 327–38
  Typeline, 326
Ulpan Davka, 397–98
ULTIMATE Professional Publishing System, 325
Varityper 6700 Series, 329–30
Vector, 24
Ventura Publisher, 280–94
VERSE BY VERSE, 381
Video display adaptors, 52–59
  Best of Both, 57–58
  FonTableaux, 58–59
  Hercules Graphics Card, 54
  Hercules Graphics Card Plus, 54–56
  IBM Color Graphics Adapter, 53
  IBM Enhanced Graphics Adapter, 56–57
  IBM Monochrome Adapter, 53
  Quadvue, 58
  Summary, 59
Vocabulary on the Attack, 417
Vuwriter, 159–61
Webster's Electronic Thesaurus, 205–6
Webster's NewWorld On-Line Thesaurus, 204–5
Webster's New World Spelling Checker, 196–97
Westminster Computer Project—Groves, 527–29. *See also* Machine-readable versions of the Masoretic Text.
WordCruncher, 270–73
WordFinder, 205
WordMill, 158–59
Word Plus, The, 196
Word processing and related programs, 39–342
  academically oriented, 74–101
  bibliography and sorting programs, 228–47
  business oriented, 102–11
  categories for evaluation, 72–73
  characters, 43–44
  dedicated multilingual, 117–76
  desktop publishing programs, 280–319
  font and printer utilities, 177–92
  introduction, 39–43
  keyboard character to screen character, 50–51
  keyboard macro utilities, 220–28
  printers, 65–68
  programs with multilingual capabilities, 73–117
  raster-scan graphics, 48–49
  resolution and character size, 49–50
  scientifically oriented, 111–17
  screen modes, 44–47

Notes

Notes

Notes

Notes

Notes

Notes

Notes

Notes

Notes

Notes

Notes

Notes

Introducing
the
BITS & BYTES REVIEW™

State-of-the-Art Reviews of Computer Products for IBM PCs and Macintoshes

BITS & BYTES REVIEW™

REVIEWS & NEWS OF COMPUTER PRODUCTS & RESOURCES FOR THE HUMANITIES

A NEW PUBLICATION FOR THE HUMANITIES

The *Bits & Bytes Review*™ provides first-hand, in-depth reviews of computer products for students and scholars in the humanities. Evaluations of software and hardware developed by individuals, universities, and commercial companies explain in detail how products work and how they can enhance academic research and increase productivity.

The *Bits & Bytes Review*™ also covers a broad spectrum of journals, newsletters, trade publications, and project reports to provide the latest, most important news about conferences, grants, on-line data bases, networks, university computer projects, and major events in the microcomputer industry.

The *Bits & Bytes Review*™ is the outgrowth of three years of intensive research, writing, and product testing. An extensive international network of contacts in universities and the computer industry (including developers of software and hardware, designers of computer systems and components, and heads of computer-assisted research programs at major universities and graduate schools) gives this publication access to the latest commercial and academic products and news.

Product Review: *Computer System*

The IBYCUS SC:
A MULTILINGUAL COMPUTER SYSTEM FOR SCHOLARS

Imagine sitting at your computer and being able to read Plato, Aeschylus, Homer, and scores of other Greek authors in flawlessly accented Greek and then switching almost instantaneously to a beautifully pointed display of any book of the Hebrew Old Testament. And consider being able to search through any of those texts at lightning speeds for several character strings at once and having matches displayed in inverse video in a context you specify. Or maybe you'd prefer to scroll through a text on-screen, page-by-page, perhaps browsing now and then for interesting linguistic patterns. Now picture yourself splitting the screen and displaying the Masoretic (Hebrew) text of Genesis on one side and the Septuagintal (Greek) text of that book on the other—or two parts of the same text in two different windows. Finally, imagine being able to move any section of any of those texts into a window where you can do multilingual word processing, using the Latin, Greek, Hebrew, and Coptic alphabets, complete with all breathing, vowel, and diacritical marks. You can stop dreaming; the IBYCUS Scholarly Computer (hereafter ISC) can do all of that and more.

The version of the ISC that I have for review purposes is a preproduction, Beta version. Key assignments, operating features, and program characteristics may be slightly different on production models. At this time, only rudimentary manuals exist. My remarks, then, should be taken as a report on an evolving product that is near completion, not as a review of a finished product. Because I do not own one of the printers the ISC supports, I am not able to

test its print functions.

Named after Ibycus, son of Phytius, of Rhegium, a lyric poet of the the sixth century B.C., the IBYCUS SC is designed as *a complete system* to process ancient texts, that is, to meet scholarly needs in the areas of multilingual text display, analysis, word processing, and printing—areas of interest to most humanists and areas where software and hardware have not kept up with scholars' needs. The ISC is best described as a *processor of ancient texts* that has multilingual word processing capabilities. The ISC is much more than just a multilingual word processor; its strength lies not in a multitude of fancy editing and formatting features but in crystal clear displays and lightning fast string searches of ancient Greek, Hebrew, Latin, and Coptic texts, especially as those texts exist on CD-ROMs. The ISC, then, is a *sui generis*, special-purpose, microcomputer system.

The ISC is fast, flexible, and powerful. Designed by David W. Packard, a Harvard Ph.D. in classics and a computer engineer, for other classicists and humanists who work with ancient texts, the multitasking ISC (1) displays up to 4,096 unique characters on-screen in a single document, (2) works with up to fifteen different windows, (3) can search texts at astonishingly high rates of speed for multiple character strings, (4) supports the latest CD-ROM and laser printing technologies, (5) is designed to work with the TLG's data base of machine-readable ancient texts (see below), and (6) prints draft and near-camera-ready-quality documents in multiple languages (when used with proper printers).

Bits & Bytes Review™ Volume, 1, Number 1. Copyright © 1986 by Bits & Bytes Computer Resources. All rights reserved. ISSN: 0891-2955. Editor and Publisher: John J. Hughes. The *Bits & Bytes Review*™ is published nine times a year (Sept.through May) by Bits & Bytes Computer Resources, Whitefish, Montana 59937. Postage paid at Whitefish, MT. **Electronic Addresses:** BITNET (XB.J24@Stanford), DIALMAIL™ (11597), MCI Mail (226-1461), CompuServe * (71056, 1715), The Source™ (BCD931), DELPHI™ (JohnHughes). **Subscriptions:** (1) *Students* $40 per year (U.S.), $47 per year (Canada), $55 per year (foreign); (2) *Faculty* $55 per year (U.S.), $62 per year (Canada), $70 per year (foreign); (3) *Institutions and Others* $70 per year (U.S.), $77 (Canada), $85 (foreign). Subscriptions in categories two and three include one hour of consultation by phone with the Editor. Address all subscription inquiries to the Editor, Bits & Bytes Computer Resources, 623 N. Iowa Ave., Whitefish, MT 59937. Subscription requests sent to an electronic address must include VISA® or MasterCard® number and expiration date, complete mailing address, and daytime telephone number. Please allow two to four weeks for subscription processing. **Reprints:** Reproduction of material appearing in the *Bits & Bytes Review*™is forbidden without written permission. Send all reprint requests to the Editor at the address above. **Editorial Offices** are located at 623 N. Iowa Avenue, Whitefish, MT 59937; telephone (406) 862-7280. Some products evaluated in this newsletter are prerelease, Beta versions. The *Bits & Bytes Review*™ makes every effort to compare production and prerelease versions of products and to report on interim changes. All product reviews in this newsletter are based on independent, first-hand evaluations.

BITS & BYTES ORDER FORM

☐ **YES!** I want to subscribe to the **Bits & Bytes Review**™ for one year (9 issues per year).

    ☐ Student Rate: $40/U.S., $47/Canada, $55/Foreign
    ☐ Faculty Rate: $55/U.S., $62/Canada, $70/Foreign
    ☐ Institutional Rate: $70/U.S., $77/Canada, $85/Foreign

☐ **YES!** Send me a free sample issue.

Name _____
                    please print full name

Title_____

Company / School _____

Address _____

City _____

State _____ Zip _____

☐ Bill me
☐ Payment enclosed (U.S. funds)
☐ Charge to my ☐ VISA®   ☐ MasterCard®

_____
                   please print full name

Card # _____ Expires _____

Signature _____

BITS & BYTES COMPUTER RESOURCES
623 Iowa Avenue
Whitefish, Montana 59937
(406) 862-7280

Bits & Bytes Review

- WHAT IS IT?

The **Bits & Bytes Review**™ is one of today's most respected high-tech newsletters for academic computing. Published nine times a year, each twenty-page issue is filled with vital information to keep readers abreast of the fast-changing world of microcomputers. An annual index issue is provided at no extra cost.

- WHAT DOES IT PROVIDE?

The **Bits & Bytes Review**™ provides moderately technical, detailed product reviews and reports on a broad spectrum of computing-related activities. First-hand reviews of software and hardware for IBM PCs and Macintoshes are unbiased, clear, and comprehensive. They explain what products do, how they work, and how they can enhance academic research and increase productivity.

Specialized products and resources are reviewed, as are programs and hardware of a more general nature. Scholars who use computers for word processing, text analysis, data base management, or related applications will find the in-depth reviews and detailed information in the **Bits & Bytes Review**™ invaluable. Past issues have included the first published reviews of David Packard's IBYCUS Scholarly Computer, Version 2 of the Nota Bene™ multilingual word processing program, the WordCruncher® text-retrieval system, and the LC BLOC Company's liquid-crystal display, multi-lingual keyboard.

The **Bits & Bytes Review**™ is abstracted and indexed by INSPEC and by Information Science Abstracts, which are available on-line through vendors such as DIALOG® Information Services.

Each issue also includes a calendar of important events, news about grants, fellowships, data bases, CD-ROMs, hardware, software, and utilities, as well as a listing of helpful bibliographical items.

- HOW TO SUBSCRIBE

Subscription information and an order form may be found on page 646 of this book. A complimentary, sample copy of the **Bits & Bytes Review**™ is available on request.

Bits & Bites Review . . .

"The *Bits & Bytes Review*™...has firmly established itself as a solid and invaluable resource....Its in-depth software and hardware evaluations, along with its reports on a broad spectrum of computing-related activities in the various humanistic disciplines, constitute a gold mine of information for the academic reader. The *Bits & Bytes Review*™ is highly recommended to any humanist concerned with computer-assisted research and teaching, as well as to any library seeking to meet the needs of humanities-based computing."

Theodore F. Brunner, Director
Thesaurus Linguae Graecae Project
University of California at Irvine

"Today's scholars require the types of detailed reviews and information provided in the...*Bits & Bytes Review*™....One is hard pressed to find a comparable publication that should be on everyone's shelf who is currently using microcomputers for publishing, research, and administration."

John R. Abercrombie
Assistant Dean for Computing, Humanities
Director of the Center for Computer Analysis of Texts
University of Pennsylvania

"Because it provides up-to-date, informed commentary on the products and resources currently available, the *Bits & Bytes Review*™ has become required reading for anyone interested in the application of computer technology to teaching and research in the humanities."

C. Stuart Hunter
Coordinator of Humanities Computing
University of Guelph

"We find it extremely useful, particularly for its thoroughness in product reviews and would recommend it highly to scholars and university administrators seeking better ways of putting technology to use in the service of humanities research."

Eleanor Selfridge-Field
Center for Computer Assisted
Research in the Humanities
Menlo Park, California

The manuscript for this book was prepared on an IBM Personal Computer.
The text files were processed and formatted using FinalWord II™.

Cover design by Art Jacobs.
Cover photo by Geoffrey Gove.
Technical illustrations by Evelyn Barnes.

Text composition in Goudy Old Style.
Typesetting by Bits and Bytes Computer Resources, using FinalWord II™ and the
Compugraphic® MCS™ 8000 digital phototypesetter.

Cover art separated by Holland Litho, Holland, Michigan.
Text stock, 45 lb. Bright White K Offset.
Book printed and bound by Eerdmans Printing Co., Grand Rapids, Michigan.